Edna Ferber,

Collection novels

In this book:

Cheerful--By Request, 1918

Fanny Herself, 1917

Buttered Side Down, 1912

Gigolo, 1922

Half Portions, 1919

Dawn O'Hara 1911

D1529894

Edna Ferber (1885 –1968) was an American novelist, short story writer and playwright. Her novels were especially popular and included the Pulitzer Prize-winning So Big (1924), Show Boat (1926; made into the celebrated 1927 musical), Cimarron (1929; made into the 1931 film which won the Academy Award for Best Picture), and Giant (1952; made into the 1956 Hollywood movie).

Ferber's novels generally featured strong female protagonists, along with a rich and diverse collection of supporting characters. She usually highlighted at least one strong secondary character who faced discrimination ethnically or for other reasons; through this technique, Ferber demonstrated her belief that people are people and that the not-so-pretty people have the best character.

In this book:

Cheerful--By Request

CHEERFUL—BY REQUEST

The editor paid for the lunch (as editors do). He lighted his seventh cigarette and leaned back. The conversation, which had zigzagged from the war to Zuloaga, and from Rasputin the Monk to the number of miles a Darrow would go on a gallon, narrowed down to the thin, straight line of business.

"Now don't misunderstand. Please! We're not presuming to dictate. Dear me, no! We have always felt that the writer should be free to express that which is in his—ah—heart. But in the last year we've been swamped with these drab, realistic stories. Strong, relentless things, you know, about dishwashers, with a lot of fine detail about the fuzz of grease on the rim of the pan. And then those drear and hopeless ones about fallen sisters who end it all in the East River. The East River must be choked up with 'em. Now, I know that life is real, life is earnest, and I'm not demanding a happy ending, exactly. But if you could—that is—would you—do you see your way at all clear to giving us a fairly cheerful story? Not necessarily Glad, but not so darned Russian, if you get me. Not pink, but not all grey either. Say—mauve." ...

That was Josie Fifer's existence. Mostly grey, with a dash of pink. Which makes mauve.

Unless you are connected (which you probably are not) with the great firm of Hahn & Lohman, theatrical producers, you never will have heard of Josie Fifer.

There are things about the theatre that the public does not know. A statement, at first blush, to be disputed. The press agent, the special writer, the critic, the magazines, the Sunday supplement, the divorce courts—what have they left untold? We know the make of car Miss Billboard drives; who her husbands are and were; how much the movies have offered her; what she wears, reads, says, thinks, and eats for breakfast. Snapshots of author writing play at place on Hudson; pictures of the play in rehearsal; of the director directing it; of the stage hands rewriting it—long before the opening night we know more about the piece than does the playwright himself, and are ten times less eager to see it.

Josie Fifer's knowledge surpassed even this. For she was keeper of the ghosts of the firm of Hahn & Lohman. Not only was she present at the birth of a play; she officiated at its funeral. She carried the keys to the closets that housed the skeletons of the firm. When a play died of inanition, old age, or—as was sometimes the case—before it was born, it was Josie Fifer who laid out its remains and followed it to the grave.

Her notification of its demise would come thus:

"Hello, Fifer! This is McCabe" (the property man of H. & L. at the phone).

"Well?"

"A little waspish this morning, aren't you, Josephine?"

"I've got twenty-five bathing suits for the No. 2 'Ataboy' company to mend and clean and press before five this afternoon. If you think I'm going to stand here wasting my—"

"All right, all right! I just wanted to tell you that 'My Mistake' closes Saturday. The stuff'll be up Monday morning early."

A sardonic laugh from Josie. "And yet they say 'What's in a name!'"

The unfortunate play had been all that its title implies. Its purpose was to star an actress who hadn't a glint. Her second-act costume alone had cost $700, but even Russian sable bands can't carry a bad play. The critics had pounced on it with the savagery of their kind and hacked it, limb from limb, leaving its carcass to rot under the pitiless white glare of Broadway. The dress with the Russian sable bands went the way of all Hahn & Lohman tragedies. Josie Fifer received it, if not reverently, still appreciatively.

"I should think Sid Hahn would know by this time," she observed sniffily, as her expert fingers shook out the silken folds and smoothed the fabulous fur, "that auburn hair and a gurgle and a Lucille dress don't make a play. Besides, Fritzi Kirke wears the biggest shoe of any actress I ever saw. A woman with feet like that"—she picked up a satin slipper, size 7½ C—"hasn't any business on the stage. She ought to travel with a circus. Here, Etta. Hang this away in D, next to the amethyst blue velvet, and be sure and lock the door."

McCabe had been right. A waspish wit was Josie's.

The question is whether to reveal to you now where it was that Josie Fifer reigned thus, queen of the cast-offs; or to take you back to the days that led up to her being there—the days when she was José Fyfer on the programme.

Her domain was the storage warehouse of Hahn & Lohman, as you may have guessed. If your business lay Forty-third Street way, you might have passed the building a hundred times without once giving it a seeing glance. It was not Forty-third Street of the small shops, the smart crowds, and the glittering motors. It was the Forty-third lying east of the Grand Central sluice gates; east of fashion; east, in a word, of Fifth Avenue—a great square brick building smoke-grimed, cobwebbed, and having the look of a cold-storage plant or a car barn fallen into disuse;

dusty, neglected, almost eerie. Yet within it lurks Romance, and her sombre sister Tragedy, and their antic brother Comedy, the cut-up.

A worn flight of wooden steps leads up from the sidewalk to the dim hallway; a musty-smelling passage wherein you are met by a genial sign which reads:

"No admittance. Keep out. This means you."

To confirm this, the eye, penetrating the gloom, is confronted by a great blank metal door that sheathes the elevator. To ride in that elevator is to know adventure, so painfully, so protestingly, with such creaks and jerks and lurchings does it pull itself from floor to floor, like an octogenarian who, grunting and groaning, hoists himself from his easy-chair by slow stages that wring a protest from ankle, knee, hip, back and shoulder. The corkscrew stairway, broken and footworn though it is, seems infinitely less perilous.

First floor—second—third—fourth. Whew! And there you are in Josie Fifer's kingdom—a great front room, unexpectedly bright and even cosy with its whir of sewing machines: tables, and tables, and tables, piled with orderly stacks of every sort of clothing, from shoes to hats, from gloves to parasols; and in the room beyond this, and beyond that, and again beyond that, row after row of high wooden cabinets stretching the width of the room, and forming innumerable aisles. All of Bluebeard's wives could have been tucked away in one corner of the remotest and least of these, and no one the wiser. All grimly shut and locked, they are, with the key in Josie's pocket. But when, at the behest of McCabe, or sometimes even Sid Hahn himself, she unlocked and opened one of these doors, what treasures hung revealed! What shimmer and sparkle and perfume—and moth balls! The long-tailed electric light bulb held high in one hand, Josie would stand at the door like a priestess before her altar.

There they swung, the ghosts and the skeletons, side by side. You remember that slinking black satin snakelike sheath that Gita Morini wore in "Little Eyolf"? There it dangles, limp, invertebrate, yet how eloquent! No other woman in the world could have worn that gown, with its unbroken line from throat to hem, its smooth, high, black satin collar, its writhing tail that went slip-slip-slipping after her. In it she had looked like a sleek and wicked python that had fasted for a long, long time.

Dresses there are that have made stage history. Surely you remember the beruffled, rose-strewn confection in which the beautiful Elsa Marriott swam into our ken in "Mississipp'"? She used to say, wistfully, that she always got a hand on her entrance in that dress. It was due to the sheer shock of delight that thrilled audience after audience as it beheld her loveliness enhanced by this floating, diaphanous tulle cloud. There it hangs, time-yellowed, its pristine freshness vanished quite, yet as fragrant with romance as is the sere and withered blossom of a dead white rose pressed within the leaves of a book of love poems. Just next it, incongruously enough, flaunt the wicked froufrou skirts and the low-cut bodice and the wasp waist of the abbreviated costume in which Cora Kassell used so generously to display her charms. A rich and portly society matron of Pittsburgh now—she whose name had been a synonym for pulchritude these thirty years; she who had had more cold creams, hats, cigars, corsets, horses, and lotions named for her than any woman in history! Her ample girth would have wrought sad havoc with that eighteen-inch waist now. Gone are the chaste curves of the slim white silk legs that used to kick so lithely from the swirl of lace and chiffon. Yet there it hangs, pertly pathetic, mute evidence of her vanished youth, her delectable beauty, and her unblushing confidence in those same.

Up one aisle and down the next—velvet, satin, lace and broadcloth—here the costume the great Canfield had worn in Richard III; there the little cocked hat and the slashed jerkin in which Maude Hammond, as Peterkins, winged her way to fame up through the hearts of a million children whose ages ranged from seven to seventy. Brocades and ginghams; tailor suits and peignoirs; puffed sleeves and tight—dramatic history, all, they spelled failure, success, hope, despair, vanity, pride, triumph, decay. Tragic ghosts, over which Josie Fifer held grim sway!

Have I told you that Josie Fifer, moving nimbly about the great storehouse, limped as she went? The left leg swung as a normal leg should. The right followed haltingly, sagging at hip and knee. And that brings us back to the reason for her being where she was. And what.

The story of how Josie Fifer came to be mistress of the cast-off robes of the firm of Hahn & Lohman is one of those stage tragedies that never have a public performance. Josie had been one of those little girls who speak pieces at chicken-pie suppers held in the basement of the Presbyterian church. Her mother had been a silly, idle woman addicted to mother hubbards and paper-backed novels about the house. Her one passion was the theatre, a passion that had very scant opportunity for feeding in Wapello, Iowa. Josie's piece-speaking talent was evidently a direct inheritance. Some might call it a taint.

Two days before one of Josie's public appearances her mother would twist the child's hair into innumerable rag curlers that stood out in grotesque, Topsy-like bumps all over her fair head. On the eventful evening each rag chrysalis would burst into a full-blown butterfly curl. In a pale-blue, lace-fretted dress over a pale-blue slip, made in what her mother called "Empire style," Josie would deliver herself of "Entertaining Big Sister's Beau" and other sophisticated classics with an incredible ease and absence of embarrassment. It wasn't a definite boldness in her. She merely liked standing there before all those people, in her blue dress and her toe slippers, speaking her pieces with enhancing gestures taught her by her mother in innumerable rehearsals.

Any one who has ever lived in Wapello, Iowa, or its equivalent, remembers the old opera house on the corner of Main and Elm, with Schroeder's drug store occupying the first floor. Opera never came within three hundred miles of Wapello, unless it was the so-called comic kind. It was before the day of the ubiquitous moving-picture theatre

4

that has since been the undoing of the one-night stand and the ten-twenty-thirty stock company. The old red-brick opera house furnished unlimited thrills for Josie and her mother. From the time Josie was seven she was taken to see whatever Wapello was offered in the way of the drama. That consisted mostly of plays of the tell-me-more-about-me-mother type.

By the time she was ten she knew the whole repertoire of the Maude La Vergne Stock Company by heart. She was *blasé* with "East Lynne" and "The Two Orphans," and even "Camille" left her cold. She was as wise to the trade tricks as is a New York first nighter. She would sit there in the darkened auditorium of a Saturday afternoon, surveying the stage with a judicious and undeceived eye, as she sucked indefatigably at a lollipop extracted from the sticky bag clutched in one moist palm. (A bag of candy to each and every girl; a ball or a top to each and every boy!) Josie knew that the middle-aged *soubrette* who came out between the first and second acts to sing a gingham-and-sunbonnet song would whisk off to reappear immediately in knee-length pink satin and curls. When the heroine left home in a shawl and a sudden snowstorm that followed her upstage and stopped when she went off, Josie was interested, but undeceived. She knew that the surprised-looking white horse used in the Civil War comedy-drama entitled "His Southern Sweetheart" came from Joe Brink's livery stable in exchange for four passes, and that the faithful old negro servitor in the white cotton wig would save somebody from something before the afternoon was over.

In was inevitable that as Josie grew older she should take part in home-talent plays. It was one of these tinsel affairs that had made clear to her just where her future lay. The Wapello *Daily Courier* helped her in her decision. She had taken the part of a gipsy queen, appropriately costumed in slightly soiled white satin slippers with four-inch heels, and a white satin dress enhanced by a red sash, a black velvet bolero, and large hoop earrings. She had danced and sung with a pert confidence, and the *Courier* had pronounced her talents not amateur, but professional, and had advised the managers (who, no doubt, read the Wapello *Courier* daily, along with their *Morning Telegraph*) to seek her out, and speedily.

Josie didn't wait for them to take the hint. She sought them out instead. There followed seven tawdry, hard-working, heartbreaking years. Supe, walk-on, stock, musical comedy—Josie went through them all. If any illusions about the stage had survived her Wapello days, they would have vanished in the first six months of her dramatic career. By the time she was twenty-four she had acquired the wisdom of fifty, a near-seal coat, a turquoise ring with a number of smoky-looking crushed diamonds surrounding it, and a reputation for wit and for decency. The last had cost the most.

During all these years of cheap theatrical boarding houses (the most soul-searing cheapness in the world), of one-night stands, of insult, disappointment, rebuff, and something that often came perilously near to want, Josie Fifer managed to retain a certain humorous outlook on life. There was something whimsical about it. She could even see a joke on herself. When she first signed her name José Fyfer, for example, she did it with, an appreciative giggle and a glint in her eye as she formed the accent mark over the e.

"They'll never stop me now," she said. "I'm made. But I wish I knew if that J was pronounced like H, in humbug. Are there any Spanish blondes?"

It used to be the habit of the other women in the company to say to her: "Jo, I'm blue as the devil to-day. Come on, give us a laugh."

She always obliged.

And then came a Sunday afternoon in late August when her laugh broke off short in the middle, and was forever after a stunted thing.

She was playing Atlantic City in a second-rate musical show. She had never seen the ocean before, and she viewed it now with an appreciation that still had in it something of a Wapello freshness.

They all planned to go in bathing that hot August afternoon after rehearsal. Josie had seen pictures of the beauteous bathing girl dashing into the foaming breakers. She ran across the stretch of glistening beach, paused and struck a pose, one toe pointed waterward, her arms extended affectedly.

"So!" she said mincingly. "So this is Paris!"

It was a new line in those days, and they all laughed, as she had meant they should. So she leaped into the water with bounds and shouts and much waving of white arms. A great floating derelict of a log struck her leg with its full weight, and with all the tremendous force of the breaker behind it. She doubled up ridiculously, and went down like a shot. Those on the beach laughed again. When she came up, and they saw her distorted face they stopped laughing, and fished her out. Her leg was broken in two places, and mashed in a dozen.

José Fyfer's dramatic career was over. (This is not the cheery portion of the story.)

When she came out of the hospital, three months later, she did very well indeed with her crutches. But the merry-eyed woman had vanished—she of the Wapello colouring that had persisted during all these years. In her place limped a wan, shrunken, tragic little figure whose humour had soured to a caustic wit. The near-seal coat and the turquoise-and-crushed-diamond ring had vanished too.

During those agonized months she had received from the others in the company such kindness and generosity as only stage folk can show—flowers, candy, dainties, magazines, sent by every one from the prima donna to the call boy. Then the show left town. There came a few letters of kind inquiry, then an occasional post card, signed by half a dozen members of the company. Then these ceased. Josie Fifer, in her cast and splints and bandages and pain, dragged out long hospital days and interminable hospital nights. She took a dreary pleasure in following the tour of her erstwhile company via the pages of the theatrical magazines.

"They're playing Detroit this week," she would announce to the aloof and spectacled nurse. Or: "One-night stands, and they're due in Muncie, Ind., to-night. I don't know which is worse—playing Muncie for one night or this moan factory for a three month's run."

When she was able to crawl out as far as the long corridor she spoke to every one she met. As she grew stronger she visited here and there, and on the slightest provocation she would give a scene ranging all the way from "Romeo and Juliet" to "The Black Crook." It was thus she first met Sid Hahn, and felt the warming, healing glow of his friendship.

Some said that Sid Hahn's brilliant success as a manager at thirty-five was due to his ability to pick winners. Others thought it was his refusal to be discouraged when he found he had picked a failure. Still others, who knew him better, were likely to say: "Why, I don't know. It's a sort of—well, you might call it charm—and yet—. Did you ever see him smile? He's got a million-dollar grin. You can't resist it."

None of them was right. Or all of them. Sid Hahn, erstwhile usher, call boy, press agent, advance man, had a genius for things theatrical. It was inborn. Dramatic, sensitive, artistic, intuitive, he was often rendered inarticulate by the very force and variety of his feelings. A little, rotund, ugly man, Sid Hahn, with the eyes of a dreamer, the wide, mobile mouth of a humourist, the ears of a comic ol'-clo'es man. His generosity was proverbial, and it amounted to a vice.

In September he had come to Atlantic City to try out "Splendour." It was a doubtful play, by a new author, starring Sarah Haddon for the first time. No one dreamed the play would run for years, make a fortune for Hahn, lift Haddon from obscurity to the dizziest heights of stardom, and become a classic of the stage.

Ten minutes before the curtain went up on the opening performance Hahn was stricken with appendicitis. There was not even time to rush him to New York. He was on the operating table before the second act was begun. When he came out of the ether he said: "How did it go?"

"Fine!" beamed the nurse. "You'll be out in two weeks."

"Oh, hell! I don't mean the operation. I mean the play."

He learned soon enough from the glowing, starry-eyed Sarah Haddon and from every one connected with the play. He insisted on seeing them all daily, against his doctor's orders, and succeeded in working up a temperature that made his hospital stay a four weeks' affair. He refused to take the tryout results as final.

"Don't be too bubbly about this thing," he cautioned Sarah Haddon. "I've seen too many plays that were skyrockets on the road come down like sticks when they struck New York."

The company stayed over in Atlantic City for a week, and Hahn held scraps of rehearsals in his room when he had a temperature of 102. Sarah Haddon worked like a slave. She seemed to realise that her great opportunity had come—the opportunity for which hundreds of gifted actresses wait a lifetime. Haddon was just twenty-eight then—a year younger than Josie Fifer. She had not yet blossomed into the full radiance of her beauty. She was too slender, and inclined to stoop a bit, but her eyes were glorious, her skin petal-smooth, her whole face reminding one, somehow, of an intelligent flower. Her voice was a golden, liquid delight.

Josie Fifer, dragging herself from bed to chair, and from chair to bed, used to watch for her. Hahn's room was on her floor. Sarah Haddon, in her youth and beauty and triumph, represented to Josie all that she had dreamed of and never realised; all that she had hoped for and never could know. She used to insist on having her door open, and she would lie there for hours, her eyes fixed on that spot in the hall across which Haddon would flash for one brief instant on her way to the room down the corridor. There is about a successful actress a certain radiant something—a glamour, a luxuriousness, an atmosphere that suggest a mysterious mixture of silken things, of perfume, of adulation, of all that is rare and costly and perishable and desirable.

Josie Fifer's stage experience had included none of this. But she knew they were there. She sensed that to this glorious artist would come all those fairy gifts that Josie Fifer would never possess. All things about her—her furs, her gloves, her walk, her hats, her voice, her very shoe ties—were just what Josie would have wished for. As she lay there she developed a certain grim philosophy.

"She's got everything a woman could wish for. Me, I haven't got a thing. Not a blamed thing! And yet they say everything works out in the end according to some scheme or other. Well, what's the answer to this, I wonder? I can't make it come out right. I guess one of the figures must have got away from me."

In the second week of Sid Hahn's convalescence he heard, somehow, of Josie Fifer. It was characteristic of him that he sent for her. She put a chiffon scarf about the neck of her skimpy little kimono, spent an hour and ten minutes on her hair, made up outrageously with that sublime unconsciousness that comes from too close familiarity with rouge pad and grease jar, and went. She was trembling as though facing a first-night audience in a part she wasn't up on. Between the crutches, the lameness, and the trembling she presented to Sid Hahn, as she stood in the doorway, a picture that stabbed his kindly, sensitive heart with a quick pang of sympathy.

He held out his hand. Josie's crept into it. At the feel of that generous friendly clasp she stopped trembling. Said Hahn:

"My nurse tells me that you can do a bedside burlesque of 'East Lynne' that made even that Boston-looking interne with the thick glasses laugh. Go on and do it for me, there's a good girl. I could use a laugh myself just now."

And Josie Fifer caught up a couch cover for a cloak, with the scarf that was about her neck for a veil, and, using Hahn himself as the ailing chee-ild, gave a biting burlesque of the famous bedside visit that brought the tears of laughter to his eyes, and the nurse flying from down the hall. "This won't do," said that austere person.

"Won't, eh? Go on and stick your old thermometer in my mouth. What do I care! A laugh like that is worth five degrees of temperature."

When Josie rose to leave he eyed her keenly, and pointed to the dragging leg.

"How about that? Temporary or permanent?"

"Permanent."

"Oh, fudge! Who's telling you that? These days they can do—"

"Not with this, though. That one bone was mashed into about twenty-nine splinters, and when it came to putting 'em together again a couple of pieces were missing. I must've mislaid 'em somewhere. Anyway, I make a limping exit—for life."

"Then no more stage for you—eh, my girl?"

"No more stage."

Hahn reached for a pad of paper on the table at his bedside, scrawled a few words on it, signed it "S.H." in the fashion which became famous, and held the paper out to her.

"When you get out of here," he said, "you come to New York, and up to my office; see? Give 'em this at the door. I've got a job for you—if you want it."

And that was how Josie Fifer came to take charge of the great Hahn & Lohman storehouse. It was more than a storehouse. It was a museum. It housed the archives of the American stage. If Hahn & Lohman prided themselves on one thing more than on another, it was the lavish generosity with which they invested a play, from costumes to carpets. A period play was a period play when they presented it. You never saw a French clock on a Dutch mantel in a Hahn & Lohman production. No hybrid hangings marred their back drop. No matter what the play, the firm provided its furnishings from the star's slippers to the chandeliers. Did a play last a year or a week, at the end of its run furniture, hangings, scenery, rugs, gowns, everything, went off in wagonloads to the already crowded storehouse on East Forty-third Street.

Sometimes a play proved so popular that its original costumes, outworn, had to be renewed. Sometimes the public cried "Thumbs down!" at the opening performance, and would have none of it thereafter. That meant that costumes sometimes reached Josie Fifer while the wounds of the dressmaker's needle still bled in them. And whether for a week or a year fur on a Hahn & Lohman costume was real fur; its satin was silk-backed, its lace real lace. No paste, or tinsel, or cardboard about H. & L.! Josie Fifer could recall the scenes in a play, step by step from noting with her keen eye the marks left on costume after costume by the ravages of emotion. At the end of a play's run she would hold up a dress for critical inspection, turning it this way and that.

"This is the dress she wore in her big scene at the end of the second act where she crawls on her knees to her wronged husband and pounds on the door and weeps. She certainly did give it some hard wear. When Marriott crawls she crawls, and when she bawls she bawls. I'll say that for her. From the looks of this front breadth she must have worn a groove in the stage at the York."

No gently sentimental reason caused Hahn & Lohman to house these hundreds of costumes, these tons of scenery, these forests of furniture. Neither had Josie Fifer been hired to walk wistfully among them like a spinster wandering in a dead rose garden. No, they were stored for a much thriftier reason. They were stored, if you must know, for possible future use. H. & L. were too clever not to use a last year's costume for a this year's road show. They knew what a coat of enamel would do for a bedroom set. It was Josie Fifer's duty not only to tabulate and care for these relics, but to refurbish them when necessary. The sewing was done by a little corps of assistants under Josie's direction.

But all this came with the years. When Josie Fifer, white and weak, first took charge of the H. & L. *lares et penates*, she told herself it was only for a few months—a year or two at most. The end of sixteen years found her still there.

When she came to New York, "Splendour" was just beginning its phenomenal three years' run. The city was mad about the play. People came to see it again and again—a sure sign of a long run. The Sarah Haddon second-act costume was photographed, copied (unsuccessfully), talked about, until it became as familiar as a uniform. That costume had much to do with the play's success, though Sarah Haddon would never admit it. "Splendour" was what is known as a period play. The famous dress was of black velvet, made with a quaint, full-gathered skirt that made Haddon's slim waist seem fairylike and exquisitely supple. The black velvet bodice outlined the delicate swell of the bust. A rope of pearls enhanced the whiteness of her throat. Her hair, done in old-time scallops about her forehead, was a gleaming marvel of simplicity, and the despair of every woman who tried to copy it. The part was that of an Italian opera singer. The play pulsated with romance and love, glamour and tragedy. Sarah Haddon, in her flowing black velvet robe and her pearls and her pallor, was an exotic, throbbing, exquisite realisation of what every woman in the audience dreamed of being and every man dreamed of loving.

Josie Fifer saw the play for the first time from a balcony seat given her by Sid Hahn. It left her trembling, red-eyed, shaken. After that she used to see it, by hook or crook whenever possible. She used to come in at the stage door and lurk back of the scenes and in the wings when she had no business there. She invented absurd errands to take her to the theatre where "Splendour" was playing. Sid Hahn always said that after the big third-act scene he liked to watch the audience swim up the aisle. Josie, hidden in the back-stage shadows, used to watch, fascinated, breathless. Then, one night, she indiscreetly was led, by her, absorbed interest, to venture too far into the wings. It was during the scene where Haddon, hearing a broken-down street singer cracking the golden notes of "Aïda" into a thousand mutilated fragments, throws open her window and, leaning far out, pours a shower of Italian and broken English and laughter and silver coin upon her amazed compatriot below.

When the curtain went down she came off raging.

"What was that? Who was that standing in the wings? How dare any one stand there! Everybody knows I can't have any one in the wings. Staring! It ruined my scene to-night. Where's McCabe? Tell Mr. Hahn I want to see him. Who was it? Staring at me like a ghost!"

Josie had crept away, terrified, contrite, and yet resentful. But the next week saw her back at the theatre, though she took care to stay in the shadows.

She was waiting for the black velvet dress. It was more than a dress to her. It was infinitely more than a stage costume. It was the habit of glory. It epitomised all that Josie Fifer had missed of beauty and homage and success.

The play ran on, and on, and on. Sarah Haddon was superstitious about the black gown. She refused to give it up for a new one. She insisted that if ever she discarded the old black velvet for a new the run of the play would stop. She assured Hahn that its shabbiness did not show from the front. She clung to it with that childish unreasonableness that is so often found in people of the stage.

But Josie waited patiently. Dozens of costumes passed through her hands. She saw plays come and go. Dresses came to her whose lining bore the mark of world-famous modistes. She hung them away, or refurbished them if necessary with disinterested conscientiousness. Sometimes her caustic comment, as she did so, would have startled the complacency of the erstwhile wearers of the garments. Her knowledge of the stage, its artifices, its pretence, its narrowness, its shams, was widening and deepening. No critic in bone-rimmed glasses and evening clothes was more scathingly severe than she. She sewed on satin. She mended fine lace. She polished stage jewels. And waited. She knew that one day her patience would be rewarded. And then, at last came the familiar voice over the phone: "Hello, Fifer! McCabe talking."

"Well?"

"'Splendour' closes Saturday. Haddon says she won't play in this heat. They're taking it to London in the autumn. The stuff'll be up Monday, early."

Josie Fifer turned away from the telephone with a face so radiant that one of her sewing women, looking up, was moved to comment.

"Got some good news, Miss Fifer?"

"'Splendour' closes this week."

"Well, my land! To look at you a person would think you'd been losing money at the box office every night it ran."

The look was still on her face when Monday morning came. She was sewing on a dress just discarded by Adelaide French, the tragédienne. Adelaide's maid was said to be the hardest-worked woman in the profession. When French finished with a costume it was useless as a dress; but it was something historic, like a torn and tattered battle flag—an emblem.

McCabe, box under his arm, stood in the doorway. Josie Fifer stood up so suddenly that the dress on her lap fell to the floor. She stepped over it heedlessly, and went toward McCabe, her eyes on the pasteboard box. Behind McCabe stood two more men, likewise box-laden.

"Put them down here," said Josie. The men thumped the boxes down on the long table. Josie's fingers were already at the strings. She opened the first box, emptied its contents, tossed them aside, passed on to the second. Her hands busied themselves among the silks and broadcloth of this; then on to the third and last box. McCabe and his men, with scenery and furniture still to unload and store, turned to go. Their footsteps echoed hollowly as they clattered down the worn old stairway. Josie snapped the cord that bound the third box. Her cheeks were flushed, her eyes bright. She turned it upside down. Then she pawed it over. Then she went back to the contents of the first two boxes, clawing about among the limp garments with which the table was strewn. She was breathing quickly. Suddenly: "It isn't here!" she cried. "It isn't here!" She turned and flew to the stairway. The voices of the men came up to her. She leaned far over the railing. "McCabe! McCabe!"

"Yeh? What do you want?"

"The black velvet dress! The black velvet dress! It isn't there."

"Oh, yeh. That's all right. Haddon, she's got a bug about that dress, and she says she wants to take it to London with her, to use on the opening night. She says if she wears a new one that first night, the play'll be a failure. Some temperament, that girl, since she's got to be a star!"

Josie stood clutching the railing of the stairway. Her disappointment was so bitter that she could not weep. She felt cheated, outraged. She was frightened at the intensity of her own sensations. "She might have let me have it," she said aloud in the dim half light of the hallway. "She's got everything else in the world. She might have let me have that."

Then she went back into the big, bright sewing room. "Splendour" ran three years in London.

During those three years she saw Sid Hahn only three or four times. He spent much of his time abroad. Whenever opportunity presented itself she would say: "Is 'Splendour' still playing in London?"

"Still playing."

The last time Hahn, intuitive as always, had eyed her curiously. "You seem to be interested in that play."

"Oh, well," Josie had replied with assumed carelessness, "it being in Atlantic City just when I had my accident, and then meeting you through that, and all, why, I always kind of felt a personal interest in it." ...

At the end of three years Sarah Haddon returned to New York with an English accent, a slight embonpoint, and a little foreign habit of rushing up to her men friends with a delighted exclamation (preferably French) and kissing them on both cheeks. When Josie Fifer, happening back stage at a rehearsal of the star's new play, first saw her do this a grim gleam came into her eyes.

"Bernhardt's the only woman who can spring that and get away with it," she said to her assistant. "Haddon's got herself sized up wrong. I'll gamble her next play will be a failure."

And it was.

The scenery, props, and costumes of the London production of "Splendour" were slow in coming back. But finally they did come. Josie received them with the calmness that comes of hope deferred. It had been three years since she last saw the play. She told herself, chidingly, that she had been sort of foolish over that play and this costume. Her recent glimpse of Haddon had been somewhat disillusioning. But now, when she finally held the gown itself in her hand—the original "Splendour" second-act gown, a limp, soft black mass: just a few yards of worn and shabby velvet—she found her hands shaking. Here was where she had hugged the toy dog to her breast. Here where she had fallen on her knees to pray before the little shrine in her hotel room. Every worn spot had a meaning for her. Every mark told a story. Her fingers smoothed it tenderly.

"Not much left of that," said one of the sewing girls, glancing up. "I guess Sarah would have a hard time making the hooks and eyes meet now. They say she's come home from London looking a little too prosperous."

Josie did not answer. She folded the dress over her arm and carried it to the wardrobe room. There she hung it away in an empty closet, quite apart from the other historic treasures. And there it hung, untouched, until the following Sunday.

On Sunday morning East Forty-third Street bears no more resemblance to the week-day Forty-third than does a stiffly starched and subdued Sabbath-school scholar to his Monday morning self. Strangely quiet it is, and unfrequented. Josie Fifer, scurrying along in the unwonted stillness, was prompted to throw a furtive glance over her shoulder now and then, as though afraid of being caught at some criminal act. She ran up the little flight of steps with a rush, unlocked the door with trembling fingers, and let herself into the cool, dank gloom of the storehouse hall. The metal door of the elevator stared inquiringly after her. She fled past it to the stairway. Every step of that ancient structure squeaked and groaned. First floor, second, third, fourth. The everyday hum of the sewing machines was absent. The room seemed to be holding its breath. Josie fancied that the very garments on the worktables lifted themselves inquiringly from their supine position to see what it was that disturbed their Sabbath rest. Josie, a tense, wide-eyed, frightened little figure, stood in the centre of the vast room, listening to she knew not what. Then, relaxing, she gave a nervous little laugh and, reaching up, unpinned her hat. She threw it on a near-by table and disappeared into the wardrobe room beyond.

Minutes passed—an hour. She did not come back. From the room beyond came strange sounds—a woman's voice; the thrill of a song; cries; the anguish of tears; laughter, harsh and high, as a desperate and deceived woman laughs—all this following in such rapid succession that Sid Hahn, puffing laboriously up the four flights of stairs leading to the wardrobe floor, entered the main room unheard. Unknown to any one, he was indulging in one of his unsuspected visits to the old wareroom that housed the evidence of past and gone successes—successes that had brought him fortune and fame, but little real happiness, perhaps. No one knew that he loved to browse among these pathetic rags of a forgotten triumph. No one would have dreamed that this chubby little man could glow and weep over the cast-off garment of a famous Cyrano, or the faded finery of a Zaza.

At the doorway he paused now, startled. He was listening with every nerve of his taut body. What? Who? He tiptoed across the room with a step incredibly light for one so stout, peered cautiously around the side of the doorway, and leaned up against it weakly. Josie Fifer, in the black velvet and mock pearls of "Splendour," with her grey-streaked blonde hair hidden under the romantic scallops of a black wig, was giving the big scene from the third act. And though it sounded like a burlesque of that famous passage, and though she limped more than ever as she reeled to an imaginary shrine in the corner, and though the black wig was slightly askew by now, and the black velvet hung with bunchy awkwardness about her skinny little body, there was nothing of mirth in Sid Hahn's face as he gazed. He shrank back now.

She was coming to the big speech at the close of the act—the big renunciation speech that was the curtain. Sid Hahn turned and tiptoed painfully, breathlessly, magnificently, out of the big front room, into the hallway, down the creaking stairs, and so to the sunshine of Forty-third Street, with its unaccustomed Sunday-morning quiet. And he was smiling that rare and melting smile of his—the smile that was said to make him look something like a kewpie, and something like a cupid, and a bit like an imp, and very much like an angel. There was little of the first three in it now, and very much of the last. And so he got heavily into his very grand motor car and drove off.

"Why, the poor little kid," said he—"the poor, lonely, stifled little crippled-up kid."

"I beg your pardon, sir?" inquired his chauffeur.

"Speak when you're spoken to," snapped Sid Hahn.

And here it must be revealed to you that Sid Hahn did not marry the Cinderella of the storage warehouse. He did not marry anybody, and neither did Josie. And yet there is a bit more to this story—ten years more, if you must know—ten years, the end of which found Josie a sparse, spectacled, and agile little cripple, as alert and caustic as ever. It found Sid Hahn the most famous theatrical man of his day. It found Sarah Haddon at the fag-end of a career that had blazed with triumph and adulation. She had never had a success like "Splendour." Indeed, there were those who said that all the plays that followed had been failures, carried to semi-success on the strength of that play's glorious past. She eschewed low-cut gowns now. She knew that it is the telltale throat which first shows the marks of age. She knew, too, why Bernhardt, in "Camille," always died in a high-necked nightgown. She took to wearing high, ruffled things about her throat, and softening, kindly chiffons.

And then, in a mistaken moment, they planned a revival of "Splendour." Sarah Haddon would again play the part that had become a classic. Fathers had told their children of it—of her beauty, her golden voice, the exquisite grace of her, the charm, the tenderness, the pathos. And they told them of the famous black velvet dress, and how in it she had moved like a splendid, buoyant bird.

So they revived "Splendour." And men and women brought their sons and daughters to see. And what they saw was a stout, middle-aged woman in a too-tight black velvet dress that made her look like a dowager. And when this woman flopped down on her knees in the big scene at the close of the last act she had a rather dreadful time of it getting up again. And the audience, resentful, bewildered, cheated of a precious memory, laughed. That laugh sealed the career of Sarah Haddon. It is a fickle thing, this public that wants to be amused; fickle and cruel and—paradoxically enough—true to its superstitions. The Sarah Haddon of eighteen years ago was one of these. They would have none of this fat, puffy, ample-bosomed woman who was trying to blot her picture from their memory. "Away with her!" cried the critics through the columns of next morning's paper. And Sarah Haddon's day was done.

"It's because I didn't wear the original black velvet dress!" cried she, with the unreasoning rage for which she had always been famous. "If I had worn it, everything would have been different. That dress had a good-luck charm. Where is it? I want it. I don't care if they do take off the play. I want it. I want it."

"Why, child," Sid Hahn said soothingly, "that dress has probably fallen into dust by this time."

"Dust! What do you mean? How old do you think I am? That you should say that to me! I've made millions for you, and now—"

"Now, now, Sally, be a good girl. That's all rot about that dress being lucky. You've grown out of this part; that's all. We'll find another play—"

"I want that dress."

Sid Hahn flushed uncomfortably. "Well, if you must know, I gave it away."

"To whom?"

"To—to Josie Fifer. She took a notion to it, and so I told her she could have it." Then, as Sarah Haddon rose, dried her eyes, and began to straighten her hat: "Where are you going?" He trailed her to the door worriedly. "Now, Sally, don't do anything foolish. You're just tired and overstrung. Where are you—"

"I am going to see Josie Fifer."

"Now, look here, Sarah!"

But she was off, and Sid Hahn could only follow after, the showman in him anticipating the scene that was to follow. When he reached the fourth floor of the storehouse Sarah Haddon was there ahead of him. The two women—one tall, imperious, magnificent in furs; the other shrunken, deformed, shabby—stood staring at each other from opposites sides of the worktable. And between them, in a crumpled, grey-black heap, lay the velvet gown.

"I don't care who says you can have it," Josie Fifer's shrill voice was saying. "It's mine, and I'm going to keep it. Mr. Hahn himself gave it to me. He said I could cut it up for a dress or something if I wanted to. Long ago." Then, as Sid Hahn himself appeared, she appealed to him. "There he is now. Didn't you, Mr. Hahn? Didn't you say I could have it? Years ago?"

"Yes, Jo," said Sid Hahn. "It's yours, to do with as you wish."

Sarah Haddon, who never had been denied anything in all her pampered life, turned to him now. Her bosom rose and fell. She was breathing sharply. "But S.H.!" she cried, "S.H., I've got to have it. Don't you see, I want it! It's all I've got left in the world of what I used to be. I want it!" She began to cry, and it was not acting.

Josie Fifer stood staring at her, her eyes wide with horror and unbelief.

"Why, say, listen! Listen! You can have it. I didn't know you wanted it as bad as that. Why, you can have it. I want you to take it. Here."

She shoved it across the table. Sarah reached out for it quickly. She rolled it up in a tight bundle and whisked off with it without a backward glance at Josie or at Hahn. She was still sobbing as she went down the stairs.

10

The two stood staring at each other ludicrously. Hahn spoke first.

"I'm sorry, Josie. That was nice of you, giving it to her like that."

But Josie did not seem to hear. At least she paid no attention to his remark. She was staring at him with that dazed and wide-eyed look of one upon whom a great truth has just dawned. Then, suddenly, she began to laugh. She laughed a high, shrill laugh that was not so much an expression of mirth as of relief.

Sid Hahn put up a pudgy hand in protest. "Josie! Please! For the love of Heaven don't *you* go and get it. I've had to do with one hysterical woman to-day. Stop that laughing! Stop it!"

Josie stopped, not abruptly, but in a little series of recurring giggles. Then these subsided and she was smiling. It wasn't at all her usual smile. The bitterness was quite gone from it. She faced Sid Hahn across the table. Her palms were outspread, as one who would make things plain. "I wasn't hysterical. I was just laughing. I've been about seventeen years earning that laugh. Don't grudge it to me."

"Let's have the plot," said Hahn.

"There isn't any. You see, it's just—well, I've just discovered how it works out. After all these years! She's had everything she wanted all her life. And me, I've never had anything. Not a thing. She's travelled one way, and I've travelled in the opposite direction, and where has it brought us? Here we are, both fighting over an old black velvet rag. Don't you see? Both wanting the same—" She broke off, with the little twisted smile on her lips again. "Life's a strange thing, Mr. Hahn."

"I hope, Josie, you don't claim any originality for that remark," replied Sid Hahn dryly.

"But," argued the editor, "you don't call this a cheerful story, I hope."

"Well, perhaps not exactly boisterous. But it teaches a lesson, and all that. And it's sort of philosophical and everything, don't you think?"

The editor shuffled the sheets together decisively, so that they formed a neat sheaf. "I'm afraid I didn't make myself quite clear. It's entertaining, and all that, but—ah—in view of our present needs, I'm sorry to say we—"

II
THE GAY OLD DOG

Those of you who have dwelt—or even lingered—in Chicago, Illinois (this is not a humorous story), are familiar with the region known as the Loop. For those others of you to whom Chicago is a transfer point between New York and San Francisco there is presented this brief explanation:

The Loop is a clamorous, smoke-infested district embraced by the iron arms of the elevated tracks. In a city boasting fewer millions, it would be known familiarly as downtown. From Congress to Lake Street, from Wabash almost to the river, those thunderous tracks make a complete circle, or loop. Within it lie the retail shops, the commercial hotels, the theatres, the restaurants. It is the Fifth Avenue (diluted) and the Broadway (deleted) of Chicago. And he who frequents it by night in search of amusement and cheer is known, vulgarly, as a Loop-hound.

Jo Hertz was a Loop-hound. On the occasion of those sparse first nights granted the metropolis of the Middle West he was always present, third row, aisle, left. When a new loop café was opened Jo's table always commanded an unobstructed view of anything worth viewing. On entering he was wont to say, "Hello, Gus," with careless cordiality to the head waiter, the while his eye roved expertly from table to table as he removed his gloves. He ordered things under glass, so that his table, at midnight or thereabouts, resembled a hot-bed that favours the bell system. The waiters fought for him. He was the kind of man who mixes his own salad dressing. He liked to call for a bowl, some cracked ice, lemon, garlic, paprika, salt, pepper, vinegar, and oil and make a rite of it. People at near-by tables would lay down their knives and forks to watch, fascinated. The secret of it seemed to lie in using all the oil in sight and calling for more.

That was Jo—a plump and lonely bachelor of fifty. A plethoric, roving-eyed and kindly man, clutching vainly at the garments of a youth that had long slipped past him. Jo Hertz, in one of those pinch-waist belted suits and a trench coat and a little green hat, walking up Michigan Avenue of a bright winter's afternoon, trying to take the curb with a jaunty youthfulness against which every one of his fat-encased muscles rebelled, was a sight for mirth or pity, depending on one's vision.

The gay-dog business was a late phase in the life of Jo Hertz. He had been a quite different sort of canine. The staid and harassed brother of three unwed and selfish sisters is an under dog. The tale of how Jo Hertz came to be a Loop-hound should not be compressed within the limits of a short story. It should be told as are the photo plays, with frequent throwbacks and many cut-ins. To condense twenty-three years of a man's life into some five or six thousand words requires a verbal economy amounting to parsimony.

At twenty-seven Jo had been the dutiful, hard-working son (in the wholesale harness business) of a widowed and gummidging mother, who called him Joey. If you had looked close you would have seen that now and then a double wrinkle would appear between Jo's eyes—a wrinkle that had no business there at twenty-seven. Then Jo's mother died, leaving him handicapped by a death-bed promise, the three sisters and a three-story-and-basement house on Calumet Avenue. Jo's wrinkle became a fixture.

Death-bed promises should be broken as lightly as they are seriously made. The dead have no right to lay their clammy fingers upon the living.

"Joey," she had said, in her high, thin voice, "take care of the girls."

"I will, Ma," Jo had choked.

"Joey," and the voice was weaker, "promise me you won't marry till the girls are all provided for." Then as Joe had hesitated, appalled: "Joey, it's my dying wish. Promise!"

"I promise, Ma," he had said.

Whereupon his mother had died, comfortably, leaving him with a completely ruined life.

They were not bad-looking girls, and they had a certain style, too. That is, Stell and Eva had. Carrie, the middle one, taught school over on the West Side. In those days it took her almost two hours each way. She said the kind of costume she required should have been corrugated steel. But all three knew what was being worn, and they wore it—or fairly faithful copies of it. Eva, the housekeeping sister, had a needle knack. She could skim the State Street windows and come away with a mental photograph of every separate tuck, hem, yoke, and ribbon. Heads of departments showed her the things they kept in drawers, and she went home and reproduced them with the aid of a two-dollar-a-day seamstress. Stell, the youngest, was the beauty. They called her Babe. She wasn't really a beauty, but some one had once told her that she looked like Janice Meredith (it was when that work of fiction was at the height of its popularity). For years afterward, whenever she went to parties, she affected a single, fat curl over her right shoulder, with a rose stuck through it.

Twenty-three years ago one's sisters did not strain at the household leash, nor crave a career. Carrie taught school, and hated it. Eva kept house expertly and complainingly. Babe's profession was being the family beauty, and it took all her spare time. Eva always let her sleep until ten.

This was Jo's household, and he was the nominal head of it. But it was an empty title. The three women dominated his life. They weren't consciously selfish. If you had called them cruel they would have put you down as mad. When you are the lone brother of three sisters, it means that you must constantly be calling for, escorting, or dropping one of them somewhere. Most men of Jo's age were standing before their mirror of a Saturday night, whistling blithely and abstractedly while they discarded a blue polka-dot for a maroon tie, whipped off the maroon for a shot-silk, and at the last moment decided against the shot-silk in favor of a plain black-and-white, because she had once said she preferred quiet ties. Jo, when he should have been preening his feathers for conquest, was saying:

"Well, my God, I *am* hurrying! Give a man time, can't you? I just got home. You girls have been laying around the house all day. No wonder you're ready."

He took a certain pride in seeing his sisters well dressed, at a time when he should have been reveling in fancy waistcoats and brilliant-hued socks, according to the style of that day, and the inalienable right of any unwed male under thirty, in any day. On those rare occasions when his business necessitated an out-of-town trip, he would spend half a day floundering about the shops, selecting handkerchiefs, or stockings, or feathers, or fans, or gloves for the girls. They always turned out to be the wrong kind, judging by their reception.

From Carrie, "What in the world do I want of a fan!"

"I thought you didn't have one," Jo would say.

"I haven't. I never go to dances."

Jo would pass a futile hand over the top of his head, as was his way when disturbed. "I just thought you'd like one. I thought every girl liked a fan. Just," feebly, "just to—to have."

"Oh, for pity's sake!"

And from Eva or Babe, "I've *got* silk stockings, Jo." Or, "You brought me handkerchiefs the last time."

There was something selfish in his giving, as there always is in any gift freely and joyfully made. They never suspected the exquisite pleasure it gave him to select these things; these fine, soft, silken things. There were many things about this slow-going, amiable brother of theirs that they never suspected. If you had told them he was a dreamer of dreams, for example, they would have been amused. Sometimes, dead-tired by nine o'clock, after a hard day down town, he would doze over the evening paper. At intervals he would wake, red-eyed, to a snatch of conversation such as, "Yes, but if you get a blue you can wear it anywhere. It's dressy, and at the same time it's quiet, too." Eva, the expert, wrestling with Carrie over the problem of the new spring dress. They never guessed that the commonplace man in the frayed old smoking-jacket had banished them all from the room long ago; had banished himself, for that matter. In his place was a tall, debonair, and rather dangerously handsome man to whom six o'clock spelled evening clothes. The kind of man who can lean up against a mantel, or propose a toast, or give an order to a man-servant, or whisper a gallant speech in a lady's ear with equal ease. The shabby old house on Calumet Avenue was transformed into a brocaded and chandeliered rendezvous for the brilliance of the city. Beauty was here, and wit. But none so beautiful and witty as She. Mrs.—er—Jo Hertz. There was wine, of course; but no vulgar display. There was music; the soft sheen of satin; laughter. And he the gracious, tactful host, king of his own domain—

"Jo, for heaven's sake, if you're going to snore go to bed!"

"Why—did I fall asleep?"

"You haven't been doing anything else all evening. A person would think you were fifty instead of thirty."

And Jo Hertz was again just the dull, grey, commonplace brother of three well-meaning sisters.

Babe used to say petulantly, "Jo, why don't you ever bring home any of your men friends? A girl might as well not have any brother, all the good you do."

Jo, conscience-stricken, did his best to make amends. But a man who has been petticoat-ridden for years loses the knack, somehow, of comradeship with men. He acquires, too, a knowledge of women, and a distaste for them, equalled only, perhaps, by that of an elevator-starter in a department store.

Which brings us to one Sunday in May. Jo came home from a late Sunday afternoon walk to find company for supper. Carrie often had in one of her school-teacher friends, or Babe one of her frivolous intimates, or even Eva a staid guest of the old-girl type. There was always a Sunday night supper of potato salad, and cold meat, and coffee, and perhaps a fresh cake. Jo rather enjoyed it, being a hospitable soul. But he regarded the guests with the undazzled eyes of a man to whom they were just so many petticoats, timid of the night streets and requiring escort home. If you had suggested to him that some of his sisters' popularity was due to his own presence, or if you had hinted that the more kittenish of these visitors were probably making eyes at him, he would have stared in amazement and unbelief.

This Sunday night it turned out to be one of Carrie's friends.

"Emily," said Carrie, "this is my brother, Jo."

Jo had learned what to expect in Carrie's friends. Drab-looking women in the late thirties, whose facial lines all slanted downward.

"Happy to meet you," said Jo, and looked down at a different sort altogether. A most surprisingly different sort, for one of Carrie's friends. This Emily person was very small, and fluffy, and blue-eyed, and sort of—well, crinkly looking. You know. The corners of her mouth when she smiled, and her eyes when she looked up at you, and her hair, which was brown, but had the miraculous effect, somehow, of being golden.

Jo shook hands with her. Her hand was incredibly small, and soft, so that you were afraid of crushing it, until you discovered she had a firm little grip all her own. It surprised and amused you, that grip, as does a baby's unexpected clutch on your patronising forefinger. As Jo felt it in his own big clasp, the strangest thing happened to him. Something inside Jo Hertz stopped working for a moment, then lurched sickeningly, then thumped like mad. It was his heart. He stood staring down at her, and she up at him, until the others laughed. Then their hands fell apart, lingeringly.

"Are you a school-teacher, Emily?" he said.

"Kindergarten. It's my first year. And don't call me Emily, please."

"Why not? It's your name. I think it's the prettiest name in the world." Which he hadn't meant to say at all. In fact, he was perfectly aghast to find himself saying it. But he meant it.

At supper he passed her things, and stared, until everybody laughed again, and Eva said acidly, "Why don't you feed her?"

It wasn't that Emily had an air of helplessness. She just made you feel you wanted her to be helpless, so that you could help her.

Jo took her home, and from that Sunday night he began to strain at the leash. He took his sisters out, dutifully, but he would suggest, with a carelessness that deceived no one, "Don't you want one of your girl friends to come along? That little What's-her-name—Emily, or something. So long's I've got three of you, I might as well have a full squad."

For a long time he didn't know what was the matter with him. He only knew he was miserable, and yet happy. Sometimes his heart seemed to ache with an actual physical ache. He realised that he wanted to do things for Emily. He wanted to buy things for Emily—useless, pretty, expensive things that he couldn't afford. He wanted to buy everything that Emily needed, and everything that Emily desired. He wanted to marry Emily. That was it. He discovered that one day, with a shock, in the midst of a transaction in the harness business. He stared at the man with whom he was dealing until that startled person grew uncomfortable.

"What's the matter, Hertz?"

"Matter?"

"You look as if you'd seen a ghost or found a gold mine. I don't know which."

"Gold mine," said Jo. And then, "No. Ghost."

For he remembered that high, thin voice, and his promise. And the harness business was slithering downhill with dreadful rapidity, as the automobile business began its amazing climb. Jo tried to stop it. But he was not that kind of business man. It never occurred to him to jump out of the down-going vehicle and catch the up-going one. He stayed on, vainly applying brakes that refused to work.

"You know, Emily, I couldn't support two households now. Not the way things are. But if you'll wait. If you'll only wait. The girls might—that is, Babe and Carrie—"

She was a sensible little thing, Emily. "Of course I'll wait. But we mustn't just sit back and let the years go by. We've got to help."

She went about it as if she were already a little match-making matron. She corralled all the men she had ever known and introduced them to Babe, Carrie, and Eva separately, in pairs, and *en masse*. She arranged parties at which Babe could display the curl. She got up picnics. She stayed home while Jo took the three about. When she was present she tried to look as plain and obscure as possible, so that the sisters should show up to advantage. She schemed, and planned, and contrived, and hoped; and smiled into Jo's despairing eyes.

And three years went by. Three precious years. Carrie still taught school, and hated it. Eva kept house, more and more complainingly as prices advanced and allowance retreated. Stell was still Babe, the family beauty; but even she knew that the time was past for curls. Emily's hair, somehow, lost its glint and began to look just plain brown. Her crinkliness began to iron out.

"Now, look here!" Jo argued, desperately, one night. "We could be happy, anyway. There's plenty of room at the house. Lots of people begin that way. Of course, I couldn't give you all I'd like to, at first. But maybe, after a while—"

No dreams of salons, and brocade, and velvet-footed servitors, and satin damask now. Just two rooms, all their own, all alone, and Emily to work for. That was his dream. But it seemed less possible than that other absurd one had been.

You know that Emily was as practical a little thing as she looked fluffy. She knew women. Especially did she know Eva, and Carrie, and Babe. She tried to imagine herself taking the household affairs and the housekeeping pocketbook out of Eva's expert hands. Eva had once displayed to her a sheaf of aigrettes she had bought with what she saved out of the housekeeping money. So then she tried to picture herself allowing the reins of Jo's house to remain in Eva's hands. And everything feminine and normal in her rebelled. Emily knew she'd want to put away her own freshly laundered linen, and smooth it, and pat it. She was that kind of woman. She knew she'd want to do her own delightful haggling with butcher and vegetable pedlar. She knew she'd want to muss Jo's hair, and sit on his knee, and even quarrel with him, if necessary, without the awareness of three ever-present pairs of maiden eyes and ears.

"No! No! We'd only be miserable. I know. Even if they didn't object. And they would, Jo. Wouldn't they?"

His silence was miserable assent. Then, "But you do love me, don't you, Emily?"

"I do, Jo. I love you—and love you—and love you. But, Jo, I—can't."

"I know it, dear. I knew it all the time, really. I just thought, maybe, somehow—"

The two sat staring for a moment into space, their hands clasped. Then they both shut their eyes, with a little shudder, as though what they saw was terrible to look upon. Emily's hand, the tiny hand that was so unexpectedly firm, tightened its hold on his, and his crushed the absurd fingers until she winced with pain.

That was the beginning of the end, and they knew it.

Emily wasn't the kind of girl who would be left to pine. There are too many Jo's in the world whose hearts are prone to lurch and then thump at the feel of a soft, fluttering, incredibly small hand in their grip. One year later Emily was married to a young man whose father owned a large, pie-shaped slice of the prosperous state of Michigan.

That being safely accomplished, there was something grimly humorous in the trend taken by affairs in the old house on Calumet. For Eva married. Of all people, Eva! Married well, too, though he was a great deal older than she. She went off in a hat she had copied from a French model at Field's, and a suit she had contrived with a home dressmaker, aided by pressing on the part of the little tailor in the basement over on Thirty-first Street. It was the last of that, though. The next time they saw her, she had on a hat that even she would have despaired of copying, and a suit that sort of melted into your gaze. She moved to the North Side (trust Eva for that), and Babe assumed the management of the household on Calumet Avenue. It was rather a pinched little household now, for the harness business shrank and shrank.

"I don't see how you can expect me to keep house decently on this!" Babe would say contemptuously. Babe's nose, always a little inclined to sharpness, had whittled down to a point of late. "If you knew what Ben gives Eva."

"It's the best I can do, Sis. Business is something rotten."

"Ben says if you had the least bit of—" Ben was Eva's husband, and quotable, as are all successful men.

"I don't care what Ben says," shouted Jo, goaded into rage. "I'm sick of your everlasting Ben. Go and get a Ben of your own, why don't you, if you're so stuck on the way he does things."

And Babe did. She made a last desperate drive, aided by Eva, and she captured a rather surprised young man in the brokerage way, who had made up his mind not to marry for years and years. Eva wanted to give her her wedding things, but at that Jo broke into sudden rebellion.

"No sir! No Ben is going to buy my sister's wedding clothes, understand? I guess I'm not broke—yet. I'll furnish the money for her things, and there'll be enough of them, too."

Babe had as useless a trousseau, and as filled with extravagant pink-and-blue and lacy and frilly things as any daughter of doting parents. Jo seemed to find a grim pleasure in providing them. But it left him pretty well pinched. After Babe's marriage (she insisted that they call her Estelle now) Jo sold the house on Calumet. He and Carrie took one of those little flats that were springing up, seemingly over night, all through Chicago's South Side.

There was nothing domestic about Carrie. She had given up teaching two years before, and had gone into Social Service work on the West Side. She had what is known as a legal mind—hard, clear, orderly—and she made a great success of it. Her dream was to live at the Settlement House and give all her time to the work. Upon the little household she bestowed a certain amount of grim, capable attention. It was the same kind of attention she would have given a piece of machinery whose oiling and running had been entrusted to her care. She hated it, and didn't hesitate to say so.

Jo took to prowling about department store basements, and household goods sections. He was always sending home a bargain in a ham, or a sack of potatoes, or fifty pounds of sugar, or a window clamp, or a new kind of paring knife. He was forever doing odd little jobs that the janitor should have done. It was the domestic in him claiming its own.

Then, one night, Carrie came home with a dull glow in her leathery cheeks, and her eyes alight with resolve. They had what she called a plain talk.

"Listen, Jo. They've offered me the job of first assistant resident worker. And I'm going to take it. Take it! I know fifty other girls who'd give their ears for it. I go in next month."

They were at dinner. Jo looked up from his plate, dully. Then he glanced around the little dining room, with its ugly tan walls and its heavy, dark furniture (the Calumet Avenue pieces fitted cumbersomely into the five-room flat).

"Away? Away from here, you mean—to live?" Carrie laid down her fork. "Well, really, Jo! After all that explanation."

"But to go over there to live! Why, that neighbourhood's full of dirt, and disease, and crime, and the Lord knows what all. I can't let you do that, Carrie."

Carrie's chin came up. She laughed a short little laugh. "Let me! That's eighteenth-century talk, Jo. My life's my own to live. I'm going."

And she went.

Jo stayed on in the apartment until the lease was up. Then he sold what furniture he could, stored or gave away the rest, and took a room on Michigan Avenue in one of the old stone mansions whose decayed splendour was being put to such purpose.

Jo Hertz was his own master. Free to marry. Free to come and go. And he found he didn't even think of marrying. He didn't even want to come or go, particularly. A rather frumpy old bachelor, with thinning hair and a thickening neck. Much has been written about the unwed, middle-aged woman; her fussiness, her primness, her angularity of mind and body. In the male that same fussiness develops, and a certain primness, too. But he grows flabby where she grows lean.

Every Thursday evening he took dinner at Eva's, and on Sunday noon at Stell's. He tucked his napkin under his chin and openly enjoyed the home-made soup and the well-cooked meats. After dinner he tried to talk business with Eva's husband, or Stell's. His business talks were the old-fashioned kind, beginning:

"Well, now, looka here. Take, f'rinstance your raw hides and leathers."

But Ben and George didn't want to "take, f'rinstance, your raw hides and leathers." They wanted, when they took anything at all, to take golf, or politics or stocks. They were the modern type of business man who prefers to leave his work out of his play. Business, with them, was a profession—a finely graded and balanced thing, differing from Jo's clumsy, downhill style as completely as does the method of a great criminal detective differ from that of a village constable. They would listen, restively, and say, "Uh-uh," at intervals, and at the first chance they would sort of fade out of the room, with a meaning glance at their wives. Eva had two children now. Girls. They treated Uncle Jo with good-natured tolerance. Stell had no children. Uncle Jo degenerated, by almost imperceptible degrees, from the position of honoured guest, who is served with white meat, to that of one who is content with a leg and one of those obscure and bony sections which, after much turning with a bewildered and investigating knife and fork, leave one baffled and unsatisfied.

Eva and Stell got together and decided that Jo ought to marry.

"It isn't natural," Eva told him. "I never saw a man who took so little interest in women."

"Me!" protested Jo, almost shyly. "Women!"

"Yes. Of course. You act like a frightened schoolboy."

So they had in for dinner certain friends and acquaintances of fitting age. They spoke of them as "splendid girls." Between thirty-six and forty. They talked awfully well, in a firm, clear way, about civics, and classes, and politics, and economics, and boards. They rather terrified Jo. He didn't understand much that they talked about, and he felt humbly inferior, and yet a little resentful, as if something had passed him by. He escorted them home, dutifully, though they told him not to bother, and they evidently meant it. They seemed capable, not only of going home quite unattended, but of delivering a pointed lecture to any highwayman or brawler who might molest them.

The following Thursday Eva would say, "How did you like her, Jo?"

"Like who?" Jo would spar feebly.

"Miss Matthews."

"Who's she?"

"Now, don't be funny, Jo. You know very well I mean the girl who was here for dinner. The one who talked so well on the emigration question.

"Oh, her! Why, I liked her all right. Seems to be a smart woman."

"Smart! She's a perfectly splendid girl."

"Sure," Jo would agree cheerfully.

"But didn't you like her?"

"I can't say I did, Eve. And I can't say I didn't. She made me think a lot of a teacher I had in the fifth reader. Name of Himes. As I recall her, she must have been a fine woman. But I never thought of her as a woman at all. She was just Teacher."

"You make me tired," snapped Eva impatiently. "A man of your age. You don't expect to marry a girl, do you? A child!"

"I don't expect to marry anybody," Jo had answered.

And that was the truth, lonely though he often was.

The following spring Eva moved to Winnetka. Any one who got the meaning of the Loop knows the significance of a move to a north-shore suburb, and a house. Eva's daughter, Ethel, was growing up, and her mother had an eye on society.

That did away with Jo's Thursday dinner. Then Stell's husband bought a car. They went out into the country every Sunday. Stell said it was getting so that maids objected to Sunday dinners, anyway. Besides, they were unhealthy, old-fashioned things. They always meant to ask Jo to come along, but by the time their friends were placed, and the lunch, and the boxes, and sweaters, and George's camera, and everything, there seemed to be no room for a man of Jo's bulk. So that eliminated the Sunday dinners.

"Just drop in any time during the week," Stell said, "for dinner. Except Wednesday—that's our bridge night—and Saturday. And, of course, Thursday. Cook is out that night. Don't wait for me to phone."

And so Jo drifted into that sad-eyed, dyspeptic family made up of those you see dining in second-rate restaurants, their paper propped up against the bowl of oyster crackers, munching solemnly and with indifference to the stare of the passer-by surveying them through the brazen plate-glass window.

And then came the War. The war that spelled death and destruction to millions. The war that brought a fortune to Jo Hertz, and transformed him, over night, from a baggy-kneed old bachelor, whose business was a failure, to a prosperous manufacturer whose only trouble was the shortage in hides for the making of his product—leather! The armies of Europe called for it. Harnesses! More harnesses! Straps! Millions of straps. More! More!

The musty old harness business over on Lake Street was magically changed from a dust-covered, dead-alive concern to an orderly hive that hummed and glittered with success. Orders poured in. Jo Hertz had inside information on the War. He knew about troops and horses. He talked with French and English and Italian buyers—noblemen, many of them—commissioned by their countries to get American-made supplies. And now, when he said to Ben or George, "Take f'rinstance your raw hides and leathers," they listened with respectful attention.

And then began the gay-dog business in the life of Jo Hertz. He developed into a Loop-hound, ever keen on the scent of fresh pleasure. That side of Jo Hertz which had been repressed and crushed and ignored began to bloom, unhealthily. At first he spent money on his rather contemptuous nieces. He sent them gorgeous fans, and watch bracelets, and velvet bags. He took two expensive rooms at a downtown hotel, and there was something more tear-compelling than grotesque about the way he gloated over the luxury of a separate ice-water tap in the bathroom. He explained it.

"Just turn it on. Ice-water! Any hour of the day or night."

He bought a car. Naturally. A glittering affair; in colour a bright blue, with pale blue leather straps and a great deal of gold fittings, and wire wheels. Eva said it was the kind of thing a soubrette would use, rather than an elderly business man. You saw him driving about in it, red-faced and rather awkward at the wheel. You saw him, too, in the Pompeian room at the Congress Hotel of a Saturday afternoon when doubtful and roving-eyed matrons in kolinsky capes are wont to congregate to sip pale amber drinks. Actors grew to recognise the semi-bald head and the shining, round, good-natured face looming out at them from the dim well of the parquet, and sometimes, in a musical show, they directed a quip at him, and he liked it. He could pick out the critics as they came down the aisle, and even had a nodding acquaintance with two of them.

"Kelly, of the *Herald*," he would say carelessly. "Bean, of the *Trib*. They're all afraid of him."

So he frolicked, ponderously. In New York he might have been called a Man About Town.

And he was lonesome. He was very lonesome. So he searched about in his mind and brought from the dim past the memory of the luxuriously furnished establishment of which he used to dream in the evenings when he dozed over his paper in the old house on Calumet. So he rented an apartment, many-roomed and expensive, with a man-servant in charge, and furnished it in styles and periods ranging through all the Louises. The living room was mostly rose colour. It was like an unhealthy and bloated boudoir. And yet there was nothing sybaritic or uncleanly in the sight of this paunchy, middle-aged man sinking into the rosy-cushioned luxury of his ridiculous home. It was a frank and naïve indulgence of long-starved senses, and there was in it a great resemblance to the rolling eyed ecstasy of a schoolboy smacking his lips over an all-day sucker.

The War went on, and on, and on. And the money continued to roll in—a flood of it. Then, one afternoon, Eva, in town on shopping bent, entered a small, exclusive, and expensive shop on Michigan Avenue. Exclusive, that is, in price. Eva's weakness, you may remember, was hats. She was seeking a hat now. She described what she sought with a languid conciseness, and stood looking about her after the saleswoman had vanished in quest of it. The room was becomingly rose-illumined and somewhat dim, so that some minutes had passed before she realised that a man seated on a raspberry brocade settee not five feet away—a man with a walking stick, and yellow gloves, and tan spats, and a check suit—was her brother Jo. From him Eva's wild-eyed glance leaped to the woman who was trying on hats before one of the many long mirrors. She was seated, and a saleswoman was exclaiming discreetly at her elbow.

Eva turned sharply and encountered her own saleswoman returning, hat-laden. "Not to-day," she gasped. "I'm feeling ill. Suddenly." And almost ran from the room.

That evening she told Stell, relating her news in that telephone pidgin-English devised by every family of married sisters as protection against the neighbours and Central. Translated, it ran thus:

"He looked straight at me. My dear, I thought I'd die! But at least he had sense enough not to speak. She was one of those limp, willowy creatures with the greediest eyes that she tried to keep softened to a baby stare, and couldn't, she was so crazy to get her hands on those hats. I saw it all in one awful minute. You know the way I do. I suppose some people would call her pretty. I don't. And her colour! Well! And the most expensive-looking hats. Aigrettes, and paradise, and feathers. Not one of them under seventy-five. Isn't it disgusting! At his age! Suppose Ethel had been with me!"

The next time it was Stell who saw them. In a restaurant. She said it spoiled her evening. And the third time it was Ethel. She was one of the guests at a theatre party given by Nicky Overton II. You know. The North Shore Overtons. Lake Forest. They came in late, and occupied the entire third row at the opening performance of "Believe Me!" And Ethel was Nicky's partner. She was glowing like a rose. When the lights went up after the first act Ethel saw that her uncle Jo was seated just ahead of her with what she afterward described as a blonde. Then her uncle had turned around, and seeing her, had been surprised into a smile that spread genially all over his plump and rubicund face. Then he had turned to face forward again, quickly.

"Who's the old bird?" Nicky had asked. Ethel had pretended not to hear, so he had asked again.

"My Uncle," Ethel answered, and flushed all over her delicate face, and down to her throat. Nicky had looked at the blonde, and his eyebrows had gone up ever so slightly.

It spoiled Ethel's evening. More than that, as she told her mother of it later, weeping, she declared it had spoiled her life.

Eva talked it over with her husband in that intimate, kimonoed hour that precedes bedtime. She gesticulated heatedly with her hair brush.

"It's disgusting, that's what it is. Perfectly disgusting. There's no fool like an old fool. Imagine! A creature like that. At his time of life."

There exists a strange and loyal kinship among men. "Well, I don't know," Ben said now, and even grinned a little. "I suppose a boy's got to sow his wild oats some time."

"Don't be any more vulgar than you can help," Eva retorted. "And I think you know, as well as I, what it means to have that Overton boy interested in Ethel."

"If he's interested in her," Ben blundered, "I guess the fact that Ethel's uncle went to the theatre with some one who wasn't Ethel's aunt won't cause a shudder to run up and down his frail young frame, will it?"

"All right," Eva had retorted. "If you're not man enough to stop it, I'll have to, that's all. I'm going up there with Stell this week."

They did not notify Jo of their coming. Eva telephoned his apartment when she knew he would be out, and asked his man if he expected his master home to dinner that evening. The man had said yes. Eva arranged to meet Stell in town. They would drive to Jo's apartment together, and wait for him there.

When she reached the city Eva found turmoil there. The first of the American troops to be sent to France were leaving. Michigan Boulevard was a billowing, surging mass: Flags, pennants, banners crowds. All the elements that make for demonstration. And over the whole—quiet. No holiday crowd, this. A solid, determined mass of people waiting patient hours to see the khaki-clads go by. Three years of indefatigable reading had brought them to a clear knowledge of what these boys were going to.

"Isn't it dreadful!" Stell gasped.

"Nicky Overton's only nineteen, thank goodness."

Their car was caught in the jam. When they moved at all it was by inches. When at last they reached Jo's apartment they were flushed, nervous, apprehensive. But he had not yet come in. So they waited.

No, they were not staying to dinner with their brother, they told the relieved houseman.

Jo's home has already been described to you. Stell and Eva, sunk in rose-coloured cushions, viewed it with disgust, and some mirth. They rather avoided each other's eyes.

"Carrie ought to be here," Eva said. They both smiled at the thought of the austere Carrie in the midst of those rosy cushions, and hangings, and lamps. Stell rose and began to walk about, restlessly. She picked up a vase and laid it down; straightened a picture. Eva got up, too, and wandered into the hall. She stood there a moment, listening. Then she turned and passed into Jo's bedroom. And there you knew Jo for what he was.

This room was as bare as the other had been ornate. It was Jo, the clean-minded and simple-hearted, in revolt against the cloying luxury with which he had surrounded himself. The bedroom, of all rooms in any house, reflects the personality of its occupant. True, the actual furniture was panelled, cupid-surmounted, and ridiculous. It had been the fruit of Jo's first orgy of the senses. But now it stood out in that stark little room with an air as incongruous and ashamed as that of a pink tarleton*danseuse* who finds herself in a monk's cell. None of those wall-pictures with which bachelor bedrooms are reputed to be hung. No satin slippers. No scented notes. Two plain-backed military brushes on the chiffonier (and he so nearly hairless!). A little orderly stack of books on the table near the bed. Eva fingered their titles and gave a little gasp. One of them was on gardening.

"Well, of all things!" exclaimed Stell. A book on the War, by an Englishman. A detective story of the lurid type that lulls us to sleep. His shoes ranged in a careful row in the closet, with a shoe-tree in every one of them. There was something speaking about them. They looked so human. Eva shut the door on them, quickly. Some bottles on the dresser. A jar of pomade. An ointment such as a man uses who is growing bald and is panic-stricken too late. An insurance calendar on the wall. Some rhubarb-and-soda mixture on the shelf in the bathroom, and a little box of pepsin tablets.

"Eats all kinds of things at all hours of the night," Eva said, and wandered out into the rose-coloured front room again with the air of one who is chagrined at her failure to find what she has sought. Stell followed her furtively.

"Where do you suppose he can be?" she demanded. "It's"—she glanced at her wrist—"why, it's after six!"

And then there was a little click. The two women sat up, tense. The door opened. Jo came in. He blinked a little. The two women in the rosy room stood up.

"Why—Eve! Why, Babe! Well! Why didn't you let me know?"

"We were just about to leave. We thought you weren't coming home."

Joe came in, slowly.

"I was in the jam on Michigan, watching the boys go by." He sat down, heavily. The light from the window fell on him. And you saw that his eyes were red.

And you'll have to learn why. He had found himself one of the thousands in the jam on Michigan Avenue, as he said. He had a place near the curb, where his big frame shut off the view of the unfortunates behind him. He waited with the placid interest of one who has subscribed to all the funds and societies to which a prosperous, middle-aged business man is called upon to subscribe in war time. Then, just as he was about to leave, impatient at the delay, the crowd had cried, with a queer dramatic, exultant note in its voice, "Here they come! Here come the boys!"

Just at that moment two little, futile, frenzied fists began to beat a mad tattoo on Jo Hertz's broad back. Jo tried to turn in the crowd, all indignant resentment. "Say, looka here!"

The little fists kept up their frantic beating and pushing. And a voice—a choked, high little voice—cried, "Let me by! I can't see! You man, you! You big fat man! My boy's going by—to war—and I can't see! Let me by!"

Jo scrooged around, still keeping his place. He looked down. And upturned to him in agonised appeal was the face of little Emily. They stared at each other for what seemed a long, long time. It was really only the fraction of a second. Then Jo put one great arm firmly around Emily's waist and swung her around in front of him. His great bulk protected her. Emily was clinging to his hand. She was breathing rapidly, as if she had been running. Her eyes were straining up the street.

"Why, Emily, how in the world!—"

"I ran away. Fred didn't want me to come. He said it would excite me too much."

"Fred?"

"My husband. He made me promise to say good-bye to Jo at home."

"Jo?"

"Jo's my boy. And he's going to war. So I ran away. I had to see him. I had to see him go."

She was dry-eyed. Her gaze was straining up the street.

"Why, sure," said Jo. "Of course you want to see him." And then the crowd gave a great roar. There came over Jo a feeling of weakness. He was trembling. The boys went marching by.

"There he is," Emily shrilled, above the din. "There be is! There he is! There he—" And waved a futile little hand. It wasn't so much a wave as a clutching. A clutching after something beyond her reach.

"Which one? Which one, Emily?"

"The handsome one. The handsome one. There!" Her voice quavered and died.

Jo put a steady hand on her shoulder. "Point him out," he commanded. "Show me." And the next instant. "Never mind. I see him."

Somehow, miraculously, he had picked him from among the hundreds. Had picked him as surely as his own father might have. It was Emily's boy. He was marching by, rather stiffly. He was nineteen, and fun-loving, and he had a girl, and he didn't particularly want to go to France and—to go to France. But more than he had hated going, he had hated not to go. So he marched by, looking straight ahead, his jaw set so that his chin stuck out just a little. Emily's boy.

Jo looked at him, and his face flushed purple. His eyes, the hard-boiled eyes of a Loop-hound, took on the look of a sad old man. And suddenly he was no longer Jo, the sport; old J. Hertz, the gay dog. He was Jo Hertz, thirty, in love with life, in love with Emily, and with the stinging blood of young manhood coursing through his veins.

Another minute and the boy had passed on up the broad street—the fine, flag-bedecked street—just one of a hundred service-hats bobbing in rhythmic motion like sandy waves lapping a shore and flowing on.

Then he disappeared altogether.

Emily was clinging to Jo. She was mumbling something, over and over. "I can't. I can't. Don't ask me to. I can't let him go. Like that. I can't."

Jo said a queer thing.

"Why, Emily! We wouldn't have him stay home, would we? We wouldn't want him to do anything different, would we? Not our boy. I'm glad he enlisted. I'm proud of him. So are you glad."

Little by little he quieted her. He took her to the car that was waiting, a worried chauffeur in charge. They said good-bye, awkwardly. Emily's face was a red, swollen mass.

So it was that when Jo entered his own hallway half an hour later he blinked, dazedly, and when the light from the window fell on him you saw that his eyes were red.

Eva was not one to beat about the bush. She sat forward in her chair, clutching her bag rather nervously.

"Now, look here, Jo. Stell and I are here for a reason. We're here to tell you that this thing's got to stop."

"Thing? Stop?"

"You know very well what I mean. You saw me at the milliner's that day. And night before last, Ethel. We're all disgusted. If you must go about with people like that, please have some sense of decency."

Something gathering in Jo's face should have warned her. But he was slumped down in his chair in such a huddle, and he looked so old and fat that she did not heed it. She went on. "You've got us to consider. Your sisters. And your nieces. Not to speak of your own—"

But he got to his feet then, shaking, and at what she saw in his face even Eva faltered and stopped. It wasn't at all the face of a fat, middle-aged sport. It was a face Jovian, terrible.

"You!" he began, low-voiced, ominous. "You!" He raised a great fist high. "You two murderers! You didn't consider me, twenty years ago. You come to me with talk like that. Where's my boy! You killed him, you two, twenty years ago. And now he belongs to somebody else. Where's my son that should have gone marching by to-day?" He flung his arms out in a great gesture of longing. The red veins stood out on his forehead. "Where's my son! Answer me that, you two selfish, miserable women. Where's my son!" Then, as they huddled together, frightened, wild-eyed. "Out of my house! Out of my house! Before I hurt you!"

They fled, terrified. The door banged behind them.

Jo stood, shaking, in the centre of the room. Then he reached for a chair, gropingly, and sat down. He passed one moist, flabby hand over his forehead and it came away wet. The telephone rang. He sat still. It sounded far away and unimportant, like something forgotten. I think he did not even hear it with his conscious ear. But it rang and rang insistently. Jo liked to answer his telephone, when at home.

"Hello!" He knew instantly the voice at the other end.

"That you, Jo?" it said.

"Yes."

"How's my boy?"

"I'm—all right."

"Listen, Jo. The crowd's coming over to-night. I've fixed up a little poker game for you. Just eight of us."

"I can't come to-night, Gert."

"Can't! Why not?"

"I'm not feeling so good."

"You just said you were all right."

"I *am* all right. Just kind of tired."

The voice took on a cooing note. "Is my Joey tired? Then he shall be all comfy on the sofa, and he doesn't need to play if he don't want to. No, sir."

Jo stood staring at the black mouth-piece of the telephone. He was seeing a procession go marching by. Boys, hundreds of boys, in khaki.

"Hello! Hello!" the voice took on an anxious note. "Are you there?"

"Yes," wearily.

"Jo, there's something the matter. You're sick. I'm coming right over."

"No!"

"Why not? You sound as if you'd been sleeping. Look here—"

"Leave me alone!" cried Jo, suddenly, and the receiver clacked onto the hook. "Leave me alone. Leave me alone." Long after the connection had been broken.

He stood staring at the instrument with unseeing eyes. Then he turned and walked into the front room. All the light had gone out of it. Dusk had come on. All the light had gone out of everything. The zest had gone out of life. The game was over—the game he had been playing against loneliness and disappointment. And he was just a tired old man. A lonely, tired old man in a ridiculous, rose-coloured room that had grown, all of a sudden, drab.

III
THE TOUGH GUY

19

You could not be so very tough in Chippewa, Wisconsin. But Buzz Werner managed magnificently with the limited means at hand. Before he was nineteen mothers were warning their sons against him, and brothers their sisters. Buzz Werner not only was tough—he looked tough. When he spoke—which was often—his speech slid sinisterly out of the extreme left corner of his mouth. He had a trick of hitching himself up from the belt—one palm on the stomach and a sort of heaving jerk from the waist, as a prize fighter does it—that would have made a Van Bibber look rough.

His name was not really Buzz, but quotes are dispensed with because no one but his mother remembered what it originally had been. His mother called him Ernie and she alone, in all Chippewa, Wisconsin, was unaware that her son was the town tough guy. But even she sometimes mildly remonstrated with him for being what she called kind of wild. Buzz had yellow hair with a glint in it, and it curled up into a bang at the front. No amount of wetting or greasing could subdue that irrepressible forelock. A boy with hair like that never grows up in his mother's eyes.

If Buzz's real name was lost in the dim mists of boyhood, the origin and fitness of his nickname were apparent after two minutes' conversation with him. Buzz Werner was called Buzz not only because he talked too much, but because he was a braggart. His conversation bristled with the perpendicular pronoun, and his pet phrase was, "I says to him—"

He buzzed.

By the time Buzz was fourteen he was stealing brass from the yards of the big paper mills down in the Flats and selling it to the junk man. How he escaped the reform school is a mystery. Perhaps it was the blond forelock. At nineteen he was running with the Kearney girl.

Twenty-five years hence Chippewa will have learned to treat the Kearney-girl type as a disease, and a public menace. Which she was. The Kearney girl ran wild in Chippewa, and Chippewa will be paying taxes on the fruit of her liberty for a hundred years to come. The Kearney girl was a beautiful idiot, with a lovely oval face, and limpid, rather wistful blue eyes, and fair, fine hair, and a long slim neck. She looked very much like those famous wantons of history, from Lucrezia Borgia to Nell Gwyn, that you see pictured in the galleries of Europe—all very mild and girlish, with moist red mouths, like a puppy's, so that you wonder if they have not been basely defamed through all the centuries.

The Kearney girl's father ran a saloon out on Second Avenue, and every few days the Chippewa paper would come out with a story of a brawl, a knifing, or a free-for-all fight following a Saturday night in Kearney's. The Kearney girl herself was forever running up and down Grand Avenue, which was the main business street. She would trail up and down from the old Armory to the post-office and back again. When she turned off into the homeward stretch on Outagamie Street there always slunk after her some stoop-shouldered, furtive, loping youth. But he never was seen with her on Grand Avenue. She had often been up before old Judge Colt for some nasty business or other. At such times the shabby office of the Justice of the Peace would be full of shawled mothers and heavy-booted, work-worn fathers, and an aunt or two, and some cousins, and always a slinking youth fumbling with the hat in his hands, his glance darting hither and thither, from group to group, but never resting for a moment within any one else's gaze. Of all these present, the Kearney girl herself was always the calmest. Old Judge Colt meted out justice according to his lights. Unfortunately, the wearing of a yellow badge on the breast was a custom that had gone out some years before.

This nymph it was who had taken a fancy to Buzz Werner. It looked very black for his future.

The strange part of it was that the girl possessed little attraction for Buzz. It was she who made all the advances. Buzz had sprung from very decent stock, as you shall see. And something about the sultry unwholesomeness of this girl repelled him, though he was hardly aware that this was so. Buzz and his gang would meet down town of a Saturday night, very moist as to hair and clean as to soft shirt. They would lounge on the corner of Grand and Outagamie, in front of Schroeder's brightly lighted drug store, watching the girls go by. They were, for the most part, a pimply-faced lot. They would shuffle their feet in a slow jig, hands in pockets. When a late comer joined them it was considered *au fait* to welcome him by assuming a fistic attitude, after the style of the pugilists pictured in the barber-shop magazines, and spar a good-natured and make-believe round with him, with much agile dancing about in a circle, head held stiffly, body crouching, while working a rapid and facetious right.

This corner, or Donovan's pool-shack, was their club, their forum. Here they recounted their exploits, bragged of their triumphs, boasted of their girls, flexed their muscles to show their strength. And all through their talk there occurred again and again a certain term whose use is common to their kind. Their remarks were prefaced and interlarded and concluded with it, so that it was no longer an oath or a blasphemy.

"Je's, I was sore at 'm. I told him where to get off at. Nobody can talk to me like that. Je's, I should say not."

So accustomed had it grown that it was not even thought of as profanity.

If Buzz's family could have heard him in his talk with his street-corner companions they would not have credited their ears. A mouthy braggart in company is often silent in his own home, and Buzz was no exception to this rule. Fortunately, Buzz's braggadocio carried with it a certain conviction. He never kept a job more than a month, and his own account of his leave-taking was always as vainglorious as it was dramatic.

"'G'wan!' I says to him, 'Who you talkin' to? I don't have to take nothin' from you nor nobody like you,' I says. 'I'm as good as you are any day, and better. You can have your dirty job,' I says. And with that I give him my time and walked out on 'm. Je's, he was sore!"

They would listen to him, appreciatively, but with certain mental reservations; reservations inevitable when a speaker's name is Buzz. One by one they would melt away as their particular girl, after flaunting by with a giggle and a sidelong glance for the dozenth time, would switch her skirts around the corner of Outagamie Street past the Brill House, homeward bound.

"Well, s'long," they would say. And lounging after her, would overtake her in the shadow of the row of trees in front of the Agassiz School.

If the Werner family had been city folk they would, perforce, have burrowed in one of those rabbit-warren tenements that line block after block of city streets. But your small-town labouring man is likely to own his two-story frame house with a garden patch in the back and a cement walk leading up to the front porch, and pork roast on Sundays. The Werners had all this, no thanks to Pa Werner; no thanks to Buzz, surely; and little to Minnie Werner who clerked in the Sugar Bowl Candy Store and tried to dress like Angie Hatton whose father owned the biggest Pulp and Paper mill in the Fox River Valley. No, the house and the garden, the porch and the cement sidewalk, and the pork roast all had their origin in Ma Werner's tireless energy, in Ma Werner's thrift; in her patience and unremitting toil, her nimble fingers and bent back, her shapeless figure and unbounded and unexpressed (verbally, that is) love for her children. Pa Werner—sullen, lazy, brooding, tyrannical—she soothed and mollified for the children's sake, or shouted down with a shrewish outburst, as the occasion required. An expert stone-mason by trade, Pa Werner could be depended on only when he was not drinking, or when he was not on strike, or when he had not quarrelled with the foreman. An anarchist, Pa—dissatisfied with things as they were, but with no plan for improving them. His evil-smelling pipe between his lips, he would sit, stocking-footed, in silence, smoking and thinking vague, formless, surly thoughts. This sullen unrest and rebellion it was that, transmitted to his son, had made Buzz the unruly braggart that he was, and which, twenty or thirty years hence, would find him just such a one as his father—useless, evil-tempered, half brutal, defiant of order.

It was in May, a fine warm sunny day, that Ma Werner, looking up from the garden patch where she was spading, a man's old battered felt hat perched grotesquely atop her white head, saw Buzz lounging homeward, cutting across lots from Bates Street, his dinner pail glinting in the sun. It was four o'clock in the afternoon. Ma Werner straightened painfully and her over-flushed face took on a purplish tinge. She wiped her moist chin with an apron-corner.

As Buzz espied her his gait became a swagger. At sight of that swagger Ma knew. She dropped her spade and plodded heavily through the freshly turned earth to the back porch as Buzz turned in at the walk. She shifted her weight ponderously as she wiped first one earth-crusted shoe and then the other.

"What's the matter, Ernie? You ain't sick, are you?"

"Naw."

"What you home so early for?"

"Because I feel like it, that's why."

He took the back steps at a bound and slammed the kitchen door behind him. Ma Werner followed heavily after. Buzz was hanging his hat up behind the kitchen door. He turned with a scowl as his mother entered. She looked even more ludicrous in the house than she had outside, with her skirts tucked up to make spading the easier, so that there was displayed an unseemly length of thick ankle rising solidly above the old pair of men's side-boots that encased her feet. The battered hat perched rakishly atop her knob of gray-white hair gave her a jaunty, sporting look, as of a ponderous, burlesque Watteau.

She abandoned pretense. "Ernie, your pa'll be awful mad. You know the way he carried on the last time."

"Let him. He aint worked five days himself this month." Then, at a sudden sound from the front of the house, "He ain't home, is he?"

"That's the shade flapping."

Buzz turned toward the inside wooden stairway that led to the half-story above. But his mother followed, with surprising agility for so heavy a woman. She put a hand on his arm. "Such a good-payin' job, Ernie. An' you said only yesterday you liked it. Somethin' must've happened."

There broke a grim little laugh from Buzz. "Believe *me* something happened good an' plenty." A little frightened look came into his eyes. "I just had a run-in with young Hatton."

The red faded from her face and a grey-white mask seemed to slip down over it. "You don't mean Hatton! Not Hatton's son. Ernie, you ain't done—"

A dash of his street-corner bravado came back to him. "Aw, keep your hair on, Ma. I didn't know it was young Hatton when I hit'm. An' anyway nobody his age is gonna tell me where to get off at. Say, w'en a guy who ain't twenty-three, hardly, and that never done a lick in his life except go to college, the sissy, tries t'—"

But the first sentence only had penetrated her brain. She grappled with it, dizzily. "Hit him! Ernie, you don't mean you hit him! Not Hatton's son! Ernie!"

"Sure I did. You oughta seen his face." But there was very little triumph or satisfaction in Buzz Werner's face or voice as he said it. "Course, I didn't know it was him when I done it. I dunno would it have made any difference if I had."

She seemed so old and so shrunken, in spite of her bulk, as she looked up at him. The look in her eyes was so strained. The way her hand brought her apron-corner up to her mouth, as though to stifle the fear that shook her, was so groping, somehow, so uncertain, that, paradoxically, the pitifulness of it reacted to make him savage.

When she quavered her next question, "What was he doin' in the mill?" he turned toward the stairway again, flinging his answer over his shoulder.

"Learnin' the business, that's what. From the ground up, see?" He turned at the first stair and leaned forward and down, one hand on the door-jamb. "Well, believe me he don't use me as no ground-dirt. An' when I'm takin' the screen off the big roll—see?—he comes up to me an' says I'm handlin' it rough an' it's a delicate piece of mechanism. 'Who're you?' I says. 'Never mind who I am' he says, 'I'm working' on this job,' he says, 'an' this is a paper mill you're workin' in,' he says, 'not a boiler factory. Treat the machinery accordin', like a real workman,' he says. The simp! I just stepped down off the platform of the big press, and I says, 'Well, you look like a kinda delicate piece of mechanism yourself,' I says, 'an' need careful handlin', so take that for a starter,' I says. An' with that I handed him one in the nose." Buzz laughed, but there was little mirth in it. "I bet he seen enough wheels an' delicate machinery that minute to set up a whole new plant."

There was nothing of mirth in the woman's drawn face. "Oh, Ernie, fr God's sake! What they goin' to do to you!"

He was half way up the narrow stairway, she at the foot of it, peering up at him. "They won't do anything. I guess old Hatton ain't so stuck on havin' his swell golf club crowd know his little boy was beat up by one of the workmen."

He was clumping about upstairs now. So she turned toward the kitchen, dazedly. She glanced at the clock. Going on toward five. Still in the absurd hat she got out a panful of potatoes and began to peel them skilfuly, automatically. The seamed and hardened fingers had come honestly by their deftness. They had twirled and peeled pecks—bushels—tons of these brown balls in their time.

At five-thirty Pa came in. At six, Minnie. She had to go back to the Sugar Bowl until nine. Five minutes later the supper was steaming on the table.

"Ernie," called Ma, toward the ceiling. "Er-nie! Supper's on." The three sat down at the table without waiting. Pa had slipped off his shoes, and was in his stockinged feet. They ate in silence. It was a good meal. A European family of the same class would have considered it a banquet. There were meat and vegetables, butter and home-made bread, preserve and cake, true to the standards of the extravagant American labouring-class household. In the summer the garden supplied them with lettuce, beans, peas, onions, radishes, beets, potatoes, corn, thanks to Ma's aching back and blistered hands. They stored enough vegetables in the cellar to last through the winter.

Buzz usually cleaned up after supper. But to-night, when he came down, he was already clean-shaven, clean-shirted, and his hair was wet from the comb. He took his place in silence. His acid-stained work shoes had been replaced by his good tan ones. Evidently he was going down town after supper. Buzz never took any exercise for the sake of his body's good. Sometimes he and the Lembke boys across the way played a game of ball in the middle of the road, or in the vacant lot, but they did it out of the game instinct, and with no thought of their muscles' gain.

But to-night, evidently, there was to be no ball. Buzz ate little. His mother, forever between the stove and the table, ate less. But that was nothing unusual in her. She waited on the others, but mostly she hovered about the boy.

"Ernie, you ain't eaten your potatoes. Look how nice an' mealy they are."

"Don't want none."

"Ernie, would you rather have a baked apple than the raspberry preserve? I fixed a pan this morning."

"Naw. Lemme alone. I ain't hungry."

He slouched from the table. Minnie, teacup in hand, regarded him over its rim with wide, malicious eyes. "I saw that Kearney girl go by here before supper, and she rubbered in like everything."

"You're a liar," said Buzz, unemotionally.

"I did so! She went by and then she came back again. I saw her both times. Say, I guess I ought to know her. Anybody in town'd know Kearney."

Buzz had been headed toward the front porch. He hesitated and turned, now, and picked up the newspaper from the sitting-room sofa. Pa Werner, in trousers, shirt and suspenders, was padding about the kitchen with his pipe and tobacco. He came into the sitting room now and stood a moment, his lips twisted about the pipe-stem. The pipe's putt-putting gave warning that he was about to break into unaccustomed speech. He regarded Buzz with beady, narrowed eyes.

"You let me see you around with that Kearney girl and I'll break every bone in your body, and hers too. The hussy!"

"Oh, you will, will you?"

Ma, who had been making countless trips from the kitchen to the back garden with water pail and sprinkling can sagging from either arm, put in a word to stay the threatening storm. "Now, Pa! Now, Ernie!" The two men subsided into bristling silence.

Suddenly, "There she is again!" shrilled Minnie, from her bedroom. Buzz shrank back in his chair. Old man Werner, with a muttered oath, went to the open doorway and stood there, puffing savage little spurts of smoke streetward. The Kearney girl stared brazenly at him as she strolled slowly by, a slim and sinister figure. Old man Werner watched her until she passed out of sight.

"You go gettin' mixed up with dirt like that," threatened he, "and I'll learn you. She'll be hangin' around the mill yet, the brass-faced thing. If I hear of it I'll get the foreman to put her off the place. You'll stay home to-night. Carry a pail of water for your ma once."

"Carry it yourself."

Buzz, with a wary eye up the street, slouched out to the front porch, into the twilight of the warm May evening. Charley Lembke, from his porch across the street, called to him: "Goin' down town?"

"Yeh, I guess so."

"Ain't you afraid of bein' pinched?" Buzz turned his head quickly toward the room just behind him. He turned to go in. Charley's voice came again, clear and far-reaching. "I hear you had a run-in with Hatton's son, and knocked him down. Some class t' you, Buzz, even if it does cost you your job."

From within the sound of a newspaper hurled to the floor. Pa Werner was at the door. "What's that! What's that he's sayin'?"

Buzz, cornered, jutted a threatening jaw at his father and brazened it out. "Can't you hear good?"

"Come on in here."

Buzz hesitated a moment. Then he turned, slowly, and walked into the little sitting room with an attempt at a swagger that failed to convince even himself. He leaned against the side of the door, hands in pockets. Pa Werner faced him, black-browed. "Is that right, what he said? Lembke? Huh?"

"Sure it's right. I had a run-in with Hatton, an' licked him, and give'm my time. What you goin' to do about it?"

Ma Werner was in the room, now. Minnie, passing through on her way to work again, caught the electric current of the storm about to break and escaped it with a parting:

"Oh, for the land's sakes! You two. Always a-fighting."

The two men faced each other. The one a sturdy man-boy nearing twenty, with a great pair of shoulders and a clear eye, a long, quick arm and a deft hand—these last his assets as a workman. The other, gnarled, prematurely wrinkled, almost gnome-like. This one took his pipe from between his lips and began to speak. The drink he had had at Wenzel's on the way home sparked his speech.

He began with a string of epithets. They flowed from his lips, an acid stream. Pick and choose as I will, there is none that can be repeated here. Old Man Werner had, perhaps, been something of a tough guy himself, in his youth. As he reviled his son now you saw that son, at fifty, just such another stocking-footed, bitter old man, smoking a glum pipe on the back porch, summer evenings, and spitting into the fresh young grass.

I don't say that this thought came to Buzz as his father flayed him with his abuse. But there was something unusual, surely, in the non-resistance with which he allowed the storm to beat about his head. Something in his steady, unruffled gaze caused the other man to falter a little in his tirade, and finally to stop, almost apprehensively. He had paid no heed to Ma Werner's attempts at pacification. "Now, Pa!" she had said, over and over, her hand on his arm, though he shook it off again and again. "Now, Pa!—" But he stopped now, fist raised in a last profane period. Buzz stood regarding him with his unblinking stare.

Finally: "You through?" said Buzz.

"Ya-as," snarled Pa, "I'm through. Get to hell out of here. You'll be hung yet, you loafer. A good-for-nothing bum, that's what. Get out o' here!"

"I'm gettin'," said Buzz. He took his hat off the hook and wiped it carefully with the lower side of his sleeve, round and round. He placed it on his head, jauntily. He stepped to the kitchen, took a tooth-pick from the little red-and-white glass holder on the table, and—with this emblem of insouciance, at an angle of ninety, between his teeth—strolled indolently, nonchalantly down the front steps, along the cement walk to the street and so toward town. The two old people, left alone in the sudden silence of the house, stared after the swaggering figure until the dim twilight blotted it out. And a sinister something seemed to close its icy grip about the heart of one of them. A vague premonition that she could only feel, not express, made her next words seem futile.

"Pa, you oughtn't to talked to him like that. He's just a little wild. He looked so kind of funny when he went out. I don'no, he looked so kind of—"

"He looked like the bum he is, that's what. No respect for nothing. For his pa, or ma, or nothing. Down on the corner with the rest of 'em, that's where he's goin'. Hatton ain't goin' to let this go by. You see."

But she, on her way to the kitchen, repeated, "I don'no, he looked so kind of funny. He looked so kind of—"

Considering all things—the happenings of the past few hours, at least—Buzz, as he strolled on down toward Grand Avenue with his sauntering, care-free gait, did undoubtedly look kind of funny. The red-hot rage of the afternoon and the white-hot rage of the evening had choked the furnace of brain and soul with clinkers so that he was thinking unevenly and disconnectedly. On the surface he was cool and unruffled. He stopped for a moment at the railroad tracks to talk with Stumpy Gans, the one-legged gateman. The little bell above Stumpy's shanty was ringing its warning, so he strolled leisurely over to the depot platform to see the 7:15 come in from Chicago. When the train pulled out Buzz went on down the street. His mind was darting here and there, planning this revenge, discarding it; seizing on another, abandoning that. He'd show'm. He'd show'm. Sick of the whole damn bunch, anyway.... Wonder was Hatton going to raise a shindy.... Let'm. Who cares?... The old man was a drunk, that's what.... Ma had looked kinda sick....

He put that uncomfortable thought out of his mind and slammed the door on it. Anyway, he'd show'm.

Out of the shadows of the great trees in front of the Agassiz School stepped the Kearney girl, like a lean and hungry cat. One hand clutched his arm.

Buzz jumped and said something under his breath. Then he laughed, shortly. "Might as well kill a guy as scare him to death!"

She thrust one hand through his arm and linked it with the other. "I've been waiting for you, Buzz."

"Yeh. Well, let me tell you something. You quit traipsing up and down in front of my house, see?"

"I wanted to see you. An' I didn't know whether you was coming down town to-night or not."

"Well, I am. So now you know." He pulled away from her, but she twined her arm the tighter about his.

"Ain't sore at me, are yuh, Buzz?"

"No. Leggo my arm."

"If you're sore because I been foolin' round with that little wart of a Donahue—" She turned wise eyes up to him, trying to make them limpid in the darkness.

"What do I care who you run with?"

"Don't you care, Buzz?" The words were soft but there was a steel edge to her utterance.

"No."

"Oh, Buzz, I'm batty about you. I can't help it, can I? H'm? Look here, you go on to Grand, and hang around for an hour, maybe, and I'll meet you here an' we'll walk a ways. Will you? I got something to tell you."

"Naw, I can't to-night. I'm busy."

And then the steel edge cut. "Buzz, if you turn me down I'll have you up."

"Up?"

"Before old Colt. I can fix up charges. He'll believe it. Say, he knows me, Judge Colt does. I can name you an'—"

"Me!" Sheer amazement rang in his voice. "Me? You must be crazy. I ain't had anything to do with you. You make me sick."

"That don't make any difference. You can't prove it. I told you I was crazy about you. I told you—"

He jerked loose from her then and was off. He ran one block. Then, after a backward glance, fell into a quick walk that brought him past the Brill House and to Schroeder's drug store corner. There was his crowd—Spider, and Red, and Bing, and Casey. They took him literally unto their breasts. They thumped him on the back. They bestowed on him the low epithets with which they expressed admiration. Red worked at one of the bleaching vats in the Hatton paper mill. The story of Buzz's fistic triumph had spread through the big plant like a flame.

"Go on, Buzz, tell 'em about it," Red urged, now. "Je's, I like to died laughing when I heard it. He must of looked a sight, the poor boob. Go on, Buzz, tell 'em how you says to him he must be a kind of delicate piece of— you know; go on, tell 'em."

Buzz hitched himself up with a characteristic gesture, and plunged into his story. His audience listened entranced, interrupting him with an occasional "Je's!" of awed admiration. But the thing seemed to lack a certain something. Perhaps Casey put his finger on that something when, at the recital's finish he asked:

"Didn't he see you was goin' to hit him?"

"No. He never see a thing."

Casey ruminated a moment. "You could of give him a chanst to put up his dukes," he said at last. A little silence fell upon the group. Honour among thieves.

Buzz shifted uncomfortably. "He's a bigger guy than I am. I bet he's over six foot. The papers was always telling how he played football at that college he went to."

Casey spoke up again. "They say he didn't wait for this here draft. He's goin' to Fort Sheridan, around Chicago somewhere, to be made a officer."

"Yeh, them rich guys, they got it all their own way," Spider spoke up, gloomily. "They—"

From down the street came a dull, muffled thud-thud-thud-thud. Already Chippewa, Wisconsin, had learned to recognise it. Grand Avenue, none too crowded on this mid-week night, pressed to the curb to see. Down the street they stared toward the moving mass that came steadily nearer. The listless group on the corner stiffened into something like interest.

"Company G," said Red. "I hear they're leavin' in a couple of days."

And down the street they came, thud-thud-thud, Company G, headed for the new red-brick Armory for the building of which they had engineered everything from subscription dances and exhibition drills to turkey raffles. Chippewa had never taken Company G very seriously until now. How could it, when Company G was made up of Willie Kemp, who clerked in Hassell's shoe store; Fred Garvey, the reporter on the Chippewa *Eagle*; Hermie Knapp, the real-estate man, and Earl Hanson who came around in the morning for your grocery order.

Thud-thud-thud-thud. And to Chippewa, standing at the curb, quite suddenly these every-day men and boys were transformed into something remote and almost terrible. Something grim. Something sacrificial. Something sacred.

Thud-thud-thud-thud. Looking straight ahead.

"The poor boobs," said Spider, and spat, and laughed.

The company passed on down the street—vanished. Grand Avenue went its way.

A little silence fell upon the street-corner group. Bing was the first to speak.

"They won't git me in this draft. I got a mother an' two kid sisters to support."

"Yeh, a swell lot of supportin' you do!"

"Who says I don't! I can prove it."

"They'll get me all right," said Casey. "I ain't kickin'."

"I'm under age," from Red.

Spider said nothing. His furtive eyes darted here and there. Spider was of age. And Spider had no family to support. But Spider had reason to know that no examining board would pass him into the army of his country. And it was a reason of which one did not speak. "You're only twenty, ain't you, Buzz?" he asked, to cover the gap in the conversation.

"Yeh." Silence fell again. Then, "But I wouldn't mind goin'. Anything for a change. This place makes me sick."

Spider laughed. "You better be a hero and go and enlist."

Buzz's head came up with a jerk. "Je's, I never thought of that!"

Red struck an attitude, one hand on his breast. "Now's your chanct, Buzz, to save your country an' your flag. Enlistment office's right over the Golden Eagle clothing store. Step up. Don't crowd gents! This way!"

Buzz was staring at him, open-mouthed. His gaze was fixed, tense. Suddenly he seemed to gather all his muscles together as for a spring. But he only threw his cigarette into the gutter, yawned elaborately, and moved away. "S'long," he said; and lounged off. The others looked after him a moment, puzzled, speculative. Buzz was not usually so laconic. But evidently he was leaving with no further speech.

"I guess maybe he ain't so dead sure that Hatton bunch won't git him for this, anyway," Casey said. Then, raising his voice: "Goin' home, Buzz?"

"Yeh."

But he did not. If they had watched him they would have seen him change his lounging gait when he reached the corner. They would have seen him stand a moment, sending a quick glance this way and that, then turn, retrace his steps almost at a run, and dart into the doorway that led to the flight of wooden stairs at the side of the Golden Eagle clothing store.

A dingy room. A man at a bare table. Another seated at the window, his chair tipped back, his feet on the sill, a pipe between his teeth. Buzz, shambling, suddenly awkward, stood in the door.

"This the place where you enlist?"

The man at the table stood up. The chair in front of the open window came down on all-fours.

"Sure," said the first man. "What's your name?"

Buzz told him.

"Meet Sergeant Keith. He's a Canadian. Been through the whole game."

Five minutes later Buzz's fine white torso rose above his trousers like a great pillar. Unconsciously his sagging shoulders had straightened. His stomach was held in. His chest jutted, shelf-like. His ribs showed through the pink-white flesh.

"Get some of that pork off of him," observed Sergeant Keith, "and he'll do in a couple of Fritzes before he's through."

"Me!" blurted Buzz, struggling now with his shirt. "A couple! Say, you don't know me. Whaddyou mean, a couple? I can lick a whole regiment of them beerheads with one hand tied behind me an' my feet in a sack." He emerged from the struggle with his shirt, his face very red, his hair rumpled.

Sergeant Keith smiled a grim little smile. "Keep your shirt on, kid," he said, "and remember, this isn't a fist fight you're going into. It's war."

Buzz, fumbling with his hat, put his question. "When—when do I go?" For he had signed his name in his round, boyish, sixth-grade scrawl.

"To-morrow. Now listen to these instructions."

"T-to-morrow?" gasped Buzz.

He was still gasping as he reached the street and struck out toward home. To-morrow! When the Kearney girl again stepped out of the tree-shadows he stared at her as at something remote and trivial.

"I thought you tried to give me the slip, Buzz. Where you been?"

"Never mind where I've been."

She fell into step beside him, but had difficulty in matching his great strides. She caught at his arm. At that Buzz turned and stopped. It was too dark to see his face, but something in his voice—something new, and hard, and resolute—reached even the choked and slimy cells of this creature's consciousness.

"Now looka here. You beat it. I got somethin' on my mind to-night and I can't be bothered with no fool girl, see? Don't get me sore. I mean it."

Her hand dropped away from his arm. "I didn't mean what I said about havin' you up, Buzz; honest t' Gawd I didn't."

"I don't care what you meant."

'Will you meet me to-morrow night? Will you, Buzz?"

"If I'm in this town to-morrow night I'll meet you. Is that good enough?"

He turned and strode away. But she was after him. "Where you goin' to-morrow?"

"I'm goin' to war, that's where."

"Yes you are!" scoffed Miss Kearney. Then, at his silence: "You didn't go and do a fool thing like that?"

"I sure did."

"When you goin'?"

"To-morrow."

"Well, of all the big boobs," sneered Miss Kearney; "what did you go and do that for?"

"Search *me*," said Buzz, dully. "Search *me*."

Then he turned and went on toward home, alone. The Kearney girl's silly, empty laugh came back to him through the darkness. It might have been called a scornful laugh if the Kearney girl had been capable of any emotion so dignified as scorn.

The family was still up. The door was open to the warm May night. The Werners, in their moments of relaxation, were as unbuttoned and highly *negligée* as one of those group pictures you see of the Robert Louis Stevenson family. Pa, shirt-sleeved, stocking-footed, asleep in his chair. Ma's dress open at the front. Minnie, in an untidy kimono, sewing.

On this flaccid group Buzz burst, bomb-like. He hung his hat on the hook, wordlessly. The noise he made woke his father, as he had meant that it should. There came a muttered growl from the old man. Buzz leaned against the stairway door, negligently. The eyes of the three were on him.

"Well," he said, "I guess you won't be bothered with me much longer." Ma Werner's head came up sharply at that.

"What you done, Ernie?"

"Enlisted."

"Enlisted—for what?"

"For the war; what do you suppose?"

Ma Werner rose at that, heavily. "Ernie! You never!"

Pa Werner was wide awake now. Out of his memory of the old country, and soldier service there, he put his next question. "Did you sign to it?"

"Yeh."

"When you goin'?"

"To-morrow."

Even Pa Werner gasped at that.

In families like the Werners emotion is rarely expressed. But now, because of something in the stricken face and starting eyes of the woman, and the open-mouthed dumbfoundedness of the old man, and the sudden tender fearfulness in the face of the girl; and because, in that moment, all these seemed very safe, and accustomed, and, somehow, dear, Buzz curled his mouth into the sneer of the tough guy and spoke out of the corner of that contorted feature.

"What did you think I was goin' to do? Huh? Stick around here and take dirt from the bunch of you! Nix! I'm through!"

There was nothing dramatic about Buzz's going. He seemed to be whisked away. One moment he was eating his breakfast at an unaccustomed hour, in his best shirt and trousers, his mother, only half understanding even now, standing over him with the coffee pot; the next he was standing with his cheap shiny suitcase in his hand. Then he was waiting on the depot platform, and Hefty Burke, the baggage man, was saying, "Where you goin', Buzz?"

"Goin' to fight the Germans."

Hefty had hooted hoarsely: "Ya-a-as you are, you big bluff!"

"Who you callin' a bluff, you baggage-smasher, you! I'm goin' to war, I'm tellin' you."

Hefty, still scoffing, turned away to his work. "Well, then, I guess it's as good as over. Give old Willie a swipe for me, will you?"

"You bet I will. Watch me!"

I think he more than half meant it.

And thus Buzz Werner went to war. He was vague about its locality. Somewhere in Europe. He was pretty sure it was France. A line from his Fourth Grade geography came back to him. "The French," it had said, "are a gay people, fond of dancing and light wines."

Well, that sounded all right.

The things that happened to Buzz Werner in the next twelve months cannot be detailed here. They would require the space of what the publishers call a 12-mo volume. Buzz himself could never have told you. Things happened too swiftly, too concentratedly.

Chicago first. Buzz had never seen Chicago. Now that he saw it, he hardly believed it. His first glimpse of it left him cowering, terrified. The noise, the rush, the glitter, the grimness, the vastness, were like blows upon his defenceless head. They beat the braggadocio and the self-confidence temporarily out of him. But only temporarily.

Then came a camp. A rough, temporary camp compared to which the present cantonments are luxurious. The United States Government took Buzz Werner by the slack of the trousers and the slack of the mind, and, holding him thus, shook him into shape—and into submission. And eventually—though it required months—into an understanding of why that submission was manly, courageous, and fine. But before he learned that he learned many other things. He learned there was little good in saying, "Aw, g'wan!" to a dapper young lieutenant if they clapped you into the guard-house for saying it. There was little point to throwing down your shovel and refusing to shovel coal if they clapped you into the guard house for doing it; and made you shovel harder than ever when you came out. He learned what it was to rise at dawn and go thud-thud-thudding down a dirt road for endless weary miles. He became an olive-drab unit in an olive-drab village. He learned what it was to wake up in the morning so sore and lame that he felt as if he had been pulled apart, limb from limb, during the night, and never put together again. He stood out with a raw squad in the dirt of No Man's Land between barracks and went through exercises that took hold of his great slack muscles and welded them into whip-cords. And in front of him, facing him, stood a slim, six-foot whipper-snapper of a lieutenant, hatless, coatless, tireless, merciless—a creature whom Buzz at first thought he could snap between thumb and finger—like that!—who made life a hell for Buzz Werner. Until his muscles became used to it.

"One—*two!*—three! One—*two*—three! One—*two*—three!" yelled this person. And, "*In*hale! *Ex*hale! *In*hale! *Ex*hale!" till Buzz's lungs were bursting, his eyes were starting from his head, his chest carried a sledge hammer inside it, his thigh-muscles screamed, and his legs, arms, neck, were no longer parts of him, but horrid useless burdens, detached, yet clinging. He learned what this person meant when he shouted (always with the rising inflection), "Comp'ny! Right! *Whup!*" Buzz whupped with the best of 'em. The whipper-snapper seemed tireless. Long after Buzz felt that another moment of it would kill him the lithe young lieutenant would be leaping about like a faun, and pride kept Buzz going though he wanted to drop with fatigue, and his shirt and hair and face were wet with sweat.

So much for his body. It soon became accustomed to the routine, then hardened. His mind was less pliable. But that, too, was undergoing a change. He found that the topics of conversation that used to interest his little crowd on the street corner in Chippewa were not of much interest, here. There were boys from every part of the great country. And they talked of the places whence they had come and speculated about the places to which they were going. And Buzz listened and learned. There was strangely little talk about girls. There usually is when muscles and mind are being driven to the utmost. But he heard men—men as big as he—speak openly of things that he had always sneered at as soft. After one of these conversations he wrote an awkward, but significant scrawl home to his mother.

"Well Ma," he wrote, "I guess maybe you would like to hear a few words from me. Well I like it in the army it is the life for me you bet. I am feeling great how are you all—"

Ma Werner wasted an entire morning showing it around the neighbourhood, and she read and reread it until it was almost pulp.

Six months of this. Buzz Werner was an intelligent machine composed of steel, cord, and iron. I think he had forgotten that the Kearney girl had ever existed. One day, after three months of camp life, the man in the next cot had thrown him a volume of Kipling. Buzz fingered it, disinterestedly. Until that moment Kipling had not existed for Buzz Werner. After that moment he dominated his leisure hours. The Y.M.C.A. hut had many battered volumes of this writer. Buzz read them all.

The week before Thanksgiving Buzz found himself on his way to New York. For some reason unexplained to him he was separated from his company in one of the great shake-ups performed for the good of the army. He never saw them again. He was sent straight to a New York camp. When he beheld his new lieutenant his limbs became fluid, and his heart leaped into his throat, and his mouth stood open, and his eyes bulged. It was young Hatton—Harry Hatton—whose aristocratic nose he had punched six months before, in the Hatton Pulp and Paper Mill.

And even as he stared young Hatton fixed him with his eye, and then came over to him and said, "It's all right, Werner."

Buzz Werner could only salute with awkward respect, while with one great gulp his heart slid back into normal place. He had not thought that Hatton was so tall, or so broad-shouldered, or so—

He no more thought of telling the other men that he had once knocked this man down than he thought of knocking him down again. He would almost as soon have thought of taking a punch at the President.

The day before Thanksgiving Buzz was told he might have a holiday. Also he was given an address and a telephone number in New York City and told that if he so desired he might call at that address and receive a bountiful Thanksgiving dinner. They were expecting him there. That the telephone exchange was Murray Hill, and the street Madison Avenue meant nothing to Buzz. He made the short trip to New York, floundered about the city, found every one willing and eager to help him find the address on the slip, and brought up, finally, in front of the house on Madison Avenue. It was a large, five-story stone place, and Buzz supposed it was a flat, of course. He stood off and surveyed it. Then he ascended the steps and rang the bell. They must have been waiting for him. The door was opened by a large amiable-looking, middle-aged man who said, "Well, well! Come in, come in, my boy!" a great deal as the folks in Chippewa, Wisconsin, might have said it. The stout old party also said he was glad to see him and Buzz believed it. They went upstairs, much to Buzz's surprise. In Buzz's experience upstairs always meant bedrooms. But in this case it meant a great bright sitting room, with books in it, and a fireplace, very cheerful. There were not a lot of people in the room. Just a middle-aged woman in a soft kind of dress, who came to him without any fuss and the first thing he knew he felt acquainted. Within the next fifteen minutes or so some other members of the family seemed to ooze in, unnoticeably. First thing you knew, there they were. They didn't pay such an awful lot of attention to you. Just took you for granted. A couple of young kids, a girl of fourteen, and a boy of sixteen who asked you easy questions about the army till you found yourself patronising him. And a tall black-haired girl who made you think of the vamps in the movies, only her eyes were different. And then, with a little rush, a girl about his own age, or maybe younger—he couldn't tell—who came right up to him, and put out her hand, and gave him a grip with her hard little fist, just like a boy, and said, "I'm Joyce Ladd."

"Pleased to meetcha," mumbled Buzz. And then he found himself talking to her quite easily. She knew a surprising lot about the army.

"I've two brothers over there," she said. "And all my friends, of course." He found out later, quite by accident, that this boyish, but strangely appealing person belonged to some sort of Motor Service League, and drove an automobile, every day, from eight to six, up and down and round and about New York, working like a man in the service of the country. He never would have believed that the world held that kind of girl.

Then four other men in uniform came in, and it turned out that three of them were privates like himself, and the other a sergeant. Their awkward entrance made him feel more than ever at ease, and ten minutes later they were all talking like mad, and laughing and joking as if they had known these people for years. They all went in to dinner. Buzz got panicky when he thought of the knives and forks, but that turned out all right, too, because they brought these as you needed them. And besides, the things they gave you to eat weren't much different from the things you had for Sunday or Thanksgiving dinner at home, and it was cooked the way his mother would have cooked it— even better, perhaps. And lots of it. And paper snappers and caps and things, and much laughter and talk. And Buzz Werner, who had never been shown any respect or deference in his life, was asked, politely, his opinion of the war, and the army, and when he thought it all would end; and he told them, politely, too.

After dinner Mrs. Ladd said, "What would you boys like to do? Would you like to drive around the city and see New York? Or would you like to go to a matinée, or a picture show? Or do you want to stay here? Some of Joyce's girl friends are coming in a little later."

And Buzz found himself saying, stumblingly, "I—I'd kind of rather stay and talk with the girls." Buzz, the tough guy, blushing like a shy schoolboy.

They did not even laugh at that. They just looked as if they understood that you missed girls at camp. Mrs. Ladd came over to him and put her hand on his arm and said, "That's splendid. We'll all go up to the ballroom and dance." And they did. And Buzz, who had learned to dance at places like Kearney's saloon, and at the mill shindigs, glided expertly about with Joyce Ladd of Madison Avenue, and found himself seated in a great cushioned window-seat, talking with her about Kipling. It was like talking to another fellow, almost, only it had a thrill in it. She said such comic things. And when she laughed she threw back her head and your eyes were dazzled by her slender white throat. They all stayed for supper. And when they left Mrs. Ladd and Joyce handed them packages that, later, turned out to be cigarettes, and chocolate, and books, and soap, and knitted things and a wallet. And when Buzz opened the wallet and found, with relief, that there was no money in it he knew that he had met and mingled with American royalty as its equal.

Three days later he sailed for France.

Buzz Werner, the Chippewa tough guy, in Paris! Buzz Werner at Napoleon's tomb, that glorious white marble poem. Buzz Werner in the Place de la Concorde. Eating at funny little Paris restaurants.

Then a new life. Life in a drab, rain-soaked, mud-choked little French village, sleeping in barns, or stables, or hen coops. If the French were "a gay people, fond of dancing and light wines," he'd like to know where it came in! Nothing but drill and mud, mud and drill, and rain, rain, rain! And old women with tragic faces, and young women with old eyes. And unbelievable stories of courage and sacrifice. And more rain, and more mud, and more drill. And then—into it!

Into it with both feet. Living in the trenches. Back home, in camp, they had refused to take the trenches seriously. They had played in them as children play bear under the piano or table, and had refused to keep their heads down. But Buzz learned to keep his down now, quickly enough. A first terrifying stretch of this, then back to the rear again. More mud and drill. Marches so long and arduous that walking was no longer walking but a dreadful mechanical motion. He learned what thirst was, did Buzz. He learned what it was to be obliged to keep your mind off the thought of pails of water—pails that slopped and brimmed over, so that you could put your head into them and lip around like a horse.

Then back into the trenches. And finally, over the top! Very little memory of what happened after that. A rush. Trampling over soft heaps that writhed. Some one yelling like an Indian with a voice somehow like his own. The German trench reached. At them with his bayonet! He remembered, automatically, how his manual had taught him to jerk out the steel, after you had driven it home. He did it. Into the very trench itself. A great six-foot German struggling with a slim figure that Buzz somehow recognised as his lieutenant, Hatton. A leap at him, like an enraged dog:

"G'wan! who you shovin', you big slob you" yelled Buzz (I regret to say). And he thrust at him, and through him. The man released his grappling hold of Hatton's throat, and grunted, and sat down. And Buzz laughed. And the two went on, Buzz behind his lieutenant, and then something smote his thigh, and he too sat down. The dying German had thrown his last bomb, and it had struck home.

Buzz Werner would never again do a double shuffle on Schroeder's drug-store corner.

Hospital days. Hospital nights. A wheel chair. Crutches. Home.

It was May once more when Buzz Werner's train came into the little red-brick depot at Chippewa, Wisconsin. Buzz, spick and span in his uniform, looked down rather nervously, and yet with a certain pride at his left leg. When he sat down you couldn't tell which was the real one. As the train pulled in at the Chippewa Junction, just before reaching the town proper, there was old Bart Ochsner ringing the bell for dinner at the Junction eating house. Well, for the love of Mike! Wouldn't that make you laugh. Ringing that bell, just like always, as if nothing had happened in the last year! Buzz leaned against the window, to see. There was some commotion in the train and some one spoke his name. Buzz turned, and there stood Old Man Hatton, and a lot of others, and he seemed to be making a speech, and kind of crying, though that couldn't be possible. And his father was there, very clean and shaved and queer. Buzz caught words about bravery, and Chippewa's pride, and he was fussed to death, and glad when the train pulled in at the Chippewa station. But there the commotion was worse than ever. There was a band, playing away like mad. Buzz's great hands grown very white, were fidgeting at his uniform buttons, and at the stripe on his sleeve, and the medal on his breast. They wouldn't let him carry a thing, and when he came out on the car platform to descend there went up a great sound that was half roar and half scream. Buzz Werner was the first of Chippewa's men to come back.

After that it was rather hazy. There was his mother. His sister Minnie, too. He even saw the Kearney girl, with her loose red mouth, and her silly eyes, and she was as a strange woman to him. He was in Hatton's glittering automobile, being driven down Grand Avenue. There were speeches, and a dinner, and, later, when he was allowed to go home, rather white, a steady stream of people pouring in and out of the house all day. That night, when he limped up the stairs to his hot little room under the roof he was dazed, spent, and not so very happy.

Next morning, though, he felt more himself, and inclined to joke. And then there was a talk with old Man Hatton; a talk that left Buzz somewhat numb, and the family breathless.

Visitors again, all that afternoon.

After supper he carried water for the garden, against his mother's outraged protests.

"What'll folks think!" she said, "you carryin' water for me?"

Afterward he took his smart visored cap off the hook and limped down town, his boots and leggings and uniform very spick and span from Ma Werner's expert brushing and rubbing. She refused to let Buzz touch them, although he tried to tell her that he had done that job for a year.

At the corner of Grand and Outagamie, in front of Schroeder's drug store, stood what was left of the gang, and some new members who had come during the year that had passed. Buzz knew them all.

They greeted him at first with a mixture of shyness and resentment. They eyed his leg, and his uniform, and the metal and ribbon thing that hung at his breast. Bing and Red and Spider were there. Casey was gone.

Finally Spider spat and said, "G'wan, Buzz, give us your spiel about how you saved young Hatton—the simp!"

"Who says he's a simp?" inquired Buzz, very quietly. But there was a look about his jaw.

"Well—anyway—the papers was full of how you was a hero. Say, is that right that old Hatton's goin' to send you to college? Huh? Je's!"

"Yeh," chorused the others, "go on, Buzz. Tell us."

Red put his question. "Tell us about the fightin', Buzz. Is it like they say?"

It was Buzz Werner's great moment. He had pictured it a thousand times in his mind as he lay in the wet trenches, as he plodded the muddy French roads, as he reclined in his wheel chair in the hospital garden. He had them in the hollow of his hand. His eyes brightened. He looked at the faces so eagerly fixed on his utterance.

"G'wan, Buzz," they urged.

Buzz opened his lips and the words he used were the words he might have used a year before, as to choice. "There's nothin' to tell. A guy didn't have no time to be scairt. Everything kind of come at once, and you got yours, or either you didn't. That's all there was to it. Je's, it was fierce!"

They waited. Nothing more. "Yeh, but tell us—"

And suddenly Buzz turned away. The little group about him fell back, respectfully. Something in his face, perhaps. A quietness, a new dignity.

"S'long, boys," he said. And limped off, toward home.

And in that moment Buzz, the bully and braggart, vanished forever. And in his place—head high, chest up, eyes clear—limped Ernest Werner, the man.

The Self-Complacent Young Cub leaned an elbow against the mantel as you've seen it done in English plays, and blew a practically perfect smoke-ring. It hurtled toward me like a discus.

"Trouble with your stuff," he began at once (we had just been introduced), "is that it lacks plot. Been meaning to meet and tell you that for a long time. Your characterization's all right, and your dialogue. In fact, I think they're good. But your stuff lacks *raison d'être*—if you know what I mean."

"But"—in feeble self-defence—"people's insides are often so much more interesting than their outsides; that which they think or feel so much more thrilling than anything they actually do. Bennett—Wells—"

"Rot!" remarked the young cub, briskly. "Plot's the thing."

There is no plot to this because there is no plot to Rose. There never was. There never will be. Compared to the drab monotony of Rose's existence a desert waste is as thrilling as a five-reel film.

They had called her Rose, fatuously, as parents do their first-born girl. No doubt she had been normally pink and white and velvety. It is a risky thing to do, however. Think back hastily on the Roses you know. Don't you find a startling majority still clinging, sere and withered, to the family bush?

In Chicago, Illinois, a city of two millions (or is it three?), there are women whose lives are as remote, as grey, as unrelated to the world about them as is the life of a Georgia cracker's woman-drudge. Rose was one of these. An unwed woman, grown heavy about the hips and arms, as houseworking women do, though they eat but little, moving dully about the six-room flat on Sangamon Street, Rose was as much a slave as any black wench of plantation days.

There was the treadmill of endless dishes, dirtied as fast as cleansed; there were beds, and beds, and beds; gravies and soups and stews. And always the querulous voice of the sick woman in the front bedroom demanding another hot water bag. Rose's day was punctuated by hot water bags. They dotted her waking hours. She filled hot water bags automatically, like a machine—water half-way to the top, then one hand clutching the bag's slippery middle while the other, with a deft twist, ejected the air within; a quick twirl of the metal stopper, the bag released, squirming, and, finally, its plump and rufous cheeks wiped dry.

"Is that too hot for you, Ma? Where'd you want it—your head or your feet?"

A spinster nearing forty, living thus, must have her memories—one precious memory, at least—or she dies. Rose had hers. She hugged it, close. The L trains roared by, not thirty feet from her kitchen door. Alley and yard and street sent up their noises to her. The life of Chicago's millions yelped at her heels. On Rose's face was the vague, mute look of the woman whose days are spent indoors, at sordid tasks.

At six-thirty every night that look lifted, for an hour. At six-thirty they came home—Floss, and Al, and Pa—their faces stamped with the marks that come from a day spent in shop and factory. They brought with them the crumbs and husks of the day's happenings, and these they flung carelessly before the life-starved Rose and she ate them, gratefully.

They came in with a rush, hungry, fagged, grimed, imperious, smelling of the city. There was a slamming of doors, a banging of drawers, a clatter of tongues, quarrelling, laughter. A brief visit to the sick woman's room. The thin, complaining voice reciting its tale of the day's discomfort and pain. Then supper.

"Guess who I waited on to-day!" Floss might demand.

Rose, dishing up, would pause, interested. "Who?"

"Gladys Moraine! I knew her the minute she came down the aisle. I saw her last year when she was playing in 'His Wives.' She's prettier off than on, I think. I waited on her, and the other girls were wild. She bought a dozen pairs of white kids, and made me give 'em to her huge, so she could shove her hand right into 'em, like a man does. Two sizes too big. All the swells wear 'em that way. And only one ring—an emerald the size of a dime."

"What'd she wear?" Rose's dull face was almost animated.

"Ah yes!" in a dreamy falsetto from Al, "what *did* she wear?"

"Oh, shut up, Al! Just a suit, kind of plain, and yet you'd notice it. And sables! And a Gladys Moraine hat. Everything quiet, and plain, and dark; and yet she looked like a million dollars. I felt like a roach while I was waiting on her, though she was awfully sweet to me."

Or perhaps Al, the eel-like, would descend from his heights to mingle a brief moment in the family talk. Al clerked in the National Cigar Company's store at Clark and Madison. His was the wisdom of the snake, the weasel, and the sphinx. A strangely silent young man, this Al, thin-lipped, smooth-cheeked, perfumed. Slim of waist, flat of hip, narrow of shoulder, his was the figure of the born fox-trotter. He walked lightly, on the balls of his feet, like an Indian, but without the Indian's dignity.

"Some excitement ourselves, to-day, down at the store, believe me. The Old Man's son started in to learn the retail selling end of the business. Back of the showcase with the rest of us, waiting on trade, and looking like a Yale yell."

Pa would put down his paper to stare over his reading specs at Al.

"Mannheim's son! The president!"

"Yep! And I guess he loves it, huh? The Old Man wants him to learn the business from the ground up. I'll bet he'll never get higher than the first floor. To-day he went out to lunch at one and never shows up again till four. Wears English collars, and smokes a brand of cigarettes we don't carry."

Thus was the world brought to Rose. Her sallow cheek would show a faint hint of colour as she sipped her tea.

At six-thirty on a Monday morning in late April (remember, nothing's going to happen) Rose smothered her alarm clock at the first warning snarl. She was wide-awake at once, as are those whose yesterdays, to-days and to-morrows are all alike. Rose never opened her eyes to the dim, tantalising half-consciousness of a something delightful or a something harrowing in store for her that day. For one to whom the wash-woman's Tuesday visitation is the event of the week, and in whose bosom the delivery boy's hoarse "Groc-rees!" as he hurls soap and cabbage on the kitchen table, arouses a wild flurry, there can be very little thrill on awakening.

Rose slept on the davenport-couch in the sitting-room. That fact in itself rises her status in the family. This Monday morning she opened her eyes with what might be called a start if Rose were any other sort of heroine. Something had happened, or was happening. It wasn't the six o'clock steam hissing in the radiator. She was accustomed to that. The rattle of the L trains, and the milkman's artillery disturbed her as little as does the chirping of the birds the farmer's daughter. A sensation new, yet familiar; delicious, yet painful, held her. She groped to define it, lying there. Her gaze, wandering over the expanse of the grey woollen blanket, fixed upon a small black object trembling there. The knowledge that came to her then had come, many weeks before, in a hundred subtle and exquisite ways, to those who dwell in the open places. Rose's eyes narrowed craftily. Craftily, stealthily, she sat up, one hand raised. Her eyes still fixed on the quivering spot, the hand descended, lightning-quick. But not quickly enough. The black spot vanished. It sped toward the open window. Through that window there came a balmy softness made up of Lake Michigan zephyr, and stockyards smell, and distant budding things. Rose had failed to swat the first fly of the season. Spring had come.

As she got out of bed and thud-thudded across the room on her heels to shut the window she glanced out into the quiet street. Her city eyes, untrained to nature's hints, failed to notice that the scraggy, smoke-dwarfed oak that sprang, somehow, miraculously, from the mangey little dirt-plot in front of the building had developed surprising things all over its scrawny branches overnight. But she did see that the front windows of the flat building across the way were bare of the Chicago-grey lace curtains that had hung there the day before. House cleaning! Well, most decidedly spring had come.

Rose was the household's Aurora. Following the donning of her limp and obscure garments it was Rose's daily duty to tear the silent family from its slumbers. Ma was always awake, her sick eyes fixed hopefully on the door. For fourteen years it had been the same.

"Sleeping?"

"Sleeping! I haven't closed an eye all night."

Rose had learned not to dispute that statement.

"It's spring out! I'm going to clean the closets and the bureau drawers to-day. I'll have your coffee in a jiffy. Do you feel like getting up and sitting out on the back porch, toward noon, maybe?"

On her way kitchenward she stopped for a sharp tattoo at the door of the room in which Pa and Al slept. A sleepy grunt of remonstrance rewarded her. She came to Floss's door, turned the knob softly, peered in. Floss was sleeping as twenty sleeps, deeply, dreamlessly, one slim bare arm outflung, the lashes resting ever so lightly on the delicate curve of cheek. As she lay there asleep in her disordered bedroom, her clothes strewing chair, dresser, floor, Floss's tastes, mental equipment, spiritual make-up, innermost thoughts, were as plainly to be read by the observer as though she had been scientifically charted by a psycho-analyst, a metaphysician and her dearest girl friend.

"Floss! Floss, honey! Quarter to seven!" Floss stirred, moaned faintly, dropped into sleep again.

Fifteen minutes later, the table set, the coffee simmering, the morning paper brought from the back porch to Ma, Rose had heard none of the sounds that proclaimed the family astir—the banging of drawers, the rush of running water, the slap of slippered feet. A peep of enquiry into the depths of the coffee pot, the gas turned to a circle of blue beads, and she was down the hall to sound the second alarm.

"Floss, you know if Al once gets into the bathroom!" Floss sat up in bed, her eyes still closed. She made little clucking sounds with her tongue and lips, as a baby does when it wakes. Drugged with sleep, hair tousled, muscles sagging, at seven o'clock in the morning, the most trying hour in the day for a woman, Floss was still triumphantly pretty. She had on one of those absurd pink muslin nightgowns, artfully designed to look like crêpe de chine. You've seen them rosily displayed in the cheaper shop windows, marked ninety-eight cents, and you may have wondered who might buy them, forgetting that there is an imitation mind for every imitation article in the world.

Rose stooped, picked up a pair of silk stockings from the floor, and ran an investigating hand through to heel and toe. She plucked a soiled pink blouse off the back of a chair, eyed it critically, and tucked it under her arm with the stockings.

"Did you have a good time last night?"

Floss yawned elaborately, stretched her slim arms high above her head; then, with a desperate effort, flung back the bed-clothes, swung her legs over the side of the bed and slipped her toes into the shabby, pomponed slippers that lay on the floor.

"I say, did you have a g—"

"Oh Lord, I don't know! I guess so," snapped Floss. Temperamentally, Floss was not at her best at seven o'clock on Monday morning. Rose did not pursue the subject. She tried another tack.

"It's as mild as summer out. I see the Werners and the Burkes are housecleaning. I thought I'd start to-day with the closets, and the bureau drawers. You could wear your blue this morning, if it was pressed."

Floss yawned again, disinterestedly, and folded her kimono about her.

"Go as far as you like. Only don't put things back in my closet so's I can't ever find 'em again. I wish you'd press that blue skirt. And wash out the Georgette crêpe waist. I might need it."

The blouse, and skirt, and stockings under her arm, Rose went back to the kitchen to prepare her mother's breakfast tray. Wafted back to her came the acrid odour of Pa's matutinal pipe, and the accustomed bickering between Al and Floss over the possession of the bathroom.

"What do you think this is, anyway? A Turkish bath?"

"Shave in your own room!"

Between Floss and Al there existed a feud that lifted only when a third member of the family turned against either of them. Immediately they about-faced and stood united against the offender.

Pa was the first to demand breakfast, as always. Very neat, was Pa, and fussy, and strangely young looking to be the husband of the grey-haired, parchment-skinned woman who lay in the front bedroom. Pa had two manias: the movies, and a passion for purchasing new and complicated household utensils—cream-whippers, egg-beaters, window-clamps, lemon-squeezers, silver-polishers. He haunted department store basements in search of them.

He opened his paper now and glanced at the head-lines and at the Monday morning ads. "I see the Fair's got a spring housecleaning sale. They advertise a new kind of extension curtain rod. And Scouro, three cakes for a dime."

"If you waste one cent more on truck like that," Rose protested, placing his breakfast before him, "when half the time I can't make the housekeeping money last through the week!"

"Your ma did it."

"Fourteen years ago liver wasn't thirty-two cents a pound," retorted Rose, "and besides—"

"Scramble 'em!" yelled Al, from the bedroom, by way of warning.

There was very little talk after that. The energies of three of them were directed toward reaching the waiting desk or counter on time. The energy of one toward making that accomplishment easy. The front door slammed once—that was Pa, on his way; slammed again—Al. Floss rushed into the dining-room fastening the waist-band of her skirt, her hat already on. Rose always had a rather special breakfast for Floss. Floss posed as being a rather special person. She always breakfasted last, and late. Floss's was a fastidiousness which shrinks at badly served food, a spotted table-cloth, or a last year's hat, while it overlooks a rent in an undergarment or the accumulated dust in a hairbrush. Her blouse was of the sheerest. Her hair shone in waves about her delicate checks. She ate her orange, and sipped her very special coffee, and made a little face over her egg that had been shirred in the oven or in some way highly specialised. Then the front door slammed again—a semi-slam, this time. Floss never did quite close a door. Rose followed her down the hall, shut and bolted it, Chicago fashion. The sick woman in the front bedroom had dropped into one of her fitful morning dozes. At eight o'clock the little flat was very still.

If you knew nothing about Rose; if you had not already been told that she slept on the sitting-room davenport; that she was taken for granted as the family drudge; that she was, in that household, merely an intelligent machine that made beds, fried eggs, filled hot water bags, you would get a characterization of her from this: She was the sort of person who never has a closet or bureau drawer all her own. Her few and negligible garments hung apologetically in obscure corners of closets dedicated to her sister's wardrobe or her brother's, or her spruce and fussy old father's. Vague personal belongings, such as combings, handkerchiefs, a spectacle case, a hairbrush, were found tucked away in a desk pigeon-hole, a table drawer, or on the top shelf in the bathroom.

As she pulled the disfiguring blue gingham dust-cap over her hair now, and rolled her sleeves to her elbows, you would never have dreamed that Rose was embarking upon her great adventure. You would never have guessed that the semi-yearly closet cleaning was to give to Rose a thrill as delicious as it was exquisitely painful. But Rose knew. And so she teased herself, and tried not to think of the pasteboard box on the shelf in the hall closet, under the pile of reserve blankets, and told herself that she would leave that closet until the last, when she would have to hurry over it.

When you clean closets and bureau drawers thoroughly you have to carry things out to the back porch and flap them, Rose was that sort of housekeeper. She leaned over the porch railing and flapped things, so that the dust motes spun and swirled in the sunshine. Rose's arms worked up and down energetically, then less energetically, finally ceased their motion altogether. She leaned idle elbows on the porch railing and gazed down into the yard below with a look in her eyes such as no squalid Chicago back yard, with its dusty débris, could summon, even in spring-time.

The woman next door came out on her back porch that adjoined Rose's. The day seemed to have her in its spell, too, for in her hand was something woolly and wintry, and she began to flap it about as Rose had done. She had lived next door since October, had that woman, but the two had never exchanged a word, true to the traditions of their city training. Rose had her doubts of the woman next door. She kept a toy dog which she aired afternoons, and her kimonos were florid and numerous. Now, as the eyes of the two women met, Rose found herself saying, "Looks like summer."

The woman next door caught the scrap of conversation eagerly, hungrily. "It certainly does! Makes me feel like new clothes, and housecleaning."

"I started to-day!" said Rose, triumphantly.

"Not already!" gasped the woman next door, with the chagrin that only a woman knows who has let May steal upon her unawares.

From far down the alley sounded a chant, drawing nearer and nearer, until there shambled into view a decrepit horse drawing a dilapidated huckster's cart. Perched on the seat was a Greek who turned his dusky face up toward the two women leaning over the porch railings. "Rhubarb, leddy. Fresh rhubarb!"

"My folks don't care for rhubarb sauce," Rose told the woman next door.

"It makes the worst pie in the world," the woman confided to Rose.

Whereupon each bought a bunch of the succulent green and red stalks. It was their offering at the season's shrine.

Rose flung the rhubarb on the kitchen table, pulled her dust-cap more firmly about her ears, and hurried back to the disorder of Floss's dim little bedroom. After that it was dust-cloth, and soapsuds, and scrub-brush in a race against recurrent water bags, insistent doorbells, and the inevitable dinner hour. It was mid-afternoon when Rose, standing a-tiptoe on a chair, came at last to the little box on the top shelf under the bedding in the hall closet. Her hand touched the box, and closed about it. A little electric thrill vibrated through her body. She stepped down from the chair, heavily, listened until her acute ear caught the sound of the sick woman's slumbrous breathing; then, box in hand, walked down the dark hall to the kitchen. The rhubarb pie, still steaming in its pan, was cooling on the kitchen table. The dishes from the invalid's lunch-tray littered the sink. But Rose, seated on the kitchen chair, her rumpled dust-cap pushed back from her flushed, perspiring face, untied the rude bit of string that bound the old candy box, removed the lid, slowly, and by that act was wafted magically out of the world of rhubarb pies, and kitchen chairs, and dirty dishes, into that place whose air is the breath of incense and myrrh, whose paths are rose-strewn, whose dwellings are temples dedicated to but one small god. The land is known as Love, and Rose travelled back to it on the magic rug of memory.

A family of five in a six-room Chicago flat must sacrifice sentiment to necessity. There is precious little space for those pressed flowers, time-yellowed gowns, and ribbon-bound packets that figured so prominently in the days of attics. Into the garbage can with yesterday's roses! The janitor's burlap sack yawns for this morning's mail; last year's gown has long ago met its end at the hands of the ol'-clo'es man or the wash-woman's daughter. That they had survived these fourteen years, and the strictures of their owner's dwelling, tells more about this boxful of letters than could be conveyed by a battalion of adjectives.

Rose began at the top of the pile, in her orderly fashion, and read straight through to the last. It took one hour. Half of that time she was not reading. She was staring straight ahead with what is mistakenly called an unseeing look, but which actually pierces the veil of years and beholds things far, far beyond the vision of the actual eye. They were the letters of a commonplace man to a commonplace woman, written when they loved each other, and so they were touched with something of the divine. They must have been, else how could they have sustained this woman through fifteen years of drudgery? They were the only tangible foundation left of the structure of dreams she had built about this man. All the rest of her house of love had tumbled about her ears fifteen years before, but with these few remaining bricks she had erected many times since castles and towers more exquisite and lofty and soaring than the original humble structure had ever been.

The story? Well, there really isn't any, as we've warned you. Rose had been pretty then in much the same delicate way that Floss was pretty now. They were to have been married. Rose's mother fell ill, Floss and Al were little more than babies. The marriage was put off. The illness lasted six months—a year—two years—became interminable. The breach into which Rose had stepped closed about her and became a prison. The man had waited, had grown impatient, finally rebelled. He had fled, probably, to marry a less encumbered lady. Rose had gone dully on, caring for the household, the children, the sick woman. In the years that had gone by since then Rose had forgiven him his faithlessness. She only remembered that he had been wont to call her his Röschen, his Rosebud, his pretty flower (being a German gentleman). She only recalled the wonder of having been first in some one's thoughts—she who now was so hopelessly, so irrevocably last.

As she sat there in her kitchen, wearing her soap-stained and faded blue gingham, and the dust-cap pushed back at a rakish angle, a simpering little smile about her lips, she was really very much like the disappointed old maids you used to see so cruelly pictured in the comic valentines. Had those letters obsessed her a little more strongly she might have become quite mad, the Freudians would tell you. Had they held less for her, or had she not been so completely the household's slave, she might have found a certain solace and satisfaction in viewing the Greek profile and marcel wave of the most-worshipped movie star. As it was, they were her ballast, her refuge, the leavening yeast in the soggy dough of her existence. This man had wanted her to be his wife. She had found favour in his eyes. She was certain that he still thought of her, sometimes, and tenderly, regretfully, as she thought of him. It helped her to live. Not only that, it made living possible.

A clock struck, a window slammed, or a street-noise smote her ear sharply. Some sound started her out of her reverie. Rose jumped, stared a moment at the letters in her lap, then hastily, almost shamefacedly, sorted them (she knew each envelope by heart) tied them, placed them in their box and bore them down the hail. There, mounting her chair, she scrubbed the top shelf with her soapy rag, placed the box in its corner, left the hall closet smelling of cleanliness, with never a hint of lavender to betray its secret treasure.

Were Rose to die and go to Heaven, there to spend her days thumbing a golden harp, her hands, by force of habit, would, drop harp-strings at quarter to six, to begin laying a celestial and unspotted table-cloth for supper. Habits as deeply rooted as that must hold, even in after-life.

To-night's six-thirty stampede was noticeably subdued on the part of Pa and Al. It had been a day of sudden and enervating heat, and the city had done its worst to them. Pa's pink gills showed a hint of purple. Al's flimsy silk shirt stuck to his back, and his glittering pompadour was many degrees less submissive than was its wont. But Floss came in late, breathless, and radiant, a large and significant paper bag in her hand. Rose, in the kitchen, was transferring the smoking supper from pot to platter. Pa, in the doorway of the sick woman's little room, had just put his fourteen-year-old question with his usual assumption of heartiness and cheer: "Well, well! And how's the old girl to-night? Feel like you could get up and punish a little supper, eh?" Al engaged at the telephone with some one whom he addressed proprietorially as Kid, was deep in his plans for the evening's diversion. Upon this accustomed scene Floss burst with havoc.

"Rose! Rose, did you iron my Georgette crêpe? Listen! Guess what!" All this as she was rushing down the hall, paper hat-bag still in hand. "Guess who was in the store to-day!"

Rose, at the oven, turned a flushed and interested face toward Floss.

"Who? What's that? A hat?"

"Yes. But listen—"

"Let's see it."

Floss whipped it out of its bag, defiantly. "There! But wait a minute! Let me tell you—"

"How much?"

Floss hesitated just a second. Her wage was nine dollars a week. Then, "Seven-fifty, trimmed." The hat was one of those tiny, head-hugging absurdities that only the Flosses can wear.

"Trimmed is right!" jeered Al, from the doorway.

Rose, thin-lipped with disapproval, turned to her stove again.

"Well, but I had to have it. I'm going to the theatre to-night. And guess who with! Henry Selz!"

Henry Selz was the unromantic name of the commonplace man over whose fifteen-year-old letters Rose had glowed and dreamed an hour before. It was a name that had become mythical in that household—to all but one. Rose heard it spoken now with a sense of unreality. She smiled a little uncertainly, and went on stirring the flour thickening for the gravy. But she was dimly aware that something inside her had suspended action for a moment, during which moment she felt strangely light and disembodied, and that directly afterward the thing began to work madly, so that there was a choked feeling in her chest and a hot pounding in her head.

"What's the joke?" she said, stirring the gravy in the pan.

"Joke nothing! Honest to God! I was standing back of the counter at about ten. The rush hadn't really begun yet. Glove trade usually starts late. I was standing there kidding Herb, the stock boy, when down the aisle comes a man in a big hat, like you see in the western pictures, hair a little grey at the temples, and everything, just like a movie actor. I said to Herb, 'Is it real?' I hadn't got the words out of my mouth when the fellow sees me, stands stock still in the middle of the aisle with his mouth open and his eyes sticking out. 'Register surprise,' I said to Herb, and looked around for the camera. And that minute he took two jumps over to where I was standing, grabbed my hands and says, 'Rose! Rose!' kind of choky. 'Not by about twenty years,' I said. 'I'm Floss, Rose's sister. Let go my hands!'"

Rose—a transfigured Rose, glowing, trembling, radiant—repeated, vibrantly, "You said, 'I'm Floss, Rose's sister. Let go my hands!' And—?"

"He looked kind of stunned, for just a minute. His face was a scream, honestly. Then he said, 'But of course. Fifteen years. But I had always thought of her as just the same.' And he kind of laughed, ashamed, like a kid. And the whitest teeth!"

"Yes, they were—white," said Rose. "Well?"

"Well, I said, 'Won't I do instead?' 'You bet you'll do!' he said. And then he told me his name, and how he was living out in Spokane, and his wife was dead, and he had made a lot of money—fruit, or real estate, or something. He talked a lot about it at lunch, but I didn't pay any attention, as long as he really has it a lot I care how—"

"At lunch?"

"Everything from grape-fruit to coffee. I didn't know it could be done in one hour. Believe me, he had those waiters jumping. It takes money. He asked all about you, and ma, and everything. And he kept looking at me and saying, 'It's wonderful!' I said, 'Isn't it!' but I meant the lunch. He wanted me to go driving this afternoon—auto and everything. Kept calling me Rose. It made me kind of mad, and I told him how you look. He said, 'I suppose so,' and asked me to go to a show to-night. Listen, did you press my Georgette? And the blue?"

"I'll iron the waist while you're eating. I'm not hungry. It only takes a minute. Did you say he was grey?"

"Grey? Oh, you mean—why, just here, and here. Interesting, but not a bit old. And he's got that money look that makes waiters and doormen and taxi drivers just hump. I don't want any supper. Just a cup of tea. I haven't got enough time to dress in, decently, as it is."

Al, draped in the doorway, removed his cigarette to give greater force to his speech. "Your story interests me strangely, little gell. But there's a couple of other people that would like to eat, even if you wouldn't. Come on with that supper, Ro. Nobody staked me to a lunch to-day."

Rose turned to her stove again. Two carmine spots had leaped suddenly to her cheeks. She served the meal in silence, and ate nothing, but that was not remarkable. For the cook there is little appeal in the meat that she has tended from its moist and bloody entrance in the butcher's paper, through the basting or broiling stage to its formal appearance on the platter. She saw that Al and her father were served. Then she went back to the kitchen, and the thud of her iron was heard as she deftly fluted the ruffles of the crêpe blouse. Floss appeared when the meal was half eaten, her hair shiningly coiffed, the pink ribbons of her corset cover showing under her thin kimono. She poured herself a cup of tea and drank it in little quick, nervous gulps. She looked deliriously young, and fragile and appealing, her delicate slenderness revealed by the flimsy garment she wore. Excitement and anticipation lent a glow to her eyes, colour to her cheeks. Al, glancing expertly at the ingenuousness of her artfully simple coiffure, the slim limpness of her body, her wide-eyed gaze, laughed a wise little laugh.

"Every move a Pickford. And so girlish withal."

Floss ignored him. "Hurry up with that waist, Rose!"

"I'm on the collar now. In a second." There was a little silence. Then: "Floss, is—is Henry going to call for you—here?"

"Well, sure! Did you think I was going to meet him on the corner? He said he wanted to see you, or something polite like that."

She finished her tea and vanished again. Al, too, had disappeared to begin that process from which he had always emerged incredibly sleek, and dapper and perfumed. His progress with shaving brush, shirt, collar and tie was marked by disjointed bars of the newest syncopation whistled with an uncanny precision and fidelity to detail. He caught the broken time, and tossed it lightly up again, and dropped it, and caught it deftly like a juggler playing with frail crystal globes that seem forever on the point of crashing to the ground.

Pa stood up, yawning. "Well," he said, his manner very casual, "guess I'll just drop around to the movie."

From the kitchen, "Don't you want to sit with ma a minute, first?"

"I will when I come back. They're showing the third installment of 'The Adventures of Aline,' and I don't want to come in in the middle of it."

He knew the selfishness of it, this furtive and sprightly old man. And because he knew it he attempted to hide his guilt under a burst of temper.

"I've been slaving all day. I guess I've got the right to a little amusement. A man works his fingers to the bone for his family, and then his own daughter nags him."

He stamped down the hall, righteously, and slammed the front door.

Rose came from the kitchen, the pink blouse, warm from the iron, in one hand. She prinked out its ruffles and pleatings as she went. Floss, burnishing her nails somewhat frantically with a dilapidated and greasy buffer, snatched the garment from her and slipped bare arms into it. The front door bell rang, three big, determined rings. Panic fell upon the household.

"It's him!" whispered Floss, as if she could be heard in the entrance three floors below. "You'll have to go."

"I can't!" Every inch of her seemed to shrink and cower away from the thought. "I can't!" Her eyes darted to and fro like a hunted thing seeking to escape. She ran to the hall. "Al! Al, go to the door, will you?"

"Can't," came back in a thick mumble. "Shaving."

The front door-bell rang again, three big, determined rings. "Rose!" hissed Floss, her tone venomous. "I can't go with my waist open. For heaven's sake! Go to the door!"

"I can't," repeated Rose, in a kind of wail. "I—can't." And went. As she went she passed one futile, work-worn hand over her hair, plucked off her apron and tossed it into; a corner, first wiping her flushed face with it.

Henry Selz came up the shabby stairs springily as a man of forty should. Rose stood at the door and waited for him. He stood in the doorway a moment, uncertainly.

"How-do, Henry."

His uncertainty became incredulity. Then, "Why, how-do, Rose! Didn't know you—for a minute. Well, well! It's been a long time. Let's see—ten—fourteen—about fifteen years, isn't it?"

His tone was cheerfully conversational. He really was interested, mathematically. He was as sentimental in his reminiscence as if he had been calculating the lapse of time between the Chicago fire and the World's Fair.

"Fifteen," said Rose, "in May. Won't you come in? Floss'll be here in a minute."

Henry Selz came in and sat down on the davenport couch and dabbed at his forehead. The years had been very kind to him—those same years that had treated Rose so ruthlessly. He had the look of an outdoor man; a man who has met prosperity and walked with her, and followed her pleasant ways; a man who has learned late in life of golf and caviar and tailors, but who has adapted himself to these accessories of wealth with a minimum of friction.

"It certainly is warm, for this time of year." He leaned back and regarded Rose tolerantly. "Well, and how've you been? Did little sister tell you how flabbergasted I was when I saw her this morning? I'm darned if it didn't take fifteen years off my age, just like that! I got kind of balled up for one minute and thought it was you. She tell you?"

"Yes, she told me," said Rose.

"I hear your ma's still sick. That certainly is tough. And you've never married, eh?"

"Never married," echoed Rose.

And so they made conversation, a little uncomfortably, until there came quick, light young steps down the hallway, and Floss appeared in the door, a radiant, glowing, girlish vision. Youth was in her eyes, her cheeks, on her lips. She radiated it. She was miraculously well dressed, in her knowingly simple blue serge suit, and her tiny hat, and her neat shoes and gloves.

"Ah! And how's the little girl to-night?" said Henry Selz.

Floss dimpled, blushed, smiled, swayed. "Did I keep you waiting a terribly long time?"

"No, not a bit. Rose and I were chinning over old times, weren't we, Rose?" A kindly, clumsy thought struck him. "Say, look here, Rose. We're going to a show. Why don't you run and put on your hat and come along. H'm? Come on!"

Rose smiled as a mother smiles at a child that has unknowingly hurt her. "No, thanks, Henry. Not to-night. You and Floss run along. Yes, I'll remember you to Ma. I'm sorry you can't see her. But she don't see anybody, poor Ma."

Then they were off, in a little flurry of words and laughter. From force of habit Rose's near-sighted eyes peered critically at the hang of Floss's blue skirt and the angle of the pert new hat. She stood a moment, uncertainly, after they had left. On her face was the queerest look, as of one thinking, re-adjusting, struggling to arrive at a conclusion in the midst of sudden bewilderment. She turned mechanically and went into her mother's room. She picked up the tray on the table by the bed.

"Who was that?" asked the sick woman, in her ghostly, devitalised voice.

"That was Henry Selz," said Rose.

The sick woman grappled a moment with memory. "Henry Selz! Henry—oh, yes. Did he go out with Rose?"

"Yes," said Rose.

"It's cold in here," whined the sick woman.

"I'll get you a hot bag in a minute, Ma." Rose carried the tray down the hall to the kitchen. At that Al emerged from his bedroom, shrugging himself into his coat. He followed Rose down the hall and watched her as she filled the bag and screwed it and wiped it dry.

"I'll take that in to Ma," he volunteered. He was up the hall and back in a flash. Rose had slumped into a chair at the dining-room table, and was pouring herself a cup of cold and bitter tea. Al came over to her and laid one white hand on her shoulder.

"Ro, lend me a couple of dollars till Saturday, will you?"

"I should say not."

Al doused his cigarette in the dregs of a convenient teacup. He bent down and laid his powdered and pale cheek against Rose's sallow one. One arm was about her, and his hand patted her shoulder.

"Oh, come on, kid," he coaxed. "Don't I always pay you back? Come on! Be a sweet ol' sis. I wouldn't ask you only I've got a date to go to the White City to-night, and dance, and I couldn't get out of it. I tried." He kissed her, and his lips were moist, and he reeked of tobacco, and though Rose shrugged impatiently away from him he knew that he had won. Rose was not an eloquent woman; she was not even an articulate one, at times. If she had been, she would have lifted up her voice to say now:

"Oh, God! I am a woman! Why have you given me all the sorrows, and the drudgery, and the bitterness and the thanklessness of motherhood, with none of its joys! Give me back my youth! I'll drink the dregs at the bottom of the cup, but first let me taste the sweet!"

But Rose did not talk or think in such terms. She could not have put into words the thing she was feeling even if she had been able to diagnose it. So what she said was, "Don't you think I ever get sick and tired of slaving for a thankless bunch like you? Well, I do! Sick and tired of it. That's what! You make me tired, coming around asking for money, as if I was a bank."

But Al waited. And presently she said, grudgingly, wearily, "There's a dollar bill and some small change in the can on the second shelf in the china closet."

Al was off like a terrier. From the pantry came the clink of metal against metal. He was up the hall in a flash, without a look at Rose. The front door slammed a third time.

Rose stirred her cold tea slowly, leaning on the table's edge and gazing down into the amber liquid that she did not mean to drink. For suddenly and comically her face puckered up like a child's. Her head came down among the supper things with a little crash that set the teacups, and the greasy plates to jingling, and she sobbed as she lay there, with great tearing, ugly sobs that would not be stilled, though she tried to stifle them as does one who lives in a paper-thin Chicago flat. She was not weeping for the Henry Selz whom she had just seen. She was not weeping for envy of her selfish little sister, or for loneliness, or weariness. She was weeping at the loss of a ghost who had become her familiar. She was weeping because a packet of soiled and yellow old letters on the top shelf in the hall closet was now only a packet of soiled and yellow old letters, food for the ash can. She was weeping because the urge of spring, that had expressed itself in her only this morning pitifully enough in terms of rhubarb, and housecleaning and a bundle of thumbed old love letters, had stirred in her for the last time.

But presently she did stop her sobbing and got up and cleared the table, and washed the dishes and even glanced at the crumpled sheets of the morning paper that she never found time to read until evening. By eight o'clock the little flat was very still.

V
THAT'S MARRIAGE

Theresa Platt (she that had been Terry Sheehan) watched her husband across the breakfast table with eyes that smouldered. When a woman's eyes smoulder at 7.30 a.m. the person seated opposite her had better look out. But Orville Platt was quite unaware of any smouldering in progress. He was occupied with his eggs. How could he know that these very eggs were feeding the dull red menace in Terry Platt's eyes?

When Orville Platt ate a soft-boiled egg he concentrated on it. He treated it as a great adventure. Which, after all, it is. Few adjuncts of our daily life contain the element of chance that is to be found in a three-minute breakfast egg.

This was Orville Platt's method of attack: First, he chipped off the top, neatly. Then he bent forward and subjected it to a passionate and relentless scrutiny. Straightening—preparatory to plunging his spoon therein—he flapped his right elbow. It wasn't exactly a flap; it was a pass between a hitch and a flap, and presented external evidence of a mental state. Orville Platt always gave that little preliminary jerk when he was contemplating a step, or when he was moved, or argumentative. It was a trick as innocent as it was maddening.

Terry Platt had learned to look for that flap—they had been married four years—to look for it, and to hate it with a morbid, unreasoning hate. That flap of the elbow was tearing Terry Platt's nerves into raw, bleeding fragments.

Her fingers were clenched tightly under the table, now. She was breathing unevenly. "If he does that again," she told herself, "if he flaps again when he opens the second egg, I'll scream. I'll scream. I'll scream! I'll sc—"

He had scooped the first egg into his cup. Now he picked up the second, chipped it, concentrated, straightened, then—up went the elbow, and down, with the accustomed little flap.

The tortured nerves snapped. Through the early morning quiet of Wetona, Wisconsin, hurtled the shrill, piercing shriek of Terry Platt's hysteria.

"Terry! For God's sake! What's the matter!"

Orville Platt dropped the second egg, and his spoon. The egg yolk trickled down his plate. The spoon made a clatter and flung a gay spot of yellow on the cloth. He started toward her.

Terry, wild-eyed, pointed a shaking finger at him. She was laughing, now, uncontrollably. "Your elbow! Your elbow!"

"Elbow?" He looked down at it, bewildered; then up, fright in his face. "What's the matter with it?"

She mopped her eyes. Sobs shook her. "You f-f-flapped it."

"F-f-f—" The bewilderment in Orville Platt's face gave way to anger. "Do you mean to tell me that you screeched like that because my—because I moved my elbow?"

"Yes."

His anger deepened and reddened to fury. He choked. He had started from his chair with his napkin in his hand. He still clutched it. Now he crumpled it into a wad and hurled it to the centre of the table, where it struck a sugar bowl, dropped back, and uncrumpled slowly, reprovingly. "You—you—" Then bewilderment closed down again like a fog over his countenance. "But why? I can't see—"

"Because it—because I can't stand it any longer. Flapping. This is what you do. Like this."

And she did it. Did it with insulting fidelity, being a clever mimic.

"Well, all I can say is you're crazy, yelling like that, for nothing."

"It isn't nothing."

"Isn't, huh? If that isn't nothing, what is?" They were growing incoherent. "What d'you mean, screeching like a maniac? Like a wild woman? The neighbours'll think I've killed you. What d'you mean, anyway!"

"I mean I'm tired of watching it, that's what. Sick and tired."

"Y'are, huh? Well, young lady, just let me tell *you* something—"

He told her. There followed one of those incredible quarrels, as sickening as they are human, which can take place only between two people who love each other; who love each other so well that each knows with cruel certainty the surest way to wound the other; and who stab, and tear, and claw at these vulnerable spots in exact proportion to their love.

Ugly words. Bitter words. Words that neither knew they knew flew between them like sparks between steel striking steel.

From him—"Trouble with you is you haven't got enough to do. That's the trouble with half you women. Just lay around the house, rotting. I'm a fool, slaving on the road to keep a good-for-nothing—"

"I suppose you call sitting around hotel lobbies slaving! I suppose the house runs itself! How about my evenings? Sitting here alone, night after night, when you're on the road."

Finally, "Well, if you don't like it," he snarled, and lifted his chair by the back and slammed it down, savagely, "if you don't like it, why don't you get out, h'm? Why don't you get out?"

And from her, her eyes narrowed to two slits, her cheeks scarlet:

"Why, thanks. I guess I will."

Ten minutes later he had flung out of the house to catch the 8.19 for Manitowoc. He marched down the street, his shoulders swinging rhythmically to the weight of the burden he carried—his black leather hand-bag and the shiny tan sample case, battle-scarred, both, from many encounters with ruthless porters and 'bus men and bell boys. For four years, as he left for his semi-monthly trip, he and Terry had observed a certain little ceremony (as had the neighbours). She would stand in the doorway watching him down the street, the heavier sample-case banging occasionally at his shin. The depot was only three blocks away. Terry watched him with fond, but unillusioned eyes, which proves that she really loved him. He was a dapper, well-dressed fat man, with a weakness for pronounced patterns in suitings, and addicted to brown derbies. One week on the road, one week at home. That was his routine. The wholesale grocery trade liked Platt, and he had for his customers the fondness that a travelling salesman has who is successful in his territory. Before his marriage to Terry Sheehan his little red address book had been overwhelming proof against the theory that nobody loves a fat man.

Terry, standing in the doorway, always knew that when he reached the corner, just where Schroeder's house threatened to hide him from view, he would stop, drop the sample case, wave his hand just once, pick up the sample case and go on, proceeding backward for a step or two, until Schroeder's house made good its threat. It was a comic scene in the eyes of the onlooker, perhaps because a chubby Romeo offends the sense of fitness. The neighbours, lurking behind their parlour curtains, had laughed at first. But after awhile they learned to look for that little scene, and to take it unto themselves, as if it were a personal thing. Fifteen-year wives whose husbands had long since abandoned flowery farewells used to get a vicarious thrill out of it, and to eye Terry with a sort of envy.

This morning Orville Platt did not even falter when he reached Schroeder's corner. He marched straight on, looking steadily ahead, the heavy bags swinging from either hand. Even if he had stopped—though she knew he wouldn't—Terry Platt would not have seen him. She remained seated at the disordered breakfast table, a dreadfully still figure, and sinister; a figure of stone and fire; of ice and flame. Over and over in her mind she was milling the things she might have said to him, and had not. She brewed a hundred vitriolic cruelties that she might have flung in his face. She would concoct one biting brutality, and dismiss it for a second, and abandon that for a third. She was too angry to cry—a dangerous state in a woman. She was what is known as cold mad, so that her mind was working clearly and with amazing swiftness, and yet as though it were a thing detached; a thing that was no part of her.

She sat thus for the better part of an hour, motionless except for one forefinger that was, quite unconsciously, tapping out a popular and cheap little air that she had been strumming at the piano the evening before, having bought it down town that same afternoon. It had struck Orville's fancy, and she had played it over and over for him. Her right forefinger was playing the entire tune, and something in the back of her head was following it accurately, though the separate thinking process was going on just the same. Her eyes were bright, and wide, and hot. Suddenly she became conscious of the musical antics of her finger. She folded it in with its mates, so that her hand became a fist. She stood up and stared down at the clutter of the breakfast table. The egg—that fateful second egg—had congealed to a mottled mess of yellow and white. The spoon lay on the cloth. His coffee, only half consumed, showed tan with a cold grey film over it. A slice of toast at the left of his plate seemed to grin at her with the semi-circular wedge that he had bitten out of it.

Terry stared down at this congealing remnant. Then she laughed, a hard, high little laugh, pushed a plate away contemptuously with her hand, and walked into the sitting room. On the piano was the piece of music (Bennie Gottschalk's great song hit, "Hicky Bloo") which she had been playing the night before. She picked it up, tore it straight across, once, placed the pieces back to back and tore it across again. Then she dropped the pieces to the floor.

"You bet I'm going," she said, as though concluding a train of thought. "You just bet I'm going. Right now!"

And Terry went. She went for much the same reason as that given by the ladye of high degree in the old English song—she who had left her lord and bed and board to go with the raggle-taggle gipsies-O! The thing that was sending Terry Platt away was much more than a conjugal quarrel precipitated by a soft-boiled egg and a flap of the arm. It went so much deeper that if psychology had not become a cant word we might drag it into the explanation. It went so deep that it's necessary to delve back to the days when Theresa Platt was Terry Sheehan to get the real significance of it, and of the things she did after she went.

When Mrs. Orville Platt had been Terry Sheehan she had played the piano, afternoons and evenings, in the orchestra of the Bijou theatre, on Cass street, Wetona, Wisconsin. Any one with a name like Terry Sheehan would, perforce, do well anything she might set out to do. There was nothing of genius in Terry, but there was something of fire, and much that was Irish. The combination makes for what is known as imagination in playing. Which meant that the Watson Team, Eccentric Song and Dance Artists, never needed a rehearsal when they played the Bijou. Ruby Watson used merely to approach Terry before the Monday performance, sheet-music in hand, and say,

"Listen, dearie. We've got some new business I want to wise you to. Right here it goes '*Tum* dee-dee *dum* dee-dee *tum dum dum*. See? Like that. And then Jim vamps. Get me?"

Terry, at the piano, would pucker her pretty brow a moment. Then, "Like this, you mean?"

"That's it! You've got it."

"All right. I'll tell the drum."

She could play any tune by ear, once heard. She got the spirit of a thing, and transmitted it. When Terry played a march number you tapped the floor with your foot, and unconsciously straightened your shoulders. When she played a home-and-mother song that was heavy on the minor wail you hoped that the man next to you didn't know you were crying (which he probably didn't, because he was weeping, too).

At that time motion pictures had not attained their present virulence. Vaudeville, polite or otherwise, had not yet been crowded out by the ubiquitous film. The Bijou offered entertainment of the cigar-box tramp variety, interspersed with trick bicyclists, soubrettes in slightly soiled pink, trained seals, and Family Fours with lumpy legs who tossed each other about and struck Goldbergian attitudes.

Contact with these gave Terry Sheehan a semi-professional tone. The more conservative of her townspeople looked at her askance. There never had been an evil thing about Terry, but Wetona considered her rather fly. Terry's hair was very black, and she had a fondness for those little, close-fitting scarlet velvet turbans. A scarlet velvet turban would have made Martha Washington look fly. Terry's mother had died when the girl was eight, and Terry's father had been what is known as easy-going. A good-natured, lovable, shiftless chap in the contracting business. He drove around Wetona in a sagging, one-seated cart and never made any money because he did honest work and charged as little for it as men who did not. His mortar stuck, and his bricks did not crumble, and his lumber did not crack. Riches are not acquired in the contracting business in that way. Ed Sheehan and his daughter were great friends. When he died (she was nineteen) they say she screamed once, like a banshee, and dropped to the floor.

After they had straightened out the muddle of books in Ed Sheehan's gritty, dusty little office Terry turned her piano-playing talent to practical account. At twenty-one she was still playing at the Bijou, and into her face was creeping the first hint of that look of sophistication which comes from daily contact with the artificial world of the footlights. It is the look of those who must make believe as a business, and are a-weary. You see it developed into its highest degree in the face of a veteran comedian. It is the thing that gives the look of utter pathos and tragedy to the relaxed expression of a circus clown.

There are, in a small, Mid-West town like Wetona, just two kinds of girls. Those who go down town Saturday nights, and those who don't. Terry, if she had not been busy with her job at the Bijou, would have come in the first group. She craved excitement. There was little chance to satisfy such craving in Wetona, but she managed to find certain means. The travelling men from the Burke House just across the street used to drop in at the Bijou for an evening's entertainment. They usually sat well toward the front, and Terry's expert playing, and the gloss of her black hair, and her piquant profile as she sometimes looked up toward the stage for a signal from one of the performers, caught their fancy, and held it.

Terry did not accept their attentions promiscuously. She was too decent a girl for that. But she found herself, at the end of a year or two, with a rather large acquaintance among these peripatetic gentlemen. You occasionally saw one of them strolling home with her. Sometimes she went driving with one of them of a Sunday afternoon. And she rather enjoyed taking Sunday dinner at the Burke Hotel with a favoured friend. She thought those small-town hotel Sunday dinners the last word in elegance. The roast course was always accompanied by an aqueous, semi-frozen concoction which the bill of fare revealed as Roman punch. It added a royal touch to the repast, even when served with roast pork. I don't say that any of these Lotharios snatched a kiss during a Sunday afternoon drive. Or that Terry slapped him promptly. But either seems extremely likely.

Terry was twenty-two when Orville Platt, making his initial Wisconsin trip for the wholesale grocery house he represented, first beheld Terry's piquant Irish profile, and heard her deft manipulation of the keys. Orville had the fat man's sense of rhythm and love of music. He had a buttery tenor voice, too, of which he was rather proud.

He spent three days in Wetona that first trip, and every evening saw him at the Bijou, first row, centre. He stayed through two shows each time, and before he had been there fifteen minutes Terry was conscious of him through the back of her head. In fact I think that, in all innocence, she rather played up to him. Orville Platt paid no more heed to the stage, and what was occurring thereon, than if it had not been. He sat looking at Terry, and waggling his head in time to the music. Not that Terry was a beauty. But she was one of those immaculately clean types. That look of fragrant cleanliness was her chief charm. Her clear, smooth skin contributed to it, and the natural pencilling of her eyebrows. But the thing that accented it, and gave it a last touch, was the way in which her black hair came down in a little point just in the centre of her forehead, where hair meets brow. It grew to form what is known as a cow-lick. (A prettier name for it is widow's peak.) Your eye lighted on it, pleased, and from it travelled its gratified way down her white temples, past her little ears, to the smooth black coil at the nape of her neck. It was a trip that rested you.

At the end of the last performance on the second night of his visit to the Bijou, Orville waited until the audience had begun to file out. Then he leaned forward over the rail that separated orchestra from audience.

"Could you," he said, his tones dulcet, "could you oblige me with the name of that last piece you played?"

Terry was stacking her music. "George!" she called, to the drum. "Gentleman wants to know the name of that last piece." And prepared to leave.

"'My Georgia Crackerjack'," said the laconic drum.

Orville Platt took a hasty side-step in the direction of the door toward which Terry was headed. "It's a pretty thing," he said, fervently. "An awful pretty thing. Thanks. It's beautiful."

Terry flung a last insult at him over her shoulder: "Don't thank *me* for it. I didn't write it."

Orville Platt did not go across the street to the hotel. He wandered up Cass street, and into the ten-o'clock quiet of Main street, and down as far as the park and back. "Pretty as a pink! And play!... And good, too. Good."

A fat man in love.

At the end of six months they were married. Terry was surprised into it. Not that she was not fond of him. She was; and grateful to him, as well. For, pretty as she was, no man had ever before asked Terry to be his wife. They had made love to her. They had paid court to her. They had sent her large boxes of stale drug-store chocolates, and called her endearing names as they made cautious declaration such as:

"I've known a lot of girls, but you've got something different. I don't know. You've got so much sense. A fellow can chum around with you. Little pal."

Orville's headquarters were Wetona. They rented a comfortable, seven-room house in a comfortable, middle-class neighbourhood, and Terry dropped the red velvet turbans and went in for picture hats and paradise aigrettes. Orville bought her a piano whose tone was so good that to her ear, accustomed to the metallic discords of the Bijou instrument, it sounded out of tune. She played a great deal at first, but unconsciously she missed the sharp spat of applause that used to follow her public performance. She would play a piece, brilliantly, and then her hands would drop to her lap. And the silence of her own sitting room would fall flat on her ears. It was better on the evenings when Orville was home. He sang, in his throaty, fat man's tenor, to Terry's expert accompaniment.

"This is better than playing for those bum actors, isn't it, hon?" And he would pinch her ear.

"Sure"—listlessly.

But after the first year she became accustomed to what she termed private life. She joined an afternoon sewing club, and was active in the ladies' branch of the U.C.T. She developed a knack at cooking, too, and Orville, after a week or ten days of hotel fare in small Wisconsin towns, would come home to sea-foam biscuits, and real soup, and honest pies and cake. Sometimes, in the midst of an appetising meal he would lay down his knife and fork and lean back in his chair, and regard the cool and unruffled Terry with a sort of reverence in his eyes. Then he would get up, and come around to the other side of the table, and tip her pretty face up to his.

"I'll bet I'll wake up, some day, and find out it's all a dream. You know this kind of thing doesn't really happen—not to a dub like me."

One year; two; three; four. Routine. A little boredom. Some impatience. She began to find fault with the very things she had liked in him: his super-neatness; his fondness for dashing suit patterns; his throaty tenor; his worship of her. And the flap. Oh, above all, that flap! That little, innocent, meaningless mannerism that made her tremble with nervousness. She hated it so that she could not trust herself to speak of it to him. That was the trouble. Had she spoken of it, laughingly or in earnest, before it became an obsession with her, that hideous breakfast quarrel, with its taunts, and revilings, and open hate, might never have come to pass. For that matter, any one of those foreign fellows with the guttural names and the psychoanalytical minds could have located her trouble in one *séance*.

Terry Platt herself didn't know what was the matter with her. She would have denied that anything was wrong. She didn't even throw her hands above her head and shriek: "I want to live! I want to live! I want to live!" like a lady in a play. She only knew she was sick of sewing at the Wetona West-End Red Cross shop; sick of marketing, of home comforts, of Orville, of the flap.

Orville, you may remember, left at 8.19. The 11.23 bore Terry Chicagoward. She had left the house as it was—beds unmade, rooms unswept, breakfast table uncleared. She intended never to come back.

Now and then a picture of the chaos she had left behind would flash across her order-loving mind. The spoon on the table-cloth. Orville's pajamas dangling over the bathroom chair. The coffee-pot on the gas stove.

"Pooh! What do I care?"

In her pocketbook she had a tidy sum saved out of the housekeeping money. She was naturally thrifty, and Orville had never been niggardly. Her meals when Orville was on the road, had been those sketchy, haphazard affairs with which women content themselves when their household is manless. At noon she went into the dining car and ordered a flaunting little repast of chicken salad and asparagus, and Neapolitan ice cream. The men in the dining car eyed her speculatively and with appreciation. Then their glance dropped to the third finger of her left hand, and wandered away. She had meant to remove it. In fact, she had taken it off and dropped it into her bag. But her hand felt so queer, so unaccustomed, so naked, that she had found herself slipping the narrow band on again, and her thumb groped for it, gratefully.

It was almost five o'clock when she reached Chicago. She felt no uncertainty or bewilderment. She had been in Chicago three or four times since her marriage. She went to a down town hotel. It was too late, she told herself, to look for a more inexpensive room that night. When she had tidied herself she went out. The things she did were the childish, aimless things that one does who finds herself in possession of sudden liberty. She walked up State Street, and stared in the windows; came back, turned into Madison, passed a bright little shop in the window of which taffy—white and gold—was being wound endlessly and fascinatingly about a double-jointed machine. She went in and bought a sackful, and wandered on down the street, munching.

She had supper at one of those white-tiled sarcophagi that emblazon Chicago's down town side streets. It had been her original intention to dine in state in the rose-and-gold dining room of her hotel. She had even thought daringly of lobster. But at the last moment she recoiled from the idea of dining alone in that wilderness of tables so obviously meant for two.

After her supper she went to a picture show. She was amazed to find there, instead of the accustomed orchestra, a pipe-organ that panted and throbbed and rumbled over lugubrious classics. The picture was about a faithless wife. Terry left in the middle of it.

She awoke next morning at seven, as usual, started up wildly, looked around, and dropped back. Nothing to get up for. The knowledge did not fill her with a rush of relief. She would have her breakfast in bed! She telephoned for it, languidly. But when it came she got up and ate it from the table, after all. Terry was the kind of woman to whom a pink gingham all-over apron, and a pink dust-cap are ravishingly becoming at seven o'clock in the morning. That sort of woman congenitally cannot enjoy her breakfast in bed.

That morning she found a fairly comfortable room, more within her means, on the north side in the boarding house district. She unpacked and hung up her clothes and drifted down town again, idly. It was noon when she came to the corner of State and Madison streets. It was a maelstrom that caught her up, and buffeted her about, and tossed her helplessly this way and that. The corner of Broadway and Forty-second streets has been exploited in song and story as the world's most hazardous human whirlpool. I've negotiated that corner. I've braved the square in front of the American Express Company's office in Paris, June, before the War. I've crossed the Strand at 11 p.m. when the theatre crowds are just out. And to my mind the corner of State and Madison streets between twelve and one, mid-day, makes any one of these dizzy spots look bosky, sylvan, and deserted.

The thousands jostled Terry, and knocked her hat awry, and dug her with unheeding elbows, and stepped on her feet.

"Say, look here!" she said, once futilely. They did not stop to listen. State and Madison has no time for Terrys from Wetona. It goes its way, pellmell. If it saw Terry at all it saw her only as a prettyish person, in the wrong kind of suit and hat, with a bewildered, resentful look on her face.

Terry drifted on down the west side of State Street, with the hurrying crowd. State and Monroe. A sound came to Terry's ears. A sound familiar, beloved. To her ear, harassed with the roar and crash, with the shrill scream of the crossing policemen's whistle, with the hiss of feet shuffling on cement, it was a celestial strain. She looked up, toward the sound. A great second-story window opened wide to the street. In it a girl at a piano, and a man, red-faced, singing through a megaphone. And on a flaring red and green sign:
BERNIE GOTTSCHALK'S MUSIC HOUSE!

COME IN! HEAR BERNIE GOTTSCHALK'S LATEST
HIT! THE HEART-THROB SONG THAT HAS GOT 'EM ALL!
THE SONG THAT MADE THE KAISER CRAWL!

"I COME FROM PARIS, ILLINOIS, BUT OH!
YOU PARIS, FRANCE!
I USED TO WEAR BLUE OVERALLS BUT
NOW ITS KHAKI PANTS."

COME IN! COME IN!
Terry accepted.

She followed the sound of the music. Around the corner. Up a little flight of stairs. She entered the realm of Euterpe; Euterpe with her back hair frizzed; Euterpe with her flowing white robe replaced by soiled white boots that failed to touch the hem of an empire-waisted blue serge; Euterpe abandoning her lyre for jazz. She sat at the piano, a red-haired young lady whose familiarity with the piano had bred contempt. Nothing else could have accounted for her treatment of it. Her fingers, tipped with sharp-pointed grey and glistening nails, clawed the keys with a dreadful mechanical motion. There were stacks of music-sheets on counters, and shelves, and dangling from overhead wires. The girl at the piano never ceased playing. She played mostly by request. A prospective purchaser would mumble something in the ear of one of the clerks. The fat man with the megaphone would bawl out, "'Hicky Bloo!' Miss Ryan." And Miss Ryan would oblige. She made a hideous rattle and crash and clatter of sound compared to which an Indian tom-tom would have seemed as dulcet as the strumming of a lute in a lady's boudoir.

Terry joined the crowds about the counter. The girl at the piano was not looking at the keys. Her head was screwed around over her left shoulder and as she played she was holding forth animatedly to a girl friend who had evidently dropped in from some store or office during the lunch hour. Now and again the fat man paused in his vocal efforts to reprimand her for her slackness. She paid no heed. There was something gruesome, uncanny, about the way her fingers went their own way over the defenceless keys. Her conversation with the frowzy little girl went on.

"Wha'd he say?" (Over her shoulder).

"Oh, he laffed."

"Well, didja go?"

"Me! Well, whutya think I yam, anyway?"

"I woulda took a chanst."

The fat man rebelled.

"Look here! Get busy! What are you paid for? Talkin' or playin'? Huh?"

The person at the piano, openly reproved thus before her friend, lifted her uninspired hands from the keys and spake. When she had finished she rose.

"But you can't leave now," the megaphone man argued. "Right in the rush hour."

"I'm gone," said the girl. The fat man looked about, helplessly. He gazed at the abandoned piano, as though it must go on of its own accord. Then at the crowd. "Where's Miss Schwimmer?" he demanded of a clerk.

"Out to lunch."

Terry pushed her way to the edge of the counter and leaned over. "I can play for you," she said.

The man looked at her. "Sight?"

"Yes."

"Come on."

Terry went around to the other side of the counter, took off her hat and coat, rubbed her hands together briskly, sat down and began to play. The crowd edged closer.

It is a curious study, this noonday crowd that gathers to sate its music-hunger on the scraps vouchsafed it by Bernie Gottschalk's Music House. Loose-lipped, slope-shouldered young men with bad complexions and slender hands. Girls whose clothes are an unconscious satire on present-day fashions. On their faces, as they listen to the music, is a look of peace and dreaming. They stand about, smiling a wistful half smile. It is much the same expression that steals over the face of a smoker who has lighted his after-dinner cigar, or of a drug victim who is being lulled by his opiate. The music seems to satisfy a something within them. Faces dull, eyes lustreless, they listen in a sort of trance.

Terry played on. She played as Terry Sheehan used to play. She played as no music hack at Bernie Gottschalk's had ever played before. The crowd swayed a little to the sound of it. Some kept time with little jerks of the shoulder—the little hitching movement of the rag-time dancer whose blood is filled with the fever of syncopation. Even the crowd flowing down State Street must have caught the rhythm of it, for the room soon filled.

At two o'clock the crowd began to thin. Business would be slack, now, until five, when it would again pick up until closing time at six.

The fat vocalist put down his megaphone, wiped his forehead, and regarded Terry with a warm blue eye. He had just finished singing "I've Wandered Far from Dear Old Mother's Knee." (Bernie Gottschalk Inc. Chicago. New York. You can't get bit with a Gottschalk hit. 15 cents each.)

"Girlie," he said, emphatically, "You sure—can—play!" He came over to her at the piano and put a stubby hand on her shoulder. "Yessir! Those little fingers—"

Terry just turned her head to look down her nose at the moist hand resting on her shoulder. "Those little fingers are going to meet your face—suddenly—if you don't move on."

"Who gave you your job?" demanded the fat man.

"Nobody. I picked it myself. You can have it if you want it."

"Can't you take a joke?"

"Label yours."

As the crowd dwindled she played less feverishly, but there was nothing slipshod about her performance. The chubby songster found time to proffer brief explanations in asides. "They want the patriotic stuff. It used to be all that Hawaiian dope, and Wild Irish Rose junk, and songs about wanting to go back to every place from Dixie to Duluth. But now seems it's all these here flag raisers. Honestly, I'm so sick of 'em I got a notion to enlist to get away from it."

Terry eyed him with, withering briefness. "A little training wouldn't ruin your figure."

She had never objected to Orville's *embonpoint*. But then, Orville was a different sort of fat man; pink-cheeked, springy, immaculate.

At four o'clock, as she was in the chorus of "Isn't There Another Joan of Arc?" a melting masculine voice from the other side of the counter said, "Pardon me. What's that you're playing?"

Terry told him. She did not look up.

"I wouldn't have known it. Played like that—a second Marseillaise. If the words—what are the words? Let me see a—"

"Show the gentleman a 'Joan'," Terry commanded briefly, over her shoulder. The fat man laughed a wheezy laugh. Terry glanced around, still playing, and encountered the gaze of two melting masculine eyes that matched the melting masculine voice. The songster waved a hand uniting Terry and the eyes in informal introduction.

"Mr. Leon Sammett, the gentleman who sings the Gottschalk songs wherever songs are heard. And Mrs.—that is—and Mrs. Sammett—"

Terry turned. A sleek, swarthy world-old young man with the fashionable concave torso, and alarmingly convex bone-rimmed glasses. Through them his darkly luminous gaze glowed upon Terry. To escape their warmth she sent her own gaze past him to encounter the arctic stare of the large blonde person who had been included so lamely in the introduction. And at that the frigidity of that stare softened, melted, dissolved.

"Why Terry Sheehan! What in the world!"

Terry's eyes bored beneath the layers of flabby fat. "It's—why, it's Ruby Watson, isn't it? Eccentric Song and Dance—"

She glanced at the concave young man and faltered. He was not Jim, of the Bijou days. From him her eyes leaped back to the fur-bedecked splendour of the woman. The plump face went so painfully red that the makeup stood out on it, a distinct layer, like thin ice covering flowing water. As she surveyed that bulk Terry realised that while Ruby might still claim eccentricity, her song and dance days were over. "That's ancient history, m'dear. I haven't been working for three years. What're you doing in this joint? I'd heard you'd done well for yourself. That you were married."

"I am. That is I—well, I am. I—"

At that the dark young man leaned over and patted Terry's hand that lay on the counter. He smiled. His own hand was incredibly slender, long, and tapering.

"That's all right," he assured her, and smiled. "You two girls can have a reunion later. What I want to know is can you play by ear?"

"Yes, but—"

He leaned far over the counter. "I knew it the minute I heard you play. You've got the touch. Now listen. See if you can get this, and fake the bass."

He fixed his sombre and hypnotic eyes on Terry. His mouth screwed up into a whistle. The tune—a tawdry but haunting little melody—came through his lips. And Terry's quick ear sensed that every note was flat. She turned back to the piano. "Of course you know you flatted every note," she said.

This time it was the blonde woman who laughed, and the man who flushed. Terry cocked her head just a little to one side, like a knowing bird, looked up into space beyond the piano top, and played the lilting little melody with charm and fidelity. The dark young man followed her with a wagging of the head and little jerks of both outspread hands. His expression was beatific, enraptured. He hummed a little under his breath and any one who was music wise would have known that he was just a half-beat behind her all the way.

When she had finished he sighed deeply, ecstatically. He bent his lean frame over the counter and, despite his swart colouring, seemed to glitter upon her—his eyes, his teeth, his very finger-nails.

"Something led me here. I never come up on Tuesdays. But something—"

"You was going to complain," put in his lady, heavily, "about that Teddy Sykes at the Palace Gardens singing the same songs this week that you been boosting at the Inn."

He put up a vibrant, peremptory hand. "Bah! What does that matter now! What does anything matter now! Listen Miss—ah—Miss?—"

"Pl—Sheehan. Terry Sheehan."

He gazed off a moment into space. "H'm. 'Leon Sammett in Songs. Miss Terry Sheehan at the Piano.' That doesn't sound bad. Now listen, Miss Sheehan. I'm singing down at the University Inn. The Gottschalk song hits. I guess you know my work. But I want to talk to you, private. It's something to your interest. I go on down at the Inn at six. Will you come and have a little something with Ruby and me? Now?"

"Now?" faltered Terry, somewhat helplessly. Things seemed to be moving rather swiftly for her, accustomed as she was to the peaceful routine of the past four years.

"Get your hat. It's your life chance. Wait till you see your name in two-foot electrics over the front of every big-time house in the country. You've got music in you. Tie to me and you're made." He turned to the woman beside him. "Isn't that so, Rube?"

"Sure. Look at *me*!" One would not have thought there could be so much subtle vindictiveness in a fat blonde.

Sammett whipped out a watch. "Just three-quarters of an hour. Come on, girlie."

His conversation had been conducted in an urgent undertone, with side glances at the fat man with the megaphone. Terry approached him now.

"I'm leaving now," she said.

"Oh, no you're not. Six o'clock is your quitting time."

In which he touched the Irish in Terry. "Any time I quit is my quitting time." She went in quest of hat and coat much as the girl had done whose place she had taken early in the day. The fat man followed her, protesting. Terry, pinning on her hat tried to ignore him. But he laid one plump hand on her arm and kept it there, though she tried to shake him off.

"Now, listen to me. That boy wouldn't mind putting his heel on your face if he thought it would bring him up a step. I know'm. Y'see that walking stick he's carrying? Well, compared to the yellow stripe that's in him, that cane is a lead pencil. He's a song tout, that's all he is." Then, more feverishly, as Terry tried to pull away: "Wait a minute. You're a decent girl. I want to—Why, he can't even sing a note without you give it to him first. He can put a song over, yes. But how? By flashin' that toothy grin, of his and talkin' every word of it. Don't you—"

But Terry freed herself with a final jerk and whipped around the counter. The two, who had been talking together in an undertone, turned to welcome her. "We've got a half hour. Come on. It's just over to Clark and up a block or so."

If you know Chicago at all, you know the University Inn, that gloriously intercollegiate institution which welcomes any graduate of any school of experience, and guarantees a post-graduate course in less time than any similar haven of knowledge. Down a flight of stairs and into the unwonted quiet that reigns during the hour of low potentiality, between five and six, the three went, and seated themselves at a table in an obscure corner. A waiter brought them things in little glasses, though no order had been given. The woman who had been Ruby Watson was so silent as to be almost wordless. But the man talked rapidly. He talked well, too. The same quality that enabled him, voiceless though he was, to boost a song to success, was making his plea sound plausible in Terry's ears now.

"I've got to go and make up in a few minutes. So get this. I'm not going to stick down in this basement eating house forever. I've got too much talent. If I only had a voice—I mean a singing voice. But I haven't. But then, neither has Georgie Cohan, and I can't see that it's wrecked his life any. Look at Elsie Janis! But she sings. And they like it! Now listen. I've got a song. It's my own. That bit you played for me up at Gottschalk's is part of the chorus. But it's the words that'll go big. They're great. It's an aviation song, see? Airship stuff. They're yelling that it's the airyoplanes that're going to win this war. Well, I'll help 'em. This song is going to put the aviator where he belongs. It's going to be the big song of the war. It's going to make 'Tipperary' sound like a Moody and Sankey hymn. It's the—"

Ruby lifted her heavy-lidded eyes and sent him a meaning look. "Get down to business, Leon. I'll tell her how good you are while you're making up."

He shot her a malignant glance, but took her advice. "Now what I've been looking for for years is somebody who has got the music knack to give me the accompaniment just a quarter of a jump ahead of my voice, see? I can follow like a lamb, but I've got to have that feeler first. It's more than a knack. It's a gift. And you've got it. I know it when I see it. I want to get away from this cabaret thing. There's nothing in it for a man of my talent. I'm gunning for vaudeville. But they won't book me without a tryout. And when they hear my voice they—Well, if me and you work together we can fool 'em. The song's great. And my makeup's one of these av-iation costumes to go with the song, see? Pants tight in the knee and baggy on the hips. And a coat with one of those full skirt whaddyoucall'ems—"

"Peplums," put in Ruby, placidly.

"Sure. And the girls'll be wild about it. And the words!" he began to sing, gratingly off-key:

"Put on your sky clothes,
Put on your fly clothes
And take a trip with me.
We'll sail so high
Up in the sky
We'll drop a bomb from Mercury."

"Why, that's awfully cute!" exclaimed Terry. Until now her opinion of Mr. Sammett's talents had not been on a level with his.

"Yeh, but wait till you hear the second verse. That's only part of the chorus. You see, he's supposed to be talking to a French girl. He says:

I'll parlez-vous in Français plain,
You'll answer, 'Cher Américain,
We'll both. . . . ."

The six o'clock lights blazed up, suddenly. A sad-looking group of men trailed in and made for a corner where certain bulky, shapeless bundles were soon revealed as those glittering and tortuous instruments which go to make a jazz band.

"You better go, Lee. The crowd comes in awful early now, with all those buyers in town."

Both hands on the table he half rose, reluctantly, still talking. "I've got three other songs. They make Gottschalk's stuff look sick. All I want's a chance. What I want you to do is accompaniment. On the stage, see? Grand piano. And a swell set. I haven't quite made up my mind to it. But a kind of an army camp room, see? And maybe you dressed as Liberty. Anyway, it'll be new, and a knock-out. If only we can get away with the voice thing. Say, if Eddie Foy, all those years never had a—"

The band opened with a terrifying clash of cymbal, and thump of drum. "Back at the end of my first turn," he said as he fled. Terry followed his lithe, electric figure. She turned to meet the heavy-lidded gaze of the woman seated opposite. She relaxed, then, and sat back with a little sigh. "Well! If he talks that way to the managers I don't see—"

Ruby laughed a mirthless little laugh. "Talk doesn't get it over with the managers, honey. You've got to deliver."

"Well, but he's—that song is a good one. I don't say it's as good as he thinks it is, but it's good."

"Yes," admitted the woman, grudgingly, "it's good."

"Well, then?"

The woman beckoned a waiter; he nodded and vanished, and reappeared with a glass that was twin to the one she had just emptied. "Does he look like he knew French? Or could make a rhyme?"

"But didn't he? Doesn't he?"

"The words were written by a little French girl who used to skate down here last winter, when the craze was on. She was stuck on a Chicago kid who went over to fly for the French."

"But the music?"

"There was a Russian girl who used to dance in the cabaret and she—"

Terry's head came up with a characteristic little jerk. "I don't believe it!"

"Better." She gazed at Terry with the drowsy look that was so different from the quick, clear glance of the Ruby Watson who used to dance so nimbly in the Old Bijou days. "What'd you and your husband quarrel about, Terry?"

Terry was furious to feel herself flushing. "Oh, nothing. He just—I—it was—Say, how did you know we'd quarrelled?"

And suddenly all the fat woman's apathy dropped from her like a garment and some of the old sparkle and animation illumined her heavy face. She pushed her glass aside and leaned forward on her folded arms, so that her face was close to Terry's.

"Terry Sheehan, I know you've quarrelled, and I know just what it was about. Oh, I don't mean the very thing it was about; but the kind of thing. I'm going to do something for you, Terry, that I wouldn't take the trouble to do for most women. But I guess I ain't had all the softness knocked out of me yet, though it's a wonder. And I guess I remember too plain the decent kid you was in the old days. What was the name of that little small-time house me and Jim used to play? Bijou, that's it; Bijou."

The band struck up a new tune. Leon Sammett—slim, sleek, lithe in his evening clothes—appeared with a little fair girl in pink chiffon. The woman reached across the table and put one pudgy, jewelled hand on Terry's arm. "He'll be through in ten minutes. Now listen to me. I left Jim four years ago, and there hasn't been a minute since then, day or night, when I wouldn't have crawled back to him on my hands and knees if I could. But I couldn't. He wouldn't have me now. How could he? How do I know you've quarrelled? I can see it in your eyes. They look just the way mine have felt for four years, that's how. I met up with this boy, and there wasn't anybody to do the turn for me that I'm trying to do for you. Now get this. I left Jim because when he ate corn on the cob he always closed his eyes and it drove me wild. Don't laugh."

"I'm not laughing," said Terry.

"Women are like that. One night—we was playing Fond du Lac; I remember just as plain—we was eating supper and Jim reached for one of those big yellow ears, and buttered and salted it, and me kind of hanging on to the edge of the table with my nails. Seemed to me if he shut his eyes when he put his teeth into that ear of corn I'd scream. And he did. And I screamed. And that's all."

Terry sat staring at her with a wide-eyed stare, like a sleep walker. Then she wet her lips, slowly. "But that's almost the very—"

"Kid, go on back home. I don't know whether it's too late or not, but go anyway. If you've lost him I suppose it ain't any more than you deserve, but I hope to God you don't get your desserts this time. He's almost through. If he sees you going he can't quit in the middle of his song to stop you. He'll know I put you wise, and he'll prob'ly half kill me for it. But it's worth it. You get."

And Terry—dazed, shaking, but grateful—fled. Down the noisy aisle, up the stairs, to the street. Back to her rooming house. Out again, with her suitcase, and into the right railroad station somehow, at last. Not another Wetona train until midnight. She shrank into a remote corner of the waiting room and there she huddled until midnight watching the entrances like a child who is fearful of ghosts in the night.

The hands of the station clock seemed fixed and immovable. The hour between eleven and twelve was endless. She was on the train. It was almost morning. It was morning. Dawn was breaking. She was home! She had the house key clutched tightly in her hand long before she turned Schroeder's corner. Suppose he had come home! Suppose he had jumped a town and come home ahead of his schedule. They had quarrelled once before, and he had done that.

Up the front steps. Into the house. Not a sound. She stood there a moment in the early morning half-light. She peered into the dining room. The table, with its breakfast débris, was as she had left it. In the kitchen the coffee pot stood on the gas stove. She was home. She was safe. She ran up the stairs, got out of her clothes and into crisp gingham morning things. She flung open windows everywhere. Down-stairs once more she plunged into an orgy of cleaning. Dishes, table, stove, floor, rugs. She washed, scoured, flapped, swabbed, polished. By eight o'clock she had done the work that would ordinarily have taken until noon. The house was shining, orderly, and redolent of soapsuds.

During all this time she had been listening, listening, with her sub-conscious ear. Listening for something she had refused to name definitely in her mind, but listening, just the same; waiting.

And then, at eight o'clock, it came. The rattle of a key in the lock. The boom of the front door. Firm footsteps.

He did not go to meet her, and she did not go to meet him. They came together and were in each other's arms. She was weeping.

"Now, now, old girl. What's there to cry about? Don't, honey; don't. It's all right."

She raised her head then, to look at him. How fresh, and rosy, and big he seemed, after that little sallow, yellow restaurant rat.

"How did you get here? How did you happen—?"

"Jumped all the way from Ashland. Couldn't get a sleeper, so I sat up all night. I had to come back and square things with you, Terry. My mind just wasn't on my work. I kept thinking how I'd talked—how I'd talked—"

"Oh, Orville, don't! I can't bear—Have you had your breakfast?"

"Why, no. The train was an hour late. You know that Ashland train."

But she was out of his arms and making for the kitchen. "You go and clean up. I'll have hot biscuits and everything in fifteen minutes. You poor boy. No breakfast!"

She made good her promise. It could not have been more than twenty minutes later when he was buttering his third feathery, golden brown biscuit. But she had eaten nothing. She watched him, and listened, and again her eyes were sombre, but for a different reason. He broke open his egg. His elbow came up just a fraction of an inch. Then he remembered, and flushed like a schoolboy, and brought it down again, carefully. And at that she gave a little tremulous cry, and rushed around the table to him.

"Oh, Orville!" She took the offending elbow in her two arms, and bent and kissed the rough coat sleeve.

"Why, Terry! Don't, honey. Don't!"

"Oh, Orville, listen—"

"Yes."

"Listen, Orville—"

"I'm listening, Terry."

"I've got something to tell you. There's something you've got to know."

"Yes, I know it, Terry. I knew you'd out with it, pretty soon, if I just waited."

She lifted an amazed face from his shoulder then, and stared at him. "But how could you know? You couldn't! How could you?"

He patted her shoulder then, gently. "I can always tell. When you have something on your mind you always take up a spoon of coffee, and look at it, and kind of joggle it back and forth in the spoon, and then dribble it back into the cup again, without once tasting it. It used to get me nervous when we were first married watching you. But now I know it just means you're worried about something, and I wait, and pretty soon—"

"Oh, Orville!" she cried, then. "Oh, Orville!"

"Now, Terry. Just spill it, hon. Just spill it to daddy. And you'll feel better."

VI

THE WOMAN WHO TRIED TO BE GOOD

Before she tried to be a good woman she had been a very bad woman—so bad that she could trail her wonderful apparel up and down Main Street, from the Elm Tree Bakery to the railroad tracks, without once having a man doff his hat to her or a woman bow. You passed her on the street with a surreptitious glance, though she was well worth looking at—in her furs and laces and plumes. She had the only full-length sealskin coat in our town, and Ganz' shoe store sent to Chicago for her shoes. Hers were the miraculously small feet you frequently see in stout women.

Usually she walked alone; but on rare occasions, especially round Christmas time, she might have been seen accompanied by some silent, dull-eyed, stupid-looking girl, who would follow her dumbly in and out of stores, stopping now and then to admire a cheap comb or a chain set with flashy imitation stones—or, queerly enough, a doll with yellow hair and blue eyes and very pink cheeks. But, alone or in company, her appearance in the stores of our town was the signal for a sudden jump in the cost of living. The storekeepers mulcted her; and she knew it and paid in silence, for she was of the class that has no redress. She owned the House With the Closed Shutters, near the freight depot—did Blanche Devine. And beneath her silks and laces and furs there was a scarlet letter on her breast.

In a larger town than ours she would have passed unnoticed. She did not look like a bad woman. Of course she used too much perfumed white powder, and as she passed you caught the oversweet breath of a certain heavy scent. Then, too, her diamond eardrops would have made any woman's features look hard; but her plump face, in spite of its heaviness, wore an expression of good-humoured intelligence, and her eyeglasses gave her somehow a look of respectability. We do not associate vice with eyeglasses. So in a large city she would have passed for a well-dressed prosperous, comfortable wife and mother, who was in danger of losing her figure from an overabundance of good living; but with us she was a town character, like Old Man Givins, the drunkard, or the weak-minded Binns girl. When she passed the drug-store corner there would be a sniggering among the vacant-eyed loafers idling there, and they would leer at each other and jest in undertones.

So, knowing Blanche Devine as we did, there was something resembling a riot in one of our most respectable neighbourhoods when it was learned that she had given up her interest in the house near the freight depot and was going to settle down in the white cottage on the corner and be good. All the husbands in the block, urged on by righteously indignant wives, dropped in on Alderman Mooney after supper to see if the thing could not be stopped. The fourth of the protesting husbands to arrive was the Very Young Husband, who lived next door to the corner cottage that Blanche Devine had bought. The Very Young Husband had a Very Young Wife, and they were the joint owners of Snooky. Snooky was three-going-on-four, and looked something like an angel—only healthier and with grimier hands. The whole neighbourhood borrowed her and tried to spoil her; but Snooky would not spoil.

Alderman Mooney was down in the cellar fooling with the furnace. He was in his furnace overalls—a short black pipe in his mouth. Three protesting husbands had just left. As the Very Young Husband, following Mrs. Mooney's directions, cautiously descended the cellar stairs, Alderman Mooney looked up from his tinkering. He peered through a haze of pipe-smoke.

"Hello!" he called, and waved the haze away with his open palm. "Come on down! Been tinkering with this blamed furnace since supper. She don't draw like she ought. 'Long toward spring a furnace always gets balky. How many tons you used this winter?"

"Oh—ten," said the Very Young Husband shortly. Alderman Mooney considered it thoughtfully. The Young Husband leaned up against the side of the cistern, his hands in his pockets. "Say, Mooney, is that right about Blanche Devine's having bought the house on the corner?"

"You're the fourth man that's been in to ask me that this evening. I'm expecting the rest of the block before bedtime. She's bought it all right."

The Young Husband flushed and kicked at a piece of coal with the toe of his boot.

"Well, it's a darned shame!" he began hotly. "Jen was ready to cry at supper. This'll be a fine neighbourhood for Snooky to grow up in! What's a woman like that want to come into a respectable street for anyway? I own my home and pay my taxes—"

Alderman Mooney looked up.

"So does she," he interrupted. "She's going to improve the place—paint it, and put in a cellar and a furnace, and build a porch, and lay a cement walk all round."

The Young Husband took his hands out of his pockets in order to emphasize his remarks with gestures.

"What's that got to do with it? I don't care if she puts in diamonds for windows and sets out Italian gardens and a terrace with peacocks on it. You're the alderman of this ward, aren't you? Well, it was up to you to keep her out of this block! You could have fixed it with an injunction or something. I'm going to get up a petition—that's what I'm going—"

Alderman Mooney closed the furnace door with a bang that drowned the rest of the threat. He turned the draft in a pipe overhead and brushed his sooty palms briskly together like one who would put an end to a profitless conversation.

"She's bought the house," he said mildly, "and paid for it. And it's hers. She's got a right to live in this neighbourhood as long as she acts respectable."

The Very Young Husband laughed.

"She won't last! They never do."

Alderman Mooney had taken his pipe out of his mouth and was rubbing his thumb over the smooth bowl, looking down at it with unseeing eyes. On his face was a queer look—the look of one who is embarrassed because he is about to say something honest.

"Look here! I want to tell you something: I happened to be up in the mayor's office the day Blanche signed for the place. She had to go through a lot of red tape before she got it—had quite a time of it, she did! And say, kid, that woman ain't so—bad."

The Very Young Husband exclaimed impatiently:

"Oh, don't give me any of that, Mooney! Blanche Devine's a town character. Even the kids know what she is. If she's got religion or something, and wants to quit and be decent, why doesn't she go to another town—Chicago or some place—where nobody knows her?"

That motion of Alderman Mooney's thumb against the smooth pipebowl stopped. He looked up slowly.

"That's what I said—the mayor too. But Blanche Devine said she wanted to try it here. She said this was home to her. Funny—ain't it? Said she wouldn't be fooling anybody here. They know her. And if she moved away, she said, it'd leak out some way sooner or later. It does, she said. Always! Seems she wants to live like—well, like other women. She put it like this: She says she hasn't got religion, or any of that. She says she's no different than she was when she was twenty. She says that for the last ten years the ambition of her life has been to be able to go into a grocery store and ask the price of, say, celery; and, if the clerk charged her ten when it ought to be seven, to be able to sass him with a regular piece of her mind—and then sail out and trade somewhere else until he saw that she didn't have to stand anything from storekeepers, any more than any other woman that did her own marketing. She's a smart woman, Blanche is! She's saved her money. God knows I ain't taking her part—exactly; but she talked a little, and the mayor and me got a little of her history."

A sneer appeared on the face of the Very Young Husband. He had been known before he met Jen as a rather industrious sower of that seed known as wild oats. He knew a thing or two, did the Very Young Husband, in spite of his youth! He always fussed when Jen wore even a V-necked summer gown on the street.

"Oh, she wasn't playing for sympathy," west on Alderman Mooney in answer to the sneer. "She said she'd always paid her way and always expected to. Seems her husband left her without a cent when she was eighteen— with a baby. She worked for four dollars a week in a cheap eating house. The two of 'em couldn't live on that. Then the baby—"

"Good night!" said the Very Young Husband. "I suppose Mrs. Mooney's going to call?"

"Minnie! It was her scolding all through supper that drove me down to monkey with the furnace. She's wild—Minnie is." He peeled off his overalls and hung them on a nail. The Young Husband started to ascend the cellar stairs. Alderman Mooney laid a detaining finger on his sleeve. "Don't say anything in front of Minnie! She's boiling! Minnie and the kids are going to visit her folks out West this summer; so I wouldn't so much as dare to say 'Good morning!' to the Devine woman. Anyway a person wouldn't talk to her, I suppose. But I kind of thought I'd tell you about her."

"Thanks!" said the Very Young Husband dryly.

In the early spring, before Blanche Devine moved in, there came stonemasons, who began to build something. It was a great stone fireplace that rose in massive incongruity at the side of the little white cottage. Blanche Devine was trying to make a home for herself. We no longer build fireplaces for physical warmth—we build them for the warmth of the soul; we build them to dream by, to hope by, to home by.

Blanche Devine used to come and watch them now and then as the work progressed. She had a way of walking round and round the house, looking up at it pridefully and poking at plaster and paint with her umbrella or fingertip. One day she brought with her a man with a spade. He spaded up a neat square of ground at the side of the cottage and a long ridge near the fence that separated her yard from that of the very young couple next door. The ridge spelled sweet peas and nasturtiums to our small-town eyes.

On the day that Blanche Devine moved in there was wild agitation among the white-ruffled bedroom curtains of the neighbourhood. Later on certain odours, as of burning dinners, pervaded the atmosphere. Blanche Devine, flushed and excited, her hair slightly askew, her diamond eardrops flashing, directed the moving, wrapped in her great fur coat; but on the third morning we gasped when she appeared out-of-doors, carrying a little household ladder, a pail of steaming water and sundry voluminous white cloths. She reared the little ladder against the side of the house mounted it cautiously, and began to wash windows: with housewifely thoroughness. Her stout figure was swathed in a grey sweater and on her head was a battered felt hat—the sort of window-washing costume that has been worn by women from time immemorial. We noticed that she used plenty of hot water and clean rags, and that she rubbed the glass until it sparkled, leaning perilously sideways on the ladder to detect elusive streaks. Our keenest housekeeping eye could find no fault with the way Blanche Devine washed windows.

By May, Blanche Devine had left off her diamond eardrops—perhaps it was their absence that gave her face a new expression. When she went down town we noticed that her hats were more like the hats the other women in our town wore; but she still affected extravagant footgear, as is right and proper for a stout woman who has cause to be vain of her feet. We noticed that her trips down town were rare that spring and summer. She used to come home laden with little bundles; and before supper she would change her street clothes for a neat, washable housedress, as is our thrifty custom. Through her bright windows we could see her moving briskly about from kitchen to sitting room; and from the smells that floated out from her kitchen door, she seemed to be preparing for her solitary supper the same homely viands that were frying or stewing or baking in our kitchens. Sometimes you could detect the delectable scent of browning hot tea biscuit. It takes a brave, courageous, determined woman to make tea biscuit for no one but herself.

Blanche Devine joined the church. On the first Sunday morning she came to the service there was a little flurry among the ushers at the vestibule door. They seated her well in the rear. The second Sunday morning a dreadful thing happened. The woman next to whom they seated her turned, regarded her stonily for a moment, then rose agitatedly and moved to a pew across the aisle. Blanche Devine's face went a dull red beneath her white powder. She never came again—though we saw the minister visit her once or twice. She always accompanied him to the door pleasantly, holding it well open until he was down the little flight of steps and on the sidewalk. The minister's wife did not call—but, then, there are limits to the duties of a minister's wife.

She rose early, like the rest of us; and as summer came on we used to see her moving about in her little garden patch in the dewy, golden morning. She wore absurd pale-blue kimonos that made her stout figure loom immense against the greenery of garden and apple tree. The neighbourhood women viewed these negligées with Puritan disapproval as they smoothed down their own prim, starched gingham skirts. They said it was disgusting—and perhaps it was; but the habit of years is not easily overcome. Blanche Devine—snipping her sweet peas; peering anxiously at the Virginia creeper that clung with such fragile fingers to the trellis; watering the flower baskets that hung from her porch—was blissfully unconscious of the disapproving eyes. I wish one of us had just stopped to call good morning to her over the fence, and to say in our neighbourly, small town way: "My, ain't this a scorcher! So early too! It'll be fierce by noon!" But we did not.

I think perhaps the evenings must have been the loneliest for her. The summer evenings in our little town are filled with intimate, human, neighbourly sounds. After the heat of the day it is infinitely pleasant to relax in the cool comfort of the front porch, with the life of the town eddying about us. We sew and read out there until it grows dusk. We call across-lots to our next-door neighbour. The men water the lawns and the flower boxes and get together in little quiet groups to discuss the new street paving. I have even known Mrs. Hines to bring her cherries out there when she had canning to do, and pit them there on the front porch partially shielded by her porch vine, but not so effectually that she was deprived of the sights and sounds about her. The kettle in her lap and the dishpan full of great ripe cherries on the porch floor by her chair, she would pit and chat and peer out through the vines, the red juice staining her plump bare arms.

I have wondered since what Blanche Devine thought of us those lonesome evenings—those evenings filled with little friendly sights and sounds. It is lonely, uphill business at best—this being good. It must have been difficult for her, who had dwelt behind closed shutters so long, to seat herself on the new front porch for all the world to stare at; but she did sit there—resolutely—watching us in silence.

She seized hungrily upon the stray crumbs of conversation that fell to her. The milkman and the iceman and the butcher boy used to hold daily conversation with her. They—sociable gentlemen—would stand on her doorstep, one grimy hand resting against the white of her doorpost, exchanging the time of day with Blanche in the doorway—a tea towel in one hand, perhaps, and a plate in the other. Her little house was a miracle of cleanliness. It was no uncommon sight to see her down on her knees on the kitchen floor, wielding her brush and rag like the rest of us. In canning and preserving time there floated out from her kitchen the pungent scent of pickled crab apples; the mouth-watering, nostril-pricking smell that meant sweet pickles; or the cloying, tantalising, divinely sticky odour that meant raspberry jam. Snooky, from her side of the fence, often used to peer through the pickets, gazing in the direction of the enticing smells next door. Early one September morning there floated out from Blanche Devine's kitchen that clean, fragrant, sweet scent of fresh-baked cookies—cookies with butter in them, and spice, and with nuts on top. Just by the smell of them your mind's eye pictured them coming from the oven—crisp brown circlets, crumbly, toothsome, delectable. Snooky, in her scarlet sweater and cap, sniffed them from afar and straightway deserted her sandpile to take her stand at the fence. She peered through the restraining bars, standing on tiptoe. Blanche Devine, glancing up from her board and rolling-pin, saw the eager golden head. And Snooky, with guile in her heart, raised one fat, dimpled hand above the fence and waved it friendlily. Blanche Devine waved back. Thus encouraged, Snooky's two hands wigwagged frantically above the pickets. Blanche Devine hesitated a moment, her floury hand on her hip. Then she went to the pantry shelf and took out a clean white saucer. She selected from the brown jar on the table three of the brownest, crumbliest, most perfect cookies, with a walnut meat perched atop of each, placed them temptingly on the saucer and, descending the steps, came swiftly across the grass to the triumphant Snooky. Blanche Devine held out the saucer, her lips smiling, her eyes tender. Snooky reached up with one plump white arm.

"Snooky!" shrilled a high voice. "Snooky!" A voice of horror and of wrath. "Come here to me this minute! And don't you dare to touch those!" Snooky hesitated rebelliously, one pink finger in her pouting mouth. "Snooky! Do you hear me?"

And the Very Young Wife began to descend the steps of her back porch. Snooky, regretful eyes on the toothsome dainties, turned away aggrieved. The Very Young Wife, her lips set, her eyes flashing, advanced and seized the shrieking Snooky by one writhing arm and dragged her away toward home and safety.

Blanche Devine stood there at the fence, holding the saucer in her hand. The saucer tipped slowly, and the three cookies slipped off and fell to the grass. Blanche Devine followed them with her eyes and stood staring at them a moment. Then she turned quickly, went into the house and shut the door.

It was about this time we noticed that Blanche Devine was away much of the time. The little white cottage would be empty for a week. We knew she was out of town because the expressman would come for her trunk. We used to lift our eyebrows significantly. The newspapers and handbills would accumulate in a dusty little heap on the porch; but when she returned there was always a grand cleaning, with the windows open, and Blanche—her head bound turbanwise in a towel—appearing at a window every few minutes to shake out a dustcloth. She seemed to put an enormous amount of energy into those cleanings—as if they were a sort of safety valve.

As winter came on she used to sit up before her grate fire long, long after we were asleep in our beds. When she neglected to pull down the shades we could see the flames of her cosy fire dancing gnomelike on the wall.

There came a night of sleet and snow, and wind and rattling hail—one of those blustering, wild nights that are followed by morning-paper reports of trains stalled in drifts, mail delayed, telephone and telegraph wires down. It must have been midnight or past when there came a hammering at Blanche Devine's door—a persistent, clamorous rapping. Blanche Devine, sitting before her dying fire half asleep, started and cringed when she heard it; then jumped to her feet, her hand at her breast—her eyes darting this way and that, as though seeking escape.

She had heard a rapping like that before. It had meant bluecoats swarming up the stairway, and frightened cries and pleadings, and wild confusion. So she started forward now, quivering. And then she remembered, being wholly awake now—she remembered, and threw up her head and smiled a little bitterly and walked toward the door. The hammering continued, louder than ever. Blanche Devine flicked on the porch light and opened the door. The half-clad figure of the Very Young Wife next door staggered into the room. She seized Blanche Devine's arm with both her frenzied hands and shook her, the wind and snow beating in upon both of them.

"The baby!" she screamed in a high, hysterical voice. "The baby! The baby—"

Blanche Devine shut the door and shook the Young Wife smartly by the shoulders.

"Stop screaming," she said quietly. "Is she sick?"

The Young Wife told her, her teeth chattering:

"Come quick! She's dying! Will's out of town. I tried to get the doctor. The telephone wouldn't—I saw your light! For God's sake—"

Blanche Devine grasped the Young Wife's arm, opened the door, and together they sped across the little space that separated the two houses. Blanche Devine was a big woman, but she took the stairs like a girl and found the right bedroom by some miraculous woman instinct. A dreadful choking, rattling sound was coming from Snooky's bed.

"Croup," said Blanche Devine, and began her fight.

It was a good fight. She marshalled her little inadequate forces, made up of the half-fainting Young Wife and the terrified and awkward hired girl.

"Get the hot water on—lots of it!" Blanche Devine pinned up her sleeves. "Hot cloths! Tear up a sheet—or anything! Got an oilstove? I want a teakettle boiling in the room. She's got to have the steam. If that don't do it we'll raise an umbrella over her and throw a sheet over, and hold the kettle under till the steam gets to her that way. Got any ipecac?"

The Young Wife obeyed orders, whitefaced and shaking. Once Blanche Devine glanced up at her sharply.

"Don't you dare faint!" she commanded.

And the fight went on. Gradually the breathing that had been so frightful became softer, easier. Blanche Devine did not relax. It was not until the little figure breathed gently in sleep that Blanche Devine sat back satisfied. Then she tucked a cover ever so gently at the side of the bed, took a last satisfied look at the face on the pillow, and turned to look at the wan, dishevelled Young Wife.

"She's all right now. We can get the doctor when morning comes—though I don't know's you'll need him."

The Young Wife came round to Blanche Devine's side of the bed and stood looking up at her.

"My baby died," said Blanche Devine simply. The Young Wife gave a little inarticulate cry, put her two hands on Blanche Devine's broad shoulders and laid her tired head on her breast.

"I guess I'd better be going," said Blanche Devine.

The Young Wife raised her head. Her eyes were round with fright.

"Going! Oh, please stay! I'm so afraid. Suppose she should take sick again! That awful—awful breathing—"

"I'll stay if you want me to."

"Oh, please! I'll make up your bed and you can rest—"

"I'm not sleepy. I'm not much of a hand to sleep anyway. I'll sit up here in the hall, where there's a light. You get to bed. I'll watch and see that every-thing's all right. Have you got something I can read out here—something kind of lively—with a love story in it?"

So the night went by. Snooky slept in her little white bed. The Very Young Wife half dozed in her bed, so near the little one. In the hall, her stout figure looming grotesque in wall-shadows, sat Blanche Devine pretending to read. Now and then she rose and tiptoed into the bedroom with miraculous quiet, and stooped over the little bed and listened and looked—and tiptoed away again, satisfied.

The Young Husband came home from his business trip next day with tales of snowdrifts and stalled engines. Blanche Devine breathed a sigh of relief when she saw him from her kitchen window. She watched the house now with a sort of proprietary eye. She wondered about Snooky; but she knew better than to ask. So she waited. The Young Wife next door had told her husband all about that awful night—had told him with tears and sobs. The Very Young Husband had been very, very angry with her—angry and hurt, he said, and astonished! Snooky could not have been so sick! Look at her now! As well as ever. And to have called such a woman! Well, really he did not want to be harsh; but she must understand that she must never speak to the woman again. Never!

So the next day the Very Young Wife happened to go by with the Young Husband. Blanche Devine spied them from her sitting-room window, and she made the excuse of looking in her mailbox in order to go to the door. She stood in the doorway and the Very Young Wife went by on the arm of her husband. She went by—rather white-faced—without a look or a word or a sign!

And then this happened! There came into Blanche Devine's face a look that made slits of her eyes, and drew her mouth down into an ugly, narrow line, and that made the muscles of her jaw tense and hard. It was the ugliest look you can imagine. Then she smiled—if having one's lips curl away from one's teeth can be called smiling.

Two days later there was great news of the white cottage on the corner. The curtains were down; the furniture was packed; the rugs were rolled. The wagons came and backed up to the house and took those things that had made a home for Blanche Devine. And when we heard that she had bought back her interest in the House With the Closed Shutters, near the freight depot, we sniffed.

"I knew she wouldn't last!" we said.

"They never do!" said we.

VII

THE GIRL WHO WENT RIGHT

There is a story—Kipling, I think—that tells of a spirited horse galloping in the dark suddenly drawing up tense, hoofs bunched, slim flanks quivering, nostrils dilated, ears pricked. Urging being of no avail the rider dismounts, strikes a match, advances a cautious step or so, and finds himself at the precipitous brink of a newly formed crevasse.

So it is with your trained editor. A miraculous sixth sense guides him. A mysterious something warns him of danger lurking within the seemingly innocent oblong white envelope. Without slitting the flap, without pausing to adjust his tortoise-rimmed glasses, without clearing his throat, without lighting his cigarette—he knows.

The deadly newspaper story he scents in the dark. Cub reporter. Crusty city editor. Cub fired. Stumbles on to a big story. Staggers into newspaper office wild-eyed. Last edition. "Hold the presses!" Crusty C.E. stands over cub's typewriter grabbing story line by line. Even foreman of pressroom moved to tears by tale. "Boys, this ain't just a story this kid's writin'. This is history!" Story finished. Cub faints. C.E. makes him star reporter.

The athletic story: "I could never marry a mollycoddle like you, Harold Hammond!" Big game of the year. Team crippled. Second half. Halfback hurt. Harold Hammond, scrub, into the game. Touchdown! Broken leg. Five to nothing. "Harold, can you ever, ever forgive me?"

The pseudo-psychological story: She had been sitting before the fire for a long, long time. The flame had flickered and died down to a smouldering ash. The sound of his departing footsteps echoed and re-echoed through her brain. But the little room was very, very still.

The shop-girl story: Torn boots and temptation, tears and sneers, pathos and bathos, all the way from Zola to the vice inquiry.

Having thus attempted to hide the deadly commonplaceness of this story with a thin layer of cynicism, perhaps even the wily editor may be tricked into taking the leap.

Four weeks before the completion of the new twelve-story addition the store advertised for two hundred experienced saleswomen. Rachel Wiletzky, entering the superintendent's office after a wait of three hours, was Applicant No. 179. The superintendent did not look up as Rachel came in. He scribbled busily on a pad of paper at his desk, thus observing rules one and two in the proper conduct of superintendents when interviewing applicants. Rachel Wiletzky, standing by his desk, did not cough or wriggle or rustle her skirts or sag on one hip. A sense of her quiet penetrated the superintendent's subconsciousness. He glanced up hurriedly over his left shoulder. Then he laid down his pencil and sat up slowly. His mind was working quickly enough though. In the twelve seconds that intervened between the laying down of the pencil and the sitting up in his chair he had hastily readjusted all his well-founded preconceived ideas on the appearance of shop-girl applicants.

Rachel Wiletzky had the colouring and physique of a dairymaid. It was the sort of colouring that you associate in your mind with lush green fields, and Jersey cows, and village maids, in Watteau frocks, balancing brimming pails aloft in the protecting curve of one rounded upraised arm, with perhaps a Maypole dance or so in the background. Altogether, had the superintendent been given to figures of speech, he might have said that Rachel was as much out of place among the preceding one hundred and seventy-eight bloodless, hollow-chested, stoop-shouldered applicants as a sunflower would be in a patch of dank white fungi.

He himself was one of those bleached men that you find on the office floor of department stores. Grey skin, grey eyes, greying hair, careful grey clothes—seemingly as void of pigment as one of those sunless things you disclose when you turn over a board that has long lain on the mouldy floor of a damp cellar. It was only when you looked closely that you noticed a fleck of golden brown in the cold grey of each eye, and a streak of warm brown forming an unquenchable forelock that the conquering grey had not been able to vanquish. It may have been a something within him corresponding to those outward bits of human colouring that tempted him to yield to a queer impulse. He whipped from his breast-pocket the grey-bordered handkerchief, reached up swiftly and passed one white corner of it down the length of Rachel Wiletzky's Killarney-rose left cheek. The rude path down which the handkerchief had travelled deepened to red for a moment before both rose-pink cheeks bloomed into scarlet. The superintendent gazed rather ruefully from unblemished handkerchief to cheek and back again.

"Why—it—it's real!" he stammered.

Rachel Wiletzky smiled a good-natured little smile that had in it a dash of superiority.

"If I was putting it on," she said, "I hope I'd have sense enough to leave something to the imagination. This colour out of a box would take a spiderweb veil to tone it down."

Not much more than a score of words. And yet before the half were spoken you were certain that Rachel Wiletzky's knowledge of lush green fields and bucolic scenes was that gleaned from the condensed-milk ads that glare down at one from billboards and street-car chromos. Hers was the ghetto voice—harsh, metallic, yet fraught with the resonant music of tragedy.

"H'm—name?" asked the grey superintendent. He knew that vocal quality.

A queer look stole into Rachel Wiletzky's face, a look of cunning and determination and shrewdness.

"Ray Willets," she replied composedly. "Double l."

"Clerked before, of course. Our advertisement stated—"

"Oh yes," interrupted Ray Willets hastily, eagerly. "I can sell goods. My customers like me. And I don't get tired. I don't know why, but I don't."

The superintendent glanced up again at the red that glowed higher with the girl's suppressed excitement. He took a printed slip from the little pile of paper that lay on his desk.

"Well, anyway, you're the first clerk I ever saw who had so much red blood that she could afford to use it for decorative purposes. Step into the next room, answer the questions on this card and turn it in. You'll be notified."

Ray Willets took the searching, telltale blank that put its questions so pertinently. "Where last employed?" it demanded. "Why did you leave? Do you live at home?"

Ray Willets moved slowly away toward the door opposite. The superintendent reached forward to press the button that would summon Applicant No. 180. But before his finger touched it Ray Willets turned and came back swiftly. She held the card out before his surprised eyes.

"I can't fill this out. If I do I won't get the job. I work over at the Halsted Street Bazaar. You know—the Cheap Store. I lied and sent word I was sick so I could come over here this morning. And they dock you for time off whether you're sick or not."

The superintendent drummed impatiently with his fingers. "I can't listen to all this. Haven't time. Fill out your blank, and if—"

All that latent dramatic force which is a heritage of her race came to the girl's aid now.

"The blank! How can I say on a blank that I'm leaving because I want to be where real people are? What chance has a girl got over there on the West Side? I'm different. I don't know why, but I am. Look at my face! Where should I get red cheeks from? From not having enough to eat half the time and sleeping three in a bed?"

She snatched off her shabby glove and held one hand out before the man's face.

"From where do I get such hands? Not from selling hardware over at Twelfth and Halsted. Look at it! Say, couldn't that hand sell silk and lace?"

Some one has said that to make fingers and wrists like those which Ray Willets held out for inspection it is necessary to have had at least five generations of ancestors who have sat with their hands folded in their laps. Slender, tapering, sensitive hands they were, pink-tipped, temperamental. Wistful hands they were, speaking hands, an inheritance, perhaps, from some dreamer ancestor within the old-world ghetto, some long-haired, velvet-eyed student of the Talmud dwelling within the pale with its squalor and noise, and dreaming of unseen things beyond the confining gates—things rare and exquisite and fine.

"Ashamed of your folks?" snapped the superintendent.

"N-no—No! But I want to be different. I am different! Give me a chance, will you? I'm straight. And I'll work. And I can sell goods. Try me."

That all-pervading greyness seemed to have lifted from the man at the desk. The brown flecks in the eyes seemed to spread and engulf the surrounding colourlessness. His face, too, took on a glow that seemed to come from within. It was like the lifting of a thick grey mist on a foggy morning, so that the sun shines bright and clear for a brief moment before the damp curtain rolls down again and effaces it.

He leaned forward in his chair, a queer half-smile on his face.

"I'll give you your chance," he said, "for one month. At the end of that time I'll send for you. I'm not going to watch you. I'm not going to have you watched. Of course your sale slips will show the office whether you're selling goods or not. If you're not they'll discharge you. But that's routine. What do you want to sell?"

"What do I want to—Do you mean—Why, I want to sell the lacy things."

"The lacy—"

Ray, very red-cheeked, made the plunge. "The—the lawnjeree, you know. The things with ribbon and handwork and yards and yards of real lace. I've seen 'em in the glass case in the French Room. Seventy-nine dollars marked down from one hundred."

The superintendent scribbled on a card. "Show this Monday morning. Miss Jevne is the head of your department. You'll spend two hours a day in the store school of instruction for clerks. Here, you're forgetting your glove."

The grey look had settled down on him again as he reached out to press the desk button. Ray Willets passed out at the door opposite the one through which Rachel Wiletzky had entered.

Some one in the department nick-named her Chubbs before she had spent half a day in the underwear and imported lingerie. At the store school she listened and learned. She learned how important were things of which Halsted Street took no cognisance. She learned to make out a sale slip as complicated as an engineering blueprint. She learned that a clerk must develop suavity and patience in the same degree as a customer waxes waspish and insulting, and that the spectrum's colours do not exist in the costume of the girl-behind-the-counter. For her there are only black and white. These things she learned and many more, and remembered them, for behind the rosy cheeks and the terrier-bright eyes burned the indomitable desire to get on. And the finished embodiment of all of Ray Willets' desires and ambitions was daily before her eyes in the presence of Miss Jevne, head of the lingerie and negligées.

Of Miss Jevne it might be said that she was real where Ray was artificial, and artificial where Ray was real. Everything that Miss Jevne wore was real. She was as modish as Ray was shabby, as slim as Ray was stocky, as artificially tinted and tinctured as Ray was naturally rosy-cheeked and buxom. It takes real money to buy clothes as real as those worn by Miss Jevne. The soft charmeuse in her graceful gown was real and miraculously draped. The cobweb-lace collar that so delicately traced its pattern against the black background of her gown was real. So was the ripple of lace that cascaded down the front of her blouse. The straight, correct, hideously modern lines of her figure bespoke a real eighteen-dollar corset. Realest of all, there reposed on Miss Jevne's bosom a bar pin of platinum and diamonds—very real diamonds set in a severely plain but very real bar of precious platinum. So if you except Miss Jevne's changeless colour, her artificial smile, her glittering hair and her undulating head-of-the-department walk, you can see that everything about Miss Jevne was as real as money can make one.

Miss Jevne, when she deigned to notice Ray Willets at all, called her "girl," thus: "Girl, get down one of those Number Seventeens for me—with the pink ribbons." Ray did not resent the tone. She thought about Miss Jevne as she worked. She thought about her at night when she was washing and ironing her other shirtwaist for next day's wear. In the Halsted Street Bazaar the girls had been on terms of dreadful intimacy with those affairs in each other's lives which popularly are supposed to be private knowledge. They knew the sum which each earned per week; how much they turned in to help swell the family coffers and how much they were allowed to keep for their own use. They knew each time a girl spent a quarter for a cheap sailor collar or a pair of near-silk stockings. Ray Willets, who wanted passionately to be different, whose hands so loved the touch of the lacy, silky garments that made up the lingerie and negligee departments, recognised the perfection of Miss Jevne's faultless realness—recognised it, appreciated it, envied it. It worried her too. How did she do it? How did one go about attaining the same degree of realness?

Meanwhile she worked. She learned quickly. She took care always to be cheerful, interested, polite. After a short week's handling of lacy silken garments she ceased to feel a shock when she saw Miss Jevne displaying a *robe-de-nuit* made up of white cloud and sea-foam and languidly assuring the customer that of course it wasn't to be expected that you could get a fine handmade lace at that price—only twenty-seven-fifty. Now if she cared to look at something really fine—made entirely by hand—why—

The end of the first ten days found so much knowledge crammed into Ray Willets' clever, ambitious little head that the pink of her cheeks had deepened to carmine, as a child grows flushed and too bright-eyed when overstimulated and overtired.

Miss Myrtle, the store beauty, strolled up to Ray, who was straightening a pile of corset covers and *brassieres*. Miss Myrtle was the store's star cloak-and-suit model. Tall, svelte, graceful, lovely in line and contour, she was remarkably like one of those exquisite imbeciles that Rossetti used to love to paint. Hers were the great cowlike eyes, the wonderful oval face, the marvellous little nose, the perfect lips and chin. Miss Myrtle could don a forty-dollar gown, parade it before a possible purchaser, and make it look like an imported model at one hundred and twenty-five. When Miss Myrtle opened those exquisite lips and spoke you got a shock that hurt. She laid one cool slim finger on Ray's ruddy cheek.

"Sure enough!" she drawled nasally. "Whereja get it anyway, kid? You must of been brought up on peaches 'n' cream and slept in a pink cloud somewheres."

"Me!" laughed Ray, her deft fingers busy straightening a bow here, a ruffle of lace there. "Me! The L-train runs so near my bed that if it was ever to get a notion to take a short cut it would slice off my legs to the knees."

"Live at home?" Miss Myrtle's grasshopper mind never dwelt long on one subject.

"Well, sure," replied Ray. "Did you think I had a flat up on the Drive?"

"I live at home too," Miss Myrtle announced impressively. She was leaning indolently against the table. Her eyes followed the deft, quick movements of Ray's slender, capable hands. Miss Myrtle always leaned when there was anything to lean on. Involuntarily she fell into melting poses. One shoulder always drooped slightly, one toe always trailed a bit like the picture on the cover of the fashion magazines, one hand and arm always followed the line of her draperies while the other was raised to hip or breast or head.

Ray's busy hands paused a moment. She looked up at the picturesque Myrtle. "All the girls do, don't they?"

"Huh?" said Myrtle blankly.

"Live at home, I mean? The application blank says—"

"Say, you've got clever hands, ain't you?" put in Miss Myrtle irrelevantly. She looked ruefully at her own short, stubby, unintelligent hands, that so perfectly reflected her character in that marvellous way hands have. "Mine are stupid-looking. I'll bet you'll get on." She sagged to the other hip with a weary gracefulness. "I ain't got no brains," she complained.

"Where do they live then?" persisted Ray.

"Who? Oh, I live at home"—again virtuously—"but I've got some heart if I am dumb. My folks couldn't get along without what I bring home every week. A lot of the girls have flats. But that don't last. Now Jevne—"

"Yes?" said Ray eagerly. Her plump face with its intelligent eyes was all aglow.

Miss Myrtle lowered her voice discreetly. "Her own folks don't know where she lives. They says she sends 'em money every month, but with the understanding that they don't try to come to see her. They live way over on the West Side somewhere. She makes her buying trip to Europe every year. Speaks French and everything. They say when she started to earn real money she just cut loose from her folks. They was a drag on her and she wanted to get to the top."

"Say, that pin's real, ain't it?"

"Real? Well, I should say it is! Catch Jevne wearing anything that's phony. I saw her at the theatre one night. Dressed! Well, you'd have thought that birds of paradise were national pests, like English sparrows. Not that she looked loud. But that quiet, rich elegance, you know, that just smells of money. Say, but I'll bet she has her lonesome evenings!"

Ray Willets' eyes darted across the long room and rested upon the shining black-clad figure of Miss Jevne moving about against the luxurious ivory-and-rose background of the French Room.

"She—she left her folks, h'm?" she mused aloud.

Miss Myrtle, the brainless, regarded the tips of her shabby boots.

"What did it get her?" she asked as though to herself. "I know what it does to a girl, seeing and handling stuff that's made for millionaires, you get a taste for it yourself. Take it from me, it ain't the six-dollar girl that needs looking after. She's taking her little pay envelope home to her mother that's a widow and it goes to buy milk for the kids. Sometimes I think the more you get the more you want. Somebody ought to turn that vice inquiry on to the tracks of that thirty-dollar-a-week girl in the Irish crochet waist and the diamond bar pin. She'd make swell readin'."

There fell a little silence between the two—a silence of which neither was conscious. Both were thinking, Myrtle disjointedly, purposelessly, all unconscious that her slow, untrained mind had groped for a great and vital truth and found it; Ray quickly, eagerly, connectedly, a new and daring resolve growing with lightning rapidity.

"There's another new baby at our house," she said aloud suddenly. "It cries all night pretty near."

"Ain't they fierce?" laughed Myrtle. "And yet I dunno—"

She fell silent again. Then with the half-sign with which we waken from day dreams she moved away in response to the beckoning finger of a saleswoman in the evening-coat section. Ten minutes later her exquisite face rose above the soft folds of a black charmeuse coat that rippled away from her slender, supple body in lines that a sculptor dreams of and never achieves.

Ray Willets finished straightening her counter. Trade was slow. She moved idly in the direction of the black-garbed figure that flitted about in the costly atmosphere of the French section. It must be a very special customer to claim Miss Jevne's expert services. Ray glanced in through the half-opened glass and ivory-enamel doors.

"Here, girl," called Miss Jevne. Ray paused and entered. Miss Jevne was frowning. "Miss Myrtle's busy. Just slip this on. Careful now. Keep your arms close to your head."

She slipped a marvellously wrought garment over Ray's sleek head. Fluffy drifts of equally exquisite lingerie lay scattered about on chairs, over mirrors, across showtables. On one of the fragile little ivory-and-rose chairs, in the centre of the costly little room, sat a large, blonde, perfumed woman who clanked and rustled and swished as she moved. Her eyes were white-lidded and heavy, but strangely bright. One ungloved hand was very white too, but pudgy and covered so thickly with gems that your eye could get no clear picture of any single stone or setting.

Ray, clad in the diaphanous folds of the *robe-de-nuit* that was so beautifully adorned with delicate embroideries wrought by the patient, needle-scarred fingers of some silent, white-faced nun in a far-away convent, paced slowly up and down the short length of the room that the critical eye of this coarse, unlettered creature might behold the wonders woven by this weary French nun, and, beholding, approve.

"It ain't bad," spake the blonde woman grudgingly. "How much did you say?"

"Ninety-five," Miss Jevne made answer smoothly. "I selected it myself when I was in France my last trip. A bargain."

She slid the robe carefully over Ray's head. The frown came once more to her brow. She bent close to Ray's ear. "Your waist's ripped under the left arm. Disgraceful!"

The blonde woman moved and jangled a bit in her chair. "Well, I'll take it," she sighed. "Look at the colour on that girl! And it's real too." She rose heavily and came over to Ray, reached up and pinched her cheek appraisingly with perfumed white thumb and forefinger.

"That'll do, girl," said Miss Jevne sweetly. "Take this along and change these ribbons from blue to pink."

Ray Willets bore the fairy garment away with her. She bore it tenderly, almost reverently. It was more than a garment. It represented in her mind a new standard of all that was beautiful and exquisite and desirable.

Ten days before the formal opening of the new twelve-story addition there was issued from the superintendent's office an order that made a little flurry among the clerks in the sections devoted to women's dress. The new store when thrown open would mark an epoch in the retail drygoods business of the city, the order began. Thousands were to be spent on perishable decorations alone. The highest type of patronage was to be catered to. Therefore the women in the lingerie, negligée, millinery, dress, suit and corset sections were requested to wear during opening week a modest but modish black one-piece gown that would blend with the air of elegance which those departments were to maintain.

Ray Willets of the lingerie and negligée sections read her order slip slowly. Then she reread it. Then she did a mental sum in simple arithmetic. A childish sum it was. And yet before she got her answer the solving of it had stamped on her face a certain hard, set, resolute look.

The store management had chosen Wednesday to be the opening day. By eight-thirty o'clock Wednesday morning the French lingerie, millinery and dress sections, with their women clerks garbed in modest but modish black one-piece gowns, looked like a levee at Buckingham when the court is in mourning. But the ladies-in-waiting, grouped about here and there, fell back in respectful silence when there paced down the aisle the queen royal in the person of Miss Jevne. There is a certain sort of black gown that is more startling and daring than scarlet. Miss Jevne's was that style. Fast black you might term it. Miss Jevne was aware of the flurry and flutter that followed her majestic progress down the aisle to her own section. She knew that each eye was caught in the tip of the little dog-eared train that slipped and slunk and wriggled along the ground, thence up to the soft drapery caught so cunningly just below the knee, up higher to the marvelously simple sash that swayed with each step, to the soft folds of black against which rested the very real diamond and platinum bar pin, up to the lace at her throat, and then stopping, blinking and staring again gazed fixedly at the string of pearls that lay about her throat, pearls rosily pink, mistily grey. An aura of self-satisfaction enveloping her, Miss Jevne disappeared behind the rose-garlanded portals of the new cream-and-mauve French section. And there the aura vanished, quivering. For standing before one of the plate-glass cases and patting into place with deft fingers the satin bow of a hand-wrought chemise was Ray Willets, in her shiny little black serge skirt and the braver of her two white shirtwaists.

Miss Jevne quickened her pace. Ray turned. Her bright brown eyes grew brighter at sight of Miss Jevne's wondrous black. Miss Jevne, her train wound round her feet like an actress' photograph, lifted her eyebrows to an unbelievable height.

"Explain that costume!" she said.

"Costume?" repeated Ray, fencing.

Miss Jevne's thin lips grew thinner. "You understood that women in this department were to wear black one-piece gowns this week!"

Ray smiled a little twisted smile. "Yes, I understood."

"Then what—"

Ray's little smile grew a trifle more uncertain. "—I had the money—last week—I was going to—The baby took sick—the heat I guess, coming so sudden. We had the doctor—and medicine—I—Say, your own folks come before black one-piece dresses!"

Miss Jevne's cold eyes saw the careful patch under Ray's left arm where a few days before the torn place had won her a reproof. It was the last straw.

"You can't stay in this department in that rig!"

"Who says so?" snapped Ray with a flash of Halsted Street bravado. "If my customers want a peek at Paquin I'll send 'em to you."

"I'll show you who says so!" retorted Miss Jevne, quite losing sight of the queen business. The stately form of the floor manager was visible among the glass showcases beyond. Miss Jevne sought him agitatedly. All the little sagging lines about her mouth showed up sharply, defying years of careful massage.

The floor manager bent his stately head and listened. Then, led by Miss Jevne, he approached Ray Willets, whose deft fingers, trembling a very little now, were still pretending to adjust the perfect pink-satin bow.

The manager touched her on the arm not unkindly. "Report for work in the kitchen utensils, fifth floor," he said. Then at sight of the girl's face: "We can't have one disobeying orders, you know. The rest of the clerks would raise a row in no time."

Down in the kitchen utensils and household goods there was no rule demanding modest but modish one-piece gowns. In the kitchenware one could don black sateen sleevelets to protect one's clean white waist without breaking the department's tenets of fashion. You could even pin a handkerchief across the front of your waist, if your job was that of dusting the granite ware.

At first Ray's delicate fingers, accustomed to the touch of soft, sheer white stuff and ribbon and lace and silk, shrank from contact with meat grinders, and aluminum stewpans, and egg beaters, and waffle irons, and pie tins. She handled them contemptuously. She sold them listlessly. After weeks of expatiating to customers on the beauties and excellencies of gossamer lingerie she found it difficult to work up enthusiasm over the virtues of dishpans and spice boxes. By noon she was less resentful. By two o'clock she was saying to a fellow clerk:

"Well, anyway, in this section you don't have to tell a woman how graceful and charming she's going to look while she's working the washing machine."

She was a born saleswoman. In spite of herself she became interested in the buying problems of the practical and plain-visaged housewives who patronised this section. By three o'clock she was looking thoughtful—thoughtful and contented.

Then came the summons. The lingerie section was swamped! Report to Miss Jevne at once! Almost regretfully Ray gave her customer over to an idle clerk and sought out Miss Jevne. Some of that lady's statuesqueness was gone. The bar pin on her bosom rose and fell rapidly. She espied Ray and met her halfway. In her hand she carried a soft black something which she thrust at Ray.

"Here, put that on in one of the fitting rooms. Be quick about it. It's your size. The department's swamped. Hurry now!"

Ray took from Miss Jevne the black silk gown, modest but modish. There was no joy in Ray's face. Ten minutes later she emerged in the limp and clinging little frock that toned down her colour and made her plumpness seem but rounded charm.

The big store will talk for many a day of that afternoon and the three afternoons that followed, until Sunday brought pause to the thousands of feet beating a ceaseless tattoo up and down the thronged aisles. On the Monday following thousands swarmed down upon the store again, but not in such overwhelming numbers. There were breathing spaces. It was during one of these that Miss Myrtle, the beauty, found time for a brief moment's chat with Ray Willets.

Ray was straightening her counter again. She had a passion for order. Myrtle eyed her wearily. Her slender shoulders had carried an endless number and variety of garments during those four days and her feet had paced weary miles that those garments might the better be displayed.

"Black's grand on you," observed Myrtle. "Tones you down." She glanced sharply at the gown. "Looks just like one of our eighteen-dollar models. Copy it?"

"No," said Ray, still straightening petticoats and corset covers. Myrtle reached out a weary, graceful arm and touched one of the lacy piles adorned with cunning bows of pink and blue to catch the shopping eye.

"Ain't that sweet!" she exclaimed. "I'm crazy about that shadow lace. It's swell under voiles. I wonder if I could take one of them home to copy it."

Ray glanced up. "Oh, that!" she said contemptuously. "That's just a cheap skirt. Only twelve-fifty. Machine-made lace. Imitation embroidery—"

She stopped. She stared a moment at Myrtle with the fixed and wide-eyed gaze of one who does not see.

"What'd I just say to you?"

"Huh?" ejaculated Myrtle, mystified.

"What'd I just say?" repeated Ray.

Myrtle laughed, half understanding. "You said that was a cheap junk skirt at only twelve-fifty, with machine lace and imitation—"

But Ray Willets did not wait to hear the rest. She was off down the aisle toward the elevator marked "Employées." The superintendent's office was on the ninth floor. She stopped there. The grey superintendent was writing at his desk. He did not look up as Ray entered, thus observing rules one and two in the proper conduct of superintendents when interviewing employees. Ray Willets, standing by his desk, did not cough or wriggle or rustle her skirts or sag on one hip. A consciousness of her quiet penetrated the superintendent's mind. He glanced up hurriedly over his left shoulder. Then he laid down his pencil and sat up slowly.

"Oh, it's you!" he said.

"Yes, it's me," replied Ray Willets simply. "I've been here a month to-day."

"Oh, yes." He ran his fingers through his hair so that the brown forelock stood away from the grey. "You've lost some of your roses," he said, and tapped his cheek. "What's the trouble?"

"I guess it's the dress," explained Ray, and glanced down at the folds of her gown. She hesitated a moment awkwardly. "You said you'd send for me at the end of the month. You didn't."

"That's all right," said the grey superintendent. "I was pretty sure I hadn't made a mistake. I can gauge applicants pretty fairly. Let's see—you're in the lingerie, aren't you?"

"Yes."

Then with a rush: "That's what I want to talk to you about. I've changed my mind. I don't want to stay in the lingeries. I'd like to be transferred to the kitchen utensils and household goods."

"Transferred! Well, I'll see what I can do. What was the name now? I forget."

A queer look stole into Ray Willets' face, a look of determination and shrewdness.

"Name?" she said. "My name is Rachel Wiletzky."

VIII
THE HOOKER-UP-THE-BACK

Miss Sadie Corn was not a charmer, but when you handed your room-key to her you found yourself stopping to chat a moment. If you were the right kind you showed her your wife's picture in the front of your watch. If you were the wrong kind, with your scant hair carefully combed to hide the bald spot, you showed her the newspaper clipping that you carried in your vest pocket. Following inspection of the first, Sadie Corn would say: "Now that's what I call a sweet face! How old is the youngest?" Upon perusal the second was returned with dignity and: "Is that supposed to be funny?" In each case Sadie Corn had you placed for life.

She possessed the invaluable gift of the floor clerk, did Sadie Corn—that of remembering names and faces. Though you had registered at the Hotel Magnifique but the night before, for the first time, Sadie Corn would look up at you over her glasses as she laid your key in its proper row, and say: "Good morning, Mr. Schultz! Sleep well?"

"Me!" you would stammer, surprised and gratified. "Me! Fine! H'm—Thanks!" Whereupon you would cross your right foot over your left nonchalantly and enjoy that brief moment's chat with Floor Clerk Number Two. You went back to Ishpeming, Michigan, with three new impressions: The first was that you were becoming a personage of considerable importance. The second was that the Magnifique realised this great truth and was grateful for your patronage. The third was that New York was a friendly little hole after all!

Miss Sadie Corn was dean of the Hotel Magnifique's floor clerks. The primary requisite in successful floor clerkship is homeliness. The second is discreet age. The third is tact. And for the benefit of those who think the duties of a floor clerk end when she takes your key when you leave your room, and hands it back as you return, it may be mentioned that the fourth, fifth, sixth and seventh requisites are diplomacy, ingenuity, unlimited patience and a comprehensive knowledge of human nature. Ambassadors have been known to keep their jobs on less than that.

She had come to the Magnifique at thirty-three, a plain, spare, sallow woman, with a quiet, capable manner, a pungent trick of the tongue on occasion, a sparse fluff of pale-coloured hair, and big, bony-knuckled hands, such as you see on women who have the gift of humanness. She was forty-eight now—still plain, still spare, still sallow. Those bony, big-knuckled fingers had handed keys to potentates, and pork-packers, and millinery buyers from Seattle; and to princes incognito, and paupers much the same—the difference being that the princes dressed down to the part, while the paupers dressed up to it.

Time, experience, understanding and the daily dealing with ever-changing humanity had brought certain lines into Sadie Corn's face. So skilfully were they placed that the unobservant put them down as wrinkles on the countenance of a homely, middle-aged woman; but he who read as he ran saw that the lines about the eyes were quizzical, shrewd lines, which come from the practice of gauging character at a glance; that the mouth-markings meant tolerance and sympathy and humour; that the forehead furrows had been carved there by those master chisellers, suffering and sacrifice.

In the last three or four years Sadie Corn had taken to wearing a little lavender-and-white crocheted shawl about her shoulders on cool days, and when Two-fifty-seven, who was a regular, caught his annual heavy cold late in the fall, Sadie would ask him sharply whether he had on his winter flannels. On his replying in the negative she would rebuke him scathingly and demand a bill of sizable denomination; and when her watch was over she would sally forth to purchase four sets of men's winter underwear. As captain of the Magnifique's thirty-four floor clerks Sadie Corn's authority extended from the parlours to the roof, but her especial domain was floor two. Ensconced behind her little desk in a corner, blocked in by mailracks, pantry signals, pneumatic-tube chutes and telephone, with a clear view of the elevators and stairway, Sadie Corn was mistress of the moods, manners and morals of the Magnifique's second floor.

It was six thirty p.m. on Monday of Automobile Show Week when Sadie Corn came on watch. She came on with a lively, well-developed case of neuralgia over her right eye and extending down into her back teeth. With its usual spitefulness the attack had chosen to make its appearance during her long watch. It never selected her short-watch days, when she was on duty only from eleven a.m. until six-thirty p.m.

Now with a peppermint bottle held close to alternately sniffing nostrils Sadie Corn was running her eye over the complex report sheet of the floor clerk who had just gone off watch. The report was even more detailed and lengthy than usual. Automobile Show Week meant that the always prosperous Magnifique was filled to the eaves and turning them away. It meant twice the usual number of inside telephone calls anent rooms too hot, rooms too cold, radiators hammering, radiators hissing, windows that refused to open, windows that refused to shut, packages undelivered, hot water not forthcoming. As the human buffers between guests and hotel management, it was the duty of Sadie Corn and her diplomatic squad to pacify the peevish, to smooth the path of the paying.

Down the hall strolled Donahue, the house detective—Donahue the leisurely. Donahue the keen-eyed, Donahue the guileless—looking in his evening clothes for all the world like a prosperous diner-out. He smiled benignly upon Sadie Corn, and Sadie Corn had the bravery to smile back in spite of her neuralgia, knowing well that men have no sympathy with that anguishing ailment and no understanding of it.

"Everything serene, Miss Corn?" inquired Donahue.

"Everything's serene," said Sadie Corn. "Though Two-thirty-three telephoned a minute ago to say that if the valet didn't bring his pants from the presser in the next two seconds he'd come down the hall as he is and get 'em. Perhaps you'd better stay round."

Donahue chuckled and passed on. Half way down the hall he retraced his steps, and stopped again before Sadie Corn's busy desk. He balanced a moment thoughtfully from toe to heel, his chin lifted inquiringly: "Keep your eye on Two-eighteen and Two-twenty-three this morning?"

"Like a lynx!" answered Sadie.

"Anything?"

"Not a thing. I guess they just scraped acquaintance in the Alley after dinner, like they sometimes do. A man with eyelashes like his always speaks to any woman alone who isn't pockmarked and toothless. Two minutes after he's met a girl his voice takes on the 'cello note. I know his kind. Why, say, he even tried waving those eyelashes of his at me first time he turned in his key; and goodness knows I'm so homely that pretty soon I'll be ripe for bachelor floor thirteen. You know as well as I that to qualify for that job a floor clerk's got to look like a gargoyle."

"Maybe they're all right," said Donahue thoughtfully. "If it's just a flirtation, why—anyway, watch 'em this evening. The day watch listened in and says they've made some date for to-night."

He was off down the hall again with his light, quick step that still had the appearance of leisureliness.

The telephone at Sadie's right buzzed warningly. Sadie picked up the receiver and plunged into the busiest half hour of the evening. From that moment until seven o'clock her nimble fingers and eyes and brain and tongue directed the steps of her little world. She held the telephone receiver at one ear and listened to the demands of incoming and outgoing guests with the other. She jotted down reports, dealt out mail and room-keys, kept her neuralgic eye on stairs and elevators and halls, her sound orb on tube and pantry signals, while through and between and above all she guided the stream of humanity that trickled past her desk—bellhops, Polish chambermaids, messenger boys, guests, waiters, parlour maids.

Just before seven there disembarked at floor two out of the cream-and-gold elevator one of those visions that have helped to make Fifth Avenue a street of the worst-dressed women in the world. The vision was Two-eighteen, and her clothes were of the kind that prepared you for the shock that you got when you looked at her face. Plume met fur, and fur met silk, and silk met lace, and lace met gold—and the whole met and ran into a riot of colour, and perfume—and little jangling, swishing sounds. Just by glancing at Two-eighteen's feet in their inadequate openwork silk and soft kid you knew that Two-eighteen's lips would be carmined.

She came down the corridor and stopped at Sadie Corn's desk. Sadie Corn had her key ready for her. Two-eighteen took it daintily between white-gloved fingers.

"I'll want a maid in fifteen minutes," she said. "Tell them to send me the one I had yesterday. The pretty one. She isn't so clumsy as some."

Sadie Corn jotted down a note without looking up.

"Oh, Julia? Sorry—Julia's busy," she lied.

Two-eighteen knew she lied, because at that moment there came round the bend in the broad, marble stairway that led up from the parlour floor the trim, slim figure of Julia herself.

Two-eighteen took a quick step forward. "Here, girl! I'll want you to hook me in fifteen minutes," she said.

"Very well, ma'am," replied Julia softly.

There passed between Sadie Corn and Two-eighteen a—well, you could hardly call it a look, it was so fleeting, so ephemeral; that electric, pregnant, meaning something that flashes between two women who dislike and understand each other. Then Two-eighteen was off down the hall to her room.

Julia stood at the head of the stairway just next to Sadie's desk and watched Two-eighteen until the bend in the corridor hid her. Julia, of the lady's-maid staff, could never have qualified for the position of floor clerk, even if she had chosen to bury herself in lavender-and-white crocheted shawls to the tip of her marvellous little Greek nose. In her frilly white cap, her trim black gown, her immaculate collar and cuffs and apron, Julia looked distractingly like the young person who, in the old days of the furniture-dusting drama, was wont to inform you that it was two years since young master went away—all but her feet. The feather-duster person was addicted to French-heeled, beaded slippers. Not so Julia. Julia was on her feet for ten hours or so a day. When you subject your feet to ten-hour tortures you are apt to pass by French-heeled effects in favour of something flat-heeled, laced, with an easy, comfortable crack here and there at the sides, and stockings with white cotton soles.

Julia, at the head of the stairway, stood looking after Two-eighteen until the tail of her silken draperies had whisked round the corner. Then, still staring, Julia spoke resentfully:

"Life for her is just one darned pair of long white kid gloves after another! Look at her! Why is it that kind of a face is always wearing the sables and diamonds?"

"Sables and diamonds," replied Sadie Corn, sniffing essence of peppermint, "seem a small enough reward for having to carry round a mug like that!"

Julia came round to the front of Sadie Corn's desk. Her eyes were brooding, her lips sullen.

"Oh, I don't know!" she said bitterly. "Being pretty don't get you anything—just being pretty! When I first came I used to wonder at those women that paint their faces and colour their hair, and wear skirts that are too tight and waists that are too low. But—I don't know! This town's so big and so—so kind of uninterested. When you see everybody wearing clothes that are more gorgeous than yours, and diamonds bigger, and limousines longer and blacker and quieter, it gives you a kind of fever. You—you want to make people look at you too."

Sadie Corn leaned back in her chair. The peppermint bottle was held at her nose. It may have been that which caused her eyes to narrow to mere slits as she gazed at the drooping Julia. She said nothing. Suddenly Julia seemed to feel the silence. She looked down at Sadie Corn. As by a miracle all the harsh, sullen lines in the girl's face vanished, to be replaced by a lovely compassion.

"Your neuralgy again, dearie?" she asked in pretty concern.

Sadie sniffed long and audibly at the peppermint bottle.

"If you ask me I think there's some imp inside of my head trying to push my right eye out with his thumb. Anyway it feels like that."

"Poor old dear!" breathed Julia. "It's the weather. Have them send you up a pot of black tea."

"When you've got neuralgy over your right eye," observed Sadie Corn grimly, "there's just one thing helps—that is to crawl into bed in a flannel nightgown, with the side of your face resting on the red rubber bosom of a hot-water bottle. And I can't do it; so let's talk about something cheerful. Seen Jo to-day?"

There crept into Julia's face a wave of colour—not the pink of pleasure, but the dull red of pain. She looked away from Sadie's eyes and down at her shabby boots. The sullen look was in her face once more.

"No; I ain't seen him," she said.

"What's the trouble?" Sadie asked.

"I've been busy," replied Julia airily. Then, with a forced vivacity: "Though it's nothing to Auto Show Week last year. I remember that week I hooked up until my fingers were stiff. You know the way the dresses fastened last winter. Some of 'em ought to have had a map to go by, they were that complicated. And now, just when I've got so's I can hook any dress that was ever intended for the human form—"

"Wasn't it Jo who said they ought to give away an engineering blueprint with every dress, when you told him about the way they hooked?" put in Sadie. "What's the trouble between you and—"

Julia rattled on, unheeding:

"You wouldn't believe what a difference there's been since these new peasant styles have come in! And the Oriental craze! Hook down the side, most of 'em—and they can do 'em themselves if they ain't too fat."

"Remember Jo saying they ought to have a hydraulic press for some of those skintight dames, when your fingers were sore from trying to squeeze them into their casings? By the way, what's the trouble between you and—"

"Makes an awful difference in my tips!" cut in Julia deftly. "I don't believe I've hooked up six this evening, and two of them sprung the haven't-anything-but-a-five-dollar-bill-see-you-to-morrow! Women are devils! I wish—"

Sadie Corn leaned forward, placed her hand on Julia's arm, and turned the girl about so that she faced her. Julia tried miserably to escape her keen eyes and failed.

"What's the trouble between you and Jo?" she demanded for the fourth time. "Out with it or I'll telephone down to the engine room and ask him myself."

"Oh, well, if you want to know—" She paused, her eyelids drooping again; then, with a rush: "Me and Jo have quarrelled again—for good, this time. I'm through!"

"What about?"

"I s'pose you'll say I'm to blame. Jo's mother's sick again. She's got to go to the hospital and have another operation. You know what that means—putting off the wedding again until God knows when! I'm sick of it—putting off and putting off! I told him we might as well quit and be done with it. We'll never get married at this rate. Soon's Jo gets enough put by to start us on, something happens. Last three times it's been his ma. Pretty soon I'll be as old and wrinkled and homely as—"

"As me!" put in Sadie calmly. "Well, I don't know's that's the worst thing that can happen to you. I'm happy. I had my plans, too, when I was a girl like you—not that I was ever pretty; but I had my trials. Funny how the thing that's easy and the thing that's right never seem to be the same!"

"Oh, I'm fond of Jo's ma," said Julia, a little shamefacedly. "We get along all right. She knows how it is, I guess; and feels—well, in the way. But when Jo told me, I was tired I guess. We had words. I told him there were plenty waiting for me if he was through. I told him I could have gone out with a real swell only last Saturday if I'd wanted to. What's a girl got her looks for if not to have a good time?"

"Who's this you were invited out by?" asked Sadie Corn.

"You must have noticed him," said Julia, dimpling. "He's as handsome as an actor. Name's Venner. He's in two-twenty-three."

There came the look of steel into Sadie Corn's eyes.

"Look here, Julia! You've been here long enough to know that you're not to listen to the talk of the men guests round here. Two-twenty-three isn't your kind—and you know it! If I catch you talking to him again I'll—"

The telephone at her elbow sounded sharply. She answered it absently, her eyes, with their expression of pain and remonstrance, still unshrinking before the onslaught of Julia's glare. Then her expression changed. A look of consternation came into her face.

"Right away, madam!" she said, at the telephone. "Right away! You won't have to wait another minute." She hung up the receiver and waved Julia away with a gesture. "It's Two-eighteen. You promised to be there in fifteen minutes. She's been waiting and her voice sounds like a saw. Better be careful how you handle her."

Julia's head, with its sleek, satiny coils of black hair that waved away so bewitchingly from the cream of her skin, came up with a jerk.

"I'm tired of being careful of other people's feelings. Let somebody be careful of mine for a change." She walked off down the hall, the little head still held high. A half dozen paces and she turned. "What was it you said you'd do to me if you caught me talking to him again?" she sneered.

A miserable twinge of pain shot through Sadie Corn's eye, to be followed by a wave of nausea that swept over her. They alone were responsible for her answer.

"I'll report you!" she snapped, and was sorry at once.

Julia turned again, walked down the corridor and round the corner in the direction of two-eighteen.

Long after Julia had disappeared Sadie Corn stared after her—miserable, regretful.

Julia knocked once at the door of two-eighteen and turned the knob before a high, shrill voice cried:

"Come!"

Two-eighteen was standing in the centre of the floor in scant satin knickerbockers and tight brassière. The blazing folds of a cerise satin gown held in her hands made a great, crude patch of colour in the neutral-tinted bedroom. The air was heavy with scent. Hair, teeth, eyes, fingernails—Two-eighteen glowed and glistened. Chairs and bed held odds and ends.

"Where've you been, girl?" shrilled Two-eighteen. "I've been waiting like a fool! I told you to be here in fifteen minutes."

"My stop-watch isn't working right," replied Julia impudently and took the cerise satin gown in her two hands.

She made a ring of the gown's opening, and through that cerise frame her eyes met those of Two-eighteen.

"Careful of my hair!" Two-eighteen warned her, and ducked her head to the practised movement of Julia's arms. The cerise gown dropped to her shoulders without grazing a hair. Two-eighteen breathed a sigh of relief. She turned to face the mirror.

"It starts at the left, three hooks; then to the centre; then back four—under the arm and down the middle again. That chiffon comes over like a drape."

She picked up a buffer from the litter of ivory and silver on the dresser and began to polish her already glittering nails, turning her head this way and that, preening her neck, biting her scarlet lips to deepen their crimson, opening her eyes wide and half closing them languorously. Julia, down on her knees in combat with the trickiest of the hooks, glanced up and saw. Two-eighteen caught the glance in the mirror. She stopped her idle polishing and preening to study the glowing and lovely little face that looked up at her. A certain queer expression grew in her eyes—a speculative, eager look.

"Tell me, little girl," she said, "What do you do round here?"

Julia turned from the mirror to the last of the hooks, her fingers working nimbly.

"Me? My regular job is working. Don't jerk, please. I've fastened this one three times."

"Working!" laughed Two-eighteen, fingering the diamonds at her throat. "What does a pretty girl like you want to do that for?"

"Hook off here," said Julia. "Shall I sew it?"

"Pin it!" snapped Two-eighteen.

Julia's tidy nature revolted.

"It'll take just a minute to catch it with thread—"

Two-eighteen whirled about in one of the sudden hot rages of her kind:

"Pin it, you fool! Pin it! I told you I was late!"

Julia paused a moment, the red surging into her face. Then in silence she knelt and wove a pin deftly in and out. When she rose from her knees her face was quite white.

"There, that's the girl!" said Two-eighteen blithely, her rage forgotten. "Just pat this over my shoulders."

She handed a powder-puff to Julia and turned her back to the broad mirror, holding a hand-glass high as she watched the powder-laden puff leaving a snowy coat on the neck and shoulders and back so generously displayed in the cherry-coloured gown. Julia's face was set and hard.

"Oh, now, don't sulk!" coaxed Two-eighteen good-naturedly, all of a sudden. "I hate sulky girls. I like people to be cheerful round me."

"I'm not used to being yelled at," Julia said resentfully.

Two-eighteen patted her cheek lightly. "You come out with me to-morrow and I'll buy you something pretty. Don't you like pretty clothes?"

"Yes; but—"

"Of course you do. Every girl does—especially pretty ones like you. How do you like this dress? Don't you think it smart?"

She turned squarely to face Julia, trying on her the tricks she had practised in the mirror. A little cruel look came into Julia's face.

"Last year's, isn't it?" she asked coolly.

"This!" cried Two-eighteen, stiffening. "Last year's! I got it yesterday on Fifth Avenue, and paid two hundred and fifty for it. What do you—"

"Oh, I believe you," drawled Julia. "They can tell a New Yorker from an out-of-towner every time. You know the really new thing is the Bulgarian effect!"

"Well, of all the nerve!" began Two-eighteen, turning to the mirror in a sort of fright. "Of all the—"

What she saw there seemed to reassure. She raised one hand to push the gown a little more off the left shoulder.

"Will there be anything else?" inquired Julia, standing aloof.

Two-eighteen turned reluctantly from the mirror and picked up a jewelled gold-mesh bag that lay on the bed. From it she extracted a coin and held it out to Julia. It was a generous coin. Julia looked at it. Her smouldering wrath burst into flame.

"Keep it!" she said savagely, and was out of the room and down the hall.

Sadie Corn, at her desk, looked up quickly as Julia turned the corner. Julia, her head held high, kept her eyes resolutely away from Sadie.

"Oh, Julia, I want to talk to you!" said Sadie Corn as Julia reached the stairway. Julia began to descend the stairs, unheeding. Sadie Corn rose and leaned over the railing, her face puckered with anxiety. "Now, Julia, girl, don't hold that up against me! I didn't mean it. You know that. You wouldn't be mad at a poor old woman that's half crazy with neuralgy!" Julia hesitated, one foot poised to take the next step. "Come on up," coaxed Sadie Corn, "and tell me what Two-eighteen's wearing this evening. I'm that lonesome, with nothing to do but sit here and watch the letter-ghosts go flippering down the mailchute! Come on!"

"What made you say you'd report me?" demanded Julia bitterly.

"I'd have said the same thing to my own daughter if I had one. You know yourself I'd bite my tongue out first!"

"Well!" said Julia slowly, and relented. She came up the stairs almost shyly. "Neuralgy any better?"

"Worse!" said Sadie Corn cheerfully.

Julia leaned against the desk sociably and glanced down the hall.

"Would you believe it," she snickered, "she's wearing red! With that hair! She asked me if I didn't think she looked too pale. I wanted to tell her that if she had any more colour, with that dress, they'd be likely to use the chemical sprinklers on her when she struck the Alley."

"Sh-sh-sh!" breathed Sadie in warning. Two-eighteen, in her shimmering, flame-coloured costume, was coming down the hall toward the elevators. She walked with the absurd and stumbling step that her scant skirt necessitated. With each pace the slashed silken skirt parted to reveal a shameless glimpse of cerise silk stocking. In her wake came Venner, of Two-twenty-three—a strange contrast in his black and white.

Sadie and Julia watched them from the corner nook. Opposite the desk Two-eighteen stopped and turned to Julia.

"Just run into my room and pick things up and hang them away, will you?" she said. "I didn't have time—and I hate things all about when I come in dead tired."

The little formula of service rose automatically to Julia's lips.

"Very well, madam," she said.

Her eyes and Sadie's followed the two figures until they had stepped into the cream-and-gold elevator and had vanished. Sadie, peppermint bottle at nose, spoke first:

"She makes one of those sandwich men with a bell, on Sixth Avenue, look like a shrinking violet!"

Julia's lower lip was caught between her teeth. The scent that had enveloped Two-eighteen as she passed was still in the air. Julia's nostrils dilated as she sniffed it. Her breath came a little quickly. Sadie Corn sat very still, watching her.

"Look at her!" said Julia, her voice vibrant. "Look at her! Old and homely, and all made up! I powdered her neck. Her skin's like tripe."

"Now Julia—" remonstrated Sadie Corn soothingly.

"I don't care," went on Julia with a rush. "I'm young. And I'm pretty too. And I like pretty things. It ain't fair! That was one reason why I broke with Jo. It wasn't only his mother. I told him he couldn't ever give me the things I want anyway. You can't help wanting 'em—seeing them all round every day on women that aren't half as good-looking as you are! I want low-cut dresses too. My neck's like milk. I want silk underneath, and fur coming up on my coat collar to make my cheeks look pink. I'm sick of hooking other women up. I want to stand in front of a mirror, looking at myself, polishing my pink nails with a silver thing and having somebody else hook me up!"

In Sadie Corn's eyes there was a mist that could not be traced to neuralgia or peppermint.

"Julia, girl," said Sadie Corn, "ever since the world began there's been hookers and hooked. And there always will be. I was born a hooker. So were you. Time was when I used to cry out against it too. But shucks! I know better now. I wouldn't change places. Being a hooker gives you such an all-round experience like of mankind. The hooked only get a front view. They only see faces and arms and chests. But the hookers—they see the necks and shoulderblades of this world, as well as faces. It's mighty broadening—being a hooker. It's the hookers that keep this world together, Julia, and fastened up right. It wouldn't amount to much if it had to depend on such as that!" She nodded her head in the direction the cerise figure had taken. "The height of her ambition is to get the cuticle of her nails trained back so perfectly that it won't have to be cut; and she don't feel decently dressed to be seen in public unless she's wearing one of those breastplates of orchids. Envy her! Why, Julia, don't you know that as you were standing here in your black dress as she passed she was envying you!"

"Envying me!" said Julia, and laughed a short laugh that had little of mirth in it. "You don't understand, Sadie!"

Sadie Corn smiled a rather sad little smile.

"Oh, yes, I do understand. Don't think because a woman's homely, and always has been, that she doesn't have the same heartaches that a pretty woman has. She's built just the same inside."

Julia turned her head to stare at her wide-eyed. It was a long and trying stare, as though she now saw Sadie Corn for the first time.

Sadie, smiling up at the girl, stood it bravely. Then, with a sudden little gesture, Julia patted the wrinkled, sallow cheek and was off down the hall and round the corner to two-eighteen.

The lights still blazed in the bedroom. Julia closed the door and stood with her back to it, looking about the disordered chamber. In that marvellous way a room has of reflecting the very personality of its absent owner, room two-eighteen bore silent testimony to the manner of woman who had just left it. The air was close and overpoweringly sweet with perfume—sachet, powder—the scent of a bedroom after a vain and selfish woman has left it. The litter of toilet articles lay scattered about on the dresser. Chairs and bed held garments of lace and silk. A bewildering negligée hung limply over a couch; and next it stood a patent-leather slipper, its mate on the floor.

Julia saw these things in one accustomed glance. Then she advanced to the middle of the room and stooped to pick up a pink wadded bedroom slipper from where it lay under the bed. And her hand touched a coat of velvet and fur that had been flung across the counterpane—touched it and rested there.

The coat was of stamped velvet and fur. Great cuffs of fur there were, and a sumptuous collar that rolled from neck to waist. There was a lining of vivid orange. Julia straightened up and stood regarding the garment, her hands on her hips.

"I wonder if it's draped in the back," she said to herself, and picked it up. It was draped in the back—bewitchingly. She held it at arm's length, turning it this way and that. Then, as though obeying some powerful force she could not resist, Julia plunged her arms into the satin of the sleeves and brought the great soft revers up about her throat. The great, gorgeous, shimmering thing completely hid her grubby little black gown. She stepped to the mirror and stood surveying herself in a sort of ecstasy. Her cheeks glowed rose-pink against the dark fur, as she had known they would. Her lovely little head, with its coils of black hair, rose flowerlike from the clinging garment. She was still standing there, lips parted, eyes wide with delight, when the door opened and closed—and Venner, of two-twenty-three, strode into the room.

"You little beauty!" exclaimed Two-twenty-three.

Julia had wheeled about. She stood staring at him, eyes and lips wide with fright now. One hand clutched the fur at her breast.

"Why, what—" she gasped.

Two-twenty-three laughed.

"I knew I'd find you here. I made an excuse to come up. Old Nutcracker Face in the hall thinks I went to my own room." He took two quick steps forward. "You raving little Cinderella beauty, you!"—And he gathered Julia, coat and all, into his arms.

"Let me go!" panted Julia, fighting with all the strength of her young arms. "Let me go!"

"You'll have coats like this," Two-twenty-three was saying in her ear—"a dozen of them! And dresses too; and laces and furs! You'll be ten times the beauty you are now! And that's saying something. Listen! You meet me to-morrow—"

There came a ring—sudden and startling—from the telephone on the wall near the door. The man uttered something and turned. Julia pushed him away, loosened the coat with fingers that shook and dropped it to the floor. It lay in a shimmering circle about the tired feet in their worn, cracked boots. And one foot was raised suddenly and kicked the silken garment into a heap.

The telephone bell sounded again. Venner, of two-twenty-three, plunged his hand into his pocket, took out something and pressed it in Julia's palm, shutting her fingers over it. Julia did not need to open them and look to see—she knew by the feel of the crumpled paper, stiff and crackling. He was making for the door, with some last instructions that she did not hear, before she spoke. The telephone bell had stopped its insistent ringing.

Julia raised her arm and hurled at him with all her might the yellow-backed paper he had thrust in her hand.

"I'll—I'll get my man to whip you for this!" she panted. "Jo'll pull those eyelashes of yours out and use 'em for couplings. You miserable little—"

The outside door opened again, striking Two-twenty-three squarely in the back. He crumpled up against the wall with an oath.

Sadie Corn, in the doorway, gave no heed to him. Her eyes searched Julia's flushed face. What she saw there seemed to satisfy her. She turned to him then grimly.

"What are you doing here?" Sadie asked briskly.

Two-twenty-three muttered something about the wrong room by mistake. Julia laughed.

"He lies!" she said, and pointed to the floor. "That bill belongs to him."

Sadie Corn motioned to him.

"Pick it up!" she said.

"I don't—want it!" snarled Two-twenty-three.

"Pick—it—up!" articulated Sadie Corn very carefully. He came forward, stooped, put the bill in his pocket. "You check out to-night!" said Sadie Corn. Then, at a muttered remonstrance from him: "Oh, yes, you will! So will Two-eighteen. Huh? Oh, I guess she will! Say, what do you think a floor clerk's for? A human keyrack? I'll give you until twelve. I'm off watch at twelve-thirty." Then, to Julia, as he slunk off: "Why didn't you answer the phone? That was me ringing!"

A sob caught Julia in the throat, but she turned it into a laugh.

"I didn't hardly hear it. I was busy promising him a licking from Jo."

Sadie Corn opened the door.

"Come on down the hall. I've left no one at the desk. It was Jo I was telephoning you for."

Julia grasped her arm with gripping fingers.

"Jo! He ain't—"

Sadie Corn took the girl's hand in hers.

"Jo's all right! But Jo's mother won't bother you any more, Sadie. You'll never need to give up your housekeeping nest-egg for her again. Jo told me to tell you."

Julia stared at her for one dreadful moment, her fist, with the knuckles showing white, pressed against her mouth. A little moan came from her that, repeated over and over, took the form of words:

"Oh, Sadie, if I could only take back what I said to Jo! If I could only take back what I said to Jo! He'll never forgive me now! And I'll never forgive myself!"

"He'll forgive you," said Sadie Corn; "but you'll never forgive yourself. That's as it should be. That, you know, is our punishment for what we say in thoughtlessness and anger."

They turned the corridor corner. Standing before the desk near the stairway was the tall figure of Donahue, house detective. Donahue had always said that Julia was too pretty to be a hotel employé.

"Straighten up, Julia!" whispered Sadie Corn. "And smile if it kills you—unless you want to make me tell the whole of it to Donahue."

Donahue, the keen-eyed, balancing, as was his wont, from toe to heel and back again, his chin thrust out inquiringly, surveyed the pair.

"Off watch?" inquired Donahue pleasantly, staring at Julia's eyes. "What's wrong with Julia?"

"Neuralgy!" said Sadie Corn crisply. "I've just told her to quit rubbing her head with peppermint. She's got the stuff into her eyes."

She picked up the bottle on her desk and studied its label, frowning. "Run along downstairs, Julia. I'll see if they won't send you some hot tea."

Donahue, hands clasped behind him, was walking off in his leisurely, light-footed way.

"Everything serene?" he called back over his big shoulder.

The neuralgic eye closed and opened, perhaps with another twinge.

"Everything's serene!" said Sadie Corn.

IX
THE GUIDING MISS GOWD

It has long been the canny custom of writers on travel bent to defray the expense of their journeyings by dashing off tales filled with foreign flavour. Dickens did it, and Dante. It has been tried all the way from Tasso to Twain; from Raskin to Roosevelt. A pleasing custom it is and thrifty withal, and one that has saved many a one but poorly prepared for the European robber in uniform the moist and unpleasant task of swimming home.

Your writer spends seven days, say, in Paris. Result? The Latin Quarter story. *Oh, mes enfants!* That Parisian student-life story! There is the beautiful young American girl—beautiful, but as earnest and good as she is beautiful, and as talented as she is earnest and good. And wedded, be it understood, to her art—preferably painting or singing. From New York! Her name must be something prim, yet winsome. Lois will do—Lois, *la belle Américaine*. Then the hero—American too. Madly in love with Lois. Tall he is and always clean-limbed—not handsome, but with one of those strong, rugged faces. His name, too, must be strong and plain, yet snappy. David is always good. The villain is French, fascinating, and wears a tiny black moustache to hide his mouth, which is cruel.

The rest is simple. A little French restaurant—Henri's. Know you not Henri's? *Tiens!* But Henri's is not for the tourist. A dim little shop and shabby, modestly tucked away in the shadows of the Rue Brie. But the food! Ah, the—whadd'you-call'ems—in the savoury sauce, that is Henri's secret! The tender, broiled *poularde*, done to a turn! The bottle of red wine! *Mais oui*; there one can dine under the watchful glare of Rosa, the plump, black-eyed wife of the *concierge*. With a snowy apron about her buxom waist, and a pot of red geraniums somewhere, and a sleek, lazy cat contentedly purring in the sunny window!

Then Lois starving in a garret. Temptation! *Sacré bleu! Zut!* Also *nom d'un nom!* Enter David. *Bon!* Oh, David, take me away! Take me back to dear old Schenectady. Love is more than all else, especially when no one will buy your pictures.

The Italian story recipe is even simpler. A pearl necklace; a low, clear whistle. Was it the call of a bird or a signal? His-s-s-st! Again! A black cape; the flash of steel in the moonlight; the sound of a splash in the water; a sickening gurgle; a stifled cry! Silence! His-st! *Vendetta!*

There is the story made in Germany, filled with students and steins and scars; with beer and blonde, blue-eyed *Mädchen* garbed—the *Mädchen*, that is—in black velvet bodice, white chemisette, scarlet skirt with two rows of black ribbon at the bottom, and one yellow braid over the shoulder. Especially is this easily accomplished if actually written in the *Vaterland*, German typewriting machines being equipped with *umlauts*.

And yet not one of these formulas would seem to fit the story of Mary Gowd. Mary Gowd, with her frumpy English hat and her dreadful English fringe, and her brick-red English cheeks, which not even the enervating Italian sun, the years of bad Italian food or the damp and dim little Roman room had been able to sallow. Mary Gowd, with her shabby blue suit and her mangy bit of fur, and the glint of humour in her pale blue eyes. Many, many times that same glint of humour had saved English Mary Gowd from seeking peace in the muddy old Tiber.

Her card read imposingly thus: Mary M. Gowd, Cicerone. Certificated and Licensed Lecturer on Art and Archaeology. Via del Babbuino, Roma.

In plain language Mary Gowd was a guide. Now, Rome is swarming with guides; but they are men guides. They besiege you in front of Cook's. They perch at the top of the Capitoline Hill, ready to pounce on you when you arrive panting from your climb up the shallow steps. They lie in wait in the doorway of St. Peter's. Bland, suave, smiling, quiet, but insistent, they dog you from the Vatican to the Catacombs.

Hundreds there are of these little men—undersized, even in this land of small men—dapper, agile, low-voiced, crafty. In his inner coat pocket each carries his credentials, greasy, thumb-worn documents, but precious. He glances at your shoes—this insinuating one—or at your hat, or at any of those myriad signs by which he marks you for his own. Then up he steps and speaks to you in the language of your country, be you French, German, English, Spanish or American.

And each one of this clan—each slim, feline little man in blue serge, white-toothed, gimlet-eyed, smooth-tongued, brisk—hated Mary Gowd. They hated her with the hate of an Italian for an outlander—with the hate of an Italian for a woman who works with her brain—with the hate of an Italian who sees another taking the bread out of his mouth. All this, coupled with the fact that your Italian is a natural-born hater, may indicate that the life of Mary Gowd had not the lyric lilt that life is commonly reputed to have in sunny Italy.

Oh, there is no formula for Mary Gowd's story. In the first place, the tale of how Mary Gowd came to be the one woman guide in Rome runs like melodrama. And Mary herself, from her white cotton gloves, darned at the fingers, to her figure, which mysteriously remained the same in spite of fifteen years of scant Italian fare, does not fit gracefully into the rôle of heroine.

Perhaps that story, scraped to bedrock, shorn of all floral features, may gain in force what it loses in artistry.

She was twenty-two when she came to Rome—twenty-two and art-mad. She had been pretty, with that pink-cheesecloth prettiness of the provincial English girl, who degenerates into blowsiness at thirty. Since seventeen she had saved and scrimped and contrived for this modest Roman holiday. She had given painting lessons—even painted on loathsome china—that the little hoard might grow. And when at last there was enough she had come to this Rome against the protests of the fussy English father and the spinster English sister.

The man she met quite casually one morning in the Sistine Chapel—perhaps he bumped her elbow as they stood staring up at the glorious ceiling. A thousand pardons! Ah, an artist too? In five minutes they were chattering like mad—she in bad French and exquisite English; he in bad English and exquisite French. He knew Rome—its pictures, its glories, its history—as only an Italian can. And he taught her art, and he taught her Italian, and he taught her love.

And so they were married, or ostensibly married, though Mary did not know the truth until three months later when he left her quite as casually as he had met her, taking with him the little hoard, and Mary's English trinkets, and Mary's English roses, and Mary's broken pride.

So! There was no going back to the fussy father or the spinster sister. She came very near resting her head on Father Tiber's breast in those days. She would sit in the great galleries for hours, staring at the wonder-works. Then, one day, again in the Sistine Chapel, a fussy little American woman had approached her, her eyes snapping. Mary was sketching, or trying to.

"Do you speak English?"

"I am English," said Mary.

The feathers in the hat of the fussy little woman quivered.

"Then tell me, is this ceiling by Raphael?"

"Ceiling!" gasped Mary Gowd. "Raphael!"

Then, very gently, she gave the master's name.

"Of course!" snapped the excited little American. "I'm one of a party of eight. We're all school-teachers And this guide"—she waved a hand in the direction of a rapt little group standing in the agonising position the ceiling demands—"just informed us that the ceiling is by Raphael. And we're paying him ten lire!"

"Won't you sit here?" Mary Gowd made a place for her. "I'll tell you."

And she did tell her, finding a certain relief from her pain in unfolding to this commonplace little woman the glory of the masterpiece among masterpieces.

"Why—why," gasped her listener, who had long since beckoned the other seven with frantic finger, "how beautifully you explain it! How much you know! Oh, why can't they talk as you do?" she wailed, her eyes full of contempt for the despised guide.

"I am happy to have helped you," said Mary Gowd.

"Helped! Why, there are hundreds of Americans who would give anything to have some one like you to be with them in Rome."

Mary Gowd's whole body stiffened. She stared fixedly at the grateful little American school-teacher.

"Some one like me—"

The little teacher blushed very red.

"I beg your pardon. I wasn't thinking. Of course you don't need to do any such work, but I just couldn't help saying—"

"But I do need work," interrupted Mary Gowd. She stood up, her cheeks pink again for the moment, her eyes bright. "I thank you. Oh, I thank you!"

"You thank me!" faltered the American.

But Mary Gowd had folded her sketchbook and was off, through the vestibule, down the splendid corridor, past the giant Swiss guard, to the noisy, sunny Piazza di San Pietro.

That had been fifteen years ago. She had taken her guide's examinations and passed them. She knew her Rome from the crypt of St. Peter's to the top of the Janiculum Hill; from the Campagna to Tivoli. She read and studied and learned. She delved into the past and brought up strange and interesting truths. She could tell you weird stories of those white marble men who lay so peacefully beneath St. Peter's dome, their ringed hands crossed on their breasts. She learned to juggle dates with an ease that brought gasps from her American clients, with their history that went back little more than one hundred years.

She learned to designate as new anything that failed to have its origin stamped B.C.; and the Magnificent Augustus, he who boasted of finding Rome brick and leaving it marble, was a mere *nouveau riche* with his miserable A.D. 14.

She was as much at home in the Thermae of Caracalla as you in your white-and-blue-tiled bath. She could juggle the history of emperors with one hand and the scandals of half a dozen kings with the other. No ruin was too unimportant for her attention—no picture too faded for her research. She had the centuries at her tongue's end. Michelangelo and Canova were her brothers in art, and Rome was to her as your back-garden patch is to you.

Mary Gowd hated this Rome as only an English woman can who has spent fifteen years in that nest of intrigue. She fought the whole race of Roman guides day after day. She no longer turned sick and faint when they hissed after her vile Italian epithets that her American or English clients quite failed to understand. Quite unconcernedly she would jam down the lever of the taximeter the wily Italian cabby had pulled only halfway so that the meter might register double. And when that foul-mouthed one crowned his heap of abuse by screaming "*Camorrista! Camor-r-rista!*" at her, she would merely shrug her shoulders and say "*Andate presto!*" to show him she was above quarrelling with a cabman.

She ate eggs and bread, and drank the red wine, never having conquered her disgust for Italian meat since first she saw the filthy carcasses, fly-infested, dust-covered, loathsome, being carted through the swarming streets.

It was six o'clock of an evening early in March when Mary Gowd went home to the murky little room in the Via Babbuino. She was too tired to notice the sunset. She was too tired to smile at the red-eyed baby of the cobbler's wife, who lived in the rear. She was too tired to ask Tina for the letters that seldom came. It had been a particularly trying day, spent with a party of twenty Germans, who had said "*Herrlich!*" when she showed them the marvels of the Vatican and "*Kolossal!*" at the grandeur of the Colosseum and, for the rest, had kept their noses buried in their Baedekers.

She groped her way cautiously down the black hall. Tina had a habit of leaving sundry brushes, pans or babies lying about. After the warmth of the March sun outdoors the house was cold with that clammy, penetrating, tomblike chill of the Italian home.

"Tina!" she called.

From the rear of the house came a cackle of voices. Tina was gossiping. There was no smell of supper in the air. Mary Gowd shrugged patient shoulders. Then, before taking off the dowdy hat, before removing the white cotton gloves, she went to the window that overlooked the noisy Via Babbuino, closed the massive wooden shutters, fastened the heavy windows and drew the thick curtains. Then she stood a moment, eyes shut. In that little room the roar of Rome was tamed to a dull humming. Mary Gowd, born and bred amid the green of Northern England, had never become hardened to the maddening noises of the Via Babbuino: The rattle and clatter of cab wheels; the clack-clack of thousands of iron-shod hoofs; the shrill, high cry of the street venders; the blasts of motor horns that seemed to rend the narrow street; the roar and rumble of the electric trams; the wail of fretful babies; the chatter of gossiping women; and above and through and below it all the cracking of the cabman's whip—that sceptre of the Roman cabby, that wand which is one part whip and nine parts crack. Sometimes it seemed to Mary Gowd that her brain was seared and welted by the pistol-shot reports of those eternal whips.

She came forward now and lighted a candle that stood on the table and another on the dresser. Their dim light seemed to make dimmer the dark little room. She looked about with a little shiver. Then she sank into the chintz-covered chair that was the one bit of England in the sombre chamber. She took off the dusty black velvet hat, passed a hand over her hair with a gesture that was more tired than tidy, and sat back, her eyes shut, her body inert, her head sagging on her breast.

The voices in the back of the house had ceased. From the kitchen came the slipslop of Tina's slovenly feet. Mary Gowd opened her eyes and sat up very straight as Tina stood in the doorway. There was nothing picturesque about Tina. Tina was not one of those olive-tinted, melting-eyed daughters of Italy that one meets in fiction. Looking at her yellow skin and her wrinkles and her coarse hands, one wondered whether she was fifty, or sixty, or one hundred, as is the way with Italian women of Tina's class at thirty-five.

Ah, the signora was tired! She smiled pityingly. Tired! Not at all, Mary Gowd assured her briskly. She knew that Tina despised her because she worked like a man.

"Something fine for supper?" Mary Gowd asked mockingly. Her Italian was like that of the Romans themselves, so soft, so liquid, so perfect.

Tina nodded vigorously, her long earrings shaking.

"*Vitello*"—she began, her tongue clinging lovingly to the double *l* sound—"*Vee-tail-loh*—"

"Ugh!" shuddered Mary Gowd. That eternal veal and mutton, pinkish, flabby, sickening!

"What then?" demanded the outraged Tina.

Mary Gowd stood up, making gestures, hat in hand.

"Clotted cream, with strawberries," she said in English, an unknown language, which always roused Tina to fury. "And a steak—a real steak of real beef, three inches thick and covered with onions fried in butter. And creamed chicken, and English hothouse tomatoes, and fresh peaches and little hot rolls, and coffee that isn't licorice and ink, and—and—"

Tina's dangling earrings disappeared in her shoulders. Her outspread palms were eloquent.

"Crazy, these English!" said the shoulders and palms. "Mad!"

Mary Gowd threw her hat on the bed, pushed aside a screen and busied herself with a little alcohol stove.

"I shall prepare an omelet," she said over her shoulder in Italian. "Also, I have here bread and wine."

"Ugh!" granted Tina.

"Ugh, veal!" grunted Mary Gowd. Then, as Tina's flapping feet turned away: "Oh, Tina! Letters?"

Tina fumbled at the bosom of her gown, thought deeply and drew out a crumpled envelope. It had been opened and clumsily closed again. Fifteen years ago Mary Gowd would have raged. Now she shrugged philosophic shoulders. Tina stole hairpins, opened letters that she could not hope to decipher, rummaged bureau drawers, rifled cupboards and fingered books; but then, so did most of the other Tinas in Rome. What use to complain?

Mary Gowd opened the thumb-marked letter, bringing it close to the candlelight. As she read, a smile appeared.

"Huh! Gregg," she said, "Americans!" She glanced again at the hotel letterhead on the stationery—the best hotel in Naples. "Americans—and rich!"

The pleased little smile lingered as she beat the omelet briskly for her supper.

The Henry D. Greggs arrived in Rome on the two o'clock train from Naples. And all the Roman knights of the waving palm espied them from afar and hailed them with whoops of joy. The season was still young and the Henry D. Greggs looked like money—not Italian money, which is reckoned in lire, but American money, which mounts grandly to dollars. The postcard men in the Piazza delle Terme sped after their motor taxi. The swarthy brigand, with his wooden box of tawdry souvenirs, marked them as they rode past. The cripple who lurked behind a pillar in the colonnade threw aside his coat with a practised hitch of his shoulder to reveal the sickeningly maimed arm that was his stock in trade.

Mr. and Mrs. Henry D. Gregg had left their comfortable home in Batavia, Illinois, with its sleeping porch, veranda and lawn, and seven-passenger car; with its two glistening bathrooms, and its Oriental rugs, and its laundry in the basement, and its Sunday fried chicken and ice cream, because they felt that Miss Eleanora Gregg ought to have the benefit of foreign travel. Miss Eleanora Gregg thought so too: in fact, she had thought so first.

Her name was Eleanora, but her parents called her Tweetie, which really did not sound so bad as it might if Tweetie had been one whit less pretty. Tweetie was so amazingly, Americanly pretty that she could have triumphed over a pet name twice as absurd.

The Greggs came to Rome, as has been stated, at two P.M. Wednesday. By two P.M. Thursday Tweetie had bought a pair of long, dangling earrings, a costume with a Roman striped collar and sash, and had learned to loll back in her cab in imitation of the dashing, black-eyed, sallow women she had seen driving on the Pincio. By Thursday evening she was teasing Papa Gregg for a spray of white aigrets, such as those same languorous ladies wore in feathery mists atop their hats.

"But, Tweet," argued Papa Gregg, "what's the use? You can't take them back with you. Custom-house regulations forbid it."

The rather faded but smartly dressed Mrs. Gregg asserted herself:

"They're barbarous! We had moving pictures at the club showing how they're torn from the mother birds. No daughter of mine—"

"I don't care!" retorted Tweetie. "They're perfectly stunning; and I'm going to have them."

And she had them—not that the aigret incident is important; but it may serve to place the Greggs in their respective niches.

At eleven o'clock Friday morning Mary Gowd called at the Gregg's hotel, according to appointment. In far-away Batavia, Illinois, Mrs. Gregg had heard of Mary Gowd. And Mary Gowd, with her knowledge of everything Roman—from the Forum to the best place at which to buy pearls—was to be the staff on which the Greggs were to lean.

"My husband," said Mrs. Gregg; "my daughter Twee—er—Eleanora. We've heard such wonderful things of you from my dear friend Mrs. Melville Peters, of Batavia."

"Ah, yes!" exclaimed Mary Gowd. "A most charming person, Mrs. Peters."

"After she came home from Europe she read the most wonderful paper on Rome before the Women's West End Culture Club, of Batavia. We're affiliated with the National Federation of Women's Clubs, as you probably know; and—"

"Now, Mother," interrupted Henry Gregg, "the lady can't be interested in your club."

"Oh, but I am!" exclaimed Mary Gowd very vivaciously. "Enormously!"

Henry Gregg eyed her through his cigar smoke with suddenly narrowed lids.

"M-m-m! Well, let's get to the point anyway. I know Tweetie here is dying to see St. Peter's, and all that."

Tweetie had settled back inscrutably after one comprehensive, disdainful look at Mary Gowd's suit, hat, gloves and shoes. Now she sat up, her bewitching face glowing with interest.

"Tell me," she said, "what do they call those officers with the long pale-blue capes and the silver helmets and the swords? And the ones in dark-blue uniform with the maroon stripe at the side of the trousers? And do they ever mingle with the—that is, there was one of the blue capes here at tea yesterday—"

Papa Gregg laughed a great, comfortable laugh.

"Oh, so that's where you were staring yesterday, young lady! I thought you acted kind of absent-minded." He got up to walk over and pinch Tweetie's blushing cheek.

So it was that Mary Gowd began the process of pouring the bloody, religious, wanton, pious, thrilling, dreadful history of Rome into the pretty and unheeding ear of Tweetie Gregg.

On the fourth morning after that introductory meeting Mary Gowd arrived at the hotel at ten, as usual, to take charge of her party for the day. She encountered them in the hotel foyer, an animated little group centred about a very tall, very dashing, very black-mustachioed figure who wore a long pale blue cape thrown gracefully over one shoulder as only an Italian officer can wear such a garment. He was looking down into the brilliantly glowing face of the pretty Eleanora, and the pretty Eleanora was looking up at him; and Pa and Ma Gregg were standing by, placidly pleased.

A grim little line appeared about Miss Gowd's mouth. Blue Cape's black eyes saw it, even as he bent low over Mary Gowd's hand at the words of introduction.

"Oh, Miss Gowd," pouted Tweetie, "it's too bad you haven't a telephone. You see, we shan't need you to-day."

"No?" said Miss Gowd, and glanced at Blue Cape.

"No; Signor Caldini says it's much too perfect a day to go poking about among old ruins and things."

Henry D. Gregg cleared his throat and took up the explanation. "Seems the—er—Signor thinks it would be just the thing to take a touring car and drive to Tivoli, and have a bite of lunch there."

"And come back in time to see the Colosseum by moonlight!" put in Tweetie ecstatically.

"Oh, yes!" said Mary Gowd.

Pa Gregg looked at his watch.

"Well, I'll be running along," he said. Then, in answer to something in Mary Gowd's eyes: "I'm not going to Tivoli, you see. I met a man from Chicago here at the hotel. He and I are going to chin awhile this morning. And Mrs. Gregg and his wife are going on a shopping spree. Say, ma, if you need any more money speak up now, because I'm—"

Mary Gowd caught his coat sleeve.

"One moment!"

Her voice was very low. "You mean—you mean Miss Eleanora will go to Tivoli and to the Colosseum alone—with—with Signor Caldini?"

Henry Gregg smiled indulgently.

"The young folks always run round alone at home. We've got our own car at home in Batavia, but Tweetie's beaus are always driving up for her in—"

Mary Gowd turned her head so that only Henry Gregg could hear what she said.

"Step aside for just one moment. I must talk to you."

"Well, what?"

"Do as I say," whispered Mary Gowd.

Something of her earnestness seemed to convey a meaning to Henry Gregg.

"Just wait a minute, folks," he said to the group of three, and joined Mary Gowd, who had chosen a seat a dozen paces away. "What's the trouble?" he asked jocularly. "Hope you're not offended because Tweet said we didn't need you to-day. You know young folks—"

"They must not go alone," said Mary Gowd.

"But—"

"This is not America. This is Italy—this Caldini is an Italian."

"Why, look here; Signor Caldini was introduced to us last night. His folks really belong to the nobility."

"I know; I know," interrupted Mary Gowd. "I tell you they cannot go alone. Please believe me! I have been fifteen years in Rome. Noble or not, Caldini is an Italian. I ask you"—she had clasped her hands and was looking pleadingly up into his face—"I beg of you, let me go with them. You need not pay me to-day. You—"

Henry Gregg looked at her very thoughtfully and a little puzzled. Then he glanced over at the group again, with Blue Cape looking down so eagerly into Tweetie's exquisite face and Tweetie looking up so raptly into Blue Cape's melting eyes and Ma Gregg standing so placidly by. He turned again to Mary Gowd's earnest face.

"Well, maybe you're right. They do seem to use chaperons in Europe—duennas, or whatever you call 'em. Seems a nice kind of chap, though."

He strolled back to the waiting group. From her seat Mary Gowd heard Mrs. Gregg's surprised exclamation, saw Tweetie's pout, understood Caldini's shrug and sneer. There followed a little burst of conversation. Then, with a little frown which melted into a smile for Blue Cape, Tweetie went to her room for motor coat and trifles that the long day's outing demanded. Mrs. Gregg, still voluble, followed.

Blue Cape, with a long look at Mary Gowd, went out to confer with the porter about the motor. Papa Gregg, hand in pockets, cigar tilted, eyes narrowed, stood irresolutely in the centre of the great, gaudy foyer. Then, with a decisive little hunch of his shoulders, he came back to where Mary Gowd sat.

"Did you say you've been fifteen years in Rome?"

"Fifteen years," answered Mary Gowd.

Henry D. Gregg took his cigar from his mouth and regarded it thoughtfully.

"Well, that's quite a spell. Must like it here." Mary Gowd said nothing. "Can't say I'm crazy about it—that is, as a place to live. I said to Mother last night: 'Little old Batavia's good enough for Henry D.' Of course it's a grand education, travelling, especially for Tweetie. Funny, I always thought the fruit in Italy was regular hothouse stuff—thought the streets would just be lined with trees all hung with big, luscious oranges. But, Lord! Here we are at the best hotel in Rome, and the fruit is worse than the stuff the pushcart men at home feed to their families—little wizened bananas and oranges. Still, it's grand here in Rome for Tweetie. I can't stay long—just ran away from business to bring 'em over; but I'd like Tweetie to stay in Italy until she learns the lingo. Sings, too—Tweetie does; and she and Ma think they'll have her voice cultivated over here. They'll stay here quite a while, I guess."

"Then you will not be here with them?" asked Mary Gowd.

"Me? No."

They sat silent for a moment.

"I suppose you're crazy about Rome," said Henry Gregg again. "There's a lot of culture here, and history, and all that; and—"

"I hate Rome!" said Mary Gowd.

Henry Gregg stared at her in bewilderment.

"Then why in Sam Hill don't you go back to England?"

"I'm thirty-seven years old. That's one reason why. And I look older. Oh, yes, I do. Thanks just the same. There are too many women in England already—too many half-starving shabby genteel. I earn enough to live on here—that is, I call it living. You couldn't. In the bad season, when there are no tourists, I live on a lire a day, including my rent."

Henry Gregg stood up.

"My land! Why don't you come to America?" He waved his arms. "America!"

Mary Gowd's brick-red cheeks grew redder.

"America!" she echoed. "When I see American tourists here throwing pennies in the Fountain of Trevi, so that they'll come back to Rome, I want to scream. By the time I save enough money to go to America I'll be an old woman and it will be too late. And if I did contrive to scrape together enough for my passage over I couldn't go to the United States in these clothes. I've seen thousands of American women here. If they look like that when they're just travelling about, what do they wear at home!"

"Clothes?" inquired Henry Gregg, mystified. "What's wrong with your clothes?"

"Everything! I've seen them look at my suit, which hunches in the back and strains across the front, and is shiny at the seams. And my gloves! And my hat! Well, even though I am English I know how frightful my hat is."

"You're a smart woman," said Henry D. Gregg.

"Not smart enough," retorted Mary Gowd, "or I shouldn't be here."

The two stood up as Tweetie came toward them from the lift. Tweetie pouted again at sight of Mary Gowd, but the pout cleared as Blue Cape, his arrangements completed, stood in the doorway, splendid hat in hand.

It was ten o'clock when the three returned from Tivoli and the Colosseum—Mary Gowd silent and shabbier than ever from the dust of the road; Blue Cape smiling; Tweetie frankly pettish. Pa and Ma Gregg were listening to the after-dinner concert in the foyer.

"Was it romantic—the Colosseum, I mean—by moonlight?" asked Ma Gregg, patting Tweetie's cheek and trying not to look uncomfortable as Blue Cape kissed her hand.

"Romantic!" snapped Tweetie. "It was as romantic as Main Street on Circus Day. Hordes of people tramping about like buffaloes. Simply swarming with tourists—German ones. One couldn't find a single ruin to sit on. Romantic!" She glared at the silent Mary Gowd.

There was a strange little glint in Mary Gowd's eyes, and the grim line was there about the mouth again, grimmer than it had been in the morning.

"You will excuse me?" she said. "I am very tired. I will say good night."

"And I," announced Caldini.

Mary Gowd turned swiftly to look at him.

"You!" said Tweetie Gregg.

"I trust that I may have the very great happiness to see you in the morning," went on Caldini in his careful English. "I cannot permit Signora Gowd to return home alone through the streets of Rome." He bowed low and elaborately over the hands of the two women.

"Oh, well; for that matter—" began Henry Gregg gallantly.

Caldini raised a protesting, white-gloved hand.

"I cannot permit it."

He bowed again and looked hard at Mary Gowd. Mary Gowd returned the look. The brick-red had quite faded from her cheeks. Then, with a nod, she turned and walked toward the door. Blue Cape, sword clanking, followed her.

In silence he handed her into the *fiacre*. In silence he seated himself beside her. Then he leaned very close.

"I will talk in this damned English," he began, "that the pig of a *fiaccheraio* may not understand. This—this Gregg, he is very rich, like all Americans. And the little Eleanora! *Bellissima!* You must not stand in my way. It is not good." Mary Dowd sat silent. "You will help me. To-day you were not kind. There will be much money— money for me; also for you."

Fifteen years before—ten years before—she would have died sooner than listen to a plan such as he proposed; but fifteen years of Rome blunts one's English sensibilities. Fifteen years of privation dulls one's moral sense. And money meant America. And little Tweetie Gregg had not lowered her voice or her laugh when she spoke that afternoon of Mary Gowd's absurd English fringe and her red wrists above her too-short gloves.

"How much?" asked Mary Gowd. He named a figure. She laughed.

"More—much more!"

He named another figure; then another.

"You will put it down on paper," said Mary Gowd, "and sign your name—to-morrow."

They drove the remainder of the way in silence. At her door in the Via Babbuino:

"You mean to marry her?" asked Mary Gowd.

Blue Cape shrugged eloquent shoulders:

"I think not," he said quite simply.

It was to be the Appian Way the next morning, with a stop at the Catacombs. Mary Gowd reached the hotel very early, but not so early as Caldini.

"Think the five of us can pile into one carriage?" boomed Henry Gregg cheerily.

"A little crowded, I think," said Mary Gowd, "for such a long drive. May I suggest that we three"—she smiled on Henry Gregg and his wife—"take this larger carriage, while Miss Eleanora and Signor Caldini follow in the single cab?"

A lightning message from Blue Cape's eyes.

"Yes; that would be nice!" cooed Tweetie.

So it was arranged. Mary Gowd rather outdid herself as a guide that morning. She had a hundred little intimate tales at her tongue's end. She seemed fairly to people those old ruins again with the men and women of a thousand years ago. Even Tweetie—little frivolous, indifferent Tweetie—was impressed and interested.

As they were returning to the carriages after inspecting the Baths of Caracalla, Tweetie even skipped ahead and slipped her hand for a moment into Mary Gowd's.

"You're simply wonderful!" she said almost shyly. "You make things sound so real. And—and I'm sorry I was so nasty to you yesterday at Tivoli."

Mary Dowd looked down at the glowing little face. A foolish little face it was, but very, very pretty, and exquisitely young and fresh and sweet. Tweetie dropped her voice to a whisper:

"You should hear him pronounce my name. It is like music when he says it—El-e-a-no-ra; like that. And aren't his kid gloves always beautifully white? Why, the boys back home—"

Mary Gowd was still staring down at her. She lifted the slim, ringed little hand which lay within her white-cotton paw and stared at that too.

Then with a jerk she dropped the girl's hand and squared her shoulders like a soldier, so that the dowdy blue suit strained more than ever at its seams; and the line that had settled about her mouth the night before faded slowly, as though a muscle too tightly drawn had relaxed.

In the carriages they were seated as before. The horses started up, with the smaller cab but a dozen paces behind. Mary Gowd leaned forward. She began to speak—her voice very low, her accent clearly English, her brevity wonderfully American.

"Listen to me!" she said. "You must leave Rome to-night!"

"Leave Rome to-night!" echoed the Greggs as though rehearsing a duet.

"Be quiet! You must not shout like that. I say you must go away."

Mamma Gregg opened her lips and shut them, wordless for once. Henry Gregg laid one big hand on his wife's shaking knees and eyed Mary Gowd very quietly.

"I don't get you," he said.

Mary Gowd looked straight at him as she said what she had to say:

"There are things in Rome you cannot understand. You could not understand unless you lived here many years. I lived here many months before I learned to step meekly off into the gutter to allow a man to pass on the narrow sidewalk. You must take your pretty daughter and go away. To-night! No—let me finish. I will tell you what happened to me fifteen years ago, and I will tell you what this Caldini has in his mind. You will believe me and forgive me; and promise me that you will go quietly away."

When she finished Mrs. Gregg was white-faced and luckily too frightened to weep. Henry Gregg started up in the carriage, his fists white-knuckled, his lean face turned toward the carriage crawling behind.

"Sit down!" commanded Mary Gowd. She jerked his sleeve. "Sit down!"

Henry Gregg sat down slowly. Then he wet his lips slightly and smiled.

"Oh, bosh!" he said. "This—this is the twentieth century and we're Americans, and it's broad daylight. Why, I'll lick the—"

"This is Rome," interrupted Mary Gowd quietly, "and you will do nothing of the kind, because he would make you pay for that too, and it would be in all the papers; and your pretty daughter would hang her head in shame forever." She put one hand on Henry Gregg's sleeve. "You do not know! You do not! Promise me you will go." The tears sprang suddenly to her English blue eyes. "Promise me! Promise me!"

"Henry!" cried Mamma Gregg, very grey-faced. "Promise, Henry!"

"I promise," said Henry Gregg, and he turned away.

Mary Gowd sank back in her seat and shut her eyes for a moment.

"*Presto!*" she said to the half-sleeping driver. Then she waved a gay hand at the carriage in the rear. "*Presto!*" she called, smiling. "*Presto!*"

At six o'clock Mary Gowd entered the little room in the Via Babbuino. She went first to the window, drew the heavy curtains. The roar of Rome was hushed to a humming. She lighted a candle that stood on the table. Its dim light emphasized the gloom. She took off the battered black velvet hat and sank into the chintz-covered English chair. Tina stood in the doorway. Mary Gowd sat up with a jerk.

"Letters, Tina?"

Tina thought deeply, fumbled at the bosom of her gown and drew out a sealed envelope grudgingly.

Mary Gowd broke the seal, glanced at the letter. Then, under Tina's startled gaze, she held it to the flaming candle and watched it burn.

"What is it that you do?" demanded Tina.

Mary Gowd smiled.

"You have heard of America?"

"America! A thousand—a million time! My brother Luigi—"

"Naturally! This, then"—Mary Gowd deliberately gathered up the ashes into a neat pile and held them in her hand, a crumpled heap—"this then, Tina, is my trip to America."

X
SOPHY-AS-SHE-MIGHT-HAVE-BEEN

The key to the heart of Paris is love. He whose key-ring lacks that open sesame never really sees the city, even though he dwell in the shadow of the Sorbonne and comprehend the *fiacre* French of the Paris cabman. Some there are who craftily open the door with a skeleton key; some who ruthlessly batter the panels; some who achieve only a wax impression, which proves to be useless. There are many who travel no farther than the outer gates. You will find them staring blankly at the stone walls; and their plaint is:

"What do they find to rave about in this town?"

Sophy Gold had been eight days in Paris and she had not so much as peeked through the key-hole. In a vague way she realised that she was seeing Paris as a blind man sees the sun—feeling its warmth, conscious of its white light beating on the eyeballs, but never actually beholding its golden glory.

This was Sophy Gold's first trip to Paris, and her heart and soul and business brain were intent on buying the shrewdest possible bill of lingerie and infants' wear for her department at Schiff Brothers', Chicago; but Sophy under-estimated the powers of those three guiding parts. While heart, soul, and brain were bent dutifully and indefatigably on the lingerie and infants'-wear job they also were registering a series of kaleidoscopic outside impressions.

As she drove from her hotel to the wholesale district, and from the wholesale district to her hotel, there had flashed across her consciousness the picture of the chic little modistes' models and *ouvrières* slipping out at noon to meet their lovers on the corner, to sit over their *sirop* or wine at some little near-by café, hands clasped, eyes glowing.

Stepping out of the lift to ask for her room key, she had come on the black-gowned floor clerk, deep in murmured conversation with the valet, and she had seemed not to see Sophy at all as she groped subconsciously for the key along the rows of keyboxes. She had seen the workmen in their absurdly baggy corduroy trousers and grimy shirts strolling along arm in arm with the women of their class—those untidy women with the tidy hair. Bareheaded and happy, they strolled along, a strange contrast to the glitter of the fashionable boulevard, stopping now and then to gaze wide-eyed at a million-franc necklace in a jeweller's window; then on again with a laugh and a shrug and a caress. She had seen the silent couples in the Tuileries Gardens at twilight.

Once, in the Bois de Boulogne, a slim, sallow *élégant* had bent for what seemed an interminable time over a white hand that was stretched from the window of a motor car. He was standing at the curb; in either greeting or parting, and his eyes were fastened on other eyes within the car even while his lips pressed the white hand.

Then one evening—Sophy reddened now at memory of it—she had turned a quiet corner and come on a boy and a girl. The girl was shabby and sixteen; the boy pale, voluble, smiling.

Evidently they were just parting. Suddenly, as she passed, the boy had caught the girl in his arms there on the street corner in the daylight, and had kissed her—not the quick, resounding smack of casual leave-taking, but a long, silent kiss that left the girl limp.

Sophy stood rooted to the spot, between horror and fascination. The boy's arm brought the girl upright and set her on her feet.

She took a long breath, straightened her hat, and ran on to rejoin her girl friend awaiting her calmly up the street. She was not even flushed; but Sophy was. Sophy was blushing hotly and burning uncomfortably, so that her eyes smarted.

Just after her late dinner on the eighth day of her Paris stay, Sophy Gold was seated in the hotel lobby. Paris thronged with American business buyers—those clever, capable, shrewd-eyed women who swarm on the city in June and strip it of its choicest flowers, from ball gowns to back combs. Sophy tried to pick them from the multitude that swept past her. It was not difficult. The women visitors to Paris in June drop easily into their proper slots.

There were the pretty American girls and their marvellously young-looking mammas, both out-Frenching the French in their efforts to look Parisian; there were rows of fat, placid, jewel-laden Argentine mothers, each with a watchful eye on her black-eyed, volcanically calm, be-powdered daughter; and there were the buyers, miraculously dressy in next week's styles in suits and hats—of the old-girl type most of them, alert, self-confident, capable.

They usually returned to their hotels at six, limping a little, dog-tired; but at sight of the brightly lighted, gay hotel foyer they would straighten up like war-horses scenting battle and achieve an effective entrance from the doorway to the lift.

In all that big, busy foyer Sophy Gold herself was the one person distinctly out of the picture. One did not know where to place her. To begin with, a woman as irrevocably, irredeemably ugly as Sophy was an anachronism in Paris. She belonged to the gargoyle period. You found yourself speculating on whether it was her mouth or her nose that made her so devastatingly plain, only to bring up at her eyes and find that they alone were enough to wreck any ambitions toward beauty. You knew before you saw it that her hair would be limp and straggling.

You sensed without a glance at them that her hands would be bony, with unlovely knuckles.

The Fates, grinning, had done all that. Her Chicago tailor and milliner had completed the work. Sophy had not been in Paris ten minutes before she noticed that they were wearing 'em long and full. Her coat was short and her skirt scant. Her hat was small. The Paris windows were full of large and graceful black velvets of the Lillian Russell school.

"May I sit here?"

Sophy looked up into the plump, pink, smiling face of one of those very women of the buyer type on whom she had speculated ten minutes before—a good-natured face with shrewd, twinkling eyes. At sight of it you forgave her her skittish white-kid-topped shoes.

"Certainly," smiled Sophy, and moved over a bit on the little French settee.

The plump woman sat down heavily. In five minutes Sophy was conscious she was being stared at surreptitiously. In ten minutes she was uncomfortably conscious of it. In eleven minutes she turned her head suddenly and caught the stout woman's eyes fixed on her, with just the baffled, speculative expression she had expected to find in them. Sophy Gold had caught that look in many women's eyes. She smiled grimly now.

"Don't try it," she said, "It's no use."

The pink, plump face flushed pinker.

"Don't try—"

"Don't try to convince yourself that if I wore my hair differently, or my collar tighter, or my hat larger, it would make a difference in my looks. It wouldn't. It's hard to believe that I'm as homely as I look, but I am. I've watched women try to dress me in as many as eleven mental changes of costume before they gave me up."

"But I didn't mean—I beg your pardon—you mustn't think—"

"Oh, that's all right! I used to struggle, but I'm used to it now. It took me a long time to realise that this was my real face and the only kind I could ever expect to have."

The plump woman's kindly face grew kinder.

"But you're really not so—"

"Oh, yes, I am. Upholstering can't change me. There are various kinds of homely women—some who are hideous in blue maybe, but who soften up in pink. Then there's the one you read about, whose features are lighted up now and then by one of those rare, sweet smiles that make her plain face almost beautiful. But once in a while you find a woman who is ugly in any colour of the rainbow; who is ugly smiling or serious, talking or in repose, hair down low or hair done high—just plain dyed-in-the-wool, sewed-in-the-seam homely. I'm that kind. Here for a visit?"

"I'm a buyer," said the plump woman.

"Yes; I thought so. I'm the lingerie and infants'-wear buyer for Schiff, Chicago."

"A buyer!" The plump woman's eyes jumped uncontrollably again to Sophy Gold's scrambled features. "Well! My name's Miss Morrissey—Ella Morrissey. Millinery for Abelman's, Pittsburgh. And it's no snap this year, with the shops showing postage-stamp hats one day and cart-wheels the next. I said this morning that I envied the head of the tinware department. Been over often?"

Sophy made the shamefaced confession of the novice: "My first trip."

The inevitable answer came:

"Your first! Really! This is my twentieth crossing. Been coming over twice a year for ten years. If there's anything I can tell you, just ask. The first buying trip to Paris is hard until you know the ropes. Of course you love this town?"

Sophy Gold sat silent a moment, hesitating. Then she turned a puzzled face toward Miss Morrissey.

"What do people mean when they say they love Paris?"

Ella Morrissey stared. Then a queer look came into her face—a pitying sort of look. The shrewd eyes softened. She groped for words.

"When I first came over here, ten years ago, I—well, it would have been easier to tell you then. I don't know— there's something about Paris—something in the atmosphere—something in the air. It—it makes you do foolish things. It makes you feel queer and light and happy. It's nothing you can put your finger on and say 'That's it!' But it's there."

"Huh!" grunted Sophy Gold. "I suppose I could save myself a lot of trouble by saying that I feel it; but I don't. I simply don't react to this town. The only things I really like in Paris are the Tomb of Napoleon, the Seine at night, and the strawberry tart you get at Vian's. Of course the parks and boulevards are a marvel, but you can't expect me to love a town for that. I'm no landscape gardener."

That pitying look deepened in Miss Morrissey's eyes.

"Have you been out in the evening? The restaurants! The French women! The life!"

Sophy Gold caught the pitying look and interpreted it without resentment; but there was perhaps an added acid in her tone when she spoke.

"I'm here to buy—not to play. I'm thirty years old, and it's taken me ten years to work my way up to foreign buyer. I've worked. And I wasn't handicapped any by my beauty. I've made up my mind that I'm going to buy the smoothest-moving line of French lingerie and infants' wear that Schiff Brothers ever had."

Miss Morrissey checked her.

"But, my dear girl, haven't you been round at all?"

"Oh, a little; as much as a woman can go round alone in Paris—even a homely woman. But I've been disappointed every time. The noise drives me wild, to begin with. Not that I'm not used to noise. I am. I can stand for a town that roars, like Chicago. But this city yelps. I've been going round to the restaurants a little. At noon I always picked the restaurant I wanted, so long as I had to pay for the lunch of the *commissionnaire* who was with me anyway. Can you imagine any man at home letting a woman pay for his meals the way those shrimpy Frenchmen do?

"Well, the restaurants were always jammed full of Americans. The men of the party would look over the French menu in a helpless sort of way, and then they'd say: 'What do you say to a nice big steak with French-fried potatoes?' The waiter would give them a disgusted look and put in the order. They might just as well have been eating at a quick lunch place. As for the French women, every time I picked what I took to be a real Parisienne coming toward me I'd hear her say as she passed: 'Henry, I'm going over to the Galerie Lafayette. I'll meet you at the American Express at twelve. And, Henry, I think I'll need some more money.'"

Miss Ella Morrissey's twinkling eyes almost disappeared in wrinkles of laughter; but Sophy Gold was not laughing. As she talked she gazed grimly ahead at the throng that shifted and glittered and laughed and chattered all about her.

"I stopped work early one afternoon and went over across the river. Well! They may be artistic, but they all looked as though they needed a shave and a hair-cut and a square meal. And the girls!"

Ella Morrissey raised a plump, protesting palm.

"Now look here, child, Paris isn't so much a city as a state of mind. To enjoy it you've got to forget you're an American. Don't look at it from a Chicago, Illinois, viewpoint. Just try to imagine you're a mixture of Montmartre girl, Latin Quarter model and duchess from the Champs Élysées. Then you'll get it."

"Get it!" retorted Sophy Gold. "If I could do that I wouldn't be buying lingerie and infants' wear for Schiffs'. I'd be crowding Duse and Bernhardt and Mrs. Fiske off the boards."

Miss Morrissey sat silent and thoughtful, rubbing one fat forefinger slowly up and down her knee. Suddenly she turned.

"Don't be angry—but have you ever been in love?"

"Look at me!" replied Sophy Gold simply. Miss Morrissey reddened a little. "As head of the lingerie section I've selected trousseaus for I don't know how many Chicago brides; but I'll never have to decide whether I'll have pink or blue ribbons for my own."

With a little impulsive gesture Ella Morrissey laid one hand on the shoulder of her new acquaintance.

"Come on up and visit me, will you? I made them give me an inside room, away from the noise. Too many people down here. Besides, I'd like to take off this armour-plate of mine and get comfortable. When a girl gets as old and fat as I am—"

"There are some letters I ought to get out," Sophy Gold protested feebly.

"Yes; I know. We all have; but there's such a thing as overdoing this duty to the firm. You get up at six to-morrow morning and slap off those letters. They'll come easier and sound less tired."

They made for the lift; but at its very gates:

"Hello, little girl!" cried a masculine voice; and a detaining hand was laid on Ella Morrissey's plump shoulder.

That lady recognised the voice and the greeting before she turned to face their source. Max Tack, junior partner in the firm of Tack Brothers, Lingerie and Infants' Wear, New York, held out an eager hand.

"Hello, Max!" said Miss Morrissey not too cordially. "My, aren't you dressy!"

He was undeniably dressy—not that only, but radiant with the self-confidence born of good looks, of well-fitting evening clothes, of a fresh shave, of glistening nails. Max Tack, of the hard eye and the soft smile, of the slim figure and the semi-bald head, of the flattering tongue and the business brain, bent his attention full on the very plain Miss Sophy Gold.

"Aren't you going to introduce me?" he demanded.

Miss Morrissey introduced them, buyer fashion—names, business connection, and firms.

"I knew you were Miss Gold," began Max Tack, the honey-tongued. "Some one pointed you out to me yesterday. I've been trying to meet you ever since."

"I hope you haven't neglected your business," said Miss Gold without enthusiasm.

Max Tack leaned closer, his tone lowered.

"I'd neglect it any day for you. Listen, little one: aren't you going to take dinner with me some evening?"

Max Tack always called a woman "Little one." It was part of his business formula. He was only one of the wholesalers who go to Paris yearly ostensibly to buy models, but really to pay heavy diplomatic court to those hundreds of women buyers who flock to that city in the interests of their firms. To entertain those buyers who were interested in goods such as he manufactured in America; to win their friendship; to make them feel under obligation at least to inspect his line when they came to New York—that was Max Tack's mission in Paris. He performed it admirably.

"What evening?" he said now. "How about to-morrow?" Sophy Gold shook her head. "Wednesday then? You stick to me and you'll see Paris. Thursday?"

"I'm buying my own dinners," said Sophy Gold.

Max Tack wagged a chiding forefinger at her.

"You little rascal!" No one had ever called Sophy Gold a little rascal before. "You stingy little rascal! Won't give a poor lonesome fellow an evening's pleasure, eh! The theatre? Want to go slumming?"

He was feeling his way now, a trifle puzzled. Usually he landed a buyer at the first shot. Of course you had to use tact and discrimination. Some you took to supper and to the naughty *revues*.

Occasionally you found a highbrow one who preferred the opera. Had he not sat through Parsifal the week before? And nearly died! Some wanted to begin at Tod Sloan's bar and work their way up through Montmartre, ending with breakfast at the Pré Catalan. Those were the greedy ones. But this one!

"What's she stalling for—with that face?" he asked himself.

Sophy Gold was moving toward the lift, the twinkling-eyed Miss Morrissey with her.

"I'm working too hard to play. Thanks, just the same. Good-night."

Max Tack, his face blank, stood staring up at them as the lift began to ascend.

"*Trazyem*," said Miss Morrissey grandly to the lift man.

"Third," replied that linguistic person, unimpressed.

It turned out to be soothingly quiet and cool in Ella Morrissey's room. She flicked on the light and turned an admiring glance on Sophy Gold.

"Is that your usual method?"

"I haven't any method," Miss Gold seated herself by the window. "But I've worked too hard for this job of mine to risk it by putting myself under obligations to any New York firm. It simply means that you've got to buy their goods. It isn't fair to your firm."

Miss Morrissey was busy with hooks and eyes and strings. Her utterance was jerky but concise. At one stage of her disrobing she breathed a great sigh of relief as she flung a heavy garment from her.

"There! That's comfort! Nights like this I wish I had that back porch of our flat to sit on for just an hour. Ma has flower boxes all round it, and I bought one of those hammock couches last year. When I come home from the store summer evenings I peel and get into my old blue-and-white kimono and lie there, listening to the girl stirring the iced tea for supper, and knowing that Ma has a platter of her swell cold fish with egg sauce!" She relaxed into an armchair. "Tell me, do you always talk to men that way?"

Sophy Gold was still staring out the open window.

"They don't bother me much, as a rule."

"Max Tack isn't a bad boy. He never wastes much time on me. I don't buy his line. Max is all business. Of course he's something of a smarty, and he does think he's the first verse and chorus of Paris-by-night; but you can't help liking him."

"Well, I can," said Sophy Gold, and her voice was a little bitter, "and without half trying."

"Oh, I don't say you weren't right. I've always made it a rule to steer clear of the ax-grinders myself. There are plenty of girls who take everything they can get. I know that Max Tack is just padded with letters from old girls, beginning 'Dear Kid,' and ending, 'Yours with a world of love!' I don't believe in that kind of thing, or in accepting things. Julia Harris, who buys for three departments in our store, drives up every morning in the French car that Parmentier's gave her when she was here last year. That's bad principle and poor taste. But—Well, you're young; and there ought to be something besides business in your life."

Sophy Gold turned her face from the window toward Miss Morrissey. It served to put a stamp of finality on what she said:

"There never will be. I don't know anything but business. It's the only thing I care about. I'll be earning my ten thousand a year pretty soon."

"Ten thousand a year is a lot; but it isn't everything. Oh, no, it isn't. Look here, dear; nobody knows better than I how this working and being independent and earning your own good money puts the stopper on any sentiment a girl might have in her; but don't let it sour you. You lose your illusions soon enough, goodness knows! There's no use in smashing 'em out of pure meanness."

"I don't see what illusions have got to do with Max Tack," interrupted Sophy Gold.

Miss Morrissey laughed her fat, comfortable chuckle.

"I suppose you're right, and I guess I've been getting a lee-tle bit nosey; but I'm pretty nearly old enough to be your mother. The girls kind of come to me and I talk to 'em. I guess they've spoiled me. They—"

There came a smart rapping at the door, followed by certain giggling and swishing. Miss Morrissey smiled.

"That'll be some of 'em now. Just run and open the door, will you, like a nice little thing? I'm too beat out to move."

The swishing swelled to a mighty rustle as the door opened. Taffeta was good this year, and the three who entered were the last in the world to leave you in ignorance of that fact. Ella Morrissey presented her new friend to the three, giving the department each represented as one would mention a title or order.

"The little plump one in black?—Ladies' and Misses' Ready-to-wear, Gates Company, Portland.... That's a pretty hat, Carrie. Get it to-day? Give me a big black velvet every time. You can wear 'em with anything, and yet they're dressy too. Just now small hats are distinctly passy.

"The handsome one who's dressed the way you always imagined the Parisiennes would dress, but don't?— Fancy Goods, Stein & Stack, San Francisco. Listen, Fan: don't go back to San Francisco with that stuff on your lips. It's all right in Paris, where all the women do it; but you know as well as I do that Morry Stein would take one look at you and then tell you to go upstairs and wash your face. Well, I'm just telling you as a friend.

"That little trick is the biggest lace buyer in the country.... No, you wouldn't, would you? Such a mite! Even if she does wear a twenty-eight blouse she's got a forty-two brain—haven't you, Belle? You didn't make a mistake with that blue crêpe de chine, child. It's chic and yet it's girlish. And you can wear it on the floor, too, when you get home. It's quiet if it is stunning."

These five, as they sat there that June evening, knew what your wife and your sister and your mother would wear on Fifth Avenue or Michigan Avenue next October. On their shrewd, unerring judgment rested the success or failure of many hundreds of feminine garments. The lace for Miss Minnesota's lingerie; the jewelled comb in Miss Colorado's hair; the hat that would grace Miss New Hampshire; the dress for Madam Delaware—all were the results of their farsighted selection. They were foragers of feminine fal-lals, and their booty would be distributed from oyster cove to orange grove.

They were marcelled and manicured within an inch of their lives. They rustled and a pleasant perfume clung about them. Their hats were so smart that they gave you a shock. Their shoes were correct. Their skirts bunched where skirts should bunch that year or lay smooth where smoothness was decreed. They looked like the essence of frivolity—until you saw their eyes; and then you noticed that that which is liquid in sheltered women's eyes was crystallised in theirs.

Sophy Gold, listening to them, felt strangely out of it and plainer than ever.

"I'm taking tango lessons, Ella," chirped Miss Laces. "Every time I went to New York last year I sat and twiddled my thumbs while every one else was dancing. I've made up my mind I'll be in it this year."

"You girls are wonders!" Miss Morrissey marvelled. "I can't do it any more. If I was to work as hard as I have to during the day and then run round the way you do in the evening they'd have to hold services for me at sea. I'm getting old."

"You—old!" This from Miss Ready-to-Wear. "You're younger now than I'll ever be. Oh, Ella, I got six stunning models at Estelle Mornet's. There's a business woman for you! Her place is smart from the ground floor up—not like the shabby old junk shops the others have. And she greets you herself. The personal touch! Let me tell you, it counts in business!"

"I'd go slow on those cape blouses if I were you; I don't think they're going to take at home. They look like regular Third Avenue style to me."

"Don't worry. I've hardly touched them."

They talked very directly, like men, when they discussed clothes; for to them a clothes talk meant a business talk.

The telephone buzzed. The three sprang up, rustling.

"That'll be for us, Ella," said Miss Fancy Goods. "We told the office to call us here. The boys are probably downstairs." She answered the call, turned, nodded, smoothed her gloves and preened her laces.

Ella Morrissey, in kimonoed comfort, waved a good-bye from her armchair. "Have a good time! You all look lovely. Oh, we met Max Tack downstairs, looking like a grand duke!"

Pert Miss Laces turned at the door, giggling.

"He says the French aristocracy has nothing on him, because his grandfather was one of the original Ten Ikes of New York."

A final crescendo of laughter, a last swishing of silks, a breath of perfume from the doorway and they were gone.

Within the room the two women sat looking at the closed door for a moment. Then Ella Morrissey turned to look at Sophy Gold just as Sophy Gold turned to look at Ella Morrissey.

"Well?" smiled Ella.

Sophy Gold smiled too—a mirthless, one-sided smile.

"I felt just like this once when I was a little girl. I went to a party, and all the other little girls had yellow curls. Maybe some of them had brown ones; but I only remember a maze of golden hair, and pink and blue sashes, and rosy cheeks, and ardent little boys, and the sureness of those little girls—their absolute faith in their power to enthrall, and in the perfection of their curls and sashes. I went home before the ice cream. And I love ice cream!"

Ella Morrissey's eyes narrowed thoughtfully.

"Then the next time you're invited to a party you wait for the ice cream, girlie."

"Maybe I will," said Sophy Gold.

The party came two nights later. It was such a very modest affair that one would hardly call it that—least of all Max Tack, who had spent seventy-five dollars the night before in entertaining an important prospective buyer.

On her way to her room that sultry June night Sophy had encountered the persistent Tack. Ella Morrissey, up in her room, was fathoms deep in work. It was barely eight o'clock and there was a wonderful opal sky—a June twilight sky, of which Paris makes a specialty—all grey and rose and mauve and faint orange.

"Somebody's looking mighty sweet to-night in her new Paris duds!"

Max Tack's method of approach never varied in its simplicity.

"They're not Paris—they're Chicago."

His soul was in his eyes.

"They certainly don't look it!" Then, with a little hurt look in those same expressive features: "I suppose, after the way you threw me down hard the other night, you wouldn't come out and play somewhere, would you—if I sat up and begged and jumped through this?"

"It's too warm for most things," Sophy faltered.

"Anywhere your little heart dictates," interrupted Max Tack ardently. "Just name it."

Sophy looked up.

"Well, then, I'd like to take one of those boats and go down the river to St.-Cloud. The station's just back of the Louvre. We've just time to catch the eight-fifteen boat."

"Boat!" echoed Max Tack stupidly. Then, in revolt: "Why, say, girlie, you don't want to do that! What is there in taking an old tub and flopping down that dinky stream? Tell you what we'll do: we'll—"

"No, thanks," said Sophy. "And it really doesn't matter. You simply asked me what I'd like to do and I told you. Thanks. Good-night."

"Now, now!" pleaded Max Tack in a panic. "Of course we'll go. I just thought you'd rather do something fussier—that's all. I've never gone down the river; but I think that's a classy little idea—yes, I do. Now you run and get your hat and we'll jump into a taxi and—"

"You don't need to jump into a taxi; it's only two blocks. We'll walk."

There was a little crowd down at the landing station. Max Tack noticed, with immense relief, that they were not half-bad-looking people either. He had been rather afraid of workmen in red sashes and with lime on their clothes, especially after Sophy had told him that a trip cost twenty centimes each.

"Twenty centimes! That's about four cents! Well, my gad!"

They got seats in the prow. Sophy took off her hat and turned her face gratefully to the cool breeze as they swung out into the river. The Paris of the rumbling, roaring auto buses, and the honking horns, and the shrill cries, and the mad confusion faded away. There was the palely glowing sky ahead, and on each side the black reflection of the tree-laden banks, mistily mysterious now and very lovely. There was not a ripple on the water and the Pont Alexandre III and the golden glory of the dome of the Hôtel des Invalides were ahead.

"Say, this is Venice!" exclaimed Max Tack.

A soft and magic light covered the shore, the river, the sky, and a soft and magic something seemed to steal over the little boat and work its wonders. The shabby student-looking chap and his equally shabby and merry little companion, both Americans, closed the bag of fruit from which they had been munching and sat looking into each other's eyes.

The long-haired artist, who looked miraculously like pictures of Robert Louis Stevenson, smiled down at his queer, slender-legged little daughter in the curious Cubist frock; and she smiled back and snuggled up and rested her cheek on his arm. There seemed to be a deep and silent understanding between them. You knew, somehow, that the little Cubist daughter had no mother, and that the father's artist friends made much of her and that she poured tea for them prettily on special days.

The bepowdered French girl who got on at the second station sat frankly and contentedly in the embrace of her sweetheart. The stolid married couple across the way smiled and the man's arm rested on his wife's plump shoulder.

So the love boat glided down the river into the night. And the shore faded and became grey, and then black. And the lights came out and cast slender pillars of gold and green and scarlet on the water.

Max Tack's hand moved restlessly, sought Sophy's, found it, clasped it. Sophy's hand had never been clasped like that before. She did not know what to do with it, so she did nothing—which was just what she should have done.

"Warm enough?" asked Max Tack tenderly.

"Just right," murmured Sophy.

The dream trip ended at St.-Cloud. They learned to their dismay that the boat did not return to Paris. But how to get back? They asked questions, sought direction—always a frantic struggle in Paris. Sophy, in the glare of the street light, looked uglier than ever.

"Just a minute," said Max Tack. "I'll find a taxi."

"Nonsense! That man said the street car passed right here, and that we should get off at the Bois. Here it is now! Come on!"

Max Tack looked about helplessly, shrugged his shoulders and gave it up.

"You certainly make a fellow hump," he said, not without a note of admiration. "And why are you so afraid that I'll spend some money?" as he handed the conductor the tiny fare.

"I don't know—unless it's because I've had to work so hard all my life for mine."

At Porte Maillot they took one of the flock of waiting *fiacres*.

"But you don't want to go home yet!" protested Max Tack.

"I—I think I should like to drive in the Bois Park—if you don't mind—that is—"

"Mind!" cried the gallant and game Max Tack.

Now Max Tack was no villain; but it never occurred to him that one might drive in the Bois with a girl and not make love to her. If he had driven with Aurora in her chariot he would have held her hand and called her tender names. So, because he was he, and because this was Paris, and because it was so dark that one could not see Sophy's extreme plainness, he took her unaccustomed hand again in his.

"This little hand was never meant for work," he murmured.

Sophy, the acid, the tart, said nothing. The Bois Park at night is a mystery maze and lovely beyond adjectives. And the horse of that particular *fiacre* wore a little tinkling bell that somehow added to the charm of the night. A waterfall, unseen, tumbled and frothed near by. A turn in the winding road brought them to an open stretch, and they saw the world bathed in the light of a yellow, mellow, roguish Paris moon. And Max Tack leaned over quietly and kissed Sophy Gold on the lips.

Now Sophy Gold had never been kissed in just that way before. You would have thought she would not know what to do; but the plainest woman, as well as the loveliest, has the centuries back of her. Sophy's mother, and her mother's mother, and her mother's mother's mother had been kissed before her. So they told her to say:

"You shouldn't have done that."

And the answer, too, was backed by the centuries:

"I know it; but I couldn't help it. Don't be angry!"

"You know," said Sophy with a little tremulous laugh, "I'm very, very ugly—when it isn't moonlight."

"Paris," spake Max Tack, diplomat, "is so full of medium-lookers who think they're pretty, and of pretty ones who think they're beauties, that it sort of rests my jaw and mind to be with some one who hasn't any fake notions to feed. They're all right; but give me a woman with brains every time." Which was a lie!

They drove home down the Bois—the cool, spacious, tree-bordered Bois—and through the Champs Élysées. Because he was an artist in his way, and because every passing *fiacre* revealed the same picture, Max Tack sat very near her and looked very tender and held her hand in his. It would have raised a laugh at Broadway and Forty-second. It was quite, quite sane and very comforting in Paris.

At the door of the hotel:

"I'm sailing Wednesday," said Max Tack. "You—you won't forget me?"

"Oh, no—no!"

"You'll call me up or run into the office when you get to New York?"

"Oh, yes!"

He walked with her to the lift, said good-bye and returned to the *fiacre* with the tinkling bell. There was a stunned sort of look in his face. The *fiacre* meter registered two francs seventy. Max Tack did a lightning mental calculation. The expression on his face deepened. He looked up at the cabby—the red-faced, bottle-nosed cabby, with his absurd scarlet vest, his mustard-coloured trousers and his glazed top hat.

"Well, can you beat that? Three francs thirty for the evening's entertainment! Why—why, all she wanted was just a little love!"

To the bottle-nosed one all conversation in a foreign language meant dissatisfaction with the meter. He tapped that glass-covered contrivance impatiently with his whip. A flood of French bubbled at his lips.

"It's all right, boy! It's all right! You don't get me!" And Max Tacked pressed a five-franc piece into the outstretched palm. Then to the hotel porter: "Just grab a taxi for me, will you? These tubs make me nervous."

Sophy, on her way to her room, hesitated, turned, then ran up the stairs to the next floor and knocked gently at Miss Morrissey's door. A moment later that lady's kimonoed figure loomed large in the doorway.

"Who is—oh, it's you! Well, I was just going to have them drag the Seine for you. Come in!"

She went back to the table. Sheets of paper, rough sketches of hat models done from memory, notes and letters lay scattered all about. Sophy leaned against the door dreamily.

"I've been working this whole mortal evening," went on Ella Morrissey, holding up a pencil sketch and squinting at it disapprovingly over her working spectacles, "and I'm so tired that one eye's shut and the other's running on first. Where've you been, child?"

"Oh, driving!" Sophy's limp hair was a shade limper than usual, and a strand of it had become loosened and straggled untidily down over her ear. Her eyes looked large and strangely luminous. "Do you know, I love Paris!"

Ella Morrissey laid down her pencil sketch and turned slowly. She surveyed Sophy Gold, her shrewd eyes twinkling.

"That so? What made you change your mind?"

The dreamy look in Sophy's eyes deepened.

"Why—I don't know. There's something in the atmosphere—something in the air. It makes you do and say foolish things. It makes you feel queer and light and happy."

Ella Morrissey's bright twinkle softened to a glow. She stared for another brief moment. Then she trundled over to where Sophy stood and patted her leathery cheek. "Welcome to our city!" said Miss Ella Morrissey.

XI
THE THREE OF THEM

For eleven years Martha Foote, head housekeeper at the Senate Hotel, Chicago, had catered, unseen, and ministered, unknown, to that great, careless, shifting, conglomerate mass known as the Travelling Public. Wholesale hostessing was Martha Foote's job. Senators and suffragists, ambassadors and first families had found ease and comfort under Martha Foote's régime. Her carpets had bent their nap to the tread of kings, and show girls, and buyers from Montana. Her sheets had soothed the tired limbs of presidents, and princesses, and prima donnas. For the Senate Hotel is more than a hostelry; it is a Chicago institution. The whole world is churned in at its revolving front door.

For eleven years Martha Foote, then, had beheld humanity throwing its grimy suitcases on her immaculate white bedspreads; wiping its muddy boots on her bath towels; scratching its matches on her wall paper; scrawling its pencil marks on her cream woodwork; spilling its greasy crumbs on her carpet; carrying away her dresser scarfs and pincushions. There is no supremer test of character. Eleven years of hotel housekeepership guarantees a knowledge of human nature that includes some things no living being ought to know about her fellow men. And inevitably one of two results must follow. You degenerate into a bitter, waspish, and fault-finding shrew; or you develop into a patient, tolerant, and infinitely understanding woman. Martha Foote dealt daily with Polack scrub girls, and Irish porters, and Swedish chambermaids, and Swiss waiters, and Halsted Street bell-boys. Italian tenors fried onions in her Louis-Quinze suite. College boys burned cigarette holes in her best linen sheets. Yet any one connected with the Senate Hotel, from Pete the pastry cook to H.G. Featherstone, lessee-director, could vouch for Martha Foote's serene unacidulation.

Don't gather from this that Martha Foote was a beaming, motherly person who called you dearie. Neither was she one of those managerial and magnificent blonde beings occasionally encountered in hotel corridors, engaged in addressing strident remarks to a damp and crawling huddle of calico that is doing something sloppy to the woodwork. Perhaps the shortest cut to Martha Foote's character is through Martha Foote's bedroom. (Twelfth floor. Turn to your left. That's it; 1246. Come in!)

In the long years of its growth and success the Senate Hotel had known the usual growing pains. Starting with walnut and red plush it had, in its adolescence, broken out all over into brass beds and birds'-eye maple. This, in turn, had vanished before mahogany veneer and brocade. Hardly had the white scratches on these ruddy surfaces been doctored by the house painter when—whisk! Away with that sombre stuff! And in minced a whole troupe of near-French furnishings; cream enamel beds, cane-backed; spindle-legged dressing tables before which it was impossible to dress; perilous chairs with raspberry complexions. Through all these changes Martha Foote, in her big, bright twelfth floor room, had clung to her old black walnut set.

The bed, to begin with, was a massive, towering edifice with a headboard that scraped the lofty ceiling. Head and foot-board were fretted and carved with great blobs representing grapes, and cornucopias, and tendrils, and knobs and other bedevilments of the cabinet-maker's craft. It had been polished and rubbed until now it shone like soft brown satin. There was a monumental dresser too, with a liver-coloured marble top. Along the wall, near the windows, was a couch; a heavy, wheezing, fat-armed couch decked out in white ruffled cushions. I suppose the mere statement that, in Chicago, Illinois, Martha Foote kept these cushions always crisply white, would make any further characterization superfluous. The couch made you think of a plump grandmother of bygone days, a beruffled white fichu across her ample, comfortable bosom. Then there was the writing desk; a substantial structure that bore no relation to the pindling rose-and-cream affairs that graced the guest rooms. It was the solid sort of desk at which an English novelist of the three-volume school might have written a whole row of books without losing his dignity or cramping his style. Martha Foote used it for making out reports and instruction sheets, for keeping accounts, and for her small private correspondence.

Such was Martha Foote's room. In a modern and successful hotel, whose foyer was rose-shaded, brass-grilled, peacock-alleyed and tessellated, that bed-sitting-room of hers was as wholesome, and satisfying, and real as a piece of home-made rye bread on a tray of French pastry; and as incongruous.

It was to the orderly comfort of these accustomed surroundings that the housekeeper of the Senate Hotel opened her eyes this Tuesday morning. Opened them, and lay a moment, bridging the morphean chasm that lay between last night and this morning. It was 6:30 A.M. It is bad enough to open one's eyes at 6:30 on Monday morning. But to open them at 6:30 on Tuesday morning, after an indigo Monday.... The taste of yesterday lingered, brackish, in Martha's mouth.

"Oh, well, it won't be as bad as yesterday, anyway. It can't." So she assured herself, as she lay there. "There never were *two* days like that, hand running. Not even in the hotel business."

For yesterday had been what is known as a muddy Monday. Thick, murky, and oozy with trouble. Two conventions, three banquets, the lobby so full of khaki that it looked like a sand-storm, a threatened strike in the laundry, a travelling man in two-twelve who had the grippe and thought he was dying, a shortage of towels (that bugaboo of the hotel housekeeper) due to the laundry trouble that had kept the linen-room telephone jangling to the tune of a hundred damp and irate guests. And weaving in and out, and above, and about and through it all, like a neuralgic toothache that can't be located, persisted the constant, nagging, maddening complaints of the Chronic Kicker in six-eighteen.

Six-eighteen was a woman. She had arrived Monday morning, early. By Monday night every girl on the switchboard had the nervous jumps when they plugged in at her signal. She had changed her rooms, and back again. She had quarrelled with the room clerk. She had complained to the office about the service, the food, the linen, the lights, the noise, the chambermaid, all the bell-boys, and the colour of the furnishings in her suite. She said she couldn't live with that colour. It made her sick. Between 8:30 and 10:30 that night, there had come a lull. Six-eighteen was doing her turn at the Majestic.

Martha Foote knew that. She knew, too, that her name was Geisha McCoy, and she knew what that name meant, just as you do. She had even laughed and quickened and responded to Geisha McCoy's manipulation of her audience, just as you have. Martha Foote knew the value of the personal note, and it had been her idea that had resulted in the rule which obliged elevator boys, chambermaids, floor clerks, doormen and waiters if possible, to learn the names of Senate Hotel guests, no matter how brief their stay.

"They like it," she had said, to Manager Brant. "You know that better than I do. They'll be flattered, and surprised, and tickled to death, and they'll go back to Burlington, Iowa, and tell how well known they are at the Senate."

When the suggestion was met with the argument that no human being could be expected to perform such daily feats of memory Martha Foote battered it down with:

"That's just where you're mistaken. The first few days are bad. After that it's easier every day, until it becomes mechanical. I remember when I first started waiting on table in my mother's quick lunch eating house in Sorghum, Minnesota. I'd bring 'em wheat cakes when they'd ordered pork and beans, but it wasn't two weeks before I could take six orders, from soup to pie, without so much as forgetting the catsup. Habit, that's all."

So she, as well as the minor hotel employés, knew six-eighteen as Geisha McCoy. Geisha McCoy, who got a thousand a week for singing a few songs and chatting informally with the delighted hundreds on the other side of the footlights. Geisha McCoy made nothing of those same footlights. She reached out, so to speak, and shook hands with you across their amber glare. Neither lovely nor alluring, this woman. And as for her voice!—And yet for ten years or more this rather plain person, somewhat dumpy, no longer young, had been singing her every-day, human songs about every-day, human people. And invariably (and figuratively) her audience clambered up over the footlights, and sat in her lap. She had never resorted to cheap music-hall tricks. She had never invited the gallery to join in the chorus. She descended to no finger-snapping. But when she sang a song about a waitress she was a waitress. She never hesitated to twist up her hair, and pull down her mouth, to get an effect. She didn't seem to be thinking about herself, at all, or about her clothes, or her method, or her effort, or anything but the audience that was plastic to her deft and magic manipulation.

Until very recently. Six months had wrought a subtle change in Geisha McCoy. She still sang her every-day, human songs about every-day, human people. But you failed, somehow, to recognise them as such. They sounded sawdust-stuffed. And you were likely to hear the man behind you say, "Yeh, but you ought to have heard her five years ago. She's about through."

Such was six-eighteen. Martha Foote, luxuriating in that one delicious moment between her 6:30 awakening, and her 6:31 arising, mused on these things. She thought of how, at eleven o'clock the night before, her telephone had rung with the sharp zing! of trouble. The voice of Irish Nellie, on night duty on the sixth floor, had sounded thick-brogued, sure sign of distress with her.

"I'm sorry to be a-botherin' ye, Mis' Phut. It's Nellie speakin'—Irish Nellie on the sixt'."

"What's the trouble, Nellie?"

"It's that six-eighteen again. She's goin' on like mad. She's carryin' on something fierce."

"What about?"

"Th'—th' blankets, Mis' Phut."

"Blankets?—"

"She says—it's her wurruds, not mine—she says they're vile. Vile, she says."

Martha Foote's spine had stiffened. "In this house! Vile!"

If there was one thing more than another upon which Martha Foote prided herself it was the Senate Hotel bed coverings. Creamy, spotless, downy, they were her especial fad. "Brocade chairs, and pink lamps, and gold snake-work are all well and good," she was wont to say, "and so are American Beauties in the lobby and white gloves on the elevator boys. But it's the blankets on the beds that stamp a hotel first or second class." And now this, from Nellie.

"I know how ye feel, an' all. I sez to 'er, I sez: 'There never was a blanket in this *house*,' I sez, 'that didn't look as if it cud be sarved up wit' whipped cr-ream,' I sez, 'an' et,' I sez to her; 'an' fu'thermore,' I sez—"

"Never mind, Nellie. I know. But we never argue with guests. You know that rule as well as I. The guest is right—always. I'll send up the linen-room keys. You get fresh blankets; new ones. And no arguments. But I want to see those—those vile—"

"Listen, Mis' Phut." Irish Nellie's voice, until now shrill with righteous anger, dropped a discreet octave. "I seen 'em. An' they *are* vile. Wait a minnit! But why? Becus that there maid of hers—that yella' hussy—give her a body massage, wit' cold cream an' all, usin' th' blankets f'r coverin', an' smearin' 'em right *an'* lift. This was afther they come back from th' theayter. Th' crust of thim people, using the iligent blankets off'n the beds t'—"

"Good night, Nellie. And thank you."

"Sure, ye know I'm that upset f'r distarbin' yuh, an' all, but—"

Martha Foote cast an eye toward the great walnut bed. "That's all right. Only, Nellie—"

"Yesm'm."

"If I'm disturbed again on that woman's account for anything less than murder—"

"Yesm'm?"

"Well, there'll *be* one, that's all. Good night."

Such had been Monday's cheerful close.

Martha Foote sat up in bed, now, preparatory to the heroic flinging aside of the covers. "No," she assured herself, "it can't be as bad as yesterday." She reached round and about her pillow, groping for the recalcitrant hairpin that always slipped out during the night; found it, and twisted her hair into a hard bathtub bun.

With a jangle that tore through her half-wakened senses the telephone at her bedside shrilled into life. Martha Foote, hairpin in mouth, turned and eyed it, speculatively, fearfully. It shrilled on in her very face, and there seemed something taunting and vindictive about it. One long ring, followed by a short one; a long ring, a short. "Ca-a-an't it? Ca-a-an't it?"

"Something tells me I'm wrong," Martha Foote told herself, ruefully, and reached for the blatant, snarling thing. "Yes?"

"Mrs. Foote? This is Healy, the night clerk. Say, Mrs. Foote, I think you'd better step down to six-eighteen and see what's—"

"I *am* wrong," said Martha Foote.

"What's that?"

"Nothing. Go on. Will I step down to six-eighteen and—?"

"She's sick, or something. Hysterics, I'd say. As far as I could make out it was something about a noise, or a sound or—Anyway, she can't locate it, and her maid says if we don't stop it right away—"

"I'll go down. Maybe it's the plumbing. Or the radiator. Did you ask?"

"No, nothing like that. She kept talking about a wail."

"A what!"

"A wail. A kind of groaning, you know. And then dull raps on the wall, behind the bed."

"Now look here, Ed Healy; I get up at 6:30, but I can't see a joke before ten. If you're trying to be funny!—"

"Funny! Why, say, listen, Mrs. Foote. I may be a night clerk, but I'm not so low as to get you out at half past six to spring a thing like that in fun. I mean it. So did she."

"But a kind of moaning! And then dull raps!"

"Those are her words. A kind of m—"

"Let's not make a chant of it. I think I get you. I'll be down there in ten minutes. Telephone her, will you?"

"Can't you make it five?"

"Not without skipping something vital."

Still, it couldn't have been a second over ten, including shoes, hair, and hooks-and-eyes. And a fresh white blouse. It was Martha Foote's theory that a hotel housekeeper, dressed for work, ought to be as inconspicuous as a steel engraving. She would have been, too, if it hadn't been for her eyes.

She paused a moment before the door of six-eighteen and took a deep breath. At the first brisk rat-tat of her knuckles on the door there had sounded a shrill "Come in!" But before she could turn the knob the door was flung open by a kimonoed mulatto girl, her eyes all whites. The girl began to jabber, incoherently but Martha Foote passed on through the little hall to the door of the bedroom.

Six-eighteen was in bed. At sight of her Martha Foote knew that she had to deal with an over-wrought woman. Her hair was pushed back wildly from her forehead. Her arms were clasped about her knees. At the left her nightgown had slipped down so that one plump white shoulder gleamed against the background of her streaming hair. The room was in almost comic disorder. It was a room in which a struggle has taken place between its occupant and that burning-eyed hag, Sleeplessness. The hag, it was plain, had won. A half-emptied glass of milk was on the table by the bed. Warmed, and sipped slowly, it had evidently failed to soothe. A tray of dishes littered another table. Yesterday's dishes, their contents congealed. Books and magazines, their covers spread wide as if they had been flung, sprawled where they lay. A little heap of grey-black cigarette stubs. The window curtain awry where she had stood there during a feverish moment of the sleepless night, looking down upon the lights of Grant Park and the sombre black void beyond that was Lake Michigan. A tiny satin bedroom slipper on a chair, its mate, sole up, peeping out from under the bed. A pair of satin slippers alone, distributed thus, would make a nun's cell look disreputable. Over all this disorder the ceiling lights, the wall lights, and the light from two rosy lamps, beat mercilessly down; and upon the white-faced woman in the bed.

She stared, hollow-eyed, at Martha Foote. Martha Foote, in the doorway, gazed serenely back upon her. And Geisha McCoy's quick intelligence and drama-sense responded to the picture of this calm and capable figure in the midst of the feverish, over-lighted, over-heated room. In that moment the nervous pucker between her eyes ironed out ever so little, and something resembling a wan smile crept into her face. And what she said was:

"I wouldn't have believed it."

"Believed what?" inquired Martha Foote, pleasantly.

"That there was anybody left in the world who could look like that in a white shirtwaist at 6:30 A.M. Is that all your own hair?"

"Strictly."

"Some people have all the luck," sighed Geisha McCoy, and dropped listlessly back on her pillows. Martha Foote came forward into the room. At that instant the woman in the bed sat up again, tense, every nerve strained in an attitude of listening. The mulatto girl had come swiftly to the foot of the bed and was clutching the footboard, her knuckles showing white.

"Listen!" A hissing whisper from the haggard woman in the bed. "What's that?"

"Wha' dat!" breathed the coloured girl, all her elegance gone, her every look and motion a hundred-year throwback to her voodoo-haunted ancestors.

The three women remained rigid, listening. From the wall somewhere behind the bed came a low, weird monotonous sound, half wail, half croaking moan, like a banshee with a cold. A clanking, then, as of chains. A s-s-swish. Then three dull raps, seemingly from within the very wall itself.

The coloured girl was trembling. Her lips were moving, soundlessly. But Geisha McCoy's emotion was made of different stuff.

"Now look here," she said, desperately, "I don't mind a sleepless night. I'm used to 'em. But usually I can drop off at five, for a little while. And that's been going on—well, I don't know how long. It's driving me crazy. Blanche, you fool, stop that hand wringing! I tell you there's no such thing as ghosts. Now you"—she turned to Martha Foote again—"you tell me, for God's sake, what *is* that!"

And into Martha Foote's face there came such a look of mingled compassion and mirth as to bring a quick flame of fury into Geisha McCoy's eyes.

"Look here, you may think it's funny but—"

"I don't. I don't. Wait a minute." Martha Foote turned and was gone. An instant later the weird sounds ceased. The two women in the room looked toward the door, expectantly. And through it came Martha Foote, smiling. She turned and beckoned to some one without. "Come on," she said. "Come on." She put out a hand, encouragingly, and brought forward the shrinking, cowering, timorous figure of Anna Czarnik, scrub-woman on the sixth floor. Her hand still on her shoulder Martha Foote led her to the centre of the room, where she stood, gazing dumbly about. She was the scrub-woman you've seen in every hotel from San Francisco to Scituate. A shapeless, moist, blue calico mass. Her shoes turned up ludicrously at the toes, as do the shoes of one who crawls her way backward, crab-like, on hands and knees. Her hands were the shrivelled, unlovely members that bespeak long and daily immersion in dirty water. But even had these invariable marks of her trade been lacking, you could not have failed to recognise her type by the large and glittering mock-diamond comb which failed to catch up her dank and stringy hair in the back.

One kindly hand on the woman's arm, Martha Foote performed the introduction.

"This is Mrs. Anna Czarnik, late of Poland. Widowed. Likewise childless. Also brotherless. Also many other uncomfortable things. But the life of the crowd in the scrub-girls' quarters on the top floor. Aren't you, Anna? Mrs. Anna Czarnik, I'm sorry to say, is the source of the blood-curdling moan, and the swishing, and the clanking, and the ghost-raps. There is a service stairway just on the other side of this wall. Anna Czarnik was performing her morning job of scrubbing it. The swishing was her wet rag. The clanking was her pail. The dull raps her scrubbing brush striking the stair corner just behind your wall."

"You're forgetting the wail," Geisha McCoy suggested, icily.

"No, I'm not. The wail, I'm afraid, was Anna Czarnik, singing."

"Singing?"

Martha Foote turned and spoke a gibberish of Polish and English to the bewildered woman at her side. Anna Czarnik's dull face lighted up ever so little.

"She says the thing she was singing is a Polish folk-song about death and sorrow, and it's called a—what was that, Anna?"

"Dumka."

"It's called a dumka. It's a song of mourning, you see? Of grief. And of bitterness against the invaders who have laid her country bare."

"Well, what's the idea!" demanded Geisha McCoy. "What kind of a hotel is this, anyway? Scrub-girls waking people up in the middle of the night with a Polish cabaret. If she wants to sing her hymn of hate why does she have to pick on me!"

"I'm sorry. You can go, Anna. No sing, remember! Sh-sh-sh!"

Anna Czarnik nodded and made her unwieldy escape.

Geisha McCoy waved a hand at the mulatto maid. "Go to your room, Blanche. I'll ring when I need you." The girl vanished, gratefully, without a backward glance at the disorderly room. Martha Foote felt herself dismissed, too. And yet she made no move to go. She stood there, in the middle of the room, and every housekeeper inch of her yearned to tidy the chaos all about her, and every sympathetic impulse urged her to comfort the nerve-tortured woman before her. Something of this must have shone in her face, for Geisha McCoy's tone was half-pettish, half-apologetic as she spoke.

"You've no business allowing things like that, you know. My nerves are all shot to pieces anyway. But even if they weren't, who could stand that kind of torture? A woman like that ought to lose her job for that. One word from me at the office and she—"

"Don't say it, then," interrupted Martha Foote, and came over to the bed. Mechanically her fingers straightened the tumbled covers, removed a jumble of magazines, flicked away the crumbs. "I'm sorry you were disturbed. The scrubbing can't be helped, of course, but there is a rule against unnecessary noise, and she shouldn't have been singing. But—well, I suppose she's got to find relief, somehow. Would you believe that woman is the cut-up of the top floor? She's a natural comedian, and she does more for me in the way of keeping the other girls happy and satisfied than—"

"What about me? Where do I come in? Instead of sleeping until eleven I'm kept awake by this Polish dirge. I go on at the Majestic at four, and again at 9.45 and I'm sick, I tell you! Sick!"

She looked it, too. Suddenly she twisted about and flung herself, face downward, on the pillow. "Oh, God!" she cried, without any particular expression. "Oh, God! Oh, God!"

That decided Martha Foote.

She crossed over to the other side of the bed, first flicking off the glaring top lights, sat down beside the shaken woman on the pillows, and laid a cool, light hand on her shoulder.

"It isn't as bad as that. Or it won't be, anyway, after you've told me about it."

She waited. Geisha McCoy remained as she was, face down. But she did not openly resent the hand on her shoulder. So Martha Foote waited. And as suddenly as Six-eighteen had flung herself prone she twisted about and sat up, breathing quickly. She passed a hand over her eyes and pushed back her streaming hair with an oddly desperate little gesture. Her lips were parted, her eyes wide.

"They've got away from me," she cried, and Martha Foote knew what she meant. "I can't hold 'em any more. I work as hard as ever—harder. That's it. It seems the harder I work the colder they get. Last week, in Indianapolis, they couldn't have been more indifferent if I'd been the educational film that closes the show. And, oh my God! They sit and knit."

"Knit!" echoed Martha Foote. "But everybody's knitting nowadays."

"Not when I'm on. They can't. But they do. There were three of them in the third row yesterday afternoon. One of 'em was doing a grey sock with four shiny needles. Four! I couldn't keep my eyes off of them. And the second was doing a sweater, and the third a helmet. I could tell by the shape. And you can't be funny, can you, when you're hypnotised by three stony-faced females all doubled up over a bunch of olive-drab? Olive-drab! I'm scared of it. It sticks out all over the house. Last night there were two young kids in uniform right down in the first row, centre, right. I'll bet the oldest wasn't twenty-three. There they sat, looking up at me with their baby faces. That's all they are. Kids. The house seems to be peppered with 'em. You wouldn't think olive-drab could stick out the way it does. I can see it farther than red. I can see it day and night. I can't seem to see anything else. I can't—"

Her head came down on her arms, that rested on her tight-hugged knees.

"Somebody of yours in it?" Martha Foote asked, quietly. She waited. Then she made a wild guess—an intuitive guess. "Son?"

"How did you know?" Geisha McCoy's head came up.

"I didn't."

"Well, you're right. There aren't fifty people in the world, outside my own friends, who know I've got a grown-up son. It's bad business to have them think you're middle-aged. And besides, there's nothing of the stage about Fred. He's one of those square-jawed kids that are just cut out to be engineers. Third year at Boston Tech."

"Is he still there, then?"

"There! He's in France, that's where he is. Somewhere—in France. And I've worked for twenty-two years with everything in me just set, like an alarm-clock, for the time when that kid would step off on his own. He always hated to take money from me, and I loved him for it. I never went on that I didn't think of him. I never came off with a half dozen encores that I didn't wish he could hear it. Why, when I played a college town it used to be a riot, because I loved every fresh-faced boy in the house, and they knew it. And now—and now—what's there in it? What's there in it? I can't even hold 'em any more. I'm through, I tell you. I'm through!"

And waited to be disputed. Martha Foote did not disappoint her.

"There's just this in it. It's up to you to make those three women in the third row forget what they're knitting for, even if they don't forget their knitting. Let 'em go on knitting with their hands, but keep their heads off it. That's your job. You're lucky to have it."

"Lucky?"

"Yes *ma'am*! You can do all the dumka stuff in private, the way Anna Czarnik does, but it's up to you to make them laugh twice a day for twenty minutes."

"It's all very well for you to talk that cheer-o stuff. It hasn't come home to you, I can see that."

Martha Foote smiled. "If you don't mind my saying it, Miss McCoy, you're too worn out from lack of sleep to see anything clearly. You don't know me, but I do know you, you see. I know that a year ago Anna Czarnik would have been the most interesting thing in this town, for you. You'd have copied her clothes, and got a translation of her sob song, and made her as real to a thousand audiences as she was to us this morning; tragic history, patient animal face, comic shoes and all. And that's the trouble with you, my dear. When we begin to brood about our own troubles we lose what they call the human touch. And that's your business asset."

Geisha McCoy was looking up at her with a whimsical half-smile. "Look here. You know too much. You're not really the hotel housekeeper, are you?"

"I am."

"Well, then, you weren't always—"

"Yes I was. So far as I know I'm the only hotel housekeeper in history who can't look back to the time when she had three servants of her own, and her private carriage. I'm no decayed black-silk gentlewoman. Not me. My father drove a hack in Sorgham, Minnesota, and my mother took in boarders and I helped wait on table. I married when I was twenty, my man died two years later, and I've been earning my living ever since."

"Happy?"

"I must be, because I don't stop to think about it. It's part of my job to know everything that concerns the comfort of the guests in this hotel."

"Including hysterics in six-eighteen?"

"Including. And that reminds me. Up on the twelfth floor of this hotel there's a big, old-fashioned bedroom. In half an hour I can have that room made up with the softest linen sheets, and the curtains pulled down, and not a sound. That room's so restful it would put old Insomnia himself to sleep. Will you let me tuck you away in it?"

Geisha McCoy slid down among her rumpled covers, and nestled her head in the lumpy, tortured pillows. "Me! I'm going to stay right here."

"But this room's—why, it's as stale as a Pullman sleeper. Let me have the chambermaid in to freshen it up while you're gone."

"I'm used to it. I've got to have a room mussed up, to feel at home in it. Thanks just the same."

Martha Foote rose, "I'm sorry. I just thought if I could help—"

Geisha McCoy leaned forward with one of her quick movements and caught Martha Foote's hand in both her own, "You have! And I don't mean to be rude when I tell you I haven't felt so much like sleeping in weeks. Just turn out those lights, will you? And sort of tiptoe out, to give the effect." Then, as Martha Foote reached the door, "And oh, say! D'you think she'd sell me those shoes?"

Martha Foote didn't get her dinner that night until almost eight, what with one thing and another. Still as days go, it wasn't so bad as Monday; she and Irish Nellie, who had come in to turn down her bed, agreed on that. The Senate Hotel housekeeper was having her dinner in her room. Tony, the waiter, had just brought it on and had set it out for her, a gleaming island of white linen, and dome-shaped metal tops. Irish Nellie, a privileged person always, waxed conversational as she folded back the bed covers in a neat triangular wedge.

"Six-eighteen kinda ca'med down, didn't she? High toime, the divil. She had us jumpin' yist'iddy. I loike t' went off me head wid her, and th' day girl th' same. Some folks ain't got no feelin', I dunno."

Martha Foote unfolded her napkin with a little tired gesture. "You can't always judge, Nellie. That woman's got a son who has gone to war, and she couldn't see her way clear to living without him. She's better now. I talked to her this evening at six. She said she had a fine afternoon."

"Shure, she ain't the only wan. An' what do you be hearin' from your boy, Mis' Phut, that's in France?"

"He's well, and happy. His arm's all healed, and he says he'll be in it again by the time I get his letter."

"Humph," said Irish Nellie. And prepared to leave. She cast an inquisitive eye over the little table as she made for the door—inquisitive, but kindly. Her wide Irish nostrils sniffed a familiar smell. "Well, fur th' land, Mis' Phut! If I was housekeeper here, an' cud have hothouse strawberries, an' swatebreads undher glass, an' sparrowgrass, an' chicken, *an'* ice crame, the way you can, whiniver yuh loike, I wouldn't be a-eatin' cornbeef an' cabbage. Not me."

"Oh, yes you would, Nellie," replied Martha Foote, quietly, and spooned up the thin amber gravy. "Oh, yes you would."

XII
SHORE LEAVE

Tyler Kamps was a tired boy. He was tired from his left great toe to that topmost spot at the crown of his head where six unruly hairs always persisted in sticking straight out in defiance of patient brushing, wetting, and greasing. Tyler Kamps was as tired as only a boy can be at 9.30 P.M. who has risen at 5.30 A.M. Yet he lay wide awake in his hammock eight feet above the ground, like a giant silk-worm in an incredible cocoon and listened to the sleep-sounds that came from the depths of two hundred similar cocoons suspended at regular intervals down the long dark room. A chorus of deep regular breathing, with an occasional grunt or sigh, denoting complete relaxation. Tyler Kamps should have been part of this chorus, himself. Instead he lay staring into the darkness, thinking mad thoughts of which this is a sample:

"Gosh! Wouldn't I like to sit up in my hammock and give one yell! The kind of a yell a movie cowboy gives on a Saturday night. Wake 'em up and stop that—darned old breathing."

Nerves. He breathed deeply himself, once or twice, because it seemed, somehow to relieve his feeling of irritation. And in that unguarded moment of unconscious relaxation Sleep, that had been lying in wait for him just around the corner, pounced on him and claimed him for its own. From his hammock came the deep, regular inhalation, exhalation, with an occasional grunt or sigh. The normal sleep-sounds of a very tired boy.

The trouble with Tyler Kamps was that he missed two things he hadn't expected to miss at all. And he missed not at all the things he had been prepared to miss most hideously.

First of all, he had expected to miss his mother. If you had known Stella Kamps you could readily have understood that. Stella Kamps was the kind of mother they sing about in the sentimental ballads; mother, pal, and sweetheart. Which was where she had made her big mistake. When one mother tries to be all those things to one son that son has a very fair chance of turning out a mollycoddle. The war was probably all that saved Tyler Kamps from such a fate.

In the way she handled this son of hers Stella Kamps had been as crafty and skilful and velvet-gloved as a girl with her beau. The proof of it is that Tyler had never known he was being handled. Some folks in Marvin, Texas, said she actually flirted with him, and they were almost justified. Certainly the way she glanced up at him from beneath her lashes was excused only by the way she scolded him if he tracked up the kitchen floor. But then, Stella Kamps and her boy were different, anyway. Marvin folks all agreed about that. Flowers on the table at meals. Sitting over the supper things talking and laughing for an hour after they'd finished eating, as if they hadn't seen each other in years. Reading out loud to each other, out of books and then going on like mad about what they'd just read, and getting all het up about it. And sometimes chasing each other around the yard, spring evenings, like a couple of fool kids. Honestly, if a body didn't know Stella Kamps so well, and what a fight she had put up to earn a living for herself and the boy after that good-for-nothing Kamps up and left her, and what a housekeeper she was, and all, a person'd think—well—

So, then, Tyler had expected to miss her first of all. The way she talked. The way she fussed around him without in the least seeming to fuss. Her special way of cooking things. Her laugh which drew laughter in its wake. The funny way she had of saying things, vitalising commonplaces with the spark of her own electricity.

And now he missed her only as the average boy of twenty-one misses the mother he has been used to all his life. No more and no less. Which would indicate that Stella Kamps, in her protean endeavours, had overplayed the parts just a trifle.

He had expected to miss the boys at the bank. He had expected to miss the Mandolin Club. The Mandolin Club met, officially, every Thursday and spangled the Texas night with their tinkling. Five rather dreamy-eyed adolescents slumped in stoop-shouldered comfort over the instruments cradled in their arms, each right leg crossed limply over the left, each great foot that dangled from the bony ankle, keeping rhythmic time to the plunketty-plink-tinketty-plunk.

He had expected to miss the familiar faces on Main Street. He had even expected to miss the neighbours with whom he and his mother had so rarely mingled. All the hundred little, intimate, trivial, everyday things that had gone to make up his life back home in Marvin, Texas—these he had expected to miss.

And he didn't.

After ten weeks at the Great Central Naval Training Station so near Chicago, Illinois, and so far from Marvin, Texas, there were two things he missed.

He wanted the decent privacy of his small quiet bedroom back home.

He wanted to talk to a girl.

He knew he wanted the first, definitely. He didn't know he wanted the second. The fact that he didn't know it was Stella Kamps' fault. She had kept his boyhood girlless, year and year, by sheer force of her own love for him, and need of him, and by the charm and magnetism that were hers. She had been deprived of a more legitimate outlet for these emotions. Concentrated on the boy, they had sufficed for him. The Marvin girls had long ago given him up as hopeless. They fell back, baffled, their keenest weapons dulled by the impenetrable armour of his impersonal gaze.

The room? It hadn't been much of a room, as rooms go. Bare, clean, asceptic, with a narrow, hard white bed and a maple dresser whose second drawer always stuck and came out zig-zag when you pulled it; and a swimmy mirror that made one side of your face look sort of lumpy, and higher than the other side. In one corner a bookshelf. He had made it himself at manual training. When he had finished it—the planing, the staining, the polishing—Chippendale himself, after he had designed and executed his first gracious, wide-seated, back-fitting chair, could have felt no finer creative glow. As for the books it held, just to run your eye over them was like watching Tyler Kamps grow up. Stella Kamps had been a Kansas school teacher in the days before she met and married Clint Kamps. And she had never quite got over it. So the book case contained certain things that a fond mother (with a teaching past) would think her small son ought to enjoy. Things like "Tom Brown At Rugby" and "Hans Brinker, Or the Silver Skates." He had read them, dutifully, but they were as good as new. No thumbed pages, no ragged edges, no creases and tatters where eager boy hands had turned a page over—hastily. No, the thumb-marked, dog's-eared, grimy ones were, as always, "Tom Sawyer" and "Huckleberry Finn" and "Marching Against the Iroquois."

A hot enough little room in the Texas summers. A cold enough little room in the Texas winters. But his own. And quiet. He used to lie there at night, relaxed, just before sleep claimed him, and he could almost feel the soft Texas night enfold him like a great, velvety, invisible blanket, soothing him, lulling him. In the morning it had been pleasant to wake up to its bare, clean whiteness, and to the tantalising breakfast smells coming up from the kitchen below. His mother calling from the foot of the narrow wooden stairway:

"Ty-ler!," rising inflection. "Ty-ler," falling inflection. "Get up, son! Breakfast'll be ready."

It was always a terrific struggle between a last delicious stolen five minutes between the covers, and the scent of the coffee and bacon.

"Ty-ler! You'll be late!"

A mighty stretch. A gathering of his will forces. A swing of his long legs over the side of the bed so that they described an arc in the air.

"Been up years."

Breakfast had won.

Until he came to the Great Central Naval Training Station Tyler's nearest approach to the nautical life had been when, at the age of six, he had sailed chips in the wash tub in the back yard. Marvin, Texas, is five hundred miles inland. And yet he had enlisted in the navy as inevitably as though he had sprung from a long line of Vikings. In his boyhood his choice of games had always been pirate. You saw him, a red handkerchief binding his brow, one foot advanced, knee bent, scanning the horizon for the treasure island from the vantage point of the woodshed roof, while the crew, gone mad with thirst, snarled and shrieked all about him, and the dirt yard below became a hungry, roaring sea. His twelve-year-old vocabulary boasted such compound difficulties as mizzentopsail-yard and main-topgallantmast. He knew the intricate parts of a full-rigged ship from the mainsail to the deck, from the jib-boom to the chart-house. All this from pictures and books. It was the roving, restless spirit of his father in him, I suppose. Clint Kamps had never been meant for marriage. When the baby Tyler was one year old Clint had walked over to where his wife sat, the child in her lap, and had tilted her head back, kissed her on the lips, and had gently pinched the boy's roseleaf cheek with a quizzical forefinger and thumb. Then, indolently, negligently, gracefully, he had strolled out of the house, down the steps, into the hot and dusty street and so on and on and out of their lives. Stella Kamps had never seen him again. Her letters back home to her folks in Kansas were triumphs of bravery and bare-faced lying. The kind of bravery, and the kind of lying that only a woman could understand. She managed to make out, somehow, at first. And later, very well indeed. As the years went on she and the boy lived together in a sort of closed corporation paradise of their own. At twenty-one Tyler, who had gone through grammar school, high school and business college had never kissed a girl or felt a love-pang. Stella Kamps kept her age as a woman does whose brain and body are alert and busy. When Tyler first went to work in the Texas State Savings Bank of Marvin the girls would come in on various pretexts just for a glimpse of his charming blondeur behind the little cage at the rear. It is difficult for a small-town girl to think of reasons for going into a bank. You have to be moneyed to do it. They say that the Davies girl saved up nickels until she had a dollar's worth and then came into the bank and asked to have a bill in exchange for it. They gave her one—a crisp, new, crackly dollar bill. She reached for it, gropingly, her eyes fixed on a point at the rear of the bank. Two days later she came in and brazenly asked to have it changed into nickels again. She might have gone on indefinitely thus if Tyler's country hadn't given him something more important to do than to change dollars into nickels and back again.

On the day he left for the faraway naval training station Stella Kamps for the second time in her life had a chance to show the stuff she was made of, and showed it. Not a whimper. Down at the train, standing at the car window, looking up at him and smiling, and saying futile, foolish, final things, and seeing only his blond head among the many thrust out of the open window.

"... and Tyler, remember what I said about your feet. You know. Dry.... And I'll send a box every week, only don't eat too many of the nut cookies. They're so rich. Give some to the other—yes, I know you will. I was just ... Won't it be grand to be right there on the water all the time! My!... I'll write every night and then send it twice a week.... I don't suppose you ... Well once a week, won't you, dear?... You're—you're moving. The train's going! Good-b—" she ran along with it for a few feet, awkwardly, as a woman runs. Stumblingly.

And suddenly, as she ran, his head always just ahead of her, she thought, with a great pang:

"O my God, how young he is! How young he is, and he doesn't know anything. I should have told him.... Things.... He doesn't know anything about ... and all those other men—"

She ran on, one arm outstretched as though to hold him a moment longer while the train gathered speed. "Tyler!" she called, through the din and shouting. "Tyler, be good! Be good!" He only saw her lips moving, and could not hear, so he nodded his head, and smiled, and waved, and was gone.

So Tyler Kamps had travelled up to Chicago. Whenever they passed a sizable town they had thrown open the windows and yelled, "Youp! Who-ee! Yow!"

People had rushed to the streets and had stood there gazing after the train. Tyler hadn't done much youping at first, but in the later stages of the journey he joined in to keep his spirits up. He, who had never been more than a two-hours' ride from home was flashing past villages, towns, cities—hundreds of them.

The first few days had been unbelievably bad, what with typhoid inoculations, smallpox vaccinations, and loneliness. The very first day, when he had entered his barracks one of the other boys, older in experience, misled by Tyler's pink and white and gold colouring, had leaned forward from amongst a group and had called in glad surprise, at the top of a leathery pair of lungs:

"Why, hello, sweetheart!" The others had taken it up with cruelty of their age. "Hello, sweetheart!" It had stuck. Sweetheart. In the hard years that followed—years in which the blood-thirsty and piratical games of his boyhood paled to the mildest of imaginings—the nickname still clung, long after he had ceased to resent it; long after he had stripes and braid to refute it.

But in that Tyler Kamps we are not interested. It is the boy Tyler Kamps with whom we have to do. Bewildered, lonely, and a little resentful. Wondering where the sea part of it came in. Learning to say "on the station" instead of "at the station," the idea being that the great stretch of land on which the station was located was not really land, but water; and the long wooden barracks not really barracks at all, but ships. Learning to sleep in a hammock (it took him a full week). Learning to pin back his sailor collar to save soiling the white braid on it (that meant scrubbing). Learning—but why go into detail? One sentence covers it.

Tyler met Gunner Moran. Moran, tattooed, hairy-armed, hairy-chested as a gorilla and with something of the sadness and humour of the gorilla in his long upper lip and short forehead. But his eyes did not bear out the resemblance. An Irish blue; bright, unravaged; clear beacon lights in a rough and storm-battered countenance. Gunner Moran wasn't a gunner at all, or even a gunner's mate, but just a seaman who knew the sea from Shanghai to New Orleans; from Liverpool to Barcelona. His knowledge of knots and sails and rifles and bayonets and fists was a thing to strike you dumb. He wasn't the stuff of which officers are made. But you should have seen him with a Springfield! Or a bayonet! A bare twenty-five, Moran, but with ten years' sea experience. Into those ten years he had jammed a lifetime of adventure. And he could do expertly all the things that Tyler Kamps did amateurishly. In a barrack, or in a company street, the man who talks the loudest is the man who has the most influence. In Tyler's barrack Gunner Moran was that man.

Because of what he knew they gave him two hundred men at a time and made him company commander, without insignia or official position. In rank, he was only a "gob" like the rest of them. In influence a captain. Moran knew how to put the weight lunge behind the bayonet. It was a matter of balance, of poise, more than of muscle.

Up in the front of his men, "G'wan," he would yell. "Whatddye think you're doin'! Tickling 'em with a straw! That's a bayonet you got there, not a tennis rackit. You couldn't scratch your initials on a Fritz that way. Put a little guts into it. Now then!"

He had been used to the old Krag, with a cam that jerked out, and threw back, and fed one shell at a time. The new Springfield, that was a gloriously functioning thing in its simplicity, he regarded with a sort of reverence and ecstasy mingled. As his fingers slid lightly, caressingly along the shining barrel they were like a man's fingers lingering on the soft curves of a woman's throat. The sight of a rookie handling this metal sweetheart clumsily filled him with fury.

"Whatcha think you got there, you lubber, you! A section o' lead pipe! You ought t' be back carryin' a shovel, where you belong. Here. Just a touch. Like that. See? Easy now."

He could box like a professional. They put him up against Slovatsky, the giant Russian, one day. Slovatsky put up his two huge hands, like hams, and his great arms, like iron beams and looked down on this lithe, agile bantam that was hopping about at his feet. Suddenly the bantam crouched, sprang, and recoiled like a steel trap. Something had crashed up against Slovatsky's chin. Red rage shook him. He raised his sledge-hammer right for a slashing blow. Moran was directly in the path of it. It seemed that he could no more dodge it than he could hope to escape an onrushing locomotive, but it landed on empty air, with Moran around in back of the Russian, and peering impishly up under his arm. It was like an elephant worried by a mosquito. Then Moran's lightning right shot out again, smartly, and seemed just to tap the great hulk on the side of the chin. A ludicrous look of surprise on Slovatsky's face before he crumpled and crashed.

This man it was who had Tyler Kamps' admiration. It was more than admiration. It was nearer adoration. But there was nothing unnatural or unwholesome about the boy's worship of this man. It was a legitimate thing, born of all his fatherless years; years in which there had been no big man around the house who could throw farther than Tyler, and eat more, and wear larger shoes and offer more expert opinion. Moran accepted the boy's homage with a sort of surly graciousness.

In Tyler's third week at the Naval Station mumps developed in his barracks and they were quarantined. Tyler escaped the epidemic but he had to endure the boredom of weeks of quarantine. At first they took it as a lark, like schoolboys. Moran's hammock was just next Tyler's. On his other side was a young Kentuckian named Dabney Courtney. The barracks had dubbed him Monicker the very first day. Monicker had a rather surprising tenor voice. Moran a salty bass. And Tyler his mandolin. The trio did much to make life bearable, or unbearable, depending on one's musical knowledge and views. The boys all sang a great deal. They bawled everything they knew, from "Oh, You Beautiful Doll" and "Over There" to "The End of a Perfect Day." The latter, *ad nauseum*. They even revived "Just Break the News to Mother" and seemed to take a sort of awful joy in singing its dreary words and mournful measures. They played everything from a saxophone to a harmonica. They read. They talked. And they grew so sick of the sight of one another that they began to snap and snarl.

Sometimes they gathered round Moran and he told them tales they only half believed. He had been in places whose very names were exotic and oriental, breathing of sandalwood, and myrrh, and spices and aloes. They were places over which a boy dreams in books of travel. Moran bared the vivid tattooing on hairy arms and chest— tattooing representing anchors, and serpents, and girls' heads, and hearts with arrows stuck through them. Each mark had its story. A broad-swathed gentleman indeed, Gunner Moran. He had an easy way with him that made you feel provincial and ashamed. It made you ashamed of not knowing the sort of thing you used to be ashamed of knowing.

Visiting day was the worst. They grew savage, somehow, watching the mothers and sisters and cousins and sweethearts go streaming by to the various barracks. One of the boys to whom Tyler had never even spoken suddenly took a picture out of his blouse pocket and showed it to Tyler. It was a cheap little picture—one of the kind they sell two for a quarter if one sitter; two for thirty-five if two. This was a twosome. The boy, and a girl. A healthy, wide-awake wholesome looking small-town girl, who has gone through high school and cuts out her own shirtwaists.

"She's vice-president of the Silver Star Pleasure Club back home," the boy confided to Tyler. "I'm president. We meet every other Saturday."

Tyler looked at the picture seriously and approvingly. Suddenly he wished that he had, tucked away in his blouse, a picture of a clear-eyed, round-cheeked vice-president of a pleasure club. He took out his mother's picture and showed it.

"Oh, yeh," said the boy, disinterestedly.

The dragging weeks came to an end. The night of Tyler's restlessness was the last night of quarantine. To-morrow morning they would be free. At the end of the week they were to be given shore leave. Tyler had made up his mind to go to Chicago. He had never been there.

Five thirty. Reveille.

Tyler awoke with the feeling that something was going to happen. Something pleasant. Then he remembered, and smiled. Dabney Courtney, in the next hammock, was leaning far over the side of his perilous perch and delivering himself of his morning speech. Tyler did not quite understand this young southern elegant. Monicker had two moods, both of which puzzled Tyler. When he awoke feeling gay he would lean over the extreme edge of his hammock and drawl, with an affected English accent:

"If this is Venice, where are the canals?"

In his less cheerful moments he would groan, heavily, "There ain't no Gawd!"

This last had been his morning observation during their many weeks of durance vile. But this morning he was, for the first time in many days, enquiring about Venetian waterways.

Tyler had no pal. His years of companionship with his mother had bred in him a sort of shyness, a diffidence. He heard the other boys making plans for shore leave. They all scorned Waukegan, which was the first sizable town beyond the Station. Chicago was their goal. They were like a horde of play-hungry devils after their confinement. Six weeks of restricted freedom, six weeks of stored-up energy made them restive as colts.

"Goin' to Chicago, kid?" Moran asked him, carelessly. It was Saturday morning.

"Yes. Are you?" eagerly.

"Kin a duck swim?"

At the Y.M.C.A. they had given him tickets to various free amusements and entertainments. They told him about free canteens, and about other places where you could get a good meal, cheap. One of the tickets was for a dance. Tyler knew nothing of dancing. This dance was to be given at some kind of woman's club on Michigan Boulevard. Tyler read the card, glumly. A dance meant girls. He knew that. Why hadn't he learned to dance?

Tyler walked down to the station and waited for the train that would bring him to Chicago at about one o'clock. The other boys, in little groups, or in pairs, were smoking and talking. Tyler wanted to join them, but he did not. They seemed so sufficient unto themselves, with their plans, and their glib knowledge of places, and amusements, and girls. On the train they all bought sweets from the train butcher—chocolate maraschinos, and nut bars, and molasses kisses—and ate them as greedily as children, until their hunger for sweets was surfeited.

Tyler found himself in the same car with Moran. He edged over to a seat near him, watching him narrowly. Moran was not mingling with the other boys. He kept aloof, his sea-blue eyes gazing out at the flat Illinois prairie. All about him swept and eddied the currents and counter-currents of talk.

"They say there's a swell supper in the Tower Building for fifty cents."

"Fifty nothing. Get all you want in the Library canteen for nix."

"Where's this dance, huh?"

"Search *me*."

"Heh, Murph! I'll shoot you a game of pool at the club."

"Naw, I gotta date."

Tyler's glance encountered Moran's, and rested there. Scorn curled the Irishman's broad upper lip. "Navy! This ain't no navy no more. It's a Sunday school, that's what! Phonographs, an' church suppers, an' pool an' dances! It's enough t' turn a fella's stomick. Lot of Sunday school kids don't know a sail from a tablecloth when they see it."

He relapsed into contemptuous silence.

Tyler, who but a moment before had been envying them their familiarity with these very things now nodded and smiled understanding at Moran. "That's right," he said. Moran regarded him a moment, curiously. Then he resumed his staring out of the window. You would never have guessed that in that bullet head there was bewilderment and resentment almost equalling Tyler's, but for a much different reason. Gunner Moran was of the old navy—the navy that had been despised and spat upon. In those days his uniform alone had barred him from decent theatres, decent halls, decent dances, contact with decent people. They had forced him to a knowledge of the burlesque houses, the cheap theatres, the shooting galleries, the saloons, the dives. And now, bewilderingly, the public had right-about faced. It opened its doors to him. It closed its saloons to him. It sought him out. It offered him amusement. It invited him to its home, and sat him down at its table, and introduced him to its daughter.

"Nix!" said Gunner Moran, and spat between his teeth. "Not f'r me. I pick me own lady friends."

Gunner Moran was used to picking his own lady friends. He had picked them in wicked Port Said, and in Fiume; in Yokohama and Naples. He had picked them unerringly, and to his taste, in Cardiff, and Hamburg, and Vladivostok.

When the train drew in at the great Northwestern station shed he was down the steps and up the long platform before the wheels had ceased revolving.

Tyler came down the steps slowly. Blue uniforms were streaming past him—a flood of them. White leggings twinkled with the haste of their wearers. Caps, white or blue, flowed like a succession of rippling waves and broke against the great doorway, and were gone.

In Tyler's town, back home in Marvin, Texas, you knew the train numbers and their schedules, and you spoke of them by name, familiarly and affectionately, as Number Eleven and Number Fifty-five. "I reckon Fifty-five'll be late to-day, on account of the storm."

Now he saw half a dozen trains lined up at once, and a dozen more tracks waiting, empty. The great train shed awed him. The vast columned waiting room, the hurrying people, the uniformed guards gave him a feeling of personal unimportance. He felt very negligible, and useless, and alone. He stood, a rather dazed blue figure, in the vastness of that shining place. A voice—the soft, cadenced voice of the negro—addressed him.

"Lookin' fo' de sailors' club rooms?"

Tyler turned. A toothy, middle-aged, kindly negro in a uniform and red cap. Tyler smiled friendlily. Here was a human he could feel at ease with. Texas was full of just such faithful, friendly types of negro.

"Reckon I am, uncle. Show me the way?"

Red Cap chuckled and led the way. "Knew you was f'om de south minute Ah see yo'. Cain't fool me. Le'ssee now. You-all f'om—?"

"I'm from the finest state in the Union. The most glorious state in the—"

"H'm—Texas," grinned Red Cap.

"How did you know!"

"Ah done heah 'em talk befoh, son. Ah done heah 'em talk be-foh."

It was a long journey through the great building to the section that had been set aside for Tyler and boys like him. Tyler wondered how any one could ever find it alone. When the Red Cap left him, after showing him the wash rooms, the tubs for scrubbing clothes, the steam dryers, the bath-tubs, the lunch room, Tyler looked after him regretfully. Then he sped after him and touched him on the arm.

"Listen. Could I—would they—do you mean I could clean up in there—as much as I wanted? And wash my things? And take a bath in a bathtub, with all the hot water I want?"

"Yo' sho' kin. On'y things look mighty grabby now. Always is Sat'days. Jes' wait aroun' an' grab yo' tu'n."

Tyler waited. And while he waited he watched to see how the other boys did things. He saw how they scrubbed their uniforms with scrubbing brushes, and plenty of hot water and soap. He saw how they hung them carefully, so that they might not wrinkle, in the dryers. He saw them emerge, glowing, from the tub rooms. And he waited, the fever of cleanliness burning in his eye.

His turn came. He had waited more than an hour, reading, listening to the phonograph and the electric piano, and watching.

Now he saw his chance and seized it. And then he went through a ceremony that was almost a ritual. Stella Kamps, could she have seen it, would have felt repaid for all her years of soap-and-water insistence.

First he washed out the stationary tub with soap, and brush, and scalding water. Then he scalded the brush. Then the tub again. Then, deliberately, and with the utter unconcern of the male biped he divested himself, piece by piece, of every stitch of covering wherewith his body was clothed. And he scrubbed them all. He took off his white leggings and his white cap and scrubbed those, first. He had seen the other boys follow that order of procedure. Then his flapping blue flannel trousers, and his blouse. Then his underclothes, and his socks. And finally he stood there, naked and unabashed, slim, and pink and silver as a mountain trout. His face, as he bent over the steamy tub, was very red, and moist and earnest. His yellow hair curled in little damp ringlets about his brow. Then he hung his trousers and blouse in the dryers without wringing them (wringing, he had been told, wrinkled them). He rinsed and wrung, and flapped the underclothes, though, and shaped his cap carefully, and spread his leggings, and hung those in the dryer, too. And finally, with a deep sigh of accomplishment, he filled one of the bathtubs in the adjoining room—filled it to the slopping-over point with the luxurious hot water, and he splashed about in this, and reclined in it, gloriously, until the waiting ones threatened to pull him out. Then he dried himself and issued forth all flushed and rosy. He wrapped himself in a clean coarse sheet, for his clothes would not be dry for another half hour. Swathed in the sheet like a Roman senator he lay down on one of the green velvet couches, relics of past Pullman glories, and there, with the rumble and roar of steel trains overhead, with the smart click of the billiard balls sounding in his ears, with the phonograph and the electric piano going full blast, with the boys dancing and larking all about the big room, he fell sound asleep as only a boy cub can sleep.

When he awoke an hour later his clothes were folded in a neat pile by the deft hand of some jackie impatient to use the drying space for his own garments. Tyler put them on. He stood before a mirror and brushed his hair until it glittered. He drew himself up with the instinctive pride and self respect that comes of fresh clean clothes against the skin. Then he placed his absurd round hat on his head at what he considered a fetching angle, though precarious, and sallied forth on the streets of Chicago in search of amusement and adventure.

He found them.

Madison and Canal streets, west, had little to offer him. He sensed that the centre of things lay to the east, so he struck out along Madison, trying not to show the terror with which the grim, roaring, clamorous city filled him. He jingled the small coins in his pocket and strode along, on the surface a blithe and carefree jackie on shore leave; a forlorn and lonely Texas boy, beneath.

It was late afternoon. His laundering, his ablutions and his nap had taken more time than he had realised. It was a mild spring day, with just a Lake Michigan evening snap in the air. Tyler, glancing about alertly, nevertheless felt dreamy, and restless, and sort of melting, like a snow-heap in the sun. He wished he had some one to talk to. He thought of the man on the train who had said, with such easy confidence, "I got a date." Tyler wished that he too had a date—he who had never had a rendezvous in his life. He loitered a moment on the bridge. Then he went on, looking about him interestedly, and comparing Chicago, Illinois, with Marvin, Texas, and finding the former sadly lacking. He passed LaSalle, Clark. The streets were packed. The noise and rush tired him, and bewildered him. He came to a moving picture theatre—one of the many that dot the district. A girl occupied the little ticket kiosk. She was rather a frowsy girl, not too young, and with a certain look about the jaw. Tyler walked up to the window and shoved his money through the little aperture. The girl fed him a pink ticket without looking up. He stood there looking at her. Then he asked her a question. "How long does the show take?" He wanted to see the colour of her eyes. He wanted her to talk to him.

"'Bout a hour," said the girl, and raised wise eyes to his.

"Thanks," said Tyler, fervently, and smiled. No answering smile curved the lady's lips. Tyler turned and went in. There was an alleged comic film. Tyler was not amused. It was followed by a war picture. He left before the show was over. He was very hungry by now. In his blouse pocket were the various information and entertainment tickets with which the Y.M.C.A. man had provided him. He had taken them out, carefully, before he had done his washing. Now he looked them over. But a dairy lunch room invited him, with its white tiling, and its pans of baked apples, and browned beans and its coffee tank. He went in and ate a solitary supper that was heavy on pie and cake.

When he came out to the street again it was evening. He walked over to State Street (the wrong side). He took the dance card out of his pocket and looked at it again. If only he had learned to dance. There'd be girls. There'd have to be girls at a dance. He stood staring into the red and tin-foil window display of a cigar store, turning the ticket over in his fingers, and the problem over in his mind.

Suddenly, in his ear, a woman's voice, very soft and low. "Hello, Sweetheart!" the voice said. His nickname! He whirled around, eagerly.

The girl was a stranger to him. But she was smiling, friendlily, and she was pretty, too, sort of. "Hello, Sweetheart!" she said, again.

"Why, how-do, ma'am," said Tyler, Texas fashion.

"Where you going, kid?" she asked.

Tyler blushed a little. "Well, nowhere in particular, ma'am. Just kind of milling around."

"Come on along with me," she said, and linked her arm in his.

"Why—why—thanks, but—"

And yet Texas people were always saying easterners weren't friendly. He felt a little uneasy, though, as he looked down into her smiling face. Something—

"Hello, Sweetheart!" said a voice, again. A man's voice, this time. Out of the cigar store came Gunner Moran, the yellow string of a tobacco bag sticking out of his blouse pocket, a freshly rolled cigarette between his lips.

A queer feeling of relief and gladness swept over Tyler. And then Moran looked sharply at the girl and said, "Why, hello, Blanche!"

"Hello yourself," answered the girl, sullenly.

"Thought you was in 'Frisco."

"Well, I ain't."

Moran shifted his attention from the girl to Tyler. "Friend o' yours?"

Before Tyler could open his lips to answer the girl put in, "Sure he is. Sure I am. We been around together all afternoon."

Tyler jerked. "Why, ma'am, I guess you've made a mistake. I never saw you before in my life. I kind of thought when you up and spoke to me you must be taking me for somebody else. Well, now, isn't that funny—"

The smile faded from the girl's face, and it became twisted with fury. She glared at Moran, her lips drawn back in a snarl. "Who're you to go buttin' into my business! This guy's a friend of mine, I tell yuh!"

"Yeh? Well, he's a friend of mine, too. Me an' him had a date to meet here right now and we're goin' over to a swell little dance on Michigan Avenoo. So it's you who's buttin' in, Blanche, me girl."

The girl stood twisting her handkerchief savagely. She was panting a little. "I'll get you for this."

"Beat it!" said Moran. He tucked his arm through Tyler's, with a little impelling movement, and Tyler found himself walking up the street at a smart gait, leaving the girl staring after them.

Tyler Kamps was an innocent, but he was not a fool. At what he had vaguely guessed a moment before, he now knew. They walked along in silence, the most ill-sorted pair that you might hope to find in all that higgledy-piggledy city. And yet with a new, strong bond between them. It was more than fraternal. It had something of the character of the feeling that exists between a father and son who understand each other.

Man-like, they did not talk of that which they were thinking.

Tyler broke the silence.

"Do you dance?"

"Me! Dance! Well, I've mixed with everything from hula dancers to geisha girls, not forgettin' the Barbary Coast in the old days, but—well, I ain't what you'd rightly call a dancer. Why you askin'?"

"Because I can't dance, either. But we'll just go up and see what it's like, anyway."

"See wot wot's like?"

Tyler took out his card again, patiently. "This dance we're going to."

They had reached the Michigan Avenue address given on the card, and Tyler stopped to look up at the great, brightly lighted building. Moran stopped too, but for a different reason. He was staring, open-mouthed, at Tyler Kamps.

"You mean t' say you thought I was goin'—"

He choked. "Oh, my Gawd!"

Tyler smiled at him, sweetly. "I'm kind of scared, too. But Monicker goes to these dances and he says they're right nice. And lots of—of pretty girls. Nice girls. I wouldn't go alone. But you—you're used to dancing, and parties and—girls."

He linked his arm through the other man's. Moran allowed himself to be propelled along, dazedly. Still protesting, he found himself in the elevator with a dozen red-cheeked, scrubbed-looking jackies. At which point Moran, game in the face of horror, accepted the inevitable. He gave a characteristic jerk from the belt.

"Me, I'll try anything oncet. Lead me to it."

The elevator stopped at the ninth floor. "Out here for the jackies' dance," said the elevator boy.

The two stepped out with the others. Stepped out gingerly, caps in hand. A corridor full of women. A corridor a-flutter with girls. Talk. Laughter. Animation. In another moment the two would have turned and fled, terrified. But in that half-moment of hesitation and bewilderment they were lost.

A woman approached them hand outstretched. A tall, slim, friendly looking woman, low-voiced, silk-gowned, inquiring.

"Good-evening!" she said, as if she had been haunting the halls in the hope of their coming. "I'm glad to see you. You can check your caps right there. Do you dance?"

Two scarlet faces. Four great hands twisting at white caps in an agony of embarrassment. "Why, no ma'am."

"That's fine. We'll teach you. Then you'll go into the ball room and have a wonderful time."

"But—" in choked accents from Moran.

"Just a minute. Miss Hall!" She beckoned a diminutive blonde in blue. "Miss Hall, this is Mr.—ah—Mr. Moran. Thanks. And Mr.?—yes—Mr. Kamps. Tyler Kamps. They want to learn to dance. I'll turn them right over to you. When does your class begin?"

Miss Hall glanced at a toy watch on the tiny wrist. Instinctively and helplessly Moran and Tyler focused their gaze on the dials that bound their red wrists. "Starting right now," said Miss Hall, crisply. She eyed the two men with calm appraising gaze. "I'm sure you'll both make wonderful dancers. Follow me."

She turned. There was something confident, dauntless, irresistible about the straight little back. The two men stared at it. Then at each other. Panic was writ large on the face of each. Panic, and mutiny. Flight was in the mind of both. Miss Hall turned, smiled, held out a small white hand. "Come on," she said. "Follow me."

And the two, as though hypnotised, followed.

A fair-sized room, with a piano in one corner and groups of fidgeting jackies in every other corner. Moran and Tyler sighed with relief at sight of them. At least they were not to be alone in their agony.

Miss Hall wasted no time. Slim ankles close together, head held high, she stood in the centre of the room. "Now then, form a circle please!"

Twenty six-foot, well-built specimens of manhood suddenly became shambling hulks. They clumped forward, breathing hard, and smiling mirthlessly, with an assumption of ease that deceived no one, least of all, themselves. "A little lively, please. Don't look so scared. I'm not a bit vicious. Now then, Miss Weeks! A fox trot."

Miss Weeks, at the piano, broke into spirited strains. The first faltering steps in the social career of Gunner Moran and Tyler Kamps had begun.

To an onlooker, it might have been mirth-provoking if it hadn't been, somehow, tear-compelling. The thing that little Miss Hall was doing might have seemed trivial to one who did not know that it was magnificent. It wasn't dancing merely that she was teaching these awkward, serious, frightened boys. She was handing them a key that would unlock the social graces. She was presenting them with a magic something that would later act as an open sesame to a hundred legitimate delights.

She was strictly business, was Miss Hall. No nonsense about her. "One-two-three-four! And a *one*-two *three*-four. One-two-three-four! And a *turn*-two, *turn*-four. Now then, all together. Just four straight steps as if you were walking down the street. That's it! One-two-three-four! Don't look at me. Look at my feet. And a *one*-two *three*-four."

Red-faced, they were. Very earnest. Pathetically eager and docile. Weeks of drilling had taught them to obey commands. To them the little dancing teacher whose white spats twinkled so expertly in the tangle of their own clumsy clumping boots was more than a pretty girl. She was knowledge. She was power. She was the commanding officer. And like children they obeyed.

Moran's Barbary Coast experience stood him in good stead now, though the stern and watchful Miss Hall put a quick stop to a certain tendency toward shoulder work. Tyler possessed what is known as a rhythm sense. An expert whistler is generally a natural dancer. Stella Kamps had always waited for the sound of his cheerful whistle as he turned the corner of Vernon Street. High, clear, sweet, true, he would approach his top note like a Tettrazini until, just when you thought he could not possibly reach that dizzy eminence he did reach it, and held it, and trilled it, bird-like, in defiance of the laws of vocal equilibrium.

His dancing was much like that. Never a half-beat behind the indefatigable Miss Weeks. It was a bit laboured, at first, but it was true. Little Miss Hall, with the skilled eye of the specialist, picked him at a glance.

"You've danced before?"

"No ma'am."

"Take the head of the line, please. Watch Mr. Kamps. Now then, all together, please."

And they were off again.

At 9.45 Tyler Kamps and Gunner Moran were standing in the crowded doorway of the ballroom upstairs, in a panic lest some girl should ask them to dance; fearful lest they be passed by. Little Miss Hall had brought them to the very door, had left them there with a stern injunction not to move, and had sped away in search of partners for them.

Gunner Moran's great scarlet hands were knotted into fists. His Adam's apple worked convulsively.

"Le's duck," he whispered hoarsely. The jackie band in the corner crashed into the opening bars of a fox trot.

"Oh, it don't seem—" But it was plain that Tyler was weakening. Another moment and they would have turned and fled. But coming toward them was little Miss Hall, her blonde head bobbing in and out among the swaying couples. At her right and left was a girl. Her bright eyes held her two victims in the doorway. They watched her approach, and were helpless to flee. They seemed to be gripped by a horrible fascination. Their limbs were fluid.

A sort of groan rent Moran. Miss Hall and the two girls stood before them, cool, smiling, unruffled.

"Miss Cunningham, this is Mr. Tyler Kamps. Mr. Moran, Miss Cunningham. Miss Drew—Mr. Moran, Mr. Kamps."

The boy and the man gulped, bowed, mumbled something.

"Would you like to dance?" said Miss Cunningham, and raised limpid eyes to Tyler's.

"Why—I—you see I don't know how. I just started to—"

"Oh, *that's* all right," Miss Cunningham interrupted, cheerfully. "We'll try it." She stood in position and there seemed to radiate from her a certain friendliness, a certain assurance and understanding that was as calming as it was stimulating. In a sort of daze Tyler found himself moving over the floor in time to the music. He didn't know that he was being led, but he was. She didn't try to talk. He breathed a prayer of thanks for that. She seemed to know, somehow, about those four straight steps and two to the right and two to the left, and four again, and turn-two, turn-four. He didn't know that he was counting aloud, desperately. He didn't even know, just then, that this was a girl he was dancing with. He seemed to move automatically, like a marionette. He never was quite clear about those first ten minutes of his ballroom experience.

The music ceased. A spat of applause. Tyler mopped his head, and his hands, and applauded too, like one in a dream. They were off again for the encore.

Five minutes later he found himself seated next Miss Cunningham in a chair against the wall. And for the first time since their meeting the mists of agony cleared before his gaze and he saw Miss Cunningham as a tall, slim, dark-haired girl, with a glint of mischief in her eye, and a mouth that looked as if she were trying to keep from smiling.

"Why don't you?" Tyler asked, and was aghast.

"Why don't I what?"

"Smile if you want to."

At which the glint in her eye and the hidden smile on her lips sort of met and sparked and she laughed. Tyler laughed, too, and then they laughed together and were friends.

Miss Cunningham's conversation was the kind of conversation that a nice girl invariably uses in putting at ease a jackie whom she has just met at a war recreation dance. Nothing could have been more commonplace or unoriginal, but to Tyler Kamps the brilliance of a Madame de Stael would have sounded trivial and uninteresting in comparison.

"Where are you from?"

"Why, I'm from Texas, ma'am. Marvin, Texas."

"Is that so? So many of the boys are from Texas. Are you out at the station or on one of the boats?"

"I'm on the Station. Yes ma'am."

"Do you like the navy?"

"Yes ma'am, I do. I sure do. You know there isn't a drafted man in the navy. No ma'am! We're all enlisted men."

"When do you think the war will end, Mr. Kamps?"

He told her, gravely. He told her many other things. He told her about Texas, at length and in detail, being a true son of that Brobdingnagian state. Your Texan born is a walking mass of statistics. Miss Cunningham made a sympathetic and interested listener. Her brown eyes were round and bright with interest. He told her that the distance from Texas to Chicago was only half as far as from here to there in the state of Texas itself. Yes *ma'am*! He had figures about tons of grain, and heads of horses and herds of cattle. Why, say, you could take little ol' meachin' Germany and tuck it away in a corner of Texas and you wouldn't any more know it was there than if it was somebody's poor no-'count ranch. Why, Big Y ranch alone would make the whole country of Germany look like a cattle grazin' patch. It was bigger than all those countries in Europe strung together, and every man in Texas would rather fight than eat. Yes ma'am. Why, you couldn't hold 'em.

"My!" breathed Miss Cunningham.

They danced again. Miss Cunningham introduced him to some other girls, and he danced with them, and they in turn asked him about the station, and Texas, and when he thought the war would end. And altogether he had a beautiful time of it, and forgot completely and entirely about Gunner Moran. It was not until he gallantly escorted Miss Cunningham downstairs for refreshments that he remembered his friend. He had procured hot chocolate for himself and Miss Cunningham; and sandwiches, and delectable chunks of caramel cake. And they were talking, and eating, and laughing and enjoying themselves hugely, and Tyler had gone back for more cake at the urgent invitation of the white-haired, pink-cheeked woman presiding at the white-clothed table in the centre of the charming room. And then he had remembered. A look of horror settled down over his face. He gasped.

"W-what's the matter?" demanded Miss Cunningham.

"My—my friend. I forgot all about him." He regarded her with stricken eyes.

"Oh, that's all right," Miss Cunningham assured him for the second time that evening. "We'll just go and find him. He's probably forgotten all about you, too."

And for the second time she was right. They started on their quest. It was a short one. Off the refreshment room was a great, gracious comfortable room all deep chairs, and soft rugs, and hangings, and pictures and shaded lights. All about sat pairs and groups of sailors and girls, talking, and laughing and consuming vast quantities of cake. And in the centre of just such a group sat Gunner Moran, lolling at his ease in a rosy velvet-upholstered chair. His little finger was crookt elegantly over his cup. A large and imposing square of chocolate cake in the other hand did not seem to cramp his gestures as he talked. Neither did the huge bites with which he was rapidly demolishing it seem in the least to stifle his conversation. Four particularly pretty girls, and two matrons surrounded him. And as Tyler and Miss Cunningham approached him he was saying, "Well, it's got so I can't sleep in anything *but* a hammick. Yessir! Why, when I was fifteen years old I was—" He caught Tyler's eye. "Hello!" he called, genially. "Meet me friend." This to the bevy surrounding him. "I was just tellin' these ladies here—"

And he was off again. All the tales that he told were not necessarily true. But that did not detract from their thrill. Moran's audience grew as he talked. And he talked until he and Tyler had to run all the way to the Northwestern station for the last train that would get them on the Station before shore leave expired. Moran, on leaving, shook hands like a presidential candidate.

"I never met up with a finer bunch of ladies," he assured them, again and again. "Sure I'm comin' back again. Ask me. I've had a elegant time. Elegant. I never met a finer bunch of ladies."

They did not talk much in the train, he and Tyler. It was a sleepy lot of boys that that train carried back to the Great Central Naval Station. Tyler was undressed and in his hammock even before Moran, the expert. He would not have to woo sleep to-night. Finally Moran, too, had swung himself up to his precarious nest and relaxed with a tired, happy grunt.

Quiet again brooded over the great dim barracks. Tyler felt himself slipping off to sleep, deliciously. She would be there next Saturday. Her first name, she had said, was Myrtle. An awful pretty name for a girl. Just about the prettiest he had ever heard. Her folks invited jackies to dinner at the house nearly every Sunday. Maybe, if they gave him thirty-six hours' leave next time—

"Hey, Sweetheart!" sounded in a hissing whisper from Moran's hammock.

"What?"

"Say, was that four steps and then turn-turn, or four and two steps t' the side? I kinda forgot."

"O, shut up!" growled Monicker, from the other side. "Let a fellow sleep, can't you! What do you think this is? A boarding school!"

"Shut up yourself!" retorted Tyler, happily. "It's four steps, and two to the right and two to the left, and four again, and turn two, turn two."

"I was pretty sure," said Moran, humbly. And relaxed again.

Quiet settled down upon the great room. There were only the sounds of deep regular breathing, with an occasional grunt or sigh. The normal sleep sounds of very tired boys.

THE END

Fanny Herself

CHAPTER ONE

You could not have lived a week in Winnebago without being aware of Mrs. Brandeis. In a town of ten thousand, where every one was a personality, from Hen Cody, the drayman, in blue overalls (magically transformed on Sunday mornings into a suave black-broadcloth usher at the Congregational Church), to A. J. Dawes, who owned the waterworks before the city bought it. Mrs. Brandeis was a super-personality. Winnebago did not know it. Winnebago, buying its dolls, and china, and Battenberg braid and tinware and toys of Mrs. Brandeis, of Brandeis' Bazaar, realized vaguely that here was some one different.

When you entered the long, cool, narrow store on Elm Street, Mrs. Brandeis herself came forward to serve you, unless she already was busy with two customers. There were two clerks—three, if you count Aloysius, the boy— but to Mrs. Brandeis belonged the privilege of docketing you first. If you happened in during a moment of business lull, you were likely to find her reading in the left-hand corner at the front of the store, near the shelf where were ranged the dolls' heads, the pens, the pencils, and school supplies.

You saw a sturdy, well-set-up, alert woman, of the kind that looks taller than she really is; a woman with a long, straight, clever nose that indexed her character, as did everything about her, from her crisp, vigorous, abundant hair to the way she came down hard on her heels in walking. She was what might be called a very definite person. But first you remarked her eyes. Will you concede that eyes can be piercing, yet velvety? Their piercingness was a mental quality, I suppose, and the velvety softness a physical one. One could only think, somehow, of wild pansies—the brown kind. If Winnebago had taken the trouble to glance at the title of the book she laid face down on the pencil boxes as you entered, it would have learned that the book was one of Balzac's, or, perhaps, Zangwill's, or Zola's. She never could overcome that habit of snatching a chapter here and there during dull moments. She was too tired to read when night came.

There were many times when the little Wisconsin town lay broiling in the August sun, or locked in the January drifts, and the main business street was as silent as that of a deserted village. But more often she came forward to you from the rear of the store, with bits of excelsior clinging to her black sateen apron. You knew that she had been helping Aloysius as he unpacked a consignment of chamber sets or a hogshead of china or glassware, chalking each piece with the price mark as it was dug from its nest of straw and paper.

"How do you do!" she would say. "What can I do for you?" And in that moment she had you listed, indexed, and filed, were you a farmer woman in a black shawl and rusty bonnet with a faded rose bobbing grotesquely atop it, or one of the patronizing East End set who came to Brandeis' Bazaar because Mrs. Brandeis' party favors, for one thing, were of a variety that could be got nowhere else this side of Chicago. If, after greeting you, Mrs. Brandeis called, "Sadie! Stockings!" (supposing stockings were your quest), you might know that Mrs. Brandeis had weighed you and found you wanting.

There had always been a store—at least, ever since Fanny could remember. She often thought how queer it would seem to have to buy pins, or needles, or dishes, or soap, or thread. The store held all these things, and many more. Just to glance at the bewildering display outside gave you promise of the variety within. Winnebago was rather ashamed of that display. It was before the day of repression in decoration, and the two benches in front of the windows overflowed with lamps, and water sets, and brooms, and boilers and tinware and hampers. Once the Winnebago Courier had had a sarcastic editorial about what they called the Oriental bazaar (that was after the editor, Lem Davis, had bumped his shin against a toy cart that protruded unduly), but Mrs. Brandeis changed nothing. She knew that the farmer women who stood outside with their husbands on busy Saturdays would not have understood repression in display, but they did understand the tickets that marked the wares in plain figures— this berry set, $1.59; that lamp, $1.23. They talked it over, outside, and drifted away, and came back, and entered, and bought.

She knew when to be old-fashioned, did Mrs. Brandeis, and when to be modern. She had worn the first short walking skirt in Winnebago. It cleared the ground in a day before germs were discovered, when women's skirts trailed and flounced behind them in a cloud of dust. One of her scandalized neighbors (Mrs. Nathan Pereles, it was) had taken her aside to tell her that no decent woman would dress that way.

"Next year," said Mrs. Brandeis, "when you are wearing one, I'll remind you of that." And she did, too. She had worn shirtwaists with a broad "Gibson" shoulder tuck, when other Winnebago women were still encased in linings and bodices. Do not get the impression that she stood for emancipation, or feminism, or any of those advanced things. They had scarcely been touched on in those days. She was just an extraordinarily alert woman, mentally and physically, with a shrewd sense of values. Molly Brandeis never could set a table without forgetting the spoons, or the salt, or something, but she could add a double column of figures in her head as fast as her eye could travel.

There she goes, running off with the story, as we were afraid she would. Not only that, she is using up whole pages of description when she should be giving us dialogue. Prospective readers, running their eyes over a printed page, object to the solid block formation of the descriptive passage. And yet it is fascinating to weave words about her, as it is fascinating to turn a fine diamond this way and that in the sunlight, to catch its prismatic hues. Besides, you want to know—do you not?—how this woman who reads Balzac should be waiting upon you in a little general store in Winnebago, Wisconsin?

In the first place, Ferdinand Brandeis had been a dreamer, and a potential poet, which is bad equipment for success in the business of general merchandise. Four times, since her marriage, Molly Brandeis had packed her household goods, bade her friends good-by, and with her two children, Fanny and Theodore, had followed her husband to pastures new. A heart-breaking business, that, but broadening. She knew nothing of the art of buying and selling at the time of her marriage, but as the years went by she learned unconsciously the things one should not do in business, from watching Ferdinand Brandeis do them all. She even suggested this change and that, but to no avail. Ferdinand Brandeis was a gentle and lovable man at home; a testy, quick-tempered one in business.

That was because he had been miscast from the first, and yet had played one part too long, even though unsuccessfully, ever to learn another. He did not make friends with the genial traveling salesmen who breezed in, slapped him on the back, offered him a cigar, inquired after his health, opened their sample cases and flirted with the girl clerks, all in a breath. He was a man who talked little, listened little, learned little. He had never got the trick of turning his money over quickly—that trick so necessary to the success of the small-town business.

So it was that, in the year preceding Ferdinand Brandeis' death, there came often to the store a certain grim visitor. Herman Walthers, cashier of the First National Bank of Winnebago, was a kindly-enough, shrewd, small-town banker, but to Ferdinand Brandeis and his wife his visits, growing more and more frequent, typified all that was frightful, presaged misery and despair. He would drop in on a bright summer morning, perhaps, with a cheerful greeting. He would stand for a moment at the front of the store, balancing airily from toe to heel, and glancing about from shelf to bin and back again in a large, speculative way. Then he would begin to walk slowly and ruminatively about, his shrewd little German eyes appraising the stock. He would hum a little absent-minded tune as he walked, up one aisle and down the next (there were only two), picking up a piece of china there, turning it over to look at its stamp, holding it up to the light, tapping it a bit with his knuckles, and putting it down carefully before going musically on down the aisle to the water sets, the lamps, the stockings, the hardware, the toys. And so, his hands behind his back, still humming, out the swinging screen door and into the sunshine of Elm Street, leaving gloom and fear behind him.

One year after Molly Brandeis took hold, Herman Walthers' visits ceased, and in two years he used to rise to greet her from his little cubbyhole when she came into the bank.

Which brings us to the plush photograph album. The plush photograph album is a concrete example of what makes business failure and success. More than that, its brief history presents a complete characterization of Ferdinand and Molly Brandeis.

Ten years before, Ferdinand Brandeis had bought a large bill of Christmas fancy-goods—celluloid toilette sets, leather collar boxes, velvet glove cases. Among the lot was a photograph album in the shape of a huge acorn done in lightning-struck plush. It was a hideous thing, and expensive. It stood on a brass stand, and its leaves were edged in gilt, and its color was a nauseous green and blue, and it was altogether the sort of thing to grace the chill and funereal best room in a Wisconsin farmhouse. Ferdinand Brandeis marked it at six dollars and stood it up for the Christmas trade. That had been ten years before. It was too expensive; or too pretentious, or perhaps even too horrible for the bucolic purse. At any rate, it had been taken out, brushed, dusted, and placed on its stand every holiday season for ten years. On the day after Christmas it was always there, its lightning-struck plush face staring wildly out upon the ravaged fancy-goods counter. It would be packed in its box again and consigned to its long summer's sleep. It had seen three towns, and many changes. The four dollars that Ferdinand Brandeis had invested in it still remained unturned.

One snowy day in November (Ferdinand Brandeis died a fortnight later) Mrs. Brandeis, entering the store, saw two women standing at the fancy-goods counter, laughing in a stifled sort of way. One of them was bowing elaborately to a person unseen. Mrs. Brandeis was puzzled. She watched them for a moment, interested. One of the women was known to her. She came up to them and put her question, bluntly, though her quick wits had already given her a suspicion of the truth.

"What are you bowing to?"

The one who had done the bowing blushed a little, but giggled too, as she said, "I'm greeting my old friend, the plush album. I've seen it here every Christmas for five years."

Ferdinand Brandeis died suddenly a little more than a week later. It was a terrible period, and one that might have prostrated a less resolute and balanced woman. There were long-standing debts, not to speak of the entire stock of holiday goods to be paid for. The day after the funeral Winnebago got a shock. The Brandeis house was besieged by condoling callers. Every member of the little Jewish congregation of Winnebago came, of course, as they had come before the funeral. Those who had not brought cakes, and salads, and meats, and pies, brought them now, as was the invariable custom in time of mourning.

Others of the townspeople called, too; men and women who had known and respected Ferdinand Brandeis. And the shock they got was this: Mrs. Brandeis was out. Any one could have told you that she should have been sitting at home in a darkened room, wearing a black gown, clasping Fanny and Theodore to her, and holding a black-bordered handkerchief at intervals to her reddened eyes. And that is what she really wanted to do, for she had loved her husband, and she respected the conventions. What she did was to put on a white shirtwaist and a black skirt at seven o'clock the morning after the funeral.

The store had been closed the day before. She entered it at seven forty-five, as Aloysius was sweeping out with wet sawdust and a languid broom. The extra force of holiday clerks straggled in, uncertainly, at eight or after, expecting an hour or two of undisciplined gossip. At eight-ten Molly Brandeis walked briskly up to the plush photograph album, whisked off its six-dollar price mark, and stuck in its place a neatly printed card bearing these figures: "To-day—79@!" The plush album went home in a farmer's wagon that afternoon.

CHAPTER TWO

Right here there should be something said about Fanny Brandeis. And yet, each time I turn to her I find her mother plucking at my sleeve. There comes to my mind the picture of Mrs. Brandeis turning down Norris Street at quarter to eight every morning, her walk almost a march, so firm and measured it was, her head high, her chin thrust forward a little, as a fighter walks, but not pugnaciously; her short gray skirt clearing the ground, her shoulders almost consciously squared. Other Winnebago women were just tying up their daughters' pigtails for school, or sweeping the front porch, or watering the hanging baskets. Norris Street residents got into the habit of timing themselves by Mrs. Brandeis. When she marched by at seven forty-five they hurried a little with the tying of the hair bow, as they glanced out of the window. When she came by again, a little before twelve, for her hasty dinner, they turned up the fire under the potatoes and stirred the flour thickening for the gravy.

Mrs. Brandeis had soon learned that Fanny and Theodore could manage their own school toilettes, with, perhaps, some speeding up on the part of Mattie, the servant girl. But it needed her keen brown eye to detect corners that Aloysius had neglected to sweep out with wet sawdust, and her presence to make sure that the counter covers were taken off and folded, the outside show dusted and arranged, the windows washed, the whole store shining and ready for business by eight o'clock. So Fanny had even learned to do her own tight, shiny, black, shoulder-length curls, which she tied back with a black bow. They were wet, meek, and tractable curls at eight in the morning. By the time school was out at four they were as wildly unruly as if charged with electric currents—which they really were, when you consider the little dynamo that wore them.

Mrs. Brandeis took a scant half hour to walk the six blocks between the store and the house, to snatch a hurried dinner, and traverse the distance to the store again. It was a program that would have killed a woman less magnificently healthy and determined. She seemed to thrive on it, and she kept her figure and her wit when other women of her age grew dull, and heavy, and ineffectual. On summer days the little town often lay shimmering in the heat, the yellow road glaring in it, the red bricks of the high school reflecting it in waves, the very pine knots in the sidewalks gummy and resinous with heat, and sending up a pungent smell that was of the woods, and yet stifling. She must have felt an almost irresistible temptation to sit for a moment on the cool, shady front porch, with its green-painted flower boxes, its hanging fern baskets and the catalpa tree looking boskily down upon it.

But she never did. She had an almost savage energy and determination. The unpaid debts were ever ahead of her; there were the children to be dressed and sent to school; there was the household to be kept up; there were Theodore's violin lessons that must not be neglected—not after what Professor Bauer had said about him.

You may think that undue stress is being laid upon this driving force in her, upon this business ability. But remember that this was fifteen years or more ago, before women had invaded the world of business by the thousands, to take their place, side by side, salary for salary, with men. Oh, there were plenty of women wage earners in Winnebago, as elsewhere; clerks, stenographers, school teachers, bookkeepers. The paper mills were full of girls, and the canning factory too. But here was a woman gently bred, untrained in business, left widowed with two children at thirty-eight, and worse than penniless—in debt.

And that was not all. As Ferdinand Brandeis' wife she had occupied a certain social position in the little Jewish community of Winnebago. True, they had never been moneyed, while the others of her own faith in the little town were wealthy, and somewhat purse-proud. They had carriages, most of them, with two handsome horses, and their houses were spacious and veranda-encircled, and set in shady lawns. When the Brandeis family came to Winnebago five years before, these people had waited, cautiously, and investigated, and then had called. They were of a type to be found in every small town; prosperous, conservative, constructive citizens, clannish, but not so much so as their city cousins, mingling socially with their Gentile neighbors, living well, spending their money freely, taking a vast pride in the education of their children. But here was Molly Brandeis, a Jewess, setting out to earn her living in business, like a man. It was a thing to stir Congregation Emanu-el to its depths. Jewish women, they would tell you, did not work thus. Their husbands worked for them, or their sons, or their brothers.

"Oh, I don't know," said Mrs. Brandeis, when she heard of it. "I seem to remember a Jewess named Ruth who was left widowed, and who gleaned in the fields for her living, and yet the neighbors didn't talk. For that matter, she seems to be pretty well thought of, to this day."

But there is no denying that she lost caste among her own people. Custom and training are difficult to overcome. But Molly Brandeis was too deep in her own affairs to care. That Christmas season following her husband's death was a ghastly time, and yet a grimly wonderful one, for it applied the acid test to Molly Brandeis and showed her up pure gold.

The first week in January she, with Sadie and Pearl, the two clerks, and Aloysius, the boy, took inventory. It was a terrifying thing, that process of casting up accounts. It showed with such starkness how hideously the Brandeis ledger sagged on the wrong side. The three women and the boy worked with a sort of dogged cheerfulness at it, counting, marking, dusting, washing. They found shelves full of forgotten stock, dust-covered and profitless. They found many articles of what is known as hard stock, akin to the plush album; glass and plated condiment casters for the dining table, in a day when individual salts and separate vinegar cruets were already the thing; lamps with straight wicks when round wicks were in demand.

They scoured shelves, removed the grime of years from boxes, washed whole battalions of chamber sets, bathed piles of plates, and bins of cups and saucers. It was a dirty, back-breaking job, that ruined the finger nails, tried the disposition, and caked the throat with dust. Besides, the store was stove-heated and, near the front door, uncomfortably cold. The women wore little shoulder shawls pinned over their waists, for warmth, and all four, including Aloysius, sniffled for weeks afterward. That inventory developed a new, grim line around Mrs. Brandeis' mouth, and carved another at the corner of each eye. After it was over she washed her hair, steamed her face over a bowl of hot water, packed two valises, left minute and masterful instructions with Mattie as to the household, and with Sadie and Pearl as to the store, and was off to Chicago on her first buying trip. She took Fanny with her, as ballast. It was a trial at which many men would have quailed. On the shrewdness and judgment of that buying trip depended the future of Brandeis' Bazaar, and Mrs. Brandeis, and Fanny, and Theodore.

Mrs. Brandeis had accompanied her husband on many of his trips to Chicago. She had even gone with him occasionally to the wholesale houses around La Salle Street, and Madison, and Fifth Avenue, but she had never bought a dollar's worth herself. She saw that he bought slowly, cautiously, and without imagination. She made up her mind that she would buy quickly, intuitively. She knew slightly some of the salesmen in the wholesale houses. They had often made presents to her of a vase, a pocketbook, a handkerchief, or some such trifle, which she accepted reluctantly, when at all. She was thankful now for these visits. She found herself remembering many details of them. She made up her mind, with a canny knowingness, that there should be no presents this time, no theater invitations, no lunches or dinners. This was business, she told herself; more than business—it was grim war.

They still tell of that trip, sometimes, when buyers and jobbers and wholesale men get together. Don't imagine that she came to be a woman captain of finance. Don't think that we are to see her at the head of a magnificent business establishment, with buyers and department heads below her, and a private office done up in mahogany, and stenographers and secretaries. No, she was Mrs. Brandeis, of Brandeis' Bazaar, to the end. The bills she bought were ridiculously small, I suppose, and the tricks she turned on that first trip were pitiful, perhaps. But they were magnificent too, in their way. I am even bold enough to think that she might have made business history, that plucky woman, if she had had an earlier start, and if she had not, to the very end, had a pack of unmanageable handicaps yelping at her heels, pulling at her skirts.

It was only a six-hour trip to Chicago. Fanny Brandeis' eyes, big enough at any time, were surely twice their size during the entire journey of two hundred miles or more. They were to have lunch on the train! They were to stop at an hotel! They were to go to the theater! She would have lain back against the red plush seat of the car, in a swoon of joy, if there had not been so much to see in the car itself, and through the car window.

"We'll have something for lunch," said Mrs. Brandeis when they were seated in the dining car, "that we never have at home, shall we?"

"Oh, yes!" replied Fanny in a whisper of excitement. "Something—something queer, and different, and not so very healthy!"

They had oysters (a New Yorker would have sniffed at them), and chicken potpie, and asparagus, and ice cream. If that doesn't prove Mrs. Brandeis was game, I should like to know what could! They stopped at the Windsor-Clifton, because it was quieter and less expensive than the Palmer House, though quite as full of red plush and walnut. Besides, she had stopped at the Palmer House with her husband, and she knew how buyers were likely to be besieged by eager salesmen with cards, and with tempting lines of goods spread knowingly in the various sample-rooms.

Fanny Brandeis was thirteen, and emotional, and incredibly receptive and alive. It is impossible to tell what she learned during that Chicago trip, it was so crowded, so wonderful. She went with her mother to the wholesale houses and heard and saw and, unconsciously, remembered. When she became fatigued with the close air of the dim showrooms, with their endless aisles piled with every sort of ware, she would sit on a chair in some obscure corner, watching those sleek, over-lunched, genial-looking salesmen who were chewing their cigars somewhat wildly when Mrs. Brandeis finished with them. Sometimes she did not accompany her mother, but lay in bed, deliciously, until the middle of the morning, then dressed, and chatted with the obliging Irish chamber maid, and read until her mother came for her at noon.

Everything she did was a delightful adventure; everything she saw had the tang of novelty. Fanny Brandeis was to see much that was beautiful and rare in her full lifetime, but she never again, perhaps, got quite the thrill that those ugly, dim, red-carpeted, gas-lighted hotel corridors gave her, or the grim bedroom, with its walnut furniture and its Nottingham curtains. As for the Chicago streets themselves, with their perilous corners (there were no czars in blue to regulate traffic in those days), older and more sophisticated pedestrians experienced various emotions while negotiating the corner of State and Madison.

That buying trip lasted ten days. It was a racking business, physically and mentally. There were the hours of tramping up one aisle and down the other in the big wholesale lofts. But that brought bodily fatigue only. It was the mental strain that left Mrs. Brandeis spent and limp at the end of the day. Was she buying wisely? Was she over-buying? What did she know about buying, anyway? She would come back to her hotel at six, sometimes so exhausted that the dining-room and dinner were unthinkable. At such times they would have dinner in their room another delicious adventure for Fanny. She would try to tempt the fagged woman on the bed with bits of this or that from one of the many dishes that dotted the dinner tray. But Molly Brandeis, harrowed in spirit and numbed in body, was too spent to eat.

But that was not always the case. There was that unforgettable night when they went to see Bernhardt the divine. Fanny spent the entire morning following standing before the bedroom mirror, with her hair pulled out in a wild fluff in front, her mother's old marten-fur scarf high and choky around her neck, trying to smile that slow, sad, poignant, tear-compelling smile; but she had to give it up, clever mimic though she was. She only succeeded in looking as though a pin were sticking her somewhere. Besides, Fanny's own smile was a quick, broad, flashing grin, with a generous glint of white teeth in it, and she always forgot about being exquisitely wistful over it until it was too late.

I wonder if the story of the china religious figures will give a wrong impression of Mrs. Brandeis. Perhaps not, if you will only remember this woman's white-lipped determination to wrest a livelihood from the world, for her children and herself. They had been in Chicago a week, and she was buying at Bauder & Peck's. Now, Bauder & Peck, importers, are known the world over. It is doubtful if there is one of you who has not been supplied, indirectly, with some imported bit of china or glassware, with French opera glasses or cunning toys and dolls, from the great New York and Chicago showrooms of that company.

Young Bauder himself was waiting on Mrs. Brandeis, and he was frowning because he hated to sell women. Young Bauder was being broken into the Chicago end of the business, and he was not taking gracefully to the process.

At the end of a long aisle, on an obscure shelf in a dim corner, Molly Brandeis' sharp eyes espied a motley collection of dusty, grimy china figures of the kind one sees on the mantel in the parlor of the small-town Catholic home. Winnebago's population was two-thirds Catholic, German and Irish, and very devout.

Mrs. Brandeis stopped short. "How much for that lot?" She pointed to the shelf. Young Bauder's gaze followed hers, puzzled. The figures were from five inches to a foot high, in crude, effective blues, and gold, and crimson, and white. All the saints were there in assorted sizes, the Pieta, the cradle in the manger. There were probably two hundred or more of the little figures. "Oh, those!" said young Bauder vaguely. "You don't want that stuff. Now, about that Limoges china. As I said, I can make you a special price on it if you carry it as an open-stock pattern. You'll find——"

"How much for that lot?" repeated Mrs. Brandeis.

"Those are left-over samples, Mrs. Brandeis. Last year's stuff. They're all dirty. I'd forgotten they were there."

"How much for the lot?" said Mrs. Brandeis, pleasantly, for the third time.

"I really don't know. Three hundred, I should say. But——"

"I'll give you two hundred," ventured Mrs. Brandeis, her heart in her mouth and her mouth very firm.

"Oh, come now, Mrs. Brandeis! Bauder & Peck don't do business that way, you know. We'd really rather not sell them at all. The things aren't worth much to us, or to you, for that matter. But three hundred——"

"Two hundred," repeated Mrs. Brandeis, "or I cancel my order, including the Limoges. I want those figures."

And she got them. Which isn't the point of the story. The holy figures were fine examples of foreign workmanship, their colors, beneath the coating of dust, as brilliant and fadeless as those found in the churches of Europe. They reached Winnebago duly, packed in straw and paper, still dusty and shelf-worn. Mrs. Brandeis and Sadie and Pearl sat on up-ended boxes at the rear of the store, in the big barn-like room in which newly arrived goods were unpacked. As Aloysius dived deep into the crate and brought up figure after figure, the three women plunged them into warm and soapy water and proceeded to bathe and scour the entire school of saints, angels, and cherubim. They came out brilliantly fresh and rosy.

All the Irish ingenuity and artistry in Aloysius came to the surface as he dived again and again into the great barrel and brought up the glittering pieces.

"It'll make an elegant window," he gasped from the depths of the hay, his lean, lengthy frame jack-knifed over the edge. "And cheap." His shrewd wit had long ago divined the store's price mark. "If Father Fitzpatrick steps by in the forenoon I'll bet they'll be gone before nighttime to-morrow. You'll be letting me do the trim, Mrs. Brandeis?"

He came back that evening to do it, and he threw his whole soul into it, which, considering his ancestry and temperament, was very high voltage for one small-town store window. He covered the floor of the window with black crepe paper, and hung it in long folds, like a curtain, against the rear wall. The gilt of the scepters, and halos, and capes showed up dazzlingly against this background. The scarlets, and pinks, and blues, and whites of the robes appeared doubly bright. The whole made a picture that struck and held you by its vividness and contrast.

Father Fitzpatrick, very tall and straight, and handsome, with his iron-gray hair and his cheeks pink as a girl's, did step by next morning on his way to the post-office. It was whispered that in his youth Father Fitzpatrick had been an actor, and that he had deserted the footlights for the altar lights because of a disappointment. The drama's loss was the Church's gain. You should have heard him on Sunday morning, now flaying them, now swaying them! He still had the actor's flexible voice, vibrant, tremulous, or strident, at will. And no amount of fasting or praying had ever dimmed that certain something in his eye—the something which makes the matinee idol.

Not only did he step by now; he turned, came back; stopped before the window. Then he entered.

"Madam," he said to Mrs. Brandeis, "you'll probably save more souls with your window display than I could in a month of hell-fire sermons." He raised his hand. "You have the sanction of the Church." Which was the beginning of a queer friendship between the Roman Catholic priest and the Jewess shopkeeper that lasted as long as Molly Brandeis lived.

By noon it seemed that the entire population of Winnebago had turned devout. The figures, a tremendous bargain, though sold at a high profit, seemed to melt away from the counter that held them.

By three o'clock, "Only one to a customer!" announced Mrs. Brandeis. By the middle of the week the window itself was ravished of its show. By the end of the week there remained only a handful of the duller and less desirable pieces—the minor saints, so to speak. Saturday night Mrs. Brandeis did a little figuring on paper. The lot had cost her two hundred dollars. She had sold for six hundred. Two from six leaves four. Four hundred dollars! She repeated it to herself, quietly. Her mind leaped back to the plush photograph album, then to young Bauder and his cool contempt. And there stole over her that warm, comfortable glow born of reassurance and triumph. Four hundred dollars. Not much in these days of big business. We said, you will remember, that it was a pitiful enough little trick she turned to make it, though an honest one. And—in the face of disapproval—a rather magnificent one too. For it gave to Molly Brandeis that precious quality, self-confidence, out of which is born success.

CHAPTER THREE

By spring Mrs. Brandeis had the farmer women coming to her for their threshing dishes and kitchenware, and the West End Culture Club for their whist prizes. She seemed to realize that the days of the general store were numbered, and she set about making hers a novelty store. There was something terrible about the earnestness with which she stuck to business. She was not more than thirty-eight at this time, intelligent, healthy, fun-loving. But she stayed at it all day. She listened and chatted to every one, and learned much. There was about her that human quality that invites confidence.

She made friends by the hundreds, and friends are a business asset. Those blithe, dressy, and smooth-spoken gentlemen known as traveling men used to tell her their troubles, perched on a stool near the stove, and show her the picture of their girl in the back of their watch, and asked her to dinner at the Haley House. She listened to their tale of woe, and advised them; she admired the picture of the girl, and gave some wholesome counsel on the subject of traveling men's lonely wives; but she never went to dinner at the Haley House.

It had not taken these debonair young men long to learn that there was a woman buyer who bought quickly, decisively, and intelligently, and that she always demanded a duplicate slip. Even the most unscrupulous could not stuff an order of hers, and when it came to dating she gave no quarter. Though they wore clothes that were two leaps ahead of the styles worn by the Winnebago young men—their straw sailors were likely to be saw-edged when the local edges were smooth, and their coats were more flaring, or their trousers wider than the coats and trousers of the Winnebago boys—they were not, for the most part, the gay dogs that Winnebago's fancy painted them. Many of them were very lonely married men who missed their wives and babies, and loathed the cuspidored discomfort of the small-town hotel lobby. They appreciated Mrs. Brandeis' good-natured sympathy, and gave her the long end of a deal when they could. It was Sam Kiser who had begged her to listen to his advice to put in Battenberg patterns and braid, long before the Battenberg epidemic had become widespread and virulent.

"Now listen to me, Mrs. Brandeis," he begged, almost tearfully. "You're a smart woman. Don't let this get by you. You know that I know that a salesman would have as much chance to sell you a gold brick as to sell old John D. Rockefeller a gallon of oil." Mrs. Brandeis eyed his samples coldly. "But it looks so unattractive. And the average person has no imagination. A bolt of white braid and a handful of buttons—they wouldn't get a mental picture of the completed piece. Now, embroidery silk——"

"Then give 'em a real picture!" interrupted Sam. "Work up one of these water-lily pattern table covers. Use No. 100 braid and the smallest buttons. Stick it in the window and they'll tear their hair to get patterns."

She did it, taking turns with Pearl and Sadie at weaving the great, lacy square during dull moments. When it was finished they placed it in the window, where it lay like frosted lace, exquisitely graceful and delicate, with its tracery of curling petals and feathery fern sprays. Winnebago gazed and was bitten by the Battenberg bug. It wound itself up in a network of Battenberg braid, in all the numbers. It bought buttons of every size; it stitched away at Battenberg covers, doilies, bedspreads, blouses, curtains. Battenberg tumbled, foamed, cascaded over Winnebago's front porches all that summer. Listening to Sam Kiser had done it.

She listened to the farmer women too, and to the mill girls, and to the scant and precious pearls that dropped from the lips of the East End society section. There was something about her brown eyes and her straight, sensible nose that reassured them so that few suspected the mischievous in her. For she was mischievous. If she had not been I think she could not have stood the drudgery, and the heartbreaks, and the struggle, and the terrific manual labor.

She used to guy people, gently, and they never guessed it. Mrs. G. Manville Smith, for example, never dreamed of the joy that her patronage brought Molly Brandeis, who waited on her so demurely. Mrs. G. Manville Smith (nee Finnegan) scorned the Winnebago shops, and was said to send to Chicago for her hairpins. It was known that her household was run on the most niggardly basis, however, and she short-rationed her two maids outrageously. It was said that she could serve less real food on more real lace doilies than any other housekeeper in Winnebago. Now, Mrs. Brandeis sold Scourine two cents cheaper than the grocery stores, using it as an advertisement to attract housewives, and making no profit on the article itself. Mrs. G. Manville Smith always patronized Brandeis' Bazaar for Scourine alone, and thus represented pure loss. Also she my-good-womaned Mrs. Brandeis. That lady, seeing her enter one day with her comic, undulating gait, double-actioned like a giraffe's, and her plumes that would have shamed a Knight of Pythias, decided to put a stop to these unprofitable visits.

She waited on Mrs. G. Manville Smith, a dangerous gleam in her eye.

"Scourine," spake Mrs. G. Manville Smith.

"How many?"

"A dozen."

"Anything else?"

"No. Send them."

Mrs. Brandeis, scribbling in her sales book, stopped, pencil poised. "We cannot send Scourine unless with a purchase of other goods amounting to a dollar or more."

Mrs. G. Manville Smith's plumes tossed and soared agitatedly. "But my good woman, I don't want anything else!"

"Then you'll have to carry the Scourine?"

"Certainly not! I'll send for it."

"The sale closes at five." It was then 4:57.

"I never heard of such a thing! You can't expect me to carry them."

Now, Mrs. G. Manville Smith had been a dining-room girl at the old Haley House before she married George Smith, and long before he made his money in lumber.

"You won't find them so heavy," Molly Brandeis said smoothly.

"I certainly would! Perhaps you would not. You're used to that sort of thing. Rough work, and all that."

Aloysius, doubled up behind the lamps, knew what was coming, from the gleam in his boss's eye.

"There may be something in that," Molly Brandeis returned sweetly. "That's why I thought you might not mind taking them. They're really not much heavier than a laden tray."

"Oh!" exclaimed the outraged Mrs. G. Manville Smith. And took her plumes and her patronage out of Brandeis' Bazaar forever.

That was as malicious as Molly Brandeis ever could be. And it was forgivable malice.

Most families must be described against the background of their homes, but the Brandeis family life was bounded and controlled by the store. Their meals and sleeping hours and amusements were regulated by it. It taught them much, and brought them much, and lost them much. Fanny Brandeis always said she hated it, but it made her wise, and tolerant, and, in the end, famous. I don't know what more one could ask of any institution. It brought her in contact with men and women, taught her how to deal with them. After school she used often to run down to the store to see her mother, while Theodore went home to practice. Perched on a high stool in some corner she heard, and saw, and absorbed. It was a great school for the sensitive, highly-organized, dramatic little Jewish girl, for, to paraphrase a well-known stage line, there are just as many kinds of people in Winnebago as there are in Washington.

It was about this time that Fanny Brandeis began to realize, actively, that she was different. Of course, other little Winnebago girls' mothers did not work like a man, in a store. And she and Bella Weinberg were the only two in her room at school who stayed out on the Day of Atonement, and on New Year, and the lesser Jewish holidays. Also, she went to temple on Friday night and Saturday morning, when the other girls she knew went to church on Sunday. These things set her apart in the little Middle Western town; but it was not these that constituted the real difference. She played, and slept, and ate, and studied like the other healthy little animals of her age. The real difference was temperamental, or emotional, or dramatic, or historic, or all four. They would be playing tag, perhaps, in one of the cool, green ravines that were the beauty spots of the little Wisconsin town.

They nestled like exquisite emeralds in the embrace of the hills, those ravines, and Winnebago's civic surge had not yet swept them away in a deluge of old tin cans, ashes, dirt and refuse, to be sold later for building lots. The Indians had camped and hunted in them. The one under the Court Street bridge, near the Catholic church and monastery, was the favorite for play. It lay, a lovely, gracious thing, below the hot little town, all green, and lush, and cool, a tiny stream dimpling through it. The plump Capuchin Fathers, in their coarse brown robes, knotted about the waist with a cord, their bare feet thrust into sandals, would come out and sun themselves on the stone bench at the side of the monastery on the hill, or would potter about the garden. And suddenly Fanny would stop quite still in the midst of her tag game, struck with the beauty of the picture it called from the past.

Little Oriental that she was, she was able to combine the dry text of her history book with the green of the trees, the gray of the church, and the brown of the monk's robes, and evolve a thrilling mental picture therefrom. The tag game and her noisy little companions vanished. She was peopling the place with stealthy Indians. Stealthy, cunning, yet savagely brave. They bore no relation to the abject, contemptible, and rather smelly Oneidas who came to the back door on summer mornings, in calico, and ragged overalls, with baskets of huckleberries on their arm, their pride gone, a broken and conquered people. She saw them wild, free, sovereign, and there were no greasy, berry-peddling Oneidas among them. They were Sioux, and Pottawatomies (that last had the real Indian sound), and Winnebagos, and Menomonees, and Outagamis. She made them taciturn, and beady-eyed, and lithe, and fleet, and every other adjectival thing her imagination and history book could supply. The fat and placid Capuchin Fathers on the hill became Jesuits, sinister, silent, powerful, with France and the Church of Rome behind them. From the shelter of that big oak would step Nicolet, the brave, first among Wisconsin explorers, and last to receive the credit for his hardihood. Jean Nicolet! She loved the sound of it. And with him was La Salle, straight, and slim, and elegant, and surely wearing ruffles and plumes and sword even in a canoe. And Tonty, his Italian friend and fellow adventurer—Tonty of the satins and velvets, graceful, tactful, poised, a shadowy figure; his menacing iron hand, so feared by the ignorant savages, encased always in a glove. Surely a perfumed g—— Slap! A rude shove that jerked her head back sharply and sent her forward, stumbling, and jarred her like a fall.

"Ya-a-a! Tag! You're it! Fanny's it!"

Indians, priests, cavaliers, coureurs de bois, all vanished. Fanny would stand a moment, blinking stupidly. The next moment she was running as fleetly as the best of the boys in savage pursuit of one of her companions in the tag game.

She was a strange mixture of tomboy and bookworm, which was a mercifully kind arrangement for both body and mind. The spiritual side of her was groping and staggering and feeling its way about as does that of any little girl whose mind is exceptionally active, and whose mother is unusually busy. It was on the Day of Atonement, known in the Hebrew as Yom Kippur, in the year following her father's death that that side of her performed a rather interesting handspring.

Fanny Brandeis had never been allowed to fast on this, the greatest and most solemn of Jewish holy days Molly Brandeis' modern side refused to countenance the practice of withholding food from any child for twenty-four hours. So it was in the face of disapproval that Fanny, making deep inroads into the steak and fried sweet potatoes at supper on the eve of the Day of Atonement, announced her intention of fasting from that meal to supper on the following evening. She had just passed her plate for a third helping of potatoes. Theodore, one lap behind her in the race, had entered his objection.

"Well, for the land's sakes!" he protested. "I guess you're not the only one who likes sweet potatoes."

Fanny applied a generous dab of butter to an already buttery morsel, and chewed it with an air of conscious virtue.

"I've got to eat a lot. This is the last bite I'll have until to-morrow night."

"What's that?" exclaimed Mrs. Brandeis, sharply.

"Yes, it is!" hooted Theodore.

Fanny went on conscientiously eating as she explained.

"Bella Weinberg and I are going to fast all day. We just want to see if we can."

"Betcha can't," Theodore said.

Mrs. Brandeis regarded her small daughter with a thoughtful gaze. "But that isn't the object in fasting, Fanny—just to see if you can. If you're going to think of food all through the Yom Kippur services——"

"I sha'n't?" protested Fanny passionately. "Theodore would, but I won't."

"Wouldn't any such thing," denied Theodore. "But if I'm going to play a violin solo during the memorial service I guess I've got to eat my regular meals."

Theodore sometimes played at temple, on special occasions. The little congregation, listening to the throbbing rise and fall of this fifteen-year-old boy's violin playing, realized, vaguely, that here was something disturbingly, harrowingly beautiful. They did not know that they were listening to genius.

Molly Brandeis, in her second best dress, walked to temple Yom Kippur eve, her son at her right side, her daughter at her left. She had made up her mind that she would not let this next day, with its poignantly beautiful service, move her too deeply. It was the first since her husband's death, and Rabbi Thalmann rather prided himself on his rendition of the memorial service that came at three in the afternoon.

A man of learning, of sweetness, and of gentle wit was Rabbi Thalmann, and unappreciated by his congregation. He stuck to the Scriptures for his texts, finding Moses a greater leader than Roosevelt, and the miracle of the Burning Bush more wonderful than the marvels of twentieth-century wizardy in electricity. A little man, Rabbi Thalmann, with hands and feet as small and delicate as those of a woman. Fanny found him fascinating to look on, in his rabbinical black broadcloth and his two pairs of glasses perched, in reading, upon his small hooked nose. He stood very straight in the pulpit, but on the street you saw that his back was bent just the least bit in the world—or perhaps it was only his student stoop, as he walked along with his eyes on the ground, smoking those slender, dapper, pale brown cigars that looked as if they had been expressly cut and rolled to fit him.

The evening service was at seven. The congregation, rustling in silks, was approaching the little temple from all directions. Inside, there was a low-toned buzz of conversation. The Brandeis' seat was well toward the rear, as befitted a less prosperous member of the rich little congregation. This enabled them to get a complete picture of the room in its holiday splendor. Fanny drank it in eagerly, her dark eyes soft and luminous. The bare, yellow-varnished wooden pews glowed with the reflection from the chandeliers. The seven-branched candlesticks on either side of the pulpit were entwined with smilax. The red plush curtain that hung in front of the Ark on ordinary days, and the red plush pulpit cover too, were replaced by gleaming white satin edged with gold fringe and finished at the corners with heavy gold tassels. How the rich white satin glistened in the light of the electric candles! Fanny Brandeis loved the lights, and the gleam, and the music, so majestic, and solemn, and the sight of the little rabbi, sitting so straight and serious in his high-backed chair, or standing to read from the great Bible. There came to this emotional little Jewess a thrill that was not born of religious fervor at all, I am afraid.

The sheer drama of the thing got her. In fact, the thing she had set herself to do to-day had in it very little of religion. Mrs. Brandeis had been right about that. It was a test of endurance, as planned. Fanny had never fasted in all her healthy life. She would come home from school to eat formidable stacks of bread and butter, enhanced by brown sugar or grape jelly, and topped off with three or four apples from the barrel in the cellar. Two hours later she would attack a supper of fried potatoes, and liver, and tea, and peach preserve, and more stacks of bread and butter. Then there were the cherry trees in the back yard, and the berry bushes, not to speak of sundry bags of small, hard candies of the jelly-bean variety, fitted for quick and secret munching during school. She liked good things to eat, this sturdy little girl, as did her friend, that blonde and creamy person, Bella Weinberg. The two girls exchanged meaningful glances during the evening service. The Weinbergs, as befitted their station, sat in the third row at the right, and Bella had to turn around to convey her silent messages to Fanny. The evening service was brief, even to the sermon. Rabbi Thalmann and his congregation would need their strength for to-morrow's trial.

The Brandeises walked home through the soft September night, and the children had to use all their Yom Kippur dignity to keep from scuffling through the piled-up drifts of crackling autumn leaves. Theodore went to the cellar and got an apple, which he ate with what Fanny considered an unnecessary amount of scrunching. It was a firm, juicy apple, and it gave forth a cracking sound when his teeth met in its white meat. Fanny, after regarding him with gloomy superiority, went to bed.

She had willed to sleep late, for gastronomic reasons, but the mental command disobeyed itself, and she woke early, with a heavy feeling. Early as it was, Molly Brandeis had tiptoed in still earlier to look at her strange little daughter. She sometimes did that on Saturday mornings when she left early for the store and Fanny slept late. This morning Fanny's black hair was spread over the pillow as she lay on her back, one arm outflung, the other at her breast. She made a rather startlingly black and white and scarlet picture as she lay there asleep. Fanny did things very much in that way, too, with broad, vivid, unmistakable splashes of color. Mrs. Brandeis, looking at the black-haired, red-lipped child sleeping there, wondered just how much determination lay back of the broad white brow. She had said little to Fanny about this feat of fasting, and she told herself that she disapproved of it. But in her heart she wanted the girl to see it through, once attempted.

Fanny awoke at half past seven, and her nostrils dilated to that most exquisite, tantalizing and fragrant of smells—the aroma of simmering coffee. It permeated the house. It tickled the senses. It carried with it visions of hot, brown breakfast rolls, and eggs, and butter. Fanny loved her breakfast. She turned over now, and decided to go to sleep again. But she could not. She got up and dressed slowly and carefully. There was no one to hurry her this morning with the call from the foot of the stairs of, "Fanny! Your egg'll get cold!"

She put on clean, crisp underwear, and did her hair expertly. She slipped an all-enveloping pinafore over her head, that the new silk dress might not be crushed before church time. She thought that Theodore would surely have finished his breakfast by this time. But when she came down-stairs he was at the table. Not only that, he had just begun his breakfast. An egg, all golden, and white, and crisply brown at the frilly edges, lay on his plate. Theodore always ate his egg in a mathematical sort of way. He swallowed the white hastily first, because he disliked it, and Mrs. Brandeis insisted that he eat it. Then he would brood a moment over the yolk that lay, unmarred and complete, like an amber jewel in the center of his plate. Then he would suddenly plunge his fork into the very heart of the jewel, and it would flow over his plate, mingling with the butter, and he would catch it deftly with little mops of warm, crisp, buttery roll.

Fanny passed the breakfast table just as Theodore plunged his fork into the egg yolk. She caught her breath sharply, and closed her eyes. Then she turned and fled to the front porch and breathed deeply and windily of the heady September Wisconsin morning air. As she stood there, with her stiff, short black curls still damp and glistening, in her best shoes and stockings, with the all-enveloping apron covering her sturdy little figure, the light of struggle and renunciation in her face, she typified something at once fine and earthy.

But the real struggle was to come later. They went to temple at ten, Theodore with his beloved violin tucked carefully under his arm. Bella Weinberg was waiting at the steps.

"Did you?" she asked eagerly.

"Of course not," replied Fanny disdainfully. "Do you think I'd eat old breakfast when I said I was going to fast all day?" Then, with sudden suspicion, "Did you?"

"No!" stoutly.

And they entered, and took their seats. It was fascinating to watch the other members of the congregation come in, the women rustling, the men subdued in the unaccustomed dignity of black on a week day. One glance at the yellow pews was like reading a complete social and financial register. The seating arrangement of the temple was the Almanach de Gotha of Congregation Emanu-el. Old Ben Reitman, patriarch among the Jewish settlers of Winnebago, who had come over an immigrant youth, and who now owned hundreds of rich farm acres, besides houses, mills and banks, kinged it from the front seat of the center section. He was a magnificent old man, with a ruddy face, and a fine head with a shock of heavy iron-gray hair, keen eyes, undimmed by years, and a startling and unexpected dimple in one cheek that gave him a mischievous and boyish look.

Behind this dignitary sat his sons, and their wives, and his daughters and their husbands, and their children, and so on, back to the Brandeis pew, third from the last, behind which sat only a few obscure families branded as Russians, as only the German-born Jew can brand those whose misfortune it is to be born in that region known as hinter-Berlin.

The morning flew by, with its music, its responses, its sermon in German, full of four- and five-syllable German words like Barmherzigkeit and Eigentumlichkeit. All during the sermon Fanny sat and dreamed and watched the shadow on the window of the pine tree that stood close to the temple, and was vastly amused at the jaundiced look that the square of yellow window glass cast upon the face of the vain and overdressed Mrs. Nathan Pereles. From time to time Bella would turn to bestow upon her a look intended to convey intense suffering and a resolute though dying condition. Fanny stonily ignored these mute messages. They offended something in her, though she could not tell what.

At the noon intermission she did not go home to the tempting dinner smells, but wandered off through the little city park and down to the river, where she sat on the bank and felt very virtuous, and spiritual, and hollow. She was back in her seat when the afternoon service was begun. Some of the more devout members had remained to pray all through the midday. The congregation came straggling in by twos and threes. Many of the women had exchanged the severely corseted discomfort of the morning's splendor for the comparative ease of second-best silks. Mrs. Brandeis, absent from her business throughout this holy day, came hurrying in at two, to look with a rather anxious eye upon her pale and resolute little daughter.

The memorial service was to begin shortly after three, and lasted almost two hours. At quarter to three Bella slipped out through the side aisle, beckoning mysteriously and alluringly to Fanny as she went. Fanny looked at her mother.

"Run along," said Mrs. Brandeis. "The air will be good for you. Come back before the memorial service begins." Fanny and Bella met, giggling, in the vestibule.

"Come on over to my house for a minute," Bella suggested. "I want to show you something." The Weinberg house, a great, comfortable, well-built home, with encircling veranda, and a well-cared-for lawn, was just a scant block away. They skipped across the street, down the block, and in at the back door. The big sunny kitchen was deserted. The house seemed very quiet and hushed. Over it hung the delicious fragrance of freshly-baked pastry. Bella, a rather baleful look in her eyes, led the way to the butler's pantry that was as large as the average kitchen. And there, ranged on platters, and baking boards, and on snowy-white napkins, was that which made Tantalus's feast seem a dry and barren snack. The Weinberg's had baked. It is the custom in the household of Atonement Day fasters of the old school to begin the evening meal, after the twenty-four hours of abstainment, with coffee and freshly-baked coffee cake of every variety. It was a lead-pipe blow at one's digestion, but delicious beyond imagining. Bella's mother was a famous cook, and her two maids followed in the ways of their mistress. There were to be sisters and brothers and out-of-town relations as guests at the evening meal, and Mrs. Weinberg had outdone herself.

"Oh!" exclaimed Fanny in a sort of agony and delight.

"Take some," said Bella, the temptress.

The pantry was fragrant as a garden with spices, and fruit scents, and the melting, delectable perfume of brown, freshly-baked dough, sugar-coated. There was one giant platter devoted wholly to round, plump cakes, with puffy edges, in the center of each a sunken pool that was all plum, bearing on its bosom a snowy sifting of powdered sugar. There were others whose centers were apricot, pure molten gold in the sunlight. There were speckled expanses of cheese kuchen, the golden-brown surface showing rich cracks through which one caught glimpses of the lemon-yellow cheese beneath—cottage cheese that had been beaten up with eggs, and spices, and sugar, and lemon. Flaky crust rose, jaggedly, above this plateau. There were cakes with jelly, and cinnamon kuchen, and cunning cakes with almond slices nestling side by side. And there was freshly-baked bread—twisted loaf, with poppy seed freckling its braid, and its sides glistening with the butter that had been liberally swabbed on it before it had been thrust into the oven.

Fanny Brandeis gazed, hypnotized. As she gazed Bella selected a plum tart and bit into it—bit generously, so that her white little teeth met in the very middle of the oozing red-brown juice and one heard a little squirt as they closed on the luscious fruit. At the sound Fanny quivered all through her plump and starved little body.

"Have one," said Bella generously. "Go on. Nobody'll ever know. Anyway, we've fasted long enough for our age. I could fast till supper time if I wanted to, but I don't want to." She swallowed the last morsel of the plum tart, and selected another—apricot, this time, and opened her moist red lips. But just before she bit into it (the Inquisition could have used Bella's talents) she selected its counterpart and held it out to Fanny. Fanny shook her head slightly. Her hand came up involuntarily. Her eyes were fastened on Bella's face.

"Go on," urged Bella. "Take it. They're grand! M-m-m-m!" The first bite of apricot vanished between her rows of sharp white teeth. Fanny shut her eyes as if in pain. She was fighting the great fight of her life. She was to meet other temptations, and perhaps more glittering ones, in her lifetime, but to her dying day she never forgot that first battle between the flesh and the spirit, there in the sugar-scented pantry—and the spirit won. As Bella's lips closed upon the second bite of apricot tart, the while her eye roved over the almond cakes and her hand still held the sweet out to Fanny, that young lady turned sharply, like a soldier, and marched blindly out of the house, down the back steps, across the street, and so into the temple.

The evening lights had just been turned on. The little congregation, relaxed, weary, weak from hunger, many of them, sat rapt and still except at those times when the prayer book demanded spoken responses. The voice of the little rabbi, rather weak now, had in it a timbre that made it startlingly sweet and clear and resonant. Fanny slid very quietly into the seat beside Mrs. Brandeis, and slipped her moist and cold little hand into her mother's warm, work-roughened palm. The mother's brown eyes, very bright with unshed tears, left their perusal of the prayer book to dwell upon the white little face that was smiling rather wanly up at her. The pages of the prayer book lay two-thirds or more to the left. Just as Fanny remarked this, there was a little moment of hush in the march of the day's long service. The memorial hour had begun.

Little Doctor Thalmann cleared his throat. The congregation stirred a bit, changed its cramped position. Bella, the guilty, came stealing in, a pink-and-gold picture of angelic virtue. Fanny, looking at her, felt very aloof, and clean, and remote.

Molly Brandeis seemed to sense what had happened.

"But you didn't, did you?" she whispered softly.

Fanny shook her head.

Rabbi Thalmann was seated in his great carved chair. His eyes were closed. The wheezy little organ in the choir loft at the rear of the temple began the opening bars of Schumann's Traumerei. And then, above the cracked voice of the organ, rose the clear, poignant wail of a violin. Theodore Brandeis had begun to play. You know the playing of the average boy of fifteen—that nerve-destroying, uninspired scraping. There was nothing of this in the sounds that this boy called forth from the little wooden box and the stick with its taut lines of catgut. Whatever it was—the length of the thin, sensitive fingers, the turn of the wrist, the articulation of the forearm, the something in the brain, or all these combined—Theodore Brandeis possessed that which makes for greatness. You realized that as he crouched over his violin to get his cello tones. As he played to-day the little congregation sat very still, and each was thinking of his ambitions and his failures; of the lover lost, of the duty left undone, of the hope deferred; of the wrong that was never righted; of the lost one whose memory spells remorse. It felt the salt taste on its lips. It put up a furtive, shamed hand to dab at its cheeks, and saw that the one who sat in the pew just ahead was doing likewise. This is what happened when this boy of fifteen wedded his bow to his violin. And he who makes us feel all this has that indefinable, magic, glorious thing known as Genius.

When it was over, there swept through the room that sigh following tension relieved. Rabbi Thalmann passed a hand over his tired eyes, like one returning from a far mental journey; then rose, and came forward to the pulpit. He began, in Hebrew, the opening words of the memorial service, and so on to the prayers in English, with their words of infinite humility and wisdom.

"Thou hast implanted in us the capacity for sin, but not sin itself!"

Fanny stirred. She had learned that a brief half hour ago. The service marched on, a moving and harrowing thing. The amens rolled out with a new fervor from the listeners. There seemed nothing comic now in the way old Ben Reitman, with his slower eyes, always came out five words behind the rest who tumbled upon the responses and scurried briskly through them, so that his fine old voice, somewhat hoarse and quavering now, rolled out its "Amen!" in solitary majesty. They came to that gem of humility, the mourners' prayer; the ancient and ever-solemn Kaddish prayer. There is nothing in the written language that, for sheer drama and magnificence, can equal it as it is chanted in the Hebrew.

As Rabbi Thalmann began to intone it in its monotonous repetition of praise, there arose certain black-robed figures from their places and stood with heads bowed over their prayer books. These were members of the congregation from whom death had taken a toll during the past year. Fanny rose with her mother and Theodore, who had left the choir loft to join them. The little wheezy organ played very softly. The black-robed figures swayed. Here and there a half-stifled sob rose, and was crushed. Fanny felt a hot haze that blurred her vision. She winked it away, and another burned in its place. Her shoulders shook with a sob. She felt her mother's hand close over her own that held one side of the book. The prayer, that was not of mourning but of praise, ended with a final crescendo from the organ, The silent black-robed figures were seated.

Over the little, spent congregation hung a glorious atmosphere of detachment. These Jews, listening to the words that had come from the lips of the prophets in Israel, had been, on this day, thrown back thousands of years, to the time when the destruction of the temple was as real as the shattered spires and dome of the cathedral at Rheims. Old Ben Reitman, faint with fasting, was far removed from his everyday thoughts of his horses, his lumber mills, his farms, his mortgages. Even Mrs. Nathan Pereles, in her black satin and bugles and jets, her cold, hard face usually unlighted by sympathy or love, seemed to feel something of this emotional wave. Fanny Brandeis was shaken by it. Her head ached (that was hunger) and her hands were icy. The little Russian girl in the seat just behind them had ceased to wriggle and squirm, and slept against her mother's side. Rabbi Thalmann, there on the platform, seemed somehow very far away and vague. The scent of clove apples and ammonia salts filled the air. The atmosphere seemed strangely wavering and luminous. The white satin of the Ark curtain gleamed and shifted.

The long service swept on to its close. Suddenly organ and choir burst into a paeon. Little Doctor Thalmann raised his arms. The congregation swept to its feet with a mighty surge. Fanny rose with them, her face very white in its frame of black curls, her eyes luminous. She raised her face for the words of the ancient benediction that rolled, in its simplicity and grandeur, from the lips of the rabbi:

"May the blessing of the Lord our God rest upon you all. God bless thee and keep thee. May God cause His countenance to shine upon thee and be gracious unto thee. May God lift up His countenance unto thee, and grant thee peace."

The Day of Atonement had come to an end. It was a very quiet, subdued and spent little flock that dispersed to their homes. Fanny walked out with scarcely a thought of Bella. She felt, vaguely, that she and this school friend were formed of different stuff. She knew that the bond between them had been the grubby, physical one of childhood, and that they never would come together in the finer relation of the spirit, though she could not have put this new knowledge into words.

Molly Brandeis put a hand on her daughter's shoulder.

"Tired, Fanchen?"

"A little."

"Bet you're hungry!" from Theodore.

"I was, but I'm not now."

"M-m-m—wait! Noodle soup. And chicken!"

She had intended to tell of the trial in the Weinberg's pantry. But now something within her—something fine, born of this day—kept her from it. But Molly Brandeis, to whom two and two often made five, guessed something of what had happened. She had felt a great surge of pride, had Molly Brandeis, when her son had swayed the congregation with the magic of his music. She had kissed him good night with infinite tenderness and love. But she came into her daughter's tiny room after Fanny had gone to bed, and leaned over, and put a cool hand on the hot forehead.

"Do you feel all right, my darling?"

"Umhmph," replied Fanny drowsily.

"Fanchen, doesn't it make you feel happy and clean to know that you were able to do the thing you started out to do?"

"Umhmph."

"Only," Molly Brandeis was thinking aloud now, quite forgetting that she was talking to a very little girl, "only, life seems to take such special delight in offering temptation to those who are able to withstand it. I don't know why that's true, but it is. I hope—oh, my little girl, my baby—I hope——"

But Fanny never knew whether her mother finished that sentence or not. She remembered waiting for the end of it, to learn what it was her mother hoped. And she had felt a sudden, scalding drop on her hand where her mother bent over her. And the next thing she knew it was morning, with mellow September sunshine.

CHAPTER FOUR

It was the week following this feat of fasting that two things happened to Fanny Brandeis—two seemingly unimportant and childish things—that were to affect the whole tenor of her life. It is pleasant to predict thus. It gives a certain weight to a story and a sense of inevitableness. It should insure, too, the readers's support to the point, at least, where the prediction is fulfilled. Sometimes a careless author loses sight altogether of his promise, and then the tricked reader is likely to go on to the very final page, teased by the expectation that that which was hinted at will be revealed.

Fanny Brandeis had a way of going to the public library on Saturday afternoons (with a bag of very sticky peanut candy in her pocket, the little sensualist!) and there, huddled in a chair, dreamily and almost automatically munching peanut brittle, her cheeks growing redder and redder in the close air of the ill-ventilated room, she would read, and read, and read. There was no one to censor her reading, so she read promiscuously, wading gloriously through trash and classic and historical and hysterical alike, and finding something of interest in them all.

She read the sprightly "Duchess" novels, where mad offers of marriage were always made in flower-scented conservatories; she read Dickens, and Thelma, and old bound Cosmopolitans, and Zola, and de Maupassant, and the "Wide, Wide World," and "Hans Brinker, or The Silver Skates," and "Jane Eyre." All of which are merely mentioned as examples of her catholicism in literature. As she read she was unaware of the giggling boys and girls who came in noisily, and made dates, and were coldly frowned on by the austere Miss Perkins, the librarian. She would read until the fading light would remind her that the short fall or winter day was drawing to a close.

She would come, shivering a little after the fetid atmosphere of the overheated library, into the crisp, cold snap of the astringent Wisconsin air. Sometimes she would stop at the store for her mother. Sometimes she would run home alone through the twilight, her heels scrunching the snow, her whole being filled with a vague and unchildish sadness and disquiet as she faced the tender rose, and orange, and mauve, and pale lemon of the winter sunset.

There were times when her very heart ached with the beauty of that color-flooded sky; there were times, later, when it ached in much the same way at the look in the eyes of a pushcart peddler; there were times when it ached, seemingly, for no reason at all—as is sometimes the case when one is a little Jew girl, with whole centuries of suffering behind one.

On this day she had taken a book from the library Miss Perkins, at sight of the title, had glared disapprovingly, and had hesitated a moment before stamping the card.

"Is this for yourself?" she had asked.

"Yes'm."

"It isn't a book for little girls," snapped Miss Perkins.

"I've read half of it already," Fanny informed her sweetly. And went out with it under her arm. It was Zola's "The Ladies' Paradise" (Au Bonheur des Dames). The story of the shop girl, and the crushing of the little dealer by the great and moneyed company had thrilled and fascinated her.

Her mind was full of it as she turned the corner on Norris Street and ran full-tilt, into a yowling, taunting, torturing little pack of boys. They were gathered in close formation about some object which they were teasing, and knocking about in the mud, and otherwise abusing with the savagery of their years. Fanny, the fiery, stopped short. She pushed into the ring. The object of their efforts was a weak-kneed and hollow-chested little boy who could not fight because he was cowardly as well as weak, and his name (oh, pity!) was Clarence—Clarence Heyl. There are few things that a mischievous group of small boys cannot do with a name like Clarence. They whined it, they catcalled it, they shrieked it in falsetto imitation of Clarence's mother. He was a wide-mouthed, sallow and pindling little boy, whose pipe-stemmed legs looked all the thinner for being contrasted with his feet, which were long and narrow. At that time he wore spectacles, too, to correct a muscular weakness, so that his one good feature—great soft, liquid eyes—passed unnoticed. He was the kind of little boy whose mother insists on dressing him in cloth-top, buttoned, patent-leather shoes for school. His blue serge suit was never patched or shiny. His stockings were virgin at the knee. He wore an overcoat on cool autumn days. Fanny despised and pitied him. We ask you not to, because in this puny, shy and ugly little boy of fifteen you behold Our Hero.

He staggered to his feet now, as Fanny came up. His school reefer was mud-bespattered. His stockings were torn. His cap was gone and his hair was wild. There was a cut or scratch on one cheek, from which the blood flowed.

"I'll tell my mother on you!" he screamed impotently, and shook with rage and terror. "You'll see, you will! You let me alone, now!"

Fanny felt a sick sensation at the pit of her stomach and in her throat. Then:

"He'll tell his ma!" sneered the boys in chorus. "Oh, mamma!" And called him the Name. And at that a she wildcat broke loose among them. She pounced on them without warning, a little fury of blazing eyes and flying hair, and white teeth showing in a snarl. If she had fought fair, or if she had not taken them so by surprise, she would have been powerless among them. But she had sprung at them with the suddenness of rage. She kicked, and scratched, and bit, and clawed and spat. She seemed not to feel the defensive blows that were showered upon her in turn. Her own hard little fists were now doubled for a thump or opened, like a claw, for scratching.

"Go on home!" she yelled to Clarence, even while she fought. And Clarence, gathering up his tattered school books, went, and stood not on the order of his going. Whereupon Fanny darted nimbly to one side, out of the way of boyish brown fists. In that moment she was transformed from a raging fury into a very meek and trembling little girl, who looked shyly and pleadingly out from a tangle of curls. The boys were for rushing at her again.

"Cowardy-cats! Five of you fighting one girl," cried Fanny, her lower lip trembling ever so little. "Come on! Hit me! Afraid to fight anything but girls! Cowardy-cats!" A tear, pearly, pathetic, coursed down her cheek.

The drive was broken. Five sullen little boys stood and glared at her, impotently.

"You hit us first," declared one boy. "What business d' you have scratching around like that, I'd like to know! You old scratch cat!"

"He's sickly," said Fanny. "He can't fight. There's something the matter with his lungs, or something, and they're going to make him quit school. Besides, he's a billion times better than any of you, anyway."

At once, "Fanny's stuck on Clar-ence! Fanny's stuck on Clar-ence!"

Fanny picked up her somewhat battered Zola from where it had flown at her first onslaught. "It's a lie!" she shouted. And fled, followed by the hateful chant.

She came in at the back door, trying to look casual. But Mattie's keen eye detected the marks of battle, even while her knife turned the frying potatoes.

"Fanny Brandeis! Look at your sweater! And your hair!"

Fanny glanced down at the torn pocket dangling untidily. "Oh, that!" she said airily. And, passing the kitchen table, deftly filched a slice of cold veal from the platter, and mounted the back stairs to her room. It was a hungry business, this fighting. When Mrs. Brandeis came in at six her small daughter was demurely reading. At supper time Mrs. Brandeis looked up at her daughter with a sharp exclamation.

"Fanny! There's a scratch on your cheek from your eye to your chin."

Fanny put up her hand. "Is there?"

"Why, you must have felt it. How did you get it?"

Fanny said nothing. "I'll bet she was fighting," said Theodore with the intuitive knowledge that one child has of another's ways.

"Fanny!" The keen brown eyes were upon her. "Some boys were picking on Clarence Heyl, and it made me mad. They called him names."

"What names?"

"Oh, names."

"Fanny dear, if you're going to fight every time you hear that name——"

Fanny thought of the torn sweater, the battered Zola, the scratched cheek. "It is pretty expensive," she said reflectively.

After supper she settled down at once to her book. Theodore would labor over his algebra after the dining-room table was cleared. He stuck his cap on his head now, and slammed out of the door for a half-hour's play under the corner arc-light. Fanny rarely brought books from school, and yet she seemed to get on rather brilliantly, especially in the studies she liked. During that winter following her husband's death Mrs. Brandeis had a way of playing solitaire after supper; one of the simpler forms of the game. It seemed to help her to think out the day's problems, and to soothe her at the same time. She would turn down the front of the writing desk, and draw up the piano stool.

All through that winter Fanny seemed to remember reading to the slap-slap of cards, and the whir of their shuffling. In after years she was never able to pick up a volume of Dickens without having her mind hark back to those long, quiet evenings. She read a great deal of Dickens at that time. She had a fine contempt for his sentiment, and his great ladies bored her. She did not know that this was because they were badly drawn. The humor she loved, and she read and reread the passages dealing with Samuel Weller, and Mr. Micawber, and Sairey Gamp, and Fanny Squeers. It was rather trying to read Dickens before supper, she had discovered. Pickwick Papers was fatal, she had found. It sent one to the pantry in a sort of trance, to ransack for food—cookies, apples, cold meat, anything. But whatever one found, it always fell short of the succulent sounding beefsteak pies, and saddles of mutton, and hot pineapple toddy of the printed page.

To-night Mrs. Brandeis, coming in from the kitchen after a conference with Mattie, found her daughter in conversational mood, though book in hand.

"Mother, did you ever read this?" She held up "The Ladies' Paradise."

"Yes; but child alive, what ever made you get it? That isn't the kind of thing for you to read. Oh, I wish I had more time to give——"

Fanny leaned forward eagerly. "It made me think a lot of you. You know—the way the big store was crushing the little one, and everything. Like the thing you were talking to that man about the other day. You said it was killing the small-town dealer, and he said some day it would be illegal, and you said you'd never live to see it."

"Oh, that! We were talking about the mail-order business, and how hard it was to compete with it, when the farmers bought everything from a catalogue, and had whole boxes of household goods expressed to them. I didn't know you were listening, Fanchen."

"I was. I almost always do when you and some traveling man or somebody like that are talking. It—it's interesting."

Fanny went back to her book then. But Molly Brandeis sat a moment, eyeing her queer little daughter thoughtfully. Then she sighed, and laid out her cards for solitaire. By eight o'clock she was usually so sleepy that she would fall, dead-tired, asleep on the worn leather couch in the sitting-room. She must have been fearfully exhausted, mind and body. The house would be very quiet, except for Mattie, perhaps, moving about in the kitchen or in her corner room upstairs. Sometimes the weary woman on the couch would start suddenly from her sleep and cry out, choked and gasping, "No! No! No!" The children would jump, terrified, and come running to her at first, but later they got used to it, and only looked up to say, when she asked them, bewildered, what it was that wakened her, "You had the no-no-nos."

She had never told of the thing that made her start out of her sleep and cry out like that. Perhaps it was just the protest of the exhausted body and the overwrought nerves. Usually, after that, she would sit up, haggardly, and take the hairpins out of her short thick hair, and announce her intention of going to bed. She always insisted that the children go too, though they often won an extra half hour by protesting and teasing. It was a good thing for them, these nine o'clock bed hours, for it gave them the tonic sleep that their young, high-strung natures demanded.

"Come, children," she would say, yawning.

"Oh, mother, please just let me finish this chapter!"

"How much?"

"Just this little bit. See? Just this."

"Well, just that, then," for Mrs. Brandeis was a reasonable woman, and she had the book-lover's knowledge of the fascination of the unfinished chapter.

Fanny and Theodore were not always honest about the bargain. They would gallop, hot-cheeked, through the allotted chapter. Mrs. Brandeis would have fallen into a doze, perhaps. And the two conspirators would read on, turning the leaves softly and swiftly, gulping the pages, cramming them down in an orgy of mental bolting, like naughty children stuffing cake when their mother's back is turned. But the very concentration of their dread of waking her often brought about the feared result. Mrs. Brandeis would start up rather wildly, look about her, and see the two buried, red-cheeked and eager, in their books.

"Fanny! Theodore! Come now! Not another minute!"

Fanny, shameless little glutton, would try it again. "Just to the end of this chapter! Just this weenty bit!"

"Fiddlesticks! You've read four chapters since I spoke to you the last time. Come now!"

Molly Brandeis would see to the doors, and the windows, and the clock, and then, waiting for the weary little figures to climb the stairs, would turn out the light, and, hairpins in one hand, corset in the other, perhaps, mount to bed.

By nine o'clock the little household would be sleeping, the children sweetly and dreamlessly, the tired woman restlessly and fitfully, her overwrought brain still surging with the day's problems. It was not like a household at rest, somehow. It was like a spirited thing standing, quivering for a moment, its nerves tense, its muscles twitching.

Perhaps you have quite forgotten that here were to be retailed two epochal events in Fanny Brandeis's life. If you have remembered, you will have guessed that the one was the reading of that book of social protest, though its writer has fallen into disfavor in these fickle days. The other was the wild and unladylike street brawl in which she took part so that a terrified and tortured little boy might escape his tormentors.

CHAPTER FIVE

There was no hard stock in Brandeis' Bazaar now. The packing-room was always littered with straw and excelsior dug from hogsheads and great crates. Aloysius lorded it over a small red-headed satellite who disappeared inside barrels and dived head first into huge boxes, coming up again with a lamp, or a doll, or a piece of glassware, like a magician. Fanny, perched on an overturned box, used to watch him, fascinated, while he laboriously completed a water set, or a tea set. A preliminary dive would bring up the first of a half dozen related pieces, each swathed in tissue paper. A deft twist on the part of the attendant Aloysius would strip the paper wrappings and disclose a ruby-tinted tumbler, perhaps. Another dive, and another, until six gleaming glasses stood revealed, like chicks without a hen mother. A final dip, much scratching and burrowing, during which armfuls of hay and excelsior were thrown out, and then the red-headed genie of the barrel would emerge, flushed and triumphant, with the water pitcher itself, thus completing the happy family.

Aloysius, meanwhile, would regale her with one of those choice bits of gossip he had always about him, like a jewel concealed, and only to be brought out for the appreciative. Mrs. Brandeis disapproved of store gossip, and frowned on Sadie and Pearl whenever she found them, their heads close together, their stifled shrieks testifying to his wit. There were times when Molly Brandeis herself could not resist the spell of his tongue. No one knew where Aloysius got his information. He had news that Winnebago's two daily papers never could get, and wouldn't have dared to print if they had.

"Did you hear about Myrtle Krieger," he would begin, "that's marryin' the Hempel boy next month? The one in the bank. She's exhibiting her trewsow at the Outagamie County Fair this week, for the handwork and embroid'ry prize. Ain't it brazen? They say the crowd's so thick around the table that they had to take down the more pers'nal pieces. The first day of the fair the grand-stand was, you might say, empty, even when they was pullin' off the trottin' races and the balloon ascension. It's funny—ain't it?—how them garmints that you wouldn't turn for a second look at on the clothesline or in a store winda' becomes kind of wicked and interestin' the minute they get what they call the human note. There it lays, that virgin lawnjerie, for all the county to look at, with pink ribbons run through everything, and the poor Krieger girl never dreamin' she's doin' somethin' indelicate. She says yesterday if she wins the prize she's going to put it toward one of these kitchen cabinets."

I wish we could stop a while with Aloysius. He is well worth it. Aloysius, who looked a pass between Ichabod Crane and Smike; Aloysius, with his bit of scandal burnished with wit; who, after a long, hard Saturday, would go home to scrub the floor of the dingy lodgings where he lived with his invalid mother, and who rose in the cold dawn of Sunday morning to go to early mass, so that he might return to cook the dinner and wait upon the sick woman. Aloysius, whose trousers flapped grotesquely about his bony legs, and whose thin red wrists hung awkwardly from his too-short sleeves, had in him that tender, faithful and courageous stuff of which unsung heroes are made. And he adored his clever, resourceful boss to the point of imitation. You should have seen him trying to sell a sled or a doll's go-cart in her best style. But we cannot stop for Aloysius. He is irrelevant, and irrelevant matter halts the progress of a story. Any one, from Barrie to Harold Bell Wright, will tell you that a story, to be successful, must march.

We'll keep step, then, with Molly Brandeis until she drops out of the ranks. There is no detouring with Mrs. Brandeis for a leader. She is the sort that, once her face is set toward her goal, looks neither to right nor left until she has reached it.

When Fanny Brandeis was fourteen, and Theodore was not quite sixteen, a tremendous thing happened. Schabelitz, the famous violinist, came to Winnebago to give a concert under the auspices of the Young Men's Sunday Evening Club.

The Young Men's Sunday Evening Club of the Congregational Church prided itself (and justifiably) on what the papers called its "auspices." It scorned to present to Winnebago the usual lyceum attractions—Swiss bell ringers, negro glee clubs, and Family Fours. Instead, Schumann-Heink sang her lieder for them; McCutcheon talked and cartooned for them; Madame Bloomfield-Zeisler played. Winnebago was one of those wealthy little Mid-Western towns whose people appreciate the best and set out to acquire it for themselves.

To the Easterner, Winnebago, and Oshkosh, and Kalamazoo, and Emporia are names invented to get a laugh from a vaudeville audience. Yet it is the people from Winnebago and Emporia and the like whom you meet in Egypt, and the Catalina Islands, and at Honolulu, and St. Moritz. It is in the Winnebago living-room that you are likely to find a prayer rug got in Persia, a bit of gorgeous glaze from China, a scarf from some temple in India, and on it a book, hand-tooled and rare. The Winnebagoans seem to know what is being served and worn, from salad to veilings, surprisingly soon after New York has informed itself on those subjects. The 7:52 Northwestern morning train out of Winnebago was always pretty comfortably crowded with shoppers who were taking a five-hour run down to Chicago to get a hat and see the new musical show at the Illinois.

So Schabelitz's coming was an event, but not an unprecedented one. Except to Theodore. Theodore had a ticket for the concert (his mother had seen to that), and he talked of nothing else. He was going with his violin teacher, Emil Bauer. There were strange stories as to why Emil Bauer, with his gift of teaching, should choose to bury himself in this obscure little Wisconsin town. It was known that he had acquaintance with the great and famous of the musical world. The East End set fawned upon him, and his studio suppers were the exclusive social events in Winnebago.

Schabelitz was to play in the evening. At half past three that afternoon there entered Brandeis' Bazaar a white-faced, wide-eyed boy who was Theodore Brandeis; a plump, voluble, and excited person who was Emil Bauer; and a short, stocky man who looked rather like a foreign-born artisan—plumber or steam-fitter—in his Sunday clothes. This was Levine Schabelitz.

Molly Brandeis was selling a wash boiler to a fussy housewife who, in her anxiety to assure herself of the flawlessness of her purchase, had done everything but climb inside it. It had early been instilled in the minds of Mrs. Brandeis's children that she was never to be approached when busy with a customer. There were times when they rushed into the store bursting with news or plans, but they had learned to control their eagerness. This, though, was no ordinary news that had blanched Theodore's face. At sight of the three, Mrs. Brandeis quietly turned her boiler purchaser over to Pearl and came forward from the rear of the store.

"Oh, Mother!" cried Theodore, an hysterical note in his voice. "Oh, Mother!"

And in that moment Molly Brandeis knew. Emil Bauer introduced them, floridly. Molly Brandeis held out her hand, and her keen brown eyes looked straight and long into the gifted Russian's pale blue ones. According to all rules he should have started a dramatic speech, beginning with "Madame!" hand on heart. But Schabelitz the great had sprung from Schabelitz the peasant boy, and in the process he had managed, somehow, to retain the simplicity which was his charm. Still, there was something queer and foreign in the way he bent over Mrs. Brandeis's hand. We do not bow like that in Winnebago.

"Mrs. Brandeis, I am honored to meet you."

"And I to meet you," replied the shopkeeper in the black sateen apron.

"I have just had the pleasure of hearing your son play," began Schabelitz.

"Mr. Bauer called me out of my economics class at school, Mother, and said that——"

"Theodore!" Theodore subsided. "He is only a boy," went on Schabelitz, and put one hand on Theodore's shoulder. "A very gifted boy. I hear hundreds. Oh, how I suffer, sometimes, to listen to their devilish scraping! To-day, my friend Bauer met me with that old plea, `You must hear this pupil play. He has genius.' `Bah! Genius!' I said, and I swore at him a little, for he is my friend, Bauer. But I went with him to his studio—Bauer, that is a remarkably fine place you have there, above that drug store; a room of exceptional proportions. And those rugs, let me tell you——"

"Never mind the rugs, Schabelitz. Mrs. Brandeis here——"

"Oh, yes, yes! Well, dear lady, this boy of yours will be a great violinist if he is willing to work, and work, and work. He has what you in America call the spark. To make it a flame he must work, always work. You must send him to Dresden, under Auer."

"Dresden!" echoed Molly Brandeis faintly, and put one hand on the table that held the fancy cups and saucers, and they jingled a little.

"A year, perhaps, first, in New York with Wolfsohn."

Wolfsohn! New York! Dresden! It was too much even for Molly Brandeis' well-balanced brain. She was conscious of feeling a little dizzy. At that moment Pearl approached apologetically. "Pardon me, Mis' Brandeis, but Mrs. Trost wants to know if you'll send the boiler special this afternoon. She wants it for the washing early to-morrow morning."

That served to steady her.

"Tell Mrs. Trost I'll send it before six to-night." Her eyes rested on Theodore's face, flushed now, and glowing. Then she turned and faced Schabelitz squarely. "Perhaps you do not know that this store is our support. I earn a living here for myself and my two children. You see what it is—just a novelty and notion store in a country town. I speak of this because it is the important thing. I have known for a long time that Theodore's playing was not the playing of the average boy, musically gifted. So what you tell me does not altogether surprise me. But when you say Dresden—well, from Brandeis' Bazaar in Winnebago, Wisconsin, to Auer, in Dresden, Germany, is a long journey for one afternoon."

"But of course you must have time to think it over. It must be brought about, somehow."

"Somehow——" Mrs. Brandeis stared straight ahead, and you could almost hear that indomitable will of hers working, crashing over obstacles, plowing through difficulties. Theodore watched her, breathless, as though expecting an immediate solution. His mother's eyes met his own intent ones, and at that her mobile mouth quirked in a sudden smile. "You look as if you expected pearls to pop out of my mouth, son. And, by the way, if you're going to a concert this evening don't you think it would be a good idea to squander an hour on study this afternoon? You may be a musical prodigy, but geometry's geometry."

"Oh, Mother! Please!"

"I want to talk to Mr. Schabelitz and Mr. Bauer, alone." She patted his shoulder, and the last pat ended in a gentle push. "Run along."

"I'll work, Mother. You know perfectly well I'll work." But he looked so startlingly like his father as he said it that Mrs. Brandeis felt a clutching at her heart.

Theodore out of the way, they seemed to find very little to discuss, after all. Schabelitz was so quietly certain, Bauer so triumphantly proud.

Said Schabelitz, "Wolfsohn, of course, receives ten dollars a lesson ordinarily."

"Ten dollars!"

"But a pupil like Theodore is in the nature of an investment," Bauer hastened to explain. "An advertisement. After hearing him play, and after what Schabelitz here will have to say for him, Wolfsohn will certainly give Theodore lessons for nothing, or next to nothing. You remember"—proudly—"I offered to teach him without charge, but you would not have it."

Schabelitz smote his friend sharply on the shoulder "The true musician! Oh, Bauer, Bauer! That you should bury yourself in this——"

But Bauer stopped him with a gesture. "Mrs. Brandeis is a busy woman. And as she says, this thing needs thinking over."

"After all," said Mrs. Brandeis, "there isn't much to think about. I know just where I stand. It's a case of mathematics, that's all. This business of mine is just beginning to pay. From now on I shall be able to save something every year. It might be enough to cover his musical education. It would mean that Fanny—my daughter—and I would have to give up everything. For myself, I should be only too happy, too proud. But it doesn't seem fair to her. After all, a girl——"

"It isn't fair," broke in Schabelitz. "It isn't fair. But that is the way of genius. It never is fair. It takes, and takes, and takes. I know. My mother could tell you, if she were alive. She sold the little farm, and my sisters gave up their dowries, and with them their hopes of marriage, and they lived on bread and cabbage. That was not to pay for my lessons. They never could have done that. It was only to send me to Moscow. We were very poor. They must have starved. I have come to know, since, that it was not worth it. That nothing could be worth it."

"But it was worth it. Your mother would do it all over again, if she had the chance. That's what we're for."

Bauer pulled out his watch and uttered a horrified exclamation. "Himmel! Four o'clock! And I have a pupil at four." He turned hastily to Mrs. Brandeis. "I am giving a little supper in my studio after the concert to-night."

"Oh, Gott!" groaned Schabelitz.

"It is in honor of Schabelitz here. You see how overcome he is. Will you let me bring Theodore back with me after the concert? There will be some music, and perhaps he will play for us."

Schabelitz bent again in his queer little foreign bow. "And you, of course, will honor us, Mrs. Brandeis." He had never lived in Winnebago.

"Oh, certainly," Bauer hastened to say. He had.

"I!" Molly Brandeis looked down at her apron, and stroked it with her fingers. Then she looked up with a little smile that was not so pleasant as her smile usually was. There had flashed across her quick mind a picture of Mrs. G. Manville Smith. Mrs. G. Manville Smith, in an evening gown whose decolletage was discussed from the Haley House to Gerretson's department store next morning, was always a guest at Bauer's studio affairs. "Thank you, but it is impossible. And Theodore is only a schoolboy. Just now he needs, more than anything else in the world, nine hours of sleep every night. There will be plenty of time for studio suppers later. When a boy's voice is changing, and he doesn't know what to do with his hands and feet, he is better off at home."

"God! These mothers!" exclaimed Schabelitz. "What do they not know!"

"I suppose you are right." Bauer was both rueful and relieved. It would have been fine to show off Theodore as his pupil and Schabelitz's protege. But Mrs. Brandeis? No, that would never do. "Well, I must go. We will talk about this again, Mrs. Brandeis. In two weeks Schabelitz will pass through Winnebago again on his way back to Chicago. Meanwhile he will write Wolfsohn. I also. So! Come, Schabelitz!"

He turned to see that gentleman strolling off in the direction of the notion counter behind which his expert eye had caught a glimpse of Sadie in her white shirtwaist and her trim skirt. Sadie always knew what they were wearing on State Street, Chicago, half an hour after Mrs. Brandeis returned from one of her buying trips. Shirtwaists had just come in, and with them those neat leather belts with a buckle, and about the throat they were wearing folds of white satin ribbon, smooth and high and tight, the two ends tied pertly at the back. Sadie would never be the saleswoman that Pearl was, but her unfailing good nature and her cheery self-confidence made her an asset in the store. Besides, she was pretty. Mrs. Brandeis knew the value of a pretty clerk.

At the approach of this stranger Sadie leaned coyly against the stocking rack and patted her paper sleevelets that were secured at wrist and elbow with elastic bands. Her method was sure death to traveling men. She prepared now to try it on the world-famous virtuoso. The ease with which she succeeded surprised even Sadie, accustomed though she was to conquest.

"Come, come, Schabelitz!" said Bauer again. "I must get along."

"Then go, my friend. Go along and make your preparations for that studio supper. The only interesting woman in Winnebago—" he bowed to Mrs. Brandeis—"will not be there. I know them, these small-town society women, with their imitation city ways. And bony! Always! I am enjoying myself. I shall stay here."

And he did stay. Sadie, talking it over afterward with Pearl and Aloysius, put it thus:

"They say he's the grandest violin player in the world. Not that I care much for the violin, myself. Kind of squeaky, I always think. But it just goes to show they're all alike. Ain't it the truth? I jollied him just like I did Sam Bloom, of Ganz & Pick, Novelties, an hour before. He laughed just where Sam did. And they both handed me a line of talk about my hair and eyes, only Sam said I was a doll, and this Schabelitz, or whatever his name is, said I was as alluring as a Lorelei. I guess he thought he had me there, but I didn't go through the seventh reader for nothing. `If you think I'm flattered,' I said to him, `you're mistaken. She was the mess who used to sit out on a rock with her back hair down, combing away and singing like mad, and keeping an eye out for sailors up and down the river. If I had to work that hard to get some attention,' I said, `I'd give up the struggle, and settle down with a cat and a teakettle.' At that he just threw back his head and roared. And when Mrs. Brandeis came up he said something about the wit of these American women. `Work is a great sharpener of wit—and wits,' Mrs. Brandeis said to him. `Pearl, did Aloysius send Eddie out with that boiler, special?' And she didn't pay any more attention to him, or make any more fuss over him, than she would to a traveler with a line of samples she wasn't interested in. I guess that's why he had such a good time."

Sadie was right. That was the reason. Fanny, coming into the store half an hour later, saw this man who had swayed thousands with his music, down on his hands and knees in the toy section at the rear of Brandeis' Bazaar. He and Sadie and Aloysius were winding up toy bears, and clowns, and engines, and carriages, and sending them madly racing across the floor. Sometimes their careening career was threatened with disaster in the form of a clump of brooms or a stack of galvanized pails. But Schabelitz would scramble forward with a shout and rescue them just before the crash came, and set them deftly off again in the opposite direction.

"This I must have for my boy in New York." He held up a miniature hook and ladder. "And this windmill that whirls so busily. My Leo is seven, and his head is full of engines, and motors, and things that run on wheels. He cares no more for music, the little savage, than the son of a bricklayer."

"Who is that man?" Fanny whispered, staring at him.

"Levine Schabelitz."

"Schabelitz! Not the—"

"Yes."

"But he's playing on the floor like—like a little boy! And laughing! Why, Mother, he's just like anybody else, only nicer."

If Fanny had been more than fourteen her mother might have told her that all really great people are like that, finding joy in simple things. I think that is the secret of their genius—the child in them that keeps their viewpoint fresh, and that makes us children again when we listen to them. It is the Schabelitzes of this world who can shout over a toy engine that would bore a Bauer to death.

Fanny stood looking at him thoughtfully. She knew all about him. Theodore's talk of the past week had accomplished that. Fanny knew that here was a man who did one thing better than any one else in the world. She thrilled to that thought. She adored the quality in people that caused them to excel. Schabelitz had got hold of a jack-in-the-box, and each time the absurd head popped out, with its grin and its squawk, he laughed like a boy. Fanny, standing behind the wrapping counter, and leaning on it with her elbows the better to see this great man, smiled too, as her flexible spirit and her mobile mind caught his mood. She did not know she was smiling. Neither did she know why she suddenly frowned in the intensity of her concentration, reached up for one of the pencils on the desk next the wrapping counter, and bent over the topmost sheet of yellow wrapping paper that lay spread out before her. Her tongue-tip curled excitedly at one corner of her mouth. Her head was cocked to one side.

She was rapidly sketching a crude and startling likeness of Levine Schabelitz as he stood there with the ridiculous toy in his hand. It was a trick she often amused herself with at school. She had drawn her school-teacher one day as she had looked when gazing up into the eyes of the visiting superintendent, who was a married man. Quite innocently and unconsciously she had caught the adoring look in the eyes of Miss McCook, the teacher, and that lady, happening upon the sketch later, had dealt with Fanny in a manner seemingly unwarranted. In the same way it was not only the exterior likeness of the man which she was catching now—the pompadour that stood stiffly perpendicular like a brush; the square, yellow peasant teeth; the strong, slender hands and wrists; the stocky figure; the high cheek bones; the square-toed, foreign-looking shoes and the trousers too wide at the instep to have been cut by an American tailor. She caught and transmitted to paper, in some uncanny way, the simplicity of the man who was grinning at the jack-in-the-box that smirked back at him. Behind the veneer of poise and polish born of success and adulation she had caught a glimpse of the Russian peasant boy delighted with the crude toy in his hand. And she put it down eagerly, wetting her pencil between her lips, shading here, erasing there.

Mrs. Brandeis, bustling up to the desk for a customer's change, and with a fancy dish to be wrapped, in her hand, glanced over Fanny's shoulder. She leaned closer. "Why, Fanny, you witch!"

Fanny gave a little crow of delight and tossed her head in a way that switched her short curls back from where they had fallen over her shoulders. "It's like him, isn't it?"

"It looks more like him than he does himself." With which Molly Brandeis unconsciously defined the art of cartooning.

Fanny looked down at it, a smile curving her lips. Mrs. Brandeis, dish in hand, counted her change expertly from the till below the desk, and reached for the sheet of wrapping paper just beneath that on which Fanny had made her drawing. At that moment Schabelitz, glancing up, saw her, and came forward, smiling, the jack-in-the-box still in his hand.

"Dear lady, I hope I have not entirely disorganized your shop. I have had a most glorious time. Would you believe it, this jack-in-the-box looks exactly—but exactly—like my manager, Weber, when the box-office receipts are good. He grins just—"

And then his eye fell on the drawing that Fanny was trying to cover with one brown paw. "Hello! What's this?" Then he looked at Fanny. Then he grasped her wrist in his fingers of steel and looked at the sketch that grinned back at him impishly. "Well, I'm damned!" exploded Schabelitz in amusement, and surprise, and appreciation. And did not apologize. "And who is this young lady with the sense of humor?"

"This is my little girl, Fanny."

He looked down at the rough sketch again, with its clean-cut satire, and up again at the little girl in the school coat and the faded red tam o' shanter, who was looking at him shyly, and defiantly, and provokingly, all at once.

"Your little girl Fanny, h'm? The one who is to give up everything that the boy Theodore may become a great violinist." He bent again over the crude, effective cartoon, then put a forefinger gently under the child's chin and tipped her glowing face up to the light. "I am not so sure now that it will work. As for its being fair! Why, no! No!"

Fanny waited for her mother that evening, and they walked home together. Their step and swing were very much alike, now that Fanny's legs were growing longer. She was at the backfisch age.

"What did he mean, Mother, when he said that about Theodore being a great violinist, and its not being fair? What isn't fair? And how did he happen to be in the store, anyway? He bought a heap of toys, didn't he? I suppose he's awfully rich."

"To-night, when Theodore's at the concert, I'll tell you what he meant, and all about it."

"I'd love to hear him play, wouldn't you? I'd just love to."

Over Molly Brandeis's face there came a curious look. "You could hear him, Fanny, in Theodore's place. Theodore would have to stay home if I told him to."

Fanny's eyes and mouth grew round with horror. "Theodore stay home! Why Mrs.—Molly—Brandeis!" Then she broke into a little relieved laugh. "But you're just fooling, of course."

"No, I'm not. If you really want to go I'll tell Theodore to give up his ticket to his sister."

"Well, my goodness! I guess I'm not a pig. I wouldn't have Theodore stay home, not for a million dollars."

"I knew you wouldn't," said Molly Brandeis as they swung down Norris Street. And she told Fanny briefly of what Schabelitz had said about Theodore.

It was typical of Theodore that he ate his usual supper that night. He may have got his excitement vicariously from Fanny. She was thrilled enough for two. Her food lay almost untouched on her plate. She chattered incessantly. When Theodore began to eat his second baked apple with cream, her outraged feelings voiced their protest.

"But, Theodore, I don't see how you can!"

"Can what?"

"Eat like that. When you're going to hear him play. And after what he said, and everything."

"Well, is that any reason why I should starve to death?"

"But I don't see how you can," repeated Fanny helplessly, and looked at her mother. Mrs. Brandeis reached for the cream pitcher and poured a little more cream over Theodore's baked apple. Even as she did it her eyes met Fanny's, and in them was a certain sly amusement, a little gleam of fun, a look that said, "Neither do I." Fanny sat back, satisfied. Here, at least, was some one who understood.

At half past seven Theodore, looking very brushed and sleek, went off to meet Emil Bauer. Mrs. Brandeis had looked him over, and had said, "Your nails!" and sent him back to the bathroom, and she had resisted the desire to kiss him because Theodore disliked demonstration. "He hated to be pawed over," was the way he put it. After he had gone, Mrs. Brandeis went into the dining-room where Fanny was sitting. Mattie had cleared the table, and Fanny was busy over a book and a tablet, by the light of the lamp that they always used for studying. It was one of the rare occasions when she had brought home a school lesson. It was arithmetic, and Fanny loathed arithmetic. She had no head for mathematics. The set of problems were eighth-grade horrors, in which A is digging a well 20 feet deep and 9 feet wide; or in which A and B are papering two rooms, or building two fences, or plastering a wall. If A does his room in 9 1/2 days, the room being 12 feet high, 20 feet long, and 15 1/2 feet wide, how long will it take B to do a room 14 feet high, 11 3/4 feet, etc.

Fanny hated the indefatigable A and B with a bitter personal hatred. And as for that occasional person named C, who complicated matters still more—!

Sometimes Mrs. Brandeis helped to disentangle Fanny from the mazes of her wall paper problems, or dragged her up from the bottom of the well when it seemed that she was down there for eternity unless a friendly hand rescued her. As a rule she insisted that Fanny crack her own mathematical nuts. She said it was good mental training, not to speak of the moral side of it. But to-night she bent her quick mind upon the problems that were puzzling her little daughter, and cleared them up in no time.

When Fanny had folded her arithmetic papers neatly inside her book and leaned back with a relieved sigh Molly Brandeis bent forward in the lamplight and began to talk very soberly. Fanny, red-cheeked and bright-eyed from her recent mental struggles, listened interestedly, then intently, then absorbedly. She attempted to interrupt, sometimes, with an occasional, "But, Mother, how—" but Mrs. Brandeis shook her head and went on. She told Fanny a few things about her early married life—things that made Fanny look at her with new eyes. She had always thought of her mother as her mother, in the way a fourteen-year-old girl does. It never occurred to her that this mother person, who was so capable, so confident, so worldly-wise, had once been a very young bride, with her life before her, and her hopes stepping high, and her love keeping time with her hopes. Fanny heard, fascinated, the story of this girl who had married against the advice of her family and her friends.

Molly Brandeis talked curtly and briefly, and her very brevity and lack of embroidering details made the story stand out with stark realism. It was such a story of courage, and pride, and indomitable will, and sheer pluck as can only be found among the seemingly commonplace.

"And so," she finished, "I used to wonder, sometimes, whether it was worth while to keep on, and what it was all for. And now I know. Theodore is going to make up for everything. Only we'll have to help him, first. It's going to be hard on you, Fanchen. I'm talking to you as if you were eighteen, instead of fourteen. But I want you to understand. That isn't fair to you either—my expecting you to understand. Only I don't want you to hate me too much when you're a woman, and I'm gone, and you'll remember—"

"Why, Mother, what in the world are you talking about? Hate you!"

"For what I took from you to give to him, Fanny. You don't understand now. Things must be made easy for Theodore. It will mean that you and I will have to scrimp and save. Not now and then, but all the time. It will mean that we can't go to the theater, even occasionally, or to lectures, or concerts. It will mean that your clothes won't be as pretty or as new as the other girls' clothes. You'll sit on the front porch evenings, and watch them go by, and you'll want to go too."

"As if I cared."

"But you will care. I know. I know. It's easy enough to talk about sacrifice in a burst of feeling; but it's the everyday, shriveling grind that's hard. You'll want clothes, and books, and beaux, and education, and you ought to have them. They're your right. You ought to have them!" Suddenly Molly Brandeis' arms were folded on the table, and her head came down on her arms and she was crying, quietly, horribly, as a man cries. Fanny stared at her a moment in unbelief. She had not seen her mother cry since the day of Ferdinand Brandeis' death. She scrambled out of her chair and thrust her head down next her mother's, so that her hot, smooth cheek touched the wet, cold one. "Mother, don't! Don't Molly dearie. I can't bear it. I'm going to cry too. Do you think I care for old dresses and things? I should say not. It's going to be fun going without things. It'll be like having a secret or something. Now stop, and let's talk about it."

Molly Brandeis wiped her eyes, and sat up, and smiled. It was a watery and wavering smile, but it showed that she was mistress of herself again.

"No," she said, "we just won't talk about it any more. I'm tired, that's what's the matter with me, and I haven't sense enough to know it. I'll tell you what. I'm going to put on my kimono, and you'll make some fudge. Will you? We'll have a party, all by ourselves, and if Mattie scolds about the milk to-morrow you just tell her I said you could. And I think there are some walnut meats in the third cocoa can on the shelf in the pantry. Use 'em all."

CHAPTER SIX

Theodore came home at twelve o'clock that night. He had gone to Bauer's studio party after all. It was the first time he had deliberately disobeyed his mother in a really big thing. Mrs. Brandeis and Fanny had nibbled fudge all evening (it had turned out deliciously velvety) and had gone to bed at their usual time. At half past ten Mrs. Brandeis had wakened with the instinctive feeling that Theodore was not in the house. She lay there, wide awake, staring into the darkness until eleven. Then she got up and went into his room, though she knew he was not there. She was not worried as to his whereabouts or his well-being. That same instinctive feeling told her where he was. She was very angry, and a little terrified at the significance of his act. She went back to bed again, and she felt the blood pounding in her head. Molly Brandeis had a temper, and it was surging now, and beating against the barriers of her self-control.

She told herself, as she lay there, that she must deal with him coolly and firmly, though she wanted to spank him. The time for spankings was past. Some one was coming down the street with a quick, light step. She sat up in bed, listening. The steps passed the house, went on. A half hour passed. Some one turned the corner, whistling blithely. But, no, he would not be whistling, she told herself. He would sneak in, quietly. It was a little after twelve when she heard the front door open (Winnebago rarely locked its doors). She was surprised to feel her heart beating rapidly. He was trying to be quiet, and was making a great deal of noise about it. His shoes and the squeaky fifth stair alone would have convicted him. The imp of perversity in Molly Brandeis made her smile, angry as she was, at the thought of how furious he must be at that stair.

"Theodore!" she called quietly, just as he was tip-toeing past her room.

"Yeh."

"Come in here. And turn on the light."

He switched on the light and stood there in the doorway. Molly Brandeis, sitting up in bed in the chilly room, with her covers about her, was conscious of a little sick feeling, not at what he had done, but that a son of hers should ever wear the sullen, defiant, hang-dog look that disfigured Theodore's face now.

"Bauer's?"

A pause. "Yes."

"Why?"

"I just stopped in there for a minute after the concert. I didn't mean to stay. And then Bauer introduced me around to everybody. And then they asked me to play, and—"

"And you played badly."

"Well, I didn't have my own violin."

"No football game Saturday. And no pocket money this week. Go to bed."

He went, breathing hard, and muttering a little under his breath. At breakfast next morning Fanny plied him with questions and was furious at his cool uncommunicativeness.

"Was it wonderful, Theodore? Did he play—oh—like an angel?"

"Played all right. Except the `Swan' thing. Maybe he thought it was too easy, or something, but I thought he murdered it. Pass the toast, unless you want it all."

It was not until the following autumn that Theodore went to New York. The thing that had seemed so impossible was arranged. He was to live in Brooklyn with a distant cousin of Ferdinand Brandeis, on a business basis, and he was to come into New York three times a week for his lessons. Mrs. Brandeis took him as far as Chicago, treated him to an extravagant dinner, put him on the train and with difficulty stifled the impulse to tell all the other passengers in the car to look after her Theodore. He looked incredibly grown up and at ease in his new suit and the hat that they had wisely bought in Chicago. She did not cry at all (in the train), and she kissed him only twice, and no man can ask more than that of any mother.

Molly Brandeis went back to Winnebago and the store with her shoulders a little more consciously squared, her jaw a little more firmly set. There was something almost terrible about her concentrativeness. Together she and Fanny began a life of self-denial of which only a woman could be capable. They saved in ways that only a woman's mind could devise; petty ways, that included cream and ice, and clothes, and candy. It was rather fun at first. When that wore off it had become a habit. Mrs. Brandeis made two resolutions regarding Fanny. One was that she should have at least a high school education, and graduate. The other that she should help in the business of the store as little as possible. To the first Fanny acceded gladly. To the second she objected.

"But why? If you can work, why can't I? I could help you a lot on Saturdays and at Christmas time, and after school."

"I don't want you to," Mrs. Brandeis had replied, almost fiercely. "I'm giving my life to it. That's enough. I don't want you to know about buying and selling. I don't want you to know a bill of lading from a sales slip when you see it. I don't want you to know whether f. o. b. is a wireless signal or a branch of the Masons." At which Fanny grinned. No one appreciated her mother's humor more than she.

"But I do know already. The other day when that fat man was selling you those go-carts I heard him say. `F. o. b. Buffalo,' and I asked Aloysius what it meant and he told me."

It was inevitable that Fanny Brandeis should come to know these things, for the little household revolved about the store on Elm Street. By the time she was eighteen and had graduated from the Winnebago high school, she knew so many things that the average girl of eighteen did not know, and was ignorant of so many things that the average girl of eighteen did know, that Winnebago was almost justified in thinking her queer. She had had a joyous time at school, in spite of algebra and geometry and physics. She took the part of the heroine in the senior class play given at the Winnebago opera house, and at the last rehearsal electrified those present by announcing that if Albert Finkbein (who played the dashing Southern hero) didn't kiss her properly when the curtain went down on the first act, just as he was going into battle, she'd rather he didn't kiss her at all.

"He just makes it ridiculous," she protested. "He sort of gives a peck two inches from my nose, and then giggles. Everybody will laugh, and it'll spoil everything."

With the rather startled elocution teacher backing her she rehearsed the bashful Albert in that kiss until she had achieved the effect of realism that she thought the scene demanded. But when, on the school sleighing parties and hay rides the boy next her slipped a wooden and uncertain arm about her waist while they all were singing "Jingle Bells, Jingle Bells," and "Good Night Ladies," and "Merrily We Roll Along," she sat up stiffly and unyieldingly until the arm, discouraged, withdrew to its normal position. Which two instances are quoted as being of a piece with what Winnebago termed her queerness.

Not that Fanny Brandeis went beauless through school. On the contrary, she always had some one to carry her books, and to take her to the school parties and home from the Friday night debating society meetings. Her first love affair turned out disastrously. She was twelve, and she chose as the object of her affections a bullet-headed boy named Simpson. One morning, as the last bell rang and they were taking their seats, Fanny passed his desk and gave his coarse and stubbly hair a tweak. It was really a love tweak, and intended to be playful, but she probably put more fervor into it than she knew. It brought the tears of pain to his eyes, and he turned and called her the name at which she shrank back, horrified. Her shock and unbelief must have been stamped on her face, for the boy, still smarting, had snarled, "Ya-as, I mean it."

It was strange how she remembered that incident years after she had forgotten important happenings in her life. Clarence Heyl, whose very existence you will have failed to remember, used to hover about her uncertainly, always looking as if he would like to walk home with her, but never summoning the courage to do it. They were graduated from the grammar school together, and Clarence solemnly read a graduation essay entitled "Where is the Horse?" Automobiles were just beginning to flash plentifully up and down Elm Street. Clarence had always been what Winnebago termed sickly, in spite of his mother's noodle soup, and coddling. He was sent West, to Colorado, or to a ranch in Wyoming, Fanny was not quite sure which, perhaps because she was not interested. He had come over one afternoon to bid her good-by, and had dangled about the front porch until she went into the house and shut the door.

When she was sixteen there was a blond German boy whose taciturnity attracted her volubility and vivacity. She mistook his stolidness for depth, and it was a long time before she realized that his silence was not due to the weight of his thoughts but to the fact that he had nothing to say. In her last year at high school she found herself singled out for the attentions of Harmon Kent, who was the Beau Nash of the Winnebago high school. His clothes were made by Schwartze, the tailor, when all the other boys of his age got theirs at the spring and fall sales of the Golden Eagle Clothing Store. It was always nip and tuck between his semester standings and his track team and football possibilities. The faculty refused to allow flunkers to take part in athletics.

He was one of those boys who have definite charm, and manner, and poise at seventeen, and who crib their exams off their cuffs. He was always at the head of any social plans in the school, and at the dances he rushed about wearing in his coat lapel a ribbon marked Floor Committee. The teachers all knew he was a bluff, but his engaging manner carried him through. When he went away to the state university he made Fanny solemnly promise to write; to come down to Madison for the football games; to be sure to remember about the Junior prom. He wrote once—a badly spelled scrawl—and she answered. But he was the sort of person who must be present to be felt. He could not project his personality. When he came home for the Christmas holidays Fanny was helping in the store. He dropped in one afternoon when she was selling whisky glasses to Mike Hearn of the Farmers' Rest Hotel.

They did not write at all during the following semester, and when he came back for the long summer vacation they met on the street one day and exchanged a few rather forced pleasantries. It suddenly dawned on Fanny that he was patronizing her much as the scion of an aristocratic line banters the housemaid whom he meets on the stairs. She bit an imaginary apron corner, and bobbed a curtsy right there on Elm Street, in front of the Courier office and walked off, leaving him staring. It was shortly after this that she began a queer line of reading for a girl—lives of Disraeli, Spinoza, Mendelssohn, Mozart—distinguished Jews who had found their religion a handicap.

The year of her graduation she did a thing for which Winnebago felt itself justified in calling her different. Each member of the graduating class was allowed to choose a theme for a thesis. Fanny Brandeis called hers "A Piece of Paper." On Winnebago's Fox River were located a number of the largest and most important paper mills in the country. There were mills in which paper was made of wood fiber, and others in which paper was made of rags. You could smell the sulphur as soon as you crossed the bridge that led to the Flats. Sometimes, when the wind was right, the pungent odor of it spread all over the town. Strangers sniffed it and made a wry face, but the natives liked it.

The mills themselves were great ugly brick buildings, their windows festooned with dust webs. Some of them boasted high detached tower-like structures where a secret acid process went on. In the early days the mills had employed many workers, but newly invented machinery had come to take the place of hand labor. The rag-rooms alone still employed hundreds of girls who picked, sorted, dusted over the great suction bins. The rooms in which they worked were gray with dust. They wore caps over their hair to protect it from the motes that you could see spinning and swirling in the watery sunlight that occasionally found its way through the gray-filmed window panes. It never seemed to occur to them that the dust cap so carefully pulled down about their heads did not afford protection for their lungs. They were pale girls, the rag-room girls, with a peculiarly gray-white pallor.

Fanny Brandeis had once been through the Winnebago Paper Company's mill and she had watched, fascinated, while a pair of soiled and greasy old blue overalls were dusted and cleaned, and put through this acid vat, and that acid tub, growing whiter and more pulpy with each process until it was fed into a great crushing roller that pressed the moisture out of it, flattened it to the proper thinness and spewed it out at last, miraculously, in the form of rolls of crisp, white paper. On the first day of the Easter vacation Fanny Brandeis walked down to the office of the Winnebago Paper Company's mill and applied at the superintendent's office for a job. She got it. They were generally shorthanded in the rag-room. When Mrs. Brandeis heard of it there followed one of the few stormy scenes between mother and daughter.

"Why did you do it?" demanded Mrs. Brandeis.

"I had to, to get it right."

"Oh, don't be silly. You could have visited the mill a dozen times."

Fanny twisted the fingers of her left hand in the fingers of her right as was her way when she was terribly in earnest, and rather excited.

"But I don't want to write about the paper business as a process."

"Well, then, what do you want?"

"I want to write about the overalls on some railroad engineer, perhaps; or the blue calico wrapper that belonged, maybe, to a scrub woman. And how they came to be spotted, or faded, or torn, and finally all worn out. And how the rag man got them, and the mill, and how the girls sorted them. And the room in which they do it. And the bins. And the machinery. Oh, it's the most fascinating, and—and sort of relentless machinery. And the acid burns on the hands of the men at the vats. And their shoes. And then the paper, so white. And the way we tear it up, or crumple it, and throw it in the waste basket. Just a piece of paper, don't you see what I mean? Just a piece of paper, and yet all that—" she stopped and frowned a little, and grew inarticulate, and gave it up with a final, "Don't you see what I mean, Mother? Don't you see what I mean?"

Molly Brandeis looked at her daughter in a startled way, like one who, walking tranquilly along an accustomed path, finds himself confronting a new and hitherto unsuspected vista, formed by a peculiar arrangement of clouds, perhaps, or light, or foliage, or all three blended. "I see what you mean," she said. "But I wish you wouldn't do it. I—I wish you didn't feel that you wanted to do it."

"But how can I make it real if I don't?"

"You can't," said Molly Brandeis. "That's just it. You can't, ever."

Fanny got up before six every morning of that Easter vacation, and went to the mill, lunch box in hand. She came home at night dead-tired. She did not take the street car to and from the mill, as she might have, because she said the other girls in the rag-room walked, some of them from the very edge of town. Mrs. Brandeis said that she was carrying things too far, but Fanny stuck it out for the two weeks, at the end of which period she spent an entire Sunday in a hair-washing, face-steaming, and manicuring bee. She wrote her paper from notes she had taken, and turned it in at the office of the high school principal with the feeling that it was not at all what she had meant it to be. A week later Professor Henning called her into his office. The essay lay on his desk.

"I've read your thesis," he began, and stopped, and cleared his throat. He was not an eloquent man. "Where did you get your information, Miss Brandeis?"

"I got it at the mill."

"From one of the employees?"

"Oh, no. I worked there, in the rag-room."

Professor Henning gave a little startled exclamation that he turned hastily into a cough. "I thought that perhaps the editor of the Courier might like to see it—it being local. And interesting."

He brought it down to the office of the little paper himself, and promised to call for it again in an hour or two, when Lem Davis should have read it. Lem Davis did read it, and snorted, and scuffled with his feet in the drift of papers under his desk, which was a way he had when enraged.

"Read it!" he echoed, at Professor Henning's question. "Read it! Yes, I read it. And let me tell you it's socialism of the rankest kind, that's what! It's anarchism, that's what! Who's this girl? Mrs. Brandeis's daughter—of the Bazaar? Let me tell you I'd go over there and tell her what I think of the way she's bringing up that girl—if she wasn't an advertiser. `A Piece of Paper'! Hell!" And to show his contempt for what he had read he wadded together a great mass of exchanges that littered his desk and hurled them, a crumpled heap, to the floor, and then spat tobacco juice upon them.

"I'm sorry," said Professor Henning, and rose; but at the door he turned and said something highly unprofessorial. "It's a darn fine piece of writing." And slammed the door. At supper that night he told Mrs. Henning about it. Mrs. Henning was a practical woman, as the wife of a small-town high school principal must needs be. "But don't you know," she said, "that Roscoe Moore, who is president of the Outagamie Pulp Mill and the Winnebago Paper Company, practically owns the Courier?"

Professor Henning passed a hand over his hair, ruefully, like a school boy. "No, Martha, I didn't know. If I knew those things, dear, I suppose we wouldn't be eating sausage for supper to-night." There was a little silence between them. Then he looked up. "Some day I'm going to brag about having been that Brandeis girl's teacher."

Fanny was in the store a great deal now. After she finished high school they sent Mattie away and Fanny took over the housekeeping duties, but it was not her milieu. Not that she didn't do it well. She put a perfect fury of energy and care into the preparation of a pot roast. After she had iced a cake she enhanced it with cunning arabesques of jelly. The house shone as it never had, even under Mattie's honest regime. But it was like hitching a high-power engine to a butter churn. There were periods of maddening restlessness. At such times she would set about cleaning the cellar, perhaps. It was a three-roomed cellar, brick-floored, cool, and having about it that indefinable cellar smell which is of mold, and coal, and potatoes, and onions, and kindling wood, and dill pickles and ashes.

Other girls of Fanny's age, at such times, cleaned out their bureau drawers and read forbidden novels. Fanny armed herself with the third best broom, the dust-pan, and an old bushel basket. She swept up chips, scraped up ashes, scoured the preserve shelves, washed the windows, cleaned the vegetable bins, and got gritty, and scarlet-cheeked and streaked with soot. It was a wonderful safety valve, that cellar. A pity it was that the house had no attic.

Then there were long, lazy summer afternoons when there was nothing to do but read. And dream. And watch the town go by to supper. I think that is why our great men and women so often have sprung from small towns, or villages. They have had time to dream in their adolescence. No cars to catch, no matinees, no city streets, none of the teeming, empty, energy-consuming occupations of the city child. Little that is competitive, much that is unconsciously absorbed at the most impressionable period, long evenings for reading, long afternoons in the fields or woods. With the cloth laid, and the bread cut and covered with a napkin, and the sauce in the glass bowl, and the cookies on a blue plate, and the potatoes doing very, very slowly, and the kettle steaming with a Peerybingle cheerfulness, Fanny would stroll out to the front porch again to watch for the familiar figure to appear around the corner of Norris Street. She would wear her blue-and-white checked gingham apron deftly twisted over one hip, and tucked in, in deference to the passers-by. And the town would go by—Hen Cody's drays, rattling and thundering; the high school boys thudding down the road, dog-tired and sweaty in their football suits, or their track pants and jerseys, on their way from the athletic field to the school shower baths; Mrs. Mosher flying home, her skirts billowing behind her, after a protracted afternoon at whist; little Ernie Trost with a napkin-covered peach basket carefully balanced in his hand, waiting for the six-fifteen interurban to round the corner near the switch, so that he could hand up his father's supper; Rudie Mass, the butcher, with a moist little packet of meat in his hand, and lurching ever so slightly, and looking about defiantly. Oh, Fanny probably never realized how much she saw and absorbed, sitting there on Brandeis' front porch, watching Winnebago go by to supper.

At Christmas time she helped in the store, afternoons and evenings. Then, one Christmas, Mrs. Brandeis was ill for three weeks with grippe. They had to have a helper in the house. When Mrs. Brandeis was able to come back to the store Sadie left to marry, not one of her traveling-men victims, but a steady person, in the paper-hanging way, whose suit had long been considered hopeless. After that Fanny took her place. She developed a surprising knack at selling. Yet it was not so surprising, perhaps, when one considered her teacher. She learned as only a woman can learn who is brought into daily contact with the outside world. It was not only contact: it was the relation of buyer and seller. She learned to judge people because she had to. How else could one gauge their tastes, temperaments, and pocketbooks? They passed in and out of Brandeis' Bazaar, day after day, in an endless and varied procession—traveling men, school children, housewives, farmers, worried hostesses, newly married couples bent on house furnishing, business men.

She learned that it was the girls from the paper mills who bought the expensive plates—the ones with the red roses and green leaves hand-painted in great smears and costing two dollars and a half, while the golf club crowd selected for a gift or prize one of the little white plates with the faded-looking blue sprig pattern, costing thirty-nine cents. One day, after she had spent endless time and patience over the sale of a nondescript little plate to one of Winnebago's socially elect, she stared wrathfully after the retreating back of the trying customer.

"Did you see that? I spent an hour with her. One hour! I showed her everything from the imported Limoges bowls to the Sevres cups and saucers, and all she bought was that miserable little bonbon dish with the cornflower pattern. Cat!"

Mrs. Brandeis spoke from the depths of her wisdom.

"Fanny, I didn't miss much that went on during that hour, and I was dying to come over and take her away from you, but I didn't because I knew you needed the lesson, and I knew that that McNulty woman never spends more than twenty-five cents, anyway. But I want to tell you now that it isn't only a matter of plates. It's a matter of understanding folks. When you've learned whom to show the expensive hand-painted things to, and when to suggest quietly the little, vague things, with what you call the faded look, why, you've learned just about all there is to know of human nature. Don't expect it, at your age."

Molly Brandeis had never lost her trick of chatting with customers, or listening to them, whenever she had a moment's time. People used to drop in, and perch themselves on one of the stools near the big glowing base burner and talk to Mrs. Brandeis. It was incredible, the secrets they revealed of business, and love and disgrace; of hopes and aspirations, and troubles, and happiness. The farmer women used to fascinate Fanny by their very drabness. Mrs. Brandeis had a long and loyal following of these women. It was before the day when every farmhouse boasted an automobile, a telephone, and a phonograph.

A worn and dreary lot, these farmer women, living a skimmed milk existence, putting their youth, and health, and looks into the soil. They used often to sit back near the stove in winter, or in a cool corner near the front of the store in summer, and reveal, bit by bit, the sordid, tragic details of their starved existence. Fanny was often shocked when they told their age—twenty-five, twenty-eight, thirty, but old and withered from drudgery, and child-bearing, and coarse, unwholesome food. Ignorant women, and terribly lonely, with the dumb, lack-luster eyes that bespeak monotony. When they smiled they showed blue-white, glassily perfect false teeth that flashed incongruously in the ruin of their wrinkled, sallow, weather-beaten faces. Mrs. Brandeis would question them gently.

Children? Ten. Living? Four. Doctor? Never had one in the house. Why? He didn't believe in them. No proper kitchen utensils, none of the devices that lighten the deadeningly monotonous drudgery of housework. Everything went to make his work easier—new harrows, plows, tractors, wind mills, reapers, barns, silos. The story would come out, bit by bit, as the woman sat there, a worn, unlovely figure, her hands—toil-blackened, seamed, calloused, unlovelier than any woman's hands were ever meant to be—lying in unaccustomed idleness in her lap.

Fanny learned, too, that the woman with the shawl, and with her money tied in a corner of her handkerchief, was more likely to buy the six-dollar doll, with the blue satin dress, and the real hair and eye-lashes, while the Winnebago East End society woman haggled over the forty-nine cent kind, which she dressed herself.

I think their loyalty to Mrs. Brandeis might be explained by her honesty and her sympathy. She was so square with them. When Minnie Mahler, out Centerville way, got married, she knew there would be no redundancy of water sets, hanging lamps, or pickle dishes.

"I thought like I'd get her a chamber set," Minnie's aunt would confide to Mrs. Brandeis.

"Is this for Minnie Mahler, of Centerville?"

"Yes; she gets married Sunday."

"I sold a chamber set for that wedding yesterday. And a set of dishes. But I don't think she's got a parlor lamp. At least I haven't sold one. Why don't you get her that? If she doesn't like it she can change it. Now there's that blue one with the pink roses."

And Minnie's aunt would end by buying the lamp.

Fanny learned that the mill girls liked the bright-colored and expensive wares, and why; she learned that the woman with the "fascinator" (tragic misnomer!) over her head wanted the finest sled for her boy. She learned to keep her temper. She learned to suggest without seeming to suggest. She learned to do surprisingly well all those things that her mother did so surprisingly well—surprisingly because both the women secretly hated the business of buying and selling. Once, on the Fourth of July, when there was a stand outside the store laden with all sorts of fireworks, Fanny came down to find Aloysius and the boy Eddie absent on other work, and Mrs. Brandeis momentarily in charge. The sight sickened her, then infuriated her.

"Come in," she said, between her teeth. "That isn't your work."

"Somebody had to be there. Pearl's at dinner. And Aloysius and Eddie were—"

"Then leave it alone. We're not starving—yet. I won't have you selling fireworks like that—on the street. I won't have it! I won't have it!"

The store was paying, now. Not magnificently, but well enough. Most of the money went to Theodore, in Dresden. He was progressing, though not so meteorically as Bauer and Schabelitz had predicted. But that sort of thing took time, Mrs. Brandeis argued. Fanny often found her mother looking at her these days with a questioning sadness in her eyes. Once she suggested that Fanny join the class in drawing at the Winnebago university—a small fresh-water college. Fanny did try it for a few months, but the work was not what she wanted; they did fruit pictures and vases, with a book, on a table; or a clump of very pink and very white flowers. Fanny quit in disgust and boredom. Besides, they were busy at the store, and needed her.

There came often to Winnebago a woman whom Fanny Brandeis admired intensely. She was a traveling saleswoman, successful, magnetic, and very much alive. Her name was Mrs. Emma McChesney, and between her and Mrs. Brandeis there existed a warm friendship. She always took dinner with Mrs. Brandeis and Fanny, and they made a special effort to give her all those delectable home-cooked dishes denied her in her endless round of hotels.

"Noodle soup!" she used to say, almost lyrically.

"With real hand-made, egg noodles! You don't know what it means. You haven't been eating vermicelli soup all through Illinois and Wisconsin."

"We've made a dessert, though, that—"

"Molly Brandeis, don't you dare to tell me what you've got for dessert. I couldn't stand it. But, oh, suppose, SUPPOSE it's homemade strawberry shortcake!"

Which it more than likely was.

Fanny Brandeis used to think that she would dress exactly as Mrs. McChesney dressed, if she too were a successful business woman earning a man-size salary. Mrs. McChesney was a blue serge sort of woman—and her blue serge never was shiny in the back. Her collar, or jabot, or tie, or cuffs, or whatever relieving bit of white she wore, was always of the freshest and crispest. Her hats were apt to be small and full of what is known as "line." She usually would try to arrange her schedule so as to spend a Sunday in Winnebago, and the three alert, humor-loving women, grown wise and tolerant from much contact with human beings, would have a delightful day together.

"Molly," Mrs. McChesney would say, when they were comfortably settled in the living-room, or on the front porch, "with your shrewdness, and experience, and brains, you ought to be one of those five or ten thousand a year buyers. You know how to sell goods and handle people. And you know values. That's all there is to the whole game of business. I don't advise you to go on the road. Heaven knows I wouldn't advise my dearest enemy to do that, much less a friend. But you could do bigger things, and get bigger results. You know most of the big wholesalers, and retailers too. Why don't you speak to them about a department position? Or let me nose around a bit for you."

Molly Brandeis shook her head, though her expressive eyes were eager and interested. "Don't you think I've thought of that, Emma? A thousand times? But I'm—I'm afraid. There's too much at stake. Suppose I couldn't succeed? There's Theodore. His whole future is dependent on me for the next few years. And there's Fanny here. No, I guess I'm too old. And I'm sure of the business here, small as it is."

Emma McChesney glanced at the girl. "I'm thinking that Fanny has the making of a pretty capable business woman herself."

Fanny drew in her breath sharply, and her face sparkled into sudden life, as always when she was tremendously interested.

"Do you know what I'd do if I were in Mother's place? I'd take a great, big running jump for it and land! I'd take a chance. What is there for her in this town? Nothing! She's been giving things up all her life, and what has it brought her?"

"It has brought me a comfortable living, and the love of my two children, and the respect of my townspeople."

"Respect? Why shouldn't they respect you? You're the smartest woman in Winnebago, and the hardest working."

Emma McChesney frowned a little, in thought. "What do you two girls do for recreation?"

"I'm afraid we have too little of that, Emma. I know Fanny has. I'm so dog-tired at the end of the day. All I want is to take my hairpins out and go to bed."

"And Fanny?"

"Oh, I read. I'm free to pick my book friends, at least."

"Now, just what do you mean by that, child? It sounds a little bitter."

"I was thinking of what Chesterfield said in one of his Letters to His Son. `Choose always to be in the society of those above you,' he wrote. I guess he lived in Winnebago, Wisconsin. I'm a working woman, and a Jew, and we haven't any money or social position. And unless she's a Becky Sharp any small town girl with all those handicaps might as well choose a certain constellation of stars in the sky to wear as a breastpin, as try to choose the friends she really wants."

From Molly Brandeis to Emma McChesney there flashed a look that said, "You see?" And from Emma McChesney to Molly Brandeis another that said, "Yes; and it's your fault."

"Look here, Fanny, don't you see any boys—men?"

"No. There aren't any. Those who have any sense and initiative leave to go to Milwaukee, or Chicago, or New York. Those that stay marry the banker's lovely daughter."

Emma McChesney laughed at that, and Molly Brandeis too, and Fanny joined them a bit ruefully. Then quite suddenly, there came into her face a melting, softening look that made it almost lovely. She crossed swiftly over to where her mother sat, and put a hand on either cheek (grown thinner of late) and kissed the tip of her nose. "We don't care—really. Do we Mother? We're poor wurkin' girruls. But gosh! Ain't we proud? Mother, your mistake was in not doing as Ruth did."

"Ruth?"

"In the Bible. Remember when What's-his-name, her husband, died? Did she go back to her home town? No, she didn't. She'd lived there all her life, and she knew better. She said to Naomi, her mother-in-law, `Whither thou goest I will go.' And she went. And when they got to Bethlehem, Ruth looked around, knowingly, until she saw Boaz, the catch of the town. So she went to work in his fields, gleaning, and she gleaned away, trying to look just as girlish, and dreamy, and unconscious, but watching him out of the corner of her eye all the time. Presently Boaz came along, looking over the crops, and he saw her. `Who's the new damsel?' he asked. `The peach?'"

"Fanny Brandeis, aren't you ashamed?"

"But, Mother, that's what it says in the Bible, actually. `Whose damsel is this?' They told him it was Ruth, the dashing widow. After that it was all off with the Bethlehem girls. Boaz paid no more attention to them than if they had never existed. He married Ruth, and she led society. Just a little careful scheming, that's all."

"I should say you have been reading, Fanny Brandeis," said Emma McChesney. She was smiling, but her eyes were serious. "Now listen to me, child. The very next time a traveling man in a brown suit and a red necktie asks you to take dinner with him at the Haley House—even one of those roast pork, queen-fritter-with-rum-sauce, Roman punch Sunday dinners—I want you to accept."

"Even if he wears an Elks' pin, and a Masonic charm, and a diamond ring and a brown derby?" "Even if he shows you the letters from his girl in Manistee," said Mrs. McChesney solemnly. "You've been seeing too much of Fanny Brandeis."

CHAPTER SEVEN

Theodore had been gone six years. His letters, all too brief, were events in the lives of the two women. They read and reread them. Fanny unconsciously embellished them with fascinating details made up out of her own imagination.

"They're really triumphs of stupidity and dullness," she said one day in disgust, after one of Theodore's long-awaited letters had proved particularly dry and sparse. "Just think of it! Dresden, Munich, Leipsic, Vienna, Berlin, Frankfort! And from his letters you would never know he had left Winnebago. I don't believe he actually sees anything of these cities—their people, and the queer houses, and the streets. I suppose a new city means nothing to him but another platform, another audience, another piano, all intended as a background for his violin. He could travel all over the world and it wouldn't touch him once. He's got his mental fingers crossed all the time."

Theodore had begun to play in concert with some success, but he wrote that there was no real money in it yet. He was not well enough known. It took time. He would have to get a name in Europe before he could attempt an American tour. Just now every one was mad over Greinert. He was drawing immense audiences. He sent them a photograph at which they gasped, and then laughed, surprisedly. He looked so awfully German, so different, somehow.

"It's the way his hair is clipped, I suppose," said Fanny. "High, like that, on the temples. And look at his clothes! That tie! And his pants! And that awful collar! Why, his very features look German, don't they? I suppose it's the effect of that haberdashery."

A month after the photograph, came a letter announcing his marriage. Fanny's quick eye, leaping ahead from line to line, took in the facts that her mind seemed unable to grasp. Her name was Olga Stumpf. (In the midst of her horror some imp in Fanny's brain said that her hands would be red, and thick, with a name like that.) An orphan. She sang. One of the Vienna concert halls, but so different from the other girls. And he was so happy. And he hated to ask them for it, but if they could cable a hundred or so. That would help. And here was her picture.

And there was her picture. One of the so-called vivacious type of Viennese of the lower class, smiling a conscious smile, her hair elaborately waved and dressed, her figure high-busted, narrow-waisted; earrings, chains, bracelets. You knew that she used a heavy scent. She was older than Theodore. Or perhaps it was the earrings.

They cabled the hundred.

After the first shock of it Molly Brandeis found excuses for him. "He must have been awfully lonely, Fanny. Often. And perhaps it will steady him, and make him more ambitious. He'll probably work all the harder now."

"No, he won't. But you will. And I will. I didn't mind working for Theodore, and scrimping, and never having any of the things I wanted, from blouses to music. But I won't work and deny myself to keep a great, thick, cheap, German barmaid, or whatever she is in comfort. I won't!"

But she did. And quite suddenly Molly Brandeis, of the straight, firm figure and the bright, alert eye, and the buoyant humor, seemed to lose some of those electric qualities. It was an almost imperceptible letting down. You have seen a fine race horse suddenly break and lose his stride in the midst of the field, and pull up and try to gain it again, and go bravely on, his stride and form still there, but his spirit broken? That was Molly Brandeis.

Fanny did much of the buying now. She bought quickly and shrewdly, like her mother. She even went to the Haley House to buy, when necessary, and Winnebagoans, passing the hotel, would see her slim, erect figure in one of the sample-rooms with its white-covered tables laden with china, or glassware, or Christmas goods, or whatever that particular salesman happened to carry. They lifted their eye-brows at first, but, somehow, it was impossible to associate this girl with the blithe, shirt-sleeved, cigar-smoking traveling men who followed her about the sample-room, order book in hand.

As time went on she introduced some new features into the business, and did away with various old ones. The overflowing benches outside the store were curbed, and finally disappeared altogether. Fanny took charge of the window displays, and often came back to the store at night to spend the evening at work with Aloysius. They would tack a piece of muslin around the window to keep off the gaze of passers-by, and together evolve a window that more than made up for the absent show benches.

This, I suppose, is no time to stop for a description of Fanny Brandeis. And yet the impulse to do so is irresistible. Personally, I like to know about the hair, and eyes, and mouth of the person whose life I am following. How did she look when she said that? What sort of expression did she wear when this happened? Perhaps the thing that Fanny Brandeis said about herself one day, when she was having one of her talks with Emma McChesney, who was on her fall trip for the Featherbloom Petticoat Company, might help.

"No ballroom would ever be hushed into admiring awe when I entered," she said. "No waiter would ever drop his tray, dazzled, and no diners in a restaurant would stop to gaze at me, their forks poised halfway, their eyes blinded by my beauty. I could tramp up and down between the tables for hours, and no one would know I was there. I'm one of a million women who look their best in a tailor suit and a hat with a line. Not that I ever had either. But I have my points, only they're blunted just now."

Still, that bit of description doesn't do, after all. Because she had distinct charm, and some beauty. She was not what is known as the Jewish type, in spite of her coloring. The hair that used to curl, waved now. In a day when coiffures were a bird's-nest of puffs and curls and pompadour, she wore her hair straight back from her forehead and wound in a coil at the neck. Her face in repose was apt to be rather lifeless, and almost heavy. But when she talked, it flashed into sudden life, and you found yourself watching her mouth, fascinated. It was the key to her whole character, that mouth. Mobile, humorous, sensitive, the sensuousness of the lower lip corrected by the firmness of the upper. She had large, square teeth, very regular, and of the yellow-white tone that bespeaks health. She used to make many of her own clothes, and she always trimmed her hats. Mrs. Brandeis used to bring home material and styles from her Chicago buying trips, and Fanny's quick mind adapted them. She managed, somehow, to look miraculously well dressed.

The Christmas following Theodore's marriage was the most successful one in the history of Brandeis' Bazaar. And it bred in Fanny Brandeis a lifelong hatred of the holiday season. In years after she always tried to get away from the city at Christmas time. The two women did the work of four men. They had a big stock on hand. Mrs. Brandeis was everywhere at once. She got an enormous amount of work out of her clerks, and they did not resent it. It is a gift that all born leaders have. She herself never sat down, and the clerks unconsciously followed her example. She never complained of weariness, she never lost her temper, she never lost patience with a customer, even the tight-fisted farmer type who doled their money out with that reluctance found only in those who have wrung it from the soil.

In the midst of the rush she managed, somehow, never to fail to grasp the humor of a situation. A farmer woman came in for a doll's head, which she chose with incredible deliberation and pains. As it was being wrapped she explained that it was for her little girl, Minnie. She had promised the head this year. Next Christmas they would buy a body for it. Molly Brandeis's quick sympathy went out to the little girl who was to lavish her mother-love on a doll's head for a whole year. She saw the head, in ghastly decapitation, staring stiffly out from the cushions of the chill and funereal parlor sofa, and the small Minnie peering in to feast her eyes upon its blond and waxen beauty.

"Here," she had said, "take this, and sew it on the head, so Minnie'll have something she can hold, at least." And she had wrapped a pink cambric, sawdust-stuffed body in with the head.

It was a snowy and picturesque Christmas, and intensely cold, with the hard, dry, cutting cold of Wisconsin. Near the door the little store was freezing. Every time the door opened it let in a blast. Near the big glowing stove it was very hot.

The aisles were packed so that sometimes it was almost impossible to wedge one's way through. The china plates, stacked high, fairly melted away, as did the dolls piled on the counters. Mrs. Brandeis imported her china and dolls, and no store in Winnebago, not even Gerretson's big department store, could touch them for value.

The two women scarcely stopped to eat in the last ten days of the holiday rush. Often Annie, the girl who had taken Mattie's place in the household, would bring down their supper, hot and hot, and they would eat it quickly up in the little gallery where they kept the sleds, and doll buggies, and drums. At night (the store was open until ten or eleven at Christmas time) they would trudge home through the snow, so numb with weariness that they hardly minded the cold. The icy wind cut their foreheads like a knife, and made the temples ache. The snow, hard and resilient, squeaked beneath their heels. They would open the front door and stagger in, blinking. The house seemed so weirdly quiet and peaceful after the rush and clamor of the store.

"Don't you want a sandwich, Mother, with a glass of beer?"

"I'm too tired to eat it, Fanny. I just want to get to bed."

Fanny grew to hate the stock phrases that met her with each customer. "I want something for a little boy about ten. He's really got everything." Or, "I'm looking for a present for a lady friend. Do you think a plate would be nice?" She began to loathe them—these satiated little boys, these unknown friends, for whom she must rack her brains.

They cleared a snug little fortune that Christmas. On Christmas Eve they smiled wanly at each other, like two comrades who have fought and bled together, and won. When they left the store it was nearly midnight. Belated shoppers, bundle-laden, carrying holly wreaths, with strange handles, and painted heads, and sticks protruding from lumpy brown paper burdens, were hurrying home.

They stumbled home, too spent to talk. Fanny, groping for the keyhole, stubbed her toe against a wooden box between the storm door and the inner door. It had evidently been left there by the expressman or a delivery boy. It was a very heavy box.

"A Christmas present!" Fanny exclaimed. "Do you think it is? But it must be." She looked at the address, "Miss Fanny Brandeis." She went to the kitchen for a crowbar, and came back, still in her hat and coat. She pried open the box expertly, tore away the wrappings, and disclosed a gleaming leather-bound set of Balzac, and beneath that, incongruously enough, Mark Twain.

"Why!" exclaimed Fanny, sitting down on the floor rather heavily. Then her eye fell upon a card tossed aside in the hurry of unpacking. She picked it up, read it hastily. "Merry Christmas to the best daughter in the world. From her Mother."

Mrs. Brandeis had taken off her wraps and was standing over the sitting-room register, rubbing her numbed hands and smiling a little.

"Why, Mother!" Fanny scrambled to her feet. "You darling! In all that rush and work, to take time to think of me! Why—" Her arms were around her mother's shoulders. She was pressing her glowing cheek against the pale, cold one. And they both wept a little, from emotion, and weariness, and relief, and enjoyed it, as women sometimes do.

Fanny made her mother stay in bed next morning, a thing that Mrs. Brandeis took to most ungracefully. After the holiday rush and strain she invariably had a severe cold, the protest of the body she had over-driven and under-nourished for two or three weeks. As a patient she was as trying and fractious as a man, tossing about, threatening to get up, demanding hot-water bags, cold compresses, alcohol rubs. She fretted about the business, and imagined that things were at a stand-still during her absence.

Fanny herself rose early. Her healthy young body, after a night's sleep, was already recuperating from the month's strain. She had planned a real Christmas dinner, to banish the memory of the hasty and unpalatable lunches they had had to gulp during the rush. There was to be a turkey, and Fanny had warned Annie not to touch it. She wanted to stuff it and roast it herself. She spent the morning in the kitchen, aside from an occasional tip-toeing visit to her mother's room. At eleven she found her mother up, and no amount of coaxing would induce her to go back to bed. She had read the papers and she said she felt rested already.

The turkey came out a delicate golden-brown, and deliciously crackly. Fanny, looking up over a drumstick, noticed, with a shock, that her mother's eyes looked strangely sunken, and her skin, around the jaws and just under the chin, where her loose wrapper revealed her throat, was queerly yellow and shriveled. She had eaten almost nothing.

"Mother, you're not eating a thing! You really must eat a little."

Mrs. Brandeis began a pretense of using knife and fork, but gave it up finally and sat back, smiling rather wanly. "I guess I'm tireder than I thought I was, dear. I think I've got a cold coming on, too. I'll lie down again after dinner, and by to-morrow I'll be as chipper as a sparrow. The turkey's wonderful, isn't it? I'll have some, cold, for supper."

After dinner the house felt very warm and stuffy. It was crisply cold and sunny outdoors. The snow was piled high except on the sidewalks, where it had been neatly shoveled away by the mufflered Winnebago sons and fathers. There was no man in the Brandeis household, and Aloysius had been too busy to perform the chores usually considered his work about the house. The snow lay in drifts upon the sidewalk in front of the Brandeis house, except where passing feet had trampled it a bit.

"I'm going to shovel the walk," Fanny announced suddenly. "Way around to the woodshed. Where are those old mittens of mine? Annie, where's the snow shovel? Sure I am. Why not?"

She shoveled and scraped and pounded, bending rhythmically to the work, lifting each heaping shovelful with her strong young arms, tossing it to the side, digging in again, and under. An occasional neighbor passed by, or a friend, and she waved at them, gayly, and tossed back their badinage. "Merry Christmas!" she called, again and again, in reply to a passing acquaintance. "Same to you!"

At two o'clock Bella Weinberg telephoned to say that a little party of them were going to the river to skate. The ice was wonderful. Oh, come on! Fanny skated very well. But she hesitated. Mrs. Brandeis, dozing on the couch, sensed what was going on in her daughter's mind, and roused herself with something of her old asperity.

"Don't be foolish, child. Run along! You don't intend to sit here and gaze upon your sleeping beauty of a mother all afternoon, do you? Well, then!"

So Fanny changed her clothes, got her skates, and ran out into the snap and sparkle of the day. The winter darkness had settled down before she returned, all glowing and rosy, and bright-eyed. Her blood was racing through her body. Her lips were parted. The drudgery of the past three weeks seemed to have been blotted out by this one radiant afternoon.

The house was dark when she entered. It seemed very quiet, and close, and depressing after the sparkle and rush of the afternoon on the river. "Mother! Mother dear! Still sleeping?"

Mrs. Brandeis stirred, sighed, awoke. Fanny flicked on the light. Her mother was huddled in a kimono on the sofa. She sat up rather dazedly now, and stared at Fanny.

"Why—what time is it? What? Have I been sleeping all afternoon? Your mother's getting old."

She yawned, and in the midst of it caught her breath with a little cry of pain.

"What is it? What's the matter?"

Molly Brandeis pressed a hand to her breast. "A stitch, I guess. It's this miserable cold coming on. Is there any asperin in the house? I'll dose myself after supper, and take a hot foot bath and go to bed. I'm dead."

She ate less for supper than she had for dinner. She hardly tasted the cup of tea that Fanny insisted on making for her. She swayed a little as she sat, and her lids came down over her eyes, flutteringly, as if the weight of them was too great to keep up. At seven she was up-stairs, in bed, sleeping, and breathing heavily.

At eleven, or thereabouts, Fanny woke up with a start. She sat up in bed, wide-eyed, peering into the darkness and listening. Some one was talking in a high, queer voice, a voice like her mother's, and yet unlike. She ran, shivering with the cold, into her mother's bedroom. She switched on the light. Mrs. Brandeis was lying on the pillow, her eyes almost closed, except for a terrifying slit of white that showed between the lids. Her head was tossing to and fro on the pillow. She was talking, sometimes clearly, and sometimes mumblingly.

"One gross cups and saucers... and now what do you think you'd like for a second prize... in the basement, Aloysius... the trains... I'll see that they get there to-day... yours of the tenth at hand..."

"Mother! Mother! Molly dear!" She shook her gently, then almost roughly. The voice ceased. The eyes remained the same. "Oh, God!" She ran to the back of the house. "Annie! Annie, get up! Mother's sick. She's out of her head. I'm going to 'phone for the doctor. Go in with her."

She got the doctor at last. She tried to keep her voice under control, and thought, with a certain pride, that she was succeeding. She ran up-stairs again. The voice had begun again, but it seemed thicker now. She got into her clothes, shaking with cold and terror, and yet thinking very clearly, as she always did in a crisis. She put clean towels in the bathroom, pushed the table up to the bed, got a glass of water, straightened the covers, put away the clothes that the tired woman had left about the room. Doctor Hertz came. He went through the usual preliminaries, listened, tapped, counted, straightened up at last.

"Fresh air," he said. "Cold air. All the windows open." They rigged up a device of screens and sheets to protect the bed from the drafts. Fanny obeyed orders silently, like a soldier. But her eyes went from the face on the pillow to that of the man bent over the bed. Something vague, cold, clammy, seemed to be closing itself around her heart. It was like an icy hand, squeezing there. There had suddenly sprung up that indefinable atmosphere of the sick-room—a sick-room in which a fight is being waged. Bottles on the table, glasses, a spoon, a paper shade over the electric light globe.

"What is it?" said Fanny, at last. "Grip?—grip?"

Doctor Hertz hesitated a moment. "Pneumonia."

Fanny's hands grasped the footboard tightly. "Do you think we'd better have a nurse?"

"Yes."

The nurse seemed to be there, somehow, miraculously. And the morning came. And in the kitchen Annie went about her work, a little more quietly than usual. And yesterday seemed far away. It was afternoon; it was twilight. Doctor Hertz had been there for hours. The last time he brought another doctor with him—Thorn. Mrs. Brandeis was not talking now. But she was breathing. It filled the room, that breathing; it filled the house. Fanny took her mother's hand, that hand with the work-hardened palm and the broken nails. It was very cold. She looked down at it. The nails were blue. She began to rub it. She looked up into the faces of the two men. She picked up the other hand—snatched at it. "Look here!" she said. "Look here!" And then she stood up. The vague, clammy thing that had been wound about her heart suddenly relaxed. And at that something icy hot rushed all over her body and shook her. She came around to the foot of the bed, and gripped it with her two hands. Her chin was thrust forward, and her eyes were bright and staring. She looked very much like her mother, just then. It was a fighting face. A desperate face.

"Look here," she began, and was surprised to find that she was only whispering. She wet her lips and smiled, and tried again, forming the words carefully with her lips. "Look here. She's dying—isn't she? Isn't she! She's dying, isn't she?"

Doctor Hertz pursed his lips. The nurse came over to her, and put a hand on her shoulder. Fanny shook her off.

"Answer me. I've got a right to know. Look at this!" She reached forward and picked up that inert, cold, strangely shriveled blue hand again.

"My dear child—I'm afraid so."

There came from Fanny's throat a moan that began high, and poignant, and quavering, and ended in a shiver that seemed to die in her heart. The room was still again, except for the breathing, and even that was less raucous.

Fanny stared at the woman on the bed—at the long, finely-shaped head, with the black hair wadded up so carelessly now; at the long, straight, clever nose; the full, generous mouth. There flooded her whole being a great, blinding rage. What had she had of life? she demanded fiercely. What? What? Her teeth came together grindingly. She breathed heavily through her nostrils, as if she had been running. And suddenly she began to pray, not with the sounding, unctions thees and thous of the Church and Bible; not elegantly or eloquently, with well-rounded phrases, as the righteous pray, but threateningly, hoarsely, as a desperate woman prays. It was not a prayer so much as a cry of defiance——a challenge.

"Look here, God!" and there was nothing profane as she said it. "Look here, God! She's done her part. It's up to You now. Don't You let her die! Look at her. Look at her!" She choked and shook herself angrily, and went on. "Is that fair? That's a rotten trick to play on a woman that gave what she gave! What did she ever have of life? Nothing! That little miserable, dirty store, and those little miserable, dirty people. You give her a chance, d'You hear? You give her a chance, God, or I'll——"

Her voice broke in a thin, cracked quaver. The nurse turned her around, suddenly and sharply, and led her from the room.

CHAPTER EIGHT

"You can come down now. They're all here, I guess. Doctor Thalmann's going to begin." Fanny, huddled in a chair in her bedroom, looked up into the plump, kindly face of the woman who was bending over her. Then she stood up, docilely, and walked toward the stairs with a heavy, stumbling step.

"I'd put down my veil if I were you," said the neighbor woman. And reached up for the black folds that draped Fanny's hat. Fanny's fingers reached for them too, fumblingly. "I'd forgotten about it," she said. The heavy crape fell about her shoulders, mercifully hiding the swollen, discolored face. She went down the stairs. There was a little stir, a swaying toward her, a sibilant murmur of sympathy from the crowded sitting-room as she passed through to the parlor where Rabbi Thalmann stood waiting, prayer book in hand, in front of that which was covered with flowers. Fanny sat down. A feeling of unreality was strong upon her. Doctor Thalmann cleared his throat and opened the book.

After all, it was not Rabbi Thalmann's funeral sermon that testified to Mrs. Brandeis's standing in the community. It was the character of the gathering that listened to what he had to say. Each had his own opinion of

Molly Brandeis, and needed no final eulogy to confirm it. Father Fitzpatrick was there, tall, handsome, ruddy, the two wings of white showing at the temples making him look more than ever like a leading man. He had been of those who had sat in what he called Mrs. Brandeis's confessional, there in the quiet little store. The two had talked of things theological and things earthy. His wit, quick though it was, was no match for hers, but they both had a humor sense and a drama sense, and one day they discovered, queerly enough, that they worshiped the same God. Any one of these things is basis enough for a friendship. Besides, Molly Brandeis could tell an Irish story inimitably. And you should have heard Father Fitzpatrick do the one about Ikey and the nickel. No, I think the Catholic priest, seeming to listen with such respectful attention, really heard very little of what Rabbi Thalmann had to say.

Herman Walthers was there, he of the First National Bank of Winnebago, whose visits had once brought such terror to Molly Brandeis. Augustus G. Gerretson was there, and three of his department heads. Emil Bauer sat just behind him. In a corner was Sadie, the erstwhile coquette, very subdued now, and months behind the fashions in everything but baby clothes. Hen Cody, who had done all of Molly Brandeis's draying, sat, in unaccustomed black, next to Mayor A. J. Dawes. Temple Emmanu-el was there, almost a unit. The officers of Temple Emanu-el Ladies' Aid Society sat in a row. They had never honored Molly Brandeis with office in the society—she who could have managed its business, politics and social activities with one hand tied behind her, and both her bright eyes shut. In the kitchen and on the porch and in the hallway stood certain obscure people—women whose finger tips stuck out of their cotton gloves, and whose skirts dipped ludicrously in the back. Only Molly Brandeis could have identified them for you. Mrs. Brosch, the butter and egg woman, hovered in the dining-room doorway. She had brought a pound of butter. It was her contribution to the funeral baked meats. She had deposited it furtively on the kitchen table. Birdie Callahan, head waitress at the Haley House, found a seat just next to the elegant Mrs. Morehouse, who led the Golf Club crowd. A haughty young lady in the dining-room, Birdie Callahan, in her stiffly starched white, but beneath the icy crust of her hauteur was a molten mass of good humor and friendliness. She and Molly Brandeis had had much in common.

But no one—not even Fanny Brandeis—ever knew who sent the great cluster of American Beauty roses that had come all the way from Milwaukee. There had been no card, so who could have guessed that they came from Blanche Devine. Blanche Devine, of the white powder, and the minks, and the diamonds, and the high-heeled shoes, and the plumes, lived in the house with the closed shutters, near the freight depot. She often came into Brandeis' Bazaar. Molly Brandeis had never allowed Sadie, or Pearl, or Fanny or Aloysius to wait on her. She had attended to her herself. And one day, for some reason, Blanche Devine found herself telling Molly Brandeis how she had come to be Blanche Devine, and it was a moving and terrible story. And now her cardless flowers, a great, scarlet sheaf of them, lay next the chaste white roses that had been sent by the Temple Emanu-el Ladies' Aid. Truly, death is a great leveler.

In a vague way Fanny seemed to realize that all these people were there. I think she must even have found a certain grim comfort in their presence. Hers had not been the dry-eyed grief of the strong, such as you read about. She had wept, night and day, hopelessly, inconsolably, torturing herself with remorseful questions. If she had not gone skating, might she not have seen how ill her mother was? Why hadn't she insisted on the doctor when her mother refused to eat the Christmas dinner? Blind and selfish, she told herself; blind and selfish. Her face was swollen and distorted now, and she was thankful for the black veil that shielded her. Winnebago was scandalized to see that she wore no other black. Mrs. Brandeis had never wanted Fanny to wear it; she hadn't enough color, she said. So now she was dressed in her winter suit of blue, and her hat with the pert blue quill. And the little rabbi's voice went on and on, and Fanny knew that it could not be true. What had all this dust-to-dust talk to do with any one as vital, and electric, and constructive as Molly Brandeis. In the midst of the service there was a sharp cry, and a little stir, and the sound of stifled sobbing. It was Aloysius the merry, Aloysius the faithful, whose Irish heart was quite broken. Fanny ground her teeth together in an effort at self-control.

And so to the end, and out past the little hushed, respectful group on the porch, to the Jewish cemetery on the state road. The snow of Christmas week was quite virgin there, except for that one spot where the sexton and his men had been at work. Then back at a smart jog trot through the early dusk of the winter afternoon, the carriage wheels creaking upon the hard, dry snow. And Fanny Brandeis said to herself (she must have been a little light-headed from hunger and weeping):

"Now I'll know whether it's true or not. When I go into the house. If she's there she'll say, `Well Fanchen! Hungry? Oh, but my little girl's hands are cold! Come here to the register and warm them.' O God, let her be there! Let her be there!"

But she wasn't. The house had been set to rights by brisk and unaccustomed hands. There was a bustle and stir in the dining-room, and from the kitchen came the appetizing odors of cooking food. Fanny went up to a chair that was out of its place, and shoved it back against the wall where it belonged. She straightened a rug, carried the waste basket from the desk to the spot near the living-room table where it had always served to hide the shabby, worn place in the rug. Fanny went up-stairs, past The Room that was once more just a comfortable, old fashioned bedroom, instead of a mysterious and awful chamber; bathed her face, tidied her hair, came down-stairs again, ate and drank things hot and revivifying. The house was full of kindly women.

Fanny found herself clinging to them—clinging desperately to these ample, broad-bosomed, soothing women whom she had scarcely known before. They were always there, those women, and their husbands too; kindly, awkward men, who patted her shoulder, and who spoke of Molly Brandeis with that sincerity of admiration such as men usually give only to men. People were constantly popping in at the back door with napkin-covered trays, and dishes and baskets. A wonderful and beautiful thing, that homely small-town sympathy that knows the value of physical comfort in time of spiritual anguish.

Two days after the funeral Fanny Brandeis went back to the store, much as her mother had done many years before, after her husband's death. She looked about at the bright, well-stocked shelves and tables with a new eye—a speculative eye. The Christmas season was over. January was the time for inventory and for replenishment. Mrs. Brandeis had always gone to Chicago the second week in January for the spring stock. But something was forming in Fanny Brandeis's mind—a resolve that grew so rapidly as to take her breath away. Her brain felt strangely clear and keen after the crashing storm of grief that had shaken her during the past week.

"What are you going to do now?" people had asked her, curious and interested. "Is Theodore coming back?"

"I don't know—yet." In answer to the first. And, "No. Why should he? He has his work."

"But he could be of such help to you."

"I'll help myself," said Fanny Brandeis, and smiled a curious smile that had in it more of bitterness and less of mirth than any smile has a right to have.

Mrs. Brandeis had left a will, far-sighted business woman that she was. It was a terse, clear-headed document, that gave "to Fanny Brandeis, my daughter," the six-thousand-dollar insurance, the stock, good-will and fixtures of Brandeis' Bazaar, the house furnishings, the few pieces of jewelry in their old-fashioned setting. To Theodore was left the sum of fifteen hundred dollars. He had received his share in the years of his musical education.

Fanny Brandeis did not go to Chicago that January. She took inventory of Brandeis' Bazaar, carefully and minutely. And then, just as carefully and minutely she took stock of Fanny Brandeis. There was something relentless and terrible in the way she went about this self-analysis. She walked a great deal that winter, often out through the drifts to the little cemetery. As she walked her mind was working, working. She held long mental conversations with herself during these walks, and once she was rather frightened to find herself talking aloud. She wondered if she had done that before. And a plan was maturing in her brain, while the fight went on within herself, thus:

"You'll never do it, Fanny. You're not built that way."

"Oh, won't I! Watch me! Give me time."

"You'll think of what your mother would have done under the same conditions, and you'll do that thing."

"I won't. Not unless it's the long-headed thing to do. I'm through being sentimental and unselfish. What did it bring her? Nothing!"

The weeks went by. Fanny worked hard in the store, and bought little. February came, and with the spring her months of private thinking bore fruit. There came to Fanny Brandeis a great resolve. She would put herself in a high place. Every talent she possessed, every advantage, every scrap of knowledge, every bit of experience, would be used toward that end. She would make something of herself. It was a worldly, selfish resolve, born of a bitter sorrow, and ambition, and resentment. She made up her mind that she would admit no handicaps. Race, religion, training, natural impulses—she would discard them all if they stood in her way. She would leave Winnebago behind. At best, if she stayed there, she could never accomplish more than to make her business a more than ordinarily successful small-town store. And she would be—nobody. No, she had had enough of that. She would crush and destroy the little girl who had fasted on that Day of Atonement; the more mature girl who had written the thesis about the paper mill rag-room; the young woman who had drudged in the store on Elm Street. In her place she would mold a hard, keen-eyed, resolute woman, whose godhead was to be success, and to whom success would mean money and position. She had not a head for mathematics, but out of the puzzling problems and syllogisms in geometry she had retained in her memory this one immovable truth:

A straight line is the shortest distance between two points.

With her mental eye she marked her two points, and then, starting from the first, made directly for the second. But she forgot to reckon with the law of tangents. She forgot, too, how paradoxical a creature was this Fanny Brandeis whose eyes filled with tears at sight of a parade—just the sheer drama of it—were the marchers G. A. R. veterans, school children in white, soldiers, Foresters, political marching clubs; and whose eyes burned dry and bright as she stood over the white mound in the cemetery on the state road. Generous, spontaneous, impulsive, warm-hearted, she would be cold, calculating, deliberate, she told herself.

Thousands of years of persecution behind her made her quick to appreciate suffering in others, and gave her an innate sense of fellowship with the downtrodden. She resolved to use that sense as a searchlight aiding her to see and overcome obstacles. She told herself that she was done with maudlin sentimentality. On the rare occasions when she had accompanied her mother to Chicago, the two women had found delight in wandering about the city's foreign quarters. When other small-town women buyers snatched occasional moments of leisure for the theater or personal shopping, these two had spent hours in the ghetto around Jefferson and Taylor, and Fourteenth Streets. Something in the sight of these people—alien, hopeful, emotional, often grotesque—thrilled and interested both the women. And at sight of an ill-clad Italian, with his slovenly, wrinkled old-young wife, turning the handle of his grind organ whilst both pairs of eyes searched windows and porches and doorsteps with a hopeless sort of hopefulness, she lost her head entirely and emptied her limp pocketbook of dimes, and nickels, and pennies. Incidentally it might be stated that she loved the cheap and florid music of the hand organ itself.

It was rumored that Brandeis' Bazaar was for sale. In the spring Gerretson's offered Fanny the position of buyer and head of the china, glassware, and kitchenware sections. Gerretson's showed an imposing block of gleaming plate-glass front now, and drew custom from a dozen thrifty little towns throughout the Fox River Valley. Fanny refused the offer. In March she sold outright the stock, good-will, and fixtures of Brandeis' Bazaar. The purchaser was a thrifty, farsighted traveling man who had wearied of the road and wanted to settle down. She sold the household goods too—those intimate, personal pieces of wood and cloth that had become, somehow, part of her life. She had grown up with them. She knew the history of every nick, every scratch and worn spot. Her mother lived again in every piece. The old couch went off in a farmer's wagon. Fanny turned away when they joggled it down the front steps and into the rude vehicle. It was like another funeral. She was furious to find herself weeping again. She promised herself punishment for that.

Up in her bedroom she opened the bottom drawer of her bureau. That bureau and its history and the history of every piece of furniture in the room bore mute testimony to the character of its occupant; to her protest against things as she found them, and her determination to make them over to suit her. She had spent innumerable Sunday mornings wielding the magic paint brush that had transformed the bedroom from dingy oak to gleaming cream enamel. She sat down on the floor now, before the bureau, and opened the bottom drawer.

In a corner at the back, under the neat pile of garments, was a tightly-rolled bundle of cloth. Fanny reached for it, took it out, and held it in her hands a moment. Then she unrolled it slowly, and the bundle revealed itself to be a faded, stained, voluminous gingham apron, blue and white. It was the kind of apron women don when they perform some very special household ritual—baking, preserving, house cleaning. It crossed over the shoulders with straps, and its generous fullness ran all the way around the waist. It was discolored in many places with the brown and reddish stains of fruit juices. It had been Molly Brandeis' canning apron. Fanny had come upon it hanging on a hook behind the kitchen door, after that week in December. And at sight of it all her fortitude and forced calm had fled. She had spread her arms over the limp, mute, yet speaking thing dangling there, and had wept so wildly and uncontrollably as to alarm even herself.

Nothing in connection with her mother's death had power to call up such poignant memories as did this homely, intimate garment. She saw again the steamy kitchen, deliciously scented with the perfume of cooking fruit, or the tantalizing, mouth-watering spiciness of vinegar and pickles. On the stove the big dishpan, in which the jelly glasses and fruit jars, with their tops and rubbers, bobbed about in hot water. In the great granite kettle simmered the cooking fruit Molly Brandeis, enveloped in the familiar blue-and-white apron, stood over it, like a priestess, stirring, stirring, slowly, rhythmically. Her face would be hot and moist with the steam, and very tired too, for she often came home from the store utterly weary, to stand over the kettle until ten or eleven o'clock. But the pride in it as she counted the golden or ruby tinted tumblers gleaming in orderly rows as they cooled on the kitchen table!

"Fifteen glasses of grape jell, Fan! And I didn't mix a bit of apple with it. I didn't think I'd get more than ten. And nine of the quince preserve. That makes—let me see—eighty-three, ninety-eight—one hundred and seven altogether."

"We'll never eat it, Mother."

"You said that last year, and by April my preserve cupboard looked like Old Mother Hubbard's."

But then, Mrs. Brandeis was famous for her preserves, as Father Fitzpatrick, and Aloysius, and Doctor Thalmann, and a dozen others could testify. After the strain and flurry of a busy day at the store there was something about this homely household rite that brought a certain sense of rest and peace to Molly Brandeis.

All this moved through Fanny Brandeis's mind as she sat with the crumpled apron in her lap, her eyes swimming with hot tears. The very stains that discolored it, the faded blue of the front breadth, the frayed buttonhole, the little scorched place where she had burned a hole when trying unwisely to lift a steaming kettle from the stove with the apron's corner, spoke to her with eloquent lips. That apron had become a vice with Fanny. She brooded over it as a mother broods over the shapeless, scuffled bit of leather that was a baby's shoe; as a woman, widowed, clings to a shabby, frayed old smoking jacket. More than once she had cried herself to sleep with the apron clasped tightly in her arms.

She got up from the floor now, with the apron in her hands, and went down the stairs, opened the door that led to the cellar, walked heavily down those steps and over to the furnace. She flung open the furnace door. Red and purple the coal bed gleamed, with little white flame sprites dancing over it. Fanny stared at it a moment, fascinated. Her face was set, her eyes brilliant. Suddenly she flung the tightly-rolled apron into the heart of the gleaming mass. She shut her eyes then. The fire seemed to hold its breath for a moment. Then, with a gasp, it sprang upon its food. The bundle stiffened, writhed, crumpled, sank, lay a blackened heap, was dissolved. The fire bed glowed red and purple as before, except for a dark spot in its heart. Fanny shivered a little. She shut the furnace door and went upstairs again.

"Smells like something burning—cloth, or something," called Annie, from the kitchen.

"It's only an old apron that was cluttering up my—my bureau drawer."

Thus she successfully demonstrated the first lesson in the cruel and rigid course of mental training she had mapped out for herself.

Leaving Winnebago was not easy. There is something about a small town that holds you. Your life is so intimately interwoven with that of your neighbor. Existence is so safe, so sane, so sure. Fanny knew that when she turned the corner of Elm Street every third person she met would speak to her. Life was made up of minute details, too trivial for the notice of the hurrying city crowds. You knew when Milly Glaenzer changed the baby buggy for a go-cart. The youngest Hupp boy—Sammy—who was graduated from High School in June, is driving A. J. Dawes's automobile now. My goodness, how time flies! Doeppler's grocery has put in plate-glass windows, and they're getting out-of-season vegetables every day now from Milwaukee. As you pass you get the coral glow of tomatoes, and the tender green of lettuces. And that vivid green? Fresh young peas! And in February. Well! They've torn down the old yellow brick National Bank, and in its place a chaste Greek Temple of a building looks rather contemptuously down its classic columns upon the farmer's wagons drawn up along the curb. If Fanny Brandeis' sense of proportion had not been out of plumb she might have realized that, to Winnebago, the new First National Bank building was as significant and epochal as had been the Woolworth Building to New York.

The very intimacy of these details, Fanny argued, was another reason for leaving Winnebago. They were like detaining fingers that grasped at your skirts, impeding your progress.

She had early set about pulling every wire within her reach that might lead, directly or indirectly, to the furtherance of her ambition. She got two offers from Milwaukee retail stores. She did not consider them for a moment. Even a Chicago department store of the second grade (one of those on the wrong side of State Street) did not tempt her. She knew her value. She could afford to wait. There was money enough on which to live comfortably until the right chance presented itself. She knew every item of her equipment, and she conned them to herself greedily: Definite charm of manner; the thing that is called magnetism; brains; imagination; driving force; health; youth; and, most precious of all, that which money could not buy, nor education provide—experience. Experience, a priceless weapon, that is beaten into shape only by much contact with men and women, and that is sharpened by much rubbing against the rough edges of this world.

In April her chance came to her; came in that accidental, haphazard way that momentous happenings have. She met on Elm Street a traveling man from whom Molly Brandeis had bought for years. He dropped both sample cases and shook hands with Fanny, eying her expertly and approvingly, and yet without insolence. He was a wise, road-weary, skillful member of his fraternity, grown gray in years of service, and a little bitter. Though perhaps that was due partly to traveling man's dyspepsia, brought on by years of small-town hotel food.

"So you've sold out."

"Yes. Over a month ago."

"H'm. That was a nice little business you had there. Your ma built it up herself. There was a woman! Gosh! Discounted her bills, even during the panic."

Fanny smiled a reflective little smile. "That line is a complete characterization of my mother. Her life was a series of panics. But she never lost her head. And she always discounted."

He held out his hand. "Well, glad I met you." He picked up his sample cases. "You leaving Winnebago?"

"Yes."

"Going to the city, I suppose. Well you're a smart girl. And your mother's daughter. I guess you'll get along all right. What house are you going with?"

"I don't know. I'm waiting for the right chance. It's all in starting right. I'm not going to hurry."

He put down his cases again, and his eyes grew keen and kindly. He gesticulated with one broad forefinger. "Listen, m' girl. I'm what they call an old-timer. They want these high-power, eight-cylinder kids on the road these days, and it's all we can do to keep up. But I've got something they haven't got—yet. I never read anybody on the Psychology of Business, but I know human nature all the way from Elm Street, Winnebago, to Fifth Avenue, New York."

"I'm sure you do," said Fanny politely, and took a little step forward, as though to end the conversation.

"Now wait a minute. They say the way to learn is to make mistakes. If that's true, I'm at the head of the class. I've made 'em all. Now get this. You start out and specialize. Specialize! Tie to one thing, and make yourself an expert in it. But first be sure it's the right thing."

"But how is one to be sure?"

"By squinting up your eyes so you can see ten years ahead. If it looks good to you at that distance—better, in fact, than it does close by—then it's right. I suppose that's what they call having imagination. I never had any. That's why I'm still selling goods on the road. To look at you I'd say you had too much. Maybe I'm wrong. But I never yet saw a woman with a mouth like yours who was cut out for business—unless it was your mother—And her eyes were different. Let's see, what was I saying?"

"Specialize."

"Oh, yes. And that reminds me. Bunch of fellows in the smoker last night talking about Haynes-Cooper. Your mother hated 'em like poison, the way every small-town merchant hates the mail-order houses. But I hear they've got an infants' wear department that's just going to grass for lack of a proper head. You're only a kid. And they have done you dirt all these years, of course. But if you could sort of horn in there—why, say, there's no limit to the distance you could go. No limit! With your brains and experience."

That had been the beginning. From then on the thing had moved forward with a certain inevitableness. There was something about the vastness of the thing that appealed to Fanny. Here was an organization whose great arms embraced the world. Haynes-Cooper, giant among mail-order houses, was said to eat a small-town merchant every morning for breakfast.

"There's a Haynes-Cooper catalogue in every farmer's kitchen," Molly Brandeis used to say. "The Bible's in the parlor, but they keep the H. C. book in the room where they live."

That she was about to affiliate herself with this house appealed to Fanny Brandeis's sense of comedy. She had heard her mother presenting her arguments to the stubborn farmer folk who insisted on ordering their stove, or dinner set, or plow, or kitchen goods from the fascinating catalogue. "I honestly think it's just the craving for excitement that makes them do it," she often said. "They want the thrill they get when they receive a box from Chicago, and open it, and take off the wrappings, and dig out the thing they ordered from a picture, not knowing whether it will be right or wrong."

Her arguments usually left the farmer unmoved. He would drive into town, mail his painfully written letter and order at the post-office, dispose of his load of apples, or butter, or cheese, or vegetables, and drive cheerfully back again, his empty wagon bumping and rattling down the old corduroy road. Express, breakage, risk, loyalty to his own region—an these arguments left him cold.

In May, after much manipulation, correspondence, two interviews, came a definite offer from the Haynes-Cooper Company. It was much less than the State Street store had offered, and there was something tentative about the whole agreement. Haynes-Cooper proffered little and demanded much, as is the way of the rich and mighty. But Fanny remembered the ten-year viewpoint that the weary-wise old traveling man had spoken about. She took their offer. She was to go to Chicago almost at once, to begin work June first.

Two conversations that took place before she left are perhaps worth recording. One was with Father Fitzpatrick of St. Ignatius Catholic Church. The other with Rabbi Emil Thalmann of Temple Emanu-el.

An impulse brought her into Father Fitzpatrick's study. It was a week before her departure. She was tired. There had been much last signing of papers, nailing of boxes, strapping of trunks. When things began to come too thick and fast for her she put on her hat and went for a walk at the close of the May day. May, in Wisconsin, is a thing all fragrant, and gold, and blue; and white with cherry blossoms; and pink with apple blossoms; and tremulous with budding things.

Fanny struck out westward through the neat streets of the little town, and found herself on the bridge over the ravine in which she had played when a little girl—the ravine that her childish imagination had peopled with such pageantry of redskin, and priests, and voyageurs, and cavaliers. She leaned over the iron railing and looked down. Where grass, and brook, and wild flower had been there now oozed great eruptions of ash heaps, tin cans, broken bottles, mounds of dirt. Winnebago's growing pains had begun. Fanny turned away with a little sick feeling. She went on across the bridge past the Catholic church. Just next the church was the parish house where Father Fitzpatrick lived. It always looked as if it had been scrubbed, inside and out, with a scouring brick. Its windows were a reproach and a challenge to every housekeeper in Winnebago.

Fanny wanted to talk to somebody about that ravine. She was full of it. Father Fitzpatrick's study over-looked it. Besides, she wanted to see him before she left Winnebago. A picture came to her mind of his handsome, ruddy face, twinkling with humor as she had last seen it when he had dropped in at Brandeis' Bazaar for a chat with her mother. She turned in at the gate and ran up the immaculate, gray-painted steps, that always gleamed as though still wet with the paint brush.

"I shouldn't wonder if that housekeeper of his comes out with a pail of paint and does 'em every morning before breakfast," Fanny said to herself as she rang the bell.

Usually it was that sparse and spectacled person herself who opened the parish house door, but to-day Fanny's ring was answered by Father Casey, parish assistant. A sour-faced and suspicious young man, Father Casey, thick-spectacled, and pointed of nose. Nothing of the jolly priest about him. He was new to the town, but he recognized Fanny and surveyed her darkly.

"Father Fitzpatrick in? I'm Fanny Brandeis."

"The reverend father is busy," and the glass door began to close.

"Who is it?" boomed a voice from within. "Who're you turning away, Casey?"

"A woman, not a parishioner." The door was almost shut now.

Footsteps down the hall. "Good! Let her in." The door opened ever so reluctantly. Father Fitzpatrick loomed up beside his puny assistant, dwarfing him. He looked sharply at the figure on the porch. "For the love of—! Casey, you're a fool! How you ever got beyond being an altar-boy is more than I can see. Come in, child. Come in! The man's cut out for a jailor, not a priest."

Fanny's two hands were caught in one of his big ones, and she was led down the hall to the study. It was the room of a scholar and a man, and the one spot in the house that defied the housekeeper's weapons of broom and duster. A comfortable and disreputable room, full of books, and fishing tackle, and chairs with sagging springs, and a sofa that was dented with friendly hollows. Pipes on the disorderly desk. A copy of "Mr. Dooley" spread face down on what appeared to be next Sunday's sermon, rough-drafted.

"I just wanted to talk to you." Fanny drifted to the shelves, book-lover that she was, and ran a finger over a half-dozen titles. "Your assistant was justified, really, in closing the door on me. But I'm glad you rescued me." She came over to him and stood looking up at him. He seemed to loom up endlessly, though hers was a medium height. "I think I really wanted to talk to you about that ravine, though I came to say good-by."

"Sit down, child, sit down!" He creaked into his great leather-upholstered desk chair, himself. "If you had left without seeing me I'd have excommunicated Casey. Between you and me the man's mad. His job ought to be duenna to a Spanish maiden, not assistant to a priest with a leaning toward the flesh."

Now, Father Fitzpatrick talked with a—no, you couldn't call it a brogue. It was nothing so gross as that. One does not speak of the flavor of a rare wine; one calls attention to its bouquet. A subtle, teasing, elusive something that just tickles the senses instead of punching them in the ribs. So his speech was permeated with a will-o'-the-wisp, a tingling richness that evaded definition. You will have to imagine it. There shall be no vain attempt to set it down. Besides, you always skip dialect.

"So you're going away. I'd heard. Where to?"

"Chicago, Haynes-Cooper. It's a wonderful chance. I don't see yet how I got it. There's only one other woman on their business staff—I mean working actually in an executive way in the buying and selling end of the business. Of course there are thousands doing clerical work, and that kind of thing. Have you ever been through the plant? It's—it's incredible."

Father Fitzpatrick drummed with his fingers on the arm of his chair, and looked at Fanny, his handsome eyes half shut.

"So it's going to be business, h'm? Well, I suppose it's only natural. Your mother and I used to talk about you often. I don't know if you and she ever spoke seriously of this little trick of drawing, or cartooning, or whatever it is you have. She used to think about it. She said once to me, that it looked to her more than just a knack. An authentic gift of caricature, she called it—if it could only be developed. But of course Theodore took everything. That worried her."

"Oh, nonsense! That! I just amuse myself with it."

"Yes. But what amuses you might amuse other people. There's all too few amusing things in the world. Your mother was a smart woman, Fanny. The smartest I ever knew."

"There's no money in it, even if I were to get on with it. What could I do with it? Who ever heard of a woman cartoonist! And I couldn't illustrate. Those pink cheesecloth pictures the magazines use. I want to earn money. Lots of it. And now."

She got up and went to the window, and stood looking down the steep green slope of the ravine that lay, a natural amphitheater, just below.

"Money, h'm?" mused Father Fitzpatrick. "Well, it's popular and handy. And you look to me like the kind of girl who'd get it, once you started out for it. I've never had much myself. They say it has a way of turning to dust and ashes in the mouth, once you get a good, satisfying bite of it. But that's only talk, I suppose."

Fanny laughed a little, still looking down at the ravine. "I'm fairly accustomed to dust and ashes by this time. It won't be a new taste to me." She whirled around suddenly. "And speaking of dust and ashes, isn't this a shame? A crime? Why doesn't somebody stop it? Why don't you stop it?" She pointed to the desecrated ravine below. Her eyes were blazing, her face all animation.

Father Fitzpatrick came over and stood beside her. His face was sad. "It's a—" He stopped abruptly, and looked down into her glowing face. He cleared his throat. "It's a perfectly natural state of affairs," he said smoothly. "Winnebago's growing. Especially over there on the west side, since the new mill went up, and they've extended the street car line. They need the land to build on. It's business. And money."

"Business! It's a crime! It's wanton! Those ravines are the most beautiful natural spots in Wisconsin. Why, they're history, and romance, and beauty!"

"So that's the way you feel about it?"

"Of course. Don't you? Can't you stop it? Petitions—"

"Certainly I feel it's an outrage. But I'm just a poor fool of a priest, and sentimental, with no head for business. Now you're a business woman, and different."

"I! You're joking."

"Say, listen, m' girl. The world's made up of just two things: ravines and dump heaps. And the dumpers are forever edging up, and squeedging up, and trying to grab the ravines and spoil 'em, when nobody's looking. You've made your choice, and allied yourself with the dump heaps. What right have you to cry out against the desecration of the ravines?"

"The right that every one has that loves them."

"Child, you're going to get so used to seeing your ravines choked up at Haynes-Cooper that after a while you'll prefer 'em that way."

Fanny turned on him passionately. "I won't! And if I do, perhaps it's just as well. There's such a thing as too much ravine. What do you want me to do? Stay here, and grub away, and become a crabbed old maid like Irma

Klein, thankful to be taken around by the married crowd, joining the Aid Society and going to the card parties on Sunday nights? Or I could marry a traveling man, perhaps, or Lee Kohn of the Golden Eagle. I'm just like any other ambitious woman with brains—"

"No you're not. You're different. And I'll tell you why. You're a Jew."

"Yes, I've got that handicap."

"That isn't a handicap, Fanny. It's an asset. Outwardly you're like any other girl of your age. Inwardly you've been molded by occupation, training, religion, history, temperament, race, into something—"

"Ethnologists have proved that there is no such thing as a Jewish race," she interrupted pertly.

"H'm. Maybe. I don't know what you'd call it, then. You can't take a people and persecute them for thousands of years, hounding them from place to place, herding them in dark and filthy streets, without leaving some sort of brand on them—a mark that differentiates. Sometimes it doesn't show outwardly. But it's there, inside. You know, Fanny, how it's always been said that no artist can became a genius until he has suffered. You've suffered, you Jews, for centuries and centuries, until you're all artists—quick to see drama because you've lived in it, emotional, oversensitive, cringing, or swaggering, high-strung, demonstrative, affectionate, generous.

"Maybe they're right. Perhaps it isn't a race. But what do you call the thing, then, that made you draw me as you did that morning when you came to ten o'clock mass and did a caricature of me in the pulpit. You showed up something that I've been trying to hide for twenty years, till I'd fooled everybody, including myself. My church is always packed. Nobody else there ever saw it. I'll tell you, Fanny, what I've always said: the Irish would be the greatest people in the world—if it weren't for the Jews."

They laughed together at that, and the tension was relieved.

"Well, anyway," said Fanny, and patted his great arm, "I'd rather talk to you than to any man in the world."

"I hope you won't be able to say that a year from now, dear girl."

And so they parted. He took her to the door himself, and watched her slim figure down the street and across the ravine bridge, and thought she walked very much like her mother, shoulders squared, chin high, hips firm. He went back into the house, after surveying the sunset largely, and encountered the dour Casey in the hall.

"I'll type your sermon now, sir—if it's done."

"It isn't done, Casey. And you know it. Oh, Casey,"—(I wish your imagination would supply that brogue, because it was such a deliciously soft and racy thing)—"Oh, Casey, Casey! you're a better priest than I am—but a poorer man."

Fanny was to leave Winnebago the following Saturday. She had sold the last of the household furniture, and had taken a room at the Haley House. She felt very old and experienced—and sad. That, she told herself, was only natural. Leaving things to which one is accustomed is always hard. Queerly enough, it was her good-by to Aloysius that most unnerved her. Aloysius had been taken on at Gerretson's, and the dignity of his new position sat heavily upon him. You should have seen his ties. Fanny sought him out at Gerretson's.

"It's flure-manager of the basement I am," he said, and struck an elegant attitude against the case of misses'-ready-to-wear coats. "And when you come back to Winnebago, Miss Fanny,—and the saints send it be soon—I'll bet ye'll see me on th' first flure, keepin' a stern but kindly eye on the swellest trade in town. Ev'ry last thing I know I learned off yur poor ma."

"I hope it will serve you here, Aloysius."

"Sarve me!" He bent closer. "Meanin' no offense, Miss Fanny; but say, listen: Oncet ye get a Yiddish business education into an Irish head, and there's no limit to the length ye can go. If I ain't a dry-goods king be th' time I'm thirty I hope a packin' case'll fall on me."

The sight of Aloysius seemed to recall so vividly all that was happy and all that was hateful about Brandeis' Bazaar; all the bravery and pluck, and resourcefulness of the bright-eyed woman he had admiringly called his boss, that Fanny found her self-control slipping. She put out her hand rather blindly to meet his great red paw (a dressy striped cuff seemed to make it all the redder), murmured a word of thanks in return for his fervent good wishes, and fled up the basement stairs.

On Friday night (she was to leave next day) she went to the temple. The evening service began at seven. At half past six Fanny had finished her early supper. She would drop in at Doctor Thalmann's house and walk with him to temple, if he had not already gone.

"Nein, der Herr Rabbi ist noch hier—sure," the maid said in answer to Fanny's question. The Thalmann's had a German maid—one Minna—who bullied the invalid Mrs. Thalmann, was famous for her cookies with walnuts on the top, and who made life exceedingly difficult for unlinguistic callers.

Rabbi Thalmann was up in his study. Fanny ran lightly up the stairs.

"Who is it, Emil? That Minna! Next Monday her week is up. She goes."

"It's I, Mrs. Thalmann. Fanny Brandeis."

"Na, Fanny! Now what do you think!"

In the brightly-lighted doorway of his little study appeared Rabbi Thalmann, on one foot a comfortable old romeo, on the other a street shoe. He held out both hands. "Only at supper we talked about you. Isn't that so, Harriet?" He called into the darkened room.

"I came to say good-by. And I thought we might walk to temple together. How's Mrs. Thalmann tonight?"

The little rabbi shook his head darkly, and waved a dismal hand. But that was for Fanny alone. What he said was: "She's really splendid to-day. A little tired, perhaps; but what is that?"

"Emil!" from the darkened bedroom. "How can you say that? But how! What I have suffered to-day, only! Torture! And because I say nothing I'm not sick."

"Go in," said Rabbi Thalmann.

So Fanny went in to the woman lying, yellow-faced, on the pillows of the dim old-fashioned bedroom with its walnut furniture, and its red plush mantel drape. Mrs. Thalmann held out a hand. Fanny took it in hers, and perched herself on the edge of the bed. She patted the dry, devitalized hand, and pressed it in her own strong, electric grip. Mrs. Thalmann raised her head from the pillow.

"Tell me, did she have her white apron on?"

"White apron?"

"Minna, the girl."

"Oh!" Fanny's mind jerked back to the gingham-covered figure that had opened the door for her. "Yes," she lied, "a white one—with crochet around the bottom. Quite grand."

Mrs. Thalmann sank back on the pillow with a satisfied sigh. "A wonder." She shook her head. "What that girl wastes alone, when I am helpless here."

Rabbi Thalmann came into the room, both feet booted now, and placed his slippers neatly, toes out, under the bed. "Ach, Harriet, the girl is all right. You imagine. Come, Fanny." He took a great, fat watch out of his pocket. "It is time to go."

Mrs. Thalmann laid a detaining hand on Fanny's arm. "You will come often back here to Winnebago?"

"I'm afraid not. Once a year, perhaps, to visit my graves."

The sick eyes regarded the fresh young face. "Your mother, Fanny, we didn't understand her so well, here in Winnebago, among us Jewish ladies. She was different."

Fanny's face hardened. She stood up. "Yes, she was different."

"She comes often into my mind now, when I am here alone, with only the four walls. We were aber dumm, we women—but how dumm! She was too smart for us, your mother. Too smart. Und eine sehr brave frau."

And suddenly Fanny, she who had resolved to set her face against all emotion, and all sentiment, found herself with her glowing cheek pressed against the withered one, and it was the weak old hand that patted her now. So she lay for a moment, silent. Then she got up, straightened her hat, smiled.

"Auf Wiedersehen," she said in her best German. "Und gute Besserung."

But the rabbi's wife shook her head. "Good-by."

From the hall below Doctor Thalmann called to her. "Come, child, come!" Then, "Ach, the light in my study! I forgot to turn it out, Fanny, be so good, yes?"

Fanny entered the bright little room, reached up to turn off the light, and paused a moment to glance about her. It was an ugly, comfortable, old-fashioned room that had never progressed beyond the what-not period. Fanny's eye was caught by certain framed pictures on the walls. They were photographs of Rabbi Thalmann's confirmation classes. Spindling-legged little boys in the splendor of patent-leather buttoned shoes, stiff white shirts, black broadcloth suits with satin lapels; self-conscious and awkward little girls—these in the minority—in white dresses and stiff white hair bows. In the center of each group sat the little rabbi, very proud and alert. Fanny was not among these. She had never formally taken the vows of her creed. As she turned down the light now, and found her way down the stairs, she told herself that she was glad this was so.

It was a matter of only four blocks to the temple. But they were late, and so they hurried, and there was little conversation. Fanny's arm was tucked comfortably in his. It felt, somehow, startlingly thin, that arm. And as they hurried along there was a jerky feebleness about his gait. It was with difficulty that Fanny restrained herself from supporting him when they came to a rough bit of walk or a sudden step. Something fine in her prompted her not to. But the alert mind in that old frame sensed what was going on in her thoughts.

"He's getting feeble, the old rabbi, h'm?"

"Not a bit of it. I've got all I can do to keep up with you. You set such a pace."

"I know. I know. They are not all so kind, Fanny. They are too prosperous, this congregation of mine. And some day, `Off with his head!' And in my place there will step a young man, with eye-glasses instead of spectacles. They are tired of hearing about the prophets. Texts from the Bible have gone out of fashion. You think I do not see them giggling, h'm? The young people. And the whispering in the choir loft. And the buzz when I get up from my chair after the second hymn. `Is he going to have a sermon? Is he? Sure enough!' Na, he will make them sit up, my successor. Sex sermons! Political lectures. That's it. Lectures." They were turning in at the temple now. "The race is to the young, Fanny. To the young. And I am old."

She squeezed the frail old arm in hers. "My dear!" she said. "My dear!" A second breaking of her new resolutions.

One by one, two by two, they straggled in for the Friday evening service, these placid, prosperous people, not unkind, but careless, perhaps, in their prosperity.

"He's worth any ten of them," Fanny said hotly to herself, as she sat in her pew that, after to-morrow, would no longer be hers. "The dear old thing. `Sex sermons.' And the race is to the young. How right he is. Well, no one can say I'm not getting an early start."

The choir had begun the first hymn when there came down the aisle a stranger. There was a little stir among the congregation. Visitors were rare. He was dark and very slim—with the slimness of steel wire. He passed down the aisle rather uncertainly. A traveling man, Fanny thought, dropped in, as sometimes they did, to say Kaddish for a departed father or mother. Then she changed her mind. Her quick eye noted his walk; a peculiar walk, with a spring in it. Only one unfamiliar with cement pavements could walk like that. The Indians must have had that same light, muscular step. He chose an empty pew halfway down the aisle and stumbled into it rather awkwardly. Fanny thought he was unnecessarily ugly, even for a man. Then he looked up, and nodded and smiled at Lee Kohn, across the aisle. His teeth were very white, and the smile was singularly sweet. Fanny changed her mind again. Not so bad-looking, after all. Different, anyway. And then—why, of course! Little Clarence Heyl, come back from the West. Clarence Heyl, the cowardy-cat.

Her mind went back to that day of the street fight. She smiled. At that moment Clarence Heyl, who had been screwing about most shockingly, as though searching for some one, turned and met her smile, intended for no one, with a startlingly radiant one of his own, intended most plainly for her. He half started forward in his pew, and then remembered, and sat back again, but with an effect of impermanence that was ludicrous. It had been years since he had left Winnebago. At the time of his mother's death they had tried to reach him, and had been unable to get in touch with him for weeks. He had been off on some mountain expedition, hundreds of miles from railroad or telegraph. Fanny remembered having read about him in the Winnebago Courier. He seemed to be climbing mountains a great deal—rather difficult mountains, evidently, from the fuss they made over it. A queer enough occupation for a cowardy-cat. There had been a book, too. About the Rockies. She had not read it. She rather disliked these nature books, as do most nature lovers. She told herself that when she came upon a flaming golden maple in October she was content to know it was a maple, and to warm her soul at its blaze.

There had been something in the Chicago Herald, though—oh, yes; it had spoken of him as the brilliant young naturalist, Clarence Heyl. He was to have gone on an expedition with Roosevelt. A sprained ankle, or some such thing, had prevented. Fanny smiled again, to herself. His mother, the fussy person who had been responsible for his boyhood reefers and too-shiny shoes, and his cowardice too, no doubt, had dreamed of seeing her Clarence a rabbi.

From that point Fanny's thoughts wandered to the brave old man in the pulpit. She had heard almost nothing of the service. She looked at him now—at him, and then at his congregation, inattentive and palpably bored. As always with her, the thing stamped itself on her mind as a picture. She was forever seeing a situation in terms of its human value. How small he looked, how frail, against the background of the massive Ark with its red velvet curtain. And how bravely he glared over his blue glasses at the two Aarons girls who were whispering and giggling together, eyes on the newcomer.

So this was what life did to you, was it? Squeezed you dry, and then cast you aside in your old age, a pulp, a bit of discard. Well, they'd never catch her that way.

Unchurchly thoughts, these. The little place was very peaceful and quiet, lulling one like a narcotic. The rabbi's voice had in it that soothing monotony bred of years in the pulpit. Fanny found her thoughts straying back to the busy, bright little store on Elm Street, then forward, to the Haynes-Cooper plant and the fight that was before her. There settled about her mouth a certain grim line that sat strangely on so young a face. The service marched on. There came the organ prelude that announced the mourners' prayer. Then Rabbi Thalmann began to intone the Kaddish. Fanny rose, prayer book in hand. At that Clarence Heyl rose too, hurriedly, as one unaccustomed to the service, and stood with unbowed head, looking at the rabbi interestedly, thoughtfully, reverently. The two stood alone. Death had been kind to Congregation Emanu-el this year. The prayer ended. Fanny winked the tears from her eyes, almost wrathfully. She sat down, and there swept over her a feeling of finality. It was like the closing of Book One in a volume made up of three parts.

She said to herself: "Winnebago is ended, and my life here. How interesting that I should know that, and feel it. It is like the first movement in one of the concertos Theodore was forever playing. Now for the second movement! It's got to be lively. Fortissimo! Presto!"

For so clever a girl as Fanny Brandeis, that was a stupid conclusion at which to arrive. How could she think it possible to shed her past life, like a garment? Those impressionable years, between fourteen and twenty-four, could never be cast off. She might don a new cloak to cover the old dress beneath, but the old would always be there, its folds peeping out here and there, its outlines plainly to be seen. She might eat of things rare, and drink of things costly, but the sturdy, stocky little girl in the made-over silk dress, who had resisted the Devil in Weinberg's pantry on that long-ago Day of Atonement, would always be there at the feast. Myself, I confess I am tired of these stories of young women who go to the big city, there to do battle with failure, to grapple with temptation, sin and discouragement. So it may as well be admitted that Fanny Brandeis' story was not that of a painful hand-over-hand climb. She was made for success. What she attempted, she accomplished. That which she strove for, she won. She was too sure, too vital, too electric, for failure. No, Fanny Brandeis' struggle went on inside. And in trying to stifle it she came near making the blackest failure that a woman can make. In grubbing for the pot of gold she almost missed the rainbow.

Rabbi Thalmann raised his arms for the benediction. Fanny looked straight up at him as though stamping a picture on her mind. His eyes were resting gently on her—or perhaps she just fancied that he spoke to her alone as he began the words of the ancient closing prayer:

"May the blessings of the Lord Our God rest upon you. God bless thee and keep thee. May He cause His countenance to shine upon thee and be gracious unto thee. May God lift up His countenance unto thee..."

At the last word she hurried up the aisle, and down the stairs, into the soft beauty of the May night. She felt she could stand no good-bys. In her hotel room she busied herself with the half-packed trunks and bags. So it was she altogether failed to see the dark young man who hurried after her eagerly, and who was stopped by a dozen welcoming hands there in the temple vestibule. He swore a deep inward "Damn!" as he saw her straight, slim figure disappear down the steps and around the corner, even while he found himself saying, politely, "Why, thanks! It's good to BE back." And, "Yes, things have changed. All but the temple, and Rabbi Thalmann."

Fanny left Winnebago at eight next morning.

CHAPTER NINE

"Mr. Fenger will see you now." Mr. Fenger, general manager, had been a long time about it. This heel-cooling experience was new to Fanny Brandeis. It had always been her privilege to keep others waiting. Still, she felt no resentment as she sat in Michael Fenger's outer office. For as she sat there, waiting, she was getting a distinct impression of this unseen man whose voice she could just hear as he talked over the telephone in his inner office. It was characteristic of Michael Fenger that his personality reached out and touched you before you came into actual contact with the man. Fanny had heard of him long before she came to Haynes-Cooper. He was the genie of that glittering lamp. All through the gigantic plant (she had already met department heads, buyers, merchandise managers) one heard his name, and felt the impress of his mind:

"You'll have to see Mr. Fenger about that."

"Yes,"—pointing to a new conveyor, perhaps,—"that has just been installed. It's a great help to us. Doubles our shipping-room efficiency. We used to use baskets, pulled by a rope. It's Mr. Fenger's idea."

Efficiency, efficiency, efficiency. Fenger had made it a slogan in the Haynes-Cooper plant long before the German nation forced it into our everyday vocabulary. Michael Fenger was System. He could take a muddle of orders, a jungle of unfilled contracts, a horde of incompetent workers, and of them make a smooth-running and effective unit. Untangling snarls was his pastime. Esprit de corps was his shibboleth. Order and management his idols. And his war-cry was "Results!"

It was eleven o'clock when Fanny came into his outer office. The very atmosphere was vibrant with his personality. There hung about the place an air of repressed expectancy. The room was electrically charged with the high-voltage of the man in the inner office. His secretary was a spare, middle-aged, anxious-looking woman in snuff-brown and spectacles; his stenographer a blond young man, also spectacled and anxious; his office boy a stern youth in knickers, who bore no relation to the slangy, gum-chewing, redheaded office boy of the comic sections.

The low-pitched, high-powered voice went on inside, talking over the long-distance telephone. Fenger was the kind of man who is always talking to New York when he is in Chicago, and to Chicago when he is in New York. Trains with the word Limited after them were invented for him and his type. A buzzer sounded. It galvanized the office boy into instant action. It brought the anxious-looking stenographer to the doorway, notebook in hand, ready. It sent the lean secretary out, and up to Fanny.

"Temper," said Fanny, to herself, "or horribly nervous and high-keyed. They jump like a set of puppets on a string."

It was then that the lean secretary had said, "Mr. Fenger will see you now."

Fanny was aware of a pleasant little tingle of excitement. She entered the inner office.

It was characteristic of Michael Fenger that he employed no cheap tricks. He was not writing as Fanny Brandeis came in. He was not telephoning. He was not doing anything but standing at his desk, waiting for Fanny Brandeis. As she came in he looked at her, through her, and she seemed to feel her mental processes laid open to him as a skilled surgeon cuts through skin and flesh and fat, to lay bare the muscles and nerves and vital organs beneath. He put out his hand. Fanny extended hers. They met in a silent grip. It was like a meeting between two men. Even as he indexed her, Fanny's alert mind was busy docketing, numbering, cataloguing him. They had in common a certain force, a driving power. Fanny seated herself opposite him, in obedience to a gesture. He crossed his legs comfortably and sat back in his big desk chair. A great-bodied man, with powerful square shoulders, a long head, a rugged crest of a nose—the kind you see on the type of Englishman who has the imagination and initiative to go to Canada, or Australia, or America. He wore spectacles, not the fashionable horn-rimmed sort, but the kind with gold ear pieces. They were becoming, and gave a certain humanness to a face that otherwise would have been too rugged, too strong. A man of forty-five, perhaps.

He spoke first. "You're younger than I thought."

"So are you."

"Old inside."

"So am I."

He uncrossed his legs, leaned forward, folded his arms on the desk.

"You've been through the plant, Miss Brandeis?"

"Yes. Twice. Once with a regular tourist party. And once with the special guide." "Good. Go through the plant whenever you can. Don't stick to your own department. It narrows one." He paused a moment. "Did you think that this opportunity to come to Haynes-Cooper, as assistant to the infants' wear department buyer was just a piece of luck, augmented by a little pulling on your part?"

"Yes."

"It wasn't. You were carefully picked by me, and I don't expect to find I've made a mistake. I suppose you know very little about buying and selling infants' wear?"

"Less than about almost any other article in the world—at least, in the department store, or mail order world."

"I thought so. And it doesn't matter. I pretty well know your history, which means that I know your training. You're young; you're ambitious, you're experienced; you're imaginative. There's no length you can't go, with these. It just depends on how farsighted your mental vision is. Now listen, Miss Brandeis: I'm not going to talk to you in millions. The guides do enough of that. But you know we do buy and sell in terms of millions, don't you? Well, our infants' wear department isn't helping to roll up the millions; and it ought to, because there are millions of babies born every year, and the golden-spoon kind are in the minority. I've decided that that department needs a woman, your kind of woman. Now, as a rule, I never employ a woman when I can use a man. There's only one other woman filling a really important position in the merchandise end of this business. That's Ella Monahan, head of the glove department, and she's a genius. She is a woman who is limited in every other respect—just average; but she knows glove materials in a way that's uncanny. I'd rather have a man in her place; but I don't happen to know any men glove-geniuses. Tell me, what do you think of that etching?"

Fanny tried—and successfully—not to show the jolt her mind had received as she turned to look at the picture to which his finger pointed. She got up and strolled over to it, and she was glad her suit fitted and hung as it did in the back.

"I don't like it particularly. I like it less than any other etching you have here." The walls were hung with them. "Of course you understand I know nothing about them. But it's too flowery, isn't it, to be good? Too many lines. Like a writer who spoils his effect by using too many words."

Fenger came over and stood beside her, staring at the black and white and gray thing in its frame. "I felt that way, too." He stared down at her, then. "Jew?" he asked.

A breathless instant. "No," said Fanny Brandeis.

Michael Fenger smiled for the first time. Fanny Brandeis would have given everything she had, everything she hoped to be, to be able to take back that monosyllable. She was gripped with horror at what she had done. She had spoken almost mechanically. And yet that monosyllable must have been the fruit of all these months of inward struggle and thought. "Now I begin to understand you," Fenger went on. "You've decided to lop off all the excrescences, eh? Well, I can't say that I blame you. A woman in business is handicapped enough by the very fact of her sex." He stared at her again. "Too bad you're so pretty."

"I'm not!" said Fanny hotly, like a school-girl.

"That's a thing that can't be argued, child. Beauty's subjective, you know."

"I don't see what difference it makes, anyway."

"Oh, yes, you do." He stopped. "Or perhaps you don't, after all. I forget how young you are. Well, now, Miss Brandeis, you and your woman's mind, and your masculine business experience and sense are to be turned loose on our infants' wear department. The buyer, Mr. Slosson, is going to resent you. Naturally. I don't know whether we'll get results from you in a month, or six months or a year. Or ever. But something tells me we're going to get them. You've lived in a small town most of your life. And we want that small-town viewpoint. D'you think you've got it?"

Fanny was on her own ground here. "If knowing the Wisconsin small-town woman, and the Wisconsin farmer woman—and man too, for that matter—means knowing the Oregon, and Wyoming, and Pennsylvania, and Iowa people of the same class, then I've got it."

"Good!" Michael Fenger stood up. "I'm not going to load you down with instructions, or advice. I think I'll let you grope your own way around, and bump your head a few times. Then you'll learn where the low places are. And, Miss Brandeis, remember that suggestions are welcome in this plant. We take suggestions all the way from the elevator starter to the president." His tone was kindly, but not hopeful.

Fanny was standing too, her mental eye on the door. But now she turned to face him squarely.

"Do you mean that?"

"Absolutely."

"Well, then, I've one to make. Your stock boys and stock girls walk miles and miles every day, on every floor of this fifteen-story building. I watched them yesterday, filling up the bins, carrying orders, covering those enormous distances from one bin to another, up one aisle and down the next, to the office, back again. Your floors are concrete, or cement, or some such mixture, aren't they? I just happened to think of the boy who used to deliver our paper on Norris Street, in Winnebago, Wisconsin. He covered his route on roller skates. It saved him an hour. Why don't you put roller skates on your stock boys and girls?"

Fenger stared at her. You could almost hear that mind of his working, like a thing on ball bearings. "Roller skates." It wasn't an exclamation. It was a decision. He pressed a buzzer—the snuff-brown secretary buzzer. "Tell Clancy I want him. Now." He had not glanced up, or taken his eyes from Fanny. She was aware of feeling a little uncomfortable, but elated, too. She moved toward the door. Fenger stood at his desk. "Wait a minute." Fanny waited. Still Fenger did not speak. Finally, "I suppose you know you've earned six months' salary in the last five minutes."

Fanny eyed him coolly. "Considering the number of your stock force, the time, energy, and labor saved, including wear and tear on department heads and their assistants, I should say that was a conservative statement." And she nodded pleasantly, and left him.

Two days later every stock clerk in the vast plant was equipped with light-weight roller skates. They made a sort of carnival of it at first. There were some spills, too, going around corners, and a little too much hilarity. That wore off in a week. In two weeks their roller skates were part of them; just shop labor-savers. The report presented to Fenger was this: Time and energy saved, fifty-five per cent; stock staff decreased by one third. The picturesqueness of it, the almost ludicrous simplicity of the idea appealed to the entire plant. It tickled the humor sense in every one of the ten thousand employees in that vast organization. In the first week of her association with Haynes-Cooper Fanny Brandeis was actually more widely known than men who had worked there for years. The president, Nathan Haynes himself, sent for her, chuckling.

Nathan Haynes—but then, why stop for him? Nathan Haynes had been swallowed, long ago, by this monster plant that he himself had innocently created. You must have visited it, this Gargantuan thing that sprawls its length in the very center of Chicago, the giant son of a surprised father. It is one of the city's show places, like the stockyards, the Art Institute, and Field's. Fifteen years before, a building had been erected to accommodate a prosperous mail order business. It had been built large and roomy, with plenty of seams, planned amply, it was thought, to allow the boy to grow. It would do for twenty-five years, surely. In ten years Haynes-Cooper was bursting its seams. In twelve it was shamelessly naked, its arms and legs sticking out of its inadequate garments. New red brick buildings another—another. Five stories added to this one, six stories to that, a new fifteen story merchandise building.

The firm began to talk in tens of millions. Its stock became gilt-edged, unattainable. Lucky ones who had bought of it diffidently, discreetly, with modest visions of four and a half per cent in their unimaginative minds, saw their dividends doubling, trebling, quadrupling, finally soaring gymnastically beyond all reason. Listen to the old guide who (at fifteen a week) takes groups of awed visitors through the great plant. How he juggles figures; how grandly they roll off his tongue. How glib he is with Nathan Haynes's millions.

"This, ladies and gentlemen, is our mail department. From two thousand to twenty-five hundred pounds of mail, comprising over one hundred thousand letters, are received here every day. Yes, madam, I said every day. About half of these letters are orders. Last year the banking department counted one hundred and thirty millions of dollars. One hundred and thirty millions!" He stands there in his ill-fitting coat, and his star, and rubs one bony hand over the other.

"Dear me!" says a lady tourist from Idaho, rather inadequately. And yet, not so inadequately. What exclamation is there, please, that fits a sum like one hundred and thirty millions of anything?

Fanny Brandeis, fresh from Winnebago, Wisconsin, slipped into the great scheme of things at the Haynes-Cooper plant like part of a perfectly planned blue print. It was as though she had been thought out and shaped for this particular corner. And the reason for it was, primarily, Winnebago, Wisconsin. For Haynes-Cooper grew and thrived on just such towns, with their surrounding farms and villages. Haynes-Cooper had their fingers on the pulse and heart of the country as did no other industry. They were close, close. When rugs began to take the place of ingrain carpets it was Haynes-Cooper who first sensed the change. Oh, they had had them in New York years before, certainly. But after all, it isn't New York's artistic progress that shows the development of this nation. It is the thing they are thinking, and doing, and learning in Backwash, Nebraska, that marks time for these United States. There may be a certain significance in the announcement that New York has dropped the Russian craze and has gone in for that quaint Chinese stuff. My dear, it makes the loveliest hangings and decorations. When Fifth Avenue takes down its filet lace and eyelet embroidered curtains, and substitutes severe shantung and chaste net, there is little in the act to revolutionize industry, or stir the art-world. But when the Haynes-Cooper company, by referring to its inventory ledgers, learns that it is selling more Alma Gluck than Harry Lauder records; when its statistics show that Tchaikowsky is going better than Irving Berlin, something epochal is happening in the musical progress of a nation. And when the orders from Noose Gulch, Nevada, are for those plain dimity curtains instead of the cheap and gaudy Nottingham atrocities, there is conveyed to the mind a fact of immense, of overwhelming significance. The country has taken a step toward civilization and good taste.

So. You have a skeleton sketch of Haynes-Cooper, whose feelers reach the remotest dugout in the Yukon, the most isolated cabin in the Rockies, the loneliest ranch-house in Wyoming; the Montana mining shack, the bleak Maine farm, the plantation in Virginia.

And the man who had so innocently put life into this monster? A plumpish, kindly-faced man; a bewildered, gentle, unimaginative and somewhat frightened man, fresh-cheeked, eye-glassed. In his suite of offices in the new Administration Building—built two years ago—marble and oak throughout—twelve stories, and we're adding three already; offices all two-toned rugs, and leather upholstery, with dim, rich, brown-toned Dutch masterpieces on the walls, he sat helpless and defenseless while the torrent of millions rushed, and swirled, and foamed about him. I think he had fancied, fifteen years ago, that he would some day be a fairly prosperous man; not rich, as riches are counted nowadays, but with a comfortable number of tens of thousands tucked away. Two or three hundred thousand; perhaps five hundred thousand!—perhaps a—but, nonsense! Nonsense!

And then the thing had started. It was as when a man idly throws a pebble into a chasm, or shoves a bit of ice with the toe of his boot, and starts a snow-slide that grows as it goes. He had started this avalanche of money, and now it rushed on of its own momentum, plunging, rolling, leaping, crashing, and as it swept on it gathered rocks, trees, stones, houses, everything that lay in its way. It was beyond the power of human hand to stop this tumbling, roaring slide. In the midst of it sat Nathan Haynes, deafened, stunned, terrified at the immensity of what he had done.

He began giving away huge sums, incredible sums. It piled up faster than he could give it away. And so he sat there in the office hung with the dim old masterpieces, and tried to keep simple, tried to keep sane, with that austerity that only mad wealth can afford—or bitter poverty. He caused the land about the plant to be laid out in sunken gardens and baseball fields and tennis courts, so that one approached this monster of commerce through enchanted grounds, glowing with tulips and heady hyacinths in spring, with roses in June, blazing with salvia and golden-glow and asters in autumn. There was something apologetic about these grounds.

This, then, was the environment that Fanny Brandeis had chosen. On the face of things you would have said she had chosen well. The inspiration of the roller skates had not been merely a lucky flash. That idea had been part of the consistent whole. Her mind was her mother's mind raised to the nth power, and enhanced by the genius she was trying to crush. Refusing to die, it found expression in a hundred brilliant plans, of which the roller skate idea was only one.

Fanny had reached Chicago on Sunday. She had entered the city as a queen enters her domain, authoritatively, with no fear upon her, no trepidation, no doubts. She had gone at once to the Mendota Hotel, on Michigan Avenue, up-town, away from the roar of the loop. It was a residential hotel, very quiet, decidedly luxurious. She had no idea of making it her home. But she would stay there until she could find an apartment that was small, bright, near the lake, and yet within fairly reasonable transportation facilities for her work. Her room was on the ninth floor, not on the Michigan Avenue side, but east, overlooking the lake. She spent hours at the windows, fascinated by the stone and steel city that lay just below with the incredible blue of the sail-dotted lake beyond, and at night, with the lights spangling the velvety blackness, the flaring blaze of Thirty-first Street's chop-suey restaurants and moving picture houses at the right; and far, far away, the red and white eye of the lighthouse winking, blinking, winking, blinking, the rumble and clank of a flat-wheeled Indiana avenue car, the sound of high laughter and a snatch of song that came faintly up to her from the speeding car of some midnight joy-riders!

But all this had to do with her other side. It had no bearing on Haynes-Cooper, and business. Business! That was it. She had trained herself for it, like an athlete. Eight hours of sleep. A cold plunge on arising. Sane food. Long walks. There was something terrible about her earnestness.

On Monday she presented herself at the Haynes-Cooper plant. Monday and Tuesday were spent in going over the great works. It was an exhausting process, but fascinating beyond belief. It was on Wednesday that she had been summoned for the talk with Michael Fenger. Thursday morning she was at her desk at eight-thirty. It was an obscure desk, in a dingy corner of the infants' wear department, the black sheep section of the great plant. Her very presence in that corner seemed to change it magically. You must remember how young she was, how healthy, how vigorous, with the freshness of the small town still upon her. It was health and youth, and vigor that gave that gloss to her hair (conscientious brushing too, perhaps), that color to her cheeks and lips, that brightness to her eyes. But crafty art and her dramatic instinct were responsible for the tailored severity of her costume, for the whiteness of her blouse, the trim common-sense expensiveness of her shoes and hat and gloves.

Slosson, buyer and head of the department, came in at nine. Fanny rose to greet him. She felt a little sorry for Slosson. In her mind she already knew him for a doomed man.

"Well, well!"—he was the kind of person who would say, well, well!—"You're bright and early, Miss—ah—"

"Brandeis."

"Yes, certainly; Miss Brandeis. Well, nothing like making a good start."

"I wanted to go through the department by myself," said Fanny. "The shelves and bins, and the numbering system. I see that your new maternity dresses have just come in."

"Oh, yes. How do you like them?"

"I think they're unnecessarily hideous, Mr. Slosson."

"My dear young lady, a plain garment is what they want. Unnoticeable."

"Unnoticeable, yes; but becoming. At such a time a woman is at her worst. If she can get it, she at least wants a dress that doesn't add to her unattractiveness."

"Let me see—you are not—ah—married, I believe, Miss Brandeis?"

"No."

"I am. Three children. All girls." He passed a nervous hand over his head, rumpling his hair a little. "An expensive proposition, let me tell you, three girls. But there's very little I don't know about babies, as you may imagine."

But there settled over Fanny Brandeis' face the mask of hardness that was so often to transform it.

The morning mail was in—the day's biggest grist, deluge of it, a flood. Buyer and assistant buyer never saw the actual letters, or attended to their enclosed orders. It was only the unusual letter, the complaint or protest that reached their desk. Hundreds of hands downstairs sorted, stamped, indexed, filed, after the letter-opening machines had slit the envelopes. Those letter-openers! Fanny had hung over them, enthralled. The unopened envelopes were fed into them. Flip! Zip! Flip! Out! Opened! Faster than eye could follow. It was uncanny. It was, somehow, humorous, like the clever antics of a trained dog. You could not believe that this little machine actually performed what your eyes beheld. Two years later they installed the sand-paper letter-opener, marvel of simplicity. It made the old machine seem cumbersome and slow. Guided by Izzy, the expert, its rough tongue was capable of licking open six hundred and fifty letters a minute.

Ten minutes after the mail came in the orders were being filled; bins, shelves, warehouses, were emptying their contents. Up and down the aisles went the stock clerks; into the conveyors went the bundles, down the great spiral bundle chute, into the shipping room, out by mail, by express, by freight. This leghorn hat for a Nebraska country belle; a tombstone for a rancher's wife; a plow, brave in its red paint; coffee, tea, tinned fruit, bound for Alaska; lace, muslin, sheeting, toweling, all intended for the coarse trousseau of a Georgia bride.

It was not remarkable that Fanny Brandeis fitted into this scheme of things. For years she had ministered to the wants of just this type of person. The letters she saw at Haynes-Cooper's read exactly as customers had worded their wants at Brandeis' Bazaar. The magnitude of the thing thrilled her, the endless possibilities of her own position.

During the first two months of her work there she was as unaggressive as possible. She opened the very pores of her mind and absorbed every detail of her department. But she said little, followed Slosson's instructions in her position as assistant buyer, and suggested no changes. Slosson's wrinkle of anxiety smoothed itself away, and his manner became patronizingly authoritative again. Fanny seemed to have become part of the routine of the place. Fenger did not send for her. June and July were insufferably hot. Fanny seemed to thrive, to expand like a flower in the heat, when others wilted and shriveled. The spring catalogue was to be made up in October, as always, six months in advance. The first week in August Fanny asked for an interview with Fenger. Slosson was to be there. At ten o'clock she entered Fenger's inner office. He was telephoning—something about dinner at the Union League Club. His voice was suave, his tone well modulated, his accent correct, his English faultless. And yet Fanny Brandeis, studying the etchings on his wall, her back turned to him, smiled to herself. The voice, the tone, the accent, the English, did not ring true They were acquired graces, exquisite imitations of the real thing. Fanny Brandeis knew. She was playing the same game herself. She understood this man now, after two months in the Haynes-Cooper plant. These marvelous examples of the etcher's art, for example. They were the struggle for expression of a man whose youth had been bare of such things. His love for them was much the same as that which impels the new made millionaire to buy rare pictures, rich hangings, tapestries, rugs, not so much in the desire to impress the world with his wealth as to satisfy the craving for beauty, the longing to possess that which is exquisite, and fine, and almost unobtainable. You have seen how a woman, long denied luxuries, feeds her starved senses on soft silken things, on laces and gleaming jewels, for pure sensuous delight in their feel and look.

Thus Fanny mused as she eyed these treasures—grim, deft, repressed things, done with that economy of line which is the test of the etcher's art.

Fenger hung up the receiver.

"So it's taken you two months, Miss Brandeis. I was awfully afraid, from the start you made, that you'd be back here in a week, bursting with ideas."

Fanny smiled, appreciatively. He had come very near the truth. "I had to use all my self-control, that first week. After that it wasn't so hard."

Fenger's eyes narrowed upon her. "Pretty sure of yourself, aren't you?"

"Yes," said Fanny. She came over to his desk.

"I wish we needn't have Mr. Slosson here this morning. After all, he's been here for years, and I'm practically an upstart. He's so much older, too. I—I hate to hurt him. I wish you'd—"

But Fenger shook his head. "Slosson's due now. And he has got to take his medicine. This is business, Miss Brandeis. You ought to know what that means. For that matter, it may be that you haven't hit upon an idea. In that case, Slosson would have the laugh, wouldn't he?"

Slosson entered at that moment. And there was a chip on his shoulder. It was evident in the way he bristled, in the way he seated himself. His fingers drummed his knees. He was like a testy, hum-ha stage father dealing with a willful child.

Fenger took out his watch.

"Now, Miss Brandeis."

Fanny took a chair facing the two men, and crossed her trim blue serge knees, and folded her hands in her lap. A deep pink glowed in her cheeks. Her eyes were very bright. All the Molly Brandeis in her was at the surface, sparkling there. And she looked almost insultingly youthful.

"You—you want me to talk?"

"We want you to talk. We have time for just three-quarters of an hour of uninterrupted conversation. If you've got anything to say you ought to say it in that time. Now, Miss Brandeis, what's the trouble with the Haynes-Cooper infants' wear department?"

And Fanny Brandeis took a long breath

"The trouble with the Haynes-Cooper infants' wear department is that it doesn't understand women. There are millions of babies born every year. An incredible number of them are mail order babies. I mean by that they are born to tired, clumsy-fingered immigrant women, to women in mills and factories, to women on farms, to women in remote villages. They're the type who use the mail order method. I've learned this one thing about that sort of woman: she may not want that baby, but either before or after it's born she'll starve, and save, and go without proper clothing, and even beg, and steal to give it clothes—clothes with lace on them, with ribbon on them, sheer white things. I don't know why that's true, but it is. Well, we're not reaching them. Our goods are unattractive. They're packed and shipped unattractively. Why, all this department needs is a little psychology—and some lace that doesn't look as if it had been chopped out with an ax. It's the little, silly, intimate things that will reach these women. No, not silly, either. Quite understandable. She wants fine things for her baby, just as the silver-spoon mother does. The thing we'll have to do is to give her silver-spoon models at pewter prices."

"It can't be done," said Slosson.

"Now, wait a minute, Slosson," Fenger put in, smoothly. "Miss Brandeis has given us a very fair general statement. We'll have some facts. Are you prepared to give us an actual working plan?"

"Yes. At least, it sounds practical to me. And if it does to you—and to Mr. Slosson—"

"Humph!" snorted that gentleman, in expression of defiance, unbelief, and a determination not to be impressed.

It acted as a goad to Fanny. She leaned forward in her chair and talked straight at the big, potent force that sat regarding her in silent attention.

"I still say that we can copy the high-priced models in low-priced materials because, in almost every case, it isn't the material that makes the expensive model; it's the line, the cut, the little trick that gives it style. We can get that. We've been giving them stuff that might have been made by prison labor, for all the distinction it had. Then I think we ought to make a feature of the sanitary methods used in our infants' department. Every article intended for a baby's use should be wrapped or boxed as it lies in the bin or on the shelf. And those bins ought to be glassed. We would advertise that, and it would advertise itself. Our visitors would talk about it. This department hasn't been getting a square deal in the catalogue. Not enough space. It ought to have not only more catalogue space, but a catalogue all its own—the Baby Book. Full of pictures. Good ones. Illustrations that will make every mother think her baby will look like that baby, once it is wearing our No. 29E798—chubby babies, curly-headed, and dimply. And the feature of that catalogue ought to be, not separate garments, but complete outfits. Outfits boxed, ready for shipping, and ranging in price all the way from twenty-five dollars to three-ninety-eight—"

"It can't be done!" yelled Slosson. "Three-ninety-eight! Outfits!"

"It can be done. I've figured it out, down to a packet of assorted size safety pins. We'll call it our emergency outfit. Thirty pieces. And while we're about it, every outfit over five dollars ought to be packed in a pink or a pale blue pasteboard box. The outfits trimmed in pink, pink boxes; the outfits trimmed in blue, blue boxes. In eight cases out of ten their letters will tell us whether it's a pink or blue baby. And when they get our package, and take out that pink or blue box, they'll be as pleased as if we'd made them a present. It's the personal note—"

"Personal slop!" growled Slosson. "It isn't business. It's sentimental slush!"

"Sentimental, yes," agreed Fanny pleasantly, "but then, we're running the only sentimental department in this business. And we ought to be doing it at the rate of a million and a quarter a year. If you think these last suggestions sentimental, I'm afraid the next one—"

"Let's have it, Miss Brandeis," Fenger encouraged her quietly.

"It's"—she flashed a mischievous smile at Slosson—"it's a mother's guide and helper, and adviser. A woman who'll answer questions, give advice. Some one they'll write to, with a picture in their minds of a large, comfortable, motherly-looking person in gray. You know we get hundreds of letters asking whether they ought to order flannel bands, or the double-knitted kind. That sort of thing. And who's been answering them? Some sixteen-year-old girl in the mailing department who doesn't know a flannel band from a bootee when she sees it. We could call our woman something pleasant and everydayish, like Emily Brand. Easy to remember. And until we can find her, I'll answer those letters myself. They're important to us as well as to the woman who writes them. And now, there's the matter of obstetrical outfits. Three grades, packed ready for shipment, practical, simple, and complete. Our drug section has the separate articles, but we ought to—"

"Oh, lord!" groaned Slosson, and slumped disgustedly in his seat.

But Fenger got up, came over to Fanny, and put a hand on her shoulder for a moment. He looked down at her. "I knew you'd do it." He smiled queerly. "Tell me, where did you learn all this?"

"I don't know," faltered Fanny happily. "Brandeis' Bazaar, perhaps. It's just another case of plush photograph album."

"Plush—?"

Fanny told him that story. Even the discomfited Slosson grinned at it.

But after ten minutes more of general discussion Slosson left. Fenger, without putting it in words, had conveyed that to him. Fanny stayed. They did things that way at Haynes-Cooper. No waste. No delay. That she had accomplished in two months that which ordinarily takes years was not surprising. They did things that way, too, at Haynes-Cooper. Take the case of Nathan Haynes himself. And Michael Fenger too who, not so many years before, had been a machine-boy in a Racine woolen mill.

For my part, I confess that Fanny Brandeis begins to lose interest for me. Big Business seems to dwarf the finer things in her. That red-cheeked, shabby little schoolgirl, absorbed in Zola and peanut brittle in the Winnebago library, was infinitely more appealing than this glib and capable young woman. The spitting wildcat of the street fight so long ago was gentler by far than this cool person who was so deliberately taking his job away from Slosson. You, too, feel that way about her? That is as it should be. It is the penalty they pay who, given genius, sympathy, and understanding as their birthright, trade them for the tawdry trinkets money brings.

Perhaps the last five minutes of that conference between Fanny and Michael Fenger reveals a new side, and presents something of interest. It was a harrowing and unexpected five minutes.

You may remember how Michael Fenger had a way of looking at one, silently. It was an intent and concentrated gaze that had the effect of an actual physical hold. Most people squirmed under it. Fanny, feeling it on her now, frowned and rose to leave.

"Shall you want to talk these things over again? Of course I've only outlined them, roughly. You gave me so little time."

Fenger, at his desk, did not answer, or turn away his gaze. A little blaze of wrath flamed into Fanny's face.

"General manager or not," she said, very low-voiced, "I wish you wouldn't sit and glower at me like that. It's rude, and it's disconcerting," which was putting it forthrightly.

"I beg your pardon!" Fenger came swiftly around the desk, and over to her. "I was thinking very hard. Miss Brandeis, will you dine with me somewhere tonight? Then to-morrow night? But I want to talk to you."

"Here I am. Talk."

"But I want to talk to—you."

It was then that Fanny Brandeis saved an ugly situation. For she laughed, a big, wholesome, outdoors sort of laugh. She was honestly amused.

"My dear Mr. Fenger, you've been reading the murky magazines. Very bad for you."

Fenger was unsmiling: "Why won't you dine with me?"

"Because it would be unconventional and foolish. I respect the conventions. They're so sensible. And because it would be unfair to you, and to Mrs. Fenger, and to me."

"Rot! It's you who have the murky magazine viewpoint, as you call it, when you imply—"

"Now, look here, Mr. Fenger," Fanny interrupted, quietly. "Let's be square with each other, even if we're not being square with ourselves. You're the real power in this plant, because you've the brains. You can make any person in this organization, or break them. That sounds melodramatic, but it's true. I've got a definite life plan, and it's as complete and detailed as an engineering blue print. I don't intend to let you spoil it. I've made a real start here. If you want to, I've no doubt you can end it. But before you do, I want to warn you that I'll make a pretty stiff fight for it. I'm no silent sufferer. I'll say things. And people usually believe me when I talk."

Still the silent, concentrated gaze. With a little impatient exclamation Fanny walked toward the door. Fenger, startlingly light and agile for his great height, followed.

"I'm sorry, Miss Brandeis, terribly sorry. You see, you interest me very much. Very much."

"Thanks," dryly.

"Don't go just yet. Please. I'm not a villain. Really. That is, not a deliberate villain. But when I find something very fine, very intricate, very fascinating and complex—like those etchings, for example—I am intrigued. I want it near me. I want to study it."

Fanny said nothing. But she thought, "This is a dangerously clever man. Too clever for you. You know so little about them." Fenger waited. Most women would have found refuge in words. The wrong words. It is only the strong who can be silent when in doubt.

"Perhaps you will dine with Mrs. Fenger and me at our home some evening? Mrs. Fenger will speak to you about it."

"I'm afraid I'm usually too tired for further effort at the end of the day. I'm sorry——"

"Some Sunday night perhaps, then. Tea."

"Thank you." And so out, past the spare secretary, the anxious-browed stenographer, the academic office boy, to the hallway, the elevator, and finally the refuge of her own orderly desk. Slosson was at lunch in one of the huge restaurants provided for employees in the building across the street. She sat there, very still, for some minutes; for more minutes than she knew. Her hands were clasped tightly on the desk, and her eyes stared ahead in a puzzled, resentful, bewildered way. Something inside her was saying over and over again:

"You lied to him on that very first day. That placed you. That stamped you. Now he thinks you're rotten all the way through. You lied on the very first day."

Ella Monahan poked her head in at the door. The Gloves were on that floor, at the far end. The two women rarely saw each other, except at lunch time.

"Missed you at lunch," said Ella Monahan. She was a pink-cheeked, bright-eyed woman of forty-one or two, prematurely gray and therefore excessively young in her manner, as women often are who have grown gray before their time.

Fanny stood up, hurriedly. "I was just about to go."

"Try the grape pie, dear. It's delicious." And strolled off down the aisle that seemed to stretch endlessly ahead.

Fanny stood for a moment looking after her, as though meaning to call her back. But she must have changed her mind, because she said, "Oh, nonsense!" aloud. And went across to lunch. And ordered grape pie. And enjoyed it.

CHAPTER TEN

The invitation to tea came in due time from Mrs. Fenger. A thin, querulous voice over the telephone prepared one for the thin, querulous Mrs. Fenger herself. A sallow, plaintive woman, with a misbehaving valve. The valve, she confided to Fanny, made any effort dangerous. Also it made her susceptible to draughts. She wore over her shoulders a scarf that was constantly slipping and constantly being retrieved by Michael Fenger. The sight of this man, a physical and mental giant, performing this task ever so gently and patiently, sent a little pang of pity through Fanny, as Michael Fenger knew it would. The Fengers lived in an apartment on the Lake Shore Drive—an apartment such as only Chicago boasts. A view straight across the lake, rooms huge and many-windowed, a glass-enclosed sun-porch gay with chintz and wicker, an incredible number of bathrooms. The guests, besides Fanny, included a young pair, newly married and interested solely in rents, hangings, linen closets, and the superiority of the Florentine over the Jacobean for dining room purposes; and a very scrubbed looking, handsome, spectacled man of thirty-two or three who was a mechanical engineer. Fanny failed to catch his name, though she learned it later. Privately, she dubbed him Fascinating Facts, and he always remained that. His conversation was invariably prefaced with, "Funny thing happened down at the works to-day." The rest of it sounded like something one reads at the foot of each page of a loose-leaf desk calendar.

At tea there was a great deal of silver, and lace, but Fanny thought she could have improved on the chicken a la king. It lacked paprika and personality. Mrs. Fenger was constantly directing one or the other of the neat maids in an irritating aside.

After tea Michael Fenger showed Fanny his pictures, not boastfully, but as one who loves them reveals his treasures to an appreciative friend. He showed her his library, too, and it was the library of a reader. Fanny nibbled at it, hungrily. She pulled out a book here, a book there, read a paragraph, skimmed a page. There was no attempt at classification. Lever rubbed elbows with Spinoza; Mark Twain dug a facetious thumb into Haeckel's ribs. Fanny wanted to sit down on the floor, legs crossed, before the open shelves, and read, and read, and read. Fenger, watching the light in her face, seemed himself to take on a certain glow, as people generally did who found this girl in sympathy with them.

They were deep in book talk when Fascinating Facts strolled in, looking aggrieved, and spoiled it with the thoroughness of one who never reads, and is not ashamed of it.

"My word, I'm having a rotten time, Fenger," he said, plaintively. "They've got a tape-measure out of your wife's sewing basket, those two in there, and they're down on their hands and knees, measuring something. It has to do with their rug, over your rug, or some such rot. And then you take Miss Brandeis and go off into the library."

"Then stay here," said Fanny, "and talk books."

"My book's a blue-print," admitted Fascinating Facts, cheerfully. "I never get time to read. There's enough fiction, and romance, and adventure in my job to give me all the thrill I want. Why, just last Tuesday—no, Thursday it was—down at the works——"

Between Fanny and Fenger there flashed a look made up of dismay, and amusement, and secret sympathy. It was a look that said, "We both see the humor of this. Most people wouldn't. Our angle is the same." Such a glance jumps the gap between acquaintance and friendship that whole days of spoken conversation cannot cover.

"Cigar?" asked Fenger, hoping to stay the flood.

"No, thanks. Say, Fenger, would there be a row if I smoked my pipe?"

"That black one? With the smell?"

"The black one, yes."

"There would." Fenger glanced in toward his wife, and smiled, dryly. Fascinating Facts took his hand out of his pocket, regretfully.

"Wouldn't it sour a fellow on marriage! Wouldn't it! First those two in there, with their damned linen closets, and their rugs—I beg your pardon, Miss Brandeis! And now your missus objects to my pipe. You wouldn't treat me like that, would you, Miss Brandeis?"

There was about him something that appealed—something boyish and likeable.

"No, I wouldn't. I'd let you smoke a nargileh, if you wanted to, surrounded by rolls of blue prints."

"I knew it. I'm going to drive you home for that."

And he did, in his trim little roadster. It is a fairy road at night, that lake drive between the north and south sides. Even the Rush street bridge cannot quite spoil it. Fanny sat back luxuriously and let the soft splendor of the late August night enfold her. She was intelligently monosyllabic, while Fascinating Facts talked. At the door of her apartment house (she had left the Mendota weeks before) Fascinating Facts surprised her.

"I—I'd like to see you again, Miss Brandeis. If you'll let me."

"I'm so busy," faltered Fanny. Then it came to her that perhaps he did not know. "I'm with Haynes-Cooper, you know. Assistant buyer in the infants' wear department."

"Yes, I know. I suppose a girl like you couldn't be interested in seeing a chap like me again, but I thought maybe——"

"But I would," interrupted Fanny, impulsively. "Indeed I would."

"Really! Perhaps you'll drive, some evening. Over to the Bismarck Gardens, or somewhere. It would rest you."

"I'm sure it would. Suppose you telephone me."

That was her honest, forthright, Winnebago Wisconsin self talking. But up in her apartment the other Fanny Brandeis, the calculating, ambitious, determined woman, said: "Now why did I say that! I never want to see the boy again.

"Use him. Experiment with him. Evidently men are going to enter into this thing. Michael Fenger has, already. And now this boy. Why not try certain tests with them as we used to follow certain formulae in the chemistry laboratory at high school? This compound, that compound, what reaction? Then, when the time comes to apply your knowledge, you'll know."

Which shows how ignorant she was of this dangerous phase of her experiment. If she had not been, she must have known that these were not chemicals, but explosives with which she proposed to play.

The trouble was that Fanny Brandeis, the creative, was not being fed. And the creative fire requires fuel. Fanny Brandeis fed on people, not things. And her work at Haynes-Cooper was all with inanimate objects. The three months since her coming to Chicago had been crowded and eventful. Haynes-Cooper claimed every ounce of her energy, every atom of her wit and resourcefulness. In return it gave—salary. Not too much salary. That would come later, perhaps. Unfortunately, Fanny Brandeis did not thrive on that kind of fare. She needed people. She craved contact. All these millions whom she served—these unseen, unheard men and women, and children—she wanted to see them. She wanted to touch them. She wanted to talk with them. It was as though a lover of the drama, eager to see his favorite actress in her greatest part, were to find himself viewing her in a badly constructed film play.

So Fanny Brandeis took to prowling. There are people who have a penchant for cities—more than that, a talent for them, a gift of sensing them, of feeling their rhythm and pulse-beats, as others have a highly developed music sense, or color reaction. It is a thing that cannot be acquired. In Fanny Brandeis there was this abnormal response to the color and tone of any city. And Chicago was a huge, polyglot orchestra, made up of players in every possible sort of bizarre costume, performing on every known instrument, leaderless, terrifyingly discordant, yet with an occasional strain, exquisite and poignant, to be heard through the clamor and din.

A walk along State street (the wrong side) or Michigan avenue at five, or through one of the city's foreign quarters, or along the lake front at dusk, stimulated her like strong wine. She was drunk with it. And all the time she would say to herself, little blind fool that she was:

"Don't let it get you. Look at it, but don't think about it. Don't let the human end of it touch you. There's nothing in it."

And meanwhile she was feasting on those faces in the crowds. Those faces in the crowds! They seemed to leap out at her. They called to her. So she sketched them, telling herself that she did it by way of relaxation, and diversion. One afternoon she left her desk early, and perched herself on one of the marble benches that lined the sunken garden just across from the main group of Haynes-Cooper buildings. She wanted to see what happened when those great buildings emptied. Even her imagination did not meet the actuality. At 5:30 the streets about the plant were empty, except for an occasional passerby. At 5:31 there trickled down the broad steps of building after building thin dark streams of humanity, like the first slow line of lava that crawls down the side of an erupting volcano. The trickle broadened into a stream, spread into a flood, became a torrent that inundated the streets, the sidewalks, filling every nook and crevice, a moving mass. Ten thousand people! A city! Fanny found herself shaking with excitement, and something like terror at the immensity of it. She tried to get a picture of it, a sketch, with the gleaming windows of the red brick buildings as a background. Amazingly enough, she succeeded in doing it. That was because she tried for broad effects, and relied on one bit of detail for her story. It was the face of a girl—a very tired and tawdry girl, of sixteen, perhaps. On her face the look that the day's work had stamped there was being wiped gently away by another look; a look that said release, and a sweetheart, and an evening at the movies. Fanny, in some miraculous way, got it.

She prowled in the Ghetto, and sketched those patient Jewish faces, often grotesque, sometimes repulsive, always mobile. She wandered down South Clark street, flaring with purple-white arc-lights, and looked in at its windows that displayed a pawnbroker's glittering wares, or, just next door, a flat-topped stove over which a white-capped magician whose face smacked of the galley, performed deft tricks with a pancake turner. "Southern chicken dinner," a lying sign read, "with waffles and real maple syrup, 35 cents each." Past these windows promenaded the

Clark street women, hard-eyed, high-heeled, aigretted; on the street corners loafed the Clark street men, blue-shaven, wearing checked suits, soiled faun-topped shoes, and diamond scarf pins. And even as she watched them, fascinated, they vanished. Clark street changed overnight, and became a business thoroughfare, lined with stately office buildings, boasting marble and gold-leaf banks, filled with hurrying clerks, stenographers, and prosperous bond salesmen. It was like a sporting man who, thriving in middle age, endeavors to live down his shady past.

Fanny discovered Cottage Grove avenue, and Halsted street, and Jefferson, and South State, where she should never have walked. There is an ugliness about Chicago's ugly streets that, for sheer, naked brutality, is equaled nowhere in the world. London has its foul streets, smoke-blackened, sinister. But they are ugly as crime is ugly—and as fascinating. It is like the ugliness of an old hag who has lived a life, and who could tell you strange tales, if she would. Walking through them you think of Fagin, of Children of the Ghetto, of Tales of Mean Streets. Naples is honeycombed with narrow, teeming alleys, grimed with the sediment of centuries, colored like old Stilton, and smelling much worse. But where is there another Cottage Grove avenue! Sylvan misnomer! A hideous street, and sordid. A street of flat-wheeled cars, of delicatessen shops and moving picture houses, of clanging bells, of frowsy women, of men who dart around corners with pitchers, their coat collars turned up to hide the absence of linen. One day Fanny found herself at Fifty-first street, and there before her lay Washington Park, with its gracious meadow, its Italian garden, its rose walk, its lagoon, and drooping willows. But then, that was Chicago. All contrast. The Illinois Central railroad puffed contemptuous cinders into the great blue lake. And almost in the shadow of the City Hall nestled Bath-House John's groggery.

Michigan Avenue fascinated her most. Here was a street developing before one's eyes. To walk on it was like being present at a birth. It is one of the few streets in the world. New York has two, Paris a hundred, London none, Vienna one. Berlin, before the war, knew that no one walked Unter den Linden but American tourists and German shopkeepers from the provinces, with their fat wives. But this Michigan Boulevard, unfinished as Chicago itself, shifting and changing daily, still manages to take on a certain form and rugged beauty. It has about it a gracious breadth. As you turn into it from the crash and thunder of Wabash there comes to you a sense of peace. That's the sweep of it, and the lake just beyond, for Michigan avenue is a one-side street. It's west side is a sheer mountain wall of office buildings, clubs, and hotels, whose ground floors are fascinating with specialty shops. A milliner tantalizes the passer-by with a single hat stuck knowingly on a carved stick. An art store shows two etchings, and a vase. A jeweler's window holds square blobs of emeralds, on velvet, and perhaps a gold mesh bag, sprawling limp and invertebrate, or a diamond and platinum la valliere, chastely barbaric. Past these windows, from Randolph to Twelfth surges the crowd: matinee girls, all white fox, and giggles and orchids; wise-eyed saleswomen from the smart specialty shops, dressed in next week's mode; art students, hugging their precious flat packages under their arms; immigrants, in corduroys and shawls, just landed at the Twelfth street station; sightseeing families, dazed and weary, from Kansas; tailored and sabled Lake Shore Drive dwellers; convention delegates spilling out of the Auditorium hotel, red-faced, hoarse, with satin badges pinned on their coats, and their hats (the wrong kind) stuck far back on their heads; music students to whom Michigan Avenue means the Fine Arts Building. There you have the west side. But just across the street the walk is as deserted as though a pestilence lurked there. Here the Art Institute rears its smoke-blackened face, and Grant Park's greenery struggles bravely against the poisonous breath of the Illinois Central engines.

Just below Twelfth street block after block shows the solid plate glass of the automobile shops, their glittering wares displayed against an absurd background of oriental rugs, Tiffany lamps, potted plants, and mahogany. In the windows pose the salesmen, no less sleek and glittering than their wares. Just below these, for a block or two, rows of sinister looking houses, fallen into decay, with slatternly women lolling at their windows, and gas jets flaring blue in dim hallways. Below Eighteenth still another change, where the fat stone mansions of Chicago's old families (save the mark!) hide their diminished heads behind signs that read:

"Marguerite. Robes et Manteaux." And, "Smolkin. Tailor."

Now, you know that women buyers for mail order houses do not spend their Saturday afternoons and Sundays thus, prowling about a city's streets. Fanny Brandeis knew it too, in her heart. She knew that the Ella Monahans of her world spent their holidays in stayless relaxation, manicuring, mending a bit, skimming the Sunday papers, massaging crows'-feet somewhat futilely. She knew that women buyers do not, as a rule, catch their breath with delight at sight of the pock-marked old Field Columbian museum in Jackson Park, softened and beautified by the kindly gray chiffon of the lake mist, and tinted by the rouge of the sunset glow, so that it is a thing of spectral loveliness. Successful mercantile women, seeing the furnace glare of the South Chicago steel mills flaring a sullen red against the lowering sky, do not draw a disquieting mental picture of men toiling there, naked to the waist, and glistening with sweat in the devouring heat of the fires.

I don't know how she tricked herself. I suppose she said it was the city's appeal to the country dweller, but she lied, and she knew she was lying. She must have known it was the spirit of Molly Brandeis in her, and of Molly Brandeis' mother, and of her mother's mother's mother, down the centuries to Sarah; repressed women, suffering women, troubled, patient, nomadic women, struggling now in her for expression.

And Fanny Brandeis went doggedly on, buying and selling infants' wear, and doing it expertly. Her office desk would have interested you. It was so likely to be littered with the most appealing bits of apparel—a pair of tiny, crocheted bootees, pink and white; a sturdy linen smock; a silken hood so small that one's doubled fist filled it.

The new catalogue was on the presses. Fanny had slaved over it, hampered by Slosson. Fenger had given her practically a free hand. Results would not come in for many days. The Christmas trade would not tell the tale, for that was always a time of abnormal business. The dull season following the holiday rush would show the real returns. Slosson was discouragement itself. His attitude was not resentful; it was pitying, and that frightened Fanny. She wished that he would storm a little. Then she read her department catalogue proof sheets, and these reassured her. They were attractive. And the new baby book had turned out very well, with a colored cover that would appeal to any one who had ever been or seen a baby.

September brought a letter from Theodore. A letter from Theodore meant just one thing. Fanny hesitated a moment before opening it. She always hesitated before opening Theodore's letters. While she hesitated the old struggle would rage in her.

"I don't owe him anything," the thing within her would say. "God knows I don't. What have I done all my life but give, and give, and give to him! I'm a woman. He's a man. Let him work with his hands, as I do. He's had his share. More than his share."

Nevertheless she had sent him one thousand of the six thousand her mother had bequeathed to her. She didn't want to do it. She fought doing it. But she did it.

Now, as she held this last letter in her hands, and stared at the Bavarian stamp, she said to herself:

"He wants something. Money. If I send him some I can't have that new tailor suit, or the furs. And I need them. I'm going to have them."

She tore open the letter.

"Dear Old Fan:

"Olga and I are back in Munich, as you see. I think we'll be here all winter, though Olga hates it. She says it isn't lustig. Well, it isn't Vienna, but I think there's a chance for a class here of American pupils. Munich's swarming with Americans—whole families who come here to live for a year or two. I think I might get together a very decent class, backed by Auer's recommendations. Teaching! Good God, how I hate it! But Auer is planning a series of twenty concerts for me. They ought to be a success, if slaving can do it. I worked six hours a day all summer. I wanted to spend the summer—most of it, that is—in Holzhausen Am Ammersee, which is a little village, or artist's colony in the valley, an hour's ride from here, and within sight of the Bavarian Alps. We had Kurt Stein's little villa for almost nothing. But Olga was bored, and she wasn't well, poor girl, so we went to Interlaken and it was awful. And that brings me to what I want to tell you.

"There's going to be a baby. No use saying I'm glad, because I'm not, and neither is Olga. About February, I think. Olga has been simply wretched, but the doctor says she'll feel better from now on. The truth of it is she needs a lot of things and I can't give them to her. I told you I'd been working on this concerto of mine. Sometimes I think it's the real thing, if only I could get the leisure and the peace of mind I need to work on it. You don't know what it means to be eaten up with ambition and to be handicapped."

"Oh, don't I!" said Fanny Brandeis, between her teeth, and crumpled the letter in her strong fingers. "Don't I!" She got up from her chair and began to walk up and down her little office, up and down. A man often works off his feelings thus; a woman rarely. Fenger, who had not been twice in her office since her coming to the Haynes-Cooper plant, chose this moment to visit her, his hands full of papers, his head full of plans. He sensed something wrong at once, as a highly organized human instrument responds to a similarly constructed one.

"What's wrong, girl?"

"Everything. And don't call me girl."

Fenger saw the letter crushed in her hand.

"Brother?" She had told him about Theodore and he had been tremendously interested.

"Yes."

"Money again, I suppose?"

"Yes, but——"

"You know your salary's going up, after Christmas."

"Catalogue or no catalogue?"

"Catalogue or no catalogue."

"Why?"

"Because you've earned it."

Fanny faced him squarely. "I know that Haynes-Cooper isn't exactly a philanthropic institution. A salary raise here usually means a battle. I've only been here three months." Fenger seated himself in the chair beside her desk and ran a cool finger through the sheaf of papers in his hand. "My dear girl—I beg your pardon. I forgot. My good woman then—if you like that better—you've transfused red blood into a dying department. It may suffer a relapse after Christmas, but I don't think so. That's why you're getting more money, and not because I happen to be tremendously interested in you, personally."

Fanny's face flamed scarlet. "I didn't mean that."

"Yes you did. Here are those comparative lists you sent me. If I didn't know Slosson to be as honest as Old Dog Tray I'd think he had been selling us to the manufacturers. No wonder this department hasn't paid. He's been giving 'em top prices for shoddy. Now what's this new plan of yours?"

In an instant Fanny forgot about Theodore, the new winter suit and furs, everything but the idea that was clamoring to be born. She sat at her desk, her fingers folding and unfolding a bit of paper, her face all light and animation as she talked.

"My idea is to have a person known as a selector for each important department. It would mean a boiling down of the products of every manufacturer we deal with, and skimming the cream off the top. As it is now a department buyer has to do the selecting and buying too. He can't do both and get results. We ought to set aside an entire floor for the display of manufacturers' samples. The selector would make his choice among these, six months in advance of the season. The selector would go to the eastern markets too, of course. Not to buy. Merely to select. Then, with the line chosen as far as style, quality, and value is concerned, the buyer would be free to deal directly with the manufacturer as to quantity, time, and all that. You know as well as I that that's enough of a job for any one person, with the labor situation what it is. He wouldn't need to bother about styles or colors, or any of that. It would all have been done for him. The selector would have the real responsibility. Don't you see the simplicity of it, and the way it would grease the entire machinery?"

Something very like jealousy came into Michael Fenger's face as he looked at her. But it was gone in an instant. "Gad! You'll have my job away from me in two years. You're a super-woman, do you know that?"

"Super nothing! It's just a perfectly good idea, founded on common sense and economy."

"M-m-m, but that's all Columbus had in mind when he started out to find a short cut to India."

Fanny laughed out at that. "Yes, but see where he landed!"

But Fenger was serious. "We'll have to have a meeting on this. Are you prepared to go into detail on it, before Mr. Haynes and the two Coopers, at a real meeting in a real mahogany directors' room? Wednesday, say?"

"I think so."

Fenger got up. "Look here, Miss Brandeis. You need a day in the country. Why don't you run up to your home town over Sunday? Wisconsin, wasn't it?"

"Oh, no! No. I mean yes it was Wisconsin, but no I don't want to go."

"Then let me send you my car."

"Car! No, thanks. That's not my idea of the country."

"It was just a suggestion. What do you call going to the country, then?"

"Tramping all day, and getting lost, if possible. Lying down under a tree for hours, and letting the ants amble over you. Dreaming. And coming back tired, hungry, dusty, and refreshed."

"It sounds awfully uncomfortable. But I wish you'd try it, this week."

"Do I look such a wreck?" Fanny demanded, rather pettishly.

"You!" Fenger's voice was vibrant. "You're the most splendidly alive looking woman I ever saw. When you came into my office that first day you seemed to spark with health, and repressed energy, and electricity, so that you radiated them. People who can do that, stimulate. That's what you are to me—a stimulant."

What can one do with a man who talks like that? After all, what he said was harmless enough. His tone was quietly sincere. One can't resent an expression of the eyes. Then, too, just as she made up her mind to be angry she remembered the limp and querulous Mrs. Fenger, and the valve and the scarf. And her anger became pity. There flashed back to her the illuminating bit of conversation with which Fascinating Facts had regaled her on the homeward drive that night of the tea.

"Nice chap, Fenger. And a wiz in business. Get's a king's salary; Must be hell for a man to be tied, hand and foot, the way he is."

"Tied?"

"Mrs. Fenger's a semi-invalid. At that I don't believe she's as helpless as she seems. I think she just holds him by that shawl of hers, that's forever slipping. You know he was a machine boy in her father's woolen mill. She met him after he'd worked his way up to an office job. He has forged ahead like a locomotive ever since."

That had been their conversation, gossipy, but tremendously enlightening for Fanny. She looked up at him now.

"Thanks for the vacation suggestion. I may go off somewhere. Just a last-minute leap. It usually turns out better, that way. I'll be ready for the Wednesday discussion."

She sounded very final and busy. The crumpled letter lay on her desk. She smoothed it out, and the crumple transferred itself to her forehead. Fenger stood a moment, looking down at her. Then he turned, abruptly and left the office. Fanny did not look up.

That was Friday. On Saturday her vacation took a personally conducted turn. She had planned to get away at noon, as most office heads did on Saturday, during the warm weather. When her 'phone rang at eleven she answered it mechanically as does one whose telephone calls mean a row with a tardy manufacturer, an argument with a merchandise man, or a catalogue query from the printer's.

The name that came to her over the telephone conveyed nothing to her.

"Who?" Again the name. "Heyl?" She repeated the name uncertainly. "I'm afraid I—O, of course! Clarence Heyl. Howdy-do."

"I want to see you," said the voice, promptly.

There rose up in Fanny's mind a cruelly clear picture of the little, sallow, sniveling school boy of her girlhood. The little boy with the big glasses and the shiny shoes, and the weak lungs.

"Sorry," she replied, promptly, "but I'm afraid it's impossible. I'm leaving the office early, and I'm swamped." Which was a lie.

"This evening?"

"I rarely plan anything for the evening. Too tired, as a rule."

"Too tired to drive?"

"I'm afraid so."

A brief silence. Then, "I'm coming out there to see you."

"Where? Here? The plant! That's impossible, Mr. Heyl. I'm terribly sorry, but I can't——"

"Yes, I know. Also terribly sure that if I ever get to you it will be over your office boy's dead body. Well, arm him. I'm coming. Good-by."

"Wait a minute! Mr. Heyl! Clarence! Hello! Hello!"

A jiggling of the hook. "Number, please?" droned the voice of the operator.

Fanny jammed the receiver down on the hook and turned to her work, lips compressed, a frown forming a double cleft between her eyes.

Half an hour later he was there. Her office boy brought in his card, as she had rehearsed him to do. Fanny noted that it was the wrong kind of card. She would show him what happened to pushers who pestered business women during office hours.

"Bring him in in twenty minutes," she said, grimly. Her office boy (and slave) always took his cue from her. She hoped he wouldn't be too rude to Heyl, and turned back to her work again. Thirty-nine seconds later Clarence Heyl walked in.

"Hello, Fan!" he said, and had her limp hand in a grip that made her wince.

"But I told——"

"Yes, I know. But he's a crushed and broken office boy by now. I had to be real harsh with him."

Fanny stood up, really angry now. She looked up at Clarence Heyl, and her eyes were flashing. Clarence Heyl looked down at her, and his eyes were the keenest, kindest, most gently humorous eyes she had ever encountered. You know that picture of Lincoln that shows us his eyes with much that expression in them? That's as near as I can come to conveying to you the whimsical pathos in this man. They were the eyes of a lonely little boy grown up. And they had seen much in the process.

Fanny felt her little blaze of anger flicker and die.

"That's the girl," said Heyl, and patted her hand. "You'll like me—presently. After you've forgotten about that sniveling kid you hated." He stepped back a pace and threw back his coat senatorially. "How do I look?" he demanded.

"Look?" repeated Fanny, feebly.

"I've been hours preparing for this. Years! And now something tells me—This tie, for instance."

Fanny bit her lip in a vain effort to retain her solemnity. Then she gave it up and giggled, frankly. "Well, since you ask me, that tie!——"

"What's the matter with it?"

Fanny giggled again. "It's red, that's what."

"Well, what of it! Red's all right. I've always considered red one of our leading colors."

"But you can't wear it."

"Can't! Why can't I?"

"Because you're the brunest kind of brunette. And dark people have a special curse hanging over them that makes them want to wear red. It's fatal. That tie makes you look like a Mafia murderer dressed for business."

"I knew it," groaned Heyl. "Something told me." He sank into a chair at the side of her desk, a picture of mock dejection. "And I chose it. Deliberately. I had black ones, and blue ones, and green ones. And I chose—this." He covered his face with a shaking hand.

Fanny Brandeis leaned back in her chair, and laughed, and laughed, and laughed. Surely she hadn't laughed like that in a year at least.

"You're a madman," she said, finally.

At that Heyl looked up with his singularly winning smile. "But different. Concede that, Fanny. Be fair, now. Refreshingly different."

"Different," said Fanny, "doesn't begin to cover it. Well, now you're here, tell me what you're doing here."

"Seeing you."

"I mean here, in Chicago."

"So do I. I'm on my way from Winnebago to New York, and I'm in Chicago to see Fanny Brandeis."

"Don't expect me to believe that."

Heyl put an arm on Fanny's desk and learned forward, his face very earnest. "I do expect you to believe it. I expect you to believe everything I say to you. Not only that, I expect you not to be surprised at anything I say. I've done such a mass of private thinking about you in the last ten years that I'm likely to forget I've scarcely seen you in that time. Just remember, will you, that like the girl in the sob song, `You made me what I am to-day?'"

"I! You're being humorous again."

"Never less so in my life. Listen, Fan. That cowardly, sickly little boy you fought for in the street, that day in Winnebago, showed every sign of growing up a cowardly, sickly man. You're the real reason for his not doing so. Now, wait a minute. I was an impressionable little kid, I guess. Sickly ones are apt to be. I worshiped you and hated you from that day. Worshiped you for the blazing, generous, whole-souled little devil of a spitfire that you were. Hated you because—well, what boy wouldn't hate a girl who had to fight for him. Gosh! It makes me sick to think of it, even now. Pasty-faced rat!"

"What nonsense! I'd forgotten all about it."

"No you hadn't. Tell me, what flashed into your mind when you saw me in Temple that night before you left Winnebago? The truth, now."

She learned, later, that people did not lie to him. She tried it now, and found herself saying, rather shamefacedly, "I thought `Why, it's Clarence Heyl, the Cowardy-Cat!'"

"There! That's why I'm here to-day. I knew you were thinking that. I knew it all the time I was in Colorado, growing up from a sickly kid, with a bum lung, to a heap big strong man. It forced me to do things I was afraid to do. It goaded me on to stunts at the very thought of which I'd break out in a clammy sweat. Don't you see how I'll have to turn handsprings in front of you, like the school-boy in the McCutcheon cartoon? Don't you see how I'll have to flex my muscles—like this—to show you how strong I am? I may even have to beat you, eventually. Why, child, I've chummed with lions, and bears, and wolves, and everything, because of you, you little devil in the red cap! I've climbed unclimbable mountains. I've frozen my feet in blizzards. I've wandered for days on a mountain top, lost, living on dried currants and milk chocolate,—and Lord! how I hate milk chocolate! I've dodged snowslides, and slept in trees; I've endured cold, and hunger and thirst, through you. It took me years to get used to the idea of passing a timber wolf without looking around, but I learned to do it—because of you. You made me. They sent me to Colorado, a lonely kid, with a pretty fair chance of dying, and I would have, if it hadn't been for you. There! How's that for a burst of speech, young woman! And wait a minute. Remember, too, my name was Clarence. I had that to live down."

Fanny was staring at him eyes round, lips parted. "But why?" she said, faintly. "Why?"

Heyl smiled that singularly winning smile of his. "Since you force me to it, I think I'm in love with that little, warm-hearted spitfire in the red cap. That's why."

Fanny sat forward now. She had been leaning back in her chair, her hands grasping its arms, her face a lovely, mobile thing, across which laughter, and pity, and sympathy and surprise rippled and played. It hardened now, and set. She looked down at her hands, and clasped them in her lap, then up at him. "In that case, you can forsake the strenuous life with a free conscience. You need never climb another mountain, or wrestle with another—er—hippopotamus. That little girl in the red cap is dead."

"Dead?"

"Yes. She died a year ago. If the one who has taken her place were to pass you on the street today, and see you beset by forty thieves, she'd not even stop. Not she. She'd say, `Let him fight it out alone. It's none of your business. You've got your own fights to handle.'"

"Why—Fanny. You don't mean that, do you? What could have made her like that?"

"She just discovered that fighting for others didn't pay. She just happened to know some one else who had done that all her life and—it killed her."

"Her mother?"

"Yes."

A little silence. "Fanny, let's play outdoors tomorrow, will you? All day."

Involuntarily Fanny glanced around the room. Papers, catalogues, files, desk, chair, typewriter. "I'm afraid I've forgotten how."

"I'll teach you. You look as if you could stand a little of it."

"I must be a pretty sight. You're the second man to tell me that in two days."

Heyl leaned forward a little. "That so? Who's the other one?"

"Fenger, the General Manager."

"Oh! Paternal old chap, I suppose. No? Well, anyway, I don't know what he had in mind, but you're going to spend Sunday at the dunes of Indiana with me."

"Dunes? Of Indiana?"

"There's nothing like them in the world. Literally. In September that combination of yellow sand, and blue lake, and the woods beyond is—well, you'll see what it is. It's only a little more than an hour's ride by train. And it will just wipe that tired look out of your face, Fan." He stood up. "I'll call for you tomorrow morning at eight, or thereabouts. That's early for Sunday, but it's going to be worth it."

"I can't. Really. Besides, I don't think I even want to. I——"

"I promise not to lecture on Nature, if that's what's worrying you." He took her hand in a parting grip. "Bring some sandwiches, will you? Quite a lot of 'em. I'll have some other stuff in my rucksack. And wear some clothes you don't mind wrecking. I suppose you haven't got a red tam o' shanter?"

"Heavens, no!"

"I just thought it might help to keep me humble." He was at the door, and so was she, somehow, her hand still in his. "Eight o'clock. How do you stand it in this place, Fan? Oh, well—I'll find that out to-morrow. Good-by."

Fanny went back to her desk and papers. The room seemed all at once impossibly stuffy, her papers and letters dry, meaningless things. In the next office, separated from her by a partition half glass, half wood, she saw the top of Slosson's bald head as he stood up to shut his old-fashioned roll-top desk. He was leaving. She looked out of the window. Ella Monahan, in hat and suit, passed and came back to poke her head in the door.

"Run along!" she said. "It's Saturday afternoon. You'll work overtime enough when the Christmas rush begins. Come on, child, and call it a day!"

And Fanny gathered papers, figures, catalogue proofs into a glorious heap, thrust them into a drawer, locked the drawer, pushed back her chair, and came.

CHAPTER ELEVEN

Fanny told herself, before she went to bed Saturday night, that she hoped it would rain Sunday morning from seven to twelve. But when Princess woke her at seven-thirty, as per instructions left in penciled scrawl on the kitchen table, she turned to the window at once, and was glad, somehow, to find it sun-flooded. Princess, if you're mystified, was royal in name only—a biscuit-tinted lady, with a very black and no-account husband whose habits made it necessary for Princess to let herself into Fanny's four-room flat at seven every morning, and let herself out at eight every evening. She had an incredibly soft and musical voice, had Princess, and a cooking hand. She kept Fanny mended, fed and comfortable, and her only cross was that Fanny's taste in blouses (ultimately her property) ran to the severe and tailored.

"Mawnin', Miss Fanny. There's a gep'mun waitin' to see yo'."

Fanny choked on a yawn. "A what!"

"Gep'mun. Says yo-all goin' picnickin'. He's in the settin' room, a-lookin' at yo' pictchah papahs. Will Ah fry yo' up a li'l chicken to pack along? San'wiches ain't no eatin' fo' Sunday."

Fanny flung back her covers, swung around to the side of the bed, and stood up, all, seemingly, in one sweeping movement. "Do you mean to tell me he's in there, now?"

From the sitting room. "I think I ought to tell you I can hear everything you're saying. Say. Fanny, those sketches of yours are——Why, Gee Whiz! I didn't know you did that kind of thing. This one here, with that girl's face in the crowd——"

"For heaven's sake!" Fanny demanded, "what are you doing here at seven-thirty? And I don't allow people to look at those sketches. You said eight-thirty."

"I was afraid you'd change your mind, or something. Besides, it's now twenty-two minutes to eight. And will you tell the lady that's a wonderful idea about the chicken? Only she'd better start now."

Goaded by time bulletins shouted through the closed door, Fanny found herself tubbed, clothed, and ready for breakfast by eight-ten. When she opened the door Clarence was standing in the center of her little sitting room, waiting, a sheaf of loose sketches in his hand.

"Say, look here! These are the real thing. Why, they're great! They get you. This old geezer with the beard, selling fish and looking like one of the Disciples. And this. What the devil are you doing in a mail order house, or whatever it is? Tell me that! When you can draw like this!"

"Good morning," said Fanny, calmly. "And I'll tell you nothing before breakfast. The one thing that interests me this moment is hot coffee. Will you have some breakfast? Oh, well, a second one won't hurt you. You must have got up at three, or thereabouts." She went toward the tiny kitchen. "Never mind, Princess. I'll wait on myself. You go on with that chicken."

Princess was the kind of person who can fry a chicken, wrap it in cool, crisp lettuce leaves, box it, cut sandwiches, and come out of the process with an unruffled temper and an immaculate kitchen. Thanks to her, Fanny and Heyl found themselves on the eight fifty-three train, bound for the dunes.

Clarence swung his rucksack up to the bundle rack. He took off his cap, and stuffed it into his pocket. He was grinning like a schoolboy. Fanny turned from the window and smiled at what she saw in his face. At that he gave an absurd little bounce in his place, like an overgrown child, and reached over and patted her hand.

"I've dreamed of this for years."

"You're just fourteen, going on fifteen," Fanny reproved him.

"I know it. And it's great! Won't you be, too? Forget you're a fair financier, or whatever they call it. Forget you earn more in a month than I do in six. Relax. Unbend. Loosen up. Don't assume that hardshell air with me. Just remember that I knew you when the frill of your panties showed below your skirt."

"Clarence Heyl!"

But he was leaning past her, and pointing out of the window. "See that curtain of smoke off there? That's the South Chicago, and the Hammond and Gary steel mills. Wait till you see those smokestacks against the sky, and the iron scaffoldings that look like giant lacework, and the slag heaps, and the coal piles, and those huge, grim tanks. Gad! It's awful and beautiful. Like the things Pennell does." "I came out here on the street car one day," said Fanny, quietly. "One Sunday."

"You did!" He stared at her.

"It was hot, and they were all spilling out into the street. You know, the women in wrappers, just blobs of flesh trying to get cool. And the young girls in their pink silk dresses and white shoes, and the boys on the street corners, calling to them. Babies all over the sidewalks and streets, and the men who weren't in the mills—you know how they look in their Sunday shirtsleeves, with their flat faces, and high cheekbones, and their great brown hands with the broken nails. Hunkies. Well, at five the motor cars began whizzing by from the country roads back to Chicago. You have to go back that way. Just then the five o'clock whistles blew and the day shift came off. There was a great army of them, clumping down the road the way they do. Their shoulders were slack, and their lunch pails dangled, empty, and they were wet and reeking with sweat. The motor cars were full of wild phlox and daisies and spiderwort."

Clarence was still turned sideways, looking at her. "Get a picture of it?"

"Yes. I tried, at least."

"Is that the way you usually spend your Sundays?"

"Well, I—I like snooping about."

"M-m," mused Clarence. Then, "How's business, Fanny?"

"Business?" You could almost feel her mind jerk back. "Oh, let's not talk about business on Sunday."

"I thought so," said Clarence, enigmatically. "Now listen to me, Fanny."

"I'll listen," interrupted she, "if you'll talk about yourself. I want to know what you're doing, and why you're going to New York. What business can a naturalist have in New York, anyway?"

"I didn't intend to be a naturalist. You can tell that by looking at me. But you can't have your very nose rubbed up against trees, and rocks, and mountains, and snow for years and years without learning something about 'em. There were whole weeks when I hadn't anything to chum with but a timber-line pine and an odd assortment of mountain peaks. We just had to get acquainted."

"But you're going back, aren't you? Don't they talk about the spell of the mountains, or some such thing?" "They do. And they're right. And I've got to have them six months in the year, at least. But I'm going to try spending the other six in the bosom of the human race. Not only that, I'm going to write about it. Writing's my job, really. At least, it's the thing I like best."

"Nature?"

"Human nature. I went out to Colorado just a lonesome little kid with a bum lung. The lung's all right, but I never did quite get over the other. Two years ago, in the mountains, I met Carl Lasker, who owns the New York Star. It's said to be the greatest morning paper in the country. Lasker's a genius. And he fries the best bacon I ever tasted. I took him on a four-weeks' horseback trip through the mountains. We got pretty well acquainted. At the end of it he offered me a job. You see, I'd never seen a chorus girl, or the Woolworth building, or a cabaret, or a broiled lobster, or a subway. But I was interested and curious about all of them. And Lasker said, `A man who can humanize a rock, or a tree, or a chipmunk ought to be able to make even those things seem human. You've got what they call the fresh viewpoint. New York's full of people with a scum over their eyes, but a lot of them came to New York from Winnebago, or towns just like it, and you'd be surprised at the number of them who still get their home town paper. One day, when I came into Lee Kohl's office, with stars, and leading men, and all that waiting outside to see him, he was sitting with his feet on the desk reading the Sheffield, Illinois, Gazette.' You see, the thing he thinks I can do is to give them a picture of New York as they used to see it, before they got color blind. A column or so a day, about anything that hits me. How does that strike you as a job for a naturalist?"

"It's a job for a human naturalist. I think you'll cover it."

If you know the dunes, which you probably don't, you know why they did not get off at Millers, with the crowd, but rode on until they were free of the Sunday picnickers. Then they got off, and walked across the tracks, past saloons, and a few huddled houses, hideous in yellow paint, and on, and on down a road that seemed endless. A stretch of cinders, then dust, a rather stiff little hill, a great length of yellow sand and—the lake! We say, the lake! like that, with an exclamation point after it, because it wasn't at all the Lake Michigan that Chicagoans know. This vast blue glory bore no relation to the sullen, gray, turbid thing that the city calls the lake. It was all the blues of which you've ever heard, and every passing cloud gave it a new shade. Sapphire. No, cobalt. No, that's too cold. Mediterranean. Turquoise. And the sand in golden contrast. Miles of sand along the beach, and back of that the dunes. Now, any dictionary or Scotchman will tell you that a dune is a hill of loose sand. But these dunes are done in American fashion, lavishly. Mountains of sand, as far as the eye can see, and on the top of them, incredibly, great pine trees that clutch at their perilous, shifting foothold with frantic root-toes. And behind that, still more incredibly, the woods, filled with wild flowers, with strange growths found nowhere else in the whole land, with trees, and vines, and brush, and always the pungent scent of the pines. And there you have the dunes—blue lake, golden sand-hills, green forest, in one.

Fanny and Clarence stood there on the sand, in silence, two ridiculously diminutive figures in that great wilderness of beauty. I wish I could get to you, somehow, the clear sparkle of it, the brilliance of it, and yet the peace of it. They stood there a long while, those two, without speaking. Then Fanny shut her eyes, and I think her lower lip trembled just a little. And Clarence patted her hand just twice.

"I thank you," he said, "in the name of that much-abused lady known as Nature."

Said Fanny, "I want to scramble up to the top of one of those dunes—the high one—and just sit there."

And that is what they did. A poor enough Sunday, I suppose, in the minds of those of you who spend yours golfing at the club, or motoring along grease-soaked roads that lead to a shore dinner and a ukulele band. But it turned Fanny Brandeis back a dozen years or more, so that she was again the little girl whose heart had ached at sight of the pale rose and, orange of the Wisconsin winter sunsets. She forgot all about layettes, and obstetrical outfits, and flannel bands, and safety pins; her mind was a blank in the matter of bootees, and catalogues, and our No. 29E8347, and those hungry bins that always yawned for more. She forgot about Michael Fenger, and Theodore, and the new furs. They scrambled up dunes, digging into the treacherous sand with heels, toes, and the side of the foot, and clutching at fickle roots with frantic fingers. Forward a step, and back two—that's dune climbing. A back-breaking business, unless you're young and strong, as were these two. They explored the woods, and Heyl had a fascinating way of talking about stones and shrubs and trees as if they were endowed with human qualities—as indeed they were for him. They found a hill-slope carpeted with dwarf huckleberry plants, still bearing tiny clusters of the blue-black fruit. Fanny's heart was pounding, her lungs ached, her cheeks were scarlet, her eyes shining. Heyl, steel-muscled, took the hills like a chamois. Once they crossed hands atop a dune and literally skated down it, right, left, right, left, shrieking with laughter, and ending in a heap at the bottom. "In the name of all that's idiotic!" shouted Heyl. "Silk stockings! What in thunder made you wear silk stockings! At the sand dunes! Gosh!"

They ate their dinner in olympic splendor, atop a dune. Heyl produced unexpected things from the rucksack—things that ranged all the way from milk chocolate to literature, and from grape juice to cigarettes. They ate ravenously, but at Heyl's thrifty suggestion they saved a few sandwiches for the late afternoon. It was he, too, who made a little bonfire of papers, crusts, and bones, as is the cleanly habit of your true woodsman. Then they stretched out, full length, in the noon sun, on the warm, clean sand.

"What's your best price on one-sixth doz. flannel vests?" inquired Heyl.

And, "Oh, shut up!" said Fanny, elegantly. Heyl laughed as one who hugs a secret.

"We'll work our way down the beach," he announced, "toward Millers. There'll be northern lights to-night; did you know that? Want to stay and see them?"

"Do I want to! I won't go home till I have."

These were the things they did on that holiday; childish, happy, tiring things, such as people do who love the outdoors.

The charm of Clarence Heyl—for he had charm—is difficult to transmit. His lovableness and appeal lay in his simplicity. It was not so much what he said as in what he didn't say. He was staring unwinkingly now at the sunset that had suddenly burst upon them. His were the eyes of one accustomed to the silent distances.

"Takes your breath away, rather, doesn't it? All that color?" said Fanny, her face toward the blaze.

"Almost too obvious for my taste. I like 'em a little more subdued, myself." They were atop a dune, and he stretched himself flat on the sand, still keeping his bright brown eyes on lake and sky. Then he sat up, excitedly. "Heh, try that! Lie flat. It softens the whole thing. Like this. Now look at it. The lake's like molten copper flowing in. And you can see that silly sun going down in jerks, like a balloon on a string."

They lay there, silent, while the scarlet became orange, the orange faded to rose, the rose to pale pink, to salmon, to mauve, to gray. The first pale star came out, and the brazen lights of Gary, far to the north, defied it. Fanny sat up with a sigh and a little shiver.

"Fasten up that sweater around your throat," said Heyl. "Got a pin?" They munched their sandwiches, rather soggy by now, and drank the last of the grape juice. "We'll have a bite of hot supper in town, at a restaurant that doesn't mind Sunday trampers. Come on, Fan. We'll start down the beach until the northern lights begin to show."

"It's been the most accommodating day," murmured Fanny. "Sunshine, sunset, northern lights, everything. If we were to demand a rainbow and an eclipse they'd turn those on, too."

They started to walk down the beach in the twilight, keeping close to the water's edge where the sand was moist and firm. It was hard going. They plunged along arm in arm, in silence. Now and again they stopped, with one accord, and looked out over the great gray expanse that lay before them, and then up at the hills and the pines etched in black against the sky. Nothing competitive here, Fanny thought, and took a deep breath. She thought of to-morrow's work, with day after to-morrow's biting and snapping at its heels.

Clarence seemed to sense her thoughts. "Doesn't this make you feel you want to get away from those damned bins that you're forever feeding? I watched those boys for a minute, the other day, outside your office. Jove!"

Fanny dug a heel into the sand, savagely. "Some days I feel that I've got to walk out of the office, and down the street, without a hat, and on, and on, walking and walking, and running now and then, till I come to the horizon. That's how I feel, some days."

"Then some day, Fanny, that feeling will get too strong for you, and you'll do it. Now listen to me. Tuck this away in your subconscious mind, and leave it there until you need it. When that time comes get on a train for Denver. From Denver take another to Estes Park. That's the Rocky Mountains, and they're your destination, because that's where the horizon lives and has its being. When you get there ask for Heyl's place. They'll just hand you from one to the other, gently, until you get there. I may be there, but more likely I shan't. The key's in the mail box, tied to a string. You'll find a fire already laid, in the fireplace, with fat pine knots that will blaze up at the touch of a match. My books are there, along the walls. The bedding's in the cedar chest, and the lamps are filled. There's tinned stuff in the pantry. And the mountains are there, girl, to make you clean and whole again. And the pines that are nature's prophylactic brushes. And the sky. And peace. That sounds like a railway folder, but it's true. I know." They trudged along in silence for a little while. "Got that?"

"M-m," replied Fanny, disinterestedly, without looking at him.

Heyl's jaw set. You could see the muscles show white for an instant. Then he said: "It has been a wonderful day, Fanny, but you haven't told me a thing about yourself. I'd like to know about your work. I'd like to know what you're doing; what your plan is. You looked so darned definite up there in that office. Whom do you play with? And who's this Fenger—wasn't that the name?—who saw that you looked tired?"

"All right, Clancy. I'll tell you all about it," Fanny agreed, briskly.

"All right—who!"

"Well, I can't call you Clarence. It doesn't fit. So just for the rest of the day let's make it Clancy, even if you do look like one of the minor Hebrew prophets, minus the beard."

And so she began to tell him of her work and her aims. I think that she had been craving just this chance to talk. That which she told him was, unconsciously, a confession. She told him of Theodore and his marriage; of her mother's death; of her coming to Haynes-Cooper, and the changes she had brought about there. She showed him the infinite possibilities for advancement there. Slosson she tossed aside. Then, rather haltingly, she told him of Fenger, of his business genius, his magnetic qualities, of his career. She even sketched a deft word-picture of the limp and irritating Mrs. Fenger.

"Is this Fenger in love with you?" asked Heyl, startlingly.

Fanny recoiled at the idea with a primness that did credit to Winnebago.

"Clancy! Please! He's married."

"Now don't sneak, Fanny. And don't talk like an ingenue. So far, you've outlined a life-plan that makes Becky Sharp look like a cooing dove. So just answer this straight, will you?"

"Why, I suppose I attract him, as any man of his sort, with a wife like that, would be attracted to a healthily alert woman, whose ideas match his. And I wish you wouldn't talk to me like that. It hurts."

"I'm glad of that. I was afraid you'd passed that stage. Well now, how about those sketches of yours? I suppose you know that they're as good, in a crude, effective sort of way, as anything that's being done to-day."

"Oh, nonsense!" But then she stopped, suddenly, and put both hands on his arm, and looked up at him, her face radiant in the gray twilight. "Do you really think they're good!"

"You bet they're good. There isn't a newspaper in the country that couldn't use that kind of stuff. And there aren't three people in the country who can do it. It isn't a case of being able to draw. It's being able to see life in a peculiar light, and to throw that light so that others get the glow. Those sketches I saw this morning are life, served up raw. That's your gift, Fanny. Why the devil don't you use it!"

But Fanny had got herself in hand again. "It isn't a gift," she said, lightly. "It's just a little knack that amuses me. There's no money in it. Besides, it's too late now. One's got to do a thing superlatively, nowadays, to be recognized. I don't draw superlatively, but I do handle infants' wear better than any woman I know. In two more years I'll be getting ten thousand a year at Haynes-Cooper. In five years——"

"Then what?"

Fanny's hands became fists, gripping the power she craved. "Then I shall have arrived. I shall be able to see the great and beautiful things of this world, and mingle with the people who possess them."

"When you might be making them yourself, you little fool. Don't glare at me like that. I tell you that those pictures are the real expression of you. That's why you turn to them as relief from the shop grind. You can't help doing them. They're you."

"I can stop if I want to. They amuse me, that's all."

"You can't stop. It's in your blood. It's the Jew in you."

"The——Here, I'll show you. I won't do another sketch for a year. I'll prove to you that my ancestors' religion doesn't influence my work, or my play."

"Dear, you can't prove that, because the contrary has been proven long ago. You yourself proved it when you did that sketch of the old fish vender in the Ghetto. The one with the beard. It took a thousand years of suffering and persecution and faith to stamp that look on his face, and it took a thousand years to breed in you the genius to see it, and put it down on paper. Fan, did you ever read Fishberg's book?"

"No," said Fanny, low-voiced.

"Sometime, when you can snatch a moment from the fascinations of the mail order catalogue, read it. Fishberg says—I wish I could remember his exact words—`It isn't the body that marks the Jew. It's his Soul. The type is not anthropological, or physical; it's social or psychic. It isn't the complexion, the nose, the lips, the head. It's his Soul which betrays his faith. Centuries of Ghetto confinement, ostracism, ceaseless suffering, have produced a psychic type. The thing that is stamped on the Soul seeps through the veins and works its way magically to the face——'"

"But I don't want to talk about souls! Please! You're spoiling a wonderful day."

"And you're spoiling a wonderful life. I don't object to this driving ambition in you. I don't say that you're wrong in wanting to make a place for yourself in the world. But don't expect me to stand by and let you trample over your own immortal soul to get there. Your head is busy enough on this infants' wear job, but how about the rest of you—

how about You? What do you suppose all those years of work, and suppression, and self-denial, and beauty-hunger there in Winnebago were meant for! Not to develop the mail order business. They were given you so that you might recognize hunger, and suppression, and self-denial in others. The light in the face of that girl in the crowd pouring out of the plant. What's that but the reflection of the light in you! I tell you, Fanny, we Jews have got a money-grubbing, loud-talking, diamond-studded, get-there-at-any-price reputation, and perhaps we deserve it. But every now and then, out of the mass of us, one lifts his head and stands erect, and the great white light is in his face. And that person has suffered, for suffering breeds genius. It expands the soul just as over-prosperity shrivels it. You see it all the way from Lew Fields to Sarah Bernhardt; from Mendelssohn to Irving Berlin; from Mischa Elman to Charlie Chaplin. You were a person set apart in Winnebago. Instead of thanking your God for that, you set out to be something you aren't. No, it's worse than that. You're trying not to be what you are. And it's going to do for you."

"Stop!" cried Fanny. "My head's whirling. It sounds like something out of `Alice in Wonderland.'"

"And you," retorted Heyl, "sound like some one who's afraid to talk or think about herself. You're suppressing the thing that is you. You're cutting yourself off from your own people—a dramatic, impulsive, emotional people. By doing those things you're killing the goose that lays the golden egg. What's that old copy-book line? `To thine own self be true,' and the rest of it."

"Yes; like Theodore, for example," sneered Fanny.

At which unpleasant point Nature kindly supplied a diversion. Across the black sky there shot two luminous shafts of lights. Northern lights, pale sisters of the chromatic glory one sees in the far north, but still weirdly beautiful. Fanny and Heyl stopped short, faces upturned. The ghostly radiance wavered, expanded, glowed palely, like celestial searchlights. Suddenly, from the tip of each shaft, there burst a cluster of slender, pin-point lines, like aigrettes set in a band of silver. Then these slowly wavered, faded, combined to form a third and fourth slender shaft of light. It was like the radiance one sees in the old pictures of the Holy Family. Together Fanny and Heyl watched it in silence until the last pale glimmer faded and was gone, and only the brazen lights of Gary, far, far down the beach, cast a fiery glow against the sky.

They sighed, simultaneously. Then they laughed, each at the other.

"Curtain," said Fanny. They raced for the station, despite the sand. Their car was filled with pudgy babies lying limp in parental arms; with lunch baskets exuding the sickly scent of bananas; with disheveled vandals whose moist palms grasped bunches of wilted wild flowers. Past the belching chimneys of Gary, through South Chicago, the back yard of a metropolis, past Jackson Park that breathed coolly upon them, and so to the city again. They looked at it with the shock that comes to eyes that have rested for hours on long stretches of sand and sky and water. Monday, that had seemed so far away, became an actuality of to-morrow.

Tired as they were, they stopped at one of those frank little restaurants that brighten Chicago's drab side streets. Its windows were full of pans that held baked beans, all crusty and brown, and falsely tempting, and of baked apples swimming in a pool of syrup. These flanked by ketchup bottles and geometrical pyramids of golden grape-fruit.

Coffee and hot roast beef sandwiches, of course, in a place like that. "And," added Fanny, "one of those baked apples. Just to prove they can't be as good as they look."

They weren't, but she was too hungry to care. Not too hungry, though, to note with quick eye all that the little restaurant held of interest, nor too sleepy to respond to the friendly waitress who, seeing their dusty boots, and the sprig of sumac stuck in Fanny's coat, said, "My, it must have been swell in the country today!" as her flapping napkin precipitated crumbs into their laps.

"It was," said Fanny, and smiled up at the girl with her generous, flashing smile. "Here's a bit of it I brought back for you." And she stuck the scarlet sumac sprig into the belt of the white apron.

They finished the day incongruously by taking a taxi home, Fanny yawning luxuriously all the way. "Do you know," she said, as they parted, "we've talked about everything from souls to infants' wear. We're talked out. It's a mercy you're going to New York. There won't be a next time."

"Young woman," said Heyl, forcefully, "there will. That young devil in the red tam isn't dead. She's alive. And kicking. There's a kick in every one of those Chicago sketches in your portfolio upstairs. You said she wouldn't fight anybody's battles to-day. You little idiot, she's fighting one in each of those pictures, from the one showing that girl's face in the crowd, to the old chap with the fish-stall. She'll never die that one. Because she's the spirit. It's the other one who's dead—and she doesn't know it. But some day she'll find herself buried. And I want to be there to shovel on the dirt."

CHAPTER TWELVE

From the first of December the floor of the Haynes-Cooper mail room looked like the New York Stock Exchange, after a panic. The aisles were drifts of paper against which a squad of boys struggled as vainly as a gang of snow-shovelers against a blizzard. The guide talked in terms of tons of mail, instead of thousands. And smacked his lips after it. The Ten Thousand were working at night now, stopping for a hasty bite of supper at six, then back to desk, or bin or shelf until nine, so that Oklahoma and Minnesota might have its Christmas box in time.

Fanny Brandeis, working under the light of her green-shaded desk lamp, wondered, a little bitterly, if Christmas would ever mean anything to her but pressure, weariness, work. She told herself that she would not think of that

Christmas of one year ago. One year! As she glanced around the orderly little office, and out to the stock room beyond, then back to her desk again, she had an odd little feeling of unreality. Surely it had been not one year, but many years—a lifetime—since she had elbowed her way up and down those packed aisles of the busy little store in Winnebago—she and that brisk, alert, courageous woman.

"Mrs. Brandeis, lady wants to know if you can't put this blue satin dress on the dark-haired doll, and the pink satin.... Well, I did tell her, but she said for me to ask you, anyway."

"Mis' Brandeis, this man says he paid a dollar down on a go-cart last month and he wants to pay the rest and take it home with him."

And then the reassuring, authoritative voice, "Coming! I'll be right there."

"Coming!" That had been her whole life. Service. And now she lay so quietly beneath the snow of the bitter northern winter.

At that point Fanny's fist would come down hard on her desk, and the quick, indrawn breath of mutinous resentment would hiss through her teeth.

She kept away from the downtown shops and their crowds. She scowled at sight of the holly and mistletoe wreaths, with their crimson streamers. There was something almost ludicrous in the way she shut her eyes to the holiday pageant all around her, and doubled and redoubled her work. It seemed that she had a new scheme for her department every other day, and every other one was a good one.

Slosson had long ago abandoned the attempt to keep up with her. He did not even resent her, as he had at first. "I'm a buyer," he said, rather pathetically, "and a pret-ty good one, too. But I'm not a genius, and I never will be. And I guess you've got to be a genius, these days, to keep up. It used to be enough for an infants' wear buyer to know muslins, cottons, woolens, silks, and embroideries. But that's old-fashioned now. These days, when you hire an office boy you don't ask him if he can read and write. You tell him he's got to have personality, magnetism, and imagination. Makes me sick!"

The Baby Book came off the presses and it was good. Even Slosson admitted it, grudgingly. The cover was a sunny, breezy seashore picture, all blue and gold, with plump, dimpled youngsters playing, digging in the sand, romping (and wearing our No. 13E1269, etc., of course). Inside were displayed the complete baby outfits, with a smiling mother, and a chubby, crowing baby as a central picture, and each piece of each outfit separately pictured. Just below this, the outfit number and price, and a list of the pieces that went to make it up. From the emergency outfit at $3.98 to the outfit de luxe (for Haynes-Cooper patrons) at $28.50, each group was comprehensive, practical, complete. In the back of the book was a personal service plea. "Use us," it said. "We are here to assist you, not only in the matter of merchandise, but with information and advice. Mothers in particular are in need of such service. This book will save you weariness and worry. Use us."

Fanny surveyed the book with pardonable pride. But she was not satisfied. "We lack style," she said. "The practical garments are all right. But what we need is a little snap. That means cut and line. And I'm going to New York to get it." That had always been Slosson's work.

She and Ella Monahan were to go to the eastern markets together. Ella Monahan went to New York regularly every three weeks. Fanny had never been east of Chicago. She envied Ella her knowledge of the New York wholesalers and manufacturers. Ella had dropped into Fanny's office for a brief moment. The two women had little in common, except their work, but they got on very well, and each found the other educating.

"Seems to me you're putting an awful lot into this," observed Ella Monahan, her wise eyes on Fanny's rather tense face.

"You've got to," replied Fanny, "to get anything out of it."

"I guess you're right," Ella agreed, and laughed a rueful little laugh. "I know I've given 'em everything I've got—and a few things I didn't know I had. It's a queer game—life. Now if my old father hadn't run a tannery in Racine, and if I hadn't run around there all the day, so that I got so the smell and feel of leather and hides were part of me, why, I'd never be buyer of gloves at Haynes-Cooper. And you——"

"Brandeis' Bazaar." And was going on, when her office boy came in with a name. Ella rose to go, but Fanny stopped her. "Father Fitzpatrick! Bring him right in! Miss Monahan, you've got to meet him. He's"—then, as the great frame of the handsome old priest filled the doorway—"he's just Father Fitzpatrick. Ella Monahan."

The white-haired Irishman, and the white-haired Irish woman clasped hands.

"And who are you, daughter, besides being Ella Monahan?"

"Buyer of gloves at Haynes-Cooper, Father."

"You don't tell me, now!" He turned to Fanny, put his two big hands on her shoulders, and swung her around to face the light. "Hm," he murmured, noncommittally, after that.

"Hm—what?" demanded Fanny. "It sounds unflattering, whatever it means." "Gloves!" repeated Father Fitzpatrick, unheeding her. "Well, now, what d'you think of that! Millions of dollars' worth, I'll wager, in your time."

"Two million and a half in my department last year," replied Ella, without the least trace of boastfulness. One talked only in terms of millions at Haynes-Cooper's.

"What an age it is! When two slips of women can earn salaries that would make the old kings of Ireland look like beggars." He twinkled upon the older woman. "And what a feeling it must be—independence, and all."

"I've earned my own living since I was seventeen," said Ella Monahan. "I'd hate to tell you how long that is." A murmur from the gallant Irishman. "Thanks, Father, for the compliment I see in your eyes. But what I mean is this: You're right about independence. It is a grand thing. At first. But after a while it begins to pall on you. Don't ask me why. I don't know. I only hope you won't think I'm a wicked woman when I say I could learn to love any man who'd hang a silver fox scarf and a string of pearls around my neck, and ask me if I didn't feel a draft."

"Wicked! Not a bit of it, my girl. It's only natural, and commendable—barrin' the pearls."

"I'd forego them," laughed Ella, and with a parting handshake left the two alone.

Father Fitzpatrick looked after her. "A smart woman, that." He took out his watch, a fat silver one. "It's eleven-thirty. My train leaves at four. Now, Fanny, if you'll get on your hat, and arrange to steal an hour or so from this Brobdingnagian place a grand word that, my girl, and nearer to swearing than any word I know—I'll take you to the Blackstone, no less, for lunch. How's that for a poor miserable old priest!"

"You dear, I couldn't think of it. Oh, yes, I could get away, but let's lunch right here at the plant, in the grill——"

"Never! I couldn't. Don't ask it of me. This place scares me. I came up in the elevator with a crowd and a guide, and he was juggling millions, that chap, the way a newsboy flips a cent. I'm but a poor parish priest, but I've got my pride. We'll go to the Blackstone, which I've passed, humbly, but never been in, with its rose silk shades and its window boxes. And we'll be waited on by velvet-footed servitors, me girl. Get your hat."

Fanny, protesting, but laughing, too, got it. They took the L. Michigan avenue, as they approached it from Wabash, was wind-swept and bleak as only Michigan avenue can be in December. They entered the warm radiance of the luxurious foyer with a little breathless rush, as wind-blown Chicagoans generally do. The head waiter must have thought Father Fitzpatrick a cardinal, at least, for he seated them at a window table that looked out upon the icy street, with Grant Park, crusted with sooty snow, just across the way, and beyond that the I. C. tracks and the great gray lake. The splendid room was all color, and perfume, and humming conversation. A fountain tinkled in the center, and upon its waters there floated lily pads and blossoms, weirdly rose, and mauve, and lavender. The tables were occupied by deliciously slim young girls and very self-conscious college boys, home for the holidays, and marcelled matrons, furred and aigretted. The pink in Fanny's cheeks deepened. She loved luxury. She smiled and flashed at the handsome old priest opposite her.

"You're a wastrel," she said, "but isn't it nice!" And tasted the first delicious sip of soup.

"It is. For a change. Extravagance is good for all of us, now and then." He glanced leisurely about the brilliant room, then out to the street, bleakly windswept. He leaned back and drummed a bit with his fingers on the satin-smooth cloth. "Now and then. Tell me, Fanny, what would you say, off-hand, was the most interesting thing you see from here? You used to have a trick of picking out what they call the human side. Your mother had it, too."

Fanny, smiling, glanced about the room, her eyes unconsciously following the track his had taken. About the room, and out, to the icy street. "The most interesting thing?" Back to the flower-scented room, with its music, and tinkle, and animation. Out again, to the street. "You see that man, standing at the curb, across the street. He's sort of crouched against the lamp post. See him? Yes, there, just this side of that big gray car? He's all drawn up in a heap. You can feel him shivering. He looks as if he were trying to crawl inside himself for warmth. Ever since we came in I've noticed him staring straight across at these windows where we're all sitting so grandly, lunching. I know what he's thinking, don't you? And I wish I didn't feel so uncomfortable, knowing it. I wish we hadn't ordered lobster thermidor. I wish—there! the policeman's moving him on."

Father Fitzpatrick reached over and took her hand, as it lay on the table, in his great grasp. "Fanny, girl, you've told me what I wanted to know. Haynes-Cooper or no Haynes-Cooper, millions or no millions, your ravines aren't choked up with ashes yet, my dear. Thank God."

CHAPTER THIRTEEN

From now on Fanny Brandeis' life became such a swift-moving thing that your trilogist would have regarded her with disgust. Here was no slow unfolding, petal by petal. Here were two processes going on, side by side. Fanny, the woman of business, flourished and throve like a weed, arrogantly flaunting its head above the timid, white flower that lay close to the soil, and crept, and spread, and multiplied. Between the two the fight went on silently.

Fate, or Chance, or whatever it is that directs our movements, was forever throwing tragic or comic little life-groups in her path, and then, pointing an arresting finger at her, implying, "This means you!" Fanny stepped over these obstructions, or walked around them, or stared straight through them.

She had told herself that she would observe the first anniversary of her mother's death with none of those ancient customs by which your pious Jew honors his dead. There would be no Yahrzeit light burning for twenty-four hours. She would not go to Temple for Kaddish prayer. But the thing was too strong for her, too anciently inbred. Her ancestors would have lighted a candle, or an oil lamp. Fanny, coming home at six, found herself turning on the shaded electric lamp in her hall. She went through to the kitchen.

"Princess, when you come in to-morrow morning you'll find a light in the hall. Don't turn it off until to-morrow evening at six."

"All day long, Miss Fan! Mah sakes, wa' foh?"

"It's just a religious custom."

"Didn't know yo' had no relijin, Miss Fan. Leastways, Ah nevah could figgah——"

"I haven't," said Fanny, shortly. "Dinner ready soon, Princess? I'm starved."

She had entered a Jewish house of worship only once in this year. It was the stately, white-columned edifice on Grand Boulevard that housed the congregation presided over by the famous Kirsch. She had heard of him, naturally. She was there out of curiosity, like any other newcomer to Chicago. The beauty of the auditorium enchanted her—a magnificently proportioned room, and restful without being in the least gloomy. Then she had been interested in the congregation as it rustled in. She thought she had never seen so many modishly gowned women in one room in all her life. The men were sleekly broadclothed, but they lacked the well-dressed air, somehow. The women were slimly elegant in tailor suits and furs. They all looked as if they had been turned out by the same tailor. An artist, in his line, but of limited imagination. Dr. Kirsch, sociologist and savant, aquiline, semi-bald, grimly satiric, sat in his splendid, high-backed chair, surveying his silken flock through half-closed lids. He looked tired, and rather ill, Fanny thought, but distinctly a personage. She wondered if he held them or they him. That recalled to her the little Winnebago Temple and Rabbi Thalmann. She remembered the frequent rudeness and open inattention of that congregation. No doubt Mrs. Nathan Pereles had her counterpart here, and the hypocritical Bella Weinberg, too, and the giggling Aarons girls, and old Ben Reitman. Here Dr. Kirsch had risen, and, coming forward, had paused to lean over his desk and, with an awful geniality, had looked down upon two rustling, exquisitely gowned late-comers. They sank into their seats, cowed. Fanny grinned. He began his lecture something about modern politics. Fanny was fascinated and resentful by turns. His brilliant satire probed, cut, jabbed like a surgeon's scalpel; or he railed, scolded, snarled, like a dyspeptic schoolmaster. Often he was in wretched taste. He mimicked, postured, sneered. But he had this millionaire congregation of his in hand. Fanny found herself smiling up at him, delightedly. Perhaps this wasn't religion, as she had been taught to look upon it, but it certainly was tonic. She told herself that she would have come to the same conclusion if Kirsch had occupied a Methodist pulpit.

There were no Kaddish prayers in Kirsch's Temple. On the Friday following the first anniversary of Molly Brandeis's death Fanny did not go home after working hours, but took a bite of supper in a neighborhood restaurant. Then she found her way to one of the orthodox Russian Jewish synagogues on the west side. It was a dim, odorous, bare little place, this house of worship. Fanny had never seen one like it before. She was herded up in the gallery, where the women sat. And when the patriarchal rabbi began to intone the prayer for the dead Fanny threw the gallery into wild panic by rising for it—a thing that no woman is allowed to do in an orthodox Jewish church. She stood, calmly, though the beshawled women to right and left of her yanked at her coat.

In January Fanny discovered New York. She went as selector for her department. Hereafter Slosson would do only the actual buying. Styles, prices, and materials would be decided by her. Ella Monahan accompanied her, it being the time for her monthly trip. Fanny openly envied her her knowledge of New York's wholesale district. Ella offered to help her.

"No," Fanny had replied, "I think not, thanks. You've your own work. And besides I know pretty well what I want, and where to go to get it. It's making them give it to me that will be hard."

They went to the same hotel, and took connecting rooms. Each went her own way, not seeing the other from morning until night, but they often found kimonoed comfort in each other's presence.

Fanny had spent weeks outlining her plan of attack. She had determined to retain the cheap grades, but to add a finer line as well. She recalled those lace-bedecked bundles that the farmer women and mill hands had born so tenderly in their arms. Here was one direction in which they allowed extravagance free rein. As a canny business woman, she would trade on her knowledge of their weakness.

At Haynes-Cooper order is never a thing to be despised by a wholesaler. Fanny, knowing this, had made up her mind to go straight to Horn & Udell. Now, Horn & Udell are responsible for the bloomers your small daughter wears under her play frock, in place of the troublesome and extravagant petticoat of the old days. It was they who introduced smocked pinafores to you; and those modish patent-leather belts for children at which your grandmothers would have raised horrified hands. They taught you that an inch of hand embroidery is worth a yard of cheap lace. And as for style, cut, line—you can tell a Horn & Udell child from among a flock of thirty.

Fanny, entering their office, felt much as Molly Brandeis had felt that January many, many years before, when she had made that first terrifying trip to the Chicago market. The engagement had been made days before. Fanny never knew the shock that her youthfully expectant face gave old Sid Udell. He turned from his desk to greet her, his polite smile of greeting giving way to a look of bewilderment.

"But you are not the buyer, are you, Miss Brandeis?"

"No, Mr. Slosson buys."

"I thought so."

"But I select for my entire department. I decide on our styles, materials, and prices, six months in advance. Then Mr. Slosson does the actual bulk buying."

"Something new-fangled?" inquired Sid Udell. "Of course, we've never sold much to you people. Our stuff is———"

"Yes, I know. But you'd like to, wouldn't you?"

"Our class of goods isn't exactly suited to your wants."

"Yes, it is. Exactly. That's why I'm here. We'll be doing a business of a million and a quarter in my department in another two years. No firm, not even Horn & Udell, can afford to ignore an account like that."

Sid Udell smiled a little. "You've made up your mind to that million and a quarter, young lady?"

"Yes."

"Well, I've dealt with buyers for a quarter of a century or more. And I'd say that you're going to get it."

Whereupon Fanny began to talk. Ten minutes later Udell interrupted her to summon Horn, whose domain was the factory. Horn came, was introduced, looked doubtful. Fanny had statistics. Fanny had arguments. She had determination. "And what we want," she went on, in her quiet, assured way, "is style. The Horn & Udell clothes have chic. Now, material can't be imitated successfully, but style can. Our goods lack just that. I could copy any model you have, turn the idea over to a cheap manufacturer, and get a million just like it, at one-fifth the price. That isn't a threat. It's just a business statement that you know to be true. I can sketch from memory anything I've seen once. What I want to know is this: Will you make it necessary for me to do that, or will you undertake to furnish us with cheaper copies of your high-priced designs? We could use your entire output. I know the small-town woman of the poorer class, and I know she'll wear a shawl in order to give her child a cloth coat with fancy buttons and a velvet collar."

And Horn & Udell, whose attitude at first had been that of two seasoned business men dealing with a precocious child, found themselves quoting prices to her, shipments, materials, quality, quantities. Then came the question of time.

"We'll get out a special catalogue for the summer," Fanny said. "A small one, to start them our way. Then the big Fall catalogue will contain the entire line."

"That doesn't give us time!" exclaimed both men, in a breath.

"But you must manage, somehow. Can't you speed up the workroom? Put on extra hands? It's worth it."

They might, under normal conditions. But there was this strike-talk, its ugly head bobbing up in a hundred places. And their goods were the kind that required high-class workers. Their girls earned all the way from twelve to twenty-five dollars. But Fanny knew she had driven home the entering wedge. She left them after making an engagement for the following day. The Horn & Udell factory was in New York's newer loft-building section, around Madison, Fifth avenue, and the Thirties. Her hotel was very near. She walked up Fifth avenue a little way, and as she walked she wondered why she did not feel more elated. Her day's work had exceeded her expectations. It was a brilliant January afternoon, with a snap in the air that was almost western. Fifth avenue flowed up, flowed down, and Fanny fought the impulse to stare after every second or third woman she passed. They were so invariably well-dressed. There was none of the occasional shabbiness or dowdiness of Michigan Avenue. Every woman seemed to have emerged fresh from the hands of masseuse and maid. Their hair was coiffed to suit the angle of the hat, and the hat had been chosen to enhance the contour of the head, and the head was carried with regard for the dark furs that encircled the throat. They were amazingly well shod. Their white gloves were white. (A fact remarkable to any soot-haunted Chicagoan.) Their coloring rivaled the rose leaf. And nobody's nose was red.

"Goodness knows I've never pretended to be a beauty," Fanny said that evening, in conversation with Ella Monahan. "But I've always thought I had my good points. By the time I'd reached Forty-second street I wouldn't have given two cents for my chances of winning a cave man on a desert island."

She made up her mind that she would go back to the hotel, get a thick coat, and ride outside one of those fascinating Fifth avenue 'buses. It struck her as an ideal way to see this amazing street. She was back at her hotel in ten minutes. Ella had not yet come in. Their rooms were on the tenth floor. Fanny got her coat, peered at her own reflection in the mirror, sighed, shook her head, and was off down the hall toward the elevators. The great hall window looked toward Fifth avenue, but between it and the avenue rose a yellow-brick building that housed tier on tier of manufacturing lofts. Cloaks, suits, blouses, petticoats, hats, dresses—it was just such a building as Fanny had come from when she left the offices of Horn & Udell. It might be their very building, for all she knew. She looked straight into its windows as she stood waiting for the lift. And window after window showed women, sewing. They were sewing at machines, and at hand-work, but not as women are accustomed to sew, with leisurely stitches, stopping to pat a seam here, to run a calculating eye along hem or ruffle. It was a dreadful, mechanical motion, that sewing, a machine-like, relentless motion, with no waste in it, no pause. Fanny's mind leaped back to Winnebago, with its pleasant porches on which leisurely women sat stitching peacefully at a fine seam.

What was it she had said to Udell? "Can't you speed up the workroom? It's worth it."

Fanny turned abruptly from the window as the door of the bronze and mirrored lift opened for her. She walked over to Fifth avenue again and up to Forty-fifth street. Then she scrambled up the spiral stairs of a Washington Square 'bus. The air was crisp, clear, intoxicating. To her Chicago eyes the buildings, the streets, the very sky looked startlingly fresh and new-washed. As the 'bus lurched down Fifth avenue she leaned over the railing to stare, fascinated, at the colorful, shifting, brilliant panorama of the most amazing street in the world. Block after block, as far as the eye could see, the gorgeous procession moved up, moved down, and the great, gleaming motor cars crept, and crawled, and writhed in and out, like nothing so much as swollen angle worms in a fishing can, Fanny thought. Her eye was caught by one limousine that stood out, even in that crush of magnificence. It was all black, as though scorning to attract the eye with vulgar color, and it was lined with white. Fanny thought it looked very much like

Siegel & Cowan's hearse, back in Winnebago. In it sat a woman, all furs, and orchids, and complexion. She was holding up to the window a little dog with a wrinkled and weary face, like that of an old, old man. He was sticking his little evil, eager red tongue out at the world. And he wore a very smart and woolly white sweater, of the imported kind—with a monogram done in black.

The traffic policeman put up his hand. The 'bus rumbled on down the street. Names that had always been remotely mythical to her now met her eye and became realities. Maillard's. And that great red stone castle was the Waldorf. Almost historic, and it looked newer than the smoke-grimed Blackstone. And straight ahead—why, that must be the Flatiron building! It loomed up like the giant prow of an unimaginable ship. Brentano's. The Holland House. Madison Square. Why there never was anything so terrifying, and beautiful, and palpitating, and exquisite as this Fifth avenue in the late winter afternoon, with the sky ahead a rosy mist, and the golden lights just beginning to spangle the gray. At Madison Square she decided to walk. She negotiated the 'bus steps with surprising skill for a novice, and scurried along the perilous crossing to the opposite side. She entered Madison Square. But why hadn't O. Henry emphasized its beauty, instead of its squalor? It lay, a purple pool of shadow, surrounded by the great, gleaming, many-windowed office buildings, like an amethyst sunk in a circle of diamonds. "It's a fairyland!" Fanny told herself. "Who'd have thought a city could be so beautiful!"

And then, at her elbow, a voice said, "Oh, lady, for the lova God!" She turned with a jerk and looked up into the unshaven face of a great, blue-eyed giant who pulled off his cap and stood twisting it in his swollen blue fingers. "Lady, I'm cold. I'm hungry. I been sittin' here hours."

Fanny clutched her bag a little fearfully. She looked at his huge frame. "Why don't you work?"

"Work!" He laughed. "There ain't any. Looka this!" He turned up his foot, and you saw the bare sole, blackened and horrible, and fringed, comically, by the tattered leather upper.

"Oh—my dear!" said Fanny. And at that the man began to cry, weakly, sickeningly, like a little boy.

"Don't do that! Don't! Here." She was emptying her purse, and something inside her was saying, "You fool, he's only a professional beggar."

And then the man wiped his face with his cap, and swallowed hard, and said, "I don't want all you got. I ain't holdin' you up. Just gimme that. I been sittin' here, on that bench, lookin' at that sign across the street. Over there. It says, `EAT.' It goes off an' on. Seemed like it was drivin' me crazy."

Fanny thrust a crumpled five-dollar bill into his hand. And was off. She fairly flew along, so that it was not until she had reached Thirty-third street that she said aloud, as was her way when moved, "I don't care. Don't blame me. It was that miserable little beast of a dog in the white sweater that did it."

It was almost seven when she reached her room. A maid, in neat black and white, was just coming out with an armful of towels.

"I just brought you a couple of extra towels. We were short this morning," she said.

The room was warm, and quiet, and bright. In her bathroom, that glistened with blue and white tiling, were those redundant towels. Fanny stood in the doorway and counted them, whimsically. Four great fuzzy bath towels. Eight glistening hand towels. A blue and white bath rug hung at the side of the tub. Her telephone rang. It was Ella.

"Where in the world have you been, child? I was worried about you. I thought you were lost in the streets of New York."

"I took a 'bus ride," Fanny explained.

"See anything of New York?"

"I saw all of it," replied Fanny. Ella laughed at that, but Fanny's face was serious.

"How did you make out at Horn & Udell's? Never mind, I'm coming in for a minute; can I?"

"Please do. I need you."

A moment later Ella bounced in, fresh as to blouse, pink as to cheeks, her whole appearance a testimony to the revivifying effects of a warm bath, a brief nap, clean clothes.

"Dear child, you look tired. I'm not going to stay. You get dressed and I'll meet you for dinner. Or do you want yours up here?"

"Oh, no!"

"'Phone me when you're dressed. But tell me, isn't it a wonder, this town? I'll never forget my first trip here. I spent one whole evening standing in front of the mirror trying to make those little spit-curls the women were wearing then. I'd seen 'em on Fifth avenue, and it seemed I'd die if I couldn't have 'em, too. And I dabbed on rouge, and touched up my eyebrows. I don't know. It's a kind of a crazy feeling gets you. The minute I got on the train for Chicago I washed my face and took my hair down and did it plain again."

"Why, that's the way I felt!" laughed Fanny. "I didn't care anything about infants' wear, or Haynes-Cooper, or anything. I just wanted to be beautiful, as they all were."

"Sure! It gets us all!"

Fanny twisted her hair into the relentless knob women assume preparatory to bathing. "It seems to me you have to come from Winnebago, or thereabouts, to get New York—really get it, I mean."

"That's so," agreed Ella. "There's a man on the New York Star who writes a column every day that everybody reads. If he isn't a small-town man then we're both wrong."

Fanny, bathward bound, turned to stare at Ella. "A column about what?"

"Oh, everything. New York, mostly. Say, it's the humanest stuff. He says the kind of thing we'd all say, if we knew how. Reading him is like getting a letter from home. I'll bet he went to a country school and wore his mittens sewed to a piece of tape that ran through his coat sleeves."

"You're right," said Fanny; "he did. That man's from Winnebago, Wisconsin."

"No!"

"Yes."

"Do you mean you know him? Honestly? What's he like?"

But Fanny had vanished. "I'm a tired business woman," she called, above the splashing that followed, "and I won't converse until I'm fed."

"But how about Horn & Udell?" demanded Ella, her mouth against the crack.

"Practically mine," boasted Fanny.

"You mean—landed!"

"Well, hooked, at any rate, and putting up a very poor struggle."

"Why, you clever little divil, you! You'll be making me look like a stock girl next."

Fanny did not telephone Heyl until the day she left New York. She had told herself she would not telephone him at all. He had sent her his New York address and telephone number months before, after that Sunday at the dunes. Ella Monahan had finished her work and had gone back to Chicago four days before Fanny was ready to leave. In those four days Fanny had scoured the city from the Palisades to Pell street. I don't know how she found her way about. It was a sort of instinct with her. She seemed to scent the picturesque. She never for a moment neglected her work. But she had found it was often impossible to see these New York business men until ten— sometimes eleven—o'clock. She awoke at seven, a habit formed in her Winnebago days. Eight-thirty one morning found her staring up at the dim vastness of the dome of the cathedral of St. John the Divine. The great gray pile, mountainous, almost ominous, looms up in the midst of the dingy commonplaceness of Amsterdam avenue and 110th street. New Yorkers do not know this, or if they know it, the fact does not interest them. New Yorkers do not go to stare up into the murky shadows of this glorious edifice. They would if it were situate in Rome. Bare, crude, unfinished, chaotic, it gives rich promise of magnificent fulfillment. In an age when great structures are thrown up to-day, to be torn down to-morrow, this slow-moving giant is at once a reproach and an example. Twenty-five years in building, twenty-five more for completion, it has elbowed its way, stone by stone, into such company as St. Peter's at Rome, and the marvel at Milan. Fanny found her way down the crude cinder paths that made an alley-like approach to the cathedral. She entered at the side door that one found by following arrows posted on the rough wooden fence. Once inside she stood a moment, awed by the immensity of the half-finished nave. As she stood there, hands clasped, her face turned raptly up to where the massive granite columns reared their height to frame the choir, she was, for the moment, as devout as any Episcopalian whose money had helped make the great building. Not only devout, but prayerful, ecstatic. That was partly due to the effect of the pillars, the lights, the tapestries, the great, unfinished chunks of stone that loomed out from the side walls, and the purple shadow cast by the window above the chapels at the far end; and partly to the actress in her that responded magically to any mood, and always to surroundings. Later she walked softly down the deserted nave, past the choir, to the cluster of chapels, set like gems at one end, and running from north to south, in a semi-circle. A placard outside one said, "St. Saviour's chapel. For those who wish to rest and pray." All white marble, this little nook, gleaming softly in the gray half-light. Fanny entered, and sat down. She was quite alone. The roar and crash of the Eighth avenue L, the Amsterdam cars, the motors drumming up Morningside hill, were softened here to a soothing hum.

For those who wish to rest and pray.

Fanny Brandeis had neither rested nor prayed since that hideous day when she had hurled her prayer of defiance at Him. But something within her now began a groping for words; for words that should follow an ancient plea beginning, "O God of my Fathers——" But at that the picture of the room came back to her mental vision—the room so quiet except for the breathing of the woman on the bed; the woman with the tolerant, humorous mouth, and the straight, clever nose, and the softly bright brown eyes, all so strangely pinched and shrunken-looking now——

Fanny got to her feet, with a noisy scraping of the chair on the stone floor. The vague, half-formed prayer died at birth. She found her way out of the dim, quiet little chapel, up the long aisle and out the great door. She shivered a little in the cold of the early January morning as she hurried toward the Broadway subway.

At nine-thirty she was standing at a counter in the infants' wear section at Best's, making mental notes while the unsuspecting saleswoman showed her how the pink ribbon in this year's models was brought under the beading, French fashion, instead of weaving through it, as heretofore. At ten-thirty she was saying to Sid Udell, "I think a written contract is always best. Then we'll all know just where we stand. Mr. Fenger will be on next week to arrange the details, but just now a very brief written understanding to show him on my return would do."

And she got it, and tucked it away in her bag, in triumph.

She tried to leave New York without talking to Heyl, but some quiet, insistent force impelled her to act contrary to her resolution. It was, after all, the urge of the stronger wish against the weaker.

When he heard her voice over the telephone Heyl did not say, "Who is this?" Neither did he put those inevitable questions of the dweller to the transient, "Where are you? How long have you been here?" What he said was, "How're you going to avoid dining with me to-night?"

To which Fanny replied, promptly, "By taking the Twentieth Century back to Chicago to-day."

A little silence. A hurt silence. Then, "When they get the Twentieth Century habit they're as good as lost. How's the infants' wear business, Fanny?"

"Booming, thank you. I want to tell you I've read the column every day. It's wonderful stuff."

"It's a wonderful job. I'm a lucky boy. I'm doing the thing I'd rather do than anything else in the world. There are mighty few who can say that." There was another silence, awkward, heavy. Then, "Fanny, you're not really leaving to-day?"

"I'll be in Chicago to-morrow, barring wrecks."

"You might have let me show you our more or less fair city."

"I've shown it to myself. I've seen Riverside Drive at sunset, and at night. That alone would have been enough. But I've seen Fulton market, too, and the Grand street stalls, and Washington Square, and Central Park, and Lady Duff-Gordon's inner showroom, and the Night Court, and the Grand Central subway horror at six p. m., and the gambling on the Curb, and the bench sleepers in Madison Square—Oh, Clancy, the misery——"

"Heh, wait a minute! All this, alone?"

"Yes. And one more thing. I've landed Horn & Udell, which means nothing to you, but to me it means that by Spring my department will be a credit to its stepmother; a real success."

"I knew it would be a success. So did you. Anything you might attempt would be successful. You'd have made a successful lawyer, or cook, or actress, or hydraulic engineer, because you couldn't do a thing badly. It isn't in you. You're a superlative sort of person. But that's no reason for being any of those things. If you won't admit a debt to humanity, surely you'll acknowledge you've an obligation to yourself."

"Preaching again. Good-by."

"Fanny, you're afraid to see me."

"Don't be ridiculous. Why should I be?"

"Because I say aloud the things you daren't let yourself think. If I were to promise not to talk about anything but flannel bands——"

"Will you promise?"

"No. But I'm going to meet you at the clock at the Grand Central Station fifteen minutes before train time. I don't care if every infants' wear manufacturer in New York had a prior claim on your time. You may as well be there, because if you're not I'll get on the train and stay on as far as Albany. Take your choice."

He was there before her. Fanny, following the wake of a redcap, picked him at once from among the crowd of clock-waiters. He saw her at the same time, and started forward with that singularly lithe, springy step which was, after all, just the result of perfectly trained muscles in coordination. He was wearing New York clothes—the right kind, Fanny noted.

Their hands met. "How well you look," said Fanny, rather lamely.

"It's the clothes," said Heyl, and began to revolve slowly, coyly, hands out, palms down, eyelids drooping, in delicious imitation of those ladies whose business it is to revolve thus for fashion.

"Clancy, you idiot! All these people! Stop it!"

"But get the grace! Get the easy English hang, at once so loose and so clinging."

Fanny grinned, appreciatively, and led the way through the gate to the train. She was surprisingly glad to be with him again. On discovering that, she began to talk rapidly, and about him.

"Tell me, how do you manage to keep that fresh viewpoint? Everybody else who comes to New York to write loses his identity. The city swallows him up. I mean by that, that things seem to strike you as freshly as they did when you first came. I remember you wrote me an amazing letter."

"For one thing, I'll never be anything but a foreigner in New York. I'll never quite believe Broadway. I'll never cease to marvel at Fifth avenue, and Cooper Union, and the Bronx. The time may come when I can take the subway for granted, but don't ask it of me just yet."

"But the other writers—and all those people who live down in Washington Square?"

"I never see them. It's sure death. Those Greenwichers are always taking out their own feelings and analyzing them, and pawing them over, and passing them around. When they get through with them they're so thumb-marked and greasy that no one else wants them. They don't get enough golf, those Greenwichers. They don't get enough tennis. They don't get enough walking in the open places. Gosh, no! I know better than to fall for that kind of thing. They spend hours talking to each other, in dim-lighted attics, about Souls, and Society, and the Joy of Life, and the Greater Good. And they know all about each other's insides. They talk themselves out, and there's nothing left to write about. A little of that kind of thing purges and cleanses. Too much of it poisons, and clogs. No, ma'am! When I want to talk I go down and chin with the foreman of our composing room. There's a chap that has what I call conversation. A philosopher, and knows everything in the world. Composing room foremen always are and do. Now, that's all of that. How about Fanny Brandeis? Any sketches? Come on. Confess. Grand street, anyway."

"I haven't touched a pencil, except to add up a column of figures or copy an order, since last September, when you were so sure I couldn't stop."

"You've done a thousand in your head. And if you haven't done one on paper so much the better. You'll jam them back, and stifle them, and screw the cover down tight on every natural impulse, and then, some day, the cover will blow off with a loud report. You can't kill that kind of thing, Fanny. It would have to be a wholesale massacre of all the centuries behind you. I don't so much mind your being disloyal to your tribe, or race, or whatever you want to call it. But you've turned your back on yourself; you've got an obligation to humanity, and I'll nag you till you pay it. I don't care if I lose you, so long as you find yourself. The thing you've got isn't merely racial. God, no! It's universal. And you owe it to the world. Pay up, Fanny! Pay up!"

"Look here!" began Fanny, her voice low with anger; "the last time I saw you I said I'd never again put myself in a position to be lectured by you, like a schoolgirl. I mean it, this time. If you have anything else to say to me, say it now. The train leaves"—she glanced at her wrist—"in two minutes, thank Heaven, and this will be your last chance."

"All right," said Heyl. "I have got something to say. Do you wear hatpins?"

"Hatpins!" blankly. "Not with this small hat, but what——"

"That means you're defenseless. If you're going to prowl the streets of Chicago alone get this: If you double your fist this way, and tuck your thumb alongside, like that, and aim for this spot right here, about two inches this side of the chin, bringing your arm back, and up, quickly, like a piston, the person you hit will go down, limp. There's a nerve right here that communicates with the brain. That blow makes you see stars, bright lights, and fancy colors. They use it in the comic papers."

"You ARE crazy," said Fanny, as though at last assured of a long-suspected truth. The train began to move, almost imperceptibly. "Run!" she cried.

Heyl sped up the aisle. At the door he turned. "It's called an uppercut," he shouted to the amazement of the other passengers. And leaped from the train.

Fanny sank into her seat, weakly. Then she began to laugh, and there was a dash of hysteria in it. He had left a paper on the car seat. It was the Star. Fanny crumpled it, childishly, and kicked it under the seat. She took off her hat, arranged her belongings, and sat back with eyes closed. After a few moments she opened them, fished about under the seat for the crumpled copy of the Star, and read it, turning at once to his column. She thought it was a very unpretentious thing, that column, and yet so full of insight, and sagacity, and whimsical humor. Not a guffaw in it, but a smile in every fifth line. She wondered if those years of illness, and loneliness, with weeks of reading, and tramping, and climbing in the Colorado mountains had kept him strangely young, or made him strangely old.

She welcomed the hours that lay between New York and Chicago. They would give her an opportunity to digest the events of the past ten days. In her systematic mind she began to range them in the order of their importance. Horn & Udell came first, of course, and then the line of maternity dresses she had selected to take the place of the hideous models carried under Slosson's regime. And then the slip-over pinafores. But somehow her thoughts became jumbled here, so that faces instead of garments filled her mind's eye. Again and again there swam into her ken the face of that woman of fifty, in decent widow's weeds, who had stood there in the Night Court, charged with drunkenness on the streets. And the man with the frost-bitten fingers in Madison Square. And the dog in the sweater. And the feverish concentration of the piece-work sewers in the window of the loft building.

She gave it up, selected a magazine, and decided to go in to lunch.

There was nothing spectacular about the welcome she got on her return to the office after this first trip. A firm that counts its employees by the thousands, and its profits in tens of millions, cannot be expected to draw up formal resolutions of thanks when a heretofore flabby department begins to show signs of red blood.

Ella Monahan said, "They'll make light of it—all but Fenger. That's their way."

Slosson drummed with his fingers all the time she was giving him the result of her work in terms of style, material, quantity, time, and price. When she had finished he said, "Well, all I can say is we seem to be going out of the mail order business and into the imported novelty line, de luxe. I suppose by next Christmas the grocery department will be putting in artichoke hearts, and truffles and French champagne by the keg for community orders."

To which Fanny had returned, sweetly, "If Oregon and Wyoming show any desire for artichokes and champagne I don't see why we shouldn't."

Fenger, strangely enough, said little. He was apt to be rather curt these days, and almost irritable. Fanny attributed it to the reaction following the strain of the Christmas rush.

One did not approach Fenger's office except by appointment. Fanny sent word to him of her return. For two days she heard nothing from him. Then the voice of the snuff-brown secretary summoned her. She did not have to wait this time, but passed directly through the big bright outer room into the smaller room. The Power House, Fanny called it.

Fenger was facing the door. "Missed you," he said.

"You must have," Fanny laughed, "with only nine thousand nine hundred and ninety-nine to look after."

"You look as if you'd been on a vacation, instead of a test trip."

"So I have. Why didn't you warn me that business, as transacted in New York, is a series of social rites? I didn't have enough white kid gloves to go round. No one will talk business in an office. I don't see what they use offices for, except as places in which to receive their mail. You utter the word `Business,' and the other person immediately says, `Lunch.' No wholesaler seems able to quote you his prices until he has been sustained by half a dozen Cape Cods. I don't want to see a restaurant or a rose silk shade for weeks."

Fenger tapped the little pile of papers on his desk. "I've read your reports. If you can do that on lunches, I'd like to see what you could put over in a series of dinners."

"Heaven forbid," said Fanny, fervently. Then, for a very concentrated fifteen minutes they went over the reports together. Fanny's voice grew dry and lifeless as she went into figures.

"You don't sound particularly enthusiastic," Fenger said, when they had finished, "considering that you've accomplished what you set out to do."

"That's just it," quickly. "I like the uncertainty. It was interesting to deal directly with those people, to stack one's arguments, and personality, and mentality and power over theirs, until they had to give way. But after that! Well, you can't expect me to be vitally interested in gross lots, and carloads and dating."

"It's part of business."

"It's the part I hate."

Fenger stacked the papers neatly. "You came in June, didn't you?"

"Yes."

"It has been a remarkable eight-months' record, even at Haynes-Cooper's, where records are the rule. Have you been through the plant since the time you first went through?"

"Through it! Goodness, no! It would take a day."

"Then I wish you'd take it. I like to have the heads of departments go through the plant at least twice a year. You'll find the fourteenth floor has been cleared and is being used entirely by the selectors. The manufacturers' samples are spread on the tables in the various sections. You'll find your place ready for you. You'll be amused at Daly's section. He took your suggestion about trying the blouses on live models instead of selecting them as he used to. You remember you said that one could tell about the lines and style of a dress merely by looking at it, but that a blouse is just a limp rag until it's on."

"It's true of the flimsy Georgette things women want now. They may be lovely in the box and hideously unbecoming when worn. If Daly's going in for the higher grade stuff he can't risk choosing unbecoming models."

"Wait till you see him!" smiled Fenger, "sitting there like a sultan while the pinks and blues, and whites and plaids parade before him." He turned to his desk again. "That's all, Miss Brandeis. Thank you." Then, at a sudden thought. "Do you know that all your suggestions have been human suggestions? I mean they all have had to do with people. Tell me, how do you happen to have learned so much about what people feel and think, in such a short time?"

The thing that Clarence Heyl had said flashed through her mind, and she was startled to find herself quoting it. "It hasn't been a short time," she said.

"It took a thousand years." And left Fenger staring, puzzled.

She took next morning for her tour of the plant as Fenger had suggested. She went through it, not as the startled, wide-eyed girl of eight months before had gone, but critically, and with a little unconscious air of authority. For, this organization, vast though it was, actually showed her imprint. She could have put her finger on this spot, and that, saying, "Here is the mark of my personality." And she thought, as she passed from department to department, "Ten thousand a year, if you keep on as you've started." Up one aisle and down the next. Bundles, bundles, bundles. And everywhere you saw the yellow order-slips. In the hands of the stock boys whizzing by on roller skates; in the filing department; in the traffic department. The very air seemed jaundiced with those clouds of yellow order-slips. She stopped a moment, fascinated as always before the main spiral gravity chute down which the bundles— hundreds of them, thousands of them daily—chased each other to—to what? Fanny asked herself. She knew, vaguely, that hands caught these bundles halfway, and redirected them toward the proper channel, where they were assembled and made ready for shipping or mailing. She turned to a stock boy.

"Where does this empty?" she asked.

"Floor below," said the boy, "on the platform."

Fanny walked down a flight of iron stairs, and around to face the spiral chute again. In front of the chute, and connected with it by a great metal lip, was a platform perhaps twelve feet above the floor and looking very much like the pilot's deck of a ship. A little flight of steps led up to it—very steep steps, that trembled a little under a repetition of shocks that came from above. Fanny climbed them warily, gained the top, and found herself standing next to the girl whose face had gleamed out at her from among those thousands in the crowd pouring out of the plant. The girl glanced up at Fanny for a second—no, for the fraction of a second. Her job was the kind that permitted no more than that. Fanny watched her for one breathless moment. In that moment she understood the look that had been stamped on the girl's face that night; the look that had cried: "Release!" For this platform, shaking under the thud of bundles, bundles, bundles, was the stomach of the Haynes-Cooper plant. Sixty per cent of the forty-five thousand daily orders passed through the hands of this girl and her assistants. Down the chutes swished the bundles, stamped with their section mark, and here they were caught deftly and hurled into one of the dozen conveyers that flowed out from this main stream. The wrong bundle into the wrong conveyer? Confusion in the shipping room. It only took a glance of the eye and a motion of the arms. But that glance and that motion had been boiled down to the very concentrated essence of economy. They seemed to be working with fury, but then, so does a pile-driver until you get the simplicity of it.

Fanny bent over the girl (it was a noisy corner) and put a question. The girl did not pause in her work as she answered it. She caught a bundle with one hand, hurled one into a conveyer with the other.

"Seven a week," she said. And deftly caught the next slithering bundle.

Fanny watched her for another moment. Then she turned and went down the steep stairs.

"None of your business," she said to herself, and continued her tour. "None of your business." She went up to the new selectors' floor, and found the plan running as smoothly as if it had been part of the plant's system for years. The elevator whisked her up to the top floor, where she met the plant's latest practical fad, the new textile chemist—a charming youth, disguised in bone-rimmed glasses, who did the honors of his little laboratory with all the manner of a Harvard host. This was the fusing oven for silks. Here was the drying oven. This delicate scale weighed every ounce of the cloth swatches that came in for inspection, to get the percentage of wool and cotton. Not a chance for the manufacturer to slip shoddy into his goods, now.

"Mm," said Fanny, politely. She hated complicated processes that had to do with scales, and weights, and pounds, and acids. She crossed over to the Administration Building, and stopped at the door marked, "Mrs. Knowles." If you had been an employee of the Haynes-Cooper company, and had been asked to define Mrs. Knowles's position the chances are that you would have found yourself floundering, wordless. Haynes-Cooper was reluctant to acknowledge the need of Mrs. Knowles. Still, when you employ ten thousand people, and more than half of these are girls, and fifty per cent of these girls are unskilled, ignorant, and terribly human you find that a Mrs. Knowles saves the equivalent of ten times her salary in wear and tear and general prevention. She could have told you tragic stories, could Mrs. Knowles, and sordid stories, and comic too; she knew how to deal with terror, and shame, and stubborn silence, and hopeless misery. Gray-haired and motherly? Not at all. An astonishingly young, pleasingly plumpish woman, with nothing remarkable about her except a certain splendid calm. Four years out of Vassar, and already she had learned that if you fold your hands in your lap and wait, quietly, asking no questions, almost any one will tell you almost anything.

"Hello!" called Fanny. "How are our morals this morning?"

"Going up!" answered Esther Knowles, "considering that it's Tuesday. Come in. How's the infant prodigy, I lunched with Ella Monahan, and she told me your first New York trip was a whirlwind. Congratulations!"

"Thanks. I can't stop. I haven't touched my desk to-day. I just want to ask you if you know the name of that girl who has charge of the main chute in the merchandise building."

"Good Lord, child! There are thousands of girls."

"But this one's rather special. She is awfully pretty, and rather different looking. Exquisite coloring, a discontented expression, and a blouse that's too low in the neck."

"Which might be a description of Fanny Brandeis herself, barring the blouse," laughed Mrs. Knowles. Then, at the startled look in Fanny's face, "Do forgive me. And don't look so horrified. I think I know which one you mean. Her name is Sarah Sapinsky—yes, isn't it a pity!—and it's queer that you should ask me about her because I've been having trouble with that particular girl."

"Trouble?"

"She knows she's pretty, and she knows she's different, and she knows she's handicapped, and that accounts for the discontented expression. That, and some other things. She gets seven a week here, and they take just about all of it at home. She says she's sick of it. She has left home twice. I don't blame the child, but I've always managed to bring her back. Some day there'll be a third time—and I'm afraid of it. She's not bad. She's really rather splendid, and she has a certain dreadful philosophy of her own. Her theory is that there are only two kinds of people in the world. Those that give, and those that take. And she's tired of giving. Sarah didn't put it just that way; but you know what she means, don't you?"

"I know what she means," said Fanny, grimly.

So it was Sarah she saw above all else in her trip through the gigantic plant; Sarah's face shone out from among the thousands; the thud-thud of Sarah's bundle-chute beat a dull accompaniment to the hum of the big hive; above the rustle of those myriad yellow order-slips, through the buzz of the busy mail room; beneath the roar of the presses in the printing building, the crash of the dishes in the cafeteria, ran the leid-motif of Sarah-at-seven-a-week. Back in her office once more Fanny dictated a brief observation-report for Fenger's perusal.

"It seems to me there's room for improvement in our card index file system. It's thorough, but unwieldy. It isn't a system any more. It's a ceremony. Can't you get a corps of system sharks to simplify things there?"

She went into detail and passed on to the next suggestion.

"If the North American Cloak & Suit Company can sell mail order dresses that are actually smart and in good taste, I don't see why we have to go on carrying only the most hideous crudities in our women's dress department. I know that the majority of our women customers wouldn't wear a plain, good looking little blue serge dress with a white collar, and some tailored buttons. They want cerise satin revers on a plum-colored foulard, and that's what we've been giving them. But there are plenty of other women living miles from anywhere who know what's being worn on Fifth avenue. I don't know how they know it, but they do. And they want it. Why can't we reach those women, as well as their shoddier sisters? The North American people do it. I'd wear one of their dresses myself. I wouldn't be found dead in one of ours. Here's a suggestion:

"Why can't we get Camille to design half a dozen models a season for us? Now don't roar at that. And don't think that the women on western ranches haven't heard of Camille. They have. They may know nothing of Mrs. Pankhurst, and Lillian Russell may be a myth to them, but I'll swear that every one of them knows that Camille is a dressmaker who makes super-dresses. She is as much a household word among them as Roosevelt used to be to their men folks. And if we can promise them a Camille-designed dress for $7.85 (which we could) then why don't we?"

At the very end, to her stenographer's mystification, she added this irrelevant line.

"Seven dollars a week is not a living wage."

The report went to Fenger. He hurdled lightly over the first suggestion, knowing that the file system was as simple as a monster of its bulk could be. He ignored the third hint. The second suggestion amused, then interested, then convinced him. Within six months Camille's name actually appeared in the Haynes-Cooper catalogue. Not that alone, the Haynes-Cooper company broke its rule as to outside advertising, and announced in full-page magazine ads the news of the $7.85 gowns designed by Camille especially for the Haynes-Cooper company. There went up a nationwide shout of amusement and unbelief, but the announcement continued. Camille (herself a frump with a fringe) whose frocks were worn by queens, and dancers and matrons with millions, and debutantes; Camille, who had introduced the slouch, revived the hoop, discovered the sunset chiffon, had actually consented to design six models every season for the mail order millions of the Haynes-Cooper women's dress department—at a price that made even Michael Fenger wince.

CHAPTER FOURTEEN

Fanny Brandeis' blouses showed real Cluny now, and her hats were nothing but line. A scant two years before she had wondered if she would ever reach a pinnacle of success lofty enough to enable her to wear blue tailor suits as smart as the well-cut garments worn by her mother's friend, Mrs. Emma McChesney. Mrs. McChesney's trig little suits had cost fifty dollars, and had looked sixty. Fanny's now cost one hundred and twenty-five, and looked one hundred and twenty-five. Her sleeves alone gave it away. If you would test the soul of a tailor you have only to glance at shoulder-seam, elbow and wrist. Therein lies the wizardry. Fanny's sleeve flowed from arm-pit to thumb-bone without a ripple. Also she moved from the South side to the North side, always a sign of prosperity or social ambition, in Chicago. Her new apartment was near the lake, exhilaratingly high, correspondingly expensive. And she was hideously lonely. She was earning a man-size salary now, and she was working like a man. A less magnificently healthy woman could not have stood the strain, for Fanny Brandeis was working with her head, not her heart. When we say heart we have come to mean something more than the hollow muscular structure that propels the blood through the veins. That, in the dictionary, is the primary definition. The secondary definition has to do with such words as emotion, sympathy, tenderness, courage, conviction. She was working, now, as Michael Fenger worked, relentlessly, coldly, indomitably, using all the material at hand as a means to an end, with never a thought of the material itself, as a builder reaches for a brick, or stone, and fits it into place, smoothly, almost without actually seeing the brick itself, except as something which will help to make a finished wall. She rarely prowled the city now. She told herself she was too tired at night, and on Sundays and holidays, and I suppose she was. Indeed, she no longer saw things with her former vision. It was as though her soul had shriveled in direct proportion to her salary's expansion. The streets seldom furnished her with a rich mental meal now. When she met a woman with a child, in the park, her keen eye noted the child's dress before it saw the child itself, if, indeed, she noticed the child at all.

Fascinating Facts, the guileless, pink-cheeked youth who had driven her home the night of her first visit to the Fengers, shortly after her coming to Haynes-Cooper's, had proved her faithful slave, and she had not abused his devotion. Indeed, she hardly considered it that. The sex side of her was being repressed with the artist side. Most men found her curt, brisk, businesslike manner a little repellent, though interesting. They never made love to her, in spite of her undeniable attractiveness. Fascinating Facts drove her about in his smart little roadster and one night he established himself in her memory forever as the first man who had ever asked her to marry him. He did it haltingly, painfully, almost grudgingly. Fanny was frankly amazed. She had enjoyed going about with him. He rested and soothed her. He, in turn, had been stimulated by her energy, her humor, her electric force. Nothing was said for a minute after his awkward declaration.

"But," he persisted, "you like me, don't you?"

"Of course I do. Immensely."

"Then why?"

"When a woman of my sort marries it's a miracle. I'm twenty-six, and intelligent and very successful. A frightful combination. Unmarried women of my type aren't content just to feel. They must analyze their feelings. And analysis is death to romance."

"Great Scott! You expect to marry somebody sometime, don't you, Fanny?"

"No one I know now. When I do marry, if I do, it will be with the idea of making a definite gain. I don't mean necessarily worldly gain, though that would be a factor, too." Fascinating Facts had been staring straight ahead, his hands gripping the wheel with unnecessary rigidity. He relaxed a little now, and even laughed, though not very successfully. Then he said something very wise, for him.

"Listen to me, girl. You'll never get away with that vampire stuff. Talons are things you have to be born with. You'll never learn to grab with these." He reached over, and picked up her left hand lying inertly in her lap, and brought it up to his lips, and kissed it, glove and all. "They're built on the open-face pattern—for giving. You can't fool me. I know."

A year and a half after her coming to Haynes-Cooper Fanny's department was doing a business of a million a year. The need had been there. She had merely given it the impetus. She was working more or less directly with Fenger now, with an eye on every one of the departments that had to do with women's clothing, from shoes to hats. Not that she did any actual buying, or selling in these departments. She still confined her actual selecting of goods to the infants' wear section, but she occupied, unofficially, the position of assistant to the General Merchandise Manager. They worked well together, she and Fenger, their minds often marching along without the necessity of a single spoken word. There was no doubt that Fenger's mind was a marvelous piece of mechanism. Under it the Haynes-Cooper plant functioned with the clockwork regularity of a gigantic automaton. System and Results—these were his twin gods. With his mind intent on them he failed to see that new gods, born of spiritual unrest, were being set up in the temples of Big Business. Their coming had been rumored for many years. Words such as Brotherhood, Labor, Rights, Humanity, Hours, once regarded as the special property of the street corner ranter, were creeping into our everyday vocabulary. And strangely enough, Nathan Haynes, the gentle, the bewildered, the uninspired, heard them, and listened. Nathan Haynes had begun to accustom himself to the roar of the flood that had formerly deafened him. He was no longer stunned by the inrush of his millions. The report sheet handed him daily had never ceased to be a wildly unexpected thing, and he still shrank from it, sometimes. It was so fantastic, so out of all reason. But he even dared, now and then, to put out a tentative hand to guide the flood. He began to realize, vaguely, that Italian Gardens, and marble pools, educational endowments and pet charities were but poor, ineffectual barriers of mud and sticks, soon swept away by the torrent. As he sat there in his great, luxurious office, with the dim, rich old portraits gleaming down on him from the walls, he began, gropingly, to evolve a new plan; a plan by which the golden flood was to be curbed, divided, and made to form a sub-stream, to be utilized for the good of the many; for the good of the Ten Thousand, who were almost Fifteen Thousand now, with another fifteen thousand in mills and factories at distant points, whose entire output was swallowed up by the Haynes-Cooper plant. Michael Fenger, Super-Manager, listened to the plan, smiled tolerantly, and went on perfecting an already miraculous System. Sarah Sapinsky, at seven a week, was just so much untrained labor material, easily replaced by material exactly like it. No, Michael Fenger, with his head in the sand, heard no talk of new gods. He only knew that the monster plant under his management was yielding the greatest possible profit under the least possible outlay.

In Fanny Brandeis he had found a stimulating, energizing fellow worker. That had been from the beginning. In the first month or two of her work, when her keen brain was darting here and there, into forgotten and neglected corners, ferreting out dusty scraps of business waste and holding them up to the light, disdainfully, Fenger had watched her with a mingling of amusement and a sort of fond pride, as one would a precocious child. As the months went on the pride and amusement welded into something more than admiration, such as one expert feels for a fellow-craftsman. Long before the end of the first year he knew that here was a woman such as he had dreamed of all his life and never hoped to find. He often found himself sitting at his office desk, or in his library at home, staring straight ahead for a longer time than he dared admit, his papers or book forgotten in his hand. His thoughts applied to her adjectives which proved her a paradox: Generous, sympathetic, warm-hearted, impulsive, imaginative; cold, indomitable, brilliant, daring, intuitive. He would rouse himself almost angrily and force himself to concentrate again upon the page before him. I don't know how he thought it all would end—he whose life-habit it was to follow out every process to its ultimate step, whether mental or mechanical. As for Fanny, there was nothing of the intriguant about her. She was used to admiration. She was accustomed to deference from men. Brandeis' Bazaar had insured that. All her life men had taken orders from her, all the way from Aloysius and the blithe traveling men of whom she bought goods, to the salesmen and importers in the Chicago wholesale houses. If they had attempted, occasionally, to mingle the social and personal with the commercial Fanny had not resented their attitude. She had accepted their admiration and refused their invitations with equal good nature, and thus retained their friendship. It is not exaggeration to say that she looked upon Michael Fenger much as she had upon these genial fellow-workers. A woman as straightforward and direct as she has what is known as a single-track mind in such matters. It is your soft and silken mollusc type of woman whose mind pursues a slimy and labyrinthine trail. But it is useless to say that she did not feel something of the intense personal attraction of the man. Often it used to puzzle and annoy her to find that as they sat arguing in the brisk, everyday atmosphere of office or merchandise room the air between them would suddenly become electric, vibrant. They met each other's eyes with effort. When their hands touched, accidentally, over papers or samples they snatched them back. Fanny found herself laughing uncertainly, at nothing, and was furious. When a silence fell between them they would pounce upon it, breathlessly, and smother it with talk.

Do not think that any furtive love-making went on, sandwiched between shop talk. Their conversation might have taken place between two men. Indeed, they often were brutally frank to each other. Fanny had the vision, Fenger the science to apply it. Sometimes her intuition leaped ahead of his reasoning. Then he would say, "I'm not sold on that," which is modern business slang meaning, "You haven't convinced me." She would go back and start afresh, covering the ground more slowly.

Usually her suggestions were practical and what might be termed human. They seemed to be founded on an uncanny knowledge of people's frailties. It was only when she touched upon his beloved System that he was adamant.

"None of that socialistic stuff," he would say. "This isn't a Benevolent Association we're running. It's the biggest mail order business in the world, and its back-bone is System. I've been just fifteen years perfecting that System. It's my job. Hands off."

"A fifteen year old system ought to be scrapped," Fanny would retort, boldly. "Anyway, the Simon Legree thing has gone out."

No one in the plant had ever dared to talk to him like that. He would glare down at Fanny for a moment, like a mastiff on a terrier. Fanny, seeing his face rage-red, would flash him a cheerful and impudent smile. The anger, fading slowly, gave way to another look, so that admiration and resentment mingled for a moment.

"Lucky for you you're not a man."

"I wish I were."

"I'm glad you're not."

Not a very thrilling conversation for those of you who are seeking heartthrobs.

In May Fanny made her first trip to Europe for the firm. It was a sudden plan. Instantly Theodore leaped to her mind and she was startled at the tumult she felt at the thought of seeing him and his child. The baby, a girl, was more than a year old. Her business, a matter of two weeks, perhaps, was all in Berlin and Paris, but she cabled Theodore that she would come to them in Munich, if only for a day or two. She had very little curiosity about the woman Theodore had married. The memory of that first photograph of hers, befrizzed, bejeweled, and asmirk, had never effaced itself. It had stamped her indelibly in Fanny's mind.

The day before she left for New York (she sailed from there) she had a letter from Theodore. It was evident at once that he had not received her cable. He was in Russia, giving a series of concerts. Olga and the baby were with him. He would be back in Munich in June. There was some talk of America. When Fanny realized that she was not to see him she experienced a strange feeling that was a mixture of regret and relief. All the family love in her, a racial trait, had been stirred at the thought of again seeing that dear blond brother, the self-centered, willful, gifted boy who had held the little congregation rapt, there in the Jewish house of worship in Winnebago. But she had recoiled a little from the meeting with this other unknown person who gave concerts in Russia, who had adopted Munich as his home, who was the husband of this Olga person, and the father of a ridiculously German looking baby in a very German looking dress, all lace and tucks, and wearing bracelets on its chubby arms, and a locket round its neck. That was what one might expect of Olga's baby. But not of Theodore's. Besides, what business had that boy with a baby, anyway? Himself a baby.

Fenger had arranged for her cabin, and she rather resented its luxury until she learned later, that it is the buyers who always occupy the staterooms de luxe on ocean liners. She learned, too, that the men in yachting caps and white flannels, and the women in the smartest and most subdued of blue serge and furs were not millionaires temporarily deprived of their own private seagoing craft, but buyers like herself, shrewd, aggressive, wise and incredibly endowed with savoir faire. Merely to watch one of them dealing with a deck steward was to know for all time the superiority of mind over matter.

Most incongruously, it was Ella Monahan and Clarence Heyl who waved good-by to her as her ship swung clear of the dock. Ella was in New York on her monthly trip. Heyl had appeared at the hotel as Fanny was adjusting her veil and casting a last rather wild look around the room. Molly Brandeis had been the kind of woman who never misses a train or overlooks a hairpin. Fanny's early training had proved invaluable more than once in the last two years. Nevertheless, she was rather flustered, for her, as the elevator took her down to the main floor. She told herself it was not the contemplation of the voyage itself that thrilled her. It was the fact that here was another step definitely marking her progress. Heyl, looking incredibly limp, was leaning against a gaudy marble pillar, his eyes on the downcoming elevators. Fanny saw him just an instant before he saw her, and in that moment she found herself wondering why this boy (she felt years older than he) should look so fantastically out of place in this great, glittering, feverish hotel lobby. Just a shy, rather swarthy Jewish boy, who wore the right kind of clothes in the wrong manner—then Heyl saw her and came swiftly toward her.

"Hello, Fan!"

"Hello, Clancy!" They had not seen each other in six months.

"Anybody else going down with you?"

"No. Ella Monahan had a last-minute business appointment, but she promised to be at the dock, somehow, before the boat leaves. I'm going to be grand, and taxi all the way."

"I've an open car, waiting."

"But I won't have it! I can't let you do that."

"Oh, yes you can. Don't take it so hard. That's the trouble with you business women. You're killing the gallantry of a nation. Some day one of you will get up and give me a seat in a subway——"

"I'll punish you for that, Clancy. If you want the Jane Austen thing I'll accommodate. I'll drop my handkerchief, gloves, bag, flowers and fur scarf at intervals of five minutes all the way downtown. Then you may scramble around on the floor of the cab and feel like a knight."

Fanny had long ago ceased to try to define the charm of this man. She always meant to be serenely dignified with him. She always ended by feeling very young, and, somehow, gloriously carefree and lighthearted. There was about him a naturalness, a simplicity, to which one responded in kind.

Seated beside her he turned and regarded her with disconcerting scrutiny.

"Like it?" demanded Fanny, pertly. And smoothed her veil, consciously.

"No."

"Well, for a man who looks negligee even in evening clothes aren't you overcritical?"

"I'm not criticizing your clothes. Even I can see that that hat and suit have the repressed note that means money. And you're the kind of woman who looks her best in those plain dark things."

"Well, then?"

"You look like a buyer. In two more years your face will have that hard finish that never comes off."

"I am a buyer."

"You're not. You're a creator. Remember, I'm not belittling your job. It's a wonderful job—for Ella Monahan. I wish I had the gift of eloquence. I wish I had the right to spank you. I wish I could prove to you, somehow, that with your gift, and heritage, and racial right it's as criminal for you to be earning your thousands at Haynes-Cooper's as it would have been for a vestal virgin to desert her altar fire to stoke a furnace. Your eyes are bright and hard, instead of tolerant. Your mouth is losing its graciousness. Your whole face is beginning to be stamped with a look that says shrewdness and experience, and success."

"I am successful. Why shouldn't I look it?"

"Because you're a failure. I'm sick, I tell you—sick with disappointment in you. Jane Addams would have been a success in business, too. She was born with a humanity sense, and a value sense, and a something else that can't be acquired. Ida Tarbell could have managed your whole Haynes-Cooper plant, if she'd had to. So could a dozen other women I could name. You don't see any sign of what you call success on Jane Addams's face, do you? You wouldn't say, on seeing her, that here was a woman who looked as if she might afford hundred-dollar tailor suits and a town car. No. All you see in her face is the reflection of the souls of all the men and women she has worked to save. She has covered her job—the job that the Lord intended her to cover. And to me she is the most radiantly beautiful woman I have ever seen."

Fanny sat silent. She was twisting the fingers of one hand in the grip of the other, as she had since childhood, when deeply disturbed. And suddenly she began to cry—silently, harrowingly, as a man cries, her shoulders shaking, her face buried in her furs.

"Fanny! Fanny girl!" He was horribly disturbed and contrite. He patted her arm, awkwardly. She shook free of his hand, childishly. "Don't cry, dear. I'm sorry. It's just that I care so much. It's just——"

She raised an angry, tear-stained face. "It's just that you have an exalted idea of your own perceptions. It's just that you've grown up from what they used to call a bright little boy to a bright young man, and you're just as tiresome now as you were then. I'm happy enough, except when I see you. I'm getting the things I starved for all those years. Why, I'll never get over being thrilled at the idea of being able to go to the theater, or to a concert, whenever I like. Actually whenever I want to. And to be able to buy a jabot, or a smart hat, or a book. You don't know how I wanted things, and how tired I got of never having them. I'm happy! I'm happy! Leave me alone!"

"It's an awful price to pay for a hat, and a jabot, and a book and a theater ticket, Fan."

Ella Monahan had taken the tube, and was standing in the great shed, watching arrivals with interest, long before they bumped over the cobblestones of Hoboken. The three descended to Fanny's cabin. Ella had sent champagne—six cosy pints in a wicker basket.

"They say it's good for seasickness," she announced, cheerfully, "but it's a lie. Nothing's good for seasickness, except death, or dry land. But even if you do feel miserable—and you probably will—there's something about being able to lie in your berth and drink champagne alone, by the spoonful, that's sort of soothing."

Heyl had fallen silent. Fanny was radiant again, and exclamatory over her books and flowers.

"Of course it's my first trip," she explained, "and an event in my life, but I didn't suppose that anybody else would care. What's this? Candy? Glace fruit." She glanced around the luxurious little cabin, then up at Heyl, impudently. "I may be a coarse commercial person, Clancy, but I must say I like this very, very much. Sorry."

They went up on deck. Ella, a seasoned traveler, was full of parting instructions. "And be sure to eat at Kempinski's, in Berlin. Twenty cents for lobster. And caviar! Big as hen's eggs, and as cheap as codfish. And don't forget to order mai-bowle. It tastes like champagne, but isn't, and it has the most delicious dwarf strawberries floating on top. This is just the season for it. You're lucky. If you tip the waiter one mark he's yours for life. Oh, and remember the plum compote. You'll be disappointed in their Wertheim's that they're always bragging about. After all, Field's makes 'em all look like country stores."

"Wertheim's? Is that something to eat, too?"

"No, idiot. It's their big department store." Ella turned to Heyl, for whom she felt mingled awe and liking. "If this trip of hers is successful, the firm will probably send her over three or four times a year. It's a wonderful chance for a kid like her."

"Then I hope," said Heyl, quietly, "that this trip may be a failure."

Ella smiled, uncertainly.

"Don't laugh," said Fanny, sharply. "He means it."

Ella, sensing an unpleasant something in which she had no part, covered the situation with another rush of conversation.

"You'll get the jolt of your life when you come to Paris and find that you're expected to pay for the lunches, and all the cab fares, and everything, of those shrimpy little commissionaires. Polite little fellows, they are, in frock coats, and mustaches, and they just stand aside, as courtly as you please, while you pay for everything. Their house expects it. I almost passed away, the first time, but you get used to it. Say, imagine one of our traveling men letting you pay for his lunch and taxi."

She rattled on, genially. Heyl listened with unfeigned delight. Ella found herself suddenly abashed before those clear, far-seeing eyes. "You think I'm a gabby old girl, don't you?"

"I think you're a wonderful woman," said Heyl. "Very wise, and very kind."

"Why—thanks," faltered Ella. "Why—thanks."

They said their good-bys. Ella hugged Fanny warm-heartedly. Then she turned away, awkwardly. Heyl put his two hands on Fanny's shoulders and looked down at her. For a breathless second she thought he was about to kiss her. She was amazed to find herself hoping that he would. But he didn't. "Good-by," he said, simply. And took her hand in his steel grip a moment, and dropped it. And turned away. A messenger boy, very much out of breath, came running up to her, a telegram in his hand.

"For me?" Fanny opened it, frowned, smiled. "It's from Mr. Fenger. Good wishes. As if all those flowers weren't enough."

"Mm," said Ella. She and Heyl descended the gang-way, and stood at the dock's edge, looking rather foolish and uncertain, as people do at such times. There followed a few moments of scramble, of absurdly shouted last messages, of bells, and frantic waving of handkerchiefs. Fanny, at the rail, found her two among the crowd, and smiled down upon them, mistily. Ella was waving energetically. Heyl was standing quite still, looking up. The ship swung clear, crept away from the dock. The good-bys swelled to a roar. Fanny leaned far over the rail and waved too, a sob in her throat. Then she saw that she was waving with the hand that held the yellow telegram. She crumpled it in the other hand, and substituted her handkerchief. Heyl still stood, hat in hand, motionless.

"Why don't you wave good-by?" she called, though he could not possibly hear. "Wave good-by!" And then the hand with the handkerchief went to her face, and she was weeping. I think it was that old drama-thrill in her, dormant for so long. But at that Heyl swung his hat above his head, three times, like a schoolboy, and, grasping Ella's plump and resisting arm, marched abruptly away.

CHAPTER FIFTEEN

The first week in June found her back in New York. That month of absence had worked a subtle change. The two weeks spent in crossing and recrossing had provided her with a let-down that had been almost jarring in its completeness. Everything competitive had seemed to fade away with the receding shore, and to loom up again only when the skyline became a thing of smoke-banks, spires, and shafts. She had had only two weeks for the actual transaction of her business. She must have been something of a revelation to those Paris and Berlin manufacturers, accustomed though they were to the brisk and irresistible methods of the American business woman. She was, after all, absurdly young to be talking in terms of millions, and she was amazingly well dressed. This last passed unnoticed, or was taken for granted in Paris, but in Berlin, home of the frump and the flour-sack figure, she was stared at, appreciatively. Her business, except for one or two unimportant side lines, had to do with two factories on whose product the Haynes-Cooper company had long had a covetous eye. Quantity, as usual, was the keynote of their demand, and Fanny's task was that of talking in six-figure terms to these conservative and over-wary foreign manufacturers. That she had successfully accomplished this, and that she had managed to impress them also with the important part that time and promptness in delivery played in a swift-moving machine like the Haynes-Cooper concern, was due to many things beside her natural business ability. Self-confidence was there, and physical vigor, and diplomacy. But above all there was that sheer love of the game; the dramatic sense that enabled her to see herself in the part. That alone precluded the possibility of failure. She knew how youthful she looked, and how glowing. She anticipated the look that came into their faces when she left polite small-talk behind and soared up into the cold, rarefied atmosphere of business. She delighted in seeing the admiring and tolerant smirk vanish and give way to a startled and defensive attentiveness.

It might be mentioned that she managed, somehow, to spend almost half a day in Petticoat Lane, and its squalid surroundings, while in London. She actually prowled, alone, at night, in the evil-smelling, narrow streets of the poorer quarter of Paris, and how she escaped unharmed is a mystery that never bothered her, because she had never known fear of streets. She had always walked on the streets of Winnebago, Wisconsin, alone. It never occurred to her not to do the same in the streets of Chicago, or New York, or London, or Paris. She found Berlin, with its

Adlon, its appalling cleanliness, its overfed populace, and its omnipresent Kaiser forever scudding up and down Unter den Linden in his chocolate-colored car, incredibly dull, and unpicturesque. Something she had temporarily lost there in the busy atmosphere of the Haynes-Cooper plant, seemed to have returned, miraculously.

New York, on her return, was something of a shock. She remembered how vividly fresh it had looked to her on the day of that first visit, months before. Now, to eyes fresh from the crisp immaculateness of Paris and Berlin, Fifth avenue looked almost grimy, and certainly shabby in spots.

Ella Monahan, cheerful, congratulatory, beaming, met her at the pier, and Fanny was startled at her own sensation of happiness as she saw that pink, good-natured face looking up at her from the crowd below. The month that had gone by since last she saw Ella standing just so, seemed to slip away and fade into nothingness.

"I waited over a day," said Ella, "just to see you. My, you look grand! I know where you got that hat. Galeries Lafayette. How much?"

"I don't expect you to believe it. Thirty-five francs. Seven dollars. I couldn't get it for twenty-five here."

They were soon clear of the customs. Ella had engaged a room for her at the hotel they always used. As they rode uptown together, happily, Ella opened her bag and laid a little packet of telegrams and letters in Fanny's lap.

"I guess Fenger's pleased, all right, if telegrams mean anything. Not that I know they're from him. But he said—"

But Fanny was looking up from one of them with a startled expression. "He's here. Fenger's here."

"In New York?" asked Ella, rather dully.

"Yes." She ripped open another letter. It was from Theodore. He was coming to New York in August. The Russian tour had been a brilliant success. They had arranged a series of concerts for him in the United States. He could give his concerto there. It was impossible in Russia, Munich, even Berlin, because it was distinctly Jewish in theme—as Jewish as the Kol Nidre, and as somber. They would have none of it in Europe. Prejudice was too strong. But in America! He was happier than he had been in years. Olga objected to coming to America, but she would get over that. The little one was well, and she was learning to talk. Actually! They were teaching her to say Tante Fanny.

"Well!" exclaimed Fanny, her eyes shining. She read bits of the letter aloud to Ella. Ella was such a satisfactory sort of person to whom to read a letter aloud. She exclaimed in all the right places. Her face was as radiant as Fanny's. They both had forgotten all about Fenger, their Chief. But they had been in their hotel scarcely a half hour, and Ella had not done exclaiming over the bag that Fanny had brought her from Paris, when his telephone call came.

He wasted very little time on preliminaries.

"I'll call for you at four. We'll drive through the park, and out by the river, and have tea somewhere."

"That would be wonderful. That is, if Ella's free. I'll ask her."

"Ella?"

"Yes. She's right here. Hold the wire, will you?" She turned away from the telephone to face Ella. "It's Mr. Fenger. He wants to take us both driving this afternoon. You can go, can't you?"

"I certainly CAN," replied Miss Monahan, with what might have appeared to be undue force.

Fanny turned back to the telephone. "Yes, thanks. We can both go. We'll be ready at four."

Fanny decided that Fenger's muttered reply couldn't have been what she thought it was.

Ella busied herself with the unpacking of a bag. She showed a disposition to spoil Fanny. "You haven't asked after your friend, Mr. Heyl. My land! If I had a friend like that—" "Oh, yes," said Fanny, vaguely. "I suppose you and he are great chums by this time. He's a nice boy."

"You don't suppose anything of the kind," Ella retorted, crisply. "That boy, as you call him—and it isn't always the man with the biggest fists that's got the most fight in him—is about as far above me as—as—" she sat down on the floor, ponderously, beside the open bag, and gesticulated with a hairbrush, at loss for a simile "as an eagle is above a waddling old duck. No, I don't mean that, either, because I never did think much of the eagle, morally. But you get me. Not that he knows it, or shows it. Heyl, I mean. Lord, no! But he's got something—something kind of spiritual in him that makes you that way, too. He doesn't say much, either. That's the funny part of it. I do all the talking, seems, when I'm with him. But I find myself saying things I didn't know I knew. He makes you think about things you're afraid to face by yourself. Big things. Things inside of you." She fell silent a moment, sitting cross-legged before the bag. Then she got up, snapped the bag shut, and bore it across the room to a corner. "You know he's gone, I s'pose."

"Gone?"

"To those mountains, or wherever it is he gets that look in his eyes from. That's my notion of a job. They let him go for the whole summer, roaming around being a naturalist, just so's he'll come back in the winter."

"And the column?" Fanny asked. "Do they let that go, too?"

"I guess he's going to do some writing for them up there. After all, he's the column. It doesn't make much difference where he writes from. Did you know it's being syndicated now, all over the country? Well, it is. That's the secret of its success, I suppose. It isn't only a column written about New York for a New York paper. It's about everything, for anybody. It's the humanest stuff. And he isn't afraid of anything. New York's crazy about him. They say he's getting a salary you wouldn't believe. I'm a tongue-tied old fool when I'm with him, but then, he likes to talk about you, mostly, so it doesn't matter."

Fanny turned swiftly from the dressing-table, where she was taking the pins out of her vigorous, abundant hair.

"What kind of thing does he say about me, Ellen girl. H'm? What kind of thing?"

"Abuse, mostly. I'll be running along to my own room now. I'll be out for lunch, but back at four, for that airing Fenger's so wild to have me take. If I were you I'd lie down for an hour, till you get your land-legs." She poked her head in at the door again. "Not that you look as if you needed it. You've got a different look, somehow. Kind of rested. After all, there's nothing like an ocean voyage."

She was gone. Fanny stood a moment, in the center of the room. There was nothing relaxed or inert about her. Had you seen her standing there, motionless, you would still have got a sense of action from her. She looked so splendidly alive. She walked to the window, now, and stood looking down upon New York in early June. Summer had not yet turned the city into a cauldron of stone and steel. From her height she could glimpse the green of the park, with a glint of silver in its heart, that was the lake. Her mind was milling around, aimlessly, in a manner far removed from its usual orderly functioning. Now she thought of Theodore, her little brother—his promised return. It had been a slow and painful thing, his climb. Perhaps if she had been more ready to help, if she had not always waited until he asked the aid that she might have volunteered—she thrust that thought out of her mind, rudely, and slammed the door on it.... Fenger. He had said, "Damn!" when she had told him about Ella. And his voice had been—well—she pushed that thought outside her mind, too.... Clarence Heyl.... "He makes you think about things you're afraid to face by yourself. Big things. Things inside of you...."

Fanny turned away from the window. She decided she must be tired, after all. Because here she was, with everything to make her happy: Theodore coming home; her foreign trip a success; Ella and Fenger to praise her and make much of her; a drive and tea this afternoon (she wasn't above these creature comforts)—and still she felt unexhilarated, dull. She decided to go down for a bit of lunch, and perhaps a stroll of ten or fifteen minutes, just to see what Fifth avenue was showing. It was half-past one when she reached that ordinarily well-regulated thoroughfare. She found its sidewalks packed solid, up and down, as far as the eye could see, with a quiet, orderly, expectant mass of people. Squads of mounted police clattered up and down, keeping the middle of the street cleared. Whatever it was that had called forth that incredible mass, was scheduled to proceed uptown from far downtown, and that very soon. Heads were turned that way. Fanny, wedged in the crowd, stood a-tiptoe, but she could see nothing. It brought to her mind the Circus Day of her Winnebago childhood, with Elm street packed with townspeople and farmers, all straining their eyes up toward Cherry street, the first turn in the line of march. Then, far away, the blare of a band. "Here they come!" Just then, far down the canyon of Fifth avenue, sounded the cry that had always swayed Elm street, Winnebago. "Here they come!"

"What is it?" Fanny asked a woman against whom she found herself close-packed. "What are they waiting for?"

"It's the suffrage parade," replied the woman. "The big suffrage parade. Don't you know?"

"No. I haven't been here." Fanny was a little disappointed. The crowd had surged forward, so that it was impossible for her to extricate herself. She found herself near the curb. She could see down the broad street now, and below Twenty-third street it was a moving, glittering mass, pennants, banners, streamers flying. The woman next her volunteered additional information.

"The mayor refused permission to let them march. But they fought it, and they say it's the greatest suffrage parade ever held. I'd march myself, only—"

"Only what?"

"I don't know. I'm scared to, I think. I'm not a New Yorker."

"Neither am I," said Fanny. Fanny always became friendly with the woman next her in a crowd. That was her mother in her. One could hear the music of the band, now. Fanny glanced at her watch. It was not quite two. Oh, well, she would wait and see some of it. Her mind was still too freshly packed with European impressions to receive any real idea of the value of this pageant, she told herself. She knew she did not feel particularly interested. But she waited.

Another surging forward. It was no longer, "Here they come!" but, "Here they are!"

And here they were.

A squad of mounted police, on very prancy horses. The men looked very ruddy, and well set-up and imposing. Fanny had always thrilled to anything in uniform, given sufficient numbers of them. Another police squad. A brass band, on foot. And then, in white, on a snow-white charger, holding a white banner aloft, her eyes looking straight ahead, her face very serious and youthful, the famous beauty and suffrage leader, Mildred Inness. One of the few famous beauties who actually was a beauty. And after that women, women, women! Hundreds of them, thousands of them, a river of them flowing up Fifth avenue to the park. More bands. More horses. Women! Women! They bore banners. This section, that section. Artists. School teachers. Lawyers. Doctors. Writers. Women in college caps and gowns. Women in white, from shoes to hats. Young women. Girls. Gray-haired women. A woman in a wheel chair, smiling. A man next to Fanny began to jeer. He was a red-faced young man, with a coarse, blotchy skin, and thick lips. He smoked a cigar, and called to the women in a falsetto voice, "Hello, Sadie!" he called. "Hello, kid!" And the women marched on, serious-faced, calm-eyed. There came floats; elaborate affairs, with girls in Greek robes. Fanny did not care for these. More solid ranks. And then a strange and pitiful and tragic and eloquent group. Their banner said, "Garment Workers. Infants' Wear Section." And at their head marched a girl, carrying a banner. I don't know how she attained that honor. I think she must have been one of those fiery, eloquent leaders in her factory clique. The banner she carried was a large one, and it flapped prodigiously in the breeze, and its pole was thick and heavy. She was a very small girl, even in that group of pale-faced, under-sized, under-fed girls. A Russian Jewess, evidently. Her shoes were ludicrous. They curled up at the toes, and the heels were run down. Her dress was a sort of parody on the prevailing fashion. But on her face, as she trudged along, hugging the pole of the great pennant that flapped in the breeze, was stamped a look.—well, you see that same look in some pictures of Joan of Arc. It wasn't merely a look. It was a story. It was tragedy. It was the history of a people. You saw in it that which told of centuries of oppression in Russia. You saw eager groups of student Intellectuals, gathered in secret places for low-voiced, fiery talk. There was in it the unspeakable misery of Siberia. It spoke eloquently of pogroms, of massacres, of Kiev and its sister-horror, Kishineff. You saw mean and narrow streets, and carefully darkened windows, and, on the other side of those windows the warm yellow glow of the seven-branched Shabbos light. Above this there shone the courage of a race serene in the knowledge that it cannot die. And illuminating all, so that her pinched face, beneath the flapping pennant, was the rapt, uplifted countenance of the Crusader, there blazed the great glow of hope. This woman movement, spoken of so glibly as Suffrage, was, to the mind of this over-read, under-fed, emotional, dreamy little Russian garment worker the glorious means to a long hoped for end. She had idealized it, with the imagery of her kind. She had endowed it with promise that it would never actually hold for her, perhaps. And so she marched on, down the great, glittering avenue, proudly clutching her unwieldy banner, a stunted, grotesque, magnificent figure. More than a figure. A symbol.

Fanny's eyes followed her until she passed out of sight. She put up her hand to her cheek, and her face was wet. She stood there, and the parade went on, endlessly, it seemed, and she saw it through a haze. Bands. More bands. Pennants. Floats. Women. Women. Women.

"I always cry at parades," said Fanny, to the woman who stood next her—the woman who wanted to march, but was scared to. "That's all right," said the woman. "That's all right." And she laughed, because she was crying, too. And then she did a surprising thing. She elbowed her way to the edge of the crowd, past the red-faced man with the cigar, out to the street, and fell into line, and marched on up the street, shoulders squared, head high.

Fanny glanced down at her watch. It was quarter after four. With a little gasp she turned to work her way through the close-packed crowd. It was an actual physical struggle, from which she emerged disheveled, breathless, uncomfortably warm, and minus her handkerchief, but she had gained the comparative quiet of the side street, and she made the short distance that lay between the Avenue and her hotel a matter of little more than a minute. In the hotel corridor stood Ella and Fenger, the former looking worried, the latter savage.

"Where in the world—" began Ella.

"Caught in the jam. And I didn't want to get out. It was—it was—glorious!" She was shaking hands with Fenger, and realizing for the first time that she must be looking decidedly sketchy and that she had lost her handkerchief. She fished for it in her bag, hopelessly, when Fenger released her hand. He had not spoken. Now he said:

"What's the matter with your eyes?"

"I've been crying," Fanny confessed cheerfully.

"Crying!"

"The parade. There was a little girl in it—" she stopped. Fenger would not be interested in that little girl. Now Clancy would have—but Ella broke in on that thought.

"I guess you don't realize that out in front of this hotel there's a kind of a glorified taxi waiting, with the top rolled back, and it's been there half an hour. I never expect to see the time when I could enjoy keeping a taxi waiting. It goes against me."

"I'm sorry. Really. Let's go. I'm ready."

"You are not. Your hair's a sight; and those eyes!"

Fenger put a hand on her arm. "Go on up and powder your nose, Miss Brandeis. And don't hurry. I want you to enjoy this drive."

On her way up in the elevator Fanny thought, "He has lost his waistline. Now, that couldn't have happened in a month. Queer I didn't notice it before. And he looks soft. Not enough exercise."

When she rejoined them she was freshly bloused and gloved and all traces of the tell-tale red had vanished from her eyelids. Fifth avenue was impossible. Their car sped up Madison avenue, and made for the Park. The Plaza was a jam of tired marchers. They dispersed from there, but there seemed no end to the line that still flowed up Fifth avenue. Fenger seemed scarcely to see it. He had plunged at once into talk of the European trip. Fanny gave him every detail, omitting nothing. She repeated all that her letters and cables had told. Fenger was more excited than she had ever seen him. He questioned, cross-questioned, criticized, probed, exacted an account of every conversation. Usually it was not method that interested him, but results. Fanny, having accomplished the thing she had set out to do, had lost interest in it now. The actual millions so glibly bandied in the Haynes-Cooper plant had never thrilled her. The methods by which they were made possible had.

Ella had been listening with the shrewd comprehension of one who admires the superior art of a fellow craftsman.

"I'll say this, Mr. Fenger. If I could make you look like that, by going to Europe and putting it over those foreign boys, I'd feel I'd earned a year's salary right there, and quit. Not to speak of the cross-examination you're putting her through."

Fenger laughed, a little self-consciously. "It's just that I want to be sure it's real. I needn't tell you how important this trick is that Miss Brandeis has just turned." He turned to Fanny, with a boyish laugh. "Now don't pose. You know you can't be as bored as you look."

"Anyway," put in Ella, briskly, "I move that the witness step down. She may not be bored, but she certainly must be tired, and she's beginning to look it. Just lean back, Fanny, and let the green of this park soak in. At that, it isn't so awfully green, when you get right close, except that one stretch of meadow. Kind of ugly, Central Park, isn't it? Bare."

Fanny sat forward. There was more sparkle in her face than at any time during the drive. They were skimming along those green-shaded drives that are so sophisticatedly sylvan.

"I used to think it was bare, too, and bony as an old maid, with no soft cuddly places like the parks at home; no gracious green stretches, and no rose gardens. But somehow, it grows on you. The reticence of it. And that stretch of meadow near the Mall, in the late afternoon, with the mist on it, and the sky faintly pink, and that electric sign— Somebody's Tires or other—winking off and on—"

"You're a queer child," interrupted Fenger. "As wooden as an Indian while talking about a million-a-year deal, and lyrical over a combination of electric sign, sunset, and moth-eaten park. Oh, well, perhaps that's what makes you as you are."

Even Ella looked a little startled at that.

They had tea at Claremont, at a table overlooking the river and the Palisades. Fenger was the kind of man to whom waiters always give a table overlooking anything that should be overlooked. After tea they drove out along the river and came back in the cool of the evening. Fanny was very quiet now. Fenger followed her mood. Ella sustained the conversation, somewhat doggedly. It was almost seven when they reached the plaza exit. And there Fanny, sitting forward suddenly, gave a little cry.

"Why—they're marching yet!" she said, and her voice was high with wonder. "They're marching yet! All the time we've been driving and teaing, they've been marching."

And so they had. Thousands upon thousands, they had flowed along as relentlessly, and seemingly as endlessly as a river. They were marching yet. For six hours the thousands had poured up that street, making it a moving mass of white. And the end was not yet. What pen, and tongue, and sense of justice had failed to do, they were doing now by sheer, crude force of numbers. The red-faced hooligan, who had stood next to Fanny in the crowd hours before, had long ago ceased his jibes and slunk away, bored, if not impressed. After all, one might jeer at ten, or fifty, or a hundred women, or even five hundred. But not at forty thousand.

Their car turned down Madison Avenue, and Fenger twisted about for a last look at the throng in the plaza. He was plainly impressed. The magnitude of the thing appealed to him. To a Haynes-Cooper-trained mind, forty thousand women, marching for whatever the cause, must be impressive. Forty thousand of anything had the respect of Michael Fenger. His eyes narrowed, thoughtfully.

"They seem to have put it over," he said. "And yet, what's the idea? Oh, I'm for suffrage, of course. Naturally. And all those thousands of women, in white—still, a thing as huge as this parade has to be reduced to a common denominator, to be really successful. If somebody could take the whole thing, boil it down, and make the country see what this huge demonstration stands for."

Fanny leaned forward suddenly. "Tell the man to stop. I want to get out."

Fenger and Ella stared. "What for?" But Fenger obeyed.

"I want to get something at this stationer's shop." She had jumped down almost before the motor had stopped at the curb.

"But let me get it."

"No. You can't. Wait here." She disappeared within the shop. She was back in five minutes, a flat, loosely wrapped square under her arm. "Cardboard," she explained briefly, in answer to their questions.

Fenger, about to leave them at their hotel, presented his plans for the evening. Fanny, looking up at him, her head full of other plans, thought he looked and sounded very much like Big Business. And, for the moment at least, Fanny Brandeis loathed Big Business, and all that it stood for.

"It's almost seven," Fenger was saying. "We'll be rubes in New York, this evening. You girls will just have time to freshen up a bit—I suppose you want to—and then we'll have dinner, and go to the theater, and to supper afterward. What do you want to see?"

Ella looked at Fanny. And Fanny shook her head, "Thanks. You're awfully kind. But—no."

"Why not?" demanded Fenger, gruffly.

"Perhaps because I'm tired. And there's something else I must do."

Ella looked relieved. Fenger's eyes bored down upon Fanny, but she seemed not to feel them. She held out her hand.

"You're going back to-morrow?" Fenger asked. "I'm not leaving until Thursday."

"To-morrow, with Ella. Good-by. It's been a glorious drive. I feel quite rested."

"You just said you were tired."

The elevator door clanged, shutting out the sight of Fenger's resentful frown.

"He's as sensitive as a soubrette," said Ella. "I'm glad you decided not to go out. I'm dead, myself. A kimono for the rest of the evening."

Fanny seemed scarcely to hear her. With a nod she left Ella, and entered her own room. There she wasted no time. She threw her hat and coat on the bed. Her suitcase was on the baggage stand. She turned on all the lights, swung the closed suitcase up to the table, shoved the table against the wall, up-ended the suitcase so that its leather side presented a smooth surface, and propped a firm sheet of white cardboard against the impromptu rack. She brought her chair up close, fumbled in her bag for the pens she had just purchased. Her eyes were on the blank white surface of the paper. The table was the kind that has a sub-shelf. It prevented Fanny from crossing her legs under it, and that bothered her. While she fitted her pens, and blocked her paper, she kept on barking her shins in unconscious protest against the uncomfortable conditions under which she must work.

She sat staring at the paper now, after having marked it off into blocks, with a pencil. She got up, and walked across the room, aimlessly, and stood there a moment, and came back. She picked up a thread on the floor. Sat down again. Picked up her pencil, rolled it a moment in her palms, then, catching her toes behind either foreleg of her chair, in an attitude that was as workmanlike as it was ungraceful, she began to draw, nervously, tentatively at first, but gaining in firmness and assurance as she went on.

If you had been standing behind her chair you would have seen, emerging miraculously from the white surface under Fanny's pencil, a thin, undersized little figure in sleazy black and white, whose face, under the cheap hat, was upturned and rapturous. Her skirts were wind-blown, and the wind tugged, too, at the banner whose pole she hugged so tightly in her arms. Dimly you could see the crowds that lined the street on either side. Vaguely, too, you saw the faces and stunted figures of the little group of girls she led. But she, the central figure, stood out among all the rest. Fanny Brandeis, the artist, and Fanny Brandeis, the salesman, combined shrewdly to omit no telling detail. The wrong kind of feet in the wrong kind of shoes; the absurd hat; the shabby skirt—every bit of grotesquerie was there, serving to emphasize the glory of the face. Fanny Brandeis' face, as the figure grew, line by line, was a glorious thing, too.

She was working rapidly. She laid down her pencil, now, and leaned back, squinting her eyes critically. She looked grimly pleased. Her hair was rather rumpled, and her cheeks very pink. She took up her pen, now, and began to ink her drawing with firm black strokes. As she worked a little crow of delight escaped her—the same absurd crow of triumph that had sounded that day in Winnebago, years and years before, when she, a school girl in a red tam o' shanter, had caught the likeness of Schabelitz, the peasant boy, under the exterior of Schabelitz, the famous. There sounded a smart little double knock at her door. Fanny did not heed it. She did not hear it. Her toes were caught behind the chair-legs again. She was slumped down on the middle of her spine. She had brought the table, with its ridiculously up-ended suitcase, very near, so that she worked with a minimum of effort. The door opened. Fanny did not turn her head. Ella Monahan came in, yawning. She was wearing an expensive looking silk kimono that fell in straight, simple folds, and gave a certain majesty to her ample figure.

"Well, what in the world—" she began, and yawned again, luxuriously. She stopped behind Fanny's chair and glanced over her shoulder. The yawn died. She craned her neck a little, and leaned forward. And the little girl went marching by, in her cheap and crooked shoes, and her short and sleazy skirt, with the banner tugging, tugging in the breeze. Fanny Brandeis had done her with that economy of line, and absence of sentimentality which is the test separating the artist from the draughtsman.

Silence, except for the scratching of Fanny Brandeis's pen.

"Why—the poor little kike!" said Ella Monahan. Then, after another moment of silence, "I didn't know you could draw like that."

Fanny laid down her pen. "Like what?" She pushed back her chair, and rose, stiffly. The drawing, still wet, was propped up against the suitcase. Fanny walked across the room. Ella dropped into her chair, so that when Fanny came back to the table it was she who looked over Ella's shoulder. Into Ella's shrewd and heavy face there had come a certain look.

"They don't get a square deal, do they? They don't get a square deal."

The two looked at the girl a moment longer, in silence. Then Fanny went over to the bed, and picked up her hat and coat. She smoothed her hair, deftly, powdered her nose with care, and adjusted her hat at the smart angle approved by the Galeries Lafayette. She came back to the table, picked up her pen, and beneath the drawing wrote, in large print:

THE MARCHER.

She picked up the drawing, still wet, opened the door, and with a smile at the bewildered Ella, was gone.

It was after eight o'clock when she reached the Star building. She asked for Lasker's office, and sent in her card. Heyl had told her that Lasker was always at his desk at eight. Now, Fanny Brandeis knew that the average young woman, standing outside the office of a man like Lasker, unknown and at the mercy of office boy or secretary, continues to stand outside until she leaves in discouragement. But Fanny knew, too, that she was not an average young woman. She had, on the surface, an air of authority and distinction. She had that quiet assurance of one accustomed to deference. She had youth, and beauty, and charm. She had a hat and suit bought in Paris, France; and a secretary is only human.

Carl Lasker's private office was the bare, bright, newspaper-strewn room of a man who is not only a newspaper proprietor, but a newspaper man. There's a difference. Carl Lasker had sold papers on the street when he was ten. He had slept on burlap sacks, paper stuffed, in the basement of a newspaper office. Ink flowed with the blood in his veins. He could operate a press. He could manipulate a linotype machine (that almost humanly intelligent piece of mechanism). He could make up a paper single handed, and had done it. He knew the newspaper game, did Carl Lasker, from the composing room to the street, and he was a very great man in his line. And so he was easy to reach, and simple to talk to, as are all great men.

A stocky man, decidedly handsome, surprisingly young, well dressed, smooth shaven, direct.

Fanny entered. Lasker laid down her card. "Brandeis. That's a good name." He extended his hand. He wore evening clothes, with a white flower in his buttonhole. He must have just come from a dinner, or he was to attend a late affair, somewhere. Perhaps Fanny, taken aback, unconsciously showed her surprise, because Lasker grinned, as he waved her to a chair. His quick mind had interpreted her thought.

"Sit down, Miss Brandeis. You think I'm gotten up like the newspaper man in a Richard Harding Davis short story, don't you? What can I do for you?"

Fanny wasted no words. "I saw the parade this afternoon. I did a picture. I think it's good. If you think so too, I wish you'd use it."

She laid it, face up, on Lasker's desk. Lasker picked it up in his two hands, held it off, and scrutinized it. All the drama in the world is concentrated in the confines of a newspaper office every day in the year, and so you hear very few dramatic exclamations in such a place. Men like Lasker do not show emotion when impressed. It is too wearing on the mechanism. Besides, they are trained to self-control. So Lasker said, now:

"Yes, I think it's pretty good, too." Then, raising his voice to a sudden bellow, "Boy!" He handed the drawing to a boy, gave a few brief orders, and turned back to Fanny. "To-morrow morning every other paper in New York will have pictures showing Mildred Inness, the beauty, on her snow-white charger, or Sophronisba A. Bannister, A.B., Ph.D., in her cap and gown, or Mrs. William Van der Welt as Liberty. We'll have that little rat with the banner, and it'll get 'em. They'll talk about it." His eyes narrowed a little. "Do you always get that angle?"

"Yes."

"There isn't a woman cartoonist in New York who does that human stuff. Did you know that?"

"Yes."

"Want a job?"

"N-no."

His knowing eye missed no detail of the suit, the hat, the gloves, the shoes.

"What's your salary now?"

"Ten thousand."

"Satisfied?"

"No."

"You've hit the heart of that parade. I don't know whether you could do that every day, or not. But if you struck twelve half the time, it would be enough. When you want a job, come back."

"Thanks," said Fanny quietly. And held out her hand.

She returned in the subway. It was a Bronx train, full of sagging faces, lusterless eyes, grizzled beards; of heavy, black-eyed girls in soiled white shoes; of stoop-shouldered men, poring over newspapers in Hebrew script; of smells and sounds and glaring light.

And though to-morrow would bring its reaction, and common sense would have her again in its cold grip, she was radiant to-night and glowing with the exaltation that comes with creation. And over and over a voice within her was saying:

These are my people! These are my people!

CHAPTER SIXTEEN

The ship that brought Theodore Brandeis to America was the last of its kind to leave German ports for years. The day after he sailed from Bremen came the war. Fanny Brandeis was only one of the millions of Americans who refused to accept the idea of war. She took it as a personal affront. It was uncivilized, it was old fashioned, it was inconvenient. Especially inconvenient. She had just come from Europe, where she had negotiated a million-dollar deal. War would mean that she could not get the goods ordered. Consequently there could be no war.

Theodore landed the first week in August. Fanny stole two days from the ravenous bins to meet him in New York. I think she must have been a very love-hungry woman in the years since her mother's death. She had never admitted it. But only emotions denied to the point of starvation could have been so shaken now at the thought of the feast before them. She had trained herself to think of him as Theodore the selfish, Theodore the callous, Theodore the voracious. "An unsuccessful genius," she told herself. "He'll be impossible. They're bad enough when they're successful."

But now her eyes, her thoughts, her longings, her long-pent emotions were straining toward the boat whose great prow was looming toward her, a terrifying bulk. The crowd awaiting the ship was enormous. A dramatic enough scene at any time, the great Hoboken pier this morning was filled with an unrehearsed mob, anxious, thrilled, hysterical. The morning papers had carried wireless news that the ship had been chased by a French gunboat and had escaped only through the timely warning of the Dresden, a German gunboat. That had added the last fillip to an already tense situation. Tears were streaming down half the faces upturned toward the crowded decks. And from every side:

"Do you see her?"

"That's Jessie. There she is! Jessie!"

"Heh! Jim, old boy! Come on down!"

Fanny's eyes were searching the packed rails. "Ted!" she called, and choked back a sob. "Teddy!" Still she did not see him. She was searching, womanlike, for a tall, blondish boy, with a sulky mouth, and humorous eyes, and an unruly lock of hair that would insist on escaping from the rest and straggling down over his forehead. I think she was even looking for a boy with a violin in his arms. A boy in knickers. Women lose all sense of time and proportion at such times. Still she did not see him. The passengers were filing down the gangplank now; rushing down as quickly as the careful hands of the crew would allow them, and hurling themselves into the arms of friends and family crowded below. Fanny strained her eyes toward that narrow passageway, anxious, hopeful, fearful, heartsick. For the moment Olga and the baby did not exist for her. And then she saw him.

She saw him through an unimaginable disguise. She saw him, and knew him in spite of the fact that the fair-haired, sulky, handsome boy had vanished, and in his place walked a man. His hair was close-cropped, German-fashion; his face careworn and older than she had ever thought possible; his bearing, his features, his whole personality stamped with an unmistakable distinction. And his clothes were appallingly, inconceivably German. So she saw him, and he was her brother, and she was his sister, and she stretched out her arms to him.

"Teddy!" She hugged him close, her face buried in his shoulder. "Teddy, you—you Spitzbube you!" She laughed at that, a little hysterically. "Not that I know what a Spitzbube is, but it's the Germanest word I can think of." That shaven head. Those trousers. That linen. The awful boots. The tie! "Oh, Teddy, and you're the Germanest thing I ever saw." She kissed him again, rapturously.

He kissed her, too, wordlessly at first. They moved aside a little, out of the crowd. Then he spoke for the first time.

"God! I'm glad to see you, Fanny." There was tragedy, not profanation in his voice. His hand gripped hers. He turned, and now, for the first time, Fanny saw that at his elbow stood a buxom, peasant woman, evidently a nurse, and in her arms a child. A child with Molly Brandeis' mouth, and Ferdinand Brandeis' forehead, and Fanny Brandeis' eyes, and Theodore Brandeis' roseleaf skin, and over, and above all these, weaving in and out through the whole, an expression or cast—a vague, undefinable thing which we call a resemblance—that could only have come from the woman of the picture, Theodore Brandeis' wife, Olga.

"Why—it's the baby!" cried Fanny, and swung her out of the nurse's protesting arms. Such a German-looking baby. Such an adorably German-looking baby. "Du kleine, du!" Fanny kissed the roseleaf cheek. "Du suszes—" She turned suddenly to Theodore. "Olga—where's Olga?"

"She did not come."

Fanny tightened her hold of the little squirming bundle in her arms. "Didn't come?"

Theodore shook his head, dumbly. In his eyes was an agony of pain. And suddenly all those inexplicable things in his face were made clear to Fanny. She placed the little Mizzi in the nurse's arms again. "Then we'll go, dear. They won't be a minute over your trunks, I'm sure. Just follow me."

Her arm was linked through Theodore's. Her hand was on his. Her head was up. Her chin was thrust out, and she never knew how startlingly she resembled the Molly Brandeis who used to march so bravely down Norris street on her way to Brandeis' Bazaar. She was facing a situation, and she recognized it. There was about her an assurance, a composure, a blithe capability that imparted itself to the three bewildered and helpless ones in her charge. Theodore felt it, and the strained look in his face began to lift just a little. The heavy-witted peasant woman felt it, and trudged along, cheerfully. The baby in her arms seemed to sense it, and began to converse volubly and unintelligibly with the blue uniformed customs inspector.

They were out of the great shed in an incredibly short time. Fanny seemed equal to every situation. She had taken the tube to Hoboken, but now she found a commodious open car, and drove a shrewd bargain with the chauffeur. She bundled the three into it. Of the three, perhaps Theodore seemed the most bewildered and helpless. He clung to his violin and Fanny.

"I feel like an immigrant," he said. "Fan, you're a wonder. You don't know how much you look and act like mother. I've been watching you. It's startling."

Fanny laughed and took his hand, and held his hand up to her breast, and crushed it there. "And you look like an illustration out of the Fliegende Blaetter. It isn't only your clothes. Your face is German. As for Mizzi here—" she gathered the child in her arms again—"you've never explained that name to me. Why, by the way, Mizzi? Of all the names in the world."

Theodore smiled a wry little smile. "Mizzi is named after Olga's chum. You see, in Vienna every other—well, chorus girl I suppose you'd call them—is named Mizzi. Like all the Gladyses and Flossies here in America. Well, Olga's special friend Mizzi—"

"I see," said Fanny quietly. "Well, anything's better than Fanny. Always did make me think of an old white horse." And at that the small German person in her arms screwed her mouth into a fascinating bunch, and then unscrewed it and, having made these preparations said, "Tante Fanny. Shecago. Tante Fanny."

"Why, Mizzi Brandeis, you darling! Teddy, did you hear that! She said `Tante Fanny' and `Chicago' just as plainly!" "Did I hear it? Have I heard anything else for weeks?"

The plump person on the opposite seat, who had been shaking her head violently all this time here threatened to burst if not encouraged to speak. Fanny nodded to her. Whereupon the flood broke.

"Wunderbar, nicht war! Ich kuss' die handt, gnadiges Fraulein." She actually did it, to Fanny's consternation. "Ich hab' ihr das gelernt, Gnadige. Selbst. Ist es nicht ganz entzuckend! Tante Fanny. Auch Shecago."

Fanny nodded a number of times, first up and down, signifying assent, then sideways, signifying unbounded wonder and admiration. She made a gigantic effort to summon her forgotten German.

"Was ist Ihre Name?" she managed to ask.

"Otti."

"Oh, my!" exclaimed Fanny, weakly. "Mizzi and Otti. It sounds like the first act of the `Merry Widow.'" She turned to Theodore. "I wish you'd sit back, and relax, and if you must clutch that violin case, do it more comfortably. I don't want you to tell me a thing, now. New York is ghastly in August. We'll get a train out of here to-morrow. My apartment in Chicago is cool, and high, and quiet, and the lake is in the front yard, practically. To-night, perhaps, we'll talk about—things. And, oh, Teddy, how glad I am to see you—to have you—to—" she put out a hand and patted his thin cheek—"to touch you."

And at that the man became a boy again. His face worked a moment, painfully and then his head came down in her lap that held the baby, and so she had them both for a moment, one arm about the child, one hand smoothing the boy's close-cropped hair. And in that moment she was more splendidly maternal than either of the women who had borne these whom she now comforted.

It was Fanny who attended to the hotel rooms, to the baby's comfort, to the railroad tickets, to the ordering of the meals. Theodore was like a stranger in a strange land. Not only that, he seemed dazed.

"We'll have it out to-night," Fanny said to herself. "He'll never get that look off his face until he has told it all. I knew she was a beast."

She made him lie down while she attended to schedules, tickets, berths. She was gone for two hours. When she returned she found him looking amused, terrified and helpless, all at once, while three men reporters and one woman special writer bombarded him with questions. The woman had brought a staff artist with her, and he was now engaged in making a bungling sketch of Theodore's face, with its ludicrous expression.

Fanny sensed the situation and saved it. She hadn't sold goods all these years without learning the value of advertising. She came forward now, graciously (but not too graciously). Theodore looked relieved. Already he had learned that one might lean on this sister who was so capable, so bountifully alive.

"Teddy, you're much too tired to talk. Let me talk for you."

"My sister, Miss Brandeis," said Teddy, and waved a rather feeble hand in an inclusive gesture at the interrogatory five.

Fanny smiled. "Do sit down," she said, "all of you. Tell me, how did you happen to get on my brother's trail?"

One of the men explained. "We had a list of ship's passengers, of course. And we knew that Mr. Brandeis was a German violinist. And then the story of the ship being chased by a French boat. We just missed him down at the pier—"

"But he isn't a German violinist," interrupted Fanny. "Please get that straight. He's American. He is THE American violinist—or will be, as soon as his concert tour here is well started. It was Schabelitz himself who discovered my brother, and predicted his brilliant career. Here"—she had been glancing over the artist's shoulder—"will you let me make a sketch for you—just for the fun of the thing? I do that kind of thing rather decently. Did you see my picture called `The Marcher,' in the Star, at the time of the suffrage parade in May? Yes, that was mine. Just because he has what we call a butcher haircut, don't think he's German, because he isn't. You wouldn't call Winnebago, Wisconsin, Germany, would you?"

She was sketching him swiftly, daringly, masterfully. She was bringing out the distinction, the suffering, the boyishness in his face, and toning down the queer little foreign air he had. Toning it, but not omitting it altogether. She was too good a showman for that. As she sketched she talked, and as she talked she drew Theodore into the conversation, deftly, and just when he was needed. She gave them what they had come for—a story. And a good one. She brought in Mizzi and Otti, for color, and she saw to it that they spelled those names as they should be spelled. She managed to gloss over the question of Olga. Ill. Detained. Last minute. Too brave to sacrifice her husband's American tour. She finished her sketch and gave it to the woman reporter. It was an amazingly compelling little piece of work—and yet, not so amazing, perhaps, when you consider the thing that Fanny Brandeis had put into it. Then she sent them away, tactfully. They left, knowing all that Fanny Brandeis had wanted them to know; guessing little that she had not wanted them to guess. More than that no human being can accomplish, without the advice of his lawyer.

"Whew!" from Fanny, when the door had closed.

"Gott im Himmel!" from Theodore. "I had forgotten that America was like that."

"But America IS like that. And Teddy, we're going to make it sit up and take notice."

At that Theodore drooped again. Fanny thought that he looked startlingly as she remembered her father had looked in those days of her childhood, when Brandeis' Bazaar was slithering downhill. The sight of him moved her to a sudden resolve. She crossed swiftly to him, and put one heartening hand on his shoulder.

"Come on, brother. Out with it. Let's have it all now."

He reached up for her hand and held it, desperately. "Oh, Fan!" began Theodore, "Fan, I've been through hell."

Fanny said nothing. She only waited, quietly, encouragingly. She had learned when not to talk. Presently he took up his story, plunging directly into it, as though sensing that she had already divined much.

"She married me for a living. You'll think that's a joke, knowing what I was earning there, in Vienna, and how you and mother were denying yourselves everything to keep me. But in a city that circulates a coin valued at a twentieth of a cent, an American dollar looms up big. Besides, two of the other girls had got married. Good for nothing officers. She was jealous, I suppose. I didn't know any of that. I was flattered to think she'd notice me. She was awfully popular. She has a kind of wit. I suppose you'd call it that. The other girls were just coarse, and heavy, and—well—animal. You can't know the rottenness of life there in Vienna. Olga could keep a whole supper table laughing all evening. I can see, now, that that isn't difficult when your audience is made up of music hall girls, and stupid, bullet-headed officers, with their damned high collars, and their gold braid, and their silly swords, and their corsets, and their glittering shoes and their miserable petty poverty beneath all the show. I thought I was a lucky boy. I'd have pitied everybody in Winnebago, if I'd ever thought of anybody in Winnebago. I never did, except once in a while of you and mother when I needed money. I kept on with my music. I had sense enough left, for that. Besides, it was a habit, by that time. Well, we were married."

He laughed, an ugly, abrupt little laugh that ended in a moan, and turned his head and buried his face in Fanny's breast. And Fanny's arm was there, about his shoulder. "Fanny, you don't—I can't—" He stopped. Another silence. Fanny's arm tightened its hold. She bent and kissed the top of the stubbly head, bowed so low now. "Fan, do you remember that woman in `The Three Musketeers'? The hellish woman, that all men loved and loathed? Well, Olga's like that. I'm not whining. I'm not exaggerating. I'm just trying to make you understand. And yet I don't want you to understand. Only you don't know what it means to have you to talk to. To have some one who"—he clutched her hand, fearfully—"You do love me, don't you, Fanny? You do, don't you, Sis?"

"More than any one in the world," Fanny reassured him, quietly. "The way mother would have, if she had lived."

A sigh escaped him, at that, as though a load had lifted from him. He went on, presently. "It would have been all right if I could have earned just a little more money." Fanny shrank at that, and shut her eyes for a sick moment. "But I couldn't. I asked her to be patient. But you don't know the life there. There is no real home life. They live in the cafes. They go there to keep warm, in the winter, and to meet their friends, and gossip, and drink that eternal coffee, and every coffee house—there are thousands—is a rendezvous. We had two rooms, comfortable ones, for Vienna, and I tried to explain to her that if I could work hard, and get into concert, and keep at the composing, we'd be rich some day, and famous, and happy, and she'd have clothes, and jewels. But she was too stupid, or too bored. Olga is the kind of woman who only believes what she sees. Things got worse all the time. She had a temper. So have I—or I used to have. But when hers was aroused it was—horrible. Words that—that—unspeakable words. And one day she taunted me with being a ——with my race. The first time she called me that I felt that I must kill her. That was my mistake. I should have killed her. And I didn't."

"Teddy boy! Don't, brother! You're tired. You're excited and worn out."

"No, I'm not. Just let me talk. I know what I'm saying. There's something clean about killing." He brooded a moment over that thought. Then he went on, doggedly, not raising his voice. His hands were clasped loosely. "You don't know about the intolerance and the anti-Semitism in Prussia, I suppose. All through Germany, for that matter. In Bavaria it's bitter. That's one reason why Olga loathed Munich so. The queer part of it is that all that opposition seemed to fan something in me; something that had been smoldering for a long time." His voice had lost its dull tone now. It had in it a new timbre. And as he talked he began to interlard his English with bits of German, the language to which his tongue had accustomed itself in the past ten years. His sentences, too, took on a German construction, from time to time. He was plainly excited now. "My playing began to improve. There would be a ghastly scene with Olga—sickening—degrading. Then I would go to my work, and I would play, but magnificently! I tell you, it would be playing. I know. To fool myself I know better. One morning, after a dreadful quarrel I got the idea for the concerto, and the psalms. Jewish music. As Jewish as the Kol Nidre. I wanted to express the passion, and fire, and history of a people. My people. Why was that? Tell me. Selbst, weiss ich nicht. I felt that if I could put into it just a millionth part of their humiliation, and their glory; their tragedy and their triumph; their sorrow, and their grandeur; their persecution, their weldtschmerz. Volkschmerz. That was it. And through it all, weaving in and out, one great underlying motif. Indestructibility. The great cry which says, `We cannot be destroyed!'"

He stood up, uncertainly. His eyes were blazing. He began to walk up and down the luxurious little room. Fanny's eyes matched his. She was staring at him, fascinated, trembling.

She moistened her lips a little with her tongue. "And you've done it? Teddy! You've done—that!"

Theodore Brandeis stood up, very straight and tall. "Yes," he said, simply. "Yes, I've done that."

She came over to him then, and put her two hands on his shoulders. "Ted—dear—will you ever forgive me? I'll try to make up for it now. I didn't know. I've been blind. Worse than blind. Criminal." She was weeping now, broken-heartedly, and he was patting her with little comforting love pats, and whispering words of tenderness.

"Forgive you? Forgive you what?"

"The years of suffering. The years you've had to spend with her. With that horrible woman—"

"Don't—" He sucked his breath between his teeth. His face had gone haggard again. Fanny, direct as always, made up her mind that she would have it all. And now.

"There's something you haven't told me. Tell me all of it. You're my brother and I'm your sister. We're all we have in the world." And at that, as though timed by some miraculous and supernatural stage manager, there came a cry from the next room; a sleepy, comfortable, imperious little cry. Mizzi had awakened. Fanny made a step in the direction of the door. Then she turned back. "Tell me why Olga didn't come. Why isn't she here with her husband and baby?"

"Because she's with another man."

"Another—"

"It had been going on for a long time. I was the last to know about it. It's that way, always, isn't it? He's an officer. A fool. He'll have to take off his silly corsets now, and his velvet collar, and his shiny boots, and go to war. Damn him! I hope they'll kill him with a hundred bayonets, one by one, and leave him to rot on the field. She had been fooling me all the time, and they had been laughing at me, the two of them. I didn't find it out until just before this American trip. And when I confronted her with it she laughed in my face. She said she hated me. She said she'd rather starve than leave him to come to America with me. She said I was a fiddling fool. She—" he was trembling and sick with the shame of it—"God! I can't tell you the things she said. She wanted to keep Mizzi. Isn't that strange? She loves the baby. She neglects her, and spoils her, and once I saw her beat her, in a rage. But she says she loves my Mizzi, and I believe she does, in her own dreadful way. I promised her, and lied to her, and then I ran away with Mizzi and her nurse."

"Oh, I thank God for that!" Fanny cried. "I thank God for that! And now, Teddy boy, we'll forget all about those miserable years. We'll forget all about her, and the life she led you. You're going to have your chance here. You're going to be repaid for every minute of suffering you've endured. I'll make it up to you. And when you see them applauding you, calling for you, adoring you, all those hideous years will fade from your mind, and you'll be Theodore Brandeis, the successful, Theodore Brandeis, the gifted, Theodore Brandeis, the great! You need never think of her again. You'll never see her again. That beast! That woman!"

And at that Theodore's face became distorted and dreadful with pain. He raised two impotent, shaking arms high above his head. "That's just it! That's just it! You don't know what love is. You don't know what hate is. You don't know how I hate myself. Loathe myself. She's all that's miserable, all that's unspeakable, all that's vile. And if she called me to-day I'd come. That's it." He covered his shamed face with his two hands, so that the words came from him slobberingly, sickeningly. "I hate her! I hate her! And I want her. I want her. I want her!"

CHAPTER SEVENTEEN

If Fanny Brandeis, the deliberately selfish, the calculatingly ambitious, was aghast at the trick fate had played her, she kept her thoughts to herself. Knowing her, I think she must have been grimly amused at finding herself saddled with a helpless baby, a bewildered peasant woman, and an artist brother both helpless and bewildered.

It was out of the question to house them in her small apartment. She found a furnished apartment near her own, and installed them there, with a working housekeeper in charge. She had a gift for management, and she arranged all these details with a brisk capability that swept everything before it. A sunny bedroom for Mizzi. But then, a bright living room, too, for Theodore's hours of practice. No noise. Chicago's roar maddened him. Otti shied at every new contrivance that met her eye. She had to be broken in to elevators, electric switches, hot and cold faucets, radiators.

"No apartment ever built could cover all the requirements," Fanny confided to Fenger, after the first harrowing week. "What they really need is a combination palace, houseboat, sanatorium, and creche."

"Look here," said Fenger. "If I can help, why—" a sudden thought struck him. "Why don't you bring 'em all down to my place in the country? We're not there half the time. It's too cool for my wife in September. Just the thing for the child, and your brother could fiddle his head off."

The Fengers had a roomy, wide-verandaed house near Lake Forest; one of the many places of its kind that dot the section known as the north shore. Its lawn sloped gently down to the water's edge. The house was gay with striped awnings, and scarlet geraniums, and chintz-covered chairs. The bright, sparkling, luxurious little place seemed to satisfy a certain beauty-sense in Fenger, as did the etchings on the walls in his office. Fanny had spent a week-end there in July, with three or four other guests, including Fascinating Facts. She had been charmed with it, and had announced that her energies thereafter would be directed solely toward the possession of just such a house as this, with a lawn that was lipped by the lake, awnings and geraniums to give it a French cafe air; books and magazines enough to belie that.

"And I'll always wear white," she promised, gayly, "and there'll be pitchers on every table, frosty on the outside, and minty on the inside, and you're all invited."

They had laughed at that, and so had she, but she had been grimly in earnest just the same.

She shook her head now at Fenger's suggestion. "Imagine Mrs. Fenger's face at sight of Mizzi, and Theodore with his violin, and Otti with her shawls and paraphernalia. Though," she added, seriously, "it's mighty kind of you, and generous—and just like a man."

"It isn't kindness nor generosity that makes me want to do things for you."

"Modest," murmured Fanny, wickedly, "as always."

Fenger bent his look upon her. "Don't try the ingenue on me, Fanny."

Theodore's manager, Kurt Stein, was to have followed him in ten days. The war changed that. The war was to change many things. Fanny seemed to sense the influx of musicians that was to burst upon the United States following the first few weeks of the catastrophe, and she set about forestalling it. Advertising. That was what Theodore needed. She had faith enough in his genius. But her business sense told her that this genius must be enhanced by the proper setting. She set about creating this setting. She overlooked no chance to fix his personality in the kaleidoscopic mind of the American public—or as much of it as she could reach. His publicity man was a dignified German-American whose methods were legitimate and uninspired. Fanny's enthusiasm and superb confidence in Theodore's genius infected Fenger, Fascinating Facts, even Nathan Haynes himself. Nathan Haynes had never posed as a patron of the arts, in spite of his fantastic millions. But by the middle of September there were few of his friends, or his wife's friends, who had not heard of this Theodore Brandeis. In Chicago, Illinois, no one lives in houses, it is said, except the city's old families, and new millionaires. The rest of the vast population is flat-dwelling. To say that Nathan Haynes' spoken praise reached the city's house-dwellers would carry with it a significance plain to any Chicagoan.

As for Fanny's method; here is a typical example of her somewhat crude effectiveness in showmanship. Otti had brought with her from Vienna her native peasant costume. It is a costume seen daily in the Austrian capital, on the Ring, in the Stadt Park, wherever Viennese nurses convene with their small charges. To the American eye it is a musical comedy costume, picturesque, bouffant, amazing. Your Austrian takes it quite for granted. Regardless of the age of the nurse, the skirt is short, coming a few inches below the knees, and built like a lamp shade, in color usually a bright scarlet, with rows of black velvet ribbon at the bottom. Beneath it are worn skirts and skirts, and skirts, so that the opera-bouffe effect is complete. The bodice is black velvet, laced over a chemise of white. The head-gear a soaring winged affair of stiffly starched white, that is a pass between the Breton peasant woman's cap and an aeroplane. Black stockings and slippers finish the costume.

Otti and Mizzi spent the glorious September days in Lincoln park, Otti garbed in staid American stripes and apron, Mizzi resplendent in smartest of children's dresses provided for her lavishly by her aunt. Her fat and dimpled hands smoothed the blue, or pink or white folds with a complacency astonishing in one of her years. "That's her mother in her," Fanny thought.

One rainy autumn day Fanny entered her brother's apartment to find Otti resplendent in her Viennese nurse's costume. Mizzi had been cross and fretful, and the sight of the familiar scarlet and black and white, and the great winged cap seemed to soothe her.

"Otti!" Fanny exclaimed. "You gorgeous creature! What is it? A dress rehearsal?" Otti got the import, if not the English.

"So gehen wir im Wien," she explained, and struck a killing pose.

"Everybody? All the nurses? Alle?"

"Aber sure," Otti displayed her half dozen English words whenever possible.

Fanny stared a moment. Her eyes narrowed thoughtfully. "To-morrow's Saturday," she said, in German. "If it's fair and warm you put on that costume and take Mizzi to the park.... Certainly the animal cages, if you want to. If any one annoys you, come home. If a policeman asks you why you are dressed that way tell him it is the costume worn by nurses in Vienna. Give him your name. Tell him who your master is. If he doesn't speak German—and he won't, in Chicago—some one will translate for you."

Not a Sunday paper in Chicago that did not carry a startling picture of the resplendent Otti and the dimpled and smiling Mizzi. The omnipresent staff photographer seemed to sniff his victim from afar. He pounced on Theodore Brandeis' baby daughter, accompanied by her Viennese nurse (in costume) and he played her up in a Sunday special that was worth thousands of dollars, Fanny assured the bewildered and resentful Theodore, as he floundered wildly through the billowing waves of the Sunday newspaper flood. Theodore's first appearance was to be in Chicago as soloist with the Chicago Symphony Orchestra, in the season's opening program in October. Any music-wise Chicagoan will tell you that the Chicago Symphony Orchestra is not only a musical organization functioning marvelously (when playing Beethoven). It is an institution. Its patrons will admit the existence, but not the superiority of similar organizations in Boston, Philadelphia and New York. On Friday afternoons, during the season, Orchestra Hall, situate on Michigan Boulevard, holds more pretty girls and fewer men than one might expect to see at any one gathering other than, perhaps, a wholesale debutante tea crush. A Friday afternoon ticket is as impossible of attainment for one not a subscriber as a seat in heaven for a sinner. Saturday night's audience is staider, more masculine, less staccato. Gallery, balcony, parquet, it represents the city's best. Its men prefer Beethoven to Berlin. Its women could wear pearl necklaces, and don't. Between the audience and the solemn black-and-white rows on the platform there exists an entente cordiale. The Konzert-Meister bows to his friend in the third row, as he tucks his violin under his chin. The fifth row, aisle, smiles and nods to the sausage-fingered 'cellist.

"Fritz is playing well to-night."

In a rarefied form, it is the atmosphere that existed between audience and players in the days of the old and famous Daly stock company.

Such was the character of the audience Theodore was to face on his first appearance in America. Fanny explained its nature to him. He shrugged his shoulders in a gesture as German as it was expressive.

Theodore seemed to have become irrevocably German during the years of his absence from America. He had a queer stock of little foreign tricks. He lifted his hat to men acquaintances on the street. He had learned to smack his heels smartly together and to bow stiffly from the waist, and to kiss the hand of the matrons—and they adored him for it. He was quite innocent of pose in these things. He seemed to have imbibed them, together with his queer German haircut, and his incredibly German clothes.

Fanny allowed him to retain the bow, and the courtly hand-kiss, but she insisted that he change the clothes and the haircut.

"You'll have to let it grow, Ted. I don't mean that I want you to have a mane, like Ysaye. But I do think you ought to discard that convict cut. Besides, it isn't becoming. And if you're going to be an American violinist you'll have to look it—with a foreign finish." He let his hair grow. Fanny watched with interest for the appearance of the unruly lock which had been wont to straggle over his white forehead in his schoolboy days. The new and well-cut American clothes effected surprisingly little change. Fanny, surveying him, shook her head.

"When you stepped off the ship you looked like a German in German clothes. Now you look like a German in American clothes. I don't know—I do believe it's your face, Ted. I wouldn't have thought that ten years or so in any country could change the shape of one's nose, and mouth and cheekbones. Do you suppose it's the umlauts?"

"Cut it out!" laughed Ted, that being his idea of modern American slang. He was fascinated by these crisp phrases, but he was ten years or so behind the times, and he sometimes startled his hearers by an exhibition of slang so old as to be almost new. It was all the more startling in contrast with his conversational English, which was as carefully correct as a born German's.

As for the rest, it was plain that he was interested, but unhappy. He practiced for hours daily. He often took Mizzi to the park and came back storming about the dirt, the noise, the haste, the rudeness, the crowds, the mismanagement of the entire city. Dummheit, he called it. They profaned the lake. They allowed the people to trample the grass. They threw papers and banana skins about. And they wasted! His years in Germany had taught him to regard all these things as sacrilege, and the last as downright criminal. He was lonesome for his Germany. That was plain. He hated it, and loved it, much as he hated and loved the woman who had so nearly spoiled his life. The maelstrom known as the southwest corner of State and Madison streets appalled him.

"Gott!" he exclaimed. "Es ist unglaublich! Aber ganz unglaublich! Ich werde bald veruckt." He somehow lapsed into German when excited.

Fanny took him to the Haynes-Cooper plant one day, and it left him dazed, and incredulous. She quoted millions at him. He was not interested. He looked at the office workers, the mail-room girls, and shook his head, dumbly. They were using bicycles now, with a bundle rack in the front, in the vast stock rooms, and the roller skates had been discarded as too slow. The stock boys skimmed around corners on these lightweight bicycles, up one aisle, and down the next, snatching bundles out of bins, shooting bundles into bins, as expertly as players in a gymkhana.

Theodore saw the uncanny rapidity with which the letter-opening machines did their work. He watched the great presses that turned out the catalogue—the catalogue whose message meant millions; he sat in Fenger's office and stared at the etchings, and said, "Certainly," with politeness, when Fenger excused himself in the midst of a conversation to pick up the telephone receiver and talk to their shoe factory in Maine. He ended up finally in Fanny's office, no longer a dingy and undesirable corner, but a quietly brisk center that sent out vibrations over the entire plant. Slosson, incidentally, was no longer of the infants' wear. He had been transferred to a subordinate position in the grocery section.

"Well," said Fanny, seating herself at her desk, and smiling radiantly upon her brother. "Well, what do you think of us?"

And then Theodore Brandeis, the careless, the selfish, the blind, said a most amazing thing.

"Fanny, I'll work. I'll soon get some of these millions that are lying about everywhere in this country. And then I'll take you out of this. I promise you."

Fanny stared at him, a picture of ludicrous astonishment.

"Why, you talk as if you were—sorry for me!"

"I am, dear. God knows I am. I'll make it up to you, somehow."

It was the first time in all her dashing and successful career that Fanny Brandeis had felt the sting of pity. She resented it, hotly. And from Theodore, the groper, the—"But at any rate," something within her said, "he has always been true to himself."

Theodore's manager arrived in September, on a Holland boat, on which he had been obliged to share a stuffy inside cabin with three others. Kurt Stein was German born, but American bred, and he had the American love of luxurious travel. He was still testy when he reached Chicago and his charge.

"How goes the work?" he demanded at once, of Theodore. He eyed him sharply. "That's better. You have lost some of the look you had when you left Wien. The ladies would have liked that look, here in America. But it is bad for the work."

He took Fanny aside before he left. His face was serious. It was plain that he was disturbed. "That woman," he began. "Pardon me, Mrs. Brandeis. She came to me. She says she is starving. She is alone there, in Vienna. Her— well, she is alone. The war is everywhere. They say it will last for years. She wept and pleaded with me to take her here."

"No!" cried Fanny. "Don't let him hear it. He mustn't know. He——"

"Yes, I know. She is a paradox, that woman. I tell you, she almost prevailed on me. There is something about her; something that repels and compels." That struck him as being a very fine phrase indeed, and he repeated it appreciatively.

"I'll send her money, somehow," said Fanny.

"Yes. But they say that money is not reaching them over there. I don't know what becomes of it. It vanishes." He turned to leave. "Oh, a message for you. On my boat was Schabelitz. It looks very much as if his great fortune, the accumulation of years, would be swept away by this war. Already they are tramping up and down his lands in Poland. His money—much of it—is invested in great hotels in Poland and Russia, and they are using them for barracks and hospitals."

"Schabelitz! You mean a message for Theodore? From him? That's wonderful."

"For Theodore, and for you, too."

"For me! I made a picture of him once when I was a little girl. I didn't see him again for years. Then I heard him play. It was on his last tour here. I wanted to speak to him. But I was afraid. And my face was red with weeping."

"He remembers you. And he means to see Theodore and you. He can do much for Theodore in this country, and I think he will. His message for you was this: `Tell her I still have the picture that she made of me, with the jack-in-the-box in my hand, and that look on my face. Tell her I have often wondered about that little girl in the red cap and the black curls. I've wondered if she went on, catching that look back of people's faces. If she did, she should be more famous than her brother.'"

"He said that! About me!"

"I am telling you as nearly as I can. He said, `Tell her it was a woman who ruined Bauer's career, and caused him to end his days a music teacher in—in—Gott! I can't remember the name of that town——"

"Winnebago."

"Winnebago. That was it. `Tell her not to let the brother spoil his life that way.' So. That is the message. He said you would understand."

Theodore's face was ominous when she returned to him, after Stein had left.

"I wish you and Stein wouldn't stand out there in the hall whispering about me as if I were an idiot patient. What were you saying?"

"Nothing, Ted. Really."

He brooded a moment. Then his face lighted up with a flash of intuition. He flung an accusing finger at Fanny.

"He has seen her."

"Ted! You promised."

"She's in trouble. This war. And she hasn't any money. I know. Look here. We've got to send her money. Cable it."

"I will. Just leave it all to me."

"If she's here, in this country, and you're lying to me——"

"She isn't. My word of honor, Ted."

He relaxed.

Life was a very complicated thing for Fanny these days. Ted was leaning on her; Mizzi, Otti, and now Fenger. Nathan Haynes was poking a disturbing finger into that delicate and complicated mechanism of System which Fenger had built up in the Haynes-Cooper plant. And Fenger, snarling, was trying to guard his treasure. He came to Fanny with his grievance. Fanny had always stimulated him, reassured him, given him the mental readjustment that he needed.

He strode into her office one morning in late September. Ordinarily he sent for her. He stood by her desk now, a sheaf of papers in his hand, palpably stage props, and lifted significant eyebrows in the direction of the stenographer busy at her typewriter in the corner.

"You may leave that, Miss Mahin," Fanny said. Miss Mahin, a comprehending young woman, left it, and the room as well. Fenger sat down. He was under great excitement, though he was quite controlled. Fanny, knowing him, waited quietly. His eyes held hers.

"It's come," Fenger began. "You know that for the last year Haynes has been milling around with a herd of sociologists, philanthropists, and students of economics. He had some scheme in the back of his head, but I thought it was just another of his impractical ideas. It appears that it wasn't. Between the lot of them they've evolved a savings and profit-sharing plan that's founded on a kind of practical universal brotherhood dream. Haynes's millions are bothering him. If they actually put this thing through I'll get out. It'll mean that everything I've built up will be torn down. It will mean that any six-dollar-a-week girl——"

"As I understand it," interrupted Fanny, "it will mean that there will be no more six-dollar-a-week girls."

"That's it. And let me tell you, once you get the ignorant, unskilled type to believing they're actually capable of earning decent money, actually worth something, they're worse than useless. They're dangerous."

"You don't believe that."

"I do."

"But it's a theory that belongs to the Dark Ages. We've disproved it. We've got beyond that."

"Yes. So was war. We'd got beyond it. But it's here. I tell you, there are only two classes: the governing and the governed. That has always been true. It always will be. Let the Socialists rave. It has never got them anywhere. I know. I come from the mucker class myself. I know what they stand for. Boost them, and they'll turn on you. If there's anything in any of them, he'll pull himself up by his own bootstraps."

"They're not all potential Fengers."

"Then let 'em stay what they are."

Fanny's pencil was tracing and retracing a tortured and meaningless figure on the paper before her. "Tell me, do you remember a girl named Sarah Sapinsky?"

"Never heard of her."

"That's fitting. Sarah Sapinsky was a very pretty, very dissatisfied girl who was a slave to the bundle chute. One day there was a period of two seconds when a bundle didn't pop out at her, and she had time to think. Anyway, she left. I asked about her. She's on the streets."

"Well?"

"Thanks to you and your system."

"Look here, Fanny. I didn't come to you for that kind of talk. Don't, for heaven's sake, give me any sociological drivel to-day. I'm not here just to tell you my troubles. You know what my contract is here with Haynes-Cooper. And you know the amount of stock I hold. If this scheme of Haynes's goes in, I go out. Voluntarily. But at my own price. The Haynes-Cooper plant is at the height of its efficiency now." He dropped his voice. "But the mail order business is in its infancy. There's no limit to what can be done with it in the next few years. Understand? Do you get what I'm trying to tell you?" He leaned forward, tense and terribly in earnest.

Fanny stared at him. Then her hand went to her head in a gesture of weariness. "Not to-day. Please. And not here. Don't think I'm ungrateful for your confidence. But—this month has been a terrific strain. Just let me pass the fifteenth of October. Let me see Theodore on the way——"

Fenger's fingers closed about her wrist. Fanny got to her feet angrily. They glared at each other a moment. Then the humor of the picture they must be making struck Fanny. She began to laugh. Fenger's glare became a frown. He turned abruptly and left the office. Fanny looked down at her wrist ruefully. Four circlets of red marked its smooth whiteness. She laughed again, a little uncertainly this time.

When she got home that night she found, in her mail, a letter for Theodore, postmarked Vienna, and stamped with the mark of the censor. Theodore had given her his word of honor that he would not write Olga, or give her his address. Olga was risking Fanny's address. She stood looking at the letter now. Theodore was coming in for dinner, as he did five nights out of the week. As she stood in the hallway, she heard the rattle of his key in the lock. She flew down the hall and into her bedroom, her letters in her hand. She opened her dressing table drawer and threw them into it, switched on the light and turned to face Theodore in the doorway.

"'Lo, Sis."

"Hello, Teddy. Kiss me. Phew! That pipe again. How'd the work go to-day?"

"So—so. Any mail for me?"

"No."

That night, when he had gone, she took out the letter and stood turning it over and over in her hands. She had no thought of reading it. It was its destruction she was contemplating. Finally she tucked it away in her handkerchief box. Perhaps, after the fifteenth of October. Everything depended on that.

And the fifteenth of October came. It had dragged for weeks, and then, at the end, it galloped. By that time Fanny had got used to seeing Theodore's picture and name outside Orchestra Hall, and in the musical columns of the papers. Brandeis. Theodore Brandeis, the violinist. The name sang in her ears. When she walked on Michigan Avenue during that last week she would force herself to march straight on past Orchestra Hall, contenting herself with a furtive and oblique glance at the announcement board. The advance programs hung, a little bundle of them, suspended by a string from a nail on the wall near the box office, so that ticket purchasers might rip one off and peruse the week's musical menu. Fanny longed to hear the comment of the little groups that were constantly forming and dispersing about the box office window. She never dreamed of allowing herself to hover near it. She thought sometimes of the woman in the businesslike gray skirt and the black sateen apron who had drudged so cheerfully in the little shop so that Theodore Brandeis' name might shine now from the very top of the program, in heavy black letters:

Soloist: MR. THEODORE BRANDEIS, Violin

The injustice of it. Fanny had never ceased to rage at that.

In the years to come Theodore Brandeis was to have that adulation which the American public, temperamentally so cold, gives its favorite, once the ice of its reserve is thawed. He was to look down on that surging, tempestuous crowd which sometimes packs itself about the foot of the platform in Carnegie Hall, demanding more, more, more, after a generous concert is concluded. He had to learn to protect himself from those hysterical, enraptured, wholly feminine adorers who swarmed about him, scaling the platform itself. But of all this there was nothing on that Friday and Saturday in October. Orchestra Hall audiences are not, as a rule, wildly demonstrative. They were no exception. They listened attentively, appreciatively. They talked, critically and favorably, on the way home. They applauded generously. They behaved as an Orchestra Hall audience always behaves, and would behave, even if it were confronted with a composite Elman-Kreisler-Ysaye soloist. Theodore's playing was, as a whole, perhaps the worst of his career. Not that he did not rise to magnificent heights at times. But it was what is known as uneven playing. He was torn emotionally, nervously, mentally. His playing showed it.

Fanny, seated in the auditorium, her hands clasped tight, her heart hammering, had a sense of unreality as she waited for Theodore to appear from the little door at the left. He was to play after the intermission. Fanny had arrived late, with Theodore, that Friday afternoon. She felt she could not sit through the first part of the program. They waited together in the anteroom. Theodore, looking very slim and boyish in his frock coat, walked up and down, up and down. Fanny wanted to straighten his tie. She wanted to pick an imaginary thread off his lapel. She wanted to adjust the white flower in his buttonhole (he jerked it out presently, because it interfered with his violin, he said). She wanted to do any one of the foolish, futile things that would have served to relieve her own surcharged feelings. But she had learned control in these years. And she yielded to none of them.

The things they said and did were, perhaps, almost ludicrous.

"How do I look?" Theodore demanded, and stood up before her.

"Beautiful!" said Fanny, and meant it.

Theodore passed a hand over his cheek. "Cut myself shaving, damn it!"

"It doesn't show."

He resumed his pacing. Now and then he stopped, and rubbed his hands together with a motion we use in washing. Finally:

"I wish you'd go out front," he said, almost pettishly. Fanny rose, without a word. She looked very handsome. Excitement had given her color. The pupils of her eyes were dilated and they shone brilliantly. She looked at her brother. He stared at her. They swayed together. They kissed, and clung together for a long moment. Then Fanny turned and walked swiftly away, and stumbled a little as she groped for the stairway.

The bell in the foyer rang. The audience strolled to the auditorium. They lagged, Fanny thought. They crawled. She told herself that she must not allow her nerves to tease her like that. She looked about her, with outward calm. Her eyes met Fenger's. He was seated, alone. It was he who had got a subscription seat for her from a friend. She had said she preferred to be alone. She looked at him now and he at her, and they did not nod nor smile. The house settled itself flutteringly.

A man behind Fanny spoke. "Who's this Brandeis?"

"I don't know. A new one. German, I guess. They say he's good. Kreisler's the boy who can play for me, though."

The orchestra was seated now. Stock, the conductor, came out from the little side door. Behind him walked Theodore. There was a little, impersonal burst of applause. Stock mounted his conductor's platform and glanced paternally down at Theodore, who stood at the left, violin and bow in hand, bowing. The audience seemed to warm to his boyishness. They applauded again, and he bowed in a little series of jerky bobs that waggled his coat-tails. Heels close together, knees close together. A German bow. And then a polite series of bobs addressed to Stock and his orchestra. Stock's long, slim hands poised in air. His fingertips seemed to draw from the men before him the first poignant strains of Theodore's concerto. Theodore stood, slim and straight. Fanny's face, lifted toward him, was a prayerful thing. Theodore suddenly jerked back the left lapel of his coat in a little movement Fanny remembered as typical in his boyish days, nuzzled his violin tenderly, and began to play.

It is the most excruciating of instruments, the violin, or the most exquisite. I think Fanny actually heard very little of his playing. Her hands were icy. Her cheeks were hot. The man before her was not Theodore Brandeis, the violinist, but Teddy, the bright-haired, knickered schoolboy who played to those people seated in the yellow wooden pews of the temple in Winnebago. The years seemed to fade away. He crouched over his violin to get the 'cello tones for which he was to become famous, and it was the same hunched, almost awkward pose that the boy had used. Fanny found herself watching his feet as his shifted his position. He was nervous. And he was not taken out of himself. She knew that because she saw the play of his muscles about the jaw-bone. It followed that he was not playing his best. She could not tell that from listening to him. Her music sense was dulled. She got it from these outward signs. The woman next to her was reading a program absorbedly, turning the pages regularly, and with care. Fanny could have killed her with her two hands. She tried to listen detachedly. The music was familiar to her. Theodore had played it for her, again and again. The last movement had never failed to shake her emotionally. It was the glorious and triumphant cry of a people tried and unafraid. She heard it now, unmoved.

And then Theodore was bowing his little jerky bows, and he was shaking hands with Stock, and with the First Violin. He was gone. Fanny sat with her hands in her lap. The applause continued. Theodore appeared again. Bowed. He bent very low now, with his arms hanging straight. There was something gracious and courtly about him. And foreign. He must keep that, Fanny thought. They like it. She saw him off again. More applause. Encores were against the house rules. She knew that. Then it meant they were pleased. He was to play again. A group of Hungarian dances this time. They were wild, gypsy things, rising to frenzy at times. He played them with spirit and poetry. To listen sent the blood singing through the veins. Fanny found herself thinking clearly and exaltedly.

"This is what my mother drudged for, and died for, and it was worth it. And you must do the same, if necessary. Nothing else matters. What he needs now is luxury. He's worn out with fighting. Ease. Peace. Leisure. You've got to give them to him. It's no use, Fanny. You lose."

In that moment she reached a mark in her spiritual career that she was to outdistance but once.

Theodore was bowing again. Fanny had scarcely realized that he had finished. The concert was over.

"... the group of dances," the man behind her was saying as he helped the girl next him with her coat, "but I didn't like that first thing. Church music, not concert."

Fanny found her way back to the ante-room. Theodore was talking to the conductor, and one or two others. He looked tired, and his eyes found Fanny's with appeal and relief in them. She came over to him. There were introductions, congratulations. Fanny slipped her hand over his with a firm pressure.

"Come, dear. You must be tired."

At the door they found Fenger waiting. Theodore received his well-worded congratulations with an ill-concealed scowl.

"My car's waiting," said Fenger. "Won't you let me take you home?"

A warning pressure from Theodore. "Thanks, no. We have a car. Theodore's very tired."

"I can quite believe that."

"Not tired," growled Theodore, like a great boy. "I'm hungry. Starved. I never eat before playing."

Kurt Stein, Theodore's manager, had been hovering over him solicitously. "You must remember to-morrow night. I should advise you to rest now, as quickly as possible." He, too, glared at Fenger.

Fenger fell back, almost humbly. "I've great news for you. I must see you Sunday. After this is over. I'll telephone you. Don't try to come to work to-morrow." All this is a hurried aside to Fanny.

Fanny nodded and moved away with Theodore.

Theodore leaned back in the car, but there was no hint of relaxation. He was as tense and vibrant as one of his own violin strings.

"It went, didn't it? They're like clods, these American audiences." It was on the tip of Fanny's tongue to say that he had professed indifference to audiences, but she wisely refrained. "Gad! I'm hungry. What makes this Fenger hang around so? I'm going to tell him to keep away, some day. The way he stares at you. Let's go somewhere to-night, Fan. Or have some people in. I can't sit about after I've played. Olga always used to have a supper party, or something."

"All right, Ted. Would you like the theater?"

For the first time in her life she felt a little whisper of sympathy for the despised Olga. Perhaps, after all, she had not been wholly to blame.

He was to leave Sunday morning for Cleveland, where he would play Monday. He had insisted on taking Mizzi with him, though Fanny had railed and stormed. Theodore had had his way.

"She's used to it. She likes to travel, don't you, Mizzi? You should have seen her in Russia, and all over Germany, and in Sweden. She's a better traveler than her dad."

Saturday morning's papers were kind, but cool. They used words such as promising, uneven, overambitious, gifted. Theodore crumpled the lot into a ball and hurled them across the room, swearing horribly. Then he smoothed them out, clipped them, and saved them carefully. His playing that night was tinged with bravado, and the Saturday evening audience rose to it. There was about his performance a glow, a spirit that had been lacking on the previous day.

Inconsistently enough, he missed the antagonism of the European critics. He was puzzled and resentful.

"They hardly say a word about the meaning of the concerto. They accept it as a piece of music, Jewish in theme. It might as well be entitled Springtime."

"This isn't France or Russia," said Fanny. "Antagonism here isn't religious. It's personal, almost. You've been away so many years you've forgotten. They don't object to us as a sect, or a race, but as a type. That's the trouble, Clarence Heyl says. We're free to build as many synagogues as we like, and worship in them all day, if we want to. But we don't want to. The struggle isn't racial any more, but individual. For some reason or other one flashy, loud-talking Hebrew in a restaurant can cause more ill feeling than ten thousand of them holding a religious mass meeting in Union Square."

Theodore pondered a moment. "Then here each one of us is responsible. Is that it?"

"I suppose so."

"But look here. I've been here ten weeks, and I've met your friends, and not one of them is a Jew. How's that?"

Fanny flushed a little. "Oh, it just worked out that way."

Theodore looked at her hard. "You mean you worked it out that way?"

"Yes."

"Fan, we're a couple of weaklings, both of us, to have sprung from a mother like ours. I don't know which is worse; my selfishness, or yours." Then, at the hurt that showed in her face, he was all contrition. "Forgive me, Sis. You've been so wonderful to me, and to Mizzi, and to all of us. I'm a good-for-nothing fiddler, that's all. You're the strong one."

Fenger had telephoned her on Saturday. He and his wife were at their place in the country. Fanny was to take the train out there Sunday morning. She looked forward to it with a certain relief. The weather had turned unseasonably warm, as Chicago Octobers sometimes do. Up to the last moment she had tried to shake Theodore's determination to take Mizzi and Otti with him. But he was stubborn.

"I've got to have her," he said.

Michael Fenger's voice over the telephone had been as vibrant with suppressed excitement as Michael Fenger's dry, hard tones could be.

"Fanny, it's done—finished," he said. "We had a meeting to-day. This is my last month with Haynes-Cooper."

"But you can't mean it. Why, you ARE Haynes-Cooper. How can they let you go?"

"I can't tell you now. We'll go over it all to-morrow. I've new plans. They've bought me out. D'you see? At a price that—well, I thought I'd got used to juggling millions at Haynes-Cooper. But this surprised even me. Will you come? Early? Take the eight-ten."

"That's too early. I'll get the ten."

The mid-October country was a lovely thing. Fanny, with the strain of Theodore's debut and leave-taking behind her, and the prospect of a high-tension business talk with Fenger ahead, drank in the beauty of the wayside woods gratefully.

Fenger met her at the station. She had never seen him so boyish, so exuberant. He almost pranced.

"Hop in," he said. He had driven down in a runabout. "Brother get off all right? Gad! He CAN play. And you've made the whole thing possible." He turned to look at her. "You're a wonder."

"In your present frame of mind and state of being," laughed Fanny, "you'd consider any one a wonder. You're so pleased with yourself you're fairly gummy."

Fenger laughed softly and sped the car on. They turned in at the gate. There was scarlet salvia, now, to take the place of the red geraniums. The gay awnings, too, were gone.

"This is our last week," Fenger explained. "It's too cold out here for Katherine. We're moving into town to-morrow. We're more or less camping out here, with only the Jap to take care of us."

"Don't apologize, please. I'm grateful just to be here, after the week I've had. Let's have the news now."

"We'll have lunch first. I'm afraid you'll have to excuse Katherine. She probably won't be down for lunch." The Jap had spread the luncheon table on the veranda, but a brisk lake breeze had sprung up, and he was busy now transferring his table from the porch to the dining room. "Would you have believed it," said Fenger, "when you left town? Good old lake. Mrs. Fenger coming down?" to the man.

The Jap shook his head. "Nossa."

Their talk at luncheon was all about Theodore and his future. Fenger said that what Theodore needed was a firm and guiding hand. "A sort of combination manager and slave-driver. An ambitious and intelligent wife would do it. That's what we all need. A woman to work for, and to make us work."

Fanny smiled. "Mizzi will have to be woman enough, I'm afraid. Poor Ted."

They rose. "Now for the talk," said Fenger. But the telephone had sounded shrilly a moment before, and the omnipresent little Jap summoned Fenger. He was back in a minute, frowning. "It's Haynes. I'm sorry. I'm afraid it'll take a half hour of telephoning. Don't you want to take a cat-nap? Or a stroll down to the lake?"

"Don't bother about me. I'll probably take a run outdoors."

"Be back in half an hour."

But when she returned he was still at the telephone. She got a book and stretched luxuriously among the cushions of one of the great lounging chairs, and fell asleep. When she awoke Fenger was seated opposite her. He was not reading. He was not smoking. He evidently had been sitting there, looking at her.

"Oh, gracious! Mouth open?"

"No."

Fanny fought down an impulse to look as cross as she felt. "What time? Why didn't you wake me?" The house was very quiet. She patted her hair deftly, straightened her collar. "Where's everybody? Isn't Mrs. Fenger down yet?"

"No. Don't you want to hear about my plans now?"

"Of course I do. That's what I came for. I don't see why you didn't tell me hours ago. You're as slow in action as a Chinese play. Out with it."

Fenger got up and began to pace the floor, not excitedly, but with an air of repression. He looked very powerful and compelling, there in the low-ceilinged, luxurious room. "I'll make it brief. We met yesterday in Haynes's office. Of course we had discussed the thing before. You know that. Haynes knew that I'd never run the plant under the new conditions. Why, it would kill every efficiency rule I've ever made. Here I had trimmed that enormous plant down to fighting weight. There wasn't a useless inch or ounce about the whole enormous billionaire bulk of it. And then to have Haynes come along, with his burdensome notions, and his socialistic slop. They'd cripple any business, no matter how great a start it had. I told him all that. We didn't waste much time on argument, though. We knew we'd never get together. In half an hour we were talking terms. You know my contract and the amount of stock I hold. Well, we threshed that out, and Haynes is settling for two million and a half."

He came to a stop before Fanny's chair.

"Two million and a half what?" asked Fanny, feebly.

"Dollars." He smiled rather grimly. "In a check."

"One—check?" "One check."

Fanny digested that in her orderly mind. "I thought I was used to thinking in millions. But this—I'd like to touch the check, just once."

"You shall." He drew up a chair near her. "Now get this, Fanny. There's nothing that you and I can't do with two millions and a half. Nothing. We know this mail order game as no two people in the world know it. And it's in its infancy. I know the technical side of it. You know the human side of it. I tell you that in five years' time you and I can be a national power. Not merely the heads of a prosperous mail order business, but figures in finance. See what's happened to Haynes-Cooper in the last five years! Why, it's incredible. It's grotesque. And it's nothing to what you and I can do, working together. You know people, somehow. You've a genius for sensing their wants, or feelings, or emotions—I don't know just what it is. And I know facts. And we have two million and a half—I can make it nearly three millions—to start with. Haynes, fifteen years ago, had a couple of hundred thousand. In five years we can make the Haynes-Cooper organization look as modern and competent as a cross-roads store. This isn't a dream. These are facts. You know how my mind works. Like a cold chisel. I can see this whole country—and Europe, too, after the war—God, yes!—stretched out before us like a patient before expert surgeons. You to attend to its heart, and I to its bones and ligaments. I can put you where no other woman has ever been. I've a hundred new plans this minute, and a hundred more waiting to be born. So have you. I tell you it's just a matter of buildings. Of bricks and stone, and machinery and people to make the machinery go. Once we get those—and it's only a matter of months—we can accomplish things I daren't even dream of. What was Haynes-Cooper fifteen years ago? What was the North American Cloak and Suit Company? The Peter Johnston Stores, of New York? Wells-Kayser? Nothing. They didn't exist. And this year Haynes-Cooper is declaring a twenty-five per cent dividend. Do you get what that means? But of course you do. That's the wonder of it. I never need explain things to you. You've a genius for understanding."

Fanny had been sitting back in her chair, crouching almost, her eyes fixed upon the man's face, so terrible in its earnestness and indomitable strength. When he stopped talking now, and stood looking down at her, she rose, too, her eyes still on his face. She was twisting the fingers of one hand in the fingers of the other, in a frightened sort of way.

"I'm not really a business woman. I—wait a minute, please—I have a knack of knowing what people are thinking and wanting. But that isn't business." "It isn't, eh? It's the finest kind of business sense. It's the thing the bugs call psychology, and it's as necessary to-day as capital was yesterday. You can get along without the last. You can't without the first. One can be acquired. The other you've got to be born with."

"But I—you know, of late, it's only the human side of it that has appealed to me. I don't know why. I seem to have lost interest in the actual mechanics of it."

Fenger stood looking at her, his head lowered. A scarlet stripe, that she had never noticed before, seemed to stand out suddenly, like a welt, on his forehead. Then he came toward her. She raised her hand in a little futile gesture. She took an involuntary step backward, encountered the chair she had just left, and sank into it coweringly. She sat there, looking up at him, fascinated. His hand, on the wing of the great chair, was shaking. So, too, was his voice.

"Fanny, Katherine's not here."

Fanny still looked up at him, wordlessly.

"Katherine left here yesterday. She's in town." Then, at the look in her face, "She was here when I telephoned you yesterday. Late yesterday afternoon she had one of her fantastic notions. She insisted that she must go into town. It was too cold for her here. Too damp. Too—well, she went. And I let her go. And I didn't telephone you again. I wanted you to come."

Fanny Brandeis, knowing him, must have felt a great qualm of terror and helplessness. But she was angry, too, a wholesome ingredient in a situation such as this. The thing she said and did now was inspired. She laughed—a little uncertainly, it is true—but still she laughed. And she said, in a matter-of-fact tone:

"Well, I must say that's a rather shabby trick. Still, I suppose the tired business man has got to have his little melodrama. What do I do? H'm? Beat my breast and howl? Or pound on the door panel?"

Fenger stood looking at her. "Don't laugh at me, Fanny."

She stood up, still smiling. It was rather a brilliant piece of work. Fenger, taken out of himself though he was, still was artist enough to appreciate it.

"Why not laugh," she said, "if I'm amused? And I am. Come now, Mr. Fenger. Be serious. And let's get back to the billions. I want to catch the five-fifteen."

"I AM serious." "Well, if you expect me to play the hunted heroine, I'm sorry." She pointed an accusing finger at him. "I know now. You're quitting Haynes-Cooper for the movies. And this is a rehearsal for a vampire film."

"You nervy little devil, you!" He reached out with one great, irresistible hand and gripped her shoulder. "You wonderful, glorious girl!" The hand that gripped her shoulder swung her to him. She saw his face with veins she had never noticed before standing out, in knots, on his temples, and his eyes were fixed and queer. And he was talking, rather incoherently, and rapidly. He was saying the same thing over and over again: "I'm crazy about you. I've been looking for a woman like you—all my life. I'm crazy about you. I'm crazy———"

And then Fanny's fine composure and self control fled, and she thought of her mother. She began to struggle, too, and to say, like any other girl, "Let me go! Let me go! You're hurting me. Let me go! You! You!"

And then, quite clearly, from that part of her brain where it had been tucked away until she should need it, came Clarence Heyl's whimsical bit of advice. Her mind released it now, complete.

"If you double your fist this way, and tuck your thumb alongside, like that, and aim for this spot right here, about two inches this side of the chin, bringing your arm back and up quickly, like a piston, the person you hit will go down, limp. There's a nerve right here that communicates with the brain. The blow makes you see stars, and bright lights———"

She went limp in his arms. She shut her eyes, flutteringly. "All men—like you—have a yellow streak," she whispered, and opened her eyes, and looked up at him, smiling a little. He relaxed his hold, in surprise and relief. And with her eyes on that spot barely two inches to the side of the chin she brought her right arm down, slowly, slowly, fist doubled, and then up like a piston—snap! His teeth came together with a sharp little crack. His face, in that second, was a comic mask, surprised, stunned, almost idiotic. Then he went down, as Clarence Heyl had predicted, limp. Not with a crash, but slowly, crumplingly, so that he almost dragged her with him.

Fanny stood looking down at him a moment. Then she wiped her mouth with the back of her hand. She walked out of the room, and down the hall. She saw the little Jap dart suddenly back from a doorway, and she stamped her foot and said, "S-s-cat!" as if he had been a rat. She gathered up her hat and bag from the hall table, and so, out of the door, and down the walk, to the road. And then she began to run. She ran, and ran, and ran. It was a longish stretch to the pretty, vine-covered station. She seemed unconscious of fatigue, or distance. She must have been at least a half hour on the way. When she reached the station the ticket agent told her there was no train until six. So she waited, quietly. She put on her hat (she had carried it in her hand all the way) and patted her hair into place. When the train came she found a seat quite alone, and sank into its corner, and rested her head against her open palm. It was not until then that she felt a stab of pain. She looked at her hand, and saw that the skin of her knuckles was bruised and bleeding.

"Well, if this," she said to herself, "isn't the most idiotic thing that ever happened to a woman outside a near-novel."

She looked at her knuckles, critically, as though the hand belonged to some one else. Then she smiled. And even as she smiled a great lump came into her throat, and the bruise blurred before her eyes, and she was crying rackingly, relievedly, huddled there in her red plush corner.

CHAPTER EIGHTEEN

It was eight o'clock when she let herself into her apartment. She had given the maid a whole holiday. When Fanny had turned on the light in her little hallway she stood there a moment, against the door, her hand spread flat against the panel. It was almost as though she patted it, lovingly, gratefully. Then she went on into the living room, and stood looking at its rosy lamplight. Then, still as though seeing it all for the first time, into her own quiet, cleanly bedroom, with its cream enamel, and the chaise longue that she had had cushioned in rose because it contrasted so becomingly with her black hair. And there, on her dressing table, propped up against the brushes and bottles, was the yellow oblong of a telegram. From Theodore of course. She opened it with a rush of happiness. It was like a loving hand held out to her in need. It was a day letter.

"We sail Monday on the St. Paul. Mizzi is with me. I broke my word to you. But you lied to me about the letters. I found them the week before the concert. I shall bring her back with me or stay to fight for Germany. Forgive me, dear sister."

Just fifty words. His thrifty German training.

"No!" cried Fanny, aloud. "No! No!" And the cry quavered and died away, and another took its place, and it, too, gave way to another, so that she was moaning as she stood there with the telegram in her shaking hand. She read it again, her lips moving, as old people sometimes read. Then she began to whimper, with her closed fist over her mouth, her whole body shaking. All her fine courage gone now; all her rigid self-discipline; all her iron determination. She was not a tearful woman. And she had wept much on the train. So the thing that wrenched and shook her now was all the more horrible because of its soundlessness. She walked up and down the room, pushing her hair back from her forehead with the flat of her hand. From time to time she smoothed out the crumpled yellow slip of paper and read it again. Her mind, if you could have seen into it, would have presented a confused and motley picture. Something like this: But his concert engagements?... That was what had happened to Bauer.... How silly he had looked when her fist met his jaw.... It had turned cold; why didn't they have steam on? The middle of October.... Teddy, how could you do it! How could you do it!... Was he still lying in a heap on the floor? But of course the sneaking little Jap had found him.... Somebody to talk to. That was what she wanted. Some one to talk to....

Some one to talk to. She stood there, in the middle of her lamp-lighted living room, and she held out her hands in silent appeal. Some one to talk to. In her mind she went over the list of those whose lives had touched hers in the last few crowded years. Fenger, Fascinating Facts, Ella Monahan, Nathan Haynes; all the gay, careless men and women she had met from time to time through Fenger and Fascinating Facts. Not one of them could she turn to now.

Clarence Heyl. She breathed a sigh of relief. Clarence Heyl. He had helped her once, to-day. And now, for the second time, something that he had said long before came from its hiding place in her subconscious mind. She had said:

"Some days I feel I've got to walk out of the office, and down the street, without a hat, and on and on, walking and walking, and running and running till I come to the horizon."

And Heyl had answered, in his quiet, reassuring way: "Some day that feeling will get too strong for you. When that time comes get on a train marked Denver. From there take another to Estes Park. That's the Rocky Mountains, where the horizon lives and has its being. Ask for Heyl's place. They'll hand you from one to the other. I may be there, but more likely I shan't. The key's in the mail box, tied to a string. You'll find a fire laid with fat pine knots. My books are there. The bedding's in the cedar chest. And the mountains will make you clean and whole again; and the pines..."

Fanny went to the telephone. Trains for Denver. She found the road she wanted, and asked for information. She was on her own ground here. All her life she had had to find her own trains, check her own trunks, plan her journeys. Sometimes she had envied the cotton-wool women who had had all these things done for them, always.

One-half of her mind was working clearly and coolly. The other half was numb. There were things to be done. They would take a day. More than a day, but she would neglect most of them. She must notify the office. There were tickets to be got. Reservations. Money at the bank. Packing. When the maid came in at eleven Fanny had suitcases and bags out, and her bedroom was strewn with shoes, skirts, coats.

Late Monday afternoon Fenger telephoned. She did not answer. There came a note from him, then a telegram. She did not read them. Tuesday found her on a train bound for Colorado. She remembered little of the first half of her journey. She had brought with her books and magazines, and she must have read hem, but her mind had evidently retained nothing of what she had read. She must have spent hours looking out of the window, for she remembered, long afterward, the endlessness and the monotony of the Kansas prairies. They soothed her. She was glad there were no bits of autumnal woodland, no tantalizing vistas, nothing to break the flat and boundless immensity of it. Here was something big, and bountiful, and real, and primal. Good Kansas dirt. Miles of it. Miles of it. She felt she would like to get out and tramp on it, hard.

"Pretty cold up there in Estes Park," the conductor had said. "Been snowing up in the mountains."

She had arranged to stop in Denver only long enough to change trains. A puffy little branch line was to take her from Denver to Loveland, and there, she had been told, one of the big mountain-road steam automobiles would take her up the mountains to her destination. For one as mentally alert as she normally was, the exact location of that destination was very hazy in her mind. Heyl's place. That was all. Ordinarily she would have found the thought ridiculous. But she concentrated on it now; clung to it.

At the first glimpse of the foot-hills Fanny's listless gaze became interested. If you have ever traveled on the jerky, cleanly, meandering little road that runs between Denver and the Park you know that it winds, and curves, so that the mountains seem to leap about, friskily, first confronting you on one side of the car window, then disappearing and seeming to taunt you from the windows of the opposite side. Fanny laughed aloud. The mountain steam-car was waiting at Loveland. There were few passengers at this time of year. The driver was a great tanned giant, pongee colored from his hair to his puttees and boots. Fanny was to learn, later, that in Estes Park the male tourist was likely to be puny, pallid, and unattractive when compared to the tall, slim, straight, khaki-clad youth, browned by the sun, and the wind, and the dust, who drives his steamer up and down the perilous mountain roads with more dexterity than the charioteering gods ever displayed on Olympus.

Fanny got the seat beside this glorious person. The steamer was a huge vehicle, boasting five rows of seats, and looking very much like a small edition of the sightseeing cars one finds in tourist-infested cities.

"Heyl's place," said Fanny. Suppose it failed to work!

Said the blond god, "Stopping at the Inn overnight, I s'pose."

"Why—I don't know," faltered Fanny. "Can't I go right on to—to—Heyl's place?"

"Can." Mountain steamer men are not loquacious. "Sure. Better not. You won't get to the Inn till dark. Better stay there over night, and go on up to Heyl's place in the morning."

Then he leaned forward, clawed about expertly among what appeared to Fanny's eyes to be a maze of handles, brakes, valves; and the great car glided smoothly off, without a bump, without a jar. Fanny took a long breath.

There is no describing a mountain. One uses words, and they are futile. And the Colorado Rockies, in October, when the aspens are turning! Well, aspens turn gold in October. People who have seen an aspen grove in October believe in fairies. And such people need no clumsy descriptive passages to aid their fancies. You others who have not seen it? There shall be no poor weaving together of words. There shall be no description of orange and mauve and flame-colored sunsets, no juggling with mists and clouds, and sunrises and purple mountains. Mountain dwellers and mountain lovers are a laconic tribe. They know the futility of words.

But the effect of the mountains on Fanny Brandeis. That is within our province. In the first place, they made her hungry. That was the crisp, heady air. The mountain road, to one who has never traveled it, is a thing of delicious thrills and near-terror. A narrow, perilous ribbon of road, cut in the side of the rock itself; a road all horseshoe curves and hairpin twists. Fanny found herself gasping. But that passed after a time. Big Thompson canyon leaves no room for petty terror. And the pongee person was so competent, so quietly sure, so angularly graceful among his brakes and levers. Fanny stole a side glance at him now and then. He looked straight ahead. When you drive a mountain steamer you do look straight ahead. A glance to the right or left is so likely to mean death, or at best a sousing in the Thompson that foams and rushes below.

Fanny ventured a question. "Do you know Mr. Heyl?"

"Heyl? Took him down day before yesterday."

"Down?"

"To the village. He's gone back east."

Fanny was not quite sure whether the pang she felt was relief or consternation.

At Estes village the blond god handed her over to a twin charioteer who would drive her up the mountain road to the Inn that nestled in a valley nine thousand feet up the mountain. It was a drive Fanny never forgot. Fenger, Ted, Haynes-Cooper, her work, her plans, her ambitions, seemed to dwindle to puny insignificance beside the vast grandeur that unfolded before her at every fresh turn in the road. Up they went, and up, and up, and the air was cold, but without a sting in it. It was dark when the lights of the Inn twinkled out at them. The door was thrown open as they swung up the curve to the porch. A great log fire glowed in the fireplace. The dining room held only a dozen people, or thereabouts—a dozen weary, healthy people, in corduroys and sweaters and boots, whose cleanly talk was all about climbing and fishing, and horseback rides and trails. And it was fried chicken night at the Inn. Fanny thought she was too utterly tired to eat, until she began to eat, and then she thought she was too hungry ever to stop. After dinner she sat, for a moment, before the log fire in the low-ceilinged room, with its log walls, its rustic benches, and its soft-toned green and brown cushions. She forgot to be unhappy. She forgot to be anything but deliciously drowsy. And presently she climbed the winding stair whose newel post was a fire-marked tree trunk, richly colored, and curiously twisted. And so to her lamp-lighted room, very small, very clean, very quiet. She opened her window and looked out at the towering mass that was Long's Peak, and at the stars, and she heard the busy little brook that scurries through the Inn yard on its way from the mountain to the valley. She undressed quickly, and crept into bed, meaning to be very, very miserable indeed. And the next thing she knew it was morning. A blue and gold October morning. And the mountains!—but there is no describing a mountain. One uses words, and they are futile. Fanny viewed them again, from her window, between pauses in dressing. And she meant, privately, to be miserable again. But she could only think, somehow, of bacon and eggs, and coffee, and muffins.

CHAPTER NINETEEN

Heyl's place. Fanny stood before it, key in hand (she had found it in the mail box, tied to a string), and she had a curious and restful feeling, as if she had come home, after long wanderings. She smiled, whimsically, and repeated her lesson to herself:

"The fire's laid in the fireplace with fat pine knots that will blaze up at the touch of a match. My books are there, along the wall. The bedding's in the cedar chest, and the lamps are filled. There's tinned stuff in the pantry. And the mountains are there, girl, to make you clean and whole again...."

She stepped up to the little log-pillared porch and turned the key in the lock. She opened the door wide, and walked in. And then she shut her eyes for a moment. Because, if it shouldn't be true——

But there was a fire laid with fat pine knots. She walked straight over to it, and took her box of matches from her bag, struck one, and held it to the wood. They blazed like a torch. Books! Along the four walls, books. Fat, comfortable, used-looking books. Hundreds of them. A lamp on the table, and beside it a pipe, blackened from much use. Fanny picked it up, smiling. She held it a moment in her hand, as though she expected to find it still warm.

"It's like one of the fairy tales," she thought, "the kind that repeats and repeats. The kind that says, `and she went into the next room, and it was as the good fairy had said.'"

There's tinned stuff in the pantry. She went into the tiny kitchen and opened the pantry door cautiously, being wary of mice. But it met her eye in spotless array. Orderly rows of tins. Orderly rows of bottles. Coffee. Condensed milk. Beans. Spaghetti. Flour. Peaches. Pears.

Off the bedroom there was an absurdly adequate little bathroom, with a zinc tub and an elaborate water-heating arrangement.

Fanny threw back her head and laughed as she hadn't laughed in months. "Wild life in the Rockies," she said aloud. She went back to the book-lined living room. The fire was crackling gloriously. It was a many-windowed room, and each window framed an enchanting glimpse of mountain, flaming with aspens up to timber-line, and snow-capped at the top. Fanny decided to wait until the fire had died down to a coal-bed. Then she banked it carefully, put on a heavy sweater and a cap, and made for the outdoors. She struck out briskly, tenderfoot that she was. In five minutes she was panting. Her heart was hammering suffocatingly. Her lungs ached. She stopped, trembling. Then she remembered. The altitude, of course. Heyl had boasted that his cabin stood at an altitude of over nine thousand feet. Well, she would have to get used to it. But she was soon striding forward as briskly as before. She was a natural mountain dweller. The air, the altitude, speeded up her heart, her lungs, sent the blood dancing through her veins. Figuratively, she was on tip-toe.

They had warned her, at the Inn, to take it slowly for the first few days. They had asked no questions. Fanny learned to heed their advice. She learned many more things in the next few days. She learned how to entice the chipmunks that crossed her path, streak o' sunshine, streak o' shadow. She learned to broil bacon over a fire, with a forked stick. She learned to ride trail ponies, and to bask in a sun-warmed spot on a wind-swept hill, and to tell time by the sun, and to give thanks for the beauty of the world about her, and to leave the wild flowers unpicked, to put out her campfire with scrupulous care, and to destroy all rubbish (your true woodsman and mountaineer is as painstakingly neat as a French housewife).

She was out of doors all day. At night she read for a while before the fire, but by nine her eyelids were heavy. She walked down to the Inn sometimes, but not often. One memorable night she went, with half a dozen others from the Inn, to the tiny one-room cabin of Oscar, the handy man about the Inn, and there she listened to one of Oscar's far-famed phonograph concerts. Oscar's phonograph had cost twenty-five dollars in Denver. It stood in one corner of his cabin, and its base was a tree stump just five hundred years old, as you could tell for yourself by counting its rings. His cabin walls were gorgeous with pictures of Maxine Elliott in her palmy days, and blonde and sophisticated little girls on vinegar calendars, posing bare-legged and self-conscious in blue calico and sunbonnets. You sat in the warm yellow glow of Oscar's lamp and were regaled with everything from the Swedish National Anthem to Mischa Elman's tenderest crooning. And Oscar sat rapt, his weather-beaten face a rich deep mahogany, his eyes bluer than any eyes could ever be except in contrast with that ruddy countenance, his teeth so white that you found yourself watching for his smile that was so gently sweet and childlike. Oh, when Oscar put on his black pants and issued invitations for a musical evening one was sure to find his cabin packed. Eight did it, with squeezing.

This, then, was the atmosphere in which Fanny Brandeis found herself. As far from Haynes-Cooper as anything could be. At the end of the first week she found herself able to think clearly and unemotionally about Theodore, and about Fenger. She had even evolved a certain rather crude philosophy out of the ruins that had tumbled about her ears. It was so crude, so unformed in her mind that it can hardly be set down. To justify one's own existence. That was all that life held or meant. But that included all the lives that touched on yours. It had nothing to do with success, as she had counted success heretofore. It was service, really. It was living as—well, as Molly Brandeis had lived, helpfully, self-effacingly, magnificently. Fanny gave up trying to form the thing that was growing in her mind. Perhaps, after all, it was too soon to expect a complete understanding of that which had worked this change in her from that afternoon in Fenger's library.

After the first few days she found less and less difficulty in climbing. Her astonished heart and lungs ceased to object so strenuously to the unaccustomed work. The Cabin Rock trail, for example, whose summit found her panting and exhausted at first, now seemed a mere stroll. She grew more daring and ambitious. One day she climbed the Long's Peak trail to timberline, and had tea at Timberline Cabin with Albert Edward Cobbins. Albert Edward Cobbins, Englishman, erstwhile sailor, adventurer and gentleman, was the keeper of Timberline Cabin, and the loneliest man in the Rockies. It was his duty to house overnight climbers bound for the Peak, sunrise parties and sunset parties, all too few now in the chill October season-end. Fanny was his first visitor in three days. He was pathetically glad to see her.

"I'll have tea for you," he said, "in a jiffy. And I baked a pan of French rolls ten minutes ago. I had a feeling."

A magnificent specimen of a man, over six feet tall slim, broad-shouldered, long-headed, and scrubbed-looking as only an Englishman can be, there was something almost pathetic in the sight of him bustling about the rickety little kitchen stove.

"To-morrow," said Fanny, over her tea, "I'm going to get an early start, reach here by noon, and go on to Boulder Field and maybe Keyhole."

"Better not, Miss. Not in October, when there's likely to be a snowstorm up there in a minute's notice."

"You'd come and find me, wouldn't you? They always do, in the books."

"Books are all very well, Miss. But I'm not a mountain man. The truth is I don't know my way fifty feet from this cabin. I got the job because I'm used to loneliness, and don't mind it, and because I can cook, d'you see, having shipped as cook for years. But I'm a seafaring man, Miss. I wouldn't advise it, Miss. Another cup of tea?"

But Long's Peak, king of the range, had fascinated her from the first. She knew that the climb to the summit would be impossible for her now, but she had an overwhelming desire to see the terrifying bulk of it from a point midway of the range. It beckoned her and intrigued her, as the difficult always did.

By noon of the following day she had left Albert Edward's cabin (he stood looking after her in the doorway until she disappeared around the bend) and was jauntily following the trail that led to Boulder Field, that sea of jagged rock a mile across. Soon she had left the tortured, wind-twisted timberline trees far behind. How pitiful Cabin Rock and Twin Sisters looked compared to this. She climbed easily and steadily, stopping for brief rests. Early in the week she had ridden down to the village, where she had bought climbing breeches and stout leggings. She laughed at Albert Edward and his fears. By one o'clock she had reached Boulder Field. She found the rocks glazed with ice. Just over Keyhole, that freakish vent in a wall of rock, the blue of the sky had changed to the gray of snow-clouds. Tenderfoot though she was, she knew that the climb over Boulder Field would be perilous, if not impossible. She went on, from rock to rock, for half an hour, then decided to turn back. A clap of thunder, that roared and crashed, and cracked up and down the canyons and over the peaks, hastened her decision. She looked about her. Peak on peak. Purple and black and yellow masses, fantastic in their hugeness. Chasms. Canyons. Pyramids and minarets. And so near. So grim. So ghastly desolate. And yet so threatening. And then Fanny Brandeis was seized with mountain terror. It is a disease recognized by mountain men everywhere, and it is panic, pure and simple. It is fear brought on by the immensity and the silence of the mountains. A great horror of the vastness and ruggedness came upon her. It was colossal, it was crushing, it was nauseating.

She began to run. A mistake, that, when one is following a mountain trail, at best an elusive thing. In five minutes she had lost the trail. She stopped, and scolded herself sternly, and looked about her. She saw the faint trail line again, or thought she saw it, and made toward it, and found it to be no trail at all. She knew that she must be not more than an hour's walk from Timberline Cabin, and Albert Edward, and his biscuits and tea. Why be frightened? It was absurd. But she was frightened, horribly, harrowingly. The great, grim rock masses seemed to be shaking with silent laughter. She began to run again. She was very cold, and a piercing wind had sprung up. She kept on walking, doggedly, reasoning with herself quite calmly, and proud of her calmness. Which proves how terrified she really was. Then the snow came, not slowly, not gradually, but a blanket of it, as it does come in the mountains, shutting off everything. And suddenly Fanny's terror vanished. She felt quite free from weariness. She was alive and tingling to her fingertips. The psychology of fear is a fascinating thing. Fanny had reached the second stage. She was quite taken out of herself. She forgot her stone-bruised feet. She was no longer conscious of cold. She ran now, fleetly, lightly, the ground seeming to spur her on. She had given up the trail completely now. She told herself that if she ran on, down, down, down, she must come to the valley sometime. Unless she was turned about, and headed in the direction of one of those hideous chasms. She stopped a moment, peering through the snow curtain, but she could see nothing. She ran on lightly, laughing a little. Then her feet met a projection, she stumbled, and fell flat over a slab of wood that jutted out of the ground. She lay there a moment, dazed. Then she sat up, and bent down to look at this thing that had tripped her. Probably a tree trunk. Then she must be near timberline. She bent closer. It was a rough wooden slab. Closer still. There were words carved on it. She lay flat and managed to make them out painfully.

"Here lies Sarah Cannon. Lay to rest, and died alone, April 26, 1893."

Fanny had heard the story of Sarah Cannon, a stern spinster who had achieved the climb to the Peak, and who had met with mishap on the down trail. Her guide had left her to go for help. When the relief party returned, hours later, they had found her dead.

Fanny sprang up, filled with a furious energy. She felt strangely light and clear-headed. She ran on, stopped, ran again. Now she was making little short runs here and there. It was snowing furiously, vindictively. It seemed to her that she had been running for hours. It probably was minutes. Suddenly she sank down, got to her feet again, stumbled on perhaps a dozen paces, and sank down again. It was as though her knees had turned liquid. She lay there, with her eyes shut.

"I'm just resting," she told herself. "In a minute I'll go on. In a minute. After I've rested."

"Hallo-o-o-o!" from somewhere on the other side of the snow blanket. "Hallo-o-o-o!" Fanny sat up, helloing shrilly, hysterically. She got to her feet, staggeringly. And Clarence Heyl walked toward her.

"You ought to be spanked for this," he said.

Fanny began to cry weakly. She felt no curiosity as to his being there. She wasn't at all sure that he actually was there, for that matter. At that thought she dug a frantic hand into his arm. He seemed to understand, for he said, "It's all right. I'm real enough. Can you walk?"

"Yes." But she tried it and found she could not. She decided she was too tired to care. "I stumbled over a thing—a horrible thing—a gravestone. And I must have hurt my leg. I didn't know——"

She leaned against him, a dead weight. "Tell you what," said Heyl, cheerfully. "You wait here. I'll go on down to Timberline Cabin for help, and come back."

"You couldn't manage it—alone? If I tried? If I tried to walk?"

"Oh, impossible." His tone was brisk. "Now you sit right down here." She sank down obediently. She felt a little sorry for herself, and glad, too, and queer, and not at all cold. She looked up at him dumbly. He was smiling. "All right?"

She nodded. He turned abruptly. The snow hid him from sight at once.

"Here lies Sarah Cannon. Lay to rest and died alone, April 26, 1893."

She sank down, and pillowed her head on her arms. She knew that this was the end. She was very drowsy, and not at all sad. Happy, if anything.

"You didn't really think I'd leave you, did you, Fan?"

She opened her eyes. Heyl was there. He reached down, and lifted her lightly to her feet. "Timberline Cabin's not a hundred yards away. I just did it to try you."

She had spirit enough left to say, "Beast."

Then he swung her up, and carried her down the trail. He carried her, not in his arms, as they do it in books and in the movies. He could not have gone a hundred feet that way. He carried her over his shoulder, like a sack of meal, by one arm and one leg, I regret to say. Any boy scout knows that trick, and will tell you what I mean. It is the most effectual carrying method known, though unromantic.

And so they came to Timberline Cabin, and Albert Edward Cobbins was in the doorway. Heyl put her down gently on the bench that ran alongside the table. The hospitable table that bore two smoking cups of tea. Fanny's lips were cracked, and the skin was peeled from her nose, and her hair was straggling and her eyes red-rimmed. She drank the tea in great gulps. And then she went into the tiny bunkroom, and tumbled into one of the shelf-bunks, and slept.

When she awoke she sat up in terror, and bumped her head against the bunk above, and called, "Clancy!"

"Yep!" from the next room. He came to the door. The acrid smell of their pipes was incense in her nostrils. "Rested?"

"What time is it?"

"Seven o'clock. Dinner time. Ham and eggs."

She got up stiffly, and bathed her roughened face, and produced a powder pad (they carry them in the face of danger, death, and dissolution) and dusted it over her scaly nose. She did her hair—her vigorous, abundant hair that shone in the lamplight, pulled down her blouse, surveyed her torn shoes ruefully, donned the khaki skirt that Albert Edward had magically produced from somewhere to take the place of her breeches. She dusted her shoes with a bit of rag, regarded herself steadily in the wavering mirror, and went in.

The two men were talking quietly. Albert Edward was moving deftly from stove to table. They both looked up as she came in, and she looked at Heyl. Their eyes held.

Albert Edward was as sporting a gentleman as the late dear king whose name he bore. He went out to tend Heyl's horse, he said. It was little he knew of horses, and he rather feared them, as does a sailing man. But he went, nevertheless.

Heyl still looked at Fanny, and Fanny at him.

"It's absurd," said Fanny. "It's the kind of thing that doesn't happen."

"It's simple enough, really," he answered. "I saw Ella Monahan in Chicago, and she told me all she knew, and something of what she had guessed. I waited a few days and came back. I had to." He smiled. "A pretty job you've made of trying to be selfish."

At that she smiled, too, pitifully enough, for her lower lip trembled. She caught it between her teeth in a last sharp effort at self-control. "Don't!" she quavered. And then, in a panic, her two hands came up in a vain effort to hide the tears. She sank down on the rough bench by the table, and the proud head came down on her arms so that there was a little clatter and tinkle among the supper things spread on the table. Then quiet.

Clarence Heyl stared. He stared, helplessly, as does a man who has never, in all his life, been called upon to comfort a woman in tears. Then instinct came to his rescue. He made her side of the table in two strides (your favorite film star couldn't have done it better), put his two hands on her shoulders and neatly shifted the bowed head from the cold, hard surface of the table top to the warm, rough, tobacco-scented comfort of his coat. It rested there quite naturally. Just as naturally Fanny's arm crept up, and about his neck. So they remained for a moment, until he bent so that his lips touched her hair. Her head came up at that, sharply, so that it bumped his chin. They both laughed, looking into each other's eyes, but at what they saw there they stopped laughing and were serious.

"Dear," said Heyl. "Dearest." The lids drooped over Fanny's eyes. "Look at me," said Heyl. So she tried to lift them again, bravely, and could not. At that he bent his head and kissed Fanny Brandeis in the way a woman wants to be kissed for the first time by the man she loves. It hurt her lips, that kiss, and her teeth, and the back of her neck, and it left her breathless, and set things whirling. When she opened her eyes (they shut them at such times) he kissed her again, very tenderly, this time, and lightly, and reassuringly. She returned that kiss, and, strangely enough, it was the one that stayed in her memory long, long after the other had faded.

"Oh, Clancy, I've made such a mess of it all. Such a miserable mess. The little girl in the red tam was worth ten of me. I don't see how you can—care for me."

"You're the most wonderful woman in the world," said Heyl, "and the most beautiful and splendid."

He must have meant it, for he was looking down at her as he said it, and we know that the skin had been peeled off her nose by the mountain winds and sun, that her lips were cracked and her cheeks rough, and that she was red-eyed and worn-looking. And she must have believed him, for she brought his cheek down to hers with such a sigh of content, though she said, "But are we at all suited to each other?"

"Probably not," Heyl answered, briskly. "That's why we're going to be so terrifically happy. Some day I'll be passing the Singer building, and I'll glance up at it and think how pitiful it would look next to Long's Peak. And then I'll be off, probably, to these mountains."

"Or some day," Fanny returned, "we'll be up here, and I'll remember, suddenly, how Fifth Avenue looks on a bright afternoon between four and five. And I'll be off, probably, to the Grand Central station."

And then began one of those beautiful and foolish conversations which all lovers have whose love has been a sure and steady growth. Thus: "When did you first begin to care," etc. And, "That day we spent at the dunes, and you said so and so, did you mean this and that?"

Albert Edward Cobbins announced his approach by terrific stampings and scufflings, ostensibly for the purpose of ridding his boots of snow. He entered looking casual, and very nipped.

"You're here for the night," he said. "A regular blizzard. The greatest piece of luck I've had in a month." He busied himself with the ham and eggs and the teapot. "Hungry?"

"Not a bit," said Fanny and Heyl, together.

"H'm," said Albert Edward, and broke six eggs into the frying pan just the same.

After supper they aided Albert Edward in the process of washing up. When everything was tidy he lighted his most malignant pipe and told them seafaring yarns not necessarily true. Then he knocked the ashes out of his pipe and fell asleep there by the fire, effacing himself as effectually as one of three people can in a single room. They talked; low-toned murmurings that they seemed to find exquisitely meaningful or witty, by turn. Fanny, rubbing a forefinger (his) along her weather-roughened nose, would say, "At least you've seen me at my worst."

Or he, mock serious: "I think I ought to tell you that I'm the kind of man who throws wet towels into the laundry hamper."

But there was no mirth in Fanny's voice when she said, "Dear, do you think Lasker will give me that job? You know he said, `When you want a job, come back.' Do you think he meant it?"

"Lasker always means it."

"But," fearfully, and shyly, too, "you don't think I may have lost my drawing hand and my seeing eye, do you? As punishment?"

"I do not. I think you've just found them, for keeps. There wasn't a woman cartoonist in the country—or man, either, for that matter—could touch you two years ago. In two more I'll be just Fanny Brandeis' husband, that's all."

They laughed together at that, so that Albert Edward Cobbins awoke with a start and tried to look as if he had not been asleep, and failing, smiled benignly and drowsily upon them.

Buttered Side Down

I
THE FROG AND THE PUDDLE

Any one who has ever written for the magazines (nobody could devise a more sweeping opening; it includes the iceman who does a humorous article on the subject of his troubles, and the neglected wife next door, who journalizes) knows that a story the scene of which is not New York is merely junk. Take Fifth Avenue as a framework, pad it out to five thousand words, and there you have the ideal short story.

Consequently I feel a certain timidity in confessing that I do not know Fifth Avenue from Hester Street when I see it, because I've never seen it. It has been said that from the latter to the former is a ten-year journey, from which I have gathered that they lie some miles apart. As for Forty-second Street, of which musical comedians carol, I know not if it be a fashionable shopping thoroughfare or a factory district.

A confession of this kind is not only good for the soul, but for the editor. It saves him the trouble of turning to page two.

This is a story of Chicago, which is a first cousin of New York, although the two are not on chummy terms. It is a story of that part of Chicago which lies east of Dearborn Avenue and south of Division Street, and which may be called the Nottingham curtain district.

In the Nottingham curtain district every front parlor window is embellished with a "Rooms With or Without Board" sign. The curtains themselves have mellowed from their original department-store-basement-white to a rich, deep tone of Chicago smoke, which has the notorious London variety beaten by several shades. Block after block the two-story-and-basement houses stretch, all grimy and gritty and looking sadly down upon the five square feet of mangy grass forming the pitiful front yard of each. Now and then the monotonous line of front stoops is broken by an outjutting basement delicatessen shop. But not often. The Nottingham curtain district does not run heavily to delicacies. It is stronger on creamed cabbage and bread pudding.

Up in the third floor back at Mis' Buck's (elegant rooms $2.50 and up a week. Gents preferred) Gertie was brushing her hair for the night. One hundred strokes with a bristle brush. Anyone who reads the beauty column in the newspapers knows that. There was something heroic in the sight of Gertie brushing her hair one hundred strokes before going to bed at night. Only a woman could understand her doing it.

Gertie clerked downtown on State Street, in a gents' glove department. A gents' glove department requires careful dressing on the part of its clerks, and the manager, in selecting them, is particular about choosing "lookers," with especial attention to figure, hair, and finger nails. Gertie was a looker. Providence had taken care of that. But you cannot leave your hair and finger nails to Providence. They demand coaxing with a bristle brush and an orangewood stick.

Now clerking, as Gertie would tell you, is fierce on the feet. And when your feet are tired you are tired all over. Gertie's feet were tired every night. About eight-thirty she longed to peel off her clothes, drop them in a heap on the floor, and tumble, unbrushed, unwashed, unmanicured, into bed. She never did it.

Things had been particularly trying to-night. After washing out three handkerchiefs and pasting them with practised hand over the mirror, Gertie had taken off her shoes and discovered a hole the size of a silver quarter in the heel of her left stocking. Gertie had a country-bred horror of holey stockings. She darned the hole, yawning, her aching feet pressed against the smooth, cool leg of the iron bed. That done, she had had the colossal courage to wash her face, slap cold cream on it, and push back the cuticle around her nails.

Seated huddled on the side of her thin little iron bed, Gertie was brushing her hair bravely, counting the strokes somewhere in her sub-conscious mind and thinking busily all the while of something else. Her brush rose, fell, swept downward, rose, fell, rhythmically.

"Ninety-six, ninety-seven, ninety-eight, ninety—— Oh, darn it! What's the use!" cried Gertie, and hurled the brush across the room with a crack.

She sat looking after it with wide, staring eyes until the brush blurred in with the faded red roses on the carpet. When she found it doing that she got up, wadded her hair viciously into a hard bun in the back instead of braiding it carefully as usual, crossed the room (it wasn't much of a trip), picked up the brush, and stood looking down at it, her under lip caught between her teeth. That is the humiliating part of losing your temper and throwing things. You have to come down to picking them up, anyway.

Her lip still held prisoner, Gertie tossed the brush on the bureau, fastened her nightgown at the throat with a safety pin, turned out the gas and crawled into bed.

Perhaps the hard bun at the back of her head kept her awake. She lay there with her eyes wide open and sleepless, staring into the darkness.

191

At midnight the Kid Next Door came in whistling, like one unused to boarding-house rules. Gertie liked him for that. At the head of the stairs he stopped whistling and came softly into his own third floor back just next to Gertie's. Gertie liked him for that, too.

The two rooms had been one in the fashionable days of the Nottingham curtain district, long before the advent of Mis' Buck. That thrifty lady, on coming into possession, had caused a flimsy partition to be run up, slicing the room in twain and doubling its rental.

Lying there Gertie could hear the Kid Next Door moving about getting ready for bed and humming "Every Little Movement Has a Meaning of Its Own" very lightly, under his breath. He polished his shoes briskly, and Gertie smiled there in the darkness of her own room in sympathy. Poor kid, he had his beauty struggles, too.

Gertie had never seen the Kid Next Door, although he had come four months ago. But she knew he wasn't a grouch, because he alternately whistled and sang off-key tenor while dressing in the morning. She had also discovered that his bed must run along the same wall against which her bed was pushed. Gertie told herself that there was something almost immodest about being able to hear him breathing as he slept. He had tumbled into bed with a little grunt of weariness.

Gertie lay there another hour, staring into the darkness. Then she began to cry softly, lying on her face with her head between her arms. The cold cream and the salt tears mingled and formed a slippery paste. Gertie wept on because she couldn't help it. The longer she wept the more difficult her sobs became, until finally they bordered on the hysterical. They filled her lungs until they ached and reached her throat with a force that jerked her head back.

"Rap-rap-rap!" sounded sharply from the head of her bed.

Gertie stopped sobbing, and her heart stopped beating. She lay tense and still, listening. Everyone knows that spooks rap three times at the head of one's bed. It's a regular high-sign with them.

"Rap-rap-rap!"

Gertie's skin became goose-flesh, and coldwater effects chased up and down her spine.

"What's your trouble in there?" demanded an unspooky voice so near that Gertie jumped. "Sick?"

It was the Kid Next Door.

"N-no, I'm not sick," faltered Gertie, her mouth close to the wall. Just then a belated sob that had stopped halfway when the raps began hustled on to join its sisters. It took Gertie by surprise, and brought prompt response from the other side of the wall.

"I'll bet I scared you green. I didn't mean to, but, on the square, if you're feeling sick, a little nip of brandy will set you up. Excuse my mentioning it, girlie, but I'd do the same for my sister. I hate like sin to hear a woman suffer like that, and, anyway, I don't know whether you're fourteen or forty, so it's perfectly respectable. I'll get the bottle and leave it outside your door."

"No you don't!" answered Gertie in a hollow voice, praying meanwhile that the woman in the room below might be sleeping. "I'm not sick, honestly I'm not. I'm just as much obliged, and I'm dead sorry I woke you up with my blubbering. I started out with the soft pedal on, but things got away from me. Can you hear me?"

"Like a phonograph. Sure you couldn't use a sip of brandy where it'd do the most good?"

"Sure."

"Well, then, cut out the weeps and get your beauty sleep, kid. He ain't worth sobbing over, anyway, believe me."

"He!" snorted Gertie indignantly. "You're cold. There never was anything in peg-tops that could make me carry on like the heroine of the Elsie series."

"Lost your job?"

"No such luck."

"Well, then, what in Sam Hill could make a woman——"

"Lonesome!" snapped Gertie. "And the floorwalker got fresh to-day. And I found two gray hairs to-night. And I'd give my next week's pay envelope to hear the double click that our front gate gives back home."

"Back home!" echoed the Kid Next Door in a dangerously loud voice. "Say, I want to talk to you. If you'll promise you won't get sore and think I'm fresh, I'll ask you a favor. Slip on a kimono and we'll sneak down to the front stoop and talk it over. I'm as wide awake as a chorus girl and twice as hungry. I've got two apples and a box of crackers. Are you on?"

Gertie snickered. "It isn't done in our best sets, but I'm on. I've got a can of sardines and an orange. I'll be ready in six minutes."

She was, too. She wiped off the cold cream and salt tears with a dry towel, did her hair in a schoolgirl braid and tied it with a big bow, and dressed herself in a black skirt and a baby blue dressing sacque. The Kid Next Door was waiting outside in the hall. His gray sweater covered a multitude of sartorial deficiencies. Gertie stared at him, and he stared at Gertie in the sickly blue light of the boarding-house hall, and it took her one-half of one second to discover that she liked his mouth, and his eyes, and the way his hair was mussed.

"Why, you're only a kid!" whispered the Kid Next Door, in surprise.

Gertie smothered a laugh. "You're not the first man that's been deceived by a pig-tail braid and a baby blue waist. I could locate those two gray hairs for you with my eyes shut and my feet in a sack. Come on, boy. These Robert W. Chambers situations make me nervous."

Many earnest young writers with a flow of adjectives and a passion for detail have attempted to describe the quiet of a great city at night, when a few million people within it are sleeping, or ought to be. They work in the clang of a distant owl car, and the roar of an occasional "L" train, and the hollow echo of the footsteps of the late passer-by. They go elaborately into description, and are strong on the brooding hush, but the thing has never been done satisfactorily.

Gertie, sitting on the front stoop at two in the morning, with her orange in one hand and the sardine can in the other, put it this way:

"If I was to hear a cricket chirp now, I'd screech. This isn't really quiet. It's like waiting for a cannon cracker to go off just before the fuse is burned down. The bang isn't there yet, but you hear it a hundred times in your mind before it happens."

"My name's Augustus G. Eddy," announced the Kid Next Door, solemnly. "Back home they always called me Gus. You peel that orange while I unroll the top of this sardine can. I'm guilty of having interrupted you in the middle of what the girls call a good cry, and I know you'll have to get it out of your system some way. Take a bite of apple and then wade right in and tell me what you're doing in this burg if you don't like it."

"This thing ought to have slow music," began Gertie. "It's pathetic. I came to Chicago from Beloit, Wisconsin, because I thought that little town was a lonesome hole for a vivacious creature like me. Lonesome! Listen while I laugh a low mirthless laugh. I didn't know anything about the three-ply, double-barreled, extra heavy brand of lonesomeness that a big town like this can deal out. Talk about your desert wastes! They're sociable and snug compared to this. I know three-fourths of the people in Beloit, Wisconsin, by their first names. I've lived here six months and I'm not on informal terms with anybody except Teddy, the landlady's dog, and he's a trained rat-and-book-agent terrier, and not inclined to overfriendliness. When I clerked at the Enterprise Store in Beloit the women used to come in and ask for something we didn't carry just for an excuse to copy the way the lace yoke effects were planned in my shirtwaists. You ought to see the way those same shirtwaist stack up here. Why, boy, the lingerie waists that the other girls in my department wear make my best hand-tucked effort look like a simple English country blouse. They're so dripping with Irish crochet and real Val and Cluny insertions that it's a wonder the girls don't get stoop-shouldered carrying 'em around."

"Hold on a minute," commanded Gus. "This thing is uncanny. Our cases dovetail like the deductions in a detective story. Kneel here at my feet, little daughter, and I'll tell you the story of my sad young life. I'm no child of the city streets, either. Say, I came to this town because I thought there was a bigger field for me in Gents' Furnishings. Joke, what?"

But Gertie didn't smile. She gazed up at Gus, and Gus gazed down at her, and his fingers fiddled absently with the big bow at the end of her braid.

"And isn't there?" asked Gertie, sympathetically.

"Girlie, I haven't saved twelve dollars since I came. I'm no tightwad, and I don't believe in packing everything away into a white marble mausoleum, but still a gink kind of whispers to himself that some day he'll be furnishing up a kitchen pantry of his own."

"Oh!" said Gertie.

"And let me mention in passing," continued Gus, winding the ribbon bow around his finger, "that in the last hour or so that whisper has been swelling to a shout."

"Oh!" said Gertie again.

"You said it. But I couldn't buy a secondhand gas stove with what I've saved in the last half-year here. Back home they used to think I was a regular little village John Drew, I was so dressy. But here I look like a yokel on circus day compared to the other fellows in the store. All they need is a field glass strung over their shoulder to make them look like a clothing ad in the back of a popular magazine. Say, girlie, you've got the prettiest hair I've seen since I blew in here. Look at that braid! Thick as a rope! That's no relation to the piles of jute that the Flossies here stack on their heads. And shines! Like satin."

"It ought to," said Gertrude, wearily. "I brush it a hundred strokes every night. Sometimes I'm so beat that I fall asleep with my brush in the air. The manager won't stand for any romping curls or hooks-and-eyes that don't connect. It keeps me so busy being beautiful, and what the society writers call 'well groomed,' that I don't have time to sew the buttons on my underclothes."

"But don't you get some amusement in the evening?" marveled Gus. "What was the matter with you and the other girls in the store? Can't you hit it off?"

"Me? No. I guess I was too woodsy for them. I went out with them a couple of times. I guess they're nice girls all right; but they've got what you call a broader way of looking at things than I have. Living in a little town all your life makes you narrow. These girls!—Well, maybe I'll get educated up to their plane some day, but——"

"No, you don't!" hissed Gus. "Not if I can help it."

"But you can't," replied Gertie, sweetly. "My, ain't this a grand night! Evenings like this I used to love to putter around the yard after supper, sprinkling the grass and weeding the radishes. I'm the greatest kid to fool around with a hose. And flowers! Say, they just grow for me. You ought to have seen my pansies and nasturtiums last summer."

The fingers of the Kid Next Door wandered until they found Gertie's. They clasped them.

"This thing just points one way, little one. It's just as plain as a path leading up to a cozy little three-room flat up here on the North Side somewhere. See it? With me and you married, and playing at housekeeping in a parlor and bedroom and kitchen? And both of us going down town to work in the morning just the same as we do now. Only not the same, either."

"Wake up, little boy," said Gertie, prying her fingers away from those other detaining ones. "I'd fit into a three-room flat like a whale in a kitchen sink. I'm going back to Beloit, Wisconsin. I've learned my lesson all right. There's a fellow there waiting for me. I used to think he was too slow. But say, he's got the nicest little painting and paper-hanging business you ever saw, and making money. He's secretary of the K. P.'s back home. They give some swell little dances during the winter, especially for the married members. In five years we'll own our home, with a vegetable garden in the back. I'm a little frog, and it's me for the puddle."

Gus stood up slowly. Gertie felt a little pang of compunction when she saw what a boy he was.

"I don't know when I've enjoyed a talk like this. I've heard about these dawn teas, but I never thought I'd go to one," she said.

"Good-night, girlie," interrupted Gus, abruptly. "It's the dreamless couch for mine. We've got a big sale on in tan and black seconds to-morrow."

II
THE MAN WHO CAME BACK

There are two ways of doing battle against Disgrace. You may live it down; or you may run away from it and hide. The first method is heart-breaking, but sure. The second cannot be relied upon because of the uncomfortable way Disgrace has of turning up at your heels just when you think you have eluded her in the last town but one.

Ted Terrill did not choose the first method. He had it thrust upon him. After Ted had served his term he came back home to visit his mother's grave, intending to take the next train out. He wore none of the prison pallor that you read about in books, because he had been shortstop on the penitentiary all-star baseball team, and famed for the dexterity with which he could grab up red-hot grounders. The storied lock step and the clipped hair effect also were missing. The superintendent of Ted's prison had been one of the reform kind.

You never would have picked Ted for a criminal. He had none of those interesting phrenological bumps and depressions that usually are shown to such frank advantage in the Bertillon photographs. Ted had been assistant cashier in the Citizens' National Bank. In a mad moment he had attempted a little sleight-of-hand act in which certain Citizens' National funds were to be transformed into certain glittering shares and back again so quickly that the examiners couldn't follow it with their eyes. But Ted was unaccustomed to these now-you-see-it-and-now-you-don't feats and his hand slipped. The trick dropped to the floor with an awful clatter.

Ted had been a lovable young kid, six feet high, and blonde, with a great reputation as a dresser. He had the first yellow plush hat in our town. It sat on his golden head like a halo. The women all liked Ted. Mrs. Dankworth, the dashing widow (why will widows persist in being dashing?), said that he was the only man in our town who knew how to wear a dress suit. The men were forever slapping him on the back and asking him to have a little something.

Ted's good looks and his clever tongue and a certain charming Irish way he had with him caused him to be taken up by the smart set. Now, if you've never lived in a small town you will be much amused at the idea of its boasting a smart set. Which proves your ignorance. The small town smart set is deadly serious about its smartness. It likes to take six-hour runs down to the city to fit a pair of shoes and hear Caruso. Its clothes are as well made, and its scandals as crisp, and its pace as hasty, and its golf club as dull as the clothes, and scandals, and pace, and golf club of its city cousins.

The hasty pace killed Ted. He tried to keep step in a set of young folks whose fathers had made our town. And all the time his pocketbook was yelling, "Whoa!" The young people ran largely to scarlet-upholstered touring cars, and country-club doings, and house parties, as small town younger generations are apt to. When Ted went to high school half the boys in his little clique spent their after-school hours dashing up and down Main street in their big, glittering cars, sitting slumped down on the middle of their spines in front of the steering wheel, their sleeves rolled up, their hair combed a militant pompadour. One or the other of them always took Ted along. It is fearfully easy to develop a taste for that kind of thing. As he grew older, the taste took root and became a habit.

Ted came out after serving his term, still handsome, spite of all that story-writers may have taught to the contrary. But we'll make this concession to the old tradition. There was a difference.

His radiant blondeur was dimmed in some intangible, elusive way. Birdie Callahan, who had worked in Ted's mother's kitchen for years, and who had gone back to her old job at the Haley House after her mistress's death, put it sadly, thus:

"He was always th' han'some divil. I used to look forward to ironin' day just for the pleasure of pressin' his fancy shirts for him. I'm that partial to them swell blondes. But I dinnaw, he's changed. Doin' time has taken the edge off his hair an' complexion. Not changed his color, do yuh mind, but dulled it, like a gold ring, or the like, that has tarnished."

Ted was seated in the smoker, with a chip on his shoulder, and a sick horror of encountering some one he knew in his heart, when Jo Haley, of the Haley House, got on at Westport, homeward bound. Jo Haley is the most eligible bachelor in our town, and the slipperiest. He has made the Haley House a gem, so that traveling men will cut half a dozen towns to Sunday there. If he should say "Jump through this!" to any girl in our town she'd jump.

Jo Haley strolled leisurely up the car aisle toward Ted. Ted saw him coming and sat very still, waiting.

"Hello, Ted! How's Ted?" said Jo Haley, casually. And dropped into the adjoining seat without any more fuss.

Ted wet his lips slightly and tried to say something. He had been a breezy talker. But the words would not come. Jo Haley made no effort to cover the situation with a rush of conversation. He did not seem to realize that there was any situation to cover. He champed the end of his cigar and handed one to Ted.

"Well, you've taken your lickin', kid. What you going to do now?"

The rawness of it made Ted wince. "Oh, I don't know," he stammered. "I've a job half promised in Chicago."

"What doing?"

Ted laughed a short and ugly laugh. "Driving a brewery auto truck."

Jo Haley tossed his cigar dexterously to the opposite corner of his mouth and squinted thoughtfully along its bulging sides.

"Remember that Wenzel girl that's kept books for me for the last six years? She's leaving in a couple of months to marry a New York guy that travels for ladies' cloaks and suits. After she goes it's nix with the lady bookkeepers for me. Not that Minnie isn't a good, straight girl, and honest, but no girl can keep books with one eye on a column of figures and the other on a traveling man in a brown suit and a red necktie, unless she's cross-eyed, and you bet Minnie ain't. The job's yours if you want it. Eighty a month to start on, and board."

"I—can't, Jo. Thanks just the same. I'm going to try to begin all over again, somewhere else, where nobody knows me."

"Oh yes," said Jo. "I knew a fellow that did that. After he came out he grew a beard, and wore eyeglasses, and changed his name. Had a quick, crisp way of talkin', and he cultivated a drawl and went west and started in business. Real estate, I think. Anyway, the second month he was there in walks a fool he used to know and bellows: 'Why if it ain't Bill! Hello, Bill! I thought you was doing time yet.' That was enough. Ted, you can black your face, and dye your hair, and squint, and some fine day, sooner or later, somebody'll come along and blab the whole thing. And say, the older it gets the worse it sounds, when it does come out. Stick around here where you grew up, Ted."

Ted clasped and unclasped his hands uncomfortably. "I can't figure out why you should care how I finish."

"No reason," answered Jo. "Not a darned one. I wasn't ever in love with your ma, like the guy on the stage; and I never owed your pa a cent. So it ain't a guilty conscience. I guess it's just pure cussedness, and a hankerin' for a new investment. I'm curious to know how'll you turn out. You've got the makin's of what the newspapers call a Leading Citizen, even if you did fall down once. If I'd ever had time to get married, which I never will have, a first-class hotel bein' more worry and expense than a Pittsburg steel magnate's whole harem, I'd have wanted somebody to do the same for my kid. That sounds slushy, but it's straight."

"I don't seem to know how to thank you," began Ted, a little husky as to voice.

"Call around to-morrow morning," interrupted Jo Haley, briskly, "and Minnie Wenzel will show you the ropes. You and her can work together for a couple of months. After then she's leaving to make her underwear, and that. I should think she'd have a bale of it by this time. Been embroidering them shimmy things and lunch cloths back of the desk when she thought I wasn't lookin' for the last six months."

Ted came down next morning at 8 A.M. with his nerve between his teeth and the chip still balanced lightly on his shoulder. Five minutes later Minnie Wenzel knocked it off. When Jo Haley introduced the two jocularly, knowing that they had originally met in the First Reader room, Miss Wenzel acknowledged the introduction icily by lifting her left eyebrow slightly and drawing down the corners of her mouth. Her air of hauteur was a triumph, considering that she was handicapped by black sateen sleevelets.

I wonder how one could best describe Miss Wenzel? There is one of her in every small town. Let me think (business of hand on brow). Well, she always paid eight dollars for her corsets when most girls in a similar position got theirs for fifty-nine cents in the basement. Nature had been kind to her. The hair that had been a muddy brown in Minnie's schoolgirl days it had touched with a magic red-gold wand. Birdie Callahan always said that Minnie was working only to wear out her old clothes.

After the introduction Miss Wenzel followed Jo Haley into the lobby. She took no pains to lower her voice.

"Well I must say, Mr. Haley, you've got a fine nerve! If my gentleman friend was to hear of my working with an ex-con I wouldn't be surprised if he'd break off the engagement. I should think you'd have some respect for the feelings of a lady with a name to keep up, and engaged to a swell fellow like Mr. Schwartz."

"Say, listen, m' girl," replied Jo Haley. "The law don't cover all the tricks. But if stuffing an order was a criminal offense I'll bet your swell traveling man would be doing a life term."

Ted worked that day with his teeth set so that his jaws ached next morning. Minnie Wenzel spoke to him only when necessary and then in terms of dollars and cents. When dinner time came she divested herself of the black sateen sleevelets, wriggled from the shoulders down a la Patricia O'Brien, produced a chamois skin, and disappeared in the direction of the washroom. Ted waited until the dining-room was almost deserted. Then he went in to dinner alone. Some one in white wearing an absurd little pocket handkerchief of an apron led him to a seat in a far corner of the big room. Ted did not lift his eyes higher than the snowy square of the apron. The Apron drew out a chair, shoved it under Ted's knees in the way Aprons have, and thrust a printed menu at him.

"Roast beef, medium," said Ted, without looking up.

"Bless your heart, yuh ain't changed a bit. I remember how yuh used to jaw when it was too well done," said the Apron, fondly.

Ted's head came up with a jerk.

"So yuh will cut yer old friends, is it?" grinned Birdie Callahan. "If this wasn't a public dining-room maybe yuh'd shake hands with a poor but proud workin' girrul. Yer as good lookin' a divil as ever, Mister Ted."

Ted's hand shot out and grasped hers. "Birdie! I could weep on your apron! I never was so glad to see any one in my life. Just to look at you makes me homesick. What in Sam Hill are you doing here?"

"Waitin'. After yer ma died, seemed like I didn't care t' work fer no other privit fam'ly, so I came back here on my old job. I'll bet I'm the homeliest head waitress in captivity."

Ted's nervous fingers were pleating the tablecloth. His voice sank to a whisper. "Birdie, tell me the God's truth. Did those three years cause her death?"

"Niver!" lied Birdie. "I was with her to the end. It started with a cold on th' chest. Have some French fried with yer beef, Mr. Teddy. They're illigent to-day."

Birdie glided off to the kitchen. Authors are fond of the word "glide." But you can take it literally this time. Birdie had a face that looked like a huge mistake, but she walked like a panther, and they're said to be the last cry as gliders. She walked with her chin up and her hips firm. That comes from juggling trays. You have to walk like that to keep your nose out of the soup. After a while the walk becomes a habit. Any seasoned dining-room girl could give lessons in walking to the Delsarte teacher of an Eastern finishing school.

From the day that Birdie Callahan served Ted with the roast beef medium and the elegant French fried, she appointed herself monitor over his food and clothes and morals. I wish I could find words to describe his bitter loneliness. He did not seek companionship. The men, although not directly avoiding him, seemed somehow to have pressing business whenever they happened in his vicinity. The women ignored him. Mrs. Dankworth, still dashing and still widowed, passed Ted one day and looked fixedly at a point one inch above his head. In a town like ours the Haley House is like a big, hospitable clubhouse. The men drop in there the first thing in the morning, and the last thing at night, to hear the gossip and buy a cigar and jolly the girl at the cigar counter. Ted spoke to them when they spoke to him. He began to develop a certain grim line about the mouth. Jo Haley watched him from afar, and the longer he watched the kinder and more speculative grew the look in his eyes. And slowly and surely there grew in the hearts of our townspeople a certain new respect and admiration for this boy who was fighting his fight.

Ted got into the habit of taking his meals late, so that Birdie Callahan could take the time to talk to him.

"Birdie," he said one day, when she brought his soup, "do you know that you're the only decent woman who'll talk to me? Do you know what I mean when I say that I'd give the rest of my life if I could just put my head in my mother's lap and have her muss up my hair and call me foolish names?"

Birdie Callahan cleared her throat and said abruptly: "I was noticin' yesterday your gray pants needs pressin' bad. Bring 'em down tomorrow mornin' and I'll give 'em th' elegant crease in the laundry."

So the first weeks went by, and the two months of Miss Wenzel's stay came to an end. Ted thanked his God and tried hard not to wish that she was a man so that he could punch her head.

The day before the time appointed for her departure she was closeted with Jo Haley for a long, long time. When finally she emerged a bellboy lounged up to Ted with a message.

"Wenzel says th' Old Man wants t' see you. 'S in his office. Say, Mr. Terrill, do yuh think they can play to-day? It's pretty wet."

Jo Haley was sunk in the depths of his big leather chair. He did not look up as Ted entered. "Sit down," he said. Ted sat down and waited, puzzled.

"As a wizard at figures," mused Jo Haley at last, softly as though to himself, "I'm a frost. A column of figures on paper makes my head swim. But I can carry a whole regiment of 'em in my head. I know every time the barkeeper draws one in the dark. I've been watchin' this thing for the last two weeks hopin' you'd quit and come and tell me." He turned suddenly and faced Ted. "Ted, old kid," he said sadly, "what'n'ell made you do it again?"

"What's the joke?" asked Ted.

"Now, Ted," remonstrated Jo Haley, "that way of talkin' won't help matters none. As I said, I'm rotten at figures. But you're the first investment that ever turned out bad, and let me tell you I've handled some mighty bad smelling ones. Why, kid, if you had just come to me on the quiet and asked for the loan of a hundred or so why——"

"What's the joke, Jo?" said Ted again, slowly.

"This ain't my notion of a joke," came the terse answer. "We're three hundred short."

The last vestige of Ted Terrill's old-time radiance seemed to flicker and die, leaving him ashen and old.

"Short?" he repeated. Then, "My God!" in a strangely colorless voice—"My God!" He looked down at his fingers impersonally, as though they belonged to some one else. Then his hand clutched Jo Haley's arm with the grip of fear. "Jo! Jo! That's the thing that has haunted me day and night, till my nerves are raw. The fear of doing it again. Don't laugh at me, will you? I used to lie awake nights going over that cursed business of the bank—over and over—till the cold sweat would break out all over me. I used to figure it all out again, step by step, until—Jo, could a man steal and not know it? Could thinking of a thing like that drive a man crazy? Because if it could—if it could—then——"

"I don't know," said Jo Haley, "but it sounds darned fishy." He had a hand on Ted's shaking shoulder, and was looking into the white, drawn face. "I had great plans for you, Ted. But Minnie Wenzel's got it all down on slips of paper. I might as well call her, in again, and we'll have the whole blamed thing out."

Minnie Wenzel came. In her hand were slips of paper, and books with figures in them, and Ted looked and saw things written in his own hand that should not have been there. And he covered his shamed face with his two hands and gave thanks that his mother was dead.

There came three sharp raps at the office door. The tense figures within jumped nervously.

"Keep out!" called Jo Haley, "whoever you are." Whereupon the door opened and Birdie Callahan breezed in.

"Get out, Birdie Callahan," roared Jo. "You're in the wrong pew."

Birdie closed the door behind her composedly and came farther into the room. "Pete th' pasthry cook just tells me that Minnie Wenzel told th' day clerk, who told the barkeep, who told th' janitor, who told th' chef, who told Pete, that Minnie had caught Ted stealin' some three hundred dollars."

Ted took a quick step forward. "Birdie, for Heaven's sake keep out of this. You can't make things any better. You may believe in me, but——"

"Where's the money?" asked Birdie.

Ted stared at her a moment, his mouth open ludicrously.

"Why—I—don't—know," he articulated, painfully. "I never thought of that."

Birdie snorted defiantly. "I thought so. D'ye know," sociably, "I was visitin' with my aunt Mis' Mulcahy last evenin'."

There was a quick rustle of silks from Minnie Wenzel's direction.

"Say, look here——" began Jo Haley, impatiently.

"Shut up, Jo Haley!" snapped Birdie. "As I was sayin', I was visitin' with my aunt Mis' Mulcahy. She does fancy washin' an' ironin' for the swells. An' Minnie Wenzel, there bein' none sweller, hires her to do up her weddin' linens. Such smears av hand embroidery an' Irish crochet she never see th' likes, Mis' Mulcahy says, and she's seen a lot. And as a special treat to the poor owld soul, why Minnie Wenzel lets her see some av her weddin' clo'es. There never yet was a woman who cud resist showin' her weddin' things to every other woman she cud lay hands on. Well, Mis' Mulcahy, she see that grand trewsow and she said she never saw th' beat. Dresses! Well, her going away suit alone comes to eighty dollars, for it's bein' made by Molkowsky, the little Polish tailor. An' her weddin' dress is satin, do yuh mind! Oh, it was a real treat for my aunt Mis' Mulcahy."

Birdie walked over to where Minnie Wenzel sat, very white and still, and pointed a stubby red finger in her face. "'Tis the grand manager ye are, Miss Wenzel, gettin' satins an' tailor-mades on yer salary. It takes a woman, Minnie Wenzel, to see through a woman's thricks."

"Well I'll be dinged!" exploded Jo Haley.

"Yuh'd better be!" retorted Birdie Callahan.

Minnie Wenzel stood up, her lip caught between her teeth.

"Am I to understand, Jo Haley, that you dare to accuse me of taking your filthy money, instead of that miserable ex-con there who has done time?"

"That'll do, Minnie," said Jo Haley, gently. "That's a-plenty."

"Prove it," went on Minnie, and then looked as though she wished she hadn't.

"A business college edjication is a grand foine thing," observed Birdie. "Miss Wenzel is a graduate av wan. They teach you everything from drawin' birds with tail feathers to plain and fancy penmanship. In fact, they teach everything in the writin' line except forgery, an' I ain't so sure they haven't got a coorse in that."

"I don't care," whimpered Minnie Wenzel suddenly, sinking in a limp heap on the floor. "I had to do it. I'm marrying a swell fellow and a girl's got to have some clothes that don't look like a Bird Center dressmaker's work. He's got three sisters. I saw their pictures and they're coming to the wedding. They're the kind that wear low-necked dresses in the evening, and have their hair and nails done downtown. I haven't got a thing but my looks. Could I go to New York dressed like a rube? On the square, Jo, I worked here six years and never took a sou. But things got away from me. The tailor wouldn't finish my suit unless I paid him fifty dollars down. I only took fifty at first, intending to pay it back. Honest to goodness, Jo, I did."

"Cut it out," said Jo Haley, "and get up. I was going to give you a check for your wedding, though I hadn't counted on no three hundred. We'll call it square. And I hope you'll be happy, but I don't gamble on it. You'll be goin' through your man's pants pockets before you're married a year. You can take your hat and fade. I'd like to know how I'm ever going to square this thing with Ted and Birdie."

"An' me standin' here gassin' while them fool girls in the dinin'-room can't set a table decent, and dinner in less than ten minutes," cried Birdie, rushing off. Ted mumbled something unintelligible and was after her.

"Birdie! I want to talk to you."

"Say it quick then," said Birdie, over her shoulder. "The doors open in three minnits."

"I can't tell you how grateful I am. This is no place to talk to you. Will you let me walk home with you to-night after your work's done?"

"Will I?" said Birdie, turning to face him. "I will not. Th' swell mob has shook you, an' a good thing it is. You was travelin' with a bunch of racers, when you was only built for medium speed. Now you're got your chance to a fresh start and don't you ever think I'm going to be the one to let you spoil it by beginnin' to walk out with a dinin'-room Lizzie like me."

"Don't say that, Birdie," Ted put in.

"It's the truth," affirmed Birdie. "Not that I ain't a perfec'ly respectable girrul, and ye know it. I'm a good slob, but folks would be tickled for the chance to say that you had nobody to go with but the likes av me. If I was to let you walk home with me to-night, yuh might be askin' to call next week. Inside half a year, if yuh was lonesome enough, yuh'd ask me to marry yuh. And b'gorra," she said softly, looking down at her unlovely red hands, "I'm dead scared I'd do it. Get back to work, Ted Terrill, and hold yer head up high, and when yuh say your prayers to-night, thank your lucky stars I ain't a hussy."

<h2 style="text-align:center">III
WHAT SHE WORE</h2>

Somewhere in your story you must pause to describe your heroine's costume. It is a ticklish task. The average reader likes his heroine well dressed. He is not satisfied with knowing that she looked like a tall, fair lily. He wants to be told that her gown was of green crepe, with lace ruffles that swirled at her feet. Writers used to go so far as to name the dressmaker; and it was a poor kind of a heroine who didn't wear a red velvet by Worth. But that has been largely abandoned in these days of commissions. Still, when the heroine goes out on the terrace to spoon after dinner (a quaint old English custom for the origin of which see any novel by the "Duchess," page 179) the average reader wants to know what sort of a filmy wrap she snatches up on the way out. He demands a description, with as many illustrations as the publisher will stand for, of what she wore from the bedroom to the street, with full stops for the ribbons on her robe de nuit, and the buckles on her ballroom slippers. Half the poor creatures one sees flattening their noses against the shop windows are authors getting a line on the advance fashions. Suppose a careless writer were to dress his heroine in a full-plaited skirt only to find, when his story is published four months later, that full-plaited skirts have been relegated to the dim past!

I started to read a story once. It was a good one. There was in it not a single allusion to brandy-and-soda, or divorce, or the stock market. The dialogue crackled. The hero talked like a live man. It was a shipboard story, and the heroine was charming so long as she wore her heavy ulster. But along toward evening she blossomed forth in a yellow gown, with a scarlet poinsettia at her throat. I quit her cold. Nobody ever wore a scarlet poinsettia; or if they did, they couldn't wear it on a yellow gown. Or if they did wear it with a yellow gown, they didn't wear it at the throat. Scarlet poinsettias aren't worn, anyhow. To this day I don't know whether the heroine married the hero or jumped overboard.

You see, one can't be too careful about clothing one's heroine.

I hesitate to describe Sophy Epstein's dress. You won't like it. In the first place, it was cut too low, front and back, for a shoe clerk in a downtown loft. It was a black dress, near-princess in style, very tight as to fit, very short as to skirt, very sleazy as to material. It showed all the delicate curves of Sophy's under-fed, girlish body, and Sophy didn't care a bit. Its most objectionable feature was at the throat. Collarless gowns were in vogue. Sophy's daring shears had gone a snip or two farther. They had cut a startlingly generous V. To say that the dress was elbow-sleeved is superfluous. I have said that Sophy clerked in a downtown loft.

Sophy sold "sample" shoes at two-fifty a pair, and from where you were standing you thought they looked just like the shoes that were sold in the regular shops for six. When Sophy sat on one of the low benches at the feet of some customer, tugging away at a refractory shoe for a would-be small foot, her shameless little gown exposed more than it should have. But few of Sophy's customers were shocked. They were mainly chorus girls and ladies of doubtful complexion in search of cheap and ultra footgear, and—to use a health term—hardened by exposure.

Have I told you how pretty she was? She was so pretty that you immediately forgave her the indecency of her pitiful little gown. She was pretty in a daringly demure fashion, like a wicked little Puritan, or a poverty-stricken Cleo de Merode, with her smooth brown hair parted in the middle, drawn severely down over her ears, framing the lovely oval of her face and ending in a simple coil at the neck. Some serpent's wisdom had told Sophy to eschew puffs. But I think her prettiness could have triumphed even over those.

If Sophy's boss had been any other sort of man he would have informed Sophy, sternly, that black princess effects, cut low, were not au fait in the shoe-clerk world. But Sophy's boss had a rhombic nose, and no instep, and the tail of his name had been amputated. He didn't care how Sophy wore her dresses so long as she sold shoes.

Once the boss had kissed Sophy—not on the mouth, but just where her shabby gown formed its charming but immodest V. Sophy had slapped him, of course. But the slap had not set the thing right in her mind. She could not forget it. It had made her uncomfortable in much the same way as we are wildly ill at ease when we dream of walking naked in a crowded street. At odd moments during the day Sophy had found herself rubbing the spot furiously with her unlovely handkerchief, and shivering a little. She had never told the other girls about that kiss.

So—there you have Sophy and her costume. You may take her or leave her. I purposely placed these defects in costuming right at the beginning of the story, so that there should be no false pretenses. One more detail. About Sophy's throat was a slender, near-gold chain from which was suspended a cheap and glittering La Valliere. Sophy had not intended it as a sop to the conventions. It was an offering on the shrine of Fashion, and represented many lunchless days.

At eleven o'clock one August morning, Louie came to Chicago from Oskaloosa, Iowa. There was no hay in his hair. The comic papers have long insisted that the country boy, on his first visit to the city, is known by his greased boots and his high-water pants. Don't you believe them. The small-town boy is as fastidious about the height of his heels and the stripe of his shift and the roll of his hat-brim as are his city brothers. He peruses the slangily worded ads of the "classy clothes" tailors, and when scarlet cravats are worn the small-town boy is not more than two weeks late in acquiring one that glows like a headlight.

Louie found a rooming-house, shoved his suitcase under the bed, changed his collar, washed his hands in the gritty water of the wash bowl, and started out to look for a job.

Louie was twenty-one. For the last four years he had been employed in the best shoe store at home, and he knew shoe leather from the factory to the ash barrel. It was almost a religion with him.

Curiosity, which plays leads in so many life dramas, led Louie to the rotunda of the tallest building. It was built on the hollow center plan, with a sheer drop from the twenty-somethingth to the main floor. Louie stationed himself in the center of the mosaic floor, took off his hat, bent backward almost double and gazed, his mouth wide open. When he brought his muscles slowly back into normal position he tried hard not to look impressed. He glanced about, sheepishly, to see if any one was laughing at him, and his eye encountered the electric-lighted glass display case of the shoe company upstairs. The case was filled with pink satin slippers and cunning velvet boots, and the newest thing in bronze street shoes. Louie took the next elevator up. The shoe display had made him feel as though some one from home had slapped him on the back.

The God of the Jobless was with him. The boss had fired two boys the day before.

"Oskaloosa!" grinned the boss, derisively. "Do they wear shoes there? What do you know about shoes, huh boy?"

Louie told him. The boss shuffled the papers on his desk, and chewed his cigar, and tried not to show his surprise. Louie, quite innocently, was teaching the boss things about the shoe business.

When Louie had finished—"Well, I try you, anyhow," the boss grunted, grudgingly. "I give you so-and-so much." He named a wage that would have been ridiculous if it had not been so pathetic.

"All right, sir," answered Louie, promptly, like the boys in the Alger series. The cost of living problem had never bothered Louie in Oskaloosa.

The boss hid a pleased smile.

"Miss Epstein!" he bellowed, "step this way! Miss Epstein, kindly show this here young man so he gets a line on the stock. He is from Oskaloosa, Ioway. Look out she don't sell you a gold brick, Louie."

But Louie was not listening. He was gazing at the V in Sophy Epstein's dress with all his scandalized Oskaloosa, Iowa, eyes.

Louie was no mollycoddle. But he had been in great demand as usher at the Young Men's Sunday Evening Club service at the Congregational church, and in his town there had been no Sophy Epsteins in too-tight princess dresses, cut into a careless V. But Sophy was a city product—I was about to say pure and simple, but I will not—wise, bold, young, old, underfed, overworked, and triumphantly pretty.

"How-do!" cooed Sophy in her best baby tones. Louie's disapproving eyes jumped from the objectionable V in Sophy's dress to the lure of Sophy's face, and their expression underwent a lightning change. There was no disapproving Sophy's face, no matter how long one had dwelt in Oskaloosa.

"I won't bite you," said Sophy. "I'm never vicious on Tuesdays. We'll start here with the misses' an' children's, and work over to the other side."

Whereupon Louie was introduced into the intricacies of the sample shoe business. He kept his eyes resolutely away from the V, and learned many things. He learned how shoes that look like six dollar values may be sold for two-fifty. He looked on in wide-eyed horror while Sophy fitted a No. 5 C shoe on a 6 B foot and assured the wearer that it looked like a made-to-order boot. He picked up a pair of dull kid shoes and looked at them. His leather-wise eyes saw much, and I think he would have taken his hat off the hook, and his offended business principles out of the shop forever if Sophy had not completed her purchase and strolled over to him at the psychological moment.

She smiled up at him, impudently. "Well, Pink Cheeks," she said, "how do you like our little settlement by the lake, huh?"

"These shoes aren't worth two-fifty," said Louie, indignation in his voice.

"Well, sure," replied Sophy. "I know it. What do you think this is? A charity bazaar?"

"But back home———" began Louie, hotly.

"Ferget it, kid," said Sophy. "This is a big town, but it ain't got no room for back-homers. Don't sour on one job till you've got another nailed. You'll find yourself cuddling down on a park bench if you do. Say, are you honestly from Oskaloosa?"

"I certainly am," answered Louie, with pride.

"My goodness!" ejaculated Sophy. "I never believed there was no such place. Don't brag about it to the other fellows."

"What time do you go out for lunch?" asked Louie.

"What's it to you?" with the accent on the "to."

"When I want to know a thing, I generally ask," explained Louie, gently.

Sophy looked at him—a long, keen, knowing look. "You'll learn," she observed, thoughtfully.

Louie did learn. He learned so much in that first week that when Sunday came it seemed as though aeons had passed over his head. He learned that the crime of murder was as nothing compared to the crime of allowing a customer to depart shoeless; he learned that the lunch hour was invented for the purpose of making dates; that no one had ever heard of Oskaloosa, Iowa; that seven dollars a week does not leave much margin for laundry and general recklessness; that a madonna face above a V-cut gown is apt to distract one's attention from shoes; that a hundred-dollar nest egg is as effective in Chicago as a pine stick would be in propping up a stone wall; and that all the other men clerks called Sophy "sweetheart."

Some of his newly acquired knowledge brought pain, as knowledge is apt to do.

He saw that State Street was crowded with Sophys during the noon hour; girls with lovely faces under pitifully absurd hats. Girls who aped the fashions of the dazzling creatures they saw stepping from limousines. Girls who starved body and soul in order to possess a set of false curls, or a pair of black satin shoes with mother-o'-pearl buttons. Girls whose minds were bounded on the north by the nickel theatres; on the east by "I sez to him"; on the south by the gorgeous shop windows; and on the west by "He sez t' me."

Oh, I can't tell you how much Louie learned in that first week while his eyes were getting accustomed to the shifting, jostling, pushing, giggling, walking, talking throng. The city is justly famed as a hot house of forced knowledge.

One thing Louie could not learn. He could not bring himself to accept the V in Sophy's dress. Louie's mother had been one of the old-fashioned kind who wore a blue-and-white checked gingham apron from 6 A.M. to 2 P.M., when she took it off to go downtown and help the ladies of the church at the cake sale in the empty window of the gas company's office, only to don it again when she fried the potatoes for supper. Among other things she had taught Louie to wipe his feet before coming in, to respect and help women, and to change his socks often.

After a month of Chicago Louie forgot the first lesson; had more difficulty than I can tell you in reverencing a woman who only said, "Aw, don't get fresh now!" when the other men put their arms about her; and adhered to the third only after a struggle, in which he had to do a small private washing in his own wash-bowl in the evening.

Sophy called him a stiff. His gravely courteous treatment of her made her vaguely uncomfortable. She was past mistress in the art of parrying insults and banter, but she had no reply ready for Louie's boyish air of deference. It angered her for some unreasonable woman-reason.

There came a day when the V-cut dress brought them to open battle. I think Sophy had appeared that morning minus the chain and La Valliere. Frail and cheap as it was, it had been the only barrier that separated Sophy from frank shamelessness. Louie's outraged sense of propriety asserted itself.

"Sophy," he stammered, during a quiet half-hour, "I'll call for you and take you to the nickel show to-night if you'll promise not to wear that dress. What makes you wear that kind of a get-up, anyway?"

"Dress?" queried Sophy, looking down at the shiny front breadth of her frock. "Why? Don't you like it?"

"Like it! No!" blurted Louie.

"Don't yuh, rully! Deah me! Deah me! If I'd only knew that this morning. As a gen'ral thing I wear white duck complete down t' work, but I'm savin' my last two clean suits fr gawlf."

Louie ran an uncomfortable finger around the edge of his collar, but he stood his ground. "It—it—shows your—neck so," he objected, miserably.

Sophy opened her great eyes wide. "Well, supposin' it does?" she inquired, coolly. "It's a perfectly good neck, ain't it?"

Louie, his face very red, took the plunge. "I don't know. I guess so. But, Sophy, it—looks so—so—you know what I mean. I hate to see the way the fellows rubber at you. Why don't you wear those plain shirtwaist things, with high collars, like my mother wears back home?"

Sophy's teeth came together with a click. She laughed a short cruel little laugh. "Say, Pink Cheeks, did yuh ever do a washin' from seven to twelve, after you got home from work in the evenin'? It's great! 'Specially when you're living in a six-by-ten room with all the modern inconveniences, includin' no water except on the third floor down. Simple! Say, a child could work it. All you got to do, when you get home so tired your back teeth ache, is to haul your water, an' soak your clothes, an' then rub 'em till your hands peel, and rinse 'em, an' boil 'em, and blue 'em, an' starch 'em. See? Just like that. Nothin' to it, kid. Nothin' to it."

Louie had been twisting his fingers nervously. Now his hands shut themselves into fists. He looked straight into Sophy's angry eyes.

"I do know what it is," he said, quite simply. "There's been a lot written and said about women's struggle with clothes. I wonder why they've never said anything about the way a man has to fight to keep up the thing they call appearances. God knows it's pathetic enough to think of a girl like you bending over a tubful of clothes. But when a man has to do it, it's a tragedy."

"That's so," agreed Sophy. "When a girl gets shabby, and her clothes begin t' look tacky she can take a gore or so out of her skirt where it's the most wore, and catch it in at the bottom, and call it a hobble. An' when her waist gets too soiled she can cover up the front of it with a jabot, an' if her face is pretty enough she can carry it off that way. But when a man is seedy, he's seedy. He can't sew no ruffles on his pants."

"I ran short last week," continued Louie. "That is, shorter than usual. I hadn't the fifty cents to give to the woman. You ought to see her! A little, gray-faced thing, with wisps of hair, and no chest to speak of, and one of those mashed-looking black hats. Nobody could have the nerve to ask her to wait for her money. So I did my own washing. I haven't learned to wear soiled clothes yet. I laughed fit to bust while I was doing it. But—I'll bet my mother dreamed of me that night. The way they do, you know, when something's gone wrong."

Sophy, perched on the third rung of the sliding ladder, was gazing at him. Her lips were parted slightly, and her cheeks were very pink. On her face was a new, strange look, as of something half forgotten. It was as though the spirit of Sophy-as-she-might-have-been were inhabiting her soul for a brief moment. At Louie's next words the look was gone.

"Can't you sew something—a lace yoke—or whatever you call 'em—in that dress?" he persisted.

"Aw, fade!" jeered Sophy. "When a girl's only got one dress it's got to have some tong to it. Maybe this gown would cause a wave of indignation in Oskaloosa, Iowa, but it don't even make a ripple on State Street. It takes more than an aggravated Dutch neck to make a fellow look at a girl these days. In a town like this a girl's got to make a showin' some way. I'm my own stage manager. They look at my dress first, an' grin. See? An' then they look at my face. I'm like the girl in the story. Muh face is muh fortune. It's earned me many a square meal; an' lemme tell you, Pink Cheeks, eatin' square meals is one of my favorite pastimes."

"Say looka here!" bellowed the boss, wrathfully. "Just cut out this here Romeo and Juliet act, will you! That there ladder ain't for no balcony scene, understand. Here you, Louie, you shinny up there and get down a pair of them brown satin pumps, small size."

Sophy continued to wear the black dress. The V-cut neck seemed more flaunting than ever.

It was two weeks later that Louie came in from lunch, his face radiant. He was fifteen minutes late, but he listened to the boss's ravings with a smile.

"You grin like somebody handed you a ten-case note," commented Sophy, with a woman's curiosity. "I guess you must of met some rube from home when you was out t' lunch."

"Better than that! Who do you think I bumped right into in the elevator going down?"

"Well, Brothah Bones," mimicked Sophy, "who did you meet in the elevator going down?"

"I met a man named Ames. He used to travel for a big Boston shoe house, and he made our town every few months. We got to be good friends. I took him home for Sunday dinner once, and he said it was the best dinner he'd had in months. You know how tired those traveling men get of hotel grub."

"Cut out the description and get down to action," snapped Sophy.

"Well, he knew me right away. And he made me go out to lunch with him. A real lunch, starting with soup. Gee! It went big. He asked me what I was doing. I told him I was working here, and he opened his eyes, and then he laughed and said: 'How did you get into that joint?' Then he took me down to a swell little shoe shop on State Street, and it turned out that he owns it. He introduced me all around, and I'm going there to work next week. And wages! Why say, it's almost a salary. A fellow can hold his head up in a place like that."

"When you leavin'?" asked Sophy, slowly.

"Monday. Gee! it seems a year away."

Sophy was late Saturday morning. When she came in, hurriedly, her cheeks were scarlet and her eyes glowed. She took off her hat and coat and fell to straightening boxes and putting out stock without looking up. She took no part in the talk and jest that was going on among the other clerks. One of the men, in search of the missing mate to the shoe in his hand, came over to her, greeting her carelessly. Then he stared.

"Well, what do you know about this!" he called out to the others, and laughed coarsely, "Look, stop, listen! Little Sophy Bright Eyes here has pulled down the shades."

Louie turned quickly. The immodest V of Sophy's gown was filled with a black lace yoke that came up to the very lobes of her little pink ears. She had got some scraps of lace from—Where do they get those bits of rusty black? From some basement bargain counter, perhaps, raked over during the lunch hour. There were nine pieces in the front, and seven in the back. She had sat up half the night putting them together so that when completed they looked like one, if you didn't come too close. There is a certain strain of Indian patience and ingenuity in women that no man has ever been able to understand.

Louie looked up and saw. His eyes met Sophy's. In his there crept a certain exultant gleam, as of one who had fought for something great and won. Sophy saw the look. The shy questioning in her eyes was replaced by a spark of defiance. She tossed her head, and turned to the man who had called attention to her costume.

"Who's loony now?" she jeered. "I always put in a yoke when it gets along toward fall. My lungs is delicate. And anyway, I see by the papers yesterday that collarless gowns is slightly passed for winter."

A BUSH LEAGUE HERO

This is not a baseball story. The grandstand does not rise as one man and shout itself hoarse with joy. There isn't a three-bagger in the entire three thousand words, and nobody is carried home on the shoulders of the crowd. For that sort of thing you need not squander fifteen cents on your favorite magazine. The modest sum of one cent will make you the possessor of a Pink 'Un. There you will find the season's games handled in masterly fashion by a six-best-seller artist, an expert mathematician, and an original-slang humorist. No mere short story dub may hope to compete with these.

In the old days, before the gentry of the ring had learned the wisdom of investing their winnings in solids instead of liquids, this used to be a favorite conundrum: When is a prize-fighter not a prize-fighter?

Chorus: When he is tending bar.

I rise to ask you Brothah Fan, when is a ball player not a ball player? Above the storm of facetious replies I shout the answer:

When he's a shoe clerk.

Any man who can look handsome in a dirty baseball suit is an Adonis. There is something about the baggy pants, and the Micawber-shaped collar, and the skull-fitting cap, and the foot or so of tan, or blue, or pink undershirt sleeve sticking out at the arms, that just naturally kills a man's best points. Then too, a baseball suit requires so much in the matter of leg. Therefore, when I say that Rudie Schlachweiler was a dream even in his baseball uniform, with a dirty brown streak right up the side of his pants where he had slid for base, you may know that the girls camped on the grounds during the season.

During the summer months our ball park is to us what the Grand Prix is to Paris, or Ascot is to London. What care we that Evers gets seven thousand a year (or is it a month?); or that Chicago's new South-side ball park seats thirty-five thousand (or is it million?). Of what interest are such meager items compared with the knowledge that "Pug" Coulan, who plays short, goes with Undine Meyers, the girl up there in the eighth row, with the pink dress and the red roses on her hat? When "Pug" snatches a high one out of the firmament we yell with delight, and even as we yell we turn sideways to look up and see how Undine is taking it. Undine's shining eyes are fixed on "Pug," and he knows it, stoops to brush the dust off his dirt-begrimed baseball pants, takes an attitude of careless grace and misses the next play.

Our grand-stand seats almost two thousand, counting the boxes. But only the snobs, and the girls with new hats, sit in the boxes. Box seats are comfortable, it is true, and they cost only an additional ten cents, but we have come to consider them undemocratic, and unworthy of true fans. Mrs. Freddy Van Dyne, who spends her winters in Egypt and her summers at the ball park, comes out to the game every afternoon in her automobile, but she never occupies a box seat; so why should we? She perches up in the grand-stand with the rest of the enthusiasts, and when Kelly puts one over she stands up and clinches her fists, and waves her arms and shouts with the best of 'em. She has even been known to cry, "Good eye! Good eye!" when things were at fever heat. The only really blase individual in the ball park is Willie Grimes, who peddles ice-cream cones. For that matter, I once saw Willie turn a languid head to pipe, in his thin voice, "Give 'em a dark one, Dutch! Give 'em a dark one!"

Well, that will do for the firsh dash of local color. Now for the story.

Ivy Keller came home June nineteenth from Miss Shont's select school for young ladies. By June twenty-first she was bored limp. You could hardly see the plaits of her white tailored shirtwaist for fraternity pins and secret society emblems, and her bedroom was ablaze with college banners and pennants to such an extent that the maid gave notice every Thursday—which was upstairs cleaning day.

For two weeks after her return Ivy spent most of her time writing letters and waiting for them, and reading the classics on the front porch, dressed in a middy blouse and a blue skirt, with her hair done in a curly Greek effect like the girls on the covers of the Ladies' Magazine. She posed against the canvas bosom of the porch chair with one foot under her, the other swinging free, showing a tempting thing in beaded slipper, silk stocking, and what the story writers call "slim ankle."

On the second Saturday after her return her father came home for dinner at noon, found her deep in Volume Two of "Les Miserables."

"Whew! This is a scorcher!" he exclaimed, and dropped down on a wicker chair next to Ivy. Ivy looked at her father with languid interest, and smiled a daughterly smile. Ivy's father was an insurance man, alderman of his ward, president of the Civic Improvement club, member of five lodges, and an habitual delegate. It generally was he who introduced distinguished guests who spoke at the opera house on Decoration Day. He called Mrs. Keller "Mother," and he wasn't above noticing the fit of a gown on a pretty feminine figure. He thought Ivy was an expurgated edition of Lillian Russell, Madame De Stael, and Mrs. Pankburst.

"Aren't you feeling well, Ivy?" he asked. "Looking a little pale. It's the heat, I suppose. Gosh! Something smells good. Run in and tell Mother I'm here."

Ivy kept one slender finger between the leaves of her book. "I'm perfectly well," she replied. "That must be beefsteak and onions. Ugh!" And she shuddered, and went indoors.

Dad Keller looked after her thoughtfully. Then he went in, washed his hands, and sat down at table with Ivy and her mother.

"Just a sliver for me," said Ivy, "and no onions."

Her father put down his knife and fork, cleared his throat, and spake, thus:

"You get on your hat and meet me at the 2:45 inter-urban. You're going to the ball game with me."

"Ball game!" repeated Ivy. "I? But I'd——"

"Yes, you do," interrupted her father. "You've been moping around here looking a cross between Saint Cecilia and Little Eva long enough. I don't care if you don't know a spitball from a fadeaway when you see it. You'll be out in the air all afternoon, and there'll be some excitement. All the girls go. You'll like it. They're playing Marshalltown."

Ivy went, looking the sacrificial lamb. Five minutes after the game was called she pointed one tapering white finger in the direction of the pitcher's mound.

"Who's that?" she asked.

"Pitcher," explained Papa Keller, laconically. Then, patiently: "He throws the ball."

"Oh," said Ivy. "What did you say his name was?"

"I didn't say. But it's Rudie Schlachweiler. The boys call him Dutch. Kind of a pet, Dutch is."

"Rudie Schlachweiler!" murmured Ivy, dreamily. "What a strong name!"

"Want some peanuts?" inquired her father.

"Does one eat peanuts at a ball game?"

"It ain't hardly legal if you don't," Pa Keller assured her.

"Two sacks," said Ivy. "Papa, why do they call it a diamond, and what are those brown bags at the corners, and what does it count if you hit the ball, and why do they rub their hands in the dust and then—er—spit on them, and what salary does a pitcher get, and why does the red-haired man on the other side dance around like that between the second and third brown bag, and doesn't a pitcher do anything but pitch, and wh——?"

"You're on," said papa.

After that Ivy didn't miss a game during all the time that the team played in the home town. She went without a new hat, and didn't care whether Jean Valjean got away with the goods or not, and forgot whether you played third hand high or low in bridge. She even became chummy with Undine Meyers, who wasn't her kind of a girl at all. Undine was thin in a voluptuous kind of way, if such a paradox can be, and she had red lips, and a roving eye, and she ran around downtown without a hat more than was strictly necessary. But Undine and Ivy had two subjects in common. They were baseball and love. It is queer how the limelight will make heroes of us all.

Now "Pug" Coulan, who was red-haired, and had shoulders like an ox, and arms that hung down to his knees, like those of an orang-outang, slaughtered beeves at the Chicago stockyards in winter. In the summer he slaughtered hearts. He wore mustard colored shirts that matched his hair, and his baseball stockings generally had a rip in them somewhere, but when he was on the diamond we were almost ashamed to look at Undine, so wholly did her heart shine in her eyes.

Now, we'll have just another dash or two of local color. In a small town the chances for hero worship are few. If it weren't for the traveling men our girls wouldn't know whether stripes or checks were the thing in gents' suitings. When the baseball season opened the girls swarmed on it. Those that didn't understand baseball pretended they did. When the team was out of town our form of greeting was changed from, "Good-morning!" or "Howdy-do!" to "What's the score?" Every night the results of the games throughout the league were posted up on the blackboard in front of Schlager's hardware store, and to see the way in which the crowd stood around it, and streamed across the street toward it, you'd have thought they were giving away gas stoves and hammock couches.

Going home in the street car after the game the girls used to gaze adoringly at the dirty faces of their sweat-begrimed heroes, and then they'd rush home, have supper, change their dresses, do their hair, and rush downtown past the Parker Hotel to mail their letters. The baseball boys boarded over at the Griggs House, which is third-class, but they used their tooth-picks, and held the postmortem of the day's game out in front of the Parker Hotel, which is our leading hostelry. The postoffice receipts record for our town was broken during the months of June, July, and August.

Mrs. Freddy Van Dyne started the trouble by having the team over to dinner, "Pug" Coulan and all. After all, why not? No foreign and impecunious princes penetrate as far inland as our town. They get only as far as New York, or Newport, where they are gobbled up by many-moneyed matrons. If Mrs. Freddy Van Dyne found the supply of available lions limited, why should she not try to content herself with a jackal or so?

Ivy was asked. Until then she had contented herself with gazing at her hero. She had become such a hardened baseball fan that she followed the game with a score card, accurately jotting down every play, and keeping her watch open on her knee.

She sat next to Rudie at dinner. Before she had nibbled her second salted almond, Ivy Keller and Rudie Schlachweiler understood each other. Rudie illustrated certain plays by drawing lines on the table-cloth with his knife and Ivy gazed, wide-eyed, and allowed her soup to grow cold.

The first night that Rudie called, Pa Keller thought it a great joke. He sat out on the porch with Rudie and Ivy and talked baseball, and got up to show Rudie how he could have got the goat of that Keokuk catcher if only he had tried one of his famous open-faced throws. Rudie looked politely interested, and laughed in all the right places. But Ivy didn't need to pretend. Rudie Schlachweiler spelled baseball to her. She did not think of her caller as a good-looking young man in a blue serge suit and a white shirtwaist. Even as he sat there she saw him as a blonde god standing on the pitcher's mound, with the scars of battle on his baseball pants, his left foot placed in front of him at right angles with his right foot, his gaze fixed on first base in a cunning effort to deceive the man at bat, in that favorite attitude of pitchers just before they get ready to swing their left leg and h'ist one over.

The second time that Rudie called, Ma Keller said:

"Ivy, I don't like that ball player coming here to see you. The neighbors'll talk."

The third time Rudie called, Pa Keller said: "What's that guy doing here again?"

The fourth time Rudie called, Pa Keller and Ma Keller said, in unison: "This thing has got to stop."

But it didn't. It had had too good a start. For the rest of the season Ivy met her knight of the sphere around the corner. Theirs was a walking courtship. They used to roam up as far as the State road, and down as far as the river, and Rudie would fain have talked of love, but Ivy talked of baseball.

"Darling," Rudie would murmur, pressing Ivy's arm closer, "when did you first begin to care?"

"Why I liked the very first game I saw when Dad——"

"I mean, when did you first begin to care for me?"

"Oh! When you put three men out in that game with Marshalltown when the teams were tied in the eighth inning. Remember? Say, Rudie dear, what was the matter with your arm to-day? You let three men walk, and Albia's weakest hitter got a home run out of you."

"Oh, forget baseball for a minute, Ivy! Let's talk about something else. Let's talk about—us."

"Us? Well, you're baseball, aren't you?" retorted Ivy. "And if you are, I am. Did you notice the way that Ottumwa man pitched yesterday? He didn't do any acting for the grandstand. He didn't reach up above his head, and wrap his right shoulder with his left toe, and swing his arm three times and then throw seven inches outside the plate. He just took the ball in his hand, looked at it curiously for a moment, and fired it—zing!—like that, over the plate. I'd get that ball if I were you."

"Isn't this a grand night?" murmured Rudie.

"But they didn't have a hitter in the bunch," went on Ivy. "And not a man in the team could run. That's why they're tail-enders. Just the same, that man on the mound was a wizard, and if he had one decent player to give him some support——"

Well, the thing came to a climax. One evening, two weeks before the close of the season, Ivy put on her hat and announced that she was going downtown to mail her letters.

"Mail your letters in the daytime," growled Papa Keller.

"I didn't have time to-day," answered Ivy. "It was a thirteen inning game, and it lasted until six o'clock."

It was then that Papa Keller banged the heavy fist of decision down on the library table.

"This thing's got to stop!" he thundered. "I won't have any girl of mine running the streets with a ball player, understand? Now you quit seeing this seventy-five-dollars-a-month bush leaguer or leave this house. I mean it."

"All right," said Ivy, with a white-hot calm. "I'll leave. I can make the grandest kind of angel-food with marshmallow icing, and you know yourself my fudges can't be equaled. He'll be playing in the major leagues in three years. Why just yesterday there was a strange man at the game—a city man, you could tell by his hat-band, and the way his clothes were cut. He stayed through the whole game, and never took his eyes off Rudie. I just know he was a scout for the Cubs."

"Probably a hardware drummer, or a fellow that Schlachweiler owes money to."

Ivy began to pin on her hat. A scared look leaped into Papa Keller's eyes. He looked a little old, too, and drawn, at that minute. He stretched forth a rather tremulous hand.

"Ivy-girl," he said.

"What?" snapped Ivy.

"Your old father's just talking for your own good. You're breaking your ma's heart. You and me have been good pals, haven't we?"

"Yes," said Ivy, grudgingly, and without looking up.

"Well now, look here. I've got a proposition to make to you. The season's over in two more weeks. The last week they play out of town. Then the boys'll come back for a week or so, just to hang around town and try to get used to the idea of leaving us. Then they'll scatter to take up their winter jobs-cutting ice, most of 'em," he added, grimly.

"Mr. Schlachweiler is employed in a large establishment in Slatersville, Ohio," said Ivy, with dignity. "He regards baseball as his profession, and he cannot do anything that would affect his pitching arm."

Pa Keller put on the tremolo stop and brought a misty look into his eyes.

"Ivy, you'll do one last thing for your old father, won't you?"

"Maybe," answered Ivy, coolly.

"Don't make that fellow any promises. Now wait a minute! Let me get through. I won't put any crimp in your plans. I won't speak to Schlachweiler. Promise you won't do anything rash until the ball season's over. Then we'll wait just one month, see? Till along about November. Then if you feel like you want to see him——"

"But how——"

"Hold on. You mustn't write to him, or see him, or let him write to you during that time, see? Then, if you feel the way you do now, I'll take you to Slatersville to see him. Now that's fair, ain't it? Only don't let him know you're coming."

"M-m-m-yes," said Ivy.

"Shake hands on it." She did. Then she left the room with a rush, headed in the direction of her own bedroom. Pa Keller treated himself to a prodigious wink and went out to the vegetable garden in search of Mother.

The team went out on the road, lost five games, won two, and came home in fourth place. For a week they lounged around the Parker Hotel and held up the street corners downtown, took many farewell drinks, then, slowly, by ones and twos, they left for the packing houses, freight depots, and gents' furnishing stores from whence they came.

October came in with a blaze of sumac and oak leaves. Ivy stayed home and learned to make veal loaf and apple pies. The worry lines around Pa Keller's face began to deepen. Ivy said that she didn't believe that she cared to go back to Miss Shont's select school for young ladies.

October thirty-first came.

"We'll take the eight-fifteen to-morrow," said her father to Ivy.

"All right," said Ivy.

"Do you know where he works?" asked he.

"No," answered Ivy.

"That'll be all right. I took the trouble to look him up last August."

The short November afternoon was drawing to its close (as our best talent would put it) when Ivy and her father walked along the streets of Slatersville. (I can't tell you what streets, because I don't know.) Pa Keller brought up before a narrow little shoe shop.

"Here we are," he said, and ushered Ivy in. A short, stout, proprietary figure approached them smiling a mercantile smile.

"What can I do for you?" he inquired.

Ivy's eyes searched the shop for a tall, golden-haired form in a soiled baseball suit.

"We'd like to see a gentleman named Schlachweiler—Rudolph Schlachweiler," said Pa Keller.

"Anything very special?" inquired the proprietor. "He's—rather busy just now. Wouldn't anybody else do? Of course, if——"

"No," growled Keller.

The boss turned. "Hi! Schlachweiler!" he bawled toward the rear of the dim little shop.

"Yessir," answered a muffled voice.

"Front!" yelled the boss, and withdrew to a safe listening distance.

A vaguely troubled look lurked in the depths of Ivy's eyes. From behind the partition of the rear of the shop emerged a tall figure. It was none other than our hero. He was in his shirt-sleeves, and he struggled into his coat as he came forward, wiping his mouth with the back of his hand, hurriedly, and swallowing.

I have said that the shop was dim. Ivy and her father stood at one side, their backs to the light. Rudie came forward, rubbing his hands together in the manner of clerks.

"Something in shoes?" he politely inquired. Then he saw.

"Ivy!—ah—Miss Keller!" he exclaimed. Then, awkwardly: "Well, how-do, Mr. Keller. I certainly am glad to see you both. How's the old town? What are you doing in Slatersville?"

"Why—Ivy——" began Pa Keller, blunderingly.

But Ivy clutched his arm with a warning hand. The vaguely troubled look in her eyes had become wildly so.

"Schlachweiler!" shouted the voice of the boss. "Customers!" and he waved a hand in the direction of the fitting benches.

"All right, sir," answered Rudie. "Just a minute."

"Dad had to come on business," said Ivy, hurriedly. "And he brought me with him. I'm—I'm on my way to school in Cleveland, you know. Awfully glad to have seen you again. We must go. That lady wants her shoes, I'm sure, and your employer is glaring at us. Come, dad."

At the door she turned just in time to see Rudie removing the shoe from the pudgy foot of the fat lady customer.

We'll take a jump of six months. That brings us into the lap of April.

Pa Keller looked up from his evening paper. Ivy, home for the Easter vacation, was at the piano. Ma Keller was sewing.

Pa Keller cleared his throat. "I see by the paper," he announced, "that Schlachweiler's been sold to Des Moines. Too bad we lost him. He was a great little pitcher, but he played in bad luck. Whenever he was on the slab the boys seemed to give him poor support."

"Fudge!" exclaimed Ivy, continuing to play, but turning a spirited face toward her father. "What piffle! Whenever a player pitches rotten ball you'll always hear him howling about the support he didn't get. Schlachweiler was a bum pitcher. Anybody could hit him with a willow wand, on a windy day, with the sun in his eyes."

V
THE KITCHEN SIDE OF THE DOOR

The City was celebrating New Year's Eve. Spelled thus, with a capital C, know it can mean but New York. In the Pink Fountain room of the Newest Hotel all those grand old forms and customs handed down to us for the occasion were being rigidly observed in all their original quaintness. The Van Dyked man who looked like a Russian Grand Duke (he really was a chiropodist) had drunk champagne out of the pink satin slipper of the lady who behaved like an actress (she was forelady at Schmaus' Wholesale Millinery, eighth floor). The two respectable married ladies there in the corner had been kissed by each other's husbands. The slim, Puritan-faced woman in white, with her black hair so demurely parted and coiled in a sleek knot, had risen suddenly from her place and walked indolently to the edge of the plashing pink fountain in the center of the room, had stood contemplating its shallows with a dreamy half-smile on her lips, and then had lifted her slim legs slowly and gracefully over its fern-fringed basin and had waded into its chilling midst, trailing her exquisite white satin and chiffon draperies after her, and scaring the goldfish into fits. The loudest scream of approbation had come from the yellow-haired, loose-lipped youth who had made the wager, and lost it. The heavy blonde in the inevitable violet draperies showed signs of wanting to dance on the table. Her companion—a structure made up of layer upon layer, and fold upon fold of flabby tissue—knew all the waiters by their right names, and insisted on singing with the orchestra and beating time with a rye roll. The clatter of dishes was giving way to the clink of glasses.

In the big, bright kitchen back, of the Pink Fountain room Miss Gussie Fink sat at her desk, calm, watchful, insolent-eyed, a goddess sitting in judgment. On the pay roll of the Newest Hotel Miss Gussie Fink's name appeared as kitchen checker, but her regular job was goddessing. Her altar was a high desk in a corner of the busy kitchen, and it was an altar of incense, of burnt-offerings, and of showbread. Inexorable as a goddess of the ancients was Miss Fink, and ten times as difficult to appease. For this is the rule of the Newest Hotel, that no waiter may carry his laden tray restaurantward until its contents have been viewed and duly checked by the eye and hand of Miss Gussie Fink, or her assistants. Flat upon the table must go every tray, off must go each silver dish-cover, lifted must be each napkin to disclose its treasure of steaming corn or hot rolls. Clouds of incense rose before Miss Gussie Fink and she sniffed it unmoved, her eyes, beneath level brows, regarding savory broiler or cunning ice with equal indifference, appraising alike lobster cocktail or onion soup, traveling from blue points to brie. Things a la and things glace were all one to her. Gazing at food was Miss Gussie Fink's occupation, and just to see the way she regarded a boneless squab made you certain that she never ate.

In spite of the I-don't-know-how-many (see ads) New Year's Eve diners for whom food was provided that night, the big, busy kitchen was the most orderly, shining, spotless place imaginable. But Miss Gussie Fink was the neatest, most immaculate object in all that great, clean room. There was that about her which suggested daisies in a field, if you know what I mean. This may have been due to the fact that her eyes were brown while her hair was gold, or it may have been something about the way her collars fitted high, and tight, and smooth, or the way her close white sleeves came down to meet her pretty hands, or the way her shining hair sprang from her forehead. Also the smooth creaminess of her clear skin may have had something to do with it. But privately, I think it was due to the way she wore her shirtwaists. Miss Gussie Fink could wear a starched white shirtwaist under a close-fitting winter coat, remove the coat, run her right forefinger along her collar's edge and her left thumb along the back of her belt and disclose to the admiring world a blouse as unwrinkled and unsullied as though it had just come from her own skilful hands at the ironing board. Miss Gussie Fink was so innately, flagrantly, beautifully clean-looking that—well, there must be a stop to this description.

She was the kind of girl you'd like to see behind the counter of your favorite delicatessen, knowing that you need not shudder as her fingers touch your Sunday night supper slices of tongue, and Swiss cheese, and ham. No girl had ever dreamed of refusing to allow Gussie to borrow her chamois for a second.

To-night Miss Fink had come on at 10 P.M., which was just two hours later than usual. She knew that she was to work until 6 A.M., which may have accounted for the fact that she displayed very little of what the fans call ginger as she removed her hat and coat and hung them on the hook behind the desk. The prospect of that all-night, eight-hour stretch may have accounted for it, I say. But privately, and entre nous, it didn't. For here you must know of Heiny. Heiny, alas! now Henri.

Until two weeks ago Henri had been Heiny and Miss Fink had been Kid. When Henri had been Heiny he had worked in the kitchen at many things, but always with a loving eye on Miss Gussie Fink. Then one wild night there had been a waiters' strike—wages or hours or tips or all three. In the confusion that followed Heiny had been pressed into service and a chopped coat. He had fitted into both with unbelievable nicety, proving that waiters are born, not made. Those little tricks and foibles that are characteristic of the genus waiter seemed to envelop him as though a fairy garment had fallen upon his shoulders. The folded napkin under his left arm seemed to have been placed there by nature, so perfectly did it fit into place. The ghostly tread, the little whisking skip, the half-simper, the deferential bend that had in it at the same time something of insolence, all were there; the very "Yes, miss," and "Very good, sir," rose automatically and correctly to his untrained lips. Cinderella rising resplendent from her ash-strewn hearth was not more completely transformed than Heiny in his role of Henri. And with the transformation Miss Gussie Fink had been left behind her desk disconsolate.

Kitchens are as quick to seize upon these things and gossip about them as drawing rooms are. And because Miss Gussie Fink had always worn a little air of aloofness to all except Heiny, the kitchen was the more eager to make the most of its morsel. Each turned it over under his tongue—Tony, the Crook, whom Miss Fink had scorned; Francois, the entree cook, who often forgot he was married; Miss Sweeney, the bar-checker, who was jealous of Miss Fink's complexion. Miss Fink heard, and said nothing. She only knew that there would be no dear figure waiting for her when the night's work was done. For two weeks now she had put on her hat and coat and gone her way at one o'clock alone. She discovered that to be taken home night after night under Heiny's tender escort had taught her a ridiculous terror of the streets at night now that she was without protection. Always the short walk from the car to the flat where Miss Fink lived with her mother had been a glorious, star-lit, all too brief moment. Now it was an endless and terrifying trial, a thing of shivers and dread, fraught with horror of passing the alley just back of Cassidey's buffet. There had even been certain little half-serious, half-jesting talks about the future into which there had entered the subject of a little delicatessen and restaurant in a desirable neighborhood, with Heiny in the kitchen, and a certain blonde, neat, white-shirtwaisted person in charge of the desk and front shop.

She and her mother had always gone through a little formula upon Miss Fink's return from work. They never used it now. Gussie's mother was a real mother—the kind that wakes up when you come home.

"That you, Gussie?" Ma Fink would call from the bedroom, at the sound of the key in the lock.

"It's me, ma."

"Heiny bring you home?"

"Sure," happily.

"There's a bit of sausage left, and some pie if——"

"Oh, I ain't hungry. We stopped at Joey's downtown and had a cup of coffee and a ham on rye. Did you remember to put out the milk bottle?"

For two weeks there had been none of that. Gussie had learned to creep silently into bed, and her mother, being a mother, feigned sleep.

To-night at her desk Miss Gussie Fink seemed a shade cooler, more self-contained, and daisylike than ever. From somewhere at the back of her head she could see that Heiny was avoiding her desk and was using the services of the checker at the other end of the room. And even as the poison of this was eating into her heart she was tapping her forefinger imperatively on the desk before her and saying to Tony, the Crook:

"Down on the table with that tray, Tony—flat. This may be a busy little New Year's Eve, but you can't come any of your sleight-of-hand stuff on me." For Tony had a little trick of concealing a dollar-and-a-quarter sirloin by the simple method of slapping the platter close to the underside of his tray and holding it there with long, lean fingers outspread, the entire bit of knavery being concealed in the folds of a flowing white napkin in the hand that balanced the tray. Into Tony's eyes there came a baleful gleam. His lean jaw jutted out threateningly.

"You're the real Weissenheimer kid, ain't you?" he sneered. "Never mind. I'll get you at recess."

"Some day," drawled Miss Fink, checking the steak, "the house'll get wise to your stuff and then you'll have to go back to the coal wagon. I know so much about you it's beginning to make me uncomfortable. I hate to carry around a burden of crime."

"You're a sorehead because Heiny turned you down and now——"

"Move on there!" snapped Miss Fink, "or I'll call the steward to settle you. Maybe he'd be interested to know that you've been counting in the date and your waiter's number, and adding 'em in at the bottom of your check."

Tony, the Crook, turned and skimmed away toward the dining-room, but the taste of victory was bitter in Miss Fink's mouth.

Midnight struck. There came from the direction of the Pink Fountain Room a clamor and din which penetrated the thickness of the padded doors that separated the dining-room from the kitchen beyond. The sound rose and swelled above the blare of the orchestra. Chairs scraped on the marble floor as hundreds rose to their feet. The sound of clinking glasses became as the jangling of a hundred bells. There came the sharp spat of hand-clapping, then cheers, yells, huzzas. Through the swinging doors at the end of the long passageway Miss Fink could catch glimpses of dazzling color, of shimmering gowns, of bare arms uplifted, of flowers, and plumes, and jewels, with the rosy light of the famed pink fountain casting a gracious glow over all. Once she saw a tall young fellow throw his arm about the shoulder of a glorious creature at the next table, and though the door swung shut before she could see it, Miss Fink knew that he had kissed her.

There were no New Year's greetings in the kitchen back of the Pink Fountain Room. It was the busiest moment in all that busy night. The heat of the ovens was so intense that it could be felt as far as Miss Fink's remote corner. The swinging doors between dining-room and kitchen were never still. A steady stream of waiters made for the steam tables before which the white-clad chefs stood ladling, carving, basting, serving, gave their orders, received them, stopped at the checking-desk, and sped dining-roomward again. Tony, the Crook, was cursing at one of the little Polish vegetable girls who had not been quick enough about the garnishing of a salad, and she was saying, over and over again, in her thick tongue:

"Aw, shod op yur mout'!"

The thud-thud of Miss Fink's checking-stamp kept time to flying footsteps, but even as her practised eye swept over the tray before her she saw the steward direct Henri toward her desk, just as he was about to head in the direction of the minor checking-desk. Beneath downcast lids she saw him coming. There was about Henri to-night a certain radiance, a sort of electrical elasticity, so nimble, so tireless, so exuberant was he. In the eyes of Miss Gussie Fink he looked heartbreakingly handsome in his waiter's uniform—handsome, distinguished, remote, and infinitely desirable. And just behind him, revenge in his eye, came Tony.

The flat surface of the desk received Henri's tray. Miss Fink regarded it with a cold and business-like stare. Henri whipped his napkin from under his left arm and began to remove covers, dexterously. Off came the first silver, dome-shaped top.

"Guinea hen," said Henri.

"I seen her lookin' at you when you served the little necks," came from Tony, as though continuing a conversation begun in some past moment of pause, "and she's some lovely doll, believe me."

Miss Fink scanned the guinea hen thoroughly, but with a detached air, and selected the proper stamp from the box at her elbow. Thump! On the broad pasteboard sheet before her appeared the figures $1.75 after Henri's number.

"Think so?" grinned Henri, and removed another cover. "One candied sweets."

"I bet some day we'll see you in the Sunday papers, Heiny," went on Tony, "with a piece about handsome waiter runnin' away with beautiful s'ciety girl. Say; you're too perfect even for a waiter."

Thump! Thirty cents.

"Quit your kiddin'," said the flattered Henri. "One endive, French dressing."

Thump! "Next!" said Miss Fink, dispassionately, yawned, and smiled fleetingly at the entree cook who wasn't looking her way. Then, as Tony slid his tray toward her: "How's business, Tony? H'm? How many two-bit cigar bands have you slipped onto your own private collection of nickel straights and made a twenty-cent rake-off?"

But there was a mist in the bright brown eyes as Tony the Crook turned away with his tray. In spite of the satisfaction of having had the last word, Miss Fink knew in her heart that Tony had "got her at recess," as he had said he would.

Things were slowing up for Miss Fink. The stream of hurrying waiters was turned in the direction of the kitchen bar now. From now on the eating would be light, and the drinking heavy. Miss Fink, with time hanging heavy, found herself blinking down at the figures stamped on the pasteboard sheet before her, and in spite of the blinking, two marks that never were intended for a checker's report splashed down just over the $1.75 after Henri's number. A lovely doll! And she had gazed at Heiny. Well, that was to be expected. No woman could gaze unmoved upon Heiny. "A lovely doll—"

"Hi, Miss Fink!" it was the steward's voice. "We need you over in the bar to help Miss Sweeney check the drinks. They're coming too swift for her. The eating will be light from now on; just a little something salty now and then."

So Miss Fink dabbed covertly at her eyes and betook herself out of the atmosphere of roasting, and broiling, and frying, and stewing; away from the sight of great copper kettles, and glowing coals and hissing pans, into a little world fragrant with mint, breathing of orange and lemon peel, perfumed with pineapple, redolent of cinnamon and clove, reeking with things spirituous. Here the splutter of the broiler was replaced by the hiss of the siphon, and the pop-pop of corks, and the tinkle and clink of ice against glass.

"Hello, dearie!" cooed Miss Sweeney, in greeting, staring hard at the suspicious redness around Miss Fink's eyelids. "Ain't you sweet to come over here in the headache department and help me out! Here's the wine list. You'll prob'ly need it. Say, who do you suppose invented New Year's Eve? They must of had a imagination like a Greek 'bus boy. I'm limp as a rag now, and it's only two-thirty. I've got a regular cramp in my wrist from checkin' quarts. Say, did you hear about Heiny's crowd?"

"No," said Miss Fink, evenly, and began to study the first page of the wine list under the heading "Champagnes of Noted Vintages."

"Well," went on Miss Sweeney's little thin, malicious voice, "he's fell in soft. There's a table of three, and they're drinkin' 1874 Imperial Crown at twelve dollars per, like it was Waukesha ale. And every time they finish a bottle one of the guys pays for it with a brand new ten and a brand new five and tells Heiny to keep the change. Can you beat it?"

"I hope," said Miss Fink, pleasantly, "that the supply of 1874 will hold out till morning. I'd hate to see them have to come down to ten dollar wine. Here you, Tony! Come back here! I may be a new hand in this department but I'm not so green that you can put a gold label over on me as a yellow label. Notice that I'm checking you another fifty cents."

"Ain't he the grafter!" laughed Miss Sweeney. She leaned toward Miss Fink and lowered her voice discreetly. "Though I'll say this for'm. If you let him get away with it now an' then, he'll split even with you. H'm? O, well, now, don't get so high and mighty. The management expects it in this department. That's why they pay starvation wages."

An unusual note of color crept into Miss Gussie Fink's smooth cheek. It deepened and glowed as Heiny darted around the corner and up to the bar. There was about him an air of suppressed excitement—suppressed, because Heiny was too perfect a waiter to display emotion.

"Not another!" chanted the bartenders, in chorus.

"Yes," answered Henri, solemnly, and waited while the wine cellar was made to relinquish another rare jewel.

"O, you Heiny!" called Miss Sweeney, "tell us what she looks like. If I had time I'd take a peek myself. From what Tony says she must look something like Maxine Elliot, only brighter."

Henri turned. He saw Miss Fink. A curious little expression came into his eyes—a Heiny look, it might have been called, as he regarded his erstwhile sweetheart's unruffled attire, and clear skin, and steady eye and glossy hair. She was looking past him in that baffling, maddening way that angry women have. Some of Henri's poise seemed to desert him in that moment. He appeared a shade less debonair as he received the precious bottle from the wine man's hands. He made for Miss Fink's desk and stood watching her while she checked his order. At the door he turned and looked over his shoulder at Miss Sweeney.

"Some time," he said, deliberately, "when there's no ladies around, I'll tell you what I think she looks like."

And the little glow of color in Miss Gussic Fink's smooth cheek became a crimson flood that swept from brow to throat.

"Oh, well," snickered Miss Sweeney, to hide her own discomfiture, "this is little Heiny's first New Year's Eve in the dining-room. Honest, I b'lieve he's shocked. He don't realize that celebratin' New Year's Eve is like eatin' oranges. You got to let go your dignity t' really enjoy 'em."

Three times more did Henri enter and demand a bottle of the famous vintage, and each time he seemed a shade less buoyant. His elation diminished as his tips grew greater until, as he drew up at the bar at six o'clock, he seemed wrapped in impenetrable gloom.

"Them hawgs sousin' yet?" shrilled Miss Sweeney. She and Miss Fink had climbed down from their high stools, and were preparing to leave. Henri nodded, drearily, and disappeared in the direction of the Pink Fountain Room.

Miss Fink walked back to her own desk in the corner near the dining-room door. She took her hat off the hook, and stood regarding it, thoughtfully. Then, with a little air of decision, she turned and walked swiftly down the passageway that separated dining-room from kitchen. Tillie, the scrub-woman, was down on her hands and knees in one corner of the passage. She was one of a small army of cleaners that had begun the work of clearing away the debris of the long night's revel. Miss Fink lifted her neat skirts high as she tip-toed through the little soapy pool that followed in the wake of Tillie, the scrub-woman. She opened the swinging doors a cautious little crack and peered in. What she saw was not pretty. If the words sordid and bacchanalian had been part of Miss Fink's vocabulary they would have risen to her lips then. The crowd had gone. The great room contained not more than half a dozen people. Confetti littered the floor. Here and there a napkin, crushed and bedraggled into an unrecognizable ball, lay under a table. From an overturned bottle the dregs were dripping drearily. The air was stale, stifling, poisonous.

At a little table in the center of the room Henri's three were still drinking. They were doing it in a dreadful and businesslike way. There were two men and one woman. The faces of all three were mahogany colored and expressionless. There was about them an awful sort of stillness. Something in the sight seemed to sicken Gussie Fink. It came to her that the wintry air outdoors must be gloriously sweet, and cool, and clean in contrast to this. She was about to turn away, with a last look at Heiny yawning behind his hand, when suddenly the woman rose unsteadily to her feet, balancing herself with her finger tips on the table. She raised her head and stared across the room with dull, unseeing eyes, and licked her lips with her tongue. Then she turned and walked half a dozen paces, screamed once with horrible shrillness, and crashed to the floor. She lay there in a still, crumpled heap, the folds of her exquisite gown rippling to meet a little stale pool of wine that had splashed from some broken glass. Then this happened. Three people ran toward the woman on the floor, and two people ran past her and out of the room. The two who ran away were the men with whom she had been drinking, and they were not seen again. The three who ran toward her were Henri, the waiter, Miss Gussie Fink, checker, and Tillie, the scrub-woman. Henri and Miss Fink reached her first. Tillie, the scrub-woman, was a close third. Miss Gussie Fink made as though to slip her arm under the poor bruised head, but Henri caught her wrist fiercely (for a waiter) and pulled her to her feet almost roughly.

"You leave her alone, Kid," he commanded.

Miss Gussie Fink stared, indignation choking her utterance. And as she stared the fierce light in Henri's eyes was replaced by the light of tenderness.

"We'll tend to her," said Henri; "she ain't fit for you to touch. I wouldn't let you soil your hands on such truck." And while Gussie still stared he grasped the unconscious woman by the shoulders, while another waiter grasped her ankles, with Tillie, the scrub-woman, arranging her draperies pityingly around her, and together they carried her out of the dining-room to a room beyond.

Back in the kitchen Miss Gussie Fink was preparing to don her hat, but she was experiencing some difficulty because of the way in which her fingers persisted in trembling. Her face was turned away from the swinging doors, but she knew when Henri came in. He stood just behind her, in silence. When she turned to face him she found Henri looking at her, and as he looked all the Heiny in him came to the surface and shone in his eyes. He looked long and silently at Miss Gussie Fink—at the sane, simple, wholesomeness of her, at her clear brown eyes, at her white forehead from which the shining hair sprang away in such a delicate line, at her immaculately white shirtwaist, and her smooth, snug-fitting collar that came up to the lobes of her little pink ears, at her creamy skin, at her trim belt. He looked as one who would rest his eyes—eyes weary of gazing upon satins, and jewels, and rouge, and carmine, and white arms, and bosoms.

"Gee, Kid! You look good to me," he said.

"Do I—Heiny?" whispered Miss Fink.

"Believe me!" replied Heiny, fervently. "It was just a case of swelled head. Forget it, will you? Say, that gang in there to-night—why, say, that gang——"

"I know," interrupted Miss Fink.

"Going home?" asked Heiny.

"Yes."

"Suppose we have a bite of something to eat first," suggested Heiny.

Miss Fink glanced round the great, deserted kitchen. As she gazed a little expression of disgust wrinkled her pretty nose—the nose that perforce had sniffed the scent of so many rare and exquisite dishes.

"Sure," she assented, joyously, "but not here. Let's go around the corner to Joey's. I could get real chummy with a cup of good hot coffee and a ham on rye."

He helped her on with her coat, and if his hands rested a moment on her shoulders who was there to see it? A few sleepy, wan-eyed waiters and Tillie, the scrub-woman. Together they started toward the door. Tillie, the scrubwoman, had worked her wet way out of the passage and into the kitchen proper. She and her pail blocked their way. She was sopping up a soapy pool with an all-encompassing gray scrub-rag. Heiny and Gussie stopped a moment perforce to watch her. It was rather fascinating to see how that artful scrub-rag craftily closed in upon the soapy pool until it engulfed it. Tillie sat back on her knees to wring out the water-soaked rag. There was something pleasing in the sight. Tillie's blue calico was faded white in patches and at the knees it was dark with soapy water. Her shoes were turned up ludicrously at the toes, as scrub-women's shoes always are. Tillie's thin hair was wadded back into a moist knob at the back and skewered with a gray-black hairpin. From her parboiled, shriveled fingers to her ruddy, perspiring face there was nothing of grace or beauty about Tillie. And yet Heiny found something pleasing there. He could not have told you why, so how can I, unless to say that it was, perhaps, for much the same reason that we rejoice in the wholesome, safe, reassuring feel of the gray woolen blanket on our bed when we wake from a horrid dream.

"A Happy New Year to you," said Heiny gravely, and took his hand out of his pocket.

Tillie's moist right hand closed over something. She smiled so that one saw all her broken black teeth.

"The same t' you," said Tillie. "The same t' you."

VI
ONE OF THE OLD GIRLS

All of those ladies who end their conversation with you by wearily suggesting that you go down to the basement to find what you seek, do not receive a meager seven dollars a week as a reward for their efforts. Neither are they all obliged to climb five weary flights of stairs to reach the dismal little court room which is their home, and there are several who need not walk thirty-three blocks to save carfare, only to spend wretched evenings washing out handkerchiefs and stockings in the cracked little washbowl, while one ear is cocked for the stealthy tread of the Lady Who Objects.

The earnest compiler of working girls' budgets would pass Effie Bauer hurriedly by. Effie's budget bulged here and there with such pathetic items as hand-embroidered blouses, thick club steaks, and parquet tickets for Maude Adams. That you may visualize her at once I may say that Effie looked twenty-four—from the rear (all women do in these days of girlish simplicity in hats and tailor-mades); her skirts never sagged, her shirtwaists were marvels of plainness and fit, and her switch had cost her sixteen dollars, wholesale (a lady friend in the business). Oh, there was nothing tragic about Effie. She had a plump, assured style, a keen blue eye, a gift of repartee, and a way of doing her hair so that the gray at the sides scarcely showed at all. Also a knowledge of corsets that had placed her at the buying end of that important department at Spiegel's. Effie knew to the minute when coral beads went out and pearl beads came in, and just by looking at her blouses you could tell when Cluny died and Irish was born. Meeting Effie on the street, you would have put her down as one of the many well-dressed, prosperous-looking women shoppers—if you hadn't looked at her feet. Veteran clerks and policemen cannot disguise their feet.

Effie Bauer's reason for not marrying when a girl was the same as that of most of the capable, wise-eyed, good-looking women one finds at the head of departments. She had not had a chance. If Effie had been as attractive at twenty as she was at—there, we won't betray confidences. Still, it is certain that if Effie had been as attractive when a young girl as she was when an old girl, she never would have been an old girl and head of Spiegel's corset department at a salary of something very comfortably over one hundred and twenty-five a month (and commissions). Effie had improved with the years, and ripened with experience. She knew her value. At twenty she had been pale, anaemic and bony, with a startled-faun manner and bad teeth. Years of saleswomanship had broadened her, mentally and physically, until she possessed a wide and varied knowledge of that great and diversified subject known as human nature. She knew human nature all the way from the fifty-nine-cent girdles to the twenty-five-dollar made-to-orders. And if the years had brought, among other things, a certain hardness about the jaw and a line or two at the corners of the eyes, it was not surprising. You can't rub up against the sharp edges of this world and expect to come out without a scratch or so.

So much for Effie. Enter the hero. Webster defines a hero in romance as the person who has the principal share in the transactions related. He says nothing which would debar a gentleman just because he may be a trifle bald and in the habit of combing his hair over the thin spot, and he raises no objections to a matter of thickness and color in the region of the back of the neck. Therefore Gabe I. Marks qualifies. Gabe was the gentleman about whom Effie permitted herself to be guyed. He came to Chicago on business four times a year, and he always took Effie to the theater, and to supper afterward. On those occasions, Effie's gown, wrap and hat were as correct in texture, lines, and paradise aigrettes as those of any of her non-working sisters about her. On the morning following these excursions into Lobsterdom, Effie would confide to her friend, Miss Weinstein, of the lingeries and negligees:

"I was out with my friend, Mr. Marks, last evening. We went to Rector's after the show. Oh, well, it takes a New Yorker to know how. Honestly, I feel like a queen when I go out with him. H'm? Oh, nothing like that, girlie. I never could see that marriage thing. Just good friends."

Gabe had been coming to Chicago four times a year for six years. Six times four are twenty-four. And one is twenty-five. Gabe's last visit made the twenty-fifth.

"Well, Effie," Gabe said when the evening's entertainment had reached the restaurant stage, "this is our twenty-fifth anniversary. It's our silver wedding, without the silver and the wedding. We'll have a bottle of champagne. That makes it almost legal. And then suppose we finish up by having the wedding. The silver can be omitted."

Effie had been humming with the orchestra, holding a lobster claw in one hand and wielding the little two-pronged fork with the other. She dropped claw, fork, and popular air to stare open-mouthed at Gabe. Then a slow, uncertain smile crept about her lips, although her eyes were still unsmiling.

"Stop your joking, Gabie," she said. "Some day you'll say those things to the wrong lady, and then you'll have a breach-of-promise suit on your hands."

"This ain't no joke, Effie," Gabe had replied. "Not with me it ain't. As long as my mother selig lived I wouldn't ever marry a Goy. It would have broken her heart. I was a good son to her, and good sons make good husbands, they say. Well, Effie, you want to try it out?"

There was something almost solemn in Effie's tone and expression. "Gabie," she said slowly, "you're the first man that's ever asked me to marry him."

"That goes double," answered Gabe.

"Thanks," said Effie. "That makes it all the nicer."

"Then——" Gabe's face was radiant. But Effie shook her head quickly.

"You're just twenty years late," she said.

"Late!" expostulated Gabe. "I ain't no dead one yet."

Effie pushed her plate away with a little air of decision, folded her plump arms on the table, and, leaning forward, looked Gabe I. Marks squarely in the eyes.

"Gabie," she said gently, "I'll bet you haven't got a hundred dollars in the bank——"

"But——" interrupted Gabe.

"Wait a minute. I know you boys on the road. Besides your diamond scarf pin and your ring and watch, have you got a cent over your salary? Nix. You carry just about enough insurance to bury you, don't you? You're fifty years old if you're a minute, Gabie, and if I ain't mistaken you'd have a pretty hard time of it getting ten thousand dollars' insurance after the doctors got through with you. Twenty-five years of pinochle and poker and the fat of the land haven't added up any bumps in the old stocking under the mattress."

"Say, looka here," objected Gabe, more red-faced than usual, "I didn't know was proposing to no Senatorial investigating committee. Say, you talk about them foreign noblemen being mercenary! Why, they ain't in it with you girls to-day. A feller is got to propose to you with his bank book in one hand and a bunch of life-insurance policies in the other. You're right; I ain't saved much. But Ma selig always had everything she wanted. Say, when a man marries it's different. He begins to save."

"There!" said Effie quickly. "That's just it. Twenty years ago I'd have been glad and willing to start like that, saving and scrimping and loving a man, and looking forward to the time when four figures showed up in the bank account where but three bloomed before. I've got what they call the home instinct. Give me a yard or so of cretonne, and a photo of my married sister down in Iowa, and I can make even a boarding-house inside bedroom look like a place where a human being could live. If I had been as wise at twenty as I am now, Gabie, I could have married any man I pleased. But I was what they call capable. And men aren't marrying capable girls. They pick little yellow-headed, blue-eyed idiots that don't know a lamb stew from a soup bone when they see it. Well, Mr. Man didn't show up, and I started in to clerk at six per. I'm earning as much as you are now. More. Now, don't misunderstand me, Gabe. I'm not throwing bouquets at myself. I'm not that kind of a girl. But I could sell a style 743 Slimshape to the Venus de Milo herself. The Lord knows she needed one, with those hips of hers. I worked my way up, alone. I'm used to it. I like the excitement down at the store. I'm used to luxuries. I guess if I was a man I'd be the kind thy call a good provider—the kind that opens wine every time there's half an excuse for it, and when he dies his widow has to take in boarders. And, Gabe, after you've worn tailored suits every year for a dozen years, you can't go back to twenty-five-dollar ready-mades and be happy."

"You could if you loved a man," said Gabe stubbornly.

The hard lines around the jaw and the experienced lines about the eyes seemed suddenly to stand out on Effie's face.

"Love's young dream is all right. But you've reached the age when you let your cigar ash dribble down onto your vest. Now me, I've got a kimono nature but a straight-front job, and it's kept me young. Young! I've got to be. That's my stock in trade. You see, Gabie, we're just twenty years late, both of us. They're not going to boost your salary. These days they're looking for kids on the road—live wires, with a lot of nerve and a quick come-back. They don't want old-timers. Why, say, Gabie, if I was to tell you what I spend in face powder and toilette water and hairpins alone, you'd think I'd made a mistake and given you the butcher bill instead. And I'm no professional beauty, either. Only it takes money to look cleaned and pressed in this town."

In the seclusion of the cafe corner, Gabe laid one plump, highly manicured hand on Effie's smooth arm. "You wouldn't need to stay young for me, Effie. I like you just as you are, with out the powder, or the toilette water, or the hair-pins."

His red, good-natured face had an expression upon it that was touchingly near patient resignation as he looked up into Effie's sparkling countenance. "You never looked so good to me as you do this minute, old girl. And if the day comes when you get lonesome—or change your mind—or———"

Effie shook her head, and started to draw on her long white gloves. "I guess I haven't refused you the way the dames in the novels do it. Maybe it's because I've had so little practice. But I want to say this, Gabe. Thank God I don't have to die knowing that no man ever wanted me to be his wife. Honestly, I'm that grateful that I'd marry you in a minute if I didn't like you so well."

"I'll be back in three months, like always," was all that Gabe said. "I ain't going to write. When I get here we'll just take in a show, and the younger you look the better I'll like it."

But on the occasion of Gabe's spring trip he encountered a statuesque blonde person where Effie had been wont to reign.

"Miss—er Bauer out of town?"

The statue melted a trifle in the sunshine of Gabe's ingratiating smile.

"Miss Bauer's ill," the statue informed him, using a heavy Eastern accent. "Anything I can do for you? I'm taking her place."

"Why—ah—not exactly; no," said Gabe. "Just a temporary indisposition, I suppose?"

"Well, you wouldn't hardly call it that, seeing that she's been sick with typhoid for seven weeks."

"Typhoid!" shouted Gabe.

"While I'm not in the habit of asking gentlemen their names, I'd like to inquire if yours happens to be Marks—Gabe I. Marks?"

"Sure," said Gabe. "That's me."

"Miss Bauer's nurse telephones down last week that if a gentleman named Marks—Gabe I. Marks—drops in and inquires for Miss Bauer, I'm to tell him that she's changed her mind."

On the way from Spiegel's corset department to the car, Gabe stopped only for a bunch of violets. Effie's apartment house reached, he sent up his card, the violets, and a message that the gentleman was waiting. There came back a reply that sent Gabie up before the violets were relieved of their first layer of tissue paper.

Effie was sitting in a deep chair by the window, a flowered quilt bunched about her shoulders, her feet in gray knitted bedroom slippers. She looked every minute of her age, and she knew it, and didn't care. The hand that she held out to Gabe was a limp, white, fleshless thing that seemed to bear no relation to the plump, firm member that Gabe had pressed on so many previous occasions.

Gabe stared at this pale wraith in a moment of alarm and dismay. Then:

"You're looking—great!" he stammered. "Great! Nobody'd believe you'd been sick a minute. Guess you've just been stalling for a beauty rest, what?"

Effie smiled a tired little smile, and shook her head slowly.

"You're a good kid, Gabie, to lie like that just to make me feel good. But my nurse left yesterday and I had my first real squint at myself in the mirror. She wouldn't let me look while she was here. After what I saw staring back at me from that glass a whole ballroom full of French courtiers whispering sweet nothings in my ear couldn't make me believe that I look like anything but a hunk of Roquefort, green spots included. When I think of how my clothes won't fit it makes me shiver."

"Oh, you'll soon be back at the store as good as new. They fatten up something wonderful after typhoid. Why, I had a friend———"

"Did you get my message?" interrupted Effie.

"I was only talking to hide my nervousness," said Gabe, and started forward. But Effie waved him away.

"Sit down," she said. "I've got something to say." She looked thoughtfully down at one shining finger nail. Her lower lip was caught between her teeth. When she looked up again her eyes were swimming in tears. Gabe started forward again. Again Effie waved him away.

"It's all right, Gabie. I don't blubber as a rule. This fever leaves you as weak as a rag, and ready to cry if any one says 'Boo!' I've been doing some high-pressure thinking since nursie left. Had plenty of time to do it in, sitting here by this window all day. My land! I never knew there was so much time. There's been days when I haven't talked to a soul, except the nurse and the chambermaid. Lonesome! Say, the amount of petting I could stand would surprise you. Of course, my nurse was a perfectly good nurse—at twenty-five per. But I was just a case to her. You can't expect a nurse to ooze sympathy over an old maid with the fever. I tell you I was dying to have some one say 'Sh-sh-sh!' when there was a noise, just to show they were interested. Whenever I'd moan the nurse would come over and stick a thermometer in my mouth and write something down on a chart. The boys and girls at the store sent flowers. They'd have done the same if I'd died. When the fever broke I just used to lie there and dream, not feeling anything in particular, and not caring much whether it was day or night. Know what I mean?"

Gabie shook a sympathetic head.

There was a little silence. Then Effie went on. "I used to think I was pretty smart, earning my own good living, dressing as well as the next one, and able to spend my vacation in Atlantic City if I wanted to. I didn't know I was missing anything. But while I was sick I got to wishing that there was somebody that belonged to me. Somebody to worry about me, and to sit up nights—somebody that just naturally felt they had to come tiptoeing into my room every three or four minutes to see if I was sleeping, or had enough covers on, or wanted a drink, or something. I got to thinking what it would have been like if I had a husband and a—home. You'll think I'm daffy, maybe."

Gabie took Effie's limp white hand in his, and stroked it gently. Effie's face was turned away from him, toward the noisy street.

"I used to imagine how he'd come home at six, stamping his feet, maybe, and making a lot of noise the way men do. And then he'd remember, and come creaking up the steps, and he'd stick his head in at the door in the funny, awkward, pathetic way men have in a sick room. And he'd say, 'How's the old girl to-night? I'd better not come near you now, puss, because I'll bring the cold with me. Been lonesome for your old man?'

"And I'd say, 'Oh, I don't care how cold you are, dear. The nurse is downstairs, getting my supper ready.'

"And then he'd come tiptoeing over to my bed, and stoop down, and kiss me, and his face would be all cold, and rough, and his mustache would be wet, and he'd smell out-doorsy and smoky, the way husbands do when they come in. And I'd reach up and pat his cheek and say, 'You need a shave, old man.'

"'I know it,' he'd say, rubbing his cheek up against mine.

"'Hurry up and wash, now. Supper'll be ready.'

"'Where are the kids?' he'd ask. 'The house is as quiet as the grave. Hurry up and get well, kid. It's darn lonesome without you at the table, and the children's manners are getting something awful, and I never can find my shirts. Lordy, I guess we won't celebrate when you get up! Can't you eat a little something nourishing for supper—beefsteak, or a good plate of soup, or something?'

"Men are like that, you know. So I'd say then: 'Run along, you old goose! You'll be suggesting sauerkraut and wieners next. Don't you let Millie have any marmalade to-night. She's got a spoiled stomach.'

"And then he'd pound off down the hall to wash up, and I'd shut my eyes, and smile to myself, and everything would be all right, because he was home."

There was a long silence. Effie's eyes were closed. But two great tears stole out from beneath each lid and coursed their slow way down her thin cheeks. She did not raise her hand to wipe them away.

Gabie's other hand reached over and met the one that already clasped Effie's.

"Effie," he said, in a voice that was as hoarse as it was gentle.

"H'm?" said Effie.

"Will you marry me?"

"I shouldn't wonder," replied Effie, opening her eyes. "No, don't kiss me. You might catch something. But say, reach up and smooth my hair away from my forehead, will you, and call me a couple of fool names. I don't care how clumsy you are about it. I could stand an awful fuss being made over me, without being spoiled any."

Three weeks later Effie was back at the store. Her skirt didn't fit in the back, and the little hollow places in her cheeks did not take the customary dash of rouge as well as when they had been plumper. She held a little impromptu reception that extended down as far as the lingeries and up as far as the rugs. The old sparkle came back to Effie's eye. The old assurance and vigor seemed to return. By the time that Miss Weinstein, of the French lingeries, arrived, breathless, to greet her Effie was herself again.

"Well, if you're not a sight for sore eyes, dearie," exclaimed Miss Weinstein. "My goodness, how grand and thin you are! I'd be willing to take a course in typhoid myself, if I thought I could lose twenty-five pounds."

"I haven't a rag that fits me," Effie announced proudly.

Miss Weinstein lowered her voice discreetly. "Dearie, can you come down to my department for a minute? We're going to have a sale on imported lawnjerie blouses, slightly soiled, from nine to eleven to-morrow. There's one you positively must see. Hand-embroidered, Irish motifs, and eyeleted from soup to nuts, and only eight-fifty."

"I've got a fine chance of buying hand-made waists, no matter how slightly soiled," Effie made answer, "with a doctor and nurse's bill as long as your arm."

"Oh, run along!" scoffed Miss Weinstein. "A person would think you had a husband to get a grouch every time you get reckless to the extent of a new waist. You're your own boss. And you know your credit's good. Honestly, it would be a shame to let this chance slip. You're not getting tight in your old age, are you?"

"N-no," faltered Effie, "but——"

213

"Then come on," urged Miss Weinstein energetically. "And be thankful you haven't got a man to raise the dickens when the bill comes in."

"Do you mean that?" asked Effie slowly, fixing Miss Weinstein with a thoughtful eye.

"Surest thing you know. Say, girlie, let's go over to Klein's for lunch this noon. They have pot roast with potato pfannkuchen on Tuesdays, and we can split an order between us."

"Hold that waist till to-morrow, will you?" said Effie. "I've made an arrangement with a—friend that might make new clothes impossible just now. But I'm going to wire my party that the arrangement is all off. I've changed my mind. I ought to get an answer to-morrow. Did you say it was a thirty-six?"

VII
MAYMEYS FROM CUBA

There is nothing new in this. It has all been done before. But tell me, what is new? Does the aspiring and perspiring summer vaudeville artist flatter himself that his stuff is going big? Then does the stout man with the oyster-colored eyelids in the first row, left, turn his bullet head on his fat-creased neck to remark huskily to his companion:

"The hook for him. R-r-r-rotten! That last one was an old Weber'n Fields' gag. They discarded it back in '91. Say, the good ones is all dead, anyhow. Take old Salvini, now, and Dan Rice. Them was actors. Come on out and have something."

Does the short-story writer felicitate himself upon having discovered a rare species in humanity's garden? The Blase Reader flips the pages between his fingers, yawns, stretches, and remarks to his wife:

"That's a clean lift from Kipling—or is it Conan Doyle? Anyway, I've read something just like it before. Say, kid, guess what these magazine guys get for a full page ad.? Nix. That's just like a woman. Three thousand straight. Fact."

To anticipate the delver into the past it may be stated that the plot of this one originally appeared in the Eternal Best Seller, under the heading, "He Asked You For Bread, and Ye Gave Him a Stone." There may be those who could not have traced my plagiarism to its source.

Although the Book has had an unprecedentedly long run it is said to be less widely read than of yore.

Even with this preparation I hesitate to confess that this is the story of a hungry girl in a big city. Well, now, wait a minute. Conceding that it has been done by every scribbler from tyro to best seller expert, you will acknowledge that there is the possibility of a fresh viewpoint—twist—what is it the sporting editors call it? Oh, yes—slant. There is the possibility of getting a new slant on an old idea. That may serve to deflect the line of the deadly parallel.

Just off State Street there is a fruiterer and importer who ought to be arrested for cruelty. His window is the most fascinating and the most heartless in Chicago. A line of open-mouthed, wide-eyed gazers is always to be found before it. Despair, wonder, envy, and rebellion smolder in the eyes of those gazers. No shop window show should be so diabolically set forth as to arouse such sensations in the breast of the beholder. It is a work of art, that window; a breeder of anarchism, a destroyer of contentment, a second feast of Tantalus. It boasts peaches, dewy and golden, when peaches have no right to be; plethoric, purple bunches of English hothouse grapes are there to taunt the ten-dollar-a-week clerk whose sick wife should be in the hospital; strawberries glow therein when shortcake is a last summer's memory, and forced cucumbers remind us that we are taking ours in the form of dill pickles. There is, perhaps, a choice head of cauliflower, so exquisite in its ivory and green perfection as to be fit for a bride's bouquet; there are apples so flawless that if the garden of Eden grew any as perfect it is small wonder that Eve fell for them.

There are fresh mushrooms, and jumbo cocoanuts, and green almonds; costly things in beds of cotton nestle next to strange and marvelous things in tissue, wrappings. Oh, that window is no place for the hungry, the dissatisfied, or the man out of a job. When the air is filled with snow there is that in the sight of muskmelons which incites crime.

Queerly enough, the gazers before that window foot up the same, year in, and year out, something after this fashion:

Item: One anemic little milliner's apprentice in coat and shoes that even her hat can't redeem.

Item: One sandy-haired, gritty-complexioned man, with a drooping ragged mustache, a tin dinner bucket, and lime on his boots.

Item: One thin mail carrier with an empty mail sack, gaunt cheeks, and an habitual droop to his left shoulder.

Item: One errand boy troubled with a chronic sniffle, a shrill and piping whistle, and a great deal of shuffling foot-work.

Item: One negro wearing a spotted tan topcoat, frayed trousers and no collar. His eyes seem all whites as he gazes.

Enough of the window. But bear it in mind while we turn to Jennie. Jennie's real name was Janet, and she was Scotch. Canny? Not necessarily, or why should she have been hungry and out of a job in January?

Jennie stood in the row before the window, and stared. The longer she stared the sharper grew the lines that fright and under-feeding had chiseled about her nose, and mouth, and eyes. When your last meal is an eighteen-hour-old memory, and when that memory has only near-coffee and a roll to dwell on, there is something in the sight of January peaches and great strawberries carelessly spilling out of a tipped box, just like they do in the fruit picture on the dining-room wall, that is apt to carve sharp lines in the corners of the face.

The tragic line dwindled, going about its business. The man with the dinner pail and the lime on his boots spat, drew the back of his hand across his mouth, and turned away with an ugly look. (Pork was up to $14.25, dressed.)

The errand boy's blithe whistle died down to a mournful dirge.

He was window-wishing. His choice wavered between the juicy pears, and the foreign-looking red things that looked like oranges, and weren't. One hand went into his coat pocket, extracting an apple that was to have formed the piece de resistance of his noonday lunch. Now he regarded it with a sort of pitying disgust, and bit into it with the middle-of-the-morning contempt that it deserved.

The mail carrier pushed back his cap and reflectively scratched his head. How much over his month's wage would that green basket piled high with exotic fruit come to?

Jennie stood and stared after they had left, and another line had formed. If you could have followed her gaze with dotted lines, as they do in the cartoons, you would have seen that it was not the peaches, or the prickly pears, or the strawberries, or the muskmelon or even the grapes, that held her eye. In the center of that wonderful window was an oddly woven basket. In the basket were brown things that looked like sweet potatoes. One knew that they were not. A sign over the basket informed the puzzled gazer that these were maymeys from Cuba.

Maymeys from Cuba. The humor of it might have struck Jennie if she had not been so Scotch, and so hungry. As it was, a slow, sullen, heavy Scotch wrath rose in her breast. Maymeys from Cuba.

The wantonness of it! Peaches? Yes. Grapes, even, and pears and cherries in snow time. But maymeys from Cuba—why, one did not even know if they were to be eaten with butter, or with vinegar, or in the hand, like an apple. Who wanted maymeys from Cuba? They had gone all those hundreds of miles to get a fruit or vegetable thing—a thing so luxurious, so out of all reason that one did not know whether it was to be baked, or eaten raw. There they lay, in their foreign-looking basket, taunting Jennie who needed a quarter.

Have I told you how Jennie happened to be hungry and jobless? Well, then I sha'n't. It doesn't really matter, anyway. The fact is enough. If you really demand to know you might inquire of Mr. Felix Klein. You will find him in a mahogany office on the sixth floor. The door is marked manager. It was his idea to import Scotch lassies from Dunfermline for his Scotch linen department. The idea was more fetching than feasible.

There are people who will tell you that no girl possessing a grain of common sense and a little nerve need go hungry, no matter how great the city. Don't you believe them. The city has heard the cry of wolf so often that it refuses to listen when he is snarling at the door, particularly when the door is next door.

Where did we leave Jennie? Still standing on the sidewalk before the fruit and fancy goods shop, gazing at the maymeys from Cuba. Finally her Scotch bump of curiosity could stand it no longer. She dug her elbow into the arm of the person standing next in line.

"What are those?" she asked.

The next in line happened to be a man. He was a man without an overcoat, and with his chin sunk deep into his collar, and his hands thrust deep into his pockets. It looked as though he were trying to crawl inside himself for warmth.

"Those? That sign says they're maymeys from Cuba."

"I know," persisted Jennie, "but what are they?"

"Search me. Say, I ain't bothering about maymeys from Cuba. A couple of hot murphies from Ireland, served with a lump of butter, would look good enough to me."

"Do you suppose any one buys them?" marveled Jennie.

"Surest thing you know. Some rich dame coming by here, wondering what she can have for dinner to tempt the jaded palates of her dear ones, see? She sees them Cuban maymeys. 'The very thing!' she says. 'I'll have 'em served just before the salad.' And she sails in and buys a pound or two. I wonder, now, do you eat 'em with a fruit knife, or with a spoon?"

Jennie took one last look at the woven basket with its foreign contents. Then she moved on, slowly. She had been moving on for hours—weeks.

Most people have acquired the habit of eating three meals a day. In a city of some few millions the habit has made necessary the establishing of many thousands of eating places. Jennie would have told you that there were billions of these. To her the world seemed composed of one huge, glittering restaurant, with myriads of windows through which one caught maddening glimpses of ketchup bottles, and nickel coffee heaters, and piles of doughnuts, and scurrying waiters in white, and people critically studying menu cards. She walked in a maze of restaurants, cafes, eating-houses. Tables and diners loomed up at every turn, on every street, from Michigan Avenue's rose-shaded Louis the Somethingth palaces, where every waiter owns his man, to the white tile mausoleums where every man is his own waiter. Everywhere there were windows full of lemon cream pies, and pans of baked apples swimming in lakes of golden syrup, and pots of baked beans with the pink and crispy slices of pork just breaking through the crust. Every dairy lunch mocked one with the sign of "wheat cakes with maple syrup and country sausage, 20 cents."

There are those who will say that for cases like Jennie's there are soup kitchens, Y. W. C. A.'s, relief associations, policemen, and things like that. And so there are. Unfortunately, the people who need them aren't up on them. Try it. Plant yourself, penniless, in the middle of State Street on a busy day, dive into the howling, scrambling, pushing maelstrom that hurls itself against the mountainous and impregnable form of the crossing policeman, and see what you'll get out of it, provided you have the courage.

Desperation gave Jennie a false courage. On the strength of it she made two false starts. The third time she reached the arm of the crossing policeman, and clutched it. That imposing giant removed the whistle from his mouth, and majestically inclined his head without turning his gaze upon Jennie, one eye being fixed on a red automobile that was showing signs of sulking at its enforced pause, the other being busy with a cursing drayman who was having an argument with his off horse.

Jennie mumbled her question.

Said the crossing policeman:

"Getcher car on Wabash, ride to 'umpty-second, transfer, get off at Blank Street, and walk three blocks south."

Then he put the whistle back in his mouth, blew two shrill blasts, and the horde of men, women, motors, drays, trucks, cars, and horses swept over him, through him, past him, leaving him miraculously untouched.

Jennie landed on the opposite curbing, breathing hard. What was that street? Umpty-what? Well, it didn't matter, anyway. She hadn't the nickel for car fare.

What did you do next? You begged from people on the street. Jennie selected a middle-aged, prosperous, motherly looking woman. She framed her plea with stiff lips. Before she had finished her sentence she found herself addressing empty air. The middle-aged, prosperous, motherly looking woman had hurried on.

Well, then you tried a man. You had to be careful there. He mustn't be the wrong kind. There were so many wrong kinds. Just an ordinary looking family man would be best. Ordinary looking family men are strangely in the minority. There are so many more bull-necked, tan-shoed ones. Finally Jennie's eye, grown sharp with want, saw one. Not too well dressed, kind-faced, middle-aged.

She fell into step beside him.

"Please, can you help me out with a shilling?"

Jennie's nose was red, and her eyes watery. Said the middle-aged family man with the kindly face:

"Beat it. You've had about enough I guess."

Jennie walked into a department store, picked out the oldest and most stationary looking floorwalker, and put it to him. The floorwalker bent his head, caught the word "food," swung about, and pointed over Jennie's head.

"Grocery department on the seventh floor. Take one of those elevators up."

Any one but a floorwalker could have seen the misery in Jennie's face. But to floorwalkers all women's faces are horrible.

Jennie turned and walked blindly toward the elevators. There was no fight left in her. If the floorwalker had said, "Silk negligees on the fourth floor. Take one of those elevators up," Jennie would have ridden up to the fourth floor, and stupidly gazed at pink silk and val lace negligees in glass cases.

Tell me, have you ever visited the grocery department of a great store on the wrong side of State Street? It's a mouth-watering experience. A department store grocery is a glorified mixture of delicatessen shop, meat market, and vaudeville. Starting with the live lobsters and crabs you work your hungry way right around past the cheeses, and the sausages, and the hams, and tongues, and head-cheese, past the blonde person in white who makes marvelous and uneatable things out of gelatine, through a thousand smells and scents—smells of things smoked, and pickled, and spiced, and baked and preserved, and roasted.

Jennie stepped out of the elevator, licking her lips. She sniffed the air, eagerly, as a hound sniffs the scent. She shut her eyes when she passed the sugar-cured hams. A woman was buying a slice from one, and the butcher was extolling its merits. Jennie caught the words "juicy" and "corn-fed."

That particular store prides itself on its cheese department. It boasts that there one can get anything in cheese from the simple cottage variety to imposing mottled Stilton. There are cheeses from France, cheeses from Switzerland, cheeses from Holland. Brick and parmesan, Edam and limburger perfumed the atmosphere.

Behind the counters were big, full-fed men in white aprons, and coats. They flourished keen bright knives. As Jennie gazed, one of them, in a moment of idleness, cut a tiny wedge from a rich yellow Swiss cheese and stood nibbling it absently, his eyes wandering toward the blonde gelatine demonstrator. Jennie swayed, and caught the counter. She felt horribly faint and queer. She shut her eyes for a moment. When she opened them a woman—a fat, housewifely, comfortable looking woman—was standing before the cheese counter. She spoke to the cheese man. Once more his sharp knife descended and he was offering the possible customer a sample. She picked it off the knife's sharp tip, nibbled thoughtfully, shook her head, and passed on. A great, glorious world of hope opened out before Jennie.

Her cheeks grew hot, and her eyes felt dry and bright as she approached the cheese counter.

"A bit of that," she said, pointing. "It doesn't look just as I like it."

"Very fine, madam," the man assured her, and turned the knife point toward her, with the infinitesimal wedge of cheese reposing on its blade. Jennie tried to keep her hand steady as she delicately picked it off, nibbled as she had seen that other woman do it, her head on one side, before it shook a slow negative. The effort necessary to keep from cramming the entire piece into her mouth at once left her weak and trembling. She passed on as the other woman had done, around the corner, and into a world of sausages. Great rosy mounds of them filled counters and cases. Sausage! Sneer, you pate de foies grasers! But may you know the day when hunger will have you. And on that day may you run into linked temptation in the form of Braunschweiger Metwurst. May you know the longing that causes the eyes to glaze at the sight of Thuringer sausage, and the mouth to water at the scent of Cervelat wurst, and the fingers to tremble at the nearness of smoked liver.

Jennie stumbled on, through the smells and the sights. That nibble of cheese had been like a drop of human blood to a man-eating tiger. It made her bold, cunning, even while it maddened. She stopped at this counter and demanded a slice of summer sausage. It was paper-thin, but delicious beyond belief. At the next counter there was corned beef, streaked fat and lean. Jennie longed to bury her teeth in the succulent meat and get one great, soul-satisfying mouthful. She had to be content with her judicious nibbling. To pass the golden-brown, breaded pig's feet was torture. To look at the codfish balls was agony. And so Jennie went on, sampling, tasting, the scraps of food acting only as an aggravation. Up one aisle, and down the next she went. And then, just around the corner, she brought up before the grocery department's pride and boast, the Scotch bakery. It is the store's star vaudeville feature. All day long the gaping crowd stands before it, watching David the Scone Man, as with sleeves rolled high above his big arms, he kneads, and slaps, and molds, and thumps and shapes the dough into toothsome Scotch confections. There was a crowd around the white counters now, and the flat baking surface of the gas stove was just hot enough, and David the Scone Man (he called them Scuns) was whipping about here and there, turning the baking oat cakes, filling the shelf above the stove when they were done to a turn, rolling out fresh ones, waiting on customers. His nut-cracker face almost allowed itself a pleased expression—but not quite. David, the Scone Man, was Scotch (I was going to add, d'ye ken, but I will not).

Jennie wondered if she really saw those things. Mutton pies! Scones! Scotch short bread! Oat cakes! She edged closer, wriggling her way through the little crowd until she stood at the counter's edge. David, the Scone Man, his back to the crowd, was turning the last batch of oat cakes. Jennie felt strangely light-headed, and unsteady, and airy. She stared straight ahead, a half-smile on her lips, while a hand that she knew was her own, and that yet seemed no part of her, stole out, very, very slowly, and cunningly, and extracted a hot scone from the pile that lay in the tray on the counter. That hand began to steal back, more quickly now. But not quickly enough. Another hand grasped her wrist. A woman's high, shrill voice (why will women do these things to each other?) said, excitedly:

"Say, Scone Man! Scone Man! This girl is stealing something!"

A buzz of exclamations from the crowd—a closing in upon her—a whirl of faces, and counter, and trays, and gas stove. Jennie dropped with a crash, the warm scone still grasped in her fingers.

Just before the ambulance came it was the blonde lady of the impossible gelatines who caught the murmur that came from Jennie's white lips. The blonde lady bent her head closer. Closer still. When she raised her face to those other faces crowded near, her eyes were round with surprise.

"'S far's I can make out, she says her name's Mamie, and she's from Cuba. Well, wouldn't that eat you! I always thought they was dark complected."

VIII
THE LEADING LADY

The leading lady lay on her bed and wept. Not as you have seen leading ladies weep, becomingly, with eyebrows pathetically V-shaped, mouth quivering, sequined bosom heaving. The leading lady lay on her bed in a red-and-blue-striped kimono and wept as a woman weeps, her head burrowing into the depths of the lumpy hotel pillow, her teeth biting the pillow-case to choke back the sounds so that the grouch in the next room might not hear.

Presently the leading lady's right hand began to grope about on the bedspread for her handkerchief. Failing to find it, she sat up wearily, raising herself on one elbow and pushing her hair back from her forehead—not as you have seen a leading lady pass a lily hand across her alabaster brow, but as a heart-sick woman does it. Her tears and sniffles had formed a little oasis of moisture on the pillow's white bosom so that the ugly stripe of the ticking showed through. She gazed down at the damp circle with smarting, swollen eyes, and another lump came up into her throat.

Then she sat up resolutely, and looked about her. The leading lady had a large and saving sense of humor. But there is nothing that blunts the sense of humor more quickly than a few months of one-night stands. Even O. Henry could have seen nothing funny about that room.

The bed was of green enamel, with fly-specked gold trimmings. It looked like a huge frog. The wall-paper was a crime. It represented an army of tan mustard plasters climbing up a chocolate-fudge wall. The leading lady was conscious of a feeling of nausea as she gazed at it. So she got up and walked to the window. The room faced west, and the hot afternoon sun smote full on her poor swollen eyes. Across the street the red brick walls of the engine-house caught the glare and sent it back. The firemen, in their blue shirt-sleeves, were seated in the shade before the door, their chairs tipped at an angle of sixty. The leading lady stared down into the sun-baked street, turned abruptly and made as though to fall upon the bed again, with a view to forming another little damp oasis on the pillow. But when she reached the center of the stifling little bedroom her eye chanced on the electric call-button near the door.

Above the electric bell was tacked a printed placard giving information on the subjects of laundry, ice-water, bell-boys and dining-room hours.

The leading lady stood staring at it a moment thoughtfully. Then with a sudden swift movement she applied her forefinger to the button and held it there for a long half-minute. Then she sat down on the edge of the bed, her kimono folded about her, and waited.

She waited until a lank bell-boy, in a brown uniform that was some sizes too small for him, had ceased to take any interest in the game of chess which Bauer and Merkle, the champion firemen chess-players, were contesting on the walk before the open doorway of the engine-house. The proprietor of the Burke House had originally intended that the brown uniform be worn by a diminutive bell-boy, such as one sees in musical comedies. But the available supply of stage size bell-boys in our town is somewhat limited and was soon exhausted. There followed a succession of lank bell-boys, with arms and legs sticking ungracefully out of sleeves and trousers.

"Come!" called the leading lady quickly, in answer to the lank youth's footsteps, and before he had had time to knock.

"Ring?" asked the boy, stepping into the torrid little room.

The leading lady did not reply immediately. She swallowed something in her throat and pushed back the hair from her moist forehead again. The brown uniform repeated his question, a trifle irritably. Whereupon the leading lady spoke, desperately:

"Is there a woman around this place? I don't mean dining-room girls, or the person behind the cigar-counter."

Since falling heir to the brown uniform the lank youth had heard some strange requests. He had been interviewed by various ladies in varicolored kimonos relative to liquid refreshment, laundry and the cost of hiring a horse and rig for a couple of hours. One had even summoned him to ask if there was a Bible in the house. But this latest question was a new one. He stared, leaning against the door and thrusting one hand into the depths of his very tight breeches pocket.

"Why, there's Pearlie Schultz," he said at last, with a grin.

"Who's she?" The leading lady sat up expectantly.

"Steno."

The expectant figure drooped. "Blonde? And Irish crochet collar with a black velvet bow on her chest?"

"Who? Pearlie? Naw. You mustn't get Pearlie mixed with the common or garden variety of stenos. Pearlie is fat, and she wears specs and she's got a double chin. Her hair is skimpy and she don't wear no rat. W'y no traveling man has ever tried to flirt with Pearlie yet. Pearlie's what you'd call a woman, all right. You wouldn't never make a mistake and think she'd escaped from the first row in the chorus."

The leading lady rose from the bed, reached out for her pocket-book, extracted a dime, and held it out to the bell-boy.

"Here. Will you ask her to come up here to me? Tell her I said please."

After he had gone she seated herself on the edge of the bed again, with a look in her eyes like that which you have seen in the eyes of a dog that is waiting for a door to be opened.

Fifteen minutes passed. The look in the eyes of the leading lady began to fade. Then a footstep sounded down the hall. The leading lady cocked her head to catch it, and smiled blissfully. It was a heavy, comfortable footstep, under which a board or two creaked. There came a big, sensible thump-thump-thump at the door, with stout knuckles. The leading lady flew to answer it. She flung the door wide and stood there, clutching her kimono at the throat and looking up into a red, good-natured face.

Pearlie Schultz looked down at the leading lady kindly and benignantly, as a mastiff might look at a terrier.

"Lonesome for a bosom to cry on?" asked she, and stepped into the room, walked to the west windows, and jerked down the shades with a zip-zip, shutting off the yellow glare. She came back to where the leading lady was standing and patted her on the cheek, lightly.

"You tell me all about it," said she, smiling.

The leading lady opened her lips, gulped, tried again, gulped again—Pearlie Schultz shook a sympathetic head.

"Ain't had a decent, close-to-nature powwow with a woman for weeks and weeks, have you?"

"How did you know?" cried the leading lady.

"You've got that hungry look. There was a lady drummer here last winter, and she had the same expression. She was so dead sick of eating her supper and then going up to her ugly room and reading and sewing all evening that it was a wonder she'd stayed good. She said it was easy enough for the men. They could smoke, and play pool, and go to a show, and talk to any one that looked good to 'em. But if she tried to amuse herself everybody'd say she was tough. She cottoned to me like a burr to a wool skirt. She traveled for a perfumery house, and she said she hadn't talked to a woman, except the dry-goods clerks who were nice to her trying to work her for her perfume samples, for weeks an' weeks. Why, that woman made crochet by the bolt, and mended her clothes evenings whether they needed it or not, and read till her eyes come near going back on her."

The leading lady seized Pearlie's hand and squeezed it.

"That's it! Why, I haven't talked—really talked—to a real woman since the company went out on the road. I'm leading lady of the 'Second Wife' company, you know. It's one of those small cast plays, with only five people in it. I play the wife, and I'm the only woman in the cast. It's terrible. I ought to be thankful to get the part these days.

And I was, too. But I didn't know it would be like this. I'm going crazy. The men in the company are good kids, but I can't go trailing around after them all day. Besides, it wouldn't be right. They're all married, except Billy, who plays the kid, and he's busy writing a vawdeville skit that he thinks the New York managers are going to fight for when he gets back home. We were to play Athens, Wisconsin, to-night, but the house burned down night before last, and that left us with an open date. When I heard the news you'd have thought I had lost my mother. It's bad enough having a whole day to kill but when I think of to-night," the leading lady's voice took on a note of hysteria, "it seems as though I'd——"

"Say," Pearlie interrupted, abruptly, "you ain't got a real good corset-cover pattern, have you? One that fits smooth over the bust and don't slip off the shoulders? I don't seem able to get my hands on the kind I want."

"Have I!" yelled the leading lady. And made a flying leap from the bed to the floor.

She flapped back the cover of a big suit-case and began burrowing into its depths, strewing the floor with lingerie, newspaper clippings, blouses, photographs and Dutch collars. Pearlie came over and sat down on the floor in the midst of the litter. The leading lady dived once more, fished about in the bottom of the suit-case and brought a crumpled piece of paper triumphantly to the surface.

"This is it. It only takes a yard and five-eighths. And fits! Like Anna Held's skirts. Comes down in a V front and back—like this. See? And no fulness. Wait a minute. I'll show you my princess slip. I made it all by hand, too. I'll bet you couldn't buy it under fifteen dollars, and it cost me four dollars and eighty cents, with the lace and all."

Before an hour had passed, the leading lady had displayed all her treasures, from the photograph of her baby that died to her new Blanche Ring curl cluster, and was calling Pearlie by her first name. When a bell somewhere boomed six o'clock Pearlie was being instructed in a new exercise calculated to reduce the hips an inch a month.

"My land!" cried Pearlie, aghast, and scrambled to her feet as nimbly as any woman can who weighs two hundred pounds. "Supper-time, and I've got a bunch of letters an inch thick to get out! I'd better reduce that some before I begin on my hips. But say, I've had a lovely time."

The leading lady clung to her. "You've saved my life. Why, I forgot all about being hot and lonely and a couple of thousand miles from New York. Must you go?"

"Got to. But if you'll promise you won't laugh, I'll make a date for this evening that'll give you a new sensation anyway. There's going to be a strawberry social on the lawn of the parsonage of our church. I've got a booth. You shed that kimono, and put on a thin dress and those curls and some powder, and I'll introduce you as my friend, Miss Evans. You don't look Evans, but this is a Methodist church strawberry festival, and if I was to tell them that you are leading lady of the 'Second Wife' company they'd excommunicate my booth."

"A strawberry social!" gasped the leading lady. "Do they still have them?" She did not laugh. "Why, I used to go to strawberry festivals when I was a little girl in——"

"Careful! You'll be giving away your age, and, anyway, you don't look it. Fashions in strawberry socials ain't changed much. Better bathe your eyes in eau de cologne or whatever it is they're always dabbing on 'em in books. See you at eight."

At eight o'clock Pearlie's thump-thump sounded again, and the leading lady sprang to the door as before. Pearlie stared. This was no tear-stained, heat-bedraggled creature in an unbecoming red-striped kimono. It was a remarkably pretty woman in a white lingerie gown over a pink slip. The leading lady knew a thing or two about the gentle art of making-up!

"That just goes to show," remarked Pearlie, "that you must never judge a woman in a kimono or a bathing suit. You look nineteen. Say, I forgot something down-stairs. Just get your handkerchief and chamois together and meet in my cubbyhole next to the lobby, will you? I'll be ready for you."

Down-stairs she summoned the lank bell-boy. "You go outside and tell Sid Strang I want to see him, will you? He's on the bench with the baseball bunch."

Pearlie had not seen Sid Strang outside. She did not need to. She knew he was there. In our town all the young men dress up in their pale gray suits and lavender-striped shirts after supper on summer evenings. Then they stroll down to the Burke House, buy a cigar and sit down on the benches in front of the hotel to talk baseball and watch the girls go by. It is astonishing to note the number of our girls who have letters to mail after supper. One would think that they must drive their pens fiercely all the afternoon in order to get out such a mass of correspondence.

The obedient Sid reached the door of Pearlie's little office just off the lobby as the leading lady came down the stairs with a spangled scarf trailing over her arm. It was an effective entrance.

"Why, hello!" said Pearlie, looking up from her typewriter as though Sid Strang were the last person in the world she expected to see. "What do you want here? Ethel, this is my friend, Mr. Sid Strang, one of our rising young lawyers. His neckties always match his socks. Sid, this is my friend, Miss Ethel Evans, of New York. We're going over to the strawberry social at the M. E. parsonage. I don't suppose you'd care about going?"

Mr. Sid Strang gazed at the leading lady in the white lingerie dress with the pink slip, and the V-shaped neck, and the spangled scarf, and turned to Pearlie.

"Why, Pearlie Schultz!" he said reproachfully. "How can you ask? You know what a strawberry social means to me! I haven't missed one in years!"

"I know it," replied Pearlie, with a grin. "You feel the same way about Thursday evening prayer-meeting too, don't you? You can walk over with us if you want to. We're going now. Miss Evans and I have got a booth."

Sid walked. Pearlie led them determinedly past the rows of gray suits and lavender and pink shirts on the benches in front of the hotel. And as the leading lady came into view the gray suits stopped talking baseball and sat up and took notice. Pearlie had known all those young men inside of the swagger suits in the days when their summer costume consisted of a pair of dad's pants cut down to a doubtful fit, and a nondescript shirt damp from the swimming-hole. So she called out, cheerily:

"We're going over to the strawberry festival. I expect to see all you boys there to contribute your mite to the church carpet."

The leading lady turned to look at them, and smiled. They were such a dapper, pink-cheeked, clean-looking lot of boys, she thought. At that the benches rose to a man and announced that they might as well stroll over right now. Whenever a new girl comes to visit in our town our boys make a concerted rush at her, and develop a "case" immediately, and the girl goes home when her visit is over with her head swimming, and forever after bores the girls of her home town with tales of her conquests.

The ladies of the First M. E. Church still talk of the money they garnered at the strawberry festival. Pearlie's out-of-town friend was garnerer-in-chief. You take a cross-eyed, pock-marked girl and put her in a white dress, with a pink slip, on a green lawn under a string of rose-colored Japanese lanterns, and she'll develop an almost Oriental beauty. It is an ideal setting. The leading lady was not cross-eyed or pock-marked. She stood at the lantern-illumined booth, with Pearlie in the background, and dispensed an unbelievable amount of strawberries. Sid Strang and the hotel bench brigade assisted. They made engagements to take Pearlie and her friend down river next day, and to the ball game, and planned innumerable picnics, gazing meanwhile into the leading lady's eyes. There grew in the cheeks of the leading lady a flush that was not brought about by the pink slip, or the Japanese lanterns, or the skillful application of rouge.

By nine o'clock the strawberry supply was exhausted, and the president of the Foreign Missionary Society was sending wildly down-town for more ice-cream.

"I call it an outrage," puffed Pearlie happily, ladling ice-cream like mad. "Making a poor working girl like me slave all evening! How many was that last order? Four? My land! that's the third dish of ice-cream Ed White's had! You'll have something to tell the villagers about when you get back to New York."

The leading lady turned a flushed face toward Pearlie. "This is more fun than the Actors' Fair. I had the photograph booth last year, and I took in nearly as much as Lil Russell; and goodness knows, all she needs to do at a fair is to wear her diamond-and-pearl stomacher and her set-piece smile, and the men just swarm around her like the pictures of a crowd in a McCutcheon cartoon."

When the last Japanese lantern had guttered out, Pearlie Schultz and the leading lady prepared to go home. Before they left, the M. E. ladies came over to Pearlie's booth and personally congratulated the leading lady, and thanked her for the interest she had taken in the cause, and the secretary of the Epworth League asked her to come to the tea that was to be held at her home the following Tuesday. The leading lady thanked her and said she'd come if she could.

Escorted by a bodyguard of gray suits and lavender-striped shirts Pearlie and her friend, Miss Evans, walked toward the hotel. The attentive bodyguard confessed itself puzzled.

"Aren't you staying at Pearlie's house?" asked Sid tenderly, when they reached the Burke House. The leading lady glanced up at the windows of the stifling little room that faced west.

"No," answered she, and paused at the foot of the steps to the ladies' entrance. The light from the electric globe over the doorway shone on her hair and sparkled in the folds of her spangled scarf.

"I'm not staying at Pearlie's because my name isn't Ethel Evans. It's Aimee Fox, with a little French accent mark over the double E. I'm leading lady of the 'Second Wife' company and old enough to be—well, your aunty, anyway. We go out at one-thirty to-morrow morning."

IX
THAT HOME-TOWN FEELING

We all have our ambitions. Mine is to sit in a rocking-chair on the sidewalk at the corner of Clark and Randolph Streets, and watch the crowds go by. South Clark Street is one of the most interesting and cosmopolitan thoroughfares in the world (New Yorkers please sniff). If you are from Paris, France, or Paris, Illinois, and should chance to be in that neighborhood, you will stop at Tony's news stand to buy your home-town paper. Don't mistake the nature of this story. There is nothing of the shivering-newsboy-waif about Tony. He has the voice of a fog-horn, the purple-striped shirt of a sport, the diamond scarf-pin of a racetrack tout, and the savoir faire of the gutter-bred. You'd never pick him for a newsboy if it weren't for his chapped hands and the eternal cold-sore on the upper left corner of his mouth.

It is a fascinating thing, Tony's stand. A high wooden structure rising tier on tier, containing papers from every corner of the world. I'll defy you to name a paper that Tony doesn't handle, from Timbuctoo to Tarrytown, from South Bend to South Africa. A paper marked Christiania, Norway, nestles next to a sheet from Kalamazoo, Michigan. You can get the War Cry, or Le Figaro. With one hand, Tony will give you the Berlin Tageblatt, and

220

with the other the Times from Neenah, Wisconsin. Take your choice between the Bulletin from Sydney, Australia, or the Bee from Omaha.

But perhaps you know South Clark Street. It is honeycombed with good copy—man-size stuff. South Clark Street reminds one of a slatternly woman, brave in silks and velvets on the surface, but ragged, and rumpled and none too clean as to nether garments. It begins with a tenement so vile, so filthy, so repulsive, that the municipal authorities deny its very existence. It ends with a brand-new hotel, all red brick, and white tiling, and Louise Quinze furniture, and sour-cream colored marble lobby, and oriental rugs lavishly scattered under the feet of the unappreciative guest from Kansas City. It is a street of signs, is South Clark. They vary all the way from "Banca Italiana" done in fat, fly-specked letters of gold, to "Sang Yuen" scrawled in Chinese red and black. Spaghetti and chop suey and dairy lunches nestle side by side. Here an electric sign blazons forth the tempting announcement of lunch. Just across the way, delicately suggesting a means of availing one's self of the invitation, is another which announces "Loans." South Clark Street can transform a winter overcoat into hamburger and onions so quickly that the eye can't follow the hand.

Do you gather from this that you are being taken slumming? Not at all. For the passer-by on Clark Street varies as to color, nationality, raiment, finger-nails, and hair-cut according to the locality in which you find him.

At the tenement end the feminine passer-by is apt to be shawled, swarthy, down-at-the-heel, and dragging a dark-eyed, fretting baby in her wake. At the hotel end you will find her blonde of hair, velvet of boot, plumed of head-gear, and prone to have at her heels a white, woolly, pink-eyed dog.

The masculine Clark Streeter? I throw up my hands. Pray remember that South Clark Street embraces the dime lodging house, pawnshop, hotel, theater, chop-suey and railway office district, all within a few blocks. From the sidewalk in front of his groggery, "Bath House John" can see the City Hall. The trim, khaki-garbed enlistment officer rubs elbows with the lodging house bum. The masculine Clark Streeter may be of the kind that begs a dime for a bed, or he may loll in manicured luxury at the marble-lined hotel. South Clark Street is so splendidly indifferent.

Copy-hunting, I approached Tony with hope in my heart, a smile on my lips, and a nickel in my hand.

"Philadelphia—er—Inquirer?" I asked, those being the city and paper which fire my imagination least.

Tony whipped it out, dexterously.

I looked at his keen blue eye, his lean brown face, and his punishing jaw, and I knew that no airy persiflage would deceive him. Boldly I waded in.

"I write for the magazines," said I.

"Do they know it?" grinned Tony.

"Just beginning to be faintly aware. Your stand looks like a story to me. Tell me, does one ever come your way? For instance, don't they come here asking for their home-town paper—sobs in their voice—grasp the sheet with trembling hands—type swims in a misty haze before their eyes—turn aside to brush away a tear—all that kind of stuff, you know?"

Tony's grin threatened his cold-sore. You can't stand on the corner of Clark and Randolph all those years without getting wise to everything there is.

"I'm on," said he, "but I'm afraid I can't accommodate, girlie. I guess my ear ain't attuned to that sob stuff. What's that? Yessir. Nossir, fifteen cents. Well, I can't help that; fifteen's the reg'lar price of foreign papers. Thanks. There, did you see that? I bet that gink give up fifteen of his last two bits to get that paper. O, well, sometimes they look happy, and then again sometimes they—Yes'm. Mississippi? Five cents. Los Vegas Optic right here. Heh there! You're forgettin' your change!—an' then again sometimes they look all to the doleful. Say, stick around. Maybe somebody'll start something. You can't never tell."

And then this happened.

A man approached Tony's news stand from the north, and a woman approached Tony's news stand from the south. They brought my story with them.

The woman reeked of the city. I hope you know what I mean. She bore the stamp, and seal, and imprint of it. It had ground its heel down on her face. At the front of her coat she wore a huge bunch of violets, with a fleshly tuberose rising from its center. Her furs were voluminous. Her hat was hidden beneath the cascades of a green willow plume. A green willow plume would make Edna May look sophisticated. She walked with that humping hip movement which city women acquire. She carried a jangling handful of useless gold trinkets. Her heels were too high, and her hair too yellow, and her lips too red, and her nose too white, and her cheeks too pink. Everything about her was "too," from the black stitching on her white gloves to the buckle of brilliants in her hat. The city had her, body and soul, and had fashioned her in its metallic cast. You would have sworn that she had never seen flowers growing in a field.

Said she to Tony:

"Got a Kewaskum Courier?"

As she said it the man stopped at the stand and put his question. To present this thing properly I ought to be able to describe them both at the same time, like a juggler keeping two balls in the air at once. Kindly carry the lady in your mind's eye. The man was tall and rawboned, with very white teeth, very blue eyes and an open-faced collar that allowed full play to an objectionably apparent Adam's apple. His hair and mustache were sandy, his gait loping. His manner, clothes, and complexion breathed of Waco, Texas (or is it Arizona?)

Said he to Tony:

"Let me have the London Times."

Well, there you are. I turned an accusing eye on Tony.

"And you said no stories came your way," I murmured, reproachfully.

"Help yourself," said Tony.

The blonde lady grasped the Kewaskum Courier. Her green plume appeared to be unduly agitated as she searched its columns. The sheet rattled. There was no breeze. The hands in the too-black stitched gloves were trembling.

I turned from her to the man just in time to see the Adam's apple leaping about unpleasantly and convulsively. Whereupon I jumped to two conclusions.

Conclusion one: Any woman whose hands can tremble over the Kewaskum Courier is homesick.

Conclusion two: Any man, any part of whose anatomy can become convulsed over the London Times is homesick.

She looked up from her Courier. He glanced away from his Times. As the novelists have it, their eyes met. And there, in each pair of eyes there swam that misty haze about which I had so earnestly consulted Tony. The Green Plume took an involuntary step forward. The Adam's Apple did the same. They spoke simultaneously.

"They're going to pave Main Street," said the Green Plume, "and Mrs. Wilcox, that was Jeri Meyers, has got another baby girl, and the ladies of the First M. E. made seven dollars and sixty-nine cents on their needle-work bazaar and missionary tea. I ain't been home in eleven years."

"Hallem is trying for Parliament in Westchester and the King is back at Windsor. My mother wears a lace cap down to breakfast, and the place is famous for its tapestries and yew trees and family ghost. I haven't been home in twelve years."

The great, soft light of fellow feeling and sympathy glowed in the eyes of each. The Green Plume took still another step forward and laid her hand on his arm (as is the way of Green Plumes the world over).

"Why don't you go, kid?" she inquired, softly.

Adam's Apple gnawed at his mustache end. "I'm the black sheep. Why don't you?"

The blonde lady looked down at her glove tips. Her lower lip was caught between her teeth.

"What's the feminine for black sheep? I'm that. Anyway, I'd be afraid to go home for fear it would be too much of a shock for them when they saw my hair. They wasn't in on the intermediate stages when it was chestnut, auburn, Titian, gold, and orange colored. I want to spare their feelings. The last time they saw me it was just plain brown. Where I come from a woman who dyes her hair when it is beginning to turn gray is considered as good as lost. Funny, ain't it? And yet I remember the minister's wife used to wear false teeth—the kind that clicks. But hair is different."

"Dear lady," said the blue-eyed man, "it would make no difference to your own people. I know they would be happy to see you, hair and all. One's own people——"

"My folks? That's just it. If the Prodigal Son had been a daughter they'd probably have handed her one of her sister's mother hubbards, and put her to work washing dishes in the kitchen. You see, after Ma died my brother married, and I went to live with him and Lil. I was an ugly little mug, and it looked all to the Cinderella for me, with the coach, and four, and prince left out. Lil was the village beauty when my brother married her, and she kind of got into the habit of leaving the heavy role to me, and confining herself to thinking parts. One day I took twenty dollars and came to the city. Oh, I paid it back long ago, but I've never been home since. But say, do you know every time I get near a news stand like this I grab the home-town paper. I'll bet I've kept track every time my sister-in-law's sewing circle has met for the last ten years, and the spring the paper said they built a new porch I was just dying to write and ask'em what they did with the Virginia creeper that used to cover the whole front and sides of the old porch."

"Look here," said the man, very abruptly, "if it's money you need, why——"

"Me! Do I look like a touch? Now you——"

"Finest stock farm and ranch in seven counties. I come to Chicago once a year to sell. I've got just thirteen thousand nestling next to my left floating rib this minute."

The eyes of the woman with the green plume narrowed down to two glittering slits. A new look came into her face—a look that matched her hat, and heels and gloves and complexion and hair.

"Thirteen thousand! Thirteen thous—— Say, isn't it chilly on this corner, h'm? I know a kind of a restaurant just around the corner where——"

"It's no use," said the sandy-haired man, gently. "And I wouldn't have said that, if I were you. I was going back to-day on the 5:25, but I'm sick of it all. So are you, or you wouldn't have said what you just said. Listen. Let's go back home, you and I. The sight of a Navajo blanket nauseates me. The thought of those prairies makes my eyes ache. I know that if I have to eat one more meal cooked by that Chink of mine I'll hang him by his own pigtail. Those rangy western ponies aren't horseflesh, fit for a man to ride. Why, back home our stables were—— Look here. I want to see a silver tea-service, with a coat-of-arms on it. I want to dress for dinner, and take in a girl with a white gown and smooth white shoulders. My sister clips roses in the morning, before breakfast, in a pink ruffled dress and garden gloves. Would you believe that, here, on Clark Street, with a whiskey sign overhead, and the stock-yard smells undernose? O, hell! I'm going home."

"Home?" repeated the blonde lady. "Home?" The sagging lines about her flaccid chin took on a new look of firmness and resolve. The light of determination glowed in her eyes.

"I'll beat you to it," she said. "I'm going home, too. I'll be there to-morrow. I'm dead sick of this. Who cares whether I live or die? It's just one darned round of grease paint, and sky blue tights, and new boarding houses and humping over to the theater every night, going on, and humping back to the room again. I want to wash up some supper dishes with egg on 'em, and set some yeast for bread, and pop a dishpan full of corn, and put a shawl over my head and run over to Millie Krause's to get her kimono sleeve pattern. I'm sour on this dirt and noise. I want to spend the rest of my life in a place so that when I die they'll put a column in the paper, with a verse at the top, and all the neighbors'll come in and help bake up. Here—why, here I'd just be two lines on the want ad page, with fifty cents extra for 'Kewaskum paper please copy.'"

The man held out his hand. "Good-bye," he said, "and please excuse me if I say God bless you. I've never really wanted to say it before, so it's quite extraordinary. My name's Guy Peel."

The white glove, with its too-conspicuous black stitching, disappeared within his palm.

"Mine's Mercedes Meron, late of the Morning Glory Burlesquers, but from now on Sadie Hayes, of Kewaskum, Wisconsin. Good-bye and—well—God bless you, too. Say, I hope you don't think I'm in the habit of talking to strange gents like this."

"I am quite sure you are not," said Guy Peel, very gravely, and bowed slightly before he went south on Clark Street, and she went north.

Dear Reader, will you take my hand while I assist you to make a one year's leap. Whoop-la! There you are.

A man and a woman approached Tony's news stand. You are quite right. But her willow plume was purple this time. A purple willow plume would make Mario Doro look sophisticated. The man was sandy-haired, raw-boned, with a loping gait, very blue eyes, very white teeth, and an objectionably apparent Adam's apple. He came from the north, and she from the south.

In story books, and on the stage, when two people meet unexpectedly after a long separation they always stop short, bring one hand up to their breast, and say: "You!" Sometimes, especially in the case where the heroine chances on the villain, they say, simultaneously: "You! Here!" I have seen people reunited under surprising circumstances, but they never said, "You!" They said something quite unmelodramatic, and commonplace, such as: "Well, look who's here!" or, "My land! If it ain't Ed! How's Ed?"

So it was that the Purple Willow Plume and the Adam's Apple stopped, shook hands, and viewed one another while the Plume said, "I kind of thought I'd bump into you. Felt it in my bones." And the Adam's Apple said:

"Then you're not living in Kewaskum—er—Wisconsin?"

"Not any," responded she, briskly. "How do you happen to be straying away from the tapestries, and the yew trees and the ghost, and the pink roses, and the garden gloves, and the silver tea-service with the coat-of-arms on it?"

A slow, grim smile overspread the features of the man. "You tell yours first," he said.

"Well," began she, "in the first place, my name's Mercedes Meron, of the Morning Glory Burlesquers, formerly Sadie Hayes of Kewaskum, Wisconsin. I went home next day, like I said I would. Say, Mr. Peel (you said Peel, didn't you? Guy Peel. Nice, neat name), to this day, when I eat lobster late at night, and have dreams, it's always about that visit home."

"How long did you stay?"

"I'm coming to that. Or maybe you can figure it out yourself when I tell you I've been back eleven months. I wired the folks I was coming, and then I came before they had a chance to answer. When the train reached Kewaskum I stepped off into the arms of a dowd in a home-made-made-over-year-before-last suit, and a hat that would have been funny if it hadn't been so pathetic. I grabbed her by the shoulders, and I held her off, and looked—looked at the wrinkles, and the sallow complexion, and the coat with the sleeves in wrong, and the mashed hat (I told you Lil used to be the village peach, didn't I?) and I says:

"'For Gawd's sakes, Lil, does your husband beat you?'

"'Steve!' she shrieks, 'beat me! You must be crazy!'

"'Well, if he don't, he ought to. Those clothes are grounds for divorce,' I says.

"Mr. Guy Peel, it took me just four weeks to get wise to the fact that the way to cure homesickness is to go home. I spent those four weeks trying to revolutionize my sister-in-law's house, dress, kids, husband, wall paper and parlor carpet. I took all the doilies from under the ornaments and spoke my mind on the subject of the hand-painted lamp, and Lil hates me for it yet, and will to her dying day. I fitted three dresses for her, and made her get some corsets that she'll never wear. They have roast pork for dinner on Sundays, and they never go to the theater, and they like bread pudding, and they're happy. I wasn't. They treated me fine, and it was home, all right, but not my home. It was the same, but I was different. Eleven years away from anything makes it shrink, if you know what I mean. I guess maybe you do. I remember that I used to think that the Grand View Hotel was a regular little oriental palace that was almost too luxurious to be respectable, and that the traveling men who stopped there were

223

gods, and just to prance past the hotel after supper had the Atlantic City board walk looking like a back alley on a rainy night. Well, everything had sort of shriveled up just like that. The popcorn gave me indigestion, and I burned the skin off my nose popping it. Kneading bread gave me the backache, and the blamed stuff wouldn't raise right. I got so I was crazy to hear the roar of an L train, and the sound of a crossing policeman's whistle. I got to thinking how Michigan Avenue looks, downtown, with the lights shining down on the asphalt, and all those people eating in the swell hotels, and the autos, and the theater crowds and the windows, and—well, I'm back. Glad I went? You said it. Because it made me so darned glad to get back. I've found out one thing, and it's a great little lesson when you get it learned. Most of us are where we are because we belong there, and if we didn't, we wouldn't be. Say, that does sound mixed, don't it? But it's straight. Now you tell yours."

"I think you've said it all," began Guy Peel. "It's queer, isn't it, how twelve years of America will spoil one for afternoon tea, and yew trees, and tapestries, and lace caps, and roses. The mater was glad to see me, but she said I smelled woolly. They think a Navajo blanket is a thing the Indians wear on the war path, and they don't know whether Texas is a state, or a mineral water. It was slow—slow. About the time they were taking afternoon tea, I'd be reckoning how the boys would be rounding up the cattle for the night, and about the time we'd sit down to dinner something seemed to whisk the dinner table, and the flowers, and the men and women in evening clothes right out of sight, like magic, and I could see the boys stretched out in front of the bunk house after their supper of bacon, and beans, and biscuit, and coffee. They'd be smoking their pipes that smelled to Heaven, and further, and Wing would be squealing one of his creepy old Chink songs out in the kitchen, and the sky would be—say, Miss Meron, did you ever see the night sky, out West? Purple, you know, and soft as soap-suds, and so near that you want to reach up and touch it with your hand. Toward the end my mother used to take me off in a corner and tell me that I hadn't spoken a word to the little girl that I had taken in to dinner, and that if I couldn't forget my uncouth western ways for an hour or two, at least, perhaps I'd better not try to mingle with civilized people. I discovered that home isn't always the place where you were born and bred. Home is the place where your everyday clothes are, and where somebody, or something needs you. They didn't need me over there in England. Lord no! I was sick for the sight of a Navajo blanket. My shack's glowing with them. And my books needed me, and the boys, and the critters, and Kate."

"Kate?" repeated Miss Meron, quickly.

"Kate's my horse. I'm going back on the 5:25 to-night. This is my regular trip, you know. I came around here to buy a paper, because it has become a habit. And then, too, I sort of felt—well, something told me that you——"

"You're a nice boy," said Miss Meron. "By the way, did I tell you that I married the manager of the show the week after I got back? We go to Bloomington to-night, and then we jump to St. Paul. I came around here just as usual, because—well—because——"

Tony's gift for remembering faces and facts amounts to genius.

With two deft movements he whisked two papers from among the many in the rack, and held them out.

"Kewaskum Courier?" he suggested.

"Nix," said Mercedes Meron, "I'll take a Chicago Scream."

"London Times?" said Tony.

"No," replied Guy Peel. "Give me the San Antonio Express."

X
THE HOMELY HEROINE

Millie Whitcomb, of the fancy goods and notions, beckoned me with her finger. I had been standing at Kate O'Malley's counter, pretending to admire her new basket-weave suitings, but in reality reveling in her droll account of how, in the train coming up from Chicago, Mrs. Judge Porterfield had worn the negro porter's coat over her chilly shoulders in mistake for her husband's. Kate O'Malley can tell a funny story in a way to make the after-dinner pleasantries of a Washington diplomat sound like the clumsy jests told around the village grocery stove.

"I wanted to tell you that I read that last story of yours," said Millie, sociably, when I had strolled over to her counter, "and I liked it, all but the heroine. She had an 'adorable throat' and hair that 'waved away from her white brow,' and eyes that 'now were blue and now gray.' Say, why don't you write a story about an ugly girl?"

"My land!" protested I. "It's bad enough trying to make them accept my stories as it is. That last heroine was a raving beauty, but she came back eleven times before the editor of Blakely's succumbed to her charms."

Millie's fingers were busy straightening the contents of a tray of combs and imitation jet barrettes. Millie's fingers were not intended for that task. They are slender, tapering fingers, pink-tipped and sensitive.

"I should think," mused she, rubbing a cloudy piece of jet with a bit of soft cloth, "that they'd welcome a homely one with relief. These goddesses are so cloying."

Millie Whitcomb's black hair is touched with soft mists of gray, and she wears lavender shirtwaists and white stocks edged with lavender. There is a Colonial air about her that has nothing to do with celluloid combs and imitation jet barrettes. It breathes of dim old rooms, rich with the tones of mahogany and old brass, and Millie in the midst of it, gray-gowned, a soft white fichu crossed upon her breast.

In our town the clerks are not the pert and gum-chewing young persons that story-writers are wont to describe. The girls at Bascom's are institutions. They know us all by our first names, and our lives are as an open book to them. Kate O'Malley, who has been at Bascom's for so many years that she is rumored to have stock in the company, may be said to govern the fashions of our town. She is wont to say, when we express a fancy for gray as the color of our new spring suit:

"Oh, now, Nellie, don't get gray again. You had it year before last, and don't you think it was just the least leetle bit trying? Let me show you that green that came in yesterday. I said the minute I clapped my eyes on it that it was just the color for you, with your brown hair and all."

And we end by deciding on the green.

The girls at Bascom's are not gossips—they are too busy for that—but they may be said to be delightfully well informed. How could they be otherwise when we go to Bascom's for our wedding dresses and party favors and baby flannels? There is news at Bascom's that our daily paper never hears of, and wouldn't dare print if it did.

So when Millie Whitcomb, of the fancy goods and notions, expressed her hunger for a homely heroine, I did not resent the suggestion. On the contrary, it sent me home in thoughtful mood, for Millie Whitcomb has acquired a knowledge of human nature in the dispensing of her fancy goods and notions. It set me casting about for a really homely heroine.

There never has been a really ugly heroine in fiction. Authors have started bravely out to write of an unlovely woman, but they never have had the courage to allow her to remain plain. On Page 237 she puts on a black lace dress and red roses, and the combination brings out unexpected tawny lights in her hair, and olive tints in her cheeks, and there she is, the same old beautiful heroine. Even in the "Duchess" books one finds the simple Irish girl, on donning a green corduroy gown cut square at the neck, transformed into a wild-rose beauty, at sight of whom a ball-room is hushed into admiring awe. There's the case of jane Eyre, too. She is constantly described as plain and mouse-like, but there are covert hints as to her gray eyes and slender figure and clear skin, and we have a sneaking notion that she wasn't such a fright after all.

Therefore, when I tell you that I am choosing Pearlie Schultz as my leading lady you are to understand that she is ugly, not only when the story opens, but to the bitter end. In the first place, Pearlie is fat. Not, plump, or rounded, or dimpled, or deliciously curved, but FAT. She bulges in all the wrong places, including her chin. (Sister, who has a way of snooping over my desk in my absence, says that I may as well drop this now, because nobody would ever read it, anyway, least of all any sane editor. I protest when I discover that Sis has been over my papers. It bothers me. But she says you have to do these things when you have a genius in the house, and cites the case of Kipling's "Recessional," which was rescued from the depths of his wastebasket by his wife.)

Pearlie Schultz used to sit on the front porch summer evenings and watch the couples stroll by, and weep in her heart. A fat girl with a fat girl's soul is a comedy. But a fat girl with a thin girl's soul is a tragedy. Pearlie, in spite of her two hundred pounds, had the soul of a willow wand.

The walk in front of Pearlie's house was guarded by a row of big trees that cast kindly shadows. The strolling couples used to step gratefully into the embrace of these shadows, and from them into other embraces. Pearlie, sitting on the porch, could see them dimly, although they could not see her. She could not help remarking that these strolling couples were strangely lacking in sprightly conversation. Their remarks were but fragmentary, disjointed affairs, spoken in low tones with a queer, tremulous note in them. When they reached the deepest, blackest, kindliest shadow, which fell just before the end of the row of trees, the strolling couples almost always stopped, and then there came a quick movement, and a little smothered cry from the girl, and then a sound, and then a silence. Pearlie, sitting alone on the porch in the dark, listened to these things and blushed furiously. Pearlie had never strolled into the kindly shadows with a little beating of the heart, and she had never been surprised with a quick arm about her and eager lips pressed warmly against her own.

In the daytime Pearlie worked as public stenographer at the Burke Hotel. She rose at seven in the morning, and rolled for fifteen minutes, and lay on her back and elevated her heels in the air, and stood stiff-kneed while she touched the floor with her finger tips one hundred times, and went without her breakfast. At the end of each month she usually found that she weighed three pounds more than she had the month before.

The folks at home never joked with Pearlie about her weight. Even one's family has some respect for a life sorrow. Whenever Pearlie asked that inevitable question of the fat woman: "Am I as fat as she is?" her mother always answered: "You! Well, I should hope not! You're looking real peaked lately, Pearlie. And your blue skirt just ripples in the back, it's getting so big for you."

Of such blessed stuff are mothers made.

But if the gods had denied Pearlie all charms of face or form, they had been decent enough to bestow on her one gift. Pearlie could cook like an angel; no, better than an angel, for no angel could be a really clever cook and wear those flowing kimono-like sleeves. They'd get into the soup. Pearlie could take a piece of rump and some suet and an onion and a cup or so of water, and evolve a pot roast that you could cut with a fork. She could turn out a surprisingly good cake with surprisingly few eggs, all covered with white icing, and bearing cunning little jelly figures on its snowy bosom. She could beat up biscuits that fell apart at the lightest pressure, revealing little pools of golden butter within. Oh, Pearlie could cook!

On week days Pearlie rattled the typewriter keys, but on Sundays she shooed her mother out of the kitchen. Her mother went, protesting faintly:

"Now, Pearlie, don't fuss so for dinner. You ought to get your rest on Sunday instead of stewing over a hot stove all morning."

"Hot fiddlesticks, ma," Pearlie would say, cheerily. "It ain't hot, because it's a gas stove. And I'll only get fat if I sit around. You put on your black-and-white and go to church. Call me when you've got as far as your corsets, and I'll puff your hair for you in the back."

In her capacity of public stenographer at the Burke Hotel, it was Pearlie's duty to take letters dictated by traveling men and beginning: "Yours of the 10th at hand. In reply would say...." or: "Enclosed please find, etc." As clinching proof of her plainness it may be stated that none of the traveling men, not even Max Baum, who was so fresh that the girl at the cigar counter actually had to squelch him, ever called Pearlie "baby doll," or tried to make a date with her. Not that Pearlie would ever have allowed them to. But she never had had to reprove them. During pauses in dictation she had a way of peering near-sightedly, over her glasses at the dapper, well-dressed traveling salesman who was rolling off the items on his sale bill. That is a trick which would make the prettiest kind of a girl look owlish.

On the night that Sam Miller strolled up to talk to her, Pearlie was working late. She had promised to get out a long and intricate bill for Max Baum, who travels for Kuhn and Klingman, so that he might take the nine o'clock evening train. The irrepressible Max had departed with much eclat and clatter, and Pearlie was preparing to go home when Sam approached her.

Sam had just come in from the Gayety Theater across the street, whither he had gone in a vain search for amusement after supper. He had come away in disgust. A soiled soubrette with orange-colored hair and baby socks had swept her practiced eye over the audience, and, attracted by Sam's good-looking blond head in the second row, had selected him as the target of her song. She had run up to the extreme edge of the footlights at the risk of teetering over, and had informed Sam through the medium of song—to the huge delight of the audience, and to Sam's red-faced discomfiture—that she liked his smile, and he was just her style, and just as cute as he could be, and just the boy for her. On reaching the chorus she had whipped out a small, round mirror and, assisted by the calcium-light man in the rear, had thrown a wretched little spotlight on Sam's head.

Ordinarily, Sam would not have minded it. But that evening, in the vest pocket just over the place where he supposed his heart to be reposed his girl's daily letter. They were to be married on Sam's return to New York from his first long trip. In the letter near his heart she had written prettily and seriously about traveling men, and traveling men's wives, and her little code for both. The fragrant, girlish, grave little letter had caused Sam to sour on the efforts of the soiled soubrette.

As soon as possible he had fled up the aisle and across the street to the hotel writing-room. There he had spied Pearlie's good-humored, homely face, and its contrast with the silly, red and-white countenance of the unlaundered soubrette had attracted his homesick heart.

Pearlie had taken some letters from him earlier in the day. Now, in his hunger for companionship, he, strolled up to her desk, just as she was putting her typewriter to bed.

"Gee I This is a lonesome town!" said Sam, smiling down at her.

Pearlie glanced up at him, over her glasses. "I guess you must be from New York," she said. "I've heard a real New Yorker can get bored in Paris. In New York the sky is bluer, and the grass is greener, and the girls are prettier, and the steaks are thicker, and the buildings are higher, and the streets are wider, and the air is finer, than the sky, or the grass, or the girls, or the steaks, or the air of any place else in the world. Ain't they?"

"Oh, now," protested Sam, "quit kiddin' me! You'd be lonesome for the little old town, too, if you'd been born and dragged up in it, and hadn't seen it for four months."

"New to the road, aren't you?" asked Pearlie.

Sam blushed a little. "How did you know?"

"Well, you generally can tell. They don't know what to do with themselves evenings, and they look rebellious when they go into the dining-room. The old-timers just look resigned."

"You've picked up a thing or two around here, haven't you? I wonder if the time will ever come when I'll look resigned to a hotel dinner, after four months of 'em. Why, girl, I've got so I just eat the things that are covered up— like baked potatoes in the shell, and soft boiled eggs, and baked apples, and oranges that I can peel, and nuts."

"Why, you poor kid," breathed Pearlie, her pale eyes fixed on him in motherly pity. "You oughtn't to do that. You'll get so thin your girl won't know you."

Sam looked up quickly. "How in thunderation did you know——?"

Pearlie was pinning on her hat, and she spoke succinctly, her hatpins between her teeth: "You've been here two days now, and I notice you dictate all your letters except the longest one, and you write that one off in a corner of the writing-room all by yourself, with your cigar just glowing like a live coal, and you squint up through the smoke, and grin to yourself."

"Say, would you mind if I walked home with you?" asked Sam.

If Pearlie was surprised, she was woman enough not to show it. She picked up her gloves and hand bag, locked her drawer with a click, and smiled her acquiescence. And when Pearlie smiled she was awful.

It was a glorious evening in the early summer, moonless, velvety, and warm. As they strolled homeward, Sam told her all about the Girl, as is the way of traveling men the world over. He told her about the tiny apartment they had taken, and how he would be on the road only a couple of years more, as this was just a try-out that the firm always insisted on. And they stopped under an arc light while Sam showed her the picture in his watch, as is also the way of traveling men since time immemorial.

Pearlie made an excellent listener. He was so boyish, and so much in love, and so pathetically eager to make good with the firm, and so happy to have some one in whom to confide.

"But it's a dog's life, after all," reflected Sam, again after the fashion of all traveling men. "Any fellow on the road earns his salary these days, you bet. I used to think it was all getting up when you felt like it, and sitting in the big front window of the hotel, smoking a cigar and watching the pretty girls go by. I wasn't wise to the packing, and the unpacking, and the rotten train service, and the grouchy customers, and the canceled bills, and the grub."

Pearlie nodded understandingly. "A man told me once that twice a week regularly he dreamed of the way his wife cooked noodle-soup."

"My folks are German," explained Sam. "And my mother—can she cook! Well, I just don't seem able to get her potato pancakes out of my mind. And her roast beef tasted and looked like roast beef, and not like a wet red flannel rag."

At this moment Pearlie was seized with a brilliant idea. "To-morrow's Sunday. You're going to Sunday here, aren't you? Come over and eat your dinner with us. If you have forgotten the taste of real food, I can give you a dinner that'll jog your memory."

"Oh, really," protested Sam. "You're awfully good, but I couldn't think of it. I——"

"You needn't be afraid. I'm not letting you in for anything. I may be homelier than an English suffragette, and I know my lines are all bumps, but there's one thing you can't take away from me, and that's my cooking hand. I can cook, boy, in a way to make your mother's Sunday dinner, with company expected, look like Mrs. Newlywed's first attempt at 'riz' biscuits. And I don't mean any disrespect to your mother when I say it. I'm going to have noodle-soup, and fried chicken, and hot biscuits, and creamed beans from our own garden, and strawberry shortcake with real——"

"Hush!" shouted Sam. "If I ain't there, you'll know that I passed away during the night, and you can telephone the clerk to break in my door."

The Grim Reaper spared him, and Sam came, and was introduced to the family, and ate. He put himself in a class with Dr. Johnson, and Ben Brust, and Gargantua, only that his table manners were better. He almost forgot to talk during the soup, and he came back three times for chicken, and by the time the strawberry shortcake was half consumed he was looking at Pearlie with a sort of awe in his eyes.

That night he came over to say good-bye before taking his train out for Ishpeming. He and Pearlie strolled down as far as the park and back again.

"I didn't eat any supper," said Sam. "It would have been sacrilege, after that dinner of yours. Honestly, I don't know how to thank you, being so good to a stranger like me. When I come back next trip, I expect to have the Kid with me, and I want her to meet you, by George! She's a winner and a pippin, but she wouldn't know whether a porterhouse was stewed or frapped. I'll tell her about you, you bet. In the meantime, if there's anything I can do for you, I'm yours to command."

Pearlie turned to him suddenly. "You see that clump of thick shadows ahead of us, where those big trees stand in front of our house?"

"Sure," replied Sam.

"Well, when we step into that deepest, blackest shadow, right in front of our porch, I want you to reach up, and put your arm around me and kiss me on the mouth, just once. And when you get back to New York you can tell your girl I asked you to."

There broke from him a little involuntary exclamation. It might have been of pity, and it might have been of surprise. It had in it something of both, but nothing of mirth. And as they stepped into the depths of the soft black shadows he took off his smart straw sailor, which was so different from the sailors that the boys in our town wear. And there was in the gesture something of reverence.

Millie Whitcomb didn't like the story of the homely heroine, after all. She says that a steady diet of such literary fare would give her blue indigestion. Also she objects on the ground that no one got married—that is, the heroine didn't. And she says that a heroine who does not get married isn't a heroine at all. She thinks she prefers the pink-cheeked, goddess kind, in the end.

XI
SUN DRIED

There come those times in the life of every woman when she feels that she must wash her hair at once. And then she does it. The feeling may come upon her suddenly, without warning, at any hour of the day or night; or its approach may be slow and insidious, so that the victim does not at first realize what it is that fills her with that sensation of unrest. But once in the clutches of the idea she knows no happiness, no peace, until she has donned a kimono, gathered up two bath towels, a spray, and the green soap, and she breathes again only when, head dripping, she makes for the back yard, the sitting-room radiator, or the side porch (depending on her place of residence, and the time of year).

Mary Louise was seized with the feeling at ten o'clock on a joyous June morning. She tried to fight it off because she had got to that stage in the construction of her story where her hero was beginning to talk and act a little more like a real live man, and a little less like a clothing store dummy. (By the way, they don't seem to be using those pink-and-white, black-mustachioed figures any more. Another good simile gone.)

Mary Louise had been battling with that hero for a week. He wouldn't make love to the heroine. In vain had Mary Louise striven to instill red blood into his watery veins. He and the beauteous heroine were as far apart as they had been on Page One of the typewritten manuscript. Mary Louise was developing nerves over him. She had bitten her finger nails, and twisted her hair into corkscrews over him. She had risen every morning at the chaste hour of seven, breakfasted hurriedly, tidied the tiny two-room apartment, and sat down in the unromantic morning light to wrestle with her stick of a hero. She had made her heroine a creature of grace, wit, and loveliness, but thus far the hero had not once clasped her to him fiercely, or pressed his lips to her hair, her eyes, her cheeks. Nay (as the story-writers would put it), he hadn't even devoured her with his gaze.

This morning, however, he had begun to show some signs of life. He was developing possibilities. Whereupon, at this critical stage in the story-writing game, the hair-washing mania seized Mary Louise. She tried to dismiss the idea. She pushed it out of her mind, and slammed the door. It only popped in again. Her fingers wandered to her hair. Her eyes wandered to the June sunshine outside. The hero was left poised, arms outstretched, and unquenchable love-light burning in his eyes, while Mary Louise mused, thus:

"It certainly feels sticky. It's been six weeks, at least. And I could sit here-by the window—in the sun—and dry it——"

With a jerk she brought her straying fingers away from her hair, and her wandering eyes away from the sunshine, and her runaway thoughts back to the typewritten page. For three minutes the snap of the little disks crackled through the stillness of the tiny apartment. Then, suddenly, as though succumbing to an irresistible force, Mary Louise rose, walked across the room (a matter of six steps), removing hairpins as she went, and shoved aside the screen which hid the stationary wash-bowl by day.

Mary Louise turned on a faucet and held her finger under it, while an agonized expression of doubt and suspense overspread her features. Slowly the look of suspense gave way to a smile of beatific content. A sigh— deep, soul-filling, satisfied—welled up from Mary Louise's breast. The water was hot.

Half an hour later, head swathed turban fashion in a towel, Mary Louise strolled over to the window. Then she stopped, aghast. In that half hour the sun had slipped just around the corner, and was now beating brightly and uselessly against the brick wall a few inches away. Slowly Mary Louise unwound the towel, bent double in the contortionistic attitude that women assume on such occasions, and watched with melancholy eyes while the drops trickled down to the ends of her hair, and fell, unsunned, to the floor.

"If only," thought Mary Louise, bitterly, "there was such a thing as a back yard in this city—a back yard where I could squat on the grass, in the sunshine and the breeze—— Maybe there is. I'll ask the janitor."

She bound her hair in the turban again, and opened the door. At the far end of the long, dim hallway Charlie, the janitor, was doing something to the floor with a mop and a great deal of sloppy water, whistling the while with a shrill abandon that had announced his presence to Mary Louise.

"Oh, Charlie!" called Mary Louise. "Charlee! Can you come here just a minute?"

"You bet!" answered Charlie, with the accent on the you; and came.

"Charlie, is there a back yard, or something, where the sun is, you know—some nice, grassy place where I can sit, and dry my hair, and let the breezes blow it?"

"Back yard!" grinned Charlie. "I guess you're new to N' York, all right, with ground costin' a million or so a foot. Not much they ain't no back yard, unless you'd give that name to an ash-barrel, and a dump heap or so, and a crop of tin cans. I wouldn't invite a goat to set in it."

Disappointment curved Mary Louise's mouth. It was a lovely enough mouth at any time, but when it curved in disappointment—ell, janitors are but human, after all.

"Tell you what, though," said Charlie. "I'll let you up on the roof. It ain't long on grassy spots up there, but say, breeze! Like a summer resort. On a clear day you can see way over 's far 's Eight' Avenoo. Only for the love of Mike don't blab it to the other women folks in the buildin', or I'll have the whole works of 'em usin' the roof for a general sun, massage, an' beauty parlor. Come on."

"I'll never breathe it to a soul," promised Mary Louise, solemnly. "Oh, wait a minute."

She turned back into her room, appearing again in a moment with something green in her hand.

"What's that?" asked Charlie, suspiciously.

Mary Louise, speeding down the narrow hallway after Charlie, blushed a little. "It—it's parsley," she faltered.

"Parsley!" exploded Charlie. "Well, what the——"

"Well, you see. I'm from the country," explained Mary Louise, "and in the country, at this time of year, when you dry your hair in the back yard, you get the most wonderful scent of green and growing things—not only of flowers, you know, but of the new things just coming up in the vegetable garden, and—and—well, this parsley happens to be the only really gardeny thing I have, so I thought I'd bring it along and sniff it once in a while, and make believe it's the country, up there on the roof."

Half-way up the perilous little flight of stairs that led to the roof, Charlie, the janitor, turned to gaze down at Mary Louise, who was just behind, and keeping fearfully out of the way of Charlie's heels.

"Wimmin," observed Charlie, the janitor, "is nothin' but little girls in long skirts, and their hair done up."

"I know it," giggled Mary Louise, and sprang up on the roof, looking, with her towel-swathed head, like a lady Aladdin leaping from her underground grotto.

The two stood there a moment, looking up at the blue sky, and all about at the June sunshine.

"If you go up high enough," observed Mary Louise, "the sunshine is almost the same as it is in the country, isn't it?"

"I shouldn't wonder," said Charlie, "though Calvary cemetery is about as near's I'll ever get to the country. Say, you can set here on this soap box and let your feet hang down. The last janitor's wife used to hang her washin' up here, I guess. I'll leave this door open, see?"

"You're so kind," smiled Mary Louise.

"Kin you blame me?" retorted the gallant Charles. And vanished.

Mary Louise, perched on the soap box, unwound her turban, draped the damp towel over her shoulders, and shook out the wet masses of her hair. Now the average girl shaking out the wet masses of her hair looks like a drowned rat. But Nature had been kind to Mary Louise. She had given her hair that curled in little ringlets when wet, and that waved in all the right places when dry.

Just now it hung in damp, shining strands on either side of her face, so that she looked most remarkably like one of those oval-faced, great-eyed, red-lipped women that the old Italian artists were so fond of painting.

Below her, blazing in the sun, lay the great stone and iron city. Mary Louise shook out her hair idly, with one hand, sniffed her parsley, shut her eyes, threw back her head, and began to sing, beating time with her heel against the soap box, and forgetting all about the letter that had come that morning, stating that it was not from any lack of merit, etc. She sang, and sniffed her parsley, and waggled her hair in the breeze, and beat time, idly, with the heel of her little boot, when——

"Holy Cats!" exclaimed a man's voice. "What is this, anyway? A Coney Island concession gone wrong?"

Mary Louise's eyes unclosed in a flash, and Mary Louise gazed upon an irate-looking, youngish man, who wore shabby slippers, and no collar with a full dress air.

"I presume that you are the janitor's beautiful daughter," growled the collarless man.

"Well, not precisely," answered Mary Louise, sweetly. "Are you the scrub-lady's stalwart son?"

"Ha!" exploded the man. "But then, all women look alike with their hair down. I ask your pardon, though."

"Not at all," replied Mary Louise. "For that matter, all men look like picked chickens with their collars off."

At that the collarless man, who until now had been standing on the top step that led up to the roof, came slowly forward, stepped languidly over a skylight or two, draped his handkerchief over a convenient chimney and sat down, hugging his long, lean legs to him.

"Nice up here, isn't it?" he remarked.

"It was," said Mary Louise.

"Ha!" exploded he, again. Then, "Where's your mirror?" he demanded.

"Mirror?" echoed Mary Louise.

"Certainly. You have the hair, the comb, the attitude, and the general Lorelei effect. Also your singing lured me to your shores."

"You didn't look lured," retorted Mary Louise. "You looked lurid."

"What's that stuff in your hand?" next demanded he. He really was a most astonishingly rude young man.

"Parsley."

"Parsley!" shouted he, much as Charlie had done. "Well, what the——"

"Back home," elucidated Mary Louise once more, patiently, "after you've washed your hair you dry it in the back yard, sitting on the grass, in the sunshine and the breeze. And the garden smells come to you—the nasturtiums, and the pansies, and the geraniums, you know, and even that clean grass smell, and the pungent vegetable odor, and there are ants, and bees, and butterflies——"

"Go on," urged the young man, eagerly.

"And Mrs. Next Door comes out to hang up a few stockings, and a jabot or so, and a couple of baby dresses that she has just rubbed through, and she calls out to you:

"'Washed your hair?'

"'Yes,' you say. 'It was something awful, and I wanted it nice for Tuesday night. But I suppose I won't be able to do a thing with it.'

"And then Mrs. Next Door stands there a minute on the clothes-reel platform, with the wind whipping her skirts about her, and the fresh smell of the growing things coming to her. And suddenly she says: 'I guess I'll wash mine too, while the baby's asleep.'"

The collarless young man rose from his chimney, picked up his handkerchief, and moved to the chimney just next to Mary Louise's soap box.

"Live here?" he asked, in his impolite way.

"If I did not, do you think that I would choose this as the one spot in all New York in which to dry my hair?"

"When I said, 'Live here,' I didn't mean just that. I meant who are you, and why are you here, and where do you come from, and do you sign your real name to your stuff, or use a nom de plume?"

"Why—how did you know?" gasped Mary Louise.

"Give me five minutes more," grinned the keen-eyed young man, "and I'll tell you what make your typewriter is, and where the last rejection slip came from."

"Oh!" said Mary Louise again. "Then you are the scrub-lady's stalwart son, and you've been ransacking my waste-basket."

Quite unheeding, the collarless man went on, "And so you thought you could write, and you came on to New York (you know one doesn't just travel to New York, or ride to it, or come to it; one 'comes on' to New York), and now you're not so sure about the writing, h'm? And back home what did you do?"

"Back home I taught school—and hated it. But I kept on teaching until I'd saved five hundred dollars. Every other school ma'am in the world teaches until she has saved five hundred dollars, and then she packs two suit-cases, and goes to Europe from June until September. But I saved my five hundred for New York. I've been here six months now, and the five hundred has shrunk to almost nothing, and if I don't break into the magazines pretty soon——"

"Then?"

"Then," said Mary Louise, with a quaver in her voice, "I'll have to go back and teach thirty-seven young devils that six times five is thirty, put down the naught and carry six, and that the French are a gay people, fond of dancing and light wines. But I'll scrimp on everything from hairpins to shoes, and back again, including pretty collars, and gloves, and hats, until I've saved up another five hundred, and then I'll try it all over again, because I—can—write."

From the depths of one capacious pocket the inquiring man took a small black pipe, from another a bag of tobacco, from another a match. The long, deft fingers made a brief task of it.

"I didn't ask you," he said, after the first puff, "because I could see that you weren't the fool kind that objects." Then, with amazing suddenness, "Know any of the editors?"

"Know them!" cried Mary Louise. "Know them! If camping on their doorsteps, and haunting the office buildings, and cajoling, and fighting with secretaries and office boys, and assistants and things constitutes knowing them, then we're chums."

"What makes you think you can write?" sneered the thin man.

Mary Louise gathered up her brush, and comb, and towel, and parsley, and jumped off the soap box. She pointed belligerently at her tormentor with the hand that held the brush.

"Being the scrub-lady's stalwart son, you wouldn't understand. But I can write. I sha'n't go under. I'm going to make this town count me in as the four million and oneth. Sometimes I get so tired of being nobody at all, with not even enough cleverness in me to wrest a living from this big city, that I long to stand out at the edge of the curbing, and take off my hat, and wave it, and shout, 'Say, you four million uncaring people, I'm Mary Louise Moss, from Escanaba, Michigan, and I like your town, and I want to stay here. Won't you please pay some slight attention to me. No one knows I'm here except myself, and the rent collector.'"

"And I," put in the rude young man.

"O, you," sneered Mary Louise, equally rude, "you don't count."

The collarless young man in the shabby slippers smiled a curious little twisted smile. "You never can tell," he grinned, "I might." Then, quite suddenly, he stood up, knocked the ash out of his pipe, and came over to Mary Louise, who was preparing to descend the steep little flight of stairs.

"Look here, Mary Louise Moss, from Escanaba, Michigan, you stop trying to write the slop you're writing now. Stop it. Drop the love tales that are like the stuff that everybody else writes. Stop trying to write about New York. You don't know anything about it. Listen. You get back to work, and write about Mrs. Next Door, and the hair-washing, and the vegetable garden, and bees, and the back yard, understand? You write the way you talked to me, and then you send your stuff in to Cecil Reeves."

"Reeves!" mocked Mary Louise. "Cecil Reeves, of The Earth? He wouldn't dream of looking at my stuff. And anyway, it really isn't your affair." And began to descend the stairs.

"Well, you know you brought me up here, kicking with your heels, and singing at the top of your voice. I couldn't work. So it's really your fault." Then, just as Mary Louise had almost disappeared down the stairway he put his last astonishing question.

"How often do you wash your hair?" he demanded.

"Well, back home," confessed Mary Louise, "every six weeks or so was enough, but——"

"Not here," put in the rude young man, briskly. "Never. That's all very well for the country, but it won't do in the city. Once a week, at least, and on the roof. Cleanliness demands it."

"But if I'm going back to the country," replied Mary Louise, "it won't be necessary."

"But you're not," calmly said the collarless young man, just as Mary Louise vanished from sight.

Down at the other end of the hallway on Mary Louise's floor Charlie, the janitor, was doing something to the windows now, with a rag, and a pail of water.

"Get it dry?" he called out, sociably.

"Yes, thank you," answered Mary Louise, and turned to enter her own little apartment. Then, hesitatingly, she came back to Charlie's window.

"There—there was a man up there—a very tall, very thin, very rude, very—that is, rather nice youngish oldish man, in slippers, and no collar. I wonder——"

"Oh, him!" snorted Charlie. "He don't show himself onct in a blue moon. None of the other tenants knows he's up there. Has the whole top floor to himself, and shuts himself up there for weeks at a time, writin' books, or some such truck. That guy, he owns the building."

"Owns the building!" said Mary Louise, faintly. "Why he looked—he looked——"

"Sure," grinned Charlie. "That's him. Name's Reeves—Cecil Reeves. Say, ain't that a divil of a name?"

XII
WHERE THE CAR TURNS AT 18TH

This will be a homing pigeon story. Though I send it ever so far—though its destination be the office of a home-and-fireside magazine or one of the kind with a French story in the back, it will return to me. After each flight its feathers will be a little more rumpled, its wings more weary, its course more wavering, until, battered, spent, broken, it will flutter to rest in the waste basket.

And yet, though its message may never be delivered, it must be sent, because—well, because——

You know where the car turns at Eighteenth? There you see a glaringly attractive billboard poster. It depicts groups of smiling, white-clad men standing on tropical shores, with waving palms overhead, and a glimpse of blue sea in the distance. The wording beneath the picture runs something like this:

"Young men wanted. An unusual opportunity for travel, education, and advancement. Good pay. No expenses."

When the car turns at Eighteenth, and I see that, I remember Eddie Houghton back home. And when I remember Eddie Houghton I see red.

The day after Eddie Houghton finished high school he went to work. In our town we don't take a job. We accept a position. Our paper had it that "Edwin Houghton had accepted a position as clerk and assistant chemist at the Kunz drugstore, where he would take up his new duties Monday."

His new duties seemed, at first, to consist of opening the store in the morning, sweeping out, and whizzing about town on a bicycle with an unnecessarily insistent bell, delivering prescriptions which had been telephoned for. But by the time the summer had really set in Eddie was installed back of the soda fountain.

There never was anything better looking than Eddie Houghton in his white duck coat. He was one of those misleadingly gold and pink and white men. I say misleadingly because you usually associate pink-and-whiteness with such words as sissy and mollycoddle. Eddie was neither. He had played quarter-back every year from his freshman year, and he could putt the shot and cut classes with the best of 'em. But in that white duck coat with the braiding and frogs he had any musical-comedy, white-flannel tenor lieutenant whose duty it is to march down to the edge of the footlights, snatch out his sword, and warble about his country's flag, looking like a flat-nosed, blue-gummed Igorrote. Kunz's soda water receipts swelled to double their usual size, and the girls' complexions were something awful that summer. I've known Nellie Donovan to take as many as three ice cream sodas and two phosphates a day when Eddie was mixing. He had a way of throwing in a good-natured smile, and an easy flow of conversation with every drink. While indulging in a little airy persiflage the girls had a great little trick of pursing their mouths into rosebud shapes over their soda straws, and casting their eyes upward at Eddie. They all knew the trick, and its value, so that at night Eddie's dreams were haunted by whole rows of rosily pursed lips, and seas of upturned, adoring eyes. Of course we all noticed that on those rare occasions when Josie Morehouse came into Kunz's her glass was heaped higher with ice cream than that of any of the other girls, and that Eddie's usually easy flow of talk was interspersed with certain stammerings and stutterings. But Josie didn't come in often. She had a lot of dignity for a girl of eighteen. Besides, she was taking the teachers' examinations that summer, when the other girls were playing tennis and drinking sodas.

Eddie really hated the soda water end of the business, as every soda clerk in the world does. But he went about it good-naturedly. He really wanted to learn the drug business, but the boss knew he had a drawing card, and insisted that Eddie go right on concocting faerie queens and strawberry sundaes, and nectars and Kunz's specials. One Saturday, when he happened to have on hand an over-supply of bananas that would have spoiled over Sunday, he invented a mess and called it the Eddie Extra, and the girls swarmed on it like flies around a honey pot.

That kind of thing would have spoiled most boys. But Eddie had a sensible mother. On those nights when he used to come home nauseated with dealing out chop suey sundaes and orangeades, and saying that there was no future for a fellow in our dead little hole, his mother would give him something rather special for supper, and set him hoeing and watering the garden.

So Eddie stuck to his job, and waited, and all the time he was saying, with a melting look, to the last silly little girl who was drinking her third soda, "Somebody looks mighty sweet in pink to-day," or while he was doping to-morrow's ball game with one of the boys who dropped in for a cigar, he was thinking of bigger things, and longing for a man-size job.

The man-size job loomed up before Eddie's dazzled eyes when he least expected it. It was at the close of a particularly hot day when it seemed to Eddie that every one in town had had everything from birch beer to peach ice cream. On his way home to supper he stopped at the postoffice with a handful of letters that old man Kunz had given him to mail. His mother had told him that they would have corn out of their own garden for supper that night, and Eddie was in something of a hurry. He and his mother were great pals.

In one corner of the dim little postoffice lobby a man was busily tacking up posters. The whitewashed walls bloomed with them. They were gay, attractive-looking posters, done in red and blue and green, and after Eddie had dumped his mail into the slot, and had called out, "Hello, Jake!" to the stamp clerk, whose back was turned to the window, he strolled idly over to where the man was putting the finishing touches to his work. The man was dressed in a sailor suit of blue, with a picturesque silk scarf knotted at his hairy chest. He went right on tacking posters.

They certainly were attractive pictures. Some showed groups of stalwart, immaculately clad young gods lolling indolently on tropical shores, with a splendor of palms overhead, and a sparkling blue sea in the distance. Others depicted a group of white-clad men wading knee-deep in the surf as they laughingly landed a cutter on the sandy beach. There was a particularly fascinating one showing two barefooted young chaps on a wave-swept raft engaged in that delightfully perilous task known as signaling. Another showed the keen-eyed gunners busy about the big guns.

Eddie studied them all.

The man finished his task and looked up, quite casually.

"Hello, kid," he said.

"Hello," answered Eddie. Then—"That's some picture gallery you're giving us."

The man in the sailor suit fell back a pace or two and surveyed his work with a critical but satisfied eye.

"Pitchers," he said, "don't do it justice. We've opened a recruiting office here. Looking for young men with brains, and muscle, and ambition. It's a great chance. We don't get to these here little towns much."

He placed a handbill in Eddie's hand. Eddie glanced down at it sheepishly.

"I've heard," he said, "that it's a hard life."

The man in the sailor suit threw back his head and laughed, displaying a great deal of hairy throat and chest. "Hard!" he jeered, and slapped one of the gay-colored posters with the back of his hand. "You see that! Well, it ain't a bit exaggerated. Not a bit. I ought to know. It's the only life for a young man, especially for a guy in a little town. There's no chance here for a bright young man, and if he goes to the city, what does he get? The city's jam full of kids that flock there in the spring and fall, looking for jobs, and thinking the city's sittin' up waitin' for 'em. And where do they land? In the dime lodging houses, that's where. In the navy you see the world, and it don't cost you a cent. A guy is a fool to bury himself alive in a hole like this. You could be seeing the world, traveling by sea from port to port, from country to country, from ocean to ocean, amid ever-changing scenery and climatic conditions, to see and study the habits and conditions of the strange races——"

It rolled off his tongue with fascinating glibness. Eddie glanced at the folder in his hand.

"I always did like the water," he said.

"Sure," agreed the hairy man, heartily. "What young feller don't? I'll tell you what. Come on over to the office with me and I'll show you some real stuff."

"It's my supper time," hesitated Eddie. "I guess I'd better not——"

"Oh, supper," laughed the man. "You come on and have supper with me, kid."

Eddie's pink cheeks went three shades pinker. "Gee! That'd be great. But my mother—that is—she——"

The man in the sailor suit laughed again—a laugh with a sting in it. "A great big feller like you ain't tied to your ma's apron strings are you?"

"Not much I'm not!" retorted Eddie. "I'll telephone her when I get to your hotel, that's what I'll do."

But they were such fascinating things, those new booklets, and the man had such marvelous tales to tell, that Eddie forgot trifles like supper and waiting mothers. There were pictures taken on board ship, showing frolics, and ball games, and minstrel shows and glee clubs, and the men at mess, and each sailor sleeping snug as a bug in his hammock. There were other pictures showing foreign scenes and strange ports. Eddie's tea grew cold, and his apple pie and cheese lay untasted on his plate.

"Now me," said the recruiting officer, "I'm a married man. But my wife, she wouldn't have it no other way. No, sir! She'll be in the navy herself, I'll bet, when women vote. Why, before I joined the navy I didn't know whether Guam was a vegetable or an island, and Culebra wasn't in my geography. Now? Why, now I'm as much at home in Porto Rico as I am in San Francisco. I'm as well acquainted in Valparaiso as I am in Vermont, and I've run around Cairo, Egypt, until I know it better than Cairo, Illinois. It's the only way to see the world. You travel by sea from port to port, from country to country, from ocean to ocean, amid ever-changing scenery and climatic conditions, to see and study the——"

And Eddie forgot that it was Wednesday night, which was the prescription clerk's night off; forgot that the boss was awaiting his return that he might go home to his own supper; forgot his mother, and her little treat of green corn out of the garden; forgot everything in the wonder of this man's tales of people and scenes such as he never dreamed could exist outside of a Jack London story. Now and then Eddie interrupted with a, "Yes, but——" that grew more and more infrequent, until finally they ceased altogether. Eddie's man-size job had come.

232

When we heard the news we all dropped in at the drug store to joke with him about it. We had a good deal to say about rolling gaits, and bell-shaped trousers, and anchors and sea serpents tattooed on the arm. One of the boys scored a hit by slapping his dime down on the soda fountain marble and bellowing for rum and salt horse. Some one started to tease the little Morehouse girl about sailors having sweethearts in every port, but when they saw the look in her eyes they changed their mind, and stopped. It's funny how a girl of twenty is a woman, when a man of twenty is a boy.

Eddie dished out the last of his chocolate ice cream sodas and cherry phosphates and root beers, while the girls laughingly begged him to bring them back kimonos from China, and scarves from the Orient, and Eddie promised, laughing, too, but with a far-off, eager look in his eyes.

When the time came for him to go there was quite a little bodyguard of us ready to escort him down to the depot. We picked up two or three more outside O'Rourke's pool room, and a couple more from the benches outside the hotel. Eddie walked ahead with his mother. I have said that Mrs. Houghton was a sensible woman. She was never more so than now. Any other mother would have gone into hysterics and begged the recruiting officer to let her boy off. But she knew better. Still, I think Eddie felt some uncomfortable pangs when he looked at her set face. On the way to the depot we had to pass the Agassiz School, where Josie Morehouse was substituting second reader for the Wilson girl, who was sick. She was standing in the window as we passed. Eddie took off his cap and waved to her, and she returned the wave as well as she could without having the children see her. That would never have done, seeing that she was the teacher, and substituting at that. But when we turned the corner we noticed that she was still standing at the window and leaning out just a bit, even at the risk of being indiscreet.

When the 10:15 pulled out Eddie stood on the bottom step, with his cap off, looking I can't tell you how boyish, and straight, and clean, and handsome, with his lips parted, and his eyes very bright. The hairy-chested recruiting officer stood just beside him, and suffered by contrast. There was a bedlam of good-byes, and last messages, and good-natured badinage, but Eddie's mother's eyes never left his face until the train disappeared around the curve in the track.

Well, they got a new boy at Kunz's—a sandy-haired youth, with pimples, and no knack at mixing, and we got out of the habit of dropping in there, although those fall months were unusually warm.

It wasn't long before we began to get postcards—pictures of the naval training station, and the gymnasium, and of model camps and of drills, and of Eddie in his uniform. His mother insisted on calling it his sailor suit, as though he were a little boy. One day Josie Morehouse came over to Mrs. Houghton's with a group picture in her hand. She handed it to Eddie's mother without comment. Mrs. Houghton looked at it eagerly, her eye selecting her own boy from the group as unerringly as a mother bird finds her nest in the forest.

"Oh, Eddie's better looking than that!" she cried, with a tremulous little laugh. "How funny those pants make them look, don't they? And his mouth isn't that way, at all. Eddie always had the sweetest mouth, from the time he was a baby. Let's see some of these other boys. Why—why———"

Then she fell silent, scanning those other faces. Presently Josie bent over her and looked too, and the brows of both women knitted in perplexity. They looked for a long, long minute, and the longer they looked the more noticeable became the cluster of fine little wrinkles that had begun to form about Mrs. Houghton's eyes.

When finally they looked up it was to gaze at one another questioningly.

"Those other boys," faltered Eddie's mother, "they—they don't look like Eddie, do they? I mean———"

"No, they don't," agreed Josie. "They look older, and they have such queer-looking eyes, and jaws, and foreheads. But then," she finished, with mock cheerfulness, "you can never tell in those silly kodak pictures."

Eddie's mother studied the card again, and sighed gently. "I hope," she said, "that Eddie won't get into bad company."

After that our postal cards ceased. I wish that there was some way of telling this story so that the end wouldn't come in the middle. But there is none. In our town we know the news before the paper comes out, and we only read it to verify what we have heard. So that long before the paper came out in the middle of the afternoon we had been horrified by the news of Eddie Houghton's desertion and suicide. We stopped one another on Main Street to talk about it, and recall how boyish and handsome he had looked in his white duck coat, and on that last day just as the 10:15 pulled out. "It don't seem hardly possible, does it?" we demanded of each other.

But when Eddie's mother brought out the letters that had come after our postal cards had ceased, we understood. And when they brought him home, and we saw him for the last time, all those of us who had gone to school with him, and to dances, and sleigh rides, and hayrack parties, and picnics, and when we saw the look on his face—the look of one who, walking in a sunny path has stumbled upon something horrible and unclean—we forgave him his neglect of us, we forgave him desertion, forgave him the taking of his own life, forgave him the look that he had brought into his mother's eyes.

There had never been anything extraordinary about Eddie Houghton. He had had his faults and virtues, and good and bad sides just like other boys of his age. He—oh, I am using too many words, when one slang phrase will express it. Eddie had been just a nice young kid. I think the worst thing he had ever said was "Damn!" perhaps. If he had sworn, it was with clean oaths, calculated to relieve the mind and feelings.

But the men that he shipped with during that year or more—I am sure that he had never dreamed that such men were. He had never stood on the curbing outside a recruiting office on South State Street, in the old levee district, and watched that tragic panorama move by—those nightmare faces, drink-marred, vice-scarred, ruined.

I know that he had never seen such faces in all his clean, hard-working young boy's life, spent in our prosperous little country town. I am certain that he had never heard such words as came from the lips of his fellow seamen—great mouth-filling, soul-searing words—words unclean, nauseating, unspeakable, and yet spoken.

I don't say that Eddie Houghton had not taken his drink now and then. There were certain dark rumors in our town to the effect that favored ones who dropped into Kunz's more often than seemed needful were privileged to have a thimbleful of something choice in the prescription room, back of the partition at the rear of the drug store. But that was the most devilish thing that Eddie had ever done.

I don't say that all crews are like that one. Perhaps he was unfortunate in falling in with that one. But it was an Eastern trip, and every port was a Port Said. Eddie Houghton's thoughts were not these men's thoughts; his actions were not their actions, his practices were not their practices. To Eddie Houghton, a Chinese woman in a sampan on the water front at Shanghai was something picturesque; something about which to write home to his mother and to Josie. To those other men she was possible prey.

Those other men saw that he was different, and they pestered him. They ill-treated him when they could, and made his life a hellish thing. Men do those things, and people do not speak of it.

I don't know all the things that he suffered. But in his mind, day by day, grew the great, overwhelming desire to get away from it all—from this horrible life that was such a dreadful mistake. I think that during the long night watches his mind was filled with thoughts of our decent little town—of his mother's kitchen, with its Wednesday and Saturday scent of new-made bread—of the shady front porch, with its purple clematis—of the smooth front yard which it was his Saturday duty to mow that it might be trim and sightly for Sunday—of the boys and girls who used to drop in at the drug store—those clear-eyed, innocently coquettish, giggling, blushing girls in their middy blouses and white skirts, their slender arms and throats browned from tennis and boating, their eyes smiling into his as they sat perched at the fountain after a hot set of tennis—those slim, clean young boys, sun-browned, laughing, their talk all of swimming, and boating, and tennis, and girls.

He did not realize that it was desertion—that thought that grew and grew in his mind. In it there was nothing of faithlessness to his country. He was only trying to be true to himself, and to the things that his mother had taught him. He only knew that he was deadly sick of these sights of disease, and vice. He only knew that he wanted to get away—back to his own decent life with the decent people to whom he belonged. And he went. He went, as a child runs home when it had tripped and fallen in the mud, not dreaming of wrong-doing or punishment.

The first few hundred miles on the train were a dream. But finally Eddie found himself talking to a man—a big, lean, blue-eyed western man, who regarded Eddie with kindly, puzzled eyes. Eddie found himself telling his story in a disjointed, breathless sort of way. When he had finished the man uncrossed his long lean legs, took his pipe out of his mouth, and sat up. There was something of horror in his eyes as he sat, looking at Eddie.

"Why, kid," he said, at last. "You're deserting! You'll get the pen, don't you know that, if they catch you? Where you going?"

"Going!" repeated Eddie. "Going! Why, I'm going home, of course."

"Then I don't see what you're gaining," said the man, "because they'll sure get you there."

Eddie sat staring at the man for a dreadful minute. In that minute the last of his glorious youth, and ambition, and zest of life departed from him.

He got off the train at the next town, and the western man offered him some money, which Eddie declined with all his old-time sweetness of manner. It was rather a large town, with a great many busy people in it. Eddie went to a cheap hotel, and took a room, and sat on the edge of the thin little bed and stared at the carpet. It was a dusty red carpet. In front of the bureau many feet had worn a hole, so that the bare boards showed through, with a tuft of ragged red fringe edging them. Eddie Houghton sat and stared at the worn place with a curiously blank look on his face. He sat and stared and saw many things. He saw his mother, for one thing, sitting on the porch with a gingham apron over her light dress, waiting for him to come home to supper; he saw his own room—a typical boy's room, with camera pictures and blue prints stuck in the sides of the dresser mirror, and the boxing gloves on the wall, and his tennis racquet with one string broken (he had always meant to have that racquet re-strung) and his track shoes, relics of high school days, flung in one corner, and his gay-colored school pennants draped to form a fresco, and the cushion that Josie Morenouse had made for him two years ago, at Christmas time, and the dainty white bedspread that he, fussed about because he said it was too sissy for a boy's room—oh, I can't tell you what he saw as he sat and stared at that worn place in the carpet. But pretty soon it began to grow dark, and at last he rose, keeping his fascinated eyes still on the bare spot, walked to the door, opened it, and backed out queerly, still keeping his eyes on the spot.

He was back again in fifteen minutes, with a bottle in his hand. He should have known better than to choose carbolic, being a druggist, but all men are a little mad at such times. He lay down at the edge of the thin little bed that was little more than a pallet, and he turned his face toward the bare spot that could just be seen in the gathering gloom. And when he raised the bottle to his lips the old-time sweetness of his smile illumined his face.

Where the car turns at Eighteenth Street there is a big, glaring billboard poster, showing a group of stalwart young men in white ducks lolling on shores, of tropical splendor, with palms waving overhead, and a glimpse of blue sea in the distance. The wording beneath it runs something like this:

"Young men wanted. An unusual opportunity for travel, education and advancement. Good pay. No expenses."

When I see that sign I think of Eddie Houghton back home. And when I think of Eddie Houghton I see red.

Gigolo

Though he rarely heeded its summons—cagy boy that he was—the telephone rang oftenest for Nick. Because of the many native noises of the place, the telephone had a special bell that was a combination buzz and ring. It sounded above the roar of outgoing cars, the splash of the hose, the sputter and hum of the electric battery in the rear. Nick heard it, unheeding. A voice—Smitty's or Mike's or Elmer's—answering its call. Then, echoing through the grey, vaulted spaces of the big garage: "Nick! Oh, Ni-ick!"

From the other side of the great cement-floored enclosure, or in muffled tones from beneath a car: "Whatcha want?"

"Dame on the wire."

"I ain't in."

The obliging voice again, dutifully repeating the message: "He ain't in.... Well, it's hard to say. He might be in in a couple hours and then again he might not be back till late. I guess he's went to Hammond on a job——" (Warming to his task now.) "Say, won't I do?... Who's fresh! Aw, say, *lady*!"

You'd think, after repeated rebuffs of this sort, she could not possibly be so lacking in decent pride as to leave her name for Smitty or Mike or Elmer to bandy about. But she invariably did, baffled by Nick's elusiveness. She was likely to be any one of a number. Miss Bauers phoned: Will you tell him, please? (A nasal voice, and haughty, with the hauteur that seeks to conceal secret fright.) Tell him it's important. Miss Ahearn phoned: Will you tell him, please? Just say Miss Ahearn. A-h-e-a-r-n. Miss Olson: Just Gertie. But oftenest Miss Bauers.

Cupid's messenger, wearing grease-grimed overalls and the fatuous grin of the dalliant male, would transmit his communication to the uneager Nick.

"'S wonder you wouldn't answer the phone once yourself. Says you was to call Miss Bauers any time you come in between one and six at Hyde Park—wait a min't'—yeh—Hyde Park 6079, and any time after six at——"

"Wha'd she want?"

"Well, how the hell should I know! Says call Miss Bauers any time between one and six at Hyde Park 6——"

"Swell chanst. *Swell* chanst!"

Which explains why the calls came oftenest for Nick. He was so indifferent to them. You pictured the patient and persistent Miss Bauers, or the oxlike Miss Olson, or Miss Ahearn, or just Gertie hovering within hearing distance of the telephone listening, listening—while one o'clock deepened to six—for the call that never came; plucking up fresh courage at six until six o'clock dragged on to bedtime. When next they met: "I bet you was there all the time. Pity you wouldn't answer a call when a person leaves their name. You could of give me a ring. I bet you was there all the time."

"Well, maybe I was."

Bewildered, she tried to retaliate with the boomerang of vituperation.

How could she know? How could she know that this slim, slick young garage mechanic was a woodland creature in disguise—a satyr in store clothes—a wild thing who perversely preferred to do his own pursuing? How could Miss Bauers know—she who cashiered in the Green Front Grocery and Market on Fifty-third Street? Or Miss Olson, at the Rialto ticket window? Or the Celtic, emotional Miss Ahearn, the manicure? Or Gertie the goof? They knew nothing of mythology; of pointed ears and pug noses and goat's feet. Nick's ears, to their fond gaze, presented an honest red surface protruding from either side of his head. His feet, in tan laced shoes, were ordinary feet, a little more than ordinarily expert, perhaps, in the convolutions of the dance at Englewood Masonic Hall, which is part of Chicago's vast South Side. No; a faun, to Miss Bauers, Miss Olson, Miss Ahearn, and just Gertie, was one of those things in the Lincoln Park Zoo.

Perhaps, sometimes, they realized, vaguely, that Nick was different. When, for example, they tried—and failed—to picture him looking interestedly at one of those three-piece bedroom sets glistening like pulled taffy in the window of the installment furniture store, while they, shy yet proprietary, clung to his arm and eyed the price ticket. Now $98.50. You couldn't see Nick interested in bedroom sets, in price tickets, in any of those settled, fixed, everyday things. He was fluid, evasive, like quicksilver, though they did not put it thus.

Miss Bauers, goaded to revolt, would say pettishly: "You're like a mosquito, that's what. Person never knows from one minute to the other where you're at."

"Yeh," Nick would retort. "When you know where a mosquito's at, what do you do to him? Plenty. I ain't looking to be squashed."

Miss Ahearn, whose public position (the Hygienic Barber Shop. Gent's manicure, 50c.) offered unlimited social opportunities, would assume a gay indifference. "They's plenty boys begging to take me out every hour in the day. Swell lads, too. I ain't waiting round for any greasy mechanic like you. Don't think it. Say, lookit your nails! They'd queer you with me, let alone what else all is wrong with you."

In answer Nick would put one hand—one broad, brown, steel-strong hand with its broken discoloured nails—on Miss Ahearn's arm, in its flimsy georgette sleeve. Miss Ahearn's eyelids would flutter and close, and a little shiver would run with icy-hot feet all over Miss Ahearn.

Nick was like that.

Nick's real name wasn't Nick at all—or scarcely at all. His last name was Nicholas, and his parents, long before they became his parents, traced their origin to some obscure Czechoslovakian province—long before we became so glib with our Czechoslovakia. His first name was Dewey, knowing which you automatically know the date of his birth. It was a patriotic but unfortunate choice on the part of his parents. The name did not fit him; was too mealy; not debonair enough. Nick. Nicky in tenderer moments (Miss Bauers, Miss Olson, Miss Ahearn, just Gertie, et al.).

His method with women was firm and somewhat stern, but never brutal. He never waited for them if they were late. Any girl who assumed that her value was enhanced in direct proportion to her tardiness in keeping an engagement with Nick found herself standing disconsolate on the corner of Fifty-third and Lake trying to look as if she were merely waiting for the Lake Park car and not peering wistfully up and down the street in search of a slim, graceful, hurrying figure that never came.

It is difficult to convey in words the charm that Nick possessed. Seeing him, you beheld merely a medium-sized young mechanic in reasonably grimed garage clothes when working; and in tight pants, tight coat, silk shirt, long-visored green cap when at leisure. A rather pallid skin due to the nature of his work. Large deft hands, a good deal like the hands of a surgeon, square, blunt-fingered, spatulate. Indeed, as you saw him at work, a wire-netted electric bulb held in one hand, the other plunged deep into the vitals of the car on which he was engaged, you thought of a surgeon performing a major operation. He wore one of those round skullcaps characteristic of his craft (the brimless crown of an old felt hat). He would deftly remove the transmission case and plunge his hand deep into the car's guts, feeling expertly about with his engine-wise fingers as a surgeon feels for liver, stomach, gall bladder, intestines, appendix. When he brought up his hand, all dripping with grease (which is the warm blood of the car), he invariably had put his finger on the sore spot.

All this, of course, could not serve to endear him to the girls. On the contrary, you would have thought that his hands alone, from which he could never quite free the grease and grit, would have caused some feeling of repugnance among the lily-fingered. But they, somehow, seemed always to be finding an excuse to touch him: his tie, his hair, his coat sleeve. They seemed even to derive a vicarious thrill from holding his hat or cap when on an outing. They brushed imaginary bits of lint from his coat lapel. They tried on his seal ring, crying: "Oo, lookit, how big it is for me, even my thumb!" He called this "pawing a guy over"; and the lint ladies he designated as "thread pickers."

No; it can't be classified, this powerful draw he had for them. His conversation furnished no clue. It was commonplace conversation, limited, even dull. When astonished, or impressed, or horrified, or amused, he said: "Ken yuh feature that!" When emphatic or confirmatory, he said: "You *tell* 'em!"

It wasn't his car and the opportunities it furnished for drives, both country and city. That motley piece of mechanism represented such an assemblage of unrelated parts as could only have been made to coördinate under Nick's expert guidance. It was out of commission more than half the time, and could never be relied upon to furnish a holiday. Both Miss Bauers and Miss Ahearn had twelve-cylinder opportunities that should have rendered them forever unfit for travel in Nick's one-lung vehicle of locomotion.

It wasn't money. Though he was generous enough with what he had, Nick couldn't be generous with what he hadn't. And his wage at the garage was $40 a week. Miss Ahearn's silk stockings cost $4.50.

His unconcern should have infuriated them, but it served to pique. He wasn't actually as unconcerned as he appeared, but he had early learned that effort in their direction was unnecessary. Nick had little imagination; a gorgeous selfishness; a tolerantly contemptuous liking for the sex. Naturally, however, his attitude toward them had been somewhat embittered by being obliged to watch their method of driving a car in and out of the Ideal Garage doorway. His own manipulation of the wheel was nothing short of wizardry.

He played the harmonica.

Each Thursday afternoon was Nick's half day off. From twelve until seven-thirty he was free to range the bosky highways of Chicago. When his car—he called it "the bus"—was agreeable, he went awheel in search of amusement. The bus being indisposed, he went afoot. He rarely made plans in advance; usually was accompanied by some successful telephonee. He rather liked to have a silken skirt beside him fluttering and flirting in the breeze as he broke the speed regulations.

On this Thursday afternoon in July he had timed his morning job to a miraculous nicety so that at the stroke of twelve his workaday garments dropped from him magically, as though he were a male (and reversed) Cinderella. There was a wash room and a rough sort of sleeping room containing two cots situated in the second story of the Ideal Garage. Here Nick shed the loose garments of labour for the fashionably tight habiliments of leisure. Private chauffeurs whose employers housed their cars in the Ideal Garage used this nook for a lounge and smoker. Smitty, Mike, Elmer, and Nick snatched stolen siestas there in the rare absences of the manager. Sometimes Nick spent the night there when forced to work overtime. His home life, at best, was a sketchy affair. Here chauffeurs, mechanics, washers lolled at ease exchanging soft-spoken gossip, motor chat, speculation, comment, and occasional verbal obscenity. Each possessed a formidable knowledge of that neighbourhood section of Chicago known as Hyde Park.

237

This knowledge was not confined to car costs and such impersonal items, but included meals, scandals, relationships, finances, love affairs, quarrels, peccadillos. Here Nick often played his harmonica, his lips sweeping the metal length of it in throbbing rendition of such sure-fire sentimentality as The Long, Long Trail, or Mammy, while the others talked, joked, kept time with tapping feet or wagging heads.

To-day the hot little room was empty except for Nick, shaving before the cracked mirror on the wall, and old Elmer, reading a scrap of yesterday's newspaper as he lounged his noon hour away. Old Elmer was thirty-seven, and Nicky regarded him as an octogenarian. Also, old Elmer's conversation bored Nick to the point of almost sullen resentment. Old Elmer was a family man. His talk was all of his family—the wife, the kids, the flat. A garrulous person, lank, pasty, dish-faced, and amiable. His half day off was invariably spent tinkering about the stuffy little flat—painting, nailing up shelves, mending a broken window shade, puttying a window, playing with his pasty little boy, aged sixteen months, and his pasty little girl, aged three years. Next day he regaled his fellow workers with elaborate recitals of his holiday hours.

"Believe me, that kid's a caution. Sixteen months old, and what does he do yesterday? He unfastens the ketch on the back-porch gate. We got a gate on the back porch, see." (This frequent "see" which interlarded Elmer's verbiage was not used in an interrogatory way, but as a period, and by way of emphasis. His voice did not take the rising inflection as he uttered it.) "What does he do, he opens it. I come home, and the wife says to me: 'Say, you better get busy and fix a new ketch on that gate to the back porch. Little Elmer, first thing I know, he'd got it open to-day and was crawling out almost.' Say, can you beat that for a kid sixteen months——"

Nick had finished shaving, had donned his clean white soft shirt. His soft collar fitted to a miracle about his strong throat. Nick's sartorial effects were a triumph—on forty a week. "Say, can't you talk about nothing but that kid of yours? I bet he's a bum specimen at that. Runt, like his pa."

Elmer flung down his newspaper in honest indignation as Nick had wickedly meant he should. "Is that so! Why, we was wrastling round—me and him, see—last night on the floor, and what does he do, he raises his mitt and hands me a wallop in the stomick it like to knock the wind out of me. That's all. Sixteen months——"

"Yeh. I suppose this time next year he'll be boxing for money."

Elmer resumed his paper. "What do *you* know." His tone mingled pity with contempt.

Nick took a last critical survey of the cracked mirror's reflection and found it good. "Nothing, only this: you make me sick with your kids and your missus and your place. Say, don't you never have no fun?"

"Fun! Why, say, last Sunday we was out to the beach, and the kid swum out first thing you know——"

"Oh, shut up!" He was dressed now. He slapped his pockets. Harmonica. Cigarettes. Matches. Money. He was off, his long-visored cloth cap pulled jauntily over his eyes.

Elmer, bearing no rancour, flung a last idle query: "Where you going?"

"How should I know? Just bumming around. Bus is outa commission, and I'm outa luck."

He clattered down the stairs, whistling.

Next door for a shine at the Greek bootblack's. Enthroned on the dais, a minion at his feet, he was momentarily monarchial. How's the boy? Good? Same here. Down, his brief reign ended. Out into the bright noon-day glare of Fifty-third Street.

A fried-egg sandwich. Two blocks down and into the white-tiled lunchroom. He took his place in the row perched on stools in front of the white slab, his feet on the railing, his elbows on the counter. Four white-aproned vestals with blotchy skins performed rites over the steaming nickel urns, slid dishes deftly along the slick surface of the white slab, mopped up moisture with a sly grey rag. No nonsense about them. This was the rush hour. Hungry men from the shops and offices and garages of the district were bent on food (not badinage). They ate silently, making a dull business of it. Coffee? What kinda pie do you want? No fooling here. "Hello, Jessie."

As she mopped the slab in front of him you noticed a slight softening of her features, intent so grimly on her task. "What's yours?"

"Bacon-and-egg sandwich. Glass of milk. Piece of pie. Blueberry."

Ordinarily she would not have bothered. But with him: "The blueberry ain't so good to-day, I noticed. Try the peach?"

"All right." He looked at her. She smiled. Incredibly, the dishes ordered seemed to leap out at her from nowhere. She crashed them down on the glazed white surface in front of him. The bacon-and-egg sandwich was served open-faced, an elaborate confection. Two slices of white bread, side by side. On one reposed a fried egg, hard, golden, delectable, indigestible. On the other three crisp curls of bacon. The ordinary order held two curls only. A dish so rich in calories as to make it food sufficient for a day. Jessie knew nothing of calories, nor did Nick. She placed a double order of butter before him—two yellow pats, moisture-beaded. As she scooped up his milk from the can you saw that the glass was but three quarters filled. From a deep crock she ladled a smaller scoop and filled the glass to the top. The deep crock held cream. Nick glanced up at her again. Again Jessie smiled. A plain damsel, Jessie, and capable. She went on about her business. What's yours? Coffee with? White or rye? No nonsense about her. And yet: "Pie all right?"

"Yeh. It's good."

She actually blushed.

He finished, swung himself off the stool, nodded to Jessie. She stacked his dishes with one lean, capable hand, mopped the slab with the other, but as she made for the kitchen she flung a glance at him over her shoulder.

"Day off?"

"Yeh."

"Some folks has all the luck."

He grinned. His teeth were strong and white and even. He walked toward the door with his light quick step, paused for a toothpick as he paid his check, was out again into the July sunlight. Her face became dull again.

Well, not one o'clock. Guessed he'd shoot a little pool. He dropped into Moriarty's cigar store. It was called a cigar store because it dealt in magazines, newspapers, soft drinks, golf balls, cigarettes, pool, billiards, chocolates, chewing gum, and cigars. In the rear of the store were four green-topped tables, three for pool and one for billiards. He hung about aimlessly, watching the game at the one occupied table. The players were slim young men like himself, their clothes replicas of his own, their faces lean and somewhat hard. Two of them dropped out. Nick took a cue from the rack, shed his tight coat. They played under a glaring electric light in the heat of the day, yet they seemed cool, aloof, immune from bodily discomfort. It was a strangely silent game and as mirthless as that of the elfin bowlers in Rip Van Winkle. The slim-waisted shirted figures bent plastically over the table in the graceful postures of the game. You heard only the click of the balls, an occasional low-voiced exclamation. A solemn crew, and unemotional.

Now and then: "What's all the shootin' fur?"

"In she goes."

Nick, winner, tired of it in less than an hour. He bought a bottle of some acidulous drink just off the ice and refreshed himself with it, drinking from the bottle's mouth. He was vaguely restless, dissatisfied. Out again into the glare of two o'clock Fifty-third Street. He strolled up a block toward Lake Park Avenue. It was hot. He wished the bus wasn't sick. Might go in swimming, though. He considered this idly. Hurried steps behind him. A familiar perfume wafted to his senses. A voice nasal yet cooing. Miss Bauers. Miss Bauers on pleasure bent, palpably, being attired in the briefest of silks, white-strapped slippers, white silk stockings, scarlet hat. The Green Front Grocery and Market closed for a half day each Thursday afternoon during July and August. Nicky had not availed himself of the knowledge.

"Well, if it ain't Nicky! I just seen you come out of Moriarty's as I was passing." (She had seen him go in an hour before and had waited a patient hour in the drug store across the street.) "What you doing around loose this hour the day, anyway?"

"I'm off 'safternoon."

"Are yuh? So'm I." Nicky said nothing. Miss Bauers shifted from one plump silken leg to the other. "What you doing?"

"Oh, nothing much."

"So'm I. Let's do it together." Miss Bauers employed the direct method.

"Well," said Nick, vaguely. He didn't object particularly. And yet he was conscious of some formless programme forming mistily in his mind—a programme that did not include the berouged, be-powdered, plump, and silken Miss Bauers.

"I phoned you this morning, Nicky. Twice."

"Yeh?"

"They said you wasn't in."

"Yeh?"

A hard young woman, Miss Bauers, yet simple: powerfully drawn toward this magnetic and careless boy; powerless to forge chains strong enough to hold him. "Well, how about Riverview? I ain't been this summer."

"Oh, that's so darn far. Take all day getting there, pretty near."

"Not driving, it wouldn't."

"I ain't got the bus. Busted."

His apathy was getting on her nerves. "How about a movie, then?" Her feet hurt. It was hot.

His glance went up the street toward the Harper, down the street toward the Hyde Park. The sign above the Harper offered Mother o' Mine. The lettering above the Hyde Park announced Love's Sacrifice.

"Gawd, no," he made decisive answer.

Miss Bauers's frazzled nerves snapped. "You make me sick! Standing there. Nothing don't suit you. Say, I ain't so crazy to go round with you. Cheap guy! Prob'ly you'd like to go over to Wooded Island or something, in Jackson Park, and set on the grass and feed the squirrels. That'd be a treat for me, that would." She laughed a high, scornful tear-near laugh.

"Why—say——" Nick stared at her, and yet she felt he did not see her. A sudden peace came into his face—the peace of a longing fulfilled. He turned his head. A Lake Park Avenue street car was roaring its way toward them. He took a step toward the roadway. "I got to be going."

Fear flashed its flame into Miss Bauers's pale blue eyes. "Going! How do you mean, going? Going where?"

"I got to be going." The car had stopped opposite them. His young face was stern, implacable. Miss Bauers knew she was beaten, but she clung to hope tenaciously, piteously. "I got to see a party, see?"

"You never said anything about it in the first place. Pity you wouldn't say so in the first place. Who you got to see, anyway?" She knew it was useless to ask. She knew she was beating her fists against a stone wall, but she must needs ask notwithstanding: "Who you got to see?"

"I got to see a party. I forgot." He made the car step in two long strides; had swung himself up. "So long!" The car door slammed after him. Miss Bauers, in her unavailing silks, stood disconsolate on the hot street corner.

He swayed on the car platform until Sixty-third Street was reached. There he alighted and stood a moment at the curb surveying idly the populous corner. He purchased a paper bag of hot peanuts from a vender's glittering scarlet and nickel stand, and crossed the street into the pathway that led to Jackson Park, munching as he went. In an open space reserved for games some boys were playing baseball with much hoarse hooting and frenzied action. He drew near to watch. The ball, misdirected, sailed suddenly toward him. He ran backward at its swift approach, leaped high, caught it, and with a long curving swing, so easy as to appear almost effortless, sent it hurtling back. The lad on the pitcher's mound made as if to catch it, changed his mind, dodged, started after it.

The boy at bat called to Nick: "Heh, you! Wanna come on and pitch?"

Nick shook his head and went on.

He wandered leisurely along the gravel path that led to the park golf shelter. The wide porch was crowded with golfers and idlers. A foursome was teed up at the first tee. Nick leaned against a porch pillar waiting for them to drive. That old boy had pretty good practise swing ... Stiff, though ... Lookit that dame. Je's! I bet she takes fifteen shots before she ever gets on to the green ... There, that kid had pretty good drive. Must of been hundred and fifty, anyway. Pretty good for a kid.

Nick, in the course of his kaleidoscopic career, had been a caddie at thirteen in torn shirt and flapping knickers. He had played the smooth, expert, scornful game of the caddie with a natural swing from the lithe waist and a follow-through that was the envy of the muscle-bound men who watched him. He hadn't played in years. The game no longer interested him. He entered the shelter lunchroom. The counters were lined with lean, brown, hungry men and lean, brown, hungry women. They were eating incredible dishes considering that the hour was 3 P. M. and the day a hot one. Corned-beef hash with a poached egg on top; wieners and potato salad; meat pies; hot roast beef sandwiches; steaming cups of coffee in thick white ware; watermelon. Nick slid a leg over a stool as he had done earlier in the afternoon. Here, too, the Hebes were of stern stuff, as they needs must be to serve these ravenous hordes of club swingers who swarmed upon them from dawn to dusk. Their task it was to wait upon the golfing male, which is man at his simplest—reduced to the least common denominator and shorn of all attraction for the female eye and heart. They represented merely hungry mouths, weary muscles, reaching fists. The waitresses served them as a capable attendant serves another woman's child—efficiently and without emotion.

"Blueberry pie à la mode," said Nick—"with strawberry ice cream."

Inured as she was to the horrors of gastronomic miscegenation, the waitress—an old girl—recoiled at this.

"Say, I don't think you'd like that. They don't mix so very good. Why don't you try the peach pie instead with the strawberry ice cream—if you want strawberry?" He looked so young and cool and fresh.

"Blueberry," repeated Nick sternly, and looked her in the eye. The old waitress laughed a little and was surprised to find herself laughing. "'S for you to say." She brought him the monstrous mixture, and he devoured it to the last chromatic crumb.

"Nothing the matter with that," he remarked as she passed, dish-laden.

She laughed again tolerantly, almost tenderly. "Good thing you're young." Her busy glance lingered a brief moment on his face. He sauntered out.

Now he took the path to the right of the shelter, crossed the road, struck the path again, came to a rustic bridge that humped high in the middle, spanning a cool green stream, willow-bordered. The cool green stream was an emerald chain that threaded its way in a complete circlet about the sylvan spot known as Wooded Island, relic of World's Fair days.

The little island lay, like a thing under enchantment, silent, fragrant, golden, green, exquisite. Squirrels and blackbirds, rabbits and pigeons mingled in Æsopian accord. The air was warm and still, held by the encircling trees and shrubbery. There was not a soul to be seen. At the far north end the two Japanese model houses, survivors of the exposition, gleamed white among the trees.

Nick stood a moment. His eyelids closed, languorously. He stretched his arms out and up deliciously, bringing his stomach in and his chest out. He took off his cap and stuffed it into his pocket. He strolled across the thick cool nap of the grass, deserting the pebble path. At the west edge of the island a sign said: "No One Allowed in the Shrubbery." Ignoring it, Nick parted the branches, stopped and crept, reached the bank that sloped down to the cool green stream, took off his coat, and lay relaxed upon the ground. Above him the tree branches made a pattern against the sky. Little ripples lipped the shore. Scampering velvet-footed things, feathered things, winged things made pleasant stir among the leaves. Nick slept.

He awoke in half an hour refreshed. He lay there, thinking of nothing—a charming gift. He found a stray peanut in his pocket and fed it to a friendly squirrel. His hand encountered the cool metal of his harmonica. He drew out the instrument, placed his coat, folded, under his head, crossed his knees, one leg swinging idly, and began to play rapturously. He was perfectly happy. He played Gimme Love, whose jazz measures are stolen from Mendelssohn's Spring Song. He did not know this. The leaves rustled. He did not turn his head.

"Hello, Pan!" said a voice. A girl came down the slope and seated herself beside him. She was not smiling.

Nick removed the harmonica from his lips and wiped his mouth with the back of his hand. "Hello who?"

"Hello, Pan."

"Wrong number, lady," Nick said, and again applied his lips to the mouth organ. The girl laughed then, throwing back her head. Her throat was long and slim and brown. She clasped her knees with her arms and looked at Nick amusedly. Nick thought she was a kind of homely little thing.

"Pan," she explained, "was a pagan deity. He played pipes in the woods."

"'S all right with me," Nick ventured, bewildered but amiable. He wished she'd go away. But she didn't. She began to take off her shoes and stockings. She went down to the water's edge, then, and paddled her feet. Nick sat up, outraged. "Say, you can't do that."

She glanced back at him over her shoulder. "Oh, yes, I can. It's so hot." She wriggled her toes ecstatically.

The leaves rustled again, briskly, unmistakably this time. A heavy tread. A rough voice. "Say, looka here! Get out of there, you! What the——" A policeman, red-faced, wroth. "You can't do that! Get outa here!"

It was like a movie, Nick thought.

The girl turned her head. "Oh, now, Mr. Elwood," she said.

"Oh, it's you, miss," said the policeman. You would not have believed it could be the same policeman. He even giggled. "Thought you was away."

"I was. In fact, I am, really. I just got sick of it and ran away for a day. Drove. Alone. The family'll be wild."

"All the way?" said the policeman, incredulously. "Say, I thought that looked like your car standing out there by the road; but I says no, she ain't in town." He looked sharply at Nick, whose face had an Indian composure, though his feelings were mixed. "Who's this?"

"He's a friend of mine. His name's Pan." She was drying her feet with an inadequate rose-coloured handkerchief. She crept crabwise up the bank, and put on her stockings and slippers.

"Why'n't you come out and set on a bench?" suggested the policeman, worriedly.

The girl shook her head. "In Arcadia we don't sit on benches. I should think you'd know that. Go on away, there's a dear. I want to talk to this—to Pan."

He persisted. "What'd your pa say, I'd like to know!" The girl shrugged her shoulders. Nick made as though to rise. He was worried. A nut, that's what. She pressed him down again with a hard brown hand.

"Now it's all right. He's going. Old Fuss!" The policeman stood a brief moment longer. Then the foliage rustled again. He was gone. The girl sighed, happily. "Play that thing some more, will you? You're a wiz at it, aren't you?"

"I'm pretty good," said Nick, modestly. Then the outrageousness of her conduct struck him afresh. "Say, who're you, anyway?"

"My name's Berry—short for Bernice.... What's yours, Pan?"

"Nick—that is—Nick."

"Ugh, terrible! I'll stick to Pan. What d'you do when you're not Panning?" Then, at the bewilderment in his face: "What's your job?"

"I work in the Ideal Garage. Say, you're pretty nosey, ain't you?"

"Yes, pretty.... That accounts for your nails, h'm?" She looked at her own brown paws. "'Bout as bad as mine. I drove one hundred and fifty miles to-day."

"Ya-as, you did!"

"I did! Started at six. And I'll probably drive back to-night."

"You're crazy!"

"I know it," she agreed, "and it's wonderful.... Can you play the Tommy Toddle?"

"Yeh. It's kind of hard, though, where the runs are. I don't get the runs so very good." He played it. She kept time with head and feet. When he had finished and wiped his lips:

"Elegant!" She took the harmonica from him, wiped it brazenly on the much-abused, rose-coloured handkerchief and began to play, her cheeks puffed out, her eyes round with effort. She played the Tommy Toddle, and her runs were perfect. Nick's chagrin was swallowed by his admiration and envy.

"Say, kid, you got more wind than a factory whistle. Who learned you to play?"

She struck her chest with a hard brown fist. "Tennis ... Tim taught me."

"Who's Tim?"

"The—a chauffeur."

Nick leaned closer. "Say, do you ever go to the dances at Englewood Masonic Hall?"

"I never have."

"'Jah like to go some time?"

"I'd love it." She grinned up at him, her teeth flashing white in her brown face.

"It's swell here," he said, dreamily. "Like the woods?"

"Yes."

"Winter, when it's cold and dirty, I think about how it's here summers. It's like you could take it out of your head and look at it whenever you wanted to."

"Endymion."

"Huh?"

"A man said practically the same thing the other day. Name of Keats."

"Yeh?"

"He said: 'A thing of beauty is a joy forever.'"

"That's one way putting it," he agreed, graciously.

Unsmilingly she reached over with one slim forefinger, as if compelled, and touched the blond hairs on Nick's wrist. Just touched them. Nick remained motionless. The girl shivered a little, deliciously. She glanced at him shyly. Her lips were provocative. Thoughtlessly, blindly, Nick suddenly flung an arm about her, kissed her. He kissed her as he had never kissed Miss Bauers—as he had never kissed Miss Ahearn, Miss Olson, or just Gertie. The girl did not scream, or push him away, or slap him, or protest, or giggle as would have the above-mentioned young ladies. She sat breathing rather fast, a tinge of scarlet showing beneath the tan.

"Well, Pan," she said, low-voiced, "you're running true to form, anyway." She eyed him appraisingly. "Your appeal is in your virility, I suppose. Yes."

"My what?"

She rose. "I've got to go."

Panic seized him. "Say, don't drive back to-night, huh? Wherever it is you've got to go. You ain't driving back to-night?"

She made no answer; parted the bushes, was out on the gravel path in the sunlight, a slim, short-skirted, almost childish figure. He followed. They crossed the bridge, left the island, reached the roadway almost in silence. At the side of the road was a roadster. Its hood was the kind that conceals power. Its lamps were two giant eyes rimmed in precious metal. Its line spelled strength. Its body was foreign. Nick's engine-wise eyes saw these things at a glance.

"That your car?"

"Yes."

"Gosh!"

She unlocked it, threw in the clutch, shifted, moved. "Say!" was wrung from Nick helplessly. She waved at him. "Good-bye, Pan." He stared, stricken. She was off swiftly, silently; flashed around a corner; was hidden by the trees and shrubs.

He stood a moment. He felt bereaved, cheated. Then a little wave of exaltation shook him. He wanted to talk to someone. "Gosh!" he said again. He glanced at his wrist. Five-thirty. He guessed he'd go home. He guessed he'd go home and get one of Ma's dinners. One of Ma's dinners and talk to Ma. The Sixty-third Street car. He could make it and back in plenty time.

Nick lived in that section of Chicago known as Englewood, which is not so sylvan as it sounds, but appropriate enough for a faun. Not only that; he lived in S. Green Street, Englewood. S. Green Street, near Seventieth, is almost rural with its great elms and poplars, its frame cottages, its back gardens. A neighbourhood of thrifty, foreign-born fathers and mothers, many children, tree-lined streets badly paved. Nick turned in at a two-story brown frame cottage. He went around to the back. Ma was in the kitchen.

Nick's presence at the evening meal was an uncertain thing. Sometimes he did not eat at home for a week, excepting only his hurried early breakfast. He rarely spent an evening at home, and when he did used the opportunity for making up lost sleep. Pa never got home from work until after six. Nick liked his dinner early and hot. On his rare visits his mother welcomed him like one of the Gracchi. Mother and son understood each other wordlessly, having much in common. You would not have thought it of her (forty-six bust, forty waist, measureless hips), but Ma was a nymph at heart. Hence Nick.

"Hello, Ma!" She was slamming expertly about the kitchen.

"Hello, yourself," said Ma. Ma had a line of slang gleaned from her numerous brood. It fell strangely from her lips. Ma had never quite lost a tinge of foreign accent, though she had come to America when a girl. A hearty, zestful woman, savouring life with gusto, undiminished by child-bearing and hard work. "Eating home, Dewey?" She alone used his given name.

"Yeh, but I gotta be back by seven-thirty. Got anything ready?"

"Dinner ain't, but I'll get you something. Plenty. Platter ham and eggs and a quick fry. Cherry cobbler's done. I'll fix you some." (Cherry cobbler is shortcake with a soul.)

He ate enormously at the kitchen table, she hovering over him.

"What's the news, Dewey?"

"Ain't none." He ate in silence. Then: "How old was you when you married Pa?"

"Me? Say, I wasn't no more'n a kid. I gotta laugh when I think of it."

"What was Pa earning?"

She laughed a great hearty laugh, dipping a piece of bread sociably in the ham fat on the platter as she stood by the table, just to bear him company.

"Say, earn! If he'd of earned what you was earning now, we'd of thought we was millionaires. Time Etty was born he was pulling down thirteen a week, and we saved on it." She looked at him suddenly, sharply. "Why?"

"Oh, I was just wondering."

242

"Look what good money he's getting now! If I was you, I wouldn't stick around no old garage for what they give you. You could get a good job in the works with Pa; first thing you know you'd be pulling down big money. You're smart like that with engines.... Takes a lot of money nowadays for feller to get married."

"You *tell* 'em," agreed Nick. He looked up at her, having finished eating. His glance was almost tender. "How'd you come to marry Pa, anyway? You and him's so different."

The nymph in Ma leaped to the surface and stayed there a moment, sparkling, laughing, dimpling. "Oh, I dunno. I kept running away and he kept running after. Like that."

He looked up again quickly at that. "Yeh. That's it. Fella don't like to have no girl chasing him all the time. Say, he likes to do the chasing himself. Ain't that the truth?"

"You *tell* 'em!" agreed Ma. A great jovial laugh shook her. Heavy-footed now, but light of heart.

Suddenly: "I'm thinking of going to night school. Learn something. I don't know nothing."

"You do, too, Dewey!"

"Aw, wha'd I know? I never had enough schooling. Wished I had."

"Who's doings was it? You wouldn't stay. Wouldn't go no more than sixth reader and quit. Nothing wouldn't get you to go."

He agreed gloomily. "I know it. I don't know what nothing is. Uh—Arcadia—or—now—vitality or nothing."

"Oh, that comes easy," she encouraged him, "when you begin once."

He reached for her hand gratefully. "You're a swell cook, Ma." He had a sudden burst of generosity, of tenderness. "Soon's the bus is fixed I'll take you joy-riding over to the lake."

Ma always wore a boudoir cap of draggled lace and ribbon for motoring. Nick almost never offered her a ride. She did not expect him to.

She pushed him playfully. "Go on! You got plenty young girls to take riding, not your ma."

"Oh, girls!" he said, scornfully. Then in another tone: "Girls."

He was off. It was almost seven. Pa was late. He caught a car back to Fifty-third Street. Elmer was lounging in the cool doorway of the garage. Nick, in sheer exuberance of spirits, squared off, doubled his fists, and danced about Elmer in a semicircle, working his arms as a prizefighter does, warily. He jabbed at Elmer's jaw playfully.

"What you been doing," inquired that long-suffering gentleman, "makes you feel so good? Where you been?"

"Oh, nowheres. Bumming round. Park."

He turned in the direction of the stairway. Elmer lounged after him. "Oh, say, dame's been calling you for the last hour and a half. Like to busted the phone. Makes me sick."

"Aw, Bauers."

"No, that wasn't the name. Name's Mary or Berry, or something like that. A dozen times, I betcha. Says you was to call her as soon as you come in. Drexel 47—wait a min't'—yeh—that's right—Drexel 473——"

"Swell chanst," said Nick. Suddenly his buoyancy was gone. His shoulders drooped. His cigarette dangled limp. Disappointment curved his lips, burdened his eyes. "*Swell* chanst!"

OLD MAN MINICK

His wife had always spoiled him outrageously. No doubt of that. Take, for example, the matter of the pillows merely. Old man Minick slept high. That is, he thought he slept high. He liked two plump pillows on his side of the great, wide, old-fashioned cherry bed. He would sink into them with a vast grunting and sighing and puffing expressive of nerves and muscles relaxed and gratified. But in the morning there was always one pillow on the floor. He had thrown it there. Always, in the morning, there it lay, its plump white cheek turned reproachfully up at him from the side of the bed. Ma Minick knew this, naturally, after forty years of the cherry bed. But she never begrudged him that extra pillow. Each morning, when she arose, she picked it up on her way to shut the window. Each morning the bed was made up with two pillows on his side of it, as usual.

Then there was the window. Ma Minick liked it open wide. Old man Minick, who rather prided himself on his modernism (he called it being up to date) was distrustful of the night air. In the folds of its sable mantle lurked a swarm of dread things—colds, clammy miasmas, fevers.

"Night air's just like any other air," Ma Minick would say, with some asperity. Ma Minick was no worm; and as modern as he. So when they went to bed the window would be open wide. They would lie there, the two old ones, talking comfortably about commonplace things. The kind of talk that goes on between a man and a woman who have lived together in wholesome peace (spiced with occasional wholesome bickerings) for more than forty years.

"Remind me to see Gerson to-morrow about that lock on the basement door. The paper's full of burglars."

"If I think of it." She never failed to.

"George and Nettie haven't been over in a week now."

"Oh, well, young folks.... Did you stop in and pay that Koritz the fifty cents for pressing your suit?"

243

"By golly, I forgot again! First thing in the morning."

A sniff. "Just smell the Yards." It was Chicago.

"Wind must be from the west."

Sleep came with reluctant feet, but they wooed her patiently. And presently she settled down between them and they slept lightly. Usually, some time during the night, he awoke, slid cautiously and with infinite stealth from beneath the covers and closed the wide-flung window to within a bare two inches of the sill. Almost invariably she heard him; but she was a wise old woman; a philosopher of parts. She knew better than to allow a window to shatter the peace of their marital felicity. As she lay there, smiling a little grimly in the dark and giving no sign of being awake, she thought, "Oh, well, I guess a closed window won't kill me either."

Still, sometimes, just to punish him a little, and to prove that she was nobody's fool, she would wait until he had dropped off to sleep again and then she, too, would achieve a stealthy trip to the window and would raise it slowly, carefully, inch by inch.

"How did that window come to be open?" he would say in the morning, being a poor dissembler.

"Window? Why, it's just the way it was when we went to bed." And she would stoop to pick up the pillow that lay on the floor.

There was little or no talk of death between this comfortable, active, sound-appearing man of almost seventy and this plump capable woman of sixty-six. But as always, between husband and wife, it was understood wordlessly (and without reason) that old man Minick would go first. Not that either of them had the slightest intention of going. In fact, when it happened they were planning to spend the winter in California and perhaps live there indefinitely if they liked it and didn't get too lonesome for George and Nettie, and the Chicago smoke, and Chicago noise, and Chicago smells and rush and dirt. Still, the solid sum paid yearly in insurance premiums showed clearly that he meant to leave her in comfort and security. Besides, the world is full of widows. Everyone sees that. But how many widowers? Few. Widows there are by the thousands; living alone; living in hotels; living with married daughters and sons-in-law or married sons and daughters-in-law. But of widowers in a like situation there are bewilderingly few. And why this should be no one knows.

So, then. The California trip never materialized. And the year that followed never was quite clear in old man Minick's dazed mind. In the first place, it was the year in which stocks tumbled and broke their backs. Gilt-edged securities showed themselves to be tinsel. Old man Minick had retired from active business just one year before, meaning to live comfortably on the fruit of a half-century's toil. He now saw that fruit rotting all about him. There was in it hardly enough nourishment to sustain them. Then came the day when Ma Minick went downtown to see Matthews about that pain right here and came home looking shrivelled, talking shrilly about nothing, and evading Pa's eyes. Followed months that were just a jumble of agony, X-rays, hope, despair, morphia, nothingness.

After it was all over: "But I was going first," old man Minick said, dazedly.

The old house on Ellis near Thirty-ninth was sold for what it would bring. George, who knew Chicago real-estate if any one did, said they might as well get what they could. Things would only go lower. You'll see. And nobody's going to have any money for years. Besides, look at the neighbourhood!

Old man Minick said George was right. He said everybody was right. You would hardly have recognized in this shrunken figure and wattled face the spruce and dressy old man whom Ma Minick used to spoil so delightfully. "You know best, George. You know best." He who used to stand up to George until Ma Minick was moved to say, "Now, Pa, you don't know everything."

After Matthews' bills, and the hospital, and the nurses and the medicines and the thousand and one things were paid there was left exactly five hundred dollars a year.

"You're going to make your home with us, Father," George and Nettie said. Alma, too, said this would be the best. Alma, the married daughter, lived in Seattle. "Though you know Ferd and I would be only too glad to have you."

Seattle! The ends of the earth. Oh, no. No! he protested, every fibre of his old frame clinging to the accustomed. Seattle, at seventy! He turned piteous eyes on his son George and his daughter-in-law Nettie. "You're going to make your home with us, Father," they reassured him. He clung to them gratefully. After it was over Alma went home to her husband and their children.

So now he lived with George and Nettie in the five-room flat on South Park Avenue, just across from Washington Park. And there was no extra pillow on the floor.

Nettie hadn't said he couldn't have the extra pillow. He had told her he used two and she had given him two the first week. But every morning she had found a pillow cast on the floor.

"I thought you used two pillows, Father."

"I do."

"But there's always one on the floor when I make the bed in the morning. You always throw one on the floor. You only sleep on one pillow, really."

"I use two pillows."

But the second week there was one pillow. He tossed and turned a good deal there in his bedroom off the kitchen. But he got used to it in time. Not used to it, exactly, but—well——

The bedroom off the kitchen wasn't as menial as it sounds. It was really rather cosy. The five-room flat held living room, front bedroom, dining room, kitchen, and maid's room. The room off the kitchen was intended as a maid's room but Nettie had no maid. George's business had suffered with the rest. George and Nettie had said, "I wish there was a front room for you, Father. You could have ours and we'd move back here, only this room's too small for twin beds and the dressing table and the chiffonier." They had meant it—or meant to mean it.

"This is fine," old man Minick had said. "This is good enough for anybody." There was a narrow white enamel bed and a tiny dresser and a table. Nettie had made gay cretonne covers and spreads and put a little reading lamp on the table and arranged his things. Ma Minick's picture on the dresser with her mouth sort of pursed to make it look small. It wasn't a recent picture. Nettie and George had had it framed for him as a surprise. They had often urged her to have a picture taken, but she had dreaded it. Old man Minick didn't think much of that photograph, though he never said so. He needed no photograph of Ma Minick. He had a dozen of them; a gallery of them; thousands of them. Lying on his one pillow he could take them out and look at them one by one as they passed in review, smiling, serious, chiding, praising, there in the dark. He needed no picture on his dresser.

A handsome girl, Nettie, and a good girl. He thought of her as a girl, though she was well past thirty. George and Nettie had married late. This was only the third year of their marriage. Alma, the daughter, had married young, but George had stayed on, unwed, in the old house on Ellis until he was thirty-six and all Ma Minick's friends' daughters had had a try at him in vain. The old people had urged him to marry, but it had been wonderful to have him around the house, just the same. Somebody young around the house. Not that George had stayed around very much. But when he was there you knew he was there. He whistled while dressing. He sang in the bath. He roared down the stairway, "Ma, where's my clean shirts?" The telephone rang for him. Ma Minick prepared special dishes for him. The servant girl said, "Oh, now, Mr. George, look what you've done! Gone and spilled the grease all over my clean kitchen floor!" and wiped it up adoringly while George laughed and gobbled his bit of food filched from pot or frying pan.

They had been a little surprised about Nettie. George was in the bond business and she worked for the same firm. A plump, handsome, eye-glassed woman with fine fresh colouring, a clear skin that old man Minick called appetizing, and a great coil of smooth dark hair. She wore plain tailored things and understood the bond business in a way that might have led you to think hers a masculine mind if she hadn't been so feminine, too, in her manner. Old man Minick had liked her better than Ma Minick had.

Nettie had called him Pop and joked with him and almost flirted with him in a daughterly sort of way. He liked to squeeze her plump arm and pinch her soft cheek between thumb and forefinger. She would laugh up at him and pat his shoulder and that shoulder would straighten spryly and he would waggle his head doggishly.

"Look out there, George!" the others in the room would say. "Your dad'll cut you out. First thing you know you'll lose your girl, that's all."

Nettie would smile. Her teeth were white and strong and even. Old man Minick would laugh and wink, immensely pleased and flattered. "We understand each other, don't we, Pop?" Nettie would say.

During the first years of their married life Nettie stayed home. She fussed happily about her little flat, gave parties, went to parties, played bridge. She seemed to love the ease, the relaxation, the small luxuries. She and George were very much in love. Before her marriage she had lived in a boarding house on Michigan Avenue. At mention of it now she puckered up her face. She did not attempt to conceal her fondness for these five rooms of hers, so neat, so quiet, so bright, so cosy. Over-stuffed velvet in the living room, with silk lampshades, and small tables holding books and magazines and little boxes containing cigarettes or hard candies. Very modern. A gate-legged table in the dining room. Caramel-coloured walnut in the bedroom, rich and dark and smooth. She loved it. An orderly woman. Everything in its place. Before eleven o'clock the little apartment was shining, spotless; cushions plumped, crumbs brushed, vegetables in cold water. The telephone. "Hello!... Oh, hello, Bess! Oh, hours ago ... Not a thing ... Well, if George is willing ... I'll call him up and ask him. We haven't seen a show in two weeks. I'll call you back within the next half hour ... No, I haven't done my marketing yet.... Yes, and have dinner downtown. Meet at seven."

Into this orderly smooth-running mechanism was catapulted a bewildered old man. She no longer called him Pop. He never dreamed of squeezing the plump arm or pinching the smooth cheek. She called him Father. Sometimes George's Father. Sometimes, when she was telephoning, there came to him—"George's father's living with us now, you know. I can't."

They were very kind to him, Nettie and George. "Now just you sit right down here, Father. What do you want to go poking off into your own room for?"

He remembered that in the last year Nettie had said something about going back to work. There wasn't enough to do around the house to keep her busy. She was sick of afternoon parties. Sew and eat, that's all, and gossip, or play bridge. Besides, look at the money. Business was awful. The two old people had resented this idea as much as George had—more, in fact. They were scandalized.

"Young folks nowdays!" shaking their heads. "Young folks nowdays. What are they thinking of! In my day when you got married you had babies."

George and Nettie had had no babies. At first Nettie had said, "I'm so happy. I just want a chance to rest. I've been working since I was seventeen. I just want to rest, first." One year. Two years. Three. And now Pa Minick.

Ma Minick, in the old house on Ellis Avenue, had kept a loose sort of larder; not lavish, but plentiful. They both ate a great deal, as old people are likely to do. Old man Minick, especially, had liked to nibble. A handful of raisins from the box on the shelf. A couple of nuts from the dish on the sideboard. A bit of candy rolled beneath the tongue. At dinner (sometimes, toward the last, even at noon-time) a plate of steaming soup, hot, revivifying, stimulating. Plenty of this and plenty of that. "What's the matter, Jo? You're not eating." But he was, amply. Ma Minick had liked to see him eat too much. She was wrong, of course.

But at Nettie's things were different. Hers was a sufficient but stern ménage. So many mouths to feed; just so many lamb chops. Nettie knew about calories and vitamines and mysterious things like that, and talked about them. So many calories in this. So many calories in that. He never was quite clear in his mind about these things said to be lurking in his food. He had always thought of spinach as spinach, chops as chops. But to Nettie they were calories. They lunched together, these two. George was, of course, downtown. For herself Nettie would have one of those feminine pick-up lunches; a dab of apple sauce, a cup of tea, and a slice of cold toast left from breakfast. This she would eat while old man Minick guiltily supped up his cup of warmed-over broth, or his coddled egg. She always pressed upon him any bit of cold meat that was left from the night before, or any remnants of vegetable or spaghetti. Often there was quite a little fleet of saucers and sauce plates grouped about his main plate. Into these he dipped and swooped uncomfortably, and yet with a relish. Sometimes, when he had finished, he would look about, furtively.

"What'll you have, Father? Can I get you something?"

"Nothing, Nettie, nothing. I'm doing fine." She had finished the last of her wooden toast and was waiting for him, kindly.

Still, this balanced and scientific fare seemed to agree with him. As the winter went on he seemed actually to have regained most of his former hardiness and vigour. A handsome old boy he was, ruddy, hale, with the zest of a juicy old apple, slightly withered but still sappy. It should be mentioned that he had a dimple in his cheek which flashed unexpectedly when he smiled. It gave him a roguish—almost boyish—effect most appealing to the beholder. Especially the feminine beholder. Much of his spoiling at the hands of Ma Minick had doubtless been due to this mere depression of the skin.

Spring was to bring a new and welcome source of enrichment into his life. But these first six months of his residence with George and Nettie were hard. No spoiling there. He missed being made much of. He got kindness, but he needed love. Then, too, he was rather a gabby old man. He liked to hold forth. In the old house on Ellis there had been visiting back and forth between men and women of his own age, and Ma's. At these gatherings he had waxed oratorical or argumentative, and they had heard him, some in agreement, some in disagreement, but always respectfully, whether he prated of real estate or social depravity; prohibition or European exchange.

"Let me tell you, here and now, something's got to be done before you can get a country back on a sound financial basis. Why, take Russia alone, why ..." Or: "Young people nowdays! They don't know what respect means. I tell you there's got to be a change and there will be, and it's the older generation that's got to bring it about. What do they know of hardship! What do they know about work—real work. Most of 'em's never done a real day's work in their life. All they think of is dancing and gambling and drinking. Look at the way they dress! Look at ..."

Ad lib.

"That's so," the others would agree. "I was saying only yesterday ..."

Then, too, until a year or two before, he had taken active part in business. He had retired only at the urging of Ma and the children. They said he ought to rest and play and enjoy himself.

Now, as his strength and good spirits gradually returned he began to go downtown, mornings. He would dress, carefully, though a little shakily. He had always shaved himself and he kept this up. All in all, during the day, he occupied the bathroom literally for hours, and this annoyed Nettie to the point of frenzy, though she said nothing. He liked the white cheerfulness of the little tiled room. He puddled about in the water endlessly. Snorted and splashed and puffed and snuffled and blew. He was one of those audible washers who emerge dripping and whose ablutions are distributed impartially over ceiling, walls, and floor.

Nettie, at the closed door: "Father, are you all right?"

Splash! Prrrf! "Yes. Sure. I'm all right."

"Well, I didn't know. You've been in there so long."

He was a neat old man, but there was likely to be a spot or so on his vest or his coat lapel, or his tie. Ma used to remove these, on or off him, as the occasion demanded, rubbing carefully and scolding a little, making a chiding sound between tongue and teeth indicative of great impatience of his carelessness. He had rather enjoyed these sounds, and this rubbing and scratching on the cloth with the fingernail and a moistened rag. They indicated that someone cared. Cared about the way he looked. Had pride in him. Loved him. Nettie never removed spots. Though infrequently she said, "Father, just leave that suit out, will you? I'll send it to the cleaner's with George's. The man's coming to-morrow morning." He would look down at himself, hastily, and attack a spot here and there with a futile fingernail.

His morning toilette completed, he would make for the Fifty-first Street L. Seated in the train he would assume an air of importance and testy haste; glance out of the window; look at his watch. You got the impression of a handsome and well-preserved old gentleman on his way downtown to consummate a shrewd business deal. He had been familiar with Chicago's downtown for fifty years and he could remember when State Street was a tree-shaded cottage district. The noise and rush and clangour of the Loop had long been familiar to him. But now he seemed to find the downtown trip arduous, even hazardous. The roar of the elevated trains, the hoarse hoots of the motor horns, the clang of the street cars, the bedlam that is Chicago's downtown district bewildered him, frightened him almost. He would skip across the street like a harried hare, just missing a motor truck's nose and all unconscious of the stream of invective directed at him by its charioteer. "Heh! Whatcha!... Look!"—Sometimes a policeman came to his aid, or attempted to, but he resented this proffered help.

"Say, look here, my lad," he would say to the tall, tired, and not at all burly (standing on one's feet directing traffic at Wabash and Madison for eight hours a day does not make for burliness) policeman, "I've been coming downtown since long before you were born. You don't need to help me. I'm no jay from the country."

He visited the Stock Exchange. This depressed him. Stocks were lower than ever and still going down. His five hundred a year was safe, but the rest seemed doomed for his lifetime, at least. He would drop in at George's office. George's office was pleasantly filled with dapper, neat young men and (surprisingly enough) dapper, slim young women, seated at desks in the big light-flooded room. At one corner of each desk stood a polished metal placard on a little standard, and bearing the name of the desk's occupant. Mr. Owens. Mr. Satterlee. Mr. James. Miss Rauch. Mr. Minick.

"Hello, Father," Mr. Minick would say, looking annoyed. "What's bringing you down?"

"Oh, nothing. Nothing. Just had a little business to tend to over at the Exchange. Thought I'd drop in. How's business?"

"Rotten."

"I should think it was!" Old man Minick would agree. "I—should—think—it—was! Hm."

George wished he wouldn't. He couldn't have it, that's all. Old man Minick would stroll over to the desk marked Satterlee, or Owens, or James. These brisk young men would toss an upward glance at him and concentrate again on the sheets and files before them. Old man Minick would stand, balancing from heel to toe and blowing out his breath a little. He looked a bit yellow and granulated and wavering, there in the cruel morning light of the big plate glass windows. Or perhaps it was the contrast he presented with these slim, slick young salesmen.

"Well, h'are you to-day, Mr.—uh—Satterlee? What's the good word?"

Mr. Satterlee would not glance up this time. "I'm pretty well. Can't complain."

"Good. Good."

"Anything I can do for you?"

"No-o-o. No. Not a thing. Just dropped in to see my son a minute."

"I see." Not unkindly. Then, as old man Minick still stood there, balancing, Mr. Satterlee would glance up again, frowning a little. "Your son's desk is over there, I believe. Yes."

George and Nettie had a bedtime conference about these visits and Nettie told him, gently, that the bond house head objected to friends and relatives dropping in. It was against office rules. It had been so when she was employed there. Strictly business. She herself had gone there only once since her marriage.

Well, that was all right. Business was like that nowadays. Rush and grab and no time for anything.

The winter was a hard one, with a record snowfall and intense cold. He stayed indoors for days together. A woman of his own age in like position could have occupied herself usefully and happily. She could have hemmed a sash-curtain; knitted or crocheted; tidied a room; taken a hand in the cooking or preparing of food; ripped an old gown; made over a new one; indulged in an occasional afternoon festivity with women of her own years. But for old man Minick there were no small tasks. There was nothing he could do to make his place in the household justifiable. He wasn't even particularly good at those small jobs of hammering, or painting, or general "fixing." Nettie could drive a nail more swiftly, more surely than he. "Now, Father, don't you bother. I'll do it. Just you go and sit down. Isn't it time for your afternoon nap?"

He waxed a little surly. "Nap! I just got up. I don't want to sleep my life away."

George and Nettie frequently had guests in the evening. They played bridge, or poker, or talked.

"Come in, Father," George would say. "Come in. You all know Dad, don't you, folks?" He would sit down, uncertainly. At first he had attempted to expound, as had been his wont in the old house on Ellis. "I want to say, here and now, that this country's got to ..." But they went on, heedless of him. They interrupted or refused, politely, to listen. So he sat in the room, yet no part of it. The young people's talk swirled and eddied all about him. He was utterly lost in it. Now and then Nettie or George would turn to him and with raised voice (he was not at all deaf and prided himself on it) would shout, "It's about this or that, Father. He was saying ..."

When the group roared with laughter at a sally from one of them he would smile uncertainly but amiably, glancing from one to the other in complete ignorance of what had passed, but not resenting it. He took to sitting more and more in his kitchen bedroom, smoking a comforting pipe and reading and re-reading the evening paper. During that winter he and Canary, the negro washwoman, became quite good friends. She washed down in the basement once a week but came up to the kitchen for her massive lunch. A walrus-waisted black woman, with a rich throaty voice, a rolling eye, and a kindly heart. He actually waited for her appearance above the laundry stairs.

"Weh, how's Mist' Minick to-day! Ah nev' did see a gemun spry's you ah fo' yo' age. No, suh! nev' did."

At this rare praise he would straighten his shoulders and waggle his head. "I'm worth any ten of these young sprats to-day." Canary would throw back her head in a loud and companionable guffaw.

Nettie would appear at the kitchen swinging door. "Canary's having her lunch, Father. Don't you want to come into the front room with me? We'll have our lunch in another half-hour." He followed her obediently enough. Nettie thought of him as a troublesome and rather pathetic child—a child who would never grow up. If she attributed any thoughts to that fine old head they were ambling thoughts, bordering, perhaps, on senility. Little did she know how expertly this old one surveyed her and how ruthlessly he passed judgment. She never suspected the thoughts that formed in the active brain.

He knew about women. He had married a woman. He had had children by her. He looked at this woman—his son's wife—moving about her little five-room flat. She had theories about children. He had heard her expound them. You didn't have them except under such and such circumstances. It wasn't fair otherwise. Plenty of money for their education. Well. He and his wife had had three children. Paul, the second, had died at thirteen. A blow, that had been. They had not always planned for the coming of the three but they always had found a way, afterward. You managed, somehow, once the little wrinkled red ball had fought its way into the world. You managed. You managed. Look at George! Yet when he was born, thirty-nine years ago, Pa and Ma Minick had been hard put to it.

Sitting there, while Nettie dismissed him as negligible, he saw her clearly, grimly. He looked at her. She was plump, but not too short, with a generous width between the hips; a broad full bosom, but firm; round arms and quick slim legs; a fine sturdy throat. The curve between arm and breast made a graceful gracious line ... Working in a bond office ... Working in a bond office ... There was nothing in the Bible about working in a bond office. Here was a woman built for child-bearing.

She thought him senile, negligible.

In March Nettie had in a sewing woman for a week. She had her two or three times a year. A hawk-faced woman of about forty-nine, with a blue-bottle figure and a rapacious eye. She sewed in the dining room and there was a pleasant hum of machine and snip of scissors and murmur of conversation and rustle of silky stuff; and hot savoury dishes for lunch. She and old man Minick became great friends. She even let him take out bastings. This when Nettie had gone out from two to four, between fittings.

He chuckled and waggled his head. "I expect to be paid regular assistant's wages for this," he said.

"I guess you don't need any wages, Mr. Minick," the woman said. "I guess you're pretty well fixed."

"Oh, well, I can't complain." (Five hundred a year.)

"Complain! I should say not! If I was to complain it'd be different. Work all day to keep myself; and nobody to come home to at night."

"Widow, ma'am?"

"Since I was twenty. Work, work, that's all I've had. And lonesome! I suppose you don't know what lonesome is."

"Oh, don't I!" slipped from him. He had dropped the bastings.

The sewing woman flashed a look at him from the cold hard eye. "Well, maybe you do. I suppose living here like this, with sons and daughters, ain't so grand, for all your money. Now me, I've always managed to keep my own little place that I could call home, to come back to. It's only two rooms, and nothing to rave about, but it's home. Evenings I just cook and fuss around. Nobody to fuss for, but I fuss, anyway. Cooking, that's what I love to do. Plenty of good food, that's what folks need to keep their strength up." Nettie's lunch that day had been rather scant.

She was there a week. In Nettie's absence she talked against her. He protested, but weakly. Did she give him egg-nogs? Milk? Hot toddy? Soup? Plenty of good rich gravy and meat and puddings? Well! That's what folks needed when they weren't so young any more. Not that he looked old. My, no. Sprier than many young boys, and handsomer than his own son if she did say so.

He fed on it, hungrily. The third day she was flashing meaning glances at him across the luncheon table. The fourth she pressed his foot beneath the table. The fifth, during Nettie's afternoon absence, she got up, ostensibly to look for a bit of cloth which she needed for sewing, and, passing him, laid a caressing hand on his shoulder. Laid it there and pressed his shoulder ever so little. He looked up, startled. The glances across the luncheon had largely passed over his head; the foot beneath the table might have been an accident. But this—this was unmistakable. He stood up, a little shakily. She caught his hand. The hawk-like face was close to his.

"You need somebody to love you," she said. "Somebody to do for you, and love you." The hawk face came nearer. He leaned a little toward it. But between it and his face was Ma Minick's face, plump, patient, quizzical, kindly. His head came back sharply. He threw the woman's hot hand from him.

"Woman!" he cried. "Jezebel!"

The front door slammed. Nettie. The woman flew to her sewing. Old man Minick, shaking, went into his kitchen bedroom.

"Well," said Nettie, depositing her bundles on the dining room table, "did you finish that faggoting? Why, you haven't done so very much, have you!"

"I ain't feeling so good," said the woman. "That lunch didn't agree with me."

"Why, it was a good plain lunch. I don't see——"

"Oh, it was plain enough, all right."

Next day she did not come to finish her work. Sick, she telephoned. Nettie called it an outrage. She finished the sewing herself, though she hated sewing. Pa Minick said nothing, but there was a light in his eye. Now and then he chuckled, to Nettie's infinite annoyance, though she said nothing.

"Wanted to marry me!" he said to himself, chuckling. "Wanted to marry me! The old rip!"

At the end of April, Pa Minick discovered Washington Park, and the Club, and his whole life was from that day transformed.

He had taken advantage of the early spring sunshine to take a walk, at Nettie's suggestion.

"Why don't you go into the Park, Father? It's really warm out. And the sun's lovely. Do you good."

He had put on his heaviest shirt, and a muffler, and George's old red sweater with the great white "C" on its front, emblem of George's athletic prowess at the University of Chicago; and over all, his greatcoat. He had taken warm mittens and his cane with the greyhound's head handle, carved. So equipped he had ambled uninterestedly over to the Park across the way. And there he had found new life.

New life in old life. For the park was full of old men. Old men like himself, with greyhound's-head canes, and mufflers and somebody's sweater worn beneath their greatcoats. They wore arctics, though the weather was fine. The skin of their hands and cheek-bones was glazed and had a tight look though it lay in fine little folds. There were splotches of brown on the backs of their hands, and on the temples and forehead. Their heavy grey or brown socks made comfortable folds above their ankles. From that April morning until winter drew on the Park saw old man Minick daily. Not only daily but by the day. Except for his meals, and a brief hour for his after-luncheon nap, he spent all his time there.

For in the park old man Minick and all the old men gathered there found a Forum—a safety valve—a means of expression. It did not take him long to discover that the Park was divided into two distinct sets of old men. There were the old men who lived with their married sons and daughters-in-law or married daughters and sons-in-law. Then there were the old men who lived in the Grant Home for Aged Gentlemen. You saw its fine red-brick façade through the trees at the edge of the Park.

And the slogan of these first was:

"My son and my da'ter they wouldn't want me to live in any public Home. No, sirree! They want me right there with them. In their own home. That's the kind of son and daughter I've got!"

The slogan of the second was:

"I wouldn't live with any son or daughter. Independent. That's me. My own boss. Nobody to tell me what I can do and what I can't. Treat you like a child. I'm my own boss! Pay my own good money and get my keep for it."

The first group, strangely enough, was likely to be spotted of vest and a little frayed as to collar. You saw them going on errands for their daughters-in-law. A loaf of bread. Spool of white No. 100. They took their small grandchildren to the duck pond and between the two toddlers hand in hand—the old and infirm and the infantile and infirm—it was hard to tell which led which.

The second group was shiny as to shoes, spotless as to linen, dapper as to clothes. They had no small errands. Theirs was a magnificent leisure. And theirs was magnificent conversation. The questions they discussed and settled there in the Park—these old men—were not international merely. They were cosmic in scope.

The War? Peace? Disarmament? China? Free love? Mere conversational bubbles to be tossed in the air and disposed of in a burst of foam. Strong meat for old man Minick who had so long been fed on pap. But he soon got used to it. Between four and five in the afternoon, in a spot known as Under The Willows, the meeting took the form of a club—an open forum. A certain group made up of Socialists, Free Thinkers, parlour anarchists, bolshevists, had for years drifted there for talk. Old man Minick learned high-sounding phrases. "The Masters ... democracy ... toil of the many for the good of the few ... the ruling class ... free speech ... the People...."

The strong-minded ones held forth. The weaker ones drifted about on the outskirts, sometimes clinging to the moist and sticky paw of a round-eyed grandchild. Earlier in the day—at eleven o'clock, say—the talk was not so general nor so inclusive. The old men were likely to drift into groups of two or three or four. They sat on sun-bathed benches and their conversation was likely to be rather smutty at times, for all they looked so mild and patriarchal and desiccated. They paid scant heed to the white-haired old women who, like themselves, were sunning in the park. They watched the young women switch by, with appreciative glances at their trim figures and slim ankles. The day of the short skirt was a grand time for them. They chuckled among themselves and made wicked comment. One saw only white-haired, placid, tremulous old men, but their minds still worked with belated masculinity like naughty small boys talking behind the barn.

Old man Minick early achieved a certain leadership in the common talk. He had always liked to hold forth. This last year had been one of almost unendurable bottling up. At first he had timidly sought the less assertive ones of his kind. Mild old men who sat in rockers in the pavilion waiting for lunch time. Their conversation irritated him. They remarked everything that passed before their eyes.

"There's a boat. Fella with a boat."

A silence. Then, heavily: "Yeh."

Five minutes.

"Look at those people laying on the grass. Shouldn't think it was warm enough for that.... Now they're getting up."

A group of equestrians passed along the bridle path on the opposite side of the lagoon. They made a frieze against the delicate spring greenery. The coats of the women were scarlet, vivid green, arresting, stimulating.

"Riders."

"Yes."

"Good weather for riding."

A man was fishing near by. "Good weather for fishing."

"Yes."

"Wonder what time it is, anyway." From a pocket, deep-buried, came forth a great gold blob of a watch. "I've got one minute to eleven."

Old man Minick dragged forth a heavy globe. "Mm. I've got eleven."

"Little fast, I guess."

Old man Minick shook off this conversation impatiently. This wasn't conversation. This was oral death, though he did not put it thus. He joined the other men. They were discussing Spiritualism. He listened, ventured an opinion, was heard respectfully and then combated mercilessly. He rose to the verbal fight, and won it.

"Let's see," said one of the old men. "You're not living at the Grant Home, are you?"

"No," old man Minick made reply, proudly. "I live with my son and his wife. They wouldn't have it any other way."

"Hm. Like to be independent myself."

"Lonesome, ain't it? Over there?"

"Lonesome! Say, Mr.—what'd you say your name was? Minick? Mine's Hughes—I never was lonesome in my life 'cept for six months when I lived with my daughter and her husband and their five children. Yes, sir. That's what I call lonesome, in an eight-room flat."

George and Nettie said, "It's doing you good, Father, being out in the air so much." His eyes were brighter, his figure straighter, his colour better. It was that day he had held forth so eloquently on the emigration question. He had to read a lot—papers and magazines and one thing and another—to keep up. He devoured all the books and pamphlets about bond issues and national finances brought home by George. In the Park he was considered an authority on bonds and banking. He and a retired real-estate man named Mowry sometimes debated a single question for weeks. George and Nettie, relieved, thought he ambled to the Park and spent senile hours with his drooling old friends discussing nothing amiably and witlessly. This while he was eating strong meat, drinking strong drink.

Summer sped. Was past. Autumn held a new dread for old man Minick. When winter came where should he go? Where should he go? Not back to the five-room flat all day, and the little back bedroom, and nothingness. In his mind there rang a childish old song they used to sing at school. A silly song:

Where   do   all   the   birdies   go?
I know. *I* know.

But he didn't know. He was terror-stricken. October came and went. With the first of November the Park became impossible, even at noon, and with two overcoats and the sweater. The first frost was a black frost for him. He scanned the heavens daily for rain or snow. There was a cigar store and billiard room on the corner across the boulevard and there he sometimes went, with a few of his Park cronies, to stand behind the players' chairs and watch them at pinochle or rum. But this was a dull business. Besides, the Grant men never came there. They had card rooms of their own.

He turned away from this smoky little den on a drab November day, sick at heart. The winter. He tried to face it, and at what he saw he shrank and was afraid.

He reached the apartment and went around to the rear, dutifully. His rubbers were wet and muddy and Nettie's living-room carpet was a fashionable grey. The back door was unlocked. It was Canary's day downstairs, he remembered. He took off his rubbers in the kitchen and passed into the dining room. Voices. Nettie had company. Some friends, probably, for tea. He turned to go to his room, but stopped at hearing his own name. Father Minick. Father Minick. Nettie's voice.

"Of course, if it weren't for Father Minick I would have. But how can we as long as he lives with us? There isn't room. And we can't afford a bigger place now, with rents what they are. This way it wouldn't be fair to the child. We've talked it over, George and I. Don't you suppose? But not as long as Father Minick is with us. I don't mean we'd use the maid's room for a—for the—if we had a baby. But I'd have to have someone in to help, then, and we'd have to have that extra room."

He stood there in the dining room, quiet. Quiet. His body felt queerly remote and numb, but his mind was working frenziedly. Clearly, too, in spite of the frenzy. Death. That was the first thought. Death. It would be easy. But he didn't want to die. Strange, but he didn't want to die. He liked Life. The Park, the trees, the Club, the talk, the whole show.... Nettie was a good girl.... The old must make way for the young. They had the right to be born.... Maybe it was just another excuse. Almost four years married. Why not three years ago?... The right to live. The right to live....

He turned, stealthily, stealthily, and went back into the kitchen, put on his rubbers, stole out into the darkening November afternoon.

In an hour he was back. He entered at the front door this time, ringing the bell. He had never had a key. As if he were a child they would not trust him with one. Nettie's women friends were just leaving. In the air you smelled a mingling of perfume, and tea, and cakes, and powder. He sniffed it, sensitively.

"How do you do, Mr. Minick!" they said. "How are you! Well, you certainly look it. And how do you manage these gloomy days?"

He smiled genially, taking off his greatcoat and revealing the red sweater with the big white "C" on it. "I manage. I manage." He puffed out his cheeks. "I'm busy moving."

"Moving!" Nettie's startled eyes flew to his, held them. "Moving, Father?"

"Old folks must make way for the young," he said, gaily. "That's the law of life. Yes, sir! New ones. New ones." Nettie's face was scarlet. "Father, what in the world——"

"I signed over at the Grant Home to-day. Move in next week." The women looked at her, smiling. Old man Minick came over to her and patted her plump arm. Then he pinched her smooth cheek with a quizzical thumb and forefinger. Pinched it and shook it ever so little.

"I don't know what you mean," said Nettie, out of breath.

"Yes, you do," said old man Minick, and while his tone was light and jesting there was in his old face something stern, something menacing. "Yes, you do."

When he entered the Grant Home a group of them was seated about the fireplace in the main hall. A neat, ruddy, septuagenarian circle. They greeted him casually, with delicacy of feeling, as if he were merely approaching them at their bench in the Park.

"Say, Minick, look here. Mowry here says China ought to have been included in the four-power treaty. He says——"

Old man Minick cleared his throat. "You take China, now," he said, "with her vast and practically, you might say, virgin country, why——"

An apple-cheeked maid in a black dress and a white apron stopped before him. He paused.

"Housekeeper says for me to tell you your room's all ready, if you'd like to look at it now."

"Minute. Minute, my child." He waved her aside with the air of one who pays five hundred a year for independence and freedom. The girl turned to go. "Uh—young lady! Young lady!" She looked at him. "Tell the housekeeper two pillows, please. Two pillows on my bed. Be sure."

"Yes, sir. Two pillows. Yes, sir. I'll be sure."

GIGOLO

In the first place, *gigolo* is slang. In the second place (with no desire to appear patronizing, but one's French conversation class does not include the *argot*), it is French slang. In the third place, the gig is pronounced zhig, and the whole is not a respectable word. Finally, it is a term of utter contempt.

A gigolo, generally speaking, is a man who lives off women's money. In the mad year 1922 A. W., a gigolo, definitely speaking, designated one of those incredible and pathetic male creatures, born of the war, who, for ten francs or more or even less, would dance with any woman wishing to dance on the crowded floors of public tea rooms, dinner or supper rooms in the cafés, hotels, and restaurants of France. Lean, sallow, handsome, expert, and unwholesome, one saw them everywhere, their slim waists and sleek heads in juxtaposition to plump, respectable American matrons and slender, respectable American flappers. For that matter, feminine respectability of almost every nationality (except the French) yielded itself to the skilful guidance of the genus gigolo in the tango or fox-trot. Naturally, no decent French girl would have been allowed for a single moment to dance with a gigolo. But America, touring Europe like mad after years of enforced absence, outnumbered all other nations atravel ten to one.

By no feat of fancy could one imagine Gideon Gory, of the Winnebago, Wisconsin, Gorys, employed daily and nightly as a gigolo in the gilt and marble restaurants that try to outsparkle the Mediterranean along the Promenade des Anglais in Nice. Gideon Gory, of Winnebago, Wisconsin! Why any one knows that the Gorys were to Winnebago what the Romanoffs were to Russia—royal, remote, omnipotent. Yet the Romanoffs went in the cataclysm, and so, too, did the Gorys. To appreciate the depths to which the boy Gideon had fallen one must have known the Gorys in their glory. It happened something like this:

The Gorys lived for years in the great, ugly, sprawling, luxurious old frame house on Cass Street. It was high up on the bluff overlooking the Fox River and, incidentally, the huge pulp and paper mills across the river in which the Gory money had been made. The Gorys were so rich and influential (for Winnebago, Wisconsin) that they didn't bother to tear down the old frame house and build a stone one, or to cover its faded front with cosmetics of stucco. In most things the Gorys led where Winnebago could not follow. They disdained to follow where Winnebago led. The Gorys had an automobile when those vehicles were entered from the rear and when Winnebago roads were a wallow of mud in the spring and fall and a snow-lined trench in the winter. The family was of the town, and yet apart from it. The Gorys knew about golf, and played it in far foreign playgrounds when the rest of us thought of it, if we thought of it at all, as something vaguely Scotch, like haggis. They had oriental rugs and hardwood floors when the town still stepped on carpets; and by the time the rest of the town had caught up on rugs the Gorys had gone back to carpets, neutral tinted. They had fireplaces in bedrooms, and used them, like characters in an English novel. Old Madame Gory had a slim patent leather foot, with a buckle, and carried a sunshade when she visited the flowers in the garden. Old Gideon was rumoured to have wine with his dinner. Gideon Junior (father of Giddy) smoked cigarettes with his monogram on them. Shroeder's grocery ordered endive for them, all blanched and delicate in a wicker basket from France or Belgium, when we had just become accustomed to head-lettuce.

Every prosperous small American town has its Gory family. Every small town newspaper relishes the savoury tid-bits that fall from the rich table of the family life. Thus you saw that Mr. and Mrs. Gideon Gory, Jr., have returned from California where Mr. Gory had gone for the polo. Mr. and Mrs. Gideon Gory, Jr., announce the birth, in New York, of a son, Gideon III (our, in a manner of speaking, hero). Mr. and Mrs. Gideon Gory, Jr., and son Gideon III, left to-day for England and the continent. It is understood that Gideon III will be placed at school in England. Mr. and Mrs. Gideon Gory, accompanied by Madame Gory, have gone to Chicago for a week of the grand opera.

Born of all this, you would have thought that young Giddy would grow up a somewhat objectionable young man; and so, in fact, he did, though not nearly so objectionable as he might well have been, considering things in general and his mother in particular. At sixteen, for example, Giddy was driving his own car—a car so exaggerated and low-slung and with such a long predatory and glittering nose that one marvelled at the expertness with which he swung its slim length around the corners of our narrow tree-shaded streets. He was a real Gory, was Giddy, with his thick waving black hair (which he tried for vain years to train into docility), his lean swart face, and his slightly hooked Gory nose. In appearance Winnebago pronounced him foreign looking—an attribute which he later turned into a doubtful asset in Nice. On the rare occasions when Giddy graced Winnebago with his presence you were likely to find him pursuing the pleasures that occupied other Winnebago boys of his age, if not station. In some miraculous way he had escaped being a snob. Still, training and travel combined to lead him into many innocent errors. When he dropped into Fetzer's pool shack carrying a malacca cane, for example. He had carried a cane every day for six months in Paris, whence he had just returned. Now it was as much a part of his street attire as his hat—more, to be exact, for the hatless head had just then become the street mode. There was a good game of Kelly in progress. Giddy, leaning slightly on his stick, stood watching it. Suddenly he was aware that all about the dim smoky little room players and loungers were standing in attitudes of exaggerated elegance. Each was leaning on a cue, his elbow crooked in as near an imitation of Giddy's position as the stick's length would permit. The figure was curved so that it stuck out behind and before; the expression on each face was as asinine as its owner's knowledge of the comic-weekly swell could make it; the little finger of the free hand was extravagantly bent. The players themselves walked with a mincing step about the table. And: "My deah fellah, what a pretty play. Mean to say, neat, don't you know," came incongruously from the lips of Reddy Lennigan, whose father ran the Lennigan House on Outagamie Street. He spatted his large hands delicately together in further expression of approval.

"Think so?" giggled his opponent, Mr. Dutchy Meisenberg. "Aw—fly sweet of you to say so, old thing." He tucked his unspeakable handkerchief up his cuff and coughed behind his palm. He turned to Giddy. "Excuse my not having my coat on, deah boy."

Just here Giddy might have done a number of things, all wrong. The game was ended. He walked to the table, and, using the offending stick as a cue, made a rather pretty shot that he had learned from Benoit in London. Then he ranged the cane neatly on the rack with the cues. He even grinned a little boyishly. "You win," he said. "My treat. What'll you have?"

Which was pretty sporting for a boy whose American training had been what Giddy's had been.

Giddy's father, on the death of old Gideon, proved himself much more expert at dispensing the paper mill money than at accumulating it. After old Madame Gory's death just one year following that of her husband, Winnebago saw less and less of the three remaining members of the royal family. The frame house on the river bluff would be closed for a year or more at a time. Giddy's father rather liked Winnebago and would have been content to spend six months of the year in the old Gory house, but Giddy's mother, who had been a Leyden, of New York, put that idea out of his head pretty effectively.

"Don't talk to me," she said, "about your duty toward the town that gave you your money and all that kind of feudal rot because you know you don't mean it. It bores you worse than it does me, really, but you like to think that the villagers are pulling a forelock when you walk down Normal Avenue. As a matter of fact they're not doing anything of the kind. They've got their thumbs to their noses, more likely."

Her husband protested rather weakly. "I don't care. I like the old shack. I know the heating apparatus is bum and that we get the smoke from the paper mills, but—I don't know—last year, when we had that punk pink palace at Cannes I kept thinking——"

Mrs. Gideon Gory raised the Leyden eyebrow. "Don't get sentimental, Gid, for God's sake! It's a shanty, and you know it. And you know that it needs everything from plumbing to linen. I don't see any sense in sinking thousands in making it livable when we don't want to live in it."

"But I do want to live in it—once in a while. I'm used to it. I was brought up in it. So was the kid. He likes it, too. Don't you, Giddy?" The boy was present, as usual, at this particular scene.

The boy worshipped his mother. But, also, he was honest. So, "Yeh, I like the ol' barn all right," he confessed.

Encouraged, his father went on: "Yesterday the kid was standing out there on the bluff-edge breathing like a whale, weren't you, Giddy? And when I asked him what he was puffing about he said he liked the smell of the sulphur and chemicals and stuff from the paper mills, didn't you, kid?"

Shame-facedly, "Yeh," said Giddy.

Betrayed thus by husband and adored son, the Leyden did battle. "You can both stay here, then," she retorted with more spleen than elegance, "and sniff sulphur until you're black in the face. I'm going to London in May."

They, too, went to London in May, of course, as she had known they would. She had not known, though, that in leading her husband to England in May she was leading him to his death as well.

"All Winnebago will be shocked and grieved to learn," said the Winnebago *Courier* to the extent of two columns and a cut, "of the sudden and violent death in England of her foremost citizen, Gideon Gory. Death was due to his being thrown from his horse while hunting."

... To being thrown from his horse while hunting. Shocked and grieved though it might or might not be, Winnebago still had the fortitude to savour this with relish. Winnebago had died deaths natural and unnatural. It had been run over by automobiles, and had its skull fractured at football, and been drowned in Lake Winnebago, and struck by lightning, and poisoned by mushrooms, and shot by burglars. But never had Winnebago citizen had the distinction of meeting death by being thrown from his horse while hunting. While hunting. Scarlet coats. Hounds in full cry. Baronial halls. Hunt breakfasts. *Vogue. Vanity Fair.*

Well! Winnebago was almost grateful for this final and most picturesque gesture of Gideon Gory the second.

The widowed Leyden did not even take the trouble personally to superintend the selling of the Gory place on the river bluff. It was sold by an agent while she and Giddy were in Italy, and if she was ever aware that the papers in the transaction stated that the house had been bought by Orson J. Hubbell she soon forgot the fact and the name. Giddy, leaning over her shoulder while she handled the papers, and signing on the line indicated by a legal forefinger, may have remarked:

"Hubbell. That's old Hubbell, the dray man. Must be money in the draying line."

Which was pretty stupid of him, because he should have known that the draying business was now developed into the motor truck business with great vans roaring their way between Winnebago and Kaukauna, Winnebago and Neenah, and even Winnebago and Oshkosh. He learned that later.

Just now Giddy wasn't learning much of anything, and, to do him credit, the fact distressed him not a little. His mother insisted that she needed him, and developed a bad heart whenever he rebelled and threatened to sever the apron-strings. They lived abroad entirely now. Mrs. Gory showed a talent for spending the Gory gold that must have set old Gideon to whirling in his Winnebago grave. Her spending of it was foolish enough, but her handling of it was criminal. She loved Europe. America bored her. She wanted to identify herself with foreigners, with foreign life. Against advice she sold her large and lucrative interest in the Winnebago paper mills and invested great sums in French stocks, in Russian enterprises, in German shares.

She liked to be mistaken for a French woman.

She and Gideon spoke the language like natives—or nearly.

She was vain of Gideon's un-American looks, and cross with him when, on their rare and brief visits to New York, he insisted that he liked American tailoring and American-made shoes. Once or twice, soon after his father's death, he had said, casually, "You didn't like Winnebago, did you? Living in it, I mean."

"*Like* it!"

"Well, these English, I mean, and French—they sort of grow up in a place, and stay with it and belong to it, see what I mean? and it gives you a kind of permanent feeling. Not patriotic, exactly, but solid and native heathy and Scots-wha-hae-wi'-Wallace and all that kind of slop."

"Giddy darling, don't be silly."

Occasionally, too, he said, "Look here, Julia"—she liked this modern method of address—"look here, Julia, I ought to be getting busy. Doing something. Here I am, nineteen, and I can't do a thing except dance pretty well, but not as well as that South American eel we met last week; mix a cocktail pretty well, but not as good a one as Benny the bartender turns out at Voyot's; ride pretty well, but not as well as the English chaps; drive a car——"

She interrupted him there. "Drive a car better than even an Italian chauffeur. Had you there, Giddy darling."

She undoubtedly had Giddy darling there. His driving was little short of miraculous, and his feeling for the intricate inside of a motor engine was as delicate and unerring as that of a professional pianist for his pet pianoforte. They motored a good deal, with France as a permanent background and all Europe as a playground. They flitted about the continent, a whirl of glittering blue-and-cream enamel, tan leather coating, fur robes, air cushions, gold-topped flasks, and petrol. Giddy knew Como and Villa D'Este as the place where that pretty Hungarian widow had borrowed a thousand lires from him at the Casino roulette table and never paid him back; London as a pleasing potpourri of briar pipes, smart leather gloves, music-hall revues, and night clubs; Berlin as a rather stuffy hole where they tried to ape Paris and failed, but you had to hand it to Charlotte when it came to the skating at the Eis Palast. A pleasing existence, but unprofitable. No one saw the cloud gathering because of cloud there was none, even of the man's-hand size so often discerned as a portent.

When the storm broke (this must be hurriedly passed over because of the let's-not-talk-about-the-war-I'm-so-sick-of-it-aren't-you feeling) Giddy promptly went into the Lafayette Escadrille. Later he learned never to mention this to an American because the American was so likely to say, "There must have been about eleven million scrappers in that outfit. Every fella you meet's been in the Lafayette Escadrille. If all the guys were in it that say they were they could have licked the Germans the first day out. That outfit's worse than the old Floradora Sextette."

Mrs. Gory was tremendously proud of him, and not as worried as she should have been. She thought it all a rather smart game, and not at all serious. She wasn't even properly alarmed about her European money, at first. Giddy looked thrillingly distinguished and handsome in his aviation uniform. When she walked in the Paris streets with him she glowed like a girl with her lover. But after the first six months of it Mrs. Gory, grown rather drawn and haggard, didn't think the whole affair quite so delightful. She scarcely ever saw Giddy. She never heard the drum of an airplane without getting a sick, gone feeling at the pit of her stomach. She knew, now, that there was more to the air service than a becoming uniform. She was doing some war work herself in an incompetent, frenzied sort of way. With Giddy soaring high and her foreign stocks and bonds falling low she might well be excused for the panic that shook her from the time she opened her eyes in the morning until she tardily closed them at night.

"Let's go home, Giddy darling," like a scared child.

"Where's that?"

"Don't be cruel. America's the only safe place now."

"Too darned safe!" This was 1915.

By 1917 she was actually in need of money. But Giddy did not know much about this because Giddy had, roughly speaking, got his. He had the habit of soaring up into the sunset and sitting around in a large pink cloud like a kid bouncing on a feather bed. Then, one day, he soared higher and farther than he knew, having, perhaps, grown careless through over-confidence. He heard nothing above the roar of his own engine, and the two planes were upon him almost before he knew it. They were not French, or English, or American planes. He got one of them and would have got clean away if the other had not caught him in the arm. The right arm. His mechanician lay limp. Even then he might have managed a landing but the pursuing plane got in a final shot. There followed a period of time that seemed to cover, say, six years but that was actually only a matter of seconds. At the end of that period Giddy, together with a tangle of wire, silk, wood, and something that had been the mechanician, lay inside the German lines, and you would hardly have thought him worth the disentangling.

They did disentangle him, though, and even patched him up pretty expertly, but not so expertly, perhaps, as they might have, being enemy surgeons and rather busy with the patching of their own injured. The bone, for example, in the lower right arm, knitted promptly and properly, being a young and healthy bone, but they rather over-looked the matter of arm nerves and muscles, so that later, though it looked a perfectly proper arm, it couldn't lift four pounds. His head had emerged slowly, month by month, from swathings of gauze. What had been quite a crevasse in his skull became only a scarlet scar that his hair pretty well hid when he brushed it over the bad place. But the surgeon, perhaps being overly busy, or having no real way of knowing that Giddy's nose had been a distinguished and aristocratically hooked Gory nose, had remoulded that wrecked feature into a pure Greek line at first sight of which Giddy stood staring weakly into the mirror; reeling a little with surprise and horror and unbelief and general misery. "Can this be I?" he thought, feeling like the old man of the bramble bush in the Mother Goose rhyme. A well-made and becoming nose, but not so fine looking as the original feature had been, as worn by Giddy.

"Look here!" he protested to the surgeon, months too late. "Look here, this isn't my nose."

"Be glad," replied that practical Prussian person, "that you have any."

With his knowledge of French and English and German Giddy acted as interpreter during the months of his invalidism and later internment, and things were not so bad with him. He had no news of his mother, though, and no way of knowing whether she had news of him. With 1918, and the Armistice and his release, he hurried to Paris and there got the full impact of the past year's events.

Julia Gory was dead and the Gory money nonexistent.

Out of the ruins—a jewel or two and some paper not quite worthless—he managed a few thousand francs and went to Nice. There he walked in the sunshine, and sat in the sunshine, and even danced in the sunshine, a dazed young thing together with hundreds of other dazed young things, not thinking, not planning, not hoping. Existing only in a state of semi-consciousness like one recovering from a blinding blow. The francs dribbled away. Sometimes he played baccarat and won; oftener he played baccarat and lost. He moved in a sort of trance, feeling nothing. Vaguely he knew that there was a sort of Conference going on in Paris. Sometimes he thought of Winnebago, recalling it remotely, dimly, as one is occasionally conscious of a former unknown existence. Twice he went to Paris for periods of some months, but he was unhappy there and even strangely bewildered, like a child. He was still sick in mind and body, though he did not know it. Driftwood, like thousands of others, tossed up on the shore after the storm; lying there bleached and useless and battered.

Then, one day in Nice, there was no money. Not a franc. Not a centime. He knew hunger. He knew terror. He knew desperation. It was out of this period that there emerged Giddy, the gigolo. Now, though, the name bristled with accent marks, thus: Gédéon Goré.

This Gédéon Goré, of the Nice dansants, did not even remotely resemble Gideon Gory of Winnebago, Wisconsin. This Gédéon Goré wore French clothes of the kind that Giddy Gory had always despised. A slim, sallow, sleek, sad-eyed gigolo in tight French garments, the pants rather flappy at the ankle; effeminate French shoes with fawn-coloured uppers and patent-leather eyelets and vamps, most despicable; a slim cane; hair with a magnificent natural wave that looked artificially marcelled and that was worn with a strip growing down from the temples on either side in the sort of cut used only by French dandies and English stage butlers. No, this was not Giddy Gory. The real Giddy Gory lay in a smart but battered suitcase under the narrow bed in his lodgings. The suitcase contained:

Item; one grey tweed suit with name of a London tailor inside.

Item; one pair Russia calf oxfords of American make.

Item; one French aviation uniform with leather coat, helmet, and gloves all bearing stiff and curious splotches of brown or rust-colour which you might not recognize as dried blood stains.

Item; one handful assorted medals, ribbons, orders, etc.

All Europe was dancing. It seemed a death dance, grotesque, convulsive, hideous. Paris, Nice, Berlin, Budapest, Rome, Vienna, London writhed and twisted and turned and jiggled. St. Vitus himself never imagined contortions such as these. In the narrow side-street dance rooms of Florence, and in the great avenue restaurants of Paris they were performing exactly the same gyrations—wiggle, squirm, shake. And over all the American jazz music boomed and whanged its syncopation. On the music racks of violinists who had meant to be Elmans or Kreislers were sheets entitled Jazz Baby Fox Trot. Drums, horns, cymbals, castanets, sandpaper. So the mannequins and marionettes of Europe tried to whirl themselves into forgetfulness.

The Americans thought Giddy was a Frenchman. The French knew him for an American, dress as he would. Dancing became with him a profession—no, a trade. He danced flawlessly, holding and guiding his partner impersonally, firmly, expertly in spite of the weak right arm—it served well enough. Gideon Gory had always been a naturally rhythmic dancer. Then, too, he had been fond of dancing. Years of practise had perfected him. He adopted now the manner and position of the professional. As he danced he held his head rather stiffly to one side, and a little down, the chin jutting out just a trifle. The effect was at the same time stiff and chic. His footwork was infallible. The intricate and imbecilic steps of the day he performed in flawless sequence. Under his masterly guidance the feet of the least rhythmic were suddenly endowed with deftness and grace. One swayed with him as naturally as with an elemental force. He danced politely and almost wordlessly unless first addressed, according to the code of his kind. His touch was firm, yet remote. The dance concluded, he conducted his partner to her seat, bowed stiffly from the waist, heels together, and departed. For these services he was handed ten francs, twenty francs, thirty francs, or more, if lucky, depending on the number of times he was called upon to dance with a partner during the evening. Thus was dancing, the most spontaneous and unartificial of the Muses, vulgarized, commercialized, prostituted. Lower than Gideon Gory, of Winnebago, Wisconsin, had fallen, could no man fall.

Sometimes he danced in Paris. During the high season he danced in Nice. Afternoon and evening found him busy in the hot, perfumed, overcrowded dance salons. The Negresco, the Ruhl, Maxim's, Belle Meunière, the Casina Municipale. He learned to make his face go a perfect blank—pale, cryptic, expressionless. Between himself and the other boys of his ilk there was little or no professional comradeship. A weird lot they were, young, though their faces were strangely lacking in the look of youth. All of them had been in the war. Most of them had been injured. There was Aubin, the Frenchman. The right side of Aubin's face was rather startlingly handsome in its Greek perfection. It was like a profile chiselled. The left side was another face—the same, and yet not the same. It was as though you saw the left side out of drawing, or blurred, or out of focus. It puzzled you—shocked you. The left side of Aubin's face had been done over by an army surgeon who, though deft and scientific, had not had a hand expert as that of the Original Sculptor. Then there was Mazzetti, the Roman. He parted his hair on the wrong side, and under the black wing of it was a deep groove into which you could lay a forefinger. A piece of shell had plowed it neatly. The Russian boy who called himself Orloff had the look in his eyes of one who has seen things upon which eyes never should have looked. He smoked constantly and ate, apparently, not at all. Among these there existed a certain unwritten code and certain unwritten signals.

You did not take away the paying partner of a fellow gigolo. If in too great demand you turned your surplus partners over to gigolos unemployed. You did not accept less than ten francs (they all broke this rule). Sometimes Gédéon Goré made ten francs a day, sometimes twenty, sometimes fifty, infrequently a hundred. Sometimes not enough to pay for his one decent meal a day. At first he tried to keep fit by walking a certain number of miles daily along the ocean front. But usually he was too weary to persist in this. He did not think at all. He felt nothing. Sometimes, down deep, deep in a long-forgotten part of his being a voice called feebly, plaintively to the man who had been Giddy Gory. But he shut his ears and mind and consciousness and would not listen.

The American girls were best, the gigolos all agreed, and they paid well, though they talked too much. Gédéon Goré was a favourite among them. They thought he was so foreign looking, and kind of sad and stern and everything. His French, fluent, colloquial, and bewildering, awed them. They would attempt to speak to him in halting and hackneyed phrases acquired during three years at Miss Pence's Select School at Hastings-on-the-Hudson. At the cost of about a thousand dollars a word they would enunciate, painfully:

"*Je pense que*—um—*que Nice est le plus belle*—uh—*ville de France.*"

Giddy, listening courteously, his head inclined as though unwilling to miss one conversational pearl falling from the pretty American's lips, would appear to consider this gravely. Then, sometimes in an unexpected burst of pure mischief, he would answer:

"You said something! *Some* burg, I'm telling the world."

The girl, startled, would almost leap back from the confines of his arms only to find his face stern, immobile, his eyes sombre and reflective.

"Why! Where did you pick that up?"

His eyebrows would go up. His face would express complete lack of comprehension. "*Pardon?*"

Afterward, at home, in Toledo or Kansas City or Los Angeles, the girl would tell about it. "I suppose some American girl taught it to him, just for fun. It sounded too queer—because his French was so wonderful. He danced divinely. A Frenchman, and so aristocratic! Think of his being a professional partner. They have them over there, you know. Everybody's dancing in Europe. And gay! Why, you'd never know there'd been a war."

Mary Hubbell, of the Winnebago Hubbells, did not find it so altogether gay. Mary Hubbell, with her father, Orson J. Hubbell, and her mother, Bee Hubbell, together with what appeared to be practically the entire white population of the United States, came to Europe early in 1922, there to travel, to play, to rest, to behold, and to turn their good hard American dollars into cordwood-size bundles of German marks, Austrian kronen, Italian lires, and French francs. Most of the men regarded Europe as a wine list. In their mental geography Rheims, Rhine, Moselle, Bordeaux, Champagne, or Würzburg were not localities but libations. The women, for the most part, went in for tortoise-shell combs, fringed silk shawls, jade earrings, beaded bags, and coral neck chains. Up and down the famous thoroughfare of Europe went the absurd pale blue tweed tailleurs and the lavender tweed cape suits of America's wives and daughters. Usually, after the first month or two, they shed these respectable, middle-class habiliments for what they fondly believed to be smart Paris costumes; and you could almost invariably tell a good, moral, church-going matron of the Middle West by the fact that she was got up like a demimondaine of the second class, in the naïve belief that she looked French and chic.

The three Hubbells were thoroughly nice people. Mary Hubbell was more than thoroughly nice. She was a darb. She had done a completely good job during the 1918-1918 period, including the expert driving of a wild and unbroken Ford up and down the shell-torn roads of France. One of those small-town girls with a big-town outlook, a well-trained mind, a slim boyish body, a good clear skin, and a steady eye that saw. Mary Hubbell wasn't a beauty by a good many measurements, but she had her points, as witness the number of bouquets, bundles, books, and bon-bons piled in her cabin when she sailed.

The well-trained mind and the steady seeing eye enabled Mary Hubbell to discover that Europe wasn't so gay as it seemed to the blind; and she didn't write home to the effect that you'd never know there'd been war.

The Hubbells had the best that Europe could afford. Orson J. Hubbell, a mild-mannered, grey-haired man with a nice flat waist-line and a good keen eye (hence Mary's) adored his women-folk and spoiled them. During the first years of his married life he had been Hubbell, the drayman, as Giddy Gory had said. He had driven one of his three drays himself, standing sturdily in the front of the red-painted wooden two-horse wagon as it rattled up and down the main business thoroughfare of Winnebago. But the war and the soaring freight-rates had dealt generously with Orson Hubbell. As railroad and shipping difficulties increased the Hubbell draying business waxed prosperous. Factories, warehouses, and wholesale business firms could be assured that their goods would arrive promptly, safely, and cheaply when conveyed by a Hubbell van. So now the three red-painted wooden horse-driven drays were magically transformed into a great fleet of monster motor vans that plied up and down the state of Wisconsin and even into Michigan and Illinois and Indiana. The Orson J. Hubbell Transportation Company, you read. And below, in yellow lettering on the red background:

Have HUBBELL Do Your HAULING.

There was actually a million in it, and more to come. The buying of the old Gory house on the river bluff had been one of the least of Orson's feats. And now that house was honeycombed with sleeping porches and linen closets and enamel fittings and bathrooms white and glittering as an operating auditorium. And there were shower baths, and blue rugs, and great soft fuzzy bath towels and little white innocent guest towels embroidered with curly H's whose tails writhed at you from all corners.

Orson J. and Mrs. Hubbell had never been in Europe before, and they enjoyed themselves enormously. That is to say, Mrs. Orson J. did, and Orson, seeing her happy, enjoyed himself vicariously. His hand slid in and out of his inexhaustible pocket almost automatically now. And "How much?" was his favourite locution. They went everywhere, did everything. Mary boasted a pretty fair French. Mrs. Hubbell conversed in the various languages of

Europe by speaking pidgin English very loud, and omitting all verbs, articles, adverbs, and other cumbersome superfluities. Thus, to the *fille de chambre*.

"Me out now you beds." The red-cheeked one from the provinces understood, in some miraculous way, that Mrs. Hubbell was now going out and that the beds could be made and the rooms tidied.

They reached Nice in February and plunged into its gaieties. "Just think!" exclaimed Mrs. Hubbell rapturously, "only three francs for a facial or a manicure and two for a marcel. It's like finding them."

"If the Mediterranean gets any bluer," said Mary, "I don't think I can stand it, it's so lovely."

Mrs. Hubbell, at tea, expressed a desire to dance. Mary, at tea, desired to dance but didn't express it. Orson J. loathed tea; and the early draying business had somewhat unfitted his sturdy legs for the lighter movements of the dance. But he wanted only their happiness. So he looked about a bit, and asked some questions, and came back.

"Seems there's a lot of young chaps who make a business of dancing with the women-folks who haven't dancing men along. Hotel hires 'em. Funny to us but I guess it's all right, and quite the thing around here. You pay 'em so much a dance, or so much an afternoon. You girls want to try it?"

"I do," said Mrs. Orson J. Hubbell. "It doesn't sound respectable. Then that's what all those thin little chaps are who have been dancing with those pretty American girls. They're sort of ratty looking, aren't they? What do they call 'em? That's a nice-looking one, over there—no, no!—dancing with the girl in grey, I mean. If that's one I'd like to dance with him, Orson. Good land, what would the Winnebago ladies say! What do they call 'em, I wonder."

Mary had been gazing very intently at the nice-looking one over there who was dancing with the girl in grey. She answered her mother's question, still gazing at him. "They call them gigolos," she said, slowly. Then, "Get that one Dad, will you, if you can? You dance with him first, Mother, and then I'll——"

"I can get two," volunteered Orson J.

"No," said Mary Hubbell, sharply.

The nice-looking gigolo seemed to be in great demand, but Orson J. succeeded in capturing him after the third dance. It turned out to be a tango, and though Mrs. Hubbell, pretty well scared, declared that she didn't know it and couldn't dance it, the nice-looking gigolo assured her, through the medium of Mary's interpretation, that Mrs. Hubbell had only to follow his guidance. It was quite simple. He did not seem to look directly at Mary, or at Orson J. or at Mrs. Hubbell, as he spoke. The dance concluded, Mrs. Hubbell came back breathless, but enchanted.

"He has beautiful manners," she said, aloud, in English. "And dance! You feel like a swan when you're dancing with him. Try him, Mary." The gigolo's face, as he bowed before her, was impassive, inscrutable.

But, "Sh!" said Mary.

"Nonsense! Doesn't understand a word."

Mary danced the next dance with him. They danced wordlessly until the dance was half over. Then, abruptly, Mary said in English, "What's your name?"

Close against him she felt a sudden little sharp contraction of the gigolo's diaphragm—the contraction that reacts to surprise or alarm. But he said, in French, "*Pardon?*"

So, "What's your name?" said Mary, in French this time.

The gigolo with the beautiful manners hesitated longer than really beautiful manners should permit. But finally, "Je m'appelle Gédéon Goré." He pronounced it in his most nasal, perfect Paris French. It didn't sound even remotely like Gideon Gory.

"My name's Hubbell," said Mary, in her pretty fair French. "Mary Hubbell. I come from a little town called Winnebago."

The Goré eyebrow expressed polite disinterestedness.

"That's in Wisconsin," continued Mary, "and I love it."

"*Naturellement*," agreed the gigolo, stiffly.

They finished the dance without further conversation. Mrs. Hubbell had the next dance. Mary the next. They spent the afternoon dancing, until dinner time. Orson J.'s fee, as he handed it to the gigolo, was the kind that mounted grandly into dollars instead of mere francs. The gigolo's face, as he took it, was not more inscrutable than Mary's as she watched him take it.

From that afternoon, throughout the next two weeks, if any girl as thoroughly fine as Mary Hubbell could be said to run after any man, Mary ran after that gigolo. At the same time one could almost have said that he tried to avoid her. Mary took a course of tango lessons, and urged her mother to do the same. Even Orson J. noticed it.

"Look here," he said, in kindly protest. "Aren't you getting pretty thick with this jigger?"

"Sociological study, Dad. I'm all right."

"Yeh, you're all right. But how about him?"

"He's all right, too."

The gigolo resisted Mary's unmaidenly advances, and yet, when he was with her, he seemed sometimes to forget to look sombre and blank and remote. They seemed to have a lot to say to each other. Mary talked about America a good deal. About her home town ... "and big elms and maples and oaks in the yard ... the Fox River valley ... Middle West ... Normal Avenue ... Cass Street ... Fox River paper mills...."

She talked in French and English. The gigolo confessed, one day, to understanding some English, though he seemed to speak none. After that Mary, when very much in earnest, or when enthusiastic, spoke in her native tongue altogether. She claimed an intense interest in European after-war conditions, in reconstruction, in the attitude toward life of those millions of young men who had actually participated in the conflict. She asked questions that might have been considered impertinent, not to say nervy.

"Now you," she said, brutally, "are a person of some education, refinement, and background. Yet you are content to dance around in these—these—well, back home a chap might wash dishes in a cheap restaurant or run an elevator in an east side New York loft building, but he'd never——"

A very faint dull red crept suddenly over the pallor of the gigolo's face. They were sitting out on a bench on the promenade, facing the ocean (in direct defiance on Mary's part of all rules of conduct of respectable girls toward gigolos). Mary Hubbell had said rather brusque things before. But now, for the first time, the young man defended himself faintly.

"For us," he replied in his exquisite French, "it is finished. For us there is nothing. This generation, it is no good. I am no good. They are no good." He waved a hand in a gesture that included the promenaders, the musicians in the cafés, the dancers, the crowds eating and drinking at the little tables lining the walk.

"What rot!" said Mary Hubbell, briskly. "They probably said exactly the same thing in Asia after Alexander had got through with 'em. I suppose there was such dancing and general devilment in Macedonia that every one said the younger generation had gone to the dogs since the war, and the world would never amount to anything again. But it seemed to pick up, didn't it?"

The boy turned and looked at her squarely for the first time, his eyes meeting hers. Mary looked at him. She even swayed toward him a little, her lips parted. There was about her a breathlessness, an expectancy. So they sat for a moment, and between them the air was electric, vibrant. Then, slowly, he relaxed, sat back, slumped a little on the bench. Over his face, that for a moment had been alight with something vital, there crept again the look of defeat, of sombre indifference. At sight of that look Mary Hubbell's jaw set. She leaned forward. She clasped her fine large hands tight. She did not look at the gigolo, but out, across the blue Mediterranean, and beyond it. Her voice was low and a little tremulous and she spoke in English only.

"It isn't finished here—here in Europe. But it's sick. Back home, in America, though, it's alive. Alive! And growing. I wish I could make you understand what it's like there. It's all new, and crude, maybe, and ugly, but it's so darned healthy and sort of clean. I love it. I love every bit of it. I know I sound like a flag-waver but I don't care. I mean it. And I know it's sentimental, but I'm proud of it. The kind of thing I feel about the United States is the kind of thing Mencken sneers at. You don't know who Mencken is. He's a critic who pretends to despise everything because he's really a sentimentalist and afraid somebody'll find it out. I don't say I don't appreciate the beauty of all this Italy and France and England and Germany. But it doesn't get me the way just the mention of a name will get me back home. This trip, for example. Why, last summer four of us—three other girls and I—motored from Wisconsin to California, and we drove every inch of the way ourselves. The Santa Fé Trail! The Ocean-to-Ocean Highway! The Lincoln Highway! The Dixie Highway! The Yellowstone Trail! The very sound of those words gives me a sort of prickly feeling. They mean something so big and vital and new. I get a thrill out of them that I haven't had once over here. Why even this," she threw out a hand that included and dismissed the whole sparkling panorama before her, "this doesn't begin to give the jolt that I got out of Walla Walla, and Butte, and Missoula, and Spokane, and Seattle, and Albuquerque. We drove all day, and ate ham and eggs at some little hotel or lunch-counter at night, and outside the hotel the drummers would be sitting, talking and smoking; and there were Western men, very tanned and tall and lean, in those big two-gallon hats and khaki pants and puttees. And there were sunsets, and sand, and cactus and mountains, and campers and Fords. I can smell the Kansas corn fields and I can see the Iowa farms and the ugly little raw American towns, and the big thin American men, and the grain elevators near the railroad stations, and I know those towns weren't the way towns ought to look. They were ugly and crude and new. Maybe it wasn't all beautiful, but gosh! it was real, and growing, and big and alive! Alive!"

Mary Hubbell was crying. There, on the bench along the promenade in the sunshine at Nice, she was crying.

The boy beside her suddenly rose, uttered a little inarticulate sound, and left her there on the bench in the sunshine. Vanished, completely, in the crowd.

For three days the Orson J. Hubbells did not see their favourite gigolo. If Mary was disturbed she did not look it, though her eye was alert in the throng. During the three days of their gigolo's absence Mrs. Hubbell and Mary availed themselves of the professional services of the Italian gigolo Mazzetti. Mrs. Hubbell said she thought his dancing was, if anything, more nearly perfect than that What's-his-name, but his manner wasn't so nice and she didn't like his eyes. Sort of sneaky. Mary said she thought so, too.

Nevertheless she was undoubtedly affable toward him, and talked (in French) and laughed and even walked with him, apparently in complete ignorance of the fact that these things were not done. Mazzetti spoke frequently of his colleague, Goré, and always in terms of disparagement. A low fellow. A clumsy dancer. One unworthy of Mary's swanlike grace. Unfit to receive Orson J. Hubbell's generous fees.

Late one evening, during the mid-week after-dinner dance, Goré appeared suddenly in the doorway. It was ten o'clock. The Hubbells were dallying with their after-dinner coffee at one of the small tables about the dance floor.

Mary, keen-eyed, saw him first. She beckoned Mazzetti who stood in attendance beside Mrs. Hubbell's chair. She snatched up the wrap that lay at hand and rose. "It's stifling in here. I'm going out on the Promenade for a breath of air. Come on." She plucked at Mazzetti's sleeve and actually propelled him through the crowd and out of the room. She saw Goré's startled eyes follow them.

She even saw him crossing swiftly to where her mother and father sat. Then she vanished into the darkness with Mazzetti. And the Mazzettis put but one interpretation upon a young woman who strolls into the soft darkness of the Promenade with a gigolo.

And Mary Hubbell knew this.

Gédéon Goré stood before Mr. and Mrs. Orson J. Hubbell. "Where is your daughter?" he demanded, in French.

"Oh, howdy-do," chirped Mrs. Hubbell. "Well, it's Mr. Goré! We missed you. I hope you haven't been sick."

"Where is your daughter?" demanded Gédéon Goré, in French. "Where is Mary?"

Mrs. Hubbell caught the word Mary. "Oh, Mary. Why, she's gone out for a walk with Mr. Mazzetti."

"Good God!" said Gédéon Goré, in perfectly plain English. And vanished.

Orson J. Hubbell sat a moment, thinking. Then, "Why, say, he talked English. That young French fella talked English."

The young French fella, hatless, was skimming down the Promenade des Anglais, looking intently ahead, and behind, and to the side, and all around in the darkness. He seemed to be following a certain trail, however. At one side of the great wide walk, facing the ocean, was a canopied bandstand. In its dim shadow, he discerned a wisp of white. He made for it, swiftly, silently. Mazzetti's voice low, eager, insistent. Mazzetti's voice hoarse, ugly, importunate. The figure in white rose. Goré stood before the two. The girl took a step toward him, but Mazzetti took two steps and snarled like a villain in a movie, if a villain in a movie could be heard to snarl.

"Get out of here!" said Mazzetti, in French, to Goré. "You pig! Swine! To intrude when I talk with a lady. You are finished. Now she belongs to me."

"The hell she does!" said Giddy Gory in perfectly plain American and swung for Mazzetti with his bad right arm. Mazzetti, after the fashion of his kind, let fly in most unsportsmanlike fashion with his feet, kicking at Giddy's stomach and trying to bite with his small sharp yellow teeth. And then Giddy's left, that had learned some neat tricks of boxing in the days of the Gory greatness, landed fairly on the Mazzetti nose. And with a howl of pain and rage and terror the Mazzetti, a hand clapped to that bleeding feature, fled in the darkness.

And, "O, Giddy!" said Mary, "I thought you'd never come."

"Mary. Mary Hubbell. Did you know all the time? You did, didn't you? You think I'm a bum, don't you? Don't you?"

Her hand on his shoulder. "Giddy, I've been stuck on you since I was nine years old, in Winnebago. I kept track of you all through the war, though I never once saw you. Then I lost you. Giddy, when I was a kid I used to look at you from the sidewalk through the hedge of the house on Cass. Honestly. Honestly, Giddy."

"But look at me now. Why, Mary, I'm—I'm no good. Why, I don't see how you ever knew———"

"It takes more than a new Greek nose and French clothes and a bum arm to fool me, Gid. Do you know, there were a lot of photographs of you left up in the attic of the Cass Street house when we bought it. I know them all by heart, Giddy. By heart.... Come on home, Giddy. Let's go home."

NOT A DAY OVER TWENTY-ONE

Any one old enough to read this is old enough to remember that favourite heroine of fiction who used to start her day by rising from her couch, flinging wide her casement, leaning out and breathing deep the perfumed morning air. You will recall, too, the pure white rose clambering at the side of the casement, all jewelled with the dew of dawn. This the lady plucked carolling. Daily she plucked it. A hardy perennial if ever there was one. Subsequently, pressing it to her lips, she flung it into the garden below, where stood her lover (likewise an early riser).

Romantic proceeding this, but unhygienic when you consider that her rush for the closed casement was doubtless due to the fact that her bedroom, hermetically sealed during the night, must have grown pretty stuffy by morning. Her complexion was probably bad.

No such idyllic course marked the matin of our heroine. Her day's beginning differed from the above in practically every detail. Thus:

A—When Harrietta rose from her couch (cream enamel, full-sized bed with double hair mattress and box springs) she closed her casement with a bang, having slept in a gale that swept her two-room-and-kitchenette apartment on the eleventh floor in Fifty-sixth Street.

B—She never leaned out except, perhaps, to flap a dust rag, because lean as she might, defying the laws of gravity and the house superintendent, she could have viewed nothing more than roofs and sky and chimneys where already roofs and sky and chimneys filled the eye (unless you consider that by screwing around and flattening one ear and the side of your jaw against the window jamb you could almost get a glimpse of distant green prominently mentioned in the agent's ad as "unexcelled view of Park").

C—The morning air wasn't perfumed for purposes of breathing deep, being New York morning air, richly laden with the smell of warm asphalt, smoke, gas, and, when the wind was right, the glue factory on the Jersey shore across the river.

D—She didn't pluck a rose, carolling, because even if, by some magic Burbankian process, Jack's bean-stalk had been made rose-bearing it would have been hard put to it to reach this skyscraper home.

E—If she had flung it, it probably would have ended its eleven-story flight in the hand cart of Messinger's butcher boy, who usually made his first Fifty-sixth Street delivery at about that time.

F—The white rose would not have been jewelled and sparkling with the dews of dawn, anyway, as at Harrietta's rising hour (between 10.30 and 11.30 A. M.) the New York City dews, if any, have left for the day.

Spartans who rise regularly at the chaste hour of seven will now regard Harrietta with disapproval. These should be told that Harrietta never got to bed before twelve-thirty nor to sleep before two-thirty, which, on an eight-hour sleep count, should even things up somewhat in their minds. They must know, too, that in one corner of her white-and-blue bathroom reposed a pair of wooden dumb-bells, their ankles neatly crossed. She used them daily. Also she bathed, massaged, exercised, took facial and electric treatments; worked like a slave; lived like an athlete in training in order to preserve her hair, skin, teeth, and figure; almost never ate what she wanted nor as much as she liked.

That earlier lady of the closed casement and the white rose probably never even heard of a dentifrice or a cold shower.

The result of Harrietta's rigours was that now, at thirty-seven, she could pass for twenty-seven on Fifth Avenue at five o'clock (flesh-pink, single-mesh face veil); twenty-five at a small dinner (rose-coloured shades over the candles), and twenty-two, easily, behind the amber footlights.

You will have guessed that Harrietta, the Heroine, is none other than Harrietta Fuller, deftest of comediennes, whom you have seen in one or all of those slim little plays in which she has made a name but no money to speak of, being handicapped for the American stage by her intelligence and her humour sense, and, as she would tell you, by her very name itself.

"Harrietta Fuller! Don't you see what I mean?" she would say. "In the first place, it's hard to remember. And it lacks force. Or maybe rhythm. It doesn't clink. It sort of humps in the middle. A name should flow. Take a name like Barrymore—or Bernhardt—or Duse—you can't forget them. Oh, I'm not comparing myself to them. Don't be funny. I just mean—why, take Harrietta alone. It's deadly. A Thackeray miss, all black silk mitts and white cotton stockings. Long ago, in the beginning, I thought of shortening it. But Harriet Fuller sounds like a school-teacher, doesn't it? And Hattie Fuller makes me think, somehow, of a burlesque actress. You know. 'Hattie Fuller and Her Bouncing Belles.'"

At thirty-seven Harrietta Fuller had been fifteen years on the stage. She had little money, a small stanch following, an exquisite technique, and her fur coat was beginning to look gnawed around the edges. People even said maddeningly: "Harrietta Fuller? I saw her when I was a kid, years ago. Why, she must be le'see—ten—twelve—why, she must be going on pretty close to forty."

A worshipper would defend her. "You're crazy! I saw her last month when she was playing in Cincinnati, and she doesn't look a day over twenty-one. That's a cute play she's in—There and Back. Not much to it, but she's so kind and natural. Made me think of Jen a little."

That was part of Harrietta's art—making people think of Jen. Watching her, they would whisper: "Look! Isn't that Jen all over? The way she sits there and looks up at him while she's sewing."

Harrietta Fuller could take lines that were stilted and shoddy and speak them in a way to make them sound natural and distinctive and real. She was a clear blonde, but her speaking voice had in it a contralto note that usually accompanies brunette colouring.

It surprised and gratified you, that tone, as does mellow wine when you have expected cider. She could walk on to one of those stage library sets that reek of the storehouse and the property carpenter, seat herself, take up a book or a piece of handiwork, and instantly the absurd room became a human, livable place. She had a knack of sitting, not as an actress ordinarily seats herself in a drawing room—feet carefully strained to show the high arch, body posed to form a "line"—but easily, as a woman sits in her own house. If you saw her in the supper scene of My Mistake, you will remember how she twisted her feet about the rungs of the straight little chair in which she sat. Her back was toward the audience throughout the scene, according to stage directions, yet she managed to convey embarrassment, fright, terror, determination, decision in the agonized twisting of those expressive feet.

Authors generally claimed these bits of business as having originated with them. For that matter, she was a favourite with playwrights, as well she might be, considering the vitality which she injected into their hackneyed situations. Every little while some young writer, fired by an inflection in her voice or a nuance in her comedy, would rush back stage to tell her that she never had had a part worthy of her, and that he would now come to her rescue. Sometimes he kept his word, and Harrietta, six months later, would look up from the manuscript to say: "This is delightful! It's what I've been looking for for years. The deftness of the comedy. And that little scene with the gardener!"

But always, after the managers had finished suggesting bits that would brighten it up, and changes that would put it over with the Western buyers, Harrietta would regard the mutilated manuscript sorrowingly. "But I can't play this now, you know. It isn't the same part at all. It's—forgive me—vulgar."

Then some little red-haired ingénue would get it, and it would run a solid year on Broadway and two seasons on the road, and in all that time Harrietta would have played six months, perhaps, in three different plays, in all of which she would score what is known as a "personal success." A personal success usually means bad business at the box office.

Now this is immensely significant. In the advertisements of the play in which Harrietta Fuller might be appearing you never read:

HARRIETTA FULLER
In
Thus and So

No. It was always:

THUS AND SO
With
Harrietta Fuller

Between those two prepositions lies a whole theatrical world of difference. The "In" means stardom; the "With" that the play is considered more important than the cast.

Don't feel sorry for Harrietta Fuller. Thousands of women have envied her; thousands of men admired, and several have loved her devotedly, including her father, the Rev. H. John Scoville (deceased). The H. stands for Harry. She was named for him, of course. When he entered the church he was advised to drop his first name and use his second as being more fitting in his position. But the outward change did not affect his inner self. He remained more Harry than John to the last. It was from him Harrietta got her acting sense, her humour, her intelligence, and her bad luck.

When Harry Scoville was eighteen he wanted to go on the stage. At twenty he entered the ministry. It was the natural outlet for his suppressed talents. In his day and family and environment young men did not go on the stage. The Scovilles were Illinois pioneers and lived in Evanston, and Mrs. Scoville (Harrietta's grandmother, you understand, though Harrietta had not yet appeared) had a good deal to say as to whether coleslaw or cucumber pickles should be served at the Presbyterian church suppers, along with the veal loaf and the scalloped oysters. And when she decided on coleslaw, coleslaw it was. A firm tread had Mother Scoville, a light hand with pastry, and a will that was adamant. She it was who misdirected Harry's gifts toward the pulpit instead of the stage. He never forgave her for it, though he made a great success of his calling and she died unsuspecting his rancour. The women of his congregation shivered deliciously when the Rev. H. John Scoville stood on his tiptoes at the apex of some fiery period and hurled the force of his eloquence at them. He, the minister, was unconsciously dramatizing himself as a minister.

The dramatic method had not then come into use in the pulpit. His method of delivery was more restrained than that of the old-time revivalist; less analytical and detached than that of the present-day religious lecturer.

Presbyterian Evanston wending its way home to Sunday roast and ice cream would say: "Wasn't Reverend Scoville powerful to-day! My!" They never guessed how Reverend Scoville had had to restrain himself from delivering Mark Antony's address to the Romans. He often did it in his study when his gentle wife thought he was rehearsing next Sunday's sermon.

As he grew older he overcame these boyish weaknesses, but he never got over his feeling for the stage. There were certain ill-natured gossips who claimed to have recognized the fine, upright figure and the mobile face with hair greying at the temples as having occupied a seat in the third row of the balcony in the old Grand Opera House during the run of Erminie. The elders put it down as spite talk and declared that, personally, they didn't believe a word of it. The Rev. H. John did rather startle them when he discarded the ministerial black broadcloth for a natty Oxford suit of almost business cut. He was a pioneer in this among the clergy. The congregation soon became accustomed to it; in time, boasted of it as marking their progressiveness.

He had a neat ankle, had the Reverend Scoville, in fine black lisle; a merry eye; a rather grim look about the mouth, as has a man whose life is a secret disappointment. His little daughter worshipped him. He called her Harry. When Harrietta was eleven she was reading Lever and Dickens and Dumas, while other little girls were absorbed in the Elsie Series and The Wide, Wide World. Her father used to deliver his sermons to her in private rehearsal, and her eager mobile face reflected his every written mood.

"Oh, Rev!" she cried one day (it is to be regretted, but that is what she always called him). "Oh, Rev, you should have been an actor!"

He looked at her queerly. "What makes you think so?"

"You're too thrilling for a minister." She searched about in her agile mind for fuller means of making her thought clear. "It's like when Mother cooks rose geranium leaves in her grape jell. She says they gives it a finer flavour, but they don't really. You can't taste them for the grapes, so they're just wasted when they're so darling and perfumy and just right in the garden." Her face was pink with earnestness.

"D'you see what I mean, Rev?"

"Yes, I think I see, Harry."

Then she surprised him. "I'm going on the stage," she said, "and be a great actress when I'm grown up."

His heart gave a leap and a lurch. "Why do you say that?"

"Because I want to. And because you didn't. It'll be as if you had been an actor instead of a minister—only it'll be me."

A bewildering enough statement to any one but the one who made it and the one to whom it was made. She was trying to say that here was the law of compensation working. But she didn't know this. She had never heard of the law of compensation.

Her gentle mother fought her decision with all the savagery of the gentle.

"You'll have to run away, Harry," her father said, sadly. And at twenty-two Harrietta ran. Her objective was New York. Her father did not burden her with advice. He credited her with the intelligence she possessed, but he did overlook her emotionalism, which was where he made his mistake. Just before she left he said: "Now listen, Harry. You're a good-looking girl, and young. You'll keep your looks for a long time. You're not the kind of blonde who'll get wishy-washy or fat. You've got quite a good deal of brunette in you. It crops out in your voice. It'll help preserve your looks. Don't marry the first man who asks you or the first man who says he'll die if you don't. You've got lots of time."

That kind of advice is a good thing for the young. Two weeks later Harrietta married a man she had met on the train between Evanston and New York. His name was Lawrence Fuller, and Harrietta had gone to school with him in Evanston. She had lost track of him later. She remembered, vaguely, people had said he had gone to New York and was pretty wild. Young as she was and inexperienced, there still was something about his face that warned her. It was pathological, but she knew nothing of pathology. He talked of her and looked at her and spoke, masterfully and yet shyly, of being with her in New York. Harrietta loved the way his hair sprang away from his brow and temples in a clean line. She shoved the thought of his chin out of her mind. His hands touched her a good deal—her shoulder, her knee, her wrist—but so lightly that she couldn't resent it even if she had wanted to. When they did this, queer little stinging flashes darted through her veins. He said he would die if she did not marry him.

They had two frightful years together and eight years apart before he died, horribly, in the sanatorium whose enormous fees she paid weekly. They had regularly swallowed her earnings at a gulp.

Naturally a life like this develops the comedy sense. You can't play tragedy while you're living it. Harrietta served her probation in stock, road companies, one-night stands before she achieved Broadway. In five years her deft comedy method had become distinctive; in ten it was unique. Yet success—as the stage measures it in size of following and dollars of salary—had never been hers.

Harrietta knew she wasn't a success. She saw actresses younger, older, less adroit, lacking her charm, minus her beauty, featured, starred, heralded. Perhaps she gave her audiences credit for more intelligence than they possessed, and they, unconsciously, resented this. Perhaps if she had read the Elsie Series at eleven, instead of Dickens, she might have been willing to play in that million-dollar success called Gossip. It was offered her. The lead was one of those saccharine parts, vulgar, false, and slyly carnal. She didn't in the least object to it on the ground of immorality, but the bad writing bothered her. There was, for example, a line in which she was supposed to beat her breast and say: "He's my mate! He's my man! And I'm his woman!! I love him, I tell you I—*love him!*"

"People don't talk like that," she told the author, in a quiet aside, during rehearsal. "Especially women. They couldn't. They use quite commonplace idiom when they're excited."

"Thanks," said the author, elaborately polite. "That's the big scene in the play. It'll be a knockout."

When Harrietta tried to speak these lines in rehearsal she began to giggle and ended in throwing up the ridiculous part. They gave it to that little Frankie Langdon, and the playwright's prophecy came true. The breast-beating scene was a knockout. It ran for two years in New York alone. Langdon's sables, chinchillas, ermines, and jewels were always sticking out from the pages of *Vanity Fair* and *Vogue*. When she took curtain calls, Langdon stood with her legs far apart, boyishly, and tossed her head and looked up from beneath her lowered lids and acted surprised and sort of gasped like a fish and bit her lip and mumbled to herself as if overcome. The audience said wasn't she a shy, young, bewildered darling!

A hard little rip if ever there was one—Langdon—and as shy as a man-eating crocodile.

This sort of sham made Harrietta sick. She, whose very art was that of pretending, hated pretense, affectation, "coy stuff." This was, perhaps, unfortunate. Your Fatigued Financier prefers the comedy form in which a spade is not only called a spade but a slab of iron for digging up dirt. Harrietta never even pretended to have a cough on an opening night so that the critics, should the play prove a failure, might say: "Harrietta Fuller, though handicapped by a severe cold, still gave her usual brilliant and finished performance in a part not quite worthy of her talents." No. The plaintive smothered cough, the quick turn aside, the heaving shoulder, the wispy handkerchief were clumsy tools beneath her notice.

There often were long periods of idleness when her soul sickened and her purse grew lean. Long hot summers in New York when awnings, window boxes geranium filled, drinks iced and acidulous, and Ken's motor car for cooling drives to the beaches failed to soothe the terror in her. Thirty ... thirty-two ... thirty-four ... thirty-six....

She refused to say it. She refused to think of it. She put the number out of her mind and slammed the door on it—on that hideous number beginning with f. At such times she was given to contemplation of her own photographs—and was reassured. Her intelligence told her that retouching varnish, pumice stone, hard pencil, and etching knife had all gone into the photographer's version of this clear-eyed, fresh-lipped blooming creature gazing back at her so limpidly. But, then, who didn't need a lot of retouching? Even the youngest of them.

All this. Yet she loved it. The very routine of it appealed to her orderly nature: a routine that, were it widely known, would shatter all those ideas about the large, loose life of the actress. Harrietta Fuller liked to know that at such and such an hour she would be in her dressing room; at such and such an hour on the stage; precisely at another hour she would again be in her dressing room preparing to go home. Then the stage would be darkened. They would be putting the scenery away. She would be crossing the bare stage on her way home. Then she would be home, undressing, getting ready for bed, reading. She liked a cup of clear broth at night, or a drink of hot cocoa. It soothed and rested her. Besides, one is hungry after two and a half hours of high-tensioned, nerve-exhausting work. She was in bed usually by twelve-thirty.

"But you can't fall asleep like a dewy babe in my kind of job," she used to explain. "People wonder why actresses lie in bed until noon, or nearly. They have to, to get as much sleep as a stenographer or a clerk or a book-keeper. At midnight I'm all keyed up and over-stimulated, and as wide awake as an all-night taxi driver. It takes two solid hours of reading to send me bye-bye."

The world did not interest itself in that phase of Harrietta's life. Neither did it find fascination in her domestic side. Harrietta did a good deal of tidying and dusting and redding up in her own two-room apartment, so high and bright and spotless. She liked to cook, too, and was expert at it. Not for her those fake pictures of actresses and opera stars in chiffon tea gowns and satin slippers and diamond chains cooking "their favourite dish of spaghetti and creamed mushrooms," and staring out at you bright-eyed and palpably unable to tell the difference between salt and paprika. Harrietta liked the ticking of a clock in a quiet room; oven smells; concocting new egg dishes; washing out lacy things in warm soapsuds. A throw-back, probably, to her grandmother Scoville.

The worst feature of a person like Harrietta is, as you already have discovered with some impatience, that one goes on and on, talking about her. And the listener at last breaks out with: "This is all very interesting, but I feel as if I know her now. What then?"

Then the thing to do is to go serenely on telling, for example, how the young thing in Harrietta Fuller's company invariably came up to her at the first rehearsal and said tremulously: "Miss Fuller, I—you won't mind—I just want to tell you how proud I am to be one of your company. Playing with you. You've been my ideal ever since I was a little g—" then, warned by a certain icy mask slipping slowly over the brightness of Harrietta's features—"ever so long, but I never even hoped——"

These young things always learned an amazing lot from watching the deft, sure strokes of Harrietta's craftsmanship. She was kind to them, too. Encouraged them. Never hogged a scene that belonged to them. Never cut their lines. Never patronized them. They usually played ingénue parts, and their big line was that uttered on coming into a room looking for Harrietta. It was: "Ah, *there* you are!"

How can you really know Harrietta unless you realize the deference with which she was treated in her own little sphere? If the world at large did not acclaim her, there was no lack of appreciation on the part of her fellow workers. They knew artistry when they saw it. Though she had never attained stardom, she still had the distinction that usually comes only to a star back stage. Unless she actually was playing in support of a first-magnitude star, her dressing room was marked "A." Other members of the company did not drop into her dressing room except by invitation. That room was neat to the point of primness. A square of white coarse sheeting was spread on the floor, under the chair before her dressing table, to gather up dust and powder. It was regularly shaken or changed. There were always flowers—often a single fine rose in a slender vase. On her dressing table, in a corner, you were likely to find three or four volumes—perhaps The Amenities of Book-Collecting; something or other of Max Beerbohm's; a book of verse (not Amy Lowell's).

These were not props designed to impress the dramatic critic who might drop in for one of those personal little theatrical calls to be used in next Sunday's "Chats in the Wings." They were there because Harrietta liked them and read them between acts. She had a pretty wit of her own. The critics liked to talk with her. Even George Jean Hathem, whose favourite pastime was to mangle the American stage with his pen and hold its bleeding, gaping fragments up for the edification of Budapest, Petrograd, Vienna, London, Berlin, Paris, and Stevens Point, Wis., said that five minutes of Harrietta Fuller's conversation was worth a lifetime of New York stage dialogue. For that matter I think that Mr. Beerbohm himself would not have found a talk with her altogether dull or profitless.

The leading man generally made love to her in an expert, unaggressive way. A good many men had tried to make love to her at one time or another. They didn't get on very well. Harrietta never went to late suppers. Some of them complained: "When you try to make love to her she laughs at you!" She wasn't really laughing at them. She was laughing at what she knew about life. Occasionally men now married, and living dully content in the prim suburban smugness of Pelham or New Rochelle, boasted of past friendship with her, wagging their heads doggishly. "Little Fuller! I used to know her well."

They lied.

Not that she didn't count among her friends many men. She dined with them and they with her. They were writers and critics, lawyers and doctors, engineers and painters. Actors almost never. They sent her books and flowers; valued her opinion, delighted in her conversation, wished she wouldn't sometimes look at them so quizzically. And if they didn't always comprehend her wit, they never failed to appreciate the contour of her face, where the thoughtful brow was contradicted by the lovely little nose, and both were drowned in the twin wells of the wide-apart, misleadingly limpid eyes that lay ensnaringly between.

"Your eyes!" these gentlemen sometimes stammered, "the lashes are reflected in them like ferns edging a pool."

"Yes. The mascara's good for them. You'd think all that black sticky stuff I have put on, would hurt them, but it really makes them grow, I believe. Sometimes I even use a burnt match, and yet it——"

"Damn your burnt matches! I'm talking about your lashes."

"So am I." She would open her eyes wide in surprise, and the lashes could almost be said to wave at him tantalizingly, like fairy fans. (He probably wished he could have thought of that.)

Ken never talked to her about her lashes. Ken thought she was the most beauteous, witty, intelligent woman in the world, but he had never told her so, and she found herself wishing he would. Ken was forty-one and Knew About Etchings. He knew about a lot of other things, too. Difficult, complex things like Harrietta Fuller, for example. He had to do with some intricate machine or other that was vital to printing, and he was perfecting something connected with it or connecting something needed for its perfection that would revolutionize the thing the machine now did (whatever it was). Harrietta refused to call him an inventor. She said it sounded so impecunious. They had known each other for six years. When she didn't feel like talking he didn't say: "What's the matter?" He never told her that women had no business monkeying with stocks or asked her what they called that stuff her dress was made of, or telephoned before noon. Twice a year he asked her to marry him, presenting excellent reasons. His name was Carrigan. You'd like him.

"When I marry," Harrietta would announce, "which will be never, it will be the only son of a rich iron king from Duluth, Minnesota. And I'll go there to live in an eighteen-room mansion and pluck roses for the breakfast room."

"There are few roses in Duluth," said Ken, "to speak of. And no breakfast rooms. You breakfast in the dining room, and in the winter you wear flannel underwear and galoshes."

"California, then. And he can be the son of a fruit king. I'm not narrow."

Harrietta was thirty-seven and a half when there came upon her a great fear. It had been a wretchedly bad season. Two failures. The rent on her two-room apartment in Fifty-sixth Street jumped from one hundred and twenty-five, which she could afford, to two hundred a month, which she couldn't. Mary—Irish Mary—her personal maid, left her in January. Personal maids are one of the superstitions of the theatrical profession, and an actress of standing is supposed to go hungry rather than maidless.

"Why don't you fire Irish Mary?" Ken had asked Harrietta during a period of stringency.

"I can't afford to."

Ken understood, but you may not. Harrietta would have made it clear. "Any actress who earns more than a hundred a week is supposed to have a maid in her dressing room. No one knows why, but it's true. I remember in The Small-Town Girl I wore the same gingham dress throughout three acts, but I was paying Mary twenty a week just the same. If I hadn't some one in the company would have told some one in another company that Harrietta Fuller was broke. It would have seeped through the director to the manager, and next time they offered me a part they'd cut my salary. It's absurd, but there it is. A vicious circle."

Irish Mary's reason for leaving Harrietta was a good one. It would have to be, for she was of that almost extinct species, the devoted retainer. Irish Mary wasn't the kind of maid one usually encounters back stage. No dapper, slim, black-and-white pert miss, with a wisp of apron and a knowledgeous eye. An ample, big-hipped, broad-bosomed woman with an apron like a drop curtain and a needle knack that kept Harrietta mended, be-ribboned, beruffled, and exquisite from her garters to her coat hangers. She had been around the theatre for twenty-five years, and her thick, deft fingers had served a long line of illustrious ladies—Corinne Foster, Gertrude Bennett, Lucille Varney. She knew all the shades of grease paint from Flesh to Sallow Old Age, and if you gained an ounce she warned you.

Her last name was Lesom, but nobody remembered it until she brought forward a daughter of fifteen with the request that she be given a job; anything—walk-on, extra, chorus. Lyddy, she called her. The girl seldom spoke. She was extremely stupid, but a marvellous mimic, and pretty beyond belief; fragile, and yet with something common about her even in her fragility. Her wrists had a certain flat angularity that bespoke a peasant ancestry, but she had a singular freshness and youthful bloom. The line of her side face from the eye socket to the chin was a delicious thing that curved with the grace of a wing. The high cheekbone sloped down so that the outline was heart-shaped. There were little indentations at the corners of her mouth. She had eyes singularly clear, like a child's, and a voice so nasal, so strident, so dreadful that when she parted her pretty lips and spoke, the sound shocked you like a peacock's raucous screech.

Harrietta had managed to get a bit for her here, a bit for her there, until by the time she was eighteen she was giving a fairly creditable performance in practically speechless parts. It was dangerous to trust her even with an "Ah, there you are!" line. The audience, startled, was so likely to laugh.

At about this point she vanished, bound for Hollywood and the movies. "She's the little fool, just," said Irish Mary. "What'll she be wantin' with the movies, then, an' her mother connected with the theayter for years an' all, and her you might say brought up in it?"

But she hadn't been out there a year before the world knew her as Lydia Lissome. Starting as an extra girl earning twenty-five a week or less, she had managed, somehow, to get the part of Betty in the screen version of The Magician, probably because she struck the director as being the type; or perhaps her gift of mimicry had something to do with it, and the youth glow that was in her face. At any rate, when the picture was finished and released, no one was more surprised than Lyddy at the result. They offered her three thousand a week on a three-year contract. She wired her mother, but Irish Mary wired back: "I don't believe a word of it hold out for five am coming." She left for the Coast. Incidentally, she got the five for Lyddy. Lyddy signed her name to the contract—Lydia Lissome—in a hand that would have done discredit to an eleven-year-old.

Harrietta told Ken about it, not without some bitterness: "Which only proves one can't be too careful about picking one's parents. If my father had been a hod carrier instead of a minister of the Gospel and a darling old dreamer, I'd be earning five thousand a week, too."

They were dining together in Harrietta's little sitting room so high up and quiet and bright with its cream enamel and its log fire. Almost one entire wall of that room was window, facing south, and framing such an Arabian Nights panorama as only a New York eleventh-story window, facing south, can offer.

Ken lifted his right eyebrow, which was a way he had when being quizzical. "What would you do with five thousand a week, just supposing?"

"I'd do all the vulgar things that other people do who have five thousand a week."

"You wouldn't enjoy them. You don't care for small dogs or paradise aigrettes or Italian villas in Connecticut or diamond-studded cigarette holders or plush limousines or butlers." He glanced comprehensively about the little room—at the baby grand whose top was pleasantly littered with photographs and bonbon dishes and flower vases; at the smart little fire snapping in the grate; at the cheerful reds and blues and ochres and sombre blues and purples and greens of the books in the open bookshelves; at the squat clock on the mantelshelf; at the gorgeous splashes of black and gold glimpsed through the many-paned window. "You've got everything you really want right here"— his gesture seemed, somehow, to include himself—"if you only knew it."

"You talk," snapped Harrietta, "as the Rev. H. John Scoville used to." She had never said a thing like that before. "I'm sick of what they call being true to my art. I'm tired of having last year's suit relined, even if it is smart enough to be good this year. I'm sick of having the critics call me an intelligent comedienne who is unfortunate in her choice of plays. Some day"—a little flash of fright was there—"I'll pick up the Times and see myself referred to as 'that sterling actress.' Then I'll know I'm through."

"You!"

"Tell me I'm young, Ken. Tell me I'm young and beautiful and bewitching."

"You're young and beautiful and bewitching."

"Ugh! And yet they say the Irish have the golden tongues."

Two months later Harrietta had an offer to go into pictures. It wasn't her first, but it undeniably was the best. The sum offered per week was what she might usually expect to get per month in a successful stage play. To accept the offer meant the Coast. She found herself having a test picture taken and trying to believe the director who said it was good; found herself expatiating on the brightness, quietness, and general desirability of the eleventh-floor apartment in Fifty-sixth Street to an acquaintance who was seeking a six months' city haven for the summer.

"She'll probably ruin my enamel dressing table with toilet water and ring my piano top with wet glasses and spatter grease on the kitchenette wall. But I'll be earning a million," Harrietta announced, recklessly, "or thereabouts. Why should I care?"

She did care, though, as a naturally neat and thrifty woman cares for her household goods which have, through years of care of them and association with them, become her household gods. The clock on the mantel wasn't a clock, but a plump friend with a white smiling face and a soothing tongue; the low, ample davenport wasn't a davenport only, but a soft bosom that pillowed her; that which lay spread shimmering beneath her window was not New York alone—it was her View. To a woman like this, letting her apartment furnished is like farming out her child to strangers.

She had told her lessee about her laundress and her cleaning woman and how to handle the balky faucet that controlled the shower. She had said good-bye to Ken entirely surrounded by his books, magazines, fruit, and flowers. She was occupying a Pullman drawing room paid for by the free-handed filmers. She was crossing farm lands, plains, desert. She was wondering if all those pink sweaters and white flannel trousers outside the Hollywood Hotel were there for the same reason that she was. She was surveying a rather warm little room shaded by a dense tree whose name she did not know. She was thinking it felt a lot like her old trouping days, when her telephone tinkled and a voice announced Mrs. Lissome. Lissome? Lesam. Irish Mary, of course. Harrietta's maid, engaged for the trip, had failed her at the last moment. Now her glance rested on the two massive trunks and the litter of smart, glittering bags that strewed the room. A relieved look crept into her eyes. A knock at the door. A resplendent figure was revealed at its opening. The look in Harrietta's eyes vanished.

Irish Mary looked like the mother of a girl who was earning five thousand a week. She was marcelled, silk-clad, rustling, gold-meshed, and, oh, how real in spite of it all as she beamed upon the dazzled Harrietta.

"Out with ye!" trumpeted this figure, brushing aside Harrietta's proffered chair. "There'll be no stayin' here for you. You're coming along with me, then, bag *and* baggage." She glanced sharply about. "Where's your maid, dearie?"

"Disappointed me at the last minute. I'll have to get someone———"

"We've plenty. You're coming up to our place."

"But, Mary, I can't. I couldn't. I'm tired. This room———"

"A hole. Wait till you see The Place. Gardens and breakfast rooms and statues and fountains and them Jap boys runnin' up and down like mice. We rented it for a year from that Goya Ciro. She's gone back East. How she ever made good in pictures I don't know, and her face like a hot-water bag for expression. Lyddy's going to build next year. They're drawin' up the plans now. The Place'll be nothin' compared to it when it's finished. Put on your hat. The boys'll see to your stuff here."

"I can't. I couldn't. You're awfully kind, Mary dear———"

Mary dear was at the telephone. "Mrs. Lissome. That's who. Send up that Jap boy for the bags."

Mrs. Lissome's name and Mrs. Lissome's commands apparently carried heavily in Hollywood. A uniformed Jap appeared immediately as though summoned by a genie. The bags seemed to spring to him, so quickly was he enveloped by their glittering surfaces. He was off with the burdens, invisible except for his gnomelike face and his sturdy bow legs in their footman's boots.

"I can't," said Harrietta, feebly, for the last time. It was her introduction to the topsy-turvy world into which she had come. She felt herself propelled down the stairs by Irish Mary, who wasn't Irish Mary any more, but a Force whose orders were obeyed. In the curved drive outside the Hollywood Hotel the little Jap was stowing the last of the bags into the great blue car whose length from nose to tail seemed to span the hotel frontage. At the wheel, rigid, sat a replica of the footman.

Irish Mary with a Japanese chauffeur. Irish Mary with a Japanese footman. Irish Mary with a great glittering car that was as commodious as the average theatre dressing room.

"Get in, dearie. Lyddy's using the big car to-day. They're out on location. Shootin' the last of Devils and Men."

Harrietta was saying to herself: "Don't be a nasty snob, Harry. This is a different world. Think of the rotten time Alice would have had in Wonderland if she hadn't been broad-minded. Take it as it comes."

Irish Mary was talking as they sped along through the hot white Hollywood sunshine.... "Stay right with us as long as you like, dearie, but if after you're workin' you want a place of your own, I know of just the thing you can rent furnished, and a Jap gardener and house man and cook right on the places besides———"

"But I'm not signed for five thousand a week, like Lydia," put in Harrietta.

"I know what you're signed for. 'Twas me put 'em up to it, an' who else! 'Easy money,' I says, 'an' why shouldn't she be gettin' some of it?' Lyddy spoke to Gans about it. What Lyddy says goes. She's a good girl, Lyddy is, an' would you believe the money an' all hasn't gone to her brains, though what with workin' like a horse an' me to steady her, an' shrewder than the lawyers themself, if I do say it, she ain't had much chance. And here's The Place."

And here was The Place. Sundials, rose gardens, gravel paths, dwarf trees, giant trees, fountains, swimming pools, tennis courts, goldfish, statues, verandas, sleeping porches, awnings, bird baths, pergolas.

Inside more Japs. Maids. Rooms furnished like the interior of movie sets that Harrietta remembered having seen. A bedroom, sitting room, dressing room, and bath all her own in one wing of the great white palace, only one of thousands of great white palaces scattered through the hills of Hollywood. The closet for dresses, silk-lined and scented, could have swallowed whole her New York bedroom.

"Lay down," said Irish Mary, "an' get easy. Lyddy won't be home till six if she's early, an' she'll prob'ly be in bed by nine now they're rushin' the end of the picture, an' she's got to be on the lot made up by nine or sooner."

"Nine—in the morning!"

"Well, sure! You soon get used to it. They've got to get all the daylight they can, an' times the fog's low earlier, or they'd likely start at seven or eight. You look a little beat, dearie. Lay down. I'll have you unpacked while we're eatin'."

But Harrietta did not lie down. She went to the window. Below a small army of pigmy gardeners were doing expert things to flower beds and bushes that already seemed almost shamelessly prolific. Harrietta thought, suddenly, of her green-painted flower boxes outside the eleventh-story south window in the New York flat. Outside her window here a great scarlet hibiscus stuck its tongue out at her. Harrietta stuck her tongue out at it, childishly, and turned away. She liked a certain reticence in flowers, as in everything else. She sat down at the desk, took up a sheet of lavender and gold paper and the great lavender plumed pen. The note she wrote to Ken was the kind of note that only Ken would understand, unless you've got into the way of reading it once a year or so, too:

Ken, dear, I almost wish I hadn't gone down that rabbit hole, and yet—and yet—it's rather curious, you know, this sort of life.

Two weeks later, when she had begun to get used to her new work, her new life, the strange hours, people, jargon, she wrote him another cryptic note:

Alice—"Well, in our country you'd generally get to somewhere else—if you ran very fast for a long time, as I've been doing."

Red Queen—"Here it takes all the running you can do to keep in the same place."

In those two weeks things had happened rather breathlessly. Harrietta had moved from the splendours of The Place to her own rose-embowered bungalow. Here, had she wanted to do any casement work with a white rose, like that earlier heroine, she could easily have managed it had not the early morning been so feverishly occupied in reaching the lot in time to be made up by nine. She soon learned the jargon. "The lot" meant the studio in which she was working, and its environs. "We're going to shoot you this morning," meant that she would be needed in to-day's scenes. Often she was in bed by eight at night, so tired that she could not sleep. She wondered what the picture was about. She couldn't make head or tail of it.

They were filming J. N. Gardner's novel, Romance of Arcady, but they had renamed it Let's Get a Husband. The heroine in the novel was the young wife of twenty-seven who had been married five years. This was Harrietta's part. In the book there had been a young girl, too—a saccharine miss of seventeen who was the minor love interest. This was Lydia Lissome's part. Slowly it dawned on Harrietta that things had been nightmarishly tampered with in the film version, and that the change in name was the least of the indignities to which the novel had been subjected.

It took Harrietta some time to realize this because they were not taking the book scenes in their sequence. They took them according to light, convenience, location. Indoor scenes were taken in one group, so that the end of the story might often be the first to be filmed.

For a week Harrietta was dressed, made up, and ready for work at nine o'clock, and for a week she wasn't used in a single scene. The hours of waiting made her frantic. The sun was white hot. Her little dressing room was stifling. She hated her face with its dead-white mask and blue-lidded eyes. When, finally, her time came she found that after being dressed and ready from nine until five-thirty daily she was required, at 4:56 on the sixth day, to cross the set, open a door, stop, turn, appear to be listening, and recross the set to meet someone entering from the opposite side. This scene, trivial as it appeared, was rehearsed seven times before the director was satisfied with it.

The person for whom she had paused, turned, and crossed was Lydia Lissome. And Lydia Lissome, it soon became evident, had the lead in this film. In the process of changing from novel to scenario, the Young Wife had become a rather middle-aged wife, and the Flapper of seventeen had become the heroine. And Harrietta Fuller, erstwhile actress of youthful comedy parts for the stage, found herself moving about in black velvet and pearls and a large plumed fan as a background for the white ruffles and golden curls and sunny scenes in which Lydia Lissome held the camera's eye.

For years Harrietta Fuller's entrance during a rehearsal always had created a little stir among the company. This one rose to give her a seat; that one made her a compliment; Sam Klein, the veteran director, patted her cheek and said: "You're going to like this part, Miss Fuller. And they're going to eat it up. *You* see." The author bent over her in mingled nervousness and deference and admiration. The Young Thing who was to play the ingénue part said shyly: "Oh, Miss Fuller, may I tell you how happy I am to be playing with you? You've been my ideal, etc."

And now Harrietta Fuller, in black velvet, was the least important person on the lot. No one was rude to her. Everyone was most kind, in fact. Kind! To Harrietta Fuller! She found that her face felt stiff and expressionless after long hours of waiting, waiting, and an elderly woman who was playing a minor part showed her how to overcome this by stretching her face, feature for feature, as a dancer goes through limbering exercises in the wings. The woman had been a trouper in the old days of one-night stands. Just before she stepped in front of the camera you saw her drawing down her face grotesquely, stretching her mouth to form an oval, dropping her jaw, twisting her lips to the right, to the left, rolling her eyes round and round. It was a perfect lesson in facial calisthenics, and Harrietta was thankful for it. Harrietta was interested in such things—interested in them, and grateful for what they taught her.

She told herself that she didn't mind the stir that Lydia Lissome made when she was driven up in the morning in her great blue limousine with the two Japs sitting so straight and immobile in front, like twin Nipponese gods. But she did. She told herself she didn't mind when the director said: "Miss Fuller, if you'll just watch Miss Lissome work. She has perfect picture tempo." But she did. The director was the new-fashioned kind, who spoke softly, rehearsed you almost privately, never bawled through a megaphone. A slim young man in a white shirt and flannel trousers and a pair of Harvard-looking glasses. Everybody was young. That was it! Not thirty, or thirty-two, or thirty-four, or thirty-seven, but young. Terribly, horribly, actually young. That was it.

Harrietta Fuller was too honest not to face this fact squarely. When she went to a Thursday-night dance at the Hollywood Hotel she found herself in a ballroom full of slim, pliant, corsetless young things of eighteen, nineteen, twenty. The men, with marcelled hair and slim feet and sunburnt faces, were mere boys. As juveniles on the stage they might have been earning seventy-five or one hundred or one hundred and fifty dollars a week. Here they owned estates, motor cars in fleets, power boats; had secretaries, valets, trainers. Their technique was perfect and simple. They knew their work. When they kissed a girl, or entered a room, or gazed after a woman, or killed a man in the presence of a woman (while working) they took off their hats. Turned slowly, and took off their hats. They were mannerly, too, outside working hours. They treated Harrietta with boyish politeness—when they noticed her at all.

"Oh, won't you have this chair, Miss Fuller? I didn't notice you were standing."

They didn't notice she was standing!

"What are you doing, Miss—ah—Fuller? Yes, you did say Fuller. Names—— Are you doing a dowager bit?"

"Dowager bit?"

"I see. You're new to the game, aren't you? I saw you working to-day. We always speak of these black-velvet parts as dowager bits. Just excuse me. I see a friend of mine——" The friend of mine would be a willow wand with golden curls, and what Harrietta rather waspishly called a Gunga Din costume. She referred to that Kipling description in which:

The uniform 'e wore
Was nothin' much before,
An' rather less than 'arf o' that be'ind.

"They're wearing them that way here in Hollywood," she wrote Ken. She wrote Ken a good many things. But there were, too, a good many things she did not write him.

At the end of the week she would look at her check—and take small comfort. "You've got everything you really want right here," Ken had said, "if you only knew it."

If only she had known it.

Well, she knew it now. Now, frightened, bewildered, resentful. Thirty-seven. Why, thirty-seven was old in Hollywood. Not middle-aged, or getting on, or well preserved, but old. Even Lydia Lissome, at twenty, always made them put one thickness of chiffon over the camera's lens before she would let them take the close-ups. Harrietta thought of that camera now as a cruel Cyclops from whose hungry eye nothing escaped—wrinkles, crow's-feet—nothing.

They had been working two months on the picture. It was almost finished. Midsummer. Harrietta's little bungalow garden was ablaze with roses, dahlias, poppies, asters, strange voluptuous flowers whose names she did not know. The roses, plucked and placed in water, fell apart, petal by petal, two hours afterward. From her veranda she saw the Sierra Madre range and the foothills. She thought of her "unexcelled view of Park" which could be had by flattening one ear and the side of your face against the window jamb.

The sun came up, hard and bright and white, day after day. Hard and white and hot and dry. "Like a woman," Harrietta thought, "who wears a red satin gown all the time. You'd wish she'd put on gingham just once, for a change." She told herself that she was parched for a walk up Riverside Drive in a misty summer rain, the water sloshing in her shoes.

"Happy, my ducky?" Irish Mary would say, beaming upon her.

"Perfectly," from Harrietta.

"It's time, too. Real money you're pullin' down here. And a paradise if ever there was one."

"I notice, though, that as soon as they've completed a picture they take the Overland back to New York and make dates with each other for lunch at the Claridge, like matinée girls."

Irish Mary flapped a negligent palm. "Ah, well, change is what we all want, now and then." She looked at Harrietta sharply. "You're not wantin' to go back, are ye?"

"N-no," faltered Harrietta. Then, brazenly, hotly: "Yes, yes!" ending, miserably, with: "But my contract. Six months."

"You can break it, if you're fool enough, when they've finished this picture, though why you should want to——" Irish Mary looked as belligerent as her kindly Celtic face could manage.

But it was not until the last week of the filming of Let's get a Husband that Harrietta came to her and said passionately: "I do! I do!"

"Do what?" Irish Mary asked, blankly.

"Do want to break my contract. You said I could after this picture."

"Sure you can. They hired you because I put Lyddy up to askin' them to. I'd thought you'd be pleased for the big money an' all. There's no pleasin' some."

"It isn't that. You don't understand. To-day——"

"Well, what's happened to-day that's so turrible, then?"

But how could Harrietta tell her? "To-day——" she began again, faltered, stopped. To-day, you must know, this had happened: It was the Big Scene of the film. Lydia Lissome, in black lace nightgown and ermine negligee, her hair in marcel waves, had just been "shot" for it.

"Now then, Miss Fuller," said young Garvey, the director, "you come into the garden, see? You've noticed Joyce go out through the French window and you suspect she's gone to meet Talbot. We show just a flash of you looking out of the drawing-room windows into the garden. Then you just glance over your shoulder to where your husband is sitting in the library, reading, and you slip away, see? Then we jump to where you find them in the garden. Wait a minute"—He consulted the sheaf of typewritten sheets in his hand—"yeh—here it says: 'Joyce is keeping her tryst under the great oak in the garden with her lover.' Yeh. Wait a minute ... 'tryst under tree with'—well, you come quickly forward—down to about here—and you say: 'Ah, *there* you are!'"

Harrietta looked at him for a long, long minute. Her lips were parted. Her breath came quickly. She spoke: "I say—*what?*"

"You say: 'Ah, *there* you are.'"

"Never!" said Harrietta Fuller, and brought her closed fist down on her open palm for emphasis. "Never!"

It was August when she again was crossing desert, plains, and farmlands. It was the tail-end of a dusty, hot, humid August in New York when Ken stood at the station, waiting. As he came forward, raising one arm, her own arm shot forward in quick protest, even while her glad eyes held his.

"Don't take it off!"

"What off?"

"Your hat. Don't take it off. Kiss me—but leave your hat on."

She clutched his arm. She looked up at him. They were in the taxi bound for Fifty-sixth Street. "She moved? She's out? She's gone? You told her I'd pay her anything—a bonus——" Then, as he nodded, she leaned back, relaxed. Something in her face prompted him.

"You're young and beautiful and bewitching," said Ken.

"Keep on saying it," pleaded Harrietta. "Make a chant of it." ...

Sam Klein, the veteran, was the first to greet her when she entered the theatre at that first September rehearsal. The company was waiting for her. She wasn't late. She had just pleasantly escaped being unpunctual. She came in, cool, slim, electric. Then she hesitated. For the fraction of a second she hesitated. Then Sam Klein greeted her: "Company's waiting, Miss Fuller, if you're ready." And the leading man came forward, a flower in his buttonhole, carefully tailored and slightly yellow as a leading man of forty should be at 10:30 A. M. "How wonderful you're looking, Harrietta," he said.

Sam Klein took her aside. "You're going to make the hit of your career in this part, Miss Fuller. Yessir, dear, the hit of your career. You mark my words."

"Don't you think," stammered Harrietta—"don't you think it will take someone—someone—younger—to play the part?"

"Younger than what?"

"Than I."

Sam Klein stared. Then he laughed. "Younger than you! Say, listen, do you want to get the Gerry Society after me?"

And as he turned away a Young Thing with worshipful eyes crept up to Harrietta's side and said tremulously: "Oh, Miss Fuller, this is my first chance on Broadway, and may I tell you how happy I am to be playing with you? You've been my ideal ever since I was a—for a long, long time."

HOME GIRL

Wilson avenue, Chicago, is not merely an avenue but a district; not only a district but a state of mind; not a state of mind alone but a condition of morals. For that matter, it is none of these things so much as a mode of existence. If you know your Chicago—which you probably don't—(*sotto voce* murmur, Heaven forbid!)—you are aware that, long ago, Wilson Avenue proper crept slyly around the corner and achieved a clandestine alliance with big glittering Sheridan Road; which escapade changed the demure thoroughfare into Wilson Avenue improper.

When one says "A Wilson Avenue girl," the mind—that is, the Chicago mind—pictures immediately a slim, daring, scented, exotic creature dressed in next week's fashions; wise-eyed; doll-faced; rapacious. When chiffon stockings are worn Wilson Avenue's hosiery is but a film over the flesh. Aigrettes and mink coats are its winter uniform. A feverish district this, all plate glass windows and delicatessen dinners and one-room-and-kitchenette apartments, where light housekeepers take their housekeeping too lightly.

At six o'clock you are likely to see Wilson Avenue scurrying about in its mink coat and its French heels and its crêpe frock, assembling its haphazard dinner. Wilson Avenue food, as displayed in the ready-cooked shops, resembles in a startling degree the Wilson Avenue ladies themselves: highly coloured, artificial, chemically treated, tempting to the eye, but unnutritious. In and out of the food emporia these dart, buying dabs of this and bits of that. Chromatic viands. Vivid scarlet, orange, yellow, green. A strip of pimento here. A mound of mayonnaise there. A green pepper stuffed with such burden of deceit as no honest green pepper ever was meant to hold. Two eggs. A quarter-pound of your best creamery butter. An infinitesimal bottle of cream. "*And* what else?" says the plump woman in the white bib-apron, behind the counter. "*And* what else?" Nothing. I guess that'll be all. Mink coats prefer to dine out.

As a cripple displays his wounds and sores, proudly, so Wilson Avenue throws open its one-room front door with a grandiloquent gesture as it boasts, "Two hundred and fifty a month!" Shylock, purchasing a paper-thin slice of pinky ham in Wilson Avenue, would know his own early Venetian transaction to have been pure philanthropy.

It took Raymond and Cora Atwater twelve years to reach this Wilson Avenue, though they carried it with them all the way. They had begun their married life in this locality before it had become a definite district. Twelve years ago the neighbourhood had shown no signs of mushrooming into its present opulence. Twelve years ago Raymond, twenty-eight, and Cora, twenty-four, had taken a six-room flat at Racine and Sunnyside. Six rooms. Modern. Light. Rental, $28.50 per month.

"But I guess I can manage it, all right," Raymond had said. "That isn't so terrible—for six rooms."

Cora's full under lip had drawn itself into a surprisingly thin straight line. Later, Raymond came to recognize the meaning of that labial warning. "We don't need all those rooms. It's just that much more work."

"I don't want you doing your own work. Not unless you want to. At first, maybe, it'd be sort of fun for you. But after a while you'll want a girl to help. That'll take the maid's room off the kitchen."

"Well, supposing? That leaves an extra room, anyway."

A look came into Raymond's face. "Maybe we'll need that, too—later. Later on." He actually could have been said to blush, then, like a boy. There was much of the boy in Raymond at twenty-eight.

Cora did not blush.

Raymond had married Cora because he loved her; and because she was what is known as a "home girl." From the first, business girls—those alert, pert, confident little sparrows of office and shop and the street at lunch hour—rather terrified him. They gave you as good as you sent. They were always ready with their own nickel for carfare. You never knew whether they were laughing at you or not. There was a little girl named Calhoun in the binoculars (Raymond's first Chicago job was with the Erwin H. Nagel Optical Company on Wabash). The Calhoun girl was smart. She wore those plain white waists. Tailored, Raymond thought they called them. They made her skin look fresh and clear and sort of downy-blooming like the peaches that grew in his own Michigan state back home. Or perhaps only girls with clear fresh skins could wear those plain white waist things. Raymond had heard that girls thought and schemed about things that were becoming to them, and then stuck to those things. He wondered how the Calhoun girl might look in a fluffy waist. But she never wore one down to work. When business was dull in the motor and sun-glasses (which was where he held forth) Raymond would stroll over to Laura Calhoun's counter and talk. He would talk about the Invention. He had no one else to talk to about it. No one he could trust, or who understood.

The Calhoun girl, polishing the great black eyes of a pair of field glasses, would look up brightly to say, "Well, how's the Invention coming on?" Then he would tell her.

The Invention had to do with spectacles. Not only that, if you are a wearer of spectacles of any kind, it has to do with you. For now, twelve years later, you could not well do without it. The little contraption that keeps the side-piece from biting into your ears—that's Raymond's.

Knowing, as we do, that Raymond's wife is named Cora we know that the Calhoun girl of the fresh clear skin, the tailored white shirtwaists, and the friendly interest in the Invention, lost out. The reason for that was Raymond's youth, and Raymond's vanity, and Raymond's unsophistication, together with Lucy Calhoun's own honesty and efficiency. These last qualities would handicap any girl in love, no matter how clear her skin or white her shirtwaist.

Of course, when Raymond talked to her about the Invention she should have looked adoringly into his eyes and said, "How perfectly*wonderful*! I don't see how you think of such things."

What she said, after studying its detail thoughtfully for a moment, was: "Yeh, but look. If this little tiny wire had a spring underneath—just a little bit of spring—it'd take all the pressure off when you wear a hat. Now women's hats are worn so much lower over their ears, d'you see? That'd keep it from pressing. Men's hats, too, for that matter."

She was right. Grudgingly, slowly, he admitted it. Not only that, he carried out her idea and perfected the spectacle contrivance as you know it to-day. Without her suggestion it would have had a serious flaw. He knew he ought to be grateful. He told himself that he was grateful. But in reality he was resentful. She was a smart girl, but—well—a fella didn't feel comfortable going with a girl that knew more than he did. He took her to the theatre—it was before the motion picture had attained its present-day virulence. She enjoyed it. So did he. Perhaps they might have repeated the little festivity and the white shirtwaist might have triumphed in the end. But that same week Raymond met Cora.

Though he had come to Chicago from Michigan almost a year before, he knew few people. The Erwin H. Nagel Company kept him busy by day. The Invention occupied him at night. He read, too, books on optometry. Don't think that he was a Rollo. He wasn't. But he was naturally somewhat shy, and further handicapped by an unusually tall lean frame which he handled awkwardly. If you had a good look at his eyes you forgot his shyness, his leanness, his awkwardness, his height. They were the keynote of his gentle, studious, kindly, humorous nature. But Chicago, Illinois, is too busy looking to see anything. Eyes are something you see with, not into.

Two of the boys at Nagel's had an engagement for the evening with two girls who were friends. On the afternoon of that day one of the boys went home at four with a well-developed case of grippe. The other approached Raymond with his plea.

"Say, Atwater, help me out, will you? I can't reach my girl because she's downtown somewheres for the afternoon with Cora. That's her girl friend. And me and Harvey was to meet 'em for dinner, see? And a show. I'm in a hole. Help me out, will you? Go along and fuss Cora. She's a nice girl. Pretty, too, Cora is. Will you, Ray? Huh?"

Ray went. By nine-thirty that evening he had told Cora about the Invention. And Cora had turned sidewise in her seat next to him at the theatre and had looked up at him adoringly, awe-struck. "Why, how perfectly *wonderful*! I don't see how you think of such things."

"Oh, that's nothing. I got a lot of ideas. Things I'm going to work out. Say, I won't always be plugging down at Nagel's, believe me. I got a lot of ideas."

"Really! Why, you're an inventor, aren't you! Like Edison and those. My, it must be wonderful to think of things out of your head. Things that nobody's ever thought of before."

Ray glowed. He felt comfortable, and soothed, and relaxed and stimulated. And too large for his clothes. "Oh, I don't know. I just think of things. That's all there is to it. That's nothing."

"Oh, isn't it! No, I guess not. I've never been out with a real inventor before ... I bet you think I'm a silly little thing."

He protested, stoutly. "I should say not." A thought struck him. "Do you do anything? Work downtown somewheres, or anything?"

She shook her head. Her lips pouted. Her eyebrows made pained twin crescents. "No. I don't do anything. I was afraid you'd ask that." She looked down at her hands—her white, soft hands with little dimples at the finger-bases. "I'm just a home girl. That's all. A home girl. Now you *will* think I'm a silly stupid thing." She flashed a glance at him, liquid-eyed, appealing.

He was surprised (she wasn't) to find his hand closed tight and hard over her soft dimpled one. He was terror-stricken (she wasn't) to hear his voice saying, "I think you're wonderful. I think you're the most wonderful girl I ever saw, that's what." He crushed her hand and she winced a little. "Home girl."

Cora's name suited her to a marvel. Her hair was black and her colouring a natural pink and white, which she abetted expertly. Cora did not wear plain white tailored waists. She wore thin, fluffy, transparent things that drew your eyes and fired your imagination. Raymond began to call her Coral in his thoughts. Then, one evening, it slipped out. Coral. She liked it. He denied himself all luxuries and most necessities and bought her a strand of beads of that name, presenting them to her stammeringly, clumsily, tenderly. Tender pink and cream, they were, like her cheeks, he thought.

"Oh, Ray, for me! How darling! You naughty boy!... But I'd rather have had those clear white ones, without any colouring. They're more stylish. Do you mind?"

When he told Laura Calhoun she said, "I hope you'll be very happy. She's a lucky girl. Tell me about her, will you?"

Would he! His home girl!

When he had finished she said, quietly, "Oh, yes."

And so Raymond and Cora were married and went to live in six-room elegance at Sunnyside and Racine. The flat was furnished sumptuously in Mission and those red and brown soft leather cushions with Indian heads stamped on them. There was a wooden rack on the wall with six monks' heads in coloured plaster, very life-like, stuck on it. This was a pipe-rack, though Raymond did not smoke a pipe. He liked a mild cigar. Then there was a print of Gustave Richter's "Queen Louise" coming down that broad marble stair, one hand at her breast, her great girlish eyes looking out at you from the misty folds of her scarf. What a lot of the world she has seen from her stairway! The shelf that ran around the dining room wall on a level with your head was filled with steins in such shapes and colours as would have curdled their contents—if they had ever had any contents.

They planned to read a good deal, evenings. Improve their minds. It was Ray's idea, but Cora seconded it heartily. This was before their marriage.

"Now, take history alone," Ray argued: "American history. Why, you can read a year and hardly know the half of it. That's the trouble. People don't know the history of their own country. And it's interesting, too, let me tell you. Darned interesting. Better'n novels, if folks only knew it."

"My, yes," Cora agreed. "And French. We could take up French, evenings. I've always wanted to study French. They say if you know French you can travel anywhere. It's all in the accent; and goodness knows I'm quick at picking up things like that."

"Yeh," Ray had said, a little hollowly, "yeh, French. Sure."

But, somehow, these literary evenings never did materialize. It may have been a matter of getting the books. You could borrow them from the public library, but that made you feel so hurried. History was something you wanted to take your time over. Then, too, the books you wanted never were in. You could buy them. But buying books like that! Cora showed her first real display of temper. Why, they came in sets and cost as much as twelve or fifteen dollars. Just for books! The literary evenings degenerated into Ray's thorough scanning of the evening paper, followed by Cora's skimming of the crumpled sheets that carried the department store ads, the society column, and the theatrical news. Raymond began to use the sixth room—the unused bedroom—as a workshop. He had perfected the spectacle contrivance and had made the mistake of selling his rights to it. He got a good sum for it.

"But I'll never do that again," he said, grimly. "Somebody'll make a fortune on that thing." He had unwisely told Cora of this transaction. She never forgave him for it. On the day he received the money for it he had brought her home a fur set of baum marten. He thought the stripe in it beautiful. There was a neckpiece known as a stole, and a large muff.

"Oh, honey!" Cora had cried. "Aren't you *fun*-ny!" She often said that, always with the same accent. "Aren't you *fun*-ny!"

"What's the matter?"

"Why didn't you let me pick it out? They're wearing Persian lamb sets."

"Oh. Well, maybe the feller'll change it. It's all paid for, but maybe he'll change it."

"Do you mind? It may cost a little bit more. You don't mind my changing it though, do you?"

"No. No-o-o-o! Not a bit."

They had never furnished the unused bedroom as a bedroom. When they moved out of the flat at Racine and Sunnyside into one of those new four-room apartments on Glengyle the movers found only a long rough work-table and a green-shaded lamp in that sixth room. Ray's delicate tools and implements were hard put to it to find a resting place in the new four-room apartment. Sometimes Ray worked in the bathroom. He grew rather to like the white-tiled place, with its look of a laboratory. But then, he didn't have as much time to work at home as he formerly had had. They went out more evenings.

The new four-room flat rented at sixty dollars. "Seems the less room you have the more you pay," Ray observed.

"There's no comparison. Look at the neighbourhood! And the living room's twice as big."

It didn't seem to be. Perhaps this was due to its furnishings. The Mission pieces had gone to the second-hand dealer. Ray was assistant manager of the optical department at Nagel's now and he was getting royalties on a new smoked glass device. There were large over-stuffed chairs in the new living room, and a seven-foot davenport, and oriental rugs, and lamps and lamps and lamps. The silk lampshade conflagration had just begun to smoulder in the American household. The dining room had one of those built-in Chicago buffets. It sparkled with cut glass. There was a large punch bowl in the centre, in which Cora usually kept receipts, old bills, moth balls, buttons, and the tarnished silver top to a syrup jug that she always meant to have repaired. Queen Louise was banished to the bedroom where she surveyed a world of cretonne.

Cora was a splendid cook. She had almost a genius for flavouring. Roast or cheese soufflé or green apple pie— your sense of taste never experienced that disappointment which comes of too little salt, too much sugar, a lack of shortening. Expert as she was at it, Cora didn't like to cook. That is, she didn't like to cook day after day. She rather liked doing an occasional meal and producing it in a sort of red-cheeked triumph. When she did this it was an epicurean thing, savoury, hot, satisfying. But as a day-after-day programme Cora would not hear of it. She had banished the maid. Four rooms could not accommodate her. A woman came in twice a week to wash and iron and clean. Often Cora did not get up for breakfast and Ray got his at one of the little lunch rooms that were springing up all over that section of the North Side. Eleven o'clock usually found Cora at the manicure's, or the dressmaker's, or shopping, or telephoning luncheon arrangements with one of the Crowd. Ray and Cora were going out a good deal with the Crowd. Young married people like themselves, living royally just a little beyond their income. The women were well-dressed, vivacious, somewhat shrill. They liked stories that were a little off-colour. "Blue," one of the men called these stories. He was in the theatrical business. The men were, for the most part, a rather drab-looking lot. Colourless, good-natured, open-handed. Almost imperceptibly the Crowd began to use Ray as a target for a certain raillery. It wasn't particularly ill-natured, and Ray did not resent it.

"Oh, come on, Ray! Don't be a wet blanket.... Lookit him! I bet he's thinking about those smoked glasses again. Eh, Atwater? He's in a daze about that new rim that won't show on the glasses. Come out of it! First thing you know you'll lose your little Cora."

There was little danger of that. Though Cora flirted mildly with the husbands of the other girls in the Crowd (they all did) she was true to Ray.

Ray was always talking of building a little place of their own. People were beginning to move farther and farther north, into the suburbs.

"Little place of your own," Ray would say, "that's the only way to live. Then you're not paying it all out in rent to the other feller. Little place of your own. That's the right idear."

But as the years went by, and Ray earned more and more money, he and Cora seemed to be getting farther and farther away from the right idear. In the $28.50 apartment Cora's morning marketing had been an orderly daily proceeding. Meat, vegetables, fruit, dry groceries. But now the maidless four-room apartment took on, in spite of its cumbersome furnishings, a certain air of impermanence.

"Ray, honey, I haven't a scrap in the house. I didn't get home until almost six. Those darned old street cars. I hate 'em. Do you mind going over Jo Bauer's to eat? I won't go, because Myrtle served a regular spread at four. I couldn't eat a thing. D'you mind?"

"Why, no." He would get into his coat again and go out into the bleak November wind-swept street to Bauer's restaurant.

Cora was always home when Raymond got there at six. She prided herself on this. She would say, primly, to her friends, "I make a point of being there when Ray gets home. Even if I have to cut a round of bridge. If a woman can't be there when a man gets home from work I'd like to know what she's good for, anyway."

The girls in the Crowd said she was spoiling Raymond. She told Ray this. "They think I'm old-fashioned. Well, maybe I am. But I guess I never pretended to be anything but a home girl."

"That's right," Ray would answer. "Say, that's the way you caught me. With that home-girl stuff."

"Caught you!" The thin straight line of the mouth. "If you think for one minute——"

"Oh, now, dear. You know what I mean, sweetheart. Why, say, I never could see any girl until I met you. You know that."

He was as honestly in love with her as he had been nine years before. Perhaps he did not feel now, as then, that she had conferred a favour upon him in marrying him. Or if he did he must have known that he had made fair return for such favour.

Cora had a Hudson seal coat now, with a great kolinsky collar. Her vivid face bloomed rosily in this soft frame. Cora was getting a little heavier. Not stout, but heavier, somehow. She tried, futilely, to reduce. She would starve herself at home for days, only to gain back the vanished pounds at one afternoon's orgy of whipped-cream salad, and coffee, and sweets at the apartment of some girl in the Crowd. Dancing had come in and the Crowd had taken it up vociferously. Raymond was not very good at it. He had not filled out with the years. He still was lean and tall and awkward. The girls in the crowd tried to avoid dancing with him. That often left Cora partnerless unless she wanted to dance again and again with Raymond.

"How can you expect the boys to ask me to dance when you don't dance with their wives! Good heavens, if they can learn, you can. And for pity's sake *don't count*! You're so *fun*-ny!"

He tried painstakingly to heed her advice, but his long legs made a sorry business of it. He heard one of the girls refer to him as "that giraffe." He had put his foot through an absurd wisp of tulle that she insisted on calling a train.

They were spending a good deal of money now, but Ray jousted the landlord, the victualler, the furrier, the milliner, the hosiery maker, valiantly and still came off the victor. He did not have as much time as he would have liked to work on the new invention. The invisible rim. It was calculated so to blend with the glass of the lens as to be, in appearance, one with it, while it still protected the eyeglass from breakage. "Fortune in it, girlie," he would say, happily, to Cora. "Million dollars, that's all."

He had been working on the invisible rim for five years. Familiarity with it had bred contempt in Cora. Once, in a temper, "Invisible is right," she had said, slangily.

They had occupied the four-room apartment for five years. Cora declared it was getting beyond her. "You can't get any decent help. The washwoman acts as if she was doing me a favour coming from eight to four, for four dollars and eighty-five cents. And yesterday she said she couldn't come to clean any more on Saturdays. I'm sick and tired of it."

Raymond shook a sympathetic head. "Same way down at the store. Seems everything's that way now. You can't get help and you can't get goods. You ought to hear our customers. Yesterday I thought I'd go clear out of my nut, trying to pacify them."

Cora inserted the entering wedge, deftly. "Goodness knows I love my home. But the way things are now ..."

"Yeh," Ray said, absently. When he spoke like that Cora knew that the invisible rim was revolving in his mind. In another moment he would be off to the little cabinet in the bathroom where he kept his tools and instruments.

She widened the opening. "I noticed as I passed to-day that those new one-room kitchenette apartments on Sheridan will be ready for occupancy October first." He was going toward the door. "They say they're wonderful."

"Who wants to live in one room, anyway?"

"It's really two rooms—and the kitchenette. There's the living room—perfectly darling—and a sort of combination breakfast room and kitchen. The breakfast room is partitioned off with sort of cupboards so that it's really another room. And so handy!"

"How'd you know?"

"I went in—just to look at them—with one of the girls."

Until then he had been unconscious of her guile. But now, suddenly, struck by a hideous suspicion—"Say, looka here. If you think——"

"Well, it doesn't hurt to look at 'em, does it!"

A week later. "Those kitchenette apartments on Sheridan are almost all gone. One of the girls was looking at one on the sixth floor. There's a view of the lake. The kitchen's the sweetest thing. All white enamel. And the breakfast room thing is done in Italian."

"What d'you mean—done in Italian?"

"Why—uh—Italian period furniture, you know. Dark and rich. The living room's the same. Desk, and table, and lamps."

"Oh, they're furnished?"

"Complete. Down to the kettle covers and the linen and all. The work there would just be play. All the comforts of a home, with none of the terrible aggravations."

"Say, look here, Coral, we don't want to go to work and live in any one room. You wouldn't be happy. Why, we'd feel cooped up. No room to stretch.... Why, say, how about the beds? If there isn't a bedroom how about the beds? Don't people sleep in those places?"

"There are Murphy beds, silly."

"Murphy? Who's he?"

"Oh, goodness, I don't know! The man who invented 'em, I suppose. Murphy."

Raymond grinned in anticipation of his own forthcoming joke. "I should think they'd call 'em Morphy beds." Then, at her blank stare. "You know—short for Morpheus, god of sleep. Learned about him at high school."

Cora still looked blank. Cora hardly ever understood Ray's jokes, or laughed at them. He would turn, chuckling, to find her face a blank. Not even bewildered, or puzzled, or questioning. Blank. Unheeding. Disinterested as a slate.

Three days later Cora developed an acute pain in her side. She said it was nothing. Just worn out with the work, and the worry and the aggravation, that's all. It'll be all right.

Ray went with her to look at the Sheridan Road apartment. It was one hundred and fifty dollars. "Phew!"

"But look at what you save? Gas. Light. Maid service. Laundry. It's really cheaper in the end."

Cora was amazingly familiar with all the advantages and features of the sixth-floor apartment. "The sun all morning." She had all the agent's patter. "Harvey-Dickson ventilated double-spring mattresses. Dressing room off the bathroom. No, it isn't a closet. Here's the closet. Range, refrigerator, combination sink and laundry tub. Living room's all panelled in ivory. Shower in the bathroom. Buffet kitchen. Breakfast room has folding-leaf Italian table. Look at the chairs. Aren't they darlings! Built-in book shelves——"

"Book shelves?"

"Oh, well, we can use them for fancy china and ornaments. Or—oh, look!—you could keep your stuff there. Tools and all. Then the bathroom wouldn't be mussy all the time."

"Beds?"

"Right here. Isn't that wonderful. Would you ever know it was there? You can work it with one hand. Look."

"Do you really like it, Coral?"

"I love it. It's heavenly."

He stood in the centre of the absurd living room, a tall, lank, awkward figure, a little stooped now. His face was beginning to be furrowed with lines—deep lines that yet were softening, and not unlovely. He made you think, somehow, as he stood there, one hand on his own coat lapel, of Saint-Gaudens' figure of Lincoln, there in the park, facing the Drive. Kindly, thoughtful, harried.

They moved in October first.

The over-stuffed furniture of the four-room apartment was sold. Cora kept a few of her own things—a rug or two, some china, silver, bric-à-brac, lamps. Queen Louise was now permanently dethroned. Cora said her own things—"pieces"—would spoil the effect of the living room. All Italian.

"No wonder the Italians sit outdoors all the time, on the steps and in the street"—more of Ray's dull humour. He surveyed the heavy gloomy pieces, so out of place in the tiny room. One of the chairs was black velvet. It was the only really comfortable chair in the room but Ray never sat in it. It reminded him, vaguely, of a coffin. The corridors of the apartment house were long, narrow, and white-walled. You traversed these like a convict, speaking to no one, and entered your own cubicle. A toy dwelling for toy people. But Ray was a man-size man. When he was working downtown his mind did not take temporary refuge in the thought of the feverish little apartment to which he was to return at night. It wasn't a place to come back to, except for sleep. A roost. Bedding for the night. As permanent-seeming as a hay-mow.

Cora, too, gave him a strange feeling of impermanence. He realized one day, with a shock, that he hardly ever saw her with her hat off. When he came in at six or six-thirty Cora would be busy at the tiny sink, or the toy stove, her hat on, a cigarette dangling limply from her mouth. Ray did not object to women smoking. That is, he had no moral objection. But he didn't think it became them. But Cora said a cigarette rested and stimulated her. "Doctors say all nervous women should smoke," she said. "Soothes them." But Cora, cooking in the little kitchen, squinting into a kettle's depths through a film of cigarette smoke, outraged his sense of fitness. It was incongruous, offensive. The time, and occupation, and environment, together with the limply dangling cigarette, gave her an incredibly rowdy look.

When they ate at home they had steak or chops, and, perhaps, a chocolate éclair for dessert; and a salad. Raymond began to eat mental meals. He would catch himself thinking of breaded veal chops, done slowly, simmeringly, in butter, so that they came out a golden brown on a parsley-decked platter. With this mashed potatoes with brown butter and onions that have just escaped burning; creamed spinach with egg grated over the top; a rice pudding, baked in the oven, and served with a tart crown of grape jell. He sometimes would order these things in a restaurant at noon, or on the frequent evenings when they dined out. But they never tasted as he had thought they would.

They dined out more and more as spring drew on and the warm weather set in. The neighbourhood now was aglitter with eating places of all sorts and degrees, from the humble automat to the proud plush of the Sheridan Plaza dining room. There were tea-rooms, cafeterias, Hungarian cafés, chop suey restaurants. At the table d'hôte places you got a soup, followed by a lukewarm plateful of meat, vegetables, salad. The meat tasted of the vegetables, the vegetables tasted of the meat, and the salad tasted of both. Before ordering Ray would sit down and peer about at the food on the near-by tables as one does in a dining car when the digestive fluids have dried in your mouth at the first whiff through the doorway. It was on one of these evenings that he noticed Cora's hat.

"What do you wear a hat for all the time?" he asked, testily.

"Hat?"

"Seems to me I haven't seen you without a hat in a month. Gone bald, or something?" He was often cross like this lately. Grumpy, Cora called it. Hats were one of Cora's weaknesses. She had a great variety of them. These added to Ray's feeling of restlessness and impermanence. Sometimes she wore a hat that came down over her head, covering her forehead and her eyes, almost. The hair he used to love to touch was concealed. Sometimes he dined with an ingénue in a poke bonnet; sometimes with a señorita in black turban and black lace veil, mysterious and provocative; sometimes with a demure miss in a wistful little turned-down brim. It was like living with a stranger who was always about to leave.

When they ate at home, which was rarely, Ray tried, at first, to dawdle over his coffee and his mild cigar, as he liked to do. But you couldn't dawdle at a small, inadequate table that folded its flaps and shrank into a corner the minute you left it. Everything in the apartment folded, or flapped, or doubled, or shot in, or shot out, or concealed something else, or pretended to be something it was not. It was very irritating. Ray took his cigar and his evening paper and wandered uneasily into the Italian living room, doubling his lean length into one of his queer, angular hard chairs.

Cora would appear in the doorway, hatted. "Ready?"

"Huh? Where you going?"

"Oh, Ray, aren't you *fun*-ny! You know this is the Crowd's poker night at Lil's."

The Crowd began to say that old Ray was going queer. Honestly, didja hear him last week? Talking about the instability of the home, and the home being the foundation of the state, and the country crumbling? Cora's face was a sight! I wouldn't have wanted to be in his boots when she got him home. What's got into him, anyway?

Cora was a Wilson Avenue girl now. You saw her in and out of the shops of the district, expensively dressed. She was almost thirty-six. Her legs, beneath the absurdly short skirt of the day, were slim and shapely in their chiffon hose, but her upper figure was now a little prominent. The scant, brief skirt fore-shortened her; gave her a stork-like appearance; a combination of girlishness and matronliness not pleasing.

There were times when Ray rebelled. A peace-loving man, and gentle. But a man. "I don't want to go out to eat. My God, I'm tired! I want to eat at home."

"Honey, dear, I haven't a thing in the house. Not a scrap."

"I'll go out and get something, then. What d'you want?"

"Get whatever looks good to you. I don't want a thing. We had tea after the matinée. That's what made me so late. I'm always nagging the girls to go home. It's getting so they tease me about it."

He would go foraging amongst the delicatessen shops of the neighbourhood. He saw other men, like himself, scurrying about with moist paper packets and bags and bundles, in and out of Leviton's, in and out of the Sunlight Bakery. A bit of ham. Some cabbage salad in a wooden boat. A tiny broiler, lying on its back, its feet neatly trussed, its skin crackly and tempting-looking, its white meat showing beneath the brown. But when he cut into it at home it tasted like sawdust and gutta-percha. "*And* what else?" said the plump woman in the white bib-apron behind the counter. "*And* what else?"

In the new apartment you rather prided yourself on not knowing your next-door neighbours. The paper-thin walls permitted you to hear them living the most intimate details of their lives. You heard them laughing, talking, weeping, singing, scolding, caressing. You didn't know them. You did not even see them. When you met in the halls or elevators you did not speak. Then, after they had lived in the new apartment about a year Cora met the woman in 618 and Raymond met the woman in 620, within the same week. The Atwaters lived in 619.

There was some confusion in the delivery of a package. The woman in 618 pressed the Atwaters' electric button for the first time in their year's residence there.

A plump woman, 618; blonde; in black. You felt that her flesh was expertly restrained in tight pink satin brassières and long-hipped corsets and many straps.

"I hate to trouble you, but did you get a package for Mrs. Hoyt? It's from Field's."

It was five-thirty. Cora had her hat on. She did not ask the woman to come in. "I'll see. I ordered some things from Field's to-day, too. I haven't opened them yet. Perhaps yours ... I'll look."

The package with Mrs. Hoyt's name on it was there. "Well, thanks so much. It's some georgette crêpe. I'm making myself one those new two-tone slip-over negligees. Field's had a sale. Only one sixty-nine a yard."

Cora was interested. She sewed rather well when she was in the mood. "Are they hard to make?"

"Oh, land, no! No trick to it at all. They just hang from the shoulder, see? Like a slip-over. And then your cord comes round——"

She stepped in. She undid the box and shook out the vivid folds of the filmy stuff, vivid green and lavender. "You wouldn't think they'd go well together but they do. Makes a perfectly stunning negligee."

Cora fingered the stuff. "I'd get some. Only I don't know if I could cut the——"

"I'll show you. Glad to." She was very friendly. Cora noticed she used expensive perfume. Her hair was beautifully marcelled. The woman folded up the material and was off, smiling. "Just let me know when you get it. I've got a lemon cream pie in the oven and I've got to run." She called back over her shoulder. "Mrs. Hoyt."

Cora nodded and smiled. "Mine's Atwater." She saw that the woman's simple-seeming black dress was one she had seen in a Michigan Avenue shop, and had coveted. Its price had been beyond her purse.

Cora mentioned the meeting to Ray when he came home. "She seems real nice. She's going to show me how to cut out a new negligee."

"What'd you say her name was?" She told him. He shrugged. "Well, I'll say this: she must be some swell cook. Whenever I go by that door at dinner time my mouth just waters. One night last week there was something must have been baked spare-ribs and sauerkraut. I almost broke in the door."

The woman in 618 did seem to cook a great deal. That is, when she cooked. She explained that Mr. Hoyt was on the road a lot of the time and when he was home she liked to fuss for him. This when she was helping Cora cut out the georgette negligee.

"I'd get coral colour if I was you, honey. With your hair and all," Mrs. Hoyt had advised her.

"Why, that's my name! That is, it's what Ray calls me. My name's really Cora." They were quite good friends now.

It was that same week that Raymond met the woman in 620. He had left the apartment half an hour later than usual (he had a heavy cold, and had not slept) and encountered the man and woman just coming out of 620.

"And guess who it was!" he exclaimed to Cora that evening. "It was a girl who used to work at Nagel's, in the binoculars, years ago, when I started there. Calhoun, her name was. Laura Calhoun. Smart little girl, she was. She's married now. And guess what! She gets a big salary fitting glasses for women at the Bazaar. She learned to be an optician. Smart girl."

Cora bridled, virtuously. "Well, I think she'd better stay home and take care of that child of hers. I should think she'd let her husband earn the living. That child is all soul alone when she comes home from school. I hear her practising. I asked Mrs. Hoyt about her. She say's she's seen her. A pindling scrawny little thing, about ten years old. She leaves her alone all day."

Ray encountered the Calhoun girl again, shortly after that, in the way encounters repeat themselves, once they have started.

"She didn't say much but I guess her husband is a nit-wit. Funny how a smart girl like that always marries one of these sap-heads that can't earn a living. She said she was working because she wanted her child to have the advantages she'd missed. That's the way she put it."

One heard the long-legged, melancholy child next door practising at the piano daily at four. Cora said it drove her crazy. But then, Cora was rarely home at four. "Well," she said now, virtuously, "I don't know what she calls advantages. The way she neglects that kid. Look at her! I guess if she had a little more mother and a little less education it'd be better for her."

"Guess that's right," Ray agreed.

It was in September that Cora began to talk about the mink coat. A combination anniversary and Christmas gift. December would mark their twelfth anniversary. A mink coat.

Raymond remembered that his mother had had a mink coat, back there in Michigan, years ago. She always had taken it out in November and put it away in moth balls and tar paper in March. She had done this for years and years. It was a cheerful yellow mink, with a slightly darker marking running through it, and there had been little mink tails all around the bottom edge of it. It had spread comfortably at the waist. Women had had hips in those days. With it his mother had carried a mink muff; a small yellow-brown cylinder just big enough for her two hands. It had been her outdoor uniform, winter after winter, for as many years as he could remember of his boyhood. When she had died the mink coat had gone to his sister Carrie, he remembered.

A mink coat. The very words called up in his mind sharp winter days; the pungent moth-bally smell of his mother's fur-coated bosom when she had kissed him good-bye that day he left for Chicago; comfort; womanliness. A mink coat.

"How much could you get one for? A mink coat."

Cora hesitated a moment. "Oh—I guess you could get a pretty good one for three thousand."

"You're crazy," said Ray, unemotionally. He was not angry. He was amused.

But Cora was persistent. Her coat was a sight. She had to have something. She never had had a real fur coat.

"How about your Hudson seal?"

"Hudson seal! Did you ever see any seals in the Hudson! Fake fur. I've never had a really decent piece of fur in my life. Always some mangy make-believe. All the girls in the Crowd are getting new coats this year. The woman next door—Mrs. Hoyt—is talking of getting one. She says Mr. Hoyt——"

"Say, who are these Hoyts, anyway?"

276

Ray came home early one day to find the door to 618 open. He glanced in, involuntarily. A man sat in the living room—a large, rather red-faced man, in his shirt-sleeves, relaxed, comfortable, at ease. From the open door came the most tantalizing and appetizing smells of candied sweet potatoes, a browning roast, steaming vegetables.

Mrs. Hoyt had run in to bring a slice of fresh-baked chocolate cake to Cora. She often brought in dishes of exquisitely prepared food thus, but Raymond had never before encountered her. Cora introduced them. Mrs. Hoyt smiled, nervously, and said she must run away and tend to her dinner. And went. Ray looked after her. He strode into the kitchenette where Cora stood, hatted, at the sink.

"Say, looka here, Cora. You got to quit seeing that woman, see?"

"What woman?"

"One calls herself Mrs. Hoyt. That woman. Mrs. Hoyt! Ha!"

"Why, Ray, what in the world are you talking about! Aren't you *fun*-ny!"

"Yeh; well, you cut her out. I won't have you running around with a woman like that. Mrs. Hoyt! Mrs. Fiddlesticks!"

They had a really serious quarrel about it. When the smoke of battle cleared away Raymond had paid the first instalment on a three thousand dollar mink coat. And, "If we could sub-lease," Cora said, "I think it would be wonderful to move to the Shoreham. Lil and Harry are going there in January. You know yourself this place isn't half respectable."

Raymond had stared. "Shoreham! Why, it's a hotel. Regular hotel."

"Yes," placidly. "That's what's so nice about it. No messing around in a miserable little kitchenette. You can have your meals sent up. Or you can go down to the dining room. Lil says it's wonderful. And if you order for one up in your room the portions are big enough for two. It's really economy, in the end."

"Nix," said Ray. "No hotel in mine. A little house of our own. That's the right idea. Build."

"But nobody's building now. Materials are so high. It'll cost you ten times as much as it would if you waited a few—a little while. And no help. No maids coming over, hardly. I think you might consider me a little. We could live at the Shoreham a while, anyway. By that time things will be better, and we'd have money saved up and then we might talk of building. Goodness knows I love my home as well as any woman——"

They looked at the Shoreham rooms on the afternoon of their anniversary. They were having the Crowd to dinner, downtown, that evening. Cora thought the Shoreham rooms beautiful, though she took care not to let the room-clerk know she thought so. Ray, always a silent, inarticulate man, was so wordless that Cora took him to task for it in a sibilant aside.

"Ray, for heaven's, sake say something. You stand there! I don't know what the man'll think."

"A hell of a lot I care what he thinks." Ray was looking about the garish room—plush chairs, heavy carpets, brocade hangings, shining table-top, silly desk.

"Two hundred and seventy-five a month," the clerk was saying. "With the yearly lease, of course. Otherwise it's three twenty-five." He seemed quite indifferent.

Ray said nothing. "We'll let you know," said Cora.

The man walked to the door. "I can't hold it for you, you know. Our apartments are practically gone. I've a party who practically has closed for this suite already. I'd have to know."

Cora looked at Ray. He said nothing. He seemed not to have heard. His face was gaunt and haggard. "We'll let you know—to-morrow," Cora said. Her full under lip made a straight thin line.

When they came out it was snowing. A sudden flurry. It was already dark. "Oh, dear," said Cora. "My hat!" Ray summoned one of the hotel taxis. He helped Cora into it. He put money into the driver's hand.

"You go on, Cora. I'm going to walk."

"Walk! Why! But it's snowing. And you'll have to dress for dinner."

"I've got a little headache. I thought I'd walk. I'll be home. I'll be home."

He slammed the door then, and turned away. He began to walk in the opposite direction from that which led toward the apartment house. The snow felt cool and grateful on his face. It stung his cheeks. Hard and swift and white it came, blinding him. A blizzard off the lake. He plunged through it, head down, hands jammed into his pockets.

So. A home girl. Home girl. God, it was funny. She was a selfish, idle, silly, vicious woman. She was nothing. Nothing. It came over him in a sudden blinding crashing blaze of light. The woman in 618 who wasn't married to her man, and who cooked and planned to make him comfortable; the woman in 620 who blindly left her home and her child every day in order to give that child the thing she called advantages—either of these was better than his woman. Honester. Helping someone. Trying to, anyway. Doing a better job than she was.

He plunged across the street, blindly, choking a little with the bitterness that had him by the throat.

Hey! Watcha!——-A shout rising to a scream.

A bump. Numbness. Silence. Nothingness.

"Well, anyway, Cora," said the girls in the Crowd, "you certainly were a wonderful wife to him. You can always comfort yourself with that thought. My! the way you always ran home so's to be there before he got in."

"I know it," said Cora, mournfully. "I always was a home girl. Why, we always had planned we should have a little home of our own some day. He always said that was the right idear—idea."

Lil wiped her eyes. "What are you going to do about your new mink coat, Cora?"

Cora brushed her hair away from her forehead with a slow, sad gesture. "Oh, I don't know. I've hardly thought of such trifling things. The woman next door said she might buy it. Hoyt, her name is. Of course I couldn't get what we paid for it, though I've hardly had it on. But money'll count with me now. Ray never did finish that invisible rim he was working on all those years. Wasting his time. Poor Ray.... I thought if she took it, I'd get a caracul, with a black fox collar. After I bought it I heard mink wasn't so good anyway, this year. Everything's black. Of course, I'd never have said anything to Raymond about it. I'd just have worn it. I wouldn't have hurt Ray for the world."

AIN'T NATURE WONDERFUL!

When a child grows to boyhood, and a boy to manhood under the soul-searing blight of a given name like Florian, one of two things must follow. He will degenerate into a weakling, crushed beneath the inevitable diminutive—Flossie; or he will build up painfully, inch by inch, a barrier against the name's corroding action. He will boast of his biceps, flexing them the while. He will brag about cold baths. He will prate of chest measurements; regard golf with contempt; and speak of the West as God's country.

Florian Sykes was five feet three and a half, and he liked to quote those red-blooded virile poems about the big open spaces out where the West begins. The biggest open space in his experience was Madison Square, New York; and Eighth Avenue spelled the Far West for him. When Florian spoke or thought of great heights it was never in terms of nature, such as mountains, but in artificial ones, like skyscrapers. Yet his job depended on what he called the great outdoors.

The call of the wild, by the time it had filtered into his city abode, was only a feeble cheep. But he answered it daily from his rooms to the store in the morning, from the store to his rooms in the evening. It must have been fully ten blocks each way. There are twenty New York blocks to the mile. He threw out his legs a good deal when he walked and came down with his feet rather flat, and he stooped ever so little with the easy slouch that came in with the one-button sack suit. It's the walk you see used by English actors of the what-what school who come over here to play gentlemanly juveniles.

Down at Inverness & Heath's they called him Nature's Rival, but that was mostly jealousy, with a strong dash of resentment. Two of the men in his department had been Maine guides, and another boasted that he knew the Rockies as he knew the palm of his hand. But Florian, whose trail-finding had all been done in the subway shuttle, and who thought that butter sauce with parsley was a trout's natural element, had been promoted above their heads half a dozen times until now he lorded it over the fifth floor.

Not one of you, unless bedridden from birth, but has felt the influence of the firm of Inverness & Heath. You may never have seen the great establishment itself, rising story on story just off New York's main shopping thoroughfare. But you have felt the call of their catalogue. Surely at one time or another, they have supplied you with tents or talcum; with sleeping-bags or skis or skates; with rubber boots, or resin or reels. On their fourth floor you can be hatted for Palm Beach or booted for Skagway. On the third, outfitted for St. Moritz or San Antonio. But the fifth floor is the pride of the store. There is the camper's dream realized. There you will find man's most ingenious devices for softening Mother Nature's flinty bosom. Mosquito-proof tents; pails that will not leak; fleece-lined sleeping-bags; cooking outfits made up of pots and pans of every size, each shaped to disappear mysteriously into the next, like a conjurer's outfit, the whole swallowed up by a magic leather case.

Here Florian reigned. If you were a regular Inverness & Heath customer you learned to ask for him as soon as the elevator tossed you up to his domain. He met you with what is known in the business efficiency guides as the strong personality greeting. It consisted in clasping your hand with a grip that drove your ring into the bone, looking you straight in the eye, registering alert magnetic force, and pronouncing your name very distinctly. Like this: hand-clasp firm—straight in the eye—"How do you do, Mr. Outertown. Haven't seen you since last June. How was the trip?" He didn't mean to be a liar. And yet he lied daily and magnificently for years, to the world and himself. When, for example, in the course of purchasing rods, flies, tents, canoes, saddles, boots, or sleeping-bags of him, you spoke of the delights of your contemplated vacation, he would say, "That's the life. I'm a Western man, myself.... God's country!" He said it with a deep breath, and an exhalation, as one who pants to be free of the city's noisome fumes. You felt he must have been born with an equipment of chaps, quirts, spurs, and sombrero. You see him flinging himself on a horse and clattering off with a flirt of hoofs as they do it in the movies. His very manner sketched in a background of plains, mountains, six-shooters, and cacti.

The truth of it was Florian Sykes had been born in Kenosha, Wisconsin. At the age of three he had been brought to New York by a pair of inexpert and migratory parents. Their reasons for migrating need not concern us. They must, indeed, have been bad reasons. For Florian, at thirteen, a spindle-legged errand-boy in over-size knickers, a cold sore on his lip, and shoes chronically in need of resoling, had started to work for the great sporting goods store of Inverness & Heath.

Now, at twenty-nine, he was head of the fifth floor. The cold sore had vanished permanently under a régime of health-food, dumb-bells, and icy plunges. The shoes were bench-made and flawless. If the legs still were somewhat spindling their correctly creased casings hid the fact.

There's little doubt that if Florian had been named Bill, and if the calves of his legs had bulged, and if, in his youth, he had gone to work for a wholesale grocer, he would never have forged for himself a coat of mail whose links were pretense and whose bolts were sham. He probably would have been frankly content with the sight of an occasional ball-game out at the Polo Grounds, and the newspaper bulletins of a prizefight by rounds. But here he was at the base that supplied America's outdoor equipment. He who outfitted mountaineers must speak knowingly of glaciers, chasms, crevices, and peaks. He who advised canoeists must assume wisdom of paddles, rapids, currents, and portages. He whose sleeping hours were spangled with the clang of the street cars must counsel such hardy ones as were preparing cheerfully to seek rest rolled in blankets before a camp-fire's dying embers. And so, slowly, year by year, in his rise from errand to stock boy, from stock boy to clerk, from clerk to assistant manager, thence to his present official position, he had built about himself a tissue of innocent lies. He actually believed them himself.

Sometimes a customer who in June had come in to purchase his vacation supplies with the city pallor upon him, returned in September, brown, hard, energized, to thank Florian for the comfort of the outfit supplied him.

"I just want to tell you, Sykes, that that was a great little outfit you sold me. Yessir! Not a thing too much, and not a thing too little, either. Remember how I kicked about that air mattress? Well, say, it saved my life! I slept like a baby every night. And the trip! You've been there, haven't you?"

Florian would smile and nod his head. His grateful customer would clap him on the shoulder. "Some pebble, that mountain!"

"Get to the top?" Florian would ask.

"Well, we didn't do the peak. That is, not right to the top. Started to a couple of times, but the girls got tired, and we didn't want to leave 'em alone. Pretty stiff climb, let me tell you, young feller."

"You should have made the top."

"Been up, have you?"

"A dozen times."

"Oh, well, that's your business, you might say. Next time, maybe, we'll do it. The missus says she wants to go back there every year."

Florian would shake his head. "Oh, you don't want to do that. Have you been out to Glacier? Have you done the Yellowstone on horseback? Ever been down the Grand Canyon?"

"Why—no—but——"

"You've got a few thrills coming to you then."

The sunburned traveller would flush mahogany. "That's all right for you to say. But I'm no chamois. But it was a great trip, just the same. I want to thank you."

Then, for example, Florian's clothes. He had adopted that careful looseness—that ease of fit—that skilful sloppiness—which is the last word in masculine sartorial smartness. In talking he dropped his final g's and said "sportin'" and "mountain climbin'" and "shootin'." From June until September he wore those Norfolk things with bow ties, and his shirt patterns were restrained to the point of austerity. A signet ring with a large scrolled monogram on the third finger of his right hand was his only ornament, and he had worn a wrist watch long before the War. He had never seen a mountain. The ocean meant Coney Island. He breakfasted at Child's. He spent two hours over the Sunday papers. He was a Tittlebat Titmouse without the whiskers. And Myra loved him.

If Florian had not pretended to be something he wasn't; and if he had not professed an enthusiastic knowledge of things of which he was ignorant, he would, in the natural course of events, have loved Myra quickly in return. In fact, he would have admitted that he had loved her first, and desperately. And there would have been no story entitled, "Ain't Nature Wonderful!"

Myra worked in the women's and misses', third floor, and she didn't care a thing about the big outdoors or the great open spaces. She didn't even pretend to—at first. A clear-eyed, white-throated, capable young woman, almost poignantly pretty. You sensed it was the kind of loveliness that fades a bit with marriage. In its place come two sturdy babies to carry on the torch of beauty. You sensed, too, that Myra would keep their noses wiped, their knees scrubbed, and their buttons buttoned and that, between a fresh blouse for herself and fresh rompers for them, the blouse would always lose.

She hated discomfort, did Myra, as does one who has always had too much of it. After you have stood all day, from 8:30 A. M. to 5:30 P. M., selling sweaters, riding togs, golf clothes, and trotteurs to athletic Dianas whose lines are more lathe than lithe, you can't work up much enthusiasm about exercising for the pure joy of it. Myra had never used a tennis-racket in her life, but daily she outfitted for the sport bronzed young ladies who packed a nasty back-hand wallop in their right. She wore (and was justly proud of) a 4-A shoe, and took a good deal of comfort in the fact as she sold 7-Cs at $22.50 a pair to behemothian damsels who possessed money in proportion to Myra's beauty. Myra was the only girl in her section who never tried to dress in imitation of the moneyed ones whom she served. The other girls were wont to wear severely tailored shirts, mannish ties, stocks, flat-heeled shoes, rough tweed skirts. Not so Myra. That delicate cup-like hollow at the base of her white throat was fittingly framed in a ruffle of frilly georgette. She did her hair in soft undulations that flowed away from forehead and temple, and she powdered her nose a hundred times a day. Her little shoes were high-heeled and her hands were miraculously white, and if you prefer Rosalind to Viola you'd better quit her now.

"Anybody who wants to wear those cross-country clothes is welcome to them," she said. "I'm a girl and I'm satisfied to be. I don't see why I should wear a hard-boiled shirt and a necktie any more than a man should wear a pink georgette trimmed with filet. By the end of the week, when I've spent six solid days selling men's clothes to women, I feel's if I'd die happy if I could take a milk bath and put on white satin and pearls and a train six yards long from the shoulders—*you* know."

Not the least of Myra's charm was a certain unexpected and pleasing humour. It was as though, on opening a chocolate box, you were to find it contained caviar.

Of course by now you know that Myra is the girl you used to see smiling out at you from the Inverness & Heath catalogue entitled Sportswomen's Apparel. The head of her department had soon discovered that Myra, posing for illustrations to be used in the spring booklet, raised that pamphlet's selling power about 100 per cent. Sunburned misses, with wind-ravaged complexions, gazing at the picture of Myra, cool, slim, luscious-looking, saw themselves as they would fain be—and bought the Knollwood sweater depicted—in silk or wool—putty, maize, navy, rose, copen, or white—$35. Myra posed in paddock coat and breeches—she who had never been nearer a horse than the distance between sidewalk and road. She smiled at you over her shoulder radiant in a white tricot Palm Beach suit, who thought palms grew in jardinières only. On page 17 she was revealed in the boyish impudence of our Aiken Polo Habit, complete, $90. She was ravishing in her golf clothes, her small feet in sturdy, flat-heeled boots planted far apart, and only the most carping would have commented on the utter impossibility of her stance. Then there was the Killiecrankie Travel Tog (background of assorted mountains) made of Scotch tweed (she would never come nearer Scotland than oatmeal for breakfast) only $140. To say nothing of motor clothes, woodland suits, trap-shooting costumes, Yellowstone Park outfits, hunting habits. She wore brogues, and boots, and skating shoes, and puttees and tennis ties; sou'westers, leather topcoats, Jersey silks, military capes. You saw her fishing, hunting, boating, riding, golfing, snow-shoeing, swimming. She was equally lovely in khaki with woollen stockings, or in a habit of white linen and the shiniest of riding-boots. And as she peeled off the one to put on the next she remarked wearily, "A kimono and felt slippers and my hair down my back will look pretty good to me to-night, after this."

You see, Myra and Florian really had so much in common that if he had been honest with himself the course of their love would have run too smooth to be true. But Florian, in his effort to register as a two-fisted, hard-riding, nature-taming male, made such a success of it that for a long time he deceived even Myra who loved him. And during that time she, too, lied in her frantic effort to match her step with his. When he talked of riding and swimming; of long, hard mountain hikes; of impenetrable woods, she looked at him with sparkling eyes. (She didn't need to throw much effort into that, nature having supplied her with the ground materials.) When, on their rare Sundays together, he suggested a long tramp up the Palisades she agreed enthusiastically, though she hated it. Not only that, she went, loathing it. The stones hurt her feet. Her slender ankles ached. The sun burned her delicate skin. The wind pierced her thin coat. Florian strode along with the exaggerated step of the short man who bitterly resents his lack of stature. Every now and then he stood still, and breathed deeply, and said, "Glorious!" And Myra looked at his straight back, and his clear-cut profile, and his well-dressed legs and said, "Isn't it!" and wished he would kiss her. But he never did.

In between times he bemoaned his miserable two weeks' vacation which made impossible the sort of thing he said he craved—a long, hard, rough trip into a mountain interior. The Rockies, preferably, in their jaggedest portions.

"That's the kind of thing that makes a fellow over. Roughing it. You forget about the city. In the saddle all day—nothing but sky and mountains. God's big open spaces! That's the life!"

Myra trudged along, painfully. "But isn't it awfully uncomfortable? You know. Cold? And tents? I don't think I'd like——"

"I wouldn't give a cent for a person who was so soft they couldn't stand roughing it a little. That's the trouble with you Easterners. Soft! No red blood. Too many street cars, and high buildings, and restaurants. Chop down a few trees and fry your own bacon, and make your own camp, and saddle your own horses—that's what I call living. I'm going back to it some day, see if I don't."

Myra looked down at her own delicate wrists, with the blue veins so exquisitely etched against the white flesh. A little look of terror and hopelessness came into her eyes.

"I—I couldn't chop down a tree," she said. She was panting a little in keeping up with him, for he was walking very fast. "I'd be afraid to saddle a horse. You have to stand right next to them, don't you? Most girls can't chop———"

Florian smiled a little superior smile. "Miss Jessie Heath can." Myra looked up at him, quickly. "She's a wonder! She was in yesterday," he went on. "Spent all of two hours up in my department, looking things over. There's nothing she can't do. She won a blue ribbon at the Horse Show in February. Saddle. She's climbed every peak that amounts to anything in Europe. Did the Alps when she was a little girl. This summer she's going to do the Rockies, because things are so mussed up in Europe, she says. I'm selecting the outfit for the party. Gad, what a trip!" He sighed, deeply.

Myra was silent. She was not ungenerous toward women, as are so many pretty girls. But she was human, after all, and she did love this Florian, and Jessie Heath was old man Heath's daughter. Whenever she came into the store she created a little furore among the clerks. Myra could not resist a tiny flash of claws.

"She's flat, like a man. And she wears 7½-C. And her face looks as if it had been rubbed with a scouring brick."

"She's a goddess!" said Florian, striding along. Myra laughed, a little high hysterical laugh. Then she bit her lip, and then she was silent for a long time. He was silent, too, until suddenly he heard a little sound that made him turn quickly to look at her stumbling along at his side. And she was crying.

"Why—what's the matter! What's!——-"

"I'm tired," sobbed Myra, and sank in a little limp heap on a convenient rock. "I'm tired. I want to go home."

"Why"—he was plainly bewildered—"why didn't you tell me you were tired!"

"I'm telling you now."

They took the nearest ferry across the river, and the Subway home. At the entrance to the noisy, crowded flat in which she lived Myra turned to face him. She was through with pretense. She was tired of make-believe. She felt a certain relief in the thought of what she had to say. She faced him squarely.

"I've lived in the city all my life and I'm crazy about it. I love it. I like to walk in the park a little maybe, Sundays, but I hate tramping like we did this afternoon, and you might as well know it. I wouldn't chop down a tree, not if I was freezing to death, and I'd hate to have to sleep in a tent, so there! I hate sunburn, and freckles, and ants in the pie, and blisters on my feet, and getting wet, and flat-heeled shoes, and I never saddled a horse. I'd be afraid to. And what's more, I don't believe you do, either."

"Don't believe I do what?" asked Florian in a stunned kind of voice.

But Myra had turned and left him. And as he stood there, aghast, bewildered, resentful, clear and fair in the back of his mind, against all the turmoil of thoughts that seethed there, was the picture of her white, slim, exquisite throat with a little delicate pulse beating in it as she cried out her rebellion. He wished—or some one inside him that he could not control wished—that he could put his fingers there on her throat, gently.

It was very warm that evening, for May. And as he sat by the window in his pajamas, just before going to bed, he thought about Myra, and he thought about himself. But when he thought about himself he slammed the door on what he saw. Florian's rooms were in Lexington Avenue in the old brownstone district that used to be the home of white-headed millionaires with gold-headed canes, who, on dying, left their millions to an Alger newsboy who had once helped them across the street. Millionaires, gold-headed canes, and newsboys had long vanished, and the old brownstone fronts were rooming houses now, interspersed with delicatessens, interior decorators, and dressmaking establishments. Florian was fond of boasting when he came down to the store in the morning, after a hot, muggy July night, "My place is like a summer resort. Breeze just sweeps through it. I have to have the covers on."

Sometimes Mrs. Pet, his landlady, made him a pitcher of lemonade and brought it up to him, and he sipped it, looking out over the city, soothed by its roar, fascinated by its glow and brilliance. Mrs. Pet said it was a pleasure to have him around, he was so neat.

Florian was neat. Not only neat, but methodical. He had the same breakfast every week-day morning at Child's; half a grapefruit, one three-minute egg, coffee, rolls. On Sunday morning he had bacon and eggs. It was almost automatic. Speaking of automatics, he never took his meals at one of those modern mechanical feeders. Though at Child's he never really beheld the waitress with his seeing eye, he liked to have her slap his dishes down before him with a genial crash. A gentleman has his little foibles, and being waited on at meal-time was one of his. Occasionally, to prove to himself that he wasn't one of those fogies who get in a rut, he ordered wheat cakes with maple syrup for breakfast. They always disagreed with him.

She was a wise young woman, Myra.

Perhaps Florian, as he sat by his window that Sunday night of Myra's outburst, thought on these things. But he would not admit to himself whither his thinking led. And presently he turned back the spread, neatly, and turned out the light, and opened the window a little wider, and felt of his chin, as men do, though the next shave is eight hours distant, and slept, and did not dream of white throats as he had secretly hoped he would.

And next morning, at eleven, a very wonderful thing began to happen. Next morning, at eleven, Miss Jessie Heath loped (well, it can't be helped. That describes it exactly) into the broad aisles of the fifth floor. She had been coming in a great deal, lately. The Western trip, no doubt.

Descriptions of people are clumsy things, at best, and stop one's story. But Jessie Heath must have her paragraph. A half-dozen lines ought to do it. Well—she was the kind of girl who always goes around with a couple of Airedales, and in woollen stockings, low shoes and mannish shirts, and shell-rimmed glasses, and you felt she wore Ferris waists. Her hair was that ashen blonde with no glint of gold in it. You knew it would become grey in middle age with no definite period of transition. She never buttoned her heavy welted gloves but wore them back over her hand, like a cuff, very English. You felt there must be a riding crop concealed about her somewhere. Perhaps up her spine.

As has been said, there was always a little flurry when she came into the big store that had made millions for her father. It would be nonsense to suppose that Jessie Heath ever deliberately set out to attract a man who was an employee in that store. But it is pleasant and soothing to be admired, and to have a fine pair of eyes look fine things into one's own (shell-rimmed) ones. And, after all, the Jessie Heaths of this world are walked with, and golfed with, and ridden with, and tennised with, and told that they're wonderful pals. But it's the Myras that are made love to. So now, when Florian Sykes looked at her, and flushed a little, and said, "I suppose there are a lot of lucky ones going along with you on this trip, Miss—Jessie," she flushed, too, and flicked her boot with her riding crop—No, no! I forgot. She didn't have a riding crop. Well, anyway she gave the effect of flicking her boot with her riding crop, and said:

"Would you like to go?"

"Would I like to go——!" He choked over it. Then he sighed, and smiled rather wistfully. "That's needlessly cruel of you, Miss Jessie."

"Maybe it's not so cruel as you think," Jessie Heath answered. "Did you make out that list?"

"I spent practically all of yesterday on it." Which we know was a lie because, look, wasn't he with Myra?

They went over the list together. Fishing tackle, tents, pocket-flashes, puttees, ponchos, chocolate, quirts, slickers, matches, medicine-case, sweaters, cooking utensils, blankets. It grew longer, and longer. Their heads came close together over it. And they trailed from department to department, laughing and talking together. And the two Maine ex-guides and the clerk who boasted he knew the Rockies like the palm of his hand, said to one another, "Get on to Nature's Rival trying to make a hit with Jessie."

Meanwhile Jessie was saying, "Of course you know the Rockies, being a Western man, and all."

Florian smiled rather deprecatingly. "Queer part of it is I don't know the Rockies so well—" with an emphasis on the word Rockies that led one to think his more noteworthy feats of altitude had been accomplished about the Alps, the Pyrenees, the Andes, and the lesser Appalachians.

"But you've climbed them, haven't you?"

He burned his bridges behind him. "Only the—ah—eastern slopes."

"Oh, that's all right, then. We're going to do the west. It'll be wonderful having you——"

"Me!"

"Nothing. Let's go on with the list. M-m-m—where were we? Oh, yes. Now trout flies. Which do you honestly think best for mountain trout? The Silver Doctor or the Gray Hackle or the Yellow Professor? U'm?"

Inspiration comes to us at such times. It could have been nothing less that prompted him to say, "Well—doesn't that depend a lot on the weather and the depth of the—ahem!—water?"

"Yes, of course. How silly of me. We'll take a lot of all kinds, and then we'll be safe."

He breathed again and smiled. He had a winning smile, Florian. Jessie Heath smiled in return and they stood there, the two of them, lips parted, eyes holding eyes.

"My God!" said the man who boasted he knew the Rockies like the palm of his own hand, "it looks as if he'd landed her, the stiff."

Certainly it looked as if he had. For next morning old Heath, red-faced, genial-looking (and not so genial as he looked) approached the head of the fifth floor and said, "How long you been with us, Sykes?"

"Well, I came here as errand boy at thirteen. That's ten—twelve—fifteen—just about sixteen years next June. Yes, sir."

"How'd Jessie—how'd my daughter get the idea you were from the West, and a regular mountain goat, and a peak-climber and all that?"

He did look a little uncomfortable then, but it was too late for withdrawal. "I am from the West, you know."

"Have you had any long vacations since you've been with us?"

"No, sir. You see, in the summer, of course—our busy season. I never can get away then. So I've taken my two weeks in the fall."

Old Heath's eyes narrowed musingly. "Well, you couldn't have done all this mountain climbing before you were thirteen. And Jessie says——" He paused, rather blankly. "You say you do know the Rockies, though, eh?"

Florian drew himself up a little. "As well as I know any mountain."

"Oh, well, then, that's all right. Seems Jessie thinks you'd be a fine fellow to have along on this trip. I can't go myself. I hate this mountain climbing, anyway. Too darned hard work. But it's all right for young folks. Well, now, what do you say? Want to go? You've earned a vacation, after sixteen years. There's about eight in Jessie's crowd. Not counting guides. What do you say? Like to go?"

For a dazed moment Florian stared at him. "Why, yessir. Yes, sir, I'd—I'd like to go—very much." And he coughed to hide his joy and terror.

And two weeks later he went.

The thing swept the store like a flame. In an hour everyone knew it from the shipping-room to the roof-restaurant. Myra saw him the day he left. She was game, that girl.

"I hope you're going to have a beautiful time, Mr. Sykes."

"Thanks, Myra." He could afford to be lenient with her, poor little girl.

She ventured a final wretched word or two. "It's—it's wonderful of Mr. Heath and—Miss Heath—isn't it?" She was rubbing salt into her own wound and taking a fierce sort of joy in it.

"Wonderful! Say, they're a couple of God's green footstools, that's what they are!" He was a little mixed, but very much in earnest. "A couple of God's green footstools." And he went.

He went, and Myra watched him go, and except for a little swelling gulp in her white throat you'd never have known she'd been hit. He was going with Jessie Heath. Now, Myra had no illusions about those things. Old man Heath's wife, now dead, had been a girl with no money and no looks, and yet he had married her. If Jessie Heath happened to take a fancy to Florian, why——

Myra's little world stood still, and in it were small voices, far away, asking for 6½-B; and have you it in brown, and other unimportant things like that.

Ten minutes after the train had started Florian Sykes knew he shouldn't have come. He had suspected it before. He kept saying to himself, over and over: "You've always wanted a mountain trip, and now you're going to have it. You're a lucky guy, that's what you are. A lucky guy." But in his heart he knew he was lying.

In the first place, they were all so glib with their altitudes, and their packs, and their trails, and their horses and their camps. It was a rather mixed and raggle-taggle group that Miss Jessie Heath had gathered about her for this expedition to the West. They ranged all the way from a little fluffy witless golden-haired girl they all called Mud, for some obscure reason, and who had been Miss Heath's room-mate at college, surprisingly enough, to a lady of stern and rock-bound countenance who looked like a stage chaperon made up for the part. She was Miss Heath's companion in lieu of Mrs. Heath, deceased. In between there were a couple of men of Florian's age; two youngsters of twenty-one or two who talked of Harvard and asked Florian what his university had been; an old girl whose name Florian never did learn; and two others of Jessie Heath's age and general style. Florian found himself as bewildered by their talk and views as though they had been jabbering a foreign language. Every now and then, though, one of them would turn to him for a bit of technical advice. If it happened to concern equipment Florian could answer it readily enough. Ten years on the fifth floor had taught him many things. But if the knowledge sought happened to be of things geographical or of nature, he floundered, struggled, sank. And it took them just about half a day to learn this. The trip out takes four, from New York.

At first they asked him things to see him suffer. But they tired of that, after a bit. It was too easy. Queerly enough, Jessie Heath, mountain-wise though she was, believed in him almost to the end. But that only made the next three weeks the bitterer for Florian Sykes. For when it came to leaping from peak to peak Jessie turned out to be the young gazelle. And she liked to have Florian with her. On the trail she was a mosquito afoot, a jockey ahorseback. A thousand times, in those three weeks of torture, he would fix his eye on a tree ten feet away, up the steep trail. And to himself he would say, "I'll struggle, somehow, as far as that tree, and then die under it." And he would stagger another ten feet, his heart pounding in the unaccustomed altitude, his lungs bursting, his lips parted, his breath coming sobbingly, his eyes starting from his head. Leaping lightly ahead of him, around the bend, was Jessie, always. She had a way of calling to the laggard—hallooing, I believe it's supposed to be. And she expected an answer. An answer! When your lungs were bursting through your chest and your heart was crowding your tonsils. When he reached her it was always to find her perched on a seemingly inaccessible rock, demanding that he join her to admire the view. Before three days had gone by the sound of that halloo with its breeziness and breath-control and power, made him sick all over. Sometimes she sang, going up the trail. He could not have croaked a note if failure to do it had meant instant death. The Harvard hellions (it is his own term) were indefatigable, simian, pitiless. At nine thousand feet they aimed at ten. At ten they would have nothing less than twelve. At twelve thousand they were all for making another drive for it and having lunch at an altitude of thirteen thousand five hundred. As he toiled painfully along hundreds of feet behind them, Florian used to take a hideous pleasure in fancying how, on reaching the ever-distant top, the Harvard hellions would be missing. And after searching and hallooing he would peer over the edge (13,500 feet, at the very least, surely) and there, at the bottom, would discern their mangled forms, distorted, crushed, and quite, quite dead.

"Yoo-o-o—hoo-oo-oo-oo!" Jessie, up the trail. His rosy dream would vanish.

He learned why seasoned mountain climbers make nothing of the ascent. He learned, in bitterness and unshed tears, that it is the descent that breaks the heart and shatters the already broken frame. That down-climb with your toes crashing through your boots at every step; with your knee-brakes refusing to work, your thighs creaking, your joints spavined. The views were wonderful. But, oh, the price he paid! The air was intoxicating. But what, he asked himself, was wine to a dead man! Miserable little cockney that he was he told himself a hundred times a day that if he ever survived this he'd never look at another view again, unless from the Woolworth Tower, on a calm day. He thought of New York as a traveller, dying of thirst in the desert, thinks of the lush green oasis. New York in July! Dear New York in July, its furs in storage, its collar unstarched, its coat unbuttoned; even its doormen and chauffeurs almost human. Would he ever see it again? And then, as if in answer to his question, there befell an incident so harrowing, so nerve-shattering, as almost to make a negative answer seem inevitable.

Florian got lost.

It was the third week of the trip. Florian had answered Jessie's eleven thousandth question about things of which he was quite, quite ignorant. His brain felt queer and tight, as though something were about to snap.

They were to climb the Peak next day. All that day they had been approaching it. Florian looked at it. And he hated it. It was like a colossal forbidding finger pointing upward, upward, taunting him, menacing him. He wished that some huge cataclysm of nature would occur, swallowing up this hideous mass of pitiless rock.

Jessie Heath's none too classic nose had peeled long ere this and her neck was like a choice cut of underdone beefsteak. Florian told himself that there was something almost indecent about a girl who cared so little about her skin, and hair, and eyes, and hands. He actually hated her sturdy legs in their boots or puttees—those tireless, pitiless legs, always twinkling ahead of him, up the trail.

On the fateful day he was tired. He had often been tired to the point of desperation during the past three weeks. But this was different. Every step was torture. Every breath was pain. Jessie was a few hundred feet up the trail, as always, and hallooing to him every dozen paces. The Harvard hellions were doing the chamois ahead of her. The rest of the party were toiling along behind. One guide was just ahead. Another, leading two horses, bringing up the rear. Suddenly, desperately, Florian knew he must rest. He would fling himself on a bed of moss by the side of the trail, in the shade, near a stunted, wind-tortured timber-line pine, and let the whole procession pass him, and then catch up with them before they disappeared.

He stepped to the side of the narrow trail, almost indiscernible at this height, flung himself down with a little groan of relief, and shut his sun-seared eyes. The voices of the others came to him. There was little conversation. He heard Jessie's accursed halloo. Then the soft thud of the pack-horses' hoofs, the creak of the saddles. He must get up and follow now. In a minute. In a minute. In a m——

He must have slept there for two hours. When he awoke the light had changed and the air was chill. He sat up, bewildered. He rose. He looked about, called, hallooed, shouted, did all the futile frenzied things that a city man does who is lost in the mountains, and, knowing he is lost, is panic-stricken. The trail, of course! He looked for it, and there was no trail, to his town-wise eyes. He ran hither and thither, and back to hither again. He went forward, seemingly, and found himself back whence he started. He looked for cairns, for tree-blazes, for any one of the signs of which he had learned in the last three weeks. He found none. He called again, shrilly. A terror seized him. Terror of those grim, menacing, towering mountain masses. He ran round and round and round; darted backward and forward; called; stumbled; fell, and subsided, beaten.

He had a tiny box of matches with him, but little else. He had found the trail difficult enough without being pack-burdened. Food? He bethought himself of a little blue tin box in his coat pocket. He took it out and looked at it. Its very name struck terror to his heart.

U. S. Emergency Ration. It was printed on the box. Just below that he made out:

Powdered   sugar
Chocolate
Cocoa   butter
Malted   milk
Egg   Albumin
Casein.

Not to be opened except on command of officer.

My God! He had come to this! He looked at it, wide-eyed. He was very hungry. The ration, in its blue tin, like a box of shaving talcum, had been handed to each of the party in a chorus of shouting and laughter. And now it was to save his life. He managed to pry open the box, and ate some of its contents, slowly. It was not agreeable.

Dusk was coming on. There were mountain lions, he knew that. Those rocks and crevices were peopled with all sorts of stealthy, snarling, slinking, four-footed creatures. He would build a fire. They were afraid of the flames, he had read somewhere, and would not come near. Perhaps the others would see the light, and come back to find him. Curse them! Why hadn't they come before now!

It was dusk by the time he had his fire built. He had crouched over it for a half-hour, blowing it, coaxing it, wheedling it. There were few twigs or sticks at this height. He was very cold. His heavy sweater was in the pack on the horse's back. Finally he was rewarded with a feeble flicker, a tiny tongue of flame. He rose from his knees and passed his hand over his forehead with a gesture of utter weariness and despair. And then he stared, transfixed. For on the plateau above him rose a great shaft of fire. The kind of fire that only Pete, the most expert among guides, could build. And as he stared there burst out at him from behind trees, rocks, crevices, a whole horde of imps shrieking with fiendish laughter.

"Ho, ho," laughed Jessie.

And "Ha, ha!" howled the Harvard hellions.

"Thought you were lost, didn'tcha?"

"Gosh, you looked funny!"

"Your face!——-"

Florian stared at them. He did not smile. He went quietly over to his tiny camp-fire and stamped it out, neatly, as he had been taught to do. He took his can of emergency ration (not to be opened except on command of officer) and hurled it far, far down the mountainside. Jessie Heath laughed, contemptuously. And Florian, looking at her, didn't care. Didn't care. Didn't care.

The nightmare was over in August. Over, that is, for Florian. The rest were to do another four weeks of it, farther into the interior. Florian sickened at the thought of it. When he bade them farewell he was so glad to be free of them that he almost loved them. When he found himself actually on the little jerkwater train that was to connect him with the main line he patted the dusty red plush seat, gratefully, as one would stroke a faithful beast. When he came into the Grand Central station he would have stooped and kissed the steps of the marble staircase if his porter had not been on the point of vanishing with his bags. That night on reaching home he stayed in the bathtub for an hour, just lying there in the warm, soothing liquid, only moving to dapple his fingers now and then as a lazy fish moves a languid fin. God's country! This was it.

"My, it's nice to have you back again, Mr. Sykes," said Mrs. Pet.

"Is your big two-room suite on the next floor vacant?" said Florian, cryptically.

Mrs. Pet stared a little, wonderingly. "Yes, that's vacant since the Ostranders left, in July. Why do you ask, Mr. Sykes?"

"Nothing," Florian answered, airily. "Not a thing. Just asked."

His train had come in at nine. It was eleven now, but he was restless, and a little hungry, and very much exhilarated. "You certainly look grand," Mrs. Pet had exclaimed, admiringly. "And my, how you're sunburned!"

He left the Lexington Avenue house, now, and strolled over to the near-by white-tiled restaurant. There, in the window, was the white-capped one, flapping pancakes. Florian could have kissed him. He sat down. A waitress approached him.

"I don't know," mused Florian. "I'm sort of hungry, but I don't just——"

"The pork and beans are elegant to-night," suggested the girl.

And "Pork and beans! NO!" thundered Florian.

The girl drew herself up icily. "I ain't deef. You don't need to yell."

Florian looked up at her contritely, and smiled his winning smile. "I'm sorry. I didn't mean—I—I never want to see beans again as long as I live!"

He was down at the store early, early next morning. His practised eye swept the department for possible slackness, for changes, for needed adjustments. The two Maine ex-guides and the chap who knew the Rockies like the palm of his hand welcomed him with Judas-like slaps on the shoulder. "Like it?" they asked him. And, "God's country—the West," he answered, mechanically. After that he ignored them. At nine he ran down the two flights of stairs to the third floor. He did not wait for the elevator.

For a moment he could not find her and his heart sank. She might be away on a vacation. Then he spied her in a corner half-hidden by a rack of covert coats. She was hanging them up. The floor was empty of customers thus early. He strode over to her. She turned. Into her eyes there leaped a look which she quickly veiled as had been taught her by a thousand thousand female ancestors.

"I got your postals," she said.

Florian said nothing.

"My, you're brown!"

Florian said nothing.

"Did you—have a good time?"

Florian said nothing.

"What—what——" Her hand went to her throat, where his eyes were fastened.

Then Florian spoke. "How white your throat is!" he said. "How white your throat is!"

Myra stepped out, then, from among the covert coats on the rack. Her head was lifted high on the creamy column that supported it. She had her pride, had Myra.

"It's no whiter than it was a month ago, that I can see."

"I know it." His tone was humble, with a little pleading note in it. "I know a lot of things that I didn't know a month ago, Myra."

THE SUDDEN SIXTIES

Hannah Winter was sixty all of a sudden, as women of sixty are. Just yesterday—or the day before, at most—she had been a bride of twenty in a wine-coloured silk wedding gown, very stiff and rich. And now here she was, all of a sudden, sixty.

The actual anniversary that marked her threescore had had nothing to do with it. She had passed that day painlessly enough—happily, in fact. But now, here she was, all of a sudden, consciously, bewilderingly, sixty. This is the way it happened!

She was rushing along Peacock Alley to meet her daughter Marcia. Any one who knows Chicago knows that smoke-blackened pile, the Congress Hotel; and any one who knows the Congress Hotel has walked down that glittering white marble crypt called Peacock Alley. It is neither so glittering nor so white, nor, for that matter, so prone to preen itself as it was in the hotel's palmy '90s. But it still serves as a convenient short cut on a day when Chicago's lake wind makes Michigan Boulevard a hazard, and thus Hannah Winter was using it. She was to have met Marcia at the Michigan Boulevard entrance at two, sharp. And here it was 2.07. When Marcia said two, there she was at two, waiting, lips slightly compressed. When you came clattering up, breathless, at 2.07, she said nothing in reproach. But within the following half hour bits of her conversation, if pieced together, would have summed up something like this:

"I had to get the children off in time and give them their lunch first because it's wash day and Lutie's busy with the woman and won't do a single extra thing; and all my marketing for to-day and to-morrow because to-morrow's Memorial Day and they close at noon; and stop at the real estate agent's on Fifty-third to see them about the wall paper before I came down. I didn't even have time to swallow a cup of tea. And yet I was here at two. You haven't a thing to do. Not a blessed thing, living at a hotel. It does seem to me ..."

So then here it was 2.07, and Hannah Winter, rather panicky, was rushing along Peacock Alley, dodging loungers, and bell-boys, and travelling salesmen and visiting provincials and the inevitable red-faced delegates with satin badges. In her hurry and nervous apprehension she looked, as she scuttled down the narrow passage, very much like the Rabbit who was late for the Duchess's dinner. Her rubber-heeled oxfords were pounding down hard on the white marble pavement. Suddenly she saw coming swiftly toward her a woman who seemed strangely familiar—a well-dressed woman, harassed looking, a tense frown between her eyes, and her eyes staring so that they protruded a little, as one who runs ahead of herself in her haste. Hannah had just time to note, in a flash, that the woman's smart hat was slightly askew and that, though she walked very fast, her trim ankles showed the inflexibility of age, when she saw that the woman was not going to get out of her way. Hannah Winter swerved quickly to avoid a collision. So did the other woman. Next instant Hannah Winter brought up with a crash against her own image in that long and tricky mirror which forms a broad full-length panel set in the marble wall at the north end of Peacock Alley. Passersby and the loungers on near-by red plush seats came running, but she was unhurt except for a forehead bump that remained black-and-blue for two weeks or more. The bump did not bother her, nor did the slightly amused concern of those who had come to her assistance. She stood there, her hat still askew, staring at this woman—this woman with her stiff ankles, her slightly protruding eyes, her nervous frown, her hat a little sideways—this stranger—this murderess who had just slain, ruthlessly and forever, a sallow, lively, high-spirited girl of twenty in a wine-coloured silk wedding gown.

Don't think that Hannah Winter, at sixty, had tried to ape sixteen. She was not one of those grisly sexagenarians who think that, by wearing pink, they can combat the ochre of age. Not at all. In dress, conduct, mode of living she was as an intelligent and modern woman of sixty should be. The youth of her was in that intangible thing called, sentimentally, the spirit. It had survived forty years of buffeting, and disappointment, and sacrifice and hard work. Inside this woman who wore well-tailored black and small close hats and clean white wash gloves (even in Chicago) was the girl, Hannah Winter, still curious about this adventure known as living; still capable of bearing its disappointments or enjoying its surprises. Still capable, even, of being surprised. And all this is often the case, all unsuspected by the Marcias until the Marcias are, themselves, suddenly sixty. When it is too late to say to the Hannah Winters, "Now I understand."

We know that Hannah Winter had been married in wine-coloured silk, very stiff and grand. So stiff and rich that the dress would have stood alone if Hannah had ever thought of subjecting her wedding gown to such indignity. It was the sort of silk of which it is said that they don't make such silk now. It was cut square at the neck and trimmed with passementerie and fringe brought crosswise from breast to skirt hem. It's in the old photograph and, curiously enough, while Marcia thinks it's comic, Joan, her nine-year-old daughter, agrees with her grandmother in thinking it very lovely. And so, in its quaintness and stiffness and bravery, it is. Only you've got to have imagination.

While wine-coloured silk wouldn't have done for a church wedding it was quite all right at home; and Hannah Winter's had been a home wedding (the Winters lived in one of the old three-story red-bricks that may still be seen, in crumbling desuetude, over on Rush Street) so that wine-coloured silk for a twenty-year-old bride was quite in the mode.

It is misleading, perhaps, to go on calling her Hannah Winter, for she married Hermie Slocum and became, according to law, Mrs. Hermie Slocum, but remained, somehow, Hannah Winter in spite of law and clergy, though with no such intent on her part. She had never even heard of Lucy Stone. It wasn't merely that her Chicago girlhood friends still spoke of her as Hannah Winter. Hannah Winter suited her—belonged to her and was characteristic. Mrs. Hermie Slocum sort of melted and ran down off her. Hermie was the sort of man who, christened Herman, is called Hermie. That all those who had known her before her marriage still spoke of her as Hannah Winter forty years later was merely another triumph of the strong over the weak.

At twenty Hannah Winter had been a rather sallow, lively, fun-loving girl, not pretty, but animated; and forceful, even then. The Winters were middle-class, respected, moderately well-to-do Chicago citizens—or had been moderately well-to-do before the fire of '71. Horace Winter had been caught in the financial funk that followed this disaster and the Rush Street household, almost ten years later, was rather put to it to supply the wine-coloured silk and the supplementary gowns, linens, and bedding. In those days you married at twenty if a decent chance to marry at twenty presented itself. And Hermie Slocum seemed a decent chance, undoubtedly. A middle-class, respected, moderately well-to-do person himself, Hermie, with ten thousand dollars saved at thirty-five and just about to invest it in business in the thriving city of Indianapolis. A solid young man, Horace Winter said. Not much given to talk. That indicated depth and thinking. Thrifty and far-sighted, as witness the good ten thousand in cash. Kind. Old enough, with his additional fifteen years, to balance the lively Hannah who was considered rather flighty and too prone to find fun in things that others considered serious. A good thing she never quite lost that fault. Hannah resolutely and dutifully put out of her head (or nearly) all vagrant thoughts of Clint Darrow with the crisp black hair and the surprising blue eyes thereto, and the hat worn rakishly a little on one side, and the slender cane and the pointed shoes. A whipper-snapper, according to Horace Winter. Not a solid business man like Hermie Slocum. Hannah did not look upon herself as a human sacrifice. She was genuinely fond of Hermie. She was fond of her father, too; the rather harassed and hen-pecked Horace Winter; and of her mother, the voluble and quick-tongued and generous Bertha Winter, who was so often to be seen going down the street, shawl and bonnet-strings flying, when she should have been at home minding her household. Much of the minding had fallen to Hannah.

And so they were married, and went to the thriving city of Indianapolis to live, and Hannah Winter was so busy with her new household goods, and the linens, and the wine-coloured silk and its less magnificent satellites, that it was almost a fortnight before she realized fully that this solid young man, Hermie Slocum, was not only solid but immovable; not merely thrifty, but stingy; not alone taciturn but quite conversationless. His silences had not proceeded from the unplumbed depths of his knowledge. He merely had nothing to say. She learned, too, that the ten thousand dollars, soon dispelled, had been made for him by an energetic and shrewd business partner with whom he had quarrelled and from whom he had separated a few months before.

There never was another lump sum of ten thousand of Hermie Slocum's earning.

Well. Forty years ago, having made the worst of it you made the best of it. No going home to mother. The word "incompatibility" had not come into wide-spread use. Incompatibility was a thing to hide, not to flaunt. The years that followed were dramatic or commonplace, depending on one's sense of values. Certainly those years were like the married years of many another young woman of that unplastic day. Hannah Winter had her job cut out for her and she finished it well, and alone. No reproaches. Little complaint. Criticism she made in plenty, being the daughter of a voluble mother; and she never gave up hope of stiffening the spine of the invertebrate Hermie.

The ten thousand went in driblets. There never was anything dashing or romantic about Hermie Slocum's failures. The household never felt actual want, nor anything so picturesque as poverty. Hannah saw to that.

You should have read her letters back home to Chicago—to her mother and father back home on Rush Street, in Chicago; and to her girlhood friends, Sarah Clapp, Vinie Harden, and Julia Pierce. They were letters that, for stiff-lipped pride and brazen boasting, were of a piece with those written by Sentimental Tommy's mother when things were going worst with her.

"My wine-coloured silk is almost worn out," she wrote. "I'm thinking of making it over into a tea-gown with one of those new cream pongee panels down the front. Hermie says he's tired of seeing me in it, evenings. He wants me to get a blue but I tell him I'm too black for blue. Aren't men stupid about clothes! Though I pretend to Hermie that I think his taste is excellent, even when he brings me home one of those expensive beaded mantles I detest."

Bald, bare-faced, brave lying.

The two children arrived with mathematical promptness—first Horace, named after his grandfather Winter, of course; then Martha, named after no one in particular, but so called because Hermie Slocum insisted, stubbornly, that Martha was a good name for a girl. Martha herself fixed all that by the simple process of signing herself Marcia in her twelfth year and forever after. Marcia was a throw-back to her grandmother Winter—quick-tongued, restless, volatile. The boy was an admirable mixture of the best qualities of his father and mother; slow-going, like Hermie Slocum, but arriving surely at his goal, like his mother. With something of her driving force mixed with anything his father had of gentleness. A fine boy, and uninteresting. It was Hannah Winter's boast that Horace never caused her a moment's sorrow or uneasiness in all his life; and so Marcia, the troublous, was naturally her pride and idol.

As Hermie's business slid gently downhill Hannah tried with all her strength to stop it. She had a shrewd latent business sense and this she vainly tried to instil in her husband. The children, stirring in their sleep in the bedroom adjoining that of their parents, would realize, vaguely, that she was urging him to try something to which he was opposed. They would grunt and whimper a little, and perhaps remonstrate sleepily at being thus disturbed, and then drop off to sleep again to the sound of her desperate murmurs. For she was desperate. She was resolved not to go to her people for help. And it seemed inevitable if Hermie did not heed her. She saw that he was unsuited for business of the mercantile sort; urged him to take up the selling of insurance, just then getting such a strong and wide hold on the country.

In the end he did take it up, and would have made a failure of that, too, if it had not been for Hannah. It was Hannah who made friends for him, sought out prospective clients for him, led social conversation into business channels whenever chance presented itself. She had the boy and girl to think of and plan for. When Hermie objected to this or that luxury for them as being stuff and nonsense Hannah would say, not without a touch of bitterness, "I want them to have every advantage I can give them. I want them to have all the advantages I never had when I was young."

"They'll never thank you for it."

"I don't want them to."

Adam and Eve doubtless had the same argument about the bringing up of Cain and Abel. And Adam probably said, after Cain's shocking crime, "Well, what did I tell you! Was I right or was I wrong? Who spoiled him in the first place!"

They had been married seventeen years when Hermie Slocum, fifty-two, died of pneumonia following a heavy cold. The thirty-seven-year-old widow was horrified (but not much surprised) to find that the insurance solicitor had allowed two of his own policies to lapse. The company was kind, but businesslike. The insurance amounted, in all, to about nine thousand dollars. Trust Hermie for never quite equalling that ten again.

They offered her the agency left vacant by her husband, after her first two intelligent talks with them.

"No," she said, "not here. I'm going back to Chicago to sell insurance. Everybody knows me there. My father was an old settler in Chicago. There'll be my friends, and their husbands, and their sons. Besides, the children will have advantages there. I'm going back to Chicago."

She went. Horace and Bertha Winter had died five years before, within less than a year of each other. The old Rush Street house had been sold. The neighbourhood was falling into decay. The widow and her two children took a little flat on the south side. Widowed, one might with equanimity admit stress of circumstance. It was only when one had a husband that it was disgraceful to show him to the world as a bad provider.

"I suppose we lived too well," Hannah said when her old friends expressed concern at her plight. "Hermie was too generous. But I don't mind working. It keeps me young."

And so, truly, it did. She sold not only insurance but coal, a thing which rather shocked her south side friends. She took orders for tons of this and tons of that, making a neat commission thereby. She had a desk in the office of a big insurance company on Dearborn, near Monroe, and there you saw her every morning at ten in her neat sailor hat and her neat tailored suit. Four hours of work lay behind that ten o'clock appearance. The children were off to school a little after eight. But there was the ordering to do; cleaning; sewing; preserving, mending. A woman came in for a few hours every day but there was no room for a resident helper. At night there were a hundred tasks. She helped the boy and girl with their home lessons, as well, being naturally quick at mathematics. The boy Horace had early expressed the wish to be an engineer and Hannah contemplated sending him to the University of Wisconsin because she had heard that there the engineering courses were particularly fine. Not only that, she actually sent him.

Marcia showed no special talent. She was quick, clever, pretty, and usually more deeply engaged in some school-girl love affair than Hannah Winter approved. She would be an early bride, one could see that. No career for Marcia, though she sketched rather well, sewed cleverly, played the piano a little, sang just a bit, could trim a hat or turn a dress, danced the steps of the day. She could even cook a commendable dinner. Hannah saw to that. She saw to it, as well, that the boy and the girl went to the theatre occasionally; heard a concert at rare intervals. There was little money for luxuries. Sometimes Marcia said, thoughtlessly, "Mother, why do you wear those stiff plain things all the time?"

Hannah, who had her own notion of humour, would reply, "The better to clothe you, my dear."

Her girlhood friends she saw seldom. Two of them had married. One was a spinster of forty. They had all moved to the south side during the period of popularity briefly enjoyed by that section in the late '90s. Hannah had no time for their afternoon affairs. At night she was too tired or too busy for outside diversions. When they met her they said, "Hannah Winter, you don't grow a day older. How do you do it!"

"Hard work."

"A person never sees you. Why don't you take an afternoon off some time? Or come in some evening? Henry was saying only yesterday that he enjoyed his talk with you so much, and that you were smarter than any man insurance agent. He said you sold him I don't know how many thousand dollars' worth before he knew it. Now I suppose I'll have to go without a new fur coat this winter."

Hannah smiled agreeably. "Well, Julia, it's better for you to do without a new fur coat this winter than for me to do without any."

The Clint Darrow of her girlhood dreams, grown rather paunchy and mottled now, and with the curling black hair but a sparse grizzled fringe, had belied Horace Winter's contemptuous opinion. He was a moneyed man now, with an extravagant wife, but no children. Hannah underwrote him for a handsome sum, received his heavy compliments with a deft detachment, heard his complaints about his extravagant wife with a sympathetic expression, but no comment—and that night spent the ten minutes before she dropped off to sleep in pondering the impenetrable mysteries of the institution called marriage. She had married the solid Hermie, and he had turned out to be quicksand. She had not married the whipper-snapper Clint, and now he was one of the rich city's rich men. Had she married him against her parents' wishes would Clint Darrow now be complaining of her extravagance, perhaps, to some woman he had known in his youth? She laughed a little, to herself, there in the dark.

"What in the world are you giggling about, Mother?" called Marcia, who slept in the bedroom near by. Hannah occupied the davenport couch in the sitting room. There had been some argument about that. But Hannah had said she preferred it; and the boy and girl finally ceased to object. Horace in the back bedroom, Marcia in the front bedroom, Hannah in the sitting room. She made many mistakes like that. So, then, "What in the world are you giggling about, Mother?"

"Only a game," answered Hannah, "that some people were playing to-day."

"A new game?"

"Oh, my, no!" said Hannah, and laughed again. "It's old as the world."

Hannah was forty-seven when Marcia married. Marcia married well. Not brilliantly, of course, but well. Edward was with the firm of Gaige & Hoe, Importers. He had stock in the company and an excellent salary, with prospects. With Horace away at the engineering school Hannah's achievement of Marcia's trousseau was an almost superhuman feat. But it was a trousseau complete. As they selected the monogrammed linens, the hand-made lingerie, the satin-covered down quilts, the smart frocks, Hannah thought, quite without bitterness, of the wine-coloured silk. Marcia was married in white. She was blonde, with a fine fair skin, in her father's likeness, and she made a picture-book bride. She and Ed took a nice little six-room apartment on Hyde Park Boulevard, near the Park and the lake. There was some talk of Hannah's coming to live with them but she soon put that right.

"No," she had said, at once. "None of that. No flat was ever built that was big enough for two families."

"But you're not a family, Mother. You're us."

Hannah, though, was wiser than that.

She went up to Madison for Horace's commencement. He was very proud of his youthful looking, well-dressed, intelligent mother. He introduced her, with pride, to the fellows. But there was more than pride in his tone when he brought up Louise. Hannah knew then, at once. Horace had said that he would start to pay back his mother for his university training with the money earned from his very first job. But now he and Hannah had a talk. Hannah hid her own pangs—quite natural pangs of jealousy and something very like resentment.

"There aren't many Louises," said Hannah. "And waiting doesn't do, somehow. You're an early marrier, Horace. The steady, dependable kind. I'd be a pretty poor sort of mother, wouldn't I, if——" etc.

Horace's first job took him out to South America. He was jubilant, excited, remorseful, eager, downcast, all at once. He and Louise were married a month before the time set for leaving and she went with him. It was a job for a young and hardy and adventurous. On the day they left, Hannah felt, for the first time in her life, bereaved, widowed, cheated.

There followed, then, ten years of hard work and rigid economy. She lived in good boarding houses, and hated them. She hated them so much that, toward the end, she failed even to find amusement in the inevitable wall pictures of plump, partially draped ladies lounging on couches and being tickled in their sleep by overfed cupids in mid-air. She saved and scrimped with an eye to the time when she would no longer work. She made some shrewd and well-advised investments. At the end of these ten years she found herself possessed of a considerable sum whose investment brought her a sufficient income, with careful management.

Life had tricked Hannah Winter, but it had not beaten her. And there, commonplace or dramatic, depending on one's viewpoint, you have the first sixty years of Hannah Winter's existence.

This is the curious thing about them. Though heavy, these years had flown. The working, the planning, the hoping, had sped them by, somehow. True, things that never used to tire her tired her now, and she acknowledged it. She was older, of course. But she never thought of herself as old. Perhaps she did not allow herself to think thus. She had married, brought children into the world, made their future sure—or as sure as is humanly possible. And yet she never said, "My work is done. My life is over." About the future she was still as eager as a girl. She was a grandmother. Marcia and Ed had two children, Joan, nine, and Peter, seven (strong simple names were the mode just then).

Perhaps you know that hotel on the lake front built during the World's Fair days? A roomy, rambling, smoke-blackened, comfortable old structure, ringed with verandas, its shabby façade shabbier by contrast with the beds of tulips or geraniums or canna that jewel its lawn. There Hannah Winter went to live. It was within five minutes' walk of Marcia's apartment. Rather expensive, but as homelike as a hotel could be and housing many old-time Chicago friends.

She had one room, rather small, with a bit of the lake to be seen from one window. The grim, old-fashioned hotel furniture she lightened and supplemented with some of her own things. There was a day bed—a narrow and spindling affair for a woman of her height and comfortable plumpness. In the daytime this couch was decked out with taffeta pillows in rose and blue, with silk fruit and flowers on them, and gold braid. There were two silk-shaded lamps, a shelf of books, the photographs of the children in flat silver frames, a leather writing set on the desk, curtains of pale tan English casement cloth at the windows. A cheerful enough little room.

There were many elderly widows like herself living in the hotel on slender, but sufficient, incomes. They were well-dressed women in trim suits or crêpes, and Field's special walking oxfords; and small smart hats. They did a little cooking in their rooms—not much, they hastened to tell you. Their breakfasts only—a cup of coffee and a roll or a slice of toast, done on a little electric grill, the coffee above, the toast below. The hotel dining room was almost free of women in the morning. There were only the men, intent on their papers, and their eggs and the 8.40 I. C. train. It was like a men's club, except, perhaps, for an occasional business woman successful enough or indolent enough to do away with the cooking of the surreptitious matutinal egg in her own room. Sometimes, if they were to lunch at home, they carried in a bit of cold ham, or cheese, rolls, butter, or small dry groceries concealed in muffs or handbags. They even had diminutive iceboxes in closets. The hotel, perforce, shut its eyes to this sort of thing. Even permitted the distribution of tiny cubes of ice by the hotel porter. It was a harmless kind of cheating. Their good dinners they ate in the hotel dining room when not invited to dine with married sons or daughters or friends.

At ten or eleven in the morning you saw them issue forth, or you saw "little" manicures going in. One spoke of these as "little" not because of their size, which was normal, but in definition of their prices. There were "little" dressmakers as well, and "little" tailors. In special session they confided to one another the names or addresses of any of these who happened to be especially deft, or cheap, or modish.

"I've found a little tailor over on Fifty-fifth. I don't want you to tell any one else about him. He's wonderful. He's making me a suit that looks exactly like the model Hexter's got this year and guess what he's charging!" The guess was, of course, always a triumph for the discoverer of the little tailor.

The great lake dimpled or roared not twenty feet away. The park offered shade and quiet. The broad veranda invited one with its ample armchairs. You would have thought that peace and comfort had come at last to this shrewd, knowledgeous, hard-worked woman of sixty. She was handsomer than she had been at twenty or thirty. The white powdering her black hair softened her face, lightened her sallow skin, gave a finer lustre to her dark eyes. She used a good powder and had an occasional facial massage. Her figure, though full, was erect, firm, neat. Around her throat she wore an inch-wide band of black velvet that becomingly hid the chords and sagging chin muscles.

Yet now, if ever in her life, Hannah Winter was a slave.

Every morning at eight o'clock Marcia telephoned her mother. The hotel calls cost ten cents, but Marcia's was an unlimited phone. The conversation would start with a formula.

"Hello—Mama?... How are you?"

"Fine."

"Sleep all right?"

"Oh, yes. I never sleep all night through any more."

"Oh, you probably just think you don't.... Are you doing anything special this morning?"

"Well, I——Why?"

"Nothing. I just wondered if you'd mind taking Joan to the dentist's. Her brace came off again this morning at breakfast. I don't see how I can take her because Elsie's giving that luncheon at one, you know, and the man's coming about upholstering that big chair at ten. I'd call up and try to get out of the luncheon, but I've promised, and there's bridge afterward and it's too late now for Elsie to get a fourth. Besides, I did that to her once before and she was furious. Of course, if you can't ... But I thought if you haven't anything to do, really, why——"

Through Hannah Winter's mind would flash the events of the day as she had planned it. She had meant to go downtown shopping that morning. Nothing special. Some business at the bank. Mandel's had advertised a sale of foulards. She hated foulards with their ugly sprawling patterns. A nice, elderly sort of material. Marcia was always urging her to get one. Hannah knew she never would. She liked the shops in their spring vividness. She had a shrewd eye for a bargain. A bite of lunch somewhere; then she had planned to drop in at that lecture at the Woman's Club. It was by the man who wrote "Your Town." He was said to be very lively and insulting. She would be home by five, running in to see the children for a minute before going to her hotel to rest before dinner.

A selfish day, perhaps. But forty years of unselfish ones had paid for it. Well. Shopping with nine-year-old Joan was out of the question. So, too, was the lecture. After the dentist had mended the brace Joan would have to be brought home for her lunch. Peter would be there, too. It was Easter vacation time. Hannah probably would lunch with them, in Marcia's absence, nagging them a little about their spinach and chop and apple sauce. She hated to see the two children at table alone, though Marcia said that was nonsense.

Hannah and Marcia differed about a lot of things. Hannah had fallen into the bad habit of saying, "When you were children I didn't——"

"Yes, but things are different now, please remember, Mother. I want my children to have all the advantages I can give them. I want them to have all the advantages I never had."

If Ed was present at such times he would look up from his paper to say, "The kids'll never thank you for it, Marsh."

"I don't want them to."

There was something strangely familiar about the whole thing as it sounded in Hannah's ears.

The matter of the brace, alone. There was a tiny gap between Joan's two front teeth and, strangely enough, between Peter's as well. Itseemed to Hannah that every well-to-do child in Hyde Park had developed this gap between the two incisors and that all the soft pink child mouths in the district parted to display a hideous and disfiguring arrangement of complicated wire and metal. The process of bringing these teeth together was a long and costly one, totalling between six hundred and two thousand dollars, depending on the reluctance with which the parted teeth met, and the financial standing of the teeths' progenitors. Peter's dental process was not to begin for another year. Eight was considered the age. It seemed to be as common as vaccination.

From Hannah: "I don't know what's the matter with children's teeth nowadays. My children's teeth never had to have all this contraption on them. You got your teeth and that was the end of it."

"Perhaps if they'd paid proper attention to them," Marcia would reply, "there wouldn't be so many people going about with disfigured jaws now."

Then there were the dancing lessons. Joan went twice a week, Peter once. Joan danced very well the highly technical steps of the sophisticated dances taught her at the Krisiloff School. Her sturdy little legs were trained at the practice bar. Her baby arms curved obediently above her head or in fixed relation to the curve of her body in the dance. She understood and carried into effect the French technical terms. It was called gymnastic and interpretive dancing. There was about it none of the spontaneity with which a child unconsciously endows impromptu dance steps. But it was graceful and lovely. Hannah thought Joan a second Pavlowa; took vast delight in watching her. Taking Joan and Peter to these dancing classes was one of the duties that often devolved upon her. In the children's early years Marcia had attended a child study class twice a week and Hannah had more or less minded the two in their mother's absence. The incongruity of this had never struck her. Or if it had she had never mentioned it to Marcia. There were a good many things she never mentioned to Marcia. Marcia was undoubtedly a conscientious mother, thinking of her children, planning for her children, hourly: their food, their clothes, their training, their manners, their education. Asparagus; steak; French; health shoes; fingernails; dancing; teeth; hair; curtseys.

"Train all the independence out of 'em," Hannah said sometimes, grimly. Not to Marcia, though. She said it sometimes to her friends Julia Pierce or Sarah Clapp, or even to Vinie Harding, the spinster of sixty, for all three, including the spinster Vinie, who was a great-aunt, seemed to be living much the same life that had fallen to Hannah Winter's lot.

Hyde Park was full of pretty, well-dressed, energetic young mothers who were leaning hard upon the Hannah Winters of their own families. You saw any number of grey-haired, modishly gowned grandmothers trundling go-carts; walking slowly with a moist baby fist in their gentle clasp; seated on park benches before which blue rompers dug in the sand or gravel or tumbled on the grass. The pretty young mothers seemed very busy, too, in another direction. They attended classes, played bridge, marketed, shopped, managed their households. Some of them had gone in for careers. None of them seemed conscious of the frequency with which they said, "Mother, will you take the children from two to five this afternoon?" Or, if they were conscious of it, they regarded it as a natural and normal request. What are grandmothers for?

Hannah Winter loved the feel of the small velvet hands in her own palm. The clear blue-white of their eyes, the softness of their hair, the very feel of their firm, strong bare legs gave her an actual pang of joy. But a half hour—an hour—with them, and she grew restless, irritable. She didn't try to define this feeling.

"You say you love the children. And yet when I ask you to be with them for half a day——"

"I do love them. But they make me nervous."

"I don't see how they can make you nervous if you really care about them."

Joan was Hannah's favourite; resembled her. The boy, Peter, was blond, like his mother. In Joan was repeated the grandmother's sallow skin, dark eyes, vivacity, force. The two, so far apart in years, were united by a strong natural bond of sympathy and alikeness. When they were together on some errand or excursion they had a fine time. If it didn't last too long.

Sometimes the young married women would complain to each other about their mothers. "I don't ask her often, goodness knows. But I think she might offer to take the children one or two afternoons during their vacation, anyway. She hasn't a thing to do. Not a thing."

Among themselves the grandmothers did not say so much. They had gone to a sterner school. But it had come to this: Hannah was afraid to plan her day. So often had she found herself called upon to forego an afternoon at bridge, a morning's shopping, an hour's mending, even, or reading.

She often had dinner at Marcia's, but not as often as she was asked. More and more she longed for and appreciated the orderly quiet and solitude of her own little room. She never analyzed this, nor did Marcia or Ed. It was a craving for relaxation on the part of body and nerves strained throughout almost half a century of intensive living.

Ed and Marcia were always doing charming things for her. Marcia had made the cushions and the silk lampshades for her room. Marcia was always bringing her jellies, and a quarter of a freshly baked cake done in black Lutie's best style. Ed and Marcia insisted periodically on her going with them to the theatre or downtown for dinner, or to one of the gardens where there was music and dancing and dining. This was known as "taking mother out." Hannah Winter didn't enjoy these affairs as much, perhaps, as she should have. She much preferred a mild spree with one of her own cronies. Ed was very careful of her at street crossings and going down steps, and joggled her elbow a good deal. This irked her, though she tried not to show it. She preferred a matinée, or a good picture or a concert with Sarah, or Vinie, or Julia. They could giggle, and nudge and comment like girls together, and did. Indeed, they were girls in all but outward semblance. Among one another they recognized this. Their sense of enjoyment was un-dulled. They liked a double chocolate ice cream soda as well as ever; a new gown; an interesting book. As for people! Why, at sixty the world walked before them, these elderly women, its mind unclothed, all-revealing. This was painful, sometimes, but interesting always. It was one of the penalties—and one of the rewards—of living.

After some such excursion Hannah couldn't very well refuse to take the children to see a Fairbanks film on a Sunday afternoon when Ed and Marcia were spending the half-day at the country club. Marcia was very strict about the children and the films. They were allowed the saccharine Pickford, and of course Fairbanks's gravity-defying feats, and Chaplin's gorgeous grotesqueries. You had to read the titles for Peter. Hannah wasn't as quick at this as were Ed or Marcia, and Peter was sometimes impatient, though politely so.

And so sixty swung round. At sixty Hannah Winter had a suitor. Inwardly she resented him. At sixty Clint Darrow, a widower now and reverent in speech of the departed one whose extravagance he had deplored, came to live at the hotel in three-room grandeur, overlooking the lake. A ruddy, corpulent, paunchy little man, and rakish withal. The hotel widows made much of him. Hannah, holding herself aloof, was often surprised to find her girlhood flame hovering near now, speaking of loneliness, of trips abroad, of a string of pearls unused. There was something virgin about the way Hannah received these advances. Marriage was so far from her thoughts; this kindly, plump little man so entirely outside her plans. He told her his troubles, which should have warned her. She gave him some shrewd advice, which encouraged him. He rather fancied himself as a Lothario. He was secretly distressed about his rotund waist line and, theoretically, never ate a bite of lunch. "I never touch a morsel from breakfast until dinner time." Still you might see him any day at noon at the Congress, or at the Athletic Club, or at one of the restaurants known for its savoury food, busy with one of the richer luncheon dishes and two cups of thick creamy coffee.

Though the entire hotel was watching her Hannah was actually unconscious of Clint Darrow's attentions, or their markedness, until her son-in-law Ed teased her about him one day. "Some gal!" said Ed, and roared with laughter. She resented this indignantly; felt that they regarded her as senile. She looked upon Clint Darrow as a fat old thing, if she looked at him at all; but rather pathetic, too. Hence her kindliness toward him. Now she avoided him. Thus goaded he actually proposed marriage and repeated the items of the European trip, the pearls, and the unused house on Woodlawn Avenue. Hannah, feeling suddenly faint and white, refused him awkwardly. She was almost indignant. She did not speak of it, but the hotel, somehow, knew. Hyde Park knew. The thing leaked out.

"But why?" said Marcia, smiling—giggling, almost. "Why? I think it would have been wonderful for you, Mother!"

Hannah suddenly felt that she need not degrade herself to explain why—she who had once triumphed over her own ordeal of marriage.

Marcia herself was planning a new career. The children were seven and nine—very nearly eight and ten. Marcia said she wanted a chance at self-expression. She announced a course in landscape gardening—"landscape architecture" was the new term.

"Chicago's full of people who are moving to the suburbs and buying big places out north. They don't know a thing about gardens. They don't know a shrub from a tree when they see it. It's a new field for women—in the country, at least—and I'm dying to try it. That youngest Fraser girl makes heaps, and I never thought much of her intelligence. Of course, after I finish and am ready to take commissions, I'll have to be content with small jobs, at first. But later I may get a chance at grounds around public libraries and hospitals and railway stations. And if I can get one really big job at one of those new-rich north shore places I'll be made."

The course required two years and was rather expensive. But Marcia said it would pay, in the end. Besides, now that the war had knocked Ed's business into a cocked hat for the next five years or more, the extra money would come in very handy for the children and herself and the household.

Hannah thought the whole plan nonsense. "I can't see that you're pinched, exactly. You may have to think a minute before you buy fresh strawberries for a meringue in February. But you do buy them." She was remembering her own lean days, when February strawberries would have been as unattainable as though she had dwelt on a desert island.

On the day of the mirror accident in Peacock Alley, Hannah was meeting Marcia downtown for the purpose of helping her select spring outfits for the children. Later, Marcia explained, there would be no time. Her class met every morning except Saturday. Hannah tried to deny the little pang of terror at the prospect of new responsibility that this latest move of Marcia's seemed about to thrust upon her. Marcia wasn't covering her own job, she told herself. Why take another! She had given up an afternoon with Sarah because of this need of Marcia's to-day. Marcia depended upon her mother's shopping judgment more than she admitted. Thinking thus, and conscious of her tardiness (she had napped for ten minutes after lunch) Hannah Winter had met, face to face, with a crash, this strange, strained, rather haggard elderly woman in the mirror.

It was, then, ten minutes later than 2.07 when she finally came up to Marcia waiting, lips compressed, at the Michigan Avenue entrance, as planned.

"I bumped into that mirror——"

"Oh, Mom! I'm sorry. Are you hurt? How in the world?... Such a morning ... wash day ... children their lunch ... marketing ... wall paper ... Fifty-third Street ... two o'clock ..."

Suddenly, "Yes, I know," said Hannah Winter, tartly. "I had to do all those things and more, forty years ago."

Marcia had a list.... Let's see ... Those smocked dresses for Joan would probably be all picked over by this time ... Light-weight underwear for Peter ... Joan's cape ...

Hannah Winter felt herself suddenly remote from all this; done with it; finished years and years ago. What had she to do with smocked dresses, children's underwear, capes? But she went in and out of the shops, up and down the aisles, automatically, gave expert opinion. By five it was over. Hannah felt tired, depressed. She was to have dinner at Marcia's to-night. She longed, now, for her own room. Wished she might go to it and stay there, quietly.

"Marcia, I don't think I'll come to dinner to-night. I'm so tired. I think I'll just go home——"

"But I got the broilers specially for you, and the sweet potatoes candied the way you like them, and a lemon cream pie."

When they reached home they found Joan, listless, on the steps. One of her sudden sore throats. Stomach, probably. A day in bed for her. By to-morrow she would be quite all right. Hannah Winter wondered why she did not feel more concern. Joan's throats had always thrown her into a greater panic than she had ever felt at her own children's illnesses. To-day she felt apathetic, indifferent.

She helped tuck the rebellious Joan in bed. Joan was spluttering about some plan for to-morrow. And Marcia was saying, "But you can't go to-morrow, Joan. You know you can't, with that throat. Mother will have to stay home with you, too, and give up her plans to go to the country club with Daddy, and it's the last chance she'll have, too, for a long, long time. So you're not the only one to suffer." Hannah Winter said nothing.

They went in to dinner at 6.30. It was a good dinner. Hannah Winter ate little, said little. Inside Hannah Winter a voice—a great, strong voice, shaking with its own earnestness and force—was shouting in rebellion. And over and over it said, to the woman in the mirror at the north end of Peacock Alley: "Three score—and ten to go. That's what it says—'and ten.' And I haven't done a thing I've wanted to do. I'm afraid to do the things I want to do. We all are, because of our sons and daughters. Ten years. I don't want to spend those ten years taking care of my daughter's children. I've taken care of my own. A good job, too. No one helped me. No one helped me. What's the matter with these modern mothers, with their newfangled methods and their efficiency and all? Maybe I'm an unnatural grandmother, but I'm going to tell Marcia the truth. Yes, I am. If she asks me to stay home with Joan and Peter to-morrow, while she and Ed go off to the country club, I'm going to say, 'No!' I'm going to say, 'Listen to me, Ed and Marcia. I don't intend to spend the rest of my life toddling children to the park and playing second assistant nursemaid. I'm too old—or too young. I've only got ten years to go, according to the Bible, and I want to have my fun. I've sown. I want to reap. My teeth are pretty good, and so is my stomach. They're better than yours will be at my age, for all your smart new dentists. So are my heart and my arteries and my liver and my nerves. Well. I don't want luxury. What I want is leisure. I want to do the things I've wanted to do for forty years, and couldn't. I want, if I feel like it, to start to learn French and read Jane Austen and stay in bed till noon. I never could stay in bed till noon, and I know I can't learn now, but I'm going to do it once, if it kills me. I'm too old to bring up a second crop of children, I want to play. It's terrible to realize that you don't learn how to live until you're ready to die; and, then it's too late. I know I sound like a selfish old woman, and I am, and I don't care. I don't care. I want to be selfish. So will you, too, when you're sixty, Martha Slocum. You think you're young. But all of a sudden you'll be sixty, like me. All of a sudden you'll realize——"

"Mother, you're not eating a thing." Ed's kindly voice.

Marcia, flushed of face, pushed her hair back from her forehead with a little frenzied familiar gesture. "Eat! Who could eat with Joan making that insane racket in there! Ed, will you tell her to stop! Can't you speak to her just once! After all, she is your child, too, you know.... Peter, eat your lettuce or you can't have any dessert."

How tired she looked, Hannah Winter thought. Little Martha. Two babies, and she only a baby herself yesterday. How tired she looked.

"I wanna go!" wailed Joan, from her bedroom prison. "I wanna go to-morrow. You promised me. You said I could. I wanna GO!"

"And I say you can't. Mother has to give up her holiday, too, because of you. And yet you don't hear me——"

"You!" shouted the naughty Joan, great-granddaughter of her great-grandmother, and granddaughter of her grandmamma. "*You* don't care. Giving up's easy for you. You're an old lady."

And then Hannah Winter spoke up. "I'll stay with her to-morrow, Marcia. You and Ed go and have a good time."

IF I SHOULD EVER TRAVEL!

The	fabric	of	my	faithful	love
No	power	shall	dim	or	ravel
Whilst	I	stay	here,—but	oh,	my	dear,
If	I	should	ever	travel!

—Millay.

If you've spent more than one day in Okoochee, Oklahoma, you've had dinner at Pardee's. Someone—a business acquaintance, a friend, a townsman—has said, "Oh, you stopping at the Okmulgee Hotel? WON—derful, isn't it? Nothing finer here to the Coast. I bet you thought you were coming to the wilderness, didn't you? You Easterners! Think we live in tents and eat jerked venison and maize, huh? Never expected, I bet, to see a twelve-story hotel with separate ice-water faucet in every bathroom and a bath to every room. What'd you think of the Peacock grill, h'm?"

"Well—uh"—hesitatingly—"very nice, but why don't you have something native ... Decorations and ... Peacock grill is New York, not Okla——"

"Z'that so! Well, let me tell you you won't find any better food or service in any restaurant, New York or I don't care where. But say, hotel meals are hotel meals. You get tired of 'em. Ever eat at Pardee's, up the street? Say, there's food! If you're going to be here in town any time why'n't you call up there some evening before six—you have to leave 'em know—and get one of Pardee's dinners? Thursday's chicken. And when I say chicken I mean——Well, just try it, that's all.... And for God's sake don't make a mistake and tip Maxine."

Pardee's you find to be a plain box-like two-story frame house in a quiet and commonplace residential district. Plainly—almost scantily—furnished as to living room and dining room. The dining room comfortably seats just twenty, but the Pardees "take" eighteen diners—no more. This because Mrs. Pardee has eighteen of everything in silver. And that means eighteen of everything from grapefruit spoons to cheese knives; and finger bowls before and after until you feel like an early Roman. As for Maxine—the friendly warning is superfluous. You would as soon have thought of slipping Hebe a quarter on Olympus—a rather severe-featured Hebe in a white silk blouse ordered through *Vogue*.

All this should have been told in the past tense, because Pardee's is no more. But Okoochee, Oklahoma, is full of paradoxes like Pardee's. Before you understand Maxine Pardee and her mother in the kitchen (dishing up) you have to know Okoochee. And before you know Okoochee you have to know Sam Pardee, missing.

There are all sorts of stories about Okoochee, Oklahoma—and almost every one of them is true. Especially are the fantastic ones true—the incredible ones. The truer they are the more do they make such Arabian knights as Aladdin and Ali Baba appear dull and worthy gentlemen in the retail lamp and oil business, respectively. Ali Baba's exploit in oil, indeed, would have appeared too trivial for recounting if compared with that of any one of a dozen Okoochee oil wizards.

Take the tale of the Barstows alone, though it hasn't the slightest bearing on this story. Thirteen years ago the Barstows had a parched little farm on the outskirts of what is now the near-metropolis of Okoochee, but what was then a straggling village in the Indian Territory. Ma Barstow was a woman of thirty-five who looked sixty; withered by child-bearing; scorched by the sun; beaten by the wind; gnarled with toil; gritty with dust. Ploughing the barren little farm one day Clem Barstow had noticed a strange oily scum. It seeped up through the soil and lay there, heavily. Oil! Weeks of suspense, weeks of disappointment, weeks of hope. Through it all Ma Barstow had washed, scrubbed, cooked as usual, and had looked after the welfare of the Barstow litter. Seventeen years of drudgery dull the imagination. When they struck the great gusher—it's still known as Barstow's Old Faithful—they came running to her with the news. She had been washing a great tubful of harsh greasy clothes—overalls, shirts, drawers. As the men came, shouting, she appeared in the doorway of the crazy wooden lean-to, wiping her hands on her apron.

"Oil!" they shouted, idiotically. "Millions! Biggest gusher yet! It'll mean millions! You're a millionaire!" Then, as she looked at them, dazedly, "What're you going to do, Mis' Barstow, huh? What're you going to do with it?"

Ma Barstow had brought one hand up to push back a straggling wisp of damp hair. Then she looked at that hand as she brought it down—looked at it and it's mate, parboiled, shrunken, big-knuckled from toil. She wiped them both on her apron again, bringing the palms down hard along her flat thighs. "Do?" The miracles that millions might accomplish burst full force on her work-numbed brain. "Do? First off I'm a-going to have the washing done out."

Last week Mrs. Clement Barstow was runner-up in the women's amateur golf tournament played on the Okoochee eighteen-hole course. She wore tweed knickers. The Barstow place on the Edgecombe Road is so honeycombed with sleeping porches, sun dials, swimming pools, bird baths, terraces, sunken gardens, and Italian marble benches that the second assistant Japanese gardener has to show you the way to the tennis courts.

That's Okoochee.

It was inevitable that Sam Pardee should hear of Okoochee; and, hearing of it, drift there. Sam Pardee was drawn to a new town, a boom town, as unerringly as a small boy scents a street fight. Born seventy-five years earlier he would certainly have been one of those intrepid Forty-niners; a fearless canvas-covered fleet crawling painfully across a continent, conquering desert and plain and mountain; starving, thirsting, fighting Indians, eating each other if necessity demanded, with equal dexterity and dispatch. Perhaps a trip like this would have satisfied his wanderlust. Probably not. He was like a child in a berry patch. The fruit just beyond was always the ripest and reddest. The Klondike didn't do it. He was one of the first up the Yukon in that mad rush. He returned minus all the money and equipment with which he had started, including the great toe of his right foot—tribute levied by the frozen North. From boom town to boom town he went. The first stampede always found him there, deep in blue-prints, engineering sheets, prospectuses. But no sooner did the town install a water-works and the First National Bank house itself in a Portland-cement Greek temple with Roman pillars and a mosaic floor than he grew restless and was on the move.

A swashbuckler, Sam Pardee, in tan shoes and a brown derby. An 1890 Villon handicapped by a home-loving wife; an incurable romantic married to a woman who judged as shiftless any housewife possessed of less than two dozen bath towels, twelve tablecloths, eighteen wash cloths, and at least three dozen dish towels, hand-hemmed.

Milly Pardee's idea of adventure was testing the recipes illustrated in the How To Use The Cheaper Cuts page in the back of the woman's magazines.

Perversely enough, they had been drawn together by the very attraction of dissimilarity. He had found her feminine home-loving qualities most appealing. His manner of wearing an invisible cloak, sword and buckler, though actually garbed in ready-mades, thrilled her. She had come of a good family; he of, seemingly, no family at all. When the two married, Milly's people went through that ablutionary process known as washing their hands of her. Thus ideally mismated they tried to make the best of it—and failed. At least, Sam Pardee failed. Milly Pardee said, "Goodness knows I tried to be a good wife to him." The plaint of all unappreciated wives since Griselda.

Theirs was a feast-and-famine existence. Sometimes Sam Pardee made sudden thousands. Mrs. Pardee would buy silver, linen, and other household furnishings ranging all the way from a grand piano to a patent washing machine. The piano and the washing machine usually were whisked away within a few weeks or months, at the longest. But she cannily had the linen and silver stamped—stamped unmistakably and irrevocably with a large, flourishing capital P, embellished with floral wreaths. Eventually some of the silver went the way of the piano and washing machine. But Milly Pardee clung stubbornly to a dozen and a half of everything. She seemed to feel that if once she had less than eighteen fish forks the last of the solid ground of family respectability would sink under her feet. For years she carried that silver about wrapped in trunks full of the precious linen, and in old underwear and cotton flannel kimonos and Sam's silk socks and Maxine's discarded baby-clothes. She clung to it desperately, as other women cling to jewels, knowing that when this is gone no more will follow.

When the child was born Milly Pardee wanted to name her Myrtle but her husband had said, suddenly, "No, call her Maxine."

"After whom?" In Mrs. Pardee's code you named a child "after" someone.

He had seen Maxine Elliott in the heyday of her cold, clear, brainless beauty, with her great, slightly protuberant eyes set so far apart, her exquisitely chiselled white nose, and her black black hair. She had thrilled him.

"After my Uncle Max that lives in—uh—Australia."

"I've never heard you talk of any Uncle Max," said Mrs. Pardee, coldly.

But the name had won. How could they know that Maxine would grow up to be a rather bony young woman who preferred these high-collared white silk blouses; and said "eyether."

Maxine had been about twelve when Okoochee beckoned Sam Pardee. They were living in Chicago at the time; had been there for almost three years—that is, Mrs. Pardee and Maxine had been there. Sam was in and out on some mysterious business of his own. His affairs were always spoken of as "deals" or "propositions." And they always, seemingly, required his presence in a city other than that in which they were living—if living can be said to describe the exceedingly impermanent perch to which they clung. They had a four-room flat. Maxine was attending a good school. Mrs. Pardee was using the linen and silver daily. There was a linen closet down the hall, just off the dining room. You could open the door and feast your eyes on orderly piles of neatly laundered towels, sheets, tablecloths, napkins, tea towels. Mrs. Pardee marketed and cooked, contentedly. She was more than a merely good cook; she was an alchemist in food stuffs. Given such raw ingredients as butter, sugar, flour, eggs, she could evolve a structure of pure gold that melted on the tongue. She could take an ocherous old hen, dredge its parts in flour, brown it in fat sizzling with onion at the bottom of an iron kettle, add water, a splash of tomato and a pinch of seasoning, and bear triumphantly to the table a platter heaped with tender fricassee over which a smooth, saddle-brown gravy simmered fragrantly. She ate little herself, as do most expert cooks, and found her reward when Sam or Maxine uttered a choked and appreciative "Mmm!"

In the midst of creature comforts such as these Sam Pardee said, one evening, "Oil."

Mrs. Pardee passed it, but not without remonstrance. "It's the same identical French dressing you had last night, Sam. I mixed enough for twice. And you didn't add any oil last night."

Sam Pardee came out of his abstraction long enough to emit a roar of laughter and an unsatisfactory explanation. "I was thinking of oil in wells, not in cruets. Millions of barrels of oil, not a spoonful. Crude, not olive."

She saw her child, her peace, her linen closet threatened. "Sam Pardee, you don't mean——"

"Oklahoma. That's what I meant by oil. It's oozing with it."

Real terror leaped into Milly Pardee's eyes. "Not Oklahoma. Sam, I couldn't stand——" Suddenly she stiffened with resolve. Maxine's report card had boasted three stars that week. Oklahoma! Why, there probably were no schools at all in Oklahoma. "I won't bring my child up in Oklahoma. Indians, that's what! Scalped in our beds."

Above Sam Pardee's roar sounded Maxine's excited treble. "Oo, Oklahoma! I'd love it."

Her mother turned on her, almost fiercely. "You wouldn't."

The child had thrown out her arms in a wide gesture. "It sounds so far away and different. I like different places. I like any place that isn't here."

Milly Pardee had stared at her. It was the father talking in the child. Any place that isn't here. Different.

Out of years of bitter experience she tried to convince the child of her error; tried, as she had striven for years to convince Sam Pardee.

"Places are just the same," she said, bitterly, "and so are people, when you get to 'em."

"They can't be," the child argued, stubbornly. "India and China and Spain and Africa."

Milly Pardee had turned accusing eyes on her amused husband. "I hope you're satisfied."

He shrugged. "Well, the kid's right. That's living."

She disputed this, fiercely. "It is not. Living's staying in a place, and helping it grow, and growing up with it and belonging. Belong!" It was the cry of the rolling stone that is bruised and weary.

Sam Pardee left for Oklahoma the following week. Milly Pardee refused to accompany him. It was the first time she had taken this stand. "If you go there, and like it, and want to settle down there, I'll come. I know the Bible says, 'Whither thou goest, I will go,' but I guess even What'shername would have given up at Oklahoma."

For three years, then, Sam Pardee's letters reeked of oil: wells, strikes, gushers, drills, shares, outfits. It was early Oklahoma in the rough. This one was getting five hundred a day out of his well. That one had sunk forty thousand in his and lost out.

"Five hundred what?" Maxine asked. "Forty thousand what?"

"Dollars, I guess," Milly Pardee answered. "That's the way your father always talks. I'd rather have twenty-five a week, myself, and know it's coming without fail."

"I wouldn't. Where's the fun in that?"

"Fun! There's more fun in twenty-five a week in a pay envelope than in forty thousand down a dry well."

Maxine was fifteen now. "I wish we could live with Father in Oklahoma. I think it's wrong not to."

Milly Pardee was beginning to think so, too. Especially since her husband's letters had grown rarer as the checks they contained had grown larger. On his occasional trips back to Chicago he said nothing of their joining him out there. He seemed to have grown accustomed to living alone. Liked the freedom, the lack of responsibility. In sudden fright and resolve Milly Pardee sold the furnishings of the four-room flat, packed the peripatetic linen and silver, and joined a surprised and rather markedly unenthusiastic husband in Okoochee, Oklahoma. A wife and a fifteen-year-old daughter take a good deal of explaining on the part of one who has posed for three years as a bachelor.

The first thing Maxine said as they rode (in a taxi) to the hotel, was: "But the streets are paved!" Then, "But it's all electric lighted with cluster lights!" And, in final and utter disgust, "Why, there's a movie sign that says, 'The Perils of Pauline.' That was showing at the Élite on Forty-third Street in Chicago just the night before we left."

Milly Pardee smiled grimly. "Palestine's paved, too," she observed. "And they're probably running that same reel there next week."

Milly Pardee and her husband had a plain talk. Next day Sam Pardee rented the two-story frame house in which, for years, the famous Pardee dinners were to be served. But that came later. The house was rented with the understanding that the rent was to be considered as payment made toward final purchase. The three lived there in comfort. Maxine went to the new pressed-brick, many-windowed high school. Milly Pardee was happier than she had been in all her wedded life. Sam Pardee had made no fortune in oil, though he talked in terms of millions. In a burst of temporary prosperity, due to a boom in some oil-stocks Sam Pardee had purchased early in the game, they had paid five thousand dollars down on the house and lot. That left a bare thousand to pay. There were three good meals a day. Milly Pardee belonged to the Okoochee Woman's Thursday Club. All the women in Okoochee seemed to have come from St. Louis, Columbus, Omaha, Cleveland, Kansas City, and they spoke of these as Back East. When they came calling they left cards, punctiliously. They played bridge, observing all the newest rulings, and speaking with great elaborateness of manner.

"Yours, I believe, Mrs. Tutwiler."

"Pardon, but didn't you notice I played the ace?"

Maxine graduated in white, with a sash. Mrs. Pardee was on the committee to beautify the grounds around the M. K. & T. railroad station. When relatives from Back East (meaning Nebraska, Kansas, or Missouri) visited an Okoocheeite cards were sent out for an "At Home," and everything was as formal as a court levee in Victoria's time. Mrs. Pardee began to talk of buying an automobile. The town was full of them. There were the flivvers and lower middle-class cars owned by small merchants, natives (any one boasting twelve year's residence) and unsuccessful adventurers of the Sam Pardee type. Then there were the big, high-powered scouting cars driven by steely-eyed, wiry, cold-blooded young men from Pennsylvania and New York. These young men had no women-folk with them. Held conferences in smoke-filled rooms at the Okmulgee Hotel. The main business street was called Broadway, and the curb on either side was hidden by lines of cars drawn up slantwise at an angle of ninety. No farmer wagons. A small town with all the airs of a big one; with none of the charming informality of the old Southern small town; none of the engaging ruggedness of the established Middle-Western town; none of the faded gentility of the old New England town. A strident dame, this, in red satin and diamonds, insisting that she is a lady. Interesting, withal, and bulging with personality and possibility.

Milly Pardee loved it. She belonged. She was chairman of this committee and secretary of that. Okoochee was always having parades, with floats, sponsored by the Chamber of Commerce of Okoochee and distinguished by schoolgirls grouped on bunting-covered motor trucks, their hair loose and lately relieved from crimpers, three or four inches of sensible shirt-sleeve showing below the flowing lines of their cheesecloth Grecian robes. Maxine was often one of these. Yes, Milly Pardee was happy.

Sam Pardee was not. He began, suddenly, to talk of Mexico. Frankly, he was bored. For the first time in his life he owned a house—or nearly. There was eleven hundred dollars in the bank. Roast on Sunday. Bathroom shelf to be nailed Sunday morning. Y.M.C.A., Rotary Club, Knights of Columbus, Kiwanis, Boy Scouts.

"Hell," said Sam Pardee, "this town's no good."

Milly Pardee took a last stand. "Sam Pardee, I'll never leave here. I'm through traipsing up and down the world with you, like a gypsy. I want a home. I want to be settled. I want to stay here. And I'm going to."

"You're sure you want to stay?"

"I've moved for the last time. I—I'm going to plant a Burbank clamberer at the side of the porch, and they don't begin to flower till after the first ten years. That's how sure I am."

There came a look into Sam Pardee's eyes. He rubbed his neat brown derby round and round with his coat sleeve. He was just going out.

"Well, that's all right. I just wanted to know. Where's Max?"

"She stayed late. They're rehearsing for the Pageant of Progress down at the Library."

Sam Pardee looked thoughtful—a little regretful, one might almost have said. Then he clapped on the brown derby, paused on the top step of the porch to light his cigar, returned the greeting of young Arnold Hatch who was sprinkling the lawn next door, walked down the street with the quick, nervous step that characterized him, boarded the outgoing train for God knows where, and was never heard from again.

"Well," said the worse-than-widowed (it was her own term), "we've got the home."

She set about keeping it. We know that she had a gift for cooking that amounted almost to culinary inspiration. Pardee's dinners became an institution in Okoochee. Mrs. Pardee cooked. Maxine served. And not even the great new stucco palaces on the Edgecombe Road boasted finer silver, more exquisite napery. As for the food—old Clem Barstow himself, who had a chef and a butler and sent east for lobster and squabs weekly, came to Pardee's when he wanted a real meal. From the first they charged one dollar and fifty cents for their dinners. Okoochee, made mellow by the steaming soup, the savoury meats, the bland sauces and rich dessert, paid it ungrudgingly. They served only eighteen—no more, though Okoochee could never understand why. On each dinner Mrs. Pardee made a minimum of seventy-five cents. Eighteen times seventy-five ... naught and carry the four ... naught ... five ... thirteen-fifty ... seven times ... well, ninety-five dollars or thereabouts each week isn't so bad. Out of this Mrs. Pardee managed to bank a neat sum. She figured that at the end of ten or fifteen years....

"I hate them," said Maxine, washing dishes in the kitchen. "Greedy pigs."

"They're nothing of the kind. They like good food, and I'm thankful they do. If they didn't I don't know where I'd be."

"We might be anywhere—so long as it could be away from here. Dull, stupid, stick-in-the-muds, all of them."

"Why, they're no such thing, Maxine Pardee! They're from all over the world, pretty nearly. Why, just last Thursday they were counting there were sixteen different states represented in the eighteen people that sat down to dinner."

"Pooh! States! That isn't the world."

"What is, then?"

Maxine threw out her arms, sprinkling dish-water from her dripping finger tips with the wide-flung gesture. "Cairo! Zanzibar! Brazil! Trinidad! Seville—uh—Samar—Samarkand."

"Where's Samarkand?"

"I don't know. And I'm going to see it all some day. And the different people. The people that travel, and know about what kind of wine with the roast and the fish. You know—the kind in the novels that say, 'You've chilled this sauterne too much, Bemish.'"

"And when you do see all these places," retorted Mrs. Pardee, with the bitterness born of long years of experience, "you'll find that in every one of them somebody's got a boarding house called Pardee's, or something like that, where the people flock same's they do here, for a good meal."

"Yes, but what kind of people?"

"Same kind that comes here." Sam Pardee had once taken his wife to see a performance of The Man From Home when that comedy was at the height of its popularity. A line from this play flashed into Mrs. Pardee's mind now, and she paraphrased it deftly. "There are just as many kinds of people in Okoochee as there are in Zanzibar."

"I don't believe it."

"Well, it's so. And I'm thankful we've got the comforts of home."

At this Maxine laughed a sharp little laugh that was almost a bark. Perhaps she was justified.

The eighteen straggled in between six and six-thirty, nightly. A mixture of townspeople and strangers. While Maxine poured the water in the dining room the neat little parlour became a mess. The men threw hats and overcoats on the backs of the chairs. Their rubbers slopped under them. They rarely troubled to take them off. While waiting avidly for dinner to be served they struck matches and lighted cigarettes and cigars. Sometimes they called in to Maxine, "Say, girlie, when'll supper be ready? I'm 'bout gone."

The women trotted upstairs, chattering, and primped and fussed in Maxine's neat and austere little bedroom. They used Maxine's powder and dropped it about on the tidy dresser and the floor. They brushed away only what had settled on the front of their dresses. They forgot to switch off the electric light, leaving Maxine to do it, thriftily, between serving courses. Every penny counted. Every penny meant release.

After dinner Maxine and her mother sat down to eat off the edge of the kitchen table. It was often nine o'clock before the last straggling diner, sprawling on the parlour davenport with his evening paper and cigar, departed, leaving Maxine to pick up the scattered newspapers, cigarette butts, ashes; straighten chairs, lock doors.

Then the dishes. The dishes!

When Arnold Hatch asked her to go to a movie she shook her head, usually. "I'm too tired. I'm going to read, in bed."

"Read, read! That's all you do. What're you reading?"

"Oh, about Italy. La bel Napoli!" She collected travel folders and often talked in their terms. In her mind she always said "brooding Vesuvius"; "blue Mediterranean"; "azure coasts"; "Egypt's golden sands."

Arnold Hatch ate dinner nightly at Pardee's. He lived in the house next door, which he owned, renting it to an Okoochee family and retaining the upstairs front bedroom for himself. A tall, thin, eye-glassed young man who worked in the offices of the Okoochee Oil and Refining Company, believed in Okoochee, and wanted to marry Maxine. He had twice kissed her. On both these occasions his eyeglasses had fallen off, taking the passion, so to speak, out of the process. When Maxine giggled, uncontrollably, he said, "Go on—laugh! But some day I'm going to kiss you and I'll take my glasses off first. Then look out!"

You have to have a good deal of humour to stand being laughed at by a girl you've kissed; especially a girl who emphasizes her aloofness by wearing those high-collared white silk blouses.

"You haven't got a goitre, have you?" said Arnold Hatch, one evening, brutally. Then, as she had flared in protest, "I know it. I love that little creamy satin hollow at the base of your throat."

"You've never s——" The scarlet flamed up. She was human.

"I know it. But I love it just the same." Pretty good for a tall thin young man who worked in the offices of the Okoochee Oil and Refining Company.

Sometimes he said, "I'm darned certain you like me"—bravely—"love me. Why won't you marry me? Cut out all this slaving. I could support you. Not in much luxury, maybe, but——"

"And settle down in Okoochee! Never see anything! Stuck in this God-forsaken hole! This drab, dull, oil-soaked village! When there are wonderful people, wonderful places, colour, romance, beauty! Damascus! Mandalay! Singapore! Hongkong!... Hongkong! It sounds like a temple bell. It thrills me."

"Over in Hongkong," said Arnold Hatch, "I expect some Chinese Maxine Pardee would say, Okoochee! It sounds like an Indian war drum. It thrills me.'"

Sometimes Maxine showed signs of melting. But she always congealed again under the influence of her resolve. One evening an out-of-town diner, on hearing her name, said, "Pardee! Hm. Probably a corruption of Pardieu. A French name originally, I suppose."

After that there was no approaching her for a week. Maxine Pardieu. Pardieu. "By God!" it meant. A chevalier he must have been, this Pardieu. A musketeer! A swashbuckler, with lace falling over his slim white hand, and his hand always ready on his sword. Red heels. Plumed hat. Pardieu!

How she hated anew the great oil tanks that rose on the town's outskirts, guarding it like giant sentinels. The new houses. The new country club. Twenty-one miles of asphalt road. Population in 1900, only 467. In 1920 over 35,000. Slogan, Watch Us Grow. Seventeen hundred oil and gas wells. Fields of corn and cotton. Skyscrapers. The Watonga Building, twelve stories. Haynes Block, fourteen stories. Come West, young man! Ugh!

Sometimes she made little rhymes in her mind.

There's	Singapore	and	Zanzibar,
And	Cairo	and	Calais.
There's	Samarkand	and	Alcazar,

Rangoon and Mandalay.

"Yeh," said Arnold Hatch, one evening, when they were talking in the Pardee back yard. It was nine o'clock. Dishes done. A moon. October. Maxine had just murmured her little quatrain. They were standing by the hedge of pampas grass that separated the Pardee yard from Hatch's next door.

"Yeh," said Arnold Hatch. "Likewise:

"There's	Seminole	and	Shawnee,
Apache,			Agawam.
There's	Agua	and	Pawnee,

Walonga, Waukeetom."

He knew his Oklahoma.

"Oh!" exclaimed Maxine, in a little burst of fury; and stamped her foot down hard. Squ-ush! said something underfoot. "Oh!" said Maxine again; in surprise this time. October was a dry month. She peered down. Her shoe was wet. A slimy something clung to it. A scummy something shone reflected in the moonlight. She had not lived ten years in Oklahoma for nothing. Arnold Hatch bent down. Maxine bent down. The greasy wet patch lay just between the two back yards. They touched it, fearfully, with their forefingers. Then they straightened and looked at each other. Oil. Oil!

Things happened like that in Oklahoma.

You didn't try to swing a thing like that yourself. You leased your land for a number of years. A well cost between forty and sixty thousand dollars. You leased to a company represented by one or two of those cold-blooded steely-eyed young men from Pennsylvania or New York. There was a good deal of trouble about it, too. This was a residence district—one of the oldest in this new town. But they bought the Pardee place and the Hatch place. And Arnold Hatch, who had learned a thing or two in the offices of the Okoochee Oil and Refining Company, drove a hard bargain for both. The yard was overrun with drillers, lawyers, engineers, superintendents, foremen, machinery.

Arnold came with papers to sign. "Five hundred a day," he said, "and a percentage." He named the percentage. Maxine and her mother repeated this after him, numbly.

Mrs. Pardee had been the book-keeper in the Pardee ménage. She tried some mathematical gymnastics now and bumped her arithmetical nose.

"Five hundred a day. Including Sundays, Arnold?"

"Including Sundays."

Her lips began to move. "Seven times five ... thirty-five hundred a ... fifty-two times thirty——"

She stopped, overcome. But she began again, wildly, as a thought came to her. "Why, I could build a house. A house, up on Edgecombe. A house like the Barstows' with lawns, and gardens, and sleeping porches, and linen closets!... Oh, Maxine! We'll live there——"

"Not I," said Maxine, crisply. Arnold, watching her, knew what she was going to say before she said it. "I'm going to see the world. I want to penetrate a civilization so old that its history wanders down the centuries and is lost in the dim mists of mythology." See Baedeker.

Sudden wealth had given Arnold a new masterfulness. "Marry me before you go."

"Not at all," replied Maxine. "On the boat going over——"

"Over where?"

"Honolulu, on my way to Japan, I'll meet a tall bearded stranger, sunburned, with the flame of the Orient in his eyes, and on his thin, cruel, sensual mouth——"

Arnold Hatch took off his glasses. Maxine stiffened. "Don't you d——" But she was too late.

"There," said Arnold, "he'll have to have some beard, and some flame, and some thin, cruel, sensual mouth to make you forget that one."

Maxine started, alone, against her mother's remonstrances. After she'd picked out her boat she changed to another because she learned, at the last minute, that the first boat was an oil-burner. Being an inexperienced traveller she took a good many trunks and was pretty unpopular with the steward before he could make her understand that one trunk to the stateroom was the rule. On the first two days out on the way to the Hawaiian Islands she spent all her time (which was twenty-four hours a day in her bed) hoping that Balboa was undergoing fitting torment in punishment for his little joke about discovering the so-called Pacific Ocean. But the swell subsided, and the wind went down, and Maxine appeared on deck and in another twelve hours had met everyone from the purser to the honeymoon couple, in the surprising way one does on these voyages. She looked for the tall bearded stranger with the sunburn of the Orient and the thin, cruel, sensual lips. But he didn't seem to be about. Strangely enough, everyone she talked to seemed to be from Nebraska, or Kansas, or Iowa, or Missouri. Not only that, they all were very glib with names and places that had always seemed mythical and glamorous.

"Oh, yes, Mr. Tannenbaum and I went to India last year, and Persia and around. Real interesting. My, but they're dirty, those towns. We used to kick about Des Moines, now that they use so much soft coal, and all the manufacturing and all. But my land, it's paradise compared to those places. And the food! Only decent meals we had in Egypt was a place in Cairo called Pardee's, run by a woman whose husband's left her or died, or something. Real home-loving woman she was. Such cooking.... Why, that's so! Your name's Pardee, too, isn't it! Well, I always say to Mr. Tannenbaum, it's a small world, after all. No relation, of course?"

"Of course not." How suddenly safe Oklahoma seemed. And Arnold Hatch.

"Where you going from Honolulu, Miss Pardee?"

"Samarkand."

"Beg pardon?"

"Samarkand."

"Oh, yeh. Samar—le' see now, where is that, exactly? I used to know, but I'm such a hand for forgetting——"

"I don't know," said Maxine, distinctly.

"Don't—but I thought you said you were going——"

"I am. But I don't know where it is."

"Then how——"

"You just go to an office, where there are folders and a man behind the desk, and you say you want to go to Samarkand. He shows you. You get on a boat. That's all."

The people from Iowa, and Kansas, and Nebraska and Missouri said, Oh, yes, and there was nothing like travel. So broadening. Maxine asked them if they knew about the Vale of Kashmir and one of them, astoundingly enough, did. A man from Milwaukee, Wisconsin, who had spent a year there superintending the erection of a dredge. A plump man, with eyeglasses and perpetually chewing a dead cigar.

Gold and sunlight, myrrh and incense, the tinkling of anklets. Maxine clung to these wildly, in her mind.

But Honolulu, the Moana Hotel on Waikiki Beach, reassured her. It was her dream come true. She knew it would be so when she landed and got her first glimpse of the dark-skinned natives on the docks, their hats and necks laden with leis of flowers. There were palm trees. There were flaming hibiscus hedges. Her bed was canopied with white netting, like that of a princess (the attendant explained it was to keep out the mosquitoes).

You ate strange fruits (they grew a little sickening, after a day or two). You saw Duke, the Hawaiian world champion swimmer, come in on a surf-board, standing straight and slim and naked like a god of bronze, balancing miraculously on a plank carried in on the crest of a wave with the velocity of a steam engine. You saw Japanese women in tight kimonos and funny little stilted flapping footgear running to catch a street car; and you laughed at the incongruity of it. You made the three-day trip to the living volcano at Hilo and sat at the crater's brink watching the molten lava lake tossing, hissing, writhing. You hung there, between horror and fascination.

"Certainly a pretty sight, isn't it?" said her fellow travellers. "Makes the Grand Canyon look sick, I think, don't you?"

"I've never seen it."

"Oh, really!"

On her return from Hilo she saw him. A Vandyke beard; smouldering eyes; thin red lips; lean nervous hands; white flannel evening clothes; sunburned a rich brown. Maxine drew a long breath as if she had been running. It was after dinner. The broad veranda was filled with gayly gowned women; uniformed officers from the fort; tourists in white. They were drinking their after-dinner coffee, smoking, laughing. The Hawaiian orchestra made ready to play for the dancing on the veranda. They began to play. Their ukeleles throbbed and moaned. The musicians sang in their rich, melodious voices some native song of a lost empire and a dead king. It tore at your heart. You ached with the savage beauty of it. It was then she saw him. He was seated alone, smoking, drinking, watching the crowd with amused, uneager glance. She had seen him before. It was a certainty, this feeling. She had known him—seen him—before. Perhaps not in this life. Perhaps only in her dreams. But they had met.

She stared at him until her eye caught his. It was brazen, but she was shameless. Nothing mattered. This was no time for false modesty. Her eyes held his. Then, slowly, she rose, picked up her trailing scarf, and walked deliberately past him, glancing down at him as she passed. He half rose, half spoke. She went down the steps leading from the veranda to the court-yard, down this walk to the pier, down the pier to the very end, where the little roofed shelter lay out in the ocean, bathed in moonlight, fairylike, unreal. The ocean was a thing of molten silver. The sound of the wailing voices in song came to her on the breeze, agonizing in its beauty. There, beyond, lay Pearl Harbour. From the other side, faintly, you heard the music and laughter from the Yacht Club.

Maxine seated herself. The after-dinner couples had not yet strolled out. They were waiting for the dancing up there on the hotel veranda. She waited. She waited. She saw the glow of his cigar as he came down the pier, a tall, slim white figure in the moonlight. It was just like a novel. It was a novel, come to life. He stood a moment at the pier's edge, smoking. Then he tossed his cigar into the water and it fell with a little s-st! He stood another moment, irresolutely. Then he came over to her.

"Nice night."

In Okoochee you would have said, "Sir!" But not here. Not now. Not Maxine Pardieu. "Yes, isn't it!"

The mellow moon fell full on him—bronzed, bearded, strangely familiar.

At his next question she felt a little faint. "Haven't we—met before?"

She toyed with the end of her scarf. "You feel that, too?"

He nodded. He took a cigarette from a flat platinum case. "Mind if I smoke? Perhaps you'll join me?" Maxine took a cigarette, uncertainly. Lighted it from the match he held. Put it to her lips. Coughed, gasped. "Maybe you're not used to those. I smoke a cheap cigarette because I like 'em. Dromedaries, those are. Eighteen cents a package."

Maxine held the cigarette in her unaccustomed fingers. Her eyes were on his face. "You said you thought—you felt—we'd met before?"

"I may be mistaken, but I never forget a face. Where are you from, may I ask?"

Maxine hesitated a moment. "Oklahoma."

He slapped his leg a resounding thwack. "I knew it! I'm hardly ever mistaken. Name's—wait a minute—Pardee, isn't it?"

"Yes. But how——"

"One of the best meals I ever had in my life, Miss Pardee. Two years ago, it was. I was lecturing on Thibet and the Far East."

"Lecturing?" Her part of the conversation was beginning to sound a good deal like the dialogue in a badly written play.

"Yes, I'm Brainerd, you know. I thought you knew, when you spoke up there on the veranda."

"Brainerd?" It was almost idiotic.

"Brainerd. Paul Brainerd, the travelogue man. I remember I gave you and your mother complimentary tickets to the lecture. I've got a great memory. Got to have, in my business. Let's see, that town was——"

"Okoochee," faintly.

"Okoochee! That's it! It's a small world after all, isn't it? Okoochee. Why, I'm on my way to Oklahoma now. I'm going to spend two months or more there, taking pictures of the vast oil fields, the oil wells. A new country. An Aladdin country; a new growth; one of the most amazing and picturesque bits in the history of our amazing country. History in the making. An empire over-night. Oklahoma! Well! What a relief, after war-torn Europe and an out-worn civilization."

"But you—you're from——?"

"I'm from East Orange, New Jersey, myself. Got a nice little place down there that I wouldn't swap for all the palaces of the kings. No sir!... Already? Well, yes, it is a little damp out here, so close to the water. Mrs. Brainerd won't risk it. I'll walk up with you. I'd like to have you meet her."

THE END

Half Portions

THE MATERNAL FEMININE

Called upon to describe Aunt Sophy you would have to coin a term or fall back on the dictionary definition of a spinster. "An unmarried woman," states that worthy work, baldly, "especially when no longer young." That, to the world, was Sophy Decker. Unmarried, certainly. And most certainly no longer young. In figure she was, at fifty, what is known in the corset ads as a "stylish stout." Well dressed in blue serge, with broad-toed health shoes and a small, astute hat. The blue serge was practical common sense. The health shoes were comfort. The hat was strictly business. Sophy Decker made and sold hats, both astute and ingenuous, to the female population of Chippewa, Wisconsin. Chippewa's East-End set bought the knowing type of hat, and the mill hands and hired girls bought the naïve ones. But whether lumpy or possessed of that indefinable thing known as line, Sophy Decker's hats were honest hats.

The world is full of Aunt Sophys, unsung. Plump, ruddy, capable women of middle age. Unwed, and rather looked down upon by a family of married sisters and tolerant, good-humoured brothers-in-law, and careless nieces and nephews.

"Poor Aunt Soph," with a significant half smile. "She's such a good old thing. And she's had so little in life, really."

She was, undoubtedly, a good old thing—Aunt Soph. Forever sending a spray of sweeping black paradise, like a jet of liquid velvet, to this pert little niece in Seattle; or taking Adele, sister Flora's daughter, to Chicago or New York, as a treat, on one of her buying trips. Burdening herself, on her business visits to these cities, with a dozen foolish shopping commissions for the idle women folk of her family. Hearing without partisanship her sisters' complaints about their husbands, and her sisters' husbands' complaints about their wives. It was always the same.

"I'm telling you this, Sophy. I wouldn't breathe it to another living soul. But I honestly think, sometimes, that if it weren't for the children—"

There is no knowing why they confided these things to Sophy instead of to each other, these wedded sisters of hers. Perhaps they held for each other an unuttered distrust or jealousy. Perhaps, in making a confidante of Sophy, there was something of the satisfaction that comes of dropping a surreptitious stone down a deep well and hearing it plunk, safe in the knowledge that it has struck no one and that it cannot rebound, lying there in the soft darkness. Sometimes they would end by saying, "But you don't know what it is, Sophy. You can't. I'm sure I don't know why I'm telling you all this."

But when Sophy answered, sagely, "I know; I know"—they paid little heed, once having unburdened themselves. The curious part of it is that she did know. She knew as a woman of fifty must know who, all her life, has given and given and in return has received nothing. Sophy Decker had never used the word inhibition in her life. I doubt if she knew what it meant. When you are busy copying French models for the fall trade you have little time or taste for Freud. She only knew (without in the least knowing she knew) that in giving of her goods, of her affections, of her time, of her energy, she found a certain relief. Her own people would have been shocked if you had told them that there was about this old maid aunt something rather splendidly Rabelaisian. Without being at all what is known as a masculine woman she had, somehow, acquired the man's viewpoint, his shrewd value sense. She ate a good deal, and enjoyed her food. She did not care for those queer little stories that married women sometimes tell, with narrowed eyes, but she was strangely tolerant of what is known as sin. So simple and direct she was that you wondered how she prospered in a line so subtle as the millinery business.

You might have got a fairly true characterization of Sophy Decker from one of fifty people: from a dapper salesman in a New York or Chicago wholesale millinery house; from Otis Cowan, cashier of the First National Bank of Chippewa; from Julia Gold, her head milliner and trimmer; from almost any one, in fact, except a member of her own family. They knew her least of all, as is often true of one's own people. Her three married sisters—Grace in Seattle, Ella in Chicago, and Flora in Chippewa—regarded her with a rather affectionate disapproval from the snug safety of their own conjugal ingle-nooks.

"I don't know. There's something—well—common about Sophy," Flora confided to Ella. Flora, on shopping bent and Sophy, seeking hats, had made the five-hour run from Chippewa to Chicago together. "She talks to everybody. You should have heard her with the porter on our train. Chums! And when the conductor took our tickets it was a social occasion. You know how packed the seven fifty-two is. Every seat in the parlour car taken. And Sophy asking the coloured porter about how his wife was getting along—she called him William—and if they were going to send her west, and all about her. I *wish* she wouldn't."

Aunt Sophy undeniably had a habit of regarding people as human beings. You found her talking to chambermaids and delivery boys, and elevator starters, and gas collectors, and hotel clerks—all that aloof, unapproachable, superior crew. Under her benign volubility they bloomed and spread and took on colour as do those tight little Japanese paper water-flowers when you cast them into a bowl. It wasn't idle curiosity in her. She was interested. You found yourself confiding to her your innermost longings, your secret tribulations, under the encouragement of her sympathetic, "You don't say!" Perhaps it was as well that sister Flora was in ignorance of the fact that the men millinery salesmen at Danowitz & Danowitz, Importers, always called Miss Decker Aunt Soph, as, with one arm flung about her plump blue serge shoulder, they revealed to her the picture of their girl in the back flap of their bill-folder.

Flora, with a firm grip on Chippewa society, as represented by the East-End set, did not find her position enhanced by a sister in the millinery business in Elm Street.

"Of course it's wonderful that she's self-supporting and successful and all," she told her husband. "But it's not so pleasant for Adele, now that she's growing up, having all the girls she knows buying their hats of her aunt. Not that I—but you know how it is."

H. Charnsworth Baldwin said yes, he knew. But perhaps you, until you are made more intimately acquainted with Chippewa, Wisconsin; with the Decker girls of twenty years ago; with Flora's husband, H. Charnsworth Baldwin; and with their children Adele and Eugene, may feel a little natural bewilderment.

The Deckers had lived in a sagging old frame house (from which the original paint had long ago peeled in great scrofulous patches) on an unimportant street in Chippewa. There was a worm-eaten russet apple tree in the yard; an untidy tangle of wild-cucumber vine over the front porch; and an uncut brush of sunburnt grass and weeds all about. From May until September you never passed the Decker place without hearing the plunketty-plink of a mandolin from somewhere behind the vines, accompanied by a murmur of young voices, laughter, and the creak-creak of the hard-worked and protesting hammock hooks. Flora, Ella, and Grace Decker had more beaux and fewer clothes than any other girls in Chippewa. In a town full of pretty young things they were, undoubtedly, the prettiest; and in a family of pretty sisters (Sophy always excepted) Flora was the acknowledged beauty. She was the kind of girl whose nose never turns red on a frosty morning. A little, white, exquisite nose, purest example of the degree of perfection which may be attained by that vulgarest of features. Under her great gray eyes were faint violet shadows which gave her a look of almost poignant wistfulness. If there is a less hackneyed way to describe her head on its slender throat than to say it was like a lovely flower on its stalk, you are free to use it. Her slow, sweet smile gave the beholder an actual physical pang. Only her family knew she was lazy as a behemoth, untidy about her person, and as sentimental as a hungry shark. The strange and cruel part of it was that, in some grotesque, exaggerated way, as a cartoon may be like a photograph, Sophy resembled Flora. It was as though Nature, in prankish mood, had given a cabbage the colour and texture of a rose, with none of its fragile reticence and grace.

It was a manless household. Mrs. Decker, vague, garrulous, and given to ice-wool shawls, referred to her dead husband, in frequent reminiscence, as poor Mr. Decker. Mrs. Decker dragged one leg as she walked—rheumatism, or a spinal affection. Small wonder, then, that Sophy, the plain, with a gift for hat-making, a knack at eggless cake-baking, and a genius for turning a sleeve so that last year's style met this year's without a struggle, contributed nothing to the sag in the centre of the old twine hammock on the front porch.

That the three girls should marry well, and Sophy not at all, was as inevitable as the sequence of the seasons. Ella and Grace did not manage badly, considering that they had only their girlish prettiness and the twine hammock to work with. But Flora, with her beauty, captured H. Charnsworth Baldwin. Chippewa gasped. H. Charnsworth Baldwin drove a skittish mare to a high-wheeled yellow runabout (this was twenty years ago); had his clothes made at Proctor Brothers in Milwaukee, and talked about a game called golf. It was he who advocated laying out a section of land for what he called links, and erecting a club house thereon.

"The section of the bluff overlooking the river," he explained, "is full of natural hazards, besides having a really fine view."

Chippewa—or that comfortable, middle-class section of it which got its exercise walking home to dinner from the store at noon, and cutting the grass evenings after supper—laughed as it read this interview in the Chippewa *Eagle*.

"A golf course," they repeated to one another, grinning. "Conklin's cow pasture, up the river. It's full of natural—wait a minute—what was?—oh, yeh, here it is—hazards. Full of natural hazards. Say, couldn't you die!"

For H. Charnsworth Baldwin had been little Henry Baldwin before he went East to college. Ten years later H. Charnsworth, in knickerbockers and gay-topped stockings, was winning the cup in the men's tournament played on the Chippewa golf-club course, overlooking the river. And his name, in stout gold letters, blinked at you from the plate-glass windows of the office at the corner of Elm and Winnebago:

NORTHERN LUMBER AND LAND COMPANY.
H. CHARNSWORTH BALDWIN, PRES.

Two blocks farther down Elm Street was another sign, not so glittering, which read:

MISS SOPHY DECKER
Millinery

Sophy's hat-making, in the beginning, had been done at home. She had always made her sisters' hats, and her own, of course, and an occasional hat for a girl friend. After her sisters had married Sophy found herself in possession of a rather bewildering amount of spare time. The hat trade grew so that sometimes there were six rather botchy little bonnets all done up in yellow paper pyramids with a pin at the top, awaiting their future wearers. After her mother's death Sophy still stayed on in the old house. She took a course in millinery in Milwaukee, came home, stuck up a home-made sign in the parlour window (the untidy cucumber vines came down), and began her hat-making in earnest. In five years she had opened a shop on a side street near Elm; had painted the old house, installed new plumbing, built a warty stucco porch, and transformed the weedy, grass-tangled yard into an orderly stretch of green lawn and bright flower-beds. In ten years she was in Elm Street, and the Chippewa *Eagle* ran a half column twice a year describing her spring and fall openings. On these occasions Aunt Sophy, in black satin, and marcel wave, and her most relentless corsets was, in all the superficial things, not a pleat, or fold, or line, or wave behind her city colleagues. She had all the catch phrases:

"This is awfully good this year."

"Here's a sweet thing. A Mornet model.... Well, but my dear, it's the style—the line—you're paying for, not the material."

"I've got the very thing for you. I had you in mind when I bought it. Now don't say you can't wear henna. Wait till you see it on."

When she stood behind you as you sat, uncrowned and expectant before the mirror, she would poise the hat four inches above your head, holding it in the tips of her fingers, a precious, fragile thing. Your fascinated eyes were held by it, and your breath as well. Then down it descended, slowly, slowly. A quick pressure. Her fingers firm against your temples. A little sigh of relieved suspense.

"That's wonderful on you!... You don't! Oh, my dear! But that's because you're not used to it. You know how you said, for years, you had to have a brim, and couldn't possibly wear a turban, with your nose, until I proved to you that if the head-size was only big ... Well, perhaps this needs just a lit-tle lift here. Ju-u-ust a nip. There! That does it."

And that did it. Not that Sophy Decker ever tried to sell you a hat against your judgment, taste, or will. She was too wise a psychologist and too shrewd a business woman for that. She preferred that you go out of her shop hatless rather than with an unbecoming hat. But whether you bought or not you took with you out of Sophy Decker's shop something more precious than any hatbox ever contained. Just to hear her admonishing a customer, her good-natured face all aglow:

"My dear, always put on your hat before you get into your dress. I do. You can get your arms above your head, and set it right. I put on my hat and veil as soon's I get my hair combed."

In your mind's eye you saw her, a stout, well-stayed figure in tight brassière and scant petticoat, bare-armed and bare-bosomed, in smart hat and veil, attired as though for the street from the neck up and for the bedroom from the shoulders down.

The East-End set bought Sophy Decker's hats because they were modish and expensive hats. But she managed, miraculously, to gain a large and lucrative following among the paper-mill girls and factory hands as well. You would have thought that any attempt to hold both these opposites would cause her to lose one or the other. Aunt Sophy said, frankly, that of the two, she would have preferred to lose her smart trade.

"The mill girls come in with their money in their hands, you might say. They get good wages and they want to spend them. I wouldn't try to sell them one of those little plain model hats. They wouldn't understand 'em, or like them. And if I told them the price they'd think I was trying to cheat them. They want a velvet hat with something good and solid on it. Their fathers wouldn't prefer caviar to pork roast, would they? It's the same idea."

Her shop windows reflected her business acumen. One was chastely, severely elegant, holding a single hat poised on a slender stick. In the other were a dozen honest arrangements of velvet and satin and plumes.

At the spring opening she always displayed one of those little toques completely covered with violets. No one ever bought a hat like that. No one ever will. That violet-covered toque is a symbol.

"I don't expect 'em to buy it," Sophy Decker explained. "But everybody feels there should be a hat like that at a spring opening. It's like a fruit centre-piece at a family dinner. Nobody ever eats it but it has to be there."

The two Baldwin children—Adele and Eugene—found Aunt Sophy's shop a treasure trove. Adele, during her doll days, possessed such boxes of satin and velvet scraps, and bits of lace, and ribbon and jet as to make her the envy of all her playmates. She used to crawl about the floor of the shop workroom and under the table and chairs like a little scavenger.

"What in the world do you do with all that truck, child?" asked Aunt Sophy. "You must have barrels of it."

Adele stuffed another wisp of tulle into the pocket of her pinafore. "I keep it," she said.

When she was ten Adele had said to her mother, "Why do you always say 'Poor Sophy'?"

"Because Aunt Sophy's had so little in life. She never has married, and has always worked."

Adele considered that. "If you don't get married do they say you're poor?"

"Well—yes—"

"Then I'll get married," announced Adele. A small, dark, eerie child, skinny and rather foreign looking.

The boy, Eugene, had the beauty which should have been the girl's. Very tall, very blond, with the straight nose and wistful eyes of the Flora of twenty years ago. "If only Adele could have had his looks," his mother used to say. "They're wasted on a man. He doesn't need them but a girl does. Adele will have to be well-dressed and interesting. And that's such hard work."

Flora said she worshipped her children. And she actually sometimes still coquetted heavily with her husband. At twenty she had been addicted to baby talk when endeavouring to coax something out of someone. Her admirers had found it irresistible. At forty it was awful. Her selfishness was colossal. She affected a semi-invalidism and for fifteen years had spent one day a week in bed. She took no exercise and a great deal of baking soda and tried to fight her fat with baths. Fifteen or twenty years had worked a startling change in the two sisters, Flora the beautiful, and Sophy the plain. It was more than a mere physical change. It was a spiritual thing, though neither knew nor marked it. Each had taken on weight, the one, solidly, comfortably; the other, flabbily, unhealthily. With the encroaching fat Flora's small, delicate features seemed, somehow, to disappear in her face, so that you saw it as a large white surface bearing indentations, ridges, and hollows like one of those enlarged photographs of the moon's surface as seen through a telescope. A self-centred face, and misleadingly placid. Aunt Sophy's large, plain features, plumply padded now, impressed you as indicating strength, courage, and a great human understanding.

From her husband and her children Flora exacted service that would have chafed a galley-slave into rebellion. She loved to lie in bed, in a lavender bed-jacket with ribbons, and be read to by Adele or Eugene, or her husband. They all hated it.

"She just wants to be waited on, and petted, and admired," Adele had stormed one day, in open rebellion, to her Aunt Sophy. "She uses it as an excuse for everything and has, ever since 'Gene and I were children. She's as strong as an ox." Not a very ladylike or daughterly speech, but shockingly true.

Years before a generous but misguided woman friend, coming in to call, had been ushered in to where Mrs. Baldwin lay propped up in a nest of pillows.

"Well, I don't blame you," the caller had gushed. "If I looked the way you do in bed I'd stay there forever. Don't tell me you're sick, with all that lovely colour!"

Flora Baldwin had rolled her eyes ceilingward. "Nobody ever gives me credit for all my suffering and ill-health. And just because all my blood is in my cheeks."

Flora was ambitious, socially, but too lazy to make the effort necessary for success in that direction.

"I love my family," she would say. "They fill my life. After all, that's a profession in itself—being a wife and mother."

She showed her devotion by taking no interest whatever in her husband's land schemes; by forbidding Eugene to play football at school for fear he might be injured; by impressing Adele with the necessity for vivacity and modishness because of what she called her unfortunate lack of beauty.

"I don't understand it," she used to say in the child's very presence. "Her father's handsome enough, goodness knows; and I wasn't such a fright when I was a girl. And look at her! Little, dark, skinny thing."

The boy Eugene grew up a very silent, handsome shy young fellow. The girl dark, voluble, and rather interesting. The husband, more and more immersed in his business, was absent from home for long periods; irritable after some of these home-comings; boisterously high-spirited following other trips. Now growling about household expenses and unpaid bills; now urging the purchase of some almost prohibitive luxury. Any one but a nagging, self-absorbed, and vain woman such as Flora would have marked these unmistakable signs. But Flora was a taker, not a giver. She thought herself affectionate because she craved affection unduly. She thought herself a fond mother because she insisted on having her children with her, under her thumb, marking their devotion as a prisoner marks time with his feet, stupidly, shufflingly, advancing not a step.

Sometimes Sophy the clear-eyed and level-headed, seeing this state of affairs, tried to stop it.

"You expect too much of your husband and children," she said one day, bluntly, to her sister.

"I!" Flora's dimpled hands had flown to her breast like a wounded thing. "I! You're crazy! There isn't a more devoted wife and mother in the world. That's the trouble. I love them too much."

"Well, then," grimly, "stop it for a change. That's half Eugene's nervousness—your fussing over him. He's eighteen. Give him a chance. You're weakening him. And stop dinning that society stuff into Adele's ears. She's got brains, that child. Why, just yesterday, in the workroom she got hold of some satin and a shape and turned out a little turban that Angie Hatton—"

"Do you mean to tell me that Angie Hatton saw my Adele working in your shop! Now, look here, Sophy. You're earning your living, and it's to your credit. You're my sister. But I won't have Adele associated in the minds of my friends with your hat store, understand. I won't have it. That isn't what I sent her away to an expensive school for. To have her come back and sit around a millinery workshop with a lot of little, cheap, shoddy sewing girls! Now understand, I won't have it! You don't know what it is to be a mother. You don't know what it is to have suffered. If you had brought two children into the world—"

So then, it had come about, during the years between their childhood and their youth, that Aunt Sophy received the burden of their confidences, their griefs, their perplexities. She seemed, somehow, to understand in some miraculous way, and to make the burden a welcome one.

"Well, now, you tell Aunt Sophy all about it. Stop crying, Della. How can Aunt Sophy hear when you're crying! That's my baby. Now, then."

This when they were children. But with the years the habit clung and became fixed. There was something about Aunt Sophy's house—the old frame house with the warty stucco porch. For that matter, there was something about the very shop downtown, with its workroom in the rear, that had a cozy, homelike quality never possessed by the big Baldwin house. H. Charnsworth Baldwin had built a large brick mansion, in the Tudor style, on a bluff overlooking the Fox River, in the best residential section of Chippewa. It was expensively and correctly furnished. The hall consol alone was enough to strike a preliminary chill to your heart.

The millinery workroom, winter days, was always bright and warm and snug. The air was a little close, perhaps, and heavy, but with a not unpleasant smell of dyes, and stuffs, and velvet, and glue, and steam, and flatiron, and a certain heady scent that Julia Gold, the head trimmer, always used. There was a sociable cat, white with a dark gray patch on his throat and a swipe of it across one flank that spoiled him for style and beauty but made him a comfortable-looking cat to have around. Sometimes, on very cold days, or in the rush reason, the girls would not go home to dinner or supper, but would bring their lunches and cook coffee over a little gas heater in the corner. Julia Gold, especially, drank quantities of coffee. Aunt Sophy had hired her from Chicago. She had been with her for five years. She said Julia was the best trimmer she had ever had. Aunt Sophy often took her to New York or Chicago on her buying trips. Julia had not much genius for original design, or she would never have been content to be head milliner in a small-town shop. But she could copy a fifty-dollar model from memory down to the last detail of crown and brim. It was a gift that made her invaluable.

The boy, Eugene, used to like to look at Julia Gold. Her hair was very black and her face was very white, and her eyebrows met in a thick, dark line. Her face, as she bent over her work, was sullen and brooding, but when she lifted her head suddenly, in conversation, you were startled by a vivid flash of teeth, and eyes, and smile. Her voice was deep and low. She made you a little uncomfortable. Her eyes seemed always to be asking something. Around the work table, mornings she used to relate the dream she had had the night before. In these dreams she was always being pursued by a lover. "And then I woke up, screaming." Neither she nor the sewing girls knew what she was revealing in these confidences of hers. But Aunt Sophy, the shrewd, somehow sensed it.

"You're alone too much, evenings. That's what comes of living in a boarding house. You come over to me for a week. The change will do you good, and it'll be nice for me, too, having somebody to keep me company."

Julia often came for a week or ten days at a time. Julia, about the house after supper, was given to those vivid splashy kimonos with big flowers embroidered on them. They made her hair look blacker and her skin whiter by contrast. Sometimes Eugene or Adele or both would drop in and the four would play bridge. Aunt Sophy played a shrewd and canny game, Adele a rather brilliant one, Julia a wild and disastrous hand, always, and Eugene so badly that only Julia would take him on as a partner. Mrs. Baldwin never knew about these evenings.

It was on one of these occasions that Aunt Sophy, coming unexpectedly into the living room from the kitchen where she and Adele were foraging for refreshments after the game, beheld Julia Gold and Eugene, arms clasped about each other, cheek to cheek. They started up as she came in and faced her, the woman defiantly, the boy bravely. Julia Gold was thirty (with reservations) at that time, and the boy not quite twenty-one.

"How long?" said Aunt Sophy, quietly. She had a mayonnaise spoon and a leaf of lettuce in her hand at the time, and still she did not look comic.

"I'm crazy about her," said Eugene. "We're crazy about each other. We're going to be married."

Aunt Sophy listened for the reassuring sound of Adele's spoons and plates in the kitchen. She came forward. "Now, listen—" she began.

"I love him," said Julia Gold, dramatically. "I love him!"

Except that it was very white and, somehow, old looking, Aunt Sophy's face was as benign as always. "Now, look here, Julia, my girl. That isn't love and you know it. I'm an old maid, but I know what love is when I see it. I'm ashamed of you, Julia. Sensible woman like you. Hugging and kissing a boy like that, and old enough to be his mother, pretty near."

"Now, look here, Aunt Soph! I'm fond of you but if you're going to talk that way—Why, she's wonderful. She's taught me what it means to really—"

"Oh, my land!" Aunt Sophy sat down, looking, suddenly, very sick and old.

And then, from the kitchen, Adele's clear young voice: "Heh! What's the idea! I'm not going to do all the work. Where's everybody?"

Aunt Sophy started up again. She came up to them and put a hand—a capable, firm, steadying hand on the arm of each. The woman drew back but the boy did not.

"Will you promise me not to do anything for a week? Just a week! Will you promise me? Will you?"

"Are you going to tell Father?"

"Not for a week if you'll promise not to see each other in that week. No, I don't want to send you away, Julia, I don't want to—You're not a bad girl. It's just—he's never had—at home they never gave him a chance. Just a week, Julia. Just a week, Eugene. We can talk things over then."

Adele's footsteps coming from the kitchen.

"Quick!"

"I promise," said Eugene. Julia said nothing.

"Well, really," said Adele, from the doorway, "you're a nervy lot, sitting around while I slave in the kitchen. 'Gene, see if you can open the olives with this fool can opener. I tried."

There is no knowing what she expected to do in that week, Aunt Sophy; what miracle she meant to perform. She had no plan in her mind. Just hope. She looked strangely shrunken and old, suddenly. But when, three days later, the news came that America was to go into the war she knew that her prayers were answered.

Flora was beside herself. "Eugene won't have to go. He isn't quite twenty-one, thank God! And by the time he is it will be over. Surely." She was almost hysterical.

Eugene was in the room. Aunt Sophy looked at him and he looked at Aunt Sophy. In her eyes was a question. In his was the answer. They said nothing. The next day Eugene enlisted. In three days he was gone. Flora took to her bed. Next day Adele, a faint, unwonted colour marking her cheeks, walked into her mother's bedroom and stood at the side of the recumbent figure. Her father, his hands clasped behind him, was pacing up and down, now and then kicking a cushion that had fallen to the floor. He was chewing a dead cigar, one side of his face twisted curiously over the cylinder in his mouth so that he had a sinister and crafty look.

"Charnsworth, won't you please stop ramping up and down like that! My nerves are killing me. I can't help it if the war has done something or other to your business. I'm sure no wife could have been more economical than I have. Nothing matters but Eugene, anyway. How could he do such a thing! I've given my whole life to my children—"

H. Charnsworth kicked the cushion again so that it struck the wall at the opposite side of the room. Flora drew her breath in between her teeth as though a knife had entered her heart.

Adele still stood at the side of the bed, looking at her mother. Her hands were clasped behind her, too. In that moment, as she stood there, she resembled her mother and her father so startlingly and simultaneously that the two, had they been less absorbed in their own affairs, must have marked it.

The girl's head came up, stiffly. "Listen. I'm going to marry Daniel Oakley."

Daniel Oakley was fifty, and a friend of her father's. For years he had been coming to the house and for years she had ridiculed him. She and Eugene had called him Sturdy Oak because he was always talking about his strength and endurance, his walks, his golf, his rugged health; pounding his chest meanwhile and planting his feet far apart. He and Baldwin had had business relations as well as friendly ones.

At this announcement Flora screamed and sat up in bed. H. Charnsworth stopped short in his pacing and regarded his daughter with a queer look; a concentrated look, as though what she had said had set in motion a whole maze of mental machinery within his brain.

"When did he ask you?"

"He's asked me a dozen times. But it's different now. All the men will be going to war. There won't be any left. Look at England and France. I'm not going to be left." She turned squarely toward her father, her young face set and hard. "You know what I mean. You know what I mean."

Flora, sitting up in bed, was sobbing. "I think you might have told your mother, Adele. What are children coming to! You stand there and say, 'I'm going to marry Daniel Oakley.' Oh, I *am* so faint ... all of a sudden ... get the spirits of ammonia...."

Adele turned and walked out of the room. She was married six weeks later. They had a regular pre-war wedding—veil, flowers, dinner, and all. Aunt Sophy arranged the folds of her gown and draped her veil. The girl stood looking at herself in the mirror, a curious half-smile twisting her lips. She seemed slighter and darker than ever.

"In all this white, and my veil, I look just like a fly in a quart of milk," she said, with a laugh. Then, suddenly, she turned to her aunt who stood behind her and clung to her, holding her tight, tight. "I can't!" she gasped. "I can't! I can't!"

Aunt Sophy held her off and looked at her, her eyes searching the girl.

"What do you mean, Della? Are you just nervous or do you mean you don't want to marry him? Do you mean that? Then what are you marrying for? Tell me! Tell your Aunt Sophy."

But Adele was straightening herself and pulling out the crushed folds of her veil. "To pay the mortgage on the old homestead, of course. Just like the girl in the play." She laughed a little. But Aunt Sophy did not laugh.

"Now look here, Delia. If you're—"

But there was a knock at the door. Adele caught up her flowers. "It's all right," she said.

Aunt Sophy stood with her back against the door. "If it's money," she said. "It is! It is, isn't it! Listen. I've got money saved. It was for you children. I've always been afraid. I knew he was sailing pretty close, with his speculations and all, since the war. He can have it all. It isn't too late yet. Adele! Della, my baby."

"Don't, Aunt Sophy. It wouldn't be enough, anyway. Daniel has been wonderful, really. Don't look like that. I'd have hated being poor, anyway. Never could have got used to it. It is ridiculous, though, isn't it? Like one of those melodramas, or a cheap movie. I don't mind. I'm lucky, really, when you come to think of it. A plain little black thing like me."

"But your mother—"

"Mother doesn't know a thing."

Flora wept mistily all through the ceremony but Adele was composed enough for two.

When, scarcely a month later, Baldwin came to Sophy Decker, his face drawn and queer, Sophy knew.

"How much?" she said.

"Thirty thousand will cover it. If you've got more than that—"

"I thought Oakley—Adele said—"

"He did, but he won't any more, and this thing's got to be met. It's this damned war that's done it. I'd have been all right. People got scared. They wanted their money. They wanted it in cash."

"Speculating with it, were you?"

"Oh, well, a woman doesn't understand these business deals."

"No, naturally," said Aunt Sophy, "a butterfly like me."

"Sophy, for God's sake don't joke now. I tell you this will cover it, and everything will be all right. If I had anybody else to go to for the money I wouldn't ask you. But you'll get it back. You know that."

Aunt Sophy got up, heavily, and went over to her desk. "It was for the children, anyway. They won't need it now."

He looked up at that. Something in her voice. "Who won't? Why won't they?"

"I don't know what made me say that. I had a dream."

"Eugene?"

"Yes."

"Oh, well, we're all nervous. Flora has dreams every night and presentiments every fifteen minutes. Now, look here, Sophy. About this money. You'll never know how grateful I am. Flora doesn't understand these things but I can talk to you. It's like this—"

"I might as well be honest about it," Sophy interrupted. "I'm doing it, not for you, but for Flora, and Delia—and Eugene. Flora has lived such a sheltered life. I sometimes wonder if she ever really knew any of you. Her husband, or her children. I sometimes have the feeling that Delia and Eugene are my children—were my children."

When he came home that night Baldwin told his wife that old Soph was getting queer. "She talks about the children being hers," he said.

"Oh, well, she's awfully fond of them," Flora explained. "And she's lived her little narrow life, with nothing to bother her but her hats and her house. She doesn't know what it means to suffer as a mother suffers—poor Sophy."

"Um," Baldwin grunted.

When the official notification of Eugene's death came from the War Department Aunt Sophy was so calm that it might have appeared that Flora had been right. She took to her bed now in earnest, did Flora, and they thought that her grief would end in madness. Sophy neglected everything to give comfort to the stricken two.

"How can you sit there like that!" Flora would rail. "How can you sit there like that! Even if you weren't his mother surely you must feel something."

"It's the way he died that comforts me," said Aunt Sophy.

"What difference does that make! What difference does that make!"

This is the letter that made a difference to Aunt Sophy. You will have to read it to understand, though you are likely to skip letters on the printed page. You must not skip this.

AMERICAN RED CROSS
(CROIX ROUGE AMÉRICAINE)

MY DEAR MRS. BALDWIN:

I am sure you must have been officially notified, by now, by the U.S. War Dept. of the death of your son Lieut. Eugene H. Baldwin. But I want to write you what I can of his last hours. I was with him much of that time as his nurse. I'm sure it must mean much to a mother to hear from a woman who was privileged to be with her boy at the last.

Your son was brought to our hospital one night badly gassed from the fighting in the Argonne Forest. Ordinarily we do not receive gassed patients, as they are sent to a special hospital near here. But two nights before the Germans wrecked this hospital, so many gassed patients have come to us.

Your son was put in the officers' ward where the doctors who examined him told me there was absolutely no hope for him, as he had inhaled the gas so much that it was only a matter of a few hours. I could scarcely believe that a man so big and strong as he was could not pull through.

The first bad attack he had, losing his breath and nearly choking, rather frightened him, although the doctor and I were both with him. He held my hand tightly in his, begging me not to leave him, and repeating, over and over, that it was good to have a woman near. He was propped high in bed and put his head on my shoulder while I fanned him until he breathed more easily. I stayed with him all that night, though I was not on duty. You see, his eyes also were badly burned. But before he died he was able to see very well. I stayed with him every minute of that night and have never seen a finer character than he showed during all that dreadful fight for life. He had several bad sinking attacks that night and came through each one simply because of his great will power and fighting spirit. After each attack he would grip my hand and say, "Well, we made it that time, didn't we, nurse? And if you'll only stay with me we'll win this fight." At intervals during the night I gave him sips of black coffee which was all he could swallow. Each time I gave it to him he would ask me if I had had some. That was only one instance of his thoughtfulness even in his suffering. Toward morning he asked me if he was going to die. I could not tell him the truth. He needed all his strength. I told him he had one chance in a thousand. He seemed to become very strong then, and sitting bolt upright in bed and shaking his fist, he said: "Then by the Lord I'll fight for it!" We kept him alive for three days, and actually thought we had won when on the third day....

But even in your sorrow you must be very proud to have been the mother of such a son....

I am a Wisconsin girl—Madison. When this is over and I come home will you let me see you so that I may tell you more than I can possibly write?

MARIAN KING.

It was in March, six months later, that Marian King came. They had hoped for it, but never expected it. And she came. Four people were waiting in the living room of the big Baldwin house overlooking the river. Flora and her husband, Adele and Aunt Sophy. They sat, waiting. Now and then Adele would rise, nervously, and go to the window that faced the street. Flora was weeping with audible sniffs. Baldwin sat in his chair frowning a little, a dead cigar in one corner of his mouth. Only Aunt Sophy sat quietly, waiting.

There was little conversation. None in the last five minutes. Flora broke the silence, dabbing at her face with her handkerchief as she spoke.

"Sophy, how can you sit there like that? Not that I don't envy you. I do. I remember I used to feel sorry for you. I used to say, 'Poor Sophy.' But you unmarried ones are the happiest, after all. It's the married woman who drinks the cup to the last bitter drop. There you sit, Sophy, fifty years old, and life hasn't even touched you. You don't know how cruel life is."

Suddenly, "There!" said Adele. The other three in the room stood up and faced the door. The sound of a motor stopping outside. Daniel Oakley's hearty voice: "Well, it only took us five minutes from the station. Pretty good."

Footsteps down the hall. Marian King stood in the doorway. They faced her, the four—Baldwin and Adele and Flora and Sophy. Marian King stood a moment, uncertainly, her eyes upon them. She looked at the two older women with swift, appraising glance. Then she came into the room, quickly, and put her two hands on Aunt Sophy's shoulders and looked into her eyes straight and sure.

"You must be a very proud woman," she said. "You ought to be a very proud woman."

APRIL 25TH, AS USUAL

Mrs. Hosea C. Brewster always cleaned house in September and April. She started with the attic and worked her purifying path down to the cellar in strict accordance with Article I, Section 1, Unwritten Rules for House Cleaning. For twenty-five years she had done it. For twenty-five years she had hated it—being an intelligent woman. For twenty-five years, towel swathed about her head, skirt pinned back, sleeves rolled up—the costume dedicated to house cleaning since the days of What's-Her-Name mother of Lemuel (see Proverbs)—Mrs. Brewster had gone through the ceremony twice a year.

Furniture on the porch, woollens on the line, mattresses in the yard—everything that could be pounded, beaten, whisked, rubbed, flapped, shaken, or aired was dragged out and subjected to one or all of these indignities. After which, completely cowed, they were dragged in again and set in their places. Year after year, in attic and in cellar, things had piled up higher and higher—useless things, sentimental things; things in trunks; things in chests; shelves full of things wrapped up in brown-paper parcels.

And boxes—oh, above all, boxes: pasteboard boxes, long and flat, square and oblong, each bearing weird and cryptic pencillings on one end; cryptic, that is, to any one except Mrs. Brewster and you who have owned an attic. Thus "H's Fshg Tckl" jabberwocked one long, slim box. Another stunned you with "Cur Ted Slpg Pch." A cabalistic third hid its contents under "Sip Cov Pinky Rm." To say nothing of such curt yet intriguing fragments as "Blk Nt Drs" and "Sun Par Val." Once you had the code key they translated themselves simply enough into such homely items as Hosey's fishing tackle, canvas curtains for Ted's sleeping porch, slip covers for Pinky's room, black net dress, sun-parlour valance.

The contents of those boxes formed a commentary on normal American household life as lived by Mr. and Mrs. Hosea C. Brewster, of Winnebago, Wisconsin. Hosey's rheumatism had prohibited trout fishing these ten years; Ted wrote from Arizona that "the li'l' ol' sky" was his sleeping-porch roof and you didn't have to worry out there about the neighbours seeing you in your pyjamas; Pinky's rose-cretonne room had lacked an occupant since Pinky left the Winnebago High School for the Chicago Art Institute, thence to New York and those amazingly successful magazine covers that stare up at you from your table—young lady, hollow chested (she'd need to be with that décolletage), carrying feather fan. You could tell a Brewster cover at sight, without the fan. That leaves the black net dress and the sun-parlour valance. The first had grown too tight under the arms (Mrs. Brewster's arms); the second had faded.

Now, don't gather from this that Mrs. Brewster was an ample, pie-baking, ginghamed old soul who wore black silk and a crushed-looking hat with a palsied rose atop it. Nor that Hosea C. Brewster was spectacled and slippered. Not at all. The Hosea C. Brewsters, of Winnebago, Wisconsin, were the people you've met on the veranda of the

Moana Hotel at Honolulu, or at the top of Pike's Peak, or peering into the restless heart of Vesuvius. They were the prosperous Middle-Western type of citizen who runs down to Chicago to see the new plays and buy a hat, and to order a dozen Wedgwood salad plates at Field's.

Mrs. Brewster knew about Dunsany and georgette and alligator pears; and Hosea Brewster was in the habit of dropping around to the Elks' Club, up above Schirmer's furniture store on Elm Street, at about five in the afternoon on his way home from the cold-storage plant. The Brewster place was honeycombed with sleeping porches and sun parlours and linen closets, and laundry chutes and vegetable bins and electric surprises, as your well-to-do Middle-Western house is likely to be.

That house had long ago grown too large for the two of them—physically, that is. But as the big frame house had expanded, so had they—in tolerance and understanding and humanness—until now, as you talked with them, you felt that here was room and to spare of sun-filled mental chambers, and shelves well stored with experience; and pantries and bins and closets for all your worries and confidences.

But the attic! And the cellar! The attic was the kind of attic every woman longs for who hasn't one and every woman loathes who has. "If I only had some place to put things in!" wails the first. And, "If it weren't for the attic I'd have thrown this stuff away long ago," complains the second. Mrs. Brewster herself had helped plan it. Hardwood floored, spacious, light, the Brewster attic revealed to you the social, æsthetic, educational, and spiritual progress of the entire family as clearly as if a sociologist had charted it.

Take, for example (before we run down to the cellar for a minute), the crayon portraits of Gran'ma and Gran'pa Brewster. When Ted had been a junior and Pinky a freshman at the Winnebago High School the crayon portraits had beamed down upon them from the living-room wall. To each of these worthy old people the artist had given a pair of hectic pink cheeks. Gran'ma Brewster especially, simpering down at you from the labyrinthian scrolls of her sextuple gold frame, was rouged like a soubrette and further embellished with a pair of gentian-blue eyes behind steel-bowed specs. Pinky—and in fact the entire Brewster household—had thought these massive atrocities the last word in artistic ornament. By the time she reached her sophomore year, Pinky had prevailed upon her mother to banish them to the dining room. Then, two years later, when the Chicago decorator did over the living room and the dining room, the crayons were relegated to the upstairs hall.

Ted and Pinky, away at school, began to bring their friends back with them for the vacations. Pinky's room had been done over in cream enamel and rose-flowered cretonne. She said the chromos in the hall spoiled the entire second floor. So the gold frames, glittering undimmed, the cheeks as rosily glowing as ever, found temporary resting place in a nondescript back chamber known as the sewing room. Then the new sleeping porch was built for Ted, and the portraits ended their journeying in the attic.

One paragraph will cover the cellar. Stationary tubs, laundry stove. Behind that, bin for potatoes, bin for carrots, bins for onions, apples, cabbages. Boxed shelves for preserves. And behind that Hosea C. Brewster's *bête noir* and plaything, tyrant and slave—the furnace. "She's eating up coal this winter," Hosea Brewster would complain. Or: "Give her a little more draft, Fred." Fred, of the furnace and lawn mower, would shake a doleful head. "She ain't drawin' good. I do' know what's got into her."

By noon of this particular September day—a blue-and-gold Wisconsin September day—Mrs. Brewster had reached that stage in the cleaning of the attic when it looked as if it would never be clean and orderly again. Taking into consideration Miz' Merz (Miz' Merz by-the-day, you understand) and Gussie, the girl, and Fred, there was very little necessity for Mrs. Brewster's official house-cleaning uniform. She might have unpinned her skirt, unbound her head, rolled down her sleeves, and left for the day, serene in the knowledge that no corner, no chandelier, no mirror, no curlicue so hidden, so high, so glittering, so ornate that it might hope to escape the rag or brush of one or the other of this relentless and expert crew.

Every year, twice a year, as this box, that trunk or chest was opened and its contents revealed, Miz' Merz would say: "You keepin' this, Miz' Brewster?"

"That? Oh, dear, yes!" Or: "Well—I don't know. You can take that home with you if you want it. It might make over for Minnie."

Yet, why in the name of all that's ridiculous did she treasure the funeral wheat wreath in the walnut frame? Nothing is more *passé* than a last summer's hat, yet the leghorn and pink-cambric-rose thing in the tin trunk was the one Mrs. Brewster had worn when a bride. Then the plaid kilted dress with the black velvet monkey jacket that Pinky had worn when she spoke her first piece at the age of seven—well, these were things that even the rapacious eye of Miz' Merz (by-the-day) passed by unbrightened by covetousness.

The smell of soap and water, and cedar, and moth balls, and dust, and the ghost of a perfumery that Pinky used to use pervaded the hot attic. Mrs. Brewster, head and shoulders in a trunk, was trying not to listen and not to seem not to listen to Miz' Merz's recital of her husband's relations' latest flagrancy.

"'Families is nix,' I says. 'I got my own fam'ly to look out fur,' I says. Like that. 'Well,' s's he, 'w'en it comes to *that*,' s's he, 'I guess I got some—'" Punctuated by thumps, spatterings, swashings, and much heavy breathing, so that the sound of light footsteps along the second-floor hallway, a young, clear voice calling, then the same footsteps, fleeter now, on the attic stairway, were quite unheard.

———

Pinky's arms were around her mother's neck and for one awful moment it looked as if both were to be decapitated by the trunk lid, so violent had been Mrs. Brewster's start of surprise.

Incoherent little cries, and sentences unfinished:

"Pinky! Why—my baby! We didn't get your telegram. Did you—"

"No; I didn't. I just thought I—Don't look so dazed, mummy—You're all smudged, too—what in the world!" Pinky straightened her hat and looked about the attic. "Why, mother! You're—you're house cleaning!" There was a stunned sort of look on her face. Pinky's last visit home had been in June, all hammocks, and roses, and especially baked things, and motor trips into the country.

"Of course. This is September. But if I'd known you were coming—Come here to the window. Let mother see you. Is that the kind of hat they're—why, it's a winter one, isn't it? Already! Dear me, I've just got used to the angle of my summer one. You must telephone father."

Miz' Merz, damply calicoed, rose from a corner and came forward, wiping a moist and parboiled hand on her skirt. "Ha' do, Pinky. Ain't forgot your old friends, have you?"

"It's Mrs. Merz!" Pinky put her cool, sweet fingers into the other woman's spongy clasp. "Why, hello, Mrs. Merz! Of course when there's house cleaning—I'd forgotten all about house cleaning—that there was such a thing, I mean."

"It's got to be done," replied Miz' Merz, severely.

Pinky, suddenly looking like one of her own magazine covers (in tailor clothes), turned swiftly to her mother. "Nothing of the kind," she said, crisply. She looked about the hot, dusty, littered room. She included and then banished it all with one sweeping gesture. "Nothing of the kind. This is—this is an anachronism."

"Mebbe so," retorted Miz' Merz with equal crispness. "But it's got to be cleaned just the same. Yessir; it's got to be cleaned."

They smiled at each other then, the mother and daughter. They descended the winding attic stairs happily, talking very fast and interrupting each other.

Mrs. Brewster's skirt was still pinned up. Her hair was bound in the protecting towel. "You must telephone father. No, let's surprise him. You'll hate the dinner—built around Miz Merz; you know—boiled. Well, you know what a despot she is."

It was hot for September, in Wisconsin. As they came out to the porch Pinky saw that there were tiny beads of moisture under her mother's eyes and about her chin. The sight infuriated her somehow. "Well, really, mother!"

Mrs. Brewster unpinned her skirt and smoothed it down; and smiled at Pinky, all unconscious that she looked like a plump, pink Sister of Mercy with that towel bound tightly about her hair. With a swift movement Pinky unpinned the towel, unwound it, dabbed with it tenderly at her mother's chin and brow, rolled it into a vicious wad, and hurled it through the open doorway.

"Now just what does that mean?" said Mrs. Brewster, equably. "Take off your hat and coat, Pinky, but don't treat them that way—unless that's the way they're doing in New York. Everything is so informal since the war." She had a pretty wit of her own, Mrs. Brewster.

Of course Pinky laughed then, and kissed her mother and hugged her hard. "It's just that it seems so idiotic—your digging around in an attic in this day and age! Why, it's—it's—" Pinky could express herself much more clearly in colours than in words. "There is no such thing as an attic. People don't clean them any more. I never realized before—this huge house. It has been wonderful to come back to, of course. But just you and dad." She stopped. She raised two young fists high in impotent anger. "Do you *like* cleaning the attic?"

"Why, no. I hate it."

"Then why in the world—"

"I've always done it, Pinky. And while they may not be wearing attics in New York, we haven't taken them off in Winnebago. Come on up to your room, dear. It looks bare. If I'd known you were coming—the slip covers—"

"Are they in the box in the attic labelled 'Slp Cov Pinky Rm'?" She succeeded in slurring it ludicrously.

It brought an appreciative giggle from Mrs. Brewster. A giggle need not be inconsistent, with fifty years, especially if one's nose wrinkles up delightfully in the act. But no smile curved the daughter's stern young lips. Together they went up to Pinky's old room (the older woman stopped to pick up the crumpled towel on the hall floor). On the way they paused at the door of Mrs. Brewster's bedroom, so cool, so spacious, all soft grays and blues.

Suddenly Pinky's eyes widened with horror. She pointed an accusing forefinger at a large, dark object in a corner near a window. "That's the old walnut desk!" she exclaimed.

"I know it."

The girl turned, half amused, half annoyed. "Oh, mother dear! That's the situation in a nutshell. Without a shadow of doubt there's an eradicable streak of black walnut in your gray-enamel make-up."

"Eradicable! That's a grand word, Pinky. Stylish! I never expected to meet it out of a book. And, fu'thermore, as Miz' Merz would say, I didn't know there was any situation."

"I meant the attic. And it's more than a situation. It's a state of mind."

Mrs. Brewster had disappeared into the depths of her clothes closet. Her voice sounded muffled. "Pinky, you're talking the way they did at that tea you gave for father and me when we visited New York last winter." She emerged with a cool-looking blue kimono. "Here. Put this on. Father'll be home at twelve-thirty, for dinner, you know. You'll want a bath, won't you, dear?"

"Yes. Mummy, is it boiled—honestly?—on a day like this?"

"With onions," said Mrs. Brewster, firmly.

Fifteen minutes later Pinky, splashing in a cool tub, heard the voice of Miz' Merz high-pitched with excitement and a certain awful joy: "Miz' Brewster! Oh, Miz' Brewster! I found a moth in Mr. Brewster's winter flannels!"

"Oh!" in choked accents of fury from Pinky; and she brought a hard young fist down in the water—spat!—so that it splashed ceiling, hair, and floor impartially.

Still, it was a cool and serene young daughter who greeted Hosea Brewster as he came limping up the porch stairs. He placed the flat of the foot down at each step instead of heel and ball. It gave him a queer, hitching gait. The girl felt a sharp little constriction of her throat as she marked that rheumatic limp. "It's the beastly Wisconsin winters," she told herself. Then, darting out at him from the corner where she had been hiding: "S'prise! S'prise!"

His plump blond face, flushed with the unwonted heat, went darkly red. He dropped his hat. His arms gathered her in. Her fresh young cheek was pressed against his dear prickly one. So they stood for a long minute—close.

"Need a shave, dad."

"Well, gosh, how did I know my best girl was coming!" He held her off. "What's the matter, Pink? Don't they like your covers any more?"

"Not a thing, Hosey. Don't get fresh. They're decorating my studio—you know—plasterers and stuff. I couldn't work. And I was lonesome for you."

Hosea Brewster went to the open doorway and gave a long whistle with a little quirk at the end. Then he came back to Pinky in the wide-seated porch swing. "You know," he said, his voice lowered confidentially, "I thought I'd take mother to New York for ten days or so. See the shows, and run around and eat at the dens of wickedness. She likes it for a change."

Pinky sat up, tense. "For a change? Dad, I want to talk to you about that. Mother needs—"

Mrs. Brewster's light footstep sounded in the hall. She wore an all-enveloping gingham apron. "How did you like your surprise, father?" She came over to him and kissed the top of his head. "I'm getting dinner so that Gussie can go on with the attic. Everything's ready if you want to come in. I didn't want to dish up until you were at the table, so's everything would be hot." She threw a laughing glance at Pinky.

But when they were seated, there appeared a platter of cold, thinly sliced ham for Pinky, and a crisp salad, and a featherweight cheese soufflé, and iced tea, and a dessert coolly capped with whipped cream.

"But, mother, you shouldn't have—" feebly.

"There are always a lot of things in the house. You know that. I just wanted to tease you."

Father Brewster lingered for an unwonted hour after the midday meal. But two o'clock found him back at the cold-storage plant. Pinky watched him go, a speculative look in her eyes.

She visited the attic that afternoon at four, when it was again neat, clean, orderly, smelling of soap and sunshine. Standing there in the centre of the big room, freshly napped, smartly coifed, blue-serged, trim, the very concentrated essence of modernity, she eyed with stern deliberation the funeral wheat wreath in its walnut frame; the trunks; the chests; the boxes all shelved and neatly inscribed with their "H's Fshg Tckl" and "Blk Nt Drs."

"Barbaric!" she said aloud, though she stood there alone. "Medieval! Mad! It has got to be stopped. Slavery!" After which she went downstairs and picked golden glow for the living-room vases and scarlet salvia for the bowl in the dining room.

Still, as one saw Mrs. Brewster's tired droop at supper that night, there is no denying that there seemed some justification for Pinky's volcanic remarks.

Hosea Brewster announced, after supper, that he and Fred were going to have a session with the furnace; she needed going over in September before they began firing up for the winter.

"I'll go down with you," said Pinky.

"No, you stay up here with mother. You'll get all ashes and coal dust."

But Pinky was firm. "Mother's half dead. She's going straight up to bed, after that darned old attic. I'll come up to tuck you in, mummy."

And though she did not descend to the cellar until the overhauling process was nearly completed she did come down in time for the last of the scene. She perched at the foot of the stairs and watched the two men, overalled, sooty, tobacco-wreathed, and happy. When, finally, Hosea Brewster knocked the ashes out of his stubby black pipe, dusted his sooty hands together briskly, and began to peel his overalls, Pinky came forward.

She put her hand on his arm. "Dad, I want to talk to you."

"Careful there. Better not touch me. I'm all dirt. G'night, Fred."

"Listen, dad. Mother isn't well."

He stopped then, with one overall leg off and the other on, and looked at her. "Huh? What d'you mean—isn't well? Mother." His mouth was open. His eyes looked suddenly strained.

"This house—it's killing her. She could hardly keep her eyes open at supper. It's too much for her. She ought to be enjoying herself—like other women. She's a slave to the attic and all those huge rooms. And you're another."

"Me?" feebly.

"Yes. A slave to this furnace. You said yourself to Fred, just now, that it was all worn out, and needed new pipes or something—I don't know what. And that coal was so high it would be cheaper using dollar bills for fuel. Oh, I know you were just being funny. But it was partly true. Wasn't it? Wasn't it?"

"Yeh, but listen here, Paula." He never called her Paula unless he was terribly disturbed, "About mother—you said—"

"You and she ought to go away this winter—not just for a trip, but to stay. You"—she drew a long breath and made the plunge—"you ought to give up the house."

"Give up—"

"Permanently. Mother and you are buried alive here. You ought to come to New York to live. Both of you will love it when you are there for a few days. I don't mean to come to a hotel. I mean to take a little apartment, a furnished apartment at first, to see how you like it—two rooms and kitchenette, like a playhouse."

Hosey Brewster looked down at his own big bulk, then around the great furnace room. "Oh, but listen—"

"No, I want you to listen first. Mother's worn out, I tell you. It isn't as if she were the old-fashioned kind; she isn't. She loves the theatres, and pretty hats, and shoes with buckles, and lobster, and concerts."

He broke in again: "Sure; she likes 'em for a change. But for a steady diet—Besides, I've got a business to 'tend to. My gosh! I've got a business to—"

"You know perfectly well that Wetzler practically runs the whole thing—or could, if you'd let him." Youth is cruel like that, when it wants its way.

He did not even deny it. He seemed suddenly old. Pinky's heart smote her a little. "It's just that you've got so used to this great barracks you don't know how unhappy it's making you. Why, mother said to-day that she hated it. I asked about the attic—the cleaning and all—and she said she hated it."

"Did she say that, Paula?"

"Yes."

He dusted his hands together, slowly, spiritlessly. His eyes looked pained and dull. "She did, h'm? You say she did?" He was talking to himself, and thinking, thinking.

Pinky, sensing victory, left him. She ran lightly up the cellar stairs, through the first-floor rooms, and up to the second floor. Her mother's bedroom door was open.

A little mauve lamp shed its glow upon the tired woman in one of the plump, gray-enamel beds. "No, I'm not sleeping. Come here, dear. What in the world have you been doing in the cellar all this time?"

"Talking to dad." She came over and perched herself on the side of the bed. She looked down at her mother. Then she bent and kissed her. Mrs. Brewster looked incredibly girlish with the lamp's rosy glow on her face and her hair, warmly brown and profuse, rippling out over the pillow. Scarcely a thread of gray in it. "You know, mother, I think dad isn't well. He ought to go away."

As if by magic the youth and glow faded out of the face on the pillow. As she sat up, clutching her nightgown to her breast, she looked suddenly pinched and old. "What do you mean, Pinky! Father—but he isn't sick. He—"

"Not sick. I don't mean sick exactly. But sort of worn out. That furnace. He's sick and tired of the thing; that's what he said to Fred. He needs a change. He ought to retire and enjoy life. He could. This house is killing both of you. Why in the world don't you close it up, or sell it, and come to New York?"

"But we do. We did. Last winter—"

"I don't mean just for a little trip. I mean to live. Take a little two-room apartment in one of the new buildings—near my studio—and relax. Enjoy yourselves. Meet new men and women. Live! You're in a rut—both of you. Besides, dad needs it. That rheumatism of his, with these Wisconsin winters—"

"But California—we could go to California for—"

"That's only a stop-gap. Get your little place in New York all settled, and then run away whenever you like, without feeling that this great hulk of a house is waiting for you. Father hates it; I know it."

"Did he ever say so?"

"Well, practically. He thinks you're fond of it. He—"

Slow steps ascending the stairs—heavy, painful steps. The two women listened in silence. Every footfall seemed to emphasize Pinky's words. The older woman turned her face toward the sound, her lips parted, her eyes anxious, tender.

"How tired he sounds," said Pinky; "and old. And he's only—why, dad's only fifty-eight."

"Fifty-seven," snapped Mrs. Brewster, sharply, protectively.

Pinky leaned forward and kissed her. "Good-night, mummy dear. You're so tired, aren't you?"

Her father stood in the doorway.

"Good-night, dear. I ought to be tucking you into bed. It's all turned around, isn't it? Biscuits and honey for breakfast, remember."

So Pinky went off to her own room (*sans* slp cov) and slept soundly, dreamlessly, as does one whose work is well done.

———————————————————————

Three days later Pinky left. She waved a good-bye from the car platform, a radiant, electric, confident Pinky, her work well done.

"*Au 'voir!* The first of November! Everything begins then. You'll love it. You'll be real New Yorkers by Christmas. Now, no changing your minds, remember."

And by Christmas, somehow, miraculously, there were they, real New Yorkers; or as real and as New York as any one can be who is living in a studio apartment (duplex) that has been rented (furnished) from a lady who turned out to be from Des Moines.

When they arrived, Pinky had four apartments waiting for their inspection. She told them this in triumph, and well she might, it being the winter after the war, when New York apartments were as scarce as black diamonds and twice as costly.

Father Brewster, on hearing the price, emitted a long, low whistle and said: "How many rooms did you say?"

"Two—and a kitchenette, of course."

"Well, then, all I can say is the furniture ought to be solid gold for that; inlaid with rubies and picked out with platinum."

But it wasn't. In fact, it wasn't solid anything, being mostly of a very impermanent structure and style. Pinky explained that she had kept the best for the last. The thing that worried Father Brewster was that, no matter at what hour of the day they might happen to call on the prospective lessor, that person was always feminine and hatted. Once it was eleven in the morning. Once five in the afternoon.

"Do these New York women wear hats in the house all the time?" demanded Hosea Brewster, worriedly. "I think they sleep in 'em. It's a wonder they ain't bald. Maybe they are. Maybe that's why. Anyway, it makes you feel like a book agent."

He sounded excited and tired, "Now, father!" said Mrs. Brewster, soothingly.

They were in the elevator that was taking them up to the fourth and (according to Pinky) choicest apartment. The building was what is known as a studio apartment, in the West Sixties. The corridors were done in red flagstones, with gray-tone walls. The metal doors were painted gray.

Pinky was snickering. "Now she'll say: 'Well, *we've* been very comfortable here.' They always do. Don't look too eager."

"No fear," put in Hosey Brewster.

"It's really lovely. And a real fireplace. Everything new and good. She's asking two hundred and twenty-five. Offer her one seventy-five. She'll take two hundred."

"You bet she will," growled Hosea.

She answered the door—hatted; hatted in henna, that being the season's chosen colour. A small, dark foyer, overcrowded with furniture; a studio living room, bright, high-ceilinged, smallish; one entire side was window. There were Japanese prints, and a baby grand piano, and a lot of tables, and a davenport placed the way they do it on the stage, with its back to the room and its arms to the fireplace, and a long table just behind it, with a lamp on it, and books, and a dull jar thing, just as you've see it in the second-act library.

Hosea Brewster twisted his head around and up to gaze at the lofty ceiling. "Feel's if I was standing at the bottom of a well," he remarked.

But the hatted one did not hear him. "No; no dining room," she was saying, briskly. "No, indeed. I always use this gate-legged table. You see? It pulls out like this. You can easily seat six—eight, in fact."

"Heaven forbid!" in fervent *sotto voce* from Father Brewster.

"It's an enormous saving in time and labour."

"The—kitchen!" inquired Mrs. Brewster.

The hat waxed playful. "You'll never guess where the kitchen is!" She skipped across the room. "You see this screen?" They saw it. A really handsome affair, and so placed at one end of the room that it looked a part of it. "Come here." They came. The reverse side of the screen was dotted with hooks, and on each hook hung a pot, a pan, a ladle, a spoon. And there was the tiny gas range, the infinitesimal ice chest, the miniature sink. The whole would have been lost in one corner of the Brewster's Winnebago china closet.

"Why, how—how wonderful!" breathed Mrs. Brewster.

"Isn't it? So complete—and so convenient. I've cooked roasts, steaks, chops, everything right here. It's just play."

A terrible fear seized upon Father Brewster. He eyed the sink and the tiny range with a suspicious eye. "The beds," he demanded, "where are the beds?"

She opened the little oven door and his heart sank. But, "They're upstairs," she said. "This is a duplex, you know."

A little flight of winding stairs ended in a balcony. The rail was hung with a gay mandarin robe. Two more steps and you were in the bedroom—a rather breathless little bedroom, profusely rose-coloured, and with whole battalions of photographs in flat silver frames standing about on dressing table, shelf, desk. The one window faced a gray brick wall.

They took the apartment. And thus began a life of ease and gayety for Mr. and Mrs. Hosea C. Brewster, of Winnebago, Wisconsin.

Pinky had dinner with them the first night, and they laughed a great deal, what with one thing and another. She sprang up to the balcony, and let down her bright hair, and leaned over the railing, *à la* Juliet, having first decked Hosey out in a sketchy but effective Romeo costume consisting of a hastily snatched up scarf over one shoulder, Pinky's little turban, and a frying pan for a lute. Mother Brewster did the Nurse, and by the time Hosea began his limping climb up the balcony, the turban over one eye and the scarf winding itself about his stocky legs, they ended by tumbling in a heap of tearful laughter.

After Pinky left there came upon them, in that cozy little two-room apartment, a feeling of desolation and vastness, and a terrible loneliness such as they had never dreamed of in the great twelve-room house in Winnebago. They kept close to each other. They toiled up the winding stairs together and stood a moment on the balcony, feigning a light-heartedness that neither of them felt.

They lay very still in the little stuffy rose-coloured room, and the street noises of New York came up to them—a loose chain flapping against the mud guard of a taxi; the jolt of a flat-wheeled Eighth Avenue street car; the roar of an L train; laughter; the bleat of a motor horn; a piano in the apartment next door, or upstairs, or down.

She thought, as she lay there, choking, of the great, gracious gray-and-blue room at home, many-windowed, sweet-smelling, quiet. Quiet!

He thought, as he lay there, choking, of the gracious gray-blue room at home, many-windowed, sweet-smelling, quiet. Quiet!

Then, as he had said that night in September: "Sleeping, mother?"

"N-no. Not yet. Just dozing off."

"It's the strange beds, I guess. This is going to be great, though. Great!"

"My, yes!" agreed Mrs. Brewster, heartily.

They awoke next morning unrefreshed. Pa Brewster, back home in Winnebago, always whistled mournfully, off key, when he shaved. The more doleful his tune the happier his wife knew him to be. Also, she had learned to mark his progress by this or that passage in a refrain. Sometimes he sang, too (also off key), and you heard his genial roar all over the house. The louder he roared, and the more doleful the tune, the happier his frame of mind. Milly Brewster knew this. She had never known that she knew it. Neither had he. It was just one of those subconscious bits of marital knowledge that make for happiness and understanding.

When he sang "The Dying Cowboy's Lament" and came to the passage, "Oh, take me to the churchyard and lay the sod o-o-over me," Mrs. Brewster used to say: "Gussie, Mr. Brewster'll be down in ten minutes. You can start the eggs."

In the months of their gay life in Sixty-Seventh Street Hosey Brewster never once sang "The Dying Cowboy's Lament," nor whistled "In the Sweet By-and-By." No; he whistled not at all, or when he did, gay bits of jazz heard at the theatre or in a restaurant the night before. He deceived no one, least of all himself. Sometimes his voice would trail off into nothingness, but he would catch the tune and toss it up again, heavily, as though it were a physical weight.

Theatres! Music! Restaurants! Teas! Shopping! The gay life!

"Enjoying yourself, Milly?" he would say.

"Time of my life, father."

She had her hair dressed in those geometrical undulations without which no New York audience feels itself clothed. They saw Pinky less frequently as time went on and her feeling of responsibility lessened. Besides, the magazine covers took most of her day. She gave a tea for her father and mother at her own studio, and Mrs. Brewster's hat, slippers, gown, and manner equalled in line, style, cut, and texture those of any other woman present, which rather surprised her until she had talked to five or six of them.

She and Hosey drifted together and compared notes. "Say, Milly," he confided, "they're all from Wisconsin—or approximately; Michigan, and Minnesota, and Iowa, and around. Far's I can make out there's only one New Yorker, really, in the whole caboodle of 'em."

"Which one?"

"That kind of plain little one over there—sensible looking, with the blue suit. I was talking to her. She was born right here in New York, but she doesn't live here—that is, not in the city. Lives in some place in the country, in a house."

A sort of look came into Mrs. Brewster's eyes. "Is that so? I'd like to talk to her, Hosey. Take me over."

She did talk to the quiet little woman in the plain blue suit. And the quiet little woman said: "Oh, dear, yes!" She ignored her r's fascinatingly, as New Yorkers do. "We live in Connecticut. You see, you Wisconsin people have crowded us out of New York; no breathing space. Besides, how can one live here? I mean to say—live. And then the children—it's no place for children, grown up or otherwise. I love it—oh, yes, indeed. I love it. But it's too difficult."

Mrs. Brewster defended it like a true Westerner. "But if you have just a tiny apartment, with a kitchenette—"

The New York woman laughed. There was nothing malicious about her. But she laughed. "I tried it. There's one corner of my soul that's still wrinkled from the crushing. Everything in a heap. Not to speak of the slavery of it. That—that deceitful, lying kitchenette."

This was the first woman who Mrs. Brewster had talked to—really talked to—since leaving Winnebago. And she liked women. She missed them. At first she had eyed wonderingly, speculatively, the women she saw on Fifth Avenue. Swathed luxuriously in precious pelts, marvellously coifed and hatted, wearing the frailest of boots and hose, exhaling a mysterious, heady scent, they were more like strange, exotic birds than women.

The clerks in the shops, too—they were so remote, so contemptuous. When she went into Gerretson's, back home, Nellie Monahan was likely to say: "You've certainly had a lot of wear out of that blue, Mrs. Brewster. Let's see, you've had it two—three years this spring? My land! Let me show you our new taupes."

Pa Brewster had taken to conversing with the doorman. That adamantine individual, unaccustomed to being addressed as a human being, was startled at first, surly and distrustful. But he mellowed under Hosey's simple and friendly advances. They became quite pals, these two—perhaps two as lonely men as you could find in all lonely New York.

"I guess you ain't a New Yorker, huh?" Mike said.

"Me? No."

"Th' most of the folks in th' buildin' ain't."

"Ain't!" Hosea Brewster was startled into it. "They're artists, aren't they? Most of 'em?"

"No! Out-of-town folks, mostly, like you. West—Iowa an' Californy an' around there. Livin' here, though. Seem t' like it better'n where they come from. I dunno."

Hosey Brewster took to eying them as Mrs. Brewster had eyed the women. He wondered about them, these tight, trim men, rather short of breath, buttoned so snugly into their shining shoes and their tailored clothes, with their necks bulging in a fold of fat above the back of their white linen collars. He knew that he would never be like them. It wasn't his square-toed shoes that made the difference, or his gray hat, or his baggy trousers. It was something inside him—something he lacked, he thought. It never occurred to him that it was something he possessed that they did not.

"Enjoying yourself, Milly?"

"I should say I am, father."

"That's good. No housework and responsibility to this, is there?"

"It's play."

She hated the toy gas stove, and the tiny ice chest, and the screen pantry. All her married life she had kept house in a big, bounteous way: apples in barrels; butter in firkins; flour in sacks; eggs in boxes; sugar in bins; cream in crocks. Sometimes she told herself, bitterly, that it was easier to keep twelve rooms tidy and habitable than one combination kitchen-dining-and-living room.

"Chops taste good, Hosey?"

"Grand. But you oughtn't to be cooking around like this. We'll eat out to-morrow night somewhere, and go to a show."

"You're enjoying it, aren't you, Hosey, h'm?"

"It's the life, mother! It's the life!"

His ruddy colour began to fade. He took to haunting department store kitchenware sections. He would come home with a new kind of cream whipper, or a patent device for the bathroom. He would tinker happily with this, driving a nail, adjusting a screw. At such times he was even known to begin to whistle some scrap of a doleful tune such as he used to hum. But he would change, quickly, into something lively. The price of butter, eggs, milk, cream, and the like horrified his Wisconsin cold-storage sensibilities. He used often to go down to Fulton Market before daylight and walk about among the stalls and shops, piled with tons of food of all kinds. He would talk to the marketmen, and the buyers and grocers, and come away feeling almost happy for a time.

Then, one day, with a sort of shock, he remembered a farmer he had known back home in Winnebago. He knew the farmers for miles around, naturally, in his business. This man had been a steady butter-and-egg acquaintance, one of the wealthy farmers in that prosperous Wisconsin farming community. For his family's sake he had moved into town, a ruddy, rufous-bearded, clumping fellow, intelligent, kindly. They had sold the farm with a fine profit and had taken a box-like house on Franklin Street. He had nothing to do but enjoy himself. You saw him out on the porch early, very early summer mornings.

You saw him ambling about the yard, poking at a weed here, a plant there. A terrible loneliness was upon him; a loneliness for the soil he had deserted. And slowly, resistlessly, the soil pulled at him with its black strength and its green tendrils down, down, until he ceased to struggle and lay there clasped gently to her breast, the mistress he had thought to desert and who had him again at last, and forever.

"I don't know what ailed him," his widow had said, weeping. "He just seemed to kind of pine away."

It was one morning in April—one soft, golden April morning—when this memory had struck Hosey Brewster. He had been down at Fulton Market. Something about the place—the dewy fresh vegetables, the crates of eggs, the butter, the cheese—had brought such a surge of homesickness over him as to amount to an actual nausea. Riding uptown in the Subway he had caught a glimpse of himself in a slot-machine mirror. His face was pale and somehow shrunken. He looked at his hands. The skin hung loose where the little pads of fat had plumped them out.

"Gosh!" he said. "Gosh, I—"

He thought, then, of the red-faced farmer who used to come clumping into the cold-storage warehouse in his big boots and his buffalo coat. A great fear swept over him and left him weak and sick.

The chill grandeur of the studio-building foyer stabbed him. The glittering lift made him dizzy, somehow, this morning. He shouldn't have gone out without some breakfast perhaps. He walked down the flagged corridor softly; turned the key ever so cautiously. She might still be sleeping. He turned the knob gently, gently; tiptoed in and, turning, fell over a heavy wooden object that lay directly in his path in the dim little hall.

A barked shin. A good, round oath.

"Hosey! What's the matter? What—" She came running to him. She led him into the bright front room.

"What was that thing? A box or something, right there in front of the door. What the—"

"Oh, I'm so sorry, Hosey. You sometimes have breakfast downtown. I didn't know—"

Something in her voice—he stopped rubbing the injured shin to look up at her. Then he straightened slowly, his mouth ludicrously open. Her head was bound in a white towel. Her skirt was pinned back. Her sleeves were rolled up. Chairs, tables, rugs, ornaments, were huddled in a promiscuous heap. Mrs. Hosea C. Brewster was cleaning house.

"Milly!" he began, sternly. "And that's just the thing you came here to get away from. If Pinky—"

"I didn't mean to, father. But when I got up this morning there was a letter—a letter from the woman who owns this apartment, you know. She asked if I'd go to the hall closet—the one she reserved for her own things, you know—and unlock it, and get out a box she told me about, and have the hall boy express it to her. And I did, and—look!"

Limping a little he followed her. She turned on the light that hung in the closet. Boxes—pasteboard boxes—each one bearing a cryptic pencilling on the end that stared out at you. "Drp Stud Win," said one; "Sum Slp Cov Bedrm," another; "Toil. Set & Pic Frms."

Mrs. Brewster turned to her husband, almost shamefacedly, and yet with a little air of defiance. "It—I don't know—it made me—not homesick, Hosey. Not homesick, exactly; but—well, I guess I'm not the only woman with a walnut streak in her modern make-up. Here's the woman—she came to the door with her hat on, and yet—"

Truth—blinding, white-hot truth—burst in upon him. "Mother," he said—and he stood up, suddenly robust, virile, alert—"mother, let's go home."

Mechanically she began to unpin the looped-back skirt. "When?"

"Now."

317

"But, Hosey! Pinky—this flat—until June—"

"Now! Unless you want to stay. Unless you like it here in this—this make-believe, double-barrelled, duplex do-funny of a studio thing. Let's go home, mother. Let's go home—and breathe."

In Wisconsin you are likely to find snow in April—snow or slush. The Brewsters found both. Yet on their way up from the station in 'Gene Buck's flivver taxi they beamed out at it as if it were a carpet of daisies.

At the corner of Elm and Jackson streets Hosey Brewster stuck his head out of the window. "Stop here a minute, will you, 'Gene?"

They stopped in front of Hengel's meat market, and Hosey went in. Mrs. Brewster leaned back without comment.

Inside the shop. "Well, I see you're back from the East," said Aug Hengel.

"Yep."

"We thought you'd given us the go-by, you stayed away so long."

"No, sir-ree! Say, Aug, give me that piece of bacon—the big piece. And send me up some corned beef to-morrow for corned beef and cabbage. I'll take a steak along for to-night. Oh, about four pounds. That's right."

It seemed to him that nothing less than a side of beef could take out of his mouth the taste of those fiddling little lamb chops and the restaurant fare of the past six months.

All through the winter Fred had kept up a little heat in the house, with an eye to frozen water pipes. But there was a chill upon the place as they opened the door now. It was late afternoon. The house was very still, with the stillness of a dwelling that has long been uninhabited. The two stood there a moment, peering into the darkened rooms. Then Hosea Brewster strode forward, jerked up this curtain, that curtain with a sharp snap, flap! He stamped his feet to rid them of slush. He took off his hat and threw it high in the air and opened his arms wide and emitted a whoop of sheer joy and relief.

"Welcome home! Home!"

She clung to him. "Oh, Hosey, isn't it wonderful? How big it looks! Huge!"

"Land, yes." He strode from hall to dining room, from kitchen to library. "I know how a jack-in-the-box feels when the lid's opened. No wonder it grins and throws out its arms."

They did little talking after that. By five o'clock he was down in the cellar. She heard him making a great sound of rattling and bumping and shaking and pounding and shovelling. She smelled the acrid odour of his stubby black pipe.

"Hosey!"—from the top of the cellar stairs. "Hosey, bring up a can of preserves when you come."

"What?"

"Can of preserves."

"What kind?"

"Any kind you like."

"Can I have two kinds?"

He brought up quince marmalade and her choicest damson plums. He put them down on the kitchen table and looked around, spatting his hands together briskly to rid them of dust. "Sh's burning pretty good now. That Fred! Don't any more know how to handle a boiler than a baby does. Is the house getting warmer?"

He clumped into the dining room, through the butler's pantry, but he was back again in a wink, his eyes round. "Why, say, mother! You've got out the best dishes, and the silver, and the candles, and all. And the tablecloth with the do-dads on it. Why—"

"I know it." She opened the oven door, took out a pan of biscuits and slid it deftly to one side. "It seems as if I can't spread enough. I'm going to use the biggest platters, and I've put two extra boards in the table. It's big enough to seat ten. I want everything big, somehow. I've cooked enough potatoes for a regiment, and I know it's wasteful, and I don't care. I'll eat in my kitchen apron, if you'll keep on your overalls. Come on."

He cut into the steak—a great, thick slice. He knew she could never eat it, and she knew she could never eat it. But she did eat it all, ecstatically. And in a sort of ecstatic Nirvana the quiet and vastness and peace of the big old frame house settled down upon them.

The telephone in the hall rang startlingly, unexpectedly.

"Let me go, Milly."

"But who in the world! Nobody knows we're—"

He was at the telephone. "Who? Who? Oh." He turned: "It's Miz' Merz. She says her little Minnie went by at six and saw a light in the house. She—Hello! What?... She says she wants to know if she's to save time for you at the end of the month for the April cleaning."

Mrs. Brewster took the receiver from him: "The twenty-fifth, as usual, Miz' Merz. The twenty-fifth, as usual. The attic must be a sight."

OLD LADY MANDLE

Old lady Mandle was a queen. Her demesne, undisputed, was a six-room flat on South Park Avenue, Chicago. Her faithful servitress was Anna, an ancient person of Polish nativity, bad teeth, and a cunning hand at cookery. Not so cunning, however, but that old lady Mandle's was more artful still in such matters as meat-soups, broad noodles, fish with egg sauce, and the like. As ladies-in-waiting, flattering yet jealous, admiring though resentful, she had Mrs. Lamb, Mrs. Brunswick, and Mrs. Wormser, themselves old ladies and erstwhile queens, now deposed. And the crown jewel in old lady Mandle's diadem was my son Hugo.

Mrs. Mandle was not only a queen but a spoiled old lady. And not only a spoiled old lady but a confessedly spoiled old lady. Bridling and wagging her white head she admitted her pampered state. It was less an admission than a boast. Her son Hugo had spoiled her. This, too, she acknowledged. "My son Hugo spoils me," she would say, and there was no proper humbleness in her voice. Though he was her only son she never spoke of him merely as "Hugo," or "My son," but always as "My son Hugo." She rolled the three words on her tongue as though they were delicious morsels from which she would extract all possible savour and sweetness. And when she did this you could almost hear the click of the stiffening spines of Mrs. Lamb, Mrs. Brunswick, and Mrs. Wormser. For they envied her her son Hugo, and resented him as only three old ladies could who were living, tolerated and dependent, with their married sons and their sons' wives.

Any pleasant summer afternoon at four o'clock you might have seen Mrs. Mandle holding court. The four old women sat, a decent black silk row, on a shady bench in Washington Park (near the refectory and afternoon coffee). Three of them complained about their daughters-in-law. One of them bragged about her son. Adjective crowding adjective, pride in her voice, majesty in her mien, she bragged about my son Hugo.

My son Hugo had no wife. Not only that, Hugo Mandle, at forty, had no thought of marrying. Not that there was anything austere or saturnine about Hugo. He made you think, somehow, of a cherubic, jovial monk. It may have been his rosy rotundity, or, perhaps, the way in which his thinning hair vanished altogether at the top of his head, so as to form a tonsure. Hugo Mandle, kindly, generous, shrewd, spoiled his old mother in the way in which women of seventy, whose middle life has been hard, like to be spoiled. First of all, of course, she reigned unchecked over the South Park Avenue flat. She quarrelled wholesomely and regularly with Polish Anna. Alternately she threatened Anna with dismissal and Anna threatened Ma Mandle with impending departure. This had been going on, comfortably, for fifteen years. Ma Mandle held the purse and her son filled it. Hugo paid everything from the rent to the iceman, and this without once making his mother feel a beneficiary. She possessed an infinitesimal income of her own, left her out of the ruins of her dead husband's money, but this Hugo always waved aside did she essay to pay for her own movie ticket or an ice cream soda. "Now, now! None of that, Ma. Your money's no good to-night."

When he returned from a New York business trip he usually brought her two gifts, one practical, the other absurd. She kissed him for the first and scolded him for the second, but it was the absurdity, fashioned of lace, or silk, or fragile stuff, that she pridefully displayed to her friends.

"Look what my son Hugo brought me. I should wear a thing like that in my old days. But it's beautiful anyway, h'm? He's got taste, my son Hugo."

In the cool of the evening you saw them taking a slow and solemn walk together, his hand on her arm. He surprised her with matinée tickets in pairs, telling her to treat one of her friends. On Anna's absent Thursdays he always offered to take dinner downtown. He brought her pound boxes of candy tied with sly loops and bands of gay satin ribbon which she carefully rolled and tucked away in a drawer. He praised her cooking, and teased her with elephantine playfulness, and told her that she looked like a chicken in that hat. Oh, yes, indeed! Mrs. Mandle was a spoiled old lady.

At half-past one she always prepared to take her nap in the quiet of her neat flat. She would select a plump, after-lunch chocolate from the box in her left-hand bureau drawer, take off her shoes, and settle her old frame in comfort. No noisy grandchildren to disturb her rest. No fault-finding daughter-in-law to bustle her out of the way. The sounds that Anna made, moving about in the kitchen at the far end of the long hall, were the subdued homely swishings and brushings that lulled and soothed rather than irritated. At half-past two she rose, refreshed, dressed herself in her dotted swiss with its rows of val, or in black silk, modish both. She was, in fact, a modish old lady as were her three friends. They were not the ultra-modern type of old lady who at sixty apes sixteen. They were neat and rather tart-tongued septuagenarians, guiltless of artifice. Their soft white hair was dressed neatly and craftily so as to conceal the thinning spots that revealed the pink scalp beneath. Their corsets and their stomachs were too high, perhaps, for fashion, and their heavy brooches and chains and rings appeared clumsy when compared to the hoar-frost tracery of the platinumsmith's exquisite art. But their skirts had pleats when pleated skirts were worn, and their sleeves were snug when snug sleeves were decreed. They were inclined to cling over-long to a favourite leather reticule, scuffed and shapeless as an old shoe, but they could hold their own at bridge on a rainy afternoon.

In matters of material and cut Mrs. Mandle triumphed. Her lace was likely to be real where that of the other three was imitation.

So there they sat on a park bench in the pleasant afternoon air, filling their lives with emptiness. They had married, and brought children into the world; sacrificed for them, managed a household, been widowed. They represented magnificent achievement, those four old women, though they themselves did not know it. They had come up the long hill, reached its apex, and come down. Their journey was over and yet they sat by the roadside. They knew that which could have helped younger travellers over the next hill, but those fleet-footed ones pressed on, wanting none of their wisdom. Ma Mandle alone still moved. She still queened it over her own household; she alone still had the delightful task of making a man comfortable. If the world passed them by as they sat there it did not pass unscathed. Their shrewd old eyes regarded the panorama, undeceived. They did not try to keep up with the procession, but they derived a sly amusement and entertainment from their observation of the modes and manners of this amazing day and age. Perhaps it was well that this plump matron in the over-tight skirt or that miss mincing on four-inch heels could not hear the caustic comment of the white-haired four sitting so mildly on the bench at the side of the path.

Their talk, stray as it might, always came back to two subjects. They seemed never to tire of them. Three talked of their daughters-in-law, and bitterness rasped their throats. One talked of her son, and her voice was unctuous with pride.

"My son's wife—" one of the three would begin. There was something terribly significant in the mock respect with which she uttered the title.

"If I had ever thought," Mrs. Brunswick would say, shaking her head, "if I had ever thought that I would live to see the day when I had to depend on strangers for my comfort, I would have wished myself dead."

"You wouldn't call your son a stranger, Mrs. Brunswick!" in shocked tones from Mrs. Mandle.

"A stranger has got more consideration. I count for nothing. Less than nothing. I'm in the way. I don't interfere in that household. I see enough, and I hear enough, but I say nothing. My son's wife, she says it all."

A silence, thoughtful, brooding. Then, from Mrs. Wormser: "What good do you have of your children? They grow up, and what do you have of them?"

More shaking of heads, and a dark murmur about the advisability of an Old People's Home as a refuge. Then:

"My son Hugo said only yesterday, 'Ma,' he said, 'when it comes to housekeeping you could teach them all something, believe me. Why,' he says, 'if I was to try and get a cup of coffee like this in a restaurant—well, you couldn't get it in a restaurant, that's all. You couldn't get it in any hotel, Michigan Avenue or I don't care where.'"

Goaded, Mrs. Lamb would look up from her knitting. "Mark my words, he'll marry yet." She was a sallow, lively woman, her hair still markedly streaked with black. Her rheumatism-twisted fingers were always grotesquely busy with some handiwork, and the finished product was a marvel of perfection.

Mrs. Wormser, plump, placid, agreed. "That's the kind always marries late. And they get it the worst. Say, my son was no spring chicken, either, when he married. And you would think the sun rises and sets in his wife. Well, I suppose it's only natural. But you wait."

"Some girl is going to have a snap." Mrs. Brunswick, eager, peering, a trifle vindictive, offered final opinion. "The girls aren't going to let a boy like your Hugo get away. Not nowadays, the way they run after them like crazy. All they think about is dress and a good time."

The three smiled grimly. Ma Mandle smiled, too, a little nervously, her fingers creasing and uncreasing a fold of her black silk skirt as she made airy answer: "If I've said once I've said a million times to my son Hugo, 'Hugo, why don't you pick out some nice girl and settle down? I won't be here always.' And he says, 'Getting tired of me, are you, Ma? I guess maybe you're looking for a younger fellow.' Only last night I said, at the table, 'Hugo, when are you going to get married?' And he laughed. 'When I find somebody that can cook dumplings like these. Pass me another, Ma'."

"That's all very well," said Mrs. Wormser.

"But when the right one comes along he won't know dumplings from mud."

"Oh, a man of forty isn't such a—"

"He's just like a man of twenty-five—only worse."

Mrs. Mandle would rise, abruptly. "Well, I guess you all know my son Hugo better than his own mother. How about a cup of coffee, ladies?"

They would proceed solemnly and eagerly to the columned coolness of the park refectory where they would drink their thick, creamy coffee. They never knew, perhaps, how keenly they counted on that cup of coffee, or how hungrily they drank it. Their minds, unconsciously, were definitely fixed on the four-o'clock drink that stimulated the old nerves.

Life had not always been so plumply upholstered for old lady Mandle. She had known its sharp corners and cruel edges. At twenty-three, a strong, healthy, fun-loving girl, she had married Herman Mandle, a dour man twenty-two years her senior. In their twenty-five years of married life together Hattie Mandle never had had a five-cent piece that she could call her own. Her husband was reputed to be wealthy, and probably was, according to the standards of that day. There were three children: Etta, the oldest; a second child, a girl, who died; and Hugo. Her husband's miserliness, and the grind of the planning, scheming, and contriving necessary to clothe and feed her two children would have crushed the spirit of many women. But hard and glum as her old husband was he never quite succeeded in subduing her courage or her love of fun. The habit of heart-breaking economy clung to her, however, even when days of plenty became hers. It showed in little hoarding ways: in the saving of burned matches, of bits of ribbon, of scraps of food, of the very furniture and linen, as though, when these were gone, no more would follow.

Ten years after her marriage her husband retired from active business. He busied himself now with his real estate, with mysterious papers, documents, agents. He was forever poking around the house at hours when a household should be manless, grumbling about the waste where there was none, peering into bread boxes, prying into corners never meant for masculine eyes. Etta, the girl, was like him, sharp-nosed, ferret-faced, stingy. The mother and the boy turned to each other. In a wordless way they grew very close, those two. It was as if they were silently matched against the father and daughter.

It was a queer household, brooding, sinister, like something created in a Brontë brain. The two children were twenty-four and twenty-two when the financial avalanche of '93 thundered across the continent sweeping Herman Handle, a mere speck, into the débris. Stocks and bonds and real estate became paper, with paper value. He clawed about with frantic, clutching fingers but his voice was lost in the shrieks of thousands more hopelessly hurt. You saw him sitting for hours together with a black tin box in front of him, pawing over papers, scribbling down figures, muttering. The bleak future that confronted them had little of terror for Hattie Mandle. It presented no contrast with the bleakness of the past. On the day that she came upon him, his head fallen at a curious angle against the black tin box, his hands, asprawl, clutching the papers that strewed the table, she was appalled, not at what she found, but at the leap her heart gave at what she found. Herman Handle's sudden death was one of the least of the tragedies that trailed in the wake of the devastating panic.

Thus it was that Hugo Handle, at twenty-three, became the head of a household. He did not need to seek work. From the time he was seventeen he had been employed in a large china-importing house, starting as a stock boy. Brought up under the harsh circumstances of Hugo's youth, a boy becomes food for the reformatory or takes on the seriousness and responsibility of middle age. In Hugo's case the second was true. From his father he had inherited a mathematical mind and a sense of material values. From his mother, a certain patience and courage, though he never attained her iron indomitability.

It had been a terrific struggle. His salary at twenty-three was most modest, but he was getting on. He intended to be a buyer, some day, and take trips abroad to the great Austrian and French and English china houses.

The day after the funeral he said to his mother, "Well, now we've got to get Etta married. But married well. Somebody who'll take care of her."

"You're a good son, Hugo," Mrs. Handle had said.

Hugo shook his head. "It isn't that. If she's comfortable and happy—or as happy as she knows how to be—she'll never come back. That's what I want. There's debts to pay, too. But I guess we'll get along."

They did get along, but at snail's pace. There followed five years of economy so rigid as to make the past seem profligate. Etta, the acid-tongued, the ferret-faced, was not the sort to go off without the impetus of a dowry. The man for Etta, the shrew, must be kindly, long-suffering, subdued—and in need of a start. He was. They managed a very decent trousseau and the miracle of five thousand dollars in cash. Every stitch in the trousseau and every penny in the dowry represented incredible sacrifice and self-denial on the part of mother and brother. Etta went off to her new home in Pittsburg with her husband. She had expressed thanks for nothing and had bickered with her mother to the last, but even Hugo knew that her suit and hat and gloves and shoes were right. She was almost handsome in them, the unwonted flush of excitement colouring her cheeks, brightening her eyes.

The next day Hugo came home with a new hat for his mother, a four-pound steak, and the announcement that he was going to take music lessons. A new era had begun in the life of Ma Mandle.

Two people, no matter how far apart in years or tastes, cannot struggle side by side, like that, in a common cause, without forging between them a bond indissoluble. Hugo, at twenty-eight, had the serious mien of a man of forty. At forty he was to revert to his slighted twenty-eight, but he did not know that then. His music lessons were his one protest against a beauty-starved youth. He played rather surprisingly well the cheap music of the day, waggling his head (already threatening baldness) in a professional vaudeville manner and squinting up through his cigar smoke, happily. His mother, seated in the room, sewing, would say, "Play that again, Hugo. That's beautiful. What's the name of that?" He would tell her, for the dozenth time, and play it over, she humming, off-key, in his wake. The relation between them was more than that of mother and son. It was a complex thing that had in it something conjugal. When Hugo kissed his mother with a resounding smack and assured her that she looked like a kid she would push him away with little futile shoves, pat her hair into place, and pretend annoyance. "Go away, you big rough thing!" she would cry. But all unconsciously she got from it a thrill that her husband's withered kisses had never given her.

Twelve years had passed since Etta's marriage. Hugo's salary was a comfortable thing now, even in these days of soaring prices. The habit of economy, so long a necessity, had become almost a vice in old lady Mandle. Hugo, with the elasticity of younger years, learned to spend freely, but his mother's thrift and shrewdness automatically swelled his savings. When he was on the road, as he sometimes was for weeks at a time, she spent only a tithe of the generous sum he left with her. She and Anna ate those sketchy meals that obtain in a manless household. When

321

Hugo was home the table was abundant and even choice, though Ma Mandle often went blocks out of her way to save three cents on a bunch of new beets. So strong is usage. She would no more have wasted his money than she would have knifed him in the dark. She ran the household capably, but her way was the old-fashioned way. Sometimes Hugo used to protest, aghast at some petty act of parsimony.

"But, Ma, what do you want to scrimp like that for! You're the worst tightwad I ever saw. Here, take this ten and blow it. You're worse than the squirrels in the park, darned if you ain't!"

She couldn't resist the ten. Neither could she resist showing it, next day, to Mrs. Brunswick, Mrs. Lamb, and Mrs. Wormser. "How my son Hugo spoils me! He takes out a ten-dollar bill, and he stuffs it into my hand and says 'Ma, you're the worst tightwad I ever saw.'" She laughed contentedly. But she did not blow the ten. As she grew older Hugo regularly lied to her about the price of theatre tickets, dainties, articles of dress, railway fares, luxuries. Her credulity increased with age, shrewd though she naturally was.

It was a second blooming for Ma Mandle. When he surprised her with an evening at the theatre she would fuss before her mirror for a full hour. "Some gal!" Hugo would shout when finally she emerged. "Everybody'll be asking who the old man is you're out with. First thing I know I'll have a police-woman after me for going around with a chicken."

"Don't talk foolishness." But she would flush like a bride. She liked a musical comedy with a lot of girls in it and a good-looking tenor. Next day you would hear her humming the catch-tune in an airy falsetto. Sometimes she wondered about him. She was, after all, a rather wise old lady, and she knew something of men. She had a secret horror of his becoming what she called fast.

"Why don't you take out some nice young girl instead of an old woman like me, Hugo? Any girl would be only too glad." But in her heart was a dread. She thought of Mrs. Lamb, Mrs. Wormser, and Mrs. Brunswick.

So they had gone on, year after year, in the comfortable flat on South Park Avenue. A pleasant thing, life.

And then Hugo married, suddenly, breathlessly, as a man of forty does.

Afterward, Ma Mandle could recall almost nothing from which she might have taken warning. That was because he had said so little. She remembered that he had come home to dinner one evening and had spoken admiringly of a woman buyer from Omaha. He did not often speak of business.

"She buys like a man," he had said at dinner. "I never saw anything like it. Knew what she wanted and got it. She bought all my best numbers at rock bottom. I sold her a four-figure bill in half an hour. And no fuss. Everything right to the point and when I asked her out to dinner she turned me down. Good looking, too. She's coming in again to-morrow for novelties."

Ma Mandle didn't even recall hearing her name until the knife descended. Hugo played the piano a great deal all that week, after dinner. Sentimental things, with a minor wail in the chorus. Smoked a good deal, too. Twice he spent a full hour in dressing, whistling absent-mindedly during the process and leaving his necktie rack looking like a nest of angry pythons when he went out, without saying where he was going. The following week he didn't touch the piano and took long walks in Washington Park, alone, after ten. He seemed uninterested in his meals. Usually he praised this dish, or that.

"How do you like the blueberry pie, Hugo?"

"'S all right." And declined a second piece.

The third week he went West on business. When he came home he dropped his bag in the hall, strode into his mother's bedroom, and stood before her like a schoolboy. "Lil and I are going to be married," he said.

Ma Mandle had looked up at him, her face a blank. "Lil?"

"Sure. I told you all about her." He hadn't. He had merely thought about her, for three weeks, to the exclusion of everything else. "Ma, you'll love her. She knows all about you. She's the grandest girl in the world. Say, I don't know why she ever fell for a dub like me. Well, don't look so stunned. I guess you kind of suspicioned, huh?"

"But who—?"

"I never thought she'd look at me. Earned her own good salary, and strictly business, but she's a real woman. Says she wants her own home an—'n everything. Says every normal woman does. Says—"

Ad lib.

They were married the following month.

Hugo sub-leased the flat on South Park and took an eight-room apartment farther east. Ma Mandle's red and green plush parlour pieces, and her mahogany rockers, and her rubber plant, and the fern, and the can of grapefruit pits that she and Anna had planted and that had come up, miraculously, in the form of shiny, thick little green leaves, all were swept away in the upheaval that followed. Gone, too, was Polish Anna, with her damp calico and her ubiquitous pail and dripping rag and her gutturals. In her place was a trim Swede who wore white kid shoes in the afternoon and gray dresses and cob-web aprons. The sight of the neat Swede sitting in her room at two-thirty in the afternoon, tatting, never failed to fill Ma Mandle with a dumb fury. Anna had been an all-day scrubber.

But Lil. Hugo thought her very beautiful, which she was not. A plump, voluble, full-bosomed woman, exquisitely neat, with a clear, firm skin, bright brown eyes, an unerring instinct for clothes, and a shrewd business head. Hugo's devotion amounted to worship.

He used to watch her at her toilette in their rose and black mahogany front bedroom. Her plump white shoulders gleamed from pink satin straps. She smelled pleasantly of sachet and a certain heady scent she affected. Seated

322

before the mirror, she stared steadily at herself with a concentration such as an artist bestows upon a work that depends, for its perfection, upon nuances of light and shade. Everything about her shone and glittered. Her pink nails were like polished coral. Her hair gleamed in smooth undulations, not a strand out of place. Her skin was clear and smooth as a baby's. Her hands were plump and white. She was always getting what she called a facial, from which process she would emerge looking pinker and creamier than ever. Lil knew when camisoles were edged with filet, and when with Irish. Instinctively she sensed when taffeta was to be superseded by foulard. The contents of her scented bureau drawers needed only a dab of whipped cream on top to look as if they might have been eaten as something soufflé.

"How do I look in it, Hugo? Do you like it?" was a question that rose daily to her lips. A new hat, or frock, or collar, or negligée. Not that she was unduly extravagant. She knew values, and profited by her knowledge.

"Le's see. Turn around. It looks great on you. Yep. That's all right."

He liked to fancy himself a connoisseur in women's clothes and to prove it he sometimes brought home an article of feminine apparel glimpsed in a shop window or showcase, but Lil soon put a stop to that. She had her own ideas on clothes. He turned to jewellery. On Lil's silken bosom reposed a diamond-and-platinum pin the size and general contour of a fish-knife. She had a dinner ring that crowded the second knuckle, and on her plump wrist sparkled an oblong so encrusted with diamonds that its utilitarian dial was almost lost.

It wasn't a one-sided devotion, however. Lil knew much about men, and she had an instinct for making them comfortable. It is a gift that makes up for myriad minor shortcomings. She had a way of laying his clean things out on the bed—fresh linen, clean white socks (Hugo was addicted to white socks and tan, low-cut shoes), silk shirt, immaculate handkerchief. When he came in at the end of a hard day downtown—hot, fagged, sticky—she saw to it that the bathroom was his own for an hour so that he could bathe, shave, powder, dress, and emerge refreshed to eat his good dinner in comfort. Lil was always waiting for him cool, interested, sweet-smelling.

When she said, "How's business, lover?" she really wanted to know. More than that, when he told her she understood, having herself been so long in the game. She gave him shrewd advice, too, so shrewdly administered that he never realized he had been advised, and so, man-like, could never resent it.

Ma Mandle's reign was over.

To Mrs. Lamb, Mrs. Brunswick, and Mrs. Wormser Ma Mandle lied magnificently. Their eager, merciless questions pierced her like knives, but she made placid answer: "Young folks are young folks. They do things different. I got my way. My son's wife has got hers." Their quick ears caught the familiar phrase.

"It's hard, just the same," Mrs. Wormser insisted, "after you've been boss all these years to have somebody else step in and shove you out of the way. Don't I know!"

"I'm glad to have a little rest. Marketing and housekeeping nowadays is no snap, with the prices what they are. Anybody that wants the pleasure is welcome."

But they knew, the three. There was, in Ma Mandle's tone, a hollow pretence that deceived no one. They knew, and she knew that they knew. She was even as they were, a drinker of the hemlock cup, an eater of ashes.

Hugo Mandle was happier and more comfortable than he had ever been in his life. It wasn't merely his love for Lil, and her love for him that made him happy. Lil set a good table, though perhaps it was not as bounteous as his mother's had been. His food, somehow, seemed to agree with him better than it used to. It was because Lil selected her provisions with an eye to their building value, and to Hugo's figure. She told him he was getting too fat, and showed him where, and Hugo agreed with her and took off twenty-five burdensome pounds, but Ma Mandle fought every ounce of it.

"You'll weaken yourself, Hugo! Eat! How can a man work and not eat? I never heard of such a thing. Fads!"

But these were purely physical things. It was a certain mental relaxation that Hugo enjoyed, though he did not definitely know it. He only knew that Lil seemed, somehow, to understand. For years his mother had trailed after him, putting away things that he wanted left out, tidying that which he preferred left in seeming disorder. Lil seemed miraculously to understand about those things. He liked, for example, a certain grimy, gritty old rag with which he was wont to polish his golf clubs. It was caked with dirt, and most disreputable, but it was of just the right material, or weight, or size, or something, and he had for it the unreasoning affection that a child has for a tattered rag doll among a whole family of golden-haired, blue-eyed beauties. Ma Mandle, tidying up, used to throw away that rag in horror. Sometimes he would rescue it, crusted as it was with sand and mud and scouring dust. Sometimes he would have to train in a new rag, and it was never as good as the old. Lil understood about that rag, and approved of it. For that matter, she had a rag of her own which she used to remove cold cream from her face and throat. It was a clean enough bit of soft cloth to start with, but she clung to it as an actress often does, until it was smeared with the pink of makeup and the black of Chicago soot. She used to search remote corners of it for an inch of unused, unsmeared space. Lil knew about not talking when you wanted to read the paper, too. Ma Mandle, at breakfast, had always had a long and intricate story to tell about the milkman, or the strawberries that she had got the day before and that had spoiled overnight in the icebox. A shame! Sometimes he had wanted to say, "Let me read my paper in peace, won't you!" But he never had. Now it was Lil who listened patiently to Ma Mandle's small grievances, and Hugo was left free to peruse the head-lines.

If you had told Ma Mandle that she was doing her best to ruin the life of the one person she loved best in all the world she would have told you that you were insane. If you had told her that she was jealous she would have denied it, furiously. But both were true.

When Hugo brought his wife a gift he brought one for his mother as well.

"You don't need to think you have to bring your old mother anything," she would say, unreasonably.

"Didn't I always bring you something, Ma?"

If seventy can be said to sulk, Ma Mandle sulked.

Lil, on her way to market in the morning, was a pleasant sight, trim, well-shod, immaculate. Ma, whose marketing costume had always been neat but sketchy, would eye her disapprovingly. "Are you going out?"

"Just to market. I thought I'd start early, before everything was picked over."

"Oh—to market! I thought you were going to a party, you're so dressy."

In the beginning Lil had offered to allow Ma Mandle to continue with the marketing but Mrs. Mandle had declined, acidly. "Oh, no," she had said. "This is your household now."

But she never failed to inspect the groceries as they lay on the kitchen table after delivery. She would press a wise and disdainful thumb into a head of lettuce; poke a pot-roast with disapproving finger; turn a plump chicken over and thump it down with a look that was pregnant with meaning.

Ma Mandle disapproved of many things. Of Lil's silken, lacy lingerie; of her social activities; of what she termed her wastefulness. Lil wore the fewest possible undergarments, according to the fashion of the day, and she worried, good-naturedly, about additional plumpness that was the result of leisure and of rich food. She was addicted to afternoon parties at the homes of married women of her own age and station—pretty, well-dressed, over-indulged women who regularly ate too much. They served a mayonnaise chicken salad, and little hot buttery biscuits, and strong coffee with sugar and cream, and there were dishes of salted almonds, and great, shining, oily, black ripe olives, and a heavy, rich dessert. When she came home she ate nothing.

"I couldn't eat a bite of dinner," she would say. "Let me tell you what we had." She would come to the table in one of her silken, lace-bedecked teagowns and talk animatedly to Hugo while he ate his dinner and eyed her appreciatively as she sat there leaning one elbow on the cloth, the sleeve fallen back so that you saw her plump white forearm. She kept her clear, rosy skin in spite of the pastry and sweets and the indolent life, and even the layers of powder with which she was forever dabbing her face had not coarsened its texture.

Hugo, man-like, was unconscious of the undercurrent of animosity between the two women. He was very happy. He only knew that Lil understood about cigar ashes; that she didn't mind if a pillow wasn't plumped and patted after his Sunday nap on the davenport; that she never complained to him about the shortcomings of the little Swede, as Ma Mandle had about Polish Anna. Even at house-cleaning time, which Ma Mandle had always treated as a scourge, things were as smooth-running and peaceful as at ordinary times. Just a little bare, perhaps, as to floors, and smelling of cleanliness. Lil applied businesslike methods to the conduct of her house, and they were successful in spite of Ma Mandle's steady efforts to block them. Old lady Mandle did not mean to be cruel. She only thought that she was protecting her son's interests. She did not know that the wise men had a definite name for the mental processes which caused her, perversely, to do just the thing which she knew she should not do.

Hugo and Lil went out a great deal in the evening. They liked the theatre, restaurant life, gayety. Hugo learned to dance and became marvellously expert at it, as does your fat man.

"Come on and go out with us this evening, Mother," Lil would say.

"Sure!" Hugo would agree, heartily. "Come along, Ma. We'll show you some night life."

"I don't want to go," Ma Mandle would mutter. "I'm better off at home. You enjoy yourself better without an old woman dragging along."

That being true, they vowed it was not, and renewed their urging. In the end she went, grudgingly. But her old eyes would droop; the late supper would disagree with her; the noise, the music, the laughter, and shrill talk bewildered her. She did not understand the banter, and resented it.

Next day, in the park, she would boast of her life of gayety to the vaguely suspicious three.

Later she refused to go out with them. She stayed in her room a good deal, fussing about, arranging bureau drawers already geometrically precise, winding endless old ribbons, ripping the trimming off hats long passé and re-trimming them with odds and ends and scraps of feathers and flowers.

Hugo and Lil used to ask her to go with them to the movies, but they liked the second show at eight-thirty while she preferred the earlier one at seven. She grew sleepy early, though she often lay awake for hours after composing herself for sleep. She would watch the picture absorbedly, but when she stepped, blinking, into the bright glare of Fifty-third Street, she always had a sense of let-down, of depression.

A wise old lady of seventy, who could not apply her wisdom for her own good. A rather lonely old lady, with hardening arteries and a dilating heart. An increasingly fault-finding old lady. Even Hugo began to notice it. She would wait for him to come home and then, motioning him mysteriously into her own room, would pour a tale of fancied insult into his ear.

"I ran a household and brought up a family before she was born. I don't have to be told what's what. I may be an old woman but I'm not so old that I can sit and let my own son be made a fool of. One girl isn't enough, she's got to have a wash woman. And now a wash woman isn't enough she's got to have a woman to clean one day a week."

An hour later, from the front bedroom, where Hugo was dressing, would come the low murmur of conversation. Lil had reached the complaining point, goaded by much repetition.

The attitude of the two women distressed and bewildered Hugo. He was a simple soul, and this was a complex situation. His mind leaped from mother to wife, and back again, joltingly. After all, one woman at a time is all that any man can handle successfully.

"What's got into you women folks!" he would say. "Always quarrelling. Why can't you get along."

One night after dinner Lil said, quite innocently, "Mother, we haven't a decent picture of you. Why don't you have one taken? In your black lace."

Old lady Mandle broke into sudden fury. "I guess you think I'm going to die! A picture to put on the piano after I'm gone, huh? 'That's my dear mother that's gone.' Well, I don't have any picture taken. You can think of me the way I was when I was alive."

The thing grew and swelled and took on bitterness as it progressed. Lil's face grew strangely flushed and little veins stood out on her temples. All the pent-up bitterness that had been seething in Ma Mandle's mind broke bounds now, and welled to her lips. Accusation, denial; vituperation, retort.

"You'll be happy when I'm gone."

"If I am it's your fault."

"It's the ones that are used to nothing that always want the most. They don't know where to stop. When you were working in Omaha—"

"The salary I gave up to marry your son was more money than you ever saw."

And through it all, like a leit-motiv, ran Hugo's attempt at pacification: "Now, Ma! Don't, Lil. You'll only excite yourself. What's got into you two women?"

It was after dinner. In the end Ma Mandle slammed out of the house, hatless. Her old legs were trembling. Her hands shook. It was a hot June night. She felt as if she were burning up. In her frantic mind there was even thought of self-destruction. There were thousands of motor cars streaming by. The glare of their lamps and the smell of the gasoline blinded and stifled her. Once, at a crossing, she almost stumbled in front of an on-rushing car. The curses of the startled driver sounded in her terrified ears after she had made the opposite curb in a frantic bound. She walked on and on for what seemed to her to be a long time, with plodding, heavy step. She was not conscious of being tired. She came to a park bench and sat down, feeling very abused, and lonely and agonized. This was what she had come to in her old days. It was for this you bore children, and brought them up and sacrificed for them. How right they were—Mrs. Lamb, Mrs. Brunswick, and Mrs. Wormser. Useless. Unconsidered. In the way.

By degrees she grew calmer. Her brain cooled as her fevered old body lost the heat of anger. Lil had looked kind of sick. Perhaps ... and how worried Hugo had looked....

Feeling suddenly impelled she got up from the bench and started toward home. Her walk, which had seemed interminable, had really lasted scarcely more than half an hour. She had sat in the park scarcely fifteen minutes. Altogether her flight had been, perhaps, an hour in duration.

She had her latchkey in her pocket. She opened the door softly. The place was in darkness. Voices from the front bedroom, and the sound of someone sobbing, as though spent. Old lady Mandle's face hardened again. The door of the front bedroom was closed. Plotting against her! She crouched there in the hall, listening. Lil's voice, hoarse with sobs.

"I've tried and tried. But she hates me. Nothing I do suits her. If it wasn't for the baby coming sometimes I think I'd—"

"You're just nervous and excited, Lil. It'll come out all right. She's an old lady—"

"I know it. I know it. I've said that a million times in the last year and a half. But that doesn't excuse everything, does it? Is that any reason why she should spoil our lives? It isn't fair. It isn't fair!"

"Sh! Don't cry like that, dear. Don't! You'll only make yourself sick."

Her sobs again, racking, choking, and the gentle murmur of his soothing endearments. Then, unexpectedly, a little, high-pitched laugh through the tears.

"No, I'm not hysterical. I—it just struck me funny. I was just wondering if I might be like that. When I grow old, and my son marries, maybe I'll think everything his wife does is wrong. I suppose if we love them too much we really harm them. I suppose—"

"Oh, it's going to be a son, is it?"

"Yes."

Another silence. Then: "Come, dear. Bathe your poor eyes. You're all worn out from crying. Why, sweetheart, I don't believe I ever saw you cry before."

"I know it. I feel better now. I wish crying could make it all right. I'm sorry. She's so old, dear. That's the trouble. They live in the past and they expect us to live in the past with them. You were a good son to her, Hughie. That's why you make such a wonderful husband. Too good, maybe. You've spoiled us both, and now we both want all of you."

Hugo was silent a moment. He was not a quick-thinking man. "A husband belongs to his wife," he said then, simply. "He's his mother's son by accident of birth. But he's his wife's husband by choice, and deliberately."

But she laughed again at that. "It isn't as easy as that, sweetheart. If it was there'd be no jokes in the funny papers. My poor boy! And just now, too, when you're so worried about business."

"Business'll be all right, Lil. Trade'll open up next winter. It's got to. We've kept going on the Japanese and English stuff. But if the French and Austrian factories start running we'll have a whirlwind year. If it hadn't been for you this last year I don't know how I'd have stood the strain. No importing, and the business just keeping its head above water. But you were right, honey. We've weathered the worst of it now."

"I'm glad you didn't tell Mother about it. She'd have worried herself sick. If she had known we both put every cent we had into the business—"

"We'll get it back ten times over. You'll see."

The sound of footsteps. "I wonder where she went. She oughtn't to be out alone. I'm kind of worried about her, Hugo. Don't you think you'd better—"

Ma Mandle opened the front door and then slammed it, ostentatiously, as though she had just come in.

"That you, Ma?" called Hugo.

He turned on the hall light. She stood there, blinking, a bent, pathetic little figure. Her eyes were averted. "Are you all right, Ma? We began to worry about you."

"I'm all right. I'm going to bed."

He made a clumsy, masculine pretence at heartiness. "Lil and I are going over to the drug store for a soda, it's so hot. Come on along, Ma."

Lil joined him in the doorway of the bedroom. Her eyes were red-rimmed behind the powder that she had hastily dabbed on, but she smiled bravely.

"Come on, Mother," she said. "It'll cool you off."

But Ma Mandle shook her head. "I'm better off at home. You run along, you two."

That was all. But the two standing there caught something in her tone. Something new, something gentle, something wise.

She went on down the hall to her room. She took off her clothes, and hung them away, neatly. But once in her nightgown she did not get into bed. She sat there, in the chair by the window. Old lady Mandle had lived to be seventy and had acquired much wisdom. One cannot live to be seventy without having experienced almost everything in life. But to crystallize that experience of a long lifetime into terms that would express the meaning of life—this she had never tried to do. She could not do it now, for that matter. But she groped around, painfully, in her mind. There had been herself and Hugo. And now Hugo's wife and the child to be. They were the ones that counted, now. That was the law of life. She did not put it into words. But something of this she thought as she sat there in her plain white nightgown, her scant white locks pinned in a neat knob at the top of her head. Selfishness. That was it. They called it love, but it was selfishness. She must tell them about it to-morrow—Mrs. Lamb, Mrs. Brunswick, and Mrs. Wormser. Only yesterday Mrs. Brunswick had waxed bitter because her daughter-in-law had let a moth get into her husband's winter suit.

"I never had a moth in my house!" Mrs. Brunswick had declared. "Never. But nowadays housekeeping is nothing. A suit is ruined. What does my son's wife care! I never had a moth in my house."

Ma Mandle chuckled to herself there in the darkness. "I bet she did. She forgets. We all forget."

It was very hot to-night. Now and then there was a wisp of breeze from the lake, but not often.... How red Lil's eyes had been ... poor girl. Moved by a sudden impulse Ma Mandle thudded down the hall in her bare feet, found a scrap of paper in the writing-desk drawer, scribbled a line on it, turned out the light, and went into the empty front room. With a pin from the tray on the dresser she fastened the note to Lil's pillow, high up, where she must see it the instant she turned on the light. Then she scuttled down the hall to her room again.

She felt the heat terribly. She would sit by the window again. All the blood in her body seemed to be pounding in her head ... pounding in her head ... pounding....

At ten Hugo and Lil came in, softly. Hugo tiptoed down the hall, as was his wont, and listened. The room was in darkness. "Sleeping, Ma?" he whispered. He could not see the white-gowned figure sitting peacefully by the window, and there was no answer. He tiptoed with painful awkwardness up the hall again.

"She's asleep, all right. I didn't think she'd get to sleep so early on a scorcher like this."

Lil turned on the light in her room. "It's too hot to sleep," she said. She began to disrobe languidly. Her eye fell on the scrap of paper pinned to her pillow. She went over to it, curiously, leaned over, read it.

"Oh, look, Hugo!" She gave a little tremulous laugh that was more than half sob. He came over to her and read it, his arm around her shoulder.

"My son Hugo and my daughter Lil they are the best son and daughter in the world."

A sudden hot haze before his eyes blotted out the words as he finished reading them.

When you try to do a story about three people like Sid Hahn and Mizzi Markis and Wallie Ascher you find yourself pawing around among the personalities helplessly. For the three of them are what is known in newspaper parlance as national figures. One n.f. is enough for any short story. Three would swamp a book. It's like one of those plays advertised as having an all-star cast. By the time each luminary has come on, and been greeted, and done his twinkling the play has faded into the background. You can't see the heavens for the stars.

Surely Sid Hahn, like the guest of honour at a dinner, needs no introduction. And just as surely will he be introduced. He has been described elsewhere and often; perhaps nowhere more concisely than on Page 16, paragraph two, of a volume that shall be nameless, though quoted, thus:

"Sid Hahn, erstwhile usher, call-boy, press agent, advance man, had a genius for things theatrical. It was inborn. Dramatic, sensitive, artistic, intuitive, he was often rendered inarticulate by the very force and variety of his feelings. A little, rotund, ugly man, with the eyes of a dreamer, the wide, mobile mouth of a humourist, the ears of a comic ol' clo'es man. His generosity was proverbial, and it amounted to a vice."

Not that that covers him. No one paragraph could. You turn a fine diamond this way and that, and as its facets catch the light you say, "It's scarlet! No—it's blue! No—rose!—orange!—lilac!—no—"

That was Sid Hahn.

I suppose he never really sat for a photograph and yet you saw his likeness in all the magazines. He was snapped on the street, and in the theatre, and even up in his famous library-study-office on the sixth and top floor of the Thalia Theatre Building. Usually with a fat black cigar—unlighted—in one corner of his commodious mouth. Everyone interested in things theatrical (and whom does that not include!) knew all about Sid Hahn—and nothing. He had come, a boy, from one of those middle-western towns with a high-falutin Greek name. Parthenon, Ohio, or something incredible like that. No one knows how he first approached the profession which he was to dominate in America. There's no record of his having asked for a job in a theatre, and received it. He oozed into it, indefinably, and moved with it, and became a part of it and finally controlled it. Satellites, fur-collared and pseudo-successful, trailing in his wake, used to talk loudly of I-knew-him-when. They all lied. It had been Augustin Daly, dead these many years, who had first recognized in this boy the genius for discovering and directing genius. Daly was, at that time, at the zenith of his career—managing, writing, directing, producing. He fired the imagination of this stocky, gargoyle-faced boy with the luminous eyes and the humorous mouth. I don't know that Sid Hahn, hanging about the theatre in every kind of menial capacity, ever said to himself in so many words:

"I'm going to be what he is. I'm going to concentrate on it. I won't let anything or anybody interfere with it. Nobody knows what I'm going to be. But I know.... And you've got to be selfish. You've got to be selfish."

Of course no one ever really made a speech like that to himself, even in the Horatio Alger books. But if the great ambition and determination running through the whole fibre of his being could have been crystallized into spoken words they would have sounded like that.

By the time he was forty-five he had discovered more stars than Copernicus. They were not all first-magnitude twinklers. Some of them even glowed so feebly that you could see their light only when he stood behind them, the steady radiance of his genius shining through. But taken as a whole they made a brilliant constellation, furnishing much of the illumination for the brightest thoroughfare in the world.

He had never married. There are those who say that he had had an early love affair, but that he had sworn not to marry until he had achieved what he called success. And by that time it had been too late. It was as though the hot flame of ambition had burned out all his other passions. Later they say he was responsible for more happy marriages contracted by people who did not know that he was responsible for them than a popular east-side shadchen. He grew a little tired, perhaps, of playing with make-believe stage characters, and directing them, so he began to play with real ones, like God. But always kind.

No woman can resist making love to a man as indifferent as Sid Hahn appeared to be. They all tried their wiles on him: the red-haired ingénues, the blonde soubrettes, the stately leading ladies, the war horses, the old-timers, the ponies, the prima donnas. He used to sit there in his great, luxurious, book-lined inner office, smiling and inscrutable as a plump joss-house idol while the fair ones burnt incense and made offering of shew-bread. Figuratively, he kicked over the basket of shew-bread, and of the incense said, "Take away that stuff! It smells!"

Not that he hated women. He was afraid of them, at first. Then, from years of experience with the femininity of the theatre, not nearly afraid enough. So, early, he had locked that corner of his mind, and had thrown away the key. When, years after, he broke in the door, lo! (as they say when an elaborate figure of speech is being used) lo! the treasures therein had turned to dust and ashes.

It was he who had brought over from Paris to the American stage the famous Renée Paterne of the incorrigible eyes. She made a fortune and swept the country with her song about those delinquent orbs. But when she turned them on Hahn, in their first interview in his office, he regarded her with what is known as a long, level look. She knew at that time not a word of English. Sid Hahn was ignorant of French. He said, very low, and with terrible calm to Wallie Ascher who was then acting as a sort of secretary, "Wallie, can't you do something to make her stop rolling her eyes around at me like that? It's awful! She makes me think of those heads you shy balls at, out at Coney. Take away my ink-well."

Renée had turned swiftly to Wallie and had said something to him in French. Sid Hahn cocked a quick ear. "What's that she said?"

"She says," translated the obliging and gifted Wallie, "that monsieur is a woman-hater."

"My God! I thought she didn't understand English!"

"She doesn't. But she's a woman. Not only that, she's a French woman. They don't need to know a language to understand it."

"Where did you get that, h'm? That wasn't included in your Berlitz course, was it?"

Wallie Ascher had grinned—that winning flash lighting up his dark, keen face. "No. I learned that in another school."

Wallie Ascher's early career in the theatre, if repeated here, might almost be a tiresome repetition of Hahn's beginning. And what Augustin Daly had been to Sid Hahn's imagination and ambition, Sid Hahn was to Wallie's. Wallie, though, had been born to the theatre—if having a tumbler for a father and a prestidigitator's foil for a mother can be said to be a legitimate entrance into the world of the theatre.

He had been employed about the old Thalia for years before Hahn noticed him. In the beginning he was a spindle-legged office boy in the upstairs suite of the firm of Hahn & Lohman, theatrical producers; the kind of office-boy who is addicted to shrill, clear whistling unless very firmly dealt with. No one in the outer office realized how faultless, how rhythmic were the arpeggios and cadences that issued from those expertly puckered lips. There was about his performance an unerring precision. As you listened you felt that his ascent to the inevitable high note was a thing impossible of achievement. Up—up—up he would go, while you held your breath in suspense. And then he took the high note—took it easily, insouciantly—held it, trilled it, tossed it.

"Now, look here," Miss Feldman would snap—Miss Feldman of the outer office typewriter—"look here, you kid. Any more of that bird warbling and you go back to the woods where you belong. This ain't a—a—"

"Aviary," suggested Wallie, almost shyly.

Miss Feldman glared. "How did you know that word?"

"I don't know," helplessly. "But it's the word, isn't it?"

Miss Feldman turned back to her typewriter. "You're too smart for your age, you are."

"I know it," Wallie had agreed, humbly.

There's no telling where or how he learned to play the piano. He probably never did learn. He played it, though, as he whistled—brilliantly. No doubt it was as imitative and as unconscious, too, as his whistling had been. They say he didn't know one note from another, and doesn't to this day.

At twenty, when he should have been in love with at least three girls, he had fixed in his mind an image, a dream. And it bore no resemblance to twenty's accepted dreams. At that time he was living in one room (rear) of a shabby rooming house in Thirty-ninth Street. And this was the dream: By the time he was—well, long before he was thirty—he would have a bachelor apartment with a Jap, Saki. Saki was the perfect servant, noiseless, unobtrusive, expert. He saw little dinners just for four—or, at the most, six. And Saki, white-coated, deft, sliding hot plates when plates should be hot; cold plates when plates should be cold. Then, other evenings, alone, when he wanted to see no one—when, in a silken lounging robe (over faultless dinner clothes, of course, and wearing the kind of collar you see in the back of the magazines) he would say, "That will do, Saki." Then, all evening, he would play softly to himself those little, intimate, wistful Schumanny things in the firelight with just one lamp glowing softly—almost sombrely—at the side of the piano (grand).

His first real meeting with Sid Hahn had had much to do with the fixing of this image. Of course he had seen Hahn hundreds of times in the office and about the theatre. They had spoken, too, many times. Hahn called him vaguely, "Heh, boy!" but he grew to know him later as Wallie. From errand-boy, office-boy, call-boy he had become, by that time, a sort of unofficial assistant stage manager. No one acknowledged that he was invaluable about the place, but he was. When a new play was in rehearsal at the Thalia, Wallie knew more about props, business, cues, lights, and lines than the director himself. For a long time no one but Wallie and the director were aware of this. The director never did admit it. But that Hahn should find it out was inevitable.

He was nineteen or thereabouts when he was sent, one rainy November evening, to deliver a play manuscript to Hahn at his apartment. Wallie might have refused to perform an errand so menial, but his worship of Hahn made him glad of any service, however humble. He buttoned his coat over the manuscript, turned up his collar, and plunged into the cold drizzle of the November evening.

Hahn's apartment—he lived alone—was in the early fifties, off Fifth Avenue. For two days he had been ill with one of the heavy colds to which he was subject. He was unable to leave the house. Hence Wallie's errand.

It was Saki—or Saki's equivalent—who opened the door. A white-coated, soft-stepping Jap, world-old looking like the room glimpsed just beyond. Someone was playing the piano with one finger, horribly.

"You're to give this to Mr. Hahn. He's waiting for it."

"Genelmun come in," said the Jap, softly.

"No, he don't want to see me. Just give it to him, see?"

"Genelmun come in." Evidently orders.

"Oh, all right. But I know he doesn't want—"

Wallie turned down his collar with a quick flip, looked doubtfully at his shoes, and passed through the glowing little foyer into the room beyond. He stood in the doorway. He was scarcely twenty then, but something in him sort of rose, and gathered, and seethed, and swelled, and then hardened. He didn't know it then but it was his great resolve.

Sid Hahn was seated at the piano, a squat, gnomelike little figure, with those big ears, and that plump face, and those soft eyes—the kindest eyes in the world. He did not stop playing as Wallie appeared. He glanced up at him, ever so briefly, but kindly, too, and went on playing the thing with one short forefinger, excruciatingly. Wallie waited. He had heard somewhere that Hahn would sit at the piano thus, for hours, the tears running down his cheeks because of the beauty of the music he could remember but not reproduce; and partly because of his own inability to reproduce it.

The stubby little forefinger faltered, stopped. He looked up at Wallie.

"God, I wish I could play!"

"Helps a lot."

"You play?"

"Yes."

"What?"

"Oh, most anything I've heard once. And some things I kind of make up."

"Compose, you mean?"

"Yes."

"Play one of those."

So Wallie Ascher played one of those. Of course you know "Good Night—Pleasant Dreams." He hadn't named it then. It wasn't even published until almost two years later, but that was what he played for Sid Hahn. Since "After The Ball" no popular song has achieved the success of that one. No doubt it was cheap, and no doubt it was sentimental, but so, too, are "The Suwanee River" and "My Old Kentucky Home," and they'll be singing those when more classical songs have long been forgotten. As Wallie played it his dark, thin face seemed to gleam and glow in the lamplight.

When he had finished Sid Hahn was silent for a moment. Then, "What're you going to do with it?"

"With what?"

"With what you've got. You know."

Wallie knew that he did not mean the song he had just played. "I'm going to—I'm going to do a lot with it."

"Yeh, but how?"

Wallie was looking down at his two lean brown hands on the keys. For a long minute he did not answer. Then: "By thinking about it all the time. And working like hell.... And you've got to be selfish ... You've got to be selfish ..."

As Sid Hahn stared at him, as though hypnotized, the Jap appeared in the doorway. Sid Hahn said, "Stay and have dinner with me," instead of what he had meant to say.

"Oh, I can't! Thanks. I—" He wanted to terribly, but the thought was too much.

"Better."

They had dinner together. Even under the influence of Hahn's encouragement and two glasses of mellow wine whose name he did not know, Wallie did not become fatuous. They talked about music—neither of them knew anything about it, really. Wallie confessed that he used it as an intoxicant and a stimulant.

"That's it!" cried Hahn, excitedly. "If I could play I'd have done more. More."

"Why don't you get one of those piano-players, What-you-call'ems?" Then, immediately, "No, of course not."

"Nah, that doesn't do it," said Hahn, quickly. "That's like adopting a baby when you can't have one of your own. It isn't the same. It isn't the same. It looks like a baby, and acts like a baby, and sounds like a baby—but it isn't yours. It isn't you. That's it! It isn't you!"

"Yeh," agreed Wallie, nodding. So perfectly did they understand each other, this ill-assorted pair.

It was midnight before Wallie left. They had both forgotten about the play manuscript whose delivery had been considered so important. The big room was gracious, quiet, soothing. A fire flickered in the grate. One lamp glowed softly—almost sombrely.

As Wallie rose at last to go he shook himself slightly like one coming out of a trance. He looked slowly about the golden, mellow room. "Gee!"

"Yes, but it isn't worth it," said Hahn, "after you've got it."

"That's what they all say"—grimly—"*after* they've got it."

The thing that had been born in Sid Hahn's mind thirty years before was now so plainly stamped on this boy's face that Hahn was startled into earnestness. "But I tell you, it's true! It's true!"

"Maybe. Some day, when I'm living in a place like this, I'll let you know if you're right."

In less than a year Wallie Ascher was working with Hahn. No one knew his official title or place. But "Ask Wallie. He'll know," had become a sort of slogan in the office. He did know. At twenty-one his knowledge of the theatre was infallible (this does not include plays unproduced; in this no one is infallible) and his feeling for it amounted to a sixth sense. There was something uncanny about the way he could talk about Lottie, for example, as if he had seen her; or Mrs. Siddons; or Mrs. Fiske when she was Minnie Maddern, the soubrette. It was as though he had the power to cast himself back into the past. No doubt it was that power which gave later to his group of historical plays (written by him between the ages of thirty and thirty-five) their convincingness and authority.

When Wallie was about twenty-three or -four Sid Hahn took him abroad on one of his annual scouting trips. Yearly, in the spring, Hahn swooped down upon London, Paris, Vienna, Berlin, seeking that of the foreign stage which might be translated, fumigated, desiccated, or otherwise rendered suitable for home use. He sent Wallie on to Vienna, alone, on the trail of a musical comedy rumoured to be a second Merry Widow in tunefulness, chic, and charm. Of course it wasn't. Merry Widows rarely repeat. Wallie wired Hahn, as arranged. The telegram is unimportant, perhaps, but characteristic.

MR.   SID.   HAHN,
Hotel   Savoy,
London,
England.

It's a second all right but not a second Merry Widow. Heard of a winner in Budapest. Shall I go. Spent to-day from eleven to five running around the Ringstrasse looking for mythical creature known as the chic Viennese. After careful investigation wish to be quoted as saying the species if any is extinct.

WALLIE.

This, remember, was in the year 1913, B.W. Wallie, obeying instructions, went to Budapest, witnessed the alleged winner, found it as advertised, wired Hahn to that effect, and was joined by that gentleman three days later.

Budapest, at that time, was still Little Paris, only wickeder. A city of magnificent buildings, and unsalted caviar, and beautiful, dangerous women, and frumpy men (civilian) and dashing officers in red pants, and Cigány music, and cafés and paprika and two-horse droshkies. Buda, low and flat, lay on one side; Pest, high and hilly, perched picturesquely on the other. Between the two rolled the Blue Danube (which is yellow).

It was here that Hahn and Wallie found Mizzi Markis. Mizzi Markis, then a girl of nineteen, was a hod carrier.

Wallie had three days in Budapest before Hahn met him there. As the manager stepped from the train, looking geometrically square in a long ulster that touched his ears and his heels, Wallie met him with a bound.

"Hello, S.H.! Great to see you! Say, listen, I've found something. I've found something big!"

Hahn had never seen the boy so excited. "Oh, shucks! No play's as good as that."

"Play! It isn't a play."

"Why, you young idiot, you said it was good! You said it was darned good! You don't mean to tell me—"

"Oh, that! That's all right. It's good—or will be when you get through with it."

"What you talking about then? Here, let's take one of these things with two horses. Gee, you ought to smoke a fat black seegar and wear a silk hat when you ride in one of these! I feel like a parade." He was like a boy on a holiday, as always when in Europe.

"But let me tell you about this girl, won't you!"

"Oh, it's a girl! What's her name? What's she do?"

"Her name's Mizzi."

"Mizzi what?"

"I don't know. She's a hod carrier. She—"

"That's all right, Wallie. I'm here now. An ice bag on your head and real quiet for two-three days. You'll come round fine."

But Wallie was almost sulking. "Wait till you see her, S.H. She sings."

"Beautiful, is she?"

"No, not particularly. No."

"Wonderful voice, h'm?"

"N-n-no. I wouldn't say it was what you'd call exactly wonderful."

Sid Hahn stood up in the droshky and waved his short arms in windmill circles. "Well, what the devil does she do then, that's so good? Carry bricks!"

"She is good at that. When she balances that pail of mortar on her head and walks off with it, her arms hanging straight at her sides—"

But Sid Hahn's patience was at an end. "You're a humourist, you are. If I didn't know you I'd say you were drunk. I'll bet you are, anyway. You've been eating paprika, raw. You make me sick."

Inelegant, but expressive of his feelings. But Wallie only said, "You wait. You'll see."

Sid Hahn did see. He saw next day. Wallie woke him out of a sound sleep so that he might see. It was ten-thirty A.M. so that his peevishness was unwarranted. They had seen the play the night before and Hahn had decided that, translated and with interpolations (it was a comic opera), it would captivate New York. Then and there he completed the negotiations which Wallie had begun. Hahn was all for taking the first train out, but Wallie was firm. "You've got to see her, I tell you. You've got to see her."

Their hotel faced the Corso. The Corso is a wide promenade that runs along the Buda bank of the Danube. Across the river, on the hill, the royal palace looks down upon the little common people. In that day the monde and the demi-monde of Budapest walked on the Corso between twelve and one. Up and down. Up and down. The women, tall, dark, flashing-eyed, daringly dressed. The men sallow, meagre, and wearing those trousers which, cut very wide and flappy at the ankles, make them the dowdiest men in the world. Hahn's room and Wallie's were on the second floor of the hotel, and at a corner. One set of windows faced the Corso, the river, and Pest on the hill. The other set looked down upon a new building being erected across the way. It was on this building that Mizzi Markis worked as hod carrier.

The war accustomed us to a million women in overalls doing the work of a million men. We saw them ploughing, juggling steel bars, making shells, running engines, stoking furnaces, handling freight. But to these two American men, at that time, the thing at which these labouring women were employed was dreadful and incredible.

Said Wallie "By the time we've dressed, and had breakfast, and walked a little and everything, it'll be almost noon. And noon's the time. After they've eaten their lunch. But I want you to see her before."

By now his earnestness had impressed Hahn who still feigned an indifference he did not feel. It was about 11:30 when Wallie propelled him by the arm to the unfinished building across the way. And there he met Mizzi.

They were just completing the foundation. The place was a busy hive. Back and forth with pails. Back and forth with loads of bricks.

"What's the matter with the men?" was Hahn's first question.

Wallie explained. "They do the dainty work. They put one brick on top of the other, with a dab of mortar between. But none of the back-breaking stuff for them. The women do that."

And it was so. They were down in the pits mixing the mortar, were the women. They were carrying great pails of it. They were hauling bricks up one ladder and down. They wore short, full skirts with a musical-comedy-chorus effect. Some of them looked seventy and some seventeen. It was fearful work for a woman. A keen wind was blowing across the river. Their hands were purple.

"Pick Mizzi," said Wallie. "If you can pick her I'll know I'm right. But I know it, anyway."

Five minutes passed. The two men stood silent. "The one with the walk and the face," said Hahn, then. Which wasn't very bright of him, because they all walked and they all had faces. "Going up the pit-ladder now. With the pail on her head." Wallie gave a little laugh of triumph. But then, Hahn wouldn't have been Hahn had he not been able to pick a personality when he saw it.

Years afterward the reviewers always talked of Mizzi's walk. They called it her superb carriage. They didn't know that you have to walk very straight, on the balls of your feet, with your hips firm, your stomach held in flat, your shoulders back, your chest out, your chin out and a little down, if you are going to be at all successful in balancing a pail of mortar on your head. After a while that walk becomes a habit.

"Watch her with that pail," said Wallie.

Mizzi filled the pail almost to the top with the heavy white mixture. She filled it quickly, expertly. The pail, filled, weighed between seventeen and twenty kilos. One kilo is equal to about two and one fifth pounds. The girl threw down her scoop, stooped, grasped the pail by its two handles, and with one superb, unbroken motion raised the pail high in her two strong arms and placed it on her head. Then she breathed deeply, once, set her whole figure, turned stiffly, and was off with it. Sid Hahn took on a long breath as though he himself had just accomplished the gymnastic feat.

"Well, so far it's pretty good. But I don't know that the American stage is clamouring for any hod carriers and mortar mixers, exactly."

A whistle blew. Twelve o'clock. Bricks, mortar, scoops, shovels were abandoned. The women, in their great clod-hopping shoes, flew chattering to the tiny hut where their lunch boxes were stored. The men followed more slowly, a mere handful of them. Not one of them wore overalls or apron. Out again with their bundles and boxes of food—very small bundles. Very tiny boxes. They ate ravenously the bread and sausage and drank their beer in great gulps. Fifteen minutes after the whistle had blown the last crumb had vanished.

"Now, then," said Wallie, and guided Hahn nearer. He looked toward Mizzi. Everyone looked toward her. Mizzi stood up, brushing crumbs from her lap. She had a little four-cornered black shawl, folded cross-wise, over her head and tied under her chin. Her face was round and her cheeks red. The shawl, framing this, made her look very young and cherubic.

She did not put her hands on her hips, or do any of those story-book things. She grinned, broadly, showing strong white teeth made strong and white through much munching of coarse black bread; not yet showing the neglect common to her class. She asked a question in a loud, clear voice.

"What's that?" asked Hahn.

"She's talking a kind of hunky Hungarian, I guess. The people here won't speak German, did you know that? They hate it."

The crowd shouted back with one voice. They settled themselves comfortably, sitting or standing. Their faces held the broad smile of anticipation.

"She asked them what they want her to sing. They told her. It's the same every day."

Mizzi Markis stood there before them in the mud, and clay, and straw of the building débris. And she sang for them a Hungarian popular song of the day which, translated, sounds idiotic and which runs something like this:

A hundred geese in a rowGoing into the coop.At the head of the processionA stick over his shoulder—

No, you can't do it. It means less than nothing that way, and certainly would not warrant the shrieks of mirth that came from the audience gathered round the girl. Still, when you recall the words of "A Hot Time":

When you hear dem bells go ding-ling-ling,All join round and sweetly you must singAnd when the words am through in the chorus all join inThere'll be a *hot time*In the *old town*To-night.MyBa-By.

And yet it swept this continent, and Europe, and in Japan they still think it's our national anthem.

When she had finished, the crowd gave a roar of delight, and clapped their hands, and stamped their feet, and shouted. She had no unusual beauty. Her voice was untrained though possessed of strength and flexibility. It wasn't what she had sung, surely. You heard the song in a hundred cafés. Every street boy whistled it. It wasn't that expressive pair of shoulders, exactly. It wasn't a certain soothing tonal quality that made you forget all the things you'd been trying not to remember.

There is something so futile and unconvincing about an attempted description of an intangible thing. Some call it personality; some call it magnetism; some a rhythm sense; and some, genius. It's all these things, and none of them. Whatever it is, she had it. And whatever it is, Sid Hahn has never failed to recognize it.

So now he said, quietly, "She's got it."

"You bet she's got it!" from Wallie. "She's got more than Renée Paterne ever had. A year of training and some clothes—"

"You don't need to tell me. I'm in the theatrical business, myself."

"I'm sorry," stiffly.

But Hahn, too, was sorry immediately. "You know how I am, Wallie. I like to run a thing off by myself. What do you know about her? Find out anything?"

"Well, a little. She doesn't seem to have any people. And she's decent. Kind of a fierce kid, I guess, and fights when offended. They say she's Polish, not Hungarian. Her mother was a peasant. Her father—nobody knows. I had a dickens of a time finding out anything. The most terrible language in the world—Hungarian. They'll stick a *b* next to a *k* and follow it up with a *z* and put an accent mark over the whole business and call it a word. Last night I followed her home. And guess what!"

"What?" said Hahn, obligingly.

"On her way she had to cross the big square—the one they call Gisela Tér, with all the shops around it. Well, when she came to Gerbeaud's—"

"What's Gerbeaud's?"

"That's the famous tea room and pastry shop where all the swells go and guzzle tea with rum in it and eat cakes—and say! It isn't like our pastry that tastes like sawdust covered with shaving soap. Marvellous stuff, this is!"

After all, he was barely twenty-four. So Hahn said, good-naturedly, "All right, all right. We'll go there this afternoon and eat an acre of it. Go on. When she came to Gerbeaud's...?"

"Well, when she came to Gerbeaud's she stopped and stood there, outside. There was a strip of red carpet from the door to the street. You know—the kind they have at home when there's a wedding on Fifth Avenue. There she stood at the edge of the carpet, waiting, her face, framed in that funny little black shawl, turned toward the window, and the tail of the little shawl kind of waggling in the wind. It was cold and nippy. I waited, too. Finally I sort of strolled over to her—I knew she couldn't any more than knock me down—and said, kind of casual, 'What's doing?' She looked up at me, like a kid, in that funny shawl. She knew I was an Englees, right away. I guess I must have a fine, open countenance. And I had motioned toward the red carpet, and the crowded windows. Anyway, she opens up with a regular burst of fireworks Hungarian, in that deep voice of hers. Not only that, she acted it out. In two seconds she had on an imaginary coronet and a court train. And haughty! Gosh! I was sort of stumped, but I said, 'You don't say!' and waited some more. And then they flung open the door of the tea shop thing. At the same moment up dashed an equipage—you couldn't possibly call it anything less—with flunkeys all over the outside, like trained monkeys. The people inside the shop stood up, with their mouths full of cake, and out came an old frump with a terrible hat and a fringe. And it was the Archduchess, and her name is Josefa."

"Your story interests me strangely, boy," Hahn said, grinning, "but I don't quite make you. Do archduchesses go to tea rooms for tea? And what's that got to do with our gifted little hod carrier?"

"This duchess does. Believe me, those tarts are good enough for the Queen of Hearts, let alone a duchess, no matter how arch. But the plot of the piece is this. The duchess person goes to Gerbeaud's about twice a week. And they always spread a red carpet for her. And Mizzi always manages to cut away in time to stand there in front of Gerbeaud's and see her come out. She's a gorgeous mimic, that little kid. And though I couldn't understand a word she said I managed to get out of it just this: That some day they're going to spread a red carpet for Mizzi and she's going to walk down it in glory. If you'd seen her face when she said it, S.H., you wouldn't laugh."

"I wouldn't laugh anyway," said Hahn, seriously.

And that's the true story of Mizzi Markis's beginning. Few people know it.

There they were, the three of them. And of the three, Mizzi's ambition seemed to be the fiercest, the most implacable. She worked like a horse, cramming English, French, singing. In some things she was like a woman of thirty; in others a child of ten. Her gratitude to Hahn was pathetic. No one ever doubted that he was in love with her almost from the first—he who had resisted the professional beauties of three decades.

You know she wasn't—and isn't—a beauty, even in that portrait of her by Sargent, with her two black-haired, stunning-looking boys, one on either side. But she was one of those gorgeously healthy women whose very presence energizes those with whom she comes in contact. And then there was about her a certain bounteousness. There's no other word for it, really. She reminded you of those gracious figures you see posed for pictures entitled "Autumn Harvest."

While she was studying she had a little apartment with a middle-aged woman to look after her, and she must have been a handful. A born cook, she was, and Hahn and Wallie used to go there to dinner whenever she would let them. She cooked it herself. Hahn would give up any engagement for a dinner at Mizzi's. When he entered her little sitting room his cares seemed to drop from him. She never got over cutting bread as the peasant women do it—the loaf held firmly against her breast, the knife cutting toward her. Hahn used to watch her and laugh. Sometimes she would put on the little black head-shawl of her Budapest days and sing the street-song about the hundred geese in a row. A delightful, impudent figure.

With the very first English she learned she told Hahn and Wallie that some day they were going to spread a fine red carpet for her to tread upon and that all the world would gaze on her with envy. It was in her mind a symbol typifying all that there was of earthly glory.

"It'll be a long time before they do any red carpeting for you, my girl," Sid Hahn had said.

She turned on him fiercely. "I will not rest—I will not eat—I will not sleep—I will not love—until I have it."

Which was, of course, an exaggerated absurdity.

"Oh, what rot!" Wallie Ascher had said, angrily, and then he had thought of his own symbol of success, and his own resolve. And his face had hardened. Sid Hahn looked at the two of them; very young, both of them, very gifted, very electric. Very much in love with each other, though neither would admit it even in their own minds. Both their stern young faces set toward the goal which they thought meant happiness.

Now, Sid Hahn had never dabbled in this new stuff—you know—complexes and fixed ideas and images. But he was a very wise man, and he did know to what an extent these two were possessed by ambition for that which they considered desirable.

He must have thought it over for weeks. He was in love with Mizzi, remember. And his fondness for Wallie was a thing almost paternal. He watched these two for a long, long time, a queer, grim little smile on his gargoyle face. And then his mind was made up. He had always had his own way. He must have had a certain terrible enjoyment in depriving himself of the one thing he wanted most in the world—the one thing he wanted more than he had ever wanted anything.

He decided that Destiny—a ponderous, slow-moving creature at best—needed a little prodding from him. His plans were simple, as all effective plans are.

Mizzi had been in America just a year and a half. Her development was amazing, but she was far from being the finished product that she became in later years. Hahn decided to chance it. Mizzi had no fear of audiences. He had tried her out on that. An audience stimulated her. She took it to her breast. She romped with it.

He found a play at last. A comedy, with music. It was frankly built for Mizzi. He called Wallie Ascher into his office.

"I wouldn't try her out here for a million. New York's too fly. Some little thing might be wrong—you know how they are. And all the rest would go for nothing. The kindest audience in the world—when they like you. And the cruelest when they don't. We'll go on the road for two weeks. Then we'll open at the Blackstone in Chicago. I think this girl has got more real genius than any woman since—since Bernhardt in her prime. Five years from now she won't be singing. She'll be acting. And it'll *be* acting."

"Aren't you forcing things just a little?" asked Wallie, coolly.

"Oh, no. No. Anyway, it's just a try-out. By the way, Wallie, I'll probably be gone almost a month. If things go pretty well in Chicago I'll run over to French Lick for eight or ten days and see if I can't get a little of this stiffness out of my old bones. Will you do something for me?"

"Sure."

"Pack a few clothes and go up to my place and live there, will you? The Jap stays on, anyway. The last time I left it alone things went wrong. You'll be doing me a favour. Take it and play the piano, and have your friends in, and boss the Jap around. He's stuck on you, anyway. Says he likes to hear you play."

He stayed away six weeks. And any one who knows him knows what hardship that was. He loved New York, and his own place, and his comfort, and his books; and hotel food gave him hideous indigestion.

Mizzi's first appearance was a moderate success. It was nothing like the sensation of her later efforts. She wasn't ready, and Hahn knew it. Mizzi and her middle-aged woman companion were installed at the Blackstone Hotel, which is just next door to the Blackstone Theatre, as any one is aware who knows Chicago. She was advertised as the Polish comedienne, Mizzi Markis, and the announcements hinted at her royal though remote ancestry. And on the night the play opened, as Mizzi stepped from the entrance of her hotel on her way to the stage door, just forty or fifty feet away, there she saw stretched on the pavement a scarlet path of soft-grained carpet for her feet to tread. From the steps of the hotel to the stage door of the theatre, there it lay, a rosy line of splendour.

The newspapers played it up as a publicity stunt. Every night, while the play lasted, the carpet was there. It was rolled up when the stage door closed upon her. It was unrolled and spread again when she came out after the performance. Hahn never forgot her face when she first saw it, and realized its significance. The look was there on the second night, and on the third, but after that it faded, vanished, and never came again. Mizzi had tasted of the golden fruit and found it dry and profitless, without nourishment or sweetness.

The show closed in the midst of a fairly good run. It closed abruptly, without warning. Together they came back to New York. Just outside New York Hahn knocked at the door of Mizzi's drawing room and stuck his round, ugly face in at the opening.

"Let's surprise Wallie," he said.

"Yes," said Mizzi, listlessly.

"He doesn't know the show's closed. We'll take a chance on his being home for dinner. Unless you're too tired."

"I'm not tired."

The Jap admitted them, and Hahn cut off his staccato exclamations with a quick and smothering hand. They tiptoed into the big, gracious, lamp-lighted room.

Wallie was seated at the piano. He had on a silk dressing gown with a purple cord. One of those dressing gowns you see in the haberdashers' windows, and wonder who buys them. He looked very tall in it, and rather distinguished, but not quite happy. He was playing as they came in. They said, "Boo!" or something idiotic like that. He stood up. And his face!

"Why, hello!" he said, and came forward, swiftly. "Hello! Hello!"

"Hello!" Hahn answered; "Not to say hello-hello."

Wallie looked at the girl. "Hello, Mizzi."

"Hello," said Mizzi.

"For God's sake stop saying 'hello!'" roared Hahn.

They both looked at him absently, and then at each other again.

Hahn flung his coat and hat at the Jap and rubbed his palms briskly together. "Well, how did you like it?" he said, and slapped Wallie on the back. "How'd you like it—the place I mean, and the Jap boy and all? H'm?"

"Very much," Wallie answered, formally. "Very nice."

"You'll be having one of your own some day, soon. That's sure."

"I suppose so," said Wallie, indifferently.

"I would like to go home," said Mizzi, suddenly, in her precise English.

At that Wallie leaped out of his lounging coat. "I'll take you! I'll—I'll be glad to take you."

Hahn smiled a little, ruefully. "We were going to have dinner here, the three of us. But if you're tired, Mizzi. I'm not so chipper myself when it comes to that." He looked about the room, gratefully. "It's good to be home."

Wallie, hat in hand, was waiting in the doorway, Mizzi, turning to go, suddenly felt two hands on her shoulders. She was whirled around. Hahn—he had to stand on tiptoe to do it—kissed her once on the mouth, hard. Then he gave her a little shove toward the door. "Tell Wallie about the red carpet," he said.

"I will not," Mizzi replied, very distinctly. "I hate red carpets."

Then they were gone. Hahn hardly seemed to notice that they had left. There were, I suppose, the proper number of Good-byes, and See-you-to-morrows, and Thank yous.

Sid Hahn stood there a moment in the middle of the room, very small, very squat, rather gnomelike, but not at all funny. He went over to the piano and seated himself, his shoulders hunched, his short legs clearing the floor. With the forefinger of his right hand he began to pick out a little tune. Not a sad little tune. A Hungarian street song. He did it atrociously. The stubby forefinger came down painstakingly on the white keys. Suddenly the little Jap servant stood in the doorway. Hahn looked up. His cheeks were wet with tears.

"God! I wish I could play!" he said.

LONG DISTANCE

Chet Ball was painting a wooden chicken yellow. The wooden chicken was mounted on a six-by-twelve board. The board was mounted on four tiny wheels. The whole would eventually be pulled on a string guided by the plump, moist hand of some blissful six-year-old.

You got the incongruity of it the instant your eye fell upon Chet Ball. Chet's shoulders alone would have loomed large in contrast with any wooden toy ever devised, including the Trojan horse. Everything about him, from the big, blunt-fingered hands that held the ridiculous chick to the great muscular pillar of his neck, was in direct opposition to his task, his surroundings, and his attitude.

Chet's proper milieu was Chicago, Illinois (the West Side); his job that of lineman for the Gas, Light and Power Company; his normal working position astride the top of a telegraph pole supported in his perilous perch by a lineman's leather belt and the kindly fates, both of which are likely to trick you in an emergency.

Yet now he lolled back among his pillows, dabbling complacently at the absurd yellow toy. A description of his surroundings would sound like Pages 3 to 17 of a novel by Mrs. Humphry Ward. The place was all greensward, and terraces, and sun dials, and beeches, and even those rhododendrons without which no English novel or country estate is complete. The presence of Chet Ball among his pillows and some hundreds similarly disposed revealed to you at once the fact that this particular English estate was now transformed into Reconstruction Hospital No. 9.

The painting of the chicken quite finished (including two beady black paint eyes) Chet was momentarily at a loss. Miss Kate had not told him to stop painting when the chicken was completed. Miss Kate was at the other end of the sunny garden walk, bending over a wheel-chair. So Chet went on painting, placidly. One by one, with meticulous nicety, he painted all his finger nails a bright and cheery yellow. Then he did the whole of his left thumb, and was starting on the second joint of the index finger when Miss Kate came up behind him and took the brush gently from his strong hands.

"You shouldn't have painted your fingers," she said.

Chet surveyed them with pride. "They look swell."

Miss Kate did not argue the point. She put the freshly painted wooden chicken on the table to dry in the sun. Her eyes fell upon a letter bearing an American postmark and addressed to Sergeant Chester Ball, with a lot of cryptic figures and letters strung out after it, such as A.E.F. and Co. 11.

"Here's a letter for you!" She infused a lot of Glad into her voice. But Chet only cast a languid eye upon it and said, "Yeh?"

"I'll read it to you, shall I? It's a nice fat One."

Chet sat back, indifferent, negatively acquiescent. And Miss Kate began to read in her clear young voice, there in the sunshine and scent of the centuries-old English garden.

It marked an epoch in Chet's life—that letter. But before we can appreciate it we'll have to know Chester Ball in his Chicago days.

Your true lineman has a daredevil way with the women, as have all men whose calling is a hazardous one. Chet was a crack workman. He could shinny up a pole, strap his emergency belt, open his tool kit, wield his pliers with expert deftness, and climb down again in record time. It was his pleasure—and seemingly the pleasure and privilege of all lineman's gangs the world over—to whistle blithely and to call impudently to any passing petticoat that caught his fancy.

Perched three feet from the top of the high pole he would cling, protected, seemingly, by some force working in direct defiance of the law of gravity. And now and then, by way of brightening the tedium of their job he and his gang would call to a girl passing in the street below, "Hoo-Hoo! Hello, sweetheart!"

There was nothing vicious in it, Chet would have come to the aid of beauty in distress as quickly as Don Quixote. Any man with a blue shirt as clean, and a shave as smooth, and a haircut as round as Chet Ball's has no meanness in him. A certain dare-deviltry went hand in hand with his work—a calling in which a careless load dispatcher, a cut wire, or a faulty strap may mean instant death. Usually the girls laughed and called back to them or went on more quickly, the colour in their cheeks a little higher.

But not Anastasia Rourke. Early the first morning of a two-weeks' job on the new plant of the Western Castings Company Chet Ball, glancing down from his dizzy perch atop an electric light pole, espied Miss Anastasia Rourke going to work. He didn't know her name nor anything about her, except that she was pretty. You could see that from a distance even more remote than Chet's. But you couldn't know that Stasia was a lady not to be trifled with. We know her name was Rourke, but he didn't.

So then: "Hoo-Hoo!" he had called. "Hello, sweetheart! Wait for me and I'll be down."

Stasia Rourke had lifted her face to where he perched so high above the streets. Her cheeks were five shades pinker than was their wont, which would make them border on the red.

"You big coward, you!" she called, in her clear, crisp voice. "If you had your foot on the ground you wouldn't dast call to a decent girl like that. If you were down here I'd slap the face of you. You know you're safe up there."

The words were scarcely out of her mouth before Chet Ball's sturdy legs were twinkling down the pole. His spurred heels dug into the soft pine of the pole with little ripe, tearing sounds. He walked up to Stasia and stood squarely in front of her, six feet of brawn and brazen nerve. One ruddy cheek he presented to her astonished gaze. "Hello, sweetheart," he said. And waited. The Rourke girl hesitated just a second. All the Irish heart in her was melting at the boyish impudence of the man before her. Then she lifted one hand and slapped his smooth cheek. It was a ringing slap. You saw the four marks of her fingers upon his face. Chet straightened, his blue eyes bluer. Stasia looked up at him, her eyes wide. Then down at her own hand, as if it belonged to somebody else. Her hand came up to her own face. She burst into tears, turned, and ran. And as she ran, and as she wept, she saw that Chet was still standing there, looking after her.

Next morning, when Stasia Rourke went by to work, Chet Ball was standing at the foot of the pole, waiting.

They were to have been married that next June. But that next June Chet Ball, perched perilously on the branch of a tree in a small woodsy spot somewhere in France, was one reason why the American artillery in that same woodsy spot was getting such a deadly range on the enemy. Chet's costume was so devised that even through field glasses (made in Germany) you couldn't tell where tree left off and Chet began.

Then, quite suddenly, the Germans got the range. The tree in which Chet was hidden came down with a crash, and Chet lay there, more than ever indiscernible among its tender foliage.

Which brings us back to the English garden, the yellow chicken, Miss Kate, and the letter.

His shattered leg was mended by one of those miracles of modern war surgery, though he never again would dig his spurred heels into the pine of a G.L. & P. Company pole. But the other thing—they put it down under the broad general head of shell shock. In the lovely English garden they set him to weaving and painting, as a means of soothing the shattered nerves. He had made everything from pottery jars to bead chains; from baskets to rugs. Slowly the tortured nerves healed. But the doctors, when they stopped at Chet's cot or chair, talked always of "the memory centre." Chet seemed satisfied to go on placidly painting toys or weaving chains with his great, square-tipped fingers—the fingers that had wielded the pliers so cleverly in his pole-climbing days.

"It's just something that only luck or an accident can mend," said the nerve specialist. "Time may do it—but I doubt it. Sometimes just a word—the right word—will set the thing in motion again. Does he get any letters?"

"His girl writes to him. Fine letters. But she doesn't know yet about—about this. I've written his letters for him. She knows now that his leg is healed and she wonders—"

That had been a month ago. To-day Miss Kate slit the envelope postmarked Chicago. Chet was fingering the yellow wooden chicken, pride in his eyes. In Miss Kate's eyes there was a troubled, baffled look as she began to read:

Chet, dear, it's raining in Chicago. And you know when it rains in Chicago, it's wetter, and muddier, and rainier than any place in the world. Except maybe this Flanders we're reading so much about. They say for rain and mud that place takes the prize.

I don't know what I'm going on about rain and mud for, Chet darling, when it's you I'm thinking of. Nothing else and nobody else. Chet, I got a funny feeling there's something you're keeping back from me. You're hurt worse than just the leg. Boy, dear, don't you know it won't make any difference with me how you look, or feel, or anything? I don't care how bad you're smashed up. I'd rather have you without any features at all than any other man with two sets. Whatever's happened to the outside of you, they can't change your insides. And you're the same man that called out to me, that day, "Hoo-hoo! Hello, sweetheart!" and when I gave you a piece of my mind climbed down off the pole, and put your face up to be slapped, God bless the boy in you—

A sharp little sound from him. Miss Kate looked up, quickly. Chet Ball was staring at the beady-eyed yellow chicken in his hand.

"What's this thing?" he demanded in a strange voice.

Miss Kate answered him very quietly, trying to keep her own voice easy and natural. "That's a toy chicken, cut out of wood."

"What'm I doin' with it?"

"You've just finished painting it."

Chet Ball held it in his great hand and stared at it for a brief moment, struggling between anger and amusement. And between anger and amusement he put it down on the table none too gently and stoop up, yawning a little.

"That's a hell of a job for a he-man!" Then in utter contrition: "Oh, beggin' your pardon! That was fierce! I didn't—"

But there was nothing shocked about the expression on Miss Kate's face. She was registering joy—pure joy.

UN MORSO DOO PANG

When you are twenty you do not patronize sunsets unless you are unhappy, in love, or both. Tessie Golden was both. Six months ago a sunset that Belasco himself could not have improved upon had wrung from her only a casual tribute such as: "My! Look how red the sky is!" delivered as unemotionally as a weather bulletin.

Tessie Golden sat on the top step of the back porch now, a slim, inert heap in a cotton kimono whose colour and design were libels on the Nipponese. Her head was propped wearily against the porch post. Her hands were limp in her lap. Her face was turned toward the west, where shone that mingling of orange and rose known as salmon pink. But no answering radiance in the girl's face met the glow in the Wisconsin sky.

Saturday night, after supper in Chippewa, Wis., Tessie Golden of the pre-sunset era would have been calling from her bedroom to the kitchen: "Ma, what'd you do with my pink georgette waist?"

And from the kitchen: "It's in your second bureau drawer. The collar was kind of mussed from Wednesday night, and I give it a little pressing while my iron was on."

At seven-thirty Tessie would have emerged from her bedroom in the pink georgette blouse that might have been considered alarmingly frank as to texture and precariously V-cut as to neck had Tessie herself not been so reassuringly unopulent; a black taffeta skirt, lavishly shirred and very brief; white kid shoes, high-laced, whose height still failed to achieve the two inches of white silk stocking that linked skirt hem to shoe top; finally, a hat with a good deal of French blue about it.

As she passed through the sitting room on her way out her mother would appear in the doorway, dish towel in hand. Her pride in this slim young thing and her love of her she concealed with a thin layer of carping criticism.

"Runnin' downtown again, I s'pose." A keen eye on the swishing skirt hem.

Tessie, the quick-tongued, would pat the arabesque of shining hair that lay coiled so submissively against either glowing cheek. "Oh, my, no! I just thought I'd dress up in case Angie Hatton drove past in her auto and picked me up for a little ride. So's not to keep her waiting."

Angie Hatton was Old Man Hatton's daughter. Any one in the Fox River Valley could have told you who Old Man Hatton was. You saw his name at the top of every letterhead of any importance in Chippewa, from the Pulp and Paper Mill to the First National Bank, and including the watch factory, the canning works, and the Mid-Western Land Company. Knowing this, you were able to appreciate Tessie's sarcasm. Angie Hatton was as unaware of Tessie's existence as only a young woman could be whose family residence was in Chippewa, Wis., but who wintered in Italy, summered in the mountains, and bought (so the town said) her very hairpins in New York. When Angie Hatton came home from the East the town used to stroll past on Mondays to view the washing on the Hatton line. Angie's underwear, flirting so audaciously with the sunshine and zephyrs, was of voile and silk and crêpe de Chine and satin—materials that we had always thought of heretofore as intended exclusively for party dresses and wedding gowns. Of course two years later they were showing practically the same thing at Megan's dry-goods store. But that was always the way with Angie Hatton. Even those of us who went to Chicago to shop never quite caught up with her.

Delivered of this ironic thrust, Tessie would walk toward the screen door with a little flaunting sway of the hips. Her mother's eyes, following the slim figure, had a sort of grudging love in them. A spare, caustic, wiry little woman, Tessie's mother. Tessie resembled her as a water colour may resemble a blurred charcoal sketch. Tessie's wide mouth curved into humour lines. She was the cut-up of the escapement department at the watch factory; the older woman's lips sagged at the corners. Tessie was buoyant and colourful with youth. The other was shrunken and faded with years and labour. As the girl minced across the room in her absurdly high-heeled white kid shoes the older woman thought: "My, but she's pretty!" But she said aloud: "Them shoes could stand a cleaning. I should think you'd stay home once in a while and not be runnin' the streets every night."

"Time enough to be sittin' home when I'm old like you."

And yet between these two there was love, and even understanding. But in families such as Tessie's demonstration is a thing to be ashamed of; affection a thing to conceal. Tessie's father was janitor of the Chippewa High School. A powerful man, slightly crippled by rheumatism, loquacious, lively, fond of his family, proud of his neat gray frame house, and his new cement sidewalk, and his carefully tended yard and garden patch. In all her life Tessie had never seen a caress exchanged between her parents.

Nowadays Ma Golden had little occasion for finding fault with Tessie's evening diversion. She no longer had cause to say: "Always gaddin' downtown, or over to Cora's or somewhere, like you didn't have a home to stay in. You ain't been in a evening this week, 'cept when you washed your hair."

Tessie had developed a fondness for sunsets viewed from the back porch—she who had thought nothing of dancing until three and rising at half-past six to go to work.

Stepping about in the kitchen after supper, her mother would eye the limp, relaxed figure on the back porch with a little pang at her heart. She would come to the screen door, or even out to the porch on some errand or other—to empty the coffee grounds; to turn the row of half-ripe tomatoes reddening on the porch railing; to flap and hang up a damp tea towel.

"Ain't you goin' out, Tess?"

"No."

"What you want to lop around here for? Such a grand evening. Why don't you put on your things and run downtown, or over to Cora's or somewhere, h'm?"

"What for?"—listlessly.

"What for! What does anybody go out for!"

"I don't know."

If they could have talked it over together, these two, the girl might have found relief. But the family shyness of their class was too strong upon them. Once Mrs. Golden had said, in an effort at sympathy: "Person'd think Chuck Mory was the only one who'd gone to war an' the last fella left in the world."

A grim flash of the old humour lifted the corners of the wide mouth. "He is. Who's there left? Stumpy Gans, up at the railroad crossing? Or maybe Fatty Weiman, driving the hack. Guess I'll doll up this evening and see if I can't make a hit with one of them."

She relapsed into bitter silence. The bottom had dropped out of Tessie Golden's world.

In order to understand the Tessie of to-day you will have to know the Tessie of six months ago; Tessie the impudent, the life-loving, the pleasureful. Tessie Golden could say things to the escapement-room foreman that any one else would have been fired for. Her wide mouth was capable of glorious insolences. Whenever you heard shrieks of laughter from the girls' wash room at noon you knew that Tessie was holding forth to an admiring group. She was a born mimic; audacious, agile, and with the gift of burlesque. The autumn that Angie Hatton came home from Europe wearing the first hobble skirt that Chippewa had ever seen Tessie gave an imitation of that advanced young woman's progress down Grand Avenue in this restricted garment. The thing was cruel in its fidelity, though containing just enough exaggeration to make it artistic. She followed it up by imitating the stricken look on the face of Mattie Haynes, cloak and suit buyer at Megan's, who, having just returned from the East with what she considered the most fashionable of the new fall styles, now beheld Angie Hatton in the garb that was the last echo of the last cry in Paris modes—and no model in Mattie's newly selected stock bore even the remotest resemblance to it.

You would know from this that Tessie was not a particularly deft worker. Her big-knuckled fingers were cleverer at turning out a shirt waist or retrimming a hat. Hers were what are known as handy hands, but not sensitive. It takes a light and facile set of fingers to fit pallet and arbour and fork together: close work and tedious. Seated on low benches along the tables, their chins almost level with the table top, the girls worked with pincers and gas flame, screwing together the three tiny parts of the watch's anatomy that was their particular specialty. Each wore a jeweller's glass in one eye. Tessie had worked at the watch factory for three years, and the pressure of the glass on the eye socket had given her the slightly hollow-eyed appearance peculiar to experienced watchmakers. It was not unbecoming, though, and lent her, somehow, a spiritual look which made her diablerie all the more piquant.

Tessie wasn't always witty, really. But she had achieved a reputation for wit which insured applause for even her feebler efforts. Nap Ballou, the foreman, never left the escapement room without a little shiver of nervous apprehension—a feeling justified by the ripple of suppressed laughter that went up and down the long tables. He knew that Tessie Golden, like a naughty schoolgirl when teacher's back is turned, had directed one of her sure shafts at him.

Ballou, his face darkling, could easily have punished her. Tessie knew it. But he never did, or would. She knew that, too. Her very insolence and audacity saved her.

"Some day," Ballou would warn her, "you'll get too gay, and then you'll find yourself looking for a job."

"Go on—fire me," retorted Tessie, "and I'll meet you in Lancaster"—a form of wit appreciated only by watchmakers. For there is a certain type of watch hand who is as peripatetic as the old-time printer. Restless, ne'er-do-well, spendthrift, he wanders from factory to factory through the chain of watchmaking towns: Springfield, Trenton, Waltham, Lancaster, Waterbury, Chippewa. Usually expert, always unreliable, certainly fond of drink, Nap Ballou was typical of his kind. The steady worker had a mingled admiration and contempt for him. He, in turn, regarded the other as a stick-in-the-mud. Nap wore his cap on one side of his curly head, and drank so evenly and steadily as never to be quite drunk and never strictly sober. He had slender, sensitive fingers like an artist's or a woman's, and he knew the parts of that intricate mechanism known as a watch from the jewel to the finishing room. It was said he had a wife or two. Forty-six, good-looking in a dissolute sort of way, possessing the charm of the wanderer, generous with his money, it was known that Tessie's barbs were permitted to prick him without retaliation because Tessie herself appealed to his errant fancy.

When the other girls teased her about this obvious state of affairs something fine and contemptuous welled up in her. "Him! Why, say, he ought to work in a pickle factory instead of a watch works. All he needs is a little dill and a handful of grape leaves to make him good eatin' as a relish."

And she thought of Chuck Mory, perched on the high seat of the American Express wagon, hatless, sunburnt, stockily muscular, shouting to his horse as he galloped clattering down Winnebago Street on his way to the depot and the 7:50 train.

I suppose there was something about the clear simplicity and uprightness of the firm little figure that appealed to Nap Ballou. He used to regard her curiously with a long, hard gaze before which she would grow uncomfortable. "Think you'll know me next time you see me?" But there was an uneasy feeling beneath her flip exterior. Not that there was anything of the beautiful, persecuted factory girl and villainous foreman about the situation. Tessie worked at watchmaking because it was light, pleasant, and well paid. She could have found another job for the asking. Her money went for white shoes and pink blouses and lacy boudoir caps which she affected Sunday mornings. She was forever buying a vivid necktie for her father and dressing up her protesting mother in gay colours that went ill with the drab, wrinkled face. "If it wasn't for me, you'd go round looking like one of those Polack women down by the tracks," Tessie would scold. "It's a wonder you don't wear a shawl!"

That was the Tessie of six months ago, gay, care-free, holding the reins of her life in her own two capable hands. Three nights a week, and Sunday, she saw Chuck Mory. When she went downtown on Saturday night it was frankly to meet Chuck, who was waiting for her on Schroeder's drug-store corner. He knew it, and she knew it. Yet they always went through a little ceremony. She and Cora, turning into Grand from Winnebago Street, would make for the post office. Then down the length of Grand with a leaping glance at Schroeder's corner before they reached it. Yes, there they were, very clean-shaven, clean-shirted, slick looking. Tessie would have known Chuck's blond head among a thousand. An air of studied hauteur and indifference as they approached the corner. Heads turned the other way. A low whistle from the boys.

"Oh, how do!"

"Good evening!"

Both greetings done with careful surprise. Then on down the street. On the way back you took the inside of the walk, and your hauteur was now stony to the point of insult. Schroeder's corner simply did not exist. On as far as Megan's which you entered and inspected, up one brightly lighted aisle and down the next. At the dress-goods counter there was a neat little stack of pamphlets entitled "In the World of Fashion." You took one and sauntered out leisurely. Down Winnebago Street now, homeward bound, talking animatedly and seemingly unconscious of quick footsteps sounding nearer and nearer. Just past the Burke House, where the residential district began, and where the trees cast their kindly shadows: "Can I see you home?" A hand slipped through her arm; a little tingling thrill.

"Oh, why, how do, Chuck! Hello, Scotty. Sure, if you're going our way."

At every turn Chuck left her side and dashed around behind her in order to place himself at her right again, according to the rigid rule of Chippewa etiquette. He took her arm only at street crossings until they reached the tracks, which perilous spot seemed to justify him in retaining his hold throughout the remainder of the stroll. Usually they lost Cora and Scotty without having been conscious of their loss.

Their talk? The girls and boys that each knew; the day's happenings at factory and express office; next Wednesday night's dance up in the Chute; and always the possibility of Chuck's leaving the wagon and assuming the managership of the office.

"Don't let this go any further, see? But I heard it straight that old Benke is goin' to be transferred to Fond du Lac. And if he is, why, I step in, see? Benke's got a girl in Fondy, and he's been pluggin' to get there. Gee, maybe I won't be glad when he does!" A little silence. "Will you be glad, Tess? H'm?"

Tess felt herself glowing and shivering as the big hand closed more tightly on her arm. "Me? Why, sure I'll be pleased to see you get a job that's coming to you by rights, and that'll get you better pay, and all."

But she knew what he meant, and he knew she knew. And the clasp tightened until it hurt her, and she was glad.

No more of that now. Chuck—gone. Scotty—gone. All the boys at the watch works, all the fellows in the neighbourhood—gone. At first she hadn't minded. It was exciting. You kidded them at first: "Well, believe me, Chuck, if you shoot the way you play ball, you're a gone goose already."

"All you got to do, Scotty, is to stick that face of yours up over the top of the trench and the Germans'll die of fright an' save you wastin' bullets."

There was a great knitting of socks and sweaters and caps. Tessie's big-knuckled, capable fingers made you dizzy, they flew so fast. Chuck was outfitted as for a polar expedition. Tess took half a day off to bid him good-bye. They marched down Grand Avenue, that first lot of them, in their everyday suits and hats, with their shiny yellow suitcases and their paste-board boxes in their hands, sheepish, red-faced, awkward. In their eyes, though, a certain look. And so off for Camp Sherman, their young heads sticking out of the car windows in clusters—black, yellow, brown, red. But for each woman on the depot platform there was just one head. Tessie saw a blurred blond one with a misty halo around it. A great shouting and waving of handkerchiefs:

"Goo'-bye! Goo'-bye! Write, now! Be sure! Mebbe you can get off in a week, for a visit. Goo'-bye! Goo—"

They were gone. Their voices came back to the crowd on the depot platform—high, clear young voices; almost like the voices of children, shouting.

Well, you wrote letters; fat, bulging letters, and in turn you received equally plump envelopes with a red triangle in one corner. You sent boxes of homemade fudge (nut variety) and cookies and the more durable forms of cake.

Then, unaccountably, Chuck was whisked all the way to California. He was furious at parting with his mates, and his indignation was expressed in his letters to Tessie. She sympathized with him in her replies. She tried to make light of it, but there was a little clutch of terror in it, too. California! My land! Might as well send a person to the end of the world while they were about it. Two months of that. Then, inexplicably again, Chuck's letters bore the astounding postmark of New York. She thought, in a panic, that he was Franceward bound, but it turned out not to be so. Not yet. Chuck's letters were taking on a cosmopolitan tone. "Well," he wrote, "I guess the little old town is as dead as ever. It seems funny you being right there all this time and I've travelled from the Atlantic to the Pacific. Everybody treats me swell. You ought to seen some of those California houses. They make Hatton's place look sick."

The girls, Cora and Tess and the rest, laughed and joked among themselves and assured one another, with a toss of the head, that they could have a good time without the fellas. They didn't need boys around. Well, I should say not!

They gave parties, and they were not a success. There was one of the type known as a stag. They dressed up in their brother's clothes, or their father's or a neighbour boy's, and met at Cora's. They looked as knock-kneed and slope-shouldered and unmasculine as girls usually do in men's attire. All except Tessie. There was something so astonishingly boyish and straight about her; she swaggered about with such a mannish swing of the leg (that was the actress in her) that the girls flushed a little and said: "Honest, Tess, if I didn't know you was a girl, I'd be stuck on you. With that hat on a person wouldn't know you from a boy."

Tessie would cross one slim leg over the other and bestow a knowing wink upon the speaker. "Some hen party!" they all said. They danced to the music of the victrola and sang "Over There." They had ice cream and chocolate layer cake and went home in great hilarity, with their hands on each other's shoulders, still singing. When they met a passer-by they giggled and shrieked and ran.

But the thing was a failure, and they knew it. Next day, at the lunch hour and in the wash room, there was a little desultory talk about the stag. But the meat of such an aftergathering is contained in phrases such as "I says t'him" and "He says t'me." They wasted little conversation on the stag. It was much more exciting to exhibit letters on blue-lined paper with the red triangle at the top. Chuck's last letter had contained the news of his sergeancy.

Angie Hatton, home from the East, was writing letters, too. Everyone in Chippewa knew that. She wrote on that new art paper with the gnawed looking edges and stiff as a newly laundered cuff. But the letters which she awaited so eagerly were written on the same sort of paper as were those Tessie had from Chuck: blue-lined, cheap in quality, a red triangle at one corner. A New York fellow, Chippewa learned; an aviator. They knew, too, that young Hatton was an infantry lieutenant somewhere in the East. These letters were not from him.

Ever since her home-coming Angie had been sewing at the Red Cross shop on Grand Avenue. Chippewa boasted two Red Cross shops. The Grand Avenue shop was the society shop. The East-End crowd sewed there, capped, veiled, aproned—and unapproachable. Were your fingers ever so deft, your knowledge of seams and basting mathematical, your skill with that complicated garment known as a pneumonia jacket uncanny; if you did not belong to the East-End set, you did not sew at the Grand Avenue shop. No matter how grossly red the blood which the Grand Avenue bandages and pads were ultimately to stanch, the liquid in the fingers that rolled and folded them was pure cerulean.

Tessie and her crowd had never thought of giving any such service to their country. They spoke of the Grand Avenue workers as "that stinkin' bunch," I regret to say. Yet each one of the girls was capable of starting a shirt waist in an emergency on Saturday night and finishing it in time for a Sunday picnic, buttonholes and all. Their help might have been invaluable. It never was asked.

Without warning Chuck came home on three days' leave. It meant that he was bound for France right enough this time. But Tessie didn't care.

"I don't care where you're goin'," she said, exultantly, her eyes lingering on the stocky, straight, powerful figure in its rather ill-fitting khaki. "You're here now. That's enough. Ain't you tickled to be home, Chuck? Gee!"

"I sh'd say," responded Chuck. But even he seemed to detect some lack in his tone and words. He elaborated somewhat shamefacedly: "Sure. It's swell to be home. But I don't know. After you've travelled around, and come back, things look so kind of little to you. I don't know—kind of—" he floundered about at a loss for expression. Then tried again: "Now, take Hatton's place, f'r example. I always used to think it was a regular palace, but, gosh, you ought to see places where I was asked in San Francisco and around there. Why, they was—were—enough to make the Hatton house look like a shack. Swimmin' pools of white marble, and acres of yard like a park, and a Jap help always bringin' you something to eat or drink. And the folks themselves—why, say! Here we are scrapin' and bowin' to Hattons and that bunch. They're pikers to what some people are that invited me to their houses in New York and Berkeley, and treated me and the other guys like kings or something. Take Megan's store, too"—he was warming to his subject, so that he failed to notice the darkening of Tessie's face—"it's a joke compared to New York and San Francisco stores. Reg'lar rube joint."

Tessie stiffened. Her teeth were set, her eyes sparkled. She tossed her head. "Well, I'm sure, Mr. Mory, it's good enough for me. Too bad you had to come home at all now you're so elegant and swell, and everything. You better go call on Angie Hatton instead of wastin' time on me. She'd probably be tickled to see you."

He stumbled to his feet, then, awkwardly. "Aw, say, Tessie, I didn't mean—why, say—you don't suppose—why, believe me, I pretty near busted out cryin' when I saw the Junction eatin' house when my train came in. And I been thinkin' of you every minute. There wasn't a day—"

"Tell that to your swell New York friends. I may be a rube, but I ain't a fool." She was perilously near to tears.

"Why, say, Tess, listen! Listen! If you knew—if you knew—a guy's got to—he's got no right to—"

And presently Tessie was mollified, but only on the surface. She smiled and glanced and teased and sparkled. And beneath was terror. He talked differently. He walked differently. It wasn't his clothes or the army. It was something else—an ease of manner, a new leisureliness of glance, an air. Once Tessie had gone to Milwaukee over Labour Day. It was the extent of her experience as a traveller. She remembered how superior she had felt for at least two days after. But Chuck! California! New York! It wasn't the distance that terrified her. It was his new knowledge, the broadening of his vision, though she did not know it and certainly could not have put it into words.

They went walking down by the river to Oneida Springs, and drank some of the sulphur water that tasted like rotten eggs. Tessie drank it with little shrieks and shudders and puckered her face up into an expression indicative of extreme disgust.

"It's good for you," Chuck said, and drank three cups of it, manfully. "That taste is the mineral qualities the water contains—sulphur and iron and so forth."

"I don't care," snapped Tessie, irritably. "I hate it!" They had often walked along the river and tasted of the spring water, but Chuck had never before waxed scientific. They took a boat at Baumann's boathouse and drifted down the lovely Fox River.

"Want to row?" Chuck asked. "I'll get an extra pair of oars if you do."

"I don't know how. Besides, it's too much work. I guess I'll let you do it."

Chuck was fitting his oars in the oarlocks. She stood on the landing looking down at him. His hat was off. His hair seemed blonder than ever against the rich tan of his face. His neck muscles swelled a little as he bent. Tessie felt a great longing to bury her face in the warm red skin. He straightened with a sigh and smiled at her. "I'll be ready in a minute." He took off his coat and turned his khaki shirt in at the throat, so that you saw the white, clean line of his untanned chest in strange contrast to his sunburnt throat. A feeling of giddy faintness surged over Tessie. She stepped blindly into the boat and would have fallen if Chuck's hard, firm grip had not steadied her. "Whoa, there! Don't you know how to step into a boat? There. Walk along the middle." She sat down and smiled up at him. "I don't know how I come to do that. I never did before."

Chuck braced his feet, rolled up his sleeves, and took an oar in each brown hand, bending rhythmically to his task. He looked about him, then at the girl, and drew a deep breath, feathering his oars. "I guess I must have dreamed about this more'n a million times."

"Have you, Chuck?"

They drifted on in silence. "Say, Tess, you ought to learn to row. It's good exercise. Those girls in California and New York, they play baseball and row and swim as good as the boys. Honest, some of 'em are wonders!"

"Oh, I'm sick of your swell New York friends! Can't you talk about something else?"

He saw that he had blundered without in the least understanding how or why. "All right. What'll we talk about?" In itself a fatal admission.

"About—you." Tessie made it a caress.

"Me? Nothin' to tell about me. I just been drillin' and studyin' and marchin' and readin' some—Oh, say, what d'you think?"

"What?"

"They been learnin' us—teachin' us, I mean—French. It's the darnedest language! Bread is pain. Can you beat that? If you want to ask for a piece of bread, you say like this: *Donnay ma un morso doo pang.* See?"

"My!" breathed Tessie, all admiration.

And within her something was screaming: "Oh, my God! Oh, my God! He knows French. And those girls that can row and everything. And me, I don't know anything. Oh, God, what'll I do?"

It was as though she could see him slipping away from her, out of her grasp, out of her sight. She had no fear of what might come to him in France. Bullets and bayonets would never hurt Chuck. He'd make it, just as he always made the 7.50 when it seemed as if he was going to miss it sure. He'd make it there and back, all right. But he—he'd be a different Chuck, while she stayed the same Tessie. Books, travel, French, girls, swell folks—

And all the while she was smiling and dimpling and trailing her hand in the water. "Bet you can't guess what I got in that lunch box."

"Chocolate cake."

"Well, of course I've got chocolate cake. I baked it myself this morning."

"Yes, you did!"

"Why, Chuck Mory, I did so! I guess you think I can't do anything, the way you talk."

"Oh, don't I! I guess you know what I think."

"Well, it isn't the cake I mean. It's something else."

"Fried chicken!"

"Oh, now you've gone and guessed it." She pouted prettily.

"You asked me to, didn't you?"

Then they laughed together, as at something exquisitely witty.

Down the river, drifting, rowing. Tessie pointed to a house half hidden among the trees on the farther shore: "There's Hatton's camp. They say they have grand times there with their swell crowd some Saturdays and Sundays. If I had a house like that, I'd live in it all the time, not just a couple of days out of the whole year." She hesitated a moment. "I suppose it looks like a shanty to you now."

Chuck surveyed it, patronizingly. "No, it's a nice little place."

They beached their boat, and built a little fire, and had supper on the river bank, and Tessie picked out the choice bits for him—the breast of the chicken, beautifully golden brown; the ripest tomato; the firmest, juiciest pickle; the corner of the little cake which would give him a double share of icing. She may not have been versed in French, Tessie, but she was wise in feminine wiles.

From Chuck, between mouthfuls: "I guess you don't know how good this tastes. Camp grub's all right, but after you've had a few months of it you get so you don't believe there is such a thing as fried chicken and chocolate cake."

"I'm glad you like it, Chuck. Here, take this drumstick. You ain't eating a thing!" His fourth piece of chicken.

Down the river as far as the danger line just above the dam, with Tessie pretending fear just for the joy of having Chuck reassure her. Then back again in the dusk, Chuck bending to the task now against the current. And so up the hill homeward bound. They walked very slowly, Chuck's hand on her arm. They were dumb with the tragic, eloquent dumbness of their kind. If she could have spoken the words that were churning in her mind, they would have been something like this:

"Oh, Chuck, I wish I was married to you. I wouldn't care if only I had you. I wouldn't mind babies or anything. I'd be glad. I want our house, with a dining-room set, and a brass bed, and a mahogany table in the parlour, and all the housework to do. I'm scared. I'm scared I won't get it. What'll I do if I don't?"

And he, wordlessly: "Will you wait for me, Tessie, and keep on loving me and thinking of me? And will you keep yourself clean in mind and body so that if I come back—"

Aloud, she said: "I guess you'll get stuck on one of those French girls. I should worry! They say wages at the watch factory are going to be raised, workers are so scarce. I'll prob'ly be as rich as Angie Hatton time you get back."

And he, miserably: "Little old Chippewa girls are good enough for Chuck. I ain't counting on taking up with those Frenchies. I don't like their jabber, from what I know of it. I saw some pictures of 'em, last week, a fellow in camp had who'd been over there. Their hair is all funny, and fixed up with combs and stuff, and they look real dark like foreigners. Nix!"

It had been reassuring enough at the time. But that was six months ago. Which brings us to the Tessie who sat on the back porch, evenings, surveying the sunset. A listless, lackadaisical, brooding Tessie. Little point to going downtown Saturday nights now. There was no familiar, beloved figure to follow you swiftly as you turned off Elm Street, homeward bound. If she went downtown now, she saw only those Saturday-night family groups which are familiar to every small town. The husband, very wet as to hair and clean as to shirt, guarding the gocart outside while the woman accomplished her Saturday-night trading at Ding's or Halpin's. Sometimes there were as many as half a dozen gocarts outside Halpin's, each containing a sleeping burden, relaxed, chubby, fat-cheeked. The waiting men smoked their pipes and conversed largely. "Hello, Ed. Th' woman's inside, buyin' the store out, I guess."

"Tha' so? Mine, too. Well, how's everything?"

Tessie knew that presently the woman would come out, bundle laden, and that she would stow these lesser bundles in every corner left available by the more important sleeping bundle—two yards of goods; a spool of 100, white; a banana for the baby; a new stewpan at the Five-and-Ten.

There had been a time when Tessie, if she thought of these women at all, felt sorry for them; worn, drab, lacking in style and figure. Now she envied them. For the maternal may be strong at twenty.

There were weeks upon weeks when no letter came from Chuck. In his last letter there had been some talk of his being sent to Russia. Tessie's eyes, large enough now in her thin face, distended with a great fear. Russia! His letter spoke, too, of French villages and châteaux. He and a bunch of fellows had been introduced to a princess or a countess or something—it was all one to Tessie—and what do you think? She had kissed them all on both cheeks! Seems that's the way they did in France.

The morning after the receipt of this letter the girls at the watch factory might have remarked her pallor had they not been so occupied with a new and more absorbing topic.

"Tess, did you hear about Angie Hatton?"

"What about her?"

"She's going to France. It's in the Milwaukee paper, all about her being Chippewa's fairest daughter, and a picture of the house, and her being the belle of the Fox River Valley, and she's giving up her palatial home and all to go to work in a Y.M.C.A. canteen for her country and bleeding France."

"Ya-as she is!" sneered Tessie, and a dull red flush, so deep as to be painful, swept over her face from throat to brow. "Ya-as she is, the doll-faced simp! Why, say, she never wiped up a floor in her life, or baked a cake, or stood on them feet of hers. She couldn't cut up a loaf of bread decent. Bleedin' France! Ha! That's rich, that is." She thrust her chin out brutally, and her eyes narrowed to slits. "She's goin' over there after that fella of hers. She's chasin' him. It's now or never, and she knows it and she's scared, same's the rest of us. On'y we got to set home and make the best of it. Or take what's left." She turned her head slowly to where Nap Ballou stood over a table at the far end of the room. She laughed a grim, unlovely little laugh. "I guess when you can't go after what you want, like Angie, why, you gotta take second choice."

All that day, at the bench, she was the reckless, insolent, audacious Tessie of six months ago. Nap Ballou was always standing over her, pretending to inspect some bit of work or other, his shoulder brushing hers. She laughed up at him so that her face was not more than two inches from his. He flushed, but she did not. She laughed a reckless little laugh.

"Thanks for helpin' teach me my trade, Mr. Ballou. 'Course I only been at it over three years now, so I ain't got the hang of it yet."

He straightened up slowly, and as he did so he rested a hand on her shoulder for a brief moment. She did not shrug it off.

That night, after supper, Tessie put on her hat and strolled down to Park Avenue. It wasn't for the walk. Tessie had never been told to exercise systematically for her body's good, or her mind's. She went in a spirit of unwholesome, brooding curiosity and a bitter resentment. Going to France, was she? Lots of good she'd do there. Better stay home and—and what? Tessie cast about in her mind for a fitting job for Angie. Guess she might's well go, after all. Nobody'd miss her, unless it was her father, and he didn't see her but about a third of the time. But in Tessie's heart was a great envy for this girl who could bridge the hideous waste of ocean that separated her from her man. Bleedin' France. Yeh! Joke!

The Hatton place, built and landscaped twenty years before, occupied a square block in solitary grandeur, the show place of Chippewa. In architectural style it was an impartial mixture of Norman castle, French château, and Rhenish Schloss, with a dash of Coney Island about its façade. It represented Old Man Hatton's realized dream of landed magnificence.

Tessie, walking slowly past it, and peering through the high iron fence, could not help noting an air of unwonted excitement about the place, usually so aloof, so coldly serene. Automobiles standing out in front. People going up and down. They didn't look very cheerful. Just as if it mattered whether anything happened to her or not!

Tessie walked around the block and stood a moment, uncertainly. Then she struck off down Grand Avenue and past Donovan's pool shack. A little group of after-supper idlers stood outside, smoking and gossiping, as she knew there would be. As she turned the corner she saw Nap Ballou among them. She had known that, too. As she passed she looked straight ahead, without bowing. But just past the Burke House he caught up to her. No half-shy "Can I walk home with you?" from Nap Ballou. No. Instead: "Hello, sweetheart!"

"Hello, yourself."

"Somebody's looking mighty pretty this evening, all dolled up in pink."

"Think so?"

She tried to be pertly indifferent, but it was good to have someone following, someone walking home with you. What if he was old enough to be her father, with graying hair? Lots of the movie heroes had graying hair at the sides. Twenty craves someone to tell it how wonderful it is. And Nap Ballou told her.

They walked for an hour. Tessie left him at the corner. She had once heard her father designate Ballou as "that drunken skunk." When she entered the sitting room her cheeks held an unwonted pink. Her eyes were brighter than they had been in months. Her mother looked up quickly, peering at her over a pair of steel-rimmed spectacles, very much askew.

"Where you been, Tessie?"

"Oh, walkin'."

"Who with?"

"Cora."

"Why, she was here, callin' for you, not more'n an hour ago."

Tessie, taking the hatpins out of her hat on her way upstairs, met this coolly. "Yeh, I ran into her comin' back."

Upstairs, lying fully dressed on her hard little bed, she stared up into the darkness, thinking, her hands limp at her sides. Oh, well, what's the diff? You had to make the best of it. Everybody makin' a fuss about the soldiers: feedin' 'em, and askin' 'em to their houses, and sendin' 'em things, and givin' dances and picnics and parties so they wouldn't be lonesome. Chuck had told her all about it. The other boys told the same. They could just pick and choose their good times. Tessie's mind groped about, sensing a certain injustice. How about the girls? She didn't put it thus squarely. Hers was not a logical mind, trained to think. Easy enough to paw over the menfolks and get silly over brass buttons and a uniform. She put it that way. She thought of the refrain of a popular song: "What Are You Going to Do to Help the Boys?" Tessie, smiling a crooked little smile up there in the darkness, parodied the words deftly: "What're you going to do to help the girls?" she demanded. "What're you going to do—" She rolled over on one side and buried her head in her arms.

There was news again next morning at the watch factory. Tessie of the old days had never needed to depend on the other girls for the latest bit of gossip. Her alert eye and quick ear had always caught it first. But of late she had led a cloistered existence, indifferent to the world about her. The Chippewa *Courier* went into the newspaper pile behind the kitchen door without a glance from Tessie's incurious eye.

She was late this morning. As she sat down at the bench and fitted her glass in her eye the chatter of the others, pitched in the high key of unusual excitement, penetrated even her listlessness.

"An' they say she never screeched or fainted or anything. She stood there, kind of quiet, lookin' straight ahead, and then all of a sudden she ran to her pa—"

"Both comin' at once, like that—"

"I feel sorry for her. She never did anything to me. She—"

Tessie spoke, her voice penetrating the staccato fragments all about her and gathering them into a whole. "Say, who's the heroine of this picture? Somebody flash me a cut-in so I can kinda follow the story. I come in in the middle of the reel, I guess."

They turned on her with the unlovely eagerness of those who have ugly news to tell. They all spoke at once, in short sentences, their voices high with the note of hysteria.

"Angie Hatton's beau was killed—"

"They say his aireoplane fell ten thousan' feet—"

"The news come only last evenin' about eight—"

"She won't see nobody but her pa—"

Eight! At eight Tessie had been standing outside Hatton's house envying Angie and hating her. So that explained the people, and the automobiles, and the excitement. Tessie was not receiving the news with the dramatic reaction which its purveyors felt it deserved. Tessie, turning from one to the other quietly, had said nothing. She was pitying Angie. Oh, the luxury of it! Nap Ballou, coming in swiftly to still the unwonted commotion in work hours, found Tessie the only one quietly occupied in that chatter-filled room. She was smiling as she worked. Nap Ballou, bending over her on some pretense that deceived no one, spoke low-voiced in her ear. But she veiled her eyes insolently and did not glance up. She hummed contentedly all the morning at her tedious work.

She had promised Nap Ballou to go picnicking with him Sunday. Down the river, boating, with supper on shore. The small, still voice within her had said: "Don't go! Don't go!" But the harsh, high-pitched, reckless overtone said: "Go on! Have a good time. Take all you can get."

She would have to lie at home and she did it. Some fabrication about the girls at the watch works did the trick. Fried chicken, chocolate cake. She packed them deftly and daintily. High-heeled white kid shoes, flimsy blouse, rustling skirt. Nap Ballou was waiting for her over in the city park. She saw him before he espied her. He was leaning against a tree idly, staring straight ahead with queer, lack-lustre eyes. Silhouetted there against the tender green of the pretty square he looked very old, somehow, and different—much older than he looked in his shop clothes, issuing orders. Tessie noticed that he sagged where he should have stuck out, and protruded where he should have been flat. There flashed across her mind a vividly clear picture of Chuck as she had last seen him: brown, fit, high of chest, flat of stomach, slim of flank.

Ballou saw her. He straightened and came toward her swiftly: "Somebody looks mighty sweet this afternoon."

Tessie plumped the heavy lunch box into his arms. "When you get a line you like you stick to it, don't you?"

Down at the boathouse even Tessie, who had confessed ignorance of boats and oars, knew that Ballou was fumbling clumsily. He stooped to adjust the oars to the oarlocks. His hat was off. His hair looked very gray in the cruel spring sunshine. He straightened and smiled up at her.

"Ready in a minute, sweetheart," he said. He took off his collar and turned in the neckband of his shirt. His skin was very white. Tessie felt a little shudder of disgust sweep over her, so that she stumbled a little as she stepped into the boat.

The river was very lovely. Tessie trailed her fingers in the water and told herself that she was having a grand time. She told Nap the same when he asked her.

"Having a good time, little beauty?" he said. He was puffing a little with the unwonted exercise. Alcohol-atrophied muscles do not take kindly to rowing.

Tessie tried some of her old-time pertness of speech. "Oh, good enough, considerin' the company."

He laughed, admiringly, at that and said she was a card.

When the early evening came on they made a clumsy landing and had supper. This time Nap fed her the titbits, though she protested. "White meat for you," he said, "with your skin like milk."

"You must of read that in a book," scoffed Tessie. She glanced around her at the deepening shadows. "We haven't got much time. It gets dark so early."

"No hurry," Nap assured her. He went on eating in a leisurely, finicking sort of way, though he consumed very little food actually.

"You're not eating much," Tessie said once, half-heartedly. She decided that she wasn't having such a very grand time, after all, and that she hated his teeth, which were very bad. Now, Chuck's strong, white double row ...

"Well," she said, "let's be going."

"No hurry," again.

Tessie looked up at that with the instinctive fear of her kind. "What d'you mean, no hurry! 'Spect to stay here till dark?" She laughed at her own joke.

"Yes."

She got up then, the blood in her face. "Well, I don't."

He rose, too. "Why not?"

"Because I don't, that's why." She stooped and began picking up the remnants of the lunch, placing spoons and glass bottles swiftly and thriftily in the lunch box. Nap stepped around behind her.

"Let me help," he said. And then his arm was about her and his face was close to hers, and Tessie did not like it. He kissed her after a little wordless struggle. And then she knew. Tessie's lips were not virgin. She had been kissed before. But not like this. Not like this! She struck at him furiously. Across her mind flashed the memory of a girl who had worked in the finishing room. A nice girl, too. But that hadn't helped her. Nap Ballou was laughing a little as he clasped her.

At that she heard herself saying: "I'll get Chuck Mory after you—you drunken bum, you! He'll lick you black and blue. He'll ..."

The face, with the ugly, broken brown teeth, was coming close again. With all the young strength that was in her she freed one hand and clawed at that face from eyes to chin. A howl of pain rewarded her. His hold loosened. Like a flash she was off. She ran. It seemed to her that her feet did not touch the earth. Over brush, through bushes, crashing against trees, on and on. She heard him following her, but the broken-down engine that was his heart refused to do the work. She ran on, though her fear was as great as before. Fear of what might have happened ... to her, Tessie Golden ... that nobody could even talk fresh to. She gave a little sob of fury and fatigue. She was stumbling now. It was growing dark. She ran on again, in fear of the overtaking darkness. It was easier now. Not so many trees and bushes. She came to a fence, climbed over it, lurched as she landed, leaned against it weakly for support, one hand on her aching heart. Before her was the Hatton summer cottage, dimly outlined in the twilight among the trees. A warm, flickering light danced in the window.

Tessie stood a moment, breathing painfully, sobbingly. Then, with a little instinctive gesture, she patted her hair, tidied her blouse, and walked uncertainly toward the house, up the steps to the door. She stood there a moment, swaying slightly. Somebody'd be there. The light. The woman who cooked for them or the man who took care of the place. Somebody'd—

She knocked at the door feebly. She'd tell 'em she had lost her way and got scared when it began to get dark. She knocked again, louder now. Footsteps. She braced herself and even arranged a crooked smile. The door opened wide. Old Man Hatton!

She looked up at him, terror and relief in her face. He peered over his glasses at her. "Who is it?" Tessie had not known, somehow, that his face was so kindly.

Tessie's carefully planned story crumbled into nothingness. "It's me!" she whimpered. "It's me!"

He reached out and put a hand on her arm and drew her inside.

"Angie! Angie! Here's a poor little kid...."

Tessie clutched frantically at the last crumbs of her pride. She tried to straighten, to smile with her old bravado. What was that story she had planned to tell?

"Who is it, dad? Who...?" Angie Hatton came into the hallway. She stared at Angie. Then: "Why, my dear!" she said. "My dear! Come in here."

Angie Hatton! Tessie began to cry weakly, her face buried in Angie Hatton's expensive blouse. Tessie remembered later that she had felt no surprise at the act.

"There, there!" Angie Hatton was saying. "Just poke up the fire, dad. And get something from the dining room. Oh, I don't know. To drink, you know. Something...."

Then Old Man Hatton stood over her, holding a small glass to her lips. Tessie drank it obediently, made a wry little face, coughed, wiped her eyes, and sat up. She looked from one to the other, like a trapped little animal. She put a hand to her tousled head.

"That's all right," Angie Hatton assured her. "You can fix it after a while."

There they were, the three of them: Old Man Hatton with his back to the fire, looking benignly down upon her; Angie seated, with some knitting in her hands, as if entertaining bedraggled, tearstained young ladies at dusk were an everyday occurrence; Tessie, twisting her handkerchief in a torment of embarrassment. But they asked no questions, these two. They evinced no curiosity about this dishevelled creature who had flung herself in upon their decent solitude.

Tessie stared at the fire. She looked up at Old Man Hatton's face and opened her lips. She looked down and shut them again. Then she flashed a quick look at Angie, to see if she could detect there some suspicion, some disdain. None. Angie Hatton looked—well, Tessie put it to herself, thus: "She looks like she'd cried till she couldn't cry no more—only inside."

And then, surprisingly, Tessie began to talk. "I wouldn't never have gone with this fella, only Chuck, he was gone. All the boys're gone. It's fierce. You get scared, sittin' home, waitin', and they're in France and everywheres, learnin' French and everything, and meetin' grand people and havin' a fuss made over 'em. So I got mad and said I didn't care, I wasn't goin' to squat home all my life, waitin'...."

Angie Hatton had stopped knitting now. Old Man Hatton was looking down at her very kindly. And so Tessie went on. The pent-up emotions and thoughts of these past months were finding an outlet at last. These things which she had never been able to discuss with her mother she now was laying bare to Angie Hatton and Old Man Hatton! They asked no questions. They seemed to understand. Once Old Man Hatton interrupted with: "So that's the kind of fellow they've got as escapement-room foreman, eh?"

Tessie, whose mind was working very clearly now, put out a quick hand. "Say, it wasn't his fault. He's a bum, all right, but I knew it, didn't I? It was me. I didn't care. Seemed to me it didn't make no difference who I went with, but it does." She looked down at her hands clasped so tightly in her lap.

"Yes, it makes a whole lot of difference," Angie agreed, and looked up at her father.

At that Tessie blurted her last desperate problem: "He's learnin' all kind of new things. Me, I ain't learnin' anything. When Chuck comes home he'll just think I'm dumb, that's all. He...."

"What kind of thing would you like to learn, Tessie, so that when Chuck comes home...."

Tessie looked up then, her wide mouth quivering with eagerness. "I'd like to learn to swim—and row a boat—and play ball—like the rich girls—like the girls that's makin' such a fuss over the soldiers."

Angie Hatton was not laughing. So, after a moment's hesitation, Tessie brought out the worst of it. "And French. I'd like to learn to talk French."

Old Man Hatton had been surveying his shoes, his mouth grim. He looked at Angie now and smiled a little. "Well, Angie, it looks as if you'd found your job right here at home, doesn't it? This young lady's just one of hundreds, I suppose. Hundreds. You can have the whole house for them, if you want it, Angie, and the grounds, and all the money you need. I guess we've kind of overlooked the girls. H'm, Angie. What d'you say?"

But Tessie was not listening. She had scarcely heard. Her face was white with earnestness.

"C'n you speak French?"

"Yes," Angie answered.

"Well," said Tessie, and gulped once, "well, how do you say in French: 'Give me a piece of bread'? That's what I want to learn first."

Angie Hatton said it correctly.

"That's it! Wait a minute! Say it again, will you?"

Angie said it again.

Tessie wet her lips. Her cheeks were smeared with tears and dirt. Her hair was wild and her blouse awry. "Donnay-ma-un-morso-doo-pang," she articulated, painfully. And in that moment, as she put her hand in that of Chuck Mory, across the ocean, her face was very beautiful to see.

They had always had two morning papers—he his, she hers. The *Times*. Both. Nothing could illustrate more clearly the plan on which Mr. and Mrs. T.A. Buck conducted their married life. Theirs was the morning calm and harmony which comes to two people who are free to digest breakfast and the First Page simultaneously with no— "Just let me see the inside sheet, will you, dear?" to mar the day's beginning.

In the days when she had been Mrs. Emma McChesney, travelling saleswoman for the T.A. Buck Featherloom Petticoat Company, New York, her perusal of the morning's news had been, perforce, a hasty process, accomplished between trains, or in a small-town hotel 'bus, jolting its way to the depot for the 7.52; or over an American-plan breakfast throughout which seven eighths of her mind was intent on the purchasing possibilities of a prospective nine o'clock skirt buyer. There was no need now of haste, but the habit of years still clung. From eight-thirty to eight thirty-five A.M. Emma McChesney Buck was always in partial eclipse behind the billowing pages of her newspaper. Only the tip of her topmost coil of bright hair was visible. She read swiftly, darting from war news to health hints, from stock market to sport page, and finding something of interest in each. For her there was nothing cryptic in a headline such as "Rudie Slams One Home"; and Do pfd followed by dotted lines and vulgar fractions were to her as easily translated as the Daily Hint From Paris. Hers was the photographic eye and the alert brain that can film a column or a page at a glance.

Across the table her husband sat turned slightly sidewise in his chair, his paper folded in a tidy oblong. He read down one column, top of the next and down that, seriously and methodically; giving to toast or coffee-cup the single-handed and groping attention of one whose interest is elsewhere. The light from the big bay window fell on the printed page and cameoed his profile. After three years of daily contact with it, Emma still caught herself occasionally gazing with appreciation at that clear-cut profile and the clean, shining line of his hair as it grew away from the temple.

"T.A.," she had announced one morning, to his mystification, "you're the Francis X. Bushman of the breakfast table. I believe you sit that way purposely."

"Francis X—?" He was not a follower of the films.

Emma elucidated. "Discoverer and world's champion exponent of the side face."

"I might punish you, Emma, by making a pun about its all being Greek to me, but I shan't." He returned to Page Two, Column Four.

Usually their conversation was comfortably monosyllabic and disjointed, as is the breakfast talk of two people who understand each other. Amicable silence was the rule, broken only by the rustle of paper, the clink of china, an occasional, "Toast, dear?" And when Buck, in a low, vibrating tone (slightly muffled by buttered corn muffin) said, "Dogs!" Emma knew he was pursuing the daily *schrecklichkeit*.

Upon this cozy scene Conservation cast his gaunt shadow. It was in June, the year of America's Great Step, that Emma, examining her household, pronounced it fattily degenerate, with complications, and performed upon it a severe and skilful surgical operation. Among the rest:

"One morning paper ought to be enough for any husband and wife who aren't living on a Boffin basis. There'll be one copy of the *Times* delivered at this house in the future, Mr. Buck. We might match pennies for it, mornings."

It lay there on the hall table that first morning, an innocent oblong, its headlines staring up at them with inky eyes.

"Paper, T.A.," she said, and handed it to him.

"You take it, dear."

"Oh, no! No."

She poured the coffee, trying to keep her gaze away from the tantalizing tail-end of the headline at whose first half she could only guess.

"By Jove, Emma! Listen to this! Pershing says if we have one m—"

"Stop right there! We've become pretty well acquainted in the last three years, T.A. But if you haven't learned that if there's one thing I can't endure, it's being fed across the table with scraps of the day's news, I shall have to consider our marriage a failure."

"Oh, very well. I merely thought you'd be—"

"I am. But there's something about having it read to you—"

On the second morning Emma, hurriedly fastening the middle button of her blouse on her way downstairs, collided with her husband, who was shrugging himself into his coat. They continued their way downstairs with considerable dignity and pronounced leisure. The paper lay on the hall table. They reached for it. There was a moment—just the fraction of a minute—when each clutched a corner of it, eying the other grimly. Then both let go suddenly, as though the paper had burned their fingers. They stared at each other, surprise and horror in their gaze. The paper fell to the floor with a little slap. Both stooped for it, apologetically. Their heads bumped. They staggered back, semi-stunned.

Emma found herself laughing, rather wildly. Buck joined in after a moment—a rueful laugh. She was the first to recover.

"That settles it. I'm willing to eat trick bread and whale meat and drink sugarless coffee, but I draw the line at hating my husband for the price of a newspaper subscription. White paper may be scarce but so are husbands. It's cheaper to get two newspapers than to set up two establishments."

They were only two among many millions who, at that time, were playing an amusing and fashionable game called Win the War. They did not realize that the game was to develop into a grim and magnificently functioning business to whose demands they would cheerfully sacrifice all that they most treasured.

Of late, Emma had spent less and less time in the offices of the Featherloom Company. For more than ten years that flourishing business, and the career of her son, Jock McChesney, had been the twin orbits about which her existence had revolved. But Jock McChesney was a man of family now, with a wife, two babies, and an uncanny advertising sense that threatened to put his name on the letterhead of the Raynor Advertising Company of Chicago. As for the Featherloom factory—it seemed to go of its own momentum. After her marriage to the firm's head, Emma's interest in the business was unflagging.

"Now look here, Emma," Buck would say. "You've given enough to this firm. Play a while. Cut up. Forget you're the 'And Company' in T.A. Buck & Co."

"But I'm so used to it. I'd miss it so. You know what happened that first year of our marriage when I tried to do the duchess. I don't know how to loll. If you take Featherlooms away from me I'll degenerate into a Madam Chairman. You'll see."

She might have, too, if the War had not come along and saved her.

By midsummer the workrooms were turning out strange garments, such as gray and khaki flannel shirts, flannelette one-piece pajamas, and woollen bloomers, all intended for the needs of women war workers going abroad.

Emma had dropped into the workroom one day and had picked up a half-finished gray flannel garment. She eyed it critically, her deft fingers manipulating the neckband. A little frown gathered between her eyes.

"Somehow a woman in a flannel shirt always looks as if she had quinsy. It's the collar. They cut them like a man's small-size. But a woman's neck is as different from a man's as her collarbone is."

She picked up a piece of flannel and smoothed it on the cutting-table. The head designer had looked on in disapproval while her employer's wife had experimented with scraps of cloth, and pins, and chalk, and scissors. But Emma had gone on serenely cutting and snipping and pinning. They made up samples of service shirts with the new neck-hugging collar and submitted them to Miss Nevins, the head of the woman's uniform department at Fyfe & Gordon's. That astute lady had been obliged to listen to scores of canteeners, nurses, secretaries, and motor leaguers who, standing before a long mirror in one of the many fitting-rooms, had gazed, frowned, fumbled at collar and topmost button, and said, "But it looks so—so lumpy around the neck."

Miss Kate Nevins's reply to this plaint was: "Oh, when you get your tie on—"

"Perhaps they'll let me wear a turn-down collar."

"Absolutely against regulations. The rules strictly forbid anything but the high, close-fitting collar."

The fair war worker would sigh, mutter something about supposing they'd shoot you at sunrise for wearing a becoming shirt, and order six, grumbling.

Kate Nevins had known Mrs. T.A. Buck in that lady's Emma McChesney days. At the end of the first day's trial of the new Featherloom shirt she had telephoned the Featherloom factory and had asked for Emma McChesney. People who had known her by that name never seemed able to get the trick of calling her by any other.

With every fitting-room in the Fyfe & Gordon establishment demanding her attention, Miss Nevins's conversation was necessarily brief. "Emma McChesney?... Kate Nevins.... Who's responsible for the collar on those Featherloom shirts?... I was sure of it.... No regular designer could cut a collar like that. Takes a genius.... H'm?... Well, I mean it. I'm going to write to Washington and have 'em vote you a distinguished service medal. This is the first day since last I-don't-know-when that hasn't found me in the last stages of nervous exhaustion at six o'clock.... All these women warriors are willing to bleed and die for their country, but they want to do it in a collar that fits, and I don't blame 'em. After I saw the pictures of that Russian Battalion of Death, I understood why.... Yes, I know I oughtn't to say that, but...."

By autumn Emma was wearing one of those Featherloom service shirts herself. It was inevitable that a woman of her executive ability, initiative, and detail sense should be pressed into active service. November saw Fifth Avenue a-glitter with uniforms, and one third of them seemed to be petticoated. The Featherloom factory saw little of Emma now. She bore the title of Commandant with feminine captains, lieutenants, and girl workers under her; and her blue uniform, as she herself put it, was so a-jingle with straps, buckles, belts, bars, and bolts that when she first put it on she felt like a jail.

She left the house at eight in the morning now. Dinner time rarely found her back in Sixty-third Street. Buck was devoting four evenings a week to the draft board. At the time of the second Liberty Loan drive in the autumn he had deserted Featherlooms for bonds. His success was due to the commodity he had for sale, the type of person to whom he sold it, and his own selling methods and personality. There was something about this slim, leisurely man, with the handsome eyes and the quiet voice, that convinced and impressed you.

"It's your complete lack of eagerness in the transaction, too," Emma remarked after watching him land a twenty-five-thousand-dollar bond pledge, the buyer a business rival of the Featherloom Petticoat Company. "You make it seem a privilege, not a favour. A man with your method could sell sandbags in the Sahara."

Sometimes the two dined downtown together. Sometimes they scarcely saw each other for days on end. One afternoon at 5.30, Emma, on duty bound, espied him walking home up Fifth Avenue, on the opposite side of the street. She felt a little pang as she watched the easy, graceful figure swinging its way up the brilliant, flag-decked avenue. She had given him so little time and thought; she had bestowed upon the house such scant attention in the last few weeks. She turned abruptly and crossed the street, dodging the late afternoon traffic with a sort of expert recklessness. She almost ran after the tall figure that was now a block ahead of her, and walking fast. She caught up with him, matched his stride, and touched his arm lightly.

"I beg your pardon, but aren't you Mr. T.A. Buck?"

"Yes."

"How do you do! I'm Mrs. Buck."

Then they had giggled together, deliciously, and he had put a firm hand on the smartly tailored blue serge sleeve.

"I thought so. That being the case, you're coming home along o' me, young 'ooman."

"Can't do it. I'm on my way to the Ritz to meet a dashing delegation from Serbia. You never saw such gorgeous creatures. All gold and green and red, with swords, and snake-work, and glittering boots. They'd make a musical-comedy soldier look like an undertaker."

There came a queer little look into his eyes. "But this isn't a musical comedy, dear. These men are—Look here, Emma. I want to talk to you. Let's walk home together and have dinner decently in our own dining room. There are things at the office—"

"S'impossible, Mr. Buck. I'm late now. And you know perfectly well there are two vice-commandants ready to snatch my shoulder-straps."

"Emma! Emma!"

At his tone the smiling animation of her face was dimmed. "What's gone wrong?"

"Nothing. Everything. At least, nothing that I can discuss with you at the corner of Fifth Avenue and Forty-fifth Street. When does this Serbian thing end? I'll call for you."

"There's no telling. Anyway, the Fannings will drive me home, thanks, dear."

He looked down at her. She was unbelievably girlish and distingué in the blue uniform; a straight, slim figure, topped by an impudent cocked hat. The flannel shirt of workaday service was replaced to-day by a severely smart affair of white silk, high-collared, stitched, expensively simple. And yet he frowned as he looked.

"Fisk got his exemption papers to-day." With apparent irrelevance.

"Yes?" She was glancing sharply up and down the thronged street. "Better call me a cab, dear. I'm awfully late. Oh, well, with his wife practically an invalid, and all the expense of the baby's illness, and the funeral—The Ritz, dear. And tell him to hurry." She stepped into the cab, a little nervous frown between her eyes.

But Buck, standing at the curb, seemed bent on delaying her. "Fisk told me the doctor said all she needs is a couple of months at a sanitarium, where she can be bathed and massaged and fed with milk. And if Fisk could go to a camp now he'd have a commission in no time. He's had training, you know. He spent his vacation last summer at Plattsburg."

"But he's due on his advance spring trip in two or three weeks, isn't he?... I really must hurry, T.A."

"Ritz," said Buck, shortly, to the chauffeur. "And hurry." He turned away abruptly, without a backward glance. Emma's head jerked over her shoulder in surprise. But he did not turn. The tall figure disappeared. Emma's taxi crept into the stream. But uppermost in her mind was not the thought of Serbians, uniforms, Fisk, or Ritz, but of her husband's right hand, which, as he turned away from the cab, had been folded tight into a fist.

She meant to ask an explanation of the clenched fingers; but the Serbians, despite their four tragic years, turned out to be as sprightly as their uniforms, and it was past midnight when the Fannings dropped her at her door. Her husband was rather ostentatiously asleep. As she doffed her warlike garments, her feminine canniness warned her that this was no time for explanations. Tomorrow morning would be better.

But next morning's breakfast turned out to be all Jock.

A letter from Grace, his wife. Grace McChesney had been Grace Gait, one of the youngest and cleverest women advertising writers in the profession. When Jock was a cub in the Raynor office she had been turning out compelling copy. They had been married four years. Now Jock ruled a mahogany domain of his own in the Raynor suite overlooking the lake in the great Michigan Avenue building. And Grace was saying, "Eat the crust, girlie. It's the crust that makes your hair grow curly."

Emma, uniformed for work, read hasty extracts from Grace's letter. Buck listened in silence.

"You wouldn't know Jock. He's restless, irritable, moody. And the queer part of it is he doesn't know it. He tries to be cheerful, and I could weep to see him. He has tried to cover it up with every kind of war work from Red Crossing to Liberty Loaning, and from writing free full-page national advertising copy to giving up his tobacco money to the smoke fund. And he's miserable. He wants to get into it. And he ought. But you know I haven't been really husky since Buddy came. Not ill, but the doctor says it will be another six months before I'm myself, really. If

I had only myself to think of—how simple! But two kiddies need such a lot of things. I could get a job at Raynor's. They need writers. Jock says, bitterly, that all the worth-while men have left. Don't think I'm complaining. I'm just trying to see my way clear, and talking to someone who understands often clears the way."

"Well!" said Emma.

And, "Well?" said T.A.

She sat fingering the letter, her breakfast cooling before her. "Of course, Jock wants to get into it. I wish he could. I'd be so proud of him. He'd be beautiful in khaki. But there's work to do right here. And he ought to be willing to wait six months."

"They can't wait six months over there, Emma. They need him now."

"Oh, come, T.A.! One man—"

"Multiplied by a million. Look at Fisk. Just such another case. Look at—"

The shrill summons of the telephone cut him short. Emma's head came up alertly. She glanced at her wrist-watch and gave a little exclamation of horror.

"That's for me! I'm half an hour late! The first time, too." She was at the telephone a second later, explanatory, apologetic. Then back in the dining-room doorway, her cheeks flushed, tugging at her gloves, poised for flight. "Sorry, dear. But this morning was so important, and that letter about Jock upset me. I'm afraid I'm a rotten soldier."

"I'm afraid you are, Emma."

She stared at that. "Why—! Oh, you're still angry at something. Listen, dear—I'll call for you at the office to-night at five, and we'll walk home together. Wait for me. I may be a few minutes late—"

She was off. The front door slammed sharply. Buck sat very still for a long minute, staring down at the coffee cup whose contents he did not mean to drink. The light from the window cameoed his fine profile. And you saw that his jaw was set. His mind was a thousand miles away, in Chicago, Illinois, with the boy who wanted to fight and couldn't.

Emma, flashing down Fifth Avenue as fast as wheels and traffic rules would permit, saw nothing of the splendid street. Her mind was a thousand miles away, in Chicago, Illinois.

And a thousand miles away, in Chicago, Illinois, Jock McChesney, three hours later, was slamming down the two big windows of his office. From up the street came the sound of a bugle and of a band playing a brisk march. And his office windows looked out upon Michigan Avenue. If you know Chicago, you know the building that housed the Raynor offices—a great gray shaft, towering even above its giant neighbours, its head in the clouds, its face set toward the blue beauty of Lake Michigan. Until very recently those windows of his office had been a source of joy and inspiration to Jock McChesney. The green of Grant Park just below. The tangle of I.C. tracks beyond that, and the great, gracious lake beyond that, as far as the eye could see. He had seen the changes the year had brought. The lake dotted with sinister gray craft. Dog tents in Grant Park, sprung up overnight like brown mushrooms. Men—mere boys, most of them—awkward in their workaday clothes of office and shop, drilling, wheeling, marching at the noon hour. And parades, and parades, and parades. At first Jock, and, in fact, the entire office staff—heads of departments, writers, secretaries, stenographers, office boys—would suspend business and crowd to the windows to see the pageant pass in the street below. Stirring music, khaki columns, flags, pennants, horses, bugles. And always the Jackie band from the Great Lakes Station, its white leggings twinkling down the street in the lead of its six-foot-six contortionistic drum-major.

By October the window-gazers, watching the parades from the Raynor windows, were mostly petticoated and exclamatory. Jock stayed away from the window now. It seemed to his tortured mind that there was a fresh parade hourly, and that bugles and bands sounded a taunting note.

"Where are *you*! (sounded the bugle)
Where are *you*?
Where are YOU?!!!
Where
are
you?
Where—are—you-u-u-u—"

He slammed down the windows, summoned a stenographer, and gave out dictation in a loud, rasping voice.

"Yours of the tenth at hand, and contents noted. In reply I wish to say—"

(Boom! Boom! And a boom-boom-boom!)

"—all copy for the Sans Scent Soap is now ready for your approval and will be mailed to you to-day under separate cover. We in the office think that this copy marks a new record in soap advertising—"

(Over there! Over there! Send the word, send the word over there!)

"Just read that last line will you, Miss Dugan?"

"Over th—I mean, 'We in the office think that this copy marks a new record in soap advertising—'"

"H'm. Yes." A moment's pause. A dreamy look on the face of the girl stenographer. Jock interpreted it. He knew that the stenographer was in the chair at the side of his desk, taking his dictation accurately and swiftly, while the spirit of the girl herself was far and away at Camp Grant at Rockford, Illinois, with an olive-drab unit in an olive-drab world.

"—and, in fact, in advertising copy of any description that has been sent out from the Raynor offices."

The girl's pencil flew over the pad. But when Jock paused for thought or breath she lifted her head and her eyes grew soft and bright, and her foot, in its absurd high-heeled gray boot, beat a smart left! Left! Left-right-left!

Something of this picture T.A. Buck saw in his untasted coffee cup. Much of it Emma visualized in her speeding motor car. All of it Grace knew by heart as she moved about the new, shining house in the Chicago suburb, thinking, planning; feeling his agony, and trying not to admit the transparency of the look about her hands and her temples. So much for Chicago.

At five o'clock Emma left the war to its own devices and dropped in at the loft building in which Featherlooms were born and grew up. Mike, the elevator man, twisted his gray head about at an unbelievable length to gaze appreciatively at the trim, uniformed figure.

"Haven't seen you around fur many the day, Mis' Buck."

"Been too busy, Mike."

Mike turned back to face the door. "Well, 'tis a great responsibility, runnin' this war, an' all." He stopped at the Featherloom floor and opened the door with his grandest flourish. Emma glanced at him quickly. His face was impassive. She passed into the reception room with a little jingling of buckles and strap hooks.

The work day was almost ended. The display room was empty of buyers. She could see the back of her husband's head in his office. He was busy at his desk. A stock girl was clearing away the piles of garments that littered tables and chairs. At the window near the door Fisk, the Western territory man, stood talking with O'Brien, city salesman. The two looked around at her approach. O'Brien's face lighted up with admiration. Into Fisk's face there flashed a look so nearly resembling resentment that Emma, curious to know its origin, stopped to chat a moment with the two.

Said O'Brien, the gallant Irishman, "I'm more resigned to war this minute, Mrs. Buck, than I've been since it began."

Emma dimpled, turned to Fisk, stood at attention. Fisk said nothing. His face was unsmiling. "Like my uniform?" Emma asked; and wished, somehow, that she hadn't.

Fisk stared. His eyes had none of the softness of admiration. They were hard, resentful. Suddenly, "Like it! God! I wish I could wear one!" He turned away, abruptly. O'Brien threw him a sharp look. Then he cleared his throat, apologetically.

Emma glanced down at her own trim self—at her stitched seams, her tailored lengths, her shining belt and buckles, her gloved hands—and suddenly and unaccountably her pride in them vanished. Something—something—

She wheeled and made for Buck's office, her colour high. He looked up, rose, offered her a chair. She felt strangely ill at ease there in the office to which she had given years of service. The bookkeeper in the glass-enclosed cubby-hole across the little hall smiled and nodded and called through the open door: "My, you're a stranger, Mrs. Buck."

"Be with you in a minute, Emma," said T.A. And turned to his desk again. She rose and strolled toward the door, restlessly. "Don't hurry." Out in the showroom again she saw Fisk standing before a long table. He was ticketing and folding samples of petticoats, pajamas, blouses, and night-gowns. His cigar was gripped savagely between his teeth and his eyes squinted, half closed through the smoke.

She strolled over to him and fingered the cotton flannel of a garment that lay under her hand. "Spring samples?"

"Yes."

"It ought to be a good trip. They say the West is dripping money, war or no war."

"'S right."

"How's Gertie?"

"Don't get me started, Mrs. Buck. That girl!—say, I knew what she was when I married her, and so did you. She was head stenographer here long enough. But I never really knew that kid until now, and we've been married two years. You know what the last year has been for her; the baby and all. And then losing him. And do you know what she says! That if there was somebody who knew the Western territory and could cover it, she'd get a job and send me to war. Yessir! That's Gert. We've been married two years, and she says herself it's the first really happy time she's ever known. You know what she had at home. Why, even when I was away on my long spring trip she used to say it wasn't so bad being alone, because there was always my home-coming to count on. How's that for a wife!"

"Gertie's splendid," agreed Emma. And wondered why it sounded so lame.

"You don't know her. Why, when it comes to patriotism, she makes T.R. look like a pacifist. She says if she could sell my line on the road, she'd make you give her the job so she could send her man to war. Gert says a travelling man's wife ought to make an ideal soldier's wife, anyway; and that if I went it would only be like my long Western trip, multiplied by about ten, maybe. That's Gertie."

Emma was fingering the cotton-flannel garment on the table.

Buck crossed the room and stood beside her. "Sorry I kept you waiting. Three of the boys were called to-day. It crippled us pretty badly in the shipping room. Ready?"

"Yes. Good-night, Charley. Give my love to Gertie."

"Thanks, Mrs. Buck." He picked up his cigar, took an apprehensive puff and went on ticketing and folding. There was a grin behind the cigar now.

Into the late afternoon glitter of Fifth Avenue. Five o'clock Fifth Avenue. Flags of every nation, save one. Uniforms of every blue from French to navy; of almost any shade save field green. Pongee-coloured Englishmen, seeming seven feet high, to a man; aviators slim and elegant, with walking sticks made of the propeller of their shattered planes, with a notch for every Hun plane bagged. Slim girls, exotic as the orchids they wore, gazing limpid-eyed at these warrior *élégants*. Women uniformed to the last degree of tailored exquisiteness. Girls, war accoutred, who brought arms up in sharp salute as they passed Emma. Buck eyed them gravely, hat and arm describing parabolas with increasing frequency as they approached Fiftieth Street, slackening as the colourful pageant grew less brilliant, thinned, and faded into the park mists.

Emma's cheeks were a glorious rose-pink. Head high, shoulders back, she matched her husband's long stride every step of the way. Her eyes were bright and very blue.

"There's a beautiful one, T.A.! The Canadian officer with the limp. They've all been gassed, and shot five times in the thigh and seven in the shoulder, and yet look at 'em! What do you suppose they were when they were new if they can look like that, damaged!"

Buck cut a vicious little semi-circle in the air with his walking stick.

"I know now how the father of the Gracchi felt, and why you never hear him mentioned."

"Nonsense, T.A. You're doing a lot." She did not intend her tone to be smug; but if she had glanced sidewise at her husband, she might have seen the pained red mount from chin to brow. She did not seem to sense his hurt. They went on, past the plaza now. Only a few blocks lay between them and their home; the old brownstone house that had been New York's definition of architectural elegance in the time of T.A. Buck, Sr.

"Tell me, Emma. Does this satisfy you—the work you're doing, I mean? Do you think you're giving the best you've got?"

"Well, of course I'd like to go to France—"

"I didn't ask you what you'd like."

"Yes, sir. Very good, sir. I don't know what you call giving the best one has got. But you know I work from eight in the morning until midnight, often and often. Oh, I don't say that someone else couldn't do my work just as well. And I don't say, either, that it doesn't include a lot of dashing up and down Fifth Avenue, and teaing at the Ritz, and meeting magnificent Missions, and being cooed over by Lady Millionaires. But if you'd like a few statistics as to the number of hundreds of thousands of soldiers we've canteened since last June, I'd be pleased to oblige." She tugged at a capacious pocket and brought forth a smart leather-bound notebook.

"Spare me! I've had all the statistics I can stand for one day at the office. I know you're working hard. I just wondered if you didn't realize—"

They turned into their own street. "Realize what?"

"Nothing. Nothing."

Emma sighed a mock sigh and glanced up at the windows of her own house. "Oh, well, everybody's difficult these days, T.A., including husbands. That second window shade is crooked. Isn't it queer how maids never do.... I'll tell you what I can realize, though. I realize that we're going to have dinner at home, reg'lar old-fashioned befo'-de-war. And I can bathe before dinner. There's richness."

But when she appeared at dinner, glowing, radiant, her hair shiningly re-coifed, she again wore the blue uniform, with the service cap atop her head. Buck surveyed her, unsmiling. She seated herself at table with a little clinking of buckles and buttons. She flung her motor gloves on a near-by chair, ran an inquiring finger along belt and collar with a little gesture that was absurdly feminine in its imitation of masculinity. Buck did not sit down. He stood at the opposite side of the table, one hand on his chair, the knuckles showing white where he gripped it.

"It seems to me, Emma, that you might manage to wear something a little less military when you're dining at home. War is war, but I don't see why you should make me feel like your orderly. It's like being married to a policewoman. Surely you can neglect your country for the length of time it takes to dine with your husband."

It was the bitterest speech he had made to her in the years of their married life. She flushed a little. "I thought you knew that I was going out again immediately after dinner. I left at five with the understanding that I'd be on duty again at 8.30."

He said nothing. He stood looking down at his own hand that gripped the chair back so tightly. Emma sat back and surveyed her trim and tailored self with a placidity that had in it, perhaps, a dash of malice. His last speech had cut. Then she reached forward, helped herself to an olive, and nibbled it, head on one side.

"D'you know, T.A., what I think? H'm? I think you're jealous of your wife's uniform."

She had touched the match to the dynamite.

He looked up. At the blaze in his eyes she shrank back a little. His face was white. He was breathing quickly.

"You're right! I am. I am jealous. I'm jealous of every buck private in the army! I'm jealous of the mule drivers! Of the veterinarians. Of the stokers in the transports. Men!" He doubled his hand into a fist. His fine eyes glowed. "Men!"

And suddenly he sat down, heavily, and covered his eyes with his hands.

Emma sat staring at him for a dull, sickening moment. Then she looked down at herself, horror in her eyes. Then up again at him. She got up and came over to him.

"Why, dear—dearest—I didn't know. I thought you were satisfied. I thought you were happy. You—"

"Honey, the only man who's happy is the man in khaki. The rest of us are gritting our teeth and pretending."

She put a hand on his shoulder. "But what do you want—what can you do that—"

He reached back over his shoulder and found her hand. He straightened. His head came up. "They've offered me a job in Bordeaux. It isn't a fancy job. It has to do with merchandising. But I think you know they're having a devil of a time with all the millions of bales of goods. They need men who know materials. I ought to. I've handled cloth and clothes enough. I know values. It would mean hard work—manual work lots of times. No pay. And happiness. For me." There was a silence. It seemed to fill the room, that silence. It filled the house. It roared and thundered about Emma's ears, that silence. When finally she broke it:

"Blind!" she said. "Blind! Deaf! Dumb! *And* crazy." She laughed, and two tears sped down her cheeks and dropped on the unblemished blue serge uniform. "Oh, T.A.! Where have I been? How you must have despised me. Me, in my uniform. In my uniform that was costing the Government three strapping men. My uniform, that was keeping three man-size soldiers out of khaki. You, Jock, and Fisk. Why didn't you tell me, dear! Why didn't you tell me!"

"I've tried. I couldn't. You've always seen things first. I couldn't ask you to go back to the factory."

"Factory! Factory nothing! I'm going back on the road. I'm taking Fisk's Western territory. I know the Middle West better than Fisk himself. I ought to. I covered it for ten years. I'll pay Gertie Fisk's salary until she's able to come back to us as stenographer. We've never had one so good. Grace can give the office a few hours a week. And we can promote O'Brien to manager while I'm on the road."

Buck was staring at her, dully. "Grace? Now wait a minute. You're travelling too fast for a mere man." His hand was gripping hers, tight, tight.

Their dinner was cooling on the table. They ignored it. She pulled a chair around to his. They sat shoulder to shoulder, elbows on the cloth.

"It took me long enough to wake up, didn't it? I've got to make up for lost time. The whole thing's clear in my mind. Now get this: Jock gets a commission. Grace and the babies pack up and come to New York, and live right here, with me, in this house. Fisk goes to war. Gertie gets well and comes back to work for Featherlooms. Mr. T.A. Buck goes to Bordeaux. Old Emmer takes off her uniform and begins to serve her country—on the road."

At that he got up and began pacing the room. "I can't have you do that, dear. Why, you left all that behind when you married me."

"Yes, but our marriage certificate didn't carry a war guarantee."

"Gad, Emma, you're glorious!"

"Glorious nothing! I'm going to earn the living for three families for a few months, until things get going. And there's nothing glorious about that, old dear. I haven't any illusions about what taking a line on the road means these days. It isn't travelling. It's exploring. You never know where you're going to land, or when, unless you're travelling in a freight train. They're cock o' the walk now. I think I'll check myself through as first-class freight. Or send my pack ahead, with natives on foot, like an African explorer. But it'll be awfully good for me character. And when I'm eating that criminal corn bread they serve on dining cars on a train that's seven hours late into Duluth I'll remember when I had my picture, in uniform, in the Sunday supplements, with my hand on the steering wheel along o' the nobility and gentry."

"Listen, dear, I can't have you—"

"Too late. Got a pencil? Let's send fifty words to Jock and Grace. They'll wire back 'No!' but another fifty'll fetch 'em. After all, it takes more than one night letter to explain a move that is going to change eight lives. Now let's have dinner, dear. It'll be cold, but filling."

Perhaps in the whirlwind ten days that followed a woman of less energy, less determination, less courage and magnificent vitality might have faltered and failed in an undertaking of such magnitude. But Emma was alert and forceful enough to keep just one jump ahead of the swift-moving times. In a less cataclysmic age the changes she wrought within a period of two weeks would have seemed herculean. But in this time of stress and change, when every household in every street in every town in all the country was feeling the tremor of upheaval, the readjustment of this little family and business group was so unremarkable as to pass unnoticed. Even the members of the group itself, seeing themselves scattered to camp, to France, to New York, to the Middle West, shuffled like pawns that the Great Game might the better be won, felt strangely unconcerned and unruffled.

It was little more than two weeks after the night of Emma's awakening that she was talking fast to keep from crying hard, as she stuffed plain, practical blue serge garments (unmilitary) into a bellows suitcase ("Can't count on trunks these days," she had said. "I'm not taking any chances on a clean shirtwaist"). Buck, standing in the doorway, tried hard to keep his gaze from the contemplation of his khaki-clad self reflected in the long mirror. At intervals he said: "Can't I help, dear?" Or, "Talk about the early Pilgrim mothers, and the Revolutionary mothers, and the Civil War mothers! I'd like to know what they had on you, Emma."

And from Emma: "Yeh, ain't I noble!" Then, after a little pause: "This house is going to be so full of wimmin folks it'll look like a Home for Decayed Gentlewomen. Buddy McChesney, aged six months, is going to be the only male protector around the place. We'll make him captain of the home guard."

"Gertie was in to-day. She says I'm a shrimp in my uniform compared to Charley. You know she always was the nerviest little stenographer we ever had about the place, but she knows more about Featherlooms than any woman in the shop except you. She's down to ninety-eight pounds, poor little girl, but every ounce of it's pure pluck, and she says she'll be as good as new in a month or two, and I honestly believe she will."

Emma was counting a neat stack of folded handkerchiefs. "Seventeen—eighteen—When she comes back we'll have to pay her twice the salary she got when she left. But, then, you have to pay an errand boy what you used to pay a shipping clerk, and a stock girl demands money that an operator used to brag about—nineteen—"

Buck came over to her and put a hand on the bright hair that was rumpled, now, from much diving into bags and suitcases and clothes closets.

"All except you, Emma. You'll be working without a salary—working like a man—like three men—"

"Working for three men, T.A. Three fighting men. I've got two service buttons already," she glanced down at her blouse, "and Charley Fisk said I had the right to wear one for him. I'll look like a mosaic, but I'm going to put 'em all on."

The day before Emma's departure for the West Grace arrived, with bags, bundles, and babies. A wan and tired Grace, but proud, too, and with the spirit of the times in her eyes.

"Jock!" she repeated, in answer to their questions. "My dears, he doesn't know I'm alive. I visited him at camp the day before I left. He thinks he'll be transferred East, as we hoped. Wouldn't that be glorious! Well, I had all sorts of intimate and vital things to discuss with him, and he didn't hear what I was saying. He wasn't even listening. He couldn't wait until I had finished a sentence so that he could cut in with something about his work. I murmured to him in the moonlight that there was something I had long meant to tell him and he answered that dammit he forgot to report that rifle that exploded. And when I said, 'Dearest, isn't this hotel a *little* like the place we spent our honeymoon in—that porch, and all?' he said, 'See this feller coming, Gracie? The big guy with the moustache. Now mash him, Gracie. He's my Captain. I'm going to introduce you. He was a senior at college when I was a fresh.'"

But the peace and the pride in her eyes belied her words.

Emma's trip, already delayed, was begun ten days before her husband's date for sailing. She bore that, too, with smiling equanimity. "When I went to school," she said, "I thought I hated the Second Peloponnesian War worse than any war I'd ever heard of. But I hate this one so that I want everyone to get into it one hundred per cent., so that it'll be over sooner; and because we've won."

They said little on their way to the train. She stood on the rear platform just before the train pulled out. They had tried frantically to get a lower berth, but unsuccessfully. "Don't look so tragic about it," she laughed. "It's like old times. These last three years have been a dream—a delusion."

He looked up at her, as she stood there in her blue suit, and white blouse, and trim blue hat and crisp veil. "Gad, Emma, it's uncanny. I believe you're right. You look exactly as you did when I first saw you, when you came in off the road after father died and I had just taken hold of the business."

For answer she hummed a few plaintive bars. He grinned as he recognized "Silver Threads Among the Gold." The train moved away, gathered speed. He followed it. They were not smiling now. She was leaning over the railing, as though to be as near to him as the fast-moving train would allow. He was walking swiftly along with the train, as though hypnotized. Their eyes held. The brave figure in blue on the train platform. The brave figure in khaki outside. The blue suddenly swam in a haze before his eyes; the khaki a mist before hers. The crisp little veil was a limp little rag when finally she went in to search for Upper Eleven.

The white-coated figure that had passed up and down the aisle unnoticed and unnoticing as she sat hidden behind the kindly folds of her newspaper suddenly became a very human being as Emma regained self-control, decided on dinner as a panacea, and informed the white coat that she desired Upper Eleven made up early.

The White Coat had said, "Yas'm," and glanced up at her. Whereupon she had said:

"Why, William!"

And he, "Well, fo' de lan'! 'F 'tain't Mis' McChesney! Well, mah sakes alive, Mis' McChesney! Ah ain't seen yo' since yo' married. Ah done heah yo' married yo' boss an' got a swell brownstone house, an' ev'thing gran'—"

"I've got everything, William, but a lower berth to Chicago. They swore they couldn't give me anything but an upper."

A speculative look crept into William's rolling eye. Emma recognized it. Her hand reached toward her bag. Then it stopped. She smiled. "No. No, William. Time was. But not these days. Four years ago I'd have slipped you fifty cents right now, and you'd have produced a lower berth from somewhere. But I'm going to fool you. My boss has gone to war, William, and so has my son. And I'm going to take that fifty cents and buy thrift stamps for Miss Emma McChesney, aged three, and Mr. Buddy McChesney, aged six months. And I'll dispose my old bones in Upper Eleven."

She went in to dinner.

At eight-thirty a soft and deferential voice sounded in her ear.

"Ah got yo' made up, Mis' McChesney."

"But this is my—"

He beckoned. He padded down the aisle with that walk which is a peculiar result of flat feet and twenty years of swaying car. Emma followed. He stopped before Lower Six and drew aside the curtain. It was that lower which can always be produced, magically, though ticket sellers, Pullman agents, porters, and train conductors swear that it does not exist. The key to it is silver, but to-night Emma McChesney Buck had unlocked it with finer metal. Gold. Pure gold. For William drew aside the curtain with a gesture such as one of his slave ancestors might have used before a queen of Egypt. He carefully brushed a cinder from the sheet with one gray-black hand. Then he bowed like any courtier.

Emma sank down on the edge of the couch with a little sigh of weariness. Gratefulness was in it, too. She looked up at him—at the wrinkled, kindly, ape-like face, and he looked down at her.

"William," she said, "war is a filthy, evil, vile thing, but it bears wonderful white flowers."

"Yas'm!" agreed William, genially, and smiled all over his rubbery, gray-black countenance. "*Yas'm!*"

And who shall say he did not understand?

FARMER IN THE DELL

Old Ben Westerveld was taking it easy. Every muscle taut, every nerve tense, his keen eyes vainly straining to pierce the blackness of the stuffy room—there lay Ben Westerveld in bed, taking it easy. And it was hard. Hard. He wanted to get up. He wanted so intensely to get up that the mere effort of lying there made him ache all over. His toes were curled with the effort. His fingers were clenched with it. His breath came short, and his thighs felt cramped. Nerves. But old Ben Westerveld didn't know that. What should a retired and well-to-do farmer of fifty-eight know of nerves, especially when he has moved to the city and is taking it easy?

If only he knew what time it was. Here in Chicago you couldn't tell whether it was four o'clock or seven unless you looked at your watch. To do that it was necessary to turn on the light. And to turn on the light meant that he would turn on, too, a flood of querulous protest from his wife, Bella, who lay asleep beside him.

When for forty-five years of your life you have risen at four-thirty daily, it is difficult to learn to loll. To do it successfully you must be a natural-born loller to begin with, and revert. Bella Westerveld was and had. So there she lay, asleep. Old Ben wasn't and hadn't. So there he lay, terribly wide-awake, wondering what made his heart thump so fast when he was lying so still. If It had been light, you could have seen the lines of strained resignation in the sagging muscles of his patient face.

They had lived in the city for almost a year, but it was the same every morning. He would open his eyes, start up with one hand already reaching for the limp, drab, work-worn garments that used to drape the chair by his bed. Then he would remember and sink back while a great wave of depression swept over him. Nothing to get up for. Store clothes on the chair by the bed. He was taking it easy.

Back home on the farm in southern Illinois he had known the hour the instant his eyes opened. Here the flat next door was so close that the bedroom was in twilight even at midday. On the farm he could tell by the feeling—an intangible thing, but infallible. He could gauge the very quality of the blackness that comes just before dawn. The crowing of the cocks, the stamping of the cattle, the twittering of the birds in the old elm whose branches were etched eerily against his window in the ghostly light—these things he had never needed. He had known. But here, in the unsylvan section of Chicago which bears the bosky name of Englewood, the very darkness had a strange quality. A hundred unfamiliar noises misled him. There were no cocks, no cattle, no elm. Above all, there was no instinctive feeling. Once, when they first came to the city, he had risen at twelve-thirty, thinking it was morning, and had gone clumping about the flat waking up everyone and loosing from his wife's lips a stream of acid vituperation that seared even his case-hardened sensibilities. The people sleeping in the bedroom of the flat next door must have heard her.

"You big rube! Getting up in the middle of the night and stomping around like cattle. You'd better build a shed in the backyard and sleep there if you're so dumb you can't tell night from day."

Even after thirty-three years of marriage he had never ceased to be appalled at the coarseness of her mind and speech—she who had seemed so mild and fragile and exquisite when he married her. He had crept back to bed, shamefacedly. He could hear the couple in the bedroom of the flat just across the little court grumbling and then laughing a little, grudgingly, and yet with appreciation. That bedroom, too, had still the power to appall him. Its nearness, its forced intimacy, were daily shocks to him whose most immediate neighbour, back on the farm, had been a quarter of a mile away. The sound of a shoe dropped on the hardwood floor, the rush of water in the bathroom, the murmur of nocturnal confidences, the fretful cry of a child in the night, all startled and distressed him whose ear had found music in the roar of the thresher and had been soothed by the rattle of the tractor and the hoarse hoot of the steamboat whistle at the landing. His farm's edge had been marked by the Mississippi rolling grandly by.

Since they had moved into town he had found only one city sound that he really welcomed: the rattle and clink that marked the milkman's matutinal visit. The milkman came at six, and he was the good fairy who released Ben Westerveld from durance vile—or had been until the winter months made his coming later and later, so that he became worse than useless as a timepiece. But now it was late March, and mild. The milkman's coming would soon again mark old Ben's rising hour. Before he had begun to take it easy six o'clock had seen the entire mechanism of his busy little world humming smoothly and sweetly, the whole set in motion by his own big work-calloused hands. Those hands puzzled him now. He often looked at them curiously and in a detached sort of way as if they belonged to someone else. So white they were, and smooth and soft, with long, pliant nails that never broke off from rough work as they used to. Of late there were little splotches of brown on the backs of his hands and around the thumbs.

"Guess it's my liver," he decided, rubbing the spots thoughtfully. "She gets kind of sluggish from me not doing anything. Maybe a little spring tonic wouldn't go bad. Tone me up."

He got a bottle of reddish-brown mixture from the druggist on Halsted Street near Sixty-third. A genial gentleman, the druggist, white-coated and dapper, stepping affably about the fragrant-smelling store. The reddish-brown mixture had toned old Ben up surprisingly—while it lasted. He had two bottles of it. But on discontinuing it he slumped back into his old apathy.

Ben Westerveld, in his store clothes, his clean blue shirt, his incongruous hat, ambling aimlessly about Chicago's teeming, gritty streets, was a tragedy. Those big, capable hands, now dangling so limply from inert wrists, had wrested a living from the soil; those strangely unfaded blue eyes had the keenness of vision which comes from scanning great stretches of earth and sky; the stocky, square-shouldered body suggested power unutilized. All these spelled tragedy. Worse than tragedy—waste.

For almost half a century this man had combated the elements, head set, eyes wary, shoulders squared. He had fought wind and sun, rain and drought, scourge and flood. He had risen before dawn and slept before sunset. In the process he had taken on something of the colour and the rugged immutability of the fields and hills and trees among which he toiled. Something of their dignity, too, though your town dweller might fail to see it beneath the drab exterior. He had about him none of the high lights and sharp points of the city man. He seemed to blend in with the background of nature so as to be almost indistinguishable from it as were the furred and feathered creatures. This farmer differed from the city man as a hillock differs from an artificial golf bunker, though form and substance are the same.

Ben Westerveld didn't know he was a tragedy. Your farmer is not given to introspection. For that matter any one knows that a farmer in town is a comedy. Vaudeville, burlesque, the Sunday supplement, the comic papers, have marked him a fair target for ridicule. Perhaps even you should know him in his overalled, stubble-bearded days, with the rich black loam of the Mississippi bottom-lands clinging to his boots.

At twenty-five, given a tasselled cap, doublet and hose, and a long, slim pipe, Ben Westerveld would have been the prototype of one of those rollicking, lusty young mynheers that laugh out at you from a Frans Hals canvas. A roguish fellow with a merry eye; red-cheeked, vigorous. A serious mouth, though, and great sweetness of expression. As he grew older the seriousness crept up and up and almost entirely obliterated the roguishness. By the time the life of ease claimed him even the ghost of that ruddy wight of boyhood had vanished.

The Westerveld ancestry was as Dutch as the name. It had been hundreds of years since the first Westerveld came to America, and they had married and intermarried until the original Holland strain had almost entirely disappeared. They had drifted to southern Illinois by one of those slow processes of migration and had settled in Calhoun County, then almost a wilderness, but magnificent with its rolling hills, majestic rivers, and gold-and-purple distances. But to the practical Westerveld mind hills and rivers and purple haze existed only in their relation to crops and weather. Ben, though, had a way of turning his face up to the sky sometimes, and it was not to scan the heavens for clouds. You saw him leaning on the plow handle to watch the whirring flight of a partridge across the meadow. He liked farming. Even the drudgery of it never made him grumble. He was a natural farmer as men are natural mechanics or musicians or salesmen. Things grew for him. He seemed instinctively to know facts about the kinship of soil and seed that other men had to learn from books or experience. It grew to be a saying in that section "Ben Westerveld could grow a crop on rock."

At picnics and neighbourhood frolics Ben could throw farther and run faster and pull harder than any of the farmer boys who took part in the rough games. And he could pick up a girl with one hand and hold her at arm's length while she shrieked with pretended fear and real ecstasy. The girls all liked Ben. There was that about his primitive strength which appealed to the untamed in them as his gentleness appealed to their softer side. He liked the girls, too, and could have had his pick of them. He teased them all, took them buggy riding, beaued them about to neighbourhood parties. But by the time he was twenty-five the thing had narrowed down to the Byers girl on the farm adjoining Westerveld's. There was what the neighbours called an understanding, though perhaps he had never actually asked the Byers girl to marry him. You saw him going down the road toward the Byers place four nights out of the seven. He had a quick, light step at variance with his sturdy build, and very different from the heavy, slouching gait of the work-weary farmer. He had a habit of carrying in his hand a little twig or switch cut from a tree. This he would twirl blithely as he walked along. The switch and the twirl represented just so much energy and animal spirits. He never so much as flicked a dandelion head with it.

An inarticulate sort of thing, that courtship.

"Hello, Emma."

"How do, Ben."

"Thought you might like to walk a piece down the road. They got a calf at Aug Tietjens with five legs."

"I heard. I'd just as lief walk a little piece. I'm kind of beat, though. We've got the threshers day after to-morrow. We've been cooking up."

Beneath Ben's bonhomie and roguishness there was much shyness. The two would plod along the road together in a sort of blissful agony of embarrassment. The neighbours were right in their surmise that there was no definite understanding between them. But the thing was settled in the minds of both. Once Ben had said: "Pop says I can have the north eighty on easy payments if—when—"

Emma Byers had flushed up brightly, but had answered equably: "That's a fine piece. Your pop is an awful good man."

Beneath the stolid exteriors of these two there was much that was fine and forceful. Emma Byers's thoughtful forehead and intelligent eyes would have revealed that in her. Her mother was dead. She kept house for her father and brother. She was known as "that smart Byers girl." Her butter and eggs and garden stuff brought higher prices at Commercial, twelve miles away, than did any in the district. She was not a pretty girl, according to the local standards, but there was about her, even at twenty-two, a clear-headedness and a restful serenity that promised well for Ben Westerveld's future happiness.

But Ben Westerveld's future was not to lie in Emma Byers's capable hands. He knew that as soon as he saw Bella Huckins. Bella Huckins was the daughter of old Red Front Huckins, who ran the saloon of that cheerful name in Commercial. Bella had elected to teach school, not from any bent toward learning, but because teaching appealed to her as being a rather elegant occupation. The Huckins family was not elegant. In that day a year or two of teaching in a country school took the place of the present-day normal-school diploma. Bella had an eye on St. Louis, forty miles from the town of Commercial. So she used the country school as a step toward her ultimate goal, though she hated the country and dreaded her apprenticeship.

"I'll get a beau," she said, "that'll take me driving and around. And Saturdays and Sundays I can come to town."

The first time Ben Westerveld saw her she was coming down the road toward him in her tight-fitting black alpaca dress. The sunset was behind her. Her hair was very golden. In a day of tiny waists hers could have been spanned by Ben Westerveld's two hands. He discovered that later. Just now he thought he had never seen anything so fairylike and dainty, though he did not put it that way. Ben was not glib of thought or speech.

He knew at once that this was the new school-teacher. He had heard of her coming, though at the time the conversation had interested him not at all. Bella knew who he was, too. She had learned the name and history of every eligible young man in the district two days after her arrival. That was due partly to her own bold curiosity and partly to the fact that she was boarding with the Widow Becker, the most notorious gossip in the county. In Bella's mental list of the neighbourhood swains Ben Westerveld already occupied a two-star position, top of column.

He felt his face redden as they approached each other. To hide his embarrassment he swung his little hickory switch gayly and called to his dog Dunder that was nosing about by the roadside. Dunder bounded forward, spied the newcomer, and leaped toward her playfully and with natural canine curiosity.

Bella screamed. She screamed and ran to Ben and clung to him, clasping her hands about his arm. Ben lifted the hickory switch in his free hand and struck Dunder a sharp cut with it. It was the first time in his life that he had done such a thing. If he had had a sane moment from that time until the day he married Bella Huckins, he would never have forgotten the dumb hurt in Dunder's stricken eyes and shrinking, quivering body.

Bella screamed again. Still clinging to him, Ben was saying: "He won't hurt you. He won't hurt you," meanwhile patting her shoulder reassuringly. He looked down at her pale face. She was so slight, so childlike, so apparently different from the sturdy country girls. From—well, from the girls he knew. Her helplessness, her utter femininity, appealed to all that was masculine in him. Bella the experienced, clinging to him, felt herself swept from head to foot by a queer, electric tingling that was very pleasant but that still had in it something of the sensation of a wholesale bumping of one's crazy bone. If she had been anything but a stupid little flirt, she would have realized that here was a specimen of the virile male with which she could not trifle. She glanced up at him now, smiling faintly. "My, I was scared!" She stepped away from him a little—very little.

"Aw, he wouldn't hurt a flea."

But Bella looked over her shoulders fearfully to where Dunder stood by the roadside, regarding Ben with a look of uncertainty. He still thought that perhaps this was a new game. Not a game that he cared for, but still one to be played if his master fancied it. Ben stooped, picked up a stone, and threw it at Dunder, striking him in the flank. "Go on home!" he commanded, sternly. "Go home!" He started toward the dog with a well-feigned gesture of menace. Dunder, with a low howl, put his tail between his legs and loped off home, a disillusioned dog.

Bella stood looking up at Ben. Ben looked down at her.

"You're the new teacher, ain't you?"

"Yes. I guess you must think I'm a fool, going on like a baby about that dog."

"Most girls would be scared of him if they didn't know he wouldn't hurt nobody. He's pretty big." He paused a moment, awkwardly. "My name's Ben Westerveld."

"Pleased to meet you," said Bella, twiddling her fingers in assumed shyness.

"Which way was you going? There's a dog down at Tietjens that's enough to scare anybody. He looks like a pony, he's so big."

"I forgot something at the school this afternoon, and I was walking over to get it." Which was a lie. "I hope it won't get dark before I get there. You were going the other way, weren't you?"

"Oh, I wasn't going no place in particular. I'll be pleased to keep you company down to the school and back." He was surprised at his own sudden masterfulness.

They set off together, chatting as freely as if they had known one another for years. Ben had been on his way to the Byers farm, as usual. The Byers farm and Emma Byers passed out of his mind as completely as if they had been whisked away on a magic rug.

Bella Huckins had never meant to marry him. She hated farm life. She was contemptuous of farmer folk. She loathed cooking and drudgery. The Huckinses lived above the saloon in Commercial and Mrs. Huckins was always boiling ham and tongue and cooking pig's feet and shredding cabbage for slaw, all these edibles being destined for the free-lunch counter downstairs. Bella had early made up her mind that there should be no boiling and stewing and frying in her life. Whenever she could find an excuse, she loitered about the saloon. There she found life and talk and colour. Old Red Front Huckins used to chase her away, but she always turned up again, somehow, with a dish for the lunch counter or with an armful of clean towels.

Ben Westerveld never said clearly to himself: "I want to marry Bella." He never dared meet the thought. He intended honestly to marry Emma Byers. But this thing was too strong for him. As for Bella, she laughed at him, but she was scared, too. They both fought the thing, she selfishly, he unselfishly, for the Byers girl, with her clear, calm eyes and her dependable ways, was heavy on his heart. Ben's appeal for Bella was merely that of the magnetic male. She never once thought of his finer qualities. Her appeal for him was that of the frail and alluring woman. But in the end they married. The neighbourhood was rocked with surprise. In fact, the only unsurprised party to the transaction was the dame known as Nature. She has a way of playing these tricks on men and women for the furtherance of her own selfish ends.

Usually in a courtship it is the male who assumes the bright colours of pretence in order to attract a mate. But Ben Westerveld had been too honest to be anything but himself. He was so honest and fundamentally truthful that he refused at first to allow himself to believe that this slovenly shrew was the fragile and exquisite creature he had married. He had the habit of personal cleanliness, had Ben, in a day when tubbing was a ceremony and in an environment that made bodily nicety difficult. He discovered that Bella almost never washed and that her appearance of fragrant immaculateness, when dressed, was due to a natural clearness of skin and eye, and to the way her blonde hair swept away in a clean line from her forehead. For the rest, she was a slattern, with a vocabulary of invective that would have been a credit to any of the habitués of Old Red Front Huckins's bar.

They had three children, a girl and two boys. Ben Westerveld prospered in spite of his wife. As the years went on he added eighty acres here, eighty acres there, until his land swept down to the very banks of the Mississippi.

There is no doubt that she hindered him greatly, but he was too expert a farmer to fail. At threshing time the crew looked forward to working for Ben, the farmer, and dreaded the meals prepared by Bella, his wife. She was notoriously the worst cook and housekeeper in the county. And all through the years, in trouble and in happiness, her plaint was the same: "If I'd thought I was going to stick down on a farm all my life, slavin' for a pack of men folks day and night, I'd rather have died. Might as well be dead as rottin' here."

Her school-teacher English had early reverted. Her speech was as slovenly as her dress. She grew stout, too, and unwieldy, and her skin coarsened from lack of care and overeating. And in her children's ears she continually dinned a hatred of farm life and farming. "You can get away from it," she counselled her daughter, Minnie. "Don't you be a rube like your pa," she cautioned John, the older boy. And they profited by her advice. Minnie went to work at Commercial when she was seventeen, an over-developed girl with an inordinate love of cheap finery. At twenty she married an artisan, a surly fellow with anarchistic tendencies. They moved from town to town. He never stuck long at one job. John, the older boy, was as much his mother's son as Minnie was her mother's daughter. Restless, dissatisfied, empty-headed, he was the despair of his father. He drove the farm horses as if they were racers, lashing them up hill and down dale. He was forever lounging off to the village or wheedling his mother for money to take him to Commercial. It was before the day of the ubiquitous automobile. Given one of those present adjuncts to farm life, John would have ended his career much earlier. As it was, they found him lying by the roadside at dawn one morning after the horses had trotted into the yard with the wreck of the buggy bumping the road behind them. He had stolen the horses out of the barn after the help was asleep, had led them stealthily down the road, and then had whirled off to a rendezvous of his own in town. The fall from the buggy might not have hurt him, but he evidently had been dragged almost a mile before his battered body became somehow disentangled from the splintered wood and the reins.

That horror might have served to bring Ben Westerveld and his wife together, but it did not. It only increased her bitterness and her hatred of the locality and the life.

"I hope you're good an' satisfied now," she repeated in endless reproach. "I hope you're good an' satisfied. You was bound you'd make a farmer out of him, an' now you finished the job. You better try your hand at Dike now for a change."

Dike was young Ben, sixteen; and old Ben had no need to try his hand at him. Young Ben was a born farmer, as was his father. He had come honestly by his nickname. In face, figure, expression, and manner he was a five-hundred-year throwback to his Holland ancestors. Apple-cheeked, stocky, merry of eye, and somewhat phlegmatic. When, at school, they had come to the story of the Dutch boy who saved his town from flood by thrusting his hand into the hole in the dike and holding it there until help came, the class, after one look at the accompanying picture in the reader, dubbed young Ben "Dike" Westerveld. And Dike he remained.

Between Dike and his father there was a strong but unspoken feeling. The boy was crop-wise, as his father had been at his age. On Sundays you might see the two walking about the farm looking at the pigs—great black fellows worth almost their weight in silver; eying the stock; speculating on the winter wheat showing dark green in April with rich patches that were almost black. Young Dike smoked a solemn and judicious pipe, spat expertly, and voiced the opinion that the winter wheat was a fine prospect. Ben Westerveld, listening tolerantly to the boy's opinions, felt a great surge of joy that he did not show. Here, at last, was compensation for all the misery and sordidness and bitter disappointment of his married life.

That married life had endured now for more than thirty years. Ben Westerveld still walked with a light, quick step—for his years. The stocky, broad-shouldered figure was a little shrunken. He was as neat and clean at fifty-five as he had been at twenty-five—a habit that requires much personal courage on a farm and that is fraught with difficulties. The community knew and respected him. He was a man of standing. When he drove into town on a bright winter morning and entered the First National Bank in his big sheepskin coat and his shaggy cap and his great boots, even Shumway, the cashier, would look up from his desk to say: "Hello, Westerveld! Hello! Well, how goes it?"

When Shumway greeted a farmer in that way you knew that there were no unpaid notes to his discredit.

All about Ben Westerveld stretched the fruit of his toil; the work of his hands. Orchards, fields, cattle, barns, silos. All these things were dependent on him for their future well-being—on him and on Dike after him. His days were full and running over. Much of the work was drudgery; most of it was back-breaking and laborious. But it was his place. It was his reason for being. And he felt that the reason was good, though he never put that thought into words, mental or spoken. He only knew that he was part of the great scheme of things and that he was functioning ably. If he had expressed himself at all, he might have said:

"Well, I got my work cut out for me, an' I do it an' do it right."

There was a tractor now, of course; a phonograph with expensive records, so that Caruso and McCormack and Elman were household words; a sturdy, middle-class automobile, in which Bella lolled red-faced in a lacy and beribboned boudoir cap when they drove into town. On a Saturday afternoon you saw more boudoir caps skimming up and down the main street in Commercial than you might see in a century of French farces.

As Ben Westerveld had prospered his shrewish wife had reaped her benefits. Ben was not the selfish type of farmer who insists on twentieth-century farm implements and medieval household equipment. He had added a bedroom here, a cool summer kitchen there, an ice house, a commodious porch, a washing machine, even a crude bathroom. But Bella remained unplaced. Her face was set toward the city. And slowly, surely, the effect of thirty-odd years of nagging was beginning to tell on Ben Westerveld. He was the finer metal, but she was the heavier, the coarser. She beat him and molded him as iron beats upon gold.

Minnie was living in Chicago now—a good-natured creature, but slack, like her mother. Her surly husband was still talking of his rights and crying down with the rich. They had two children. Minnie wrote of them, and of the delights of city life. Movies every night. Halsted Street just around the corner. The big stores. State Street. The L took you downtown in no time. Something going on all the while. Bella Westerveld, after one of those letters, was more than a chronic shrew; she became a terrible termagant.

When Ben Westerveld decided to concentrate on hogs and wheat he didn't dream that a world would be clamouring for hogs and wheat for four long years. When the time came he had them, and sold them fabulously. But wheat and hogs and markets became negligible things on the day that Dike with seven other farm boys from the district left for the nearest training camp that was to fit them for France and war.

Bella made the real fuss, wailing and mouthing and going into hysterics. Old Ben took it like a stoic. He drove the boy to town that day. When the train pulled out, you might have seen, if you had looked close, how the veins and cords swelled in the lean brown neck above the clean blue shirt. But that was all. As the weeks went on the quick, light step began to lag a little.

He had lost more than a son; his right-hand helper was gone. There were no farm helpers to be had. Old Ben couldn't do it all. A touch of rheumatism that winter half crippled him for eight weeks. Bella's voice seemed never to stop its plaint.

"There ain't no sense in you trying to make out alone. Next thing you'll die on me, and then I'll have the whole shebang on my hands." At that he eyed her dumbly from his chair by the stove. His resistance was wearing down. He knew it. He wasn't dying. He knew that, too. But something in him was. Something that had resisted her all these years. Something that had made him master and superior in spite of everything.

In those days of illness, as he sat by the stove, the memory of Emma Byers came to him often. She had left that district twenty-eight years ago, and had married, and lived in Chicago somewhere, he had heard, and was prosperous. He wasted no time in idle regrets. He had been a fool, and he paid the price of fools. Bella, slamming noisily about the room, never suspected the presence in the untidy place of a third person—a sturdy girl of twenty-two or three, very wholesome to look at, and with honest, intelligent eyes and a serene brow.

"It'll get worse an' worse all the time," Bella's whine went on. "Everybody says the war'll last prob'ly for years an' years. You can't make out alone. Everything's goin' to rack and ruin. You could rent out the farm for a year, on trial. The Burdickers'd take it and glad. They got those three strappin' louts that's all flat-footed or slab-sided or cross-eyed or somethin', and no good for the army. Let them run it on shares. Maybe they'll even buy, if things turn out. Maybe Dike'll never come b—"

But at the look on his face then, and at the low growl of unaccustomed rage that broke from him, even she ceased her clatter.

They moved to Chicago in the early spring. The look that had been on Ben Westerveld's face when he drove Dike to the train that carried him to camp was stamped there again—indelibly this time, it seemed. Calhoun County, in the spring, has much the beauty of California. There is a peculiar golden light about it, and the hills are a purplish haze. Ben Westerveld, walking down his path to the gate, was more poignantly dramatic than any figure in a rural play. He did not turn to look back, though, as they do in a play. He dared not.

They rented a flat in Englewood, Chicago, a block from Minnie's. Bella was almost amiable these days. She took to city life as though the past thirty years had never been. White kid shoes, delicatessen stores, the movies, the haggling with peddlers, the crowds, the crashing noise, the cramped, unnatural mode of living necessitated by a four-room flat—all these urban adjuncts seemed as natural to her as though she had been bred in the midst of them.

She and Minnie used to spend whole days in useless shopping. Theirs was a respectable neighbourhood of well-paid artisans, bookkeepers, and small shopkeepers. The women did their own housework in drab garments and soiled boudoir caps that hid a multitude of unkempt heads. They seemed to find a deal of time for amiable, empty gabbling. Any time from seven to four you might see a pair of boudoir caps leaning from opposite bedroom windows, conversing across back porches, pausing in the task of sweeping front steps, standing at a street corner, laden with grocery bundles. Minnie wasted hours in what she called "running over to ma's for a minute." The two quarrelled a great deal, being so nearly of a nature. But the very qualities that combated each other seemed, by some strange chemical process, to bring them together as well.

"I'm going downtown to-day to do a little shopping," Minnie would say. "Do you want to come along, ma?"

"What you got to get?"

"Oh, I thought I'd look at a couple of little dresses for Pearlie."

"When I was your age I made every stitch you wore."

"Yeh, I bet they looked like it, too. This ain't the farm. I got all I can do to tend to the house, without sewing."

"I did it. I did the housework and the sewin' and cookin', an' besides—"

"A swell lot of housekeepin' you did. You don't need to tell me."

The bickering grew to a quarrel. But in the end they took the downtown L together. You saw them, flushed of face, with twitching fingers, indulging in a sort of orgy of dime spending in the five-and-ten-cent store on the wrong side of State Street. They pawed over bolts of cheap lace and bins of stuff in the fetid air of the crowded place. They would buy a sack of salted peanuts from the great mound in the glass case, or a bag of the greasy pink candy piled in vile profusion on the counter, and this they would munch as they went.

They came home late, fagged and irritable, and supplemented their hurried dinner with hastily bought and so-called food from the near-by delicatessen.

Thus ran the life of ease for Ben Westerveld, retired farmer. And so we find him lying impatiently in bed, rubbing a nervous forefinger over the edge of the sheet and saying to himself that, well, here was another day. What day was it? Le'see now. Yesterday was—yesterday—a little feeling of panic came over him. He couldn't remember what yesterday had been. He counted back laboriously and decided that to-day must be Thursday. Not that it made any difference.

They had lived in the city almost a year now. But the city had not digested Ben. He was a leathery morsel that could not be assimilated. There he stuck in Chicago's crop, contributing nothing, gaining nothing. A rube in a comic collar ambling aimlessly about Halsted Street, or State downtown. You saw him conversing hungrily with the gritty and taciturn Swede who was janitor for the block of red-brick flats. Ben used to follow him around pathetically, engaging him in the talk of the day. Ben knew no men except the surly Gus, Minnie's husband. Gus, the firebrand, thought Ben hardly worthy of his contempt. If Ben thought, sometimes, of the respect with which he had always been greeted when he clumped down the main street of Commercial, Ill.—if he thought of how the farmers for miles around had come to him for expert advice and opinion—he said nothing.

Sometimes the janitor graciously allowed Ben to attend to the furnace of the building in which he lived. He took out ashes, shovelled coal. He tinkered and rattled and shook things. You heard him shovelling and scraping down there, and smelled the acrid odour of his pipe. It gave him something to do. He would emerge sooty and almost happy.

"You been monkeying with that furnace again!" Bella would scold. "If you want something to do, why don't you plant a garden in the backyard and grow something. You was crazy enough about it on the farm."

His face flushed a slow, dull red at that. He could not explain to her that he lost no dignity in his own eyes in fussing about an inadequate little furnace, but that self-respect would not allow him to stoop to gardening—he who had reigned over six hundred acres of bountiful soil.

On winter afternoons you saw him sometimes at the movies, whiling away one of his many idle hours in the dim, close-smelling atmosphere of the place. Tokyo and Petrograd and Gallipoli came to him. He saw beautiful tiger women twining fair, false arms about the stalwart but yielding forms of young men with cleft chins. He was only mildly interested. He talked to any one who would talk to him, though he was naturally a shy man. He talked to the barber, to the grocer, the druggist, the street-car conductor, the milkman, the iceman. But the price of wheat did not interest these gentlemen. They did not know that the price of wheat was the most vital topic of conversation in the world.

"Well, now," he would say, "you take this year's wheat crop with about 917,000,000 bushels of wheat harvested, why, that's what's going to win the war! Yes, sirree! No wheat, no winning, that's what I say."

"Ya-as, it is!" the city men would scoff. But the queer part of it is that Farmer Ben was right.

Minnie got into the habit of using him as a sort of nursemaid. It gave her many hours of unearned freedom for gadding and gossiping.

"Pa, will you look after Pearlie for a little while this morning? I got to run downtown to match something and she gets so tired and mean-acting if I take her along. Ma's goin' with me."

He loved the feel of Pearlie's, small, velvet-soft hand in his big fist. He called her "little feller," and fed her forbidden dainties. His big brown fingers were miraculously deft at buttoning and unbuttoning her tiny garments, and wiping her soft lips, and performing a hundred tender offices. I think that he was playing a sort of game with himself, and that he pretended this was Dike become a baby again. Once the pair managed to get over to Lincoln Park, where they spent a glorious day looking at the animals, eating popcorn, and riding on the miniature railway.

They returned, tired, dusty, and happy, to a double tirade.

Bella engaged in a great deal of what she called worrying about Dike. Ben spoke of him seldom, but the boy was always present in his thoughts. They had written him of their move, but he had not seemed to get the impression of its permanence. His letters indicated that he thought they were visiting Minnie, or taking a vacation in the city. Dike's letters were few. Ben treasured them, and read and reread them. When the armistice news came, and with it the possibility of Dike's return, Ben tried to fancy him fitting into the life of the city. And his whole being revolted at the thought.

He saw the pimply-faced, sallow youths in their one-button suits and striped shirts standing at the corner of Halsted and Sixty-Third, spitting languidly and handling their limp cigarettes with an amazing labial dexterity. Their conversation was low-voiced, sinister, and terse, and their eyes narrowed as they watched the over-dressed, scarlet-lipped girls go by. A great fear clutched at Ben Westerveld's heart.

The lack of exercise and manual labour began to tell on Ben. He did not grow fat from idleness. Instead his skin seemed to sag and hang on his frame, like a garment grown too large for him. He walked a great deal. Perhaps that had something to do with it. He tramped miles of city pavements. He was a very lonely man. And then, one day, quite by accident, he came upon South Water Street. Came upon it, stared at it as a water-crazed traveller in a desert gazes upon the spring in the oasis, and drank from it, thirstily, gratefully.

South Water Street feeds Chicago. Into that close-packed thoroughfare come daily the fruits and vegetables that will supply a million tables. Ben had heard of it, vaguely, but had never attempted to find it. Now he stumbled upon it and standing there felt at home in Chicago for the first time in more than a year. He saw ruddy men walking about in overalls and carrying whips in their hands—wagon whips, actually. He hadn't seen men like that since he left the farm. The sight of them sent a great pang of homesickness through him. His hand reached out and he ran an accustomed finger over the potatoes in a barrel on the walk. His fingers lingered and gripped them, and passed over them lovingly.

At the contact something within him that had been tight and hungry seemed to relax, satisfied. It was his nerves, feeding on those familiar things for which they had been starving.

He walked up one side and down the other. Crates of lettuce, bins of onions, barrels of apples. Such vegetables!

The radishes were scarlet globes. Each carrot was a spear of pure orange. The green and purple of fancy asparagus held his expert eye. The cauliflower was like a great bouquet, fit for a bride; the cabbages glowed like jade.

And the men! He hadn't dreamed there were men like that in this big, shiny-shod, stiffly laundered, white-collared city. Here were rufous men in overalls—worn, shabby, easy-looking overalls and old blue shirts, and mashed hats worn at a careless angle. Men jovial, good-natured, with clear blue eyes and having about them some of the revivifying freshness and wholesomeness of the products they handled.

Ben Westerveld breathed in the strong, pungent smell of onions and garlic and of the good earth that seemed to cling to the vegetables, washed clean though they were. He breathed deeply, gratefully, and felt strangely at peace.

It was a busy street. A hundred times he had to step quickly to avoid hand truck, or dray, or laden wagon. And yet the busy men found time to greet him friendlily: "H'are you!" they said, genially. "H'are you this morning!"

He was market-wise enough to know that some of these busy people were commission men, and some grocers, and some buyers, stewards, clerks. It was a womanless thoroughfare. At the busiest business corner, though, in front of the largest commission house on the street, he saw a woman. Evidently she was transacting business, too, for he saw the men bringing boxes of berries and vegetables for her inspection. A woman in a plain blue skirt and a small black hat.

He caught a glimpse of white-streaked hair beneath the hat. A funny job for a woman. What weren't they mixing into nowadays! He turned sidewise in the narrow, crowded space in order to pass her little group. And one of the men—a red-cheeked, merry-looking young fellow in white apron—laughed and said: "Well, Emma, you win. When it comes to driving a bargain with you, I quit. It can't be did!"

Even then he didn't know her. He did not dream that this straight, slim, tailored, white-haired woman, bargaining so shrewdly with these men, was the Emma Byers of the old days. But he stopped there a moment, in frank curiosity, and the woman looked up. She looked up, and he knew those intelligent eyes and that serene brow. He had carried the picture of them in his mind for more than thirty years, so it was not so surprising. And time deals kindly with women who have intelligent eyes and serene brows.

He did not hesitate. He might have if he had thought a moment, but he acted automatically. He stood before her. "You're Emma Byers, ain't you?"

She did not know him at first. Small blame to her, so completely had the roguish, vigorous boy vanished in this sallow, sad-eyed old man. Then: "Why, Ben!" she said, quietly. And there was pity in her voice, though she did not mean to have it there. She put out one hand—that capable, reassuring hand—and gripped his and held it a moment. It was queer and significant that it should be his hand that lay within hers.

"Well, what in all get-out are you doing around here, Emma?" He tried to be jovial and easy. She turned to the aproned man with whom she had been dealing and smiled.

"What am I doing here, Joe?" she said.

Joe grinned, waggishly. "Nothin'; only beatin' every man on the street at his own game, and makin' so much money that—"

But she stopped him there. "I guess I'll do my own explaining." She turned to Ben again. "And what are you doing here in Chicago?"

Ben passed a faltering hand across his chin. "Me? Well, I'm—we're livin' here, I s'pose. Livin' here."

She glanced at him, sharply. "Left the farm, Ben?"

"Yes."

"Wait a minute." She concluded her business with Joe; finished it briskly and to her own satisfaction. With her bright brown eyes and her alert manner and her quick little movements she made you think of a wren—a business-like little wren—a very early wren that is highly versed in the worm-catching way.

At her next utterance he was startled but game. "Have you had your lunch?"

"Why, no; I—"

"I've been down here since seven, and I'm starved. Let's go and have a bite at the little Greek restaurant around the corner. A cup of coffee and a sandwich, anyway."

Seated at the bare little table, she surveyed him with those intelligent, understanding, kindly eyes, and he felt the years slip from him. They were walking down the country road together, and she was listening quietly and advising him.

She interrogated him, gently. But something of his old masterfulness came back to him. "No, I want to know about you first. I can't get the rights of it, you being here on South Water, tradin' and all."

So she told him, briefly. She was in the commission business. Successful. She bought, too, for such hotels as the Blackstone and the Congress, and for half a dozen big restaurants. She gave him bare facts, but he was shrewd enough and sufficiently versed in business to know that here was a woman of wealth and established commercial position.

"But how does it happen you're keepin' it up, Emma, all this time? Why, you must be anyway—it ain't that you look it—but—" He floundered, stopped.

She laughed. "That's all right, Ben. I couldn't fool you on that. And I'm working because it keeps me happy. I want to work till I die. My children keep telling me to stop, but I know better than that. I'm not going to rust out. I want to wear out." Then, at an unspoken question in his eyes: "He's dead. These twenty years. It was hard at first when the children were small. But I knew garden stuff if I didn't know anything else. It came natural to me. That's all."

So then she got his story from him bit by bit. He spoke of the farm and of Dike, and there was a great pride in his voice. He spoke of Bella, and the son who had been killed, and of Minnie. And the words came falteringly. He was trying to hide something, and he was not made for deception. When he had finished:

"Now, listen, Ben. You go back to your farm."

"I can't. She—I can't."

She leaned forward, earnestly. "You go back to the farm."

He turned up his palms with a little gesture of defeat. "I can't."

"You can't stay here. It's killing you. It's poisoning you. Did you ever hear of toxins? That means poisons, and you're poisoning yourself. You'll die of it. You've got another twenty years of work in you. What's ailing you? You go back to your wheat and your apples and your hogs. There isn't a bigger job in the world than that."

For a moment his face took on a glow from the warmth of her own inspiring personality. But it died again. When they rose to go his shoulders drooped again, his muscles sagged. At the doorway he paused a moment, awkward in farewell. He blushed a little, stammered.

"Emma—I always wanted to tell you. God knows it was luck for you the way it turned out—but I always wanted to—"

She took his hand again in her firm grip at that, and her kindly, bright brown eyes were on him. "I never held it against you, Ben. I had to live a long time to understand it. But I never held a grudge. It just wasn't to be, I suppose. But listen to me, Ben. You do as I tell you. You go back to your wheat and your apples and your hogs. There isn't a bigger man-size job in the world. It's where you belong."

Unconsciously his shoulders straightened again. Again they sagged. And so they parted, the two.

He must have walked almost all the long way home, through miles and miles of city streets. He must have lost his way, too, for when he looked up at a corner street sign it was an unfamiliar one.

So he floundered about, asked his way, was misdirected. He took the right street car at last and got off at his own corner at seven o'clock, or later. He was in for a scolding, he knew.

But when he came to his own doorway he knew that even his tardiness could not justify the bedlam of sound that came from within. High-pitched voices. Bella's above all the rest, of course, but there was Minnie's, too, and Gus's growl, and Pearlie's treble, and the boy Ed's, and—

At the other voice his hand trembled so that the key rattled in the lock, and he could not turn it. But finally he did turn it, and stumbled in, breathing hard. And that other voice was Dike's.

He must just have arrived. The flurry of explanation was still in progress. Dike's knapsack was still on his back, and his canteen at his hip, his helmet slung over his shoulder. A brown, hard, glowing Dike, strangely tall and handsome and older, too. Older.

All this he saw in less than one electric second. Then he had the boy's two shoulders in his hands, and Dike was saying: "Hello, pop."

Of the roomful, Dike and old Ben were the only quiet ones. The others were taking up the explanation and going over it again and again, and marvelling, and asking questions.

"He come in to—what's that place, Dike?—Hoboken—yesterday only. An' he sent a dispatch to the farm. Can't you read our letters, Dike, that you didn't know we was here now? And then he's only got an hour more here. They got to go to Camp Grant to be, now, demobilized. He come out to Minnie's on a chance. Ain't he big!"

But Dike and his father were looking at each other quietly. Then Dike spoke. His speech was not phlegmatic, as of old. He had a new clipped way of uttering his words:

"Say, pop, you ought to see the way the Frenchies farm! They got about an acre each, and, say, they use every inch of it. If they's a little dirt blows into the crotch of a tree, they plant a crop in there. I never see nothin' like it. Say, we waste enough stuff over here to keep that whole country in food for a hundred years. Yessir. And tools! Outta the ark, believe me. If they ever saw our tractor, they'd think it was the Germans comin' back. But they're smart at that. I picked up a lot of new ideas over there. And you ought to see the old birds—womenfolks and men about eighty years old—runnin' everything on the farm. They had to. I learned somethin' off of them about farmin'."

"Forget the farm," said Minnie.

"Yeh," echoed Gus, "forget the farm stuff. I can get you a job here out at the works for four a day, and six when you learn it right."

Dike looked from one to the other, alarm and unbelief on his face. "What d'you mean, a job? Who wants a job! What you all—"

Bella laughed, jovially. "F'r Heaven's sakes, Dike, wake up! We're livin' here. This is our place. We ain't rubes no more."

Dike turned to his father. A little stunned look crept into his face. A stricken, pitiful look. There was something about it that suddenly made old Ben think of Pearlie when she had been slapped by her quick-tempered mother.

"But I been countin' on the farm," he said, miserably. "I just been livin' on the idea of comin' back to it. Why, I—The streets here, they're all narrow and choked up. I been countin' on the farm. I want to go back and be a farmer. I want—"

And then Ben Westerveld spoke. A new Ben Westerveld—no, not a new, but the old Ben Westerveld. Ben Westerveld, the farmer, the monarch over six hundred acres of bounteous bottomland.

"That's all right, Dike," he said. "You're going back. So'm I. I've got another twenty years of work in me. We're going back to the farm."

Bella turned on him, a wildcat. "We ain't! Not me! We ain't! I'm not agoin' back to the farm."

But Ben Westerveld was master again in his own house. "You're goin' back, Bella," he said, quietly. "An' things are goin' to be different. You're goin' to run the house the way I say, or I'll know why. If you can't do it, I'll get them in that can. An' me and Dike, we're goin' back to our wheat and our apples and our hogs. Yessir! There ain't a bigger man-size job in the world."

THE DANCING GIRLS

When, on opening a magazine, you see a picture of a young man in uniform with a background of assorted star-shells in full flower; a young man in uniform gazing into the eyes of a young lady (in uniform); a young man in uniform crouching in a trench, dugout, or shell-hole, this happens:

You skip lightly past the story of the young man in uniform; you jump hurriedly over the picture; and you plunge into the next story, noting that it is called "The Crimson Emerald" and that, judging from the pictures, all the characters in it wear evening clothes all the time.

Chug Scaritt took his dose of war with the best of them, but this is of Chug before and after taking. If, inadvertently, there should sound a faintly martial note it shall be stifled at once with a series of those stylish dots ... indicative of what the early Victorian writers conveniently called a drawn veil.

Nothing could be fairer than that.

Chug Scaritt was (and is) the proprietor and sole owner of the Elite Garage, and he pronounced it with a long i. Automobile parties, touring Wisconsin, used to mistake him for a handy man about the place and would call to him, "Heh, boy! Come here and take a look at this engine. She ain't hitting." When Chug finished with her she was hitting, all right. A medium-sized young fellow in the early twenties with a serious mouth, laughing eyes, and a muscular grace pretty well concealed by the grease-grimed grotesquerie of overalls. Out of the overalls and in his tight-fitting, belted green suit and long-visored green cap and flat russet shoes he looked too young and insouciant to be the sole owner—much less the proprietor—of anything so successful and established as the Elite Garage.

In a town like Chippewa, Wisconsin—or in any other sort of town, for that matter—a prosperous garage knows more about the scandals of the community than does a barber-shop, a dressmaker-by-the-day, or a pool-room habitue. It conceals more skeletons than the catacombs. Chug Scaritt, had he cared to open his lips and speak, might have poured forth such chronicles as to make Spoon River sound a pæan of sweetness and light. He knew how much Old Man Hatton's chauffeur knocked down on gas and repairs; he knew just how much the Tillotsons had gone into debt for their twin-six, and why Emil Sauter drove to Oshkosh so often on business, and who supplied the flowers for Mrs. Gurnee's electric. Chug didn't encourage gossip in his garage. Whenever possible he put his foot down on its ugly head in a vain attempt to crush it. But there was something about the very atmosphere of the place that caused it to thrive and flourish. It was like a combination newspaper office and Pullman car smoker. Chug tried to keep the thing down but there might generally be seen lounging about the doorway or perched on the running board of an idle car a little group of slim, flat-heeled, low-voiced young men in form-fitting, high-waisted suits of that peculiarly virulent shade of green which makes its wearer look as if he had been picked before he was ripe.

They were a lean, slim-flanked crew with a feline sort of grace about them; terse of speech, quick of eye, engine-wise, and, generally, nursing a boil just above the collar of their soft shirt. Not vicious. Not even tough. Rather bored, though they didn't know it. In their boredom resorting to the only sort of solace afforded boys of their class in a town of Chippewa's size: cheap amusements, cheap girls, cheap talk. This last unless the topic chanced to be of games or of things mechanical. Baseball, or a sweet-running engine brought out the best that was in them. At their worst, perhaps, they stood well back in the dim, cool shade of the garage doorway to watch how, when the girls went by in their thin summer dresses, the strong sunlight made a transparency of their skirts. At supper time they would growl to their surprised sisters:

"Put on some petticoats, you. Way you girls run around it's enough to make a person sick."

Chug Scaritt escaped being one of these by a double margin. There was his business responsibility on one side; his very early history on the other. Once you learn the derivation of Chug's nickname you have that history from the age of five to twenty-five, inclusive.

Chug had been christened Floyd (she had got it out of a book) but it was an appendix rather then an appellation. No one ever dreamed of addressing him by that misnomer, unless you except his school teachers. Once or twice the boys had tried to use his name as a weapon, shrieking in a shrill falsetto and making two syllables of it. He put a stop to that soon enough with fists and feet. His virility could have triumphed over a name twice as puerile. For that matter, I once knew a young husky named Fayette who—but that's another story.

The Scaritts lived the other side of the tracks. If you know Chippewa, or its equivalent, you get the significance of that. Nobodys. Not only did they live the other side of the tracks; they lived so close to them that the rush and rumble of the passing trains shook the two-story frame cottage and rattled the crockery on the pantry shelves. The first intelligible sound the boy made was a chesty chug-chug-chug in imitation of a panting engine tugging its freight load up the incline toward the Junction. When Chug ran away—which was on an average of twice daily— he was invariably to be found at the switchman's shanty or roaming about the freight yards. It got so that Stumpy Gans, the one-legged switchman, would hoist a signal to let Mrs. Scaritt know that Chug was safe.

He took his first mechanical toy apart, piece by piece. "Wait till your pa comes home!" his mother had said, with terrible significance. Chug, deep in the toy's wreckage, seemed undismayed, so Mrs. Scaritt gave him a light promissory slap and went on about her housework. That night, before supper, Len Scaritt addressed his son with a sternness quite at variance with his easy-going nature.

"Come here to me! Now, then, what's this about your smashing up good toys? Huh? Whatdya mean! Christmas not two days back and here you go smashing—"

The culprit trotted over to a corner and returned with the red-painted tin thing in his hand. It was as good as new. There may even have been some barely noticeable improvement in its locomotive powers. Chug had merely taken it apart in order to put it together again, and he had been too absorbed to pause long enough to tell his mother so. After that, nothing that bore wheels, internally or externally, was safe from his investigating fingers.

It was his first velocipede that really gave him his name. As he rode up and down, his short legs working like piston-rods gone mad, pedestrians would scatter in terror. His onrush was as relentless as that of an engine on a track, and his hoarse, "Chug-chug! Da-r-r-n-ng! Da-r-r-n-ng!" as he bore down upon a passerby caused that one to sidestep precipitously into the gutter (and none too soon).

Chug earned his first real bicycle carrying a paper route for the Chippewa *Eagle*. It took him two years. By the time he had acquired it he knew so much about bicycles, from ball-bearings to handle-bars, that its possession roused very little thrill in him. It was as when a lover has had to wait over-long for his bride. As Chug whizzed about Chippewa's streets, ringing an unnecessarily insistent bell, you sensed that a motorcycle was already looming large in his mechanism-loving mind. By the time he was seventeen Chug's motorcycle was spitting its way venomously down Elm Street. And the sequence of the seasons was not more inevitable than that an automobile should follow the motorcycle. True, he practically built it himself, out of what appeared to be an old wash-boiler, some wire, and an engine made up of parts that embraced every known car from Ford to Fiat. He painted it an undeniable red, hooded it like a demon racer, and shifted to first. The thing went.

He was a natural mechanic. He couldn't spend a day with a piece of mechanism without having speeded it up, or in some way done something to its belt, gears, wheels, motor. He was almost never separated from a monkey-wrench or pliers, and he was always turning a nut or bolt or screw in his grease-grimed fingers.

Right here it should be understood that Chug never became a Steinmetz or a Wright. He remained just average-plus to the end, with something more than a knack at things mechanical; a good deal of grease beneath his nails; and, generally, a smudge under one eye or a swipe of black across a cheek that gave him a misleadingly sinister and piratical look. There's nothing very magnificent, surely, in being the proprietor of a garage, even if it is the best-paying garage in Chippewa, where six out of ten families own a car, and summer tourists are as locusts turned beneficent.

Some time between Chug's motorcycle and the home-made automobile Len Scaritt died. The loss to the household was social more than economic. Len had been one of those good-natured, voluble, walrus-moustached men who make such poor providers. A carpenter by trade, he had always been a spasmodic worker and a steady talker. His high, hollow voice went on endlessly above the fusillade of hammers at work and the clatter of dishes at home. Politics, unions, world events, local happenings, neighbourhood gossip, all fed the endless stream of his loquacity.

"Well, now, looka here. Take, f'rins'ance, one these here big concerns—"

After he was gone Mrs. Scaritt used to find herself listening to the silence. His ceaseless talk had often rasped her nerves to the point of hysteria, but now she missed it as we miss a dull ache to which we have grown accustomed.

Chug was in his second year at the Chippewa high school. He had always earned some money, afternoons and Saturdays. Now he quit to go to work in earnest. His mother took it hard.

"I wanted you to have an education," she said. "Not just schooling. An education." Mittie Scaritt had always had ambition and a fierce sort of pride. She had needed them to combat Len's shiftlessness and slack good nature. They had kept the two-story frame cottage painted and tidy, had her pride and ambition; they had managed a Sunday suit, always, for Chug; money for the contribution box; pork roast on Sundays; and a sitting room, chill but elegant, with its plump pyramids of pillows, embroidered with impossible daisies and carnations and violets, filling every corner.

Mrs. Scaritt had had to fight for Chug's two years of high school. "He don't need no high school," Len Scaritt had argued, in one of the rare quarrels between the two. "I never had none."

The retort to this was so obvious that his wife refrained from uttering it. Len continued: "He don't go with none of my money. His age I was working 'n' had been for three years and more. You'll be fixing to send him to college, next."

"Well, if I do? Then what?"

"Then you're crazy," said Len, without heat, as one would state a self-evident fact.

That afternoon Mrs. Scaritt went down to the office of the *Eagle* and inserted a neat ad.

LACE CURTAINS DONE UP LIKE NEW. 25
CENTS A PR. MRS. SCARITT, 639 OUTAGAMIE ST.

For years afterward you never passed the Scaritt place without seeing the long skeleton frames of wooden curtain stretchers propped up against the back porch in the sun. Mrs. Scaritt became famous for her curtains as an artist is known for his middle distances, his woodland green, or his flesh tones. In time even the Hattons, who had always heretofore sent their fine curtains to Milwaukee to be cleaned, trusted their lacy treasures to Mrs. Scaritt's expert hands.

Chug went to high school on those lace curtains. He used to call for and deliver them. He rigged up a shelf-like device on his bicycle handlebars. On this the freshly laundered curtains reposed in their neat paper wrappings as unwrinkled as when they had come from the stretching frame.

At seventeen he went to work in the Elite Garage. He hadn't been there a month before the owner was saying, "Say, Chug, take a look at this here bus, will you? She don't run right but I can't find out what's got into her."

Chug would put his ear to the heart of the car, and tap its vitals, and count its pulse-beats as a doctor sounds you with his stethoscope. The look on his face was that of a violinist who tries his G-string.

For the rest, he filled gas tanks, changed and pumped up tires, tested batteries, oiled tappets. But the thing that fascinated him was the engine. An oily, blue-eyed boy in spattered overalls, he was always just emerging from beneath a car, or crawling under it. When a new car came in, en route—a proud, glittering affair—he always managed to get a chance at it somehow, though the owner or chauffeur guarded it ever so jealously. The only thing on wheels that he really despised was an electric brougham. Chippewa's well-paved streets made these vehicles possible. Your true garage man's feeling for electrics is unprintable. The least that they called them was juice-boxes.

At home Chug was forever rigging up labour-saving devices for his mother. The Scaritt's window-shades always rolled; their doorbell always rang with a satisfactory zing; their suction-pump never stuck. By the time he was twenty Chug was manager of the garage and his mother was saying, "You're around that garage sixteen hours a day. When you're home you're everlastingly reading those engineering papers and things. Your pa at your age had a girl for every night in the week and two on Sundays."

"Another year or so and I can buy out old Behnke and own the place. Soon's I do I'm going to come home in the speediest boat in the barn, and I'm going to bust up those curtain frames into kindling wood, over my knee, and pile 'em in the backyard and make a bonfire out of 'em."

"They've been pretty good friends to us, Chug—those curtain frames."

"Um." He glanced at her parboiled fingers. "Just the same, it'll be nix with the lace curtains for you."

Glancing back on what has been told of Chug he sounds, somehow, so much like a modern Rollo, with a dash of Alger, that unless something is told of his social side he may be misunderstood.

Chug was a natural born dancer. There are young men who, after the music has struck up, can start out incredibly enough by saying: "What is this, anyway—waltz or fox trot?" This was inconceivable to Chug. He had never had a dancing lesson in his life, but he had a sense of rhythm that was infallible. He could no more have danced out of time than he could have started a car on high, or confused a flivver with a Twelve. He didn't look particularly swanlike as he danced, having large, sensible feet, but they were expert at not being where someone else's feet happened to be, and he could time a beat to the fraction of a second.

When you have practically spent your entire day sprawled under a balky car, with a piece of dirty mat between you and the cement floor, your view limited to crank-case, transmission, universal, fly-wheel, differential, pan, and brake-rods you can do with a bit of colour in the evening. And just here was where Chippewa failed Chug.

He had a grave problem confronting him in his search for an evening's amusement. Chippewa, Wisconsin, was proud of its paved streets, its thirty thousand population, its lighting system, and the Greek temple that was the new First National Bank. It boasted of its interurban lines, its neat houses set well back among old elms, its paper mills, its plough works, and its prosperity. If you had told Chippewa that it was criminally ignoring Chug's crying need it would have put you down as mad.

Boiled down, Chug Scaritt's crying need was girls. At twenty-two or three you must have girls in your life if you're normal. Chug was, but Chippewa wasn't. It had too many millionaires at one end and too many labourers at the other for a town of thirty thousand. Its millionaires had their golf club, their high-powered cars, their smart social functions. They were always running down to Chicago to hear Galli-Curci; and when it came to costume— diamond bracelet, daring decolletage, large feather fans, and brilliant-buckled slippers—you couldn't tell their women from the city dwellers. There is much money in paper mills and plough works.

The mill hands and their families were well-paid, thrifty, clannish Swedes, most of them, with a liberal sprinkling of Belgians and Slavs. They belonged to all sorts of societies and lodges to which they paid infinitesimal dues and swore lifelong allegiance.

Chug Scaritt and boys of his kind were left high and dry. So, then, when Chug went out with a girl it was likely to be by way of someone's kitchen; or with one of those who worked in the rag room at the paper and pulp mill. They were the very girls who switched up and down in front of the garage evenings and Saturday afternoons. Many of them had been farm girls in Michigan or northern Wisconsin or even Minnesota. In Chippewa they did housework. Big, robust girls they were, miraculously well dressed in good shoes and suits and hats. They had bad teeth, for the most part, with a scum over them; over-fond of coffee; and were rather dull company. But they were good-natured, and hearty, and generous.

The paper-mill girls were quite another type. Theirs was a grayish pallor due to lungs dust-choked from work in the rag room. That same pallor promised ill for future generations in Chippewa. But they had a rather appealing, wistful fragility. Their eyes generally looked too big for their faces. They possessed, though, a certain vivacity and diablerie that the big, slower-witted Swede girls lacked.

When Chug felt the need of a dash of red in the evening he had little choice. In the winter he often went up to Woodman's Hall. The dances at Woodman's Hall were of the kind advertised at fifty cents a couple. Extra lady, twenty-five cents. Ladies without gents, thirty-five cents. Bergstrom's two-piece orchestra. Chug usually went alone, but he escorted home one of the ladies-without-gents. It was not that he begrudged the fifty cents. Chug was free enough with his money. He went to these dances on a last-minute impulse, almost against his will, and out of sheer boredom. Once there he danced every dance and all the encores. The girls fought for him. Their manner of dancing was cheek to cheek, in wordless rhythm. His arm about the ample waist of one of the Swedish girls, or clasping close the frail form of one of the mill hands, Chug would dance on and on, indefatigably, until the music played "Home Sweet Home." The conversation, if any, varied little.

"The music's swell to-night," from the girl.

"Yeh."

"You're some little dancer, Chug, I'll say. Honest, I could dance with you forever." This with a pressure of the girl's arm, and spoken with a little accent, whether Swedish, Belgian, or Slavic.

"They all say that."

"Crazy about yourself, ain't you!"

"Not as crazy as I am about you," with tardy gallantry.

He was very little stirred, really.

"Yeh, you are. I wish you was. It makes no never minds to you who you're dancing with, s'long's you're dancing."

This last came one evening as a variant in the usual formula. It startled Chug a little, so that he held the girl off the better to look at her. She was Wanda something-or-other, and anybody but Chug would have been alive to the fact that she had been stalking him for weeks with a stolid persistence.

"Danced with you three times to-night, haven't I?" he demanded. He was rather surprised to find that this was so.

"Wisht it was thirty."

That was Wanda. Her very eagerness foiled her. She cheapened herself. When Chug said, "Can I see you home?" he knew the answer before he put the question. Too easy to get along with, Wanda. Always there ahead of time, waiting, when you made a date with her. Too ready to forgive you when you failed to show up. Telephoned you when you were busy. Didn't give a fellow a chance to come half way, but went seven eighths of it herself. An ignorant, kindly, dangerous girl, with the physical development of a woman and the mind of a child. There were dozens like her in Chippewa.

If the girls of his own class noticed him at all it was the more to ignore him as a rather grimy mechanic passing briefly before their vision down Outagamie Street on his way to and from dinner. He was shy of them. They had a middle-class primness which forbade their making advances even had they been so inclined. Chug would no more have scraped acquaintance with them than he would have tried to flirt with Angie Hatton, Old Man Hatton's daughter, and the richest girl in Chippewa—so rich that she drove her own car with the chauffeur stuck up behind.

You didn't have to worry about Wanda and her kind. There they were, take them or leave them. They expected you to squeeze their waist when you danced with them, and so you did. You didn't have to think about what you were going to say to them.

Mrs. Scaritt suspected in a vague sort of way that Chug was "running with the hired girls." The thought distressed her. She was too smart a woman to nag him about it. She tried diplomacy.

"Why don't you bring some young folks home to eat, Chug? I like to fuss around for company." She was a wonderful cook, Mrs. Scaritt, and liked to display her skill.

"Who is there to bring?"

"The boys and girls you go around with. Who is it you're always fixing up for, evenings?"

"Nobody."

Mrs. Scaritt tried another tack.

"I s'pose this house isn't good enough for 'em? Is that it?"

"Good enough!" Chug laughed rather grimly. "I'd like to know what's the matter with it!"

There was, as a matter of fact, nothing the matter with it. It was as spick and span as paint and polish could make it. The curtain-stretching days were long past. There had even been talk of moving out of the house by the tracks, but at the last moment Mrs. Scaritt had rebelled.

"I'll miss the sound of the trains. I'm used to 'em. It's got so I can tell just where my right hand'll be when the seven fifty-two goes by in the morning, and I've got used to putting on the potatoes when I hear the 'leven-forty. Let's stay, Chug."

So they had stayed. Gradually they had added an improvement here, a convenience there, as Chug's prosperity grew, until now the cottage by the tracks was newly painted, bathroomed, electric-lighted, with a cement walk front and back and a porch with a wicker swing and flower baskets. Chug gave his mother more housekeeping money than she needed, though she, in turn, served him meals that would have threatened the waist-line of an older and less active man. There was a banana pie, for instance (it sounds sickish, but wait!) which she baked in a deep pan, and over which she poured a golden-brown custard all flecked with crusty melted sugar. You took a bite and lo! it had vanished like a sweet dewdrop, leaving in your mouth a taste as of nectar, and clover-honey, and velvet cream.

Mrs. Scaritt learned to gauge Chug's plans for the evening by his ablutions. Elaborate enough at any time, on dance nights they amounted to a rite. In the old days Chug's father had always made a brief enough business of the process he called washing up. A hand-basin in the kitchen sink or on the back-porch bench sufficed. The noises he made were out of all proportion to the results obtained. His snufflings, and snortings, and splashings were like those of a grampus at play. When he emerged from them you were surprised to find that he had merely washed his face.

Chug had grease to fight. He had learned how in his first days at the garage. His teacher had been old Rudie, a mechanic who had tinkered around automobiles since their kerosene days, and who knew more about them than their inventor. Soap and water alone were powerless against the grease and carbon and dust that ground themselves into Chug's skin. First, he lathered himself with warm, soapy water. Then, while arms, neck, and face were still wet, he covered them with oil—preferably lubricating oil, medium. Finally he rubbed sawdust over all; great handfuls of it. The grease rolled out then, magically, leaving his skin smooth and white. Old Rudie, while advocating this process, made little use of it. He dispatched the whole grimy business by the simple method of washing in gasoline guaranteed to take the varnish off a car fender. It seemed to leave Rudie's tough hide undevastated.

At twenty-four Chug Scaritt was an upstanding, level-headed, and successful young fellow who worked hard all day and found himself restless and almost irritable toward evening. He could stay home and read, or go back to the garage, though after eight things were very quiet. For amusement there were the pool shack, the cheap dances, the street corner, the Y.M.C.A. This last had proved a boon. The swimming pool, the gym, the reading room, had given Chug many happy, healthful hours. But, after all, there was something—

Chug didn't know it was girls—girls you could talk to, and be with, and take around. But it was. After an hour in the pool, or around the reading table, or talking and smoking, he usually drifted out into the quiet street. He could go home. Or there was Wanda. If he went home he found himself snapping rather irritably at his mother, for no reason at all. Ashamed of doing it. Powerless, somehow, to stop.

He took to driving in the evening: long drives along the country roads, his cap pulled low over his eyes, the wind blowing fresh in his face. He used to cover mile on mile, sitting slumped low on his spine, his eyes on the road; the engine running sweet and true. Sometimes he took Wanda along, or one of the mill girls. But not often. They were disappointed if you didn't drive with one arm around them. He liked being alone. It soothed him.

It was thus that he first met the Weld girl. The Weld girl was the plain daughter of the Widow Weld. The Widow Weld was a musical-comedy sort of widow in French-heeled, patent-leather slippers and girlish gowns. When you met her together with her daughter Elizabeth you were supposed to say, "Not mother and daughter! Surely not! Sisters, of course." Elizabeth was twenty-four and not a success. At the golf-club dances on Saturday night she would sit, unsought, against the wall while her skittish mother tripped it with the doggish bachelors. Sometimes a man would cross the floor toward her and her heart would give a little leap, but he always asked the girl seated two chairs away. Elizabeth danced much better than her mother—much better than most girls, for that matter. But she was small, and dark, and rather shy, and wore thick glasses that disguised the fineness of her black-lashed gray eyes. Now and then her mother, flushed and laughing, would come up and say, "Is my little girl having a good time?" The Welds had no money, but they belonged to Chippewa's fashionable set. There were those who lifted significant eyebrows at mention of the Widow Weld's name, and it was common knowledge that no maid would stay with her for any length of time because of the scanty provender. The widow kowtowed shamelessly to the moneyed ones of Chippewa, flattering the women, flirting with the men. Elizabeth had no illusions about her mother, but she was stubbornly loyal to her. Her manner toward her kittenish parent was rather sternly maternal. But she was the honest sort that congenitally hates sham and pretence. She was often deliberately rude to the very people toward whom her mother was servile. Her strange friendship with Angie Hatton, the lovely and millioned, was the one thing in Elizabeth's life of which her Machiavellian mother approved.

"Betty, you practically stuck out your tongue at Mr. Oakley!" This after a dance at which Elizabeth had been paired off, as usual, with the puffy and red-eyed old widower of that name.

"I don't care. His hands are fat and he creaks when he breathes."

"Next to Hatton, he's the richest man in Chippewa. And he likes you."

"He'd better not!" She spat it out, and the gray eyes blazed behind the glasses. "I'd rather be plastered up against the wall all my life than dance with him. Fat!"

"Well, my dear, you're no beauty, you know," with cruel frankness.

"I'm not much to look at," replied Elizabeth, "but I'm beautiful inside."

"Rot!" retorted the Widow Weld, inelegantly.

Had you lived in Chippewa all this explanation would have been unnecessary. In that terrifying way small towns have, it was known that of all codfish aristocracy the Widow Weld was the piscatorial pinnacle.

When Chug Scaritt first met the Weld girl she was standing out in the middle of the country road at ten-thirty P.M., her arms outstretched and the blood running down one cheek. He had been purring along the road toward home, drowsy and lulled by the motion and the April air. His thoughts had been drowsy, too, and disconnected.

"If I can rent Bergstrom's place next door when their lease is up I'll knock down the partition and put in auto supplies. There's big money in 'em.... Guess if it keeps on warm like this we can plant the garden next week.... That was swell cake Ma had for supper.... What's that in the road! What's!—"

Jammed down the foot-brake. Jerked back the emergency. A girl standing in the road. A dark mass in the ditch by the road-side. He was out of his car. He recognized her as the Weld girl.

"'S'matter?"

"In the ditch. She's hurt. Quick!"

"Whose car?" Chug was scrambling down the banks.

"Hatton's. Angie Hatton's."

"Gosh!"

Over by the fence, where she had been flung, Angie Hatton was found sitting up, dizzily, and saying, "Betty! Betty!" in what she supposed was a loud cry but which was really a whisper.

"I'm all right, dear. I'm all right. Oh, Angie, are you—"

She was cut and bruised, and her wrist had been broken. The two girls clung to each other, wordlessly. The thing was miraculous, in view of the car that lay perilously tipped on its fender.

"You're a lucky bunch," said Chug. "Who was driving?"

"I was," said Angie Hatton.

"It wasn't her fault," the Weld girl put in, quickly. "We were coming from Winnebago. She's a wonderful driver. We met a farm-wagon coming toward us. One of those big ones. The middle of the road. Perhaps he was asleep. He didn't turn out. We thought he would, of course. At the last minute we had to try for the ditch. It was too steep."

"Anyway, you're nervy kids, both of you. I'll have you both home in twenty minutes. We'll have to leave five thousand dollars' worth of car in the road till morning. It'll be all right."

He did get them home in twenty minutes and the five thousand dollars' worth of car was still lying repentantly in the ditch when morning came. Old Man Hatton himself came into the garage to thank Chug the following day. Chug met him in overalls, smudge-faced as he was. Old Man Hatton put out his hand. Chug grinned and looked at his own grease-grimed paw.

"That's all right," said Old Man Hatton, and grasped it firmly. "Want to thank you."

"That's all right," said Chug. "Didn't do a thing."

"No business driving alone that hour of the night. Girls nowadays—" He looked around the garage. "Work here, I suppose?"

"Yessir."

"If there's anything I can do for you? Over at the mill."

"Guess not," said Chug.

"Treat you right here, do they?"

"Fine."

"Let's see. Who owns this place?"

"I do."

Old Man Hatton's face broke into a sunburst of laugh-wrinkles. He threw back his head and went the scale from roar to chuckle. "One on me. Pretty good. Have to tell Angie that one."

Chug walked to the street with him. "Your daughter, she's got a lot of nerve, all right. And that girl with her— Weld. Say, not a whimper out of her and the blood running down her face. She all right?"

"Cut her head a little. They're both all right. Angie wouldn't even stay in bed. Well, as I say, if there's anything—?"

Chug flushed a little. "Tell you what, Mr. Hatton. I'm working on a thing that'll take the whine out of the Daker."

Old Man Hatton owned the Daker Motor plant among other things. The Daker is the best car for the money in the world. Not much for looks but everything in the engine. And everyone who has ever owned one knows that its only fault is the way its engine moans. Daker owners hate that moan. When you're going right it sounds a pass between a peanut roaster and a banshee with bronchitis. Every engineer in the Daker plant had worked over it.

"Can't be done," said Old Man Hatton.

"Another three months and I'll show you."

"Hope you do, son. Hope you do."

But in another three months Chug Scaritt was one of a million boys destined to take off a pink-striped shirt, a nobby belted suit, and a long-visored cap to don a rather bob-tailed brown outfit. It was some eighteen months later before he resumed the chromatic clothes with an ardour out of all proportion to their style and cut. But in the interval between doffing pink-striped shirt and donning pink-striped shirt....

No need to describe Camp Sibley, two miles outside Chippewa, and the way it grew miraculously, overnight, into a khaki city. No going into detail concerning the effective combination formed by Chug and a machine gun. These things were important and interesting. But perhaps not more interesting than the seemingly unimportant fact that in July following that April Chug was dancing blithely and rhythmically with Elizabeth Weld, and saying, "Angie Hatton's a smooth little dancer, all right; but she isn't in it with you."

For Chippewa, somehow, had fused. Chippewa had forgotten sets, sections, cliques, factions, and parties, and formed a community. It had, figuratively, wiped out the railroad tracks, together with all artificial social boundaries. Chug Scaritt, in uniform, must be kept happy. He must be furnished with wholesome recreation, fun, amusement, entertainment. There sprang up, seemingly overnight, a great wooden hall in Elm Street, on what had been a vacant lot. And there, by day or by night, were to be had music, and dancing, and hot cakes, and magazines, and hot coffee, and ice cream and girls. Girls! Girls who were straight, and slim, and young, and bright-eyed, and companionable. Girls like Angie Hatton. Girls like Betty Weld. Betty Weld, who no longer sat against the wall at the golf-club dances and prayed in her heart that fat old Oakley wasn't coming to ask her to dance.

Betty Weld was so popular now that the hostess used to have to say to her, in a tactful aside, "My dear, you've danced three times this evening with the Scaritt boy. You know that's against the rules."

Betty knew it. So did Chug. Betty danced so lightly that Chug could hardly feel her in his arms. He told her that she ran sweet and true like the engine of a high-powered car, and with as little apparent effort. She liked that, and understood.

It was wonderful how she understood. Chug had never known that girls could understand like that. She talked to you, straight. Looked at you, straight. Was interested in the things that interested you. No waist-squeezing here. No cheap banter. You even forgot she wore glasses.

"I'm going to try to get over."

"Say, you don't want to do that."

"I certainly do. Why not?"

"You're—why, you're too young. You're a girl. You're—"

"I'm as old as you, or almost. They're sending heaps of girls over to work in the canteens, and entertain the boys. If they'll take me. I'll have to lie six months on my age."

Rudie was in charge of the garage now. "That part of it's all right," Chug confided to the Weld girl. "Only thing that worries me is Ma. She hasn't peeped, hardly, but I can see she's pretty glum, all right."

"I don't know your mother," said the Weld girl.

"Thasso," absent-mindedly, from Chug.

"I'd—like to."

Chug woke up. "Why, say, that'd be fine! Listen, why don't you come for Sunday dinner. I've got a hunch we'll shove off next week, and this'll be my last meal away from camp. They haven't said so, but I don't know—maybe you wouldn't want to, though. Maybe you—we live the other side of the tracks—"

"I'd love to," said the Weld girl. "If you think your mother would like to have me."

"Would she! And cook! Say!"

The Widow Weld made a frightful fuss. Said that patriotism was all right, but that there were limits. Betty put on her organdie and went.

It began with cream soup and ended with shortcake. Even Chug realized that his mother had outdone herself. After his second helping of shortcake he leaned back and said, "Death, where is thy sting?" But his mother refused to laugh at that. She couldn't resist telling Miss Weld that it was plain food but that she hoped she'd enjoyed it.

Elizabeth Weld leaned forward. "Mrs. Scaritt, it's the best dinner I've ever eaten."

Mrs. Scaritt flushed a little, but protested, politely: "Oh, now! You folks up in the East End—"

"Not the Welds. Mother and I are as poor as can be. Everybody knows that. We have lots of doylies and silver on the table, but very little to eat. We never could afford a meal like this. We're sort of crackers-and-tea codfish, really."

"Oh, now, Miss Weld!" Chug's mother was aghast at such frankness. But Chug looked at the girl. She looked at him. They smiled understandingly at each other.

An hour or so later, after Elizabeth had admired the vegetable garden, the hanging flower-baskets, the new parlour curtains ("I used to do 'em up for folks in town," said Mrs. Scaritt, "so's Chug could go to high school." And "I know it. That's what I call splendid," from the girl), she went home, escorted by Chug.

Chug's hunch proved a good one. In a week he was gone. Thirteen months passed before he saw Elizabeth Weld again. When he did, Chippewa had swung back to normal. The railroad tracks were once more boundary lines.

Chug Scaritt went to France to fight. Three months later Elizabeth Weld went to France to dance. They worked hard at their jobs, these two. Perhaps Elizabeth's task was the more trying. She danced indefatigably, tirelessly, magnificently. Miles, and miles, and miles of dancing. She danced on rough plank floors with cracks an inch wide between the boards. She danced in hospitals, châteaux, canteens, huts; at Bordeaux, Verdun, Tours, Paris. Five girls, often, to five hundred boys. Every two weeks she danced out a pair of shoes. Her feet, when she went to bed at night, were throbbing, burning, aching, swollen. No hot water. You let them throb, and burn, and ache, and swell until you fell asleep. She danced with big blond bucks, and with little swarthy doughboys from New York's East Side. She danced with privates, lieutenants, captains; and once with a general. But never a dance with Chug.

Once or twice she remembered those far-away Chippewa golf-club dances. She was the girl who used to sit there against the wall! She used to look away with pretended indifference when a man crossed the floor toward her—her heart leaping a little. He would always go to the girl next to her. She would sit there with a set smile on her face, and the taste of ashes in her mouth. And those shoddy tulle evening dresses her mother had made her wear! Girlish, she had called them. A girl in thick-lensed glasses should not wear tulle evening frocks with a girlish note. Elizabeth had always felt comic in them. Yet there she had sat, shrinking lest the odious Oakley, of the fat white fingers and the wheezy breath, should ask her to dance.

She reflected, humorously, that if the miles of dancing she had done in the past year were placed end to end, as they do it in the almanac's fascinating facts, they must surely reach to Mars and return.

Whenever the hut door opened to admit a tall, graceful, lean brown figure her heart would give a little leap and a skip. As the door did this on an average of a thousand times daily her cardiac processes might be said to have been alarmingly accelerated.

Sometimes—though they did not know it—she and Chug were within a half hour's ride of each other. In all those months they never once met.

Elizabeth Weld came back to Chippewa in June. The First National Bank Building seemed to have shrunk; and she thought her mother looked old in that youthful hat. But she was glad to be home and said so.

"It has been awful here," said the Widow Weld. "Nothing to do but sew at the Red Cross shop; and no sugar or white bread."

"It must have been," agreed Elizabeth.

"They're giving a dance for you—and dinner—a week from Saturday, at the golf club. In your honour."

"Dance!" Elizabeth closed her eyes, faintly. Then, "Who is?"

"Well, Mr. Oakley's really giving it—that is, it was his idea. But the club wanted to tender some fitting—"

"I won't go."

"Oh, yes, you will."

Elizabeth did not argue the point. She had two questions to ask.

"Have the boys come back?"

"What boys?"

"The—the boys."

"Some of them. You know about dear Harry Hatton, of course. Croix de—"

"What have they done with the Khaki Club, where they used to give the dances?"

"Closed. Long ago. There was some talk of keeping it open for a community centre, or something, but it fell through. Now, Betty, you'll have to have a dress for Saturday night, I wonder if that old chiffon, with a new—"

Chug Scaritt came home in September. The First National Bank Building seemed, somehow, to have shrunk. And his mother hadn't had all that gray hair when he left. He put eager questions about the garage. Rudie had made out, all right, hadn't he? Good old scout.

"The boys down at the garage are giving some kind of a party for you. Old Rudie was telling me about it. I've got a grand supper for you to-night, Chug."

"Where's this party? I don't want any party."

"Woodman's Hall, I think they said. There was some girl called up yesterday. Wanda, her name sounded like. I couldn't—"

"Don't they give dances any more at the Soldiers' Club down on Elm?"

"Oh, that's closed, long. There was some talk of using it for what they called a community club. The *Eagle* was boosting for a big new place. What they called a Community Memorial Centre. But I don't know. It kind of fell through, I guess."

"I won't go," said Chug, suddenly.

"Go where, Chug?"

But instead of answering, Chug put his second question.

"Have you seen—is that—I wonder if that Weld girl's back."

"My, yes. Papers were full of it. Old Oakley gave her a big dance, and all, at the Country Club. They say—"

A week later, his arm about Wanda's big, yielding waist, he was dancing at Woodman's Hall. There was about her a cheap, heavy scent. She had on a georgette blouse and high-heeled shoes. She clung to Chug and smiled up at him. Wanda had bad teeth—yellow, with a sort of scum over them.

"I sure was lonesome for you, Chug. You're some dancer, I'll say. Honest, I could dance with you all night." A little pressure of her arm.

Somewhere in the recesses of his brain a memory cell broke. Dimly he heard himself saying, "Oh, they all tell me that."

"Crazy about yourself, ain't you!"

"Not as crazy as I am about you," with tardy gallantry.

Then, suddenly, Chug stopped dancing. He stopped, and stepped back from Wanda's arms. Bergstrom's two-piece orchestra was in the throes of its jazziest fox-trot number. Chug stood there a moment, in the centre of the floor, staring at Wanda's face that was staring back at him in vacuous surprise. He turned, without a word, and crossed the crowded floor, bumping couples blindly as he went. And so down the rickety wooden stairs, into the street, and out into the decent darkness of Chippewa's night.

THE END

Dawn O'Hara,

The Girl Who Laughed

CHAPTER I. THE SMASH-UP

There are a number of things that are pleasanter than being sick in a New York boarding-house when one's nearest dearest is a married sister up in far-away Michigan.

Some one must have been very kind, for there were doctors, and a blue-and-white striped nurse, and bottles and things. There was even a vase of perky carnations—scarlet ones. I discovered that they had a trick of nodding their heads, saucily. The discovery did not appear to surprise me.

"Howdy-do!" said I aloud to the fattest and reddest carnation that overtopped all the rest. "How in the world did you get in here?"

The striped nurse (I hadn't noticed her before) rose from some corner and came swiftly over to my bedside, taking my wrist between her fingers.

"I'm very well, thank you," she said, smiling, "and I came in at the door, of course."

"I wasn't talking to you," I snapped, crossly, "I was speaking to the carnations; particularly to that elderly one at the top—the fat one who keeps bowing and wagging his head at me."

"Oh, yes," answered the striped nurse, politely, "of course. That one is very lively, isn't he? But suppose we take them out for a little while now."

She picked up the vase and carried it into the corridor, and the carnations nodded their heads more vigorously than ever over her shoulder.

I heard her call softly to some one. The some one answered with a sharp little cry that sounded like, "Conscious!"

The next moment my own sister Norah came quietly into the room, and knelt at the side of my bed and took me in her arms. It did not seem at all surprising that she should be there, patting me with reassuring little love pats, murmuring over me with her lips against my check, calling me a hundred half-forgotten pet names that I had not heard for years. But then, nothing seemed to surprise me that surprising day. Not even the sight of a great, red-haired, red-faced, scrubbed looking man who strolled into the room just as Norah was in the midst of denouncing newspapers in general, and my newspaper in particular, and calling the city editor a slave-driver and a beast. The big, red-haired man stood regarding us tolerantly.

"Better, eh?" said he, not as one who asks a question, but as though in confirmation of a thought. Then he too took my wrist between his fingers. His touch was very firm and cool. After that he pulled down my eyelids and said, "H'm." Then he patted my cheek smartly once or twice. "You'll do," he pronounced. He picked up a sheet of paper from the table and looked it over, keen-eyed. There followed a clinking of bottles and glasses, a few low-spoken words to the nurse, and then, as she left the room the big red-haired man seated himself heavily in the chair near the bedside and rested his great hands on his fat knees. He stared down at me in much the same way that a huge mastiff looks at a terrier. Finally his glance rested on my limp left hand.

"Married, h'm?"

For a moment the word would not come. I could hear Norah catch her breath quickly. Then—"Yes," answered I.

"Husband living?" I could see suspicion dawning in his cold gray eye.

Again the catch in Norah's throat and a little half warning, half supplicating gesture. And again, "Yes," said I.

The dawn of suspicion burst into full glow.

"Where is he?" growled the red-haired doctor. "At a time like this?"

I shut my eyes for a moment, too sick at heart to resent his manner. I could feel, more than see, that Sis was signaling him frantically. I moistened my lips and answered him, bitterly.

"He is in the Starkweather Hospital for the insane."

When the red-haired man spoke again the growl was quite gone from his voice.

"And your home is—where?"

"Nowhere," I replied meekly, from my pillow. But at that Sis put her hand out quickly, as though she had been struck, and said:

"My home is her home."

"Well then, take her there," he ordered, frowning, "and keep her there as long as you can. Newspaper reporting, h'm? In New York? That's a devil of a job for a woman. And a husband who... Well, you'll have to take a six months' course in loafing, young woman. And at the end of that time, if you are still determined to work, can't you pick out something easier—like taking in scrubbing, for instance?"

I managed a feeble smile, wishing that he would go away quickly, so that I might sleep. He seemed to divine my thoughts, for he disappeared into the corridor, taking Norah with him. Their voices, low-pitched and carefully guarded, could be heard as they conversed outside my door.

Norah was telling him the whole miserable business. I wished, savagely, that she would let me tell it, if it must be told. How could she paint the fascination of the man who was my husband? She had never known the charm of him as I had known it in those few brief months before our marriage. She had never felt the caress of his voice, or the magnetism of his strange, smoldering eyes glowing across the smoke-dimmed city room as I had felt them fixed on me. No one had ever known what he had meant to the girl of twenty, with her brain full of unspoken dreams—dreams which were all to become glorious realities in that wonder-place, New York.

How he had fired my country-girl imagination! He had been the most brilliant writer on the big, brilliant sheet—and the most dissolute. How my heart had pounded on that first lonely day when this Wonder-Being looked up from his desk, saw me, and strolled over to where I sat before my typewriter! He smiled down at me, companionably. I'm quite sure that my mouth must have been wide open with surprise. He had been smoking a cigarette an expensive-looking, gold-tipped one. Now he removed it from between his lips with that hand that always shook a little, and dropped it to the floor, crushing it lightly with the toe of his boot. He threw back his handsome head and sent out the last mouthful of smoke in a thin, lazy spiral. I remember thinking what a pity it was that he should have crushed that costly-looking cigarette, just for me.

"My name's Orme," he said, gravely. "Peter Orme. And if yours isn't Shaughnessy or Burke at least, then I'm no judge of what black hair and gray eyes stand for."

"Then you're not," retorted I, laughing up at him, "for it happens to be O'Hara—Dawn O'Hara, if ye plaze."

He picked up a trifle that lay on my desk—a pencil, perhaps, or a bit of paper—and toyed with it, absently, as though I had not spoken. I thought he had not heard, and I was conscious of feeling a bit embarrassed, and very young. Suddenly he raised his smoldering eyes to mine, and I saw that they had taken on a deeper glow. His white, even teeth showed in a half smile.

"Dawn O'Hara," said he, slowly, and the name had never sounded in the least like music before, "Dawn O'Hara. It sounds like a rose—a pink blush rose that is deeper pink at its heart, and very sweet."

He picked up the trifle with which he had been toying and eyed it intently for a moment, as though his whole mind were absorbed in it. Then he put it down, turned, and walked slowly away. I sat staring after him like a little simpleton, puzzled, bewildered, stunned. That had been the beginning of it all.

He had what we Irish call "a way wid him." I wonder now why I did not go mad with the joy, and the pain, and the uncertainty of it all. Never was a girl so dazzled, so humbled, so worshiped, so neglected, so courted. He was a creature of a thousand moods to torture one. What guise would he wear to-day? Would he be gay, or dour, or sullen, or teasing or passionate, or cold, or tender or scintillating? I know that my hands were always cold, and my cheeks were always hot, those days.

He wrote like a modern Demosthenes, with all political New York to quiver under his philippics. The managing editor used to send him out on wonderful assignments, and they used to hold the paper for his stuff when it was late. Sometimes he would be gone for days at a time, and when he returned the men would look at him with a sort of admiring awe. And the city editor would glance up from beneath his green eye-shade and call out:

"Say, Orme, for a man who has just wired in about a million dollars' worth of stuff seems to me you don't look very crisp and jaunty."

"Haven't slept for a week," Peter Orme would growl, and then he would brush past the men who were crowded around him, and turn in my direction. And the old hot-and-cold, happy, frightened, laughing, sobbing sensation would have me by the throat again.

Well, we were married. Love cast a glamour over his very vices. His love of drink? A weakness which I would transform into strength. His white hot flashes of uncontrollable temper? Surely they would die down at my cool, tender touch. His fits of abstraction and irritability? Mere evidences of the genius within. Oh, my worshiping soul was always alert with an excuse.

And so we were married. He had quite tired of me in less than a year, and the hand that had always shaken a little shook a great deal now, and the fits of abstraction and temper could be counted upon to appear oftener than any other moods. I used to laugh, sometimes, when I was alone, at the bitter humor of it all. It was like a Duchess novel come to life.

His work began to show slipshod in spots. They talked to him about it and he laughed at them. Then, one day, he left them in the ditch on the big story of the McManus indictment, and the whole town scooped him, and the managing editor told him that he must go. His lapses had become too frequent. They would have to replace him with a man not so brilliant, perhaps, but more reliable.

I daren't think of his face as it looked when he came home to the little apartment and told me. The smoldering eyes were flaming now. His lips were flecked with a sort of foam. I stared at him in horror. He strode over to me, clasped his fingers about my throat and shook me as a dog shakes a mouse.

"Why don't you cry, eh?" he snarled. "Why don't you cry!"

And then I did cry out at what I saw in his eyes. I wrenched myself free, fled to my room, and locked the door and stood against it with my hand pressed over my heart until I heard the outer door slam and the echo of his footsteps die away.

Divorce! That was my only salvation. No, that would be cowardly now. I would wait until he was on his feet again, and then I would demand my old free life back once more. This existence that was dragging me into the gutter—this was not life! Life was a glorious, beautiful thing, and I would have it yet. I laid my plans, feverishly, and waited. He did not come back that night, or the next, or the next, or the next. In desperation I went to see the men at the office. No, they had not seen him. Was there anything that they could do? they asked. I smiled, and thanked them, and said, oh, Peter was so absent-minded! No doubt he had misdirected his letters, or something of the sort. And then I went back to the flat to resume the horrible waiting.

One week later he turned up at the old office which had cast him off. He sat down at his former desk and began to write, breathlessly, as he used to in the days when all the big stories fell to him. One of the men reporters strolled up to him and touched him on the shoulder, man-fashion. Peter Orme raised his head and stared at him, and the man sprang back in terror. The smoldering eyes had burned down to an ash. Peter Orme was quite bereft of all reason. They took him away that night, and I kept telling myself that it wasn't true; that it was all a nasty dream, and I would wake up pretty soon, and laugh about it, and tell it at the breakfast table.

Well, one does not seek a divorce from a husband who is insane. The busy men on the great paper were very kind. They would take me back on the staff. Did I think that I still could write those amusing little human interest stories? Funny ones, you know, with a punch in 'em.

Oh, plenty of good stories left in me yet, I assured them. They must remember that I was only twenty-one, after all, and at twenty-one one does not lose the sense of humor.

And so I went back to my old desk, and wrote bright, chatty letters home to Norah, and ground out very funny stories with a punch in 'em, that the husband in the insane asylum might be kept in comforts. With both hands I hung on like grim death to that saving sense of humor, resolved to make something of that miserable mess which was my life—to make something of it yet. And now—

At this point in my musings there was an end of the low-voiced conversation in the hall. Sis tiptoed in and looked her disapproval at finding me sleepless.

"Dawn, old girlie, this will never do. Shut your eyes now, like a good child, and go to sleep. Guess what that great brute of a doctor said! I may take you home with me next week! Dawn dear, you will come, won't you? You must! This is killing you. Don't make me go away leaving you here. I couldn't stand it."

She leaned over my pillow and closed my eyelids gently with her sweet, cool fingers. "You are coming home with me, and you shall sleep and eat, and sleep and eat, until you are as lively as the Widow Malone, ohone, and twice as fat. Home, Dawnie dear, where we'll forget all about New York. Home, with me."

I reached up uncertainly, and brought her hand down to my lips and a great peace descended upon my sick soul. "Home—with you," I said, like a child, and fell asleep.

CHAPTER II. MOSTLY EGGS

Oh, but it was clean, and sweet, and wonderfully still, that rose-and-white room at Norah's! No street cars to tear at one's nerves with grinding brakes and clanging bells; no tramping of restless feet on the concrete all through the long, noisy hours; no shrieking midnight joy-riders; not one of the hundred sounds which make night hideous in the city. What bliss to lie there, hour after hour, in a delicious half-waking, half-sleeping, wholly exquisite stupor, only rousing myself to swallow egg-nogg No. 426, and then to flop back again on the big, cool pillow!

New York, with its lights, its clangor, its millions, was only a far-away, jumbled nightmare. The office, with its clacking typewriters, its insistent, nerve-racking telephone bells, its systematic rush, its smoke-dimmed city room, was but an ugly part of the dream.

Back to that inferno of haste and scramble and clatter? Never! Never! I resolved, drowsily. And dropped off to sleep again.

And the sheets. Oh, those sheets of Norah's! Why, they were white, instead of gray! And they actually smelled of flowers. For that matter, there were rosebuds on the silken coverlet. It took me a week to get chummy with that rosebud-and-down quilt. I had to explain carefully to Norah that after a half-dozen years of sleeping under doubtful boarding-house blankets one does not so soon get rid of a shuddering disgust for coverings which are haunted by the ghosts of a hundred unknown sleepers. Those years had taught me to draw up the sheet with scrupulous care, to turn it down, and smooth it over, so that no contaminating and woolly blanket should touch my skin. The habit stuck even after Norah had tucked me in between her fragrant sheets. Automatically my hands groped about, arranging the old protecting barrier.

"What's the matter, Fuss-fuss?" inquired Norah, looking on. "That down quilt won't bite you; what an old maid you are!"

"Don't like blankets next to my face," I elucidated, sleepily, "never can tell who slept under 'em last—"

"You cat!" exclaimed Norah, making a little rush at me. "If you weren't supposed to be ill I'd shake you! Comparing my darling rosebud quilt to your miserable gray blankets! Just for that I'll make you eat an extra pair of eggs."

There never was a sister like Norah. But then, who ever heard of a brother-in-law like Max? No woman—not even a frazzled-out newspaper woman—could receive the love and care that they gave me, and fail to flourish under it. They had been Dad and Mother to me since the day when Norah had tucked me under her arm and carried me away from New York. Sis was an angel; a comforting, twentieth-century angel, with white apron strings for wings, and a tempting tray in her hands in place of the hymn books and palm leaves that the picture-book angels carry. She coaxed the inevitable eggs and beef into more tempting forms than Mrs. Rorer ever guessed at. She could disguise those two plain, nourishing articles of diet so effectually that neither hen nor cow would have suspected either of having once been part of her anatomy. Once I ate halfway through a melting, fluffy, peach-bedecked plate of something before I discovered that it was only another egg in disguise.

"Feel like eating a great big dinner to-day, Kidlet?" Norah would ask in the morning as she stood at my bedside (with a glass of egg-something in her hand, of course).

"Eat!"—horror and disgust shuddering through my voice—"Eat! Ugh! Don't s-s-speak of it to me. And for pity's sake tell Frieda to shut the kitchen door when you go down, will you? I can smell something like ugh!—like pot roast, with gravy!" And I would turn my face to the wall.

Three hours later I would hear Sis coming softly up the stairs, accompanied by a tinkling of china and glass. I would face her, all protest.

"Didn't I tell you, Sis, that I couldn't eat a mouthful? Not a mouthf—um-m-m-m! How perfectly scrumptious that looks! What's that affair in the lettuce leaf? Oh, can't I begin on that divine-looking pinky stuff in the tall glass? H'm? Oh, please!"

"I thought—" Norah would begin; and then she would snigger softly.

"Oh, well, that was hours ago," I would explain, loftily. "Perhaps I could manage a bite or two now."

Whereupon I would demolish everything except the china and doilies.

It was at this point on the road to recovery, just halfway between illness and health, that Norah and Max brought the great and unsmiling Von Gerhard on the scene. It appeared that even New York was respectfully aware of Von Gerhard, the nerve specialist, in spite of the fact that he lived in Milwaukee. The idea of bringing him up to look at me occurred to Max quite suddenly. I think it was on the evening that I burst into tears when Max entered the room wearing a squeaky shoe. The Weeping Walrus was a self-contained and tranquil creature compared to me at that time. The sight of a fly on the wall was enough to make me burst into a passion of sobs.

"I know the boy to steady those shaky nerves of yours, Dawn," said Max, after I had made a shamefaced apology for my hysterical weeping, "I'm going to have Von Gerhard up here to look at you. He can run up Sunday, eh, Norah?"

"Who's Von Gerhard?" I inquired, out of the depths of my ignorance. "Anyway, I won't have him. I'll bet he wears a Vandyke and spectacles."

"Von Gerhard!" exclaimed Norah, indignantly. "You ought to be thankful to have him look at you, even if he wears goggles and a flowing beard. Why, even that red-haired New York doctor of yours cringed and looked impressed when I told him that Von Gerhard was a friend of my husband's, and that they had been comrades at Heidelberg. I must have mentioned him dozens of times in my letters."

"Never."

"Queer," commented Max, "he runs up here every now and then to spend a quiet Sunday with Norah and me and the Spalpeens. Says it rests him. The kids swarm all over him, and tear him limb from limb. It doesn't look restful, but he says it's great. I think he came here from Berlin just after you left for New York, Dawn. Milwaukee fits him as if it had been made for him."

"But you're not going to drag this wonderful being up here just for me!" I protested, aghast.

Max pointed an accusing finger at me from the doorway. "Aren't you what the bromides call a bundle of nerves? And isn't Von Gerhard's specialty untying just those knots? I'll write to him to-night."

And he did. And Von Gerhard came. The Spalpeens watched for him, their noses flattened against the window-pane, for it was raining. As he came up the path they burst out of the door to meet him. From my bedroom window I saw him come prancing up the walk like a boy, with the two children clinging to his coat-tails, all three quite unmindful of the rain, and yelling like Comanches.

Ten minutes later he had donned his professional dignity, entered my room, and beheld me in all my limp and pea-green beauty. I noted approvingly that he had to stoop a bit as he entered the low doorway, and that the Vandyke of my prophecy was missing.

He took my hand in his own steady, reassuring clasp. Then he began to talk. Half an hour sped away while we discussed New York—books—music—theatres—everything and anything but Dawn O'Hara. I learned later that as we chatted he was getting his story, bit by bit, from every twitch of the eyelids, from every gesture of the hands that had grown too thin to wear the hateful ring; from every motion of the lips; from the color of my nails; from each convulsive muscle; from every shadow, and wrinkle and curve and line of my face.

Suddenly he asked: "Are you making the proper effort to get well? You try to conquer those jumping nerfs, yes?"

I glared at him. "Try! I do everything. I'd eat woolly worms if I thought they might benefit me. If ever a girl has minded her big sister and her doctor, that girl is I. I've eaten everything from pate de foie gras to raw beef, and I've drunk everything from blood to champagne."

"Eggs?" queried Von Gerhard, as though making a happy suggestion.

"Eggs!" I snorted. "Eggs! Thousands of 'em! Eggs hard and soft boiled, poached and fried, scrambled and shirred, eggs in beer and egg-noggs, egg lemonades and egg orangeades, eggs in wine and eggs in milk, and eggs au naturel. I've lapped up iron-and-wine, and whole rivers of milk, and I've devoured rare porterhouse and roast beef day after day for weeks. So! Eggs!"

"Mein Himmel!" ejaculated he, fervently, "And you still live!" A suspicion of a smile dawned in his eyes. I wondered if he ever laughed. I would experiment.

"Don't breathe it to a soul," I whispered, tragically, "but eggs, and eggs alone, are turning my love for my sister into bitterest hate. She stalks me the whole day long, forcing egg mixtures down my unwilling throat. She bullies me. I daren't put out my hand suddenly without knocking over liquid refreshment in some form, but certainly with an egg lurking in its depths. I am so expert that I can tell an egg orangeade from an egg lemonade at a distance of twenty yards, with my left hand tied behind me, and one eye shut, and my feet in a sack."

"You can laugh, eh? Well, that iss good," commented the grave and unsmiling one.

"Sure," answered I, made more flippant by his solemnity. "Surely I can laugh. For what else was my father Irish? Dad used to say that a sense of humor was like a shillaly—an iligent thing to have around handy, especially when the joke's on you."

The ghost of a twinkle appeared again in the corners of the German blue eyes. Some fiend of rudeness seized me.

"Laugh!" I commanded.

Dr. Ernst von Gerhard stiffened. "Pardon?" inquired he, as one who is sure that he has misunderstood.

"Laugh!" I snapped again. "I'll dare you to do it. I'll double dare you! You dassen't!"

But he did. After a moment's bewildered surprise he threw back his handsome blond head and gave vent to a great, deep infectious roar of mirth that brought the Spalpeens tumbling up the stairs in defiance of their mother's strict instructions.

After that we got along beautifully. He turned out to be quite human, beneath the outer crust of reserve. He continued his examination only after bribing the Spalpeens shamefully, so that even their rapacious demands were satisfied, and they trotted off contentedly.

There followed a process which reduced me to a giggling heap but which Von Gerhard carried out ceremoniously. It consisted of certain raps at my knees, and shins, and elbows, and fingers, and certain commands to—"look at my finger! Look at the wall! Look at my finger! Look at the wall!"

"So!" said Von Gerhard at last, in a tone of finality. I sank my battered frame into the nearest chair. "This—this newspaper work—it must cease." He dismissed it with a wave of the hand.

"Certainly," I said, with elaborate sarcasm. "How should you advise me to earn my living in the future? In the stories they paint dinner cards, don't they? or bake angel cakes?"

"Are you then never serious?" asked Von Gerhard, in disapproval.

"Never," said I. "An old, worn-out, worked-out newspaper reporter, with a husband in the mad-house, can't afford to be serious for a minute, because if she were she'd go mad, too, with the hopelessness of it all." And I buried my face in my hands.

The room was very still for a moment. Then the great Von Gerhard came over, and took my hands gently from my face. "I—I do beg your pardon," he said. He looked strangely boyish and uncomfortable as he said it. "I was thinking only of your good. We do that, sometimes, forgetting that circumstances may make our wishes impossible of execution. So. You will forgive me?"

"Forgive you? Yes, indeed," I assured him. And we shook hands, gravely. "But that doesn't help matters much, after all, does it?"

"Yes, it helps. For now we understand one another, is it not so? You say you can only write for a living. Then why not write here at home? Surely these years of newspaper work have given you a great knowledge of human nature. Then too, there is your gift of humor. Surely that is a combination which should make your work acceptable to the magazines. Never in my life have I seen so many magazines as here in the United States. But hundreds! Thousands!"

"Me!" I exploded—"A real writer lady! No more interviews with actresses! No more slushy Sunday specials! No more teary tales! Oh, my! When may I begin? To-morrow? You know I brought my typewriter with me. I've almost forgotten where the letters are on the keyboard."

"Wait, wait; not so fast! In a month or two, perhaps. But first must come other things outdoor things. Also housework."

"Housework!" I echoed, feebly.

"Naturlich. A little dusting, a little scrubbing, a little sweeping, a little cooking. The finest kind of indoor exercise. Later you may write a little—but very little. Run and play out of doors with the children. When I see you again you will have roses in your cheeks like the German girls, yes?"

"Yes," I echoed, meekly, "I wonder how Frieda will like my elephantine efforts at assisting with the housework. If she gives notice, Norah will be lost to you."

But Frieda did not give notice. After I had helped her clean the kitchen and the pantry I noticed an expression of deepest pity overspreading her lumpy features. The expression became almost one of agony as she watched me roll out some noodles for soup, and delve into the sticky mysteries of a new kind of cake.

Max says that for a poor working girl who hasn't had time to cultivate the domestic graces, my cakes are a distinct triumph. Sis sniffs at that, and mutters something about cups of raisins and nuts and citron hiding a multitude of batter sins. She never allows the Spalpeens to eat my cakes, and on my baking days they are usually sent from the table howling. Norah declares, severely, that she is going to hide the Green Cook Book. The Green Cook Book is a German one. Norah bought it in deference to Max's love of German cookery. It is called Aunt Julchen's cook book, and the author, between hints as to flour and butter, gets delightfully chummy with her pupil. Her cakes are proud, rich cakes. She orders grandly:

"Now throw in the yolks of twelve eggs; one-fourth of a pound of almonds; two pounds of raisins; a pound of citron; a pound of orange-peel."

As if that were not enough, there follow minor instructions as to trifles like ounces of walnut meats, pounds of confectioner's sugar, and pints of very rich cream. When cold, to be frosted with an icing made up of more eggs, more nuts, more cream, more everything.

The children have appointed themselves official lickers and scrapers of the spoons and icing pans, also official guides on their auntie's walks. They regard their Aunt Dawn as a quite ridiculous but altogether delightful old thing.

And Norah—bless her! looks up when I come in from a romp with the Spalpeens and says: "Your cheeks are pink! Actually! And you're losing a puff there at the back of your ear, and your hat's on crooked. Oh, you are beginning to look your old self, Dawn dear!"

At which doubtful compliment I retort, recklessly: "Pooh! What's a puff more or less, in a worthy cause? And if you think my cheeks are pink now, just wait until your mighty Von Gerhard comes again. By that time they shall be so red and bursting that Frieda's, on wash day, will look anemic by comparison. Say, Norah, how red are German red cheeks, anyway?"

CHAPTER III. GOOD AS NEW

So Spring danced away, and Summer sauntered in. My pillows looked less and less tempting. The wine of the northern air imparted a cocky assurance. One blue-and-gold day followed the other, and I spent hours together out of doors in the sunshine, lying full length on the warm, sweet ground, to the horror of the entire neighborhood. To be sure, I was sufficiently discreet to choose the lawn at the rear of the house. There I drank in the atmosphere, as per doctor's instructions, while the genial sun warmed the watery blood in my veins and burned the skin off the end of my nose.

All my life I had envied the loungers in the parks—those silent, inert figures that lie under the trees all the long summer day, their shabby hats over their faces, their hands clasped above their heads, legs sprawled in uncouth comfort, while the sun dapples down between the leaves and, like a good fairy godmother, touches their frayed and wrinkled garments with flickering figures of golden splendor, while they sleep. They always seemed so blissfully care-free and at ease—those sprawling men figures—and I, to whom such simple joys were forbidden, being a woman, had envied them.

Now I was reveling in that very joy, stretched prone upon the ground, blinking sleepily up at the sun and the cobalt sky, feeling my very hair grow, and health returning in warm, electric waves. I even dared to cross one leg over the other and to swing the pendant member with nonchalant air, first taking a cautious survey of the neighboring back windows to see if any one peeked. Doubtless they did, behind those ruffled curtains, but I grew splendidly indifferent.

Even the crawling things—and there were myriads of them—added to the enjoyment of my ease. With my ear so close to the ground the grass seemed fairly to buzz with them. Everywhere there were crazily busy ants, and I, patently a sluggard and therefore one of those for whom the ancient warning was intended, considered them lazily. How they plunged about, weaving in and out, rushing here and there, helter-skelter, like bargain-hunting women darting wildly from counter to counter!

"O, foolish, foolish antics!" I chided them, "stop wearing yourselves out this way. Don't you know that the game isn't worth the candle, and that you'll give yourselves nervous jim-jams and then you'll have to go home to be patched up? Look at me! I'm a horrible example."

But they only bustled on, heedless of my advice, and showed their contempt by crawling over me as I lay there like a lady Gulliver.

Oh, I played what they call a heavy thinking part. It was not only the ants that came in for lectures. I preached sternly to myself.

"Well, Dawn old girl, you've made a beautiful mess of it. A smashed-up wreck at twenty-eight! And what have you to show for it? Nothing! You're a useless pulp, like a lemon that has been squeezed dry. Von Gerhard was right. There must be no more newspaper work for you, me girl. Not if you can keep away from the fascination of it, which I don't think you can."

Then I would fall to thinking of those years of newspapering—of the thrills of them, and the ills of them. It had been exhilarating, and educating, but scarcely remunerative. Mother had never approved. Dad had chuckled and said that it was a curse descended upon me from the terrible old Kitty O'Hara, the only old maid in the history of the O'Haras, and famed in her day for a caustic tongue and a venomed pen. Dad and Mother—what a pair of children they had been! The very dissimilarity of their natures had been a bond between them. Dad, light-hearted, whimsical, care-free, improvident; Mother, gravely sweet, anxious-browed, trying to teach economy to the handsome Irish husband who, descendant of a long and royal line of spendthrift ancestors, would have none of it.

It was Dad who had insisted that they name me Dawn. Dawn O'Hara! His sense of humor must have been sleeping. "You were such a rosy, pinky, soft baby thing," Mother had once told me, "that you looked just like the first flush of light at sunrise. That is why your father insisted on calling you Dawn."

Poor Dad! How could he know that at twenty-eight I would be a yellow wreck of a newspaper reporter—with a wrinkle between my eyes. If he could see me now he would say:

"Sure, you look like the dawn yet, me girl but a Pittsburgh dawn."

At that, Mother, if she were here, would pat my check where the hollow place is, and murmur: "Never mind, Dawnie dearie, Mother thinks you are beautiful just the same." Of such blessed stuff are mothers made.

At this stage of the memory game I would bury my face in the warm grass and thank my God for having taken Mother before Peter Orme came into my life. And then I would fall asleep there on the soft, sweet grass, with my head snuggled in my arms, and the ants wriggling, unchided, into my ears.

On the last of these sylvan occasions I awoke, not with a graceful start, like the story-book ladies, but with a grunt. Sis was digging me in the ribs with her toe. I looked up to see her standing over me, a foaming tumbler of something in her hand. I felt that it was eggy and eyed it disgustedly.

"Get up," said she, "you lazy scribbler, and drink this."

I sat up, eyeing her severely and picking grass and ants out of my hair.

"D' you mean to tell me that you woke me out of that babe-like slumber to make me drink that goo? What is it, anyway? I'll bet it's another egg-nogg."

"Egg-nogg it is; and swallow it right away, because there are guests to see you."

I emerged from the first dip into the yellow mixture and fixed on her as stern and terrible a look at any one can whose mouth is encircled by a mustache of yellow foam.

"Guests!" I roared, "not for me! Don't you dare to say that they came to see me!"

"Did too," insists Norah, with firmness, "they came especially to see you. Asked for you, right from the jump."

I finished the egg-nogg in four gulps, returned the empty tumbler with an air of decision, and sank upon the grass.

"Tell 'em I rave. Tell 'em that I'm unconscious, and that for weeks I have recognized no one, not even my dear sister. Say that in my present nerve-shattered condition I—"

"That wouldn't satisfy them," Norah calmly interrupts, "they know you're crazy because they saw you out here from their second story back windows. That's why they came. So you may as well get up and face them. I promised them I'd bring you in. You can't go on forever refusing to see people, and you know the Whalens are—"

"Whalens!" I gasped. "How many of them? Not—not the entire fiendish three?"

"All three. I left them champing with impatience."

The Whalens live just around the corner. The Whalens are omniscient. They have a system of news gathering which would make the efforts of a New York daily appear antiquated. They know that Jenny Laffin feeds the family on soup meat and oat-meal when Mr. Laffin is on the road; they know that Mrs. Pearson only shakes out her rugs once in four weeks; they can tell you the number of times a week that Sam Dempster comes home drunk; they know that the Merkles never have cream with their coffee because little Lizzie Merkle goes to the creamery every day with just one pail and three cents; they gloat over the knowledge that Professor Grimes, who is a married man, is sweet on Gertie Ashe, who teaches second reader in his school; they can tell you where Mrs. Black got her seal coat, and her husband only earning two thousand a year; they know who is going to run for mayor, and how long poor Angela Sims has to live, and what Guy Donnelly said to Min when he asked her to marry him.

The three Whalens—mother and daughters—hunt in a group. They send meaning glances to one another across the room, and at parties they get together and exchange bulletins in a corner. On passing the Whalen house one is uncomfortably aware of shadowy forms lurking in the windows, and of parlor curtains that are agitated for no apparent cause.

Therefore it was with a groan that I rose and prepared to follow Norah into the house. Something in my eye caused her to turn at the very door. "Don't you dare!" she hissed; then, banishing the warning scowl from her face, and assuming a near-smile, she entered the room and I followed miserably at her heels.

The Whalens rose and came forward effusively; Mrs. Whalen, plump, dark, voluble; Sally, lean, swarthy, vindictive; Flossie, pudgy, powdered, over-dressed. They eyed me hungrily. I felt that they were searching my features for signs of incipient insanity.

"Dear, DEAR girl!" bubbled the billowy Flossie, kissing the end of my nose and fastening her eye on my ringless left hand.

Sally contented herself with a limp and fishy handshake. She and I were sworn enemies in our school-girl days, and a baleful gleam still lurked in Sally's eye. Mrs. Whalen bestowed on me a motherly hug that enveloped me in an atmosphere of liquid face-wash, strong perfumery and fried lard. Mrs. Whalen is a famous cook. Said she:

"We've been thinking of calling ever since you were brought home, but dear me! you've been looking so poorly I just said to the girls, wait till the poor thing feels more like seeing her old friends. Tell me, how are you feeling now?"

The three sat forward in their chairs in attitudes of tense waiting.

I resolved that if err I must it should be on the side of safety. I turned to sister Norah.

"How am I feeling anyway, Norah?" I guardedly inquired.

Norah's face was a study. "Why Dawn dear," she said, sugar-sweet, "no doubt you know better than I. But I'm sure that you are wonderfully improved—almost your old self, in fact. Don't you think she looks splendid, Mrs. Whalen?"

The three Whalens tore their gaze from my blank countenance to exchange a series of meaning looks.

"I suppose," purred Mrs. Whalen, "that your awful trouble was the real cause of your—a-a-a-sickness, worrying about it and grieving as you must have."

She pronounces it with a capital T, and I know she means Peter. I hate her for it.

"Trouble!" I chirped. "Trouble never troubles me. I just worked too hard, that's all, and acquired an awful 'tired.' All work and no play makes Jill a nervous wreck, you know."

At that the elephantine Flossie wagged a playful finger at me. "Oh, now, you can't make us believe that, just because we're from the country! We know all about you gay New Yorkers, with your Bohemian ways and your midnight studio suppers, and your cigarettes, and cocktails and high jinks!"

Memory painted a swift mental picture of Dawn O'Hara as she used to tumble into bed after a whirlwind day at the office, too dog-tired to give her hair even one half of the prescribed one hundred strokes of the brush. But in turn I shook a reproving forefinger at Flossie.

"You've been reading some naughty society novel! One of those millionaire-divorce-actress-automobile novels. Dear, dear! Shall I, ever forget the first New York actress I ever met; or what she said!"

I felt, more than saw, a warning movement from Sis. But the three Whalens had hitched forward in their chairs.

"What did she say?" gurgled Flossie. "Was it something real reezk?"

"Well, it was at a late supper—a studio supper given in her honor," I confessed.

"Yes-s-s-s," hissed the Whalens.

"And this actress—she was one of those musical comedy actresses, you know; I remember her part called for a good deal of kicking about in a short Dutch costume—came in rather late, after the performance. She was wearing a regal-looking fur-edged evening wrap, and she still wore all her make-up"—out of the corner of my eye I saw Sis sink back with an air of resignation—"and she threw open the door and said—

"Yes-s-s-s!" hissed the Whalens again, wetting their lips.

"—said: 'Folks, I just had a wire from mother, up in Maine. The boy has the croup. I'm scared green. I hate to spoil the party, but don't ask me to stay. I want to go home to the flat and blubber. I didn't even stop to take my make-up off. My God! If anything should happen to the boy!—Well, have a good time without me. Jim's waiting outside.'" A silence.

Then—"Who was Jim?" asked Flossie, hopefully.

"Jim was her husband, of course. He was in the same company."

Another silence.

"Is that all?" demanded Sally from the corner in which she had been glowering.

"All! You unnatural girl! Isn't one husband enough?"

Mrs. Whalen smiled an uncertain, wavering smile. There passed among the three a series of cabalistic signs. They rose simultaneously.

"How quaint you are!" exclaimed Mrs. Whalen, "and so amusing! Come girls, we mustn't tire Miss—ah—Mrs.—er—" with another meaning look at my bare left hand.

"My husband's name is still Orme," I prompted, quite, quite pleasantly.

"Oh, certainly. I'm so forgetful. And one reads such queer things in the newspapers nowa-days. Divorces, and separations, and soul-mates and things." There was a note of gentle insinuation in her voice.

Norah stepped firmly into the fray. "Yes, doesn't one? What a comfort it must be to you to know that your dear girls are safe at home with you, and no doubt will be secure, for years to come, from the buffeting winds of matrimony."

There was a tinge of purple in Mrs. Whalen's face as she moved toward the door, gathering her brood about her. "Now that dear Dawn is almost normal again I shall send my little girlies over real often. She must find it very dull here after her—ah—life in New York."

"Not at all," I said, hurriedly, "not at all. You see I'm—I'm writing a book. My entire day is occupied."

"A book!" screeched the three. "How interesting! What is it? When will it be published?"

I avoided Norah's baleful eye as I answered their questions and performed the final adieux.

As the door closed, Norah and I faced each other, glaring.

"Hussies!" hissed Norah. Whereupon it struck us funny and we fell, a shrieking heap, into the nearest chair. Finally Sis dabbed at her eyes with her handkerchief, drew a long breath, and asked, with elaborate sarcasm, why I hadn't made it a play instead of a book, while I was about it.

"But I mean it," I declared. "I've had enough of loafing. Max must unpack my typewriter to-night. I'm homesick for a look at the keys. And to-morrow I'm to be installed in the cubbyhole off the dining-room and I defy any one to enter it on peril of their lives. If you value the lives of your offspring, warn them away from that door. Von Gerhard said that there was writing in my system, and by the Great Horn Spoon and the Beard of the Prophet, I'll have it out! Besides, I need the money. Norah dear, how does one set about writing a book? It seems like such a large order."

CHAPTER IV. DAWN DEVELOPS A HEIMWEH

It's hard trying to develop into a real Writer Lady in the bosom of one's family, especially when the family refuses to take one seriously. Seven years of newspaper grind have taught me the fallacy of trying to write by the inspiration method. But there is such a thing as a train of thought, and mine is constantly being derailed, and wrecked and pitched about.

Scarcely am I settled in my cubby-hole, typewriter before me, the working plan of a story buzzing about in my brain, when I hear my name called in muffled tones, as though the speaker were laboring with a mouthful of hairpins. I pay no attention. I have just given my heroine a pair of calm gray eyes, shaded with black lashes and hair to match. A voice floats down from the upstairs regions.

"Dawn! Oh, Dawn! Just run and rescue the cucumbers out of the top of the ice-box, will you? The iceman's coming, and he'll squash 'em."

A parting jab at my heroine's hair and eyes, and I'm off to save the cucumbers.

Back at my typewriter once more. Shall I make my heroine petite or grande? I decide that stateliness and Gibsonesque height should accompany the calm gray eyes. I rattle away happily, the plot unfolding itself in some mysterious way. Sis opens the door a little and peers in. She is dressed for the street.

"Dawn dear, I'm going to the dressmaker's. Frieda's upstairs cleaning the bathroom, so take a little squint at the roast now and then, will you? See that it doesn't burn, and that there's plenty of gravy. Oh, and Dawn—tell the milkman we want an extra half-pint of cream to-day. The tickets are on the kitchen shelf, back of the clock. I'll be back in an hour."

"Mhmph," I reply.

Sis shuts the door, but opens it again almost immediately.

"Don't let the Infants bother you. But if Frieda's upstairs and they come to you for something to eat, don't let them have any cookies before dinner. If they're really hungry they'll eat bread and butter."

I promise, dreamily, my last typewritten sentence still running through my head. The gravy seems to have got into the heroine's calm gray eyes. What heroine could remain calm-eyed when her creator's mind is filled with roast beef? A half-hour elapses before I get back on the track. Then appears the hero—a tall blond youth, fair to behold. I make him two yards high, and endow him with a pair of clothing-advertisement shoulders.

There assails my nostrils a fearful smell of scorching. The roast! A wild rush into the kitchen. I fling open the oven door. The roast is mahogany-colored, and gravyless. It takes fifteen minutes of the most desperate first-aid-to-the-injured measures before the roast is revived.

Back to the writing. It has lost its charm. The gray-eyed heroine is a stick; she moves like an Indian lady outside a cigar shop. The hero is a milk-and-water sissy, without a vital spark in him. What's the use of trying to write, anyway? Nobody wants my stuff. Good for nothing except dubbing on a newspaper!

Rap! Rap! Rappity-rap-rap! Bing! Milk!

I dash into the kitchen. No milk! No milkman! I fly to the door. He is disappearing around the corner of the house.

"Hi! Mr. Milkman! Say, Mr. Milkman!" with frantic beckonings.

He turns. He lifts up his voice. "The screen door was locked so I left youse yer milk on top of the ice-box on the back porch. Thought like the hired girl was upstairs an' I could git the tickets to-morra."

I explain about the cream, adding that it is wanted for short-cake. The explanation does not seem to cheer him. He appears to be a very gloomy and reserved milkman. I fancy that he is in the habit of indulging in a little airy persiflage with Frieda o' mornings, and he finds me a poor substitute for her red-cheeked comeliness.

The milk safely stowed away in the ice-box, I have another look at the roast. I am dipping up spoonfuls of brown gravy and pouring them over the surface of the roast in approved basting style, when there is a rush, a scramble, and two hard bodies precipitate themselves upon my legs so suddenly that for a moment my head pitches forward into the oven. I withdraw my head from the oven, hastily. The basting spoon is immersed in the bottom of the pan. I turn, indignant. The Spalpeens look up at me with innocent eyes.

"You little divils, what do you mean by shoving your old aunt into the oven! It's cannibals you are!"

The idea pleases them. They release my legs and execute a savage war dance around me. The Spalpeens are firm in the belief that I was brought to their home for their sole amusement, and they refuse to take me seriously. The Spalpeens themselves are two of the finest examples of real humor that ever were perpetrated upon parents. Sheila is the first-born. Norah decided that she should be an Irish beauty, and bestowed upon her a name that reeks of the bogs. Whereupon Sheila, at the age of six, is as flaxen-haired and blue-eyed and stolid a little German madchen as ever fooled her parents, and she is a feminine reproduction of her German Dad. Two years later came a sturdy boy, and they named him Hans, in a flaunt of defiance. Hans is black-haired, gray-eyed and Irish as Killarny.

"We're awful hungry," announces Sheila.

"Can't you wait until dinner time? Such a grand dinner!"

Sheila and Hans roll their eyes to convey to me that, were they to wait until dinner for sustenance we should find but their lifeless forms.

"Well then, Auntie will get a nice piece of bread and butter for each of you."

"Don't want bread an' butty!" shrieks Hans. "Want tooky!"

"Cooky!" echoes Sheila, pounding on the kitchen table with the rescued basting spoon.

"You can't have cookies before dinner. They're bad for your insides."

"Can too," disputes Hans. "Fwieda dives us tookies. Want tooky!" wailingly.

"Please, ple-e-e-ease, Auntie Dawnie dearie," wheedles Sheila, wriggling her soft little fingers in my hand.

"But Mother never lets you have cookies before dinner," I retort severely. "She knows they are bad for you."

"Pooh, she does too! She always says, 'No, not a cooky!' And then we beg and screech, and then she says, 'Oh, for pity's sake, Frieda, give 'em a cooky and send 'em out. One cooky can't kill 'em.'" Sheila's imitation is delicious.

Hans catches the word screech and takes it as his cue. He begins a series of ear-piercing wails. Sheila surveys him with pride and then takes the wail up in a minor key. Their teamwork is marvelous. I fly to the cooky jar and extract two round and sugary confections. I thrust them into the pink, eager palms. The wails cease. Solemnly they place one cooky atop the other, measuring the circlets with grave eyes.

"Mine's a weeny bit bigger'n yours this time," decides Sheila, and holds her cooky heroically while Hans takes a just and lawful bite out of his sister's larger share.

"The blessed little angels!" I say to myself, melting. "The dear, unselfish little sweeties!" and give each of them another cooky.

Back to my typewriter. But the words flatly refuse to come now. I make six false starts, bite all my best finger-nails, screw my hair into a wilderness of cork-screws and give it up. No doubt a real Lady Writer could write on, unruffled and unhearing, while the iceman squashed the cucumbers, and the roast burned to a frazzle, and the Spalpeens perished of hunger. Possessed of the real spark of genius, trivialities like milkmen and cucumbers could not dim its glow. Perhaps all successful Lady Writers with real live sparks have cooks and scullery maids, and need not worry about basting, and gravy, and milkmen.

This book writing is all very well for those who have a large faith in the future and an equally large bank account. But my future will have to be hand-carved, and my bank account has always been an all too small pay envelope at the end of each week. It will be months before the book is shaped and finished. And my pocketbook is empty. Last week Max sent money for the care of Peter. He and Norah think that I do not know.

Von Gerhard was here in August. I told him that all my firm resolutions to forsake newspaperdom forever were slipping away, one by one.

"I have heard of the fascination of the newspaper office," he said, in his understanding way. "I believe you have a heimweh for it, not?"

"Heimweh! That's the word," I had agreed. "After you have been a newspaper writer for seven years—and loved it—you will be a newspaper writer, at heart and by instinct at least, until you die. There's no getting away from it. It's in the blood. Newspaper men have been known to inherit fortunes, to enter politics, to write books and become famous, to degenerate into press agents and become infamous, to blossom into personages, to sink into nonentities, but their news-nose remained a part of them, and the inky, smoky, stuffy smell of a newspaper office was ever sweet in their nostrils."

But, "Not yet," Von Gerhard had said, "It unless you want to have again this miserable business of the sick nerfs. Wait yet a few months."

And so I have waited, saying nothing to Norah and Max. But I want to be in the midst of things. I miss the sensation of having my fingers at the pulse of the big old world. I'm lonely for the noise and the rush and the hard work; for a glimpse of the busy local room just before press time, when the lights are swimming in a smoky haze, and the big presses downstairs are thundering their warning to hurry, and the men are breezing in from their runs with the grist of news that will be ground finer and finer as it passes through the mill of copy-readers' and editors' hands. I want to be there in the thick of the confusion that is, after all, so orderly. I want to be there when the telephone bells are zinging, and the typewriters are snapping, and the messenger boys are shuffling in and out, and the office kids are scuffling in a corner, and the big city editor, collar off, sleeves rolled up from his great arms, hair bristling wildly above his green eye-shade, is swearing gently and smoking cigarette after cigarette, lighting each fresh one at the dying glow of the last. I would give a year of my life to hear him say:

"I don't mind tellin' you, Beatrice Fairfax, that that was a darn good story you got on the Millhaupt divorce. The other fellows haven't a word that isn't re-hash."

All of which is most unwomanly; for is not marriage woman's highest aim, and home her true sphere? Haven't I tried both? I ought to know. I merely have been miscast in this life's drama. My part should have been that of one who makes her way alone. Peter, with his thin, cruel lips, and his shaking hands, and his haggard face and his smoldering eyes, is a shadow forever blotting out the sunny places in my path. I was meant to be an old maid, like the terrible old Kitty O'Hara. Not one of the tatting-and-tea kind, but an impressive, bustling old girl, with a double chin. The sharp-tongued Kitty O'Hara used to say that being an old maid was a great deal like death by drowning—a really delightful sensation when you ceased struggling.

Norah has pleaded with me to be more like other women of my age, and for her sake I've tried. She has led me about to bridge parties and tea fights, and I have tried to act as though I were enjoying it all, but I knew that I wasn't getting on a bit. I have come to the conclusion that one year of newspapering counts for two years of ordinary, existence, and that while I'm twenty-eight in the family Bible I'm fully forty inside. When one day may bring under one's pen a priest, a pauper, a prostitute, a philanthropist, each with a story to tell, and each requiring to be bullied, or cajoled, or bribed, or threatened, or tricked into telling it; then the end of that day's work finds one looking out at the world with eyes that are very tired and as old as the world itself.

I'm spoiled for sewing bees and church sociables and afternoon bridges. A hunger for the city is upon me. The long, lazy summer days have slipped by. There is an autumn tang in the air. The breeze has a touch that is sharp.

Winter in a little northern town! I should go mad. But winter in the city! The streets at dusk on a frosty evening; the shop windows arranged by artist hands for the beauty-loving eyes of women; the rows of lights like jewels strung on an invisible chain; the glitter of brass and enamel as the endless procession of motors flashes past; the smartly-gowned women; the keen-eyed, nervous men; the shrill note of the crossing policeman's whistle; every smoke-grimed wall and pillar taking on a mysterious shadowy beauty in the purple dusk, every unsightly blot obscured by the kindly night. But best of all, the fascination of the People I'd Like to Know. They pop up now and then in the shifting crowds, and are gone the next moment, leaving behind them a vague regret. Sometimes I call them the People I'd Like to Know and sometimes I call them the People I Know I'd Like, but it means much the same. Their faces flash by in the crowd, and are gone, but I recognize them instantly as belonging to my beloved circle of unknown friends.

Once it was a girl opposite me in a car—a girl with a wide, humorous mouth, and tragic eyes, and a hole in her shoe. Once it was a big, homely, red-headed giant of a man with an engineering magazine sticking out of his coat pocket. He was standing at a book counter reading Dickens like a schoolboy and laughing in all the right places, I know, because I peaked over his shoulder to see. Another time it was a sprightly little, grizzled old woman, staring into a dazzling shop window in which was displayed a wonderful collection of fashionably impossible hats and gowns. She was dressed all in rusty black, was the little old lady, and she had a quaint cast in her left eye that gave her the oddest, most sporting look. The cast was working overtime as she gazed at the gowns, and the ridiculous old sprigs on her rusty black bonnet trembled with her silent mirth. She looked like one of those clever, epigrammatic, dowdy old duchesses that one reads about in English novels. I'm sure she had cardamon seeds in her shabby bag, and a carriage with a crest on it waiting for her just around the corner. I ached to slip my hand through her arm and ask her what she thought of it all. I know that her reply would have been exquisitely witty and audacious, and I did so long to hear her say it.

No doubt some good angel tugs at my common sense, restraining me from doing these things that I am tempted to do. Of course it would be madness for a woman to address unknown red-headed men with the look of an engineer about them and a book of Dickens in their hands; or perky old women with nutcracker faces; or girls with wide humorous mouths. Oh, it couldn't be done, I suppose. They would clap me in a padded cell in no time if I were to say:

"Mister Red-headed Man, I'm so glad your heart is young enough for Dickens. I love him too—enough to read him standing at a book counter in a busy shop. And do you know, I like the squareness of your jaw, and the way your eyes crinkle up when you laugh; and as for your being an engineer—why one of the very first men I ever loved was the engineer in 'Soldiers of Fortune.'"

I wonder what the girl in the car would have said if I had crossed over to her, and put my hand on her arm and spoken, thus:

"Girl with the wide, humorous mouth, and the tragic eyes, and the hole in your shoe, I think you must be an awfully good sort. I'll wager you paint, or write, or act, or do something clever like that for a living. But from that hole in your shoe which you have inked so carefully, although it persists in showing white at the seams, I fancy you are stumbling over a rather stony bit of Life's road just now. And from the look in your eyes, girl, I'm afraid the stones have cut and bruised rather cruelly. But when I look at your smiling, humorous mouth I know that you are trying to laugh at the hurts. I think that this morning, when you inked your shoe for the dozenth time, you hesitated between tears and laughter, and the laugh won, thank God! Please keep right on laughing, and don't you dare stop for a minute! Because pretty soon you'll come to a smooth easy place, and then won't you be glad that you didn't give up to lie down by the roadside, weary of your hurts?"

Oh, it would never do. Never. And yet no charm possessed by the people I know and like can compare with the fascination of those People I'd Like to Know, and Know I Would Like.

Here at home with Norah there are no faces in the crowds. There are no crowds. When you turn the corner at Main street you are quite sure that you will see the same people in the same places. You know that Mamie Hayes will be flapping her duster just outside the door of the jewelry store where she clerks. She gazes up and down Main street as she flaps the cloth, her bright eyes keeping a sharp watch for stray traveling men that may chance to be passing. You know that there will be the same lounging group of white-faced, vacant-eyed youths outside the pool-room. Dr. Briggs's patient runabout will be standing at his office doorway. Outside his butcher shop Assemblyman Schenck will be holding forth on the subject of county politics to a group of red-faced, badly dressed, prosperous looking farmers and townsmen, and as he talks the circle of brown tobacco juice which surrounds the group closes in upon them, nearer and nearer. And there, in a roomy chair in a corner of the public library reference room, facing the big front window, you will see Old Man Randall. His white hair forms a halo above his pitiful drink-marred face. He was to have been a great lawyer, was Old Man Randall. But on the road to fame he met Drink, and she grasped his arm, and led him down by-ways, and into crooked lanes, and finally into ditches, and he never arrived at his goal. There in that library window nook it is cool in summer, and warm in winter. So he sits and dreams, holding an open volume, unread, on his knees. Some times he writes, hunched up in his corner, feverishly scribbling at ridiculous plays, short stories, and novels which later he will insist on reading to the tittering schoolboys and girls who come into the library to do their courting and reference work. Presently, when it grows dusk, Old Man Randall will put away his book, throw his coat over his shoulders, sleeves dangling, flowing white locks sweeping the frayed velvet collar. He will march out with his soldierly tread, humming a bit of a tune, down the street and into Vandermeister's saloon, where he will beg a drink and a lunch, and some man will give it to him for the sake of what Old Man Randall might have been.

All these things you know. And knowing them, what is left for the imagination? How can one dream dreams about people when one knows how much they pay their hired girl, and what they have for dinner on Wednesdays?

CHAPTER V. THE ABSURD BECOMES SERIOUS

I can understand the emotions of a broken-down war horse that is hitched to a vegetable wagon. I am going to Milwaukee to work! It is a thing to make the gods hold their sides and roll down from their mountain peaks with laughter. After New York—Milwaukee!

Of course Von Gerhard is to blame. But I think even he sees the humor of it. It happened in this way, on a day when I was indulging in a particularly greenery-yallery fit of gloom. Norah rushed into my room. I think I was mooning over some old papers, or letters, or ribbons, or some such truck in the charming, knife-turning way that women have when they are blue.

"Out wid yez!" cried Norah. "On with your hat and coat! I've just had a wire from Ernst von Gerhard. He's coming, and you look like an under-done dill pickle. You aren't half as blooming as when he was here in August, and this is October. Get out and walk until your cheeks are so red that Von Gerhard will refuse to believe that this fiery-faced puffing, bouncing creature is the green and limp thing that huddled in a chair a few months ago. Out ye go!"

And out I went. Hatless, I strode countrywards, leaving paved streets and concrete walks far behind. There were drifts of fallen leaves all about, and I scuffled through them drearily, trying to feel gloomy, and old, and useless, and failing because of the tang in the air, and the red-and-gold wonder of the frost-kissed leaves, and the regular pump-pump of good red blood that was coursing through my body as per Norah's request.

In a field at the edge of the town, just where city and country begin to have a bowing acquaintance, the college boys were at football practice. Their scarlet sweaters made gay patches of color against the dull gray-brown of the autumn grass.

"Seven-eighteen-two-four!" called a voice. There followed a scuffle, a creaking of leather on leather, a thud. I watched them, a bit enviously, walking backwards until a twist in the road hid them from view. That same twist transformed my path into a real country road—a brown, dusty, monotonous Michigan country road that went severely about its business, never once stopping to flirt with the blushing autumn woodland at its left, or to dally with the dimpling ravine at its right.

"Now if that were an English country road," thought I, "a sociably inclined, happy-go-lucky, out-for-pleasure English country road, one might expect something of it. On an English country road this would be the psychological moment for the appearance of a blond god, in gray tweed. What a delightful time of it Richard Le Gallienne's hero had on his quest! He could not stroll down the most innocent looking lane, he might not loiter along the most out-of-the-way path, he never ambled over the barest piece of country road, that he did not come face to face with some witty and lovely woman creature, also in search of things unconventional, and able to quote charming lines from Chaucer to him."

Ah, but that was England, and this is America. I realize it sadly as I step out of the road to allow a yellow milk wagon to rattle past. The red letters on the yellow milk cart inform the reader that it is the property of August Schimmelpfennig, of Hickory Grove. The Schimmelpfennig eye may be seen staring down upon me from the bit of glass in the rear as the cart rattles ahead, doubtless being suspicious of hatless young women wandering along country roads at dusk, alone. There was that in the staring eye to which I took exception. It wore an expression which made me feel sure that the mouth below it was all a-grin, if I could but have seen it. It was bad enough to be stared at by the fishy Schimmelpfennig eye, but to be grinned at by the Schimmelpfennig mouth!—I resented it. In order to show my resentment I turned my back on the Schimmelpfennig cart and pretended to look up the road which I had just traveled.

I pretended to look up the road, and then I did look in earnest. No wonder the Schimmelpfennig eye and mouth had worn the leering expression. The blond god in gray tweed was swinging along toward me! I knew that he was blond because he wore no hat and the last rays of the October sun were making a little halo effect about his head. I knew that his-gray clothes were tweed because every well regulated hero on a country road wears tweed. It's almost a religion with them. He was not near enough to make a glance at his features possible. I turned around and continued my walk. The yellow cart, with its impudent Schimmelpfennig leer, was disappearing in a cloud of dust. Shades of the "Duchess" and Bertha M. Clay! How does one greet a blond god in gray tweed on a country road, when one has him!

The blond god solved the problem for me.

"Hi!" he called. I did not turn. There was a moment's silence. Then there came a shrill, insistent whistle, of the kind that is made by placing four fingers between the teeth. It is a favorite with the gallery gods. I would not have believed that gray tweed gods stooped to it.

"Hi!" called the voice again, very near now. "Lieber Gott! Never have I seen so proud a young woman!"

I whirled about to face Von Gerhard; a strangely boyish and unprofessional looking Von Gerhard.

"Young man," I said severely, "have you been a-follerin' of me?"

"For miles," groaned he, as we shook hands. "You walk like a grenadier. I am sent by the charming Norah to tell you that you are to come home to mix the salad dressing, for there is company for supper. I am the company."

I was still a bit dazed. "But how did you know which road to take? And when—"

"Wunderbar, nicht wahr?" laughed Von Gerhard. "But really quite simple. I come in on an earlier train than I had expected, chat a moment with sister Norah, inquire after the health of my patient, and am told that she is running away from a horde of blue devils!—quote your charming sister—that have swarmed about her all day. What direction did her flight take? I ask. Sister Norah shrugs her shoulders and presumes that it is the road which shows the reddest and yellowest autumn colors. That road will be your road. So!"

"Pooh! How simple! That is the second disappointment you have given me to-day."

"But how is that possible? The first has not had time to happen."

"The first was yourself," I replied, rudely.

"I had been longing for an adventure. And when I saw you 'way up the road, such an unusual figure for our Michigan country roads, I forgot that I was a disappointed old grass widder with a history, and I grew young again, and my heart jumped up into my throat, and I sez to mesilf, sez I: 'Enter the hero!' And it was only you."

Von Gerhard stared a moment, a curious look on his face. Then he laughed one of those rare laughs of his, and I joined him because I was strangely young, light, and happy to be alive.

"You walk and enjoy walking, yes?" asked Von Gerhard, scanning my face. "Your cheeks they are like—well, as unlike the cheeks of the German girls as Diana's are unlike a dairy maid's. And the nerfs? They no longer jump, eh?"

"Oh, they jump, but not with weariness. They jump to get into action again. From a life of too much excitement I have gone to the other extreme. I shall be dead of ennui in another six months."

"Ennui?" mused he, "and you are—how is it?—twenty-eight years, yes? H'm!"

There was a world of exasperation in the last exclamation.

"I am a thousand years old," it made me exclaim, "a million!"

"I will prove to you that you are sixteen," declared Von Gerhard, calmly.

We had come to a fork in the road. At the right the narrower road ran between two rows of great maples that made an arch of golden splendor. The frost had kissed them into a gorgeous radiance.

"Sunshine Avenue," announced Von Gerhard. "It beckons us away from home, and supper and salad dressing and duty, but who knows what we shall find at the end of it!"

"Let's explore," I suggested. "It is splendidly golden enough to be enchanted."

We entered the yellow canopied pathway.

"Let us pretend this is Germany, yes?" pleaded Von Gerhard. "This golden pathway will end in a neat little glass-roofed restaurant, with tables and chairs outside, and comfortable German papas and mammas and pig-tailed children sitting at the tables, drinking coffee or beer. There will be stout waiters, and a red-faced host. And we will seat ourselves at one of the tables, and I will wave my hand, and one of the stout waiters will come flying. 'Will you have coffee, *Fraulein*, or beer?' It sounds prosaic, but it is very, very good, as you will see. Pathways in Germany always end in coffee and Kuchen and waiters in white aprons."

But, "Oh, no!" I exclaimed, for his mood was infectious. "This is France. Please! The golden pathway will end in a picturesque little French farm, with a dairy. And in the doorway of the farmhouse there will be a red-skirted peasant woman, with a white cap! and a baby on her arm! and sabots! Oh, surely she will wear sabots!"

"Most certainly she will wear sabots," Von Gerhard said, heatedly, "and blue knitted stockings. And the baby's name is Mimi!"

We had taken hands and were skipping down the pathway now, like two excited children.

"Let's run," I suggested. And run we did, like two mad creatures, until we rounded a gentle curve and brought up, panting, within a foot of a decrepit rail fence. The rail fence enclosed a stubbly, lumpy field. The field was inhabited by an inquiring cow. Von Gerhard and I stood quite still, hand in hand, gazing at the cow. Then we turned slowly and looked at each other.

"This pathway of glorified maples ends in a cow," I said, solemnly. At which we both shrieked with mirth, leaning on the decrepit fence and mopping our eyes with our handkerchiefs.

"Did I not say you were sixteen?" taunted Von Gerhard. We were getting surprisingly well acquainted.

"Such a scolding as we shall get! It will be quite dark before we are home. Norah will be tearing her hair."

It was a true prophecy. As we stampeded up the steps the door was flung open, disclosing a tragic figure.

"Such a steak!" wailed Norah, "and it has been done for hours and hours, and now it looks like a piece of fried ear. Where have you two driveling idiots been? And mushrooms too."

"She means that the ruined steak was further enhanced by mushrooms," I explained in response to Von Gerhard's bewildered look. We marched into the house, trying not to appear like sneak thieves. Max, pipe in mouth, surveyed us blandly.

"Fine color you've got, Dawn," he remarked.

"There is such a thing as overdoing this health business," snapped Norah, with a great deal of acidity for her. "I didn't tell you to make them purple, you know."

Max turned to Von Gerhard. "Now what does she mean by that do you suppose, eh Ernst?"

"Softly, brother, softly!" whispered Von Gerhard. "When women exchange remarks that apparently are simple, and yet that you, a man, cannot understand, then know there is a woman's war going on, and step softly, and hold your peace. Aber ruhig!"

Calm was restored with the appearance of the steak, which was found to have survived the period of waiting, and to be incredibly juicy and tender. Presently we were all settled once more in the great beamed living room, Sis at the piano, the two men smoking their after-dinner cigars with that idiotic expression of contentment which always adorns the masculine face on such occasions.

I looked at them—at those three who had done so much for my happiness and well being, and something within me said: "Now! Speak now!" Norah was playing very softly, so that the Spalpeens upstairs might not be disturbed. I took a long breath and made the plunge.

"Norah, if you'll continue the slow music, I'll be much obliged. 'The time has come, the Walrus said, to talk of many things.'"

"Don't be absurd," said Norah, over her shoulder, and went on playing.

"I never was more serious in my life, good folkses all. I've got to be. This butterfly existence has gone on long enough. Norah, and Max, and Mr. Doctor Man, I am going away."

Norah's hands crashed down on the piano keys with a jangling discord. She swung about to face me.

"Not New York again, Dawn! Not New York!"

"I am afraid so," I answered.

Max—bless his great, brotherly heart—rose and came over to me and put a hand on my shoulder.

"Don't you like it here, girlie? Want to be hauled home on a shutter again, do you? You know that as long as we have a home, you have one. We need you here."

But I shook my head. From his chair at the other side of the room I could feel Von Gerhard's gaze fixed upon us. He had said nothing.

"Need me! No one needs me. Don't worry; I'm not going to become maudlin about it. But I don't belong here, and you know, it. I have my work to do. Norah is the best sister that a woman ever had. And Max, you're an angel brother-in-law. But how can I stay on here and keep my self-respect?" I took Max's big hand in mine and gathered courage from it.

"But you have been working," wailed Norah, "every morning. And I thought the book was coming on beautifully. And I'm sure it will be a wonderful book, Dawn dear. You are so clever."

"Oh, the book—it is too uncertain. Perhaps it will go, but perhaps it won't. And then—what? It will be months before the book is properly polished off. And then I may peddle it around for more months. No; I can't afford to trifle with uncertainties. Every newspaper man or woman writes a book. It's like having the measles. There is not a newspaper man living who does not believe, in his heart, that if he could only take a month or two away from the telegraph desk or the police run, he could write the book of the year, not to speak of the great American Play. Why, just look at me! I've only been writing seriously for a few weeks, and already the best magazines in the country are refusing my manuscripts daily."

"Don't joke," said Norah, coming over to me, "I can't stand it."

"Why not? Much better than weeping, isn't it? And anyway, I'm no subject for tears any more. Dr. von Gerhard will tell you how well and strong I am. Won't you, Herr Doktor?"

"Well," said Von Gerhard, in his careful, deliberate English, "since you ask me, I should say that you might last about one year, in New York."

"There! What did I tell you!" cried Norah.

"What utter blither!" I scoffed, turning to glare at Von Gerhard.

"Gently," warned Max. "Such disrespect to the man who pulled you back from the edge of the yawning grave only six months ago!"

"Yawning fiddlesticks!" snapped I, elegantly. "There was nothing wrong with me except that I wanted to be fussed over. And I have been. And I've loved it. But it must stop now." I rose and walked over to the table and faced Von Gerhard, sitting there in the depths of a great chair. "You do not seem to realize that I am not free to come and go, and work and play, and laugh and live like other women. There is my living to make. And there is—Peter Orme. Do you think that I could stay on here like this? Oh, I know that Max is not a poor man. But he is not a rich man, either. And there are the children to be educated, and besides, Max married Norah O'Hara, not the whole O'Hara tribe. I want to go to work. I am not a free woman, but when I am working, I forget, and am almost, happy. I tell you I must be well again! I will be well! I am well!"

At the end of which dramatic period I spoiled the whole effect by bowing my head on the table and giving way to a fit of weeping such as I had not had since the days of my illness.

"Looks like it," said Max, at which I decided to laugh, and the situation was saved.

It was then that Von Gerhard proposed the thing that set us staring at him in amused wonder. He came over and stood looking down at us, his hands outspread upon the big library table, his body bent forward in an attitude of eager intentness. I remember thinking what wonderful hands they were, true indexes of the man's character; broad, white, surgeonly hands; the fingers almost square at the tips. They were hands as different from those slender, nervous, unsteady, womanly hands of Peter Orme as any hands could be, I thought. They were hands made for work that called for delicate strength, if such a paradox could be; hands to cling to; to gain courage from; hands that spelled power and reserve. I looked at them, fascinated, as I often had done before, and thought that I never had seen such SANE hands.

"You have done me the honor to include me in this little family conclave," began Ernst von Gerhard. "I am going to take advantage of your trust. I shall give you some advice—a thing I usually keep for unpleasant professional occasions. Do not go back to New York."

"But I know New York. And New York—the newspaper part of it—knows me. Where else can I go?"

"You have your book to finish. You could never finish it there, is it not so?"

I'm afraid I shrugged my shoulders. It was all so much harder than I had expected. What did they want me to do? I asked myself, bitterly.

Von Gerhard went on. "Why not go where the newspaper work will not be so nerve-racking? where you still might find time for this other work that is dear to you, and that may bring its reward in time." He reached out and took my hand, into his great, steady clasp. "Come to the happy, healthy, German town called Milwaukee, yes? Ach, you may laugh. But newspaper work is newspaper work the world over, because men and women are just men and women the world over. But there you could live sanely, and work not too hard, and there would be spare hours for the book that is near your heart. And I—I will speak of you to Norberg, of the Post. And on Sundays, if you are good, I may take you along the marvelous lake drives in my little red runabout, yes? Aber wunderbar, those drives are! So."

Then—"Milwaukee!" shrieked Max and Norah and I, together. "After New York—Milwaukee!"

"Laugh," said Von Gerhard, quite composedly. "I give you until to-morrow morning to stop laughing. At the end of that time it will not seem quite so amusing. No joke is so funny after one has contemplated it for twelve hours."

The voice of Norah, the temptress, sounded close to my ear. "Dawn dear, just think how many million miles nearer you would be to Max, and me, and home."

"Oh, you have all gone mad! The thing is impossible. I shan't go back to a country sheet in my old age. I suppose that in two more years I shall be editing a mothers' column on an agricultural weekly."

"Norberg would be delighted to get you," mused Von Gerhard, "and it would be day work instead of night work."

"And you would send me a weekly bulletin on Dawn's health, wouldn't you, Ernst?" pleaded Norah. "And you'd teach her to drink beer and she shall grow so fat that the Spalpeens won't know their auntie."

At last—"How much do they pay?" I asked, in desperation. And the thing that had appeared so absurd at first began to take on the shape of reality.

Von Gerhard did speak to Norberg of the Post. And I am to go to Milwaukee next week. The skeleton of the book manuscript is stowed safely away in the bottom of my trunk and Norah has filled in the remaining space with sundry flannels, and hot water bags and medicine flasks, so that I feel like a schoolgirl on her way to boarding-school, instead of like a seasoned old newspaper woman with a capital PAST and a shaky future. I wish that I were chummier with the Irish saints. I need them now.

CHAPTER VI. STEEPED IN GERMAN

I am living at a little private hotel just across from the court house square with its scarlet geraniums and its pretty fountain. The house is filled with German civil engineers, mechanical engineers, and Herr Professors from the German academy. On Sunday mornings we have Pfannkuchen with currant jelly, and the Herr Professors come down to breakfast in fearful flappy German slippers. I'm the only creature in the place that isn't just over from Germany. Even the dog is a dachshund. It is so unbelievable that every day or two I go down to Wisconsin Street and gaze at the stars and stripes floating from the government building, in order to convince myself that this is America. It needs only a Kaiser or so, and a bit of Unter den Linden to be quite complete.

The little private hotel is kept by Herr and Frau Knapf. After one has seen them, one quite understands why the place is steeped in a German atmosphere up to its eyebrows.

I never would have found it myself. It was Doctor von Gerhard who had suggested Knapf's, and who had paved the way for my coming here.

"You will find it quite unlike anything you have ever tried before," he warned me. "Very German it is, and very, very clean, and most inexpensive. Also I think you will find material there—how is it you call it?—copy, yes? Well, there should be copy in plenty; and types! But you shall see."

From the moment I rang the Knapf doorbell I saw. The dapper, cheerful Herr Knapf, wearing a disappointed Kaiser Wilhelm mustache, opened the door. I scarcely had begun to make my wishes known when he interrupted with a large wave of the hand, and an elaborate German bow.

"Ach yes! You would be the lady of whom the Herr Doktor has spoken. Gewiss! Frau Orme, not? But so a young lady I did not expect to see. A room we have saved for you—aber wunderhubsch! It makes me much pleasure to show. Folgen Sie mir, bitte."

"You—you speak English?" I faltered, with visions of my evenings spent in expressing myself in the sign language.

"Englisch? But yes. Here in Milwaukee it gives aber mostly German. And then too, I have been only twenty years in this country. And always in Milwaukee. Here is it gemutlich—and mostly it gives German."

I tried not to look frightened, and followed him up to the "but wonderfully beautiful" room. To my joy I found it high-ceilinged, airy, and huge, with a great vault of a clothes closet bristling with hooks, and boasting an unbelievable number of shelves. My trunk was swallowed up in it. Never in all my boarding-house experience have I seen such a room, or such a closet. The closet must have been built for a bride's trousseau in the days of hoopskirts and scuttle bonnets. There was a separate and distinct hook for each and every one of my most obscure garments. I tried to spread them out. I used two hooks to every petticoat, and three for my kimono, and when I had finished there were rows of hooks to spare. Tiers of shelves yawned for hat-boxes which I possessed not. Bluebeard's wives could have held a family reunion in that closet and invited all of Solomon's spouses. Finally, in desperation, I gathered all my poor garments together and hung them in a sociable bunch on the hooks nearest the door. How I should have loved to have shown that closet to a select circle of New York boarding-house landladies!

After wrestling in vain with the forest of hooks, I turned my attention to my room. I yanked a towel thing off the center table and replaced it with a scarf that Peter had picked up in the Orient. I set up my typewriter in a corner near a window and dug a gay cushion or two and a chafing-dish out of my trunk. I distributed photographs of Norah and Max and the Spalpeens separately, in couples, and in groups. Then I bounced up and down in a huge yellow brocade chair and found it unbelievably soft and comfortable. Of course, I reflected, after the big veranda, and the apple tree at Norah's, and the leather-cushioned comfort of her library, and the charming tones of her Oriental rugs and hangings—

"Oh, stop your carping, Dawn!" I told myself. "You can't expect charming tones, and Oriental do-dads and apple trees in a German boarding-house. Anyhow there's running water in the room. For general utility purposes that's better than a pink prayer rug."

There was a time when I thought that it was the luxuries that made life worth living. That was in the old Bohemian days.

"Necessities!" I used to laugh, "Pooh! Who cares about the necessities! What if the dishpan does leak? It is the luxuries that count."

Bohemia and luxuries! Half a dozen lean boarding-house years have steered me safely past that. After such a course in common sense you don't stand back and examine the pictures of a pink Moses in a nest of purple bullrushes, or complain because the bureau does not harmonize with the wall paper. Neither do you criticize the blue and saffron roses that form the rug pattern. 'Deedy not! Instead you warily punch the mattress to see if it is rock-stuffed, and you snoop into the clothes closet; you inquire the distance to the nearest bath room, and whether the payments are weekly or monthly, and if there is a baby in the room next door. Oh, there's nothing like living in a boarding-house for cultivating the materialistic side.

But I was to find that here at Knapf's things were quite different. Not only was Ernst von Gerhard right in saying that it was "very German, and very, very clean;" he recognized good copy when he saw it. Types! I never dreamed that such faces existed outside of the old German woodcuts that one sees illustrating time-yellowed books.

I had thought myself hardened to strange boarding-house dining rooms, with their batteries of cold, critical women's eyes. I had learned to walk unruffled in the face of the most carping, suspicious and the fishiest of these batteries. Therefore on my first day at Knapf's I went down to dinner in the evening, quite composed and secure in the knowledge that my collar was clean and that there was no flaw to find in the fit of my skirt in the back.

As I opened the door of my room I heard sounds as of a violent altercation in progress downstairs. I leaned over the balusters and listened. The sounds rose and fell and swelled and boomed. They were German sounds that started in the throat, gutturally, and spluttered their way up. They were sounds such as I had not heard since the night I was sent to cover a Socialist meeting in New York. I tip-toed down the stairs, although I might have fallen down and landed with a thud without having been heard. The din came from the direction of the dining room. Well, come what might, I would not falter. After all, it could not be worse than that awful time when I had helped cover the teamsters' strike. I peered into the dining room.

The thunder of conversation went on as before. But there was no bloodshed. Nothing but men and women sitting at small tables, eating and talking. When I say eating and talking I do not mean that those acts were carried on separately. Not at all. The eating and the talking went on simultaneously, neither interrupting the other. A fork full of food and a mouthful of ten-syllabled German words met, wrestled, and passed one another, unscathed. I stood in the doorway, fascinated, until Herr Knapf spied me, took a nimble skip in my direction, twisted the discouraged mustaches into temporary sprightliness, and waved me toward a table in the center of the room.

Then a frightful thing happened. When I think of it now I turn cold. The battery was not that of women's eyes, but of men's. And conversation ceased! The uproar and the booming of vowels was hushed. The silence was appalling. I looked up in horror to find that what seemed to be millions of staring blue eyes were fixed on me. The stillness was so thick that you could cut it with a knife. Such men! Immediately I dubbed them the aborigines, and prayed that I might find adjectives with which to describe their foreheads.

It appeared that the aborigines were especially favored in that they were all placed at one long, untidy table at the head of the room. The rest of us sat at small tables. Later I learned that they were all engineers. At meals they discuss engineering problems in the most awe-inspiring German. After supper they smoke impossible German pipes and dozens of cigarettes. They have bulging, knobby foreheads and bristling pompadours, and some of the rawest of them wear wild-looking beards, and thick spectacles, and cravats and trousers that Lew Fields never even dreamed of. They are all graduates of high-sounding foreign universities and are horribly learned and brilliant, but they are the worst mannered lot I ever saw.

In the silence that followed my entrance a red-cheeked maid approached me and asked what I would have for supper. Supper? I asked. Was not dinner served in the evening? The aborigines nudged each other and sniggered like fiendish little school-boys.

The red-cheeked maid looked at me pityingly. Dinner was served in the middle of the day, naturlich. For supper there was Wienerschnitzel, and kalter Aufschnitt, also Kartoffel Salat, and fresh Kaffeekuchen.

The room hung breathless on my decision. I wrestled with a horrible desire to shriek and run. Instead I managed to mumble an order. The aborigines turned to one another inquiringly.

"Was hat sie gesagt?" they asked. "What did she say?" Whereupon they fell to discussing my hair and teeth and eyes and complexion in German as crammed with adjectives as was the rye bread over which I was choking with caraway. The entire table watched me with wide-eyed, unabashed interest while I ate, and I advanced by quick stages from red-faced confusion to purple mirth. It appeared that my presence was the ground for a heavy German joke in connection with the youngest of the aborigines. He was a very plump and greasy looking aborigine with a doll-like rosiness of cheek and a scared and bristling pompadour and very small pig-eyes. The other aborigines clapped him on the back and roared:

"Ai Fritz! Jetzt brauchst du nicht zu weinen! Deine Lena war aber nicht so huebsch, eh?"

Later I learned that Fritz was the newest arrival and that since coming to this country he had been rather low in spirits in consequence of a certain flaxen-haired Lena whom he had left behind in the fatherland.

An examination of the dining room and its other occupants served to keep my mind off the hateful long table. The dining room was a double one, the floor carpetless and clean. There was a little platform at one end with hardy-looking plants in pots near the windows. The wall was ornamented with very German pictures of very plump, bare-armed German girls being chucked under the chin by very dashing, mustachioed German lieutenants. It was all very bare, and strange and foreign to my eyes, and yet there was something bright and comfortable about it. I felt that I was going to like it, aborigines and all. The men drink beer with their supper and read the Staats-Zeitung and the Germania and foreign papers that I never heard of. It is uncanny, in these United States. But it is going to be bully for my German.

After my first letter home Norah wrote frantically, demanding to know if I was the only woman in the house. I calmed her fears by assuring her that, while the men were interesting and ugly with the fascinating ugliness of a bulldog, the women were crushed looking and uninteresting and wore hopeless hats. I have written Norah and Max reams about this household, from the aborigines to Minna, who tidies my room and serves my meals, and admires my clothes. Minna is related to Frau Knapf, whom I have never seen. Minna is inordinately fond of dress, and her remarks anent my own garments are apt to be a trifle disconcerting, especially when she intersperses her recital of dinner dishes with admiring adjectives directed at my blouse or hat. Thus:

"Wir haben roast beef, und spareribs mit Sauerkraut, und schicken—ach, wie schon, Frau Orme! Aber ganz prachtvoll!" Her eyes and hands are raised toward heaven.

"What's prachtful?" I ask, startled. "The chicken?"

"Nein; your waist. Selbst gemacht?"

I am even becoming hardened to the manners of the aborigines. It used to fuss me to death to meet one of them in the halls. They always stopped short, brought heels together with a click, bent stiffly from the waist, and thundered: "Nabben', Fraulein!"

I have learned to take the salutation quite calmly, and even the wildest, most spectacled and knobby-browed aborigine cannot startle me. Nonchalantly I reply, "Nabben'," and wish that Norah could but see me in the act.

When I told Ernst von Gerhard about them, he laughed a little and shrugged his shoulders and said:

"Na, you should not look so young, and so pretty, and so unmarried. In Germany a married woman brushes her hair quite smoothly back, and pins it in a hard knob. And she knows nothing of such bewildering collars and fluffy frilled things in the front of the blouse. How do you call them—jabots?"

Von Gerhard has not behaved at all nicely. I did not see him until two weeks after my arrival in Milwaukee, although he telephoned twice to ask if there was anything that he could do to make me comfortable.

"Yes," I had answered the last time that I heard his voice over the telephone. "It would be a whole heap of comfort to me just to see you. You are the nearest thing to Norah that there is in this whole German town, and goodness knows you're far from Irish."

He came. The weather had turned suddenly cold and he was wearing a fur-lined coat with a collar of fur. He looked most amazingly handsome and blond and splendidly healthy. The clasp of his hands was just as big and sure as ever.

"You have no idea how glad I am to see you," I told him. "If you had, you would have been here days ago. Aren't you rather ill-mannered and neglectful, considering that you are responsible for my being here?"

"I did not know whether you, a married woman, would care to have me here," he said, in his composed way. "In a place like this people are not always kind enough to take the trouble to understand. And I would not have them raise their eyebrows at you, not for—"

"Married!" I laughed, some imp of willfulness seizing me, "I'm not married. What mockery to say that I am married simply because I must write madam before my name! I am not married, and I shall talk to whom I please."

And then Von Gerhard did a surprising thing. He took two great steps over to my chair, and grasped my hands and pulled me to my feet. I stared up at him like a silly creature. His face was suffused with a dull red, and his eyes were unbelievably blue and bright. He had my hands in his great grip, but his voice was very quiet and contained.

"You are married," he said. "Never forget that for a moment. You are bound, hard and fast and tight. And you are for no man. You are married as much as though that poor creature in the mad house were here working for you, instead of the case being reversed as it is. So."

"What do you mean!" I cried, wrenching myself away indignantly. "What right have you to talk to me like this? You know what my life has been, and how I have tried to smile with my lips and stay young in my heart! I thought you understood. Norah thought so too, and Max—"

"I do understand. I understand so well that I would not have you talk as you did a moment ago. And I said what I said not so much for your sake, as for mine. For see, I too must remember that you write madam before your name. And sometimes it is hard for me to remember."

"Oh," I said, like a simpleton, and stood staring after him as he quietly gathered up his hat and gloves and left me standing there.

CHAPTER VII. BLACKIE'S PHILOSOPHY

I did not write Norah about Von Gerhard. After all, I told myself, there was nothing to write. And so I was the first to break the solemn pact that we had made.

"You will write everything, won't you, Dawn dear?" Norah had pleaded, with tears, in her pretty eyes. "Promise me. We've been nearer to each other in these last few months than we have been since we were girls. And I've loved it so. Please don't do as you did during those miserable years in New York, when you were fighting your troubles alone and we knew nothing of it. You wrote only the happy things. Promise me you'll write the unhappy ones too—though the saints forbid that there should be any to write! And Dawn, don't you dare to forget your heavy underwear in November. Those lake breezes!—Well, some one has to tell you, and I can't leave those to Von Gerhard. He has promised to act as monitor over your health."

And so I promised. I crammed my letters with descriptions of the Knapf household. I assured her that I was putting on so much weight that the skirts which formerly hung about me in limp, dejected folds now refused to meet in the back, and all the hooks and eyes were making faces at each other. My cheeks, I told her, looked as if I were wearing plumpers, and I was beginning to waddle and puff as I walked.

Norah made frantic answer:

"For mercy's sake child, be careful or you'll be FAT!"

To which I replied: "Don't care if I am. Rather be hunky and healthy than skinny and sick. Have tried both."

It is impossible to avoid becoming round-cheeked when one is working on a paper that allows one to shut one's desk and amble comfortably home for dinner at least five days in the week. Everybody is at least plump in this comfortable, gemutlich town, where everybody placidly locks his shop or office and goes home at noon to dine heavily on soup and meat and vegetables and pudding, washed down by the inevitable beer and followed by forty winks on the dining room sofa with the German Zeitung spread comfortably over the head as protection against the flies.

There is a fascination about the bright little city. There is about it something quaint and foreign, as though a cross-section of the old world had been dumped bodily into the lap of Wisconsin. It does not seem at all strange to hear German spoken everywhere—in the streets, in the shops, in the theaters, in the street cars. One day I chanced upon a sign hung above the doorway of a little German bakery over on the north side. There were Hornchen and Kaffeekuchen in the windows, and a brood of flaxen-haired and sticky children in the back of the shop. I stopped, open-mouthed, to stare at the worn sign tacked over the door.

"Hier wird Englisch gesprochen," it announced.

I blinked. Then I read it again. I shut my eyes, and opened them again suddenly. The fat German letters spoke their message as before—"English spoken here."

On reaching the office I told Norberg, the city editor, about my find. He was not impressed. Norberg never is impressed. He is the most soul-satisfying and theatrical city editor that I have ever met. He is fat, and unbelievably nimble, and keen-eyed, and untiring. He says, "Hell!" when things go wrong; he smokes innumerable cigarettes, inhaling the fumes and sending out the thin wraith of smoke with little explosive sounds between tongue and lips; he wears blue shirts, and no collar to speak of, and his trousers are kept in place only by a miracle and an inefficient looking leather belt.

When he refused to see the story in the little German bakery sign I began to argue.

"But man alive, this is America! I think I know a story when I see it. Suppose you were traveling in Germany, and should come across a sign over a shop, saying: 'Hier wird Deutsch gesprochen.' Wouldn't you think you were dreaming?"

Norberg waved an explanatory hand. "This isn't America. This is Milwaukee. After you've lived here a year or so you'll understand what I mean. If we should run a story of that sign, with a two-column cut, Milwaukee wouldn't even see the joke."

But it was not necessary that I live in Milwaukee a year or so in order to understand its peculiarities, for I had a personal conductor and efficient guide in the new friend that had come into my life with the first day of my work on the Post. Surely no woman ever had a stronger friend than little "Blackie" Griffith, sporting editor of the Milwaukee Post. We became friends, not step by step, but in one gigantic leap such as sometimes triumphs over the gap between acquaintance and liking.

I never shall forget my first glimpse of him. He strolled into the city room from his little domicile across the hall. A shabby, disreputable, out-at-elbows office coat was worn over his ultra-smart street clothes, and he was puffing at a freakish little pipe in the shape of a miniature automobile. He eyed me a moment from the doorway, a fantastic, elfin little figure. I thought that I had never seen so strange and so ugly a face as that of this little brown Welshman with his lank, black hair and his deep-set, uncanny black eyes. Suddenly he trotted over to me with a quick little step. In the doorway he had looked forty. Now a smile illumined the many lines of his dark countenance, and in some miraculous way he looked twenty.

"Are you the New York importation?" he, asked, his great black eyes searching my face.

"I'm what's left of it," I replied, meekly.

"I understand you've been in for repairs. Must of met up with somethin' on the road. They say the goin' is full of bumps in N' York."

"Bumps!" I laughed, "it's uphill every bit of the road, and yet you've got to go full speed to get anywhere. But I'm running easily again, thank you."

He waved away a cloud of pipe-smoke, and knowingly squinted through the haze. "We don't speed up much here. And they ain't no hill climbin' t' speak of. But say, if you ever should hit a nasty place on the route, toot your siren for me and I'll come. I'm a regular little human garage when it comes to patchin' up those aggravatin' screws that need oilin'. And, say, don't let Norberg bully you. My name's Blackie. I'm goin' t' like you. Come on over t' my sanctum once in a while and I'll show you my scrapbook and let you play with the office revolver."

And so it happened that I had not been in Milwaukee a month before Blackie and I were friends.

Norah was horrified. My letters were full of him. I told her that she might get a more complete mental picture of him if she knew that he wore the pinkest shirts, and the purplest neckties, and the blackest and whitest of black-and-white checked vests that ever aroused the envy of an office boy, and beneath them all, the gentlest of hearts. And therefore one loves him. There is a sort of spell about the illiterate little slangy, brown Welshman. He is the presiding genius of the place. The office boys adore him. The Old Man takes his advice in selecting a new motor car; the managing editor arranges his lunch hour to suit Blackie's and they go off to the Press club together, arm in arm. It is Blackie who lends a sympathetic ear to the society editor's tale of woe. He hires and fires the office boys; boldly he criticizes the news editor's makeup; he receives delegations of tan-coated, red-faced prizefighting-looking persons; he gently explains to the photographer why that last batch of cuts make their subjects look as if afflicted with the German measles; he arbitrates any row that the newspaper may have with such dignitaries as the mayor or the chief of police; he manages boxing shows; he skims about in a smart little roadster; he edits the best sporting page in the city; and at four o'clock of an afternoon he likes to send around the corner for a chunk of devil's food cake with butter filling from the Woman's Exchange. Blackie never went to school to speak of. He doesn't know was from were. But he can "see" a story quicker, and farther and clearer than any newspaper man I ever knew— excepting Peter Orme.

There is a legend about to the effect that one day the managing editor, who is Scotch and without a sense of humor, ordered that Blackie should henceforth be addressed by his surname of Griffith, as being a more dignified appellation for the use of fellow reporters, hangers-on, copy kids, office boys and others about the big building.

The day after the order was issued the managing editor summoned a freckled youth and thrust a sheaf of galley proofs into his hand.

"Take those to Mr. Griffith," he ordered without looking up.

"T' who?"

"To Mr. Griffith," said the managing editor, laboriously, and scowling a bit.

The boy took three unwilling steps toward the door. Then he turned a puzzled face toward the managing editor.

"Say, honest, I ain't never heard of dat guy. He must be a new one. W'ere'll I find him?"

"Oh, damn! Take those proofs to Blackie!" roared the managing editor. And thus ended Blackie's enforced flight into the realms of dignity.

All these things, and more, I wrote to the scandalized Norah. I informed her that he wore more diamond rings and scarf pins and watch fobs than a railroad conductor, and that his checked top-coat shrieked to Heaven.

There came back a letter in which every third word was underlined, and which ended by asking what the morals of such a man could be.

Then I tried to make Blackie more real to Norah who, in all her sheltered life, had never come in contact with a man like this.

"... As for his morals—or what you would consider his morals, Sis—they probably are a deep crimson; but I'll swear there is no yellow streak. I never have heard anything more pathetic than his story. Blackie sold papers on a down-town corner when he was a baby six years old. Then he got a job as office boy here, and he used to sharpen pencils, and run errands, and carry copy. After office hours he took care of some horses in an alley barn near by, and after that work was done he was employed about the pressroom of one of the old German newspaper offices. Sometimes he would be too weary to crawl home after working half the night, and so he would fall asleep, a worn, tragic little figure, on a pile of old papers and sacks in a warm corner near the presses. He was the head of a household, and every penny counted. And all the time he was watching things, and learning. Nothing escaped those keen black eyes. He used to help the photographer when there was a pile of plates to develop, and presently he knew more about photography than the man himself. So they made him staff photographer. In some marvelous way he knew more ball players, and fighters and horsemen than the sporting editor. He had a nose for news that was nothing short of wonderful. He never went out of the office without coming back with a story. They used to use him in the sporting department when a rush was on. Then he became one of the sporting staff; then assistant sporting editor; then sporting editor. He knows this paper from the basement up. He could operate a linotype or act as managing editor with equal ease.

"No, I'm afraid that Blackie hasn't had much time for morals. But, Norah dear, I wish that you could hear him when he talks about his mother. He may follow doubtful paths, and associate with questionable people, and wear restless clothes, but I wouldn't exchange his friendship for that of a dozen of your ordinary so-called good men. All these years of work and suffering have made an old man of little Blackie, although he is young in years. But they haven't spoiled his heart any. He is able to distinguish between sham and truth because he has been obliged to do it ever since he was a child selling papers on the corner. But he still clings to the office that gave him his start, although he makes more money in a single week outside the office than his salary would amount to in half a year. He says that this is a job that does not interfere with his work."

Such is Blackie. Surely the oddest friend a woman ever had. He possesses a genius for friendship, and a wonderful understanding of suffering, born of those years of hardship and privation. Each learned the other's story, bit by bit, in a series of confidences exchanged during that peaceful, beatific period that follows just after the last edition has gone down. Blackie's little cubby-hole of an office is always blue with smoke, and cluttered with a thousand odds and ends—photographs, souvenirs, boxing-gloves, a litter of pipes and tobacco, a wardrobe of dust-covered discarded coats and hats, and Blackie in the midst of it all, sunk in the depths of his swivel chair, and looking like an amiable brown gnome, or a cheerful little joss-house god come to life. There is in him an uncanny wisdom which only the streets can teach. He is one of those born newspaper men who could not live out of sight of the ticker-tape, and the copy-hook and the proof-sheet.

"Y' see, girl, it's like this here," Blackie explained one day. "W're all workin' for some good reason. A few of us are workin' for the glory of it, and most of us are workin' t' eat, and lots of us are pluggin' an' savin' in the hopes that some day we'll have money enough to get back at some people we know; but there is some few workin' for the pure love of the work—and I guess I'm one of them fools. Y' see, I started in at this game when I was such a little runt that now it's a ingrowing habit, though it is comfortin' t' know you got a place where you c'n always come in out of the rain, and where you c'n have your mail sent."

"This newspaper work is a curse," I remarked. "Show me a clever newspaper man and I'll show you a failure. There is nothing in it but the glory—and little of that. We contrive and scheme and run about all day getting a story. And then we write it at fever heat, searching our souls for words that are cleancut and virile. And then we turn it in, and what is it? What have we to show for our day's work? An ephemeral thing, lacking the first breath of life; a thing that is dead before it is born. Why, any cub reporter, if he were to put into some other profession the same

393

amount of nerve, and tact, and ingenuity and finesse, and stick-to-it-iveness that he expends in prying a single story out of some unwilling victim, could retire with a fortune in no time."

Blackie blew down the stem of his pipe, preparatory to re-filling the bowl. There was a quizzical light in his black eyes. The little heap of burned matches at his elbow was growing to kindling wood proportions. It was common knowledge that Blackie's trick of lighting pipe or cigarette and then forgetting to puff at it caused his bill for matches to exceed his tobacco expense account.

"You talk," chuckled Blackie, "like you meant it. But sa-a-ay, girl, it's a lonesome game, this retirin' with a fortune. I've noticed that them guys who retire with a barrel of money usually dies at the end of the first year, of a kind of a lingerin' homesickness. You c'n see their pictures in th' papers, with a pathetic story of how they was just beginnin' t' enjoy life when along comes the grim reaper an' claims 'em."

Blackie slid down in his chair and blew a column of smoke ceilingward.

"I knew a guy once—newspaper man, too—who retired with a fortune. He used to do the city hall for us. Well, he got in soft with the new administration before election, and made quite a pile in stocks that was tipped off to him by his political friends. His wife was crazy for him to quit the newspaper game. He done it. An' say, that guy kept on gettin' richer and richer till even his wife was almost satisfied. But sa-a-ay, girl, was that chap lonesome! One day he come up here looking like a dog that's run off with the steak. He was just dyin' for a kind word, an' he sniffed the smell of the ink and the hot metal like it was June roses. He kind of wanders over to his old desk and slumps down in the chair, and tips it back, and puts his feet on the desk, with his hat tipped back, and a bum stogie in his mouth. And along came a kid with a bunch of papers wet from the presses and sticks one in his hand, and—well, girl, that fellow, he just wriggled he was so happy. You know as well as I do that every man on a morning paper spends his day off hanging around the office wishin' that a mob or a fire or somethin' big would tear lose so he could get back into the game. I guess I told you about the time Von Gerhard sent me abroad, didn't I?"

"Von Gerhard!" I repeated, startled. "Do you know him?"

"Well, he ain't braggin' about it none," Blackie admitted. "Von Gerhard, he told me I had about five years or so t' live, about two, three years ago. He don't approve of me. Pried into my private life, old Von Gerhard did, somethin' scand'lous. I had sort of went to pieces about that time, and I went t' him to be patched up. He thumps me fore 'an' aft, firing a volley of questions, lookin' up the roof of m' mouth, and squintin' at m' finger nails an' teeth like I was a prize horse for sale. Then he sits still, lookin' at me for about half a minute, till I begin t' feel uncomfortable. Then he says, slow: 'Young man, how old are you?'

"'O, twenty-eight or so,' I says, airy.

"'My Gawd!' said he. 'You've crammed twice those years into your life, and you'll have to pay for it. Now you listen t' me. You got t' quit workin', an' smokin', and get away from this. Take a ocean voyage,' he says, 'an' try to get four hours sleep a night, anyway.'

"Well say, mother she was scared green. So I tucked her under m' arm, and we hit it up across the ocean. Went t' Germany, knowin' that it would feel homelike there, an' we took in all the swell baden, and chased up the Jungfrau—sa-a-ay, that's a classy little mountain, that Jungfrau. Mother, she had some swell time I guess. She never set down except for meals, and she wrote picture postals like mad. But sa-a-ay, girl, was I lonesome! Maybe that trip done me good. Anyway, I'm livin' yet. I stuck it out for four months, an' that ain't so rotten for a guy who just grew up on printer's ink ever since he was old enough to hold a bunch of papers under his arm. Well, one day mother an' me was sittin' out on one of them veranda cafes they run to over there, w'en somebody hits me a crack on the shoulder, an' there stands old Ryan who used t' do A. P. here. He was foreign correspondent for some big New York syndicate papers over there.

"'Well if it ain't Blackie!' he says. 'What in Sam Hill are you doing out of your own cell when Milwaukee's just got four more games t' win the pennant?'

"'Sa-a-a-ay, girl, w'en I got through huggin' him around the neck an' buyin' him drinks I knew it was me for the big ship. 'Mother,' I says, 'if you got anybody on your mind that you neglected t' send picture postals to, now's' your last chance. 'F I got to die I'm going out with m' scissors in one mitt, and m' trusty paste-pot by m' side!' An' we hits it up for old Milwaukee. I ain't been away since, except w'en I was out with the ball team, sending in sportin' extry dope for the pink sheet. The last time I was in at Baumbach's in comes Von Gerhard an'—"

"Who are Baumbach's?" I interrupted.

Blackie regarded me pityingly. "You ain't never been to Baumbach's? Why girl, if you don't know Baumbach's, you ain't never been properly introduced to Milwaukee. No wonder you ain't hep to the ways of this little community. There ain't what the s'ciety editor would call the proper ontong cordyal between you and the natives if you haven't had coffee at Baumbach's. It ain't hardly legal t' live in Milwaukee all this time without ever having been inside of B—"

"Stop! If you do not tell me at once just where this wonderful place may be found, and what one does when one finds it, and how I happened to miss it, and why it is so necessary to the proper understanding of the city—"

"I'll tell you what I'll do," said Blackie, grinning, "I'll romp you over there to-morrow afternoon at four o'clock. Ach Himmel! What will that for a grand time be, no?"

"Blackie, you're a dear to be so polite to an old married cratur' like me. Did you notice—that is, does Ernst von Gerhard drop in often at Baumbach's?"

394

I have visited Baumbach's. I have heard Milwaukee drinking its afternoon Kaffee.

O Baumbach's, with your deliciously crumbling butter cookies and your kaffee kuchen, and your thick cream, and your thicker waitresses and your cockroaches, and your dinginess and your dowdy German ladies and your black, black Kaffee, where in this country is there another like you!

Blackie, true to his promise, had hailed me from the doorway on the afternoon of the following day. In the rush of the day's work I had quite forgotten about Blackie and Baumbach's.

"Come, Kindchen!" he called. "Get your bonnet on. We will by Baumbach's go, no?"

Ruefully I gazed at the grimy cuffs of my blouse, and felt of my dishevelled hair. "Oh, I'm afraid I can't go. I look so mussy. Haven't had time to brush up."

"Brush up!" scoffed Blackie, "the only thing about you that will need brushin' up is your German. I was goin' t' warn you to rumple up your hair a little so you wouldn't feel overdressed w'en you got there. Come on, girl."

And so I came. And oh, I'm so glad I came!

I must have passed it a dozen times without once noticing it—just a dingy little black shop nestling between two taller buildings, almost within the shadow of the city hall. Over the sidewalk swung a shabby black sign with gilt letters that spelled, "Franz Baumbach."

Blackie waved an introductory hand in the direction of the sign. "There he is. That's all you'll ever see of him."

"Dead?" asked I, regretfully, as we entered the narrow doorway.

"No; down in the basement baking Kaffeekuchen."

Two tiny show-windows faced the street—such queer, old-fashioned windows in these days of plate glass. At the back they were quite open to the shop, and in one of them reposed a huge, white, immovable structure—a majestic, heavy, nutty, surely indigestible birthday cake. Around its edge were flutings and scrolls of white icing, and on its broad breast reposed cherries, and stout butterflies of jelly, and cunning traceries of colored sugar. It was quite the dressiest cake I had ever beheld. Surely no human hand could be wanton enough to guide a knife through all that magnificence. But in the center of all this splendor was an inscription in heavy white letters of icing: "Charlottens Geburtstag."

Reluctantly I tore my gaze from this imposing example of the German confectioner's art, for Blackie was tugging impatiently at my sleeve.

"But Blackie," I marveled, "do you honestly suppose that that structure is intended for some Charlotte's birthday?"

"In Milwaukee," explained Blackie, "w'en you got a birthday you got t' have a geburtstag cake, with your name on it, and all the cousins and aunts and members of the North Side Frauen Turner Verein Gesellchaft, in for the day. It ain't considered decent if you don't. Are you ready to fight your way into the main tent?"

It was holiday time, and the single narrow aisle of the front shop was crowded. It was not easy to elbow one's way through the packed little space. Men and women were ordering recklessly of the cakes of every description that were heaped in cases and on shelves.

Cakes! What a pale; dry name to apply to those crumbling, melting, indigestible German confections! Blackie grinned with enjoyment while I gazed. There were cakes the like of which I had never seen and of which I did not even know the names. There were little round cup cakes made of almond paste that melts in the mouth; there were Schnecken glazed with a delicious candied brown sugar; there were Bismarcks composed of layer upon layer of flaky crust inlaid with an oozy custard that evades the eager consumer at the first bite, and that slides down one's collar when chased with a pursuing tongue. There were Pfeffernusse; there, were Lebkuchen; there were cheese-kuchen; plum-kuchen, peach-kuchen, Apfelkuchen, the juicy fruit stuck thickly into the crust, the whole dusted over with powdered sugar. There were Torten, and Hornchen, and butter cookies.

Blackie touched my arm, and I tore my gaze from a cherry-studded Schaumtorte that was being reverently packed for delivery.

"My, what a greedy girl! Now get your mind all made up. This is your chance. You know you're supposed t' take a slant at th' things an' make up your mind w'at you want before you go back w'ere th' tables are. Don't fumble this thing. When Olga or Minna comes waddlin' up t' you an' says: 'Nu, Fraulein?' you gotta tell her whether your heart says plum-kuchen oder Nusstorte, or both, see? Just like that. Now make up your mind. I'd hate t' have you blunder. Have you decided?"

"Decided! How can I?" I moaned, watching a black-haired, black-eyed Alsatian girl behind the counter as she rolled a piece of white paper into a cone and dipped a spoonful of whipped cream from a great brown bowl heaped high with the snowy stuff. She filled the paper cone, inserted the point of it into one end of a hollow pastry horn, and gently squeezed. Presto! A cream-filled Hornchen!

"Oh, Blackie!" I gasped. "Come on. I want to go in and eat."

As we elbowed our way to the rear room separated from the front shop only by a flimsy wooden partition, I expected I know not what.

But surely this was not Blackie's much-vaunted Baumbach's! This long, narrow, dingy room, with its bare floor and its iron-legged tables whose bare marble tops were yellow with age and use! I said nothing as we seated ourselves. Blackie was watching me out of the tail of his eye. My glance wandered about the shabby, smoke-filled room, and slowly and surely the charm of that fusty, dingy little cafe came upon me.

A huge stove glowed red in one corner. On the wall behind the stove was suspended a wooden rack, black with age, its compartments holding German, Austrian and Hungarian newspapers. Against the opposite wall stood an ancient walnut mirror, and above it hung a colored print of Bismarck, helmeted, uniformed, and fiercely mustached. The clumsy iron-legged tables stood in two solemn rows down the length of the narrow room. Three or four stout, blond girls plodded back and forth, from tables to front shop, bearing trays of cakes and steaming cups of coffee. There was a rumble and clatter of German. Every one seemed to know every one else. A game of chess was in progress at one table, and between moves each contestant would refresh himself with a long-drawn, sibilant mouthful of coffee. There was nothing about the place or its occupants to remind one of America. This dim, smoky, cake-scented cafe was Germany.

"Time!" said Blackie. "Here comes Rosie to take our order. You can take your choice of coffee or chocolate. That's as fancy as they get here."

An expansive blond girl paused at our table smiling a broad welcome at Blackie.

"Wie geht's, Roschen?" he greeted her. Roschen's smile became still more pervasive, so that her blue eyes disappeared in creases of good humor. She wiped the marble table top with a large and careless gesture that precipitated stray crumbs into our laps. "Gut!" murmured she, coyly, and leaned one hand on a portly hip in an attitude of waiting.

"Coffee?" asked Blackie, turning to me. I nodded.

"Zweimal Kaffee?" beamed Roschen, grasping the idea.

"Now's your time to speak up," urged Blackie. "Go ahead an' order all the cream gefillte things that looked good to you out in front."

But I leaned forward, lowering my voice discreetly. "Blackie, before I plunge in too recklessly, tell me, are their prices very—"

"Sa-a-ay, child, you just can't spend half a dollar here if you try. The flossiest kind of thing they got is only ten cents a order. They'll smother you in whipped cream fr a quarter. You c'n come in here an' eat an' eat an' put away piles of cakes till you feel like a combination of Little Jack Horner an' old Doc Johnson. An' w'en you're all through, they hand yuh your check, an', say—it says forty-five cents. You can't beat it, so wade right in an' spoil your complexion."

With enthusiasm I turned upon the patient Rosie. "O, bring me some of those cunning little round things with the cream on 'em, you know—two of those, eh Blackie? And a couple of those with the flaky crust and the custard between, and a slice of that fluffy-looking cake and some of those funny cocked-hat shaped cookies—"

But a pall of bewilderment was slowly settling over Rosie's erstwhile smiling face. Her plump shoulders went up in a helpless shrug, and she turned her round blue eyes appealingly to Blackie.

"Was meint sie alles?" she asked.

So I began all over again, with the assistance of Blackie. We went into minute detail. We made elaborate gestures. We drew pictures of our desired goodies on the marble-topped table, using a soft-lead pencil. Rosie's countenance wore a distracted look. In desperation I was about to accompany her to the crowded shop, there to point out my chosen dainties when suddenly, as they would put it here, a light went her over.

"Ach, yes-s-s-s! Sie wollten vielleicht abgeruhrter Gugelhopf haben, und auch Schaumtorte, und Bismarcks, und Hornchen mit cream gefullt, nicht?"

"Certainly," I murmured, quite crushed. Roschen waddled merrily off to the shop.

Blackie was rolling a cigarette. He ran his funny little red tongue along the edge of the paper and glanced up at me in glee. "Don't bother about me," he generously observed. "Just set still and let the atmosphere soak in."

But already I was lost in contemplation of a red-faced, pompadoured German who was drinking coffee and reading the Fliegende Blatter at a table just across the way. There were counterparts of my aborigines at Knapf's— thick spectacled engineers with high foreheads—actors and actresses from the German stock company—reporters from the English and German newspapers—business men with comfortable German consciences—long-haired musicians—dapper young lawyers—a giggling group of college girls and boys—a couple of smartly dressed women nibbling appreciatively at slices of Nusstorte—low-voiced lovers whose coffee cups stood untouched at their elbows, while no fragrant cloud of steam rose to indicate that there was warmth within. Their glances grow warmer as the neglected Kaffee grows colder. The color comes and goes in the girl's face and I watch it, a bit enviously, marveling that the old story still should be so new.

At a large square table near the doorway a group of eight men were absorbed in an animated political discussion, accompanied by much waving of arms, and thundering of gutturals. It appeared to be a table of importance, for the high-backed bench that ran along one side was upholstered in worn red velvet, and every newcomer paused a moment to nod or to say a word in greeting. It was not of American politics that they talked, but of the politics of Austria and Hungary. Finally the argument resolved itself into a duel of words between a handsome, red-faced German whose rosy skin seemed to take on a deeper tone in contrast to the whiteness of his hair and mustache, and a swarthy young fellow whose thick spectacles and heavy mane of black hair gave him the look of a caricature out of an illustrated German weekly. The red-faced man argued loudly, with much rapping of bare knuckles on the table top. But the dark man spoke seldom, and softly, with a little twisted half-smile on his lips; and whenever he spoke the red-faced man grew redder, and there came a huge laugh from the others who sat listening.

"Say, wouldn't it curdle your English?" Blackie laughed.

Solemnly I turned to him. "Blackie Griffith, these people do not even realize that there is anything unusual about this."

"Sure not; that's the beauty of it. They don't need to make no artificial atmosphere for this place; it just grows wild, like dandelions. Everybody comes here for their coffee because their aunts an' uncles and Grossmutters and Grosspapas used t' come, and come yet, if they're livin'! An', after all, what is it but a little German bakery?"

"But O, wise Herr Baumbach down in the kitchen! O, subtle Frau Baumbach back of the desk!" said I. "Others may fit their shops with mirrors, and cut-glass chandeliers and Oriental rugs and mahogany, but you sit serenely by, and you smile, and you change nothing. You let the brown walls grow dimmer with age; you see the marble-topped tables turning yellow; you leave bare your wooden floor, and you smile, and smile, and smile."

"Fine!" applauded Blackie. "You're on. And here comes Rosie."

Rosie, the radiant, placed on the table cups and saucers of an unbelievable thickness. She set them down on the marble surface with a crash as one who knows well that no mere marble or granite could shatter the solidity of those stout earthenware receptacles. Napkins there were none. I was to learn that fingers were rid of any clinging remnants of cream or crumb by the simple expedient of licking them.

Blackie emptied his pitcher of cream into his cup of black, black coffee, sugared it, stirred, tasted, and then, with a wicked gleam in his black eyes he lifted the heavy cup to his lips and took a long, gurgling mouthful.

"Blackie," I hissed, "if you do that again I shall refuse to speak to you!"

"Do what?" demanded he, all injured innocence.

"Snuffle up your coffee like that."

"Why, girl, that's th' proper way t' drink coffee here. Listen t' everybody else." And while I glared he wrapped his hand lovingly about his cup, holding the spoon imprisoned between first and second fingers, and took another sibilant mouthful. "Any more of your back talk and I'll drink it out of m' saucer an' blow on it like the hefty party over there in the earrings is doin'. Calm yerself an' try a Bismarck."

I picked up one of the flaky confections and eyed it in despair. There were no plates except that on which the cakes reposed.

"How does one eat them?" I inquired.

"Yuh don't really eat 'em. The motion is more like inhalin'. T' eat 'em successful you really ought t' get into a bath-tub half-filled with water, because as soon's you bite in at one end w'y the custard stuff slides out at the other, an' no human mouth c'n be two places at oncet. Shut your eyes girl, an' just wade in."

I waded. In silence I took a deep delicious bite, nimbly chased the coy filling around a corner with my tongue, devoured every bit down to the last crumb and licked the stickiness off my fingers. Then I investigated the interior of the next cake.

"I'm coming here every day," I announced.

"Better not. Ruin your complexion and turn all your lines into bumps. Look at the dame with the earrings. I've been keepin' count an' I've seen her eat three Schnecken, two cream puffs, a Nusshornchen and a slice of Torte with two cups of coffee. Ain't she a horrible example! And yet she's got th' nerve t' wear a princess gown!"

"I don't care," I replied, recklessly, my voice choked with whipped cream and butteriness. "I can just feel myself getting greasy. Haven't I done beautifully for a new hand? Now tell me about some of these people. Who is the funny little man in the checked suit with the black braid trimming, and the green cravat, and the white spats, and the tan hat and the eyeglasses?"

"Ain't them th' dizzy habiliments?" A note of envy crept into Blackie's voice. "His name is Hugo Luders. Used t' be a reporter on the Germania, but he's reformed and gone into advertisin', where there's real money. Some say he wears them clo'es on a bet, and some say his taste in dress is a curse descended upon him from Joseph, the guy with the fancy coat, but I think he wears'em because he fancies 'em. He's been coming here ever' afternoon for twelve years, has a cup of coffee, game of chess, and a pow-wow with a bunch of cronies. If Baumbach's ever decide to paint the front of their shop or put in cut glass fixtures and handpainted china, Hugo Luders would serve an injunction on 'em. Next!"

"Who's the woman with the leathery complexion and the belt to match, and the untidy hair and the big feet? I like her face. And why does she sit at a table with all those strange-looking men? And who are all the men? And who is the fur-lined grand opera tenor just coming in—Oh!"

Blackie glanced over his shoulder just as the tall man in the doorway turned his face toward us. "That? Why, girl, that's Von Gerhard, the man who gives me one more year t' live. Look at everybody kowtowing to him. He don't favor Baumbach's often. Too busy patching up the nervous wrecks that are washed up on his shores."

The tall figure in the doorway was glancing from table to table, nodding here and there to an acquaintance. His eyes traveled the length of the room. Now they were nearing us. I felt a sudden, inexplicable tightening at heart and throat, as though fingers were clutching there. Then his eyes met mine, and I felt the blood rushing to my face as he came swiftly over to our table and took my hand in his.

"So you have discovered Baumbach's," he said. "May I have my coffee and cigar here with you?"

"Blackie here is responsible for my being initiated into the sticky mysteries of Baumbach's. I never should have discovered it if he had not offered to act as personal conductor. You know one another, I believe?"

The two men shook hands across the table. There was something forced and graceless about the act. Blackie eyed Von Gerhard through a misty curtain of cigarette smoke. Von Gerhard gazed at Blackie through narrowed lids as he lighted his cigar. "I'm th' gink you killed off two or three years back," Blackie explained.

"I remember you perfectly," Von Gerhard returned, courteously. "I rejoice to see that I was mistaken."

"Well," drawled Blackie, a wicked gleam in his black eyes, "I'm some rejoiced m'self, old top. Angel wings and a white kimono, worn bare-footy, would go some rotten with my Spanish style of beauty, what? Didn't know that you and m'dame friend here was acquainted. Known each other long?"

I felt myself flushing again.

"I knew Dr. von Gerhard back home. I've scarcely seen him since I have been here. Famous specialists can't be bothered with middle-aged relatives of their college friends, can they, Herr Doktor?"

And now it was Von Gerhard's face that flushed a deep and painful crimson. He looked at me, in silence, and I felt very little, and insignificant, and much like an impudent child who has stuck out its tongue at its elders. Silent men always affect talkative women in that way.

"You know that what you say is not true," he said, slowly.

"Well, we won't quibble. We—we were just about to leave, weren't we Blackie?"

"Just," said Blackie, rising. "Sorry t' see you drinkin' Baumbach's coffee, Doc. It ain't fair t' your patients."

"Quite right," replied Von Gerhard; and rose with us. "I shall not drink it. I shall walk home with Mrs. Orme instead, if she will allow me. That will be more stimulating than coffee, and twice as dangerous, perhaps, but—"

"You know how I hate that sort of thing," I said, coldly, as we passed from the warmth of the little front shop where the plump girls were still filling pasteboard boxes with holiday cakes, to the brisk chill of the winter street. The little black-and-gilt sign swung and creaked in the wind. Whimsically, and with the memory of that last cream-filled cake fresh in my mind, I saluted the letters that spelled "Franz Baumbach."

Blackie chuckled impishly. "Just the same, try a pinch of soda bicarb'nate when you get home, Dawn," he advised. "Well, I'm off to the factory again. Got t' make up for time wasted on m' lady friend. Auf wiedersehen!"

And the little figure in the checked top-coat trotted off.

"But he called you—Dawn," broke from Von Gerhard.

"Mhum," I agreed. "My name's Dawn."

"Surely not to him. You have known him but a few weeks. I would not have presumed—"

"Blackie never presumes," I laughed. "Blackie's just—Blackie. Imagine taking offense at him! He knows every one by their given name, from Jo, the boss of the pressroom, to the Chief, who imports his office coats from London. Besides, Blackie and I are newspaper men. And people don't scrape and bow in a newspaper office—especially when they're fond of one another. You wouldn't understand."

As I looked at Von Gerhard in the light of the street lamp I saw a tense, drawn look about the little group of muscles which show when the teeth are set hard. When he spoke those muscles had relaxed but little.

"One man does not talk ill of another. But this is different. I want to ask you—do you know what manner of man this—this Blackie is? I ask you because I would have you safe and sheltered always from such as he—because I—"

"Safe! From Blackie? Now listen. There never was a safer, saner, truer, more generous friend. Oh, I know what his life has been. But what else could it have been, beginning as he did? I have no wish to reform him. I tried my hand at reforming one man, and made a glorious mess of it. So I'll just take Blackie as he is, if you please—slang, wickedness, pink shirt, red necktie, diamond rings and all. If there's any bad in him, we all know it, for it's right down on the table, face up. You're just angry because he called you Doc."

"Small one," said Von Gerhard, in his quaint German idiom, "we will not quarrel, you and I. If I have been neglectful it was because edged tools were never a chosen plaything of mine. Perhaps your little Blackie realizes that he need have no fear of such things, for the Great Fear is upon him."

"The Great Fear! You mean!—"

"I mean that there are too many fine little lines radiating from the corners of the sunken eyes, and that his hand-clasp leaves a moisture in the palm. Ach! you may laugh. Come, we will change the subject to something more cheerful, yes? Tell me, how grows the book?"

"By inches. After working all day on a bulletin paper whose city editor is constantly shouting: 'Boil it now, fellows! Keep it down! We're crowded!' it is too much of a wrench to find myself seated calmly before my own typewriter at night, privileged to write one hundred thousand words if I choose. I can't get over the habit of crowding the story all into the first paragraph. Whenever I flower into a descriptive passage I glance nervously over my shoulder, expecting to find Norberg stationed behind me, scissors and blue pencil in hand. Consequently the book, thus far, sounds very much like a police reporter's story of a fire four minutes before the paper is due to go to press."

Von Gerhard's face was unsmiling. "So," he said, slowly. "You burn the candle at both ends. All day you write, is it not so? And at night you come home to write still more? Ach, Kindchen!—Na, we shall change all that. We will be better comrades, we two, yes? You remember that gay little walk of last autumn, when we explored the Michigan country lane at dusk? I shall be your Sunday Schatz, and there shall be more rambles like that one, to bring the roses into your cheeks. We shall be good Kameraden, as you and this little Griffith are—what is it they say—good fellows? That is it—good fellows, yes? So, shall we shake hands on it?"

But I snatched my hand away. "I don't want to be a good fellow," I cried. "I'm tired of being a good fellow. I've been a good fellow for years and years, while every other married woman in the world has been happy in her own home, bringing up her babies. When I am old I want some sons to worry me, too, and to stay awake nights for, and some daughters to keep me young, and to prevent me from doing my hair in a knob and wearing bonnets! I hate good-fellow women, and so do you, and so does every one else! I—I—"

"Dawn!" cried Von Gerhard. But I ran up the steps and into the house and slammed the door behind me, leaving him standing there.

CHAPTER IX. THE LADY FROM VIENNA

Two more aborigines have appeared. One of them is a lady aborigine. They made their entrance at supper and I forgot to eat, watching them. The new-comers are from Vienna. He is an expert engineer and she is a woman of noble birth, with a history. Their combined appearance is calculated to strike terror to the heart. He is daringly ugly, with a chin that curves in under his lip and then out in a peak, like pictures of Punch. She wore a gray gown of a style I never had seen before and never expect to see again. It was fastened with huge black buttons all the way down the breathlessly tight front, and the upper part was composed of that pre-historic garment known as a basque. She curved in where she should have curved out, and she bulged where she should have had "lines." About her neck was suspended a string of cannon-ball beads that clanked as she walked. On her forehead rested a sparse fringe.

"Mein Himmel!" thought I. "Am I dreaming? This isn't Wisconsin. This is Nurnberg, or Strassburg, with a dash of Heidelberg and Berlin thrown in. Dawn, old girl, it's going to be more instructive than a Cook's tour."

That turned out to be the truest prophecy I ever made.

The first surprising thing that the new-comers did was to seat themselves at the long table with the other aborigines, the lady aborigine being the only woman among the twelve men. It was plain that they had known one another previous to this meeting, for they became very good friends at once, and the men grew heavily humorous about there being thirteen at table.

At that the lady aborigine began to laugh. Straightway I forgot the outlandish gown, forgot the cannon-ball beads, forgot the sparse fringe, forgave the absence of "lines." Such a voice! A lilting, melodious thing. She broke into a torrent of speech, with bewildering gestures, and I saw that her hands were exquisitely formed and as expressive as her voice. Her German was the musical tongue of the Viennese, possessing none of the gutturals and sputterings. When she crowned it with the gay little trilling laugh my views on the language underwent a lightning change. It seemed the most natural thing in the world to see her open the flat, silver case that dangled at the end of the cannon-ball chain, take out a cigarette, light it, and smoke it there in that little German dining room. She wore the most gracefully nonchalant air imaginable as she blew little rings and wreaths, and laughed and chatted brightly with her husband and the other men. Occasionally she broke into French, her accent as charmingly perfect as it had been in her native tongue. There was a moment of breathless staring on the part of the respectable middle-class Frauen at the other tables. Then they shrugged their shoulders and plunged into their meal again. There was a certain little high-born air of assurance about that cigarette-smoking that no amount of staring could ruffle.

Watching the new aborigines grew to be a sort of game. The lady aborigine of the golden voice, and the ugly husband of the peaked chin had a strange fascination for me. I scrambled downstairs at meal time in order not to miss them, and I dawdled over the meal so that I need not leave before they. I discovered that when the lady aborigine was animated, her face was that of a young woman, possessing a certain high-bred charm, but that when in repose the face of the lady aborigine was that of a very old and tired woman indeed. Also that her husband bullied her, and that when he did that she looked at him worshipingly.

Then one evening, a week or so after the appearance of the new aborigines, there came a clumping at my door. I was seated at my typewriter and the book was balkier than usual, and I wished that the clumper at the door would go away.

"Come!" I called, ungraciously enough. Then, on second thought: "Herein!"

The knob turned slowly, and the door opened just enough to admit the top of a head crowned with a tight, moist German knob of hair. I searched my memory to recognize the knob, failed utterly and said again, this time with mingled curiosity and hospitality:

"Won't you come in?"

The apparently bodiless head thrust itself forward a bit, disclosing an apologetically smiling face, with high check bones that glistened with friendliness and scrubbing.

"Nabben', Fraulein," said the head.

"Nabben'," I replied, more mystified than ever. "Howdy do! Is there anything—"

The head thrust itself forward still more, showing a pair of plump shoulders as its support. Then the plump shoulders heaved into the room, disclosing a stout, starched gingham body.

"Ich bin Frau Knapf," announced the beaming vision.

Now up to this time Frau Knapf had maintained a Mrs. Harris-like mysteriousness. I had heard rumors of her, and I had partaken of certain crispy dishes of German extraction, reported to have come from her deft hands, but I had not even caught a glimpse of her skirts whisking around a corner.

Therefore: "Frau Knapf!" I repeated. "Nonsense! There ain't no sich person—that is, I'm glad to see you. Won't you come in and sit down?"

"Ach, no!" smiled the substantial Frau Knapf, clinging tightly to the door knob. "I got no time. It gives much to do to-night yet. Kuchen dough I must set, und ich weiss nicht was. I got no time."

Bustling, red-cheeked Frau Knapf! This was why I had never had a glimpse of her. Always, she got no time. For while Herr Knapf, dapper and genial, welcomed new-comers, chatted with the diners, poured a glass of foaming Doppel-brau for Herr Weber or, dexterously carved fowl for the aborigines' table, Frau Knapf was making the wheels go round. I discovered that it was she who bakes the melting, golden German Pfannkuchen on Sunday mornings; she it is who fries the crisp and hissing Wienerschnitzel; she it is who prepares the plump ducklings, and the thick gravies, and the steaming lentil soup and the rosy sausages nestling coyly in their bed of sauerkraut. All the week Frau Knapf bakes and broils and stews, her rosy cheeks taking on a twinkling crimson from the fire over which she bends. But on Sunday night Frau Knapf sheds her huge apron and rolls down the sleeves from her plump arms. On Sunday evening she leaves pots and pans and cooking, and is a transformed Frau Knapf. Then does she don a bright blue silk waist and a velvet coat that is dripping with jet, and a black bonnet on which are perched palpitating birds and weary-looking plumes. Then she and Herr Knapf walk comfortably down to the Pabst theater to see the German play by the German stock company. They applaud their favorite stout, blond, German comedienne as she romps through the acts of a sprightly German comedy, and after the play they go to their favorite Wein-stube around the corner. There they have sardellen and cheese sandwiches and a great deal of beer, and for one charmed evening Frau Knapf forgets all about the insides of geese and the thickening for gravies, and is happy.

Many of these things Frau Knapf herself told me, standing there by the door with the Kuchen heavy on her mind. Some of them I got from Ernst von Gerhard when I told him about my visitor and her errand. The errand was not disclosed until Frau Knapf had caught me casting a despairing glance at my last typewritten page.

"Ach, see! you got no time for talking to, ain't it?" she apologized.

"Heaps of time," I politely assured her, "don't hurry. But why not have a chair and be comfortable?"

Frau Knapf was not to be deceived. "I go in a minute. But first it is something I like to ask you. You know maybe Frau Nirlanger?"

I shook my head.

"But sure you must know. From Vienna she is, with such a voice like a bird."

"And the beads, and the gray gown, and the fringe, and the cigarettes?"

"And the oogly husband," finished Frau Knapf, nodding.

"Oogly," I agreed, "isn't the name for it. And so she is Frau Nirlanger? I thought there would be a Von at the very least."

Whereupon my visitor deserted the doorknob, took half a dozen stealthy steps in my direction and lowered her voice to a hissing whisper of confidence.

"It is more as a Von. I will tell you. Today comes Frau Nirlanger by me and she says: 'Frau Knapf, I wish to buy clothes, aber echt Amerikanische. Myself, I do not know what is modish, and I cannot go alone to buy.'"

"That's a grand idea," said I, recalling the gray basque and the cannon-ball beads.

"Ja, sure it is," agreed Frau Knapf. "Soo-o-o, she asks me was it some lady who would come with her by the stores to help a hat and suit and dresses to buy. Stylish she likes they should be, and echt Amerikanisch. So-o-o-o, I say to her, I would go myself with you, only so awful stylish I ain't, and anyway I got no time. But a lady I know who is got such stylish clothes!" Frau Knapf raised admiring hands and eyes toward heaven. "Such a nice lady she is, and stylish, like anything! And her name is Frau Orme."

"Oh, really, Frau Knapf—" I murmured in blushing confusion.

"Sure, it is so," insisted Frau Knapf, coming a step nearer, and sinking her, voice one hiss lower. "You shouldn't say I said it, but Frau Nirlanger likes she should look young for her husband. He is much younger as she is—aber much. Anyhow ten years. Frau Nirlanger does not tell me this, but from other people I have found out." Frau Knapf shook her head mysteriously a great many times. "But maybe you ain't got such an interest in Frau Nirlanger, yes?"

"Interest! I'm eaten up with curiosity. You shan't leave this room alive until you've told me!"

Frau Knapf shook with silent mirth. "Now you make jokings, ain't? Well, I tell you. In Vienna, Frau Nirlanger was a widow, from a family aber hoch edel—very high born. From the court her family is, and friends from the Emperor, und alles. Sure! Frau Nirlanger, she is different from the rest. Books she likes, und meetings, und all such komisch things. And what you think!"

"I don't know," I gasped, hanging on her words, "what DO I think?"

"She meets this here Konrad Nirlanger, and falls with him in love. Und her family is mad! But schrecklich mad! Forty years old she is, and from a noble family, and Konrad Nirlanger is only a student from a university, and he comes from the Volk. Sehr gebildet he is, but not high born. So-o-o-o-o, she runs with him away and is married."

Shamelessly I drank it all in. "You don't mean it! Well, then what happened? She ran away with him—with that chin! and then what?"

Frau Knapf was enjoying it as much as I. She drew a long breath, felt of the knob of hair, and plunged once more into the story.

"Like a story-book it is, nicht? Well, Frau Nirlanger, she has already a boy who is ten years old, and a fine sum of money that her first husband left her. Aber when she runs with this poor kerl away from her family, and her first husband's family is so schrecklich mad that they try by law to take from her her boy and her money, because she has her highborn family disgraced, you see? For a year they fight in the courts, and then it stands that her money Frau Nirlanger can keep, but her boy she cannot have. He will be taken by her highborn family and educated, and he must forget all about his mamma. To cry it is, ain't it? Das arme Kind! Well, she can stand it no longer to live where her boy is, and not to see him. So-o-o-o, Konrad Nirlanger he gets a chance to come by Amerika where there is a big engineering plant here in Milwaukee, and she begs her husband he should come, because this boy she loves very much—Oh, she loves her young husband too, but different, yes?"

"Oh, yes," I agreed, remembering the gay little trilling laugh, and the face that was so young when animated, and so old and worn in repose. "Oh, yes. Quite, quite different."

Frau Knapf smoothed her spotless skirt and shook her head slowly and sadly. "So-o-o-o, by Amerika they come. And Konrad Nirlanger he is maybe a little cross and so, because for a year they have been in the courts, and it might have been the money they would lose, and for money Konrad Nirlanger cares—well, you shall see. But Frau Nirlanger must not mourn and cry. She must laugh and sing, and be gay for her husband. But Frau Nirlanger has no grand clothes, for first she runs away with Konrad Nirlanger, and then her money is tied in the law. Now she has again her money, and she must be young—but young!"

With a gesture that expressed a world of pathos and futility Frau Knapf flung out her arms. "He must not see that she looks different as the ladies in this country. So Frau Nirlanger wants she should buy here in the stores new dresses—echt Amerikanische. All new and beautiful things she would have, because she must look young, ain't it? And perhaps her boy will remember her when he is a fine young man, if she is yet young when he grows up, you see? And too, there is the young husband. First, she gives up her old life, and her friends and her family for this man, and then she must do all things to keep him. Men, they are but children, after all," spake the wise Frau Knapf in conclusion. "They war and cry and plead for that which they would have, and when they have won, then see! They are amused for a moment, and the new toy is thrown aside."

"Poor, plain, vivacious, fascinating little Frau Nirlanger!" I said. "I wonder just how much of pain and heartache that little musical laugh of hers conceals?"

"Ja, that is so," mused Frau Knapf. "Her eyes look like eyes that have wept much, not? And so you will be so kind and go maybe to select the so beautiful clothes?"

"Clothes?" I repeated, remembering the original errand. "But dear lady! How, does one select clothes for a woman of forty who would not weary her husband? That is a task for a French modiste, a wizard, and a fairy godmother all rolled into one."

"But you will do it, yes?" urged Frau Knapf.

"I'll do it," I agreed, a bit ruefully, "if only to see the face of the oogly husband when his bride is properly corseted and shod."

Whereupon Frau Knapf, in a panic, remembered the unset Kuchen dough and rushed away, with her hand on her lips and her eyes big with secrecy. And I sat staring at the last typewritten page stuck in my typewriter and I found that the little letters on the white page were swimming in a dim purple haze.

CHAPTER X. A TRAGEDY OF GOWNS

From husbands in general, and from oogly German husbands in particular may Hymen defend me! Never again will I attempt to select "echt Amerikanische" clothes for a woman who must not weary her young husband. But how was I to know that the harmless little shopping expedition would resolve itself into a domestic tragedy, with Herr Nirlanger as the villain, Frau Nirlanger as the persecuted heroine, and I as—what is it in tragedy that corresponds to the innocent bystander in real life? That would be my role.

The purchasing of the clothes was a real joy. Next to buying pretty things for myself there is nothing I like better than choosing them for some one else. And when that some one else happens to be a fascinating little foreigner who coos over the silken stuffs in a delightful mixture of German and English; and especially when that some one else must be made to look so charming that she will astonish her oogly husband, then does the selecting of those pretty things cease to be a task, and become an art.

It was to be a complete surprise to Herr Nirlanger. He was to know nothing of it until everything was finished and Frau Nirlanger, dressed in the prettiest of the pretty Amerikanisch gowns, was ready to astound him when he should come home from the office of the vast plant where he solved engineering problems.

"From my own money I buy all this," Frau Nirlanger confided to me, with a gay little laugh of excitement, as we started out. "From Vienna it comes. Always I have given it at once to my husband, as a wife should. Yesterday it came, but I said nothing, and when my husband said to me, 'Anna, did not the money come as usual to-day? It is time,' I told a little lie—but a little one, is it not? Very amusing it was. Almost I did laugh. Na, he will not be cross when he see how his wife like the Amerikanische ladies will look. He admires very much the ladies of Amerika. Many times he has said so."

("I'll wager he has—the great, ugly boor!" I thought, in parenthesis.) "We'll show him!" I said, aloud. "He won't know you. Such a lot of beautiful clothes as we can buy with all this money. Oh, dear Frau Nirlanger, it's going to be slathers of fun! I feel as excited about it as though it were a trousseau we were buying."

"So it is," she replied, a little shadow of sadness falling across the brightness of her face. "I had no proper clothes when we were married—but nothing! You know perhaps my story. In America, everyone knows everything. It is wonderful. When I ran away to marry Konrad Nirlanger I had only the dress which I wore; even that I borrowed from one of the upper servants, on a pretext, so that no one should recognize me. Ach Gott! I need not have worried. So! You see, it will be after all a trousseau."

Why, oh, why should a woman with her graceful carriage and pretty vivacity have been cursed with such an ill-assorted lot of features! Especially when certain boorish young husbands have expressed an admiration for pink-and-white effects in femininity.

"Never mind, Mr. Husband, I'll show yez!" I resolved as the elevator left us at the floor where waxen ladies in shining glass cases smiled amiably all the day.

There must be no violent pinks or blues. Brown was too old. She was not young enough for black. Violet was too trying. And so the gowns began to strew tables and chairs and racks, and still I shook my head, and Frau Nirlanger looked despairing, and the be-puffed and real Irish-crocheted saleswoman began to develop a baleful gleam about the eyes.

And then we found it! It was a case of love at first sight. The unimaginative would have called it gray. The thoughtless would have pronounced it pink. It was neither, and both; a soft, rosily-gray mixture of the two, like the sky that one sometimes sees at winter twilight, the pink of the sunset veiled by the gray of the snow clouds. It was of a supple, shining cloth, simple in cut, graceful in lines.

"There! We've found it. Let's pray that it will not require too much altering."

But when it had been slipped over her head we groaned at the inadequacy of her old-fashioned stays. There followed a flying visit to the department where hips were whisked out of sight in a jiffy, and where lines miraculously took the place of curves. Then came the gown once more, over the new stays this time. The effect was magical. The Irish-crocheted saleswoman and I clasped hands and fell back in attitudes of admiration. Frau Nirlanger turned this way and that before the long mirror and chattered like a pleased child. Her adjectives grew into words of six syllables. She cooed over the soft-shining stuff in little broken exclamations in French and German.

Then came a straight and simple street suit of blue cloth, a lingerie gown of white, hats, shoes and even a couple of limp satin petticoats. The day was gone before we could finish.

I bullied them into promising the pinky-gray gown for the next afternoon.

"Sooch funs!" giggled Frau Nirlanger, "and how it makes one tired. So kind you were, to take this trouble for me. Me, I could never have warred with that Fraulein who served us—so haughty she was, nicht? But it is good again pretty clothes to have. Pretty gowns I lofe—you also, not?"

"Indeed I do lofe 'em. But my money comes to me in a yellow pay envelope, and it is spent before it reaches me, as a rule. It doesn't leave much of a margin for general recklessness."

A tiny sigh came from Frau Nirlanger. "There will be little to give to Konrad this time. So much money they cost, those clothes! But Konrad, he will not care when he sees the so beautiful dresses, is it not so?"

"Care!" I cried with a great deal of bravado, although a tiny inner voice spake in doubt. "Certainly not. How could he?"

Next day the boxes came, and we smuggled them into my room. The unwrapping of the tissue paper folds was a ceremony. We reveled in the very crackle of it. I had scuttled home from the office as early as decency would permit, in order to have plenty of time for the dressing. It must be quite finished before Herr Nirlanger should arrive. Frau Nirlanger had purchased three tickets for the German theater, also as a surprise, and I was to accompany the happily surprised husband and the proud little wife of the new Amerikanische clothes.

I coaxed her to let me do things to her hair. Usually she wore a stiff and ugly coiffure that could only be described as a chignon. I do not recollect ever having seen a chignon, but I know that it must look like that. I was thankful for my Irish deftness of fingers as I stepped back to view the result of my labors. The new arrangement of the hair gave her features a new softness and dignity.

We came to the lacing of the stays, with their exaggerated length. "Aber!" exclaimed Frau Nirlanger, not daring to laugh because of the strange snugness. "Ach!" and again, "Aber to laugh it is!"

We had decided the prettiest of the new gowns must do honor to the occasion. "This shade is called ashes of roses," I explained, as I slipped it over her head.

"Ashes of roses!" she echoed. "How pretty, yes? But a little sad too, is it not so? Like rosy hopes that have been withered. Ach, what a foolish talk! So, now you will fasten it please. A real trick it is to button such a dress—so sly they are, those fastenings."

When all the sly fastenings were secure I stood at gaze.

"Nose is shiny," I announced, searching in a drawer for chamois and powder.

Frau Nirlanger raised an objecting hand. "But Konrad does not approve of such things. He has said so. He has—"

"You tell your Konrad that a chamois skin isn't half as objectionable as a shiny one. Come here and let me dust this over your nose and chin, while I breathe a prayer of thanks that I have no overzealous husband near to forbid me the use of a bit of powder. There! If I sez it mesilf as shouldn't, yez ar-r-re a credit t' me, me darlint."

"You are satisfied. There is not one small thing awry? Ach, how we shall laugh at Konrad's face."

"Satisfied! I'd kiss you if I weren't afraid that I should muss you up. You're not the same woman. You look like a girl! And so pretty! Now skedaddle into your own rooms, but don't you dare to sit down for a moment. I'm going down to get Frau Knapf before your husband arrives."

"But is there then time?" inquired Frau Nirlanger. "He should be here now."

"I'll bring her up in a jiffy, just for one peep. She won't know you! Her face will be a treat! Don't touch your hair—it's quite perfect. And fr Jawn's sake! Don't twist around to look at yourself in the back or something will burst, I know it will. I'll be back in a minute. Now run!"

The slender, graceful figure disappeared with a gay little laugh, and I flew downstairs for Frau Knapf. She was discovered with a spoon in one hand and a spluttering saucepan in the other. I detached her from them, clasped her big, capable red hands and dragged her up the stairs, explaining as I went.

"Now don't fuss about that supper! Let 'em wait. You must see her before Herr Nirlanger comes home. He's due any minute. She looks like a girl. So young! And actually pretty! And her figure—divine! Funny what a difference a decent pair of corsets, and a gown, and some puffs will make, h'm?"

Frau Knapf was panting as I pulled her after me in swift eagerness. Between puffs she brought out exclamations of surprise and unbelief such as: "Unmoglich! (Puff! Puff!) Aber—wunderbar! (Puff! Puff!)"

We stopped before Frau Nirlanger's door. I struck a dramatic pose. "Prepare!" I cried grandly, and threw open the door with a bang.

Crouched against the wall at a far corner of the room was Frau Nirlanger. Her hands were clasped over her breast and her eyes were dilated as though she had been running. In the center of the room stood Konrad Nirlanger, and on his oogly face was the very oogliest look that I have ever seen on a man. He glanced at us as we stood transfixed in the doorway, and laughed a short, sneering laugh that was like a stinging blow on the cheek.

"So!" he said; and I would not have believed that men really said "So!" in that way outside of a melodrama. "So! You are in the little surprise, yes? You carry your meddling outside of your newspaper work, eh? I leave behind me an old wife in the morning and in the evening, presto! I find a young bride. Wonderful!—but wonderful!" He laughed an unmusical and mirthless laugh.

"But—don't you like it?" I asked, like a simpleton.

Frau Nirlanger seemed to shrink before our very eyes, so that the pretty gown hung in limp folds about her.

I stared, fascinated, at Konrad Nirlanger's cruel face with its little eyes that were too close together and its chin that curved in below the mouth and out again so grotesquely.

"Like it?" sneered Konrad Nirlanger. "For a young girl, yes. But how useless, this belated trousseau. What a waste of good money! For see, a young wife I do not want. Young women one can have in plenty, always. But I have an old woman married, and for an old woman the gowns need be few—eh, Frau Orme? And you too, Frau Knapf?"

Frau Knapf, crimson and staring, was dumb. There came a little shivering moan from the figure crouched in the corner, and Frau Nirlanger, her face queerly withered and ashen, crumpled slowly in a little heap on the floor and buried her shamed head in her arms.

Konrad Nirlanger turned to his wife, the black look on his face growing blacker.

"Come, get up Anna," he ordered, in German. "These heroics become not a woman of your years. And too, you must not ruin the so costly gown that will be returned to-morrow."

Frau Nirlanger's white face was lifted from the shelter of her arms. The stricken look was still upon it, but there was no cowering in her attitude now. Slowly she rose to her feet. I had not realized that she was so tall.

"The gown does not go back," she said.

"So?" he snarled, with a savage note in his voice. "Now hear me. There shall be no more buying of gowns and fripperies. You hear? It is for the wife to come to the husband for the money; not for her to waste it wantonly on gowns, like a creature of the streets. You," his voice was an insult, "you, with your wrinkles and your faded eyes in a gown of—" he turned inquiringly toward me—"How does one call it, that color, Frau Orme?"

There came a blur of tears to my eyes. "It is called ashes of roses," I answered. "Ashes of roses."

Konrad Nirlanger threw back his head and laughed a laugh as stinging as a whip-lash. "Ashes of roses! So? It is well named. For my dear wife it is poetically fit, is it not so? For see, her roses are but withered ashes, eh Anna?"

Deliberately and in silence Anna Nirlanger walked to the mirror and stood there, gazing at the woman in the glass. There was something dreadful and portentous about the calm and studied deliberation with which she critically viewed that reflection. She lifted her arms slowly and patted into place the locks that had become disarranged, turning her head from side to side to study the effect. Then she took from a drawer the bit of chamois skin that I had given her, and passed it lightly over her eyelids and cheeks, humming softly to herself the while. No music ever sounded so uncanny to my ears. The woman before the mirror looked at the woman in the mirror with a long, steady, measuring look. Then, slowly and deliberately, the long graceful folds of her lovely gown trailing behind her, she walked over to where her frowning husband stood. So might a queen have walked, head held high, gaze steady. She stopped within half a foot of him, her eyes level with his. For a long half-minute they stood thus, the faded blue eyes of the wife gazing into the sullen black eyes of the husband, and his were the first to drop, for all the noble blood in Anna Nirlanger's veins, and all her long line of gently bred ancestors were coming to her aid in dealing with her middle-class husband.

"You forget," she said, very slowly and distinctly. "If this were Austria, instead of Amerika, you would not forget. In Austria people of your class do not speak in this manner to those of my caste."

"Unsinn!" laughed Konrad Nirlanger. "This is Amerika."

"Yes," said Anna Nirlanger, "this is Amerika. And in Amerika all things are different. I see now that my people knew of what they spoke when they called me mad to think of wedding a clod of the people, such as you."

For a moment I thought that he was going to strike her. I think he would have, if she had flinched. But she did not. Her head was held high, and her eyes did not waver.

"I married you for love. It is most comical, is it not? With you I thought I should find peace, and happiness and a re-birth of the intellect that was being smothered in the splendor and artificiality and the restrictions of my life there. Well, I was wrong. But wrong. Now hear me!" Her voice was tense with passion. "There will be gowns—as many and as rich as I choose. You have said many times that the ladies of Amerika you admire. And see! I shall be also one of those so-admired ladies. My money shall go for gowns! For hats! For trifles of lace and velvet and fur! You shall learn that it is not a peasant woman whom you have married. This is Amerika, the land of the free, my husband. And see! Who is more of Amerika than I? Who?"

She laughed a high little laugh and came over to me, taking my hands in her own.

"Dear girl, you must run quickly and dress. For this evening we go to the theater. Oh, but you must. There shall be no unpleasantness, that I promise. My husband accompanies us—with joy. Is it not so, Konrad? With joy? So!"

Wildly I longed to decline, but I dared not. So I only nodded, for fear of the great lump in my throat, and taking Frau Knapf's hand I turned and fled with her. Frau Knapf was muttering:

"Du Hund! Du unverschamter Hund du!" in good Billingsgate German, and wiping her eyes with her apron. And I dressed with trembling fingers because I dared not otherwise face the brave little Austrian, the plucky little aborigine who, with the donning of the new Amerikanische gown had acquired some real Amerikanisch nerve.

CHAPTER XI. VON GERHARD SPEAKS

Of Von Gerhard I had not had a glimpse since that evening of my hysterical outburst. On Christmas day there had come a box of roses so huge that I could not find vases enough to hold its contents, although I pressed into service everything from Mason jars from the kitchen to hand-painted atrocities from the parlor. After I had given posies to Frau Nirlanger, and fastened a rose in Frau Knapf's hard knob of hair, where it bobbed in ludicrous discomfort, I still had enough to fill the washbowl. My room looked like a grand opera star's boudoir when she is expecting the newspaper reporters. I reveled in the glowing fragrance of the blossoms and felt very eastern and luxurious and popular. It had been a busy, happy, work-filled week, in which I had had to snatch odd moments for the selecting of certain wonderful toys for the Spalpeens. There had been dolls and doll-clothes and a marvelous miniature kitchen for the practical and stolid Sheila, and ingenious bits of mechanism that did unbelievable things when wound up, for the clever, imaginative Hans. I was not to have the joy of seeing their wide-eyed delight, but I knew that there would follow certain laboriously scrawled letters, filled with topsy-turvy capitals and crazily leaning words of thanks to the doting old auntie who had been such good fun the summer before.

Boarding-house Christmases had become an old story. I had learned to accept them, even to those obscure and foreign parts of turkey which are seen only on boarding-house plates, and which would be recognized nowhere else as belonging to that stately bird.

Christmas at Knapf's had been a happy surprise; a day of hearty good cheer and kindness. There had even been a Christmas tree, hung with stodgy German angels and Pfeffernuesse and pink-frosted cakes. I found myself the bewildered recipient of gifts from everyone—from the Knapfs, and the aborigines and even from one of the crushed-looking wives. The aborigine whom they called Fritz had presented me with a huge and imposing Lebkuchen, reposing in a box with frilled border, ornamented with quaint little red-and-green German figures in sugar, and labeled Nurnberg in stout letters, for it had come all the way from that kuchen-famous city. The Lebkuchen I placed on my mantel shelf as befitted so magnificent a work of art. It was quite too elaborate and imposing to be sent the way of ordinary food, although it had a certain tantalizingly spicy scent that tempted one to break off a corner here and there.

On the afternoon of Christmas day I sat down to thank Dr. von Gerhard for the flowers as prettily as might be. Also I asked his pardon, a thing not hard to do with the perfume of his roses filling the room.

"For you," I wrote, "who are so wise in the ways of those tricky things called nerves, must know that it was only a mild hysteria that made me say those most unladylike things. I have written Norah all about it. She has replied, advising me to stick to the good-fellow role but not to dress the part. So when next you see me I shall be a perfectly safe and sane comrade in petticoats. And I promise you—no more outbursts."

So it happened that on the afternoon of New Year's day Von Gerhard and I gravely wished one another many happy and impossible things for the coming year, looking fairly and squarely into each other's eyes as we did so.

"So," said Von Gerhard, as one who is satisfied. "The nerfs are steady to-day. What do you say to a brisk walk along the lake shore to put us in a New Year frame of mind, and then a supper down-town somewhere, with a toast to Max and Norah?"

"You've saved my life! Sit down here in the parlor and gaze at the crepe-paper oranges while I powder my nose and get into some street clothes. I have such a story to tell you! It has made me quite contented with my lot."

The story was that of the Nirlangers; and as we struggled against a brisk lake breeze I told it, and partly because of the breeze, and partly because of the story, there were tears in my eyes when I had finished. Von Gerhard stared at me, aghast.

"But you are—crying!" he marveled, watching a tear slide down my nose.

"I'm not," I retorted. "Anyway I know it. I think I may blubber if I choose to, mayn't I, as well as other women?"

"Blubber?" repeated Von Gerhard, he of the careful and cautious English. "But most certainly, if you wish. I had thought that newspaper women did not indulge in the luxury of tears."

"They don't—often. Haven't the time. If a woman reporter were to burst into tears every time she saw something to weep over she'd be going about with a red nose and puffy eyelids half the time. Scarcely a day passes that does not bring her face to face with human suffering in some form. Not only must she see these things, but she must write of them so that those who read can also see them. And just because she does not wail and tear her hair and faint she popularly is supposed to be a flinty, cigarette-smoking creature who rampages up and down the land, seeking whom she may rend with her pen and gazing, dry-eyed, upon scenes of horrid bloodshed."

"And yet the little domestic tragedy of the Nirlangers can bring tears to your eyes?"

"Oh, that was quite different. The case of the Nirlangers had nothing to do with Dawn O'Hara, newspaper reporter. It was just plain Dawn O'Hara, woman, who witnessed that little tragedy. Mein Himmel! Are all German husbands like that?"

"Not all. I have a very good friend named Max—"

"O, Max! Max is an angel husband. Fancy Max and Norah waxing tragic on the subject of a gown! Now you—"

"I? Come, you are sworn to good-fellowship. As one comrade to another, tell me, what sort of husband do you think I should make, eh? The boorish Nirlanger sort, or the charming Max variety. Come, tell me—you who always have seemed so—so damnably able to take care of yourself." His eyes were twinkling in the maddening way they had.

I looked out across the lake to where a line of white-caps was piling up formidably only to break in futile wrath against the solid wall of the shore. And there came over me an equally futile wrath; that savage, unreasoning instinct in women which prompts them to hurt those whom they love.

"Oh, you!" I began, with Von Gerhard's amused eyes laughing down upon me. "I should say that you would be more in the Nirlanger style, in your large, immovable, Germansure way. Not that you would stoop to wrangle about money or gowns, but that you would control those things. Your wife will be a placid, blond, rather plump German Fraulein, of excellent family and no imagination. Men of your type always select negative wives. Twenty years ago she would have run to bring you your Zeitung and your slippers. She would be that kind, if Zeitung-and-slipper husbands still were in existence. You will be fond of her, in a patronizing sort of way, and she will never know the difference between that and being loved, not having a great deal of imagination, as I have said before. And you will go on becoming more and more famous, and she will grow plumper and more placid, and less and less understanding of what those komisch medical journals have to say so often about her husband who is always discovering things. And you will live happily ever after—"

A hand gripped my shoulder. I looked up, startled, into two blue eyes blazing down into mine. Von Gerhard's face was a painful red. I think that the hand on my shoulder even shook me a little, there on that bleak and deserted lake drive. I tried to wrench my shoulder free with a jerk.

"You are hurting me!" I cried.

A quiver of pain passed over the face that I had thought so calmly unemotional. "You talk of hurts! You, who set out deliberately and maliciously to make me suffer! How dare you then talk to me like this! You stab with a hundred knives—you, who know how I—"

"I'm sorry," I put in, contritely. "Please don't be so dreadful about it. After all, you asked me, didn't you? Perhaps I've hurt your vanity. There, I didn't mean that, either. Oh, dear, let's talk about something impersonal. We get along wretchedly of late."

The angry red ebbed away from Von Gerhard's face. The blaze of wrath in his eyes gave way to a deeper, brighter light that held me fascinated, and there came to his lips a smile of rare sweetness. The hand that had grasped my shoulder slipped down, down, until it met my hand and gripped it.

"Na, 's ist schon recht, Kindchen. Those that we most care for we would hurt always. When I have told you of my love for you, although already you know it, then you will tell me. Hush! Do not deny this thing. There shall be no more lies between us. There shall be only the truth, and no more about plump, blonde German wives who run with Zeitung and slippers. After all, it is no secret. Three months ago I told Norah. It was not news to her. But she trusted me."

I felt my face to be as white and as tense as his own. "Norah—knows!"

"It is better to speak these things. Then there need be no shifting of the eyes, no evasive words, no tricks, no subterfuge."

We had faced about and were retracing our steps, past the rows of peculiarly home-like houses that line Milwaukee's magnificent lake shore. Windows were hung with holiday scarlet and holly, and here and there a face was visible at a window, looking out at the man and woman walking swiftly along the wind-swept heights that rose far above the lake.

A wretched revolt seized me as I gazed at the substantial comfort of those normal, happy homes.

"Why did you tell me! What good can that do? At least we were make-believe friends before. Suppose I were to tell you that I care, then what."

"I do not ask you to tell me," Von Gerhard replied, quietly.

"You need not. You know. You knew long, long ago. You know I love the big quietness of you, and your sureness, and the German way you have of twisting your sentences about, and the steady grip of your great firm hands, and the rareness of your laugh, and the simplicity of you. Why I love the very cleanliness of your ruddy skin, and the way your hair grows away from your forehead, and your walk, and your voice and—Oh, what is the use of it all?"

"Just this, Dawn. The light of day sweetens all things. We have dragged this thing out into the sunlight, where, if it grows, it will grow sanely and healthily. It was but an ugly, distorted, unsightly thing, sending out pale unhealthy shoots in the dark, unwholesome cellars of our inner consciences. Norah's knowing was the cleanest, sweetest thing about it."

"How wonderfully you understand her, and how right you are! Her knowing seems to make it as it should be, doesn't it? I am braver already, for the knowledge of it. It shall make no difference between us?"

"There is no difference, Dawn," said he.

"No. It is only in the story-books that they sigh, and groan and utter silly nonsense. We are not like that. Perhaps, after a bit, you will meet some one you care for greatly—not plump, or blond, or German, perhaps, but still—"

"Doch you are flippant?"

"I must say those things to keep the tears back. You would not have me wailing here in the street. Tell me just one thing, and there shall be no more fluttering breaths and languishing looks. Tell me, when did you begin to care?"

We had reached Knapfs' door-step. The short winter day was already drawing to its close. In the half-light Von Gerhard's eyes glowed luminous.

"Since the day I first met you at Norah's," he said, simply.

I stared at him, aghast, my ever-present sense of humor struggling to the surface. "Not—not on that day when you came into the room where I sat in the chair by the window, with a flowered quilt humped about my shoulders! And a fever-sore twisting my mouth! And my complexion the color of cheese, and my hair plastered back from my forehead, and my eyes like boiled onions!"

"Thank God for your gift of laughter," Von Gerhard said, and took my hand in his for one brief moment before he turned and walked away.

Quite prosaically I opened the big front door at Knapfs' to find Herr Knapf standing in the hallway with his: "Nabben', Frau Orme."

And there was the sane and soothing scent of Wienerschnitzel and spluttering things in the air. And I ran upstairs to my room and turned on all the lights and looked at the starry-eyed creature in the mirror. Then I took the biggest, newest photograph of Norah from the mantel and looked at her for a long, long minute, while she looked back at me in her brave true way.

"Thank you, dear," I said to her. "Thank you. Would you think me stagey and silly if I were to kiss you, just once, on your beautiful trusting eyes?"

A telephone bell tinkled downstairs and Herr Knapf stationed himself at the foot of the stairs and roared my name.

When I had picked up the receiver: "This is Ernst," said the voice at the other end of the wire. "I have just remembered that I had asked you down-town for supper."

"I would rather thank God fasting," I replied, very softly, and hung the receiver on its hook.

CHAPTER XII. BENNIE THE CONSOLER

In a corner of Frau Nirlanger's bedroom, sheltered from draughts and glaring light, is a little wooden bed, painted blue and ornamented with stout red roses that are faded by time and much abuse. Every evening at eight o'clock three anxious-browed women hold low-spoken conclave about the quaint old bed, while its occupant sleeps and smiles as he sleeps, and clasps to his breast a chewed-looking woolly dog. For a new joy has come to the sad little Frau Nirlanger, and I, quite by accident, was the cause of bringing it to her. The queer little blue bed, with its faded roses, was brought down from the attic by Frau Knapf, for she is one of the three foster mothers of the small occupant of the bed. The occupant of the bed is named Bennie, and a corporation formed for the purpose of bringing him up in the way he should go is composed of: Dawn O'Hara Orme, President and Distracted Guardian; Mrs. Konrad Nirlanger, Cuddler-in-chief and Authority on the Subject of Bennie's Bed-time; Mr. Blackie Griffith, Good Angel, General Cut-up and Monitor off'n Bennie's Neckties and Toys; Dr. Ernst von Gerhard, Chief Medical Adviser, and Sweller of the Exchequer, with the Privilege of Selecting All Candies. Members of the corporation meet with great frequency evenings and Sundays, much to the detriment of a certain Book-in-the-making with which Dawn O'Hara Orme was wont to struggle o' evenings.

Bennie had been one of those little tragedies that find their way into juvenile court. Bennie's story was common enough, but Bennie himself had been different. Ten minutes after his first appearance in the court room everyone, from the big, bald judge to the newest probation officer, had fallen in love with him. Somehow, you wanted to smooth the hair from his forehead, tip his pale little face upward, and very gently kiss his smooth, white brow. Which alone was enough to distinguish Bennie, for Juvenile court children, as a rule, are distinctly not kissable.

Bennie's mother was accused of being unfit to care for her boy, and Bennie was temporarily installed in the Detention Home. There the superintendent and his plump and kindly wife had fallen head over heels in love with him, and had dressed him in a smart little Norfolk suit and a frivolous plaid silk tie. There were delays in the case, and postponement after postponement, so that Bennie appeared in the court room every Tuesday for four weeks. The reporters, and the probation officers and policemen became very chummy with Bennie, and showered him with bright new pennies and certain wonderful candies. Superintendent Arnett of the Detention Home was as proud of the boy as though he were his own. And when Bennie would look shyly and questioningly into his face for permission to accept the proffered offerings, the big superintendent would chuckle delightedly. Bennie had a strangely mobile face for such a baby, and the whitest, smoothest brow I have ever seen.

The comedy and tears and misery and laughter of the big, white-walled court room were too much for Bennie. He would gaze about with puzzled blue eyes; then, giving up the situation as something too vast for his comprehension, he would fall to drawing curly-cues on a bit of paper with a great yellow pencil presented him by one of the newspaper men.

Every Tuesday the rows of benches were packed with a motley crowd of Poles, Russians, Slavs, Italians, Greeks, Lithuanians—a crowd made up of fathers, mothers, sisters, brothers, aunts, uncles, neighbors, friends, and enemies of the boys and girls whose fate was in the hands of the big man seated in the revolving chair up in front. But Bennie's mother was not of this crowd; this pitiful, ludicrous crowd filling the great room with the stifling, rancid odor of the poor. Nor was Bennie. He sat, clear-eyed and unsmiling, in the depths of a great chair on the court side of the railing and gravely received the attentions of the lawyers, and reporters and court room attaches who had grown fond of the grave little figure.

Then, on the fifth Tuesday, Bennie's mother appeared. How she had come to be that child's mother God only knows—or perhaps He had had nothing to do with it. She was terribly sober and frightened. Her face was swollen and bruised, and beneath one eye there was a puffy green-and-blue swelling. Her sordid story was common enough as the probation officer told it. The woman had been living in one wretched room with the boy. Her husband had deserted her. There was no food, and little furniture. The queer feature of it, said the probation officer, was that the woman managed to keep the boy fairly neat and clean, regardless of her own condition, and he generally had food of some sort, although the mother sometimes went without food for days. Through the squalor and misery and degradation of her own life Bennie had somehow been kept unsullied, a thing apart.

"H'm!" said judge Wheeling, and looked at Bennie. Bennie was standing beside his mother. He was very quiet, and his eyes were smiling up into those of the battered creature who was fighting for him. "I guess we'll have to take you out of this," the judge decided, abruptly. "That boy is too good to go to waste."

The sodden, dazed woman before him did not immediately get the full meaning of his words. She still stood there, swaying a bit, and staring unintelligently at the judge. Then, quite suddenly, she realized it. She took a quick step forward. Her hand went up to her breast, to her throat, to her lips, with an odd, stifled gesture.

"You ain't going to take him away! From me! No, you wouldn't do that, would you? Not for—not for always! You wouldn't do that—you wouldn't—"

Judge Wheeling waved her away. But the woman dropped to her knees.

"Judge, give me a chance! I'll stop drinking. Only don't take him away from me! Don't, judge, don't! He's all I've got in the world. Give me a chance. Three months! Six months! A year!"

"Get up!" ordered judge Wheeling, gruffly, "and stop that! It won't do you a bit of good."

And then a wonderful thing happened. The woman rose to her feet. A new and strange dignity had come into her battered face. The lines of suffering and vice were erased as by magic, and she seemed to grow taller, younger, almost beautiful. When she spoke again it was slowly and distinctly, her words quite free from the blur of the barroom and street vernacular.

"I tell you you must give me a chance. You cannot take a child from a mother in this way. I tell you, if you will only help me I can crawl back up the road that I've traveled. I was not always like this. There was another life, before—before—Oh, since then there have been years of blackness, and hunger, and cold and—worse! But I never dragged the boy into it. Look at him!"

Our eyes traveled from the woman's transfigured face to that of the boy. We could trace a wonderful likeness where before we had seen none. But the woman went on in her steady, even tone.

"I can't talk as I should, because my brain isn't clear. It's the drink. When you drink, you forget. But you must help me. I can't do it alone. I can remember how to live straight, just as I can remember how to talk straight. Let me show you that I'm not all bad. Give me a chance. Take the boy and then give him back to me when you are satisfied. I'll try—God only knows how I'll try. Only don't take him away forever, Judge! Don't do that!"

Judge Wheeling ran an uncomfortable finger around his collar's edge.

"Any friends living here?"

"No! No!"

"Sure about that?"

"Quite sure."

"Now see here; I'm going to give you your chance. I shall take this boy away from you for a year. In that time you will stop drinking and become a decent, self-supporting woman. You will be given in charge of one of these probation officers. She will find work for you, and a good home, and she'll stand by you, and you must report to her. If she is satisfied with you at the end of the year, the boy goes back to you."

"She will be satisfied," the woman said, simply. She stooped and taking Bennie's face between her hands kissed him once. Then she stepped aside and stood quite still, looking after the little figure that passed out of the court room with his hand in that of a big, kindly police officer. She looked until the big door had opened and closed upon them.

Then—well, it was just another newspaper story. It made a good one. That evening I told Frau Nirlanger about it, and she wept, softly, and murmured: "Ach, das arme baby! Like my little Oscar he is, without a mother." I told Ernst about him too, and Blackie, because I could not get his grave little face out of my mind. I wondered if those who had charge of him now would take the time to bathe the little body, and brush the soft hair until it shone, and tie the gay plaid silk tie as lovingly as "Daddy" Arnett of the Detention Home had done.

Then it was that I, quite unwittingly, stepped into Bennie's life.

There was an anniversary, or a change in the board of directors, or a new coat of paint or something of the kind in one of the orphan homes, and the story fell to me. I found the orphan home to be typical of its kind—a big, dreary, prison-like structure. The woman at the door did not in the least care to let me in. She was a fish-mouthed woman with a hard eye, and as I told my errand her mouth grew fishier and the eye harder. Finally she led me down a long, dark, airless stretch of corridor and departed in search of the matron, leaving me seated in the unfriendly reception room, with its straight-backed chairs placed stonily against the walls, beneath rows of red and blue and yellow religious pictures.

Just as I was wondering why it seemed impossible to be holy and cheerful at the same time, there came a pad-padding down the corridor. The next moment the matron stood in the doorway. She was a mountainous, red-faced woman, with warts on her nose.

"Good-afternoon," I said, sweetly. ("Ugh! What a brute!") I thought. Then I began to explain my errand once more. Criticism of the Home? No indeed, I assured her. At last, convinced of my disinterestedness she reluctantly guided me about the big, gloomy building. There were endless flights of shiny stairs, and endless stuffy, airless rooms, until we came to a door which she flung open, disclosing the nursery. It seemed to me that there were a hundred babies—babies at every stage of development, of all sizes, and ages and types. They glanced up at the opening of the door, and then a dreadful thing happened.

Every child that was able to walk or creep scuttled into the farthest corners and remained quite, quite still with a wide-eyed expression of fear and apprehension on every face.

For a moment my heart stood still. I turned to look at the woman by my side. Her thin lips were compressed into a straight, hard line. She said a word to a nurse standing near, and began to walk about, eying the children sharply. She put out a hand to pat the head of one red-haired mite in a soiled pinafore; but before her hand could descend I saw the child dodge and the tiny hand flew up to the head, as though in defense.

"They are afraid of her!" my sick heart told me. "Those babies are afraid of her! What does she do to them? I can't stand this. I'm going."

I mumbled a hurried "Thank you," to the fat matron as I turned to leave the big, bare room. At the head of the stairs there was a great, black door. I stopped before it—God knows why!—and pointed toward it.

"What is in that room?" I asked. Since then I have wondered many times at the unseen power that prompted me to put the question.

The stout matron bustled on, rattling her keys as she walked.

"That—oh, that's where we keep the incorrigibles."

"May I see them?" I asked, again prompted by that inner voice.

"There is only one." She grudgingly unlocked the door, using one of the great keys that swung from her waist. The heavy, black door swung open. I stepped into the bare room, lighted dimly by one small window. In the farthest corner crouched something that stirred and glanced up at our entrance. It peered at us with an ugly look of terror and defiance, and I stared back at it, in the dim light. During one dreadful, breathless second I remained staring, while my heart stood still. Then—"Bennie!" I cried. And stumbled toward him. "Bennie—boy!"

The little unkempt figure, in its soiled knickerbocker suit, the sunny hair all uncared for, the gay plaid tie draggled and limp, rushed into my arms with a crazy, inarticulate cry.

Down on my knees on the bare floor I held him close—close! and his arms were about my neck as though they never should unclasp.

"Take me away! Take me away!" His wet cheek was pressed against my own streaming one. "I want my mother! I want Daddy Arnett! Take me away!"

I wiped his cheeks with my notebook or something, picked him up in my arms, and started for the door. I had quite forgotten the fat matron.

"What are you doing?" she asked, blocking the doorway with her huge bulk.

"I'm going to take him back with me. Please let me! I'll take care of him until the year is up. He shan't bother you any more."

"That is impossible," she said, coldly. "He has been sent here by the court, for a year, and he must stay here. Besides, he is a stubborn, uncontrollable child."

"Uncontrollable! He's nothing of the kind! Why don't you treat him as a child should be treated, instead of like a little animal? You don't know him! Why, he's the most lovable—I And he's only a baby! Can't you see that? A baby!"

She only stared her dislike, her little pig eyes grown smaller and more glittering.

"You great—big—thing!" I shrieked at her, like an infuriated child. With the tears streaming down my cheeks I unclasped Bennie's cold hands from about my neck. He clung to me, frantically, until I had to push him away and run.

The woman swung the door shut, and locked it. But for all its thickness I could hear Bennie's helpless fists pounding on its panels as I stumbled down the stairs, and Bennie's voice came faintly to my ears, muffled by the heavy door, as he shrieked to me to take him away to his mother, and to Daddy Arnett.

I blubbered all the way back in the car, until everyone stared, but I didn't care. When I reached the office I made straight for Blackie's smoke-filled sanctum. When my tale was ended he let me cry all over his desk, with my head buried in a heap of galley-proofs and my tears watering his paste-pot. He sat calmly by, smoking. Finally he began gently to philosophize. "Now girl, he's prob'ly better off there than he ever was at home with his mother soused all the time. Maybe he give that warty matron friend of yours all kinds of trouble, yellin' for his ma."

I raised my head from the desk. "Oh, you can talk! You didn't see him. What do you care! But if you could have seen him, crouched there—alone—like a little animal! He was so sweet—and lovable—and—and—he hadn't been decently washed for weeks—and his arms clung to me—I can feel his hands about my neck!—"

I buried my head in the papers again. Blackie went on smoking. There was no sound in the little room except the purr-purring of Blackie's pipe. Then:

"I done a favor for Wheeling once," mused he.

I glanced up, quickly. "Oh, Blackie, do you think—"

"No, I don't. But then again, you can't never tell. That was four or five years ago, and the mem'ry of past favors grows dim fast. Still, if you're through waterin' the top of my desk, why I'd like t' set down and do a little real brisk talkin' over the phone. You're excused."

Quite humbly I crept away, with hope in my heart.

To this day I do not know what secret string the resourceful Blackie pulled. But the next afternoon I found a hastily scrawled note tucked into the roll of my typewriter. It sent me scuttling across the hall to the sporting editor's smoke-filled room. And there on a chair beside the desk, surrounded by scrap-books, lead pencils, paste-pot and odds and ends of newspaper office paraphernalia, sat Bennie. His hair was parted very smoothly on one side, and under his dimpled chin bristled a very new and extremely lively green-and-red plaid silk tie.

The next instant I had swept aside papers, brushes, pencils, books, and Bennie was gathered close in my arms. Blackie, with a strange glow in his deep-set black eyes regarded us with an assumed disgust.

"Wimmin is all alike. Ain't it th' truth? I used t' think you was different. But shucks! It ain't so. Got t' turn on the weeps the minute you're tickled or mad. Why say, I ain't goin' t' have you comin' in here an' dampenin' up the whole place every little while! It's unhealthy for me, sittin' here in the wet."

"Oh, shut up, Blackie," I said, happily. "How in the world did you do it?"

"Never you mind. The question is, what you goin' t' do with him, now you've got him? Goin' t' have a French bunny for him, or fetch him up by hand? Wheeling appointed a probation skirt to look after the crowd of us, and we got t' toe the mark."

"Glory be!" I ejaculated. "I don't know what I shall do with him. I shall have to bring him down with me every morning, and perhaps you can make a sporting editor out of him."

"Nix. Not with that forehead. He's a high-brow. We'll make him dramatic critic. In the meantime, I'll be little fairy godmother, an' if you'll get on your bonnet I'll stake you and the young 'un to strawberry shortcake an' chocolate ice cream."

So it happened that a wondering Frau Knapf and a sympathetic Frau Nirlanger were called in for consultation an hour later. Bennie was ensconced in my room, very wide-eyed and wondering, but quite content. With the entrance of Frau Nirlanger the consultation was somewhat disturbed. She made a quick rush at him and gathered him in her hungry arms.

"Du baby du!" she cried. "Du Kleiner! And she was down on her knees, and somehow her figure had melted into delicious mother-curves, with Bennie's head just fitting into that most gracious one between her shoulder and breast. She cooed to him in a babble of French and German and English, calling him her lee-tel Oscar. Bennie seemed miraculously to understand. Perhaps he was becoming accustomed to having strange ladies snatch him to their breasts.

"So," said Frau Nirlanger, looking up at us. "Is he not sweet? He shall be my lee-tel boy, nicht? For one small year he shall be my own boy. Ach, I am but lonely all the long day here in this strange land. You will let me care for him, nicht? And Konrad, he will be very angry, but that shall make no bit of difference. Eh, Oscar?"

And so the thing was settled, and an hour later three anxious-browed women were debating the weighty question of eggs or bread-and-milk for Bennie's supper. Frau Nirlanger was for soft-boiled eggs as being none too heavy after orphan asylum fare; I was for bread-and-milk, that being the prescribed supper dish for all the orphans and waifs that I had ever read about, from "The Wide, Wide World" to "Helen's Babies," and back again. Frau Knapf was for both eggs and bread-and-milk with a dash of meat and potatoes thrown in for good measure, and a slice or so of Kuchen on the side. We compromised on one egg, one glass of milk, and a slice of lavishly buttered bread, and jelly. It was a clean, sweet, sleepy-eyed Bennie that we tucked between the sheets. We three women stood looking down at him as he lay there in the quaint old blue-painted bed that had once held the plump little Knapfs.

"You think anyway he had enough supper? mused the anxious-browed Frau Knapf.

"To school he will have to go, yes?" murmured Frau Nirlanger, regretfully.

I tucked in the covers at one side of the bed, not that they needed tucking, but because it was such a comfortable, satisfying thing to do.

"Just at this minute," I said, as I tucked, "I'd rather be a newspaper reporter than anything else in the world. As a profession 'tis so broadenin', an' at the same time, so chancey."

CHAPTER XIII. THE TEST

Some day the marriageable age for women will be advanced from twenty to thirty, and the old maid line will be changed from thirty to forty. When that time comes there will be surprisingly few divorces. The husband of whom we dream at twenty is not at all the type of man who attracts us at thirty. The man I married at twenty was a brilliant, morbid, handsome, abnormal creature with magnificent eyes and very white teeth and no particular appetite at mealtime. The man whom I could care for at thirty would be the normal, safe and substantial sort who would come in at six o'clock, kiss me once, sniff the air twice and say: "Mm! What's that smells so good, old girl? I'm as hungry as a bear. Trot it out. Where are the kids?"

These are dangerous things to think upon. So dangerous and disturbing to the peace of mind that I have decided not to see Ernst von Gerhard for a week or two. I find that seeing him is apt to make me forget Peter Orme; to forget that my duty begins with a capital D; to forget that I am dangerously near the thirty year old mark; to forget Norah, and Max, and the Spalpeens, and the world, and everything but the happiness of being near him, watching his eyes say one thing while his lips say another.

At such times I am apt to work myself up into rather a savage frame of mind, and to shut myself in my room evenings, paying no heed to Frau Nirlanger's timid knocking, or Bennie's good-night message. I uncover my typewriter and set to work at the thing which may or may not be a book, and am extremely wretched and gloomy and pessimistic, after this fashion:

"He probably wouldn't care anything about you if you were free. It is just a case of the fruit that is out of reach being the most desirable. Men don't marry frumpy, snuffy old things of thirty, or thereabouts. Men aren't marrying now-a-days, anyway. Certainly not for love. They marry for position, or power, or money, when they do marry. Think of all the glorious creatures he meets every day—women whose hair, and finger-nails and teeth and skin are a religion; women whose clothes are a fine art; women who are free to care only for themselves; to rest, to enjoy, to hear delightful music, and read charming books, and eat delicious food. He doesn't really care about you, with your rumpled blouses, and your shabby gloves and shoes, and your somewhat doubtful linen collars. The last time you saw him you were just coming home from the office after a dickens of a day, and there was a smudge on the end of your nose, and he told you of it, laughing. But you didn't laugh. You rubbed it off, furiously, and you wanted to cry. Cry! You, Dawn O'Hara! Begorra! 'Tis losin' your sense av humor you're after doin'! Get to work."

After which I would fall upon the book in a furious, futile fashion, writing many incoherent, irrelevant paragraphs which I knew would be cast aside as worthless on the sane and reasoning to-morrow.

Oh, it had been easy enough to talk of love in a lofty, superior impersonal way that New Year's day. Just the luxury of speaking of it at all, after those weeks of repression, sufficed. But it is not so easy to be impersonal and lofty when the touch of a coat sleeve against your arm sends little prickling, tingling shivers racing madly through thousands of too taut nerves. It is not so easy to force the mind and tongue into safe, sane channels when they are forever threatening to rush together in an overwhelming torrent that will carry misery and destruction in its wake. Invariably we talk with feverish earnestness about the book; about my work at the office; about Ernst's profession, with its wonderful growth; about Norah, and Max and the Spalpeens, and the home; about the latest news; about the weather; about Peter Orme—and then silence.

At our last meeting things took a new and startling turn. So startling, so full of temptation and happiness-that-must-not-be, that I resolved to forbid myself the pain and joy of being, near him until I could be quite sure that my grip on Dawn O'Hara was firm, unshakable and lasting.

Von Gerhard sports a motor-car, a rakish little craft, built long and low, with racing lines, and a green complexion, and a nose that cuts through the air like the prow of a swift boat through water. Von Gerhard had promised me a spin in it on the first mild day. Sunday turned out to be unexpectedly lamblike, as only a March day can be, with real sunshine that warmed the end of one's nose instead of laughing as it tweaked it, as the lying February sunshine had done.

"But warmly you must dress yourself," Von Gerhard warned me, "with no gauzy blouses or sleeveless gowns. The air cuts like a knife, but it feels good against the face. And a little road-house I know, where one is served great steaming plates of hot oyster stew. How will that be for a lark, yes?"

And so I had swathed myself in wrappings until I could scarcely clamber into the panting little car, and we had darted off along the smooth lake drives, while the wind whipped the scarlet into our cheeks, even while it brought the tears to our eyes. There was no chance for conversation, even if Von Gerhard had been in talkative mood, which he was not. He seemed more taciturn than usual, seated there at the wheel, looking straight ahead at the ribbon of road, his eyes narrowed down to mere keen blue slits. I realized, without alarm, that he was driving furiously and lawlessly, and I did not care. Von Gerhard was that sort of man. One could sit quite calmly beside him while he pulled at the reins of a pair of runaway horses, knowing that he would conquer them in the end.

Just when my face began to feel as stiff and glazed as a mummy's, we swung off the roadway and up to the entrance of the road-house that was to revive us with things hot and soupy.

"Another minute," I said, through stiff lips, as I extricated myself from my swathings, "and I should have been what Mr. Mantalini described as a demnition body. For pity's sake, tell 'em the soup can't be too hot nor too steaming for your lady friend. I've had enough fresh air to last me the remainder of my life. May I timidly venture to suggest that a cheese sandwich follow the oyster stew? I am famished, and this place looks as though it might make a speciality of cheese sandwiches."

"By all means a cheese sandwich. Und was noch? That fresh air it has given you an appetite, nicht wahr?" But there was no sign of a smile on his face, nor was the kindly twinkle of amusement to be seen in his eyes—that twinkle that I had learned to look for.

"Smile for the lady," I mockingly begged when we had been served. "You've been owlish all the afternoon. Here, try a cheese sandwich. Now, why do you suppose that this mustard tastes so much better than the kind one gets at home?"

Von Gerhard had been smoking a cigarette, the first that I had ever seen in his fingers. Now he tossed it into the fireplace that yawned black and empty at one side of the room. He swept aside the plates and glasses that stood before him, leaned his arms on the table and deliberately stared at me.

"I sail for Europe in June, to be gone a year—probably more," he said.

"Sail!" I echoed, idiotically; and began blindly to dab clots of mustard on that ridiculous sandwich.

"I go to study and work with Gluck. It is the opportunity of a lifetime. Gluck is to the world of medicine what Edison is to the world of electricity. He is a wizard, a man inspired. You should see him—a little, bent, grizzled, shabby old man who looks at you, and sees you not. It is a wonderful opportunity, a—"

The mustard and the sandwich and the table and Von Gerhard's face were very indistinct and uncertain to my eyes, but I managed to say: "So glad—congratulate you—very happy—no doubt fortunate—"

Two strong hands grasped my wrists. "Drop that absurd mustard spoon and sandwich. Na, I did not mean to frighten you, Dawn. How your hands tremble. So, look at me. You would like Vienna, Kindchen. You would like the gayety, and the brightness of it, and the music, and the pretty women, and the incomparable gowns. Your sense of humor would discern the hollowness beneath all the pomp and ceremony and rigid lines of caste, and military glory; and your writer's instinct would revel in the splendor, and color and romance and intrigue."

I shrugged my shoulders in assumed indifference. "Can't you convey all this to me without grasping my wrists like a villain in a melodrama? Besides, it isn't very generous or thoughtful of you to tell me all this, knowing that it is not for me. Vienna for you, and Milwaukee and cheese sandwiches for me. Please pass the mustard."

But the hold on my wrists grew firmer. Von Gerhard's eyes were steady as they gazed into mine. "Dawn, Vienna, and the whole world is waiting for you, if you will but take it. Vienna—and happiness—with me—"

I wrenched my wrists free with a dreadful effort and rose, sick, bewildered, stunned. My world—my refuge of truth, and honor, and safety and sanity that had lain in Ernst von Gerhard's great, steady hands, was slipping away from me. I think the horror that I felt within must have leaped to my eyes, for in an instant Von Gerhard was beside me, steadying me with his clear blue eyes. He did not touch the tips of my fingers as he stood there very near me. From the look of pain on his face I knew that I had misunderstood, somehow.

"Kleine, I see that you know me not," he said, in German, and the saying it was as tender as is a mother when she reproves a child that she loves. "This fight against the world, those years of unhappiness and misery, they have made you suspicious and lacking in trust, is it not so? You do not yet know the perfect love that casts out all doubt.

Dawn, I ask you in the name of all that is reasoning, and for the sake of your happiness and mine, to divorce this man Peter Orme—this man who for almost ten years has not been your husband—who never can be your husband. I ask you to do something which will bring suffering to no one, and which will mean happiness to many. Let me make you happy—you were born to be happy—you who can laugh like a girl in spite of your woman's sorrows—"

But I sank into a chair and hid my face in my hands so that I might be spared the beauty and the tenderness of his eyes. I tried to think of all the sane and commonplace things in life. Somewhere in my inner consciousness a cool little voice was saying, over and over again:

"Now, Dawn, careful! You've come to the crossroads at last. Right or left? Choose! Now, Dawn, careful!" and the rest of it all over again.

When I lifted my face from my hands at last it was to meet the tenderness of Von Gerhard's gaze with scarcely a tremor.

"You ought to know," I said, very slowly and evenly, "that a divorce, under these circumstances, is almost impossible, even if I wished to do what you suggest. There are certain state laws—"

An exclamation of impatience broke from him. "Laws! In some states, yes. In others, no. It is a mere technicality—a trifle! There is about it a bit of that which you call red tape. It amounts to nothing—to that!" He snapped his fingers. "A few months' residence in another state, perhaps. These American laws, they are made to break."

"Yes; you are quite right," I said, and I knew in my heart that the cool, insistent little voice within had not spoken in vain. "But there are other laws—laws of honor and decency, and right living and conscience—that cannot be broken with such ease. I cannot marry you. I have a husband."

"You can call that unfortunate wretch your husband! He does not know that he has a wife. He will not know that he has lost a wife. Come, Dawn—small one—be not so foolish. You do not know how happy I will make you. You have never seen me except when I was tortured with doubts and fears. You do not know what our life will be together. There shall be everything to make you forget—everything that thought and love and money can give you. The man there in the barred room—"

At that I took his dear hands in mine and held them close as I miserably tried to make him hear what that small, still voice had told me.

"There! That is it! If he were free, if he were able to stand before men that his actions might be judged fairly and justly, I should not hesitate for one single, precious moment. If he could fight for his rights, or relinquish them, as he saw fit, then this thing would not be so monstrous. But, Ernst, can't you see? He is there, alone, in that dreadful place, quite helpless, quite incapable, quite at our mercy. I should as soon think of hurting a little child, or snatching the pennies from a blind man's cup. The thing is inhuman! It is monstrous! No state laws, no red tape can dissolve such a union."

"You still care for him!"

"Ernst!"

His face was very white with the pallor of repressed emotion, and his eyes were like the blue flame that one sees flashing above a bed of white-hot coals.

"You do care for him still. But yes! You can stand there, quite cool—but quite—and tell me that you would not hurt him, not for your happiness, not for mine. But me you can hurt again and again, without one twinge of regret."

There was silence for a moment in the little bare dining-room—a miserable silence on my part, a bitter one for Ernst. Then Von Gerhard seated himself again at the table opposite and smiled one of the rare smiles that illumined his face with such sweetness.

"Come, Dawn, almost we are quarreling—we who were to have been so matter-of-fact and sensible. Let us make an end of this question. You will think of what I have said, will you not? Perhaps I was too abrupt, too brutal. Ach, Dawn, you know not how I—Very well, I will not."

With both hands I was clinging to my courage and praying for strength to endure this until I should be alone in my room again.

"As for that poor creature who is bereft of reason, he shall lack no care, no attention. The burden you have borne so long I shall take now upon my shoulders."

He seemed so confident, so sure. I could bear it no longer. "Ernst, if you have any pity, any love for me, stop! I tell you I can never do this. Why do you make it so terribly hard for me! So pitilessly hard! You always have been so strong, so sure, such a staff of courage."

"I say again, and again, and again, you do not care."

It was then that I took my last vestige of strength and courage together and going over to him, put my two hands on his great shoulders, looking up into his drawn face as I spoke.

"Ernst, look at me! You never can know how much I care. I care so much that I could not bear to have the shadow of wrong fall upon our happiness. There can be no lasting happiness upon a foundation of shameful deceit. I should hate myself, and you would grow to hate me. It always is so. Dear one, I care so much that I have the strength to do as I would do if I had to face my mother, and Norah tonight. I don't ask you to understand. Men are not made to understand these things; not even a man such as you, who are so beautifully understanding. I only ask that you believe in me—and think of me sometimes—I shall feel it, and be helped. Will you take me home now, Dr. von Gerhard?"

The ride home was made in silence. The wind was colder, sharper. I was chilled, miserable, sick. Von Gerhard's face was quite expressionless as he guided the little car over the smooth road. When we had stopped before my door, still without a word, I thought that he was going to leave me with that barrier of silence unbroken. But as I stepped stiffly to the curbing his hands closed about mine with the old steady grip. I looked up quickly, to find a smile in the corners of the tired eyes.

"You—you will let me see you—sometimes?"

But wisdom came to my aid. "Not now. It is better that we go our separate ways for a few weeks, until our work has served to adjust the balance that has been disturbed. At the end of that time I shall write you, and from that time until you sail in June we shall be just good comrades again. And once in Vienna—who knows?—you may meet the plump blond Fraulein, of excellent family—"

"And no particular imagination—"

And then we both laughed, a bit hysterically, because laughter is, after all, akin to tears. And the little green car shot off with a whir as I turned to enter my new world of loneliness.

CHAPTER XIV. BENNIE AND THE CHARMING OLD MAID

There followed a blessed week of work—a "human warious" week, with something piquant lurking at every turn. A week so busy, so kaleidoscopic in its quick succession of events that my own troubles and grievances were pushed into a neglected corner of my mind and made to languish there, unfed by tears or sighs.

News comes in cycles. There are weeks when a city editor tears his hair in vain as he bellows for a first-page story. There follow days so bristling with real, live copy that perfectly good stuff which, in the ordinary course of events might be used to grace the front sheet, is sandwiched away between the marine intelligence and the Elgin butter reports.

Such a week was this. I interviewed everything from a red-handed murderer to an incubator baby. The town seemed to be running over with celebrities. Norberg, the city editor, adores celebrities. He never allows one to escape uninterviewed. On Friday there fell to my lot a world-famous prima donna, an infamous prize-fighter, and a charming old maid. Norberg cared not whether the celebrity in question was noted for a magnificent high C, or a left half-scissors hook, so long as the interview was dished up hot and juicy, with plenty of quotation marks, a liberal sprinkling of adjectives and adverbs, and a cut of the victim gracing the top of the column.

It was long past the lunch hour when the prima donna and the prize-fighter, properly embellished, were snapped on the copy hook. The prima donna had chattered in French; the prize-fighter had jabbered in slang; but the charming old maid, who spoke Milwaukee English, was to make better copy than a whole chorus of prima donnas, or a ring full of fighters. Copy! It was such wonderful stuff that I couldn't use it.

It was with the charming old maid in mind that Norberg summoned me.

"Another special story for you," he cheerfully announced.

No answering cheer appeared upon my lunchless features. "A prize-fighter at ten-thirty, and a prima donna at twelve. What's the next choice morsel? An aeronaut with another successful airship? or a cash girl who has inherited a million?"

Norberg's plump cheeks dimpled. "Neither. This time it is a nice German old maid."

"Eloped with the coachman, no doubt?"

"I said a nice old maid. And she hasn't done anything yet. You are to find out how she'll feel when she does it."

"Charmingly lucid," commented I, made savage by the pangs of hunger.

Norberg proceeded to outline the story with characteristic vigor, a cigarette waggling from the corner of his mouth.

"Name and address on this slip. Take a Greenfield car. Nice old maid has lived in nice old cottage all her life. Grandfather built it himself about a hundred years ago. Whole family was born in it, and married in it, and died in it, see? It's crammed full of spinning-wheels and mahogany and stuff that'll make your eyes stick out. See? Well, there's no one left now but the nice old maid, all alone. She had a sister who ran away with a scamp some years ago. Nice old maid has never heard of her since, but she leaves the gate ajar or the latch-string open, or a lamp in the window, or something, so that if ever she wanders back to the old home she'll know she's welcome, see?"

"Sounds like a moving picture play," I remarked.

"Wait a minute. Here's the point. The city wants to build a branch library or something on her property, and the nice old party is so pinched for money that she'll have to take their offer. So the time has come when she'll have to leave that old cottage, with its romance, and its memories, and its lamp in the window, and go to live in a cheap little flat, see? Where the old four-poster will choke up the bedroom—"

"And the parlor will be done in red and green," I put in, eagerly, "and where there will be an ingrowing sideboard in the dining-room that won't fit in with the quaint old dinner-set at all, and a kitchenette just off that, in which the great iron pots and kettles that used to hold the family dinners will be monstrously out of place—"

"You're on," said Norberg.

Half an hour later I stood before the cottage, set primly in the center of a great lot that extended for half a square on all sides. A winter-sodden, bare enough sight it was in the gray of that March day. But it was not long before Alma Pflugel, standing in the midst of it, the March winds flapping her neat skirts about her ankles, filled it with a blaze of color. As she talked, a row of stately hollyhocks, pink, and scarlet, and saffron, reared their heads against the cottage sides. The chill March air became sweet with the scent of heliotrope, and Sweet William, and pansies, and bridal wreath. The naked twigs of the rose bushes flowered into wondrous bloom so that they bent to the ground with their weight of crimson and yellow glory. The bare brick paths were overrun with the green of growing things. Gray mounds of dirt grew vivid with the fire of poppies. Even the rain-soaked wood of the pea-frames miraculously was hidden in a hedge of green, over which ran riot the butterfly beauty of the lavender, and pink, and cerise blossoms. Oh, she did marvelous things that dull March day, did plain German Alma Pflugel! And still more marvelous were the things that were to come.

But of these things we knew nothing as the door was opened and Alma Pflugel and I gazed curiously at one another. Surprise was writ large on her honest face as I disclosed my errand. It was plain that the ways of newspaper reporters were foreign to the life of this plain German woman, but she bade me enter with a sweet graciousness of manner.

Wondering, but silent, she led the way down the dim narrow hallway to the sitting-room beyond. And there I saw that Norberg had known whereof he spoke.

A stout, red-faced stove glowed cheerfully in one corner of the room. Back of the stove a sleepy cat opened one indolent eye, yawned shamelessly, and rose to investigate, as is the way of cats. The windows were aglow with the sturdy potted plants that flower-loving German women coax into bloom. The low-ceilinged room twinkled and shone as the polished surfaces of tables and chairs reflected the rosy glow from the plethoric stove. I sank into the depths of a huge rocker that must have been built for Grosspapa Pflugel's generous curves. Alma Pflugel, in a chair opposite, politely waited for this new process of interviewing to begin, but relaxed in the embrace of that great armchair I suddenly realized that I was very tired and hungry, and talk-weary, and that here; was a great peace. The prima donna, with her French, and her paint, and her pearls, and the prizefighter with his slang, and his cauliflower ear, and his diamonds, seemed creatures of another planet. My eyes closed. A delicious sensation of warmth and drowsy contentment stole over me.

"Do listen to the purring of that cat!" I murmured. "Oh, newspapers have no place in this. This is peace and rest."

Alma Pflugel leaned forward in her chair. "You—you like it?"

"Like it! This is home. I feel as though my mother were here in this room, seated in one of those deep chairs, with a bit of sewing in her hand; so near that I could touch her cheek with my fingers."

Alma Pflugel rose from her chair and came over to me. She timidly placed her hand on my arm. "Ah, I am so glad you are like that. You do not laugh at the low ceilings, and the sunken floors, and the old-fashioned rooms. You do not raise your eyes in horror and say: 'No conveniences! And why don't you try striped wall paper? It would make those dreadful ceilings seem higher.' How nice you are to understand like that!"

My hand crept over to cover her own that lay on my arm. "Indeed, indeed I do understand," I whispered. Which, as the veriest cub reporter can testify, is no way to begin an interview.

A hundred happy memories filled the little low room as Alma Pflugel showed me her treasures. The cat purred in great content, and the stove cast a rosy glow over the scene as the simple woman told the story of each precious relic, from the battered candle-dipper on the shelf, to the great mahogany folding table, and sewing stand, and carved bed. Then there was the old horn lantern that Jacob Pflugel had used a century before, and in one corner of the sitting-room stood Grossmutter Pflugel's spinning-wheel. Behind cupboard doors were ranged the carefully preserved blue-and-white china dishes, and on the shelf below stood the clumsy earthen set that Grosspapa Pflugel himself had modeled for his young bride in those days of long ago. In the linen chest there still lay, in neat, fragrant folds, piles of the linen that had been spun on that time-yellowed spinning-wheel. And because of the tragedy in the honest face bent over these dear treasures, and because she tried so bravely to hide her tears, I knew in my heart that this could never be a newspaper story.

"So," said Alma Pflugel at last, and rose and walked slowly to the window and stood looking out at the wind-swept garden. That window, with its many tiny panes, once had looked out across a wilderness, with an Indian camp not far away. Grossmutter Pflugel had sat at that window many a bitter winter night, with her baby in her arms, watching and waiting for the young husband who was urging his ox-team across the ice of Lake Michigan in the teeth of a raging blizzard.

The little, low-ceilinged room was very still. I looked at Alma Pflugel standing there at the window in her neat blue gown, and something about the face and figure—or was it the pose of the sorrowful head?—seemed strangely familiar. Somewhere in my mind the resemblance haunted me. Resemblance to—what? Whom?

"Would you like to see my garden?" asked Alma Pflugel, turning from the window. For a moment I stared in wonderment. But the honest, kindly face was unsmiling. "These things that I have shown you, I can take with me when I—go. But there," and she pointed out over the bare, wind-swept lot, "there is something that I cannot take. My flowers! You see that mound over there, covered so snug and warm with burlap and sacking? There my tulips and hyacinths sleep. In a few weeks, when the covering is whisked off—ah, you shall see! Then one can be quite sure that the spring is here. Who can look at a great bed of red and pink and lavender and yellow tulips and hyacinths, and doubt it? Come."

With a quick gesture she threw a shawl over her head, and beckoned me. Together we stepped out into the chill of the raw March afternoon. She stood a moment, silent, gazing over the sodden earth. Then she flitted swiftly down the narrow path, and halted before a queer little structure of brick, covered with the skeleton of a creeping vine. Stooping, Alma Pflugel pulled open the rusty iron door and smiled up at me.

"This was my grandmother's oven. All her bread she baked in this little brick stove. Black bread it was, with a great thick crust, and a bitter taste. But it was sweet, too. I have never tasted any so good. I like to think of Grossmutter, when she was a bride, baking her first batch of bread in this oven that Grossvater built for her. And because the old oven was so very difficult to manage, and because she was such a young thing—only sixteen!—I like to think that her first loaves were perhaps not so successful, and that Grosspapa joked about them, and that the little bride wept, so that the young husband had to kiss away the tears."

She shut the rusty, sagging door very slowly and gently. "No doubt the workmen who will come to prepare the ground for the new library will laugh and joke among themselves when they see the oven, and they will kick it with their heels, and wonder what the old brick mound could have been."

There was a little twisted smile on her face as she rose—a smile that brought a hot mist of tears to my eyes. There was tragedy itself in that spare, homely figure standing there in the garden, the wind twining her skirts about her.

"You should but see the children peering over the fence to see my flowers in the summer," she said. The blue eyes wore a wistful, far-away look. "All the children know my garden. It blooms from April to October. There I have my sweet peas; and here my roses—thousands of them! Some are as red as a drop of blood, and some as white as a bridal wreath. When they are blossoming it makes the heart ache, it is so beautiful."

She had quite forgotten me now. For her the garden was all abloom once more. It was as though the Spirit of the Flowers had touched the naked twigs with fairy fingers, waking them into glowing life for her who never again was to shower her love and care upon them.

"These are my poppies. Did you ever come out in the morning to find a hundred poppy faces smiling at you, and swaying and glistening and rippling in the breeze? There they are, scarlet and pink, side by side as only God can place them. And near the poppies I planted my pansies, because each is a lesson to the other. I call my pansies little children with happy faces. See how this great purple one winks his yellow eye, and laughs!"

Her gray shawl had slipped back from her face and lay about her shoulders, and the wind had tossed her hair into a soft fluff about her head.

"We used to come out here in the early morning, my little Schwester and I, to see which rose had unfolded its petals overnight, or whether this great peony that had held its white head so high only yesterday, was humbled to the ground in a heap of ragged leaves. Oh, in the morning she loved it best. And so every summer I have made the garden bloom again, so that when she comes back she will see flowers greet her.

"All the way up the path to the door she will walk in an aisle of fragrance, and when she turns the handle of the old door she will find it unlocked, summer and winter, day and night, so that she has only to turn the knob and enter."

She stopped, abruptly. The light died out of her face. She glanced at me, half defiantly, half timidly, as one who is not quite sure of what she has said. At that I went over to her, and took her work-worn hands in mine, and smiled down into the faded blue eyes grown dim with tears and watching.

"Perhaps—who knows?—the little sister may come yet. I feel it. She will walk up the little path, and try the handle of the door, and it will turn beneath her fingers, and she will enter."

With my arm about her we walked down the path toward the old-fashioned arbor, bare now except for the tendrils that twined about the lattice. The arbor was fitted with a wooden floor, and there were rustic chairs, and a table. I could picture the sisters sitting there with their sewing during the long, peaceful summer afternoons. Alma Pflugel would be wearing one of her neat gingham gowns, very starched and stiff, with perhaps a snowy apron edged with a border of heavy crochet done by the wrinkled fingers of Grossmutter Pflugel. On the rustic table there would be a bowl of flowers, and a pot of delicious Kaffee, and a plate of German Kaffeekuchen, and through the leafy doorway the scent of the wonderful garden would come stealing.

I thought of the cheap little flat, with the ugly sideboard, and the bit of weedy yard in the rear, and the alley beyond that, and the red and green wall paper in the parlor. The next moment, to my horror, Alma Pflugel had dropped to her knees before the table in the damp little arbor, her face in her hands, her spare shoulders shaking.

"Ich kann's nicht thun!" she moaned. "Ich kann nicht! Ach, kleine Schwester, wo bist du denn! Nachts und Morgens bete ich, aber doch kommst du nicht."

A great dry sob shook her. Her hand went to her breast, to her throat, to her lips, with an odd, stifled gesture.

"Do that again!" I cried, and shook Alma Pflugel sharply by the shoulder. "Do that again!"

Her startled blue eyes looked into mine. "What do you mean?" she asked.

"That—that gesture. I've seen it—somewhere—that trick of pressing the hand to the breast, to the throat, to the lips—Oh!"

Suddenly I knew. I lifted the drooping head and rumpled its neat braids, and laughed down into the startled face.

"She's here!" I shouted, and started a dance of triumph on the shaky floor of the old arbor. "I know her. From the moment I saw you the resemblance haunted me." And then as Alma Pflugel continued to stare, while the stunned bewilderment grew in her eyes, "Why, I have one-fourth interest in your own nephew this very minute. And his name is Bennie!"

Whereupon Alma Pflugel fainted quietly away in the chilly little grape arbor, with her head on my shoulder.

I called myself savage names as I chafed her hands and did all the foolish, futile things that distracted humans think of at such times, wondering, meanwhile, if I had been quite mad to discern a resemblance between this simple, clear-eyed gentle German woman, and the battered, ragged, swaying figure that had stood at the judge's bench.

Suddenly Alma Pflugel opened her eyes. Recognition dawned in them slowly. Then, with a jerk, she sat upright, her trembling hands clinging to me.

"Where is she? Take me to her. Ach, you are sure—sure?"

"Lordy, I hope so! Come, you must let me help you into the house. And where is the nearest telephone? Never mind; I'll find one."

When I had succeeded in finding the nearest drug store I spent a wild ten minutes telephoning the surprised little probation officer, then Frau Nirlanger, and finally Blackie, for no particular reason. I shrieked my story over the wire in disconnected, incoherent sentences. Then I rushed back to the little cottage where Alma Pflugel and I waited with what patience we could summon.

Blackie was the first to arrive. He required few explanations. That is one of the nicest things about Blackie. He understands by leaps and bounds, while others crawl to comprehension. But when Frau Nirlanger came, with Bennie in tow, there were tears, and exclamations, followed by a little stricken silence on the part of Frau Nirlanger when she saw Bennie snatched to the breast of this weeping woman. So it was that in the midst of the confusion we did not hear the approach of the probation officer and her charge. They came up the path to the door, and there the little sister turned the knob, and it yielded under her fingers, and the old door swung open; and so she entered the house quite as Alma Pflugel had planned she should, except that the roses were not blooming along the edge of the sunken brick walk.

She entered the room in silence, and no one could have recognized in this pretty, fragile creature the pitiful wreck of the juvenile court. And when Alma Pflugel saw the face of the little sister—the poor, marred, stricken face—her own face became terrible in its agony. She put Bennie down very gently, rose, and took the shaking little figure in her strong arms, and held it as though never to let it go again. There were little broken words of love and pity. She called her "Lammchen" and "little one," and so Frau Nirlanger and Blackie and I stole away, after a whispered consultation with the little probation officer.

Blackie had come in his red runabout, and now he tucked us into it, feigning a deep disgust.

"I'd like to know where I enter into this little drayma," he growled. "Ain't I got nothin' t' do but run around town unitin' long lost sisters an' orphans!"

"Now, Blackie, you know you would never have forgiven me if I had left you out of this. Besides, you must hustle around and see that they need not move out of that dear little cottage. Now don't say a word! You'll never have a greater chance to act the fairy godmother."

Frau Nirlanger's hand sought mine and I squeezed it in silent sympathy. Poor little Frau Nirlanger, the happiness of another had brought her only sorrow. And she had kissed Bennie good-by with the knowledge that the little blue-painted bed, with its faded red roses, would again stand empty in the gloom of the Knapf attic.

Norberg glanced up quickly as I entered the city room. "Get something good on that south side story?" he asked.

"Why, no," I answered. "You were mistaken about that. The—the nice old maid is not going to move, after all."

CHAPTER XV. FAREWELL TO KNAPFS

Consternation has corrugated the brows of the aborigines. Consternation twice confounded had added a wrinkle or two to my collection. We are homeless. That is, we are Knapfless—we, to whom the Knapfs spelled home.

Herr Knapf, mustache aquiver, and Frau Knapf, cheek bones glistening, broke the news to us one evening just a week after the exciting day which so changed Bennie's life. "Es thut uns sehr, sehr leid," Herr Knapf had begun. And before he had finished, protesting German groans mingled with voluble German explanations. The aborigines were stricken down. They clapped pudgy fists to knobby foreheads; they smote their breasts, and made wild gestures with their arms. If my protests were less frenzied than theirs, it was only because my knowledge of German stops at words of six syllables.

Out of the chaos of ejaculations and interrogation the reason for our expulsion at last was made clear. The little German hotel had not been remunerative. Our host and hostess were too hospitable and too polite to state the true reason for this state of affairs. Perhaps rents were too high. Perhaps, thought I, Frau Knapf had been too liberal with the butter in the stewed chicken. Perhaps there had been too many golden Pfannkuchen with real eggs and milk stirred into them, and with toothsome little islands of ruddy currant jelly on top. Perhaps there had been too much honest, nourishing food, and not enough boarding-house victuals. At any rate, the enterprise would have to be abandoned.

It was then that the bare, bright little dining room, with its queer prints of chin-chucking lieutenants, and its queerer faces, and its German cookery became very dear to me. I had grown to like Frau Knapf, of the shining cheek bones, and Herr Knapf, of the heavy geniality. A close bond of friendship had sprung up between Frau Nirlanger and me. I would miss her friendly visits, and her pretty ways, and her sparkling conversation. She and I had held many kimonoed pow-wows, and sometimes—not often—she had given me wonderful glimpses of that which she had left—of Vienna, the opera, the court, the life which had been hers. She talked marvelously well, for she had all the charm and vivacity of the true Viennese. Even the aborigines, bristling pompadours, thick spectacles, terrifying manner, and all, became as dear as old friends, now that I knew I must lose them.

The great, high-ceilinged room upstairs had taken on the look of home. The Blue-beard closet no longer appalled me. The very purpleness of the purple roses in the rug had grown beautiful in my eyes because they were part of that little domain which spelled peace and comfort and kindness. How could I live without the stout yellow brocade armchair! Its plethoric curves were balm for my tired bones. Its great lap admitted of sitting with knees crossed, Turk-fashion. Its cushioned back stopped just at the point where the head found needed support. Its pudgy arms offered rest for tired elbows; its yielding bosom was made for tired backs. Given the padded comfort of that stout old chair—a friendly, time-tried book between my fingers—a dish of ruddy apples twinkling in the fire-light; my mundane soul snuggled in content. And then, too, the book-in-the-making had grown in that room. It had developed from a weak, wobbling uncertainty into a lusty full-blooded thing that grew and grew until it promised soon to become mansize.

Now all this was to be changed. And I knew that I would miss the easy German atmosphere of the place; the kindness they had shown me; the chattering, admiring Minna; the taffy-colored dachshund; the aborigines with their ill-smelling pipes and flappy slippers; the Wienerschnitzel; the crushed-looking wives and the masterful German husbands; the very darns in the table-cloths and the very nicks in the china.

We had a last family gathering in token of our appreciation of Herr and Frau Knapf. And because I had not seen him for almost three weeks; and because the time for his going was drawing so sickeningly near; and because I was quite sure that I had myself in hand; and because he knew the Knapfs, and was fond of them; and because-well, I invited Von Gerhard. He came, and I found myself dangerously glad to see him, so that I made my greeting as airy and frivolous as possible. Perhaps I overdid the airy business, for Von Gerhard looked at me for a long, silent minute, until the nonsense I had been chattering died on my lips, and I found myself staring up at him like a child that is apprehensive of being scolded for some naughtiness.

"Not so much chatter, small one," he said, unsmilingly. "This pretense, it is not necessary between you and me. So. You are ein bischen blasz, nicht? A little pale? You have not been ill, Dawn?"

"Ill? Never felt more chipper in my life," I made flippant answer, "and I adore these people who are forever telling one how unusually thin, or pale, or scrawny one is looking."

"Na, they are not to be satisfied, these women! If I were to tell you how lovely you look to me to-night you would draw yourself up with chill dignity and remind me that I am not privileged to say these things to you. So I discreetly mention that you are looking, interestingly pale, taking care to keep all tenderness out of my tones, and still you are not pleased." He shrugged despairing shoulders.

"Can't you strike a happy medium between rudeness and tenderness? After all, I haven't had a glimpse of your blond beauty for three weeks. And while I don't ask you to whisper sweet nothings, still, after twenty-one days—"

"You have been lonely? If only I thought that those weeks have been as wearisome to you—"

"Not lonely exactly," I hurriedly interrupted, "but sort of wishing that some one would pat me on the head and tell me that I was a good doggie. You know what I mean. It is so easy to become accustomed to thoughtfulness and devotion, and so dreadfully hard to be happy without it, once one has had it. This has been a sort of training for what I may expect when Vienna has swallowed you up."

"You are still obstinate? These three weeks have not changed you? Ach, Dawn! Kindchen!—"

But I knew that these were thin spots marked "Danger!" in our conversational pond. So, "Come," said I. "I have two new aborigines for you to meet. They are the very shiniest and wildest of all our shiny-faced and wild aborigines. And you should see their trousers and neckties! If you dare to come back from Vienna wearing trousers like these!—"

"And is the party in honor of these new aborigines?" laughed Von Gerhard. "You did not explain in your note. Merely you asked me to come, knowing that I cared not if it were a lawn fete or a ball, so long as I might again be with you."

We were on our way to the dining room, where the festivities were to be held. I stopped and turned a look of surprise upon him.

"Don't you know that the Knapfs are leaving? Did I neglect to mention that this is a farewell party for Herr and Frau Knapf? We are losing our home, and we have just one week in which to find another."

"But where will you go? And why did you not tell me this before?"

"I haven't an idea where I shall lay my poor old head. In the lap of the gods, probably, for I don't know how I shall find the time to interview landladies and pack my belongings in seven short days. The book will have to suffer for it. Just when it was getting along so beautifully, too."

There was a dangerous tenderness in Von Gerhard's eyes as he said: "Again you are a wanderer, eh—small one? That you, with your love of beautiful things, and your fastidiousness, should have to live in this way—in these boarding-houses, alone, with not even the comforts that should be yours. Ach, Kindchen, you were not made for that. You were intended for the home, with a husband, and kinder, and all that is truly worth while."

I swallowed a lump in my throat as I shrugged my shoulders. "Pooh! Any woman can have a husband and babies," I retorted, wickedly. "But mighty few women can write a book. It's a special curse."

"And you prefer this life—this existence, to the things that I offer you! You would endure these hardships rather than give up the nonsensical views which you entertain toward your—"

"Please. We were not to talk of that. I am enduring no hardships. Since I have lived in this pretty town I have become a worshiper of the goddess Gemutlichkeit. Perhaps I shan't find another home as dear to my heart as this has been, but at least I shan't have to sleep on a park bench, and any one can tell you that park benches have long been the favored resting place of genius. There is Frau Nirlanger beckoning us. Now do stop scowling, and smile for the lady. I know you will get on beautifully with the aborigines."

He did get on with them so beautifully that in less than half an hour they were swapping stories of Germany, of Austria, of the universities, of student life. Frau Knapf served a late supper, at which some one led in singing Auld Lang Syne, although the sounds emanating from the aborigines' end of the table sounded suspiciously like Die Wacht am Rhein. Following that the aborigines rose en masse and roared out their German university songs, banging their glasses on the table when they came to the chorus until we all caught the spirit of it and banged our glasses like rathskeller veterans. Then the red-faced and amorous Fritz, he of the absent Lena, announced his intention of entertaining the company. Made bold by an injudicious mixture of Herr Knapf's excellent beer, and a wonderful punch which Von Gerhard had concocted, Fritz mounted his chair, placed his plump hand over the spot where he supposed his heart to be, fastened his watery blue eyes upon my surprised and blushing countenance, and sang "Weh! Dass Wir Scheiden Mussen!" in an astonishingly beautiful barytone. I dared not look at Von Gerhard, for I knew that he was purple with suppressed mirth, so I stared stonily at the sardine sandwich and dill pickle on my plate, and felt myself growing hot and hysterical, and cold and tearful by turns.

At the end of the last verse I rose hastily and brought from their hiding-place the gifts which we of Knapfs' had purchased as remembrances for Herr and Frau Knapf. I had been delegated to make the presentation speech, so I grasped in one hand the too elaborate pipe that was to make Herr Knapf unhappy, and the too fashionable silk umbrella that was to appall Frau Knapf, and ascended the little platform at the end of the dining room, and began to speak in what I fondly thought to be fluent and highsounding German. Immediately the aborigines went off into paroxysms of laughter. They threw back their heads and roared, and slapped their thighs, and spluttered. It appeared that they thought I was making a humorous speech. At that discovery I cast dignity aside and continued my speech in the language of a German vaudeville comedian, with a dash of Weber and Field here and there. With the presentation of the silk umbrella Frau Knapf burst into tears, groped about helplessly for her apron, realized that it was missing from its accustomed place, and wiped her tears upon her cherished blue silk sleeve in the utter abandon of her sorrow. We drank to the future health and prosperity of our tearful host and hostess, and some one suggested drei mal drei, to which we responded in a manner to make the chin-chucking lieutenant tremble in his frame on the wall.

When it was all over Frau Nirlanger beckoned me, and she, Dr. von Gerhard and I stole out into the hall and stood at the foot of the stairway, discussing our plans for the future, and trying to smile as we talked of this plan and that. Frau Nirlanger, in the pretty white gown, was looking haggard and distrait. The oogly husband was still in the dining room, finishing the beer and punch, of which he had already taken too much.

"A tiny apartment we have taken," said Frau Nirlanger, softly. "It is better so. Then I shall have a little housework, a little cooking, a little marketing to keep me busy and perhaps happy." Her hand closed over mine. "But that shall us not separate," she pleaded. "Without you to make me sometimes laugh what should I then do? You will bring her often to our little apartment, not?" she went on, turning appealingly to Von Gerhard.

"As often as Mrs. Orme will allow me," he answered.

"Ach, yes. So lonely I shall be. You do not know what she has been to me, this Dawn. She is brave for two. Always laughing she is, and merry, nicht wahr? Meine kleine Soldatin, I call her.

"Soldatin, eh?" mused Von Gerhard. "Our little soldier. She is well named. And her battles she fights alone. But quite alone." His eyes, as they looked down on me from his great height had that in them which sent the blood rushing and tingling to my finger-tips. I brought my hand to my head in stiff military salute.

"Inspection satisfactory, sir?"

He laughed a rueful little laugh. "Eminently. Aber ganz befriedigend."

He was very tall, and straight and good to look at as he stood there in the hall with the light from the newel-post illuminating his features and emphasizing his blondness. Frau Nirlanger's face wore a drawn little look of pain as she gazed at him, and from him to the figure of her husband who had just emerged from the dining room, and was making unsteady progress toward us. Herr Nirlanger's face was flushed and his damp, dark hair was awry so that one lock straggled limply down over his forehead. As he approached he surveyed us with a surly frown that changed slowly into a leering grin. He lurched over and placed a hand familiarly on my shoulder.

"We mus' part," he announced, dramatically. "O, weh! The bes' of frien's m'z part. Well, g'by, li'l interfering Teufel. F'give you, though, b'cause you're such a pretty li'l Teufel." He raised one hand as though to pat my check and because of the horror which I saw on the face of the woman beside me I tried to smile, and did not shrink from him. But with a quick movement Von Gerhard clutched the swaying figure and turned it so that it faced the stairs.

"Come Nirlanger! Time for hard-working men like you and me to be in bed. Mrs. Orme must not nod over her desk to-morrow, either. So good-night. Schlafen Sie wohl."

Konrad Nirlanger turned a scowling face over his shoulder. Then he forgot what he was scowling for, and smiled a leering smile.

"Pretty good frien's, you an' the li'l Teufel, yes? Guess we'll have to watch you, huh, Anna? We'll watch 'em, won't we?"

He began to climb the stairs laboriously, with Frau Nirlanger's light figure flitting just ahead of him. At the bend in the stairway she turned and looked down on us a moment, her eyes very bright and big. She pressed her fingers to her lips and wafted a little kiss toward us with a gesture indescribably graceful and pathetic. She viewed her husband's laborious progress, not daring to offer help. Then the turn in the stair hid her from sight.

In the dim quiet of the little hallway Von Gerhard held out his hands—those deft, manual hands—those steady, sure, surgeonly hands—hands to cling to, to steady oneself by, and because I needed them most just then, and because I longed with my whole soul to place both my weary hands in those strong capable ones and to bring those dear, cool, sane fingers up to my burning cheeks, I put one foot on the first stair and held out two chilly fingertips. "Good-night, Herr Doktor," I said, "and thank you, not only for myself, but for her. I have felt what she feels to-night. It is not a pleasant thing to be ashamed of one's husband."

Von Gerhard's two hands closed over that one of mine. "Dawn, you will let me help you to find comfortable quarters? You cannot tramp about from place to place all the week. Let us get a list of addresses, and then, with the machine, we can drive from one to the other in an hour. It will at least save you time and strength."

"Go boarding-house hunting in a stunning green automobile!" I exclaimed. From my vantage point on the steps I could look down on him, and there came over me a great longing to run my fingers gently through that crisp blond hair, and to bring his head down close against my breast for one exquisite moment. So—"Landladies and oitermobiles!" I laughed. "Never! Don't you know that if they got one glimpse, through the front parlor windows, of me stepping grand-like out of your green motor car, they would promptly over-charge me for any room in the house? I shall go room-hunting in my oldest hat, with one finger sticking out of my glove."

Von Gerhard shrugged despairing shoulders.

"Na, of what use is it to plead with you. Sometimes I wonder if, after all, you are not merely amusing yourself. Getting copy, perhaps, for the book, or a new experience to add to your already varied store."

Abruptly I turned to hide my pain, and began to ascend the stairs. With a bound Von Gerhard was beside me, his face drawn and contrite.

"Forgive me, Dawn! I know that you are wisest. It is only that I become a little mad, I think, when I see you battling alone like this, among strangers, and know that I have not the right to help you. I knew not what I was saying. Come, raise your eyes and smile, like the little Soldatin that you are. So. Now I am forgiven, yes?"

I smiled cheerily enough into his blue eyes. "Quite forgiven. And now you must run along. This is scandalously late. The aborigines will be along saying 'Morgen!' instead of 'Nabben'!' if we stay here much longer. Good-night."

"You will give me your new address as soon as you have found a satisfactory home?"

"Never fear! I probably shall be pestering you with telephone calls, urging you to have pity upon me in my loneliness. Now goodnight again. I'm as full of farewells as a Bernhardt." And to end it I ran up the stairs. At the bend, just where Frau Nirlanger had turned, I too stopped and looked over my shoulder. Von Gerhard was standing as I had left him, looking up at me. And like Frau Nirlanger, I wafted a little kiss in his direction, before I allowed the bend in the stairs to cut off my view. But Von Gerhard did not signify by look or word that he had seen it, as he stood looking up at me, one strong white hand resting on the broad baluster.

CHAPTER XVI. JUNE MOONLIGHT, AND A NEW BOARDINGHOUSE

There was a week in which to scurry about for a new home. The days scampered by, tripping over one another in their haste. My sleeping hours were haunted by nightmares of landladies and impossible boarding-house bedrooms. Columns of "To Let, Furnished or Unfurnished" ads filed, advanced, and retreated before my dizzy eyes. My time after office hours was spent in climbing dim stairways, interviewing unenthusiastic females in kimonos, and peering into ugly bedrooms papered with sprawly and impossible patterns and filled with the odors of dead-and-gone dinners. I found one room less impossible than the rest, only to be told that the preference was to be given to a man who had "looked" the day before.

"I d'ruther take gents only," explained the ample person who carried the keys to the mansion. "Gents goes early in the morning and comes in late at night, and that's all you ever see of 'em, half the time. I've tried ladies, an' they get me wild, always yellin' for hot water to wash their hair, or pastin' handkerchiefs up on the mirr'r or wantin' to butt into the kitchen to press this or that. I'll let you know if the gent don't take it, but I got an idea he will."

He did. At any rate, no voice summoned me to that haven for gents only. There were other landladies— landladies fat and German; landladies lean and Irish; landladies loquacious (regardless of nationality); landladies reserved; landladies husbandless, wedded, widowed, divorced, and willing; landladies slatternly; landladies prim; and all hinting of past estates wherein there had been much grandeur.

At last, when despair gripped me, and I had horrid visions of my trunk, hat-box and typewriter reposing on the sidewalk while I, homeless, sat perched in the midst of them, I chanced upon a room which commanded a glorious view of the lake. True, it was too expensive for my slim purse; true, the owner of it was sour of feature; true, the room itself was cavernous and unfriendly and cold-looking, but the view of the great, blue lake triumphed over all these, although a cautious inner voice warned me that that lake view would cover a multitude of sins. I remembered, later, how she of the sour visage had dilated upon the subject of the sunrise over the water. I told her at the time that while I was passionately fond of sunrises myself, still I should like them just as well did they not occur so early in the morning. Whereupon she of the vinegar countenance had sniffed. I loathe landladies who sniff.

My trunk and trusty typewriter were sent on to my new home at noon, unchaperoned, for I had no time to spare at that hour of the day. Later I followed them, laden with umbrella, boxes, brown-paper parcels, and other unfashionable moving-day paraphernalia. I bumped and banged my way up the two flights of stairs that led to my lake view and my bed, and my heart went down as my feet went up. By the time the cavernous bedroom was gained I felt decidedly quivery-mouthed, so that I dumped my belongings on the floor in a heap and went to the window to gaze on the lake until my spirits should rise. But it was a gray day, and the lake looked large, and wet and unsociable. You couldn't get chummy with it. I turned to my great barn of a room. You couldn't get chummy with that, either. I began to unpack, with furious energy. In vain I turned every gas jet blazing high. They only cast dim shadows in the murky vastness of that awful chamber. A whole Fourth of July fireworks display, Roman candles, sky-rockets, pin-wheels, set pieces and all, could not have made that room take on a festive air.

As I unpacked I thought of my cosy room at Knapfs', and as I thought I took my head out of my trunk and sank down on the floor with a satin blouse in one hand, and a walking boot in the other, and wanted to bellow with loneliness. There came to me dear visions of the friendly old yellow brocade chair, and the lamplight, and the fireplace, and Frau Nirlanger, and the Pfannkuchen. I thought of the aborigines. In my homesick mind their bumpy faces became things of transcendent beauty. I could have put my head on their combined shoulders and wept down their blue satin neckties. In my memory of Frau Knapf it seemed to me that I could discern a dim, misty halo hovering above her tightly wadded hair. My soul went out to her as I recalled the shining cheek-bones, and the apron, and the chickens stewed in butter. I would have given a year out of my life to have heard that good-natured, "Nabben'." One aborigine had been wont to emphasize his after-dinner arguments with a toothpick brandished fiercely between thumb and finger. The brandisher had always annoyed me. Now I thought of him with tenderness in my heart and reproached myself for my fastidiousness. I should have wept if I had not had a walking boot in one hand, and a satin blouse in the other. A walking boot is but a cold comfort. And my thriftiness denied my tears the soiling of the blouse. So I sat up on my knees and finished the unpacking.

Just before dinner time I donned a becoming gown to chirk up my courage, groped my way down the long, dim stairs, and telephoned to Von Gerhard. It seemed to me that just to hear his voice would instill in me new courage and hope. I gave the number, and waited.

"Dr. von Gerhard?" repeated a woman's voice at the other end of the wire. "He is very busy. Will you leave your name?"

"No," I snapped. "I'll hold the wire. Tell him that Mrs. Orme is waiting to speak to him."

"I'll see." The voice was grudging.

Another wait; then—"Dawn!" came his voice in glad surprise.

"Hello!" I cried, hysterically. "Hello! Oh, talk! Say something nice, for pity's sake! I'm sorry that I've taken you away from whatever you were doing, but I couldn't help it. Just talk please! I'm dying of loneliness."

"Child, are you ill?" Von Gerhard's voice was so satisfyingly solicitous. "Is anything wrong? Your voice is trembling. I can hear it quite plainly. What has happened? Has Norah written—"

"Norah? No. There was nothing in her letter to upset me. It is only the strangeness of this place. I shall be all right in a day or so."

"The new home—it is satisfactory? You have found what you wanted? Your room is comfortable?"

"It's—it's a large room," I faltered. "And there's a—a large view of the lake, too."

There was a smothered sound at the other end of the wire. Then—"I want you to meet me down-town at seven o'clock. We will have dinner together," Von Gerhard said, "I cannot have you moping up there all alone all evening."

"I can't come."

"Why?"

"Because I want to so very much. And anyway, I'm much more cheerful now. I am going in to dinner. And after dinner I shall get acquainted with my room. There are six corners and all the space under the bed that I haven't explored yet."

"Dawn!"

"Yes?"

"If you were free to-night, would you marry me? If you knew that the next month would find you mistress of yourself would you—"

"Ernst!"

"Yes?"

"If the gates of Heaven were opened wide to you, and they had 'Welcome!' done in diamonds over the door, and all the loveliest angel ladies grouped about the doorway to receive you, and just beyond you could see awaiting you all that was beautiful, and most exquisite, and most desirable, would you enter?"

And then I hung up the receiver and went in to dinner. I went in to dinner, but not to dine. Oh, shades of those who have suffered in boarding-houses—that dining room! It must have been patterned after the dining room at Dotheboys' hall. It was bare, and cheerless, and fearfully undressed looking. The diners were seated at two long, unsociable, boarding-housey tables that ran the length of the room, and all the women folks came down to dine with white wool shawls wrapped snugly about their susceptible black silk shoulders. The general effect was that of an Old People's Home. I found seat after seat at table was filled, and myself the youngest thing present. I felt so criminally young that I wondered they did not strap me in a high chair and ram bread and milk down my throat. Now and then the door would open to admit another snuffly, ancient, and be-shawled member of the company. I learned that Mrs. Schwartz, on my right, did not care mooch for shteak for breakfast, aber a leedle l'mb ch'p she likes. Also that the elderly party on my left and the elderly party on my right resented being separated by my person. Conversation between E. P. on right, and E. P. on left scintillated across my soup, thus:

"How you feel this evening Mis' Maurer, h'm?"

"Don't ask me."

"No wonder you got rheumatism. My room was like a ice-house all day. Yours too?"

"I don't complain any more. Much good it does. Barley soup again? In my own home I never ate it, and here I pay my good money and get four time a week barley soup. Are those fresh cucumbers? M-m-m-m. They haven't stood long enough. Look at Mis' Miller. She feels good this evening. She should feel good. Twenty-five cents she won at bridge. I never seen how that woman is got luck."

I choked, gasped, and fled.

Back in my own mausoleum once more I put things in order, dragged my typewriter stand into the least murky corner under the bravest gas jet and rescued my tottering reason by turning out a long letter to Norah. That finished, my spirits rose. I dived into the bottom of my trunk for the loose sheets of the book-in-the-making, glanced over the last three or four, discovered that they did not sound so maudlin as I had feared, and straightway forgot my gloomy surroundings in the fascination of weaving the tale.

In the midst of my fine frenzy there came a knock at the door. In the hall stood the anemic little serving maid who had attended me at dinner. She was almost eclipsed by a huge green pasteboard box.

"You're Mis' Orme, ain't you? This here's for you."

The little white-cheeked maid hovered at the threshold while I lifted the box cover and revealed the perfection of the American beauty buds that lay there, all dewy and fragrant. The eyes of the little maid were wide with wonder as she gazed, and because I had known flower-hunger I separated two stately blossoms from the glowing cluster and held them out to her.

"For me!" she gasped, and brought her lips down to them, gently. Then—"There's a high green jar downstairs you can have to stick your flowers in. You ain't got nothin' big enough in here, except your water pitcher. An' putting these grand flowers in a water pitcher—why, it'd be like wearing a silk dress over a flannel petticoat, wouldn't it?"

When the anemic little boarding-house slavey with the beauty-loving soul had fetched the green jar, I placed the shining stems in it with gentle fingers. At the bottom of the box I found a card that read: "For it is impossible to live in a room with red roses and still be traurig."

How well he knew! And how truly impossible to be sad when red roses are glowing for one, and filling the air with their fragrance!

The interruption was fatal to book-writing. My thoughts were a chaos of red roses, and anemic little maids with glowing eyes, and thoughtful young doctors with a marvelous understanding of feminine moods. So I turned out all the lights, undressed by moonlight, and, throwing a kimono about me, carried my jar of roses to the window and sat down beside them so that their exquisite scent caressed me.

The moonlight had put a spell of white magic upon the lake. It was a light-flooded world that lay below my window. Summer, finger on lip, had stolen in upon the heels of spring. Dim, shadowy figures dotted the benches of the park across the way. Just beyond lay the silver lake, a dazzling bar of moonlight on its breast. Motors rushed along the roadway with a roar and a whir and were gone, leaving a trail of laughter behind them. From the open window of the room below came the slip-slap of cards on the polished table surface, and the low buzz of occasional conversation as the players held postmortems. Under the street light the popcorn vender's cart made a blot on the mystic beauty of the scene below. But the perfume of my red roses came to me, and their velvet caressed my check, and beyond the noise and lights of the street lay that glorious lake with the bar of moonlight on its soft breast. I gazed and forgave the sour-faced landlady her dining room; forgave the elderly parties their shawls and barley soup; forgot for a moment my weary thoughts of Peter Orme; forgot everything except that it was June, and moonlight and good to be alive.

All the changes and events of that strange, eventful year came crowding to my mind as I crouched there at the window. Four new friends, tried and true! I conned them over joyously in my heart. What a strange contrast they made! Blackie, of the elastic morals, and the still more elastic heart; Frau Nirlanger, of the smiling lips and the lilting voice and the tragic eyes—she who had stooped from a great height to pluck the flower of love blooming below, only to find a worthless weed sullying her hand; Alma Pflugel, with the unquenchable light of gratefulness in her honest face; Von Gerhard, ready to act as buffer between myself and the world, tender as a woman, gravely thoughtful, with the light of devotion glowing in his steady eyes.

"Here's richness," said I, like the fat boy in Pickwick Papers. And I thanked God for the new energy which had sent me to this lovely city by the lake. I thanked Him that I had not been content to remain a burden to Max and Norah, growing sour and crabbed with the years. Those years of work and buffeting had made of me a broader, finer, truer type of womanhood—had caused me to forget my own little tragedy in contemplating the great human comedy. And so I made a little prayer there in the moon-flooded room.

"O dear Lord," I prayed, and I did not mean that it should sound irreverent. "O dear Lord, don't bother about my ambitions! Just let me remain strong and well enough to do the work that is my portion from day to day. Keep me faithful to my standards of right and wrong. Let this new and wonderful love which has come into my life be a staff of strength and comfort instead of a burden of weariness. Let me not grow careless and slangy as the years go by. Let me keep my hair and complexion and teeth, and deliver me from wearing soiled blouses and doing my hair in a knob. Amen."

I felt quite cheerful after that—so cheerful that the strange bumps in the new bed did not bother me as unfamiliar beds usually did. The roses I put to sleep in their jar of green, keeping one to hold against my cheek as I slipped into dreamland. I thought drowsily, just before sleep claimed me:

"To-morrow, after office hours, I'll tuck up my skirt, and wrap my head in a towel and have a housecleaning bee. I'll move the bed where the wash-stand is now, and I'll make the chiffonnier swap places with the couch. One feels on friendlier terms with furniture that one has shoved about a little. How brilliant the moonlight is! The room is flooded with it. Those roses—sweet!—sweet!—"

When I awoke it was morning. During the days that followed I looked back gratefully upon that night, with its moonlight, and its roses, and its great peace.

CHAPTER XVII. THE SHADOW OF TERROR

Two days before the date set for Von Gerhard's departure the book was finished, typed, re-read, packed, and sent away. Half an hour after it was gone all its most glaring faults seemed to marshall themselves before my mind's eye. Whole paragraphs, that had read quite reasonably before, now loomed ludicrous in perspective. I longed to snatch it back; to tidy it here, to take it in there, to smooth certain rough places neglected in my haste. For almost a year I had lived with this thing, so close that its faults and its virtues had become indistinguishable to me. Day and night, for many months, it had been in my mind. Of late some instinct had prompted me to finish it. I had worked at it far into the night, until I marveled that the ancient occupants of the surrounding rooms did not enter a combined protest against the clack-clacking of my typewriter keys. And now that it was gone I wondered, dully, if I could feel Von Gerhard's departure more keenly.

No one knew of the existence of the book except Norah, Von Gerhard, Blackie and me. Blackie had a way of inquiring after its progress in hushed tones of mock awe. Also he delighted in getting down on hands and knees and guiding a yard-stick carefully about my desk with a view to having a fence built around it, bearing an inscription which would inform admiring tourists that here was the desk at which the brilliant author had been wont to sit when grinding out heart-throb stories for the humble Post. He took an impish delight in my struggles with my hero and heroine, and his inquiries after the health of both were of such a nature as to make any earnest writer person rise in wrath and slay him. I had seen little of Blackie of late. My spare hours had been devoted to the work in hand. On the day after the book was sent away I was conscious of a little shock as I strolled into Blackie's sanctum and took my accustomed seat beside his big desk. There was an oddly pinched look about Blackie's nostrils and lips, I thought. And the deep-set black eyes appeared deeper and blacker than ever in his thin little face.

A week of unseasonable weather had come upon the city. June was going out in a wave of torrid heat such as August might have boasted. The day had seemed endless and intolerably close. I was feeling very limp and languid. Perhaps, thought I, it was the heat which had wilted Blackie's debonair spirits.

"It has been a long time since we've had a talk-talk, Blackie. I've missed you. Also you look just a wee bit green around the edges. I'm thinking a vacation wouldn't hurt you."

Blackie's lean brown forefinger caressed the bowl of his favorite pipe. His eyes, that had been gazing out across the roofs beyond his window, came back to me, and there was in them a curious and quizzical expression as of one who is inwardly amused.

"I've been thinkin' about a vacation. None of your measly little two weeks' affairs, with one week on salary, and th' other without. I ain't goin' t' take my vacation for a while—not till fall, p'raps, or maybe winter. But w'en I do take it, sa-a-ay, girl, it's goin' t' be a real one."

"But why wait so long?" I asked. "You need it now. Who ever heard of putting off a vacation until winter!"

"Well, I dunno," mused Blackie. "I just made my arrangements for that time, and I hate t' muss 'em up. You'll say, w'en the time comes, that my plans are reasonable."

There was a sharp ring from the telephone at Blackie's elbow. He answered it, then thrust the receiver into my hand. "For you," he said.

It was Von Gerhard's voice that came to me. "I have something to tell you," he said. "Something most important. If I call for you at six we can drive out to the bay for supper, yes? I must talk to you."

"You have saved my life," I called back. "It has been a beast of a day. You may talk as much and as importantly as you like, so long as I am kept cool."

"That was Von Gerhard," said I to Blackie, and tried not to look uncomfortable.

"Mm," grunted Blackie, pulling at his pipe. "Thoughtful, ain't he?"

I turned at the door. "He—he's going away day after to-morrow, Blackie," I explained, although no explanation had been asked for, "to Vienna. He expects to stay a year—or two—or three—"

Blackie looked up quickly. "Goin' away, is he? Well, maybe it's best, all around, girl. I see his name's been mentioned in all the medical papers, and the big magazines, and all that, lately. Gettin' t' be a big bug, Von Gerhard is. Sorry he's goin', though. I was plannin' t' consult him just before I go on my—vacation. But some other guy'll do. He don't approve of me, Von Gerhard don't."

For some reason which I could never explain I went back into the room and held out both my hands to Blackie. His nervous brown fingers closed over them. "That doesn't make one bit of difference to us, does it, Blackie?" I said, gravely. "We're—we're not caring so long as we approve of one another, are we?"

"Not a bit, girl," smiled Blackie, "not a bit."

When the green car stopped before the Old Folks' Home I was in seraphic mood. I had bathed, donned clean linen and a Dutch-necked gown. The result was most soul-satisfying. My spirits rose unaccountably. Even the sight of Von Gerhard, looking troubled and distrait, did not quiet them. We darted away, out along the lake front, past the toll gate, to the bay road stretching its flawless length along the water's side. It was alive with swift-moving motor cars swarming like twentieth-century pilgrims toward the mecca of cool breezes and comfort. There were proud limousines; comfortable family cars; trim little roadsters; noisy runabouts. Not a hoof-beat was to be heard. It was as though the horseless age had indeed descended upon the world. There was only a hum, a rush, a roar, as car after car swept on.

Summer homes nestled among the trees near the lake. Through the branches one caught occasional gleams of silvery water. The rush of cool air fanned my hot forehead, tousled my hair, slid down between my collar and the back of my neck, and I was grandly content.

"Even though you are going to sail away, and even though you have the grumps, and refuse to talk, and scowl like a jabberwock, this is an extremely nice world. You can't spoil it."

"Behute!" Von Gerhard's tone was solemn.

"Would you be faintly interested in knowing that the book is finished?"

"So? That is well. You were wearing yourself thin over it. It was then quickly perfected."

"Perfected!" I groaned. "I turn cold when I think of it. The last chapters got away from me completely. They lacked the punch."

Von Gerhard considered that a moment, as I wickedly had intended that he should. Then—"The punch? What is that then—the punch?"

Obligingly I elucidated. "A book may be written in flawless style, with a plot, and a climax, and a lot of little side surprises. But if it lacks that peculiar and convincing quality poetically known as the punch, it might as well never have been written. It can never be a six-best-seller, neither will it live as a classic. You will never see it advertised on the book review page of the Saturday papers, nor will the man across the aisle in the street car be so absorbed in its contents that he will be taken past his corner."

Von Gerhard looked troubled. "But the literary value? Does that not enter—"

"I don't aim to contribute to the literary uplift," I assured him. "All my life I have cherished two ambitions. One of them is to write a successful book, and the other to learn to whistle through my teeth—this way, you know, as the gallery gods do it. I am almost despairing of the whistle, but I still have hopes of the book."

Whereupon Von Gerhard, after a moment's stiff surprise, gave vent to one of his heartwarming roars.

"Thanks," said I. "Now tell me the important news."

His face grew serious in an instant. "Not yet, Dawn. Later. Let us hear more about the book. Not so flippant, however, small one. The time is past when you can deceive me with your nonsense."

"Surely you would not have me take myself seriously! That's another debt I owe my Irish forefathers. They could laugh—bless 'em!—in the very teeth of a potato crop failure. And let me tell you, that takes some sense of humor. The book is my potato crop. If it fails it will mean that I must keep on drudging, with a knot or two taken in my belt. But I'll squeeze a smile out of the corner of my mouth, somehow. And if it succeeds! Oh, Ernst, if it succeeds!"

"Then, Kindchen?"

"Then it means that I may have a little thin layer of jam on my bread and butter. It won't mean money—at least, I don't think it will. A first book never does. But it will mean a future. It will mean that I will have something solid to stand on. It will be a real beginning—a breathing spell—time in which to accomplish something really worth while—independence—freedom from this tread-mill—"

"Stop!" cried Von Gerhard, sharply. Then, as I stared in surprise—"I do ask your pardon. I was again rude, nicht wahr? But in me there is a queer vein of German superstition that disapproves of air castles. Sich einbilden, we call it."

The lights of the bay pavilion twinkled just ahead. The green car poked its nose up the path between rows of empty machines. At last it drew up, panting, before a vacant space between an imposing, scarlet touring car and a smart, cream-colored runabout. We left it there and walked up the light-flooded path.

Inside the great, barn-like structure that did duty as pavilion glasses clinked, chairs scraped on the wooden floor; a burst of music followed a sharp fusillade of applause. Through the open doorway could be seen a company of Tyrolese singers in picturesque costumes of scarlet and green and black. The scene was very noisy, and very bright, and very German.

"Not in there, eh?" said Von Gerhard, as though divining my wish. "It is too brightly lighted, and too noisy. We will find a table out here under the trees, where the music is softened by the distance, and our eyes are not offended by the ugliness of the singers. But inexcusably ugly they are, these Tyrolese women."

We found a table within the glow of the pavilion's lights, but still so near the lake that we could hear the water lapping the shore. A cadaverous, sandy-haired waiter brought things to eat, and we made brave efforts to appear hungry and hearty, but my high spirits were ebbing fast, and Von Gerhard was frankly distraught. One of the women singers appeared suddenly in the doorway of the pavilion, then stole down the steps, and disappeared in the shadow of the trees beyond our table. The voices of the singers ceased abruptly. There was a moment's hushed silence. Then, from the shadow of the trees came a woman's voice, clear, strong, flexible, flooding the night with the bird-like trill of the mountain yodel. The sound rose and fell, and swelled and soared. A silence. Then, in a great burst of melody the chorus of voices within the pavilion answered the call. Again a silence. Again the wonder of the woman's voice flooded the stillness, ending in a note higher, clearer, sweeter than any that had gone before. Then the little Tyrolese, her moment of glory ended, sped into the light of the noisy pavilion again.

When I turned to Von Gerhard my eyes were wet. "I shall have that to remember, when you are gone."

Von Gerhard beckoned the hovering waiter. "Take these things away. And you need not return." He placed something in the man's palm—something that caused a sudden whisking away of empty dishes, and many obsequious bows.

Von Gerhard's face was turned away from me, toward the beauty of the lake and sky. Now, as the last flirt of the waiter's apron vanished around the corner he turned his head slowly, and I saw that in his eyes which made me catch my breath with apprehension.

"What is it?" I cried. "Norah? Max? The children?"

He shook his head. "They are well, so far, as I know. I—perhaps first I should tell you—although this is not the thing which I have to say to you—"

"Yes?" I urged him on, impatiently. I had never seen him like this.

"I do not sail this week. I shall not be with Gluck in Vienna this year. I shall stay here."

"Here! Why? Surely—"

"Because I shall be needed here, Dawn. Because I cannot leave you now. You will need—some one—a friend—"

I stared at him with eyes that were wide with terror, waiting for I knew not what.

"Need—some one—for—what?" I stammered. "Why should you—"

In the kindly shadow of the trees Von Gerhard's hands took my icy ones, and held them in a close clasp of encouragement.

"Norah is coming to be with you—"

"Norah! Why? Tell me at once! At once!"

"Because Peter Orme has been sent home—cured," said he.

The lights of the pavilion fell away, and advanced, and swung about in a great sickening circle. I shut my eyes. The lights still swung before my eyes. Von Gerhard leaned toward me with a word of alarm. I clung to his hands with all my strength.

"No!" I said, and the savage voice was not my own. "No! No! No! It isn't true! It isn't—Oh, it's some joke, isn't it? Tell me, it's—it's something funny, isn't it? And after a bit we'll laugh—we'll laugh—of course—see! I am smiling already—"

"Dawn—dear one—it is true. God knows I wish that I could be happy to know it. The hospital authorities pronounce him cured. He has been quite sane for weeks."

"You knew it—how long?"

"You know that Max has attended to all communications from the doctors there. A few weeks ago they wrote that Orme had shown evidences of recovery. He spoke of you, of the people he had known in New York, of his work on the paper, all quite rationally and calmly. But they must first be sure. Max went to New York a week ago. Peter was gone. The hospital authorities were frightened and apologetic. Peter had walked away quite coolly one day. He had gone into the city, borrowed money of some old newspaper cronies, and vanished. He may be there still. He may be—"

"Here! Ernst! Take me home! O God; I can't do it! I can't! I ought to be happy, but I'm not. I ought to be thankful, but I'm not, I'm not! The horror of having him there was great enough, but it was nothing compared to the horror of having him here. I used to dream that he was well again, and that he was searching for me, and the dreadful realness of it used to waken me, and I would find myself shivering with terror. Once I dreamed that I looked up from my desk to find him standing in the doorway, smiling that mirthless smile of his, and I heard him say, in his mocking way: 'Hello, Dawn my love; looking wonderfully well. Grass widowhood agrees with you, eh?'"

"Dawn, you must not laugh like that. Come, we will go. You are shivering! Don't, dear, don't. See, you have Norah, and Max, and me to help you. We will put him on his feet. Physically he is not what he should be. I can do much for him."

"You!" I cried, and the humor of it was too exquisite for laughter.

"For that I gave up Vienna," said Von Gerhard, simply. "You, too, must do your share."

"My share! I have done my share. He was in the gutter, and he was dragging me with him. When his insanity came upon him I thanked God for it, and struggled up again. Even Norah never knew what that struggle was. Whatever I am, I am in spite of him. I tell you I could hug my widow's weeds. Ten years ago he showed me how horrible and unclean a thing can be made of this beautiful life. I was a despairing, cowering girl of twenty then—I am a woman now, happy in her work, her friends; growing broader and saner in thought, quicker to appreciate the finer things in life. And now—what?"

They were dashing off a rollicking folk-song indoors. When it was finished there came a burst of laughter and the sharp spat of applauding hands, and shouts of approbation. The sounds seemed seared upon my brain. I rose and ran down the path toward the waiting machine. There in the darkness I buried my shamed face in my hands and prayed for the tears that would not come.

It seemed hours before I heard Von Gerhard's firm, quick tread upon the gravel path. He moved about the machine, adjusting this and that, then took his place at the wheel without a word. We glided out upon the smooth white road. All the loveliness of the night seemed to have vanished. Only the ugly, distorted shadows remained. The terror of uncertainty gripped me. I could not endure the sight of Von Gerhard's stern, set face. I grasped his arm suddenly so that the machine veered and darted across the road. With a mighty wrench Von Gerhard righted it. He stopped the machine at the road-side.

"Careful, Kindchen," he said, gravely.

"Ernst," I said, and my breath came quickly, chokingly, as though I had been running fast, "Ernst, I can't do it. I'm not big enough. I can't. I hate him, I tell you, I hate him! My life is my own. I've made it what it is, in the face of a hundred temptations; in spite of a hundred pitfalls. I can't lay it down again for Peter Orme to trample. Ernst, if you love me, take me away now. To Vienna—anywhere—only don't ask me to take up my life with him again. I can't—I can't—"

"Love you?" repeated Ernst, slowly, "yes. Too well—"

"Too well—"

"Yes, too well for that, Gott sei dank, small one. Too well for that."

CHAPTER XVIII. PETER ORME

A man's figure rose from the shadows of the porch and came forward to meet us as we swung up to the curbing. I stifled a scream in my throat. As I shrank back into the seat I heard the quick intake of Von Gerhard's breath as he leaned forward to peer into the darkness. A sick dread came upon me.

"Sa-a-ay, girl," drawled the man's voice, with a familiar little cackling laugh in it, "sa-a-ay, girl, the policeman on th' beat's got me spotted for a suspicious character. I been hoofin' it up an' down this block like a distracted mamma waitin' for her daughter t' come home from a boat ride."

"Blackie! It's only you!"

"Thanks, flatterer," simpered Blackie, coming to the edge of the walk as I stepped from the automobile. "Was you expectin' the landlady?"

"I don't know just whom I expected. I—I'm nervous, I think, and you startled me. Dr. Von Gerhard was taken back for a moment, weren't you, Doctor?"

Von Gerhard laughed ruefully. "Frankly, yes. It is not early. And visitors at this hour—"

"What in the world is it, Blackie?" I put in. "Don't tell me that Norberg has been seized with one of his fiendish inspirations at this time of night."

Blackie struck a match and held it for an instant so that the flare of it illuminated his face as he lighted his cigarette. There was no laughter in the deep-set black eyes.

"What is it Blackie?" I asked again. The horror of what Von Gerhard had told me made the prospect of any lesser trial a welcome relief.

"I got t' talk to you for a minute. P'raps Von Gerhard 'd better hear it, too. I telephoned you an hour ago. Tried to get you out to the bay. Waited here ever since. Got a parlor, or somethin', where a guy can talk?"

I led the way indoors. The first floor seemed deserted. The bare, unfriendly boarding-house parlor was unoccupied, and one dim gas jet did duty as illumination.

"Bring in the set pieces," muttered Blackie, as he turned two more gas jets flaring high. "This parlor just yells for a funeral."

Von Gerhard was frowning. "Mrs. Orme is not well," he began. "She has had a shock—some startling news concerning—"

"Her husband?" inquired Blackie, coolly. I started up with a cry. "How could you know?"

A look of relief came into Blackie's face. "That helps a little. Now listen, kid. An' w'en I get through, remember I'm there with the little helpin' mitt. Have a cigarette, Doc?"

"No," said Von Gerhard, shortly.

Blackie's strange black eyes were fastened on my face, and I saw an expression of pity in their depths as he began to talk.

"I was up at the Press Club to-night. Dropped in for a minute or two, like I always do on the rounds. The place sounded kind of still when I come up the steps, and I wondered where all the boys was. Looked into the billiard room—nothin' doin'. Poked my head in at the writin' room—same. Ambled into the readin' room—empty. Well, I steered for the dining room, an' there was the bunch. An' just as I come in they give a roar, and I started to investigate. Up against the fireplace, with one hand in his pocket, and the other hanging careless like on the mantel, stood a man—stranger t' me. He was talkin' kind of low, and quick, bitin' off his words like a Englishman. An' the boys, they was starin' with their eyes, an' their mouths, and forgettin' t' smoke, an' lettin' their pipes an' cigars go dead in their hands, while he talked. Talk! Sa-a-ay, girl, that guy, he could talk the leads right out of a ruled, locked form. I didn't catch his name. Tall, thin, unearthly lookin' chap, with the whitest teeth you ever saw, an' eyes—well, his eyes was somethin' like a lighted pipe with a little fine ash over the red, just waitin' for a sudden pull t' make it glow."

"Peter!" I moaned, and buried my face in my hands. Von Gerhard put a quick hand on my arm. But I shook it off. "I'm not going to faint," I said, through set teeth. "I'm not going to do anything silly. I want to think. I want to... Go on, Blackie."

"Just a minute," interrupted Von Gerhard. "Does he know where Mrs. Orme is living?"

"I'm coming t' that," returned Blackie, tranquilly. "Though for Dawn's sake I'll say right here he don't know. I told him later, that she was takin' a vacation up at her folks' in Michigan."

"Thank God!" I breathed.

"Wore a New York Press Club button, this guy did. I asked one of the boys standin' on the outer edge of the circle what the fellow's name was, but he only says: 'Shut up Black! An' listen. He's seen every darn thing in the world.' Well, I listened. He wasn't braggin'. He wasn't talkin' big. He was just talkin'. Seems like he'd been war correspondent in the Boer war, and the Spanish-American, an' Gawd knows where. He spoke low, not usin' any big words, either, an' I thought his eyes looked somethin' like those of the Black Cat up on the mantel just over his head—you know what I mean, when the electric lights is turned on in-inside{sic} the ugly thing. Well, every time he showed signs of stoppin', one of the boys would up with a question, and start him goin' again. He knew everybody, an' everything, an' everywhere. All of a sudden one of the boys points to the Roosevelt signature on the wall—the one he scrawled up there along with all the other celebrities first time he was entertained by the Press Club boys. Well this guy, he looked at the name for a minute. 'Roosevelt?' he says, slow. 'Oh, yes. Seems t' me I've heard of him.' Well, at that the boys yelled. Thought it was a good joke, seein' that Ted had been smeared all over the first page of everything for years. But kid, I seen th' look in that man's eyes when he said it, and he wasn't jokin', girl. An' it came t' me, all of a sudden, that all the things he'd been talkin' about had happened almost ten years back. After he'd made that break about Roosevelt he kind of shut up, and strolled over to the piano and began t' play. You know that bum old piano, with half a dozen dead keys, and no tune?"

I looked up for a moment. "He could make you think that it was a concert grand, couldn't he? He hasn't forgotten even that?"

"Forgotten? Girl, I don't know what his accomplishments was when you knew him, but if he was any more fascinatin' than he is now, then I'm glad I didn't know him. He could charm the pay envelope away from a reporter that was Saturday broke. Somethin' seemed t' urge me t' go up t' him an' say: 'Have a game of billiards?'

"'Don't care if I do,' says he, and swung his long legs off the piano stool and we made for the billiard room, with the whole gang after us. Sa-a-ay, girl, I'm a modest violet, I am, but I don't mind mentionin' that the general opinion up at the club is that I'm a little wizard with the cue. Well, w'en he got through with me I looked like little sister when big brother is tryin' t' teach her how to hold the cue in her fingers. He just sent them balls wherever he thought they'd look pretty. I bet if he'd held up his thumb and finger an' said, 'jump through this!' them balls would of jumped."

Von Gerhard took a couple of quick steps in Blackie's direction. His eyes were blue steel.

"Is this then necessary?" he asked. "All this leads to what? Has not Mrs. Orme suffered enough, that she should undergo this idle chatter? It is sufficient that she knows this—this man is here. It is a time for action, not for words."

"Action's comin' later, Doc," drawled Blackie, looking impish. "Monologuin' ain't my specialty. I gener'ly let the other gink talk. You never can learn nothin' by talkin'. But I got somethin' t' say t' Dawn here. Now, in case you're bored the least bit, w'y don't hesitate one minnit t'—"

"Na, you are quite right, and I was hasty," said Von Gerhard, and his eyes, with the kindly gleam in them, smiled down upon the little man. "It is only that both you and I are over-anxious to be of assistance to this unhappy lady. Well, we shall see. You talked with this man at the Press Club?"

"He talked. I listened."

"That would be Peter's way," I said, bitterly. "How he used to love to hold forth, and how I grew to long for blessed silence—for fewer words, and more of that reserve which means strength!"

"All this time," continued Blackie, "I didn't know his name. When we'd finished our game of billiards he hung up his cue, and then he turned around like lightning, and faced the boys that were standing around with their hands in their pockets. He had a odd little smile on his face—a smile with no fun it, if you know what I mean. Guess you do, maybe, if you've seen it.

"'Boys,' says he, smilin' that twisted kind of smile, 'boys, I'm lookin' for a job. I'm not much of a talker, an' I'm only a amateur at music, and my game of billiards is ragged. But there's one thing I can do, fellows, from abc up to xyz, and that's write. I can write, boys, in a way to make your pet little political scribe sound like a high school paper. I don't promise to stick. As soon as I get on my feet again I'm going back to New York. But not just yet. Meanwhile, I'm going to the highest bidder.'

"Well, you know since Merkle left us we haven't had a day when we wasn't scooped on some political guff. 'I guess we can use you—some place,' I says, tryin' not t' look too anxious. If your ideas on salary can take a slump be tween New York and Milwaukee. Our salaries around here is more what is elegantly known as a stipend. What's your name, Bo?'

"'Name?' says he, smiling again, 'Maybe it'll be familiar t' you. That is, it will if my wife is usin' it. Orme's my name—Peter Orme. Know a lady of that name? Good.'

"I hadn't said I did, but those eyes of his had seen the look on my face.

"'Friends in New York told me she was here,' he says. 'Where is she now? Got her address?' he says.

"'She expectin' you?' I asked.

"'N-not exactly,' he says, with that crooked grin.

"'Thought not,' I answered, before I knew what I was sayin'. 'She's up north with her folks on a vacation.'

"'The devil she is!' he says. 'Well, in that case can you let me have ten until Monday?'"

Blackie came over to me as I sat cowering in my chair. He patted my shoulder with one lean brown hand. "Now kid, you dig, see? Beat it. Go home for a week. I'll fix it up with Norberg. No tellin' what a guy like that's goin' t' do. Send your brother-in-law down here if you want to make it a family affair, and between us, we'll see this thing through."

I looked up at Von Gerhard. He was nodding approval. It all seemed so easy, so temptingly easy. To run away! Not to face him until I was safe in the shelter of Norah's arms! I stood up, resolve lending me new strength and courage.

"I am going. I know it isn't brave, but I can't be brave any longer. I'm too tired—too old—"

I grasped the hand of each of those men who had stood by me so staunchly in the year that was past. The words of thanks that I had on my lips ended in dry, helpless sobs. And because Blackie and Von Gerhard looked so pathetically concerned and so unhappy in my unhappiness my sobs changed to hysterical laughter, in which the two men joined, after one moment's bewildered staring.

So it was that we did not hear the front door slam, or the sound of footsteps in the hall. Our overstrained nerves found relief in laughter, so that Peter Orme, a lean, ominous figure in the doorway looked in upon a merry scene.

I was the first to see him. And at the sight of the emaciated figure, with its hollow cheeks and its sunken eyes all terror and hatred left me, and I felt only a great pity for this wreck of manhood. Slowly I went up to him there in the doorway.

"Well, Peter?" I said.

"Well, Dawn old girl," said he "you're looking wonderfully fit. Grass widowhood seems to agree with you, eh?"

And I knew then that my dread dream had come true.

Peter advanced into the room with his old easy grace of manner. His eyes glowed as he looked at Blackie. Then he laughed, showing his even, white teeth. "Why, you little liar!" he said, in his crisp, clear English. "I've a notion to thwack you. What d' you mean by telling me my wife's gone? You're not sweet on her yourself, eh?"

Von Gerhard stifled an exclamation, and Orme turned quickly in his direction. "Who are you?" he asked. "Still another admirer? Jolly time you were having when I interrupted." He stared at Von Gerhard deliberately and coolly. A little frown of dislike came into his face. "You're a doctor, aren't you? I knew it. I can tell by the hands, and the eyes, and the skin, and the smell. Lived with 'em for ten years, damn them! Dawn, tell these fellows they're excused, will you? And by the way, you don't seem very happy to see me?"

I went up to him then, and laid my hand on his arm. "Peter, you don't understand. These two gentlemen have been all that is kind to me. I am happy to know that you are well again. Surely you do not expect me to be joyful at seeing you. All that pretense was left out of our lives long before your—illness. It hasn't been all roses for me since then, Peter. I've worked until I wanted to die with weariness. You know what this newspaper game is for a woman. It doesn't grow easier as she grows older and tireder."

"Oh, cut out the melodrama, Dawn," sneered Peter. "Have either of you fellows the makin's about you? Thanks. I'm famished for a smoke."

The worrying words of ten years ago rose automatically to my lips. "Aren't you smoking too much, Peter?" The tone was that of a harassed wife.

Peter stared. Then he laughed his short, mirthless little laugh. "By Jove! Dawn, I believe you're as much my wife now as you were ten years ago. I always said, you know, that you would have become a first-class nagger if you hadn't had such a keen sense of humor. That saved you." He turned his mocking eyes to Von Gerhard. "Doesn't it beat the devil, how these good women stick to a man, once they're married! There's a certain dog-like devotion about it that's touching."

There was a dreadful little silence. For the first time in my knowledge of him I saw a hot, painful red dyeing Blackie's sallow face. His eyes had a menace in their depths. Then, very quietly, Von Gerhard stepped forward and stopped directly before me.

"Dawn," he said, very softly and gently, "I retract my statement of an hour ago. If you will give me another chance to do as you asked me, I shall thank God for it all my life. There is no degradation in that. To live with this man—that is degradation. And I say you shall not suffer it."

I looked up into his face, and it had never seemed so dear to me. "The time for that is past," I said, my tone as calm and even as his own. "A man like you cannot burden himself with a derelict like me—mast gone, sails gone, water-logged, drifting. Five years from now you'll thank me for what I am saying now. My place is with this other wreck—tossed about by wind and weather until we both go down together." There came a sharp, insistent ring at the door-bell. No answering sound came from the regions above stairs. The ringing sounded again, louder than before.

"I'll be the Buttons," said Blackie, and disappeared into the hallway.

"Oh, yes, I've heard about you," came to our ears a moment later, in a high, clear voice—a dear, beloved voice that sent me flying to the door in an agony of hope.

"Norah!" I cried, "Norah! Norah! Norah!" And as her blessed arms closed about me the tears that had been denied me before came in a torrent of joy.

"There, there!" murmured she, patting my shoulder with those comforting mother-pats. "What's all this about? And why didn't somebody meet me? I telegraphed. You didn't get it? Well, I forgive you. Howdy-do, Peter? I suppose you are Peter. I hope you haven't been acting devilish again. That seems to be your specialty. Now don't smile that Mephistophelian smile at me. It doesn't frighten me. Von Gerhard, take him down to his hotel. I'm dying for my kimono and bed. And this child is trembling like a race-horse. Now run along, all of you. Things that look greenery-yallery at night always turn pink in the morning. Great Heavens! There's somebody calling down from the second-floor landing. It sounds like a landlady. Run, Dawn, and tell her your perfectly respectable sister has come. Peter! Von Gerhard! Mr. Blackie! Shoo!"

CHAPTER XIX. A TURN OF THE WHEEL

"You who were ever alert to befriend a man You who were ever the first to defend a man, You who had always the money to lend a man Down on his luck and hard up for a V, Sure you'll be playing a harp in beatitude (And a quare sight you will be in that attitude) Some day, where gratitude seems but a platitude, You'll find your latitude."

From my desk I could see Peter standing in the doorway of the news editor's room. I shut my eyes for a moment. Then I opened them again, quickly. No, it was not a dream. He was there, a slender, graceful, hateful figure, with the inevitable cigarette in his unsteady fingers—the expensive-looking, gold-tipped cigarette of the old days. Peter was Peter. Ten years had made little difference. There were queer little hollow places in his cheeks, and under the jaw-bone, and at the base of the head, and a flabby, parchment-like appearance about the skin. That was all that made him different from the Peter of the old days.

The thing had adjusted itself, as Norah had said it would. The situation that had filled me with loathing and terror the night of Peter's return had been transformed into quite a matter-of-fact and commonplace affair under Norah's deft management. And now I was back in harness again, and Peter was turning out brilliant political stuff at spasmodic intervals. He was not capable of any sustained effort. He never would be again; that was plain. He was growing restless and dissatisfied. He spoke of New York as though it were Valhalla. He said that he hadn't seen a pretty girl since he left Forty-second street. He laughed at Milwaukee's quaint German atmosphere. He sneered at our journalistic methods, and called the newspapers "country sheets," and was forever talking of the World, and the Herald, and the Sun, until the men at the Press Club fought shy of him. Norah had found quiet and comfortable quarters for Peter in a boarding-house near the lake, and just a square or two distant from my own boarding-house. He hated it cordially, as only the luxury-loving can hate a boarding-house, and threatened to leave daily.

"Let's go back to the big town, Dawn, old girl," he would say. "We're buried alive in this overgrown Dutch village. I came here in the first place on your account. Now it's up to you to get me out of it. Think of what New York means! Think of what I've been! And I can write as well as ever."

But I always shook my head. "We would not last a month in New York, Peter. New York has hurried on and left us behind. We're just two pieces of discard. We'll have to be content where we are."

"Content! In this silly hole! You must be mad!" Then, with one of his unaccountable changes of tone and topic, "Dawn, let me have some money. I'm strapped. If I had the time I'd get out some magazine stuff. Anything to get a little extra coin. Tell me, how does that little sport you call Blackie happen to have so much ready cash? I've never yet struck him for a loan that he hasn't obliged me. I think he's sweet on you, perhaps, and thinks he's doing you a sort of second-hand favor."

At times such as these all the old spirit that I had thought dead within me would rise up in revolt against this creature who was taking, from me my pride, my sense of honor, my friends. I never saw Von Gerhard now. Peter had refused outright to go to him for treatment, saying that he wasn't going to be poisoned by any cursed doctor, particularly not by one who had wanted to run away with his wife before his very eyes.

Sometimes I wondered how long this could go on. I thought of the old days with the Nirlangers; of Alma Pflugel's rose-encircled cottage; of Bennie; of the Knapfs; of the good-natured, uncouth aborigines, and their many kindnesses. I saw these dear people rarely now. Frau Nirlanger's resignation to her unhappiness only made me rebel more keenly against my own.

If only Peter could become well and strong again, I told myself, bitterly. If it were not for those blue shadows under his eyes, and the shrunken muscles, and the withered skin, I could leave him to live his life as he saw fit. But he was as dependent as a child, and as capricious. What was the end to be? I asked myself. Where was it all leading me?

And then, in a fearful and wonderful manner, my question was answered.

There came to my desk one day an envelope bearing the letter-head of the publishing house to which I had sent my story. I balanced it for a moment in my fingers, woman-fashion, wondering, hoping, surmising.

"Of course they can't want it," I told myself, in preparation for any disappointment that was in store for me. "They're sending it back. This is the letter that will tell me so."

And then I opened it. The words jumped out at me from the typewritten page. I crushed the paper in my hands, and rushed into Blackie's little office as I had been used to doing in the old days. He was at his desk, pipe in mouth. I shook his shoulder and flourished the letter wildly, and did a crazy little dance about his chair.

"They want it! They like it! Not only that, they want another, as soon as I can get it out. Think of it!"

Blackie removed his pipe from between his teeth and wiped his lips with the back of his hand. "I'm thinkin'," he said. "Anything t' oblige you. When you're through shovin' that paper into my face would you mind explainin' who wants what?"

"Oh, you're so stupid! So slow! Can't you see that I've written a real live book, and had it accepted, and that I am going to write another if I have to run away from a whole regiment of husbands to do it properly? Blackie, can't you see what it means! Oh, Blackie, I know I'm maudlin in my joy, but forgive me. It's been so long since I've had the taste of it."

"Well, take a good chew while you got th'chance an' don't count too high on this first book business. I knew a guy who wrote a book once, an' he planned to take a trip to Europe on it, and build a house when he got home, and maybe a yacht or so, if he wasn't too rushed. Sa-a-ay, girl, w'en he got through gettin' those royalties for that book they'd dwindled down to fresh wall paper for the dinin'-room, and a new gas stove for his wife, an' not enough left over to take a trolley trip to Oshkosh on. Don't count too high."

"I'm not counting at all, Blackie, and you can't discourage me."

"Don't want to. But I'd hate to see you come down with a thud." Suddenly he sat up and a grin overspread his thin face. "Tell you what we'll do, girlie. We'll celebrate. Maybe it'll be the last time. Let's pretend this is six months ago, and everything's serene. You get your bonnet. I'll get the machine. It's too hot to work, anyway. We'll take a spin out to somewhere that's cool, and we'll order cold things to eat, and cold things to drink, and you can talk about yourself till you're tired. You'll have to take it out on somebody, an' it might as well be me."

Five minutes later, with my hat in my hand, I turned to find Peter at my elbow.

"Want to talk to you," he said, frowning.

"Sorry, Peter, but I can't stop. Won't it do later?"

"No. Got an assignment? I'll go with you."

"N-not exactly, Peter. The truth is, Blackie has taken pity on me and has promised to take me out for a spin, just to cool off. It has been so insufferably hot."

Peter turned away. "Count me in on that," he said, over his shoulder.

"But I can't, Peter," I cried. "It isn't my party. And anyway—"

Peter turned around, and there was an ugly glow in his eyes and an ugly look on his face, and a little red ridge that I had not noticed before seemed to burn itself across his forehead. "And anyway, you don't want me, eh? Well, I'm going. I'm not going to have my wife chasing all over the country with strange men. Remember, you're not the giddy grass widdy you used to be. You can take me, or stay at home, understand?"

His voice was high-pitched and quavering. Something in his manner struck a vague terror to my heart. "Why, Peter, if you care that much I shall be glad to have you go. So will Blackie, I am sure. Come, we'll go down now. He'll be waiting for us."

Blackie's keen, clever mind grasped the situation as soon as he saw us together. His dark face was illumined by one of his rare smiles. "Coming with us, Orme? Do you good. Pile into the tonneau, you two, and hang on to your hair. I'm going to smash the law."

Peter sauntered up to the steering-wheel. "Let me drive," he said. "I'm not bad at it."

"Nix with the artless amateur," returned Blackie. "This ain't no demonstration car. I drive my own little wagon when I go riding, and I intend to until I take my last ride, feet first."

Peter muttered something surly and climbed into the front seat next to Blackie, leaving me to occupy the tonneau in solitary state.

Peter began to ask questions—dozens of them, which Blackie answered, patiently and fully. I could not hear all that they said, but I saw that Peter was urging Blackie to greater speed, and that Blackie was explaining that he must first leave the crowded streets behind. Suddenly Peter made a gesture in the direction of the wheel, and said something in a high, sharp voice. Blackie's answer was quick and decidedly in the negative. The next instant Peter Orme rose in his place and leaning forward and upward, grasped the wheel that was in Blackie's hands. The car swerved sickeningly. I noticed, dully, that Blackie did not go white as novelists say men do in moments of horror. A dull red flush crept to the very base of his neck. With a twist of his frail body he tried to throw off Peter's hands. I remember leaning over the back of the seat and trying to pull Peter back as I realized that it was a madman with whom we were dealing. Nothing seemed real. It was ridiculously like the things one sees in the moving picture theaters. I felt no fear.

"Sit down, Orme!" Blackie yelled. "You'll ditch us! Dawn! God!—"

We shot down a little hill. Two wheels were lifted from the ground. The machine was poised in the air for a second before it crashed into the ditch and turned over completely, throwing me clear, but burying Blackie and Peter under its weight of steel and wood and whirring wheels.

I remember rising from the ground, and sinking back again and rising once more to run forward to where the car lay in the ditch, and tugging at that great frame of steel with crazy, futile fingers. Then I ran screaming down the road toward a man who was tranquilly working in a field nearby.

CHAPTER XX. BLACKIE'S VACATION COMES

The shabby blue office coat hangs on the hook in the little sporting room where Blackie placed it. No one dreams of moving it. There it dangles, out at elbows, disreputable, its pockets burned from many a hot pipe thrust carelessly into them, its cuffs frayed, its lapels bearing the marks of cigarette, paste-pot and pen.

It is that faded old garment, more than anything else, which makes us fail to realize that its owner will never again slip into its comfortable folds. We cannot believe that a lifeless rag like that can triumph over the man of flesh and blood and nerves and sympathies. With what contempt do we look upon those garments during our lifetime! And how they live on, defying time, long, long after we have been gathered to our last rest.

In some miraculous manner Blackie had lived on for two days after that ghastly ride. Peter had been killed instantly, the doctors said. They gave no hope for Blackie. My escape with but a few ridiculous bruises and scratches was due, they said, to the fact that I had sat in the tonneau. I heard them all, in a stupor of horror and grief, and wondered what plan Fate had in store for me, that I alone should have been spared. Norah and Max came, and took things in charge, and I saw Von Gerhard, but all three appeared dim and shadowy, like figures in a mist. When I closed my eyes I could see Peter's tense figure bending over Blackie at the wheel, and heard his labored breathing as he struggled in his mad fury, and felt again the helpless horror that had come to me as we swerved off the road and into the ditch below, with Blackie, rigid and desperate, still clinging to the wheel. I lived it all over and over in my mind. In the midst of the blackness I heard a sentence that cleared the fog from my mind, and caused me to raise myself from my pillows.

Some one—Norah, I think—had said that Blackie was conscious, and that he was asking for some of the men at the office, and for me. For me! I rose and dressed, in spite of Norah's protests. I was quite well, I told them. I must see him. I shook them off with trembling fingers and when they saw that I was quite determined they gave in, and Von Gerhard telephoned to the hospital to learn the hour at which I might meet the others who were to see Blackie for a brief moment.

I met them in the stiff little waiting room of he hospital—Norberg, Deming, Schmidt, Holt—men who had known him from the time when they had yelled, "Heh, boy!" at him when they wanted their pencils sharpened. Awkwardly we followed the fleet-footed nurse who glided ahead of us down the wide hospital corridors, past doorways through which we caught glimpses of white beds that were no whiter than the faces that lay on the pillows. We came at last into a very still and bright little room where Blackie lay.

Had years passed over his head since I saw him last? The face that tried to smile at us from the pillow was strangely wizened and old. It was as though a withering blight had touched it. Only the eyes were the same. They glowed in the sunken face, beneath the shock of black hair, with a startling luster and brilliancy.

I do not know what pain he suffered. I do not know what magic medicine gave him the strength to smile at us, dying as he was even then.

"Well, what do you know about little Paul Dombey?" he piped in a high, thin voice. The shock of relief was too much. We giggled hysterically, then stopped short and looked at each other, like scared and naughty children.

"Sa-a-ay, boys and girls, cut out the heavy thinking parts. Don't make me do all the social stunts. What's the news? What kind of a rotten cotton sportin' sheet is that dub Callahan gettin' out? Who won to-day—Cubs or Pirates? Norberg, you goat, who pinned that purple tie on you?"

He was so like the Blackie we had always known that we were at our ease immediately. The sun shone in at the window, and some one laughed a little laugh somewhere down the corridor, and Deming, who is Irish, plunged into a droll description of a brand-new office boy who had arrived that day.

"S'elp me, Black, the kid wears spectacles and a Norfolk suit, and low-cut shoes with bows on 'em. On the square he does. Looks like one of those Boston infants you see in the comic papers. I don't believe he's real. We're saving him until you get back, if the kids in the alley don't chew him up before that time."

An almost imperceptible shade passed over Blackie's face. He closed his eyes for a moment. Without their light his countenance was ashen, and awful.

A nurse in stripes and cap appeared in the doorway. She looked keenly at the little figure in the bed. Then she turned to us.

"You must go now," she said. "You were just to see him for a minute or two, you know."

Blackie summoned the wan ghost of a smile to his lips. "Guess you guys ain't got th' stimulatin' effect that a bunch of live wires ought to have. Say, Norberg, tell that fathead, Callahan, if he don't keep the third drawer t' the right in my desk locked, th' office kids'll swipe all the roller rink passes surest thing you know."

"I'll—tell him, Black," stammered Norberg, and turned away.

They said good-by, awkwardly enough. Not one of them that did not owe him an unpayable debt of gratitude. Not one that had not the memory of some secret kindness stored away in his heart. It was Blackie who had furnished the money that had sent Deming's sick wife west. It had been Blackie who had rescued Schmidt time and again when drink got a strangle-hold. Blackie had always said: "Fire Schmidt! Not much! Why, Schmidt writes better stuff drunk than all the rest of the bunch sober." And Schmidt would be granted another reprieve by the Powers that Were.

Suddenly Blackie beckoned the nurse in the doorway. She came swiftly and bent over him.

"Gimme two minutes more, that's a good nursie. There's something I want to say t' this dame. It's de rigger t' hand out last messages, ain't it?"

The nurse looked at me, doubtfully. "But you're not to excite yourself."

"Sa-a-ay, girl, this ain't goin' t' be no scene from East Lynne. Be a good kid. The rest of the bunch can go."

And so, when the others had gone, I found myself seated at the side of his bed, trying to smile down at him. I knew that there must be nothing to excite him. But the words on my lips would come.

"Blackie," I said, and I struggled to keep my voice calm and emotionless, "Blackie, forgive me. It is all my fault—my wretched fault."

"Now, cut that," interrupted Blackie. "I thought that was your game. That's why I said I wanted t' talk t' you. Now, listen. Remember my tellin' you, a few weeks ago, 'bout that vacation I was plannin'? This is it, only it's come sooner than I expected, that's all. I seen two three doctor guys about it. Your friend Von Gerhard was one of 'em. They didn't tell me t' take no ocean trip this time. Between 'em, they decided my vacation would come along about November, maybe. Well, I beat 'em to it, that's all. Sa-a-ay, girl, I ain't kickin'. You can't live on your nerves and expect t' keep goin'. Sooner or later you'll be suein' those same nerves for non-support. But, kid, ain't it a shame that I got to go out in a auto smashup, in these days when even a airship exit don't make a splash on the front page!"

The nervous brown hand was moving restlessly over the covers. Finally it met my hand, and held it in a tense little grip.

"We've been good pals, you and me, ain't we, kid?"

"Yes, Blackie."

"Ain't regretted it none?"

"Regretted it! I am a finer, truer, better woman for having known you, Blackie."

He gave a little contented sigh at that, and his eyes closed. When he opened them the old, whimsical smile wrinkled his face.

"This is where I get off at. It ain't been no long trip, but sa-a-ay, girl, I've enjoyed every mile of the road. All kinds of scenery—all kinds of lan'scape—plain—fancy—uphill—downhill—"

I leaned forward, fearfully.

"Not—yet," whispered Blackie. "Say Dawn—in the story books—they—always—are strong on the—good-by kiss, what?"

And as the nurse appeared in the doorway again, disapproval on her face, I stooped and gently pressed my lips to the pain-lined cheek.

CHAPTER XXI. HAPPINESS

We laid Peter to rest in that noisy, careless, busy city that he had loved so well, and I think his cynical lips would have curled in a bitterly amused smile, and his somber eyes would have flamed into sudden wrath if he could have seen how utterly and completely New York had forgotten Peter Orme. He had been buried alive ten years before—

and Newspaper Row has no faith in resurrections. Peter Orme was not even a memory. Ten years is an age in a city where epochs are counted by hours.

Now, after two weeks of Norah's loving care, I was back in the pretty little city by the lake. I had come to say farewell to all those who had filled my life so completely in that year. My days of newspaper work were over. The autumn and winter would be spent at Norah's, occupied with hours of delightful, congenial work, for the second book was to be written in the quiet peace of my own little Michigan town. Von Gerhard was to take his deferred trip to Vienna in the spring, and I knew that I was to go with him. The thought filled my heart with a great flood of happiness.

Together Von Gerhard and I had visited Alma Pflugel's cottage, and the garden was blooming in all its wonder of color and scent as we opened the little gate and walked up the worn path. We found them in the cool shade of the arbor, the two women sewing, Bennie playing with the last wonderful toy that Blackie had given him. They made a serene and beautiful picture there against the green canopy of the leaves. We spoke of Frau Nirlanger, and of Blackie, and of the strange snarl of events which had at last been unwound to knit a close friendship between us. And when I had kissed them and walked for the last time in many months up the flower-bordered path, the scarlet and pink, and green and gold of that wonderful garden swam in a mist before my eyes.

Frau Nirlanger was next. When we spoke of Vienna she caught her breath sharply.

"Vienna!" she repeated, and the longing in her voice was an actual pain. "Vienna! Gott! Shall I ever see it again? Vienna! My boy is there. Perhaps—"

"Perhaps," I said, gently. "Stranger things have happened. Perhaps if I could see them, and talk to them—if I could tell them—they might be made to understand. I haven't been a newspaper reporter all these years without acquiring a golden gift of persuasiveness. Perhaps—who knows?—we may meet again in Vienna. Stranger things have happened."

Frau Nirlanger shook her head with a little hopeless sigh. "You do not know Vienna; you do not know the iron strength of caste, and custom and stiff-necked pride. I am dead in Vienna. And the dead should rest in peace."

It was late in the afternoon when Von Gerhard and I turned the corner which led to the building that held the Post. I had saved that for the last.

"I hope that heaven is not a place of golden streets, and twanging harps and angel choruses," I said, softly. "Little, nervous, slangy, restless Blackie, how bored and ill at ease he would be in such a heaven! How lonely, without his old black pipe, and his checked waistcoats, and his diamonds, and his sporting extra. Oh, I hope they have all those comforting, everyday things up there, for Blackie's sake." "How you grew to understand him in that short year," mused Von Gerhard. "I sometimes used to resent the bond between you and this little Blackie whose name was always on your tongue." "Ah, that was because you did not comprehend. It is given to very few women to know the beauty of a man's real friendship. That was the bond between Blackie and me. To me he was a comrade, and to him I was a good-fellow girl—one to whom he could talk without excusing his pipe or cigarette. Love and love-making were things to bring a kindly, amused chuckle from Blackie."

Von Gerhard was silent. Something in his silence held a vague irritation for me. I extracted a penny from my purse, and placed it in his hand. "I was thinking," he said, "that none are so blind as those who will not see." "I don't understand," I said, puzzled. "That is well," answered Von Gerhard, as we entered the building. "That is as it should be." An he would say nothing more. The last edition of the paper had been run off for the day. I had purposely waited until the footfalls of the last departing reporter should have ceased to echo down the long corridor. The city room was deserted except for one figure bent over a pile of papers and proofs. Norberg, the city editor, was the last to leave, as always. His desk light glowed in the darkness of the big room, and his typewriter alone awoke the echoes.

As I stood in the doorway he peered up from beneath his green eye-shade, and waved a cloud of smoke away with the palm of his hand.

"That you, Mrs. Orme?" he called out. "Lord, we've missed you! That new woman can't write an obituary, and her teary tales sound like they were carved with a cold chisel. When are you coming back?"

"I'm not coming back," I replied. "I've come to say good-by to you and—Blackie."

Norberg looked up quickly. "You feel that way, too? Funny. So do the rest of us. Sometimes I think we are all half sure that it is only another of his impish tricks, and that some morning he will pop open the door of the city room here and call out, 'Hello, slaves! Been keepin' m' memory green?'"

I held out my hand to him, gratefully. He took it in his great palm, and a smile dimpled his plump cheeks. "Going to blossom into a regular little writer, h'm? Well, they say it's a paying game when you get the hang of it. And I guess you've got it. But if ever you feel that you want a real thrill—a touch of the old satisfying newspaper feeling—a sniff of wet ink—the music of some editorial cussing—why come up here and I'll give you the hottest assignment on my list, if I have to take it away from Deming's very notebook."

When I had thanked him I crossed the hall and tried the door of the sporting editor's room. Von Gerhard was waiting for me far down at the other end of the corridor. The door opened and I softly entered and shut it again. The little room was dim, but in the half-light I could see that Callahan had changed something—had shoved a desk nearer the window, or swung the typewriter over to the other side. I resented it. I glanced up at the corner where the shabby old office coat had been wont to hang. There it dangled, untouched, just as he had left it. Callahan had not dared to change that. I tip-toed over to the corner and touched it gently with my fingers. A light pall of dust had settled over the worn little garment, but I knew each worn place, each ink-spot, each scorch or burn from pipe or cigarette. I passed my hands over it reverently and gently, and then, in the dimness of that quiet little room I laid my cheek against the rough cloth, so that the scent of the old black pipe came back to me once more, and a new spot appeared on the coat sleeve—a damp, salt spot. Blackie would have hated my doing that. But he was not there to see, and one spot more or less did not matter; it was such a grimy, disreputable old coat.

"Dawn!" called Von Gerhard softly, outside the door. "Dawn! Coming, Kindchen?"

I gave the little coat a parting pat. "Goodby," I whispered, under my breath, and turned toward the door. "Coming!" I called, aloud.

CPSIA information can be obtained
at www.ICGtesting.com
Printed in the USA
BVHW011133251118
533921BV00018B/375/P